MANAGEMENT:
A Book of Readings

McGRAW HILL-SERIES IN MANAGEMENT
Keith Davis, Consulting Editor

Allen Management and Organization
Allen The Management Profession
Argyris Management and Organizational Development: The Path from XA to YB
Beckett Management Dynamics: The New Synthesis
Bennis Changing Organizations
Benton Supervision and Management
Bergen and Haney Organizational Relations and Management Action
Blough International Business: Environment and Adaptation
Bowman Management: Organization and Planning
Brown Judgment in Administration
Campbell, Dunnette, Lawler, and Weick Managerial Behavior, Performance, and Effectiveness
Cleland and King Management: A Systems Approach
Cleland and King Systems Analysis and Project Management
Cleland and King Systems, Organizations, Analysis, Management: A Book of Readings
Dale Management: Theory and Practice
Dale Readings in Management: Landmarks and New Frontiers
Davis Human Behavior at Work: Human Relations and Organizational Behavior
Davis Organizational Behavior: A Book of Readings
Davis and Blomstrom Business and Society: Environment and Responsibility
DeGreene Systems Psychology
Dunn and Rachel Wage and Salary Administration: Total Compensation Systems
Dunn and Stephens Management of Personnel: Manpower Management and Organizational Behavior
Edmunds and Letey Environmental Administration
Fiedler A Theory of Leadership Effectiveness
Finch, Jones, and Litterer Managing for Organizational Effectiveness: An Experiential Approach
Flippo Principles of Personnel Management
Glueck Business Policy: Strategy Formation and Management Action
Golembiewski Men, Management, and Morality
Hicks and Gullett The Management of Organizations
Hicks and Gullett Modern Business Management: A Systems and Environmental Approach
Hicks and Gullett Organizations: Theory and Behavior
Johnson, Kast, and Rosenzweig The Theory and Management of Systems
Kast and Rosenzweig Organization and Management: A Systems Approach
Knudson, Woodworth, and Bell Management: An Experiential Approach
Koontz Toward a Unified Theory of Management
Koontz and O'Donnell Essentials of Management
Koontz and O'Donnell Management: A Book of Readings
Koontz and O'Donnell Management: A Systems and Contingency Analysis of Managerial Functions
Levin, McLaughlin, Lamone, and Kottas Production/Operations Management: Contemporary Policy for Managing Operating Systems
Luthans Contemporary Readings in Organizational Behavior
Luthans Introduction to Management: A Contingency Approach
Luthans Organizational Behavior
McNichols Policy Making and Executive Action
Maier Problem-solving Discussions and Conferences: Leadership Methods and Skills
Margulies and Raia Organizational Development: Values, Process, and Technology
Mayer Production and Operations Management
Miles Theories of Management: Implications for Organization Behavior and Development

Mundel A Conceptual Framework for the Management Sciences
Newstrom, Reif, and Monczka A Contingency Approach to Management: Readings
Petit The Moral Crisis in Management
Petrof, Carusone, and McDavid Small Business Management: Concepts and Techniques for Improving Decisions
Pigors and Pigors Case Method in Human Relations
Porter, Lawler, and Hackman Behavior in Organizations
Prasow and Peters Arbitration and Collective Bargaining: Conflict Resolution in Labor Relations
Ready The Administrator's Job
Reddin Managerial Effectiveness
Richman and Copen International Management and Economic Development
Sartain and Baker The Supervisor and His Job
Schrieber, Johnson, Meier, Fischer, and Newell Cases in Manufacturing Management
Shore Operations Management
Shull, Delbecq, and Cummings Organizational Decision Making
Steers and Porter Motivation and Work Behavior
Steiner Managerial Long-Range Planning
Sutermeister People and Productivity
Tannenbaum, Weschler, and Massarik Leadership and Organization
Vance Industrial Administration

MANAGEMENT: A Book of Readings

Fourth Edition

Harold Koontz

Graduate School of Management
University of California, Los Angeles

Cyril O'Donnell

Graduate School of Management
University of California, Los Angeles

McGRAW-HILL BOOK COMPANY

New York St. Louis San Francisco
Auckland Düsseldorf Johannesburg
Kuala Lumpur London Mexico
Montreal New Delhi Panama
Paris São Paulo Singapore
Sydney Tokyo Toronto

MANAGEMENT: A Book of Readings

1 2 3 4 5 6 7 8 9 0 WHWH 7 9 8 7 6 5

This book was set in Times Roman by Monotype Composition Company, Inc. The editors were William J. Kane, Sonia Sheldon, and Matthew Cahill; the cover was designed by Joseph Gillians; the production supervisor was Judi Allen. New drawings were done by Tek/Nek, Inc.
The Whitlock Press, Inc., was printer and binder.

Library of Congress Cataloging in Publication Data

Koontz, Harold, date ed.
Management, a book of readings.

(McGraw-Hill series in management)
First published in 1959 under title: Readings in management.
Includes bibliographical references.
1. Management—Addresses, essays, lectures.
I. O'Donnell, Cyril, date, joint ed. II. Title.
HD31.K599 1976 658'.008 75-23189
ISBN 0-07-035353-0
ISBN 0-07-035352-2 pbk.

Contents

Preface

One of the difficulties encountered by all who read or teach in the area of management theory and policy is that much of the best thought and experience in the field is in widely scattered sources. Moreover, the great interest in management in recent years has led to a deluge of materials on the subject. The reader who tries to wade through this mass of information has difficulty selecting the most pertinent and representative selections. Even guided by a well-compiled bibliography, the reader has to cope with the limitations of libraries and the understandable desire to have the material conveniently at hand.

A book of selected readings in management has seemed to us especially worthwhile, particularly for students, but also for the practicing manager who would like to have some of this material readily available. None of the books devoted to an analysis of management can do much more than refer to some of the more significant literature. The tendency for such books to be rather narrow in approach and to deal with the subject matter summarily, rather than broadly, is unavoidable. This is not the choice or the fault of those who write such books; rather, it naturally results from the restrictions of space imposed by the publishers and the size limitations of such a book from the standpoint of the reader.

This situation appears to be especially serious in the area of general management. It is compounded because the source material is widely scattered in books and journals devoted to the social sciences, in business and management association publications, and in journals concerned with business and other kinds of enterprise activities.

The editors, in attempting to collect the more significant and useful writings on general management for this volume and to include a meaningful sample of writing in a number of important management areas, have found that the task of selecting appropriate material from hundreds of important journal articles and other sources is monumental. It was so when earlier editions of this book were published. It is even more true now, since the volume and quality of writing in the field have increased so tremendously. Although this collection of readings remains larger than comparable books, it was found necessary to reduce the number somewhat in this edition. The editors regretfully and painfully found it necessary to omit some valuable items which were in the previous editions, both to shorten this book and to make way for many new readings. Thus, despite the retention of many classics in the field, nearly one-third of the readings are new.

The materials have been grouped primarily according to a very widely accepted theory of management; that is, the book has a general introductory part followed by five parts in the areas of the principal management functions: planning, organizing, staffing, directing and leading, and controlling. This framework is flexible and inclusive enough to permit presentation of a wide variety of selections written from many different points of view. Users will find these selections effective in almost any classroom situation (the "principles" or any other basic management courses, graduate courses, seminars, management development programs), as well as in the practicing manager's office.

In making the selections, the editors thought it best to cover most subjects in as thorough a way as the originals, rather than give brief excerpts as is often done. While in a very few cases we have used excerpts and omitted sentences and even paragraphs, almost all the material is essentially as it was when originally published.

We are indebted to the authors of these selections and to their publishers for permission to reprint. Their cooperation has been both prompt and courteous, and we trust that our readers will appreciate having such a wide selection of the best management literature available in one volume.

Harold Koontz
Cyril O'Donnell

MANAGEMENT: A Book of Readings

Part 1
THE BASIS OF A THEORY OF MANAGEMENT

This introductory section contains a selection of readings in four areas. The first group deals with the subject of managing and management science and attempts to give some insights into what managing is, how systems and contingency management relates to operational management theory, and how the development of a science, given structure by theory, can relate to it. The second group contains selections from systems theory, since management as theory and science does and should utilize the guidelines of systems theory and managers clearly operate in an open social system. The third section samples literature on the role of the manager in his environmental setting, and the final section includes a paper on comparative management with the purpose of differentiating the science of management from enterprise sciences and clarifying the impact of cultural variables on management practice.

In the section on managing and management science, the editors have chosen an excerpt from the writing of the great Henri Fayol, generally regarded as the father of modern operational management theory. Fayol, like many other pioneers, viewed theory as a means for giving substance to the subject of management so that it could be more effectively taught. It is interesting to note that Fayol's central thesis was that principles, or theory, became the means by which light is shed on the understanding and improvement of management practice.

To develop understanding and distill fundamental truths of use to practitioners in any field, one must recognize what a theory is, how it contributes to the development of science, and why it must be based on a conceptual scheme that "makes sense." The editors have selected for this purpose excerpts from the writings of social theorist George C. Homans.

The various approaches that have been made toward study and research in management, particularly in recent years, are discussed in Harold Koontz's provocative article "The Management Theory Jungle." Koontz attempts to distill, from the deluge of writings, research, and statements of philosophy on this subject, a classification of approaches, or "schools," of management theory. In doing so, he outlines the differences among these schools and suggests how the various approaches can be integrated into a useful and systematic theory of management.

The article by William T. Greenwood, "Future Management Theory: A Comparative Evolution to a General Theory," has been selected because it skillfully traces the development of various approaches to management theory and suggests how a comparative approach might lead to their synthesis. Pointing out that he is not using "comparative" in the sense of different management styles and approaches in varying cultures and societies, Greenwood believes that the evolution of a basic management theory will be achieved from the analysis of the various theories and approaches concurrently being developed and the selecting from each the most pertinent elements.

In the section on systems theory and management, the classic description of the nature of systems by Kenneth Boulding, entitled "General Systems Theory—The Skeleton of Science," has been selected. Boulding sees systems theory as the means of integrating findings of various disciplines into a single science and identifies various levels of systems complexity and sophistication. To this is added the article by Robert J. Mockler, "The Systems Approach to Organization and Decision Making," in which the current state of systems theory is summarized and suggestions are made for its application to management.

Because managers act in formally organized enterprises, and these are, of course, social systems, an excerpt from *Social Psychology of Organizations* by Daniel Katz and Robert L. Kahn is included on this subject. While these writers look upon social systems through the eyes of social psychologists, their clear analysis of systems is applicable to management.

Since all enterprises are open social systems and managers must necessarily be responsive to their external environment, the third section of this part includes three articles on the environment of managing. Although it is recognized that this environment, to which managers must in their own self interest be responsive, includes many elements—economic, technological, political, social, and ethical—space permits only including a sample of papers on the social, ethical, and technological elements of this environment. The first paper is from John J. Corson's and George A. Steiner's study for the Committee for Economic Development, the first chapter of which outlines the nature of social responsibility. Father John W. Clark's "A Tentative Statement of Ethical Guides" is an extraordinarily clear and perceptive treatment of this difficult subject. Vaclav Smil's paper on "Energy and the Environment: Scenarios for 1985–2000" has been selected as a good example of the various studies being made to foresee the future technological environment enterprises face.

One article is reprinted on comparative management. This is the paper by Harold Koontz, "A Model for Analyzing the Universality and Transferability of Management." In this, the pioneering models by Richman and Farmer and by Negandhi and Estafen are examined, and revisions of these are suggested to bring out more clearly the impact of cultural variables on managing and to distinguish between contributions of management science and the enterprise sciences.

A. MANAGING AND MANAGEMENT SCIENCE

1 THE NEED FOR AND POSSIBILITY OF MANAGEMENT TEACHING*

Henri Fayol

The real reason for the absence of management teaching in our vocational schools is absence of theory; without theory no teaching is possible. Now there exists no generally accepted theory of management emanating from general discussion. There is no shortage of personal theorizing, but failing any accepted theory each one thinks that he has the best methods and everywhere there may be observed—in industry, the army, the home, the State—the most contradictory practices under the aegis of the same principle. Whereas in the technical sphere a head would not dare to infringe certain established rules without risking total loss of prestige, in the managerial one the most undesirable practices may be indulged in with impunity. The methods used are judged not on their own merits but on their results, which often are very remote and mostly difficult to relate to their causes. The situation might be quite otherwise were there an accepted theory, that is to say, a collection of principles, rules, methods, procedures, tried and checked by general experience. It is not principles which are lacking: were it sufficient to proclaim them to have them prevail we should enjoy the best possible management everywhere. Who has not heard proclaimed a hundred times the need for the grand principles of authority, discipline, subordination of individual interest to the common good, unity of direction, co-ordination of effort, foresight, etc.? It must be admitted that proclamation is not enough. The fact is that the light of principles, like that of lighthouses, guides only those who already know the way into port, and a principle bereft of the means of putting it into practice is of no avail.

Nor is there any lack of methods: their name is legion, but good and bad are to be found side by side at the same time in the home, workshop and State, with a persistence only to be explained by lack of theory. The general public is not in a position to pass judgment on managerial activity, hence the importance of establishing a theory of management as soon as possible. It would be neither lengthy nor difficult if a few industrial leaders decided to set forth their personal views on the general principles which they consider most calculated to promote smooth running and on the means most conducive to the realization of such principles. Light would soon be thrown on the subject as the result of comparison and discussion. But the majority of higher managers have neither time nor inclination for writing and most often depart without leaving either doctrine or disciples. Hence too much reliance must not be placed on help from this quarter.

Fortunately there is no need to be concerned with the running of a large-scale undertaking or to proffer a masterly treatise in order to make useful contribution to the building up of theory. The slightest comment appropriately made is of value, and since there is no limit to the possible number of commentators it is to be hoped that once the stream has started to flow it will not be stemmed. It is a case of setting it going, starting general discussion—that is what I am trying to do by publishing this survey, and I hope that a theory will emanate from it. This done, there is the question of teaching to be solved. Everyone needs some concepts of management; in the home, in affairs of State, the need for managerial ability is in keeping with the importance of the undertaking, and for individual people the need is everywhere greater in accordance with the position occupied. Hence there should be some

* Reprinted by permission of the publisher from Henri Fayol, *General and Industrial Management*, Pitman Publishing Corporation, New York, 1949, pp. 14–16. Mr. Fayol was a highly successful French industrialist who perceived the universality of management and the need for management principles. This excerpt was originally published in 1916 and was based, in part, on lectures delivered in 1908.

generalized teaching of management; elementary in the primary schools, somewhat wider in the post-primary schools, and quite advanced in higher educational establishments. This teaching will no more make good managers out of all its pupils than technical teaching makes excellent technicians out of its trainees. All that would be asked of it would be services analogous to those rendered by technical education. And why not? It is chiefly a matter of putting young people in the way of understanding and using the lessons of experience. At present the beginner has neither management theory nor method, and in this respect some remain beginners all their lives. Hence an effort must be made to spread management ideas throughout all ranks of the population. Obviously school has a large part to play in this teaching. In establishments for higher education teachers will be well able to work out their courses the day when management forms part of their teaching. It is more difficult to conceive what primary school teaching of management should be. On this point I have made an attempt which I shall set out, without claiming anything for it, in the conviction that a good primary teacher will be better able than I am to select from theory and put within his pupils' reach what is suitable to teach them.

2 A THEORY IN SOCIAL SCIENCE*

George C. Homans

The behavior of men, usually in small numbers, has inspired the largest part of human literature and eloquence. If we investigated no further than we have today, we should have plenty of material to study. But until recently this great mass of observation has led to nothing. Some leaders, perhaps those of the past more than those of the present, have shown great capacity for handling men in groups, but their know-how could not easily be communicated in words from one man to another. There have been a few maxims of practical wisdom, always at odds with one another because the limits of any single maxim were never stated. Whatever a man did, he could always find a rule to back him up. But until recently there has been little growth. Our knowledge is Babylonian. Our proverbs are carved on the pyramids. A new fact in physics or biology fits into an old theory, or by not fitting starts a new theory. Either way one can build on it. Think of the mass of old work summarized and new work suggested by the periodic table of the elements. But every adventurer in the science of human behavior from Aristotle to Freud has had to make a fresh start, or something like it.

If the outlook has changed since the opening of this century, the reason is that we have begun to sketch out systematic theories of human behavior and to use them. Einstein taught the world, what it ought to have known long ago, that no theory is permanent. If an old theory survives new conquests of science, it survives as a slave. But even the most fragile theory has its uses. In its lowest form, as a classification, it provides a set of pigeonholes, a filing cabinet, in which fact can accumulate. For nothing is more lost than a loose fact. The empty folders of the file demand filling. In time the accumulation makes necessary a more economical filing system, with more cross references, and a new theory is born. . . .

The group will be described as an organic whole, surviving and evolving in an environment. We do not want just to get the feel of this whole. We want to be men and *understand*. We want to build up in detail the articulation of the whole, and in these mazes we shall certainly go astray unless we have a method of

* Excerpts reprinted by permission from George C. Homans, *The Human Group*, Harcourt, Brace, & World, Inc., New York, 1950, pp. 4–5, 10–12, 13–17, 21–22. Copyright 1950 by Harcourt, Brace & World, Inc. Mr. Homans is professor of sociology, Harvard University.

attacking our problem, a method that we can apply patiently, repeatedly, and systematically, at whatever risk of dullness. The question then is: How shall we go about constructing our theory of the group?

We shall begin with semantics, the science of tracing words back to their references in observed fact. In sociology we are devoted to "big" words: status, culture, function, heuristic, particularistic, methodology, integration, solidarity, authority. Too often we work with these words and not with observations. Or rather, we do not wed the two. No one will make progress with this book who does not train himself to extensionalize, who does not habitually catch himself as he mouths one of the big abstractions and ask: What does this mouthful mean in terms of actual human behavior that someone has seen and reported? Just what, in human behavior, do we *see?* The question is devastating, and we do not ask it half often enough. Carefully working out the referents of existing concepts will help us to reach a simple method of classifying what we see, and in the classification itself we shall gain a new set of concepts more adequate than some of the old ones for the purposes we have in mind.

Let us take an example. Let us take the concepts *status* and *role,* which are commonly used in social science. What do they mean? Ralph Linton, the anthropologist, who gave these concepts an important place in his social theory, has this to say: "A *status,* in the abstract, is a position in a particular pattern [of social behavior] . . . A status, as distinct from the individual who may occupy it, is simply a collection of rights and duties . . . A *role* represents the dynamic aspects of a status. The individual is socially assigned to a status and occupies it with relation to other statuses. When he puts the rights and duties which constitute the status into effect, he is performing a role. Role and status are quite inseparable, and the distinction between them is of only academic interest. There are no roles without statuses or statuses without roles."[1]

Now let us try, if we can, to translate these words into observations, and, leaving out of consideration the fact that a person may hold several statuses—he may be a *father,* an *officer* of a lodge, a *deacon* of a church—let us consider only a single status, that of *foreman.* Foreman is a status in that the position may be occupied by a number of individuals in succession; the position does not disappear when an individual leaves it. Let us suppose that a man is foreman in a factory, and that we are watching him at work. What do we see and hear? We watch him, perhaps, overseeing a battery of punch presses, going from one man to another as they tend the machines, answering their questions and showing them, if they have made mistakes, where they have gone wrong. We see him also at his desk making out records. That is, we see that he has a certain kind of job, that he carries on certain activities. We see also that he deals with certain men in the plant and not with others. He goes to certain men and talks to them; others come to his desk and talk to him. He gets his orders from a boss and passes on the orders to members of his own department. That is, he communicates or, as we shall say in this book, interacts with certain persons and not with others, and this communication from person to person often takes place in a certain order—for instance, from the boss to the foreman and then from the foreman to the workers—, so that we can say, in Linton's words, that the foreman occupies a position in a chain of communications. If, moreover, we stay in the factory and listen sharply, we shall hear remarks to the effect that a foreman's job is lower or worse than the president's but higher or better than the ordinary workingman's. That is, the foreman's job is given an emotional evaluation. We shall also hear statements of one kind or another about the way the foreman ought to behave, statements that may come both from the boss he works for and from the men who work for him. That is, we hear norms of behavior being expressed. These make up "the collection of rights and duties" that Linton speaks of: notions of what the foreman's behavior ought to be, not necessarily what it really is. And finally, if the foreman's behavior departs outrageously from the norms, we shall see his boss and even his own men take action to bring him back into line. That is, we see men acting so as to control the behavior of others.

No doubt we could make other observations, but we have cited enough to illustrate our point. We do not directly observe *status* and *role.* What we do observe are activities, interactions, evaluations, norms, and controls. Status and role are names we give to a complex of many different kinds of observations. Or, as an expert in semantics would say, a word like *interaction* is a first-order abstraction: it is a name given to a single class of observations; whereas a word like *status* is a second-order abstraction: it is a name given to several classes of observation combined. Second-order abstractions are useful for some purposes but for others have serious drawbacks. They spare us the pain of analysis when we should not be spared. To speak of a man's status as if it were an indivisible unit is a convenient kind of short-

[1] R. Linton, *The Study of Man,* pp. 113–114.

hand, but to think of status in this way may prevent our seeing the relations between its components. It may prevent us, for instance, from seeing that as a man's position in a chain of communications changes, so the way he is evaluated by his fellows will change. Since it is just this kind of relation that we shall be examining in this book, the concepts that enter our theories will be, so far as possible, first-order abstractions. At least we shall not use the higher abstractions until we have established the lower ones.[2] . . .

THE PROBLEM OF ABSTRACTION

Let no one be deceived by our systematic attack. It means that we shall study methodically the aspects of social life we choose to take up; it does not mean that we shall study every aspect of social life. There are always more observations than can possibly be summed up in any one theory; or rather, if the theory is to be formulated at all, it must leave many observations out of account. Galileo took a fateful step for science when he left friction out of the study of motion. He framed, for instance, his law describing the motion of a ball rolling down an inclined plane on the assumption that there was no friction between the ball and the plane. He was justified in doing so because he could set up his experiments in such a way that they approximated this ideal state more and more closely, although they never quite got there. And he could not have framed a simple, general law if he had not used this method. It is, in fact, the necessary method, but its victories are abstract. As every one of us knows, friction always does exist in any piece of machinery and for practical purposes must be taken into account, often by methods far from elegant. Abstraction is the price paid for generalization.

The method of abstraction seems to create no such mental conflict in physics as it does in sociology. Electrons are members of a group—the atom—, and if we were electrons and knew man's theory of the atom, we might be amused by it, as an educated Hindu might be amused by a missionary's picture of Hindu culture. The theory would seem so gross, so statistical, so simplified, even if it was adequate enough to show man how to split electrons out of the group. But we are not electrons; we study the atom from the outside; we have no way of comparing the theory with the reality, and therefore our shortcomings create no mental conflict in us. This is not true of our social theory. We have inside knowledge of our own society, and this immediate familiarity with group behavior is at once an asset and a liability. It is an asset because we always have our experience to check our theories against. They must be in some degree true to experience. It is a liability because people are too easily able to say of any social theory, "You have left such and such out." They are quite right: we always leave something out. We must if we are to make theories at all. But such people make no attempt to see what we have got in. For them, the social equivalent of friction is a ghost at the table. They do not understand that a theory may be true, and yet not the whole truth.

CLINICAL AND ANALYTICAL SCIENCE

It is high time we knew the difference between clinical and analytical science. Clinical science is what a doctor uses at his patient's bedside. There, the doctor cannot afford to leave out of account anything in the patient's condition that he can see or test. He cannot leave it out either in itself or in its relation to the whole picture of a sick human being. It may be the clue to the complex. Of course the doctor has some general theories at the back of his mind, theories of the connections between a limited number of physiological factors: what the others will do when one is changed. These doctrines may turn out to be useful, but he cannot, at the outset, let them master his thinking. They may not take into consideration, and so may prevent his noticing, the crucial fact in the case before him.

In action we must always be clinical. An analytical science is for understanding but not for action, at least not directly. It picks out a few of the factors at work in particular situations and describes systematically the relations between these factors. Only by cutting down the number of factors considered can it achieve this systematic description. It is general, but it is abstract. As soon as he left friction out of account, Galileo's science became analytical. To return to our medical illustration, a description of particular cases of anemia is clinical science, whereas a theory of blood chemistry is analytical. When progress is rapid, clinical and analytical science help one another. The clinicians tell the analysts what the latter have left out. The analysts need the most brutal reminders because they are always so charmed with their pictures they mistake them for the real thing. On the other hand, the analysts' generalizations often suggest where the clinicians should look more closely. Both the clinician and the analyst are needed. We ought to

[2] See G. C. Homans, "The Strategy of Industrial Sociology," *American Journal of Sociology*, vol. 54, p. 336, 1949.

be sick and tired of boasts that one is better than the other. This is a book of analysis, but it relies heavily on work that is clinical, as the word is used here, and this work was stimulated by earlier analyses.

Elton Mayo, a pioneer in the field of industrial psychology and sociology, used to say that it was better to have a complex body of fact and a simple theory—a working hypothesis—than a simple body of fact and a complex theory. Of course it is better, and many a social scientist has damned himself by taking the second course. Yet you can be just as damned by the first. You may become a man who is sensitive and intuitive about people, and yet incapable of communicating any but your most obvious intuitions; or one who theorizes in spite of his theories but always at the highest level, never among those middle-level generalizations that Francis Bacon felt were the most fruitful.[3] But we need not, unless we insist, be impaled on a nonexistent dilemma. There are always more choices than two. What we need is a theory neither more nor less complex than the facts it subsumes, but adequate to them. If we hesitate to generalize, we lose both our generalization and the observation it might have suggested. If there is a body of fact crying for theoretical synthesis, no doctrinaire stand need stop us from making it. Let us follow Rabelais' advice and do what we like. Above all, let us not be merely sensitive souls; let us be men and understand.

RULES OF THEORY-BUILDING

All these ideas can be summed up in a set of rules that, as experience seems to show, are wisely followed in setting up a theory of the kind we propose. A theory, we will remember, is a form in which the results of observation may be expressed. The rules are:

1. Look first at the obvious, the familiar, the common. In a science that has not established its foundations, these are the things that best repay study.
2. State the obvious in its full generality. Science is an economy of thought only if its hypotheses sum up in a simple form a large number of facts.
3. Talk about one thing at a time. That is, in choosing your words (or, more pedantically, concepts) see that they refer not to several classes of fact at the same time but to one and one only. Corollary: Once you have chosen your words, always use the same words when referring to the same things.
4. Cut down as far as you dare the number of things you are talking about. "As few as you may; as many as you must," is the rule governing the number of classes of fact you take into account.
5. Once you have started to talk, do not stop until you have finished. That is, describe systematically the relationships between the facts designated by your words.
6. Recognize that your analysis must be abstract, because it deals with only a few elements of the concrete situation. Admit the dangers of abstraction, especially when action is required, but do not be afraid of abstraction.[4] . . .

THE HUMAN QUALITIES NEEDED

Finally, something must be said about the human qualities we shall need in this undertaking. We shall need, first, the innocence of the child, not the good little boy or girl but the *enfant terrible* who stops the conversation by asking the wrong questions. For we shall have to ask, "What do I actually see?" And, as we have said, no question is more devastating.

We shall also need the sophistication of the man of the world in order to make use of the past experience of the intellectual disciplines in dealing with problems of complicated fact. As Mary Follett said, "I do wish that when a principle has been worked out, say in ethics, it didn't have to be discovered all over again in psychology, in economics, in government, in business, in biology, and in sociology. It's such a waste of time."[5] The critical attitude is the heart of sophistication. We must recognize that many of the methods we should like to follow were late products of old sciences such as physics, sciences, moreover, whose problems can be made to look as if they brought in only a few variables. The study of the group is not an advanced science and can seldom pretend to manage with a small number of variables. Let us get what help we can, without feeling that we must imitate everything.

Sophistication includes knowing when not to be sophisticated. No one is more a creature of fashion than the average intellectual. He is quite ready to believe, at any moment, that certain kinds of work are the only respectable ones to go into. We are told, for instance, that our data in sociology should be quantitative, that is, should be cast in numerical form, and of course they should. But good observation

[3] *Novum Organum*, book I, aphorisms lxvi, civ.

[4] See G. C. Homans, "A Conceptual Scheme for the Study of Social Organization," *American Sociological Review* XII (1947), 13. Many of the ideas developed in this book were stated briefly in this paper.

[5] *Dynamic Administration*, p. 16.

ought not to be discarded just because it is not numerical. Sociology may miss a great deal if it tries to be too quantitative too soon. Data are not nobler because they are quantitative, nor thinking more logical because mathematical. The old-fashioned naturalist, who used only his eyes, was also a scientist, and his counterpart in sociology is very useful in the stage the science has reached. Let us make the important quantitative, and not the quantitative important.

3 THE MANAGEMENT THEORY JUNGLE*

Harold Koontz

Although students of management would readily agree that there have been problems of management since the dawn of organized life, most would also agree that systematic examination of management, with few exceptions, is the product of the present century and more especially of the past two decades. Moreover, until recent years almost all of those who have attempted to analyze the management process and look for some theoretical underpinnings to help improve research, teaching, and practice were alert and perceptive practitioners of the art who reflected on many years of experience. Thus, at least in looking at *general* management as an intellectually based art, the earliest meaningful writing came from such experienced practitioners as Fayol, Mooney, Alvin Brown, Sheldon, Barnard, and Urwick. Certainly not even the most academic worshipper of empirical research can overlook the

* Reprinted by permission of the publisher from the *Journal of the Academy of Management*, vol. 4, no. 3, pp. 174–188, December, 1961. Mr. Koontz is Mead Johnson Professor of Management in the Graduate School of Management, University of California, Los Angeles.

empiricism involved in distilling fundamentals from decades of experience by such discerning practitioners as these. Admittedly done without questionnaires, controlled interviews, or mathematics, observations by such men can hardly be accurately regarded as *a priori* or "armchair."

The noteworthy absence of academic writing and research in the formative years of modern management theory is now more than atoned for by a deluge of research and writing from the academic halls. What is interesting and perhaps nothing more than a sign of the unsophisticated adolescence of management theory is how the current flood has brought with it a wave of great differences and apparent confusion. From the orderly analysis of management at the shop-room level by Frederick Taylor and the reflective distillation of experience from the general management point of view of Henri Fayol, we now see these and other early beginnings overgrown and entangled by a jungle of approaches and approachers to management theory.

There are the behavioralists, born of the Hawthorne experiments and the awakened interest in human relations during the 1930's and 1940's, who see management as a complex of interpersonal relationships and the basis of management theory the tentative tenets of the new and undeveloped science of psychology. There are also those who see management theory as simply a manifestation of the institutional and cultural aspects of sociology. Still others, observing that the central core of management is decision-making, branch in all directions from this core to encompass everything in organization life. Then, there are mathematicians who think of management primarily as an exercise in logical relationships expressed in symbols and the omnipresent and ever revered model. But the entanglement of growth reaches its ultimate when the study of management is regarded as a study of one of a number of systems and subsystems, with an understandable tendency for the researcher to be dissatisfied until he has encompassed the entire physical and cultural universe as a management system.

With the recent discovery of an ages-old problem area by social, physical, and biological scientists, and with the supersonic increase in interest by all types of enterprise managers, the apparent impenetrability of the present thicket which we call management theory is not difficult to comprehend. One can hardly be surprised that psychologists, sociologists, anthropologists, sociometricists, economists, mathematicians, physicists, biologists, political scientists, business administration scholars, and even practicing managers, should hop on this interesting, challenging, and profitable band wagon.

This welling of interest from every academic and practicing corner should not upset anyone concerned with seeing the frontiers of knowledge pushed back and the intellectual base of practice broadened. But what is rather upsetting to the practitioner and the observer, who sees great social potential from improved management, is that the variety of approaches to management theory has led to a kind of confused and destructive jungle warfare. Particularly among academic disciplines and their disciples, the primary interests of many would-be cult leaders seem to be to carve out a distinct (and hence "original") approach to management. And to defend this originality, and thereby gain a place in posterity (or at least to gain a publication which will justify academic status or promotion), it seems to have become too much the current style to downgrade, and sometimes misrepresent, what anyone else has said, or thought, or done.

In order to cut through this jungle and bring to light some of the issues and problems involved in the present management theory area so that the tremendous interest, intelligence, and research results may become more meaningful, it is my purpose here to classify the various "schools" of management theory, to identify briefly what I believe to be the major source of differences, and to offer some suggestions for disentangling the jungle. It is hoped that a movement for clarification can be started so at least we in the field will not be a group of blind men identifying the same elephant with our widely varying and sometimes viciously argumentative theses.

THE MAJOR "SCHOOLS" OF MANAGEMENT THEORY

In attempting to classify the major schools of management theory into six main groups, I am aware that I may overlook certain approaches and cannot deal with all the nuances of each approach. But it does seem that most of the approaches to management theory can be classified in one of these so-called "schools."

The Management Process School This approach to management theory perceives management as a process of getting things done through and with people operating in organized groups. It aims to analyze the process, to establish a conceptual framework for it, to identify principles underlying it, and to build up a theory of management from them. It regards management as a universal process, regardless of the type of enterprise, or the level in a given enterprise, although recognizing, obviously, that the environment of management differs widely between enterprises and levels. It looks upon management theory as a way of organizing experience so that practice can be improved through research, empirical testing of principles, and teaching of fundamentals involved in the management process.[1]

Often referred to, especially by its critics, as the "traditional" or "universalist" school, this school can be said to have been fathered by Henri Fayol, although many of his offspring did not know of their parent, since Fayol's work was eclipsed by the bright light of his contemporary, Frederick Taylor, and clouded by the lack of a widely available English translation until 1949. Other than Fayol, most of the early contributors to this school dealt only with the organization portion of the management process, largely because of their greater experience with this facet of management and the simple fact that planning and control, as well as the function of staffing, were given little attention by managers before 1940.

This school bases its approach to management theory on several fundamental beliefs:

1. that managing is a process and can best be dissected intellectually by analyzing the functions of the manager;
2. that long experience with management in a variety of enterprise situations can be grounds for distillation of certain fundamental truths or generalizations—usually referred to as principles—which have a clarifying and predictive value in the understanding and improvement of managing;
3. that these fundamental truths can become focal points for useful research both to ascertain their validity and to improve their meaning and applicability in practice;
4. that such truths can furnish elements, at least until disproved, and certainly until sharpened, of a useful theory of management;
5. that managing is an art, but one like medicine or engineering, which can be improved by reliance on the light and understanding of principles;
6. that principles in management, like principles in the biological and physical sciences, are nonetheless true even if a prescribed treatment or design by a practitioner in a given case situation chooses to ignore a principle and the costs involved, or attempts to do something else to offset the costs incurred (this is, of course, not new in medicine, engineering, or any other art, for art is the creative task of compromising fundamentals to attain a desired result); and
7. that, while the totality of culture and of the physical and biological universe has varying effects on the manager's environment and subjects, as indeed they do in every other field of science and art, the theory of management does not need to encompass the field of all knowledge in order for it to serve as a scientific or theoretical foundation.

The basic approach of this school, then, is to look, first, to the functions of managers. As a second step in this approach, many of us have taken the functions of managers and further dissected them by distilling what we see as fundamental truths in the understandably complicated practice of management. I have found it useful to classify my analysis of these functions around the essentials involved in the following questions:

1. What is the nature of the function?
2. What is the purpose of the function?
3. What explains the structure of the function?
4. What explains the process of the function?

Perhaps there are other more useful approaches, but I have found that I can place everything pertaining to management (even some of the rather remote research and concepts) in this framework.

Also, purely to make the area of management theory intellectually manageable, those who subscribe to this school do not usually attempt to include in the theory the entire areas of sociology, economics, biology, psychology, physics, chemistry, or others. This is done not because these other areas of knowledge are unimportant and have no bearing on management, but merely because no real progress has ever been made in science or art without significant partitioning of knowledge. Yet, anyone would be foolish not to realize that a function which deals with people in their various activities of producing and marketing

[1] It is interesting that one of the scholars strongly oriented to human relations and behavioral approaches to management has recently noted that "theory can be viewed as a way of organizing experience" and that "once initial sense is made out of experienced environment, the way is cleared for an even more adequate organization of this experience." See Robert Dubin in "Psyche, Sensitivity, and Social Structure," critical comment in Robert Tannenbaum, I. R. Weschler, and Fred Massarik, *Leadership and Organization: A Behavioral Science Approach,* McGraw-Hill Book Company, New York, 1961, p. 401.

anything from money to religion and education is completely independent of the physical, biological, and cultural universe in which we live. And, are there not such relationships in other "compartments" of knowledge and theory?

The Empirical School A second approach to management I refer to as the "empirical" school. In this, I include those scholars who identify management as a study of experience, sometimes with intent to draw generalizations but usually merely as a means of teaching experience and transferring it to the practitioner or student. Typical of this school are those who see management or "policy" as the study and analysis of cases and those with such approaches as Ernest Dale's "comparative approach."[2]

This approach seems to be based upon the premise that, if we study the experience of successful managers, or the mistakes made in management, or if we attempt to solve management problems, we will somehow understand and learn to apply the most effective kinds of management techniques. This approach, as often applied, assumes that, by finding out what worked or did not work in individual circumstances, the student or the practitioner will be able to do the same in comparable situations.

No one can deny the importance of studying experience through such study, or of analyzing the "how-it-was-done" of management. But management, unlike law, is not a science based on precedent, and situations in the future exactly comparable to the past are exceedingly unlikely to occur. Indeed, there is a positive danger of relying too much on past experience and on undistilled history of managerial problem-solving for the simple reason that a technique or approach found "right" in the past may not fit a situation of the future.

Those advocating the empirical approach are likely to say that what they really do in analyzing cases or history is to draw from certain generalizations which can be applied as useful guides to thought or action in future case situations. As a matter of fact, Ernest Dale, after claiming to find "so little practical value" from the principles enunciated by the "universalists," curiously drew certain "generalizations" or "criteria" from his valuable study of a number of great practitioners of management.[3] There is some question as to whether Dale's "comparative" approach is not really the same as the "universalist" approach he decries, except with a different distiller of basic truths.

By the emphasis of the empirical school on study of experience, it does appear that the research and thought so engendered may assist in hastening the day for verification of principles. It is also possible that the proponents of this school may come up with a more useful framework of principles than that of the management process school. But, to the extent that the empirical school draws generalizations from its research, and it would seem to be a necessity to do so unless its members are satisfied to exchange meaningless and structureless experience, this approach tends to be and do the same as the management process school.

The Human Behavior School This approach to the analysis of management is based on the central thesis that, since managing involves getting things done with and through people, the study of management must be centered on interpersonal relations. Variously called the "human relations," "leadership," or "behavioral sciences" approach, this school brings to bear "existing and newly developed theories, methods, and techniques of the relevant social sciences upon the study of inter- and intrapersonal phenomena, ranging fully from the personality dynamics of individuals at one extreme to the relations of cultures at the other."[4] In other words, this school concentrates on the "people" part of management and rests on the principle that, where people work together as groups in order to accomplish objectives, "people should understand people."

The scholars in this school have a heavy orientation to psychology and social psychology. Their primary focus is the individual as a socio-psychological being and what motivates him. The members of this school vary from those who see it as a portion of the manager's job, a tool to help him understand and get the best from people by meeting their needs and responding to their motivations, to those who see the psychological behavior of individuals and groups as the total of management.

In this school are those who emphasize human relations as an art that the manager should advantageously understand and practice. There are those who focus attention on the manager as a leader and sometimes equate management to leadership, thus, in effect, tending to treat all group activities as "managed" situations. There are those who see the study

[2] Ernest Dale, *The Great Organizers: Theory and Practice of Organization*, McGraw-Hill Book Company, New York, 1960, pp. 11–28.

[3] *Ibid.*, pp. 11, 26–28, 62–66.

[4] Tannenbaum, Weschler, and Massarik, *op. cit.*, p. 9.

of group dynamics and interpersonal relationships as simply a study of socio-psychological relationships and seem, therefore, merely to be attaching the term "management" to the field of social psychology.

That management must deal with human behavior can hardly be denied. That the study of human interactions, whether in the environment of management or in unmanaged situations, is important and useful one could not dispute. And it would be a serious mistake to regard good leadership as unimportant to good managership. But whether the field of human behavior is the equivalent of the field of management is quite another thing. Perhaps it is like calling the study of the human body the field of cardiology.

The Social System School Closely related to the human behavior school and often confused or intertwined with it is one which might be labeled the social system school. This includes those researchers who look upon management as a social system, that is, a system of cultural interrelationships. Sometimes, as in the case of March and Simon,[5] the system is limited to formal organizations, using the term "organization" as equivalent to enterprise, rather than the authority-activity concept used most often in management. In other cases, the approach is not to distinguish the formal organization, but rather to encompass any kind of system of human relationships.

Heavily sociological in flavor, this approach to management does essentially what any study of sociology does. It identifies the nature of the cultural relationships of various social groups and attempts to show these as a related, and usually an integrated, system.

Perhaps the spiritual father of this ardent and vocal school of management theorists is Chester Barnard.[6] In searching for an answer to fundamental explanations underlying the managing process, this thoughtful business executive developed a theory of cooperation grounded in the needs of the individual to solve, through cooperation, the biological, physical, and social limitations of himself and his environment. Barnard then carved from the total of cooperative systems so engendered one set of interrelationships which he defines as "formal organization." His formal organization concept, quite unlike that usually held by management practitioners, is any cooperative system in which there are persons able to communicate with each other and who are willing to contribute action toward a conscious common purpose.

The Barnard concept of cooperative systems pervades the work of many contributors to the social system school of management. For example, Herbert Simon at one time defined the subject of organization theory and the nature of human organizations as "systems of interdependent activity, encompassing at least several primary groups and usually characterized, at the level of consciousness of participants, by a high degree of rational direction of behavior toward ends that are objects of common knowledge."[7] Simon and others have subsequently seemed to have expanded this concept of social systems to include any cooperative and purposeful group interrelationship or behavior.

This school has made many noteworthy contributions to management. The recognition of organized enterprise as a social organism, subject to all the pressures and conflicts of the cultural environment, has been helpful to the management theorist and the practitioner alike. Among some of the more helpful aspects are the awareness of the institutional foundations of organization authority, the influence of informal organization, and such social factors as those Wight Bakke has called the "bonds of organization."[8] Likewise, many of Barnard's helpful insights, such as his economy of incentives and his theory of opportunism, have brought the power of sociological understanding into the realm of management practice.

Basic sociology, analysis of concepts of social behavior, and the study of group behavior in the framework of social systems do have great value in the field of management. But one may well ask the question whether this *is* management. Is the field of management coterminous with the field of sociology? Or is sociology an important underpinning like language, psychology, physiology, mathematics, and other fields of knowledge? Must management be defined in terms of the universe of knowledge?

[5] J. G. March and H. A. Simon, *Organizations*, John Wiley & Sons, Inc., New York, 1958.

[6] Chester Barnard, *The Functions of the Executive*, Harvard University Press, Cambridge, Mass., 1938.

[7] "Comments on the Theory of Organizations," *American Political Science Review, vol.* 46, no. 4, p. 1130, December, 1952.

[8] Wight Bakke, *Bonds of Organization*, Harper & Row, Publishers, Incorporated, New York, 1950. These "bonds" or "devices" of organization are identified by Bakke as (1) the functional specifications system (a system of teamwork arising from job specifications and arrangements for association); (2) the status system (a vertical hierarchy of authority); (3) the communications system; (4) the reward and penalty system; and (5) the organization charter (ideas and means which give character and individuality to the organization, or enterprise).

The Decision Theory School Another approach to management theory, undertaken by a growing and scholarly group, might be referred to as the decision theory school. This group concentrates on rational approach to decision—the selection from among possible alternatives of a course of action or of an idea. The approach of this school may be to deal with the decision itself, or to the persons or organizational group making the decision, or to an analysis of the decision process. Some limit themselves fairly much to the economic rationale of the decision, while others regard anything which happens in an enterprise the subject of their analysis, and still others expand decision theory to cover the psychological and sociological aspect and environment of decisions and decision-makers.

The decision-making school is apparently an outgrowth of the theory of consumer's choice with which economists have been concerned since the days of Jeremy Bentham early in the nineteenth century. It has arisen out of such economic problems and analyses as utility maximization, indifference curves, marginal utility, and economic behavior under risks and uncertainties. It is, therefore, no surprise that one finds most of the members of this school to be economic theorists. It is likewise no surprise to find the content of this school to be heavily oriented to model construction and mathematics.

The decision theory school has tended to expand its horizon considerably beyond the process of evaluating alternatives. That point has become for many only a springboard for examination of the entire sphere of human activity, including the nature of the organization structure, psychological and social reactions of individuals and groups, the development of basic information for decisions, an analysis of values and particularly value considerations with respect to goals, communications networks, and incentives. As one would expect, when the decision theorists study the small, but central, area of decision *making,* they are led by this keyhole look at management to consider the entire field of enterprise operation and its environment. The result is that decision theory becomes no longer a neat and narrow concentration on decision, but rather a broad view of the enterprise as a social system.

There are those who believe that, since management is characterized by its concentration on decisions, the future development of management theory will tend to use the decision as its central focus and the rest of management theory will be hung on this structural center. This may occur and certainly the study of the decision, the decision process, and the decision maker can be extended to cover the entire field of management as anyone might conceive it. Nevertheless, one wonders whether this focus cannot also be used to build around it the entire area of human knowledge. For, as most decision theorists recognize, the problem of choice is individual, as well as organizational, and most of what has been said that is pure decision theory can be applied to the existence and thinking of a Robinson Crusoe.

The Mathematical School Although mathematical methods can be used by any school of management theory, and have been, I have chosen to group under a school those theorists who see management as a system of mathematical models and processes. Perhaps the most widely known group I arbitrarily so lump are the operations researchers or operations analysts, who have sometimes anointed themselves with the rather pretentious name of "management scientists." The abiding belief of this group is that, if management, or organization, or planning, or decision making is a logical process, it can be expressed in terms of mathematical symbols and relationships. The central approach of this school is the model, for it is through these devices that the problem is expressed in its basic relationships and in terms of selected goals or objectives.

There can be no doubt of the great usefulness of mathematical approaches to any field of inquiry. It forces upon the researcher the definition of a problem or problem area, it conveniently allows the insertion of symbols for unknown data, and its logical methodology, developed by years of scientific application and abstraction, furnishes a powerful tool for solving or simplifying complex phenomena.

But it is hard to see mathematics as a truly separate school of management theory, any more than it is a separate "school" in physics, chemistry, engineering, or medicine. I only deal with it here as such because there has appeared to have developed a kind of cult around mathematical analysts who have subsumed to themselves the area of management.

In pointing out that mathematics is a tool, rather than a school, it is not my intention to underestimate the impact of mathematics on the science and practice of management. By bringing to this immensely important and complex field the tools and techniques of the physical sciences, the mathematicians have already made an immense contribution to orderly thinking. They have forced on people in management the means and desirability of seeing many problems more clearly, they have pressed on scholars and practitioners the need for establishing goals and measures of effectiveness, they have been extremely helpful in getting the management area seen as a logical system of relationships, and they have caused people in management to review and occasionally reorganize information sources and systems so that mathematics can be given sensible quantitative meaning. But with all this meaningful contribution and the greater sharpness and sophistication of planning which is resulting, I cannot see that mathematics is management theory any more than it is astronomy.

THE MAJOR SOURCES OF MENTAL ENTANGLEMENT IN THE JUNGLE

In outlining the various schools, or approaches, of management theory, it becomes clear that these intellectual cults are not drawing greatly different inferences from the physical and cultural environment surrounding us. Why, then, have there been so many differences between them and why such a struggle, particularly among our academic brethren to obtain a place in the sun by denying the approaches of others? Like the widely differing and often contentious denominations of the Christian religion, all have essentially the same goals and deal with essentially the same world.

While there are many sources of the mental entanglement in the management theory jungle, the major ones are the following:

The Semantics Jungle As is so often true when intelligent men argue about basic problems, some of the trouble lies in the meaning of key words. The semantics problem is particularly severe in the field of management. There is even a difference in the meaning of the word "management." Most people would agree that it means getting things done through and with people, but is it people in formal organizations, or in all group activities? Is it governing, leading, or teaching?

Perhaps the greatest single semantics confusion lies in the word "organization." Most members of the management process school use it to define the activity-authority structure of an enterprise and certainly most practitioners believe that they are "organizing" when they establish a framework of activity groupings and authority relationships. In this case, organization represents the formal framework within an enterprise that furnishes the environment in which people perform. Yet a large number of "organization" theorists conceive of organization as the sum total of human relationships in any group activity; they thus seem to make it equivalent to *social* structure. And some use "organization" to mean "enterprise."

If the meaning of organization cannot be clarified and a standard use of the term adopted by management theorists, understanding and criticism should not be based on this difference. It hardly seems to me to be accurate for March and Simon, for example, to criticize the organization theories of the management process, or "universalist," school for not considering the management planning function as part of organizing, when they have chosen to treat it separately. Nor should those who choose to treat the training, selecting, guiding or leading of people under staffing and direction be criticized for a tendency to "view the employee as an inert instrument" or a "given rather than a variable."[9] Such accusations, proceeding from false premises, are clearly erroneous.

Other semantic entanglements might be mentioned. By some, decision-making is regarded as a process of choosing from among alternatives; by others, the total managerial task and environment. Leadership is often made synonymous with managership and is analytically separated by others. Communications may mean everything from a written or oral report to a vast network of formal and informal relationships. Human relations to some implies a psychiatric manipulation of people, but to others the study and art of understanding people and interpersonal relationships.

Differences in Definition of Management as a Body of Knowledge As was indicated in the discussion of semantics, "management" has far from a standard meaning, although most agree that it at least involves getting things done through and with people. But, does it mean the dealing with all human relationships? Is a street peddler a manager? Is a parent a manager? Is a leader of a disorganized mob a manager? Does the field of management equal the fields of sociology and social psychology combined? Is it the equivalent of the entire system of social relationships?

While I recognize that sharp lines cannot be drawn in management any more than they are in medicine or engineering, there surely can be a sharper distinction drawn than at present. With the plethora of management writing and experts, calling almost everything under the sun "management," can one expect management theory to be regarded as very useful or scientific to the practitioner?

[9] March and Simon, *op. cit.*, pp. 29–33.

The *a priori* Assumption Confusion in management theory has also been heightened by the tendency for many newcomers in the field to cast aside significant observations and analyses of the past on the grounds that they are *a priori* in nature. This is an often-met accusation made by those who wish to cast aside the work of Fayol, Mooney, Brown, Urwick, Gulick, and others who are branded as "universalists." To make the assumption that the distilled experiences of men such as these represent *a priori* reasoning is to forget that experience in and with managing *is* empirical. While the conclusions that perceptive and experienced practitioners of the art of management are not infallible, they represent an experience which is certainly real and not "armchair." No one could deny, I feel sure, that the ultimate test of accuracy of management theory must be practice and management theory and science must be developed from reality.

The Misunderstanding of Principles
Those who feel that they gain caste or a clean slate for advancing a particular notion or approach often delight in casting away anything which smacks of management principles. Some have referred to them as platitudes, forgetting that a platitude is still a truism and a truth does not become worthless because it is familiar. (As Robert Frost has written, "Most of the changes we think we see in life are merely truths going in or out of favor.") Others cast away principles of Fayol and other practitioners, only to draw apparently different generalizations from their study of management; but many of the generalizations so discovered are often the same fundamental truths in different words that certain criticized "universalists" have discovered.

One of the favorite tricks of the managerial theory trade is to disprove a whole framework of principles by reference to one principle which the observer sees disregarded in practice. Thus, many critics of the universalists point to the well-known cases of dual subordination in organized enterprise, coming to the erroneous conclusion that there is no substance to the principle of unity of command. But this does not prove that there is no cost to the enterprise by designing around, or disregarding, the principle of unity of command; nor does it prove that there were not other advantages which offset the costs, as there often are in cases of establishing functional authorities in organization.

Perhaps the almost hackneyed stand-by for those who would disprove the validity of all principles by referring to a single one is the misunderstanding around the principle of span of management (or span of control). The usual source of authority quoted by those who criticize is Sir Ian Hamilton, who never intended to state a universal principle, but rather to make a personal observation in a book of reflections on his Army experience, and who did say, offhand, that he found it wise to limit his span to 3 to 6 subordinates. No modern universalist relies on this single observation, and, indeed, few can or will state an absolute or universal numerical ceiling. Since Sir Ian was not a management theorist and did not intend to be, let us hope that the ghost of his innocent remark may be laid to deserved rest!

What concerns those who feel that a recognition of fundamental truths, or generalizations, may help in the diagnosis and study of management, and who know from managerial experience that such truths or principles do serve an extremely valuable use, is the tendency for some researchers to prove the wrong things through either misstatement or misapplication of principles. A classic case of such misunderstanding and misapplication is in Chris Argyris' interesting book on *Personality and Organization.*[10] This author, who in this book and his other works has made many noteworthy contributions to management, concludes that "formal organization principles make demands on relatively healthy individuals that are incongruent with their needs," and that "frustration, conflict, failure, and short-time perspective are predicted as results of this basic incongruency."[11] This startling conclusion—the exact opposite of what "good" formal organization based on "sound" organization principles should cause, is explained when one notes that, of four "principles" Argyris quotes, one is not an organization principle at all but the economic principle of specialization and three other "principles" are quoted incorrectly.[12] With such a postulate, and with no attempt to recognize, correctly or incorrectly, any other organization and management principles, Argyris has simply proved that wrong principles badly applied will lead to frustration; and every management practitioner knows this to be true!

The Inability or Unwillingness of Management Theorists to Understand Each Other
What has been said above leads one to the conclusion that much of the management

[10] Chris Argyris, *Personality and Organization,* Harper & Row, Publishers, Incorporated, New York, 1957.
[11] *Ibid.,* p. 74.
[12] *Ibid.,* pp. 58–66.

theory jungle is caused by the unwillingness or inability of the management theorists to understand each other. Doubting that it is inability, because one must assume that a person interested in management theory is able to comprehend, at least in concept and framework, the approaches of the various "schools," I can only come to the conclusion that the roadblock to understanding is unwillingness.

Perhaps this unwillingness comes from the professional "walls" developed by learned disciplines. Perhaps the unwillingness stems from a fear that someone or some new discovery will encroach on professional and academic status. Perhaps it is fear of professional or intellectual obsolescence. But whatever the cause, it seems that these walls will not be torn down until it is realized that they exist, until all cultists are willing to look at the approach and content of other schools, and until, through exchange and understanding of ideas some order may be brought from the present chaos.

DISENTANGLING THE MANAGEMENT THEORY JUNGLE

It is important that steps be taken to disentangle the management theory jungle. Perhaps, it is too soon and we must expect more years of wandering through a thicket of approaches, semantics, thrusts, and counterthrusts. But in any field as important to society where the many blunders of an unscientifically based managerial art can be so costly, I hope that this will not be long.

There do appear to be some things that can be done. Clearly, meeting what I see to be the major sources of the entanglement should remove much of it. The following considerations are important:

1. *The need for definition of a body of knowledge.* Certainly, if a field of knowledge is not to get bogged down in a quagmire of misunderstandings, the first need is for definition of the field. Not that it need be defined in sharp, detailed, and inflexible lines, but rather along lines which will give it fairly specific content. Because management is reality, life, practice, my suggestion would be that it be defined in the light of the able and discerning practitioner's frame of reference. A science unrelated to the art for which it is to serve is not likely to be a very productive one.

Although the study of managements in various enterprises, in various countries, and at various levels made by many persons, including myself, may neither be representative nor adequate, I have come to the conclusion that management is the art of getting things done through and with people in *formally organized groups,* the art of creating an environment in such an organized group where people can perform as individuals and yet cooperate toward attainment of group goals, the art of removing blocks to such performance, the art of optimizing efficiency in effectively reaching goals. If this kind of definition of the field is unsatisfactory, I suggest at least an agreement that the area should be defined to reflect the field of the practitioner and that further research and study of practice be done to this end.

In defining the field, too, it seems to me imperative to draw some limits for purposes of analysis and research. If we are to call the entire cultural, biological, and physical universe the field of management, we can no more make progress than could have been done if chemistry or geology had not carved out a fairly specific area and had, instead studied all knowledge.

In defining the body of knowledge, too, care must be taken to distinguish between tools and content. .Thus mathematics, operations research, accounting, economic theory, sociometry, and psychology, to mention a few, are significant *tools* of management but are not, in themselves, a part of the *content* of the field. This is not to mean that they are unimportant or that the practicing manager should not have them available to him, nor does it mean that they may not be the means of pushing back the frontiers of knowledge of management. But they should not be confused with the basic content of the field.

This is not to say that fruitful study should not continue on the underlying disciplines affecting management. Certainly knowledge of sociology, social systems, psychology, economics, political science, mathematics, and other areas, pointed toward contributing to the field of management, should be continued and encouraged. And significant findings in these and other fields of knowledge might well cast important light on, or change concepts in, the field of management. This has certainly happened in other sciences and in every other art based upon significant science.

2. *Integration of management and other disciplines.* If recognition of the proper content of the field were made, I believe that the present crossfire of misunderstanding might tend to disappear. Management would be regarded as a specific discipline and other disciplines would be looked upon as important bases of the field. Under these circumstances, the allied and underlying disciplines would be welcomed

by the business and public administration schools, as well as by practitioners, as loyal and helpful associates. Integration of management and other disciplines would then not be difficult.

3. *The clarification of management semantics.* While I would expect the need for clarification and uniformity of management semantics would largely be satisfied by definition of the field as a body of knowledge, semantics problems might require more special attention. There are not too many places where semantics are important enough to cause difficulty. Here again, I would suggest the adoption of the semantics of the intelligent practitioners, unless words are used by them so inexactly as to require special clarification. At least, we should not complicate an already complex field by developing a scientific or academic jargon which would build a language barrier between the theorist and the practitioner.

Perhaps the most expeditious way out of this problem is to establish a commission representing academic societies immediately concerned and associations of practicing managers. This would not seem to be difficult to do. And even if it were, the results would be worth the efforts.

4. *Willingness to distill and test fundamentals.* Certainly, the test of maturity and usefulness of a science is the sharpness and validity of the principles underlying it. No science, now regarded as mature, started out with a complete statement of incontrovertibly valid principles. Even the oldest sciences, such as physics, keep revising their underlying laws and discovering new principles. Yet any science has proceeded, and more than that has been useful, for centuries on the basis of generalizations, some laws, some principles, and some hypotheses.

One of the understandable sources of inferiority of the social sciences is the recognition that they are inexact sciences. On the other hand, even the so-called exact sciences are subject to a great deal of inexactness, have principles which are not completely proved, and use art in the design of practical systems and components. The often-encountered defeatist attitude of the social sciences, of which management is one, overlooks the fact that management may be explained, practice may be improved, and the goals of research may be more meaningful if we encourage attempts at perceptive distillation of experience by stating principles (or generalizations) and placing them in a logical framework. As two scientists recently said on this subject:

> The reason for this defeatist point of view regarding the social sciences may be traceable to a basic misunderstanding of the nature of scientific endeavor. What matters is not whether or to what extent inexactitudes in procedures and predictive capability can eventually be removed . . . : rather it is *objectivity,* i.e., the intersubjectivity of findings independent of any one person's intuitive judgment, which distinguishes science from intuitive guesswork however brilliant. . . . But once a new fact or a new idea has been conjectured, no matter how intuitive a foundation, it must be capable of objective test and confirmation by anyone. And it is this crucial standard of scientific objectivity rather than any purported criterion of exactitude to which the social sciences must conform.[13]

In approaching the clarification of management theory, then, we should not forget a few criteria:

1. The theory should deal with an area of knowledge and inquiry that is "manageable"; no great advances in knowledge were made so long as man contemplated the whole universe;
2. The theory should be *useful* in improving practice and the task and person of the practitioner should not be overlooked;
3. The theory should not be lost in semantics, especially useless jargon not understandable to the practitioner;
4. The theory should give direction and efficiency to research and teaching; and
5. The theory must recognize that it is a part of a larger universe of knowledge and theory.

[13] O. Helmer and N. Rescher, "On the Epistemology of the Inexact Sciences," The Rand Corporation, P-1513, Santa Monica, Calif., pp. 4–5.

4 FUTURE MANAGEMENT THEORY: A "COMPARATIVE" EVOLUTION TO A GENERAL THEORY*

William T. Greenwood

Management theory has been in a rapid ferment of evolution over the past decade of time. But prior to the mid-1950s there was no universally developed and taught theory, as attested to by the many Departments of Production and Personnel Management at that time.

Ever since the management theory jungle was defined by Koontz in 1961,[48] a wide array of developments has taken place, in both a concurrent and sequential fashion. In the decade of the 1960s a number of concurrently developing theories came into their own, with many tending to be substituted for traditional "process" theory, and others as more "in-depth" studies of different management functions. An overview of management theory today would include the following: Production and Personnel Management; Management "Process" Principles and Theory; Human Relations, Organizational Behavior and Organization Theories; Management Science; Decision Theory; Operations Research; Quantitative Methods and Models; Systems Theory; Management Philosophy—Business and Society Environment; Comparative Theory—International and Intercultural; and a General Theory of Administration. These may be reduced to the four major sequential streams of management theory development, many of which have concurrently evolved over the past two decades.

PRODUCTION MANAGEMENT AND MANAGEMENT SCIENCE (DECISION THEORY, OPERATIONS RESEARCH, QUANTITATIVE METHODS, SYSTEMS THEORY, AND CYBERNETICS)

Evolving from Frederick W. Taylor's scientific management and the industrial engineering influence on production operations, an early production-organization-management theory was presented by Anderson and Schwenning[2] which gave both an organizational theory for the firm as well as the production function and also included a treatment of some management functions. Following this came a strong managerial orientation toward production management by Timms,[84] followed more recently by new trends toward operations research and quantitative models by Buffa.[14]

Concurrently with the questionable survival of production as a field of management theory has been the rapid evolution of the management sciences. First under this heading, but only recently receiving significant emphasis, is the field of decision theory. This field emerged from the statistical decision theories of Chernoff and Moses[15] and of Pratt, Raiffa, and Schlaifer,[70] but the label "decision theory" has also been applied to the contributions toward decision models and processes by Bross,[13] the interdisciplinary analyses of the decision process as in the field of psychology by Edwards,[25] and particular applications of the decision process to organizations by Simon.[78,79] Decision theory, now becoming a field unto itself, has been approached in a number of ways; for example, (a) as an overlay or restructuring of the management process by Newman and Summer,[67] and (b) as compiled for organizations by Alexis and Wilson[1] and by Shull, Delbecq and Cummings.[77]

Operations research theory, the major development in the management sciences, can be dated from the late 1950s by Churchman, Arnoff, and Ackoff;[16] and the equation of operations research with management science, more recently by Brambilla.[12] The mathematical and computer applied models integral to operations research brought about the concurrent developments of quantitative methods and models with a new orientation toward the quantitative analysis of business-management problems by Fetter.[30]

Last, but certainly not least, has been the concurrent development of systems theory. This can be traced historically from the analysis of production control systems, systems analyses in motion and time studies, the emergence of systems theory by Johnson, Kast, and Rosenzweig[44] and management systems by Young,[91]

* Reprinted by permission of the publisher from *Academy of Management Journal,* vol. 17, no. 4, pp. 739–754 (December 1974). Mr. Greenwood is research professor of management, University of Georgia. This paper was originally presented at the Academy of Management, Western Division, meeting, Yosemite, California, April 1972.

and from an earlier and more basic work on systems analysis by Optner.[69] Other applications of systematic approaches to both the firm and management have been found in attempts to appraise or audit management scientifically by Martindell[62] and in management audit systems applied to the decisions of the firm and the functions of managers by Greenwood.[38] The epitome of the systems approach is found in the totally automated factory or total system of cybernetics by Beer.[6]

The developments in these fields or subfields of management have evolved to the development of different systems and models: (a) Production control systems, (b) Systems and/or operations research analyses leading to the development of problem, department, and companywide mathematical-quantitative method models, and (c) Management (sometimes organizational) systems theories and models. These developments are increasingly identified as Management Science developments—in search of a theory.

PERSONNEL MANAGEMENT, HUMAN RELATIONS, ORGANIZATIONAL BEHAVIOR, AND ORGANIZATION THEORIES

The full sweep of history of personnel management as an integral part of management theory fortunately has been developed by Ling,[54] and the research findings have been made available for over 30 years by Yoder,[90] followed by a strong managerial approach since the late 1940s by Jucius.[46]

The human relations function emerged as part of the personnel management problems of both general managers and staff personnel managers, dating from the 1930s in the work of Mayo[63] and of Roethlisberger.[72] It became an integral part of the management department curricula in the late 1950s, especially with the delineation of the field by Keith Davis[20] and its evaluation in the latter part of the decade by Scott.[74]

The concurrently emerging organizational behavior and organization theories have attempted to supplant human relations as an integral part of management theory. The study of organizational, individual, and group conflicts ran parallel to human relations problems, but emerged in a stronger theory position in the decade of the 1960s by Lawrence et al.;[52] and some attempts were made toward the development of a theory of organizational behavior by Presthus.[71] But the more significant developments occurred in the field within the new organization theories, discussed below.

Traditional management "process" theory serves as "traditional" organization theory with definitive works in the field by Dale[19] and the emergence of principles of management in the mid-1950s by Terry[82] and by Koontz and O'Donnell.[51] But these early traditional treatments of business organizational structures became the target of critiques by the newly emerging organization theories, not restricted to business organizations. The more important of these include observations of the business organization as a social system by Barnard;[4] analogies of traditional organizations with bureaucracy by Weber;[88] and the search for a theory for all types of organizations, business or nonbusiness, by March and Simon.[61] These have been followed by well-known critiques of contemporary business organizational management in terms of its dehumanizing influence by Argyris,[3] authoritarian leadership by McGregor,[58] failures to consider group interaction and adaptive behavior patterns by Likert,[53] lack of attention to coordination problems by Sayles,[73] and a systems analysis of these organizations by Thompson.[83]

It is significant to note that the concurrent evolutionary developments in the fields of personnel, human relations, organizational behavior, and organization theories marked a number of achievements. First, personnel management still survives as an integral field in terms of the pervasive problems in the management of this function in the overwhelming majority of business organizations today. While human relations as a theory appears to have been absorbed in organizational behavior or organization theories, the necessity of providing training and education in organizational conflicts should insure that the study of human relations problems be maintained for the preparation of the management practitioner. And, finally, the emergence of organization theories, now being treated in a highly comparative fashion, for business and nonbusiness organizations and for different types of business organizations, gives us the first insight toward the evolution of perhaps a general theory of administration, comparatively derived.

BASIC MANAGEMENT THEORY AND PHILOSOPHY: PROCESS, BUSINESS AND SOCIETY, AND COMPARATIVE MANAGEMENT THEORY AND PRACTICE

Management process and principles have been in evolution since the turn of the century, as is well documented in three historical analyses by George,[34] by Mee,[64] and by Wren.[89] A first comparative analysis of different approaches to the formulation of the management functions and process by Urwick[85] preceded other delineations of the process by R. C. Davis[22] and by Newman,[66] but the development of the principles approach by Terry[82] and by Koontz and O'Donnell[51] established the management process as the basic theory of the field. This process has been supported by management practitioners, training for management by the American Management Association, and the writings of practitioners such as Cordiner[17] and Houser[42] as well as theoretician-consultants such as Drucker,[24] and a comparative analysis of management by Dale.[19] Since the turn of the decade of the 1960s, theory refinements primarily have been through contributions from the behavioral and quantitative sciences, resulting in eclectic modifications of management process theory. This has resulted in an evolutionary refinement of management process theory with varying approximations of syntheses of the concurrently and sequentially developing theories.

Management philosophy has a very spotty record, but nevertheless a very necessary one if management theory is ever to become complete. The field still relies on a rather dated but significant approach to the subject by Sheldon,[76] but some notable writings have been done in more recent years by R. C. Davis[22] and by Gast,[33] who gave a philosophical derivation of a philosophy and principles of management. The present and future state of management philosophy by Jones[45] and by Mee[65] tend to parallel the present and future development of management theory in general, as outlined throughout this paper. Fortunately, at least one philosophical history of business, by Eells and Walton,[26] does provide a broad sweep of the philosophical issues for the management theory literature.

The philosophical questions of management and business have been treated in the decade of the 1960s under the headings of "Business and Society" by Smith[80] and by McGuire,[59] "Business and Its Environment" by Davis and Blomstrom,[21] and the "Social Responsibilities of the Businessman" by Bowen,[11] rather than under the heading of business or management philosophy.

The survival of any management theory tends to rest upon its universality of practice and study. Unfortunately, the practice of management theory is overwhelmingly oriented to the management process, while the study, writing, and development of theories in the field have almost abandoned this approach. The question of universality of application of American management philosophy abroad by Gonzalez and McMillan[35] has brought about the emergence of comparative management practices as a new field of study in management theory. In general, the universality and transferability of American management theory has been affirmed at a very high level for management concepts, principles, and theory that constitute the science versus the art of management by Koontz.[50] "Comparative Management," as the term is most widely used by Richman and Farmer,[29] has been applied to management practices in different countries and cultures. Earlier studies of management practice in other countries by Harbison and Myers[41] point out their general evolution toward management practice and theory as found in the United States, or as found in the more industrialized countries. The different international-intercultural influences on management practice and theory by Webber[87] have led to the study of management in different areas of the world as, for example, in Europe by Nowotny,[68] the Soviet Union by Berliner,[8] Latin America by McCann,[57] Japan by Froomkin,[32] and many other particular nations throughout the world.

Comparative management practice and theory may also be applied to the management of nonbusiness institutions. This would include educational administration by Halpin,[39] army management by Beishline[7] and by Hanson,[40] political or public administrative theory by Kaufman,[47] religious administration,[60] etc. Other management theories have been developed or modified for particular applications to institutionalized fields within the economy, such as hospitals by Coser[18] and bank management by Litzinger.[56] When the point of management theory maturity is reached, practitioners may be found testing and refining academic theories and the theoreticians submitting new theory formulations for application testing in the actual business environment. This may be the point in time when the management science theory becomes more universal, from a more common body of knowledge, resulting in a General Theory and Science of Management. One of the first steps in this direction should be a comparative and exclusive study of management theory effectiveness by excluding all nonmanagerial factors, such as diverse business functions and external environmental (including cultural) factors as in Koontz.[50]

Management theories may also be developed and refined in their applications to many particular industries and institutions. Practitioner applications could include agriculture, mining, contract construction, the different manufacturing industries, public utilities, wholesale and retail industries, financial institutions, the rapidly growing consumer and business services, and governmental administration. This, therefore, presents a more comprehensive challenge for comparative management theory formulation and testing than does a mere international comparison.

The comparative approach to the study of business by Boddewyn[9] has been evaluated by a comparative administration task force within the Academy of Management by Ericson,[28] and a statement on these developments toward a possible synthesis of administrative theory via the comparative administrative approach also has been provided by Ericson.[27] Unfortunately, the so-called comparative approach is most often interpreted today as an international or intercultural analysis of management in the different nations of the world. Since comparative analyses have been made at different stages in the development of management theory by Urwick[85] and by Dale[19] and since many organization theories have been evaluated on a comparative basis, it is most likely that the evolutionary development of management theory will inescapably be achieved through the comparative analysis of the many concurrently developing theories. As these theories are pitted against each other, some will pass away, with the good parts abstracted and incorporated in the surviving theories.

In conclusion, therefore, it appears that management theory will evolve through comparative theory evaluations and universality application tests of management practices in:

1. Differing business and nonbusiness organizations,
2. Different nations and cultures, and
3. Different industries and institutions.

A GENERAL THEORY OF ADMINISTRATION

The first approximation of a general theory of administration was presented for the field as early as the year 1956 by Litchfield[55] and reconstructed in the following year by Green and Redmond[36] in a schematic model of the general theory. A general theory as the next development in management science has been forecast by Frederick,[31] and its development via a comparative administration theory synthesis has been predicted by Ericson.[27] The most significant step taken toward the evaluation of a general theory was a symposium held on this subject in the early 1960s by Koontz,[49] but no consensus was reached by the group. Nevertheless, it was reported that such a theory synthesis should be achieved through an interdisciplinary approach. This perspective was supported by another analysis, by Mee,[65] made against the framework of a twentieth century history of management thought, in which it was expected that future management philosophy and a general theory of administration would most likely evolve in an interdisciplinary fashion.

The interdisciplinary approach has been developing, especially in the past decade, with contributions from many different disciplines in increasing numbers. But the interdisciplinary approach may also be (a) intercontextual, as in Ericson,[28] in which the different theories from different disciplines are analytically compared and eventually integrated and synthesized; or (b) it may be taken from the start of a general theory, as in Huff and McGuire,[43] in which all of the disciples are initially synthesized in the development of the general system. A third alternative would be to integrate those interdisciplinary contributions into the management process theory which has been most universally developed, studied, and applied by management practitioners since the turn of the century, as in Greenwood.[37]

These three approaches probably will be pursued concurrently in the immediate future and, hopefully, by the end of this decade a complete statement of a general theory of administration will have emerged.

Based upon these findings, the following conclusions-hypotheses may be considered for the future:

FUTURE MANAGEMENT THEORY

1. Production and personnel management will continue concurrent developments as sub or applied fields to the field of management theory. They probably will incorporate the new contributions from many disciplines, but it is unlikely that they will be substituted for these fields because of the continuing professional needs of industry.
2. The comparative study of management theories will become the dominant approach in the decade of the 1970s. This will mean that "comparative" will no longer simply mean international or intercultural, as it has been until now. The comparative approach will include:
   a. Many theories from different academic disciplines,
   b. The application and testing of theory in different nations and cultures,
   c. The application of theory to business and nonbusiness organizations, and

   d. The comparative application of management theory to different industries and institutions.
3. Management process theory will remain the standard against which all other theories will be compared. The possibility exists that systems theory may take over and subsume this process theory, but this remains to be seen, possibly within the coming decade. In the meantime, process theory should continue to be refined by comparative analyses with other theories, and especially theories from other disciplines.
4. A general theory of administration appears as the ultimate point of the evolutionary development of both management theory and practice comparisons, and leaves the following alternatives:
   a. An evolutionary integration of intercontexual and interdisciplinary theories,
   b. The development of a completely new and all embracing general management systems theory, evolving from general systems theory, and
   c. A continuing refinement of traditional management process theory and practice by the voluntary integration of theories of other disciplines.

REFERENCES

1. Alexis, Marcus, and Charles Z. Wilson. *Organizational Decision Making* (Englewood Cliffs, N.J.: Prentice-Hall, 1967).
2. Anderson, E. H., and G. T. Schwenning. *The Science of Production Organization* (New York: Wiley, 1938).
3. Argyris, Chris. *Personality and Organization: The Conflict Between the System and the Individual* (New York: Harper and Row, 1957).
4. Barnard, Chester I. *The Functions of the Executive* (Cambridge, Mass.: Harvard University Press, 1938).
5. Barnes, Ralph M. *Motion and Time Study* (New York: Wiley, 1937), revised 1968.
6. Beer, Stafford, *Cybernetics and Management* (New York: Wiley, 1959).
7. Beishline, J. R. *Military Management for National Defense* (Englewood Cliffs, N.J.: Prentice-Hall, 1950).
8. Berliner, Joseph. "Managerial Incentives and Decision Making: A Comparison of the United States and the Soviet Union," *Comparisons of the United States and Soviet Economies,* Joint Economic Committee, Congress of the United States, 1959.
9. Boddewyn, J. "The Comparative Approach to the Study of Business Administration," *Academy of Management Journal,* Vol. 8 (1965), 261–267.
10. Boulding, Kenneth. "General Systems Theory: The Skeleton of Science," *Management Science,* Vol. 3 (1956), 197–208.
11. Bowen, Howard R. *Social Responsibilities of the Businessman* (New York: Harper, 1953).
12. Brambilla, Francesio. "Operations Research as a Management Science," *Management International,* Vol. 1, No. 4 (1961).
13. Bross, Irwin D. J. *Design for Decision* (New York: Macmillan, 1953).
14. Buffa, Elwood S. *Models for Production and Operations Management* (New York: Wiley, 1963).
15. Chernoff, Herman, and Leonard E. Moses. *Elementary Decision Theory* (New York: Wiley, 1959).
16. Churchman, West, Russel L. Ackoff, and Leonard Arnoff. *Introduction to Operations Research* (New York: Wiley, 1957).
17. Cordiner, Ralph J. *New Frontiers for Professional Managers* (New York: McGraw-Hill, 1956).
18. Coser, Rose L. "Authority and Decision Making in a Hospital: A Comparative Analysis," *American Sociological Review,* Vol. 23, (1958), 56–63.
19. Dale, Ernest. *The Great Organizers* (New York: McGraw-Hill, 1960).
20. Davis, Keith. *Human Relations in Business* (New York: McGraw-Hill, 1954).
21. Davis, Keith, and Robert Blomstrom. *Business and Its Environment* (New York: McGraw-Hill, 1966).
22. Davis, Ralph C. *The Fundamentals of Top Management* (New York: Harper, 1951).
23. Davis, Ralph C. "A Philosophy of Management," *Journal of the Academy of Management,* Vol. 1, No. 3 (1958), 37–40.
24. Drucker, Peter. *The Practice of Management* (New York: Harper and Row, 1954).
25. Edwards, Ward. "The Theory of Decision Making," *Psychological Bulletin,* Vol. 51 (1954), 380–417.
26. Eells, Richard, and Clarence C. Walton. *Conceptual Foundations of Business* (Homewood, Ill.: Irwin, 1961).
27. Ericson, Richard F. "Comparative Administration Synthesis—Research Scholars Views on Administrative Theory," *Academy of Management Proceedings,* 1965, pp. 56–76.
28. Ericson, Richard F. "Report of the Comparative Administration Task Force," *Academy of Management Proceedings,* 1967, pp. 219–227.

29. Farmer, Richard N., and Barry M. Richman. *Comparative Management and Economic Progress* (Homewood, Ill.: Irwin, 1965).

30. Fetter, Robert B. "Management Science: The Quantitative Analysis of Management Problems," *The Manager's Key,* May, 1957.

31. Frederick, William C. "The Next Development for Management Science: A General Theory," *Journal of the Academy of Management,* Vol. 6 (1963), 212–219.

32. Froomkin, Joseph N. "Management and Organization in Japanese Industry," *Journal of the Academy of Management,* Vol. 7 (1964), 71–76.

33. Gast, Walter F. *Principles of Business Management* (St. Louis, Mo.: St. Louis University, 1953).

34. George, Claude S., Jr. *The History of Management Thought* (Englewood Cliffs, N.J.: Prentice-Hall, 1968).

35. Gonzales, Richard R., and Claude McMillan, Jr. "The Universality of Management Philosophy," *Journal of the Academy of Management,* Vol. 4 (1961), 33–42.

36. Green, Edward J., and Gover H. Redmond. "Comments on a General Theory of Administration," *Administrative Science Quarterly,* Vol. 2 (1957).

37. Greenwood, William T. *Management and Organizational Behavior Theories* (Cincinnati, Ohio: South-Western, 1965).

38. Greenwood, William T. *A Management Audit System* (Carbondale, Ill.: Southern Illinois University, 1967).

39. Halpin, Andrew W. *Theory and Research in Administration* (New York: Macmillan, 1966).

40. Hanson, Floyd A. "Management Theory in (Army) Practice," *Army Management Views,* Vol. 10 (1965), U.S. Army Management School, Fort Belvoir, Va.

41. Harbison, Frederich, and Clark A. Myers. *Management in the Industrial World* (New York: McGraw-Hill, 1959).

42. Houser, Theodore V. *Big Business and Human Values* (New York: McGraw-Hill, 1957).

43. Huff, David L., and Joseph W. McGuire. "The Interdisciplinary Approach to the Study of Business," *University of Washington Business Review,* Vol. 19, No. 9 (1960).

44. Johnson, Richard A., Fremont E. Kast, and James E. Rosenzweig. *The Theory and Management of Systems* (New York: McGraw-Hill, 1963).

45. Jones, Manley, Jr. "Evolving a Business Philosophy," *Journal of the Academy of Management,* Vol. 3 (1960), 93–98.

46. Jucius, Michael J. *Personnel Management* (Homewood, Ill.: Irwin, 1947).

47. Kaufman, Herbert. "Organization Theory and Political Theory," *American Political Science Review,* Vol. 58 (1964), 5–14.

48. Koontz, Harold. "The Management Theory Jungle," *Journal of the Academy of Management,* Vol. 4 (1961), 174–188.

49. Koontz, Harold. *Toward a Unified Theory of Management* (New York: McGraw-Hill, 1964).

50. Koontz, Harold. "A Model for Analyzing the Universality and Transferability of Management," *Academy of Management Journal,* Vol. 12 (1969), 415–430.

51. Koontz, Harold, and Cyril O'Donnell. *Principles of Management* (New York: McGraw-Hill, 1955).

52. Lawrence, Paul R., Joseph C. Bailey, Robert L. Katz, John A. Seiler, Charles D. Orth, James V. Clark, Louis B. Barnes, and Arthur N. Turner. *Organizational Behavior and Administration: Cases, Concepts, and Research Findings* (Homewood, Ill.: Irwin, 1961).

53. Likert, Rensis. *New Patterns of Management* (New York: McGraw-Hill, 1961).

54. Ling, Cyril C. *The Management of Personnel Relations: History and Origin* (Homewood, Ill.: Irwin, 1965).

55. Litchfield, Edward H. "Notes on a General Theory of Administration," *Administrative Science Quarterly,* Vol. 1, 1956.

56. Litzinger, William D. "Entrepreneurial Prototype in Bank Management: A Comparative Study of Branch Bank Managers," *Journal of the Academy of Management,* Vol. 6 (1963), 36–45.

57. McAnn, Eugene C. "An Aspect of Management Philosophy in the United States and Latin America," *Academy of Management Journal,* Vol. 7 (1964), 149–152.

58. McGregor, Douglas. *The Human Side of Enterprise* (New York: McGraw-Hill, 1960).

59. McGuire, Joseph W. *Business and Society* (New York: McGraw-Hill, 1963).

60. "Management Audit of the Catholic Church," *America,* February 25, 1956.

61. March, James G., and Herbert A. Simon. *Organizations* (New York: Wiley, 1958).

62. Martindell, Jackson. *The Scientific Appraisal of Management* (New York: Harper, 1950).

63. Mayo, Elton. *The Human Problems of an Industrial Civilization* (New York: Macmillan, 1933).

64. Mee, John F. *A History of Twentieth Cen-*

tury Management Thought (Columbus, Ohio: Ohio State University, 1959).

65. Mee, John F. *Management Thought in a Dynamic Economy* (New York: New York University Press, 1963).
66. Newman, William H. *Administrative Action: The Techniques of Organization and Management* (Englewood Cliffs, N.J.: Prentice-Hall, 1950).
67. Newman, William H., and Charles E. Summer. *The Process of Management: Concepts, Behavior, and Practice* (Englewood Cliffs, N.J.: Prentice-Hall, 1961).
68. Nowotny, Otto. "American Versus European Management Philosophy," *Harvard Business Review,* Vol. 42, No. 2 (1964), 101–108.
69. Optner, Stanford L. *Systems Analysis for Business Management* (Englewood Cliffs, N.J.: Prentice-Hall, 1960).
70. Pratt, John, Howard Raiffa, and Robert Schlaifer. *Introduction to Statistical Decision Theory* (Homewood, Ill.: Irwin, 1965).
71. Presthus, Robert. "Toward a Theory of Organizational Behavior," *Administrative Science Quarterly,* Vol. 3 (1958).
72. Roethlisberger, R. J., and W. Dickson. *Management and the Worker* (Cambridge, Mass.: Harvard University Press, 1956).
73. Sayles, Leonard R. *Managerial Behavior: Administration in Complex Organizations* (New York: McGraw-Hill, 1964).
74. Scott, William G. "Modern Human Relations in Perspective," *Personnel Administration,* Vol. 22, No. 6 (1959).
75. Scott, William G. "Organization Theory: An Overview and an Appraisal," *Journal of the Academy of Management,* Vol. 4 (1961), 7–26.
76. Sheldon, Oliver. *The Philosophy of Management* (New York: Pitman, 1923).
77. Shull, Fremont A., Jr., Andre L. Delbecq, and L. L. Cummings. *Organizational Decision Making* (New York: McGraw-Hill, 1970).
78. Simon, Herbert A. *Administrative Behavior* (New York: Macmillan, 1945).
79. Simon, Herbert A. *The Shape of Automation for Men and Management* (New York: Harper and Row, 1965).
80. Smith, George Albert, Jr. *Business, Society, and the Individual* (Homewood, Ill.: Irwin, 1962).
81. Starr, Martin K. "Evolving Concepts in Production Management," *Academy of Management Proceedings,* 1964, pp. 128–133.
82. Terry, George R. *Principles of Management* (Homewood, Ill.: Irwin, 1953).
83. Thompson, James D. *Organizations in Action* (New York: McGraw-Hill, 1967).
84. Timms, Howard L. *The Production Function in Business* (Homewood, Ill.: Irwin, 1962).
85. Urwick, L. *The Elements of Administration* (New York: Harper, 1943).
86. von Bertalanffy, Ludwig. "General Systems Theory: A New Approach to Unity of Science," *Human Biology,* Vol. 23 (1961), 302–361.
87. Webber, Ross A. *Culture and Management* (Homewood, Ill.: Irwin, 1969).
88. Weber, Max. "The Theory of Social and Economic Organization," translated by A. M. Henderson and Talcott Parsons (New York: Oxford University Press, 1947).
89. Wren, Daniel A. *The Evolution of Management Thought* (New York: Ronald, 1972).
90. Yoder, Dale. *Personnel Management and Industrial Relations* (Englewood Cliffs, N.J.: Prentice-Hall, 1938).
91. Young, Stanley. *Management: A Systems Analysis* (Glenview, Ill.: Scott, Foresman, 1966).

B. SYSTEMS THEORY AND MANAGEMENT

5 GENERAL SYSTEMS THEORY—THE SKELETON OF SCIENCE*

Kenneth E. Boulding

General Systems Theory[1] is a name which has come into use to describe a level of theoretical model-building which lies somewhere between the highly generalized constructions of pure mathematics and the specific theories of the specialized disciplines. Mathematics attempts to organize highly general relationships into a coherent system, a system however which does not have any necessary connections with the "real" world around us. It studies all thinkable relationships abstracted from any concrete situation or body of empirical knowledge. It is not even confined to "quantitative" relationships narrowly defined—indeed, the development of a mathematics of quality and structure is already on the way, even though it is not as far advanced as the "classical" mathematics of quantity and number. Nevertheless because in a sense mathematics contains all theories it contains none; it is the language of theory, but it does not give us the content. At the other extreme we have the separate disciplines and sciences, with their separate bodies of theory. Each discipline corresponds to a certain segment of the empirical world, and each develops theories which have particular applicability to its own empirical segment. Physics, Chemistry, Biology, Psychology, Sociology, Economics and so on all carve out for themselves certain elements of the experience of man and develop theories and patterns of activity (research) which yield satisfaction in understanding, and which are appropriate to their special segments.

In recent years increasing need has been felt for a body of systematic theoretical constructs which will discuss the general relationships of the empirical world. This is the quest of General Systems Theory. It does not seek, of course, to establish a single, self-contained "general theory of practically everything" which will replace all the special theories of particular disciplines. Such a theory would be almost without content, for we always pay for generality by sacrificing content, and all we can say about practically everything is almost nothing. Somewhere however between the specific that has no meaning and the general that has no content there must be, for each purpose and at each level of abstraction, an optimum degree of generality. It is the contention of the General Systems Theorists that this optimum degree of generality in theory is not always reached by the particular sciences. The objectives of General Systems Theory then can be set out with varying degrees of ambition and confidence. At a low level of ambition but with a high degree of confidence it aims to point out similarities in the theoretical constructions of different disciplines, where these exist, and to develop theoretical models having applicability to at least two different fields of study. At a higher level of ambition, but with perhaps a lower degree of confidence it hopes to develop something like a "spectrum" of theories—a system of systems which may perform the function of a "gestalt" in theoretical construction. Such "gestalts" in special fields have been of great value in directing research towards the gaps which they reveal. Thus the periodic table of elements in chemistry directed research for many decades towards the discovery of unknown elements to fill gaps in the table until the table was completely filled. Similarly a "system of systems" might be of value in directing the attention of theorists towards gaps in theoretical models, and might even be of value in pointing towards methods of filling them.

The need for general systems theory is accentuated by the present sociological situation in science. Knowledge is not something which exists and grows in the abstract. It is a function of human organisms and of social organization. Knowledge, that is to say, is always what some-

* Reprinted by permission of the publisher from *Management Science*, vol. 2, no. 3, pp. 197–208, April, 1956. Mr. Boulding is professor of economics at the University of Colorado.

[1] The name and many of the ideas are to be credited to L. von Bertalanffy, who is not, however, to be held accountable for the ideas of the present author! For a general discussion of Bertalanffy's ideas see "General System Theory: A New Approach to Unity of Science," *Human Biology*, Dec., 1951, Vol. 23, pp. 302–361.

body knows: the most perfect transcript of knowledge in writing is not knowledge if nobody knows it. Knowledge however grows by the receipt of meaningful information—that is, by the intake of messages by a knower which are capable of reorganizing his knowledge. We will quietly duck the question as to what reorganizations constitute "growth" of knowledge by defining "semantic growth" of knowledge as those reorganizations which can profitably be talked about, in writing or speech, by the Right People. Science, that is to say, is what can be talked about profitably by scientists in their role as scientists. The crisis of science today arises because of the increasing difficulty of such profitable talk among scientists as a whole. Specialization has outrun Trade, communication between the disciples becomes increasingly difficult, and the Republic of Learning is breaking up into isolated subcultures with only tenuous lines of communication between them—a situation which threatens intellectual civil war. The reason for this breakup in the body of knowledge is that in the course of specialization the receptors of information themselves become specialized. Hence physicists only talk to physicists, economists to economists—worse still, nuclear physicists only talk to nuclear physicists and econometricians to econometricians. One wonders sometimes if science will not grind to a stop in an assemblage of walled-in hermits, each mumbling to himself words in a private language that only he can understand. In these days the arts may have beaten the sciences to this desert of mutual unintelligibility, but that may be merely because the swift intuitions of art reach the future faster than the plodding leg work of the scientist. The more science breaks into sub-groups, and the less communication is possible among the disciplines, however, the greater chance there is that the total growth of knowledge is being slowed down by the loss of relevant communications. The spread of specialized deafness means that someone who ought to know something that someone else knows isn't able to find it out for lack of generalized ears.

It is one of the main objectives of General Systems Theory to develop these generalized ears, and by developing a framework of general theory to enable one specialist to catch relevant communications from others. Thus the economist who realizes the strong formal similarity between utility theory in economics and field theory in physics[2] is probably in a better position to learn from the physicists than one who does not. Similarly a specialist who works with the growth concept—whether the crystallographer, the virologist, the cytologist, the physiologist, the psychologist, the sociologist or the economist—will be more sensitive to the contributions of other fields if he is aware of the many similarities of the growth process in widely different empirical fields.

There is not much doubt about the demand for general systems theory under one brand name or another. It is a little more embarrassing to inquire into the supply. Does any of it exist, and if so where? What is the chance of getting more of it, and if so, how? The situation might be described as promising and in ferment, though it is not wholly clear what is being promised or brewed. Something which might be called an "interdisciplinary movement" has been abroad for some time. The first signs of this are usually the development of hybrid disciplines. Thus physical chemistry emerged in the third quarter of the nineteenth century, social psychology in the second quarter of the twentieth. In the physical and biological sciences the list of hybrid disciplines is now quite long—biophysics, biochemistry, astrophysics are all well established. In the social sciences social anthropology is fairly well established, economic psychology and economic sociology are just beginning. There are signs, even, that Political Economy, which died in infancy some hundred years ago, may have a re-birth.

In recent years there has been an additional development of great interest in the form of "multisexual" interdisciplines. The hybrid disciplines, as their hyphenated names indicate, come from two respectable and honest academic parents. The newer interdisciplines have a much more varied and occasionally even obscure ancestry, and result from the reorganization of material from many different fields of study. Cybernetics, for instance, comes out of electrical engineering, neurophysiology, physics, biology, with even a dash of economics. Information theory, which originated in communications engineering, has important applications in many fields stretching from biology to the social sciences. Organization theory comes out of economics, sociology, engineering, physiology, and Management Science itself is an equally multidisciplinary product.

On the more empirical and practical side the interdisciplinary movement is reflected in the development of interdepartmental institutes of many kinds. Some of these find their basis of unity in the empirical field which they study, such as institutes of industrial relations, of public administration, of international affairs,

[2] See A. G. Pikler, "Utility Theories in Field Physics and Mathematical Economics," *British Journal for the Philosophy of Science*, 1955, Vol. 5, p. 47 and 303.

and so on. Others are organized around the application of a common methodology to many different fields and problems, such as the Survey Research Center and the Group Dynamics Center at the University of Michigan. Even more important than these visible developments, perhaps, though harder to perceive and identify, is a growing dissatisfaction in many departments, especially at the level of graduate study, with the existing traditional theoretical backgrounds for the empirical studies which form the major part of the output of Ph.D. theses. To take but a single example from the field with which I am most familiar. It is traditional for studies of labor relations, money and banking, and foreign investment to come out of departments of economics. Many of the needed theoretical models and frameworks in these fields, however, do not come out of "economic theory" as this is usually taught, but from sociology, social psychology, and cultural anthropology. Students in the department of economics however rarely get a chance to become acquainted with these theoretical models, which may be relevant to their studies, and they become impatient with economic theory, much of which may not be relevant.

It is clear that there is a good deal of interdisciplinary excitement abroad. If this excitement is to be productive, however, it must operate within a certain framework of coherence. It is all too easy for the interdisciplinary to degenerate into the undisciplined. If the interdisciplinary movement, therefore, is not to lose that sense of form and structure which is the "discipline" involved in the various separate disciplines, it should develop a structure of its own. This I conceive to be the great task of general systems theory. For the rest of this paper, therefore, I propose to look at some possible ways in which general systems theory might be structured.

Two possible approaches to the organization of general systems theory suggest themselves, which are to be thought of as complementary rather than competitive, or at least as two roads each of which is worth exploring. The first approach is to look over the empirical universe and to pick out certain general *phenomena* which are found in many different disciplines, and to seek to build up general theoretical models relevant to these phenomena. The second approach is to arrange the empirical fields in a hierarchy of complexity of organization of their basic "individual" or unit of behavior, and to try to develop a level of abstraction appropriate to each.

Some examples of the first approach will serve to clarify it, without pretending to be exhaustive. In almost all disciplines, for instance, we find examples of populations—aggregates of individuals conforming to a common definition, to which individuals are added (born) and subtracted (die) and in which the age of the individual is a relevant and identifiable variable. These populations exhibit dynamic movements of their own, which can frequently be described by fairly simple systems of difference equations. The populations of different species also exhibit dynamic interactions among themselves, as in the theory of Volterra. Models of population change and interaction cut across a great many different fields—ecological systems in biology, capital theory in economics which deals with populations of "goods," social ecology, and even certain problems of statistical mechanics. In all these fields population change, both in absolute numbers and in structure, can be discussed in terms of birth and survival functions relating numbers of births and of deaths in specific age groups to various aspects of the system. In all these fields the interaction of population can be discussed in terms of competitive, complementary, or parasitic relationships among populations of different species, whether the species consist of animals, commodities, social classes or molecules.

Another phenomenon of almost universal significance for all disciplines is that of the interaction of an "individual" of some kind with its environment. Every discipline studies some kind of "individual"—electron, atom, molecule, crystal, virus, cell, plant, animal, man, family, tribe, state, church, firm, corporation, university, and so on. Each of these individuals exhibits "behavior," action, or change, and this behavior is considered to be related in some way to the environment of the individual—that is, with other individuals with which it comes into contact or into some relationship. Each individual is thought of as consisting of a structure or complex of individuals of the order immediately below it—atoms are an arrangement of protons and electrons, molecules of atoms, cells of molecules, plants, animals and men of cells, social organizations of men. The "behavior" of each individual is "explained" by the structure and arrangement of the lower individuals of which it is composed, or by certain principles of equilibrium or homeostasis according to which certain "states" of the individual are "preferred." Behavior is described in terms of the restoration of these preferred states when they are disturbed by changes in the environment.

Another phenomenon of universal significance is growth. Growth theory is in a sense a subdivision of the theory of individual "behavior," growth being one important aspect of behavior. Nevertheless there are important differences between equilibrium theory and growth theory, which perhaps warrant giving growth theory a special category. There is hardly a science in which the growth phenomenon does not have some importance, and though there is a great difference in complexity between the growth of crystals, embryos, and societies, many of the principles and concepts which are important at the lower levels are also illuminating at higher levels. Some growth phenomena can be dealt with in terms of relatively simple population models, the solution of which yields growth curves of single variables. At the more complex levels structural problems become dominant and the complex interrelationships between growth and form are the focus of interest. All growth phenomena are sufficiently alike however to suggest that a general theory of growth is by no means an impossibility.[3]

Another aspect of the theory of the individual and also of interrelationships among individuals which might be singled out for special treatment is the theory of information and communication. The information concept as developed by Shannon has had interesting applications outside its original field of electrical engineering. It is not adequate, of course, to deal with problems involving the semantic level of communication. At the biological level however the information concept may serve to develop general notions of structuredness and abstract measures of organization which give us, as it were, a third basic dimension beyond mass and energy. Communication and information processes are found in a wide variety of empirical situations, and are unquestionably essential in the development of organization, both in the biological and the social world.

These various approaches to general systems through various aspects of the empirical world may lead ultimately to something like a general field theory of the dynamics of action and interaction. This, however, is a long way ahead.

A second possible approach to general systems theory is through the arrangement of theoretical systems and constructs in a hierarchy of complexity, roughly corresponding to the complexity of the "individuals" of the various empirical fields. This approach is more systematic than the first, leading towards a "system of systems." It may not replace the first entirely, however, as there may always be important theoretical concepts and constructs lying outside the systematic framework. I suggest below a possible arrangement of "levels" of theoretical discourse.

(i) The first level is that of the static structure. It might be called the level of *frameworks*. This is the geography and anatomy of the universe—the patterns of electrons around a nucleus, the pattern of atoms in a molecular formula, the arrangement of atoms in a crystal, the anatomy of the gene, the cell, the plant, the animal, the mapping of the earth, the solar system, the astronomical universe. The accurate description of these frameworks is the beginning of organized theoretical knowledge in almost any field, for without accuracy in this description of static relationships no accurate functional or dynamic theory is possible. Thus the Copernican revolution was really the discovery of a new static framework for the solar system which permitted a simpler description of its dynamics.

(ii) The next level of systematic analysis is that of the simple dynamic system with predetermined, necessary motions. This might be called the level of *clockworks*. The solar system itself is of course the great clock of the universe from man's point of view, and the deliciously exact predictions of the astronomers are a testimony to the excellence of the clock which they study. Simple machines such as the lever and the pulley, even quite complicated machines like steam engines and dynamos fall mostly under this category. The greater part of the theoretical structure of physics, chemistry, and even of economics falls into this category. Two special cases might be noted. Simple equilibrium systems really fall into the dynamic category, as every equilibrium system must be considered as a limiting case of a dynamic system, and its stability cannot be determined except from the properties of its parent dynamic system. Stochastic dynamic systems leading to equilibria, for all their complexity, also fall into this group of systems; such is the modern view of the atom and even of the molecule, each position or part of the system being given with a certain degree of probabil-

[3] See "Towards a General Theory of Growth" by K. E. Boulding, *Canadian Journal of Economics and Political Science*, 19 Aug. 1953, 326–340.

ity, the whole nevertheless exhibiting a determinate structure. Two types of analytical method are important here, which we may call, with the usage of the economists, comparative statics and true dynamics. In comparative statics we compare two equilibrium positions of the system under different values for the basic parameters. These equilibrium positions are usually expressed as the solution of a set of simultaneous equations. The method of comparative statics is to compare the solutions when the parameters of the equations are changed. Most simple mechanical problems are solved in this way. In true dynamics on the other hand we exhibit the system as a set of difference or differential equations, which are then solved in the form of an explicit function of each variable with time. Such a system may reach a position of stationary equilibrium, or it may not—there are plenty of examples of explosive dynamic systems, a very simple one being the growth of a sum at compound interest! Most physical and chemical reactions and most social systems do in fact exhibit a tendency to equilibrium—otherwise the world would have exploded or imploded long ago.

(iii) The next level is that of the control mechanism or cybernetic system, which might be nicknamed the level of the *thermostat.* This differs from the simple stable equilibrium system mainly in the fact that the transmission and interpretation of information is an essential part of the system. As a result of this the equilibrium position is not merely determined by the equations of the system, but the system will move to the maintenance of any *given* equilibrium, within limits. Thus the thermostat will maintain *any* temperature at which it can be set; the equilibrium temperature of the system is not determined solely by its equations. The trick here of course is that the essential variable of the dynamic system is the *difference* between an "observed" or "recorded" value of the maintained variable and its "ideal" value. If this difference is not zero the system moves so as to diminish it; thus the furnace sends up heat when the temperature as recorded is "too cold" and is turned off when the recorded temperature is "too hot." The homeostasis model, which is of such importance in physiology, is an example of a cybernetic mechanism, and such mechanisms exist through the whole empirical world of the biologist and the social scientist.

(iv) The fourth level is that of the "open system," or self-maintaining structure. This is the level at which life begins to differentiate itself from not-life: it might be called the level of the *cell.* Something like an open system exists, of course, even in physico-chemical equilibrium systems; atomic structures maintain themselves in the midst of a throughput of electrons, molecular structures maintain themselves in the midst of a throughput of atoms. Flames and rivers likewise are essentially open systems of a very simple kind. As we pass up the scale of complexity of organization towards living systems, however, the property of self-maintenance of structure in the midst of a throughput of material becomes of dominant importance. An atom or a molecule can presumably exist without throughput: the existence of even the simplest living organism is inconceivable without ingestion, excretion and metabolic exchange. Closely connected with the property of self-maintenance is the property of self-reproduction. It may be, indeed, that self-reproduction is a more primitive or "lower level" system than the open system, and that the gene and the virus, for instance, may be able to reproduce themselves without being open systems. It is not perhaps an important question at what point in the scale of increasing complexity "life" begins. What is clear, however, is that by the time we have got to systems which both reproduce themselves and maintain themselves in the midst of a throughput of material and energy, we have something to which it would be hard to deny the title of "life."

(v) The fifth level might be called the genetic-societal level; it is typified by the *plant,* and it dominates the empirical world of the botanist. The outstanding characteristics of these systems are first, a division of labor among cells to form a cell-society with differentiated and mutually dependent parts (roots, leaves, seeds, etc.), and second, a sharp differentiation between the genotype and the phenotype, associated with the phenomenon of equifinal or "blueprinted" growth. At this level there are no highly specialized sense organs and information receptors are diffuse and incapable of much throughput of information—it is doubtful whether a tree can distinguish much more than light from dark, long days from short days, cold from hot.

(vi) As we move upward from the plant world towards the animal kingdom we gradually pass over into a new level, the "animal" level, characterized by increased mobility, teleological behavior, and self-awareness. Here we have the development of specialized information-receptors (eyes, ears, etc.) leading to an enormous increase in the intake of information; we have also a great development of nervous systems, leading ultimately to the brain, as an organizer of the information intake into a knowledge structure or "image." Increasingly as we ascend the scale of animal life, behavior is response not to a specific stimulus but to an "image" or knowledge structure or view of the environment as a whole. This image is of course determined ultimately by information received into the organism; the relation between the receipt of information and the building up of an image however is exceedingly complex. It is not a simple piling up or accumulation of information received, although this frequently happens, but a structuring of information into something essentially different from the information itself. After the image structure is well established most information received produces very little change in the image—it goes through the loose structure, as it were, without hitting it, much as a sub-atomic particle might go through an atom without hitting anything. Sometimes however the information is "captured" by the image and added to it, and sometimes the information hits some kind of a "nucleus" of the image and a reorganization takes place, with far reaching and radical changes in behavior in apparent reponse to what seems like a very small stimulus. The difficulties in the prediction of the behavior of these systems arise largely because of this intervention of the image between the stimulus and the response.

(vii) The next level is the "human" level, that is of the individual human being considered as a system. In addition to all, or nearly all, of the characteristics of animal systems man possesses self-consciousness, which is something different from mere awareness. His image, besides being much more complex than that even of the higher animals, has a self-reflexive quality—he not only knows, but knows that he knows. This property is probably bound up with the phenomenon of language and symbolism. It is the capacity for speech—the ability to produce, absorb, and interpret *symbols*, as opposed to mere signs like the warning cry of an animal—which most clearly marks man off from his humbler brethren. Man is distinguished from the animals also by a much more elaborate image of time and relationship; man is probably the only organization that knows that it dies, that contemplates in its behavior a whole life span, and more than a life span. Man exists not only in time and space but in history, and his behavior is profoundly affected by his view of the time process in which he stands.

(viii) Because of the vital importance for the individual man of symbolic images and behavior based on them it is not easy to separate clearly the level of the individual human organism from the next level, that of social organizations. In spite of the occasional stories of feral children raised by animals, man isolated from his fellows is practically unknown. So essential is the symbolic image in human behavior that one suspects that a truly isolated man would not be "human" in the usually accepted sense, though he would be potentially human. Nevertheless it is convenient for some purposes to distinguish the individual human as a system from the social systems which surround him, and in this sense social organizations may be said to constitute another level of organization. The unit of such systems is not perhaps the person—the individual human as such—but the "role"—that part of the person which is concerned with the organization or situation in question, and it is tempting to define social organizations, or almost any social system, as a set of roles tied together with channels of communication. The interrelations of the role and the person however can never be completely neglected—a square person in a round role may become a little rounder, but he also makes the role squarer, and the perception of a role is affected by the personalities of those who have occupied it in the past. At this level we must concern ourselves with the content and meaning of messages, the nature and dimensions of value systems, the transcription of images into a historical record, the subtle symbolizations of art, music, and poetry, and the complex gamut of human emotion. The empirical universe here is human life and society in all its complexity and richness.

(ix) To complete the structure of systems we should add a final turret for transcendental systems, even if we may be accused at this point of having built Babel to the clouds. There are however the ultimates and absolutes and the inescapable unknowables, and they also exhibit systematic structure and relationship. It will be a sad day for man when nobody is allowed to ask questions that do not have any answers.

One advantage of exhibiting a hierarchy of systems in this way is that it gives us some idea of the present gaps in both theoretical and empirical knowledge. Adequate theoretical models extend up to about the fourth level, and not much beyond. Empirical knowledge is deficient at practically all levels. Thus at the level of the static structure, fairly adequate descriptive models are available for geography, chemistry, geology, anatomy, and descriptive social science. Even at this simplest level, however, the problem of the adequate description of complex structures is still far from solved. The theory of indexing and cataloguing, for instance, is only in its infancy. Librarians are fairly good at cataloguing books, chemists have begun to catalogue structural formulae, and anthropologists have begun to catalogue culture traits. The cataloguing of events, ideas, theories, statistics, and empirical data has hardly begun. The very multiplication of records however as time goes on will force us into much more adequate cataloguing and reference systems than we now have. This is perhaps the major unsolved theoretical problem at the level of the static structure. In the empirical field there are still great areas where static structures are very imperfectly known, although knowledge is advancing rapidly, thanks to new probing devices such as the electron microscope. The anatomy of that part of the empirical world which lies between the large molecule and the cell however, is still obscure at many points. It is precisely this area however—which includes, for instance, the gene and the virus—that holds the secret of life, and until its anatomy is made clear the nature of the functional systems which are involved will inevitably be obscure.

The level of the "clockwork" is the level of "classical" natural science, especially physics and astronomy, and is probably the most completely developed level in the present state of knowledge, especially if we extend the concept to include the field theory and stochastic models of modern physics. Even here however there are important gaps, especially at the higher empirical levels. There is much yet to be known about the sheer mechanics of cells and nervous systems, of brains and of societies.

Beyond the second level adequate theoretical models get scarcer. The last few years have seen great developments at the third and fourth levels. The theory of control mechanisms ("thermostats") has established itself as the new discipline of cybernetics, and the theory of self-maintaining systems or "open systems" likewise has made rapid strides. We could hardly maintain however that much more than a beginning had been made in these fields. We know very little about the cybernetics of genes and genetic systems, for instance, and still less about the control mechanisms involved in the mental and social world. Similarly the processes of self-maintenance remain essentially mysterious at many points, and although the theoretical possibility of constructing a self-maintaining machine which would be a true open system has been suggested, we seem to be a long way from the actual construction of such a mechanical similitude of life.

Beyond the fourth level it may be doubted whether we have as yet even the rudiments of theoretical systems. The intricate machinery of growth by which the genetic complex organizes the matter around it is almost a complete mystery. Up to now, whatever the future may hold, only God can make a tree. In the face of living systems we are almost helpless; we can occasionally cooperate with systems which we do not understand: we cannot even begin to reproduce them. The ambiguous status of medicine, hovering as it does uneasily between magic and science, is a testimony to the state of systematic knowledge in this area. As we move up the scale the absence of the appropriate theoretical systems becomes ever more noticeable. We can hardly conceive ourselves constructing a system which would be in any recognizable sense "aware," much less self-conscious. Nevertheless as we move towards the human and societal level a curious thing happens: the fact that we have, as it were, an inside track, and that we ourselves *are* the systems which we are studying, enables us to utilize systems which we do not really understand. It is almost inconceivable that we should make a machine that would make a poem: nevertheless, poems *are* made by fools like us by processes which are largely hidden from us. The kind of knowledge and skill that we have at the symbolic level is very different from that which we have at lower levels—it is like, shall we say, the "knowhow" of the gene as compared with the knowhow of the biologist. Nevertheless it is a real kind of knowledge and it is the source of the creative achievements of man as artist, writer, architect, and composer.

Perhaps one of the most valuable uses of the above scheme is to prevent us from accepting as final a level of theoretical analysis which is below the level of the empirical world which we are investigating. Because, in a sense, each level incorporates all those below it, much valuable information and insights can be obtained by applying low-level systems to high-level subject matter. Thus most of the theoretical schemes of the social sciences are still at level (ii), just rising now to (iii), although the subject matter clearly involves level (viii). Economics, for instance, is still largely a "mechanics of utility and self-interest," in Jevons' masterly phrase. Its theoretical and mathematical base is drawn largely from the level of simple equilibrium theory and dynamic mechanisms. It has hardly begun to use concepts such as information which are appropriate at level (iii), and makes no use of higher level systems. Furthermore, with this crude apparatus it has achieved a modicum of success, in the sense that anybody trying to manipulate an economic system is almost certain to be better off if he knows some economics than if he doesn't. Nevertheless at some point progress in economics is going to depend on its ability to break out of these low-level systems, useful as they are as first approximations, and utilize systems which are more directly appropriate to its universe—when, of course, these systems are discovered. Many other examples could be given—the wholly inappropriate use in psychoanalytic theory, for instance, of the concept of energy, and the long inability of psychology to break loose from a sterile stimulus-response model.

Finally, the above scheme might serve as a mild word of warning even to Management Science. This new discipline represents an important breakaway from overly simple mechanical models in the theory of organization and control. Its emphasis on communication systems and organizational structure, on principles of homeostasis and growth, on decision processes under uncertainty, is carrying us far beyond the simple models of maximizing behavior of even ten years ago. This advance in the level of theoretical analysis is bound to lead to more powerful and fruitful systems. Nevertheless we must never quite forget that even these advances do not carry us much beyond the third and fourth levels, and that in dealing with human personalities and organizations we are dealing with systems in the empirical world far beyond our ability to formulate. We should not be wholly surprised, therefore, if our simpler systems, for all their importance and validity, occasionally let us down.

I chose the subtitle of my paper with some eye to its possible overtones of meaning. General Systems Theory is the skeleton of science in the sense that it aims to provide a framework or structure of systems on which to hang the flesh and blood of particular disciplines and particular subject matters in an orderly and coherent corpus of knowledge. It is also, however, something of a skeleton in a cupboard—the cupboard in this case being the unwillingness of science to admit the very low level of its successes in systematization, and its tendency to shut the door on problems and subject matters which do not fit easily into simple mechanical schemes. Science, for all its successes, still has a very long way to go. General Systems Theory may at times be an embarrassment in pointing out how very far we still have to go, and in deflating excessive philosophical claims for overly simple systems. It also may be helpful however in pointing out to some extent *where* we have to go. The skeleton must come out of the cupboard before its dry bones can live.

6 THE SYSTEMS APPROACH TO BUSINESS ORGANIZATION AND DECISION MAKING*

Robert J. Mockler

Systems theory has had a revolutionary effect on business operations. Many an executive has found the revolution chaotic, for it has come in the form of the intrusion of the computer and computer personnel into his operations. He has felt his authority and control slowly stripped away by a movement he little understands and because of this has resisted it.

The computer is not, however, the villain. What normally happens is that the introduction of the computer sets in motion a systematic re-evaluation of what the business is and how it can operate most efficiently. This re-evaluation exposes the real problem—the gradual fragmentation of decision-making systems within a company over the years. The exposure of the problem in turn leads to an effort to re-establish smoothly working, fully coordinated decision-making systems for the business.

Systems theory provides a conceptual basis, as well as principles and guidelines, for establishing a more efficient system for planning, control, and operational decision making.

The Theory of Systems A system may be defined as an orderly grouping of separate but interdependent components for the purpose of attaining some predetermined objective.[1] Three important aspects of systems are implied by this definition:

- The arrangement of components must be orderly and hierarchical, no matter how complex it is.
- Since the components of the system are interdependent, there must be communication among them.
- Since a system is oriented toward an objective, any interaction among the components must be designed to achieve that objective.

A number of authorities working in diverse fields of specialization have contributed to the development of systems theory. Four of the better known are Ludwig von Bertalanffy, Kenneth Boulding, Norbert Wiener, and Herbert Simon.

A biologist, von Bertalanffy, is considered the originator of the general systems theory.[2] Disturbed by the increasing fragmentation and specialization of knowledge in this century, he attempted to find a unifying framework for the separate scientific disciplines. His work led to the development of a general theory of systems, which he felt provided such an integrating approach to the study and development of a wide range of scientific disciplines: "The notion of a 'system' being defined as 'any arrangement or combination, as of parts or elements, in a whole' applies to a cell, a human being, a society, as well as to an atom, a planet or a galaxy."[3]

Kenneth Boulding carried the general systems theory a step further by defining nine levels of systems, starting with the most simple and static (the anatomy and geography of the universe) and ending with the most dynamic (transcendental systems).[4] He thus conceived of a hierarchical arrangement of separate systems, which are in turn components of larger systems.

Both Boulding and von Bertalanffy recognized the dangers that resulted from the increasing fragmentation of science into more and more subgroups and the growing difficulty of communicating among the scientific disciplines. One of the main objectives of the general systems theory was to develop "a framework of general theory to enable one specialist to catch relevant communications from others."[5]

Since systems theory focuses on the dynamic interrelationship and interaction of entities, information and communication theory are important to the development of systems theory. In his study of information theory and communication, Norbert Wiener drew many parallels between the communication processes in living beings and in the newer communication machines, such as computers. Both have spe-

* Reprinted by permission of the publisher from *California Management Review*, vol. 11, no. 2, pp. 53–58, Winter, 1968. Copyright, 1968 by The Regents of the University of California. Mr. Mockler is professor of management at St. John's University.

cial apparatuses for collecting information from the outside world, storing it, and using it as a basis for action. Through this mechanism both human beings and information-processing machines have the capacity to compare actual performance to expected performance and to correct any deviations by "the sending of messages which effectively change the behavior of the recipient."[6] Thus, Wiener saw communication and information theory as a basis for understanding and explaining the planning, control, and decision-making processes.[7]

Herbert Simon, in his study of business management, considered "decision making" and "managing" as synonymous.[8] He saw the business organization within which the manager works as a decision-making information system. Simon thus extended the scope of Wiener's information and communication theory and von Bertalanffy's general systems theory by applying them to business operations, where they can be viewed as vehicles for effectively achieving corporate objectives.

Systems theory and the various applications of it explored by these four men are important to business managers primarily for these reasons:[9]

- Since the systems concept is objective-oriented, systems organization automatically centers attention upon the objectives for which the firm has been established and helps to generate concerted and coordinated activity toward attainment of these objectives.
- Systems theory stresses the interdependence of elements, so that a manager is continually forced to view the business firm as a component of the over-all operating economy.

From a systems theory viewpoint, therefore, a business organization can be viewed on one level as a complete, integrated decision-making system designed to achieve some specific objective, such as producing automobiles or paper products. On another level this internal business system can be viewed as a component or subsystem of a larger system—the economic, social, and competitive environment within which the business operates.

The Environmental System Looking upon the social, economic, and competitive environment as an integrated system, of which a particular business is a subsystem, aids management planning and decision making.

1 / In planning and operating a particular company its managers are led to give greater consideration to the political and social values of the environment and potential impact that these values, and the legislation they produce, have on the business.

2 / Managers become more aware of the economic forces influencing the business. The company's long- and short-range planning is thus influenced to a greater degree by such economic factors as supply and demand; population growth and labor force trends; gross national product and income estimates; technological development; trends in governmental receipts and expenditures; fluctuations in industrial production, price levels, business, and the economy in general; and seasonal factors.[10]

3 / A company's managers are made more aware of the specific influences of the competitive system on their operations. As a result, a company's sales forecasting is improved, for greater consideration is given to such market and industry factors as anticipated market standing and share, competitive strategy and action, and new product and market development. Projected profit levels, rates of return on investment, and specific production, marketing, and financial plans are also developed with more precise estimates of competitive conditions in mind.

The effects of these external factors can then be weighed with other information on internal company resources—the strengths and weaknesses of the particular business under study—to develop final corporate plans and to make operating decisions.

A business manager acquires such an approach to planning and decision making by following the principles of scientific business planning.[11] However, the systems approach supplements and reinforces the disciplines laid down in scientific planning by impressing upon the manager the relationship between his internal business operation and its economic and social environment.

The Relation of Systems Theory to Business Organization for Decision Making Systems theory has had an even greater impact on the internal organization of, and the decision-making processes within, individual business enterprises.

The systems approach forces the manager to look upon his business organization as an information network, with the flow of information providing the decision makers at varying management levels with the information needed to make decisions of all types. As a result, business information systems, which were once considered mainly accounting record-keeping systems, are now being called upon to support all the planning, control, and operational decision-making processes within a company. As such, these systems are required to store and process not only information concerning internal operations, but also information concerning competitor plans, strategies, programs, and performance, as well as significant information on the economic and social environment—in short, all the information needed for executive decision making.

These information-communication systems necessarily link together the components needed to operate a business successfully, i.e., the people, plants, and machines assembled for the purpose of achieving both the general corporate objective of making money and the individual corporate objective of making money by engaging in a specific type of profit-making business enterprise.

In organizing the components of a business to achieve its objectives, traditional business organization theory has emphasized the relationships between people by focusing on the tasks to be performed, the job positions related to performing these tasks, and the appropriate authority and responsibility for each job position.

In *Management Systems,* McDonough and Garrett[12] give some of the principles of organization that show the traditional, people-oriented approach to organization:

1 / Be sure that adequate provision is made for all activities.

2 / Group (departmentalize) activities on some logical basis.

3 / Limit the number of subordinates reporting to each executive.

4 / Define the responsibilities of each department, division, and subdivision.

5 / Delegate authority to subordinates wherever practicable.

6 / Make authority and responsibility equal.

7 / Provide for controls over those to whom authority is delegated.

8 / Avoid dual subordination.

9 / Distinguish clearly between line authority, functional authority, and staff relationships.

10 / Develop methods of coordination.

These principles clearly focus on the person-to-person relationships within an organization, and on the physical and functional departmentalization of the business unit. The commonplace block-diagram organization chart reflects this concept. Such relationships are, of course, important in thinking about organizations, but overemphasis of these relationships can obscure the information and communication links so vital to effective decision making within the corporation.

When changes are introduced within the traditional organization structure, new departments or units are normally added or new responsibilities given to existing departments. Sometimes these additions or changes are made to meet new business needs, sometimes to take maximum advantage of an individual executive's particular combination of talents, and sometimes merely to adjust to the personalities of individual executives. Such a fragmented development process almost invariably leads to some decrease in the effectiveness of the decision-making processes within an organization.

The systems concept of organization attempts to avoid this problem by focusing on the dynamic interaction and intercommunication among components of the system. Systems theory subordinates the separate units or departments of a business to decision-making information and communication networks. Understanding this difference is fundamental to understanding how systems theory has affected business organization and decision making.

The initial chart picturing a business organization restructured around the information flows, instead of around the authority and responsibility units, does not look substantially different, for during the first phases of the changeover only a few departments have been added and some job responsibilities shifted. The change in basic organization philosophy has a profound effect, however, for it creates major changes in the way an organization functions—changes that affect the lives of all the individuals operating within the business system and changes that after a period of time produce major adjustments in the structure of the business organization. Both in theory and in practice, therefore, the theory of systems is revolutionary for an established business.

The revolution has in fact occurred in most larger companies, for the introduction of electronic data processing, with its enormous capacity for storing and processing information and its enormous expense, is forcing business to use a systems approach to organization development. The computer has in a sense been the catalyst for re-evalution and change. For some companies the transition has been smooth; for others it has been chaotic.

When introducing a computer, many companies tend to approach the changeover in the traditional way—piecemeal, department by department. Such an approach only reinforces the fragmentation and disruption of information and decision-making systems.

THE CATALYST FOR CHANGE

Instead, as most companies sooner or later discover, before major decisions concerning computerization are made, management must step back and re-evaluate the entire flow of business, not merely the individual operations being computerized, in order to isolate the major decision-making areas, their interrelations, and the information needed to make these decisions most effectively. In other words, the systems approach has proved in practice to be the best one.

For example, in a large mail-order business which has recently been changing to computerized order processing and information handling, the first inclination was to write programs in steps, first for marketing, then for order processing, billing, inventory control, and so on, for each of the components or departments currently operating in the company.

It soon became apparent that this was not the best approach. At this time management directed the systems group to study the nature of the business in which the company was then engaged, the business in which the company hoped to be engaged within the next five years, and the environment in which the company would operate in the future.

The group next constructed a chart of the flow of the business operation, starting with the coupon-advertisement offering the product and asking for the order, and following the customer's order through processing and billing until the product is shipped, the merchandise restocked, and the bill paid. For each phase in the flow chart a supplemental list was made of the significant planning, control, and operational decisions necessary to perform that phase well. The information needed to make these decisions and the form in which this information was needed was then determined.

Only after the above studies were completed was a decision made as to which aspects of the business process could most economically be computerized, which would best be done clerically, and which were of sufficiently minor importance to the over-all functioning of the business that they would be done in a less than ideal way or not be done at all.

As a final step, the actual organization of the operation was restructured around the picture of the business which had been developed in the systems studies.

The diagram of the restructured organization may have looked to the casual observer like the traditional organization chart of the former organization, for there were departments for marketing, order processing, billing and credit, product procurement and inventory control, and liaison among all these operations. But the changes made to bring the organization into line with the known decision-making needs of the business were enormous.

On closer examination it was clear that the new organization set up to handle the business had little relation to the old organization. Pockets of personal strength had been wiped out, and antiquated reporting relationships had been changed drastically. Major adjustments had been made in the daily interworkings between departments and in the groupings of functions within each department. For example, advertising was now a marketing department, order processing included customer service, and product procurement and warehousing were combined. In other words, what is commonly called an "authority" organization structure had given way to a "systems" organization structure.

The re-evaluation showed that the organization had not grown dynamically with the business but was a conglomeration of old operating procedures, compromises made to accommodate personality differences, and the like. Although the changeover was painful, it revitalized the operation.

The advantages of following the systems approach may seem obvious to the reader. Yet it is still an approach rarely followed in practice. In an existing business concern the tendency is to look at the business as a series of departments, with department heads who perform various functions, the totality of which is the "business." What this business is, how it flows, and how its parts interrelate is likely to be known only by those who grew up with the business and now head it. And even they may not have a clear understanding of some of the newer aspects of the business.

The mail-order company cited in the example above was fortunate. In spite of the problems caused by the introduction of systems thinking into the organization, the company finally adjusted to and profited from the systems approach. Many companies faced with computerization have taken the easy way out. Instead of starting with a thorough re-evaluation of their businesses from a systems viewpoint, they have computerized their operations piecemeal. Letting presently established organizational structures control the systems study and development creates problems, among them: it leaves the antiquated organization structure intact and hinders the development of an effective mechanism for improved decision making; and it leads to inefficient use of the new, automated, computerized processing equipment.

The systems approach is revolutionizing business decision making, for it can provide more comprehensive information, faster, at the point and in the form it is needed to make better business decisions. Adapting the organization to the information systems needed for effective planning, control, and operational decision making enables a company to take advantage of new facilities for storing and processing information, which can in turn lead to competitive advantages and greater profits.

CONTROL AND EXPANSION

Conclusion Drastic organizational changes do not necessarily have to occur at the time a study of the business system is made, for a company may have grown and developed in tune with its growing business. But this is the exception. Some changes will always occur, and over the long run they are usually major.

The executive familiar with the fundamental changes in business philosophy forced upon business by the introduction of electronic data processing and the development of systems theory will be better prepared to meet the challenges they present. He will not be confused by the continuing change brought about by the systems approach to organization and decision making, nor will he consider electronic data processing a threat to his position. Instead, he will be able to control and guide that change in the most profitable directions and at the same time expand his capacity for more effective management performance.

REFERENCES

1. Many variations of this definition exists, e.g., Warren Brown, "Systems, Boundaries, and Information Flow," *Academy of Management Journal,* IX:4 (Dec. 1966), 318, defines a system as "a group or complex of parts (such as people, machines, etc.) interrelated in their actions towards some goal," and Richard A. Johnson, Fremont E. Kast, and James E. Rosenzweig, *The Theory and Management of Systems* (New York: McGraw-Hill Book Company, Inc., 1963), p. vii, state that "a system may be defined as an array of components designed to achieve an objective according to plan."
2. Johnson, Kast, and Rosenzweig, p. 6, n. 1, assert that von Bertalanffy was the first to use this term. For further information on von Bertalanffy's systems theory, see his *Problems of Life: An Evaluation of Modern Biological and Scientific Thought* (London: C. A. Watts and Co., Ltd., 1952) and a series of papers by von Bertalanffy, Carl G. Hempel, Robert E. Bass, and Hans Jonas, published as "General Systems Theory: A New Approach to Unity of Science," in *Human Biology,* XXIII:4 (Dec. 1951), 302–361.
3. von Bertalanffy, "General Systems Theory," 303.
4. Kenneth E. Boulding, "General Systems Theory—The Skeleton of Science," *Management Science,* II:3 (April 1956), 197–208.
5. *Ibid.,* p. 199.
6. Norbert Wiener, *The Human Use of Human Beings: Cybernetics and Society* (Boston: Houghton Mifflin Company, 1950), p. 8.
7. *Ibid.,* p. 15.
8. Herbert A. Simon, *The New Science of Management Decision* (New York: Harper & Row, Publishers, 1960), p. 1.
9. A number of recent authors have studied the applicaton of systems theory to business operations: Robert N. Anthony, John Dearden, and Richard F. Vancil, *Management Control Systems: Cases and Readings* (Homewood, Ill.: Richard D. Irwin, Inc., 1965); John Dearden and F. Warren McFarlan (*Management Information Systems: Text and Cases* (Homewood, Ill.: Richard D. Irwin, Inc., 1966); Daniel O. Dommasch and Charles W. Laudeman, *Principles Underlying Systems Engineering* (New York: Pitman Publishing Corp., 1962); Donald G. Malcolm and Alan J. Rowe, *Management Control Systems* (New York: John Wiley & Sons, Inc., 1960); Adrian M. McDonough and Leonard J. Garrett, *Management Systems: Working Concepts and Practices* (Homewood, Ill.: Richard D. Irwin, Inc., 1965); Henry M. Paynter, *Analysis and Design of Engineering Systems* (Cambridge, Mass.: M.I.T. Press, 1961); and Thomas R. Prince, *Information Systems for Management Planning and Control* (Homewood, Ill.: Richard D. Irwin, Inc., 1966).
10. A review of the kinds of environmental information needed for business planning, control, and operational decision making can be found in the following: V. Lewis Bassie, *Economic Forecasting* (New York: McGraw-Hill Book Company, Inc., 1958); Elmer Clark Bratt, *Business and Cycles and Forecasting* (5th ed.; Homewood, Ill.: Richard D. Irwin, Inc., 1961); John F. Due and Robert W. Clower, *Intermediate Economic Analysis: Resource Allocation, Factor Pricing, and Welfare* (5th ed.; Homewood, Ill.: Richard D. Irwin, Inc., 1966); and Milton H. Spencer, Colin G. Clark, and Peter W. Hoguet, *Business and Economic Forecasting* (Homewood, Ill.: Richard D. Irwin, Inc. 1961).
11. The following is a simplified statement of the planning process: (1) Define specifically what the company's planning effort is expected to achieve and to what use the plans will be put; develop an approach (including organization and management planning policies) to carry out the planning function within the

corporation. (2) Determine the key factors (planning premises) which will have a major influence on planning, through a study of both the environment (the economy, society, public policy, industry, and market) and the company's strengths and weaknesses. (3) In the light of the planning premises, develop and evaluate alternative directions the company might follow over the long range and select the corporate objective (i.e., kind of company) which will enable the company to most profitably exploit the market opportunities identified during the premising stage of planning. (4) After developing the evaluating alternative policies and programs which will achieve the objective, determine the policies, programs, and procedures that best fulfill the corporate objective and still meet market, industry, and company criteria (premises), and establish a suitable organization structure and adequate budgetary and operational controls. (5) Review and refine the program periodically.

For further information on the approach to scientific planning, see: Melville C. Branch, *The Corporate Planning Process* (New York: American Management Association, 1962); Preston P. LeBreton and Dale A. Henning, *Planning Theory* (Englewood Cliffs, N.J.: Prentice-Hall, Inc., 1961); Bruce Payne, *Planning for Company Growth* (New York: McGraw-Hill Book Company, 1963); and Brian W. Scott, *Long-Range Planning in American Industry* (New York: American Management Association, 1965).

12. McDonough and Garrett, p. 9.

7 ORGANIZATIONS AND THE SYSTEM CONCEPT*

Daniel Katz and *Robert L. Kahn*

The aims of social science with respect to human organizations are like those of any other science with respect to the events and phenomena of its domain. The social scientist wishes to understand human organizations, to describe what is essential in their form, aspects, and functions. He wishes to explain their cycles of growth and decline, to predict their effects and effectiveness. Perhaps he wishes as well to test and apply such knowledge by introducing purposeful changes into organizations—by making them, for example, more benign, more responsive to human needs.

Such efforts are not solely the prerogative of social science, however; common sense approaches to understanding and altering organizations are ancient and perpetual. They tend, on the whole, to rely heavily on two assumptions: that the location and nature of an organization are given by its name; and that an organization is possessed of built-in goals—because such goals were implanted by its founders, decreed by its present leaders, or because they emerged mysteriously as the purposes of the organizational system itself. These assumptions scarcely provide an adequate basis for the study of organizations and at times can be misleading and even fallacious. We propose, however, to make use of the information to which they point.

The first problem in understanding an organization or a social system is its location and identification. How do we know that we are dealing with an organization? What are its boundaries? What behavior belongs to the organization and what behavior lies outside it? Who are the individuals whose actions are to be studied and what segments of their behavior are to be included?

The fact that popular names exist to label social organizations is both a help and a hindrance. These popular labels represent the socially accepted stereotypes about organizations and do not specify their role structure, their psychological nature, or their boundaries. On the other hand, these names help in locating the area of behavior in which we are interested. Moreover, the fact that people both within and without an organization accept stereotypes about its nature and functioning is one determinant of its character.

The second key characteristic of the common sense approach to understanding an organization is to regard it simply as the epitome of the purposes of its designer, its leaders, or its key members. The teleology of this approach is again both a help and a hindrance. Since human purpose is deliberately built into organizations and is specifically recorded in the social compact, the by-laws, or other formal protocol of the undertaking, it would be inefficient not to utilize these sources of information. In the early development of a group, many processes are generated which have little to do with its rational purpose, but over time there is a cumulative recognition of the devices for ordering group life and a deliberate use of these devices.

Apart from formal protocol, the primary mission of an organization as perceived by its leaders furnishes a highly informative set of clues for the researcher seeking to study organizational functioning. Nevertheless, the stated purposes of an organization as given by its by-laws or in the reports of its leaders can be misleading. Such statements of objectives may idealize, rationalize, distort, omit, or even conceal some essential aspects of the functioning of the organization. Nor is there always agreement about the mission of the organization among its leaders and members. The university president may describe the purpose of his institution as one of turning out national leaders; the academic dean sees it as imparting the cultural heritage of the past, the academic vice-president as enabling students to move toward self-actualization and development, the graduate dean as creating new knowledge, the dean of men as training youngsters in technical and professional skills which will enable them to earn their living, and the editor of the student newspaper as inculcating the conservative

* Reprinted by permission of the publisher from *The Social Psychology of Organizations,* John Wiley & Sons, Inc., New York, 1966, chap. 2. Mr. Katz and Mr. Kahn are professors of psychology, University of Michigan.

values which will preserve the status quo of an outmoded capitalistic society.

The fallacy here is one of equating the purposes or goals of organizations with the purposes and goals of individual members. The organization as a system has an output, a product or an outcome, but this is not necessarily identical with the individual purposes of group members. Though the founders of the organization and its key members do think in teleological terms about organizational objectives, we should not accept such practical thinking, useful as it may be, in place of a theoretical set of constructs for purposes of scientific analysis. Social science, too frequently in the past, has been misled by such short-cuts and has equated popular phenomenology with scientific explanation.

In fact, the classic body of theory and thinking about organizations has assumed a teleology of this sort as the easiest way of identifying organizational structures and their functions. From this point of view an organization is a social device for efficiently accomplishing through group means some stated purpose; it is the equivalent of the blueprint for the design of the machine which is to be created for some practical objective. The essential difficulty with this purposive or design approach is that an organization characteristically includes more and less than is indicated by the design of its founder or the purpose of its leader. Some of the factors assumed in the design may be lacking or so distorted in operational practice as to be meaningless, while unforeseen embellishments dominate the organizational structure. Moreover, it is not always possible to ferret out the designer of the organization or to discover the intricacies of the design which he carried in his head. The attempt by Merton (1957) to deal with the latent function of the organization in contrast with its manifest function is one way of dealing with this problem. The study of unanticipated consequences as well as anticipated consequences of organizational functioning is a similar way of handling the matter. Again, however, we are back to the purposes of the creator or leader, dealing with unanticipated consequences on the assumption that we can discover the consequences anticipated by him and can lump all other outcomes together as a kind of error variance.

It would be much better theoretically, however, to start with concepts which do not call for identifying the purposes of the designers and then correcting for them when they do not seem to be fulfilled. The theoretical concepts should begin with the input, output, and functioning of the organization as a system and not with the rational purposes of its leaders. We may want to utilize such purposive notions to lead us to sources of data or as subjects of special study, but not as our basic theoretical constructs for understanding organizations.

Our theoretical model for the understanding of organizations is that of an energic input-output system in which the energic return from the output reactivates the system. Social organizations are flagrantly open systems in that the input of energies and the conversion of output into further energic input consist of transactions between the organization and its environment.

All social systems, including organizations, consist of the patterned activities of a number of individuals. Moreover, these patterned activities are complementary or interdependent with respect to some common output or outcome; they are repeated, relatively enduring and bounded in space and time. If the activity pattern occurs only once or at unpredictable intervals, we could not speak of an organization. The stability or recurrence of activities can be examined in relation to the *energic input* into the system, the *transformation of energies within the system,* and the *resulting product or energic output.* In a factory the raw materials and the human labor are the energic input, the patterned activities of production the transformation of energy, and the finished product the output. To maintain this patterned activity requires a continued renewal of the inflow of energy. This is guaranteed in social systems by the energic return from the product or outcome. Thus the outcome of the cycle of activities furnishes new energy for the initiation of a renewed cycle. The company which produces automobiles sells them and by doing so obtains the means of securing new raw materials, compensating its labor force, and continuing the activity pattern.

In many organizations outcomes are converted into money and new energy is furnished through this mechanism. Money is a convenient way of handling energy units both on the output and input sides, and buying and selling represent one set of social rules for regulating the exchange of money. Indeed, these rules are so effective and so widespread that there is some danger of mistaking the business of buying and selling for the defining cycles of organization. It is a commonplace executive observation that businesses exist to make money, and the observation is usually allowed to go unchallenged. It is, however, a very limited statement about the purposes of business.

Some human organizations do not depend on the cycle of selling and buying to maintain themselves. Universities and public agencies depend rather on bequests and legislative appropriations, and in so-called voluntary organizations the output reenergizes the activity of organization members in a more direct fashion. Member activities and accomplishments are rewarding in themselves and tend therefore to be continued, without the mediation of the outside environment. A society of bird watchers can wander into the hills and engage in the rewarding activities of identifying birds for their mutual edification and enjoyment. Organizations thus differ on this important dimension of the source of energy renewal, with the great majority utilizing both intrinsic and extrinsic sources in varying degree. Most large-scale organizations are not as self-contained as small voluntary groups and are very dependent upon the social effects of their output for energy renewal.

Our two basic criteria for identifying social systems and determining their functions are (1) tracing the pattern of energy exchange or activity of people as it results in some output and (2) ascertaining how the output is translated into energy which reactivates the pattern. We shall refer to organizational functions or objectives not as the conscious purposes of group leaders or group members but as the outcomes which are the energic source for a maintenance of the same type of output.

This model of an energic input-output system is taken from the open system theory as promulgated by von Bertalanffy (1956). Theorists have pointed out the applicability of the system concepts of the natural sciences to the problems of social science. It is important, therefore, to examine in more detail the constructs of system theory and the characteristics of open systems.

System theory is basically concerned with problems of relationships, of structure, and of interdependence rather than with the constant attributes of objects. In general approach it resembles field theory except that its dynamics deal with temporal as well as spatial patterns. Older formulations of system constructs dealt with the closed systems of the physical sciences, in which relatively self-contained structures could be treated successfully as if they were independent of external forces. But living systems, whether biological organisms or social organizations, are acutely dependent upon their external environment and so must be conceived of as open systems.

Before the advent of open-system thinking, social scientists tended to take one of two approaches in dealing with social structures; they tended either (1) to regard them as closed systems to which the laws of physics applied or (2) to endow them with some vitalistic concept like entelechy. In the former case they ignored the environmental forces affecting the organization and in the latter case they fell back upon some magical purposiveness to account for organizational functioning. Biological theorists, however, have rescued us from this trap by pointing out that the concept of the open system means that we neither have to follow the laws of traditional physics, nor in deserting them do we have to abandon science. The laws of Newtonian physics are correct generalizations but they are limited to closed systems. They do not apply in the same fashion to open systems which maintain themselves through constant commerce with their environment, i.e., a continuous inflow and outflow of energy through permeable boundaries.

One example of the operation of closed versus open systems can be seen in the concept of entropy and the second law of thermodynamics. According to the second law of thermodynamics, a system moves toward equilibrium; it tends to run down, that is, its differentiated structures tend to move toward dissolution as the elements composing them become arranged in random disorder. For example, suppose that a bar of iron has been heated by the application of a blow-torch on one side. The arrangement of all the fast (heated) molecules on one side and all the slow molecules on the other is an unstable state, and over time the distribution of molecules becomes in effect random, with the resultant cooling of one side and heating of the other, so that all surfaces of the iron approach the same temperature. A similar process of heat exchange will also be going on between the iron bar and its environment, so that the bar will gradually approach the temperature of the room in which it is located, and in so doing will elevate somewhat the previous temperature of the room. More technically, entropy increases toward a maximum and equilibrium occurs as the physical system attains the state of the most probable distribution of its elements. In social systems, however, structures tend to become more elaborated rather than less differentiated. The rich may grow richer and the poor may grow poorer. The open system does not run down, because it can import energy from the world around it. Thus the operation of entropy is counteracted by the importation of energy and the living system is characterized by negative rather than positive entropy.

COMMON CHARACTERISTICS OF OPEN SYSTEMS

Though the various types of open systems have common characteristics by virtue of being open systems, they differ in other characteristics. If this were not the case, we would be able to obtain all our basic knowledge about social organizations through studying the biological organisms or even through the study of a single cell.

The following nine characteristics seem to define all open systems.

1. Importation of Energy. Open systems import some form of energy from the external environment. The cell receives oxygen from the blood stream; the body similarly takes in oxygen from the air and food from the external world. The personality is dependent upon the external world for stimulation. Studies of sensory deprivation show that when a person is placed in a darkened soundproof room, where he has a minimal amount of visual and auditory stimulation, he develops hallucinations and other signs of mental stress (Solomon et al., 1961). Deprivation of social stimulation also can lead to mental disorganization (Spitz, 1945). Köhler's (1944, 1947) studies of the figural after-effects of continued stimulation show the dependence of perception upon its energic support from the external world. Animals deprived of visual experience from birth for a prolonged period never fully recover their visual capacities (Melzack and Thompson, 1956). In other words, the functioning personality is heavily dependent upon the continuous inflow of stimulation from the external environment. Similarly, social organizations must also draw renewed supplies of energy from other institutions, or people, or the material environment. No social structure is self-sufficient or self-contained.

2. The Through-put. Open systems transform the energy available to them. The body converts starch and sugar into heat and action. The personality converts chemical and electrical forms of stimulation into sensory qualities, and information into thought patterns. The organization creates a new product, or processes materials, or trains people, or provides a service. These activities entail some reorganization of input. Some work gets done in the system.

3. The Output. Open systems export some product into the environment, whether it be the invention of an inquiring mind or a bridge constructed by an engineering firm. Even the biological organism exports physiological products such as carbon dioxide from the lungs which helps to maintain plants in the immediate environment.

4. Systems As Cycles of Events. The pattern of activities of the energy exchange has a cyclic character. The product exported into the environment furnishes the sources of energy for the repetition of the cycle of activities. The energy reinforcing the cycle of activities can derive from some exchange of the product in the external world or from the activity itself. In the former instance, the industrial concern utilizes raw materials and human labor to turn out a product which is marketed, and the monetary return is used to obtain more raw materials and labor to perpetuate the cycle of activities. In the latter instance, the voluntary organization can provide expressive satisfactions to its members so that the energy renewal comes directly from the organizational activity itself.

The problem of structure, or the relatedness of parts, can be observed directly in some physical arrangement of things where the larger unit is physically bounded and its subparts are also bounded within the larger structure. But how do we deal with social structures, where physical boundaries in this sense do not exist? It was the genius of F. H. Allport (1962) which contributed the answer, namely that the structure is to be found in an interrelated set of events which return upon themselves to complete and renew a cycle of activities. It is events rather than things which are structured, so that social structure is a dynamic rather than a static concept. Activities are structured so that they comprise a unity in their completion or closure. A simple linear stimulus-response exchange between two people would not constitute social structure. To create structure, the responses of A would have to elicit B's reactions in such a manner that the responses of the latter would stimulate A to further responses. Of course the chain of events may involve many people, but their behavior can be characterized as showing structure only when there is some closure to the chain by a return to its point of origin with the probability that the chain of events will then be repeated. The repetition of the cycle does not have to involve the same set of phenotypical happenings. It may expand to include more sub-events of exactly the same kind or it may involve similar activities directed toward the same outcomes. In the individual organism the eye may move in such a way as to have the point of light fall upon the center of the retina. As the point of light moves, the movements of the eye may also change but to complete the same cycle of activity, i.e., to focus upon the point of light.

A single cycle of events of a self-closing character gives us a simple form of structure. But such single cycles can also combine to give a larger structure of events or an event system. An event system may consist of a circle of smaller cycles or hoops, each one of which makes contact with several others. Cycles may also be tangential to one another from other types of subsystems. The basic method for the identification of social structures is to follow the energic chain of events from the input of energy through its transformation to the point of closure of the cycle.

5. Negative Entropy. To survive, open systems must move to arrest the entropic process; they must acquire negative entropy. The entropic process is a universal law of nature in which all forms of organization move toward disorganization or death. Complex physical systems move toward simple random distribution of their elements and biological organisms also run down and perish. The open system, however, by importing more energy from its environment than it expends, can store energy and can acquire negative entropy. There is then a general trend in an open system to maximize its ratio of imported to expended energy, to survive and even during periods of crisis to live on borrowed time. Prisoners in concentration camps on a starvation diet will carefully conserve any form of energy expenditure to make the limited food intake go as far as possible (Cohen, 1954). Social organizations will seek to improve their survival position and to acquire in their reserves a comfortable margin of operation.

The entropic process asserts itself in all biological systems as well as in closed physical systems. The energy replenishment of the biological organism is not of a qualitative character which can maintain indefinitely the complex organizational structure of living tissue. Social systems, however, are not anchored in the same physical constancies as biological organisms and so are capable of almost indefinite arresting of the entropic process. Nevertheless the number of organizations which go out of existence every year is large.

6. Information Input, Negative Feedback, and the Coding Process. The inputs into living systems consist not only of energic materials which become transformed or altered in the work that gets done. Inputs are also informative in character and furnish signals to the structure about the environment and about its own functioning in relation to the environment. Just as we recognize the distinction between cues and drives in individual psychology, so must we take account of information and energic inputs for all living systems.

The simplest type of information input found in all systems is negative feedback. Information feedback of a negative kind enables the system to correct its deviations from course. The working parts of the machine feed back information about the effects of their operation to some central mechanism or subsystem which acts on such information to keep the system on target. The thermostat which controls the temperature of the room is a simple example of a regulatory device which operates on the basis of negative feedback. The automated power plant would furnish more complex examples. Miller (1955) emphasizes the critical nature of negative feedback in his proposition: *"When a system's negative feedback discontinues, its steady state vanishes, and at the same time its boundary disappears and the system terminates"* (p. 529). If there is no corrective device to get the system back on its course, it will expend too much energy or it will ingest too much energic input and no longer continue as a system.

The reception of inputs into a system is selective. Not all energic inputs are capable of being absorbed into every system. The digestive system of living creatures assimilates only those inputs to which it is adapted. Similarly, systems can react only to those information signals to which they are attuned. The general term for the selective mechanisms of a system by which incoming materials are rejected or accepted and translated for the structure is coding. Through the coding process the "blooming, buzzing confusion" of the world is simplified into a few meaningful and simplified categories for a given system. The nature of the functions performed by the system determines its coding mechanisms, which in turn perpetuate this type of functioning.

7. The Steady State and Dynamic Homeostasis. The importation of energy to arrest entropy operates to maintain some constancy in energy exchange, so that open systems which survive are characterized by a steady state. A steady state is not motionless or a true equilibrium. There is a continuous inflow of energy from the external environment and a continuous export of the products of the system, but the character of the system, the ratio of the energy exchanges and the relations between parts, remains the same. The catabolic and anabolic processes of tissue breakdown and restoration within the body preserve a steady state so that the organism from time to time is not the identical organism it was but a highly similar organism. The steady state is seen in clear form in the homeostatic processes for the regulation of body temperature; external conditions of humidity and temperature may vary, but the temperature of the body remains the same. The endocrine glands are a regulatory mechanism for preserving an evenness of physiological functioning. The general principle here is that of Le Châtelier (see Bradley and Calvin, 1956) who maintains that any internal or external factor making for disruption of the system is countered by forces which restore the system as closely as possible to its previous state. Krech and Crutchfield (1948) similarly hold, with respect to psychological organization, that cognitive structures will react to influences in such a way as to absorb them with minimal change to existing cognitive integration.

The homeostatic principle does not apply literally to the functioning of all complex living systems, in that in counteracting entropy they move toward growth and expansion. This apparent contradiction can be resolved, however, if we recognize the complexity of the subsystems and their interaction in anticipating changes necessary for the maintenance of an overall steady state. Stagner (1951) has pointed out that the initial disturbance of a given tissue constancy within the biological organism will result in mobilization of energy to restore the balance, but that recurrent upsets will lead to actions to anticipate the disturbance:

> We eat before we experience intense hunger pangs. . . . energy mobilization for forestalling tactics must be explained in terms of a *cortical tension* which reflects the visceral-proprioceptive pattern of the original biological disequilibration. . . . *Dynamic homeostasis* involves the maintenance of tissue constancies by establishing a constant physical environment—by reducing the variability and disturbing effects of external stimulation. Thus the organism does not simply restore the prior equilibrium. A new, more complex and more comprehensive equilibrium is established. (p. 5)

Though the tendency toward a steady state in its simplest form is homeostatic, as in the preservation of a constant body temperature, the basic principle is *the preservation of the character of the system*. The equilibrium which complex systems approach is often that of a quasi-stationary equilibrium, to use Lewin's concept (1947). An adjustment in one direction is countered by a movement in the opposite direction and both movements are approximate rather than precise in their compensatory nature. Thus a temporal chart of activity will show a series of ups and downs rather than a smooth curve.

In preserving the character of the system, moreover, the structure will tend to import more energy than is required for its output, as we have already noted in discussing negative entropy. To insure survival, systems will operate to acquire some margin of safety beyond the immediate level of existence. The body will store fat, the social organization will build up reserves, the society will increase its technological and cultural base. Miller (1955) has formulated the proposition that the rate of growth of a system—within certain ranges—is exponential if it exists in a medium which makes available unrestricted amounts of energy for input.

In adapting to their environment, systems will attempt to cope with external forces by ingesting them or acquiring control over them. The physical boundedness of the single organism means that such attempts at control over the environment affect the behavioral system rather than the biological system of the individual. Social systems will move, however, towards incorporating within their boundaries the external resources essential to survival. Again the result is an expansion of the original system.

Thus, the steady state which at the simple level is one of homeostasis over time, at more complex levels becomes one of preserving the character of the system through growth and expansion. The basic type of system does not change directly as a consequence of expansion. The most common type of growth is a multiplication of the same type of cycles or subsystems—a change in quantity rather than in quality. Animal and plant species grow by multiplication. A social system adds more units of the same essential type as it already has. Haire (1959) has studied the ratio between the sizes of different subsystems in growing business organizations. He found that though the number of people increased in both the production subsystem and the subsystem concerned with the external world, the ratio of the two groups remained constant. Qualitative change does occur, however, in two ways. In the first place, quantitative growth calls for supportive subsystems of a specialized character not necessary when the system was smaller. In the second place, there is a point where quantitative changes produce a qualitative difference in the functioning of a system. A small college which triples its size is no longer the same institution in terms of the relation between its administration and faculty, relations among the various academic departments, or the nature of its instruction.

In fine, living systems exhibit a growth or expansion dynamic in which they maximize their basic character. They react to change or they anticipate change through growth which assimilates the new energic inputs to the nature of their structure. In terms of Lewin's quasi-stationary equilibrium the ups and downs of the adjustive process do not always result in a return to the old level. Under certain circumstances a solidification or freezing occurs during one of the adjustive cycles. A new base line level is thus established and successive movements fluctuate around this plateau which may be either above or below the previous plateau of operation.

8. Differentiation. Open systems move in the direction of differentiation and elaboration. Diffuse global patterns are replaced by more specialized functions. The sense organs and the nervous system evolved as highly differentiated structures from the primitive nervous tissues. The growth of the personality proceeds from primitive, crude organizations of mental functions to hierarchically structured and well-differentiated systems of beliefs and feelings. Social organizations move toward the multiplication and elaboration of roles with greater specialization of function. In the United States today medical specialists now outnumber the general practitioners.

One type of differentiated growth in systems is what von Bertalanffy (1956) terms progressive mechanization. It finds expression in the way in which a system achieves a steady state. The early method is a process which involves an interaction of various dynamic forces, whereas the later development entails the use of a regulatory feedback mechanism. He writes:

> It can be shown that the *primary* regulations in organic systems, that is, those which are most fundamental and primitive in embryonic development as well as in evolution, are of such nature of dynamic interaction. . . . Superimposed are those regulations which we may call *secondary*, and which are controlled by fixed arrangements, especially of the feedback type. This state of affairs is a consequence of a general principle of organization which may be called progressive mechanization. At first, systems—biological, neurological, psychological or social—are governed by dynamic interaction of their components; later on, fixed arrangements and conditions of constraint are established which render the system and its parts more efficient, but also gradually diminish and eventually abolish its equipotentiality. (p. 6)

9. Equifinality. Open systems are further characterized by the principle of equifinality, a principle suggested by von Bertalanffy in 1940. According to this principle, a system can reach the same final state from differing initial conditions and by a variety of paths. The well-known biological experiments on the sea urchin show that a normal creature of that species can develop from a complete ovum, from each half of a divided ovum, or from the fusion product of two whole ova. As open systems move toward regulatory mechanisms to control their operations, the amount of equifinality may be reduced.

SOME CONSEQUENCES OF VIEWING ORGANIZATIONS AS OPEN SYSTEMS

In the following chapter we shall inquire into the specific implications of considering organizations as open systems and into the ways in which social organizations differ from other types of living systems. At this point, however, we should call attention to some of the misconceptions which arise both in theory and practice when social organizations are regarded as closed rather than open systems.

The major misconception is the failure to recognize fully that the organization is continually dependent upon inputs from the environment and that the inflow of materials and human energy is not a constant. The fact that organizations have built-in protective devices to maintain stability and that they are notoriously difficult to change in the direction of some reformer's desires should not obscure the realities of the dynamic interrelationships of any social structure with its social and natural environment. The very efforts of the organization to maintain a constant external environment produce changes in organizational structure. The reaction to changed inputs to mute their possible revolutionary implications also results in changes.

The typical models in organizational theorizing concentrate upon principles of internal functioning as if these problems were independent of changes in the environment and as if they did not affect the maintenance inputs of motivation and morale. Moves toward tighter integration and coordination are made to insure stability, when flexibility may be the more important requirement. Moreover, coordination and control become ends in themselves rather than means to an end. They are not seen in full perspective as adjusting the system to its environment but as desirable goals within a closed system. In fact, however, every attempt at coordination which is not functionally required may produce a host of new organizational problems.

One error which stems from this kind of misconception is the failure to recognize the equifinality of the open system, namely that there are more ways than one of producing a given outcome. In a closed physical system the same initial conditions must lead to the same final result. In open systems this is not true even at the biological level. It is much less true at the social level. Yet in practice we insist that there is one best way of assembling a gun for all recruits, one best way for the baseball player to hurl the ball in from the outfield, and that we standardize and teach these best methods. Now it is true under certain conditions that there is one best way, but these conditions must first be established. The general principle, which characterizes all open systems, is that there does not have to be a single method for achieving an objective.

A second error lies in the notion that irregularities in the functioning of a system due to environmental influences are error variances and should be treated accordingly. According to this conception, they should be controlled out of studies of organizations. From the organization's own operations they should be excluded as irrelevant and should be guarded against. The decisions of officers to omit a consideration of external factors or to guard against such influences in a defensive fashion, as if they would go away if ignored, is an instance of this type of thinking. So is the now outmoded "public be damned" attitude of businessmen toward the clientele upon whose support they depend. Open system theory, on the other hand, would maintain that environmental influences are not sources of error variance but are integrally related to the functioning of a social system, and that we cannot understand a system without a constant study of the forces that impinge upon it.

Thinking of the organization as a closed system, moreover, results in a failure to develop the intelligence or feedback function of obtaining adequate information about the changes in environmental forces. It is remarkable how weak many industrial companies are in their market research departments when they are so dependent upon the market. The prediction can be hazarded that organizations in our society will increasingly move toward the improvement of the facilities for research in assessing environmental forces. The reason is that we are in the process of correcting our misconception of the organization as a closed system.

Emery and Trist (1960) have pointed out how current theorizing on organizations still reflects the older closed system conceptions. They write:

> In the realm of social theory, however, there has been something of a tendency to continue thinking in terms of a "closed" system, that is, to regard the enterprise as sufficiently independent to allow most of its problems to be analyzed with reference to its internal structure and without reference to its external environment. . . . In practice the system theorists in social science . . . did "tend to focus on the statics of social structure and to neglect the study of structural change." In an attempt to overcome this bias, Merton suggested that "the concept of dysfunction, which implied the concept of strain, stress and tension on the structural level, provides an analytical approach to the study of dynamics and change." This concept has been widely accepted by system theorists but while it draws attention to sources of imbalance within an organization it does not conceptually reflect the mutual permeation of an organization and its environment that is the cause of such imbalance. It still retains the limiting perspectives of "closed system" theorizing. In the administrative field the same limitations may be seen in the otherwise invaluable contributions of Barnard and related writers. (p. 84)

SUMMARY

The open-system approach to organizations is contrasted with common-sense approaches, which tend to accept popular names and stereotypes as basic organizational properties and to identify the purpose of an organization in terms of the goals of its founders and leaders.

The open-system approach, on the other hand, begins by identifying and mapping the repeated cycles of input, transformation, output, and renewed input which comprise the organizational pattern. This approach to organizations represents the adaptation of work in biology and in the physical sciences by von Bertalanffy and others.

Organizations as a special class of open systems have properties of their own, but they share other properties in common with all open systems. These include the importation of energy from the environment, the through-put or transformation of the imported energy into some product form which is characteristic of the system, the exporting of that product into the environment, and the reenergizing of the system from sources in the environment.

Open systems also share the characteristics of negative entropy, feedback, homeostasis, differentiation, and equifinality. The law of negative entropy states that systems survive and maintain their characteristic internal order only so long as they import from the environment more energy than they expend in the process of transformation and exportation. The feedback principle has to do with information input, which is a special kind of energic importation, a kind of signal to the system about environmental conditions and about the functioning of the system in relation to its environment. The feedback of such information enables the system to correct for its own malfunctioning or for changes in the environment, and thus to maintain a steady state or homeostasis. This is a dynamic rather than a static balance, however. Open systems are not at rest but tend toward differentiation and elaboration, both because of subsystem dynamics and because of the relationship between growth and survival. Finally, open systems are characterized by the principle of equifinality, which asserts that systems can reach the same final state from different initial conditions and by different paths of development.

Traditional organizational theories have tended to view the human organization as a closed system. This tendency has led to a disregard of differing organizational environments and the nature of organizational dependency on environment. It has led also to an overconcentration on principles of internal organizational functioning, with consequent failure to develop and understand the processes of feedback which are essential to survival.

C. THE ENVIRONMENT OF MANAGING

8 SOCIAL RESPONSIBILITY: A NEW DIMENSION OF CORPORATE ACCOUNTABILITY*

John J. Corson and *George A. Steiner*

American business enterprises—from the self-employed appliance repairman to the billion-dollar corporation—are being held responsible for their performance in a more precise and thorough fashion than has ever occurred.[1] The quality and reliability of the services and products offered for sale must meet steadily rising standards. The truthfulness and completeness of the information given consumers about the services or products through labeling of advertising is subject to continually exacting standards. The degree to which investors must be informed as to the details of a corporation's financial operations, even its projections of revenues and earnings, is greater today than at any previous time. From August 1971 to May 1974 prices charged for many services and products were subject to formal control by the federal government. Even before this, however, the prices of some services (e.g., medical care) and of some products (e.g., automobiles and steel) were increasingly subject to informal control in the court of public opinion.

Of more recent origin but part and parcel of this extended demand for accountability is a growing insistence that corporations, particularly the larger ones, shall measure up to a proliferating variety of social responsibilities. There is substantial evidence that "the public wants business to contribute a good deal more to achieving the goals of a good society"[2] and that individuals and groups (e.g., minorities, consumers, investors) alike want evidence with which to measure the contribution of business —positive or negative—to the well-being of society.

* Reprinted by permission from the publisher from *Measuring Business's Social Performance: The Corporate Social Audit,* Committee for Economic Development, New York, 1974, chap. 1, pp. 1–20. Mr. Corson is a director of several companies, a former management consultant, and a former professor at Princeton University. Mr. Steiner is professor of management and public policy, University of California, Los Angeles.

There agreement ends. There is no consensus on what is meant by the social actions of business, what social responsibilities it shall be expected to bear, how its performance in discharging them is to be appraised or audited, by whom the appraisal or social audit will be made, or to whom the findings shall be reported.

What is clear is that it is generally recognized that many of the actions of business firms (e.g., how many and who are employed, how scarce raw materials are utilized, the reliability and the safety of the products sold) affect the well-being of the society, and thus can be described as social actions. It is also clear that "business is being asked to assume broader responsibilities to society than ever before and to serve a wider range of human values"[3] (e.g., to employ the physically handicapped; to provide advancement opportunities for minorities; to assist in overcoming urban blight; to support educational, health, art, and other cultural institutions); these and similar expectations have come to be called social responsibilities. And the evolving means by which the corporation and others have striven to appraise the impact of its actions on the society and the manner in which it has discharged its social responsibilities have generally been described as a social audit.

The nature of these concepts and the evolution of the corporation's accountability for the discharge of social responsibilities is the subject of this book. Specifically, the variety of pressures for greater accountability and their sources are examined in this first chapter. The ways in which corporations are responding to these pressures are shown by a recently completed survey of 284 companies; that survey was undertaken to reveal what responsibilities corporations have assumed and how and to what extent they are taking stock of these activities. The third chapter assesses the logic and feasibility of meeting the growing demand for accountability through a social audit. The final chapter presents a series of steps that a firm may consider taking into account in assessing its social performance.

GUARDIANS OF THE PUBLIC INTEREST

Among those who advance the notion of corporate accountability are the self-appointed guardians of the public interest. Several are prominent leaders in this community. Ralph Nader, the crusading lawyer and consumer advocate; Robert A. Dahl, professor of political science, Yale University; and Neil H. Jacoby, professor of business economics and policy, University of California, Los Angeles, articulate the underlying logic on which the views of this group are based.

Nader contends that what is needed is "a great national debate on the whole question of corporate accountability." The reason for this, he argues, is that:

> We're heading into a greater and greater portion of the economy taking on the characterization of corporate socialism, which is basically corporate power utilizing government power to protect it from competition, for example, oil import quotas; to grant large subsidies, for example, to the maritime industry; or to socialize the risk and costs of a lot of corporate activities through the tax mechanism or through inflated and constantly renegotiated contracts, for example, Lockheed.[4]

To assure that the concentrated corporate power he envisions is used in the public interest, Nader argues that the disclosure requirements of the Securities and Exchange Commission should be broadened to cover the whole impact of the corporation on society. He asks rhetorically: "Why shouldn't we know in the annual report how much U.S. Steel dumps into the water, air, and land—and where—as part of its social cost accounting?" Nader would supplement such disclosure with the requirement that each corporation maintain a complaint procedure and that each complaint be "fed into a national computerized system where it would be instantaneously available to the citizen."[5]

Professor Dahl has advanced views that imply the need for an assessment of the corporation's performance on an even broader front. Every large corporation, he contends, should be thought of as a social enterprise and as a political system that exercises "great power, influence, and control over other human beings." Dahl further states that "since 'external controls' on the behavior of large firms through markets and competition . . . are virtually worthless," and since neither stockholders nor management can be relied upon to ensure socially responsible behavior, other controls must be established.[6]

In proposing a remedy, Dahl goes far beyond Nader's basic requirement of disclosure. He recommends that a major investigation be launched by Congress to determine "the most appropriate ways to govern the large United States corporation in the foreseeable future." That is, Dahl asks, should the corporation be governed from without by the market, by the market supplemented by government controls, or from within by stockholders, by workers, by consumers, or by some combination of these groups? "What is the most appropriate form of ownership to achieve and maintain the kind of corporate government desired?" Congress should attempt to determine this as well as "the comparative efficiencies of different alternatives" of government and ownership; for example, can an enterprise be operated more efficiently under managerial control than under cooperative control? Finally, Congress should ascertain the advantages and disadvantages of scale. That is, "are large firms necessary in order to benefit from the advantages of scale?"[7]

The thrust of these questions is that such an investigation might demonstrate the need for the exercise of some greater control over corporate managements by government, stockholders, consumers, and employees. An even more likely result is that such an investigation would emphasize the necessity of providing each of these groups with fuller information about corporate affairs.

A rationale, which leads to less radical conclusions, for how the corporation may be made to serve the public interest, has been formulated by Neil H. Jacoby. He believes that the conventional theories of the past, which held that corporate behavior was dictated by "short-run profit maximization" or by the "security and business volume," are no longer tenable. It is now essential to recognize that "corporate behavior is responsive to political forces, public opinion, and governmental pressure." These forces, which are "all non-market forces," have "induced large companies to allocate resources to a variety of social purposes." Reciprocally, it follows that "political forces, public opinion, and governmental agencies are guided in their exercise of substantial power by such information and its accuracy as is made available (or is not made available) by the corporation itself."[8]

The observations and demands of these observers of contemporary corporate performance are certainly subject to debate. Their views are not presented here because they have general acceptance. Nor are their views set forth because they specifically call for a corporate social audit. They do not. Rather, these views are noted here because they demonstrate a growing demand for fuller information so that firms can be held accountable for the roles that different groups contend they should perform. We believe such demands will expand rather than diminish. The following discussion adds support to this contention.

ADVOCATES FOR THE CONSUMER

Closely affiliated with those concerned with guarding the public interest are the official and unofficial representatives of perhaps the most vocal group that now insists upon an evaluation of the social performance of business enterprises, namely, the consumers. The increased recognition of the rights and the strength of the consumer in the American economy is reflected in: (1) the accumulation of consumer protection legislation, for example, Flammable Fabrics Act (1953), Fair Packaging and Labeling Act (1966), Truth-in-Lending Act (1968), and Consumer Product Safety Act (1972); (2) the existence of governmental machinery, for example, the special assistant to the President for consumer affairs and similar units in at least twenty-nine states and nine major cities or counties; (3) the new federal Consumer Product Safety Commission; and (4) a continuing volume of literature presenting the plight of the consumer or urging consumers to exercise their presumed economic power.[9]

The consumer is said to have four rights: to safety, to choose, to be heard, and to be informed. Implicit in the first three rights is the fourth. The presumption that the consumer will, if informed, act to protect his own safety, make wise and economic decisions, and voice his own views to producers is often challenged by evidence that consumers may still buy a shoddy product or service because it is the least expensive and remain silent about the lack of quality. Still, it is clear that if the consumer is to protect himself, let alone rule in the marketplace, he needs to be informed. Hence, each statute cited in the preceding paragraph specifically provides for the disclosure of information, and each governmental agency established to protect the consumer devotes much of its effort to forcing the disclosure of fuller and more reliable information. Much consumer-focused literature emphasizes that in a complex technological society advertising messages do not enable the average buyer to make intelligent choices between, for example, clothing made of Dacron or Fortrel, or competing automobiles, refrigerators, tires, or television sets.[10]

INVESTOR'S NEED TO KNOW

Corporate investors (a group that includes mutual funds, insurance companies, trust companies, trust departments of banks, pension funds, university or foundation endowments, and individuals) and their advisors are being confronted with both moral and economic pressures by some whose funds they handle and by social critics. Those who make investment decisions are increasingly being pressed to form moral judgments on the behavior of the corporations in which they might invest. They are now required to give recognition to the prospective impact on future costs and earnings of "unfunded past and future social costs" that society has imposed or is expected to impose on the corporations in which they would invest.[11]

The moral pressures bear with special force on those responsible for investing the funds of churches, universities, foundations, and other nonprofit institutions with similar social orientations. Together, these investors manage funds worth many billions of dollars. The executives responsible for these funds take various stands on the degree of pressure they should place upon corporations in which they are stockholders "to meet human needs and to ameliorate many kinds of current social problems, such as pollution, discrimination, unsafe conditions, and urban blight."[12] Some church, university, and foundation investors have stated that they do not condone particular activities engaged in by companies whose stock they hold, notably corporate operations in South Africa and the production of weapons with which the war in Vietnam was prosecuted.* Moreover, they have said that they will use their shares of stock to put ownership pressure on executives to engage in what they believe to be more socially responsive behavior.[13]

These investors seek information not generally made available upon which to base judgments about corporate behavior. The creation in December 1972 of the Investor Responsibility Research Center signaled an organized effort on the part of a number of large uni-

* An example was provided by the World Council of Churches when it announced on January 22, 1973, that it had liquidated investments valued at about $1.5 million in British, Swiss, and Dutch companies doing business with white-ruled African countries. These investments represented 30 to 40 percent of the council's total shareholdings.

versities, foundations, and other endowed institutions to establish a basis for a more informed appraisal of the social behavior of corporations in which they and others have invested or contemplate investing. The essential function of the center is to offer those who subscribe to its research and information services an audit of the social behavior of corporations.

Economic pressures confronting investors are recognized by a small but increasing number of their spokesmen. The guidelines set by the American Bankers Association for use by the trust officers of banks reflect this awareness. These guidelines advise:

> A bank fiduciary should make every effort to make relative judgments on social and environmental issues [but] it would be improper . . . unless directed by its customer, to invest in the securities of a corporation solely because it has a good performance record in dealing with social and environmental problems, if investments in other securities . . . will produce a better financial reward.[14]

The Dreyfus Third Century Fund, one of the few mutual funds that focuses attention on corporations that avow an acceptance of social responsibilities, specifies what it takes into account in evaluations of the companies in which it invests. Its prospectus of March 1972 stated:

> The Fund will invest in companies which not only meet traditional investment standards but also show evidence in the conduct of their business relative to other companies in the same industry or industries of contributing to the enhancement of the quality of life in America. . . . The Fund intends to consider performance by companies in the areas of (1) the protection and improvement of the environment and the proper use of our natural resources, (2) occupational health and safety, (3) consumer protection and product purity, and (4) equal employment opportunity [and] special consideration will be given to those companies which have, or are developing, technology products or services which . . . will contribute to the enhancement of the quality of life.

The rationale for considering these factors is founded in the belief by managers of the Fund that performance at high standards in these areas "will generally indicate that these companies are well managed and, therefore, present opportunities for capital growth."

Three other mutual funds (First Spectrum Fund, Pax World Fund, and Social Dimensions Fund) have announced substantially similar policies. If these funds persist in their efforts, they will tend to promote more socially responsive corporate behavior. Yet the managers of these funds have not made clear what guides they use in answering such basic questions as: What is socially responsive behavior? What standards exist against which the behavior of corporations can be measured? Is adequate information about corporate practice available?

To aid institutional and individual investors in formulating judgments regarding corporate social performance, the Council on Economic Priorities was established in 1970 by Alice Tepper Marlin to make in-depth studies of the policies and practices of particular companies and industries. The council serves both the investors who seek to weigh corporate social performance in considering investments and consumers who want to weigh such performance in choosing which products or services to purchase. The council's focus is indicated by the studies it has issued to date. One early report, *Paper Profits,*[15] assessed the extent to which each of twenty-four pulp and paper producers have installed antipollution devices and processes. A second report described activities of companies in the petroleum industry, and a third examined the environmental pollution practices of electric utility companies. Two further reports told subscribers of the involvement of a number of major corporations in the production of war matériel.

REPORTING TO GOVERNMENT

Governments, especially the federal government, are now requiring an accounting from corporations about their performance in a number of social program areas. However, reporting is piecemeal in the sense that each of a number of governmental agencies requires separate pieces of information about individual products, operational practices, employment practices, and financial operations. The consumer or the investor who desires to form an overall judgment of the social performance of a particular company can expect little help in integrating the various reports so that he can form that judgment, even if he could get the information.

Both the Food and Drug Administration and the Federal Trade Commission have required producers of products over which they have authority either to report the characteristics of products (e.g., through tests showing the safety or purity of drugs or the flammability of textiles) or to disclose specified information to the consumer (e.g., by labeling drugs, giving warnings on cigarette packages, and providing data concerning interest charges in consumer loan agreements). The information about product safety reported to these agencies has been supplemented since 1972 by the National Electronic Injury Surveillance System established by the Bureau of Product Safety in the Food and Drug Administration. This system, known as NEISS, provides periodic reports on the number of injuries to individuals in which a product was the cause.

The Environmental Protection Agency has set air pollution standards and has stimulated the state governments to establish water-quality standards. Corporations whose operations are covered must report periodically on their conformance with these standards.

The Equal Employment Opportunity Commission investigates the employment practices of corporations and requires the submission of data on employment of minority group members. The Department of Labor requires every establishment covered by the Occupational Safety and Health Act of 1970 to maintain a log of each occupational injury or illness suffered by an employee. This log must be available when the department's inspectors visit the establishment.

In June 1971 the Securities and Exchange Commission instituted new disclosure rules that require corporations to set forth in their financial statements the accounting principles that were used and the effect these principles had on the financial results reported.[16] Other new rules broadened the conventional areas of disclosure by adding requirements that each corporation disclose any prospective impact on capital outlays or earnings as a result of compliance with environmental control or civil rights legislation.[17] The commission is now being prodded by public-interest groups to force companies to include public-interest proposals suggested by shareholders in their proxy statements (e.g., the creation of a committee of General Motors Corporation shareholders to review the public impact of the company's management decisions).

Finally, the contracts signed by companies that do business with the federal government require them to perform various socially responsible actions and, in several instances, to report on their performance.[18] Firms that sell products or services to the federal government are required to maintain "fair employment practices," to provide "safe and healthful" working conditions, to pay "prevailing wages," to curb the pollution of the air and water, and to facilitate the employment and training of handicapped persons and of former prisoners seeking rehabilitation.

ROLE OF THE ACCOUNTANT

As the growth of corporate enterprise has increased the impact of major corporations on investors, employees, consumers, other business firms, and the public, accountants have been pressed to accept steadily broadening responsibility for informing the society generally as well as their clients. They have, thus, "been caught in the bind between their public responsibilities and the pressure of clients who pay their fees."[19] Their response to this pressure has been manifested in the issuances of the former Accounting Principles Board, the establishment of the new Financial Accounting Standards Board, and the promulgation of guidelines by the American Institute of Certified Public Accountants. Their issuances have been reaffirmed by SEC rulings, and the courts have vigorously sought ways of providing all who read corporate annual reports with a fuller knowledge of the workings and projects of audited companies. One manifestation of this effort has been the development of what some now call socioeconomic accounting, a concept that embraces the assessment of corporate social performance.[20]

Accountants, like other observers of the current scene, have witnessed society's heightened concern with the quality of life. First, in noticing the vast sums being spent by governments for social programs, some accountants have come to believe that waste could be reduced by the application of their skills to the management of these programs.[21] Second, accountants have noted the emergence of the idea of indicators of social change, that is, measures of gain or loss in such areas as crime, education, health, and poverty reduction. Again, as professionals skilled in quantification and evaluation, they have visualized a role that they might play in refining the idea of indicators.[22] Third, and most relevant to this discussion, some have been considering how they can help a business firm to equip itself to cope with increasing demands for information about its social performance.

Each of the three professional associations of accountants has now established a committee to consider how they should go about measuring corporate social performance.† The work of the Committee on Social Measurement established by the American Institute of Certified Public Accountants is illustrative of these efforts. The chairman of this committee explains that "when business is being accused of

† The American Institute of Certified Public Accountants, the American Accounting Association, and the National Association of Accountants.

an overpreoccupation with economic results at the expense of society at large, more and better information about social performance is clearly desirable." Hence, this committee is considering how accountants can:

1. Aid business to make plans and to formulate decisions that do a better job of taking external social impacts into account.
2. Help business to make its own *pro bono publico* expenditures more productive
3. Report to the business's various publics, including the government and regulatory agencies, on its performance as a corporate citizen
4. Enable investors, if and when they desire, to take social responsibility into account in selecting where to place their funds[23]

Even before this committee and the analogous committees of other professional associations report on their deliberations, some individual accountants experimented with the preparation of social audits for operating companies. One such experiment called a *social responsibility annual report (SRAR)* includes a summary statement describing the company and its operations. Also presented are factual data concerning "the social impact in the community," "the pollution of air and water," "occupational health and safety," "minorities recruitment and promotion," and "funds flow for socially relevant activities."[24] Another is described as a *socioeconomic operating statement (SEOS)*. It is "a tabulation of those expenditures made voluntarily to improve the welfare of employees and the public, product safety, or environmental conditions." Set against these pluses are certain "detriments," that is, the estimated costs of actions the company did not take and that, as a consequence, employees of the community had to bear; for example, the cost of safety devices or of pollution purification equipment the company did *not* install. Additionally the author of this proposal suggests that those businesses publishing a SEOS be allowed an extra tax deduction or credit for the net investment in social activities during the year.[25]

These prototypes are the initial attempts by accountants to apply their skills and experience in measuring corporate financial performance to the appraisal of a company's social performance. However, these prototypes may also be limited in their effectiveness because accountants' addiction to quantification and their limited familiarity with emerging social standards may handicap them in developing fruitful approaches to meeting the demands for information that reformers, consumers, investors, government, and responsible corporate executives will require in order to assess and compare social performance.

EXECUTIVE LEADERSHIP

Business executives have led the way in the recognition of the social responsibilities of corporations. Despite their closeness to the daily problems of operating their various enterprises profitably, which might be expected to influence their judgments, they have come to see that corporations must meet the noneconomic expectations of society. Indeed, read in the light of questions being debated in the early 1970s, the words and actions of Owen D. Young of the General Electric Company in the 1920s, of George Eastman and Marion B. Folsom of the Eastman Kodak Company in the 1930s, of Paul G. Hoffman of the Studebaker Corporation in the late 1940s, of Frank W. Abrams of Standard Oil Company (New Jersey) [now the Exxon Corporation] in the 1950s, and of J. Irwin Miller of the Cummins Engine Company, and Arjay Miller, then president of the Ford Motor Company in the 1960s, were prescient.

The views of these early executives were updated in June 1971 by their modern-day counterparts in a statement on national policy by the Committee for Economic Development, *Social Responsibilities of Business Corporations,* which stated:

> Today it is clear that the terms of the contract between society and business are, in fact, changing in substantial and important ways. Business is being asked to assume broader responsibilities to society than ever before and to serve a wider range of human values.... Inasmuch as business exists to serve society, its future will depend on the quality of management's response to the changing expectations of the public.[26]
>
> As the corporation adapts to the changing requirements of society, and moves into uncharted social terrain, there is a clear need to develop better methods for determining corporate goals and evaluating performance.[27]

Why do these business leaders propose that corporations should accept these additional responsibilities, although they would not result in any profits, and should accept the obligation of reporting to stockholders and to the public about their performance? A look back at the reasons voiced by those business leaders who (in their respective decades) assumed responsibilities for their companies that were not generally accepted and a look at recent happenings suggest three explanations for the course business leaders have taken.

The first explanation is that society's expectations of business have expanded over the years. Recent evidence of this is provided by a summary of public opinion polls conducted by Louis Harris over a six-year period. In February 1973 the Harris poll reported its findings as to what a sample of Americans stated as their expectations at three points in time (listed on p. 55). As can be seen in the list, nationwide cross-sections of the public have been asked this same question periodically since 1966, and there has been a steady rise in the proportion of respondents that expect business to take the lead in resolving the problems indicated.

The second explanation for the more socially responsive behavior of business leaders is that many of them believe that if business does not itself resolve those social problems that it is equipped to cope with, government will enter the picture and assume the responsibility. A frequently cited example is the employment of ex-convicts, drug addicts, and persons similarly handicapped in finding jobs.

The third and most frequently cited reason businessmen give for their assumption of social responsibilities is that it is in their enlightened self-interest‡ to maintain a society in which private property is respected, private profits are permitted, and which is equitable, just, productive, rewarding, and secure. It is reasoned that the majority of the people are content to continue with laws and regulations that are hospitable to corporate operations when business leaders assume nonprofit responsibilities voluntarily.

Few would contend today that business has no responsibility for providing for those employees who after serving for many years are too old to work, for ensuring the safety and purity of the products it sells, for preventing the pollution of the environment, or for contributing to the maintenance of educational and social institutions. Even Milton Friedman, the most vocal opponent of business assumption of social responsibilities, has stated that business firms must "stay within the rules of the game."[28]

‡ "*Enlightened* self-interest is responsive to basic shifts in public attitudes (it is the wise bamboo which bends with the wind), consistently sensitive to human values, alert to subtle and indirect effects, and long in view. It is responsive to increasing expectations of openness and accountability." ("What Should a Corporation Do?" *Roper Report,* no. 2 [October 1971], p. 3. This appears in an excerpt of the philosophy and goals of the Standard Oil Company [N.J.], now the Exxon Corporation.)

Indeed, these social responsibilities have become accepted rules. Differences of opinion nevertheless do arise when it is proposed that businesses take on the additional responsibility of reporting to the public concerning its performance in the roles that it has assumed (at least in the first instance) voluntarily.

Viewed in the perspective of changes that have taken place in the last fifty years, it becomes clear that business has assumed large responsibilities for the welfare, safety, and equitable treatment of all employees; for safeguarding the interests of consumers; for protecting the environment; and for contributing to the well-being of society as a whole.

Everyone realizes, of course, that there are limits to the assumption of social responsibilities of business in general and for particular companies, whether they are government imposed or voluntarily undertaken. This is a very complex subject about which there is controversy, and this is not the place to examine it in any detail. Our views on this subject have been expressed elsewhere.[29]

BROADENING ACCOUNTABILITY

Accountability is not new for American corporations. In 1971 the Standard Oil Company (N.J.), now the Exxon Corporation, stated: "Historically we have had a responsibility to account financially to our shareholders. Now there is growing pressure for a broader accounting to a wider audience."[30] The demand for broader accounting has been described by one group of businessmen as "a fundamental shift from the principle that all business is essentially private and accountable only to stockholders and the free marketplace to legal doctrines that make large enterprises, in particular, more and more accountable to the general public."[31]

Pressures for accountability reflect the fundamental trend that Daniel Bell has termed "the subordination of the corporation."[32] He contends that, whereas the corporation was long judged in terms of individual contributions, it is being judged increasingly in terms of its contributions to, and the costs it imposes on, society as a whole. Individual satisfactions—those enjoyed by employees, consumers, and investors—can be assessed by the market. The satisfaction or dissatisfaction afforded society—stable, accident-free employment; safe, pure, and utilitarian products; and profitable, growing enterprises mindful of their impact on the physical and the social environment—cannot be evaluated in the marketplace.[33] Therefore, new means of appraisal are sought.

"Do you think (READ LIST) is a problem that businessmen and companies should give some special leadership to, or not?"

	SHOULD GIVE LEADERSHIP		
	1972	1971	1966
Controlling air and water pollution	92%	89%	69%
Eliminating economic depressions	88	83	76
Rebuilding our cities	85	84	74
Enabling people to use their creative talents fully	85	85	73
Eliminating racial discrimination	84	81	69
Wiping out poverty	83	81	69
Raising living standards around the world	80	74	43
Finding cures for disease	76	70	63
Giving a college education to all qualified	75	70	71
Controlling crime	73	64	42
Cutting down highway accidents	72	67	50
Raising moral standards	70	64	48
Reducing threat of war	68	61	55
Eliminating religious prejudice	63	52	37
Cutting out government red tape	57	50	34
Controlling too rapid population growth	44	43	17

CONCEPTS OF THE SOCIAL AUDIT

There are many different ideas about what a social audit is, and consensus on the subject is limited to the agreement that, at a high level of abstraction, the social audit is concerned with the social performance of a business in contrast to its economic performance as measured in the financial audit. Since all the definitions cannot be presented here, five basic types will be described.

First, some businessmen have concentrated on identifying and totaling expenditures for social activities. This concept, described as the "cost or outlay approach," involves the recognition of costs and the search for ways to reduce such costs. The application of this concept poses difficult problems of cost allocation. For example, what part of the cost of orienting and training a new employee should be attributed to the regular costs of doing business, and what part, such as the reduction of unemployment among black youths, should be attributed to the employer's undertaking of a social activity? The cost approach concentrates on inputs and makes no attempt to measure outputs—that is, how much social good and/or favorable public reaction toward the corporation have the dollars expended actually produced? It provides information needed to guide operating officials within the corporation but offers no measures of accomplishment that will satisfy the demands for information by consumers, the public at large, and government.

Second, the "human asset valuation approach to the social audit" is designed to measure the "value of the productive capability of the firm's human organization" and the "value of shareholder loyalty, banker and finance community goodwill, customer loyalty, supplier loyalty, and loyalty in the communities where plants or offices are located."[34] That these factors have values and that these values are influenced by the corporation's social behavior (e.g., the environment the firm provides for employees; the reputation for integrity it builds with customers, suppliers, and financiers; and the image it establishes in the minds of citizens) are ideas that are generally accepted. Hence, some students of the idea of a social audit propose the fulfillment of these values as a justification for the costs of social activities that the corporation carries on.

Those espousing this concept contend that it offers a "positive evaluation" of the worth of social activities and is preferable to a negative approach that focuses on costs and perhaps measures of what is done (e.g., number of women promoted above the supervisory level or the abandonment of billboard advertising). Critics of this concept, while accepting it as an aid to executive decision making and stockholder understanding, fault this approach on the grounds that it measures social accomplishments in terms that are not meaningful to constituents outside the corporation.

A third concept of the social audit has been described as the "program management" approach, which focuses on measuring only those activities in which a particular company is involved largely for social reasons. With respect to each such activity (e.g., the student loan program of a bank or the provision of scholarships for the children of employees of a corporation) this approach would involve (1) an approximation of the costs and (2) an evaluation of the effectiveness of the activity. The Bank of America has used this approach in assessing its activities, and its spokesmen argue for this concept in very pragmatic terms: Such "an audit appraises what can be appraised."[35] Thus, this kind of social audit serves the needs of corporate officials and provides some measures of accomplishment that meet the demands of certain external constituents.

A fourth concept, generally called the "inventory approach," involves the cataloging and narrative description of what the corporation is doing in each area where it recognizes that society (or articulate segments of society) expects it to do something. The results of this approach may be a massive descriptive listing of the corporation's activities with little or no analysis of results or costs. This approach does not provide a measure of the aggregate costs entailed; of the value to the company in terms of morale, goodwill, and public image; or of the benefits contributed to the society. It serves to inform the corporation's management and directors but provides less than is required to meet the demands of many outside the company who seek an evaluative accounting.

A fifth concept of the social audit can be called the cost/benefit approach. There are a number of possible types of cost/benefit analysis. One may be called the "balance sheet approach." This tries to quantify values contributed to society (assets) and detriments to society for actions taken or not taken (liabilities) and arrays them in a fashion comparable to the typical financial balance sheet.[36, 37] This is fundamentally an accounting approach to making a social audit and entails difficult and costly calculations. Very few companies have tried this approach. Another, simpler approach is to calculate costs of social programs and benefits, to the company and/or society, for programs undertaken, in either quantitative or qualitative terms. A number of companies have done this.

In actual practice, we have found no type of social audit that predominates either conceptually or operationally. There are combinations of approaches ranging from highly simplified descriptive statements to substantial documentation and quantification. The pressures for accountability suggest that a concept of the social audit that most businessmen may accept will likely evolve and that a standard operational format will be developed. That time, however, is far off.

Nonetheless, a surprising amount of interest and activity about the social audit is found in American business today, especially among the larger corporations. This is revealed in a survey of the business social audit completed in late 1973 by the authors.

NOTES

1. *Du Pont Cavalcade of Television Plans Exciting 1973–74 Season,* a leaflet distributed to stockholders by the Stockholder Relations Division of the E. I. du Pont de Nemours and Company with the quarterly dividend payment in September 1973.
2. Committee for Economic Development, *Social Responsibilities of Business Corporations,* A Statement on National Policy by the Research and Policy Committee of the Committee for Economic Development (New York, June 1971), p. 15.
3. Ibid., p. 16.
4. *New York Times,* 24 January 1971, sec. 3, pp. 1, 9.
5. Ibid. Theodore J. Jacobs makes the further point that "neither the regulator's zeal nor the business executive's conscience is a substitute for continual monitoring and participation by those affected by corporate power, the voluntary and involuntary consumers." "Pollution, Consumerism, Accountability," *Center Magazine* 5, no. 1 (January–February 1972): 46.
6. Robert A. Dahl, "A Prelude to Corporate Reform," *Business and Society Review,* no. 1 (Spring 1972), pp. 17–23.
7. Ibid., pp. 21–23.
8. Neil H. Jacoby, "The Business Corporation in Social Service: Its Role as Problem Solver for Government" (Paper presented to the Conference on the Corporation and the Quality of Life, Center for the Study of Democratic Institutions, Santa Barbara, Calif., September 27–October 1, 1971).
9. For example, see Vance O. Packard, *The Waste Makers* (New York: David McKay Co., 1960).
10. For a discussion, in well-reasoned detail, of the need and the growing insistence of consumers for timely, intelligible, relevant, truthful, and complete information, see John A. Howard and James Hulbert, "Advertising and the Public Interest" (Staff report prepared for the Federal Trade Commission, April 1973). This recommends actions by the Federal Trade Commission, the Food and Drug Administra-

tion, the Federal Communications Commission, the Executive Office of the President, Congress, the courts, and consumer interest groups that would ensure the availability of such information.

11. For development of this reasoning, see William H. Donaldson (Address delivered at the Annual Convention of the National Council on Teacher Retirement, Louisville, Ky., October 7, 1971). Donaldson is chairman and chief executive officer of Donaldson, Lufkin and Jenrette.
12. For a statement on investment philosophy, see Russell Sage Foundation, *Annual Report 70–71* (New York, 1972), p. 71.
13. For an analysis and recommendations concerning the role the university should play as an investor, see John G. Simon, Charles W. Powers, and Jon P. Gunnemann, *The Ethical Investor: Universities and Corporate Responsibility* (New Haven: Yale University Press, 1972).
14. "Principles for the Guidance of Bank Fiduciaries in Dealing with Issues of Corporate Social Responsibility," in American Bankers Association, Trust Division, *Trust Principles and Policies* (Washington, D.C., 1973).
15. Council on Economic Priorities, *Paper Profits: Pollution in the Pulp and Paper Industry* (New York, 1972).
16. U.S. Securities and Exchange Commission, SEC Release No. 33-5343 (Washington, D.C., December 1972); and a revised Release No. 33-5427, which contained proposed amendments to Rule 3-08 of Regulation 5-X.
17. SEC Release No. 33-5120 (July 1971).
18. Murray L. Weidenbaum, "Social Responsibility Is Closer Than You Think," *Michigan Business Review* 25, no. 4 (July 1973): 32–40.
19. *Wall Street Journal,* 30 October 1973, p. 18. See also the decision in Stephen Fischer et al. *v.* Michael Kletz et al., 249 F. Supp. 539 (1966), in which the U.S. District Court, S.D. New York, stated that "the public accountant must report fairly on the facts as he finds them whether favorable or unfavorable to his client. His duty is to safeguard the public interest, not that of his client."
20. For an enumeration and description of ten principles of socioeconomic accounting, see David F. Linowes, "The Accounting Profession and Social Progress," *Journal of Accountancy* 136, no. 1 (July 1973): 32–40.
21. David F. Linowes, "Socio-Economic Accounting," *Journal of Accountancy* 126, no. 5 (November 1968): 37–42.
22. Ibid.
23. Arthur B. Toan, "Social Information and Social Measurement" (Paper presented to the Committee on Social Measurement, American Institute of Certified Public Accountants, Denver, Colo., September 7, 1972).
24. Steven C. Dilley and Jerry J. Weygandt, "Measuring Social Responsibility: An Empirical Test," *Journal of Accountancy* 136, no. 3 (September 1973): 62–70.
25. David F. Linowes, "Let's Get on with the Social Audit: A Specific Proposal," *Business and Society Review/Innovation,* no. 4 (Winter 1972–73), pp. 39–42.
26. Committee for Economic Development, *Social Responsibilities of Business Corporations,* p. 16.
27. Ibid., p. 46.
28. *New York Times Magazine,* 13 September 1970, p. 126.
29. John J. Corson, *Business in the Humane Society* (New York: McGraw-Hill Book Company, 1971); George A. Steiner, "Social Policies for Business," *California Management Review* 15, no. 2 (Winter 1972): 17–24; and George A. Steiner, *Business and Society,* 2d ed. (New York: Random House, 1974).
30. "What Should a Corporation Do?" *Roper Report,* no. 2 (October 1971), p. 2.
31. U.S. Chamber of Commerce, *Business and the Consumer—A Program for the Seventies* (Washington, D.C., 1970), p. 3.
32. Daniel Bell, *The Coming of Post-Industrial Society: A Venture in Social Forecasting* (New York: Basic Books, 1973), pp. 269–298.
33. A very recent volume (Robin Marris, ed., *The Corporate Society,* New York: Halsted Press, 1974), which presents the views of ten economists and sociologists prominent in this country and Great Britain, stresses two characteristics of the American society in the seventies: (1) In today's highly urbanized, technological society publicly supplied goods (e.g., education, police protection, urban transportation, consumer protection, and protection of the environment) are of large and growing importance; (2) there has been "an extraordinary growth of problems [as the public goods cited illustrate] that are *not* spontaneously solved by market mechanisms" (pp. 302–303).
34. For a description of three methods for approximating the value of a firm's human organization and various forms of goodwill, see Rensis Likert, "The Influence of Social Research on Corporate Responsibility," in William J. Baumol et al., *A New Rationale for Corporate Social Policy* (New York: Committee for Economic Development, 1970), pp. 20–38. For an approximation by a consulting

firm of social benefits and costs to four categories (to the staff, to the community, to the general public, and to the firm's clients), see Abt Associates, "Social Income Statement" (Cambridge, Mass.: December 31, 1971).

35. For a description of this approach, see Bernard L. Butcher, "The Program Management Approach to the Corporate Social Audit," in *The Unstable Ground: Corporate Social Policy in a Dynamic Society*, ed. S. Prakash Sethi (Los Angeles: Melville Publishing Company, 1974), pp. 98–106.

36. Clark Abt, "Social Audits—The State of the Art" (Presented at Conference on Corporate Social Responsibility, New York, October 1972).

37. David F. Linowes, "Measuring Social Programs in Business," *Social Audit Seminar—Selected Proceedings* (Washington, D.C.: Public Affairs Council, July 1972).

9 A TENTATIVE STATEMENT OF ETHICAL GUIDES*

John W. Clark, S.J.

DESCRIPTION OF THE TENTATIVE STATEMENT

A General Description This formulation consists of the organization of ethical guides on two levels of understanding. The first level includes a series of primary guides which are most basic and theoretical. These primary guides may be looked upon as the foundation of the ethical theory and correspond roughly to the objective level of the function of planning.[1] The second level of guides, the middle guides, as they will be called, are somewhat more directed to concrete problems, but are still quite broad in their content and are concerned more with the formation of ethical thinking than with the direct problems of ethical conduct. These middle guides correspond to the policy level of planning.

The Tentative Statement as a Model Exhibit XVII illustrates the relationship of these two levels of guides to the concrete decision-making process. Primary guides are seen as underlying the individual's ethical code and as the foundation of the code itself. These guides are most general in nature and probably are the most widely accepted of the guides. The middle guides are norms which are established as means of achieving the ethical goals expressed by the primary guides. These norms, like the primary guides, are general in nature and are directed to helping the executive in the formation of his attitudes or his thinking toward the ethical dimensions of business decisions. Nevertheless, they are more specific than the primary guides and represent a bridge between the goals of business as a social institution and the activity of the individual businessman. They attempt to express the values of the primary guides as they have bearing on the individual executive. Thus the step from the primary to the middle guides, while remaining on the theoretical level, represents a transfer from the goals of society to the norms for individual ethical thinking. The middle guides are meant to assure that the action and decisions of the individual are in accord with the broader goals of business as a social institution.

Exhibit XVII also reveals an area between the guides and the ethical decision based upon these guides. This "area of prudential judgment" is an attempt to illustrate the gap which exists between abstract norms and concrete situations which businessmen face. Several factors contribute to the existence of this gap. First, circumstances surrounding decisions are constantly changing, and these circumstances demand consideration by executives. Circumstances may be so important that they vitally affect the ethical direction of the decision. Further, it is possible that in some business decisions two ethical guides may be in conflict, one supporting each alternative of any given decision. This is an area that cannot be charted perfectly by theory. Rather, it represents the point where individual judgment needs to weigh and balance the relevancy of theory to the specific situation.

This area of prudential judgment illustrates an important point with regard to this model.

EXHIBIT XVII The Structure of an Ethical Decision

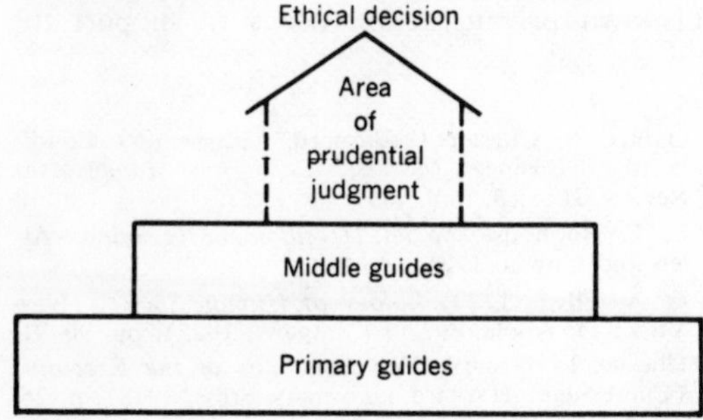

* Reprinted by permission of the publisher from *Religion and the Moral Standards of American Businessmen*, South-Western Publishing Company, Cincinnati, 1966, pp. 149–177. Father Clark is Vice-President of Loyola University, Los Angeles.

[1] Harold Koontz and Cyril O'Donnell, *Principles of Management* (New York: McGraw-Hill Book Co., 1964), pp. 74–75.

It is not proposed—indeed, it would be foolish to propose—that guides or principles can supply automatic or mechanical solutions to ethical problems so that, given any particular ethical problem, some particular guide will remove all doubt about the ethical direction of a given decision.[2] This type of model may have its place in the physical or engineering sciences, but not here. Rather, the present model illustrates that ethical guides somewhat resemble the backlog of knowledge which a surgeon brings to the operating table. Such knowledge is of considerable value, and yet it must be applied with attention to the unique and specific circumstances of each case.

If the following exploratory effort toward the formulation of ethical guides be viewed in this light, its true usefulness becomes apparent. It is not a system for removing the judgment or the evaluative process from the decisions of the businessman. Rather it is an aid, another instrument at hand to make his decision more likely to conform with his own and with society's ethical ideals.

THE PRIMARY GUIDES

The primary guides of business are probably few in number, but they are undoubtedly the most important influences on the ethical character of business conduct. They are very broad in content, and at the same time they are remote from the immediate decision-making process. But for all that, they are still a most important influence on business ethics. They lie at the roots of the American value system, for they are to a great extent widely accepted and are almost self-evident. In this sense they may be regarded as similar to mathematical axioms. Nevertheless, any logical framework of ethical norms will need to begin with these basic and pervasive guides.

These guides are capable of formulation in several modes. In the present expression of ethical guides, the primary norms will be described in three formulas.

The Guide of Social Institutions Ethical action is based upon the support of the social institutions which are generally accepted by a given society.

Meaning of the Guide. Alfred North Whitehead has observed that "a sense of responsibility for the continuance of a social system is basic to any morality."[3] This truth is so fundamental that it is placed at the beginning of the present synthesis. In a certain sense it forms the basis of all the guides to follow, for to a certain degree the other guides are developed from this basic value.

The term "social institutions" is itself somewhat ambiguous. Hobhouse has observed that "The term is so variously used that it is doubtful if it has a single root meaning common to all its applications."[4] In the sense that it is used in this first guide, the meaning is rather broad. C. A. Ellwood has given expression to the meaning of institutions as used in this first guide. As he describes them, "Institutions may be defined as habitual ways of living together which have been sanctioned, systematized, and established by the authority of communities."[5] In this sense, institutions are the outgrowth of social habits established by groups. Usually they have stronger sanctions attached to them than do customs.

The first guide expresses the need of the ethical man to support the social institutions which have been established in the society of which he is a part. Fundamentally the need for such support is rooted in the very purpose of human society. Chester Barnard, in his penetrating analysis of formal organizations, has expressed the primary purpose of such organizations as the attempt to overcome the biological limitation of man by means of cooperation.[6] In a very effective way, social institutions, especially when supported by ethical guides, make cooperation possible by providing a relatively stable environment in which human cooperation can take place. It establishes, by common agreement, an area in which an individual can reasonably predict the response of others to his actions, and thus it makes possible cooperative effort with some degree of certainty and stability.

It is especially the relation of social institutions to values that makes them the subject of this first guide. Social institutions are in reality an embodiment and concrete expression of the values which a particular civilization has come to accept. The individual who recognizes that his own private action needs to support the

[2] This point has been discussed at length by William C. Frederick, "The Growing Concern over Business Responsibility," *California Management Review*, II: 4, Summer, 1960; cf. especially p. 61.

[3] Quoted in Chester I. Barnard, "Elementary Conditions of Business Morals," *California Management Review*, I(1): 3, Fall, 1959.

[4] L. T. Hobhouse, *Social Development* (London: Allen and Unwin. 1924), p. 48.

[5] C. A. Ellwood, *Psychology of Human Society* (New York: D. Appleton and Company, 1925), pp. 90–91.

[6] Chester I. Barnard, *The Functions of the Executive* (Cambridge: Harvard University Press, 1938), p. 26.

commonly accepted social institutions of his culture is in fact acknowledging the need to contribute to the cooperation which is the basic purpose of human society. Accepted social institutions are a mirror of a society's functioning ethics. There are, of course, conventionally taboo social institutions which serve criminals and similar underground groups, which do not set the tone of society as a whole. Thus social institutions, as understood in this guide, are limited to those which are commonly accepted. Fundamentally, then, this first guide expresses the need for individual human action to be related to the objectives and the goals of society itself.

Support of the Guide in the Present Study. As has been observed, the guides have not been derived exclusively from the research embodied in the present study. Rather, they draw upon a number of studies concerned with business ethics. Nevertheless, since the guides do represent important hypotheses for contemporary business society, support of these guides should be evidenced in the previous sections of the present study.

The guide of social institutions can find support in both the historical and empirical sections of the present study. The religious values of all three major faiths manifest a deep respect for the social institutions of man. The Protestant ethic itself directly reflects values which are associated more with an individual rather than with social orientation. Yet it is clear that a responsible support of existing social institutions is implicitly contained in its value hierarchy. Early Puritan communities in Colonial America reflect the concern of the early settlers for civil harmony. It would be difficult to understand such concern apart from the values of the Protestant ethic of which it is a natural part. Jewish religious values even more explicitly support this guide, as it is, indeed, a corollary of the Jewish religious value of social consciousness. The guide is also closely related to the Catholic emphasis on the social nature of man.

Empirical support of this guide can also be found in the present study. Executive responses to the questionnaire reflected a high degree of personal responsibility for social order. The electrical-equipment price-fixing case (A) and the case dealing with a political bribe (S), discussed in Chapter 6, manifest a strong willingness to sacrifice personal gain to support widely accepted social institutions. Other cases less directly reflect this same viewpoint (e.g., F and E). Thus, empirically executives show an inclination to embrace values which reflect this guide.

Application of the Guide. The guide has special significance for the businessman, for the business system itself is a social institution, and as such as a part of another, larger social system. Responsibility for the vitality of the macro-system is fundamental to the existence of civilization itself and to the security of all members of society. The businessman, then, needs to act in such a way that his decisions contribute to the welfare of the social system, or at least do the social system no overall harm. This is the condition of his living in society and of his sharing in the fruits of cooperative effort. If at times this norm demands of the individual businessman substantial sacrifices, these must be regarded as the "cost" of living in society.

In its general expression this guide probably enjoys wide, if not universal, acceptance by the business community. As it is developed more explicitly and applied to the area of middle guides, it touches on areas of controversy. But even in its general expression, it has rather far-reaching implications for the businessman.

First of all, this guide expresses the public nature of every business. It is by reason of this orientation to the public good that business itself receives its *raison d'etre* and the legitimacy of the power which it exercises. Fundamentally, the existence of the American institution of business is dependent upon public acceptance of its usefulness to personal, national, and social goals of the American people as a whole. The basis of this acceptance is the conviction on the part of the American people that business serves or contributes to this common welfare. Hence this guide lies at the very roots of the business system itself. And the recognition of its existence by businessmen is of the greatest importance for the survival of the business system.

In another respect this norm is of great importance because it is the basis of the modern discussion concerning the social responsibilities of the businessman. Fundamentally, such responsibility lies in the recognition by the businessman of his commitment to other values of the American people which are outside the business system. Thus if the business system is not closed, but rather one which is influenced by and influences other social systems, then the businessman, in order to understand properly his role in society and his relationship with other segments of society, needs to recognize the validity of this guide and to condition his activities to the reality which it expresses.

The Guide of Respect for Others A proper support of social institutions includes a recognition of the rights and the obligations of others.

Meaning of the Guide. Just as the first primary guide laid the basis for the businessman's need to view his function with respect to social institutions, the present guide has its objective to provide a basic norm for the businessman's relationship with other individuals. Social institutions are built upon interpersonal relationships. In the cooperative effort that is implied in any organization, the harmonious relationships among individuals are fundamental to the achievement of organizational objectives. Thus there is need to establish a general guide relevant to interpersonal relations both within and without the firm in a comprehensive synthesis of ethical norms. This second guide is directed to this need.

A word of clarification is needed in regard to the use of the word "obligation." If it is basic to the support of social institutions that an individual respect the rights of others, it is equally fundamental to understand the mutuality of this relationship. Indeed, it is impossible for one to act in recognition of the rights of others unless he can reasonably surmise that others will treat him in a like manner. Upon such an assumption are the interpersonal relationships of society based. Human cooperation would be impossible if individuals could not reasonably expect others to recognize one another's rights. Thus in a real sense the very acceptance of membership in society implies a certain obligation to respect the rights of others. And this is the obligation which is referred to in this second guide.[7]

Support of the Guide in the Present Study. Little needs to be said about the support of this guide in the research sections of this study. Certainly the presence of values embodied in this guide were patently manifest in both the historical and empirical phases of the research. The guide is so basic to the values of the Protestant ethic that it can almost be identified as a postulate of this religious creed. It is less evident in Jewish religious values,[8] though certainly respect for the individual is an integral part of the value of attachment to life described in Chapter 2. Catholic thought expresses this value in the concept of the dignity of the individual. In the empirical research, executives frequently manifested an appreciation of the rights and obligations of other individuals (Cases T, W, G, K, X, and V).

Applications to Business. The guide of respect for others is fundamental to a wide variety of business activities which are related to ethical values. All those activities which imply a *quid pro quo* relationship and are concerned with questions of justice are rooted in this primary norm. Thus the simple honesty which is implied in a business exchange, the payment of debts, fidelity to commitments, truthfulness in communications—all these and many other business activities are founded on the conviction that businessmen will recognize in others a basic human dignity which lies at the roots of the rights and privileges of others. This in turn puts responsibility on the shoulders of the businessman.

It is interesting to note that the vast majority of businessmen give public support to this guide. Businessmen are quick to explain how their own dealings do not infringe upon or abuse the rights of others. Business history contains some remarkable examples of the extremes some executives will go to in order to show that their dealings have not been unjust.[9] This ritual of defending one's action as just is religiously practiced precisely because businessmen do recognize the indispensable requirement that individuals recognize the rights of others in modern industrial society.[10] Undoubtedly, this practice can be traced to the almost universal recognition of justice as a traditional value in Western civilization.

The Guide of Individual Integrity A proper support of social institutions supposes a personal commitment to individual integrity.

Meaning of the Guide. This third primary guide is directed to the relationship of the support of social institutions to individual integrity. Integrity as used in this study has reference to a certain moral unity or wholeness in the character of individuals. This wholeness is expressed by a consistency between the moral standards and ideals of the individual and his conduct. In this sense, a person who possesses such integrity directs his conduct in accordance with the ethical standards which he has ac-

[7] C. H. Waddington has developed the idea of ethics as functionally related to man's effort to live in social relations with other men. Cf. his *The Ethical Animal* (London: George Allen & Unwin, Ltd., 1960), especially pp. 60–61.

[8] Alfred Kutzik in *Social Work and Jewish Values* (Washington, D.C.: Public Affairs Press, 1959), pp. 13, 24; quoted on p. 35 of the present work.

[9] Typical of this attitude was the observation of a General Electric executive involved in the 1961 electrical-equipment price-fixing scandal: "Sure, collusion was illegal, but it wasn't unethical." From Richard Austin Smith, "The Incredible Electrical Conspiracy," *Fortune,* LXIII(4): 135, April, 1961.

[10] Bernard W. Dempsey, S. J., "The Roots of Business Responsibility," *Harvard Business Review,* XXVII (4): 395, July, 1949.

cepted on an intellectual or theoretical level. Frequently, he is regarded by his acquaintances as a "man of principle" because he makes a sincere effort to apply known ethical standards to his everyday activity.

This norm is also axiomatic in character and is widely accepted in our culture without the need for a strictly scientific proof of its validity. In this respect it is probably an immediate corollary of Western man's appreciation of the dignity of the individual. Regardless of one's belief concerning the nature of man, Western civilization has traditionally recognized the individual as something more than a sophisticated complex of electrons, and this high esteem of the individual is in no small part based on the moral responsibility implied in this guide of personal integrity.

Indeed, acceptance of this guide of individual integrity can be regarded as the recognition of personal responsibility for one's own conduct, and such recognition is fundamental to the very possibility of an ethical theory. For, unless businessmen perceive the presence of an obligation, a moral responsibility to avoid what they themselves consider unethical, ethical standards will have no practical meaning.

Support of the Guide in Present Research. The present guide can be observed as operational in both the religious and the personal value systems explored in the previous sections of this study. Integrity plays a basic role in the ethical content of almost all religions, and evidence of its esteemed position in the three major religious faiths is ample. In the limited discussion of religious values of Chapters 1, 2, and 3, no explicit treatment of integrity was included because attention was given to less obvious aspects of these religious creeds. However, evidence of the Protestant, Jewish, and Catholic acceptance of the value embodied in this guide hardly requires testimonial support in a study of the present character. The conclusions of other scholars[11] can be readily accepted in the interest of devoting full attention to other aspects of the ethical content of religious creeds.

A number of cases in the empirical phase of the present study support the conclusion that the guide of integrity is operational in the personal value systems of the majority of the respondents. In a sense, every case reflects the influence of this value, for executive approval or disapproval implies a belief that a man's conduct should be consistent with his moral beliefs. But the guide is particularly operative in Cases S (campaign contribution for a construction contract) and K (recommending inferior bonds). In each of these cases the respondents were asked their evaluation of a situation in which profit maximization was chosen at the sacrifice of personal moral convictions. In each of these cases the respondents were in relative agreement in their disapproval of such activity, thus revealing support of this guide.

Applications to Business. This is a truth that has been recognized by the business community on both a practical and a theoretical level. Francis X. Sutton relates individual integrity to the concept of individualism, which is a recurring theme in business creeds:

> Individualism has two main aspects, an injunction of responsibility and an affirmation of freedom. First, it involves individual moral responsibility in the sense that each individual must direct his actions according to moral norms and be prepared to accept the consequences of his action.[12]

The same guide has been expressed frequently in corporate statements of policies. One of the oldest of these is the policy statement of Armco Steel Corporation, adopted in 1919. In part it reads:

> 1. To do business guided and governed by the highest standards of conduct and ethics, striving always for that sort of an ending in all things affecting the conduct of the business as would make "reputation" an invaluable and permanent asset.[13]

Kaiser Aluminum and Chemical Corporation has embodied this same guide of individual integrity in a statement of ethical policy for purchasing:

> All purchasing personnel will adhere to the highest standards of integrity and personal conduct and thereby maintain and promote our

[11] For a development of this point by a Protestant scholar, see: Wesley H. Hager, "Ethics in Business in the Judeo-Christian Tradition." For a similar treatment by a Jewish scholar, see Philip S. Gershon, "The Jewish Approach to Business Ethics." A Catholic expression of this value is found in Thomas F. Divine, S.J., "The Catholic Tradition in Economic and Business Ethics." All these essays are found in Joseph W. Towle, (ed.) *Ethics and Standards in American Business* (Boston: Houghton-Mifflin Company, 1964).

[12] Francis X. Sutton, Seymour E. Harris, Carl Kaysen, and James Tobin, *The American Business Creed* (Cambridge, Mass.: Harvard University Press, 1956), p. 251.

[13] Towle, *op. cit., p.* 267.

reputation as an outstanding company with which to do business.[14]

THE MIDDLE NORMS

Henry M. Oliver has observed that what is most lacking in the present structure of ethical norms for business is a set of middle principles.[15] There is wide agreement as to the nature of the ultimate moral truths expressed in the primary guides, but it is the application of these truths to the circumstances of the business environment which seems to be missing. Probably, as Oliver views the situation, the following guides fit his description of middle principles. These guides, while remaining theoretical, nevertheless are more specific than the primary guides; and by this reason to some degree they are more controversial.

The Guide of Official Legislation Ethical conduct by executives requires observance of legislation imposed by legitimate civil authority.

Relation to the Primary Guides. This fourth guide is an application of the primary guide of support of social institutions. The legal structure of a given society expresses the specific and concrete acts to which citizens are obliged for the support and furtherance of basic social institutions which society as a whole has accepted. Laws in this respect are initiated and enacted to reinforce the basic social institutions which are prevalent in a given society. Thus a commitment to the social institutions of a given society necessarily implies a concomitant commitment to the embodiment of these social institutions as they are found in statutes.

Meaning of the Guide. The guide as expressed above calls for the observance of the law in the conduct of the businessman. It does not prohibit opposition to the law by legal means, such as lobbying for its removal or amendment, or for legislation which is more in accord with the convictions or the persuasions of the businessman. It is undoubtedly true that many laws in our statutes seem to impose restrictions which some businessmen feel are detrimental to a well-functioning free-enterprise system. They feel the need to work intelligently toward the revision of such laws. This is, of course, the legitimate manner of modifying or changing laws in a democratic society; and such activity should not be regarded as in opposition to the present guide. What the present guide does proscribe is a deliberate and intentional violation of a law which has been legitimately enacted.

Special consideration must be given to the case in which there is widespread disregard of a particular law by the general populace. In some cases, this disregard is condoned and even tacitly approved by civil authorities. In such cases, care needs to be exercised in the application of the present guide. The businessman should not be bound by what is generally recognized to be an inoperable law. In such cases he should be at liberty to follow what is the customary practice in his area. A case in point might be certain "blue laws" which are still in the statutes of several states. Such laws frequently prohibit the operation of business establishments on Sundays or certain religious holidays. Often such laws are generally disregarded; and, indeed, the case can sometimes be made that strict observance of the law could lead to a widespread social disutility. If amusement and entertainment firms could not operate on such days, much of the purpose of the day would be defeated.

Yet if such cases do provide an exception to the literal interpretation of this guide, it is important to note that this exception does not provide an escape hatch from civil obedience which the individual businessman can open up at will. The criterion for determining the applicability of this excuse from civil obedience does not rest in the private judgment of the individual businessman. Rather, the criterion is the objective and known fact that the law is presently not enforced by the civil authority. If such a condition is verified, it would seem to impose a grave and inappropriate burden on the businessman to exact from him a strict observance of such a law. But it is not for the individual businessman to decide whether or not he is to observe each particular law. This guide affirms the moral obligation of executives to observe laws even though they consider them in need of modification or repeal.

A more difficult situation occurs in the case of a law whose precise meaning or application is doubtful. Does the present guide bind the executive to obedience to such a doubtful law? In his observance of the law, must he avoid any action which might conceivably be considered a violation of the law? For instance, in the observance of federal antitrust laws, must the executive avoid any type of activity which is not certainly permitted by such legislation? The present researcher is of the opinion that

[14] *Ibid.*, pp. 273–74.

[15] Henry M. Oliver, "Trends toward a New Moral Philosophy for Business," *Business Horizons*, I(2): 41, Spring, 1958.

such a demand would put an excessively and intolerably severe burden on the shoulders of the executive. There are many instances in which there have been strong disagreements between Justice Department officials and corporate lawyers concerning the legality of certain mergers. Often enough the courts have vindicated the opinions of the corporate lawyers. Thus another clarification of this guide is necessary. Where there is a genuine doubt by competent men concerning the meaning or application of the law, the executive should not be bound to follow the strictest interpretation of the law, but should be free to act in either direction as long as he is willing to abide by subsequent clarification of the judicial branch of government.

Support of the Guide in the Present Study. Religious values implicitly support this norm. Within the context of the Protestant values, observance of legitimate legislation is fundamental to personal honesty and integrity, explicit components of the Protestant ethic. From a viewpoint of Jewish values, the guide is probably more closely related to the concept of social order than to personal honesty. Study of the law (Torah), it was observed, was basic to the concept of the Jewish people as the chosen people of God. By observing law (first the law of God, and later legitimate civil law), the individual Jew shares in the religious heritage of his people.

The empirical investigation provides strong evidence that executives support this guide, though, as was observed previously, the respondents reserved to themselves the right to judge the relevance of the law to concrete circumstances. In four cases relating to the legal system, A (electrical-equipment price fixing), F (padding the expense account), E (use of inferior materials in a construction contract) and S (campaign bribe in exchange for a contract award), the executives were in relative agreement concerning support of the law. In two cases (C, use of insider information, and I, concealment of a bribe in an auditor's report), the executives manifested balanced disagreement concerning the obligation to support the law. Of these two cases, Case I seemed to represent a situation in which literal obedience of the law would work a real injustice; hence the judgment of the respondents was probably that the incident represented a legitimate exception to the law. This leaves only Case C in possible conflict with the guide of support of legitimate legislation, and in this case the damage to society could be judged remote and small compared to the immediate and catastrophic effects of choosing the alternative.[16]

Applications of the Guide. In a number of areas this guide might provide ethical direction to the confused businessman. The recent electrical-equipment price conspiracy is a case in point.[17] Here the executives of several large firms found themselves faced with a very difficult dilemma. They were faced with the choice of deliberately violating the law by entering illegal price agreements with competitors or avoiding such illegal tactics and facing a chaotic price situation (cutthroat competition) which would result in considerable damage to the majority of companies in their industry. One who reads an account of their problems can sympathize with the difficulty of their position. Indeed, there is a history of government intervention and market control simply to avoid the kind of evils which these companies faced. Nevertheless, their decision deliberately and knowingly to violate the law in order to maintain a viable (and profitable) situation for their own companies clearly runs counter to the norm under discussion.

The National Electrical Manufacturers' Association has given apt expression to the values of this guide in the Preamble of its *Statement of Principles:*

> It is the responsibility and privilege of the members of the business community, as it is of all citizens, to observe the laws of the land. While all men, and all organizations, have the right to petition the Congress for a change in the laws, no man, and no organization, has a right to substitute individual judgments for those principles of behavior which are to be found in the law. Any other course can lead only to a collapse of order and to a deterioration of that system of government by law which is the foundation-stone of the United States.[18]

The Guide of Representative Authority Ethically responsible executives recognize their power and authority as representative, i.e., held in the interest of others.

Meaning of the Guide. Chester I. Barnard showed considerable discernment when he observed that:

> One of the most important, if not dominant, characteristics of modern Western society, as

16 These cases were discussed at length above [in *Religion and the Moral Standards of American Businessmen*], p. 101, and following.

17 Smith, *op. cit.*, pp. 132 ff.

18 Quoted in Towle, *op. cit.*, p. 277.

> contrasted with ancient, or with Western societies of one hundred or two hundred years [ago], is the extent to which concrete behavior of individuals has become representative rather than personal.[19]

This is especially true of business society. The pervasiveness of this representative character in executive activity can hardly be exaggerated. The executive, as leader of a highly complex organization, exercises his authority in behalf of interests other than his own. Management authority in this respect has the fundamental character of trusteeship, and the executive himself the character of a trustee who acts in accordance with the aims or goals of others.

This representative character of modern executive activity is especially significant with reference to the ethical parameters of business decisions. While the personal element can never be divorced from the executive process, nevertheless, it is precisely by reason of his official capacity as representative of the organization that the executive acts. Indeed, Barnard asserts that "every act of a trustee, director, officer, or employee is officially representative action."[20] In such a capacity, decisions motivated solely by personal advantage or gain, especially if adverse to representative interests, are inconsistent with the responsibilities which the executive assumes when he accepts a management position with a business concern.

The present guide attempts to express the proper relationship between personal and representative interests of the executive. It is important to recognize on the theoretical level the twofold aspect of every executive decision. With regard to its personal aspect, the executive needs to consider the demands of personal integrity, and it is hard to see how any action in violation of such integrity can be regarded as ethical. But consideration of this aspect is not enough. Further limitations may be imposed upon executive conduct by the fact of trusteeship, by reason of accountability for other legitimate interests, and by conflicts between competing interests of the business enterprise.

Support of the Guide in Present Research. Both the historical and empirical phases of the present research lend support to the guide of representative authority. The concept of trusteeship, common to both Protestant and Jewish value systems, approaches the guide inasmuch as it affirms the manager may not exercise power and control of wealth solely for personal advantage. While modern theories of representative authority have attempted to spell out who are the beneficiaries of this trusteeship relationship, these theories remain but applications of a value concept common to both Protestant and Jewish religious faiths.

Empirical evidence also tends to confirm the presence of this guide in value standards of contemporary business executives. Most of the cases relevant to this guide are within the social responsibility scale.[21] By considering such cases as W (executive's community activities), V (hiding a plant shutdown from employees), and P (corporate contributions to colleges), it is possiblé to discern an implicit support of this guide.

Applications of the Guide. Central to this guide is the question of whom management represents in its official capacity. Unfortunately, there is no consensus in responding to the question, and thus it must be admitted that the guide, in its present state of development, leaves much to be desired.

A number of scholars see management's main role in the guardianship of stockholder rights and in the protection of stockholder interests.[22] Stockholders with the legal vestiges of private ownership are regarded as the true masters of the corporation. It is they who approve the broad objectives of the enterprise, select the officers, and through their board of directors, control in some detail the more important corporate policies. And it is in the name of the stockholders that the corporate executives act. Their responsibility is to represent these stockholder interests. Chiefly, this responsibility is fulfilled by means of directing corporate policy toward the financial benefit of stockholders, but even this goal is deceptively simple. Whether stockholder benefit is best achieved by profit objectives, dividend objectives, or by the maximization of the present worth of stockholder investment is still an unsettled question.

Other scholars have insisted that the representative character of management implies that they need to look to much more than stockholder interests alone. Thus Richard Eells[23]

[19] Barnard, "Elementary Conditions of Business Morals," p. 6.

[20] Barnard, *loc. cit.*

[21] Cases included in this scale are listed on p. 89 [in *Religion and the Moral Standards of American Businessmen*].

[22] J. A. Livingston, *The American Stockholder* (Philadelphia: J. B. Lippincott, Inc., 1958), passim. See also Louis O. Kelso and Mortimer J. Adler, *The Capitalist Manifesto* (New York: Random House, 1958), pp. 77–94.

[23] Richard Eells, *The Meaning of Modern Business* (New York: Columbia University Press, 1960). Cf. especially Chapter X: "Claimants on the Corporation," pp. 211–16.

has enumerated the categories of contributor-claimants whose interests are to be protected by management. Besides stockholders, these claimants include customers, employees, suppliers, competitors, the business community as a whole, local communities, and finally the general public.[24] The manager, according to this theory, becomes a balancer of interests, a representative of several heterogeneous groups, and arbitrator and a judge of conflicting claims. Indeed, Adolph A. Berle, Jr., and Gardiner C. Means seem to suggest that the manager needs to divide the income of the corporation among its claimants according to some idea of public welfare rather than according to stockholder interest:

> [It] seems almost essential if the corporate system is to survive, that the "control" of the great corporations should develop into a purely neutral technocracy, balancing a variety of claims by various groups in the community and assigning to each a portion of the income stream as the basis of public policy rather than private cupidity.[25]

While it may be too early to settle in a definite manner this controversy, the present writer feels that there is a middle ground between these two positions. Without going so far as to regard the corporation as a "constellation of interests,"[26] it is possible to recognize that different groups have some legitimate stakes in corporate policies. To a certain degree the manager needs to respect the interests of several classes of claimants. As Chester I. Barnard has remarked:

> The responsibilities of corporations, aside from the obligation to conform to their charters and to the law, are of two kinds: (1) those which may be called internal, relating to the equitable interests of the stockholders, creditors, directors, officers, and employees; and (2) those relating to the interests of competitors, communities, government, and society in general.[27]

At the same time, this writer feels it necessary to recognize in corporate decisions a primacy of stockholder interests. After the basic responsibility to conform to the corporation charter and to the law, the corporate officer needs to recognize that his trusteeship is held in the name of the stockholder and that in his official capacity he needs to give high priority to the stockholder interests. Far from simply distributing the income stream among various claimants according to his concept of equity, the manager must be fully cognizant of the legal position of the stockholder, who has an exclusive title to all net income. It must be remembered that it is the basic function of business to produce economic goods This it could not do without stockholder investment. Thus it would seem that the legal position of the stockholder is supported by the simple exigencies of investment market: Without an exclusive claim to the net income of the corporation, the stockholder would be unwilling to risk his capital in business venture. Thus, as trustee, the manager may be called upon to look to the long-term interests of the stockholder rather than to short-run profit-maximization. He may even see stockholder benefits in the investment of corporate funds in nonbusiness activities such as Community Chest contributions or civic-improvement programs. Such contributions may indeed actually contribute to profit-maximizing objectives, for the recognition of the legitimate claims of others on the corporation and the treatment of such claimants with equity and empathy often have a business-getting and business-retaining effect. Nevertheless, this writer believes that even such contributions as these need to be regarded as investments, or at least as expenditures made in the name of ownership interests. It is believed that this position differs from the Berle and Means opinion inasmuch as here it is suggested that the surplus created by the corporation is not to be regarded as an unattached fund to be divided among worthy claimants, but rather is to be regarded as the property of ownership interests, to be used in their name and for their interest.

This discussion should suggest that the guide of representative authority has not yet been sufficiently clarified to describe precisely the total breadth of executive responsibilities. Yet it is believed that it can, even in its present state of tentative formulation, provide a useful guide to ethical action. At least, as Robert W. Austin has observed,[28] inasmuch as it proscribes executive activity which is exclusively directed toward the executive's own personal and private benefit at the cost of company

[24] *Ibid.*, pp. 213–15.

[25] Adolph A. Berle, Jr., and Gardiner C. Means, *The Modern Corporation and Private Property* (New York: The Macmillan Company, 1932), p. 356.

[26] Cf. Richard Eells and Clarence Walton, *Conceptual Foundations of Business* (Homewood, Ill.: Richard D. Irwin, Inc., 1961), pp. 147–71.

[27] Barnard, "Elementary Conditions of Business Morals," p. 7.

[28] Robert W. Austin, quoted in "A Positive Code of Ethics," *Business Week*, June 17, 1961, p. 166.

objectives, the guide provides a valuable rule. The executive who uses his position for his own personal interests without any regard for stockholder interest is certainly acting in a way which is repugnant to both the Livingston and the Eells positions.

Another contemporary problem of business philosophy is closely related to this guide. This problem concerns the legitimacy of business power, a subject which has been so much the concern of Adolf A. Berle, Jr., in recent years.[29] Berle finds the justification of the present power structure of American business in the fact that it exists by the public consensus, i.e., that the general public sees that business power is being used to meet the economic needs of the country as a whole. And this public consensus as expressed by widespread approval of the American private-enterprise system would immediately cease to exist if management lost its representative character. Paul Harbrecht[30] has carried this concept even further to state as a general social law that economic power will tend to gravitate toward those who will use it in a representative manner for the common benefit. Thus these authors related the legitimacy of business power to its representative character. It is quite possible, then, that this guide of representative authority will become the subject of intensified scrutiny as the parameters of business philosophy are explored further.

The Guide of Parity between Authority and Moral Responsibility Moral responsibility is coextensive with authority; that is, in his decision-making capacity, an executive is morally responsible for all the effects of his decisions within his control.

Meaning of the Guide. Keith Davis has observed[31] that the idea of power and responsibility going hand in hand is as old as civilization itself. Responsibility in this context has reference to the obligation to use such power in a manner beneficial to all over whom it is exercised. First expressions of the relationship between these two ideas were probably found in the political area, where authority to rule was coupled with responsibility to raise taxes, levy troops, and provide for the peace. Indeed, it might be argued that the very understanding of the terms of power and responsibility leads to the conclusion that they are coextensive. Responsibility without power is unreasonable; power without responsibility is despotic or arbitrary.

One of the most significant contributions of management theory has been to spell out the application of this idea to the organizational relationships within the individual business firm. The principle of parity of authority and responsibility as it has been expressed in management theory is fundamental to basic departmentation, the assignment of activities, the delegation of authority, and the function of control.[32] No small number of organization deficiencies can undoubtedly be traced to the failure to heed the basic relationships described by this principle. The exaction of responsibility without corresponding authority and the acceptance of authority without the corresponding recognition of responsibility still remain frequent in many business concerns.

Support of the Guide in the Present Study. Even a limited treatment of the Protestant, Jewish, and Catholic faiths reveals that the value embodied in the present guide is shared by these religious traditions. The Protestant ethic, as has been seen, reflects this value in the concept of the stewardship of wealth. The individual who has achieved the possession of economic wealth, or authority over its use, must regard his wealth and authority as held in trust to be used for the benefit of all society.[33] Though the Jewish religious tradition also shares the concept of stewardship of wealth, the basis of the present guide is also closely related to the value of *Zedakah* discussed in Chapter 2.[34] Personal responsibility for action has been associated with the recognition of the individual's role as a member of society; and, consequently, more is expected of the individual who has authority or wealth than is expected of his less fortunate neighbor.[35] Catholic tradition also supports this guide through the concept of the social aspect of property.

[29] Adolph A. Berle, Jr., *Economic Power and the Free Society* (Santa Barbara: Center for the Study of Democratic Institutions, 1957); see also *Power Without Property* (New York: Harcourt, Brace and Company, 1959).

[30] Paul Harbrecht, S.J., *Toward the Paraproprietal Society* (New York: The Twentieth Century Fund, 1960), 45 pp.

[31] Keith Davis, "Can Business Afford to Ignore Social Responsibilities?" *California Management Review*, II(3): 71, Spring, 1960.

[32] Koontz and O'Donnell, *op. cit.*, Chapters 13, 14, and 17.

[33] See Kenneth E. Boulding's expression of this viewpoint in "Our Lost Economic Gospel," *The Christian Century*, LXVII (33) (August 16, 1950), p. 970. Quoted in Chapter 1, p. 21.

[34] Cf. Chapter 2, pp. 35 and following.

[35] Cf. Chapter 2, pp. 42–43.

The empirical study of the present work does not directly manifest the presence of this guide among the values accepted by the respondents. Indeed, since the guide expresses a coextensiveness of two somewhat abstract concepts, it would be conceptually difficult to devise an empirical instrument which would verify such a guide. However, the questionnaire does give some indication that this guide would not be repugnant to a good number of the respondents. In Case T, 96 of the respondents approved of the use of company funds fòr the purchase of an expensive chemical filter. In Case V, the executives (91 percent) disapproved of hiding a plant shutdown from employees. Without attempting a measure of their willingness to affirm the coextensiveness of authority and responsibility, these cases seem to point to some degree of parallelism.

Applications of the Guide. The application of this principle to the area of business morality seems both necessary and reasonable. Indeed, the affirmation of the existence of individual responsibility is a frequent ingredient of business creeds.[36] What is often lacking in these creeds is the precise statement of the coextensiveness of this responsibility with effective power. It is, in effect, an extension or an application of the primary guide of personal integrity. For if an individual recognizes the need for moral consistency in his activities, he will see the relationship between his own actions and the results of those actions.

The full implications of this guide must not be overlooked. It is deceptively simple. Most managers would probably accept its logic; the problems come in its application to specific issues. Business decisions have such a pervasive influence that it has been argued that the acceptance of total responsibility for all the effects of business decisions will so complicate the process of decision making that management is likely to lose its effectiveness.[37] Theodore Levitt, for example, in his argument against social responsibilities, has made the point that if business is to become involved in all the noneconomic dimensions of its decisions, it will lose its vitality as a profit-making and economizing institution:

> The power which the corporation gains as a sort of demi-church it will lose as an agency of profit-motive capitalism. Indeed, as the profit motive becomes increasingly sublimated, capitalism will become only a shadow—the torpid remains of creative dynamism which was and might have been.[38]

Benjamin Selekman[39] has also voiced a fear that the assumption of a wide variety of noneconomic responsibilities will debilitate the main objective of all business activity, which he sees as the efficient provision of goods and services to society.

These opinions at first glance appear as serious objections to the guide expressed above; and, indeed, they do point to a fundamental controversy in current business literature. It may be that considerably more research is needed before this guide can achieve complete acceptance. Nevertheless, there are a number of business authorities who respond to the opinions above by suggesting that a rejection of responsibility for noneconomic aspects of business decisions will ultimately result in the public withdrawal of business power.[40] More precisely, it is frequently argued that if businessmen reject these noneconomic considerations, government legislation will effectively check business power in such areas. Thus Admiral Ben Moreell, former Chairman of the Board of Jones and Laughlin Steel Corporation, has put it this way:

> I am convinced that unless we do accept social responsibilities, the vacuum created by our unwillingness will be filled by those who would take us down the road to complete statism and inevitable moral and social collapse.[41]

This controversy represents a wide split in the business community—one which cannot be resolved here. However, the point of interest is that the defense of social responsibilities for business has taken the direction of the defense of the guide now under discussion. And it becomes apparent that, while the guide may lack universal acceptance, there are many who feel that one of the most vital controversies of business morality is now being fought precisely in the area of this guide.

The Guide of the Private Enterprise Support of social institutions in the United States

[36] Sutton et. al, *op. cit.*, pp. 251–55.

[37] Bernard Nossiter, "The Troubled Conscience of American Business," *Harper's Magazine*, 227(1, 360): 42, September, 1963.

[38] Theodore Levitt, "The Dangers of Social Responsibility," *Harvard Business Review*, XXXVI(5): 46, September–October, 1958.

[39] Benjamin M. Selekman, *A Moral Philosophy for Business* (New York: McGraw-Hill Book Company, 1959), especially Chapter 27.

[40] Davis, *op. cit.*, pp. 73–74.

[41] Quoted in *ibid.*, p. 73.

includes support of private enterprise as a legitimate and essential system of economic organization.

The Meaning of the Guide. The private-enterprise system, with its focus on the profit motive, has been characterized as the most productive economic system known to modern man.[42] But apart from the case for the economic superiority of private enterprise, it may also be regarded as a social value which is supported by a large majority of the American people. In this respect it is related to the first primary guide of social institutions; and, therefore, its support takes on a moral character. Because the American people are so strongly committed to private enterprise as a social value, the businessman himself needs to support it as a basic social value.

Undoubtedly, this commitment is rooted in a respect for the individual. It is not just that the individual, when motivated by the opportunity to make a profit, will produce more efficiently. Even more important is the belief that society is an institution whose major objective is to further the welfare of its members, and this welfare is achieved, at least in part, by providing the individual with the freedom and the opportunity to seek his own betterment through his own private industry. Private enterprise, in this respect, is intimately bound up with the American concept of liberty and human dignity.

Support of the Guide in the Present Study. Much has been written on the relationship of the Protestant, Hebrew, and Catholic faiths to the private-enterprise system. Indeed, the first two chapters of the present work investigate the contributions of Max Weber and Werner Sombart, who defend a holy alliance between religion and capitalism; and the whole of these chapters may be considered as support for the present guide. Nevertheless, the present writer thinks it important to note that the value of this guide is not primarily a religious one, but rather it is a value economic and political in nature. Especially in the case of this guide, the implication that a religious influence explains the existence of this value must carefully be avoided. Certainly religious faith has been part of the *Weltanschauung* in which the private-enterprise system has flourished. It would be equally erroneous to deny any influence to religious factors in the evolution of the private-enterprise system as it would be to ascribe to these religious factors the total influence. The true measure of their influence must lie between these extremes.

It is likewise difficult to find specific confirmation of this guide in the empirical section of the present study. Rather than being the object of a specific set of cases, support of the private-enterprise system seems to run through the whole questionnaire as a fundamental supposition. Indeed, acceptance of this guide by the vast majority of businessmen is so apparent that it needs no specific empirical confirmation in the present work.[43]

Application of the Guide. This guide suggests an inclination or mood which should be found in an executive rather than a hard-fast, concrete law. What it implies is that the businessman should show a propensity to favor the private-enterprise system as the most suitable means of providing economic goods and services in the American environment. Only when there is reasonable evidence that some particular public need cannot be satisfied by private enterprise should the businessman advocate government intervention in the private-enterprise system. Such governmental influence should be based on a need which is unable to be met by private initiative. And when such intervention is necessary, it should be such a character as to affect least the individual-business-enterprise system.

George Steiner has proposed a similar guide as a principle to be considered in introducing new economic controls into the American economy. He views the private-enterprise system as a fundamental commitment which is almost unanimously accepted by the American people. Thus governmental economic controls need to take cognizance of it as a basic social value. As he expresses and explains this principle:

> The control should be instituted within the framework of the basic institutions of the individual enterprise system. This principle, of course, is anchored in the fundamental policy commitment which the American people almost unanimously accept to preserve the basic institutions of the present-day economic system. It means . . . that controls ought not subvert the institution of private property, freedom of consumer choice, freedom of choosing an occupation, the profit motive, individual incentives, and so on.[44]

[42] This is a commonly held opinion, though one which has been challenged with some merit. Cf. Henry Wallich, *The Cost of Freedom* (New York: Harper and Brothers, 1960), p. 40 and following.

[43] If desired, a more explicit and comprehensive treatment of the acceptance of the private-enterprise system by the business community can be found in Sutton *et. al.*, *op. cit.*, Chapters 3, 4, and 8.

[44] George A. Steiner, *Governments' Role in Economic Life* (New York: McGraw-Hill Book Company, 1953), p. 395.

And Robert W. Austin has included support of the profit motive as among the four principles embodied in his code of conduct for executives. He expresses the businessman's commitment to the profit motive in the following words:

> The professional business manager affirms that when business managers follow this code of conduct, the profit motive is the best incentive for the development of a sound, expanding, and dynamic economy.[45]

[45] Robert W. Austin, "Code of Conduct for Executives," *Harvard Business Review*, XXIX (5), 60, September-October, 1961.

10 ENERGY AND THE ENVIRONMENT: SCENARIOS FOR 1985 AND 2000*

Vaclav Smil

Forecasting the future of energy production is imperative, because power plants, dams, and mines now under construction will operate well beyond the year 2000. At the same time, new methods of energy generation will require decades to research and develop.

To find out what may happen in the energy and closely related environmental fields during the coming years. I polled a group of recognized experts by means of the Delphi interview method developed by Olaf Helmer and Norman Dalkey at the RAND Corporation in Santa Monica, California. Under the Delphi method, experts are interviewed separately, so that they are not subject to influence by the others in the group. Through repeated rounds of questioning, the interviewer can arrive at a reasonably clear-cut and useful consensus of expert opinion.

My investigation began with an intensive reading of leading energy, environmental, and general scientific journals and publications. I identified 118 people who were experts in the energy-environmental field, and sent them questionnaires. Eventually, I had responses from a total of 40 senior energy and environment experts residing in seven nations. The experts ranged from inventors to editors of top journals in the energy and environmental field.

The first questionnaire sent to the participants asked them to list all major scientific, technological, and management inventions, breakthroughs and changes that they regarded as both urgently needed and feasible within the next 50 years. After getting back the questionnaires, I made a list of the developments that the experts suggested and sent this list to the respondents asking them to indicate when each development might be expected to occur.

* Reprinted by permission of the publisher from *The Futurist* (published by the World Future Society), vol. 8, no. 1, pp. 4–12 (February 1974). Mr. Smil is assistant professor of geography, University of Manitoba, Winnipeg, Canada.

The poll resulted in a schedule for events that may occur in the energy and environment fields. The tables accompanying this article summarize some of the results of the poll. (The complete report will be published in April by the University of Manitoba under the title *Energy and the Environment*.)

TECHNOLOGIES FOLLOW LAW OF GROWTH

To interpret these forecasts, we must understand the phenomenal growth of energy consumption in recent decades. An ever increasing consumption of energy naturally leads to the growth of power plants, transmission lines, tankers, mining machines, and other facilities. The growth of these technologies is governed by the basic law which applies to all growth phenomena: As stated by Edward R. Dewey, an authority on periodicity, this law is as follows:

> As a rule things grow slowly, then fast, then slowly . . . It matters not whether we record the growth of a pumpkin, a white rat, a group of yeast cells, a group of fruit-flies, a group of Swedes, or a group of Frenchmen—all behave in the same way.

Though the growth of a particular technology proceeds according to this rule, we must be aware that the similarities to biological growth are far from exact. As technological forecaster Robert U. Ayres has said, "The biological analogy carries with it the erroneous implication that each technology has 'a life of its own,' and that its evolution is governed by some internal dynamical law, with stages of (relatively) fixed length or proportions. In fact the transition from one stage to another may in some cases be so rapid as to be almost unnoticeable, and in others it may be very protracted or never occur at all."

Technological growth curves are rarely

smooth and one should not be surprised when they do not satisfy exactly the properties of biological growth and can be fitted only exceptionally into the orderly pattern of natural growth equations. Nevertheless, the growth of energy technologies closely resembles that of natural processes. When compared with biological equations, some technological growth curves show only slight deviations.

The growth curves for energy technologies suggest that the inflection points have been reached or soon will be reached and that the late 1960s and 1970s is a period of transition toward slower growth rates. The experts' estimates of growth limits made it possible to put the current steep slopes of exponential curves into broader perspective and indicate that the development of energy generation cannot continue indefinitely at high compound interest rates, as it has in recent years.

COAL AND NUCLEAR PLANTS EXPAND

The capacity of fossil-fueled power plants has expanded enormously in the past two decades. Substantial economies of scale made larger capacities justifiable and desirable. Larger units can be installed at much lower cost per kilowatt, and are also cheaper to operate. During the last 30 years, the quest for increased power production has resulted in a tenfold increase in the size of the average U.S. power plant. Announcements of new giant projects come at a fast rate and it is almost impossible to compile in a review of the world's largest projects which would not be obsolete before being printed.

But the impressive growth of fossil-fueled power generation is overshadowed by recent advances in nuclear power generation. Despite serious doubts about its practicality, nuclear power developed steadily in the late 1950s and early 1960s. In the single year of 1966, U.S. orders for nuclear power plants increased by 400%. The effort slowed in 1968 and 1969, due mainly to construction delays that resulted from the flood of orders in previous years, lack of skilled labor, more stringent specifications, and environmentalists' obstructions. But new orders have picked up strongly since 1970. Since 1957, the capacity of the largest nuclear power plant in operation has doubled every three years. Economies of scale have made possible swift improvements in the competitive position of nuclear fission.

A crucial problem that will largely determine the future trends of steam power generation is the relative positions of fossil and nuclear fuels as they compete for usage in the years ahead. In the U.S., the most important fossil fuel for power generation is coal. In the early 1960s, oil and gas displaced coal to some extent as a fuel for new electric power stations, but in recent years coal has strengthened its position as the principal fuel in fossil-fueled power stations. This trend is very likely to continue.

COAL ENJOYS COMEBACK BUT LONG-TERM FUTURE IS UNCERTAIN

In view of the indisputable success of nuclear reactors in generating electricity, one basic question seems to be: What are the chances that coal will continue to be a major source of power generation in the United States? Answering this question requires a brief review of some past trends and critical problems.

Hardly predictable 20 years ago, the comeback of coal was one of the most important changes in the U.S. energy scene during the 1960s. The process started slowly in the late 1950s, and changes became noticeable in the early 1960s. Coal's importance continued to grow and in 1967 the president of the National Coal Association confidently asserted that "The news is the go-ahead outlook for the nation's most dependable power fuel."

Innovations in three broad areas made this growth possible:

1. Modernization of underground mines: the automation of mine operations and the loading of coal into transport vehicles.
2. Tremendous progress in surface mining (strip mining with giant shovels, draglines, trucks, auger mining, and "push-button" technology).
3. Changes in transportation: unitization of trains, elimination of layovers and turnarounds, increased utilization and growth of carrying capacity.

Meanwhile, power generation provides an increasingly expanding market for bituminous coal whose increasing sales to utilities more than made up the decreased use of coal by railroads, industries, and households. Though the gains are likely to slow down later on, a realistic estimate is that close to 400 million tons of coal will be sold in 1975 and 450 million tons in 1980. (Some estimates go up to 540 million tons in 1980.)

All this leads the coal industry to believe it has a bright future, and that coal—not atomic power—is the fuel of the future. Nonetheless, the coal industry is in a peculiar position today: Demand for coal is outrunning current productive capacity and causing steep price increases, but the long-run outlook is quite uncertain. A number of complex factors account for this situation: First of all, the traditional competition between the coal and oil industry in the United States entered a new phase in 1966 with unlimited imports of residual fuel oil on the East Coast, rendering coal uncompetitive in most of the Northeastern region. Import quota restrictions, the high cost of overland transportation and the potential for oil spill contamination of harbors has limited the more widespread use of residual fuel oil, but the abundance of foreign supplies (when not embargoed), the availability of desulfurized oil from the Caribbean, the low cost of overwater transportation of low-sulfur African oils, and stricter air pollution regulations are strongly favorable factors, which might be eliminated only by protracted supply embargo or excessive price increases.

Nuclear power, the strongest long-range competitor, has already started to challenge the dominance of coal in the coal regions themselves. The Tennessee Valley Authority, the country's largest coal burning utility, took a historic step in 1967 by ordering a giant nuclear power plant in the center of coal country (Browns Ferry, Alabama) and more recently (1970) TVA ordered four more reactors.

Naturally, nuclear power plants are not without problems. Construction difficulties, numerous schedule delays, cost increases, labor shortages and environmental conflicts have somewhat lessened the competitiveness of fission generation between 1966 and the present, and though the market recovered in 1970, the situation is still subject to fluctuations. With shorter construction time and low-priced fuel in the low-cost coal fields, coal-fired power plants might still be the best power source for some time to come.

Environmental considerations added a whole new set of problems in the late 1960s. Ultimately, the ability of the coal industry to cope economically with ecology may determine the growth or decline of the coal market. Surface mining has disturbed more than three million acres of land in the United States and demands to restore this land plus continuing, immediate reclaiming of new strip sites could seriously blunt the competitive edge of the booming surface coal industry.

New health and safety laws are an even greater threat to the coal industry. During the first 10 days that these laws were in existence, 272 mines closed down. While lowering the respirable dust concentration to three milligrams per cubic meter is not an easy task, the future target of only two milligrams per cubic meter is extremely difficult to achieve, and, if insisted upon, the resulting increase in coal prices might almost completely ruin the competitive position of underground coal.

But the most widespread and urgent environmental challenge to the coal industry is the demand for strict air quality standards: Especially difficult for the industry are requirements for control of sulfur dioxide emissions.

These difficulties, combined with a chronically low attraction of the coal industry for young people, labor unrest in coal unions, and the necessity of increased capital investment per ton of capacity make it hard to believe the coal industry's forecast: "the era of the 1970s will be the decade in which the coal industry . . . finally attains its natural birthright as the principal future source of energy for the nation."

Though coal will not be *the* principal supplier of future power needs in the U.S., and though its relative decline as a major source of energy seems inevitable, there is still room for growth in the next two or three decades.

MAKING COAL CLEANER

The energy-environment experts recognized air pollution as the leading environmental problem, and power generation remains among its major causes. Fossil-fueled power plants are the third biggest source of pollutants in the United States, in terms of the mass of pollutants entering the air. (The first and second are motor vehicles and the processing and manufacturing industries, respectively.)

A modern, 1,000-megawatt power plant annually burning about 2.5 million tons of coal with a moderate 2% sulfur content emits to the atmosphere about 880 pounds of sulfur dioxide each minute. To dilute this amount of harmful gas to below 0.5 parts per million—about 17 times higher than the U.S. national air quality standard for sulfur dioxide—requires more than 325 million cubic yards of fresh air. Sulfur dioxide is converted relatively quickly to sulfur trioxide and then to sulfuric acid and sulfates, which are washed down by precipitation, but the amount of air needed to dilute sulfur dioxide from a single source during favorable atmospheric conditions is still huge. In an area with multiple sources of pollution and a limited supply of fresh air, high concentrations of sulfur oxides build up very quickly.

The gasification and liquefaction of coal may be considered as the most thorough way to remove noxious matter from fuel before combustion. Synthetic fuels will help tremendously in maintaining the quality of air, and the experts confirm the widespread feeling that the commercial, large-scale processes for production of high calorie synthetic gas from coal are very likely to appear soon. The consensus indicated a 90% probability that these processes will be available by the year 1989. Such expectations are justified by the advanced research and pilot plant stage of several methods of producing synthetic pipeline gas, most notably the Chicago Institute of Gas Technology's HY-GAS process, the Consolidation Coal Company's carbon dioxide acceptor process, and the U.S. Bureau of Mines' steam-oxygen fluidized bed combustion. More advanced technology may also realize the old plans for integrated chemical extraction and power production based on coal.

These "coalplex" schemes would start with coal "distillation," that is, the high-temperature pyrolysis, or heating of the coal to produce coke and volatile matter, which is converted to pipeline gas and liquid fuel. Advances in the coalplex technologies will require considerable funding of coal and combustion research, a demand voiced more and more vigorously by the coal industry, which points to the heavy government subsidization of nuclear research and relative neglect of advanced coal research.

Atomic energy experts, meanwhile, have developed the concept of the "nuplex," a nuclear-based complex that would desalt water as well as produce power. Nuplexes, which must operate on a giant scale to produce cheap water, might open up large parts of the world that now lack energy. Nuplexes could substantially increase the production of energy, fertilizers, and valuable crops in such underdeveloped areas as India and North Africa. Although still only in the feasibility appraisal stage, these multi-purpose projects could save about 25% of the total costs of production and shipping as compared with dispersed systems. With two crops per year, they could make profits at water costs ranging as high as 20 cents per 1,000 gallons. Oak Ridge National Laboratory is continuing to evaluate these promising schemes, the first of which should be in operation in the next decade.

Cheaply available waste heat from giant nuclear power plants could also attract various industries to the neighborhood. Hot air might be used in gigantic greenhouses and special warm-water ponds might become aquacultural farming areas, growing shrimp, lobster, and other species that mature faster when their water is moderately warm.

UNCONVENTIONAL MEANS OF GENERATING ELECTRICITY

Besides the technological advances of proven, traditional methods of electricity production, the coming decades will witness the development of unconventional systems. Some have been practically proven, or are even on the verge of full-scale application. Others still sound highly speculative but might assume some importance during the next century. The future success of a particular method depends not only on its characteristics, but to a very high degree on the state of competitive systems.

The most promising system so far is small-scale power generation by fuel cells, which directly convert chemical to electrical energy. Fuel cells are quiet, reliable, (since they have no moving parts), and cause negligible air and water pollution. The Delphi experts believe that there is a 90% probability that fuel cells will be widely used by the year 2000.

Great uncertainty surrounds the use of solar energy for power production. Numerous schemes for collecting and converting the sun's energy have been proposed, constructed, and tested, but none of the techniques seems to be applicable to efficient, base-load generation of electricity. The main obstacles are the irregular flow of energy (seasonal differences, cloudiness) and the necessity of large collecting surfaces. (Solar energy can, of course, be used economically in some areas for other purposes, such as cooking, heating, cooling, and desalination.)

The Delphi experts forecast an eventual breakthrough in the development of simple solar furnaces for home power generation at isolated spots in tropical or subtropical areas before the end of the century. Terrestrial solar devices for bulk power generation are considered unlikely during the next 50 years, if ever. So far, the French eight-story-high parabolic reflector at Odeillo in the Pyrenees has the capacity of a bare one megawatt. More likely ways to harness solar energy on a large scale are the use of satellites and microwave transmission from space. This sounds like a science fiction idea, but it could become reality surprisingly soon. The median view of the experts is that a possible breakthrough might come in the second decade of the next century. (Optimists see this development just 30 years ahead.) A satellite system of solar energy collection would beam microwaves to a receiving antenna on the earth, where the power would be distributed to users. But such a system may have to compete with fusion as a source of energy, and the experts doubted that it could do so successfully.

Tidal power has a potential about seven times larger than that of the world's rivers and lakes, but only a small part of this immense capacity is ever likely to be used, the experts indicated. Even in regions with very high tides, suitable bays to build dams are hard to find and almost any such dam is a very expensive structure. The feasibility of large-scale production was successfully proven in the Rance River plant near Saint Malo, France, which has operated since 1966. But high investment costs will block most of the projected developments such as the old U.S. Passamaquoddy scheme, the British Severn, and the Australian Kimberleys. The Russians have bold plans for the White Sea and a few large tidal power plants may be built before the end of the century, but the experts believe that they will remain rather isolated examples.

Geothermal power plants also failed to evoke much enthusiasm among the experts as a source of electricity. According to reports at the United Nations sponsored session on geothermal energy (Pisa, Italy, September 1970), a total of 677.6 megawatts is now installed in geothermal power plants in six countries (Italy, New Zealand, Japan, Mexico, Soviet Union, and United States). The technology is still in its infancy. Wells are shallow, steam pressure and temperature are low, and only about 10% of the heat is used for power generation.

The experts showed distrust in the practicality of using the thermal difference in tropical seas to produce power. Even more unlikely, in their view, is the use of gravitational energy in the form of anti-gravity as a practical source of energy.

SOCIAL CHANGES NEEDED TO SOLVE ENERGY PROBLEMS

The main focus of my study was on the technological aspects of future energy production and environmental protection. But technological innovations without parallel social changes would be wholly insufficient to bring about the badly needed compromise between energy and environment. The complexity of the problem excludes any solution based solely on engineering advances or only on social reforms.

Among the social changes needed during the coming decades, effective control of population was deemed essential. An unchecked increase of high-level consumers in advanced countries and very high population gains in developing countries would make wholly insufficient even very determined and costly efforts to balance energy needs with environmental quality. Said one Delphi participant: "If population equilibrium is not attained in about the next 100–150 years, what difference will it make how well—or poorly—we have solved our energy problems?"

An obvious certainty is that the present rate of population growth must and will come to an end. An analysis of world population during the past 2000 years indicates that each successive doubling required only half the time necessary for the prior doubling. If this trend were to continue, the time would come when each successive doubling would require an infinitely short period of time. By the year 6500 the world population would spherically expand at the speed of light into the universe.

The crucial question, thus, is not whether the world's population will level off, but what kind of development will bring about such a result. Will it be overcrowding, starvation, psychic overload, violence, destruction of the environment, global war, or some other disaster? Or will it be the intervention of human and hopefully humane decision-making? The Delphi experts seem to favor the more optimistic view. They indicated, for example, that the 1990s might be the breakthrough decade in achieving effective population control. However, if the breakthrough in population control is not achieved before the end of the century and population problems are not brought under control, the experts believe man may largely destroy his ability to survive in great numbers and in great cities.

THE AUTOMOBILE AS PRIME CULPRIT

Important behavioral changes are most likely to be required in solving the urgent problems of automotive pollution. The 90 million motor vehicles in the United States (90% powered by internal combustion engines using gasoline) are both major consumers of energy and principal sources of gaseous air pollution. Almost two-thirds of the carbon monoxide, well over half the hydrocarbons and half the nitrogen oxides emitted into the atmosphere in the U.S. are the result of imperfect automotive combustion. The importance of these emissions was fully recognized by the experts, who selected them as the most urgent environmental problem.

U.S. restrictions of air pollution from light-duty vehicles have already reduced the total amounts of pollutants significantly, but the effects of the new standards will be short-lived unless they are further tightened. There is se-

TIMETABLE FOR ENERGY DEVELOPMENTS

Experts in the energy and environment fields were asked to indicate what developments may be anticipated in the production, transmission, and transportation of energy. After collecting their suggestions, the author asked the experts to estimate the year when there would be a 50-50 chance that the development would have occurred. Their median estimates result in the following timetable.

1980 Fuel cells for small scale power generation.

1980 Use of nuclear explosives in the production of natural gas and oil, geothermal heat, etc.

1982 Coal gasification or liquefaction.

1983 "Fail-safe" nuclear power generation.

1984 High temperature gas reactors (Ackeret-Keller cycle).

1985 Extra high voltage transmission on very long distances (at least 1,000 kilowatts and 1,000 kilometers).

1985 Fast breeder reactors.

1985 Cryogenic transmission systems using underground superconducting cables.

1986 Large-scale shale oil recovery.

1988 Fossil fuel fired magnetohydrodynamics.

1988 Development of all practically feasible hydroelectric sites in populated regions.

1988 Techniques for economical recovery of additional 25% of crude oil from known resources.

1988 Fully automated underground coalmining.

1988 Cryogenic pipeline transportation of natural gas.

1990 Simple solar furnace for home power generation in tropical and subtropical regions.

1990 Low-cost high-voltage underground transmission.

1993 Microwave power transmission.

1995 "Fail-safe" systems for drilling and producing hydrocarbons at any water depth.

1998 Direct conversion of heat to electricity (thermionics).

1999 Utilization of low thermal difference systems.

2000 Controlled thermonuclear power.

2000 Efficient storage of electric energy in large quantities.

2000 Laser power transmission.

2000 Large and efficient tidal power plants.

2010 High temperature gas reactors with thermal cycle other than helium.

2020 Widespread use of geothermal power.

2020 Relay of solar energy via satellite collectors.

After 2020: Earth-based solar energy devices for bulk power generation.

After 2020: Cryogenic superfluid transportation of mechanical energy on long distances.

After 2020: Utilization of gravitational energy (antigravity).

rious disagreement between car manufacturers and environmentalists as to whether the proposed new standards for 1975 can be met. The Delphi experts, though not pessimistic, indicated some caution: A virtually non-polluting internal combustion engine may come between 1976 and 1980, but it might take another decade to achieve a significant breakthrough. In any case, the cars will be appreciably more expensive and—even with low emission rates—some major changes in individual transportation patterns in large American cities seem inevitable to comply with new air quality standards. The necessity of new, fast and safe mass transit systems is evident and many new schemes will be introduced in coming decades.

The environmental impact of individual transportation is not limited to air pollution. Today's 3.6 million miles of U.S. roads and streets consume 24,000 square miles of land, an area about twice as large as the Netherlands, and accelerate soil erosion, sedimentation and storm water runoff. Side effects come from chemicals used to melt ice, herbicides to control vegetation, and accidental oil spills and litter. Detrimental impacts on the environment will inevitably contribute to the suppression of many highways sometime in the future. Similarly, expansion of airports and concomitant increased aircraft air pollution and noise will ultimately result in limitations on air travel. The experts' median forecast was 1990, which testifies to the urgency of such development. Many recent actions such as the numerous conflicts concerning urban freeways in Philadelphia, New Orleans, Nashville, New York, and other cities, the blocking of the Everglades jet airport, and the vote in the U.S. Congress to stop financing the supersonic transport (SST) show the emergence of determined opposition to the unchecked growth of transportation corridors.

Private cars, the Delphi forecast strongly indicated, may always be with us: The 50% likelihood of banning their use ranged from the year 2017 to never. "New" cars, powered by batteries, fuel cells, gas turbines, steam or some novel methods, might significantly reduce environmental impact of individual transportation, but they are not likely to appear very soon. The breakthrough time will be about 1985, the experts estimated. The emergence of such new cars does not exclude, of course, the possibility of traffic bans in some city centers, recreational regions, and areas of outstanding natural beauty.

INTERNATIONAL COOPERATION TO SOLVE ENERGY PROBLEMS

There can be no doubt that the problems of energy supplies and environmental pollution are not confined by national boundaries, but their solution by a coordinated worldwide effort does not look too promising. In the first place, there are no worldwide standards for air and water quality, nor any consensus concerning the most common, virtually omnipresent pollutants. For instance, the basic standard for sulfur dioxide ambient air concentration (in parts per million per 24 hours) is 0.03 in the U.S., 0.05 in the Netherlands and Sweden, 0.06 in the Soviet Union, 0.09 in Romania, 0.12 in Poland and 0.2 in Switzerland. Binding international agreements are necessary, but the Delphi experts did not envision a breakthrough sooner than the latter half of the 1980s.

The establishment of a worldwide environmental surveillance and warning agency may come about the year 1990, the experts felt. Such an organization would have both archival and warning responsibilities, serving as the data bank (centralized storage of environmental measurements, evaluations of past trends, research into causes of pollution variations and interactions) and warning center (forecasts of high air pollution meteorological potential, warnings for tankers, offshore drilling rigs). The necessary know-how to start such activities immediately already exists, and satellite technology will make such activities much easier.

The prospects of coordinated international planning of energy production and development are still worse, in the experts' view. They estimated that a breakthrough in this area might come by 1995. Almost two-thirds of the respondents feel that energy resources have become the great pawn in international politics. A great many barriers in foreign relations will have to be dismantled and a new climate of mutual confidence established before some kind of coordinated international energy policy can be born.

Closely related to this problem is eventual conservation of fossil fuels for other needs. The use of fossil fuels for combustion, rather than as a raw material for chemicals, was identified by the group as one of the 25 leading energy-environment problems. To achieve any meaningful results, conservation measures would have to be undertaken on an international scale. Still another growing problem of international character and profound environmental and political implications is the export of modern Western technology to the developing countries of Asia, Africa, and Latin America without much concern about what this will do to their relatively unpolluted environment.

The finite nature of the earth, the necessity to control population, and a multitude of environmental considerations will also bring about a modification and later a rejection of the widespread belief in growth for growth's sake. This shift in attitude might point toward an absolute decrease in per capita energy consumption. But only about one fifth of the world's population now could cut down its consumption of energy and still be fairly well off. The rest of the world desperately needs to increase consumption quite substantially to feed people, create jobs, build houses, and provide medical care. Many conservationists would argue that the "over-developed" countries should start decreasing their per capita production right now, but regional and social inequalities within these nations, and social and military considerations are major blocks toward such a goal. Not unexpectedly, the experts did not see much probability of such an action for a very long time—if ever.

If these important social changes gradually become reality within the next two or three decades—and there are steady advances in crucial technological processes—there is a substantial chance for the future compatibility of increased energy production and a clean and healthy environment.

ENERGY AND THE ENVIRONMENT IN 1985 AND 2000

Based on the results of the poll we can now assemble a general picture of what the energy-environment situation might be like in the years 1985 and 2000.

TIMETABLE FOR THE ENVIRONMENT

The author also asked the experts to estimate when significant developments might occur in the field of environmental protection, planning, and management. Following is their timetable, showing the year by which time there is a 50-50 chance the event will have occurred.

1971 Energy sources become the great pawn of international politics.

1978 Environmentally motivated higher price for energy.

1978 Acceptance of the idea that all consumers share responsibility for pollution and its cost.

1980 Safe, large-scale disposal of radioactive wastes.

1980 Abolition of "growth for growth's sake" concept.

1980 Effective, harmless control of accidental oil spills.

1981 Dry cooling power plant towers.

1983 Development of waste heat utilization (desalting, heating, sewage treatment, etc.).

1983 Control of thermal pollution in water.

1983 Control of nitrogen oxides.

1985 New car (batteries, fuel cells, steam, etc.).

1985 Offshore siting of large power plants.

1986 Removal of noxious matter from fossil fuels before combustion.

1988 Establishment of worldwide environmental quality standards (air and water).

1990 Taxes to alleviate pollution problems (effluent taxes, tax incentives for dispersal of people from large cities).

1990 Establishment of worldwide environmental surveillance and warning agency.

1990 Suppression of sound along highways and airways.

1992 New, fast, and safe mass transit systems.

1995 Coordinated international planning of energy consumption.

1995 Application of Brayton power cycles to eliminate necessity of water cooling.

2000 Planned decrease of per capita energy demand and consumption.

2000 Effective population control.

2005 Conservation of fossil fuels for other future needs.

2010 Man will largely destroy his ability to survive in great numbers and in great cities.

2020 Utilization of heat sinks other than atmosphere and surface waters.

After 2020: Polar siting of large power plants.

After 2020: Application of new thermodynamic cycles (other than Brayton) to eliminate water cooling.

After 2020: Elimination of all generators using fossil fuel.

Never: No private powered cars allowed.

1985 Significant breakthroughs have been achieved in nuclear power generation. Breeder reactors have started full-scale operation both in North America and Europe, and advancing fusion research has closely approached the containment time and temperature required for controlled thermonuclear reaction. Nuclear generation has achieved a virtually "fail-safe" status, with multiple protective systems that are continuously monitored by computers to discover the slightest deviation.

The standards for release of radioactive emissions into air and water are set at a level 1,000 times lower than in 1970; actual emissions are still lower. Large-scale disposal of radioactive wastes is performed under much stricter regulations.

Since the early 1980s, nuclear energy has also been used as an explosive for peaceful purposes. Carefully-controlled nuclear blasts now are employed in the construction of natural gas reservoirs and in the production of hydrocarbons.

Meanwhile, the capacities of fossil-fueled power plants have significantly increased. Mine-mouth power plants in sparsely populated areas still burn relatively high sulfur coal, and electricity is transmitted by extra high voltage lines over long distances. Many coal-fired power plants burn low-sulfur coal transported by trains with total capacities up to 30,000 tons. Large surface mines supply several plants simultaneously; at the same time, underground coal mines have increased capacity, thanks to steady advances in mining and loading automation.

The coal industry's greatest achievement has been the breakthrough in low-cost gasification and liquefaction. The economic and environmental implications of this development are enormous. The efficient and clean use of coal has widened the perspectives of the coal industry.

The oil and gas industry has continued its worldwide search for new supplies on all continents, and, most significantly, in the shelf waters of the world's oceans. Almost one third of the world's oil now comes from the ocean. Offshore rigs can drill in water depths up to two kilometers, and the drilling capacity of special ships is virtually unlimited. Preparations are underway for the large-scale recovery of shale oil. World movements of oil and natural gas have intensified. The largest crude oil tanker has a half-million dead weight tons and dozens of ships have more than 250,000 dead weight tons. Floating refineries are manufacturing oil products while on their way from the Middle East to Japan. Stringent precautions are taken to prevent accidental spills, above all in such heavily frequented waters as the English Channel and the Ormuz and Malacca Straits.

The world's liquefied natural gas tanker fleet has well over 100 ships, carrying methane from Africa, USSR, and the Middle East to Europe, North America, and Japan. Oil and gas pipelines have grown larger, with diameters up to 1.5 meters for crude oil and 2.5 meters for natural gas. The capacity of refineries has doubled compared to the early 1970s. The largest have annual inputs of about 40 million tons of crude oil.

The energy industries, as well as the public, have paid increasing attention to the environment. The idea that all consumers must share responsibility for pollution and the cost of preventing it now is generally accepted. The cost of almost all forms of energy has increased compared to what it was 15–20 years ago.

To deal with the thermal pollution of water, a number of techniques have been devised. Waste heat from power production now is used for a variety of purposes ranging from desalting water to treating sewage; thus the thermal pollution problem is now under control.

2000 The last decades of the 20th century witnessed worldwide activity aimed at increasing the effectiveness and performance of the fossil fuel industries. These efforts have proven largely successful: Fossil fuels have attained record sales, and the industry's production and conversion processes are highly efficient. Nonetheless, coal, oil, and natural gas now are generally on the retreat. Limits on their use have been reached in many cases. The automation of underground coal mining has gone as far as practical. Surface mining is despoiling more land than it is possible to reclaim effectively and economically. "Coalplex" methods of gasification and liquefaction allow the energy of coal to be extracted with great efficiency, but the handling of large quantities of coal and waste has become a pressing problem.

The use of nuclear explosions and other sophisticated methods has now pushed the recovery of additional oil and gas to its limits. The large-scale recovery of shale oil, now underway for over a decade, faces serious environmental problems, due to its devastation of land. Drilling for hydrocarbons proceeds on all continents and virtually at all sea depths. But despite improved drilling systems and effective methods for oil spill control, the oceans continue to be polluted by ocean drilling and accidental oil leaks. Giant tankers jam transport routes, which have become closely watched corridors monitored in the same fashion as air traffic lanes. All practical, feasible hydroelectric sites in the world's populated regions now have been developed.

Nuclear generation accounts for well over three-quarters of the total electric energy production in some European countries; in the United States, nuclear reactors produce more than 50% of the electric power. Large pressurized water reactors in large power plants are still operating, but no new ones are being built. Instead, construction efforts now focus on fast breeders, many in nuclear parks that combine power generation with water desalination, the production of chemicals, and agriculture.

The top technological breakthrough of the 1990s has been the successful full-scale demonstration of a thermonuclear power plant. The next two decades should see the steady development and widespread application of fusion power. Only fusion, with its great efficiency and low levels of radioactive and heat waste, can produce the needed quantities of energy without adverse environmental consequences. Electricity transmitted by extra high voltage lines, and later, between continents by means of satellites, and the encouraging worldwide efforts to control population growth help to form the basis for an optimistic outlook.

D. COMPARATIVE MANAGEMENT

11 A MODEL FOR ANALYZING THE UNIVERSALITY AND TRANSFERABILITY OF MANAGEMENT*

Harold Koontz

As the area of management has increasingly commanded world wide interest and recognition, the question whether management is a science with universal application has concerned scholars and practitioners alike. It is now fairly generally recognized that effective management is the critical element in national economic growth and enterprise success. But it is far from generally agreed that management, as an emerging science, has universal application.

Obviously, if it does not, it is hardly even an embryonic science. For the role of science is to organize basic knowledge. A real science should explain phenomena regardless of national or cultural environments. Thus, the science of mechanics knows no boundaries providing it applies to the reality being considered. Principles of the building sciences are no different if applied to a small house or a large building and whether these structures are built in the tropics or the arctic.

Moreover, unless basic management science can be useful for practitioners in varying circumstances, it is certainly suspect. For the task of an *operational* science is so to organize pertinent knowledge as to make it applicable, and thereby useful, to those who would utilize it for accomplishing real results.

Certainly, if managing is the critical element in economic success, the best possible and most widely useful underlying science is a social "must." Nor should it be forgotten that effective management goes beyond what is usually regarded as the economic, or business, sphere. It is my firm conviction that it really does not matter what is being managed, whether business, governments, charitable or religious organizations, or even universities, the task of every manager at every level is so to manage as to accomplish group purposes with the least expenditure of material or human resources.

* Reprinted by permission of the publisher from *Academy of Management Journal*, vol. 12, no. 4, pp. 415–430, December, 1969. Mr. Koontz is Mead Johnson Professor of Management at the University of California, Los Angeles.

MANAGEMENT: THE CRITICAL ELEMENT IN ECONOMIC SUCCESS

It is a striking fact of life that per capita income varies widely in countries. In 1966, for example, only 18 countries were found to have Gross National Product per capita of more than $1,000 per year, while 33 had GNP per capita of $201–$1,000 per year, and 66 had GNP per capita of less than $200 per year.[1]

Because of these wide differences in per capita national incomes and product, attention of world leaders and development economists has naturally turned to the need for increasing productivity. One author has even referred to this concern and the many programs undertaken in the past quarter century as "one of the great world crusades of our time."[2] Until fairly recently, assuring development was thought to be one of transferring capital, technology, and education from the developed to the underdeveloped countries. But, as important as these are, it has come to be widely recognized now that managerial know-how[3] is almost certainly the most critical ingredient for growth. As one Chilean executive has put it:

> Perhaps it is time to alter our concept of underdevelopment and think in terms of management. This would focus our attention on helping mismanaged areas to improve their organizations and knowledge. No amount of capital investment will succeed in furthering human progress if such wealth producing resources

[1] R. N. Farmer and B. M. Richman, *International Business: An Operational Theory* (Homewood, Ill.: Richard D. Irwin, 1966), p. 39.

[2] M. D. Bryce, *Industrial Development* (New York: McGraw-Hill, 1960), p. 3.

[3] "Know-how" is defined here as the ability to apply knowledge to practice; it therefore includes both knowledge of underlying science and the ability to apply it to reality to gain desired results.

> are mishandled or undermined through lack of fundamental concepts. This lack of knowledge exists and the modern tools of finance, marketing, etc. are not common knowledge in underdeveloped areas and their absence prevents the rapid and successful expansion of areas. Capital alone will not replace this information, but likewise the lack of such capital will make it impossible to bring about the looked for development.[4]

Many who have worked with and studied the problems of economic development have come to similar conclusions. Rostow clearly had this in mind when he noted that "A small professional elite [of entrepreneurs and executives] can go a long way toward initiating economic growth."[5] Sayles has expressed the same viewpoint even more strongly when he concludes that "In the world race for economic growth and for the allegiance and stability of lesser-developed sections of the globe, United States management 'know-how' is a crucial factor."[6]

Conclusions such as these are not difficult for a person knowledgeable in management to understand. As pointed out above, the goal and *raison d'etre* of managing is to make it possible for people operating in groups to cooperate most effectively and gain the most in terms of goals sought with resources available. In other words, resources—whether human or material—will almost surely be wasted without effective management.

While emphasizing the critical role of managing, the importance of having technical knowledge, capital, and needed natural, physical and human resources should not be overlooked. But note that these are usually relatively easily transferred. No nation holds a monopoly on technical knowledge. Even so sophisticated a technology as the atomic bomb whose secrecy was so carefully protected by the United States did not remain a monopoly possession long. Most advances in technology, which are not nearly as complex or well-guarded, can be transferred from one country to another without great difficulty since only a few people need to have this knowledge to make it available for general use. Even capital can be fairly easily transferred, as can many other natural resources. Moreover, there are few underdeveloped areas of the world where the basic shortage is one of natural physical resources.

On the other hand, a cultural factor such as the level of education, particularly knowledge of skills, has an important impact on economic progress. Constraining on economic progress may be a large number of political factors, such as labor regulations, fiscal policy, business restrictions, and foreign policy. These and many other constraints in the environment where an enterprise must operate will necessarily influence management effectiveness. However, qualified managers can do much to bring economic progress by identifying them and by designing a managerial approach or technique to take them into account. This is the essence of "design" as engineers have found who must design a "black box" to operate in difficult environments.

This point was well identified by two specialists on international management when they said:

> We view management as the single most critical activity in connection with economic progress. Physical, financial, and manpower resources are by themselves but passive agents; they must be effectively combined and coordinated through sound, active management if a country is to experience a level of economic growth and development. A country can have sizeable natural and manpower resources including plentiful skilled labor and substantial capital but still be relatively poor because very few competent managers are available to put these resources efficiently togethe, in the production and distribution of useful goods and services.[7]

In speaking of the critical role of management, there is no implication that one is referring to *American* management. It is true that the United States has a much higher per-capita Gross National Product than any other country. It is also true that Americans are generally credited with having the most advanced management competence. It is likewise believed that there is some correlation between these two developments, although nonmanagerial environmental factors have also played a part. But the essential point is that competent management is a basic phenomenon and,

[4] J. Ross, "The Profit Motive and Its Potential for New Economics," *Proceedings, International Management Congress*, CIOS XIII (New York: Council for International Progress in Management (U.S.A.), Inc., 1963).

[5] W. W. Rostow, *The Stages of Economic Growth* (Cambridge, Mass.: Harvard University Press, 1962), p. 52.

[6] L. R. Sayles, *Managerial Behavior* (New York: McGraw-Hill, 1964), p. 17.

[7] R. N. Farmer and B. M. Richman, *Comparative Management and Economic Progress* (Homewood, Ill.: Richard D. Irwin, 1965), p. 1.

as any scholar and international practitioner knows, the underlying knowledge of management is international and many countries in the world have and are producing knowledgeable managerial practitioners.

IS MANAGEMENT CULTURE BOUND?

A considerable amount of difference has been expressed on the question whether management is culture bound. Those who take the position that management is culture bound reason that, since management practices differ and people and their cultural environments vary, management theory and principles—the framework by which management knowledge can be organized—that apply to a developed economy like the United States are not applicable in materially different cultural environments. It is even sometimes argued that within the same national culture, the fundamentals of management may apply to business, but not to government or universities, or between different sizes of businesses, or businesses in different industries.

The findings of Gonzalez and McMillan are among those that are often quoted to the effect that management is culture bound. These scholars, on the basis of a two-year study in Brazil, concluded that "American management experience abroad provides evidence that our uniquely American philosophy of management is not universally applicable but is a rather special case."[8] It is worth noting that these authors refer to "philosophy" and not to "science" or "theory" or "principles." They also point out that "that aspect of management which lacks universality has to do with interpersonal relationships, including those between management and workers, management and suppliers, management and the customer, the community, competition and government."[9]

On the basis of similar research, Oberg appears to agree with Gonzalez and McMillan. He doubts that the "game" of management in Brazil, being so different from that played in the United States, would permit application of management principles successfully employed in the United States to Brazil.[10] Oberg even expresses the belief that management principles may not only be inapplicable between cultures, but also between subcultures, such as those between rural businesses and large corporations in the United States.[11] From these observations he concludes that, since the applicability of management principles is limited to a particular culture or situation, it may be fruitless to search for a common set of principles or "determinate solutions."

However, even those who question the transferability of managerial knowledge and the universality of management principles admit that the application of American management knowledge in other countries has often been successful. Gonzalez and McMillan, for example, while concluding that the American philosophy of management is culture bound, admitted that:

> Transferred abroad, this know-how is first viewed with skepticism. Foreign national employees and partners are slow to respond and understand the American scientific approach to management problems. However, once fully indoctrinated, they accept and support this way of doing things. The superiority of this more objective, systematic, orderly and controlled approach to problems is seen and appreciated. For the host country, for American international relations, and for the American parent firm itself the export of American managerial know-how as well as technological know-how has yielded great dividends.[12]

Similar conclusions have been reached by Harbison and Myers in their study of management in a number of countries around the world. They not only found a common "logic of industrialization" but also that "organization building has its logic, too, which rests upon the development of management" and that "there is a general logic of management development which has applicability both to advanced and industrializing companies in the modern world."[13]

Interesting and consistent findings were made in another study in which the behavior of some 3600 managers in 14 countries was probed. This study, undertaken by Haire, Ghiselli and Porter, found a high degree of similarity in managerial behavior patterns and that many of

[8] R. F. Gonzalez and C. McMillan, Jr., "The Universality of American Management Philosophy," *Journal of the Academy of Management*, IV, No. 1 (April, 1961), 41.

[9] *Ibid.*, p. 39.

[10] W. Oberg, "Cross-Cultural Perspectives on Management Principles," *Academy of Management Journal*, VI, No. 2 (June, 1963), 120.

[11] *Ibid.*, pp. 142–143.

[12] Gonzalez and McMillan, p. 39.

[13] F. Harbison and C. A. Myers, *Management in the Industrial World* (New York: McGraw-Hill, 1959), p. 117.

the variations disclosed were due to identifiable cultural differences.[14] It is interesting, also, that Richman, in reporting on the developing interest in management in the Soviet Union in 1965, found that the evolving Soviet approach to management utilized the functions of managers—planning, organizing, coordination, control, direction, leadership, motivation, and staffing—which were essentially the same as long-held American concepts.[15] Other evidence pointing to universality has been found in various studies.[16]

THE IMPORTANCE OF DISTINGUISHING BETWEEN THE SCIENCE AND ART OF MANAGEMENT

It has often been argued whether managing is an art or a science. This is, of course, a fruitless and an absurd line of argument. Managing is an art, but so are engineering, medicine, accounting, and baseball. For art is the application of knowledge to reality with a view to accomplishing some concrete results, ordinarily with compromise, blend, or design to get the best total results. As can be readily recognized, the best art arises where the artist possesses a store of organized and applicable knowledge and understands how to apply it to reality. Thus, engineers have long understood that the best designers are those who are well grounded in the underlying sciences and who have an ability to conceptualize a problem in the light of goals sought and the further ability to *design* a solution to the problem to accomplish goals at the lowest system cost.

The same can be said of the task of managing. As an art, there is every reason to believe that it will succeed best if the practitioner has a store of applicable and organized knowledge to serve him. This knowledge, when organized, is science. When it is organized in such a way as to serve practice best, it becomes a truly *operational* science. It is the job of theory to act, as Homans has said so well, as "a classification, it provides a set of pigeonholes, a filing cabinet, in which fact can accumulate. For nothing is more lost than a loose fact. The empty folders of the file demand filling. In time the accumulation makes necessary a more economical filing system, with more cross references, and a new theory is born."[17]

In order to develop a theory, clear concepts are imperative. Likewise, the task of principles is to help in organizing knowledge by explaining relationships between two or more sets of variables, relationships believed to be generally true and, therefore, to have a predictive value. But, as every scientist knows, principles only describe and predict. They do not become normative (i.e., state or imply what "ought" to be) until the user applies them with a system of values (for example efficiency or effectiveness of a group effort) in mind. Moreover, no one should be surprised to see principles apparently disregarded in practice. The fact that, for example, many cases of disunity of command exist in practice does not mean that this practice has not tended to lead to confusion and splitting of responsibility. It is only to be hoped that the designer has taken into account the costs of disunity in creating his system. To say that existence of disunity of command in practice proves the invalidity of the principle is like saying that a space satellite invalidates the law of gravity.

It is exactly in the failure to distinguish between science and art where many of those who doubt the universality of management, as an organized body of knowledge, make their mistake. In a very real sense, one might say that there is a *practice* of managing and a *science* (no matter how crude it may be) of management.

Moreover, many who have written and studied managing in various cultures have erred on the very first requirement of science, the utilization of clear concepts or definitions. In reviewing the research and analysis that have been made in the field of comparative management, one is struck with how many of the differing conclusions as to the transferability of management are due to problems of semantics. The concepts of "management philosophy," "management know-how," "management theory," "management principles," and "management knowledge" are usually left either undefined or not clearly defined. One of the most widely used concepts, "management philosophy," almost defies clear definition. Strictly speaking, philosophy is the love, study, or pursuit of knowledge and is sometimes used as the

[14] M. Haire, E. E. Ghiselli, and L. W. Porter, *Managerial Thinking: An International Study* (New York: John Wiley and Sons, 1966).

[15] B. M. Richman, "The Soviet Educational and Research Revolution: Implications for Management Development," *California Management Review*, IX, No. 4 (Summer, 1967), 12.

[16] See studies referred to in footnotes 22–30.

[17] G. C. Homans, *The Human Group* (New York: Harcourt, Brace & World, 1950), p. 5.

equivalent of science. On the other hand, looking at studies of comparative management, one finds such definitions of "mangement philosophy" as "the expressed and implied attitude or relationships of a firm with some of its external and internal agents" such as consumers, stockholders, suppliers, distributors, employee unions, community, and local, state, and federal governments.[18]

In other places the term "management philosophy" is taken to mean a combination of management theory and principles, along with cultural attitudes and beliefs. Obviously, if philosophy includes such cultural beliefs as attitudes toward property rights and individuals, actual management *practice* would be expected to vary between certain cultures. Indeed, concepts such as this, particularly if they represent a composite of management fundamentals and cultural factors, can hardly have any universality. No one can argue that cultural differences exist between various societies, sometimes to a marked degree. There are even subcultural differences of an important nature in the same country or society.

It is clear then, by making the distinction between science and art, that the only generally comparative and transferable aspects of management are those which can be classified as science. When the distinction is made between management fundamentals, as expressed in basic concepts, theory and principles, and management practice—the application of management fundamentals to a given situation—progress can be made in determining the extent of management universality and the transferability of management fundamentals.

However, this does not necessarily mean that a given management technique or approach successful in one society may not work with few, if any, modifications in another. But it does mean that, if a manager borrows a technique from one society where it has worked well, he should be aware that some change may be required to make it workable in another cultural environment. At the same time, some management techniques can be surprisingly easily transferred from a well developed economy to a much less developed one. The author has found this possible, for example, with such techniques as variable budgeting, utilization of rate-of-return-on-investment, and network planning, even though less sophisticated applications of these techniques were often necessary. This is really not too surprising. These and other management techniques are so completely reflections of underlying proved principles that cultural differences often have little effect on their applicability, although they may not permit a very sophisticated approach because of limitations of information and understanding.

MANAGING AND ITS ENVIRONMENT

The above distinction between science and art necessarily means certain things that any perceptive practicing manager has long recognized. In the first place, while the principal task of the manager is to design an *internal* environment for performance, he must necessarily do so within the constraints and influences of the enterprise's external environment—whether economic, technological, social, political, or ethical. Thus, managing as an art has never assumed a closed system. It would certainly come as a surprise to practitioners to find recent writers accusing "traditional" (whoever they are) managers of having managed without recognizing interchange of influences between the enterprise and its environment. Obviously, anyone who has utilized human and material resources or who has ever attempted to engineer and market a product understands well the openness of the system in which he is operating.

However, it is true that recent researches have clarified the science, as well as the practice, of management by placing increasing emphasis on the environment. This has been particularly noteworthy in the increasing recognition of cultural factors. Many are the American multinational companies that have found they must vary their managerial approaches and techniques when they move to the management of an operation in a foreign country where they are forced to take into account different sets of customs and mores, as well as more obvious differences in government and labor rules, capital and equipment availability, and levels of learning of available workers.

But, as differences in cultural environments are better understood and considered by the intelligent manager, this does not mean that the fundamentals of management are different. However, it does mean that, in studying the universality of management or undertaking comparative management analyses, the researcher must carefully distinguish between these fundamentals and their application.

[18] A. R. Negandhi and B. D. Estafen, "A Research Model to Determine the Applicability of American Know-How in Differing Cultures and/or Environments," *Academy of Management Journal*, VIII, No. 4 (December, 1965), 312.

ATTEMPTS AT SEPARATING ENVIRONMENTAL FACTORS FROM MANAGEMENT FUNDAMENTALS: THE FARMER-RICHMAN MODEL

The meaningful study of comparative management may be regarded as starting from several important attempts to separate environmental factors from management fundamentals. One of the pioneering approaches for doing so is the model developed by Professors Farmer and Richman.[19] In this model, the approach is, first, to identify the critical elements in the management process and attempt to evaluate their operation in individual firms in varying cultures. A second feature of the model is to identify various environmental factors that have been found to have a significant impact on the operations and effectiveness of managers; these factors have been classified among (1) educational variables, (2) sociological-cultural variables, (3) political and legal variables, and (4) economic variables.

As may be noted, what these scholars have done is to postulate that environmental factors affect the elements of the management process, the way in which managing is done, and its effectiveness. They thus attempt to segregate environmental factors from the basics of management.[20] But they do not do so entirely. By including actual policies with the basics of the managerial functions, the authors have, unfortunately, not made their model as useful as it might have been for distilling from different environments the universals of management. In other words, while the fundamental concept of a policy as a guide to action in decision making is universal, as are the role of policies in planning and the relationship of policies to delegation, an actual policy may differ considerably in varying environments. Thus, a make-or-buy production policy would be heavily dependent on national import regulations or on the availability of suppliers in a country. And policies with respect to sources of capital and distribution of earnings would be completely different in a socialized economy and a private-enterprise economy.

The Farmer-Richman model is graphically shown at the top of p. 87.

But, despite this mixing of environmentally resultant policy considerations with the basics of management in the Farmer-Richman model, these scholars have made an exceptionally important contribution to the separation of environmental and management factors. If those policies so dependent on environmental factors were separated from the fundamentals of policy making and other elements of management, we could then have a model which would be very useful in distilling the transferable universals of management.

ATTEMPTS AT SEPARATING ENVIRONMENTAL FACTORS FROM MANAGEMENT FUNDAMENTALS: THE NEGANDHI-ESTAFEN MODEL

Another model designed to separate the influence of the external environment from an analysis of the basics of management is the model first offered by Professors Negandhi and Estafen in 1965[21] and somewhat modified since and used as a research device by the senior author.[22] This model differs somewhat from the Farmer-Richman model although it does focus on the task of separating environmental variables from managerial practice. The major difference in the Negandhi-Estafen model is the introduction of a major independent (or at least mostly so) variable in the form of management philosophy—an expressed or implied attitude of the firm toward such important internal and external agents as consumers, employees, distributors, stockholders, government, and the community.

The Negandhi-Estafen model is graphically depicted at the bottom of p. 87.

[19] R. N. Farmer and B. M. Richman, *Comparative Management and Economic Progress* (Homewood, Ill.: Richard D. Irwin, 1965). See also "A Model for Research in Comparative Management," *California Management Review*, VII, No. 2 (Winter, 1964), 58–68.

[20] The authors break down educational-cultural variables into 6 variables (such as literacy level and attitude toward education), the sociological-cultural variables into 9 items (such as attitude toward achievement and work and attitude toward change), the political and legal variables into 6 items (such as political stability and type of political organization), and the economic variables into 8 classes (such as fiscal policy and social overhead capital). Likewise, the elements of the management process are broken down into a number of basic factors under both the process items (planning, organizing, staffing, directing, and controlling) and various policy areas (marketing policies pursued, production and procurement policies, research and development policies, financial policies, and policies with respect to public and external relations). For a complete description of these factors, see *Comparative Management and Economic Progress*, pp. 20–21, 29–30.

[21] A. R. Negandhi and B. D. Estafen, *op. cit.*

[22] See A. R. Negandhi, "A Model for Analyzing Organizations in Cross-Cultural Settings: A Conceptual Scheme and Some Research Findings," in Negandhi et. al, *Comparative Administration and Management Conference* (Kent, Ohio: Bureau of Economic and Business Research, Kent State University, 1969.)

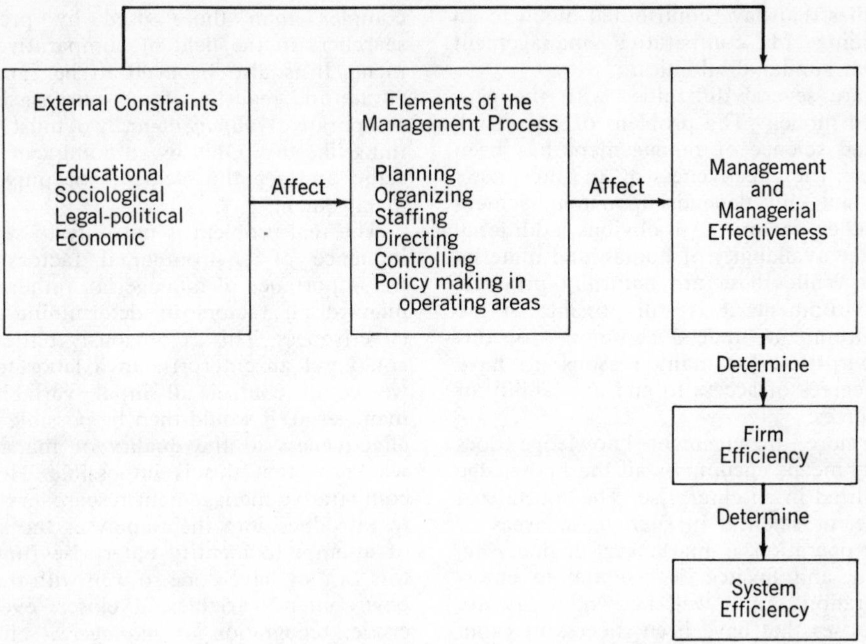

As can be seen, in this model, both management philosophy and environmental factors are seen as having influence on the practice of management and environmental factors are seen as also independently affecting management and enterprise effectiveness. Thus, the Negandhi-Estafen model does not make the error, from the standpoint of separating management universals, that the Richman-Farmer model does. However, one does have difficulty in seeing the area of management philosophy (attitudes and beliefs) as being independent of environmental factors. Also, the model itself does not make sure that management techniques or approaches can be separated between basics and environmentally influenced practices.

SEPARATING ENVIRONMENTAL FACTORS FROM MANAGEMENT FUNDAMENTALS: A PROPOSED MODEL

From the point of view of studying comparative management to determine the universality and transferability of the basics of management and thus to make a start in separating science from practice in this field, neither of the above models seems to be suitable. Both make major contributions in recognizing the importance of environmental factors and in attempting to show how they affect the practice of management, but both are not as useful as they might be in dealing with the problem of transferability. Likewise, many

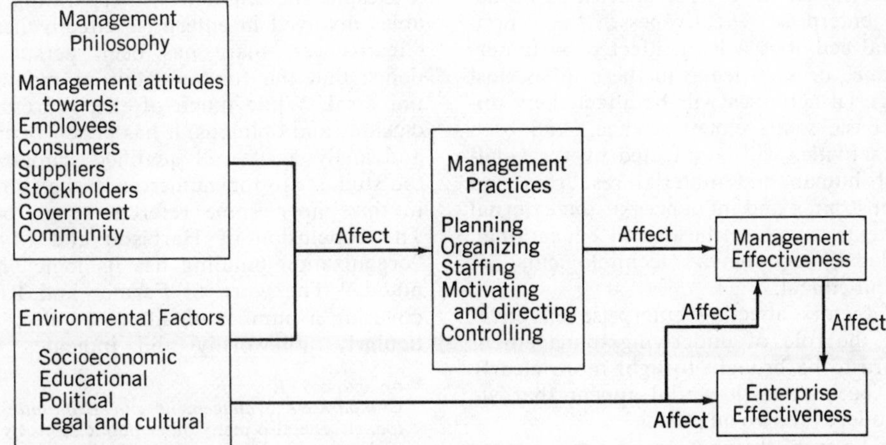

other studies that have contributed much to an understanding of comparative management suffer from similar disabilities.

There are several difficulties with the generally used models. The problem of separating the art and science of management has been noted. Also, the effectiveness of an enterprise's operation not only depends upon management but on other factors. An obvious additional factor is the availability of human and material resources. While these are naturally products of an environment, it is still possible in the same environment—indeed common—for different enterprises, for many reasons, to have varying degrees of access to and availability of such resources.

Furthermore, management knowledge does not by any means encompass all the knowledge that is utilized in an enterprise. The specialized knowledge, or science, in such basic areas of enterprise operation as marketing, engineering, production, and finance, is essential to enterprise operation. As is well known, many are the enterprises that have been successful (and, therefore, at least apparently effective) despite poor management, because of brilliant marketing, strong engineering, well organized and operated production, or astute financing. Even though it is the writer's firm judgment, based on an analysis of the histories of many companies, that effectiveness of management will ultimately make the difference between continued success and decline, at least in a competitive economy, it is still true that enterprises have for a time succeeded entirely through nonmanagerial factors. It is also probably true that, if an enterprise has excellent capabilities in nonmanagerial areas, effective managing would greatly enhance and would surely assure this success.

In total, then, if we look at enterprise activities, they fall into two broad categories, managerial and nonmanagerial. Either or both can be the causal factors for at least some degree of enterprise effectiveness. Also, nonmanagerial activities will be affected by underlying science or knowledge in these areas, just as managerial activities will be affected by underlying basic management science. And both types of activities will be affected by the availability of human and material resources and by the constraints and influences of the external environment, whether these are educational, political-legal, economic, technological, or sociological-ethical.

If the factors affecting enterprise effectiveness and the role of underlying management science are to be brought to light more clearly than has been done, it would appear that we need a model as shown on p. 89.

As can be seen, the above model is far more complex than those used by previous researchers in the field of comparative management. It is also believed to be far more accurate and realistic. If our purpose is to study comparative *management*, we must do something like this. Only by so doing can we understand and see the elements of universality in management.

The real problem is not only to separate the influence of environmental factors but also the importance of managerial, rather than nonmanagerial, factors in determining enterprise effectiveness. This is obviously difficult. If we could put an enterprise in a laboratory where we could control all input variables except managerial, it would then be possible to ascribe effectiveness to the quality of managing. But we know that this is impossible. However, if comparative management researchers would try to introduce into their analyses the same kind of attempt to identify enterprise function factors as they have done so well with the external environment variables, a closer, even though crude, recognition of *managerial* effectiveness could be made.

This may not be as difficult as it appears. If we could take enterprises (whether business, government, or other) operating in essentially the same external environment and trace their primary causes of effectiveness to managerial and nonmanagerial factors, we might be surprised at what would be disclosed. The author has had the occasion to analyze several companies in the United States that had had a profitable growth only to find in some instances the quality of managing was rather poor and the success—often erroneously ascribed to astute managing—was really due to genius in marketing or in engineering, or in clever financial manipulation.

EVIDENCES OF UNIVERSALITY

Despite the difficulties in separating the variables involved in enterprise effectiveness or ineffectiveness, there has been persuasive evidence that the fundamentals of managing are universal. While much of this represents conclusions and opinions, it has arisen from studies and analyses of well qualified scholars. While the studies are too numerous to be summarized in this paper, some references can be noted. The conclusion of Harbison and Myers that "organization building has its logic" has been noted.[23] The work of Farmer and Richman[24] covering a number of different cultures is particularly noteworthy and indicates the uni-

[23] *op. cit.*, p. 117.

[24] *Comparative Management and Economic Progress, loc. cit.* See also many other publications by the same authors, either jointly or individually presented.

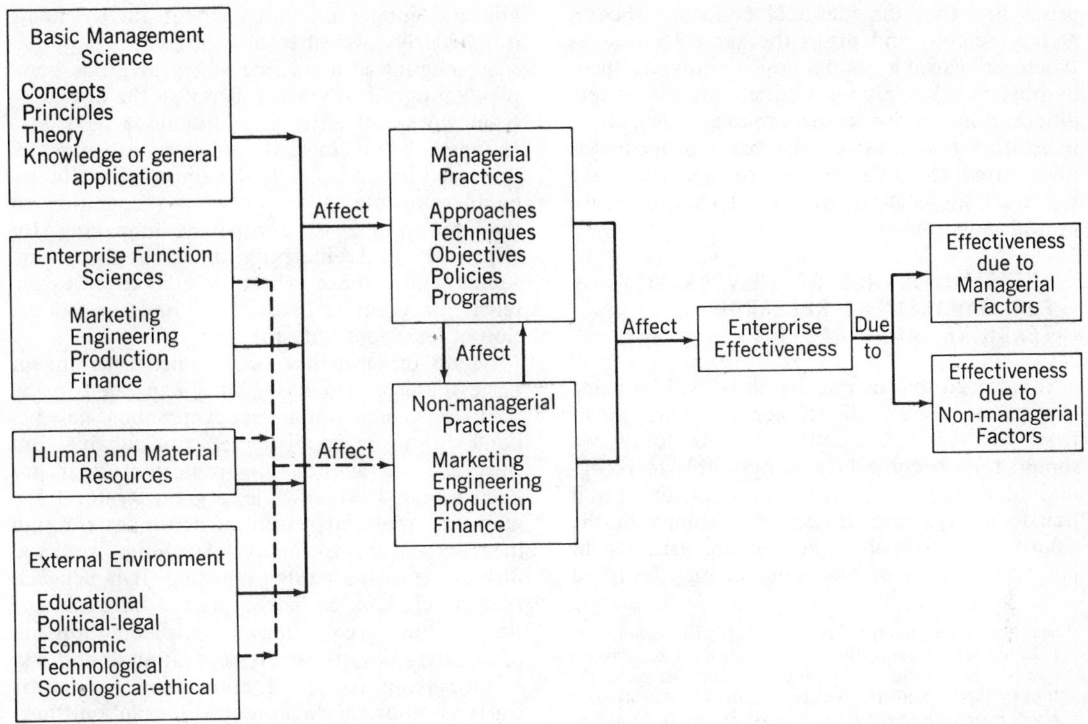

versality of basic management theory and principles. Likewise, the work of Negandhi points in the same direction.[25] The same kind of inferences can clearly be drawn from the work of Fayerweather on Mexico,[26] the various publications of the National Planning Association,[27] the work of Abegglen on Japan,[28] the studies of Prasad,[29] and many others.

Also, a number of studies on comparative management have been made in recent years by doctoral students. Most of these have indicated a high degree of universality in the application of management concepts and principles. For example, a series of studies undertaken at the University of California, Los Angeles, indicate pretty persuasively that well-managed American-owned companies, operating in less developed countries, have generally shown superiority in management and economic effectiveness.[30]

The universal nature of management fundamentals has also been apparent by examination of specialized books on administration for business, government, and other types of enterprises. While semantic differences may exist, one finds that, at the fundamental level, authors are talking about the same phenomena.

Persons like the author who have led management seminars for various types of enter-

[25] See, for example, his paper on "A Model for Organizations in Cross-Cultural Settings: A Conceptual Scheme and Some Research Findings," *loc. cit.*

[26] J. Fayerweather, *The Executive Overseas* (Syracuse: Syracuse University Press, 1959).

[27] See, for example, F. Brandenberg, *The Development of Latin American Private Enterprise* (1964); T. Geiger, *The General Electric Company in Brazil* (1961); T. Geiger and W. Armstrong, *The Development of African Private Enterprise* (1961); and S. Kannappan and E. Burgess, *Aluminum Ltd. in India* (1967).

[28] *The Japanese Factory* (New York: The Free Press of Glencoe, 1958).

[29] See, for example, "New Managerialism in Czechoslovakia and the Soviet Union," *Academy of Management Journal*, IX, No. 4 (December, 1966), 328–336.

[30] These include such unpublished dissertations as B. D. Estafen, "An Empirical Experiment in Comparative Management: A Study of the Transferability of American Management Policies and Practices into Firms Operating in Chile" (1967); A. J. Papageorge, "Transferability of Management: A Case Study of the United States and Greece" (1967); F. C. Flores, Jr., "Applicability of American Management Know-How to Developing Countries: Case Studies of U.S. Firms Operating Both in the United States and the Philippines in Comparison with Domestic Firms in the Philippines" (1967); John Jaeger, "A Comparative Management Study: Organization Patterns and Processes of Hotels in Four Countries" (1965).

prises find that the identical concepts, theory, and principles, and often the same techniques (such as variable budgeting or management by objectives) apply with equal force in widely different enterprise environments. Also, it is interesting that most of the basic propositions inventoried from the behavioral sciences have universal application where relevant to managerial situations.[31]

THE SIGNIFICANCE OF UNIVERSALITY FOR MANAGEMENT RESEARCH, TEACHING, AND PRACTICE

It is hoped that increasing effort will be made to separate underlying science of management from the art of managing. By so doing, we should then become increasingly able to recognize fundamentals of universal application and transferability. And, in doing so, many of the clouds that have obscured the analysis, teaching, and practice of management may be lifted and the jungle of management theory made into orderly rows of trees at last.

Managing as a science and practice is complex enough. But when it is put in the operating framework of enterprise functions and surrounded by a myriad of environmental influences, its complexity becomes virtually incomprehensible. With growing recognition of the importance of competent managing for effectively and efficiently reaching group and social goals, those whose role is to research, teach, or practice in the field have an obligation at least to clarify the field.

Much research has been done. Teaching of basic management has greatly expanded in the past 15 years. Management practice has become far more sophisticated and capable. But only the surface of this important field has been touched. Meanwhile, a great waste of human and material resources continues through inept research, ineffective teaching, and too much seat-of-the-pants managing. It is believed that much can be accomplished through the simple, but largely unaccomplished, approach of clearly and purposively separating underlying science from its artful application to reality. Early attempts to do so may be crude, but they, at least, should not be confusing.

[31] See, for example, the inventory of propositions in J. L. Pierce, *Organizational Effectiveness: An Inventory of Propositions* (Homewood, Ill.: Richard D. Irwin, 1968) and B. Berelson and G. A. Steiner, *Human Behavior: An Inventory of Scientific Findings* (New York: Harcourt, Brace & World, 1964).

Part 2
PLANNING

All but the first section of this book of readings are concerned with the functions of the manager—planning, organizing, staffing, directing and leading, and controlling. While these functions are regarded as fairly and accurately descriptive of broad categories of what managers actually do, the main purpose of using them is to provide a first major classification into which pertinent knowledge and techniques relating to managing may be placed. The reader will recognize of course that, in practice, these functions tend to be intertwined. This is as it should be since managing must involve a systematic approach to an enterprise and its problems.

This part undertakes to cast light on planning, regarded as the most basic of the functions of managers, since all other activities must necessarily be related to and contribute toward the accomplishment of objectives and plans. Defined as the selection from alternatives of courses of future action, planning is the function by which managers determine (within the constraints of their role) what goals are to be accomplished and how and when they are to be reached. Accordingly, the readings in this part have been grouped under the headings "Nature and Purpose of Planning," "Objectives," "Planning Premises," "Decision Making and Operations Research," and "Strategies and Policies."

Of particular importance in the development of thought about the nature and purpose of planning are two classics: the extraordinarily perceptive description of this function by Henri Fayol, a description which, although written over sixty years ago, is as up to date as today; and the original contribution of Billy E. Goetz, who crisply and accurately codified the types of basic plans and pointed to their interdependence. To these is added an excerpt from the recent research by Henry C. Egerton and James K. Brown on how executives regard planning. As will be noted, there is still considerable variation and confusion concerning the planning process.

It has long been recognized that objectives lie at the base of planning and even of managing itself, simply because we must plan toward something. Yet, despite this obvious fact, systems of formally managing by meaningful and verifiable objectives have only come into actual practice in recent years. One of the pioneers who emphasized the role of managing by objectives was Peter F. Drucker in his *Practice of Management*, published in 1954. An excerpt from this book has been reprinted here. In addition, the approach to developing objectives is treated in Cyril O'Donnell's paper "Planning Objectives." The problems encountered in actual practice have been summarized in Harold Koontz' paper on "Shortcomings and Pitfalls in Managing by Objectives."

Because plans necessarily operate in the future, forecasting is essential. One of the most important of all forecasts useful to guide planning in business is the sales forecast. This is discussed in William Lazer's article "Sales Forecasts: Key to Integrated Management." Until recent years, forecasts have been based largely upon an analysis of the future economic environment. More recently, sophisticated managers have attempted to forecast technological, political, and social factors as well. An article illustrating one of these areas and showing how special forecasts can be undertaken and related to planning is D. D. Roman's "Technological Forecasting in the Decision Process." Although technological forecasting has been increasingly undertaken, especially by high technology companies, many companies have encountered difficulty in getting it actually effective in planning. The problem is dealt with in Philip H. Thurston's "Make TF Serve Corporate Planning."

Decision making has generally been regarded as central to planning and, indeed, to all management. There are even those who view it as the total task of managers. However, the editors look upon decision making as playing a more limited but still immensely important role—that of rational selection of the best possible alternative in the light of goals sought and against the background of the future environment to be encountered. In the view of the editors, the excerpt from the late Chester I. Barnard's classic, *The Functions of the Executive,* in which he deals with the occasion and the environment of the decision, is still the best concise writing on this subject.

The systems and quantitative sciences have had their greatest impact on management in the area of decision making. This is understandable in the light of the logic of selecting from among alternatives. Not only have new tools been developed and applied but new decision theory has sharpened approaches to decision making as well. As an introduction to this subject, the editors have selected an excerpt from David Hertz' book *New Power for Management.* One of the most important of these decision tools or approaches has been operations research. As an introduction to this, the first chapter of William D. Brinkloe's book on *Managerial Operations Research,* where the essential nature of this tool is described, has been included. Among the newer techniques for improving decision making is the decision tree; on this subject, there is reprinted the paper by F. A. McCreary, "How to Grow a Decision Tree."

The important planning subject of strategies and policies is introduced by an excerpt from the excellent book of J. T. Cannon, *Business Strategy and Policy.* The author of this book presents one of the clearest and most practical discussions of the nature, elements, and purposes of strategies and policies that has yet been written. Policies, which are guides to thinking in decision making and thus furnish a framework for managerial planning, are often confused with rules that require specific action or inaction in a certain matter. The nature of policies and rules and their importance to managers are dealt with in M. Valliant Higginson's summary, "Management by Rule and by Policy," excerpted from her study of management policies made for the American Management Association.

Since strategies should be designed to shape decision making, their clarity and accuracy are obviously important. Yet many enterprises are not aware of the role of strategies in ensuring effective direction of plans made throughout the enterprise. This subject is ably handled by Louis V. Gerstner, Jr., in his paper "Can Strategic Planning Pay Off?"

The final article in this section is George A. Steiner's "How To Improve Your Long-Range Planning." Steiner deals with an important and widely attempted area of planning, analyzing what long-range planning is and making valuable suggestions to ensure that it is done, is done well, and contributes to effective operations.

A. NATURE AND PURPOSE OF PLANNING

12 PLANNING*

Henri Fayol

The maxim, "managing means looking ahead," gives some idea of the importance attached to planning in the business world, and it is true that if foresight is not the whole of management at least it is an essential part of it. To foresee, in this context, means both to assess the future and make provision for it; that is, foreseeing is itself action already. Planning is manifested on a variety of occasions and in a variety of ways, its chief manifestation, apparent sign and most effective instrument being the plan of action. The plan of action is, at one and the same time, the result envisaged, the line of action to be followed, the stages to go through, and methods to use. It is a kind of future picture wherein proximate events are outlined with some distinctness, whilst remote events appear progressively less distinct, and it entails the running of the business as foreseen and provided against over a definite period.

The plan of action rests: (1) On the firm's resources (buildings, tools, raw materials, personnel, productive capacity, sales outlets, public relations, etc.). (2) On the nature and importance of work in progress. (3) On future trends which depend partly on technical, commercial, financial and other conditions, all subject to change, whose importance and occurrence cannot be pre-determined. The preparation of the plan of action is one of the most difficult and most important matters of every business and brings into play all departments and all functions, especially the management function. It is, in effect, in order to carry out his managerial function that the manager takes the initiative for the plan of action, that he indicates its objective and scope, fixes the share of each department in the communal task, coordinates the parts and harmonizes the whole; that he decides, in fine, the line of conduct to be followed. In this line of conduct it is not only imperative that nothing should clash with principles and rules of good management, but also that the arrangement adopted should facilitate application of these principles and rules. Therefore, to the divers technical, commercial, financial and other abilities necessary on the part of a business head and his assistants, there must be added considerable managerial ability.

GENERAL FEATURES OF A GOOD PLAN OF ACTION

No one disputes the usefulness of a plan of action. Before taking action it is most necessary to know what is possible and what is wanted. It is known that absence of plan entails hesitation, false steps, untimely changes of direction, which are so many causes of weakness, if not of disaster, in business. The question of and necessity for a plan of action, then, does not arise and I think that I am voicing the general opinion in saying that a plan of action is indispensable. But there are plans and plans, there are simple ones, complex ones, concise ones, detailed ones, long- or short-term ones; there are those studied with meticulous attention, those treated lightly; there are good, bad, and indifferent ones. How are the good ones to be singled out from among the others? Experience is the only thing that finally determines the true value of a plan, i.e., on the services it can render to the firm, and even then the manner of its application must be taken into account. There is both instrument and player. Nevertheless, there are certain broad characteristics on which general agreement may be reached beforehand without waiting for the verdict of experience.

Unity of plan is an instance. Only one plan can be put into operation at a time; two different plans would mean duality, confusion, disorder. But a plan may be divided into several parts. In large concerns, there is found alongside the general plan a technical, commercial,

* Reprinted by permission of the publisher from Henri Fayol, *General and Industrial Administration*, Pitman Publishing Corporation, New York, 1949, pp. 43–52. Henri Fayol was a French industrialist who probably earlier than anyone else saw management as a universal, pervasive task based upon principles. His book, based largely on lectures delivered in 1900 and 1908, first appeared in French in 1916.

and a financial one, or else an overall one with a specific one for each department. But all these plans are linked, welded, so as to make up one only, and every modification brought to bear on any one of them is given expression in the whole plan. The guiding action of the plan must be continuous. Now the limitations of human foresight necessarily set bounds to the duration of plans, so, in order to have no break in the guiding action, a second plan must follow immediately upon the first, a third upon the second, and so on. In large businesses the annual plan is more or less in current use. Other plans of shorter or longer term, always in close accord with the annual plan, operate simultaneously with this latter. The plan should be flexible enough to bend before such adjustments, as it is considered well to introduce, whether from pressure or circumstances or from any other reason. First as last, it is the law to which one bows. Another good point about a plan is to have as much accuracy as is compatible with the unknown factors bearing on the fate of the concern. Usually it is possible to mark out the line of proximate action fairly accurately, while a simple general indication does for remote activities, for before the moment for their execution has arrived sufficient enlightenment will have been forthcoming to settle the line of action more precisely. When the unknown factor occupies a relatively very large place there can be no preciseness in the plan, and then the concern takes on the name of venture.

Unity, continuity, flexibility, precision: such are the broad features of a good plan of action.

As for other specific points which it should have, and which turn on the nature, importance and condition of the business for which the plan is drawn up, there could be no possibility of settling them beforehand save by comparison with other plans already recognized as effective in similar businesses. In each case, then, comparable elements and models must be sought in business practice, after the fashion of the architect with a building to construct. But the architect, better served than the manager, can call upon books, courses in architecture, whereas there are no books on plans of action, no lessons in foresight, for management theory has yet to be formulated.

There is no lack of good plans, they can be guessed at from the externals of a business but not seen at sufficiently close quarters to be known and judged. Nevertheless, it would be most useful for those whose concern is management to know how experienced managers go about drawing up their plans. By way of information or sample, I am going to set out the method which has long been followed in a great mining and metallurgical concern with which I am well acquainted.

Method of Drawing up the Plan of Action in a Large Mining and Metallurgical Firm

This company includes several separate establishments and employs about ten thousand personnel. The entire plan is made up of a series of separate plans called forecasts; and there are yearly forecasts, ten-yearly forecasts, monthly, weekly, daily forecasts, long-term forecasts, special forecasts, and all merge into a single programme which operates as a guide for the whole concern.

(i) *Yearly Forecasts.* Each year, two months after the end of the budgetary period, a general report is drawn up of the work and results of this period. The report deals especially with production, sales, technical, commercial, financial position, personnel, economic consequences, etc. The report is accompanied by forecasts dealing with those same matters, the forecasts being a kind of anticipatory summary of the activities and results of the new budgetary period. The two months of the new plan which have elapsed are not left without plan, because of provisional forecasts drawn up fifteen days before the end of the previous period. In a large mining and metallurgical firm not many activities are quite completed during the course of one year. Co-operative projects of a technical, commercial, and financial nature, which provide the business with its activities, need more time for their preparation and execution. From another aspect, account must be taken of the repercussions which proximate activities must have on ultimate ones and of the obligation to prepare far ahead sometimes for a requisite state of affairs.

Finally, thought must be given to constant modifications operating on the technical, commercial, financial and social condition of the industrial world in general and of the business in particular, to avoid being overtaken by circumstances. These various circumstances come outside the framework of yearly forecasts and lead on to longer-term ones.

(ii) *Ten-yearly Forecasts.* Ten-yearly forecasts deal with the same matters as yearly ones. At the outset these two types of forecast are identical, the yearly forecast merging into the first year of the ten-yearly one, but from the second year onwards notable divergences make their appearance. To maintain unity of plan each year the ten-yearly forecasts must be reconciled with annual ones so that at the end of some years the ten-yearly forecasts are generally so modified and transformed as to be

Yearly and Ten-yearly Forecasts

CONTENTS

Technical Section

Mining rights. Premises. Plant.
Extraction. Manufacture. Output.
New workings. Improvements.
Maintenance of plant and buildings.
Production costs.

Commercial Section

Sales outlets.
Marketable goods.
Agencies. Contracts.
Customer importance. Credit standing.
Selling price.

Financial Section

Capital. Loans. Deposits.
Circulating assets { Supplies in hand. Finished goods. Debtors. Liquid assets.
Available assets.
Reserves and sundry appropriations.
Creditors { Wages. Suppliers. Sundry.
Sinking funds. Dividends. Bankers.

Accounting

Balance sheet. Profit and Loss account. Statistics.

Security

Accident precautions.
Works police. Claims. Health service.
Insurance.

Management

Plan of action.
Organization of personnel. Selection.
Command.
Co-ordination. Conferences.
Control.

no longer clear and need re-drafting. In effect the custom of re-drafting every five years has become established. It is the rule that ten-yearly forecasts always embrace a decade, and that they are revised every five years. Thus there is always a line of action marked out in advance for five years at least.

(iii) *Special Forecasts.* There are some activities whose full cycle exceeds one or even several ten-yearly periods, there are others which, occurring suddenly, must sensibly affect the conditions of the business. Both the one and the other are the object of special forecasts whose findings necessarily have a place in the yearly and ten-yearly forecasts. But it must never be lost sight of that there is one plan only.

These three sorts of forecasts, yearly, ten-yearly, and special, merged and harmonized, constitute the firm's general plan.

So, having been prepared with meticulous care by each regional management, with the help of departmental management, and then revised, modified, and completed by general management and then submitted for scrutiny and approval to the Board of Directors, these forecasts become the plan which, so long as no other has been put in its place, shall serve as guide, directive, and law for the whole staff.

Fifty years ago I began to use this system of forecasts, when I was engaged in managing a colliery, and it rendered me such good service that I had no hesitation in subsequently applying it to various industries whose running was entrusted to me. I look upon it as a precious managerial instrument and have no hesitation in recommending its use to those who have no better instrument available. It has necessarily some shortcomings, but its shortcomings are very slight compared with the advantages it offers. Let us glance at these advantages and shortcomings.

ADVANTAGES AND SHORTCOMINGS OF FORECASTS

(a) The study of resources, future possibilities, and means to be used for attaining the objective call for contributions from all departmental heads within the framework of their mandate, each one brings to this study the contribution of his experience together with recognition of the responsibility which will fall upon him in executing the plan.

Those are excellent conditions for ensuring that no resource shall be neglected and that future possibilities shall be prudently and courageously assessed and that means shall be appropriate to ends. Knowing what are its capabilities and its intentions, the concern goes boldly on, confidently tackles current problems and is prepared to align all its forces against accidents and surprises of all kinds which may occur.

(b) Compiling the annual plan is always a delicate operation and especially lengthy and laborious when done for the first time, but each repetition brings some simplification and when the plan has become a habit the toil and difficulties are largely reduced. Conversely, the interest it offers increases. The attention demanded for executing the plan, the indispensable comparison between predicted and actual facts, the recognition of mistakes made and successes attained, the search for means of repeating the one and avoiding the other—all go to make the new plan a work of increasing interest and increasing usefulness.

Also, by doing this work the personnel increases in usefulness from year to year, and at the end is considerably superior to what it was in the beginning. In truth, this result is not due solely to the use of planning but everything goes together; a well-thought-out plan is rarely found apart from sound organizational, command, co-ordination, and control practices. This management element exerts an influence on all the rest.

(c) Lack of sequence in activity and unwarranted changes of course are dangers constantly threatening businesses without a plan. The slightest contrary wind can turn from its course a boat which is unfitted to resist. When serious happenings occur, regrettable changes of course may be decided upon under the influence of profound but transitory disturbance. Only a programme carefully pondered at an undisturbed time permits of maintaining a clear view of the future and of concentrating maximum possible intellectual ability and material resources upon the danger.

It is in difficult moments above all that a plan is necessary. The best of plans cannot anticipate all unexpected occurrences which may arise, but it does include a place for these events and prepare the weapons which may be needed at the moment of being surprised. The plan protects the business not only against undesirable changes of course which may be produced by grave events, but also against those arising simply from changes on the part of higher authority. Also, it protects against deviations, imperceptible at first, which end by deflecting it from its objective.

CONDITIONS AND QUALITIES ESSENTIAL FOR DRAWING UP A GOOD PLAN OF ACTION

To sum up: the plan of action facilitates the utilization of the firm's resources and the choice of best methods to use for attaining the objective. It suppresses or reduces hesitancy, false steps, unwarranted changes of course, and helps to improve personnel. It is a precious managerial instrument.

The question may be asked as to why such an instrument is not in general use and everywhere developed to the farthest extent. The reason is that its compilation demands of managerial personnel a certain number of qualities and conditions rarely to be found in combination. The compilation of a good plan demands for the personnel in charge—

1. The art of handling men.
2. Considerable energy.
3. A measure of moral courage.
4. Some continuity of tenure.
5. A given degree of competence in the specialized requirements of the business.
6. A certain general business experience.

(i) *The Art of Handling Men.* In a large firm the majority of departmental managers take part in the compiling of the working arrangements. The execution of this task from time to time is in addition to ordinary everyday work and includes a certain responsibility and does not normally carry any special remuneration. So, to have in such conditions loyal and active co-operation from departmental heads an able manager of men is needed who fears neither trouble nor responsibility. The art of handling men is apparent from keenness of subordinates and confidence of superiors.

(ii) *Energy.* Yearly and ten-yearly forecasts and special forecasts demand constant vigilance on the part of management.

(iii) *Moral Courage.* It is well known that the best-thought-out plan is never exactly carried out. Forecasts are not prophecies, their function is to minimize the unknown factor. Nevertheless, the public generally, and even shareholders best informed about the running of a business, are not kindly disposed towards a manager who has raised unfulfilled hopes, or allowed them to be raised. Whence the need for a certain prudence which has to be reconciled with the obligation of making every preparation and seeking out optimum possible results.

The timid are tempted to suppress the plan

or else whittle it down to nothing in order not to expose themselves to criticism, but it is a bad policy even from the point of view of self-interest. Lack of plan, which compromises smooth running, also exposes the manager to infinitely graver charges than that of having to explain away imperfectly executed forecasts.

(iv) *Continuity of Tenure.* Some time goes by before a new manager is able to take sufficient cognizance of the course of affairs, its general set-up and future possibilities, so as usefully to undertake the compiling of the plan. If, at such a moment, he feels that he will not have enough time to complete the work or only enough to start putting it into execution, or if, on the other hand, he is convinced that such work, condemned to bear no fruit, will only draw criticism upon him, is it to be thought that he will carry it out enthusiastically or even undertake it unless obliged? Human nature must be reckoned with. Without continuity of tenure on the part of management personnel there can be no good plan of action.

(v and vi) *Professional Competence and General Business Knowledge.* These are abilities just as necessary for drawing up a plan as for carrying it out.

Such are the conditions essential for compiling a good plan. They presuppose intelligent and experienced management. Lack of plan or a bad plan is a sign of managerial incompetence. To safeguard business against such incompetence—

1. A plan must be compulsory.
2. Good specimen plans must be made generally available. (Successful businesses could be asked to furnish such specimens. Experience and general discussion would single out the best.)
3. Planning (as a subject) must be introduced into education. Thus could general opinion be better informed and react upon management personnel, so that the latter's inefficiency would be less to be feared—a state of affairs which would in no wise detract from the importance of men of proven worth.

13 MANAGERIAL PLANNING*

Billy E. Goetz

Plans alone cannot make an enterprise successful. Action is required; the enterprise must operate. Plans can, however, focus action on purposes. They can forecast which actions will tend toward the ultimate objective of economic efficiency, which tend away, which will likely offset one another, and which are merely irrelevant. Managerial planning attempts to achieve a consistent, coordinated structure of operations focused on desired ends. Without plans, action must become merely random activity, producing nothing but chaos.

Various segments of an enterprise have repeated contacts with the same other economic and social units. Each of these other units also has managers who plan its operations in terms of its environment. These managers are inconvenienced and antagonized and their cooperation lost if the enterprise's contacts lack consistency, either through lack of coordination among its personnel or through vacillation. All points of contact should be coordinated; e.g., advertising, salesmen, product design and quality, packaging, credit arrangements, repair service, and delivery should all be fused into a team conveying a unified impression of quality and service.

The sequence and timing of events are parts of the master plan formulated by management. Failure in timing may mean congested shop

* Reprinted by permission from ***Managerial Planning and Control: A Managerial Approach to Industrial*** *Accounting,* McGraw-Hill Book Company, New York, 1949, pp. 63–68, 83–89. Copyright 1949 by McGraw-Hill, Inc. Mr. Goetz is emeritus professor of management at the Massachusetts Institute of Technology.

departments, shutdowns, delayed deliveries, excessive carrying charges. Even the managerial activity of planning is itself subject to planning in which sequence and timing are important. For example, a company decided to formalize its compensation structure. Its management analyzed each position as to job content and as to knowledge, skill, responsibility, judgment, and experience required of the job incumbent. The study incidentally revealed much duplication of effort and some activities directed at cross-purposes. A complete procedural analysis was undertaken, which resulted in major changes in assignment of duties to departments and persons. Many job descriptions and analyses were rendered obsolete, and the job analysis and evaluation study has to be repeated.

The broader and more permanent plans, i.e., policies and procedures, reduce management cost by eliminating recurrent decisions. Once a policy or procedure is adopted, recurrent problems are met by automatic, routine application of the rule adopted. For example, a company may work out the economic lot to purchase for each separate item needed. It may later discover that economic purchase lots for castings tend strongly to be approximately 3 months' usage while those for screw machine parts approximate a 6 months' supply. Starting from these facts, investigation may show that the cost of calculating each purchase lot separately is not justified by the minor savings resulting from the precision of separate calculations. A policy of buying 3 months' supply of castings and 6 of screw machine parts loses the minor savings of precision but avoids the costs of recurrent analyses and decisions.

Interdependence of Plans The plans of an enterprise should constitute an integrated program. Necessarily all current plans of a single management share a common environment. They should all be directed toward a single consistent pattern of objectives. The plans should reinforce one another; they should mesh in an articulated sequence.

Perhaps the best illustration of a complete program of plans, internally consistent and properly articulated, is the budget produced by a well-conceived budgetary procedure. Typically, the sales department furnishes estimates of sales volumes and selling expenses, both broken down to show component elements. On the basis of these sales estimates, the planning department plans inventories and production. These plans serve as a basis for estimates of purchases of materials, of employment of labor, and of needs for machinery and equipment. These estimates, in turn, supply a basis for forecasting purchasing and employment department activities and thus for estimating the expenses of these two departments. Data concerning machinery needs and aggregate personnel requirements furnish the starting point for calculations of floor space, locker- and washroom facilities, heating, electricity, etc., required to maintain over-all operations. All these plans are reduced to anticipated cash revenues and expenditures, leads and lags are estimated, and a cash budget calculated. Finally, estimated financial statements are prepared. The whole procedure provides a complete, internally consistent, integrated program of enterprise operations.

Structure of Managerial Plans We have assumed that the ultimate objective of management is economic efficiency, i.e., maximization of the ratio of output to input. This objective is implemented by major policies formulated by stockholders or board of directors. These major policies largely determine the general form of the operating organization, i.e., the division of the enterprise into major departments. Each department head, with some collaboration by his colleagues, with some assistance from his subordinates, and subject to review by president and board of directors, formulates departmental policies directed at carrying out the major policies imposed from above. These departmental policies largely determine departmental organization. Both the processes of policy formulation and of organizational design are repeated on the division level and so on down to the terminal operational level.[1] The number, elaborateness, and specific detail of these plans increase rapidly as the operation level is approached. This terminus is represented by a mass of specifications, drawings, dimensions, and standard-practice instructions. Perhaps the penultimate is reached in motion studies, such as those of surgical operations wherein every motion of each finger is planned and prescribed.

In a large enterprise, the activities of thousands of employees are directed and coordinated by this elaborate hierarchy of plans. A few broad plans are implemented by policies of several levels, and these are supported by a multitude of almost as permanent procedures.

[1] In a sense, policies are sometimes generated at the operating and first-line supervisory levels and imposed upward. If certain matters are not recognized or provided for by the set of policies adopted, or if regularly adopted policies are not enforced, customs may gradually emerge and achieve the generality, permanence, and authority of true policies.

The whole governs almost numberless specific detailed decisions. For example, a company is formed to manufacture and sell road machinery (stockholder-level decision). Policies are formulated by the board of directors as to the scope to be given this general plan: Will the company manufacture road scrapers, steam shovels, ditchers, pavement finishers, rollers, snowplows, or sweepers? These decisions are implemented at the departmental level by policies governing the sizes and styles of each line included in the program, materials to be purchased, processes to be performed, and items to be subcontracted. Many procedures for handling customers' orders, for routing and scheduling production, for keeping the score of the profit-seeking game. Finally, a multitude of detailed decisions are made within the permanent general frame: should a specific customer order be accepted? Should a particular part be a casting or a forging? Should the company buy a turret lathe or an engine lathe?

POLICIES

Major Policies Some policies are considered important enough to be imbedded in the corporate charter or in its by-laws. These can be changed only by vote of its stockholders and are the broadest and most fundamental of corporate policies. Typically, the choice of industry is stated in the purpose clause, and the scale of operations vaguely fixed by the authorized capital structure. The composition and organization of the board of directors is usually stated in the by-laws. Many companies refer other matters to annual stockholders' meetings, e.g., pension plans, plans for major financing operations, and profit-sharing plans.

Somewhat less significant (or more urgent) plans and choices are made by the board of directors. These policies tend to be companywide in scope, crossing departmental lines, although a few departmental matters may reach the board through financial importance alone. Choice of industry is perhaps the most fundamental of company policies, underlying and limiting all departmental policies. In its broadest sense, this choice is usually written into the corporate charter and thereby reserved to the stockholders' discretion. However, within these broad limits the board may decide to take on a new line or to discontinue an old one. For example, the board of directors of a manufacturer of plastic firebrick may decide to bring out a line of air-setting materials or a manufacturer of thermostatic controls may add a line of recording thermometers. The new line presents new problems to sales, production, and finance departments. Prospect lists must be revised with the new products in mind; new sales stories must sing the praises of the new line; perhaps additional sales force will have to be recruited and trained to give the new line effective representation. The engineering department will have to prepare new formulas or designs. The factory will have to buy new tools, dies, and fixtures and possibly new machinery; radical changes may become necessary in the system of production scheduling and cost control. New financing may be necessary, and credit policies may need revising, as the new line is sold to new types of customers. Both the importance and the interdepartmental character of the change make it a subject for consideration by the board of directors. After its decision is made, all departments will have to revise their policies to conform.

Selection of the competitive level is a similarly all-pervasive issue, properly the prerogative of the board. If the board decides to seek the quality market, the engineering department must specify close tolerances and fine finishes, the purchasing department must buy good materials from dependable sources, the personnel department must hire and train workmen able to produce the desired quality product, the production department must acquire high-grade equipment and provide adequate inspection, the sales department must stress a quality appeal in its advertising copy and in the type of salesperson employed, and the financial department should arrange credit terms appropriate for the quality trade. Every department must orientate its plans and operations with regard to this major policy imposed by the board of directors.

A third all-pervasive basic set of decisions fixes the company's policy as to venturesomeness, aggressiveness, and expansion. Closely related are policies regarding dilution of stockholders' equity and disposition of earnings. Aggressive expansion suggests extensive borrowing and plowing back of profits. Implications of these policies with respect to departmental plans are too obvious to require detailed comment.

In addition to formulating such fundamental policies, the board coordinates departmental plans through review and approval of the master budgets. This gives the board an opportunity to review departmental plans and ascertain that such plans are designed to implement the broader policies set by the board. Also, the board reviews and approves major expenditures before departments are allowed to proceed with their plans. Later the board compares performance with plans and passes on explanations and new plans growing out of experience with the old.

Within the frame imposed by the board of directors, all departments of whatever type formulate more specific policies to give effect to those set by the board. This will be true whether the major departments follow commodity or functional lines. Thus Chevrolet policies may differ substantially from Cadillac, and both will necessarily differ widely from Frigidaire or Electromotive: the variety of styles and sizes offered, the financing of sales, the channels of distribution will all differ profoundly. General Foods can appeal to coffee lovers with Maxwell House, to coffee haters with Postum, and to limbo with Sanka. Since no two enterprises have the same commodity divisions, commodity departmental policies must be discussed with reference to a specific company. However, many enterprises are divided into substantially similar functional departments, and commodity departments themselves are divided into similar patterns of functional divisions. This affords opportunity to investigate and partially catalogue the wide range of policies formulated by functional departments.

PROCEDURES

Nature of Procedures Procedures are a species of managerial planning. As such, they share with policies and organizational configuration the objectives and techniques of managerial planning. Procedures, in common with other forms of planning, seek to avoid the chaos of random activity by directing, coordinating, and articulating the operations of an enterprise. They help direct all enterprise activities toward common goals, they help impose consistency across the organization and through time, and they seek economy by enabling management to avoid the costs of recurrent investigations and to delegate authority to subordinates to make decisions within a frame of policies and procedures devised by management.

Procedures also share the techniques of managerial planning. Many alternate procedures may implement the same policy complex. The managerial technique for devising procedures, as for all other planning, is one of analysis of alternate possibilities and selection of the most desirable. For example, professional firms are jealous of the accuracy of their reports. The final copy must be carefully checked to eliminate errors of typing. Columns of figures may be checked by reading back, figure by figure, to check against the original, or they may be checked by footing and comparing the total with that of the original column. The two procedures can be checked for effectiveness in catching errors and for cost.

Policies are relatively general, reasonably permanent managerial plans. Procedures are less general but comparably permanent. A policy maps out a field of action. It determines objectives and limits the area of action. Procedures are stipulated sequences of definite acts. Procedures mark a path through the area of policy. They may fork, generally with adequate clues to determine clerical choice of path; they may contain trivial gaps to be filled in at the discretion of a clerk; but there is little that resembles the extension of a policy. Procedures are not multidimensional; they do not cover areas of behavior; they have only chronological sequence.

Procedures implement policies. Specific routings of salesmen embody a policy concerning territories within which sales shall be sought. Scheduling of work through the shop gives effect to policies regarding size of inventories and balancing of load factors. As already noted production planning procedures may, as a matter of policy, be based on estimated shipping requirements, on stock limits, or on customer orders. Similarly, purchasing procedures may implement a policy of shopping the market for bargains or one of selecting a few reliable sources. Policy always sets an objective or delimits an area of action, while procedures fix a path toward the objective or through the area. Sequence is the *sine qua non* of procedure.

Structure of Procedures Since a great objective can be analyzed into partial objectives or a large area divided into smaller areas, a major policy can be sub-divided into a number of minor policies. Thus policy has structure—usually paralleling the organizational configuration. Procedures also have structure. Many important procedures cross departmental lines, binding the activities of all into a common effort. Thus, a typical sales order procedure is initiated by receipt of an order from a customer. The sales department interprets the order and prepares multiple copies on the company's own standard forms. One copy may be sent to the engineering department as instructions covering necessary designs and estimates. Another may later be sent to the factory as an order directing the factory to produce the articles required for shipment to the customer. A third may be sent to the shipping department directing it to make shipment of the goods when received from the factory. A fourth may be sent to the bookkeeping department as an original evidence to be journalized and posted. A fifth may be sent to the customer as an invoice. These procedures obviously supply an important part of the connective tissue that holds the enterprise together.

Such all-pervasive procedures are main arteries tying together a great many branch paths. Many of these subordinate procedures are intradepartmental in character, but not necessarily so. Thus a complete sequence of cues and acts touched off by receipt of a customer's order could include all details of interpretation and write-up of the order by the sales department, origin and issuance of a series of shop orders with all their supporting documents and posting of production control records by the planning department, origin and return of reports of shop performance with more posting of production control and cost records, and all billing and collection procedures in the accounting department. Automatically instigated ramifications may lead through virtually all purchasing and disbursing procedures, into all pay-roll procedures, etc.

There are also a large number of relatively independent procedures tending to be largely intradepartmental in nature. Among these are procedures governing assignment and payment of second or swing shifts, employee bidding on job vacancies, the settling of employee grievances, seniority rights, handling of customer complaints, taking physical inventory counts, and many more. Though adding little to the coordinative machinery of the enterprise, these procedures are of great importance in achieving the objectives of consistency and economy.

All these procedures are implemented by a great mass of detailed procedures pertaining to single operations—often called "standard-practice instructions." For example, the operation sheet charts a series of acts by a number of employees necessary to production of articles ordered by a customer or needed for stock. Each operation listed is defined and described by blueprints and standard-practice instructions detailing setup, tooling, fixtures, feeds and speeds, and motion patterns. Standard-practice instructions govern such activities as issuance of new telephone directories, the routes of plant messengers, follow-up of delayed purchase orders, the posting of journal entries to the ledgers. Some companies produce "manuals of style" to govern preparation of letters, reports, and other written documents used by the company.[2] Similar manuals may regulate various accounting or tabulating procedures.

Recurrent Procedural Problems A number of problems recur persistently in the course of procedural design. Among the most common are (1) relevance of the procedure, (2) duplication of effort, and (3) use of clerical substitutes.

Relevance of Procedure. Perhaps most frequent and most important of recurrent procedural problems is the problem of relevance. Does the procedure do a useful job? Is it worth what it costs? There are several major sources of useless procedures. Clerks and minor supervisors may attempt to build up their prestige and bolster their security by devising intricate and obscure rituals. Or procedures may become obsolete without being discontinued. For example, material shortages may plague a company. Reports may be instituted to inform a number of executives as to condition of inventories and probable delivery dates on outstanding purchase orders. Later the supply situation eases. One by one the executives no longer need or use the report. None orders it discontinued, as each believes that others use it. But the law of clerical procedures inexorably produces and submits the report until positive orders are issued to discontinue it.

Many procedures are traditional or copied from other enterprises where they may or may not be useful. Perhaps many cost procedures illustrate this possibility. Some costs are computed because "all businesses should figure costs," not because someone is going to use the figures obtained. It is customary for cost accounts to "tie in" with general ledger controls, but many cost systems have gradually been converted to standard cost systems in which clerical errors and deviations of performance from standard are merged in the variance accounts. Yet extra clerical costs are incurred to figure costs on trivial nonrepetitive jobs or to obtain redundant data on repetitive work to secure the tie-in that no longer serves its prime purpose of proving arithmetic accuracy.

Procedures may lose relevancy by getting hopelessly behind. Data produced may be altogether obsolete, and yet reports continue. For example, one cost department was reporting

[2] For example, among a multiplicity of other procedures governing its educational processes, e.g., matriculation, registration, the University of Chicago issues a 61-page booklet of detailed rules governing the physical appearance of dissertations submitted by candidates for higher degrees. A typical detail is the insistence on the use of Roman numerals to designate chapters.

costs of producing tools some 9 months after tools were completed and in use. By the time facts regarding excessive costs of tool production became known, it was much too late for the superintendent to take remedial action. Finally, the superintendent issued instructions to skip 9 months of figuring tool costs and so got on a current and useful basis. Had he worshipped the tie-in with general ledger controls, he would have put on extra clerical help to produce useless cost data at an accelerated rate until the data were brought to a current basis.

Duplication of Effort. Many procedures are heedlessly duplicated because of a desire for secrecy or through ignorance. Foremen often keep private records of departmental production because they have no access to or knowledge of duplicate records kept by the planning department. The cost department may keep records of material prices charged by different vendors that duplicate records kept by the purchasing department. Stock-room records, cost records, and planning department records may maintain a useless triple watch over inventory balances. Avoidance of such duplication is one major reason for centralizing responsibility for design of forms and procedures and for conducting periodic reviews of procedural configurations.

Duplication often stems from a desire for "protection." Private, duplicate records are maintained to protect individuals rather than through mere ignorance of existing similar records. Forms may be routed to a long succession of persons or duplicate copies sent each for the legitimate purpose of informing each of certain activities or to provide each with expensive but useless protection. The game may be played to the extent of requiring virtually every person touching a form to initial it to prove he has seen it. He may be required to date his initials to protect himself from a charge of delaying vital procedures.

Skillful design of procedures may eliminate clerical copy work by provision of duplicate forms. For example, copies of sales invoices filed chronologically may serve as the sales journal, eliminating traditional methods of journalizing. In some instances, another copy filed alphabetically may serve as customer's ledger, substituting filing for more expensive forms of posting. Such multiple use has resulted in many companies producing tens or even hundreds of copies of basic documents. So many companies are requesting duplicate or triplicate copies of invoices that provision of such copies is becoming standard practice. Some procurement divisions of the federal government require as many as 21 copies of invoices. The principle involved is sound. Why should clerks in one company copy documents prepared by clerks in another if the first can produce the required number of forms with little or no extra effort?

Sometimes accuracy is sought through verification by duplication. Thus, extensions may be computed on the customer's order and recomputed on the sales invoice to prove the accuracy of the original computation and of the subsequent typing. When possible, it is usually cheaper and better to verify by juncture rather than by duplication. An illustration is the checking of total hours reported on job time tickets against the total shown on employees' gate cards. Another illustration is verification of detail carried in subsidiary ledgers by comparison of trial balances of such ledgers with the balances of corresponding general ledger controls.

Use of Clerical Substitutes. Taylor and his disciples revolted against the rule of tradition. Trade mysteries, long carried in the memories of skilled craftsmen, were subjected to scientific test, standardized, and made a matter of record. Policies and procedures were reviewed and reduced to writing. Routing and scheduling were taken from foremen and made subjects of elaborate clerical rituals. Taylor's functional foremen became whole departments: planning, personnel, cost, toolroom, maintenance, stock room, and materials handling. The ratio of indirect to direct labor rose spectacularly.

In general, the new technique proved amazingly effective. Clerical work became important and hence the subject of inventive activity and intensive development. Clerical aids of all kinds were vastly improved. Duplicating devices, calculating machines, visible records, and tabulating equipment were invented or improved to conserve clerical time and reduce clerical errors. Today, determination of the extent to which clerical procedures should be mechanized and selection of the most effective types of equipment are major problems of the procedural analyst.

At times, paper work has been overelaborated. Too many managers at all levels have attempted to use reports to the exclusion of direct observation. For example, a shop superintendent attempted to install planning procedures that would virtually be automatic. Provision was made for reporting all irregularities. There appeared to be no remaining reasons why the man should ever leave his comfortable office. Two disadvantages gradually emerged. The superintendent lost all feeling for intangibles, which resulted in foolish decisions and the antagonism of all foremen, and several clerks were required to keep all records posted currently and to originate the multitude of required reports. A successor superintendent found that one planning clerk armed with a simple memorandum record of shop orders could visit every machine in the shop and ascertain progress of every order in less than 2 hours. The simple memorandum served adequately both as progress record and as report to the superintendent.

Dependence on paper work and the accounting fetish of a tie-in with general ledger controls often produce needlessly elaborate inventory records. There is seldom sufficient reason for carrying extensions and dollar values in such records. Receipts and withdrawals can be entered in physical units, and balances priced and extended whenever financial statements are to be prepared. Furthermore, trivial items can be controlled by physical means rather than by paper procedures. Stock limits can be set, and minimum quantities separately packaged. Each minimum package is thrown into the corresponding bin of parts. When the bin is emptied, the minimum package is broken, and an attached tag bearing the part number is sent to the purchasing or planning department as an indication that a new order should be released for the part.

14 PERSPECTIVES ON PLANNING*

Henry C. Egerton and *James K. Brown*

Much of the literature of business planning is concerned to define planning, and to delineate the proper role of top management, line management, and staff executives in the planning process. Yet in eliciting from chief executives their views of what planning is and what it is not, and how they personally participate in planning, one is struck by the heterogeneity of their experiences and opinions. Thus it is necessary at the outset to set down two disclaimers that some executives voice about the study of planning.

The first disclaimer is that planning cannot be usefully distinguished from the rest of the management process—from, in a common formulation, organizing, directing, motivating, and controlling. Although it is acknowledged that each of these functions or elements can be formally defined and contrasted with one another, in terms of the chief executive's daily, weekly, even annual routine it is not realistic from his point of view to break up his job into parts and examine each as a discrete phenomenon. For his role as planner is meshed with his role as organizer, director, and so on, in a seamless web of management; for instance, the thought he devotes to what might be termed planning questions, and decisions he makes about them, have implications for his exercise of control; and vice versa. It is the whole of his job that must be looked at, the interaction of the elements of the management process rather than the individual elements.

The second disclaimer is that, although it can be constructively analyzed in isolation from the chief executive's full job, planning offers little opportunity for generalization. For planning and the chief executive's role in it, the argument goes, must necessarily be highly individualistic, because they depend on a host of factors whose specific combination is unique in any given company.

The chief executive himself is of course singular. He brings to his job a distinctive personality and set of interests that have been shaped importantly by his education and his career experience. He has developed a style of management and has his own conception of the company's needs and what he himself should do to fulfill them. Such influences as these determine whether he is issue-oriented or people-oriented, for instance, whether he will concentrate on "foreign policy" (Antony Jay's phrase in *Management and Machiavelli*[1]), on technical matters, on management development, or on corporate strategy, and whether in his leadership role he will function as a coach, an umpire, a team captain, an inspirer, a needler, and so on.

The traditions and circumstances of the company also have a vital bearing on planning and the chief executive's participation in it: the company's size, its geographical dispersion, its diversity of interests, the relative contribution of internal development and of acquisitions in its evolution, its procedures and routines (including of course those pertaining to planning), and the quality of its management. So too does the nature of the business or businesses in which it is engaged—characteristics such as capital intensity, natural time frames (months for manufacturers of fashion goods, decades for extractive industries), the pace of technological change, the dynamics of the marketplace, the extent of competition, the ease or difficulty of forecasting the future, the extent of government regulation, and the extent of public concern with industry practices.

* Reprinted by permission of the publisher from *Planning and the Chief Executive,* The Conference Board, 1972, pp. 1–11. Mr. Egerton and Mr. Brown are members of the management research staff of the Conference Board.

[1] Antony Jay, *Management and Machiavelli: An Inquiry Into The Politics of Corporate Life,* New York: Holt, Rinehart and Winston, 1967.

The impact of all this is that the interaction of (1) a particular executive leading (2) a particular company (3) involved in one or more particular businesses is unique; and in important respects, therefore, so too is each chief executive's approach to planning. Hence such comments by study participants as these: "There are many ways to plan. The way I'm doing it works best for me." "A company can take our planning setup and not make it work."

Yet analysis of the experiences and opinions, the philosophies and practices, of those who have contributed to this inquiry indicates that there are useful things to say about planning as distinct from the chief executive's job as a whole, and that there is enough commonality in chief executives' perspectives on planning, their involvement in and assessment of it, to warrant description and interpretation.

PLANNING DEFINED AND CHARACTERIZED

What do chief executives understand by the term "planning"? From an analysis of written definitions in planning manuals and statements in interviews several key concepts emerge:

- Planning is a systematic method for the effective and efficient management of change in the best interests of the corporation.
- It includes determining where the company is to go as well as how it is to get there; or, more formally, the setting of objectives and goals and the formulation and selection of alternative strategies and courses of action to reach the goals and objectives. (The inclusion of objective-and-goal setting within the compass of planning is challenged by some writers on the subject. They argue that while this task must of course be done, everything a company does, and not just planning, proceeds, or should proceed, from a definition of objectives and goals. And so, they hold, this definition is not properly a part of the planning process.)
- Planning identifies and analyzes opportunities, strengths, weaknesses, problems, and threats, and sets priorities for capitalizing on or overcoming them so that company resources will be put to the best uses.
- Planning is incomplete if it does not entail regular measurement of progress toward objectives and goals and the execution of strategies and action programs. Yet at the same time it is clearly recognized that plans often have to be altered, sometimes on very short notice, in the light of new circumstances.
- Planning is, or should be, a continuing process, and not a once-a-year exercise, involving all those whose jobs have a significant effect on the fortunes of the company.
- It is clearly distinct from forecasting, although quite a few respondents confess that they have had difficulty in making their subordinates understand the difference. A consensus statement would be phrased something like this: Forecasting, one of the essential elements of planning, is a prediction of what *will* happen on the basis of certain assumptions; planning is an attempt to determine what *should* happen (in very specific terms) and then to take steps that will make it *likely* to happen.

DIFFERENT KINDS OF PLANNING

Not only conceptually but also in practice most chief executives recognize at least two different kinds of planning—and, as Chapter 3 [in *Planning and the Chief Executive*] indicates, the chief executive plays a different role in each.

The most common distinction drawn is between operating planning (or profit planning) and strategic planning. Typically covering a one-year frame, the former has as its core action programs designed to accomplish particular objectives or goals by the end of that period, and specifies the resources needed to accomplish them. It tends to have a greater degree of formality than strategic planning, and, in some companies, to entail contributions from greater numbers of people, and the plans that emerge are supposed to foreshadow quite accurately the results or accomplishments during the period the plans cover. In a number of firms, supplementary compensation for execu-

Elements of Planning Identified by An Airline

PHASE I—PRE-DECISION	
Information	Missions
Statistics	Objectives
Trends	Goals
Premises	Strategies
Constraints	Alternatives
Forecasts	Decisions
Plans	
PHASE II—POST-DECISION	
Program	Resolution
Project	Problems, Threats,
Events	and Constraints
Tracking	Reevaluation

tives is influenced by the fit between performance and operating plans.[2]

Strategic planning, sometimes called long-range planning, on the other hand, has a longer time horizon (while five years is the most common one encountered, the range is from two to twenty[3]) and, as "strategic" implies, centers on the directions in which the company should go—for example, the relative emphasis that will be given to development of existing products and markets versus that given to the development of new products and markets. One company defines strategic planning as the process of deciding the basic mission of the company, the objectives it wishes to achieve, and the major strategies governing the use of company resources to achieve objectives. Strategic plans are much more tentative in nature, much more susceptible of revision, than operating plans. In terms of managerial input, as compared with operating planning, "strategic planning calls for a very different kind of thinking," one study participant states. "It deals with more uncertainties, requiring research into new areas. It calls for greater exercise of judgment in evaluating trends and possibilities. It requires more active imagination envisioning new combinations of resources. It must grow out of creativity in conceiving needs and functions that have not existed before. It takes more boldness and involves more risk."

This duality does not, of course, mean that strategic planning is done, so to speak, by the chief executive's left hand and operating planning by his right hand, with no contact between the two. One of his functions in planning is to make sure that operating plans are in consonance with the strategic plan. In fact the operating planning process and strategic planning process are often integrated, with the plan flowing from the former becoming the first year of the strategic plan. The oft-stated purpose of such an arrangement is to prevent planning from becoming a "blue sky" speculation, to ensure, in other words, its realism—and its credibility. On the other hand, in a number of companies the preparation of operating and of strategic plans is deliberately separated in time, the aim being to ensure that managers will do an adequate job of strategic planning, that they will apply a truly long-term perspective to the firm's future, a perspective not distorted by, as one study participant phrases it, "the control psychology that surrounds the planning for operations and that inhibits the imagination, creativity, and boldness a manager must bring to the consideration of new business directions."

In some companies, except for the setting of broad objectives, planning is confined to operating planning. The head of one of these firms, a concern engaged in the manufacture, wholesaling, and retailing of apparel, impugns the value of strategic planning; although the operating divisions of his company have a "sense of the future," they make no formal commitment to it beyond reaching six-month and one-year volume, profit, and inventory-control goals. This executive is concerned that the company remain "nimble" in the constantly shifting world of fashion, being always ready to capitalize quickly on new opportunities for profit. And since it has enjoyed a very high rate of return on equity over the years and has a relatively modest investment in fixed assets, it is in a good position to do so.

One view widely held by contributors to this study: It is essential to get a firm grip on operating planning before strategic planning can be successfully undertaken.

Other Distinctions Other distinctions regarding types of planning or plans are made by chief executives. Mining and construction company heads surveyed use a three-way split. In a mining company with worldwide operations, for example, there are:

- Short-term plans extending from one to three years, which provide control for operations and authority for making expenditures on projects.
- Project plans that cover the development of individual mines from start to full-scale production.
- Strategic plans that center first on the continents, and then on the countries within

[2] *Profit plan vs. budgets.* Some firms term their one-year operating or profit plans budgets. But several respondents draw a sharp distinction between the two terms. A budget, they say, is essentially a mechanism for control, consisting essentially of financial or other quantitative data, perhaps supplemented with narrative explanations; the essence of an operating plan is the specification of a course of action, with perhaps a consideration of alternatives, that will be undertaken in pursuit of goals or objectives for the period in question. Such a document usually defines what will be done, when, and by whom.

[3] The time frame used in strategic planning is heavily influenced by the volatility of the marketing environment, lead times needed to put new productive facilities on stream, and similar factors. Achieving the proper time frame has proved troublesome to several companies, entailing experimental trial and error. To illustrate: one large integrated oil company found that five years was too long a period for its planning, so it pared its horizons down to three years. A competitor of about the same size, on the other hand, concluded that five years was too short for certain crucial decisions, so it has adopted a 10-year span for plotting its strategies.

those continents, where new mines will be developed, on the political complexities that may be encountered, on the location of investment-partners-and-customers for each mine (as a rule the company engages in joint ventures with ore users), on transportation arrangements, and on the securing of necessary financing. The chief executive and his immediate subordinates are themselves deeply immersed in strategic planning, and hardly at all in project or short-term planning.

The head of one manufacturing company has found another threefold classification useful: *Conceptual planning* determines what businesses the company should be in. *Strategic planning* focuses on the changes the company must undergo or make to satisfy the goals specified in conceptual plans and embraces guideline objectives and programs for achieving conceptual goals. *Annual operating planning* yields a blueprint for achieving the results desired in the next year. Through its successive conceptual plans, the company has evolved from a manufacturer of lithographic printing presses to one of "total printing" equipment to one whose charter is the production and sale of communications and information-handling equipment.

Several chief executives have adopted yet another tripartite classification proposed by a research and consulting firm. According to this taxonomy, there are strategic, development, and operating plans. The chart on page 108 shows how one firm has spelled out the responsibilities of operating-unit management with respect to each type of plan.

Quite a different distinction from any so far described is that between *corporate* planning and *divisional* or *profit-center* planning. This distinction can, however, be more usefully discussed in terms of the chief executive's involvement in the planning process [in Chapter 3 of *Planning and the Chief Executive*] rather than in terms of his definition of planning.

INFORMALITY VS. FORMALITY

The relative weight of informality and of formality in the planning process is a matter of deep interest to many chief executives.

Every company surveyed has some element of formality in its planning—at the very least an established procedure for consideration of capital expenditures and expense budgets. And some go far beyond this. Yet it is clear that much planning—indeed, in some companies, practically all planning—is accomplished outside the context of a formal planning routine. At a large one-bank holding company, for instance, "large questions of strategy are not encompassed in the [planning] routine but are resolved by judgments reached by the policy committee."

A number of chief executives make a point of keeping planning as informal as possible, in the belief that planning must be continuous if it is to be successful, that speed in capitalizing on opportunities or in overcoming major problems is essential, and that a high degree of fruitful personal interaction is an essential ingredient in the planning process. A maximum amount of informality, they maintain, will help to ensure the realization of these ends, will encourage communication among executives representing different functions and at different levels of management, and will stimulate them to unfettered, imaginative reflection about the firm's future.

How is the chief executive's role in the informal aspect of planning manifested? It is, first of all, almost universal practice for him to meet frequently with his top executives, line and staff, to review the affairs of the company and to give it future direction. In some firms there are trappings of formality to these meetings; e.g., they occur at fixed times, they follow to a large extent a written agenda, their substance is recorded in minutes, and those participating in them are designated as a committee. (On the other hand, in one company with worldwide operations top executives travel so often that many such meetings take place as the chief executive and his colleagues are flying between headquarters and a distant operation.) But the essential points are (1) that this group is the chief executive's primary mechanism for running the company, and (2) that its deliberations are far-reaching in terms of subject matter, ranging from immediate crises and operating results to near-term prospects and longer-term problems and opportunities. As one company head puts it, "these sessions are involved with the past, present, and future in varying mixtures." Not only do such meetings produce decisions that have important consequences for the company's future, they also generate information and raise issues that are fed into the formal planning process.

The chief executive's periodic discussions with operating executives both at headquarters and in the field constitute a second element in the informal part of the planning process. These exchanges often are taken up in part with planning, with the chief executive inquiring about the status of current plans, about the operating unit's prospects, possible shifts in its emphasis and direction, and so forth. In one

Management Responsibilities

	RESPONSIBILITY OF CORPORATE MANAGEMENT	RESPONSIBILITY OF OPERATING UNIT MANAGEMENT
STRATEGIC PLAN	Set desired ends Specify business methods and fields of activity	Set unit's goals and practices within bounds set at corporate level
DEVELOPMENT PLAN	Select and assign evaluation of major company alterations and alternatives	Generate, evaluate, and select changes applicable to the division
OPERATING PLAN	Determine organizational structure and major capital use	Develop divisional and departmental tactical plans for engineering, production, sales, marketing, capital, and profits

company the chief executive makes it a point to take with him portions of an operating division's five-year plan whenever he visits that division's headquarters and to review the contents with the division head. In another, whenever a new divisional manager is appointed, the chief executive spends a good deal of time with him going over his responsibilities, with emphasis on those pertaining to planning.

Another manifestation of informal planning is found in firms whose chief executives reserve to themselves the prime responsibility for conceiving of new ventures or making acquisitions (one sees this as his primary task), rather than assign it to operating units. Although he may extend his eyes and ears by appointing *ad hoc* task forces to evaluate new businesses, he is nevertheless the central figure in his firm's diversification efforts and he pursues these efforts pragmatically.

The sheer size or geographical dispersion of their firms or the complexity or rapid change that characterizes the businesses in which the firms are engaged or the markets they serve, has led most chief executives to introduce a measure of formality into the planning process. Formality is reflected in such devices and procedures as the periodic convening of planning meetings attended by a considerable body of line and staff executives; the constitution of a top management planning committee; the designation of an annual planning cycle, with a timetable specifying who will do what and when; preparation of written plans following prescribed formats; and the creation of a corporate planning unit.

As noted, strategic or long-range planning tends to be more informal than operating planning. One other conclusion can be distilled from the observations made by study participants: planning is more informal at the higher than at the lower levels of the organizational hierarchy.

The distinction between formal and informal aspects of planning, while useful for analysis and significant in practice, can be pressed too far, some study praticipants observe. The line between them is far from clear and, necessarily, is ever shifting because of the interplay of personal relationships among, and the individual interests and capacities of, managers, and the dynamics of the economic, social, and political environment in which business functions. Furthermore, what counts in the end is the effectiveness of the total planning process rather than its admixture of formality and informality. Yet one study participant maintains that striking the proper balance between formality and informality is one of his crucial planning responsibilities. In this connection another chief executive observes: "Planning must be formalized to provide adequate communication and to promote a sense of accountability and responsibility; but the formal system must be continuously scrutinized to keep the planning process from becoming burdensome beyond the value it brings the business."

PLANNING VS. PLANS

Apropos of the proper balance between informality and formality in planning, a number of chief executives contrast the value of planning and plans. Planning, they say, has no inherent limitation if it is conceived of as a continuous process of thought; indeed, it plays an indispensable part in the intelligent direction of the company's affairs. But while acknowledging that written plans often serve an essential purpose, they express reservations about plans and their use.

The general value of preparing plans, it is said, is that it entails putting decisions and commitments in writing: doing so facilitates communication, coordination, and control, establishes authority, and fixes accountability. Says the head of a scientific equipment company: "Plans give me and other top executives the knowledge of what should be happening at all times and the assurance that if anything does not go according to plan we will be made aware of it early." (On the other hand, the former head of a mining company liked to avoid written plans wherever possible. "An executive can get himself into more trouble with a typewriter than by any other means," he remarked.)

Elaborate plans do not however, necessarily guarantee sound planning, several study participants insist. "I am suspicious of planning systems that produce big, handsome books of plans," one comments. Another makes a similar observation: "Voluminous books of plans and back-up details are for me signs of poor planning. Good plans can be presented very simply. I do not believe in planning formalities beyond the needs of basic communication."

Nor is it a question of the expense of preparing plans, though this can get out of hand. What can be more deleterious is uncritical acceptance of plans by the organization, whereas inevitably they will be rendered in part inaccurate or obsolete by the march of events. It is essential to understand the limitations of plans. "The biggest danger in planning," states one chief executive, "is to believe the plans that result." In contrast, another study participant cites as a weakness of his company's planning system management's unwillingness to believe the signals it throws off, "All plans can do is point to the proper (at the time they are made) direction for the business," asserts the head of a rubber products manufacturer. And there are other comments to this effect:

"Plans are no more than tentative statements about the future."

"Plans are only a base line of reference against which a business opportunity or problem can be understood and a suitable response developed."

"A plan is not a Bible. All it can do is give long-range direction to a company. It should have the function of screening things out, not of screening them in."

Two company heads define what they consider to be the proper and improper function of plans in relation to the planning process. "If plans are presented as predictions of end results, they will never have much value—they will always be wrong," the president of a metals fabricating company insists. He adds: "But plans developed as directions will show the way and chart the course of planning as a continuous process of thought." And in the opinion of the head of a scientific equipment company, "Successive plans provide for the continual renewal of the planning process, so that either the validity of decisions is confirmed, or the need for corrective action is detected. But these plans must not be allowed to become 'frozen in concrete' so that they are no longer capable of alerting the manager to a change in the situation that requires a change in response."

OBJECTIVES AND GOALS

It has been noted that the consensus of study participants is that planning does properly include the setting of objectives and goals. "Objectives," says one chief executive, "are at the heart of the planning process." "I think about objectives most of the time," claims another in describing his involvement in planning. And as other chief executives speak of planning, sooner or later they refer to objectives or goals. Yet the diverse perceptions of the cooperating executives in themselves hinder analysis and synthesis of objectives and goals. Nevertheless some general observations are in order.

Some Definitions To start with, a number of the companies represented in this study have established, for planning purposes, explicit working definitions of goals and objectives, or they have drawn distinctions between different kinds of objectives.

An analysis of the differences between objectives and goals shows that, as in the formal literature of business planning, there is no general agreement on terminology. For example, some firms define goals as quantitative statements of objectives. By contrast, one firm has given the following meanings to these terms in an introduction to its written planning procedures:

1. Goal—this is a statement of the basic purpose of our business efforts. It is a broad and general goal which has long-term validity and meaning.
2. Objectives—these are specific and more concrete steps along the way to the achievement of our broader goal. These are objectives

toward which we can focus our specific work effort. Responsibility and accountability for their achievement are assigned to individual departments.

Time is what separates objectives and goals, according to an apparel manufacturer. This company considers a goal a target that is to be reached in one year or less; an objective, a target whose attainment lies over a year in the future.

Time is also the crucial element in distinctions made by several companies between objectives. At a large petroleum refiner, for example, long-term objectives ("long term" means three years for this company) are understood to be statements of the general direction the company will move in—statements whose aim is to give management a sense of the future. But objectives set forth in the annual plans of the operating subsidiaries are couched in profit and expense terms essentially.

Profit/Sales Objectives Indeed, quantitative profit/sales objectives—those pertaining to ROI, revenues, product volume, deliveries—and related objectives like expense control seem to be an integral part of operating planning. For example, a manufacturer of drugs and personal care products expects its largely autonomous division managers to develop operating plans that will result in a 10% annual growth in sales and profits. The importance of such objectives in strategic planning, however, is less pervasive. In some firms they serve as a keystone to the planning effort; in others they are much more secondary or tentative—"A general guideline and not an actuator of management decisions," "Management won't break its neck to achieve them"; and in still others they are regarded as primarily for external consumption—especially by the investment community (which, one chief executive notes, puts some pressure on companies to at least go through the motions of formal planning).

Other Objectives Objectives of a more action-oriented nature—sometimes stated in quantitative terms, sometimes not—commonly play an essential role in strategic planning and often in operating planning as well. They do not, some study participants point out, stand in lieu of profit/sales objectives. Rather they are seen as means to achieving such objectives—or, if profit/sales objectives are not explicitly spelled out, to guide the firm to improved profits or revenues.

Here is a listing of the matters to which this group of objectives is addressed:

- Geographical markets (e.g., expand business abroad), market share and customer mix (e.g., reduced dependence on government business)
- Expansion of retail outlets (e.g., number of new store openings each year)
- Innovation (e.g., creativity, new products, better processes, improved management systems)
- Management recruitment and development (e.g., in a company that has acquired many businesses recently, "reach 100% professional management at the division president level in 10 years")
- Labor (e.g., reduce labor content of products)
- Compensation
- Pricing
- Facilities
- Productivity (per man, per square foot of store space, etc.)
- Research and development
- Inventory
- Capital and financing (e.g., reduce the cost of capital)
- Diversification (e.g., get into new businesses whose economic cycles differ from those of present businesses)
- Composition of growth—the balance between internal development and acquisition
- Acquisitions (defining the character of firms the business will consider buying—for example, those in fields in which the company has competence, with good management and established trade names)
- Supplier relations
- Company relationships with and posture with respect to its total external environment
- Capital expenditures
- Organization

Public Statements Several chief executives believe that they must articulate basic company objectives and principles to their organizations' various publics—customers, employees, stockholders, suppliers and members of the communities where it does business—so that these groups have a clear understanding of what management conceives to be the company's mission. These executives utilize such media as annual reports, special brochures, presentations to security analysts, and informal conversations to put across their messages. Here are two examples:

> The company plans to focus on the discovery and development of major deposits of natural resources—oil, gas, copper, coal, and uranium—

needed for the advancement of industrial society. Also the company wants to avoid overdependence on the whims of any one or two political regimes.

—*From the annual report of an international petroleum company*

1. Emphasize the search for gas and oil in North America.
2. Build up the oil and gas business outside the U.S.
3. Become a factor in the chemical business.
4. Achieve a growth in earnings of 8%–10% a year.
5. Reach a return of 10% on investment as soon as possible.
6. Compare favorably with other companies in the business according to a whole host of traditional industry measures.

—*From a talk by the chief executive of another international petroleum company to security analysts*

It can be seen that for each company some —but not all—of the objectives are highly pertinent to planning.

Revision of Objectives The most common practice is for operating and strategic objectives to be reviewed and, as necessary, revised each year. But some chief executives think that review need be undertaken only when circumstances so dictate. Others, like the head of the second petroleum company whose objectives are set forth above, have set a 10-year period for their basic objectives to run.

In most companies, once objectives are set they are considered inviolate until they are scheduled for review. But in an insurance company the two-year corporate objectives can be, and have been, altered or suspended in the course of the period to which they apply as business conditions render them inappropriate.

Other Insights Other insights on objectives as they relate to planning offered by study participants include:

- The objectives of the company's different businesses necessarily vary. For example, a key objective for a mature, established business is to generate cash efficiently, whereas for a new, growing business it is to use cash efficiently.
- Whatever objectives a company deems suitable for its planning, they must be mutually consistent—and, in many companies, they often are not.
- An objective should be neither so "far out" that there is little chance it can be met, nor too easy of accomplishment. If it falls on either side of what must be a fragile balance between feasibility and challenge, it will not gain the support or commitment of the organization.
- An organization should have a hierarchy of objectives corresponding to the organizational hierarchy.
- In an important sense objectives act as constraints, ruling out or at least delaying some plausible courses of action with respect to a threat, an opportunity, or a problem. To put it another way: for every explicit "Thou shalt" embodied in an objective, there are a host of implicit "Thou shalt not's"—which can compromise the needed adaptability of the organization to changes in its environment.

STRATEGIES

Adopting appropriate strategies to reach objectives is, in the opinion of some chief executives, the most demanding part of planning. First, the act of making a strategic choice implies the commitment of resources, the exposure to risk. It is, in other words, a bridge from thought to action. Second, such a choice often does not mean opting for one alternative and discarding others but rather arriving at a sound combination of strategies. In terms of products, for example, a typical set of strategic questions would be: *To what extent* should the firm press for new products (and to what extent should this be done by internal development, by joint ventures, by licensing, by acquisition)? *To what extent* should it emphasize improvement of present products? *To what extent* should it replace or modernize facilities so that present products can be made more efficiently? For many firms the number of plausible combinations of such strategies is very large; selecting the most promising one is a formidable task; and whether the combination chosen turns out to be the most salutary may not be known for years—if ever.

One study participant has developed a list of questions to appraise strategies:

- Will the strategy capitalize on company strengths?
- Will it tend to minimize competitors' advantages?
- Is it internally consistent—e.g., if it calls for sales volume increases, is manufacturing capacity adequate?
- Does it conflict with other strategies?

- What is its weakest element?
- What part of it will be most difficult to implement?

SUCCESSFUL PLANNING: A JOURNEY, NOT A DESTINATION

Achieving an approach to planning that is satisfactory to the chief executive, many study participants note, can be an ardous process, involving considerable trial and error, causing frustration if not trauma, and often taking more time than expected. Further, in an important respect success will be ephemeral if not elusive. For as the company's situation and needs change, as familiar faces disappear and new ones appear in the managerial roster, inevitably there will be shifts in the emphasis or methodology of planning.

B. OBJECTIVES

15 THE OBJECTIVES OF A BUSINESS*

Peter F. Drucker

Most of today's lively discussion of management by objectives is concerned with the search for the one right objective. This search is not only likely to be as unproductive as the quest for the philosopher's stone; it is certain to do harm and to misdirect.

To emphasize only profit, for instance, misdirects managers to the point where they may endanger the survival of the business. To obtain profit today they tend to undermine the future. They may push the most easily saleable product lines and slight those that are the market of tomorrow. They tend to short-change research, promotion and other postponable investments. Above all, they shy away from any capital expenditure that may increase the invested-capital base against which profits are measured; and the result is dangerous obsolescence of equipment. In other words, they are directed into the worst practices of management.

To manage a business is to balance a variety of needs and goals. This requires judgment. The search for the one objective is essentially a search for a magic formula that will make judgment unnecessary. But the attempt to replace judgment by formula is always irrational; all that can be done is to make judgment possible by narrowing its range and the available alternatives, giving it clear focus, a sound foundation in facts and reliable measurements of the effects and validity of actions and decisions. And this, by the very nature of business enterprise, requires multiple objectives.

What should these objectives be, then? There is only one answer: *Objectives are needed in every area where performance and results directly and vitally affect the survival and prosperity of the business.* These are the areas which are affected by every management decision and which therefore have to be considered in every management decision. They decide what it means concretely to manage the business. They spell out what results the business must aim at and what is needed to work effectively toward these targets.

Objectives in these key areas should enable us to do five things: to organize and explain the whole range of business phenomena in a small number of general statements; to test these statements in actual experience; to predict behavior; to appraise the soundness of decisions when they are still being made; and to enable practicing businessmen to analyze their own experience and, as a result, improve their performance. It is precisely because the traditional theorem of the maximization of profits cannot meet any of these tests—let alone all of them—that it has to be discarded.

At first sight it might seem that different businesses would have entirely different key areas—so different as to make impossible any general theory. It is indeed true that different key areas require different emphasis in different businesses—and different emphasis at different stages of the development of each business. But the areas are the same, whatever the business, whatever the economic conditions, whatever the business's size or stage of growth.

There are eight areas in which objectives of performance and results have to be set:

Market standing; innovation; productivity; physical and financial resources; profitability; manager performance and development; worker performance and attitude; public responsibility.

There should be little dispute over the first five objectives. But there will be real protest against the inclusion of the intangibles: manager performance and development; worker performance and attitude; and public responsibility.

Yet, even if managing were merely the application of economics, we would have to in-

* Reprinted by permission of the publisher from Peter F. Drucker, *The Practice of Management*, Harper & Row, Publishers, Incorporated, New York, 1954, pp. 62–65, 126–129. Copyright 1954 by Peter F. Drucker. (Also published by William Heinemann, Ltd., London.) Mr. Drucker is a well-known management consultant, lecturer, teacher, and author, and is professor of social science, Claremont University.

clude these three areas and would have to demand that objectives be set for them. They belong in the most purely formal economic theory of the business enterprise. For neglect of manager performance and development, worker performance and public responsibility soon results in the most practical and tangible loss of market standing, technological leadership, productivity and profit—and ultimately in the loss of business life. That they look so different from anything the economist—especially the modern economic analyst—is wont to deal with, that they do not readily submit to quantification and mathematical treatment, is the economist's bad luck; but it is no argument against their consideration.

The very reason for which economist and accountant consider these areas impractical—that they deal with principles and values rather than solely with dollars and cents—makes them central to the management of the enterprise, as tangible, as practical—and indeed as measurable—as dollars and cents.

For the enterprise is a community of human beings. Its performance is the performance of human beings. And a human community must be founded on common beliefs, must symbolize its cohesion in common principles. Otherwise it becomes paralyzed, unable to act, unable to demand and to obtain effort and performance from its members.

If such considerations are intangible, it is management's job to make them tangible by its deeds. To neglect them is to risk not only business incompetence but labor trouble or at least loss of worker productivity, and public restrictions on business provoked by irresponsible business conduct. It also means risking lackluster, mediocre, time-serving managers—managers who are being conditioned to "look out for themselves" instead of for the common good of the enterprise, managers who become mean, narrow and blind for lack of challenge, leadership and vision.

HOW TO SET OBJECTIVES

The real difficulty lies indeed not in determining what objectives we need, but in deciding how to set them.

There is only one fruitful way to make this decision: by determining what shall be measured in each area and what the yardstick of measurement should be. For the measurement used determines what one pays attention to. It makes things visible and tangible. The things included in the measurement become relevant; the things omitted are out of sight and out of mind. "Intelligence is what the Intelligence Test measures"—that well worn quip is used by the psychologist to disclaim omniscience and infallibility for his gadget. Parents or teachers, however, including those well aware of the shakiness of its theory and its mode of calculation, sometimes tend to see that precise-looking measurement of the "I.Q." every time they look at little Susie—to the point where they may no longer see little Susie at all.

Unfortunately the measurements available to us in the key area of business enterprise are, by and large, even shakier than the I.Q. We have adequate concepts only for measuring market standing. For something as obvious as profitability we have only a rubber yardstick, and we have no real tools at all to determine how much profitability is necessary. In respect to innovation and, even more, to productivity, we hardly know more than what ought to be done. And in the other areas—including physical and financial resources—we are reduced to statements of intentions rather than goals and measurements for their attainment.

For the subject is brand new. It is one of the most active frontiers of thought, research and invention in American business today. Company after company is working on the definition of the key areas, on thinking through what should be measured and on fashioning the tools of measurement.

Within a few years our knowledge of what to measure and our ability to do so should therefore be greatly increased. After all, twenty-five years ago we knew less about the basic problems in market standing than we know today about productivity or even about the efficiency and attitudes of workers. Today's relative clarity concerning market standing is the result not of anything inherent in the field, but of hard, concentrated and imaginative work.

WHAT SHOULD THE OBJECTIVES OF A MANAGER BE?

Each manager, from the "big boss" down to the production foreman or the chief clerk, needs clearly spelled-out objectives. These objectives should lay out what performance the man's own managerial unit is supposed to produce. They should lay out what contribution he and his unit are expected to make to help other units obtain their objectives. Finally, they should spell out what contribution the manager can expect from other units toward the attainment of his own objectives. Right from the start, in other words, emphasis should be on teamwork and team results.

These objectives should always derive from the goals of the business enterprise. In one company, I have found it practicable and effective to provide even a foreman with a detailed statement of not only his own objectives but those of the company and of the manufacturing department. Even though the company is so large as to make the distance between the individual foreman's production and the company's total output all but astronomical, the result has been a significant increase in production. Indeed, this must follow if we mean it when we say that the foreman is "part of management." For it is the definition of a manager that in what he does he takes responsibility for the whole—that, in cutting stone, he "builds the cathedral."

The objectives of every manager should spell out his contribution to the attainment of company goals in *all areas* of the business. Obviously, not every manager has a direct contribution to make in every area. The contribution which marketing makes to productivity, for example, may be very small. But if a manager and his unit are not expected to contribute toward any one of the areas that significantly affect prosperity and survival of the business, this fact should be clearly brought out. For managers must understand that business results depend on a balance of efforts and results in a number of areas. This is necessary both to give full scope to the craftsmanship of each function and specialty, and to prevent the empire-building and clannish jealousies of the various functions and specialties. It is necessary also to avoid overemphasis on any one key area.

To obtain balanced efforts the objectives of all managers on all levels and in all areas should also be keyed to both short-range and long-range considerations. And, of course, all objectives should always contain both the tangible business objectives and the intangible objectives for manager organization and development, worker performance and attitude and public responsibility. Anything else is shortsighted and impractical.

MANAGEMENT BY "DRIVES"

Proper management requires balanced stress on objectives, especially by top management. It rules out the common and pernicious business malpractice: management by "crisis" and "drives."

There may be companies in which management people do not say: "The only way we ever get anything done around here is by making a drive on it." Yet, "management by drive" is the rule rather than the exception. That things always collapse into the *status quo ante* three weeks after the drive is over, everybody knows and apparently expects. The only result of an "economy drive" is likely to be that messengers and typists get fired, and that $15,000 executives are forced to do $50-a-week work typing their own letters. And yet many managements have not drawn the obvious conclusion that drives are, after all, not the way to get things done.

But over and above its ineffectiveness, management by drive misdirects. It puts all emphasis on one phase of the job to the inevitable detriment of everything else. "For four weeks we cut inventories," a case-hardened veteran of management by crisis once summed it up. "Then we have four weeks of cost-cutting, followed by four weeks of human relations. We have just time to push customer service and courtesy for a month. And then the inventory is back where it was when we started. We don't even try to do our job. All management talks about, thinks about, preaches about, is last week's inventory figure or this week's customer complaints. How we do the rest of the job they don't even want to know."

In an organization which manages by drives people either neglect their job to get on with the current drive, or silently organize for collective sabotage of the drive to get their work done. In either event they become deaf to the cry of "wolf." And when the real crisis comes, when all hands should drop everything and pitch in, they treat it as just another case of management-created hysteria.

Management by drive, like management by "bellows and meat ax," is a sure sign of confusion. It is an admission of incompetence. It is a sign that management does not know how to plan. But above all, it is a sign that the company does not know what to expect of its managers—that, not knowing how to direct them, it misdirects them.

HOW SHOULD MANAGERS' OBJECTIVES BE SET AND BY WHOM?

By definition, a manager is responsible for the contribution that his component makes to the larger unit above him and eventually to the enterprise. His performance aims upward rather than downward. This means that the goals of each manager's job must be defined by the contribution he has to make to the success of the larger unit of which he is a part. The objectives of the district sales manager's job should be defined by the contribution he and his district sales force have to make to the sales department, the objectives of the project engineer's job by the contribution he, his engineers and draftsmen make to the engineering department. The objectives of the general manager of a decentralized division should be defined by the contribution his division has to make to the objectives of the parent company.

This requires each manager to develop and set the objectives of his unit himself. Higher management must, of course, reserve the power to approve or disapprove these objectives. But their development is part of a manager's responsibility; indeed, it is his first responsibility. It means, too, that every manager should responsibly participate in the development of the objectives of the higher unit of which his is a part. To "give him a sense of participation" (to use a neat phrase of the "human relations" jargon) is not enough. Being a manager demands the assumption of a genuine responsibility. Precisely because his aims should reflect the objective needs of the business, rather than merely what the individual manager wants, he must commit himself to them with a positive act of assent. He must know and understand the ultimate business goals, what is expected of him and why, what he will be measured against and how. There must be a "meeting of minds" within the entire management of each unit. This can be achieved only when each of the contributing managers is expected to think through what the unit objectives are, is led, in other words, to participate actively and responsibly in the work of defining them. And only if his lower managers participate in this way can the higher manager know what to expect of them and can make exacting demands.

16 PLANNING OBJECTIVES*

Cyril O'Donnell

So important is the need to select proper planning objectives that one would think that their nature and specification would be thoroughly understood and practiced with skill. But such is far from the case. Anyone who takes the trouble to examine enterprise "plans" will find that few of them qualify as true plans. Their chief fault lies in a misunderstanding of the planning process, and especially in vague statements of objective. This opens the door to vagaries of consistency, logic, and data, and invites pertinent questions concerning the need or the reason for "planning" in the first place.

The identification and description of objectives—the first step in planning—is absolutely essential to the success of any plan. One cannot specify how he will accomplish a vague and indeterminate purpose. It is not possible to develop a plan to enjoy oneself without identifying the parameters of enjoyment; neither can a firm develop a plan to improve its community relations, nor a bureau or agency make a plan to improve its image until it has described its purpose in such a way that ultimate success or failure can be determined with certitude.

Faulty specification and improper selection of a planning objective will vitiate the use of planning time and cost. The former will result in futility and bring the entire planning activity into disrepute. The latter will cause undesirable expenditures for a plan to accomplish unimportant or unrelated objectives, or objectives which are contrary to the social interest. Planning can be a most useful executive function, but it will not be if objectives are poorly or improperly selected.[1]

It is the purpose of this article to clarify the hierarchy of relationships between social purposes and enterprise goals and to inquire into the nature of the goal-setting process.

ENVIRONMENT

Enterprises are not free to plan in isolation. They must operate in a social environment of enormous scope, complexity, and change. Our planet, its peoples, and their institutions affect, in varying degree, the choice of objectives made by each enterprise. This environment may be viewed in terms of a scalar chain of authority, the degree of influence exercised over others, or the degree of freedom with which the enterprise can act. Internationally, there is a community of supposedly independent states which influence but do not control each other. Intranationally, the ultimate power rests in a political institution, democratic or authoritarian, which determines the degree of retained freedom of its peoples to act. There can be no doubt that the social purposes of the governing institution have top priority in the community. Ideally, if these are generally known and understood, all subordinate institutions should adopt, or will be constrained to adopt, purposes and objectives whose achievement will be consistent with them.

Organized societies, whether they be prehistoric villages, city-states, or nations, have certain purposes which they wish to achieve. Sometimes these are known and can be described. Archeologists suggest that the earliest organized group, simple though it probably was, had safety as its chief purpose. Cities are a social invention[2] whose prerequisites include a relatively dense population and availability of transportation facilities for bulk products. The original purpose of this organization is not known. It may have merely reflected a human preference for gregarious living; it certainly did provide an opportunity for extensive division of labor, and it had a power potential. The purposes of national states are equally uncertain. Despite the speculation on this subject by political historians, with their stress on natural boundaries, common language, etc., we really do not know why nations emerged. Per-

* Reprinted by permission of the publisher from the *California Management Review*, vol. 6, no. 3, pp. 3–10, Winter, 1963. Mr. O'Donnell is professor of business organization and policy, emeritus, at the University of California, Los Angeles.

haps success breeds power: The successful chief enjoyed the power which came by expanding his holding to a point where he was counterbalanced by other distant successes.

PURPOSE

We do have in our possession statements of purpose in the organization of the United States. This may be due to the great facility of our founding fathers in written expression happily combined with a world cultural stage highlighted by a relatively literate population, low cost of printing and distribution, and the discovery (much earlier) of the power of the written word. Whatever the explanations, statements of our national purposes are set forth in the Declaration of Independence and in the Constitution. Jefferson asserted that governments are instituted to secure to their peoples the rights of life, liberty, and the pursuit of happiness. The preamble of our Constitution states:

> We, the people of the United States, in order to form a more perfect union, establish justice, insure domestic tranquility, provide for the common defense, promote the general welfare, and secure the blessings of liberty to ourselves and our posterity, do ordain and establish this Constitution for the United States of America.

This is a formulation generally agreed upon at the time of its adoption and comes down to us as an inclusive statement. Undoubtedly there existed then, and there exist now, variant conceptions of our national purposes. Words mean different things to each person; priority issues must be faced; and there is no single authority with the power to determine exclusively, and require universal adherence to, a set of multiple purposes.

These uncertainties make it really difficult for a subordinate enterprise to adopt supportive or complementary purposes even if it would; they also permit wide latitude for conflicting, low priority, and even subversive purposes.

There are always various means by which the over-all social purposes can be attained. In the United States the chief reliance is upon political and economic freedom, characterized by free enterprise, a system in which entrepreneurs are free to organize cooperative effort to produce goods and services whose (ultimate) consumption helps our people achieve certain aspects of the social purpose. Within limits, the what, who, how, when, and where are left to individuals to decide. It should be noted that not all enterprises are intended to provide entrepreneurial profit. Persons who develop many political, welfare, educational, religious, and specialized social groups, such as a trade association, may not have profit in mind, even potentially. They exchange their services for income which is begged or taxed from contributors, or which is obtained from the non-profit sale of services.

While most enterprise is undertaken with freedom, there has been an expanding area of cooperative action in which freedom is limited. Even originally, the federal government obtained from the states exclusive rights to maintain defense, establish a supreme court, levy certain types of taxes, and conduct certain businesses, such as the post office. These functions, identified by Adam Smith as the legitimate activities of government, have not been subject to question. With the passage of time, additional restrictions and prohibitions on free enterprise have multiplied as complainants against certain aspects of free enterprise behavior have gained political power. These restrictive acts are familiar to students of economics, finance, agriculture, transportation, and trade. The power to tax business income at rates which many scholars think are confiscatory has an important effect in limiting the scope of free enterprise. It is intended that private enterprise, of whatever nature, will adopt purposes which square with regulations that are designed, we hope, to realize generally accepted social purposes. Enterprises which ignore this concept create enormous risks of losing all their resources. From a social viewpoint, this is as it should be if the regulations concerning government ownership and control are themselves consistent with social purposes.

Under the umbrella of social purposes, and contributory or complementary to them, every enterprise should face up to the problem of spelling out its own purposes. Failure to do this will result in an undertaking battered by coincidence of events and helpless because it is likely to have inconsistent and unrealistic plans or none at all. Further, to the extent that its purposes are vague, inconsistent, or unspecified, there will be no way of testing the degree to which its plans or behavior contribute toward the accomplishment of ends. On the other hand, clarity of purpose permits the identification of planning objectives, and planning, as we know, can greatly increase the probability of accomplishment, if properly executed. As L. Gulick has stated, "A clear statement of purpose universally understood is the outstanding guarantee of effective administration."[3]

NEW ENTERPRISES

In the United States each year several thousand enterprises are established. For what purpose? What is it that the entrepreneur, the prime mover, hopes to accomplish? Clearly it is to provide a product or service for exchange. He may have a variety of reasons in mind. Immediately, of course, he must see a need for the enterprise, and unless he is correct and unless the need to be served contributes to our social purposes, there is a high prospect of failure. But are we sure that the prime mover is really concerned about fulfilling others' needs? Certain men do wish to satisfy the need of the lowly for economic relief, health care, or religious service. Compassion and charity seem to be their driving power.

On the other hand many, and probably most, entrepreneurs see the fulfillment of others' needs merely as a means of satisfying personal desires for a way to make a living, achieve freedom, and perhaps acquire power. Nonprofit enterprises can and do provide very satisfactory standards of living for their employees; they can also provide freedom and power for the prime mover. Profit-making enterprises are the rule, however. Their variety is as diverse as the needs of men. It covers not merely what is generally called business: it includes hospitals, firms organized to raise money for charities, educational institutions, and even some sidelines of religious enterprise. In every case they have the potential for satisfying the income, freedom, and power needs of their founders.

It is chiefly the responsibility of the Board of Directors or its equivalent to establish and to review the enterprise's purposes. At this level, it is essential to consider whether the purposes are really complementary to the social purpose and not questionable. At the minimum, their responsibility is to avoid the risks of antisocial purposes, direct or indirect. Furthermore, there is a need to review purposes occasionally to make sure they conform to newly interpreted aspects of the social purpose. For instance, collusion is now forbidden in domestic trade but encouraged in foreign trade. Ambivalent as the social purpose is in this instance, directors must ensure that enterprise purpose will be achieved within the known or assumed confines of this legislation, and they should be alert to any modifications in the future.

Although it is perfectly clear that some enterprises are organized to achieve a short-run purpose and then be dissolved, this is unusual. Men tend to found enterprises for the indefinite long run and, if they use the corporate form, for perpetuity. Undoubtedly their hope is to realize purposes quickly, but they are more likely to be resigned to strive for them during their active years. Consequently the long-run purposes are likely to be spelled out with considerable vagueness and perhaps dissembled into terms considered inoffensive to their fellowman. Rather than admit to freedom and power as included in their long-run purpose, they may specify only a profit purpose. But even this purpose will normally be buried under a ponderous statement about fulfilling the needs of customers. In reality, the needs of customers are but the means to acquiring profit, freedom, and power. Hiding these long-run purposes for political reasons is incomprehensible if one understands our society and its component of human beings. Our society depends on people to strive for these real purposes, knowing full well that in the striving the needs of man will be served within the safeguards built into our social system.

The formulation of purposes is undertaken in a studied attempt to establish an image, ideal though it may be, of the enterprise as it will be when it reaches maturity. If this is not done, the firm is subject to the vagaries of chance. If it is, all plans for achievement can be directed toward a unifying concept.

Since an enterprise has ultimate purposes to achieve, usually much beyond the objectives of even long-range plans, experienced managers realize that general rather than specific descriptions are inevitable. The parameters of the image are spelled out on the assumption that it may take twenty, fifty, or a hundred years to mold the enterprise. To quantify purposes so far in the future is extremely hazardous. For instance, it would be much more sensible to establish one purpose as the earning of the competitive rate of return on investment rather than select an arbitrary figure. We do not know whether the specific figure will be reasonable in a distant future when the free enterprise system may be assaulted, capital scarce or plentiful, or inflation may bury the dollar under tons of paper. Specific figures should be used only at the stage where planning objectives are established.

MULTIPLE PURPOSES

These enterprises have multiple purposes. An educational enterprise may be thought of as having the purpose of educating students, but such a conception is inadequate because it does not develop the image sought. The image would become much more clear if it were stated that the purposes of the educational enterprise are to attract highly qualified graduate students to be trained in the liberal arts and sciences, to grant the Ph.D. degree to successful candidates, to attract only the most highly regarded faculty, to operate as a private school in the Spartan tradition, and be supported entirely by tuition fees and gifts of alumni and friends. Similarly, a business enterprise might spell out its multiple purposes to include earning a competitive rate of profit and return on investment, emphasizing research as a basis for a continuing flow of proprietary products, having public ownership, financing both by earnings plow-back and debt, distributing products internationally, pricing superior quality electronic products competitively, striving for stability and growth to a dominant position in the industry, and adhering as far as possible to the generally supported values of our society. Statements of purposes such as these would enable anyone to visualize the kind of enterprise the regents or directors would like to mold. They also establish several essential premises for the planning that must be done to accomplish each step on the way.

There are two sets of circumstances which could require the statement of purposes to be changed. The first is the technical matter of limiting the purposes so that change may be inevitable, due to changing circumstances. If one of the purposes is to retail or to manufacture kerosene oil lamps, any decision to manufacture or wholesale in the first case or to broaden the product line in the second would entail amendment to the enterprise charter. In some political circumstances this could easily spell trouble for incorporated enterprises.

There is another kind of circumstance which causes directors to modify statements of purpose. This includes changes in the law, elimination of free enterprise in the activity, radical technological innovations, changes in consumer living standards, reduction of the death rate, and higher literacy levels. Our society is highly dynamic, and therefore it is incumbent upon directors to review and modify purposes as seems wise. They are not absolved from this duty merely because the purposes are very distantly realizable. Purposes must be kept consistent with social change if the guided effort to achieve them is to be applied effectively and efficiently.

AN IMPORTANT FACTOR

One of the most important factors which influences the choice of purposes is the environment in which the enterprise will operate. All of its elements cannot be considered here, but they would include the nature of the economic order, affluence of the people in the society, national and international political stability, tax policies, competition, and state of the arts. One would not engage in the design and manufacture of fine furniture if he were intending to sell it to aborigines.

A second factor is technical skill and knowledge. People normally select an activity they know something about, particularly in product areas where technology is important. A truck driver is not likely to found a university or a corner grocer to establish a firm to produce power plants for space travel. There is, of course, the possibility of hiring the needed technical skill. This is often done, but the disparity between the technical knowledge of the founder and that required for operations is usually not as great as in the above examples. Even when it is, the difference normally occurs at the top level of management. It is also absolutely necessary that employees with technical ability be available. A movie queen might found a new university, but it would fail unless she could recruit a qualified staff.

Another element in the need for technical skill is the availability of satellite industries. Many firms have considered establishing a business in seemingly favorable places only to find that essential auxiliary industry—power, raw materials, refrigeration, finance, or transportation—is not available. Thus, the state of the art employed by the enterprise must be consonant with that of the environment.

A third factor in the choice of purpose concerns the creativity of founders or directors. The risks as well as the rewards for creative enterprise are well recognized. The firm that can command the services of really creative people is most likely to stress the purpose of gaining a recognized place at the forward fringe of the arts. It would concentrate on its potential for research, design, and development. Such a purpose is risky, not only because of the danger of creating unmarketable products, but especially because the services of creative employees may be lost. At the other extreme is the non-creative, tired imitator of existing firms. In between is the firm that chooses a purpose closely related to skill in innovation such as was reflected in the development of the supermarket, integrated functional operations, or new and unusual sites for an activity.

PRIMARY MOTIVATION

Finally, it should be remarked that some founders are primarily motivated by compassion for others. These men would be likely to establish a welfare purpose, among others, for this is their main interest. Tom Dooley and his enterprise for improving the health of Southeast Asians is a good example; the American hospital ship, *Hope,* is another.

There would be little need to design the purposes of enterprise if there were no intention of planning to achieve them. Without plans, the firm's history would have only an accidental relationship to purposes. Plans and their effective execution are an absolute requirement for the realization of enterprise purpose.

The objectives of long-range plans are quite different from enterprise purposes, especially in timing and specific detail. While the achievement of purpose may be thought of as a matter of decades or of continual striving, the accomplishment of long-range objectives is planned within a matter of a few years. There are, of course, a few firms—notably utilities[4]—that develop plans for building fixed assets whose life expectancy is 25 to 100 years, but most long-range planning is probably confined to a five-year span. This means, of course, that long-range objectives are not and cannot be identical to purposes. The latter perform a valuable function when used as planning premises. The objectives of the plan are merely pieces of the distant purposes, which, if achieved successfully in five-year series, eventually become equated with purposes.

In approaching the problem of defining long-range objectives, it is necessary to consider certain basic prerequisites and to select the enterprise image.

One obvious prerequisite to specifying long-range planning objectives is that their achievement must support the realization of enterprise purpose. It is as faulty to select an objective which makes no contribution to purpose as it is to select objectives which conflict with them. In both cases, effort is expended inefficiently or nonproductively. A positive contribution to purpose must be planned if it is to have more than a coincidental effect.

A second prerequisite concerns the practicality of achievement. This is no easy quality to attain. For most people, practicality and planning may seem to be contradictory concepts. They fail to see that the long-range objective sought is not a matter of guessing where the enterprise will be in five years but is a specific which proper planning and execution is most likely to make occur. As a practical matter, it can never occur unless the objective can be achieved. It is surely apparent that a five-year objective of a professional football team to obtain a monopoly in this type of entertainment is unreal. But an objective to reach the championship of the league in that time is practical.

In setting practical objectives managers must face up to the problem of whether to be conservative or expansive. For instance, should a firm set its five-year sales objective at a figure easily accomplished, or should it be optimistic and double the conservative figure? Much depends on what is occurring in the industry, what competitors are doing, estimates of economic, political, and technological factors. Managers may feel that a conservative objective will avoid the risk of discouraging employees; or they may estimate that employees will work hard to exceed the low objective. Other managers may feel that high objectives act chiefly as a challenge, believing that great achievement results from striving for high goals. In the United States we seem to prefer the second approach.

There are many other elements to be considered in settling upon practical objectives. Innovation and creativity play very important parts. So do the state of the arts, the availability of investment funds, premises concerning family-owned firms, and the growth of resources that obey laws of nature rather than synthetic processes.

A third prerequisite concerns the logical relationships between long-range objectives and enterprise purpose. The objectives of the first plan to be made must be those on whose achievement the realization of the objectives of second and third generations of plans depends. This requirement is simply common sense, but the application in practical situations is not nearly so clear. For instance, in pursuing the purposes of the educational enterprise visualized above, should the objective of the first five-year plan be to raise a fund, hire a faculty, and/or recruit students? A business firm whose objective is to double its sales in five years cannot hope to do so entirely through internal expansion. It has such options as buying established firms, producing others' products under license, integrating vertically, or combining all types of approaches. Which step is first? If planners only knew!

BUILDING BLOCKS

Conceptualization of the enterprise image as it approaches maturity makes it possible to visualize in it the achieved objectives of successive long-range plans. These objectives may be viewed as building blocks in numbered order which, when appropriately arranged, become the integrated structure. The objectives of the earliest long-term plans provide the foundation blocks and succeeding plans yield the walls and roof of the mature structure.

Since each enterprise image is unique and surely changes with men, time, and circumstance, it follows that no generalization concerning the "right" objectives can be made and that the potentiality of achievement of the image itself is likely to be ephemeral. As a consequence, managers are forced to identify *de nova* the elements of the firm's ultimate image, determine the required order of their achievement, and establish a long-term plan to accomplish the objectives with top priority. Because the inherited and modified aspects of the image may require several generations of managers to realize, each manager should enjoy the satisfaction of having made a partial contribution and not be disappointed because the realization of the grand design is beyond his time and capability. Each generation of Americans should be happy in its contribution to Jefferson's vision of our society's purpose rather than feel frustrated in the little progress it really makes.

It is of utmost importance that the selected objectives should be quantified. Vague statements such as improvement in sales, increased profit, or high morale are simply useless for planning purposes. There is a need to know "how much" in order to determine what resource commitment is necessary and whether the objective is achieved. One cannot know how to plan for an increase in sales, but one certainly does know how to plan for a 10 per cent increase. With this target, the manager will ultimately know for certain the degree of success he achieved.

NO PROBLEM

For many objectives, quantification does not present a difficult physical problem. Such things as profits, sales, output, or quality are customarily stated in dollars or units or transactions. The only problem arises in persuading managers to select a quantified objective. This issue is psychological in nature. Some men shy away because they tend to stress the many unknowns in the picture. Others refuse because they do not wish their performance to be measured against specific objectives. Perhaps these fears can be overcome by education.

There will be some objectives which are difficult or impossible to quantify directly. Examples would include morale, developing and training managers, social responsibility, creativity, quality, and public image. Assuming that it is reasonable and desirable to select one or more of these objectives for planning purposes, it is advantageous to quantify them indirectly if possible. The objective should be analyzed to discover some quantifiable element which is closely related with the qualitative objective. For instance, since absenteeism closely correlates with low morale, the determination to cut absenteeism by 50 per cent provides a substitute quantified objective for improvement in morale. Frequently a manager can find more than one correlative of the intended objective. The difficulty of this approach to indirect quantification is no excuse for avoiding these types of planning objectives. They should give impetus to the search because abandonment is a costly alternative. Unsought objectives cannot be realized beyond an occasional coincidence.

Important as it is to quantify, even by indirection, it is realistic to understand that such procedure is often frustrated by the press of continuing operations and by the difficulty of getting managerial agreement on a precise statement of objectives. While earnest attempts can, in time, reduce inchoate qualitative ends to more manageable proportions, it is fortunately true that the enterprise can still operate effectively when there is only agreement on broad objectives.

Short-range objectives support the hierarchy of long-range objectives, enterprise purposes, and social purposes. They are the one area where managers feel at home. It is difficult to project the distant future. So intangible are many elements and so rare is the talent to deal with them that most operating managers turn with relief to short-run specifications. They feel that here at last they can operate in a familiar environment.

Long-range plans, drawn to plot the accomplishment of objectives, are notably more vague for distant years than for the immediate future. This means that what is planned for accomplishment in the fifth year, if this is the length of the planning period, is more uncertain than what is planned for the fourth, third, second, and first year. Short-range objectives, typically to be realized in the first year of a long-range plan, are both comprehensive and specific. The approach to them should always be from the distant (fifth) year to the present and not vice versa. What is to be done in the immediate year must provide a foundation for the objectives of each successive year and this can only be guaranteed if short-range plans are part of the long-range plan.

The selection of short-range objectives proceeds from an evaluation of priorities relating to long-range objectives. Some things simply need to be done first either because they are a prerequisite to other objectives or because of lead time considerations. For instance, as a new firm is established to accomplish certain purposes, the raising of capital is a prime requisite when compared with any other objective. It must have capital for fixed and operating expenses and a plan is needed to secure it. Conceivably this may be the sole short-run objective. If so, the objectives visualized for the second year might be hiring managers for engineering, production, and sales; leasing space and equipment; and manning the organization. At the same time, if a three-year lead time is necessary, say for installing a piece of specialized equipment, then writing specifications and placing the order would also be an objective of the immediate year.

Thus, short-range objectives are identical with the objectives of the first year in a long-range plan. The problem becomes one of defining, clarifying, quantifying, and timing them. It is necessary to draw a plan for accomplishing each objective and combining these in a master plan for review in terms of logic, consistency, and practicality.

AFTER APPROVAL

Once the master plan is approved, the individual plans which are its elements are assigned to one or more subordinate managers for execution. Accomplishment of these several but separate objectives may be the duty of one manager or it may be the combined duty of several. The objective of raising funds to meet the requirements of operating activities may reasonably be assigned to the finance manager. But objectives relating to public relations, executive succession, or quality are clearly assignable to nearly every manager because each, willy-nilly, will make his individual contribution.

The logic of developing subsidiary plans is clear. The agreed objectives of the short-range plan are parcelled out to the chief executive's immediate subordinates. They, in turn, will assign elements of these objectives to their subordinates. This process of fractionation continues to the level of the front-line supervisor. Thus, every manager should have a group of assigned, quantified objectives to accomplish during the immediate year. For each of these he will develop specific plans.

Ideally, each manager may be viewed as executing several plans simultaneously, making consistent progress toward the realization of several objectives. It is difficult in practice to maintain this perspective for several reasons. The objectives themselves are quite diverse. For a sales manager they may range from rearranging sales territories, recruiting salesmen, manager development, service review and improvement, opening new markets, minimizing transportation and warehousing costs, and marketing research to securing new engineering or product design. It is difficult to apply simultaneous effort to these objectives. As a human being, the sales manager, for instance, will find he makes more progress by concentrating attention on each objective one after another. As he does so, planned accomplishment of all objectives is bound to suffer. Furthermore, every man tends to invest time in the objectives relating to his peculiar interests. This leads inevitably to neglected objectives.

Balance is difficult in the face of shifting priorities and changing costs—inevitable occurrences in any dynamic environment. For instance, market strategy may call for shifting to an alternative distribution plan, or advancing the predetermined shift by two years as a response to improperly evaluated competitive pressures. Executing this kind of decision may place second priority on an objective to complete a new product design. Similarly, a new research program, blithely adopted by naive managers, may have to be dropped entirely or modified drastically because its accumulating costs are gradually depriving other functions of their life-giving operating dollars, or even threatening the financial stability of the firm long before any substantial benefits can be converted to realized revenue.

Another difficulty in balancing objectives arises when unforeseen circumstances throw a plan out of phase. The loss of a key subordinate, a fire, bankruptcy of a vendor, a strike, and many similar occurrences have this effect. They may even jeopardize the planned action and force replanning.

Finally, managers give prime attention to those objectives in which their superiors show marked interest. A superior who is more interested in sales than in manager training will inquire into the former with regularity but perhaps never inquire into the latter. The reaction of subordinate managers is to attend particularly to the sales objective even though this means stealing time from the supervision of progress toward other objectives.

From these considerations it may be concluded that maintaining balanced progress toward accomplishing all objectives is almost insuperable. This need not be true. A sophisticated manager counters his own weaknesses and understands that all objectives are important, not only for their own sakes but especially because their proper accomplishment is a prerequisite to the success of the long-range plan. This type of manager understands his environment and himself, the responsibility resting upon his shoulders, and he will take intelligent action.

Planning objectives are seen in a hierarchical framework, logically based on social purposes. The discussion has been entirely in terms of logic and principle. Those readers who look for specific rules spelling out what objectives to select are bound to be disappointed. The basic point is that every manager must do his own thinking. He must, if he would be successful, be an educated man: He must know our history, understand his environment, know the principles of planning, and finally draw on his store of personal wisdom to select socially useful objectives.

REFERENCES

1. Although semantic problems are not too serious in this area, there are such terms as purpose, goal, and target which are often used synonymously. Perhaps greater clarity can be achieved by reserving "purpose" to describe the reason for the existence of an enterprise or any of its divisions and departments; "goal" and "target," terms borrowed from games, to describe the aims of minor or informal plans such as a salesman's goal; and "objective" to describe the end for which a plan is designed.
2. After R. Linton, *The Tree of Culture* (New York: Vintage Books, Inc., 1958), p. 37.
3. *Administrative Reflections from World War II* (University: University of Alabama Press, 1948), p. 77.
4. R. P. O'Brien, "Electrical Utility Planning," a paper presented to the Seminar on Long-Range Planning (University of California, Los Angeles: Research Division, Graduate School of Business Administration, Sept., 1962).

17 SHORTCOMINGS AND PITFALLS IN MANAGING BY OBJECTIVES*

Harold Koontz

Perhaps the most powerful tool of managing that has so far been put into practice is the system of managing by objectives. It is simple common sense in that it is a reflection of the purpose of managing itself. Without clear goals, managing is haphazard and random and no group or individual can expect to perform effectively. The system also has received much impetus from the need for better managerial appraisal. Disillusionment with traditional appraisal methods, still too widely used, with their emphasis on subjective standards of personality and work habits, has been a major practical reason for the current interest in managing by objectives.

The necessity for any organized group of individuals to work together for the accomplishment of a purpose has long been recognized. Yet, it is one of those strange phenomena of human history that only in recent years have more alert managers come to realize that, if objectives are to be actionable, they must be clear and verifiable to those who pursue them. As basic as this is, it is still proving difficult to accomplish in practice. As simple as the concept is, too few businesses are really so managing and it is only an exceedingly rare non-business operation that is even attempting to do so.

Experience with many companies and government enterprises, both directly and through investigation, indicates that, even now, there is far more talk and religious zeal than meaningful action. Many who talk of having programmes of managing and appraising by objectives do not really have systems that operate effectively. What is most distressing is that, if, through poor implementation, managing by objectives comes to be regarded as a personnel or training department gimmick, disenchantment by those operating personnel whose co-operation is so necessary will surely follow. People may go through the motions and the paperwork, but the spirit and meaning will be gone. This has already happened in many enterprises. And like all such programmes involving people, when this happens, a programme is discredited and top management may not be given a chance to reintroduce it for some years.

Because of the tremendous impact a programme of managing by objectives can have on profitability, accomplishment of enterprise goals and personal satisfaction, disillusionment from failure, or even partial success, must be avoided if possible. It is with the hope of giving responsible practising managers some danger signals and suggestions to avoid them that this paper is written.

BETTER MANAGING: THE STRENGTH OF MANAGING BY OBJECTIVES

The most important advantage of managing by objectives is that it can result in much improved managing. Actionable objectives cannot be established without planning and results-oriented planning is the only kind that makes sense. It forces managers to think of planning for *results,* rather than merely planning *activities* or *work.* To assure that objectives are realistic, it also requires the manager to think of the way he will accomplish given results, the organization and personnel he will need to do it, and the resources and interdepartmental assistance he will require. Also, there is no better way to know what the standards of control are than for a manager to have a clear goal before him.

It is, then, an approach to managing, and not another personnel programme added to the burdens of a manager. At the same time, it should not be forgotten that there are other things in managing, and the necessarily limited

* Reprinted by permission of the publisher from *Management by Objectives,* vol. 1, no. 3, pp. 6–12 (January 1972). Mr. Koontz is Mead Johnson Professor of Management, University of California, Los Angeles.

number of important objectives should not camouflage other work that must be done.

Clarifying Organization A major strength of a system of managing by objectives is the clarification of organizational roles and structure which should occur. Objectives must fit key result areas and both, to the extent possible, should be reflected in a position that carries responsibility for them. Thus, a marketing manager with a goal to accomplish a given volume of sales in a new product line should ideally have adequate authority in some way to see that products desired are available when wanted and at a price to make them attractive to a customer. Even where this authority must be shared with others (production, for example), the exact sharing should be clear.

Companies that have seriously embarked on a programme of managing by objectives have often discovered organizational deficiencies. The most common one is that the company has not come face to face with the basic principle of delegation—to delegate by results expected. As an executive of Honeywell, Incorporated said: "There are two things that might be considered fundamental creed at Honeywell: decentralized management is needed to make Honeywell work and management by objectives is needed to make decentralization work."

An Effective Way to Sharpen Planning Planning is basic to managing and the other functions of the manager have little significance without it. Yet every practising manager knows that today's crises and "fires" will almost invariably push out planning for tomorrow. It is, therefore, a happy thing when a technique or approach establishes an environment that forces planning.

Any competent system of managing by objectives does just that. Managers soon find that they cannot pull goals out of the air and are not likely to do so if setting and achieving of goals are major standards of their performance appraisal. If actionable objectives are to be set, they must necessarily reflect the future operating environment facing the manager; they must take into account the resources and assistance needed and available; they should be supportive of the goals of a manager's superior and of those in other departments who contribute to, or benefit from, the performance of a certain manager.

Elicits Commitment One of the major advantages of a system of managing by objectives is that it elicits commitment for performance. No longer is man just doing work or following instructions, waiting for guidance and decisions; he is now an individual with a clearly defined set of supported purposes. He has hopefully had a part in setting his objectives, has had an opportunity to put his ideas into planning, now understands his authority to make decisions and utilize resources, and has presumably been able to get decisions and commitment of resources from his superior.

These are the elements that make for a feeling of commitment. Where a programme works as it can and should, a man becomes largely a master of his fate. It is in this system that a man can experience one of the most powerful of all human drives, the desire to accomplish and do so largely on his own.

Gives the Best Guides and Reasons for Control Managers have long had difficulties in undertaking control effectively and in getting the information they need to manage because they often do not know clearly what to watch. Most control systems suffer from lack of identification of critical control points and information on progress being made. With effective managing by objectives, a manager now knows what he should watch. He has standards against which to measure his progress.

Appraising managers on their ability to set and achieve objectives becomes operational in the sense that appraisal is an easy derivative from what a manager actually does. Appraisals are not apart from his job and are not based upon personal characteristics and work qualities that are almost invariably subjective. Moreover, appraisal takes place in an atmosphere of the superior working with and helping his subordinate—not sitting in remote judgment on him.

WEAKNESSES IN THE SYSTEM

In the almost religious zeal with which managing by objectives has been embraced by some companies, it is often overlooked that there are many significant shortcomings and pitfalls. As a system of managing, it cannot do everything and indeed there are shortcomings in the programme itself that the successful user would do well to recognize. Moreover, analysis of practice has shown even more difficulties which could be avoided by intelligent and careful implementation of the system. First, let us look at the shortcomings in even a well operated programme of managing by objectives.

Goals Are Difficult To Set Even with the best practice, goals with the right degree of "stretch" or "pull" are difficult to set, quarter in and quarter out, year in and year out. Since goals are set for the future and the future has inevitable uncertainties, it is not easy to establish meaningful and actionable goals. To be sure, this is true of all planning, but it is especially true for goals in that they involve end-points of work accomplishment and not, as in many plans, only laying out work to be done.

One major problem is to set goals that are reasonably attainable and yet not easily so. Particularly in the initial stages of managing by objectives, people are inclined to fix goals that are too high. Anything seems possible in a year, almost anything in three months, but next week is far more difficult.

This means that the system does not replace the skillful art of management in using judgment of what is reasonably attainable. The astute superior will never wish goals to be set so that all can be easily met, nor will he wish to risk the frustration that comes when his subordinate regularly misses most of his goals. Perhaps a useable rule of thumb would be that the really good subordinate should accomplish approximately three-quarters of his goals.

Tendency of Goals To Be Short Term It is natural that in almost all systems of managing by objectives, goals are set for the short term, seldom more than a year and often quarterly, or less. There is clearly the danger of emphasizing the short term at the expense of the longer range.

Perhaps this shortcoming might more appropriately be looked on as one arising from practice, rather than the system itself. There is theoretically no reason that goals should not be set for the long term. And occasionally they are. One company, for example, insists on the establishment of five-year objectives in the same verifiable terms that the annual and quarterly objectives are set. In the actual review of short-term objectives, emphasis is placed on justifying them as being consistent with long-range goals.

While this shortcoming can be modified, and should be, by tying all goals into a longer term framework, this is difficult. Emphasis is understandably placed on performance for the nearer term and usually made consistent with accounting periods. Also, where used for appraisal purposes, as is usually the case, managers usually want evaluations on performance in shorter periods.

Danger in Overemphasizing Objectives There is always the danger that a system of managing by objectives will lead to so much attention being paid toward the setting and achieving of a few major objectives that managers will overlook the other aspects of a job or may push his own objectives at the expense of the company. A sales manager, for example, may be so driven to increase sales that he will concentrate on easier-to-sell low-profit items. Or a manager may forget that his job involves many tasks not directly related to achieving a few major goals for a current period of time.

This is a weakness in the system and it is also a weakness due to poor practice. Obviously, no system of managing by objectives can cover every detail of a man's job. Management by objectives is not all there is to managing; it is a tool of managing, and not a substitute. Moreover, goals must be looked on as a network of coordinated and interrelated end-results, with the goals of one manager fitting in with those of another.

May Not Be An Accurate Measure of Performance One of the great weaknesses of using performance against objectives as the standard of measuring managerial action is that it is entirely possible for a manager to meet or miss goals through no fault of his own. Luck often does play a part in meeting or missing goals. A marketing programme may succeed beyond expectations because of change in public tastes which the marketing manager had no part in influencing. Cost targets might be missed through unexpected inflationary influences beyond any manager's control.

Although those who evaluate progress usually claim that they take these external factors into account in appraising individuals, it is rare indeed that the brilliant performer is not regarded as a "fair haired boy" and the non-performer has a cloud cast over him. The facts are that external influences are difficult to evaluate and success or failure, from whatever causes, much more apparent.

SHORTCOMINGS AND PITFALLS IN PRACTICE

What is most disturbing about managing by objectives, particularly in view of the tremendous potential it has for more effective managing, are the many shortcomings and pitfalls one finds in practice. Sometimes one gets the impression that a chief executive has heard of this approach to managing, looks on it as an automatic palliative for all managerial problems, merely orders his personnel manager to install it, and then wonders why the programme yields disappointing results. Even when a system is given a strong send-off, it can wither and die from the common malady of executive malnutrition. It is a system both difficult to install and to maintain. But it is one very worthwhile doing well.

Learning the System Is Difficult Despite the unassailable and simple logic of managing by objectives, experience has shown that it is not easy for people to learn and is not self-teachable. For one thing, even those who are accustomed to giving effort to planning find it difficult to shift from planning *work* to planning for the accomplishment of clear *end-results*. Also, the meaning and practice of verifiability are not easy. For still another thing, maintaining an environment to make it work throughout a company or even a large department requires patient effort. As a matter of fact, any enterprise or any department should be happy if the system operates well in three years, and five years of careful teaching and operating may be necessary.

In view of the practical difficulties in learning the system and approach of managing by objectives, it is astonishing how many enterprises have "installed" the programme by issuing instructions and providing for the necessary forms. For the harried top executive who understandably has more problems than solutions, one can understand the desire to put the programme into effect with the minimum of time and effort.

But this will not work. People will give lip service and fill out forms for any programme the top executive orders. However, unless there is a complete understanding of what the system is, what the philosophy is underlying it, the paper may flow but the results are not likely to be impressive. Patient and thorough explanation of the entire programme, what it is, how it works, why it is being done, and how everyone can benefit from it must be made available to every person involved. While this can and often should be done by specialists inside or outside the company, there can be no substitute for the personal leadership and involvement of the top executives.

Failure To Give Goal Setters Guidelines One of the major reasons for ineffectual managing by objectives is the failure to give goal setters guidelines. No one can set a meaningful goal, either for himself or others, unless he knows several simple and fundamental things. First, he must understand the end-result area for which he is responsible and how this contributes to corporate objectives. A research and development manager must know, for example, what part of the new products programme he is responsible for, and what the corporate objectives and product strategies are. In the second place, every manager must know what the planning assumptions, or premises, of the company are. The research and development manager must know, for example, what level of research effort is assumed, what market factors, required cost and price levels for the product, whether completely new products are desired or whether the company is only interested in product improvements, and many other elements that effectively define the environment for him to set his goals and undertake his activities.

No one can set goals and plan in a vacuum. The question always will be: does the goal setter fill this vacuum with premises his enterprise believes should be followed or does he fill it with his own estimates and predilections? Certainly no network of plans can be consistent, or "fit," without consistent planning premises.

Failure To Assure A Network of Goals In the obsession to set goals, there is ever the danger that one man's objectives may be inconsistent with those of another. The production manager's goals for low cost might be non-supportive to the marketing manager's goal of product availability or quality, or the financial manager's of low inventory. An enterprise is a system. If goals, like all other plans, are not inter-connected and mutually supportive, people will tend to pursue paths that seem best for their own operations but may be detrimental to the company as a whole.

The assurance of a network of mutually supportive goals is not easy. First, it requires seeing planning programmes as a network of programme elements. As may be readily seen from figure 1, showing the network of programmes comprising a typical new product programme, this is likely to be fairly complex, and if any single part misses, the total programme will be adversely affected.

In the second place, action is required to see that individual goals and their programmes fit the desired niche in a network. This necessitates careful definition of end-result areas, dissemination of consistent planning premises, and careful review of the various goals, by those responsible for them. This, in turn, makes desirable group discussions to assure that the network is, in fact, being woven together.

Setting Arbitrary Goals One of the sure causes of failure is for the boss to set arbitrary goals for his subordinates. While the superior must take final authority for approving the objectives of those who report to him, by foisting goals on subordinates, he can destroy the feeling of commitment on the part of those who

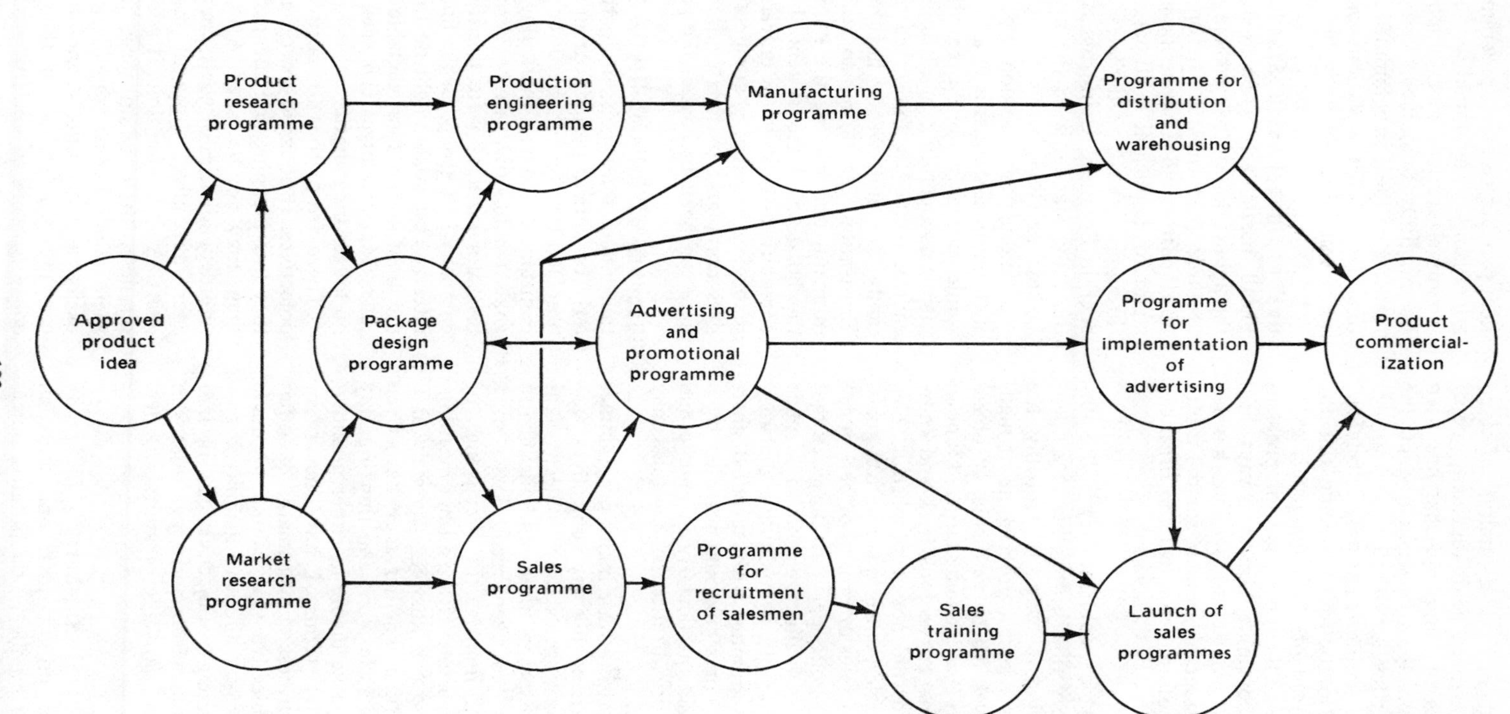

FIGURE 1 Network of Programmes Comprising a Typical New Product Programme

must achieve them. As a matter of fact, arbitrary and pressured goals represent one of the major causes of complaint that has been expressed by managers, particularly at the middle and lower levels.

Arbitrary goal setting is not only self-defeating, but it is also foolish. By doing this the superior is deprived of the intelligence, experience, and, often, the know-how of problem solution the subordinate almost always has. Experience with goal setting sessions has led me to have considerable respect for the useful knowledge that often lies down the organization.

Failure To Insist on Verifiability Requiring that goals be verifiable, whether in a quantitative or qualitative way, is probably the major key to a successful programme of managing by objectives. To be verifiable, an objective must be such that, at some targeted time in the future, a manager can look back and know whether he did or did not accomplish it. This is, of course, easiest with quantitative goals, such as dollars of sales or profits, or percentage reduction of man-hours per unit. But goals that might be termed as qualitative can also be made verifiable. For example, a qualitative goal may be a certain programme with specified characteristics to be completed and installed by a given date. In fact, particularly in middle and upper levels of organization, many goals may be of this nature.

Yet, it is surprising how many programmes that pass as managing by objectives are grounded on fuzzy goals. Such objectives as "to be alert to customers' needs and qualified to serve them," or "to keep credit losses to a minimum," or "to improve the effectiveness of the personnel department" are all but meaningless since no one can answer accurately at a given point of time whether they have been achieved. With a little work and thinking, any goal can be made verifiable in either quantitative or qualitative terms. I have never encountered in business, government, or other enterprise an objective that cannot be made verifiable. Certainly, without verifiability, a programme of managing by objectives can slip into an exercise in pious wishes and generalities with little meaning for managing or appraising performance.

Overinsistence on Numbers In many otherwise strong programmes, one finds an overinsistence on numbers—quantitative objectives—in order to make the approach rigorously verifiable. But, there are too many important objectives that simply cannot be expressed in numbers. Many of the important elements of a new product research programme, a sales and advertising programme, or one for making personnel services more important cannot be meaningfully quantified. Yet, by spelling out features of these programmes and emphasizing due dates for the various parts, programme goals can be made verifiable.

Use of Inapplicable Standards Another pitfall, particularly when used for appraisal, is the application of inapplicable standards for acceptable performance. In one company, the headquarters office has set desired performance standards applicable to all parts of the company throughout the United States. Thus, the manager in Southern California is gauged against the same standards as the manager in North Dakota or Georgia.

A moment's reflection would indicate that such national standards in a far-flung operation would probably not be equally applicable to managers operating in dissimilar markets and environments. In this case, they almost certainly are not. What has been the result? Frustration, resistance, no real sense of commitment, and playing the numbers game with the bosses and the system. It is true in this company, as it is almost universally, that, when managing becomes a numbers game, the self-preserving and reasonably intelligent subordinate can beat his boss at the game.

Dangers of Inflexibility There is always the danger that goals, ordinarily set for quarterly or annual periods, or more, will become obsolete through changed or unforeseen circumstances. Thus, a marketing manager's sales goals would obviously be obsoleted if part of his sales territory were transferred to another company in a group. Or the financial manager's interest cost goals might no longer be valid in the light of an unpredictable shift of money rates. Many changes can occur to make goals no longer meaningful.

There are reasons for not wishing to change objectives. If changed too often and too easily, they lose meaning and adequate care in setting them may not be taken. Also, because of the interdependencies of goals, change by one manager may affect those of many other managers. At the same time, if goals are materially obsolete, there is no sense in not changing them. But changes should not be made too easily, and certainly cannot be made without careful consideration of their effects on the entire network of goals.

Failure of Adequate Review, Counselling and Control There is always the danger in a system of managing by objectives that, once objectives are agreed upon, progress toward goal accomplishment will not be adequately monitored by the superior. One of the major advantages to managing of utilizing objectives is that a man has a charter for accomplishment, the appropriate resources and discretion allocated, and he can be given a high degree of freedom of work toward goal achievement. One would not expect his superior to meddle or constantly look over his shoulder. By the same token, however, the superior should not sit back and assume that everything is going well and not check on progress until the date goal achievement is due.

The superior, as well as the subordinate, should have regular information available to him as to how well a subordinate's goal performance is progressing. He should regularly review progress through this information and through personal consultation, and he should make himself available for counselling to help any of his subordinates in meeting goals. This is not, and should not be, taking over the task from his subordinate. It is merely following through with his own job as a manager. Most subordinates will welcome follow up, counselling, assistance with their problems, and aid in removing obstructions to their successful performance.

APPRAISAL OF MANAGERS AGAINST SETTING AND ACHIEVING OBJECTIVES IS NOT ENOUGH

One of the great advantages of a programme of managing by objectives is that, at long last, it gives a device for appraising the performance of managers that is objective, meaningful, and operational. Unlike traditional appraisal systems long used by all types of enterprises, where personal traits and work qualities are the standards of appraisal, evaluating performance against objectives appraises what a man *does* rather than what someone *thinks* of him. As Douglas McGregor pointed out some years ago, traditional appraisals have required "the manager to pass on the personal worth of his subordinates" and thereby be placed in the role of "playing God."[1] While managing by objectives removes much of the subjectivity of appraisal, there is naturally an area of judgment remaining, particularly in determining whether goals are proper and adequate, how adequate goal performance is, and whether reasons for non-performance are acceptable.

As pointed out earlier, goal achievement alone is not an adequate measure of performance of a person in a managerial role. Not only is there the element of luck in achieving goals, there is also the question of other factors to appraise, notably an individual's *managerial* abilities. If it can be conceded that, at least in the long run, the quality and vigour of managing makes the basic difference for the success of an enterprise, then appraisal of performance against objectives is just not enough. We need also means of appraising performance as a *manager*. To be sure, no one should want a manager who has the knowledge and capabilities to manage but cannot perform in the sense of leading his group toward achievement of objectives; nor should we want, for the long run at least, a person in a managerial role who can perform but not know how to manage.

In other words, adequate managerial appraisal should be two pronged: an appraisal of performance against objectives and appraisal of performance as a manager. While a few companies have recognized this, the standards thus far used have been too broad and too susceptible to general judgment. The author has developed and applied for five years in a multinational company a programme to appraise managerial aspects of a man's performance by utilizing key fundamentals of management as checkpoints. It employs a total of 73 checklist questions, grouped under the functions of managing—planning, organizing, staffing, directing, and controlling. Even though these are not completely free of subjectivity, their nature and number open the way to far more objectivity than the more general broad questions usually asked. They at least focus attention on what may be expected of a manager *as a manager*.

While the total programme and the list of questions are too extensive to be dealt with here,[2] some samples can be given. In planning, for example, a manager may be rated by such questions as the following:

- Does he set for his departmental unit both short-term and long-term goals in verifiable terms that are related in a positive way to those of his superior and his company?
- Does he understand the role of company policies in his decision making and assure that his subordinates do likewise?
- Does he check his plans periodically to see if they are consistent with current expectations?

In the area of organizing, such questions are asked as the following:

- Does he delegate authority to his subordi-

[1] "An Uneasy Look at Performance Appraisal," *Harvard Business Review*, vol. 35, no. 3, pp. 89–94 (May–June 1957).

[2] For the complete programme and experience with it, see Harold Koontz, *Appraising Managers as Managers* (New York: McGraw-Hill Book Company, 1971).

nates on the basis of results expected of them?

- Does he teach his subordinates or otherwise make sure they understand the nature and operation of line and staff relationships?
- Does he distinguish in his operations between lines of authority and lines of information?

While this programme is still experimental, it has been a start, at least, in filling the gap in appraisal left by even a good system of managing by objectives. Even though there have been certain difficulties and shortcomings in the programme, it has had the advantage of emphasizing the basics of management in appraisal, of serving as a development tool, and as a device for clarifying communication on management concepts and problems. Above all, of course, it has highlighted the cases of goal performers who succeeded despite poor management.

MAKING MANAGING BY OBJECTIVES EFFECTIVE

By way of summarizing how to make a system of managing by objectives work, a number of suggestions might be given.

1. *Teach the nature and philosophy of the entire system.* Without doing this as a first step for everyone who is in any way involved in the programme, managing by objectives will become a fruitless technique without purpose.
2. *Give managers adequate tools.* In addition to the more obvious requirements of human and material resources to do the job, those who are expected to achieve objectives need clear organization and adequate delegation of authority, planning premises and other guidelines, an understanding of company objectives and strategies, and a clear understanding of the superior's goals and problems.
3. *Recognize the network nature and needs of goals.* Unless goals are seen as an interlocked system, poor co-ordination will surely result. This is an urgent task for every superior.
4. *Insist on verifiability of objectives.* As difficult as this may be, there is no such thing as an actionable and meaningful objective without the highest possible degree of verifiability.
5. *Make goals realistic and attainable.* Goals that are too easy neither command respect nor elicit the best possible performance. Goals that are too difficult or impossible of attainment cause frustration, the slovenly habit of missing targets and disinterest in the system. Perhaps a reasonable rule of thumb is that the "right" level of attainability exists when 75 per cent of goals are achieved.
6. *Recognize time spans in goals.* Some goals should be achieved in a week, others in a month, some in three months, some in a year, and still others for longer periods. Goal setting and accomplishment should not be slavishly forced to coincide with accounting and budgetary periods, but rather with the time span of attainment.
7. *Make goal setting joint.* Although the superior must have the final word on his subordinate's goals, the process of setting them should involve the co-operative working together of both. This is the key to intelligent objectives and the indispensable feeling of commitment to them.
8. *Be willing to change goals.* When circumstances occur to make a goal obsolete, it should be changed to one realistic and actionable, although care must be taken to make sure that the change is accompanied by consideration of its impact on interlocking goals of others.
9. *Institute and maintain a reasonably formal and rigorous review of goals.* Whether at the time goals are set or when performance is appraised, there is benefit of review by an appropriate small group or committee, with the immediate superior having the approval role in the group. Doing this gives an aura of importance to goal setting and performance appraisal, tends to create an environment where the subordinate will feel compelled to do his utmost in preparation, provides a means of having technical assistance available, and can make easier obtaining immediate decisions in problem areas.
10. *See managing by objectives as a system.* Even though the primary force behind managing by objectives may be appraisal, participative management, budgetary assistance, or something else, it should always be regarded as a system or style of managing with many facets and applications.
11. *Be aware that managing by objectives is not all there is to managing.* As crucial as the setting and achieving of objectives is, one should never forget that it does not encompass all there is to managing.

C. PLANNING PREMISES

18 SALES FORECASTING: KEY TO INTEGRATED MANAGEMENT*

William Lazer

Business organizations are increasingly adopting the marketing management concept. This philosophy of business operation places greater emphasis on marketing planning and forces business executives to design marketing strategies and program marketing effort to achieve realistic and predetermined objectives.

Sales forecasting can aid management greatly in implementing the marketing management approach. It is a basis for developing co-ordinated and goal-directed systems of marketing action. The sales forecast is one of the vital tools of marketing planning since adequate planning and the effective deployment of marketing resources are based on sales forecasting data.

Sales forecasting promotes and facilitates the proper functioning of the many segments of a firm's total spectrum of business and marketing activities. It influences almost every other prediction of business operations. It is used in establishing budgets and marketing controls. Sales forecasts help determine various limiting conditions for management decisions and programs and are useful tools for co-ordinating the integral aspects of business operations. They provide bases for evaluating the functioning and productivity of various segments of business activity. They can guide marketing and other business action toward the achievement of implicit and explicit objectives.

This article investigates three aspects of sales forecasting as a key to integrated management action: (1) sales forecasting as a component of the marketing planning process, (2) sales forecasting as a focus for integrative planning, and (3) the basic components and procedures of a comprehensive sales forecasting program.

* Reprinted by permission from *Business Horizons*, Indiana University, vol. 2, no. 3, pp. 61–67, Fall, 1959. Mr. Lazer is professor of marketing in the College of Business and Public Service, Michigan State University.

IN MARKETING PLANNING

Figure 1 illustrates the strategic role of sales forecasting in gathering information for marketing planning. Effective planning of marketing activities can be achieved only if adequate marketing-related information is available. Marketing planning is concerned with the application of analysis and judgment to available information and the prediction of likely occurrences and trends during some future period.

Marketing-related information can refer to either the past or the future. Information about past activities is often referred to as factual information. Information about the future is

FIGURE 1 Sales Forecasting's Role in Marketing Planning

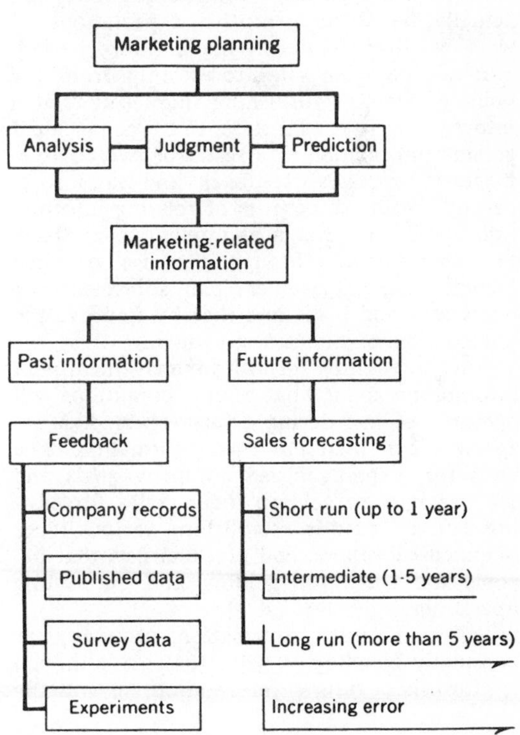

anything but factual, and might be characterized as assumptive. Past information is available to every business if it has an adequate record-keeping process. It is also available from other secondary data sources, such as information reported by governmental bureaus, university research bureaus, and trade associations. Past information may also be assembled through the use of various primary data-gathering research tools, such as surveys and experiments.

Future information requires the utilization of forecasting techniques and processes. Nevertheless, it is based on past data and is usually the result of the application of predictive tools to available past information.

Whenever a business gathers future data, varying degrees of error are bound to exist. Regardless of the forecasting techniques used and the degree of sophistication achieved, future conditions will always deviate to some degree from the predictions of the forecasters. Thus, management must expect future information to contain some error.

For effective marketing planning, both types of information must be available for executive use. From a planning and decision-making point of view, future, or nonfactual, information may be more significant than information about the past. This becomes clear if one considers that plans and decisions made today are actually based on executive expectations of what will happen during some future period.

If we consider sales forecasting from the point of view of furnishing marketing-related information, we can state that management gathers information as a result of two complementary processes: feedback and sales forecasting. Feedback consists of relating information about past events and relationships back to management. Through the use of such factual data, management can adjust existing operations and plans and thereby improve the effectiveness of all business action.

Sales forecasting furnishes management with information about what market conditions will probably be like during a future period. Management can then use this information as a basis for planning broad company goals and the strategies to achieve them. Sales forecasting data are used in establishing various types of potential volume and profit targets that become the bases for guiding and controlling operations.

Past and future information, however, are constantly blending. A sales forecast, although it furnishes future information, eventually takes the form of feedback information. Once this happens, a comparison may be made between actual and forecast sales for a specific period. Through such an audit, deviations may be noted and explanations sought for them. This information can, in turn, help refine the assumptions about future sales forecasts and increase the total effectiveness of the forecasting procedure.

The various predictions made may take the form of short-run sales forecasts of less than a year, intermediate forecasts of from one to five years, and long-run forecasts for periods of more than five years. Generally, the longer range the predictions, the greater the forecasting error.

IN INTEGRATIVE PLANNING

Another facet of sales forecasting and its role in marketing planning is its position in the integrative planning process. A sales forecast is a useful tool for integrating the external business environment with the internal forces of the company. It reduces to workable management dimensions the external business environment over which management has relatively little control. It delimits those constraints that establish the boundaries within which a company must make decisions and operate and translates them into company programs.

Figure 2 portrays sales forecasting as an aid to integrative planning. It indicates the controllable, partially controllable, and noncontrollable factors that management should integrate and take into account in making effective sales forecasts.

The noncontrollable forces determine the broad environmental limits within which the company will operate. These factors include cultural forces, the economic environment, demographic forces, political factors, ethical and social forces, and various international conditions. They cannot be influenced to any degree by company action; at best, they may be recognized and appraised in an intelligent manner.

On Figure 2, broken lines separate the competitive environment and technological factors from other noncontrollable factors. This is to indicate that management action may have some influence over at least these two external forces, which are considered partially controllable factors. However, even though company action can affect competition and technology, the forces *beyond* company control generally have a more significant impact.

FIGURE 2 Sales Forecasting: A Focus for Integrative Planning

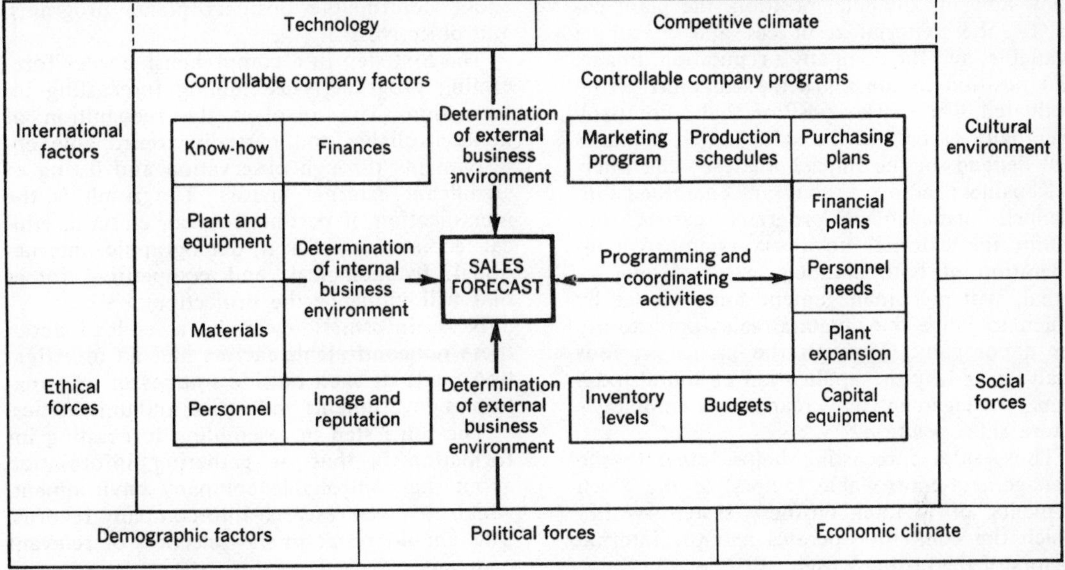

BUSINESS HORIZONS

As forecasts become longer run in nature, the necessity of recording the existing external climate becomes more imperative since, in the future, it will be these noncontrollable factors that set the over-all constraints and boundaries within which companies survive and grow or fail. Through an evaluation and projection of external forces, management attempts to make realistic assumptions about the future environment. These assumptions about noncontrollable and partially controllable factors are the foundations of sales forecasts, and intelligent sales predictions can be made only by implicitly or explicitly assuming relationships about these factors.

Management should not consider this initial step of determining the external company environment as merely a theoretical exercise that is of little use in practical sales forecasting. The external variables are factors that must be dealt with practically and realistically. Their influence cannot be ignored.

As an example of the importance of external forces, consider the development of a controlled shopping center. Several years may elapse from the initiation of the original idea and the first inquiry concerning site location until the actual opening of the center. Choices must be made from among alternative sites, and considerable negotiations may follow to obtain the property and construct and finance the center. Then there are a host of operating details to attend to, including the actual leasing of stores.

The profitability of the total investment and the sales realized by retail stores in the shopping center will be affected by external forces. Existing and potential competition, for example, can have great influence on future sales. Demographic and economic forces in the form of population shifts and income trends will shape the retail sales potential of the center. Existing and potential industrial development of the surrounding territory will influence employment and income and will be reflected in marketing opportunity.

Municipal, state, and federal regulations will have an impact on future pricing tactics, on the use of various promotional devices including trading stamps, on store hours, and even on the types of merchandise that may be sold in particular kinds of stores.

Other examples could be presented concerning such industries as wood products, chemicals, mining, petroleum, transportation, the power industry, and communications.

After determining the external business climate for a future period, the sales forecaster must estimate the impact that internal business factors will make on potential markets. This involves an evaluation of those factors over which the company has direct control. They can be adjusted over the longer run by the company itself.

For an effective forecast, the company's know-how, its financial position, the plant capacity, the material resources and personnel available, and the company's reputation, image, and position in the market place must all be evaluated. The market position that a company eventually earns and the sales that it achieves will depend on the impact made by the internal business factors as they are combined into planned management programs carried out within the external business system. A consideration of both climates, external and internal, will give management some guides by which to judge the potential sales opportunity for a company. Through the use of various analyses and by the application of sound judgment, management may map out a company's future sales position.

Thus, sales forecasting helps integrate the management-controllable factors, or the given elements of a total business system within which the company operates and the internal factors of the business itself.

The sales forecast is also a device by means of which management may integrate its objectives, its operating programs, and its targets with potential market opportunity. This can be done by translating the sales forecast into specific profit and sales-volume goals to be realized in a given future period of time. The sales forecast thus becomes a basis for marketing programs, purchasing plans, financial budgets, personnel needs, production schedules, plant and equipment requirements, expansion programs, and perhaps most other aspects of management programming.

The right half of Figure 2 presents sales forecasting as a vehicle for translating the noncontrollable, partially controllable, and internal business environments into specific controllable management programs. The figure also emphasizes the interrelationships between sales forecasts and company programs.

FORECASTING PROGRAM

Figure 3 outlines the elements of a total sales forecasting program. Four major stages of forecasting, the specific procedures to be followed, and their sequence are presented. These stages are: assembling the forecasting information; evaluating and projecting the data; applying the sales forecast operationally; and auditing the forecast. These four steps are broken down further, and some of the techniques that may be utilized at each stage and the results achieved are described. Figure 3 starts with the noncontrollable business environment and internal business climate and works down through the various predictions about controllable business plans, programs, and objectives.

The first step in a comprehensive sales forecasting program is assembling forecasting information. This involves the recognition of noncontrollable and partially controllable environments through observation and listing of significant external factors. The result is the identification of pertinent social, cultural, ethical, economic, political, demographic, international, technological, and competitive forces that will influence the projections.

Next, information can be assembled about these noncontrollable factors and an investigation made of such outside sources of information as governments, industries, and universities

The third step in assembling forecasting information is that of gathering information about the controllable company environment, which involves research into company records. This should result in the selection of relevant company forecasting information.

After forecasting information has been assembled, the data must be evaluated and projected. This activity has two components: analyzing the data and making the actual forecast. To analyze the data, such analytical tools as time series analysis, least squares methods of fitting a straight line, fitting curves, simple and multiple correlation, the use of input-output tables, and breakeven charts may be used. This leads to the determination of patterns and relationships through lead and lag indicators, cycles, seasonal indexes, trend lines, and measures of covariation.

The actual sales projections may be made through extrapolation, a straight percentage increase in sales, executive opinion polls, end-use analysis, historical analogy, a panel of experts, the grass-roots approach, samples and surveys, models, experiments, hunches, judgments, and the oft-used crystal ball. After these projections have been made, the prediction and definition of future dollar and unit sales, and maximum and minimum sales ranges is possible.

Then the forecast must be applied operationally, which involves refining the sales forecast. This is done by breaking it down on the basis of volume and profit control units by product lines, salesmen, customers, territories, and other managerial units. Specific sales targets can thus be established, and sales forecasting data become the basis for programming marketing, production, purchasing, finance, plant expansion, capital equipment acquisition,

FIGURE 3 A Total Sales Forecasting Program

STAGES OF PROCESS	TECHNIQUES	RESULTS
Assembling information		
Recognize noncontrollable and partially controllable business environment.	Observe and list significant external factors	Identification of pertinent cultural, social, economic, political, demographic, competitive, ethical, international, technological forces
Gather information about noncontrollable and partially controllable forces	Investigate outside sources of information	Selection and gathering of data from government, industry, university research, Federal Reserve Board, company records.
Gather information about controllable forces.	Investigate company records	Selection of relevant company forecasting information
Evaluating and projecting data		
Analyze data	Apply analytical tools: time series analysis, least squares, simple correlation, multiple correlation, input-output tables, break-even charts	Determination of patterns and relationships: lead and lag indicators, cycles, seasonal indexes, trend lines, covariation
Forecast future sales	Employ extrapolation, constant percentage of increase, end-use analysis, executive opinion, historical analogy, panel of experts, grass-roots techniques, surveys, models, experiments, samples, hunches, judgment, and crystal ball	Prediction and definition of future dollar sales, unit sales, maximum and minimum ranges
Operationally applying forecast		
Refine sales forecast	Break sales down by volume and profit control units: product lines, territories, customers, salesmen	Establishment of specific sales targets
Translate specific targets into operational programs	Establish and co-ordinate plans: marketing program, production schedules, purchasing plans, financial requirements, personnel needs, plant expansion, capital equipment budgets, inventory levels	Identification of controllable business environment

FIGURE 3 A Total Sales Forecasting Program (Continued)

STAGES OF PROCESS	TECHNIQUES	RESULTS
Auditing the forecast		
Review forecast	Compare actual and forecast sales regularly and analyze discrepancies	Determination of reasons for deviations
Modify forecast and forecasting procedures	Re-evaluate projections and adjust forecasting techniques	More accurate sales forecasting

personnel, and inventory needs. Controllable business programs have now been really determined.

The last step in a comprehensive sales forecasting program is that of auditing the forecast. This involves reviewing the forecast by comparing actual and forecast sales and analyzing any deviations or discrepancies. The purpose here is to determine the reasons for the deviations. Then future forecasts and even the forecasting techniques can be modified. The end result is more accurate sales forecasts.

The total sales forecasting process is one of refinement. It starts with the more general factors—the external noncontrollable environment and the internal business environment—quantifies them, and finally establishes specific operational goals and targets.

Marketing planning often suffers because management does not develop an effective sales forecasting program. One of the great inducements to ignore or neglect sales forecasting is the difficulty of making predictions. It is a trying task for anyone to try to determine future relationships and their implications for potential sales. It is much more comfortable to turn to the consideration of current operating problems, which are more concrete, are somewhat easier to grasp, and for which some corrective action may be initiated almost immediately.

However, professional marketing management cannot afford to neglect the sales forecasting process. It must become concerned with the development of well co-ordinated, planned, and forceful systems of business action. It must plan the use of company resources so that a firm can establish itself in the market place and grow.

The future marketing climate is likely to be one of keener competition, an exhilarating pace of market change, heavier fixed costs, and an increasing emphasis on innovation. Adequate marketing planning will become the foundation for integrated marketing action. Since one of the basic components of effective marketing planning is sales forecasting, it seems obvious that in the future an increasing amount of time and resources will be spent by companies in developing more adequate sales forecasts.

19 TECHNOLOGICAL FORECASTING IN THE DECISION PROCESS*

Daniel D. Roman

INTRODUCTION

The New Technology Companies in the United States are spending billions of dollars each year to research and develop new products. Technological expansion has vital economic, sociological and political implications.

The economic impact of technology is so great that some industries derive most of their current business from products which did not exist 20 years ago.[1] A study of 11 industries indicated that somewhere from 46 to 100 percent of anticipated short-term corporate growth could be attributed to new products.[2] It is now commonplace for major companies to derive 50 percent or more of current sales from products developed and introduced in the past 10 years.[3]

In a dynamic technology there must be recognition of potential human and capital obsolescence. Productive utilization of new knowledge will affect the demand and supply of present skills and new occupations not yet identifiable will emerge. Additionally, it is reasonably safe to assume that technological pressures will encourage increased interdisciplinary communication.

It is difficult to isolate the economic, sociological and political consequences of technology. It is obvious that economic and sociological factors could not be disassociated from political factors. It is also difficult to do justice to the full range of economic, sociological and political possibilities in a paper of this nature. However, recognition of the extent and direction of technological expansion can help provide the means to minimize disruption, lead to an orderly transition and assist in maximizing the positive aspects of technology.

The impact of technical developments such as lasers, jet aircraft, atomic energy and communication devices, to name a few, has been significant. On the horizon are such developments as new rapid transit systems, mechanical devices to replace human organs,[4] undersea farming and mining, economically useful desalinization of sea water, new synthetic materials for ultra-light construction, automatic language translators, and reliable weather forecasts. Other major technological breakthroughs are not so remote as to preclude planning for integration of these developments.[5]

As we move into a "post industrial society" phase, science and technology will be compelling forces for change.[6] In some environ-

* Reprinted by permission of the publisher from the *Academy of Management Journal*, vol. 13, no. 2, pp. 127–138, June, 1970. Mr. Roman is professor of management science at George Washington University.

[1] *Investing in Scientific Progress, 1961–1970*, Report NSF 61-27 (Washington, D.C: National Science Foundation, 1961), p. 7.

[2] *Management of New Products, 4th ed.*, (New York: Booz, Allen and Hamilton, Inc., 1964), p. 6.

[3] *Ibid.*, p. 2, and *Report of the Joint Economic Committee*, U.S. Congress, 88th Congress, 2nd session, (1964), p. 56.

[4] In the November 1969 issue of *Industrial Research* there is an interesting discussion of the potential use of glassy materials in product design, specifically glass that won't clot blood which could be used for producing artificial organs.

[5] Olaf Helmer, *Social Technology (New York-London:* Basic Books, Incorporated, 1966), pp. 56–57, and "New Products—Setting a Time Table," *Business Week* (May 27, 1967), pp. 52–61. Bright identifies seven technological trends: (1) increasing capability in transportation, (2) increased mastery of energy, (3) increased ability to control the life of animate and inanimate things, (4) increased ability to alter the characteristics of materials, (5) extension of man's sensory capabilities, (6) growing mechanization of physical activities, and (7) increasing mechanization of intellectual processes. James R. Bright, "Directions of Technological Change and Some Business Consequences," appearing in *Automation and Technological Change*, Report of the Assembly Jointly Sponsored by Battelle Memorial Institute and the American Assembly (May 9–11, 1963), pp. 9–22. Also, P. Michael Sinclair, "10 Years Ahead," *Industrial Research* (January 1969), pp. 68–72. Also, William O. Craig, "The Technology of Space—Earth," *Transportation & Distribution Management* (October 1969), pp. 22–26.

[6] Editorial, "Managing Technology," *Science and Technology* (January 1969), pp. 72–73.

ments managers must be alert and plan to compensate for change; in other situations a prime managerial function is to instigate technological change.[7]

In either case the manager must be aware of technological impact and be sensitive to the need for more precise planning for the future. Technological forecasting has been a response to this need.

TECHNOLOGICAL FORECASTING

Technological Forecasting—A Distinction

Technological forecasting, as distinct from general forecasting activity, has been described as "the probabilistic assessment, on a relatively high confidence level, of future technology transfer."[8] According to Jantsch, technology transfer is usually a complex process taking place at different technology transfer levels. These levels can be segregated into development and impact levels and are composed of vertical and horizontal technology transfer components. Vertical transfer of technology progresses through a discovery phase, a creative phase, a substantiate phase, a development phase and an engineering phase. The engineering phase leads to a functional, technological system that could involve a hardware product, a process, or an intellectual concept. Jantsch feels that the extension of the vertical transfer by substantial subsequent horizontal technology transfer represents technological innovation.[9]

Cetron essentially supports Jantsch's definition. He cautions that a technological forecast is not a picture of what the future will bring; it is a prediction, based on confidence, that certain technical developments can occur within a specified time period with a given level of resource allocation. According to Cetron, "the foundation underlying technological forecasting is the level that individual R&D events are susceptible to influence." The periods where these events occur, if they are possible, can be significantly affected by the diversion of resources. Another fundamental of technological forecasting is that many futures can be achieved and the route to these occurrences can be determined.[10]

Exploratory and Normative Forecasting

It is important to recognize the two fundamental types of technological forecasts—exploratory and normative. The exploratory technological forecast starts from the existing base of knowledge and proceeds to the future on the assumption of logical technological progress. Exploratory technological forecasting is passive and primarily an analysis and reporting of anticipations. As a simple illustration, technological development in electronics can be cited. Starting with the post World War II period, transistors have evolved from an expensive and qualitatively unpredictable commodity to a modestly priced, reliable component. If exploratory forecasting were used in the 1940's to target in on this phase of technology, it would have been possible to predict increasing availability, lower price and more extensive use of transistors. The anticipations suggested would have been miniaturization of electronic systems and the potential for a vast number of new products resulting from application, such as portable radios, home appliances, etc.

It would seem that most industrial firms could effectively use exploratory forecasting. Reasonable identification of emerging technology and analysis of technological implications could provide clues for the firm as to competition, possible expansion of existing product lines, related product lines—which the firm should ease into, and new product areas where a foothold could provide a competitive edge. In short, a look into the future would enable better planning, more effective use of resources and considerable avoidance of human and capital obsolescence.

Normative forecasting represents a different approach; it is mission- or goal-oriented. As distinct from exploratory forecasting, normative forecasting is an active or action-directed process.

In the normative method, future objectives are identified exclusive of the fact that technological gaps may currently exist that might act as constraints to attainment of these technological objectives. Normative technological forecasting can provide incentive to technological progress by focusing on the problems to be surmounted and solved. Perhaps the supersonic transport (SST) can be used to demonstrate normative forecasting. At a given time the state of the art for aircraft technology can be determined. It is decided that a need

[7] Marvin J. Cetron and Alan L. Weiser, "Technological Change, Technological Forecasting and Planning R&D —A View From the R&D Manager's Desk," *The George Washington Law Review*, Vol. 36, No. 5, (July 1968), p. 1079.

[8] E. Jantsch, *Technological Forecasting in Perspective*, (Paris: Organization for Economic Cooperation and Development, 1967), p. 15.

[9] *Ibid.*

[10] M. Cetron, "Prescription for the Military R&D Manager: Learn the Three Rx's," unpublished paper presented to The NATO Defense Research Group Seminar on Technological Forecasting and its Application to Defense Research (Teddington, Middlesex, England: (November 12, 1968), p. 2.)

will exist five years from the base period for an aircraft incorporating the SST specifications. On a logical technological progression using exploratory forecasting some technical advancements can be predicted. However, technical gaps appear which indicate that the SST will not be an evolutionary development by the time the need or market will require the product. There are many problems beyond the technical expertise of this author which must be surmounted but some examples could be the development of materials necessary to make flying at supersonic speeds economical, safe and technically feasible.[11] Also, ways must be found to cope with sonic booms so the SST can be used over land routes.

In normative forecasting situations, the analyst works backward from the planned mission operational date and determines the technical obstacles. Normative forecasting could act as a directional force to channel effort and resources. In the example used, these resources would be diverted to solving such problems as the sonic boom or developing new materials. Since resources are limited, normative forecasting could be used in deciding priorities and decisions could be made in conjunction with cost effectiveness studies to determine whether the mission requirements are as critical as presented, are possible within the stipulated time and if the ultimate accomplishment of the mission is worth the resource expenditure.

Normative forecasting has been used primarily by the military, but industrial organizations could possibly use it. With the normative approach, the firm could examine the market potential, explore the technical feasibility, look at its expertise in the area, estimate the cost to accomplish product development and then decide whether the project should be undertaken.

Jantsch contends that presently the most difficult technological forecasting problem is establishing the correct time-frame in normative forecasting. In exploratory forecasting difficulty exists in conceiving an end-effect in the future due to the time covered, but it is relatively simple to prognosticate compared to the normative forecast difficulties. In the normative method the forecast is predicated on objectives, requirements, and sociological factors; the problem is the assumption that present requirements or anticipations are representative of the future.[12]

[11] One such material emerging as a possibility is boron filament which has remarkable strength for its weight. See "Tough Featherweight Plays Hard to Get," *Business Week* (November 15, 1969), p. 38.

[12] Jantsch, *op. cit.* pp. 29–32.

Methodologies of Technological Forecasting

Technological forecasting methods range from naive intuitive approaches to ultra sophisticated procedures.[13] Most of the methods are academic with limited practical adoption. Essentially, the methods can be refined to intuitive, extrapolative and correlative, and logical sequence or network type techniques.

Intuitive forecasting, the most common method employed, can be done individually by genius forecasting or by consensus. Generally this method represents an "educated guess" approach. It can vary from a very naive approach in a localized situation to a broad sampling and consensus of authoritative opinion. Delphi, the best known method under this classification, was developed by Olaf Helmer of the Rand Corporation.

A plethora of methods exist which are essentially variations of PERT. Relevance trees, graphic models, Planning-Programming-Budgeting Systems (PPBS), Mission networks, Decision Trees and Systems Analysis all use network construction to derive technological forecasts.

If numbers are any criteria it would seem that after some variation of Delphi, the network technique is the most popular avenue to technological forecasting. Networks help in identifying and establishing a logical pattern from an existing point to an anticipated goal. An intuitive method, regardless of individual technological perception, might ignore or minimize a significant obstacle to technological attainment. On the other hand, the network system is vulnerable in that all critical events might not be recognized, parallel technology might be ignored or unknown, information may be inaccurate, fragmentary, or misinterpreted (leading to wrong conclusions) and, finally, optimism or pessimism might permeate the forecast.

After examining the multitude of techniques available for technological forecasting, the author is of the opinion that while some methods appear quite scientific on the surface, minute examination almost invariably shows reliance on non-quantifiable and subjective factors before reaching conclusions. Additionally, the rationale of seemingly more sophisticated methods is often difficult to follow and the cost compared to ultimate value of the forecast could also be questioned, all of which

[13] Extensive treatment of technological forecasting methodologies can be found in: M. J. Cetron, *Technological Forecasting* (New York: Gordon and Breach, 1969), Jantsch, *op. cit.*, and J. R. Bright (Ed.), *Technological Forecasting For Industry and Government* (Englewood Cliffs, N.J: Prentice-Hall, Inc., 1968).

might explain the popularity of the Delphi method or its derivatives.

TECHNOLOGICAL FORECASTING AS A MANAGEMENT TOOL

Some General Observations Technological forecasting as an organized management concept is relatively new. The model depicted in Figure 1 shows how technological forecasting might be integrated into the management process. Objectives which represent the initial *raison d'etre* generally become fluid as the organization moves through its operational life cycle. The degree of modification of objectives and the extent of operational flexibility can be dictated by external and internal factors.

In the model, technological forecasting is shown as a prelude to operational activity. Technological forecasting, depending on the nature of the operation, can encompass the universe or it can be used to focus on a relatively small segment of the universe. It can be used by management in probing the general environment and then be refined to help in determining the implications for the industry and the specific organization. As each technological phase is explored, objectives should be reviewed and modified for compatibility with potential accomplishment. From this, procedure strategy can be derived to guide planning, programming, authorization, implementation, control and evaluation.

Advantages and Application The incorporation of technological forecasting into the process of management is an extension of existing methodology. In the past it would appear that management has often intuitively drifted in this direction. Evidence can be advanced to support this contention from the information in Table 1 which shows a condensation of the time gap from innovation to application.

To be useful, technological forecasting does not have to be precise. If an innovation can be identified, and if the innovation can be translated into constructive action within a reasonable and discernible time frame, it can substantially contribute to the decision-making process.

Often, long-term commitments are undertaken on the basis of short-term technology. In many cases inability to anticipate technology leads to built-in obsolescence. Attendant to obsolescence are high modification costs to update facilites and operations, difficulty in selling change to entrenched interests and failure to exploit market potential.

An illustration of potential benefit from technological forecasting would be in product development. The technological forecasters have not yet developed the precise refinement of being able to localize specific innovations within a technological continuum. However, most technologies follow an "S" shaped curve and evaluation of existing and anticipated status of the technology can be meaningful in the decision to undergo or forego investment in product development. The technical scope, cost and time to develop a new product may be attractive or unattractive after technological forecasting information is assembled.

FIGURE 1

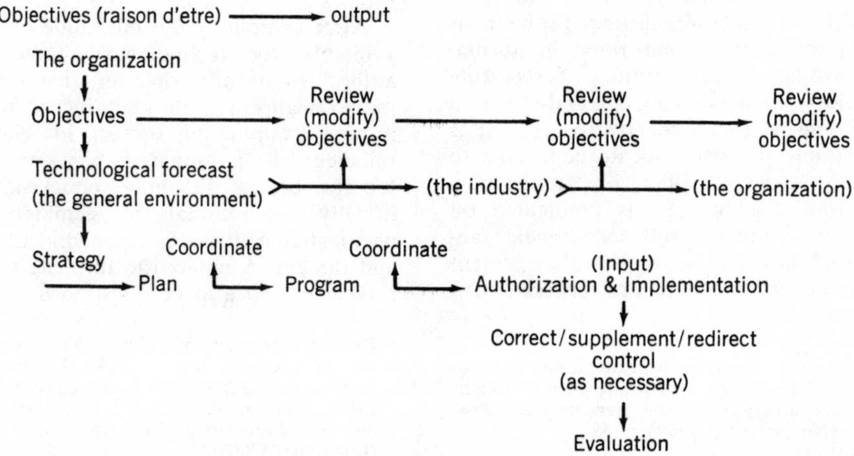

TABLE 1*

INNOVATION	YEAR OF DISCOVERY	YEAR OF APPLICATION
Electric motor	1821	1886
Vacuum tube	1882	1915
Radio broadcasting	1887	1922
X-ray tubes	1895	1913
Nuclear reactor	1932	1942
Radar	1935	1940
Atomic bomb	1938	1945
Transistor	1948	1951
Solar battery	1953	1955
Stereospecific rubbers & plastics	1955	1958

* Seymour L. Wolfbein, "The Pace of Technological Change and the Factors Affecting It," *Manpower Implications of Automation*, Papers presented by U.S. Department of Labor at the O.E.C.D. North American Regional Conference on Manpower Implications of Automation (Washington, D.C.: December 8-10, 1964), p. 19.

Generally, technological forecasting can assist management in several ways. It can represent an organized approach to a selective search for information. It can provoke thought by expanding horizons. It can help provide perspective and facilitate interdisciplinary communication. It can encourage operational sensitivity. It can assist management in determining the magnitude of anticipated change and provide a basis for estimating costs and requirements for people, facilities, equipment, etc. It can aid in giving direction to product development and market penetration. It can assist in recognizing competition and other possible restraints such as natural resources or technological limitations. It can be used to help determine sociological and economic trends.

Limitations Several limitations to technological forecasting should be apparent to the discerning reader. The fact that limitations exist in technological forecasting just as there are limitations in other techniques should not discourage management; awareness should lead to more critical and productive application.

Information may be the greatest limitation to contributive technological forecasting. The information problem is extensive. For instance: What information is needed? How much information is required? Is the information accurate? Have related and unrelated disciplines been explored for possible information transfer or possible technological fallout?

Information interpretation is a vital ingredient in technological forecasting. No mechanical process presently exists which will evaluate the information in terms of available technical solutions, cost and value, product applicability and market potential. Human judgement is a factor in interpreting information and interpretation can be colored by optimism or pessimism and courage or conservatism. Information analysis can also differ due to the competence of the analyst and his functional orientation. Augmenting the difficulties cited is the fact that often pertinent information may not be available due to security restrictions and trade secrets. The unavailability of essential information may negate the entire process by establishing the technological forecast on incomplete or erroneous premises.

Forecasting is far from an exact science, so much so that standard methods and procedures have not been generally established. Although the literature abounds with methodology, in practice, it appears that variations of the Delphi technique and network construction are most commonly used. More exact and understandable techniques must be developed which are practical and provide management with reasonable confidence in their accuracy. However, a standard method may not be feasible since each organization based on its size and mission must develop forecasting techniques to suit its own operational environment.

Another limitation is that unanticipated discovery can lead to demand for a family of products which were previously inconceivable. Good examples are the transistor and the laser. A major discovery can instigate derived demand for related and supporting products and technology and give rise to satellite industries.[14]

Quinn points out that the interaction of many technological breakthroughs could lead to unforeseen prospects which would have a negating effect on all forecasts. He says,

> Similarly, one cannot at present anticipate specifically how biological studies of cellular and molecular coding will interact with extremely high-polymer investigations which are beginning to produce synthetic molecules with many of the characteristics of living organisms. In such advanced areas one can only recognize that there is a strong probability of potential interactions which will increase the importance of both fields, and therefore do more extensive research or monitor such activities more closely.[15]

ORGANIZING FOR TECHNOLOGICAL FORECASTING

Many functions survive in organizations because of defensive management attitudes. Most managements desire a progressive image and as a consequence may install publicized new techniques without really embracing the concept. Utilization failures can often be attributed to management's unwillingness to get involved with things about which they are not familiar, and subsequently have misgivings about. Contributing to this attitude are the practitioners who lose themselves in technique and take little or no pains to translate their work into understandable terms and useful concepts which management would be willing to implement. This represents a very real threat to expanded management acceptance of technological forecasting.

A review of the literature leaves the impression of enamorment with technique. This can be disastrous if substance is sacrificed for method.

Some Organizational Considerations

There are several factors management must consider before commiting itself to technological forecasting. It must look at the type of operation in which it is involved. Is the organization in a technologically sensitive environment? Is the organization a leader or follower in its operational environment? Are operations large and diverse enough to justify commitment to a technological forecasting activity? How extensive a commitment should be made in terms of people, facilities and budget? Would management want sporadic technological forecasts on an informal basis or would there be formal reviews at set intervals? The answer to the last question could dictate the extent of commitment management is willing to make and the type of people it will have to train or recruit. In line with the aforementioned, management will have to select people with compatible skills to achieve technological forecasting objectives. Does management want a group of specialists in a range of technical areas? Does management want a group composed of multi-viewed individuals with broad perspective and minimal functional allegiance? Or is a combination of generalists and specialists more desirable? The range of possibilities is not exhausted because management can use in-house functional specialists in concert with management types to act as a technological forecasting advisory board. Finally, management may not want any internal commitment and may prefer to use outside specialists or consulting organizations to bring in fresh views to reconcile against internal prognostications.

Organizational Location Technological forecasting can be a function or an activity within a function. Several organizational affiliations appear logical such as placement in long-range planning, marketing, materials management or in the research and development group. Technological forecasting can also be elevated to functional status with independent identity.

There are no clear cut answers or universal solutions to organizational location of technological forecasting. Strong arguments can be advanced for affiliation with each of the functions indicated or for independent status. The ultimate answer of placement might be dictated by factors such as functional utilization of the technological forecast or management's orientation. Functional affiliation may lead to high utilization but it can also mean that the technological forecasting activity is functionally captive and narrow in its perspective. A danger in this situation is that technological forecasting may be slanted to support the functional parent rather than provide general direction more compatible with the objectives of the total organization.

There are some compelling advantages to having technological forecasting as an independent operation and functional entity if the size and scope of the organization warrants

[14] J. B. Quinn, "Technological Forecasting," *Harvard Business Review* (March-April 1967), pp. 101–103.

[15] *Ibid.*, p. 102.

technological forecasting. As a non-captive operation it can be used by management for organizational checks and balances and as a directional force in assessing the validity of long-range planning and objectives. It can help in determining what emphasis to place in research and development and to give management insight into the reality of marketing goals. What must be guarded against if technological forecasting has functional independence is excessive cost generated by operational practice inconsistent with the organization's need and capacity.

CONCLUSIONS

Several significant theories and techniques have been incorporated into management practice in the past quarter of a century. Often these ideas have been accepted without critical examination. Adoption without adequate evaluation has, in many instances, initially led to disillusionment and obscured the true value. Uncritical acceptance and over commitment frequently can be attributed to the disciples of innovations who oversell a concept. The fact that all tools are not applicable in all situations, or, where applicable, have differing degrees of utility should not minimize the potential contribution. Management must recognize that no single panacea exists and must judiciously exploit ideas with consideration of the operational environment.

Technological forecasting as a formal concept can be traced back to the mid-1940's. Its present structure and direction took shape around 1960.[16] To date the greatest application and methodology development has been military-oriented. The military services have had encouraging success and indications are for intensification of effort in this area.

The idea of technological forecasting is relatively unknown in business circles. Professor Bright has probably been the most active disciple in promoting technological forecasting to industry. Indications are that inroads are being made. There has generally been enthusiastic reception from those industrial executives exposed to technological forecasting.

Technological forecasting in proper context should seriously be considered as an addition to the management process. As Jantsch so aptly stated,

> Technological forecasting is not yet a science but an art, and is characterized today by attitudes, not tools; human judgment is enhanced, not substituted by it. The development of auxiliary techniques, gradually attaining higher degrees of sophistication (and complexity) since 1960, is oriented towards ultimate integration with evolving information technology.[17]

[16] Jantsch, p. 17.
[17] Jantsch, p. 17.

20 MAKE TF SERVE CORPORATE PLANNING*

Philip H. Thurston

Technological forecasting and corporate planning have one inherent characteristic in common; namely, both seek to improve management decisions in dealing with the uncertainty of future events. And this quickly brings us to the broad purpose of this article: to examine the existing and potential linkage between these two activities.

Although technological forecasting has been well described in the literature, at the outset I should like to emphasize two points:

1. TF is concerned not only with changes that may come from the scientific interests of people but also, and more importantly, with the forces in the environment such as social advances, government regulations, and actions of other corporations that will influence technology.
2. TF can be distinguished from something called "an awareness of technological changes in the environment" inasmuch as it involves the systematic handling of information components so that the combined data may disclose more than the separate parts.

But, in truth, I hold no great brief for definitions. Many business managers have dealt skillfully with technological uncertainty in major, forward-looking decisions without knowledge of what authors have had to say about technological forecasting.

Nevertheless, the fact remains that both practitioners and theoreticians are feeling their way to determine how foresight and technology on the one hand, and formal planning, on the other, may be brought together to improve business decisions. Two recent articles illustrate the growing emphasis on this relationship. In the one, Henry M. Boettinger stated:

> . . . even though individual technological events are unpredictable, one can discern forces shaping probable future developments which will affect the affairs of organizations and persons. Even if they deplore such developments, reasonable men should select strategies which at least prevent severe harm to their enterprises, or, more hopefully, let them harness these forces to positive causes and purposes.[1]

In the other article, Donald R. Schoen included this statement:

> The concept of technological forecasting is beginning to take its place as a promising management tool, to be integrated with long-term planning, market forecasting, and financial forecasting.[2]

In short, these and other writers are in effect stressing the need to "Make TF Serve Corporate Planning." And this article looks at problems and practical ways of doing just that.

NINE FINDINGS

My data come from interviews with executives, planners, and specialists in forecasting; from observation of how some of these managers are doing their jobs; and from my own business experience. As I have gathered this information over time, I have drawn nine tentative findings from it.

1. Infrequent Use *TF is experiencing major difficulties in gaining acceptance as a useful tool in planning and decision making.*

* Reprinted by permission from the *Harvard Business Review,* vol. 49, no. 5, pp. 98–102 (September–October 1971). Mr. Thurston is professor of business administration, Harvard Business School.

[1] "Technology in the Manager's Future," HBR November–December 1970, p. 4.

[2] "Managing Technological Innovation," HBR May–June 1969, p. 167.

The large majority of companies, it appears, are not using technological forecasting; many simply are unaware of the subject, and others see no promise in what they have heard of it. Still other companies have tried technological forecasting but found it to be both expensive and of questionable value.

The small minority of firms—i.e., those that have tried and stuck with technological forecasting and appear to be benefiting, exhibit these characteristics:

- The company's competitive position depends on leadership in technology to a significant degree. Hence foresight about technological matters may be critical.
- The company has done a good job—or has been fortunate—in respect to where the technological forecasting effort fits into the organization and how the men responsible relate to the rest of the organization.
- The technological forecasting itself is kept relatively simple. The more complicated tools either have not been tried or have been replaced by simpler versions.

To illustrate, one planner explained, "We call ours a Delphi forecast, but in fact it is little more than a polling of a panel of experts. The one feature of our approach that may justify the Delphi name is that we do go back to our experts a second time with feedback to see if they wish to modify or carry their opinions further after hearing what others are saying."

Even though technological forecasting is not found broadly, two things are worth noting. First, most companies are making major decisions which carry the implications that judgments have been—or should have been—made about the future of technologies. Second, at a number of companies there is expressed concern with the frequency, as one manager put it, in which "the company is surprised by technological changes—some of these surprises being quite costly."

In short, there is need for technological foresight. But technological forecasting, as practiced, in responding to only a fraction of that need.

2. Sketchy Linkage *Where TF is found, there sometimes is too little interconnection between it and planning.*

More broadly, there is too little linkage between technological forecasting and the decision-making process. In one corporate case, for example, a company engaged in these activities:

- Long-range planning with ten-year horizon.
- Technological forecasting.
- The making of important decisions in the area of technology. (These included choices in research and development work and investments in physical facilities based upon technological processes.)

There were only loose interconnections to be found among the three activities described. At worst, the long-range plan appeared to be used in some instances as a screen behind which unrelated engineering decisions were made. The technological forecasting was conducted by a strong advocate of that approach, but his ideas and findings were discounted to varying degrees or ignored completely. Although extreme in this case, I have found other instances of isolation and distrust of technological forecasting in companies using this tool.

This finding does not pass on the merit of technological forecasting. I simply note that the company cited and some others I am familiar with spend money for technological forecasting and then, to a considerable degree, fail to take the seemingly logical step of relating TF to long-range planning and decision making on technological matters.

3. To-and-fro Relationship *If and when TF is found to be a useful tool at a company, there is need for back-and-forth coordination between it and corporate planning.*

The direction of first influence should be from the corporate planning toward the technological forecasting. It is possible to start forecasts of a technical nature in a great variety of areas. A company should limit such efforts to inquiries which have a chance of influencing the management decision-making process.

The technological forecast itself should subsequently influence the planning process, modifying the overall plan, and suggesting areas of further technological inquiry. This is the back-and-forth relationship expected.

Field observation suggests that in some cases this interrelationship does not exist. At one company, there are corporate planners and technological forecasters who do not communicate with each other. Dysfunctional? Yes. Hard to understand? No. The R&D department undertakes the technological forecasts; the vice president for administration and planning heads the corporate planning function; and no executive insists that the forecasters and the planners work together.

In sum, if technological forecasting is to be of value, it should affect the corporation's decisions. The time dimensions of technological forecasting suggest that this influence should come, in part, by way of corporate planning.

4. Forward-looking Focus *In the planning process, it is of major importance to recognize the decisions which must be made.*

The process, then, is one of working backward to see which tools will improve the quality of these decisions. This approach has wide applicability, but my interest here is in decisions which have, in part, a technological base. For example, if an oil company is considering committing tens of millions of dollars for additional petroleum-processing capacity, this potential action provides a specific focus for forecasts about technological matters.

Further, the time dimensions incorporated in the tools used should be congruent with the time dimensions covered in the decision to be made. Thus in a company where the decisions covering the technological base do not exceed ten years, the technological forecasts should give major emphasis within that time frame.

In a somewhat similar approach, a manager may ask: "What are the key 'sensitivity points' to the success of my existing business (or proposed venture)?" For example, such questioning might have been useful to a canner of tuna fish who suddenly found that he had a plentiful market but only limited supplies of tuna which would pass government inspection for mercury content. After the fact, he asked, "How could I possibly have anticipated this problem?"

The answer: "There is no guaranteed way, but you might have asked, 'What are the realistic major threats to my canning operation?' Failure to meet government inspection standards might then have emerged as one potential threat. That would pinpoint for you a specific area for close scrutiny, monitoring, or forecasting."

Taking this closer to technology, at another company the question becomes: "What are the major assumptions about the future in the area of technology on which the corporation's operations and plans are based?" And the answer pinpoints specific areas requiring careful forward looking analysis. Ansoff and Stewart expressed similar ideas when they advocated a "systematic analysis of what might be termed the technological profile of the company."[3]

5. Broader Opportunities *Not all TF should necessarily be hinged to the company's existing technologies and markets.*

In company after company, one can observe major discontinuities in the technological base —some shifts are highly profitable and others are necessary steps for survival. The new technological directions seem to come (a) through the insight of managers who are sensitive to opportunities, (b) through "bootleg" research and the tinkering of men close to products and operations, and particularly (c) through market pressures and opportunities.

With respect to marketing products based on new technologies, one manager described the difference between "technology-forward" and "market-back" by saying, "Working from technology forward to the market, we filled a whole warehouse with product ideas based on what technology could do. But none sold. Then, we worked from market opportunities back to what could be developed and came up with several successful products."

What all this means for technological forecasting is that in addition to emphasis on the future of a company's existing technological base and market, there may be some small forecasting effort which searches more broadly for technological opportunities.

I believe that the payoff from such broader forecasting comes not through the systematic study of the many possible areas of analysis; that would be too expensive. Rather, the payoff comes through a heightened sensitivity to, and judgment about, technological opportunities which a small amount of systematic study may develop in managers. This is a way of leaving the door open a little wider for "technological breakthroughs."

6. Individual Advocacy *The acceptance and useful application of TF currently results largely from individual advocacy, rather than from broad acceptance of the idea within an organization.*

This reflects the state of the art, particularly the limited understanding of technological forecasting and the varying abilities of different individuals interested in it. The idea of individual advocacy is not new. Industry has relied in part on individual advocacy in judging the values of research and development projects. In contrast, industry has seen broad acceptance in the adoption of some tools such as cash budgeting, and may be seeing broad acceptance of others such as the application of probabilities in business decision making.

Technological forecasting, a more complex and in some ways a subjective approach, is not being embraced equally warmly. Individual advocacy continues to be important.

But it seems to make a difference who the advocate is or how he relates his work to other corporate activities. In a company where a division general manager had an interest in tech-

[3] H. Igor Ansoff and John M. Stewart, "Strategies for a Technology-Based Business," HBR November–December 1967, p. 83.

nological forecasting, this tool contributed, as might be expected, to the division's planning activity.

In another company, a staff man engaged in technological forecasting learned the lesson of phrasing his findings in the language and from the point of view of the company's chief line managers. The acceptance and use of his staff work was well above that of technological forecasts made at other companies by men who focused on the tools they were using and paid less attention to communications.

7. More Line Emphasis *The writers on TF have done a better job in communicating to specialists than to line managers, and the latter are poorly informed on this subject.*

Understanding of technological forecasting by line managers is important. One reason is that the specialists' skills do not appear to be used to good advantage until the line managers understand the specialists' work and can better direct, participate in, and evaluate the forecasting effort.

There is also a more important reason. I too doubt the value of more than a very small *staff* effort committed to technological forecasting—perhaps in some cases as little as part time of one staff man. The returns do not seem to justify high costs. But at the same time I feel that men with *line* responsibility must develop their skills in dealing more systematically, with a more open mind, and hence more effectively with future technological considerations.

A few line managers are looking to the tools of technological forecasting as important resources to this end. They appear interested in some instances in the rigorous application of tools, particularly the simpler tools such as curve fitting. In other instances, line managers appear to study the methodologies of technological forecasting in order to translate these rigorous approaches into their own nonrigorous approach (I prefer to call this a "more objective judgmental approach") to their own unique technological problems.

Why more line, and not more staff, emphasis? The line managers I am talking about are responsible for very high cash flows closely related to the technologies used and anticipated. For these men, it is critical to make informed decisions on technical matters reaching into the future.

Naturally, these line managers are closer to the technological problems. They can screen data more quickly, and they may improve their sense for judging interrelationships. With a little effort these men can "scan" for input data as a logical part of their regular work.

8. Better Communication *Forward-looking judgments about technology are best understood by particular "islands" of people within an organization.*

Communication of their feeling for future technological events is more difficult than is communication of judgments on other business matters.

Many business judgments are reducible to dollar figures, and these may be modified by probability statements to yield expected values. Such information is readily understandable as it moves to different decision-making points in a company. This is not equally true when dealing with technological uncertainties. It is difficult to communicate the feelings about uncertainties that exist throughout a complicated "matrix" of interrelated technical and market questions, on which the major technological uncertainty rests.

This suggests two paths for further inquiry: (a) developing and improving the communication means; and (b) reducing the need for communication outside the island of knowledgeable people by more effectively involving them in reaching the decision which is in question.

9. Stronger Motivation *The corporate reward and penalty system makes insufficient allowance for contributions in long-range assessment of technological changes.*

Usually, corporations pay men on the basis of their performance in a single or a very few years. When passing out rewards, the company often has a very short memory as to who foresaw, or who failed to foresee, technological changes.

Hence the reward and penalty system gives a man little incentive to devote his energies to developing technological foresight. This is not to say that there is negative motivation. Rather, there simply is lack of strong positive motivation for anticipating technological changes well in advance.

CONCLUDING NOTE

In these nine tentative findings, I do not see a major call for much effort (and expense) in technological forecasting related to corporate planning. Rather, I see a cautious movement with some growing momentum. Of course, the end product is not technological forecasts; it is better decisions. Technological forecasting is a set of tools—partly proven and partly promising—which to varying degrees are influencing and replacing the judgments of managers.

In fact, a great deal of "technological forecasting" is actually occurring in the guise of "managerial judgment." This is a highly appropriate way of dealing with the uncertainty of future technological events, until managerial judgment may be *supplemented* reliably by more rigorous approaches.

My closing comment looks not forward but to the past. There is a need to study more closely the technological content of key corporate decisions—a crude audit of completed decisions. Study both the affirmative decisions that may show in the corporate records and decisions made by default that are implied by failure to take action. The last step in the audit is for the executives concerned to decide if they are satisfied with how well the planning process in their organization deals with technological uncertainties.

D. DECISION MAKING AND OPERATIONS RESEARCH

21 THE ENVIRONMENT OF DECISION*

Chester I. Barnard

The acts of individuals may be distinguished in principle as those which are the result of deliberation, calculation, thought, and those which are unconscious, automatic, responsive, the results of internal or external conditions present or past. In general, whatever processes precede the first class of acts culminate in what may be termed "decision." Involved in acts which are ascribed to decision are many subsidiary acts which are themselves automatic, the processes of which are usually unknown to the actor.

When decision is involved there are consciously present two terms—the end to be accomplished and the means to be used. The end itself may be the result of logical processes in which the end is in turn a means to some broader or more remote end; or the immediate end, and generally the ultimate end, may not be a result of logical processes, but "given"—that is, unconsciously impressed—by conditions, including social conditions past or present, including orders or organizations. But whenever the end has been determined, by whatever process, the decision as to means is itself a logical process of discrimination, analysis, choice—however defective either the factual basis for choice or the reasoning related to these facts. . . .

I. THE OCCASIONS OF DECISION

The making of decisions, as everyone knows from personal experience, is a burdensome task. Offsetting the exhilaration that may result from correct and successful decision and the relief that follows the terminating of a struggle to determine issues is the depression that comes from failure or error of decision and the frustration which ensues from uncertainty. Accordingly, it will be observed that men generally try to avoid making decisions, beyond a limited degree when they are rather uncritical responses to conditions. The capacity of most men to make decisions is quite narrow, although it is a capacity that may be considerably developed by training and especially by experience.

The executive is under the obligation of making decisions usually within approximately defined limits related to the position he has accepted; and is under the necessity of keeping within the limits of his capacity if he is continuously to discharge this obligation. He must, therefore, to be successful, distinguish between the occasions of decision in order to avoid the acceptance of more than he can undertake without neglecting the fields to which his position relates. For the natural reluctance of other men to decide, their persistent disposition to avoid responsibility, and their fear of criticism, will lead them to overwhelm the executive who does not protect himself from excessive burdens of decisions if he is not already protected by a well regulated and habitual distribution of responsibilities.

It is for this reason necessary in the making of decisions to maintain a balance between the fields from which the occasions of them arise. I suppose this is rarely a matter of conscious selection, and is probably subject to no general rules. It involves in itself important decisions. For our purposes, however, it may be helpful to note that the occasions for decision originate in three distinct fields: (a) from authoritative communications from superiors; (b) from cases referred for decision by subordinates; (c) from cases originating in the initiative of the executive concerned.

(a) Occasions for decisions are frequently furnished by instructions or by general requirements of superior authority. Such decisions

* Reprinted by permission of the publisher from Chester I. Barnard, *The Functions of the Executive* Harvard University Press, Cambridge, Mass., 1938, pp. 185, 189–198, 201–205. Copyright 1938 by the President and Fellows of Harvard College; 1966 by Grace F. Noera Barnard. Mr. Barnard was formerly president of the New Jersey Bell Telephone Company and the Rockefeller Foundation; before his death in 1961, he was also a member of the New York City Board of Education and a director of several business corporations and foundations.

relate to the interpretation, application, and distribution of instructions. These occasions cannot be avoided, though the burden may be reduced by delegation of responsibility to subordinates. They involve serious decisions when the instructions seem morally wrong, harmful to the organization, or impossible of execution.

(b) The cases referred for decision may be called appellate cases. They arise from incapacity of subordinates, uncertainty of instructions, novelty of conditions, conflict of jurisdiction or conflicts of orders, or failure of subjective authority. The control of the number of appellate cases lies in adequacy of executive organization, of personnel, of previous decision; and the development of the processes of informal organization. The test of executive action is to make these decisions when they are important, or when they cannot be delegated reasonably, and to decline the others.

(c) The occasions of decision on the initiative of the executive are the most important test of his capacity. Out of his understanding of the situation, which depends upon his ability and initiative, and on the character of the communication system of his organization, it is to be determined whether something needs to be done or corrected. To decide that question involves not merely the ordinary elements but the executive's specific justification for deciding. For when the occasions for decision arise from above or below the position of the executive, others have in advance granted him authority; but when made on his own initiative, this always may be (and generally is) questioned, at least tacitly (in the form whether decision was necessary, or related to scope of obligations, etc.). Moreover, failure to decide is usually not specifically subject to attack, except under extreme conditions. Hence there is much incentive to avoid decision. Pressure of other work is the usual self-justification. Yet it is clear that the most important obligation is to raise and decide those issues which no one else is in a position to raise effectively.

From the point of view of the *relative* importance of specific decisions, those of executives properly call for first attention. From the point of view of *aggregate* importance, it is not decisions of executives but of non-executive participants in organization which should enlist major interest. Indeed it is precisely for this reason that many executive decisions are necessary—they relate to the facilitation of correct action involving appropriate decisions among others. In large measure this is a process of providing for the clear presentment of the issues or choices. At any event, it is easily evident merely from the inspection of the action of the non-executive participants in organization that coordination of action requires repeated organization decisions "on the spot" where the effective action of organization takes place. It is here that the final and most concrete objectives of purposes are found, with the maximum of definiteness. There is no further stage of organization action. The final selection of means takes place at this point.

It should be noted, however, that the types of decisions as well as the conditions change in character as we descend from the major executive to the non-executive positions in organization. At the upper limit decisions relating to ends to be pursued generally require the major attention, those relating to means being secondary, rather general, and especially concerned with personnel, that is, the development and protection of organization itself. At intermediate levels the breaking of broad purposes into more specific ends and the technical and technological problems, including economic problems, of action become prominent. At the low levels decisions characteristically relate to technologically correct conduct, so far as the action is organization action. But it is at these low levels, where ultimate authority resides, that the *personal* decisions determining willingness to contribute become of relatively greatest aggregate importance.

II. THE EVIDENCES OF DECISION

Not the least of the difficulties of appraising the executive functions or the relative merits of executives lies in the fact that there is little direct opportunity to observe the essential operations of decision. It is a perplexing fact that most executive decisions produce no direct evidence of themselves and that knowledge of them can only be derived from the cumulation of indirect evidence. They must largely be inferred from general results in which they are merely one factor, and from symptomatic indications of roundabout character.

Those decisions which are most directly known result in the emission of authoritative communications, that is, orders. Something is or is not to be done. Even in such cases the basic decision may not be evidence; for the decision to attempt to achieve a certain result or condition may require several communications to different persons which appear to be complete in themselves but in which the controlling general decision may not be disclosed.

Again, a firm decision may be taken that does not result in any communication whatever for the time being. A decision properly timed must be made in advance of communicating it, either because the action involved must wait anticipated developments or because it cannot be authoritative without educational or persuasive preparation.

Finally, the decision may be not to decide. This is a most frequent decision, and from some points of view probably the most important. For every alert executive continually raises in his own mind questions for determination. As a result of his consideration he may determine that the question is not pertinent. He may determine that it is not now pertinent. He may determine that it is pertinent now but that there are lacking adequate data upon which to base a final decision. He may determine that the question is pertinent, can be decided, will not be decided except by himself, and yet it would be better that it be not decided because his competence is insufficient.

The fine art of executive decision consists in not deciding questions that are not now pertinent, in not deciding prematurely, in not making decisions that cannot be made effective, and in not making decisions that others should make. Not to decide questions that are not pertinent at the time is uncommon good sense, though to raise them may be uncommon perspicacity. Not to decide questions prematurely is to refuse commitment or attitude or the development of prejudice. Not to make decisions that cannot be made effective is to refrain from destroying authority. Not to make decisions that others should make is to preserve morale, to develop competence, to fix responsibility, and to preserve authority.

From this it may be seen that decisions fall into two major classes, positive decisions—to do something, to direct action, to cease action, to prevent action; and negative decisions, which are decisions not to decide. Both are inescapable; but the negative decisions are often largely unconscious, relatively non-logical, "instinctive," "good sense." It is because of the rejections that the selection is good. The best of moves may be offset by a false move. This is why time is usually necessary to appraise the executive. There is no current evidence of the all-important negative decisions. The absence of effective moves indicates failure of initiative in decision, but error of action probably often means absence of good negative decisions. The success of action through a period of time denotes excellence of selection and of rejection of possible actions.

III. THE NATURE OF THE ENVIRONMENT

Whatever the occasions or the evidences of decision, it is clear that decisions are constantly being made. What is the nature of the environment of decisions, the materials with which they deal, the field to which they relate? It consists of two parts: (a) purpose; and (b) the physical world, the social world, the external things and forces and circumstances of the moment. All of these, including purpose, constitute the objective field of decision; but the two parts are of radically different nature and origin. The function of decision is to regulate the relations between these two parts. This regulation is accomplished either by changing the purpose or by changing the remainder of the environment.

(a) We may consider purpose first. It may seem strange perhaps that purpose should be included in the objective environment, since purpose of all things seems personal, subjective, internal, the expression of desire. This is true; but *at the moment of a new decision,* an existing purpose, the result of a previous decision under previous conditions, is an objective fact, and it is so treated at that moment in so far as it is a factor in new decision.

This is especially true because organization decisions do not relate to personal purposes, but to organization purposes. The purpose which concerns an organization decision may have been given as a fact to and accepted as such by the person who is responsible for making a new decision. But no matter how arrived at, when decision is in point, the purpose is fact already determined; its making is a matter of history; it may be as objective as another man's emotions may be to an observer.

We must next note, however, that purpose is essential to give any meaning to the rest of the environment.[1] The environment must be looked at from *some* point of view to be intelligible. A mere mass of things, atoms, movements, forces, noises, lights, could produce some response from a sensitive creature or certainly would have some

[1] I am under the impression that in a general way both the form of expression and the concepts stated in the next several paragraphs were derived from or influenced by A. N. Whitehead's *Process and Reality.*

effect on it, or on other things, but the reduction of this mass of everything to something significant requires a basis for discrimination, for picking out this and that as pertinent, relevant, and interesting. This basis is that in *this* situation something is or is not to be done. The situation aids, obstructs, or is neutral from *this* point of view. The basis for this discrimination is a purpose, an end, an object to be accomplished.

Purpose itself has no meaning, however, except in an environment. It can only be defined in terms of an environment.[2] Even to want to go somewhere, anywhere, supposes some kind of environment. A very general purpose supposes a very general undifferentiated environment; and if the purpose is stated or thought of it must be in terms of that general environment. But when formed, it immediately (if it is not in suspense or dormant, so to speak) serves for reducing that environment to more definite features; and the immediate result is to change purpose into a more specific purpose. Thus when I decide I want to go from A to B my idea of terrain is vague. But as soon as I have decided, the terrain becomes less vague; I immediately see paths, rocks, obstacles that are significant; and this finer discrimination results in detailed and smaller purposes. I not only want to go from A to B, but I want to go this way, that way, etc. This constant refinement of purpose is the effect of repeated decisions, in finer and finer detail, until eventually detailed purpose is contemporaneous accomplishment. But similarly with each new edition of purposes, a new discrimination of the environment is involved, until finally the last obstacle of progressive action represents a breaking up of a general purpose into many concrete purposes, each as it is made almost simultaneously associated with the action. The thing is done as soon as decided; it becomes a matter of history; it constitutes a single step in the process of experience.

Thus back and forth purpose and environment react in successive steps through successive decisions in greater and greater detail. A series of final decisions, each apparently trivial, is largely accomplished unconsciously and sums up into an effected general purpose and a route of experience.

(b) We may now consider the environment of decision exclusive of purpose. It consists of atoms and molecules, agglomerations of things in motion, alive; of men and emotions; of physical laws and social laws; social ideas; norms of actions, of forces and resistances. Their number is infinite and they are all always present. They are also always changing. They are meaningless in their variety and changes except as discriminated in the light of purpose. They are viewed as static facts, if the change is not significant from the viewpoint of the purpose, or as both static and dynamic facts.

This discrimination divides the world into two parts; the facts that are immaterial, irrelevant, mere background; and the part that contains the facts that apparently aid or prevent the accomplishment of purpose. As soon as that discrimination takes place, decision is in bud. It is in the state of selecting among alternatives. These alternatives are either to utilize favorable factors, to eliminate or circumvent unfavorable ones, or to change the purpose. Note that if the decision is to deal with the environment, this automatically introduces new but more detailed purposes, the progeny, as it were, of the parent purpose; but if the decision is to change the purpose rather than deal with the environment, the parent is sterile. It is abandoned, and a new purpose is selected, thereby creating a *new* environment in the light of *that* purpose.

This looks like metaphysical speculation if one thinks of it as individual and personal—undemonstrable assumptions, speculative reasoning. But it can be observed in an organization, at least sufficiently to corroborate it roughly. Thus if the president of a telephone company for good reasons orders[3] two poles carrying a cable removed from the north side of First Street between A and B Streets to the opposite side of First Street, it can, I think, be approximately demonstrated that carrying out

[2] Care should be taken to keep in mind that environment throughout does not mean merely physical aspects of the environment, but explicitly includes social aspects, although physical rather than other aspects are used for illustration as simpler. In many organizations, however, the physical aspects are constant and it is the social aspects which are pertinent. This is the case especially when the purpose is a concrete expression of social ideas or attitudes, as, for example, in ritualistic types of action whether religious or political.

[3] Partly to illustrate several statements in this essay I may say that it is necessary to imagine extreme conditions to suppose he would issue such an order. Ordinarily what he would do would be to inquire whether it would be feasible to take the action suggested, or what would be involved in doing so, or he would state the problem and ask for its solution, etc. The executive art is nine-tenths inducing those who have authority to use it in taking pertinent action.

that order involves perhaps 10,000 decisions of 100 men located at 15 points, requiring successive analyses of several environments, including social, moral, legal, economic, and physical facts of the environment, and requiring 9000 redefinitions and refinements of purpose, and 1000 changes of purpose. If inquiry be made of those responsible, probably not more than a half-a-dozen decisions will be recalled or deemed worthy of mention—those that seemed at the moment difficult or momentous, or that were subject to question or proved erroneous. The others will be "taken for granted," all a part of the business or knowing one's business. However, a large part of the decisions, purposes, and descriptions and analyses of the various environments will be a matter of record—short-cut, abbreviated, to be sure, but marking the routes of decisions with fair definiteness. Only in the case of individual workmen shall we be almost completely reduced to speculation as to the number and character of the decisions required, because many of them certainly will relate to the physiological action. . . .

IV. THE THEORY OF OPPORTUNISM

The opportunistic element refers to the objective field within which action must take place. The process of decision so far as it relates to this objective field is essentially one of analysis, even though in practice much of the process will be intuitive or not conscious. The analysis of present circumstances is in part the definition of purpose in immediate terms; but it is also the process of finding what present circumstances are significant with reference to that purpose. What events, what objects, what conditions aid, what prevent, the attainment of purpose?

This analysis will lead to the rejection from present interest or attention of most of the innumerable events, objects, details, circumstances of the situation, since under the conditions they are irrelevant to the purpose. This, of course, is sometimes an easy, sometimes a difficult task. It is easy if it has been done before for similar circumstances, if it yields to an established technique of analysis, if it is a solved scientific problem. It is difficult if it is novel, if there is no technique, or no science. For then the analysis is in effect partly unaided surmise, hypothesis, assumption. This fact, even when the decider is aware of it, does not permit escape from decision, though it may lead to negative decision, that is, to decision not to decide the question for the present. Hence, there is no escape from *some* decision once the process of setting up purpose against environment has begun.

The analysis required for decision is in effect a search for the "strategic factors." The notion of the "strategic factor," a term I borrow from Professor John R. Commons,[4] is related to the term "limiting factor" which is common in scientific work. Professor Commons' use of the word is restricted to certain aspects of managerial and bargaining operations in economic systems, but the restriction to this field is unnecessary; the principle involved is the same in whatever circumstances decision is required. The theory of the strategic factor is necessary to an appreciation of the process of decision, and therefore to the understanding of organization and the executive functions as well as, perhaps, individual purposive conduct. As generally as I can state it, this theory is as follows:

If we take any system, or set of conditions, or conglomeration of circumstances existing at a given time, we recognize that it consists of elements, or parts, or factors, which together make up the whole system, set of conditions, or circumstances. Now, if we approach this system or set of circumstances, with a view to the accomplishment of a purpose (and only when we so approach it), the elements or parts become distinguished into two classes: those which if absent or changed would accomplish the desired purpose, provided the others remain unchanged; and these others. The first kind are often called limiting factors, the second, complementary factors. Moreover, when we concentrate our attention upon a *restricted* or subsidiary system or set of circumstances, we often find, on the basis of previous experience or knowledge, that the circumstances fail to satisfy the requirements of purpose because they lack an additional element or elements, that is, elements which are known to exist in the *larger* environment. These are likewise limiting factors.

The limiting (strategic) factor is the one whose control, in the right form, at the right place and time, will establish a new system or set of conditions which meets the purpose. Thus if we wish to increase the yield of grain in a certain field and on analysis it appears that the soil lacks potash, potash may be said to be the strategic (or limiting) factor. If a tank of water is to be used for cleaning purposes, and is found to contain sediment, the sediment is the strategic (limiting) factor in the use of the water for cleaning. If a machine

[4] John R. Commons, *Institutional Economics*, The Macmillan Company, New York, 1934, *passim*, but especially chap. 9, pp. 627–633.

is not operable because a screw is missing, the screw is the strategic (limiting) factor.[5]

Where the crucial element or part present or absent is a thing or physical element or compound or ingredient it is convenient to call it "limiting" factor; but when personal or organizational action is the crucial element, *as it ultimately is in all purposive effort,* the word "strategic" is preferable. This preference relates to a distinction in the use of the analysis. If its purpose is knowledge for its own sake, that is, if the purpose is immediately scientific, the term "limiting factor" conveys the relatively static situation of the analyst. If the purpose is not knowledge but decision as to action, "strategic factor" conveys the relatively changing position of the analyst, in which the subjective aspects of decision interact with the objective field in which it is developed.

The fact that a strategic factor is always involved is overlooked because the personal or organization action required often seems trivial; the necessary effort is less than that required to analyze the situation or system. For example, it may require great effort to determine that the land needs potash, but little effort to get the potash. Nevertheless, when the need has been determined, a new situation has arisen because of the fact of knowledge or the assumption that potash is the limiting factor; and instead of potash, the limiting factor *obtaining* potash then becomes the strategic factor; and this will change progressively into *obtaining* the money to *buy* potash, then *finding* John to *go* after potash, then *getting* machines and men to *spread* potash, etc., etc. Thus the determination of the strategic factor is itself the decision which at once reduces purpose to a new level, compelling search for a new strategic factor in the new situation. Says Commons:

> But the limiting and complementary factors are continually changing places. What was the limiting factor becomes complementary, when once it has come under control; then another factor is the limiting one. The limiting factor, in the operation of an automobile, at one time may be the electric spark; at another the gasoline; at another the man at the wheel. This is the meaning of efficiency—the control of the changeable limiting factors at the right time, right place, right amount, and right form in order to enlarge the total output by the expected operation of complementary factors.[6]

If we rephrase this last sentence to accord with our terminology and our broader subject, it will read: "This is the meaning of effective decision—the control of the changeable strategic factors, that is, the exercise of control at the right time, right place, right amount, and right form so that purpose is properly redefined and accomplished."

Professor Commons continues:

> But out of the complex happenings, man selects the limiting factors for his purposes. If he can control these, then the other factors work out the effects intended. The "cause" is volitional control of the limiting or strategic factors. . . . The "effects" are the operations of the complementary factors. . . .

With the distinctions in phraseology which Commons makes for his purposes we are not concerned. I think it sound to say that the strategic factor always determines the *action* that is controlling, even in the case of what he calls the limiting factor. It is not the element that is missing but the action that could procure the missing element that is the controlling factor. To determine what element should be changed or is missing is the first step in defining the *action* required. Decision relates to *action,* whether it be in the field of business transactions, political transactions, mechanical operations, chemical combinations, scientific experimentation, or whatever relates to accomplishment of intention.

The strategic factor is, then, the center of the environment of decision. It is the point at which choice applies. To *do* or not to do *this,* that is the question. Often there are tentatively several strategic factors, any one of which meets the immediate situation or satisfies the necessity of immediate purpose. This expands the horizon into the less immediate future, increases the objective field. The final strategic selection will be made on the basis of the estimate of less immediate future consequences.

[5] There may be more than one limiting factor, in which they may all be taken as a limiting set, or broken down to single factors for action in some order.

[6] Commons, *op. cit.,* p. 629.

22 NEW TOOLS FOR DECISION MAKING*

David B. Hertz

The effective use of management science greatly changes the content and structure of the management decision-making process in business and government. This can have an almost traumatic effect on some executives, giving them the unsettling feeling that decision making is being taken out of their experienced hands and turned over to an impersonal machine. Even more unsettling, even to those who understand that scientific decision procedures increase rather than reduce the scope of creative intuition, is the sheer range of problems to which management science can be applied—a range so great that it ultimately takes in virtually all of a company's or institution's activities.

Experienced executives are indeed justified in believing that increasing use of management science methods will substantially change the way decisions are made in their companies. Some decisions they used to make will no longer be worth their time. On the other hand, careful reflection will make it abundantly clear that man-made decisions have not become obsolete. On the contrary, there will be more human decisions, even more comprehensive and exciting, to be made. These decisions will have greater significance and will require greater effort and more creativity than ever before. The creative executive's scope of operation will be expanded, not diminished. Further, the ability of the hard-hitting, results-oriented organization to achieve its objectives effectively and efficiently will be enormously enhanced. And such organizations will be more exciting places to work than those that have ignored the potential of the management sciences and computer systems.

Because fear among executives can so easily balk a company's efforts to benefit from management science, it is important to understand how management sciences and computers actually do affect corporate decision making. Scientific, nonintuitive methods can gradually change the structure of decisions at the executive level, making some routine and eliminating them from successively higher management levels, and substituting for them entirely new and potentially more creative decisions. Thus, the executive is freed to devote himself to decisions of more significance and scope.

Continuous load dispatching in an electric utility provides a good historical example. In an electric utility, boilers and generators are cut in and out and turbines are loaded or shut down as actual and projected loads change from hour to hour, or even from minute to minute. The profitability of a utility company is directly affected by load dispatching decisions. Yet it is not likely that management would make these load dispatching decisions today because they are being made much better by automated methods. It will be instructive to examine how load dispatching has evolved from "executive" to "automated" decisions.

In the era of the small, local electric utility with a few generators and power units, changes in load were met (or not met) by imprecise adjustments, often after consultation or discussion with management. As systems grew larger and more complex, economic and engineering analyses of the profitability of various kinds of load control became common, and the load dispatchers began to assume more and more of the prerogative of deciding how to accommodate the changes. Management simply indicated the objectives, restrictions, and policies that it desired the load dispatchers to meet or follow.

Using tools similar to those of today's management scientists, utility managements soon began to develop means to record and analyze the results of past decisions and to better define the economics—thermal and electrical—of alternative choices in a given situation. The development and codification of these methods suggested that the load dispatcher could be replaced in part by a computer. The result was one of the earliest computerized management applications.

* Reprinted by permission of the publisher from *New Power for Management*, McGraw-Hill Book Company, New York, 1969, pp. 15–29. Copyright 1969 by McGraw-Hill, Inc. Mr. Hertz is a principal and director of McKinsey and Company, International Management Consultants.

The next step was for the load dispatcher's job to become simply the supplying of the necessary parameters into a computer that, acting on current operating data, either indicates or actually makes the best load allocations under the circumstances. Management no longer even suggests the parameters. The new, important management task is, of course, to decide whether to buy a bigger and better automatic load analyzer and to tie more units into an integrated network. Such decisions, based on the ability to analyze the pattern of probable demands and evaluate the probable economic and technical effects on a very complex system, are of a higher order than earlier ones.

Some of the important management science techniques actually stem from work done in utility and communications systems analysis. The phrase "systems analysis," commonly used to describe some applications of management science, probably owes its origin to this field (rather than to the area of office "systems and procedures").

Gradually up until World War II and very rapidly since, quantitative methods have been extended to ever larger areas of management decision making. Empirical knowledge of cost/revenue relationships has been increasing; so has theoretical understanding of the economic effects of decisions. Analytical methods, or *algorithms,* have been developed for quantitative evaluation of alternative decisions. Computers programmed for management science approaches have begun to be routinely applied to specific situations. And, as a result, management has begun to get greater profit leverage from better and more timely decisions.

Together, these developments are slowly shifting the emphasis of top-management decision making from simply deciding upon specific operating alternatives to the more complex and more rewarding approach of selecting the means for applying methods of analyzing decisions problems, choosing among alternative analyses, and finally determining ways of implementing the results of the analyses. Since the manner in which these analyses result in algorithms, or "rules," for decision making seems to be the key to improved decisions, examples will be helpful.

ALGORITHMS FOR DECISION MAKING

An algorithm is simply a set of rules for carrying out some numerical calculation that is intended to yield the same result no matter by whom or when applied. Thus, rules for ordinary arithmetic—e.g., addition, subtraction, division—are algorithms. There can, of course, be different algorithms for the same operation: for example, performing long division and finding square roots. Computers are generally used to apply algorithms to decision problems.

The choice among algorithms that accomplish exactly the same numerical operation is a matter of convenience and efficiency, but the choice among those management science algorithms aimed at providing decision rules for the same management objective can be a serious decision that will require an understanding of the underlying problem and of the management science process.[1]

The important factors from the business point of view are:

- The application of the underlying operation or process
- The existence of an algorithm or set of decision rules for handling the operation

Consider a simple and familiar example. Addition is an operation for which an effective set of rules (an algorithm) provides swift and consistent results. It is also a very useful and important operation for the businessman. The addition algorithm is so much a part of our thinking that we are hardly aware of its effect on decision making, but it provides a good example through which to consider the possibility of improving management decisions.

We all know that addition and subtraction form an integral part of an accounting system. Business decisions would be difficult indeed without some means of measuring resources and liabilities, which is fundamentally what accounting systems do. Thus, addition (or subtraction, its logical equivalent) enables a businessman to determine, for example, whether a spending decision is feasible and how much of a drain upon his resources it will be. He cannot find *conceptual* answers to this general kind of problem without the *idea* of addition or subtraction, and he cannot find the actual or *concrete* answers without rules—algorithms. The addition process applied in the accounting system thus furnishes both significant concepts and key information about the state of one's affairs and provides a basis for decision. It illustrates the importance of the development of

[1] A simple example might be alternative decision rules (algorithms) for determining how much inventory to stock. Rule 1 might be: "Replenish each month end to the maximum monthly demand of the past 6 months." Rule 2: "Replenish to four times the average of the two peak weekly demands whenever stock falls to a preset minimum." The determination of cost difference between these two sets of rules in terms of inventory carrying costs, out-of-stock penalties, and production and procurement costs, is clearly not a matter of simple intuition.

the ideas about decision rules and the basic processes underlying quantification in decision making.

Imagine, if you can, doing business without using addition and subtraction.[2] Every time a businessman wanted to make a purchase, he would have to devise somehow a way of determining whether the price would or would not exceed his resources! Such a situation is virtually impossible to conceive because the modern business world is so dependent on the use of reasonably common accounting *concepts* and *algorithms* for handling double-entry bookkeeping. The algorithms used in accounting go considerably beyond addition and subtraction and are worth pursuing one step further to gain additional insight into the process of combining experience and algorithms (decision rules) into *models* that describe some aspect of the physical world.

Accounting ideas have evolved more or less continuously for 5,000 years. Almost five hundred years ago, Pacioli, the father of modern accounting, wrote the definitive treatise on double-entry bookkeeping and how it provides a detailed representation of the business situation. His stated purpose was "to give the trader without delay information on his assets and liabilities." Double-entry bookkeeping was then a profound concept for decision makers and thus a great social invention. Prior to that point in time, each decision for a commitment, division of profits, or other significant problem required the businessman to laboriously figure out where he stood. Double-entry bookkeeping is, of course, still with us in much the same form, and the concept remains basic to business accounting almost everywhere.

Herein lies the key point: the importance of really significant new concepts is not so much that they may be applied effectively in several situations but that they can, like double-entry bookkeeping, be used by all businesses. Management science plays a unique and critical role, representing generally applicable abstractions of real-life structural interrelationships and economic concepts. These ideas can thus serve as versatile, easily handled tools whose use can become nearly automatic.

KEY FACTORS IN THE DECISION PROCESS

Representations of key business processes, implemented by algorithms and applied to specific operations activities or parts of a business—models—are the fundamental building blocks of management sciences and computer systems. To use a model to help make decisions, it is of course essential to quantify the elements of the decision process included in the model: what we hope to achieve is essentially a statement of the profit and loss consequences of alternative courses of actions. A look at the total decision process shows what management has to do to quantify its elements.

Key factors underlying business decisions are:

- Resources at hand
- Possible alternatives
- Commitments required for alternatives
- Results (costs incurred, revenues or benefits received) to be achieved from alternatives
- Interactions between alternatives chosen and prior and later choices

Pacioli's algorithm for double-entry bookkeeping was a major step in quantifying the first element—resources at hand. Over the intervening 500 years, businessmen, assisted by economists and other specialists, have labored to give expression to concepts and algorithms that would attach consistent and reliable numbers to the other elements. They have succeeded in limited areas of specific business operations, as the example of electric power load dispatching illustrates. But until recently, very few new universals have been developed. Break-even analysis, cost accounting, and quality control are among the few examples of the type of conceptual and quantifiable tools that lend themselves to more or less universal use.

The inherent difficulties involved in quantifying alternatives, the results to be achieved from choices, and the interaction of past and future choices can hardly be exaggerated. Assuming that the resources and the commitments required for a set of available alternatives could be clearly described, the real problem for the business decision maker still remains. He needs to be able to analyze *consistently* and *quantitatively* the net effects of applying his resources.

This does not mean that the description will be either deterministic or final. Ultimately it will (and must) be dynamic and have characteristics of uncertainty. As Matthew Arnold put it, "They who await no gift from chance have conquered fate." Changes in the environment and changes in the uncertainty with which the future is viewed will determine the parameters or guiding variables that must be fed into analytical procedures for modern decision making through computer-based management science models. Thus, the feedback relationship between the organization and its environment will

[2] It has been done in some cultures!

always be an integral part of these problem-solving approaches.

Finally, complete dependence on analytical methods is a dangerous course. The successful executive's job is to provide a synthesis using the most accurate, complete, and precise results of analysis possible but also including still unquantifiable elements (and there always will be some!).

Before proceeding to what *can* be quantified in the decision process, the kinds of resources, commitments, and results that are difficult to measure in consistent numerical terms should be examined.

FACTORS THAT ARE DIFFICULT TO QUANTIFY

The effective decision maker cannot neglect the difficult but critically important measurement of such resources as:

- Executive talent
- Research and development
- Advertising
- Management information systems
- Inertia of the company relative to the economy

Meaningful estimates of the potential results of critical decisions require some evaluation of those elements. Attempts to describe these kinds of variables quantitatively have yet to prove completely rewarding. In these areas the executive is caught up in a web of personal, psychological actions and reactions that limit his ability to establish meaningful hypotheses. Plans are usually judged by results. Thus, little or nothing can be known about the future value of the plans themselves. In planning for management succession, for example, a company may hire many management trainees and rely on statistical odds to produce a highly competent president some years later—or it may wish to take its chances on developing one through hiring three new vice-presidents. The difference to the company of either plan may be very great, but it cannot yet be predicted quantitatively through a meaningful model—since either plan will produce *a* president.

In any case, the development of algorithms for decision making cannot be effectively carried into areas where satisfactory measurements do not apply. Business is a part of life, and as Justice Hughes wrote: "Life is a painting, not a sum." However, the fact that ultimate decisions are human, not mechanical, should not preclude management's exploration of those areas of business where inputs, relationships, and consequences can be analyzed and measured and thus understood.

FACTORS THAT CAN BE QUANTIFIED

Managers often feel that alternatives in some of the areas in which they can make decisions are so few that they have little or no choice when decision problems arise. In other words, their decisions are already dictated by the restraints placed upon them internally and externally. When this is true, the restrictions can usually be described quantitatively and often precisely. When quantitative restrictions dictate alternative courses of action, decision making becomes an automatic process and there is no need for managerial intervention. Very often, proven models with well-developed algorithms exist for such restricted problems; an example is inventory reorder policy in simple demand situations.

However, in most cases, even where executives feel that few improvements can be made in the decision process, a detailed analysis of the problem area in which the decision is to be made reveals a surprising number of alternative choices.

When the problem is complex, and the outcome of one's choices is uncertain, many managers feel that the best one can do is a common-sense guess. Yet these are precisely the circumstances where management science techniques are most valuable. When basic inputs are readily measurable, models using some tested algorithms can take both characteristics into account. A manager's belief that he can rely on sheer intuition may therefore needlessly keep him from achieving the best possible economic performance for his business.

The effects of uncertainty can frequently be reduced significantly and occasionally the amount of uncertainty as well. A simple example is a company that was considering entrance into a new market. Instead of making a difficult and uncertain forecast of the market share it was likely to win, management set out to determine what share of market would be needed to earn a satisfactory return on the investment. Analysis showed that the answer was close to 40 percent—a far larger share of market than the company was at all likely to attain for the money it was prepared to allot to the venture. The idea was therefore abandoned.

Where the problem of uncertainty cannot be significantly reduced, it can usually be attacked through a careful analysis of the "true" uncertainty surrounding the outcomes of individual courses of action.[3] This kind of analysis is illustrated in the development of information to help decide on an investment in new facilities. To develop this data, a broad range and mix of many variable factors must be analyzed. This work can be done by management of the divisions involved; e.g., marketing, engineering, and production. The problem, however, is that while the studies will indicate various factors of uncertainty, they will not show how these factors can be combined to permit realistic evaluation of the several probable end results of the investment. The estimates of the many variables that significantly influence the outcome of an investment will, at best, fall within some range of error, even if the estimates are not biased in one direction or the other. Statistically speaking, a good estimate of any one of these variables is what might be called "a 50 percent estimate," that is, an estimate in which the chances are 50-50 that the actual result will fall above or below the estimated quantity. For example, if the cost of introducing a new product line is estimated at $2.3 million, there would be 1 chance in 2 that the actual cost would be greater than $2.3 million and 1 chance in 2 that it would be less. The cost would only coincidentally turn out to be exactly $2.3 million.

Such a 50 percent estimate is perhaps the "best" single estimate that can be made under the circumstances,[4] although from a management point of view, it may be an undesirable estimate on which to base a decision. Whether or not this estimate is useful for management decision making depends on three things: (1) the range of possible error in the estimates; (2) the odds of being above or below the estimate by specified amounts; and (3) the gain or penalty attached to being above or below the estimate by a given amount. For example, suppose that a company estimates annual sales of a new plant at $100 million. If the annual sales estimate is needed for making a management decision, the 50 percent estimate will be a suitable basis for the decision only if the following conditions are approximated: (1) the chances of deviating from the estimates by specified amounts are approximately the same in either direction (for example, the odds of achieving at least $90 million in sales are the same as the odds of achieving $110 million); and (2) the penalty for achieving sales of $90 million is the same as the gain for $110 million (for example, profit is reduced by $1 million if the lower figure is achieved and is increased by $1 million if the higher figure is achieved).

However, to continue with this example, the 50 percent estimate will not provide a satisfactory basis for a management decision under other conditions. Suppose that (1) the chances of achieving at least $90 million in sales are 6 out of 10, and the chance of achieving at least $110 million is only 1 out of 10; (2) if sales of $90 million are achieved a break even point is reached; and (3) if $110 million is achieved, $1.5 million in profits is gained over the $10 million profits estimated for sales of $100 million. [Assume] a $10 million profit at the $100 million level. [See the table below.]

Under these circumstances, a management decision based on the 50 percent estimate could be very risky. There is a 40 percent chance of not selling more than $90 million; the chances of achieving $110 million in sales are small; and even if a $110 million sales level were reached, the added profits would be only $1.5 million. For each of the major variables entering into an investment decision—production cost, sales price, etc.—such uncertainties usually exist.

In such situations, rules can be developed and computer programs applied to aid management in consistently and quantitatively analyzing the likely outcomes of various courses of action. This method simulates the possible courses of future events in a computer and analyzes the results. The simulation method of analyzing potential decisions, which can take both uncertainty and complexity into account, is be-

[3] This is equivalent to estimating the odds that a specific event or class of events will occur: e.g., figuring that there is a 1-out-of-5 chance that the dollar will be devalued, or that there is a 2-out-of-3 chance that a given project will do better than break even.

[4] Note that it is not necessarily the most likely result; thus, if the possible costs ranged from $1 million to $3.6 million and each of the values between these ranges was equally likely to occur, the 50 percent estimate would still be $2.3 million, but there would be no single most likely value.

Sales estimate	$90 million	$100 million	$110.0 million
Profit	0	$ 10 million	$ 11.5 million
Odds	6/10	5/10	1/10
Chance of achieving or bettering estimate	60%	50%	10%

coming widely known and used. In this case, a "model" of the capital investment decision process is developed to help management to choose the best alternative under the particular conditions of uncertainty.

Where there are known interactions among the variables and where there are significant restrictions on the resources available to management, the best ways to use the resources to attain specific objectives can be found by other important concepts and models—of which linear programming is a most important and widely used example.

In one sense, linear programming can be considered an extension and extraordinary development of double-entry bookkeeping, because linear programming keeps track in a completely balanced manner of all quantified inputs and outputs of the production or economic system under consideration. However, linear programming is far more than this. In another sense, it may be described as a way of analyzing the use (not merely the existence) of resources to find the combinations that would produce results to fit specific management objectives, such as profit maximization or cost minimization (for example, the lowest cost raw materials mix to produce a given product in a chemical plant).

A linear programming description of a management problem makes it possible to explore the profit and loss consequences of a large number of alternative interacting decisions. Given the basic assumptions of an allocation-of-resources problem, it is possible to show by linear programming what the best allocation would be and then to demonstrate, by conventional profit and loss accounting, that there is no better allocation.

Consider the example of an oil company that purchases crude oil from a number of sources, processes this oil at a number of refineries, and delivers the product from the refineries to a number of locations geographically dispersed. Such a company faces a continuing set of decision problems. The oil it can purchase is of varying composition and price. The refineries that can process the oil have various kinds of equipment in various states of repair. Hence, they can produce different end products from the different crudes with varying degrees of efficiency. The refineries can also deliver to a number of points, each of which has its own particular combination of product requirements.

The use of a linear programming model, an algorithm to solve the numerous equations involved, and a computer to do the necessary arithmetic provides management with a tool very similar to that discussed earlier in connection with the load analyzer for electric power plants. With the changing input of prices, demands, and efficiencies, it is possible to calculate the following important variables on an instantaneous or on a projected basis: (1) the marginal value of a particular type of crude; (2) the marginal value of any specific kind of equipment in the refineries; and (3) the marginal cost of any product at any specific location. As indicated earlier, refinery managements today use the model, various algorithms, and computers to make such calculations and to control refinery operations accordingly.

Until the linear programming model and the algorithm to solve it were available, such calculations were literally impossible. Linear programming and similar models base their strength on the fundamental concept of efficient allocations of resources to meet management objectives and to satisfy other constraints and requirements imposed on the system. The power and utility of these computer-based analyses are essentially the same as the power and utility of ordinary arithmetic. Without these tools decision making is awkward and perhaps inefficient. With them, management can weigh key decisions in a rigorous and scientific manner.

MANAGEMENT'S CONTINUING ROLE IN DECISIONS

In the oil company example just cited, the fact that the relative value of a specific crude or the relative cost of a specific product can be determined at any given time certainly would be influential in the making of specific decisions. There is a competitive advantage in knowing these facts because they show certain decisions to be inevitable. The company that knows these facts and can recognize the decisions that are inevitable will move ahead. In the ordinary economic sense, this will force others to follow. Therefore, management can look forward to an inevitably continuing and growing use of profit-making tools such as this.

But the question remains whether management decision making has in fact been automated when such tools are used. The answer to this is "no"; rather, the environment in which decisions are made has changed. Decision making moves to a new and perhaps more difficult level. Management, then, has increased its theoretical understanding of the economics of decision making and has available for continuing use some models and algorithms that apply these understandings to specific problems.

Management now faces the job of making choices among models and improving the use of these models, much as it improved the use of addition and double-entry bookkeeping.

Will management decision making be entirely automated in the future? The answer is simply that a decision which can be truly automated is no longer really a management function. Management will continue to "make decisions" no matter what algorithms are supplied by the management scientist. In all effective leadership there will be decision making; this will be apparent both to the decision maker and to those who are affected by the decision. Management will retain the power of choice, of having and using preferences (for specific models, for example), and of resolving to apply specific results of model analyses in given situations. In a sense, its power will be even greater, for its understanding will be deeper and its grasp of situations more comprehensive.

On the other hand, with management inevitably utilizing these new decision-making concepts, models, and calculating mechanisms, the environment in which management analyzes and chooses is changed; the language that management speaks is changed; and even familiar events, seen in new perspective, seem different. A refinery manager using a linear programming model to schedule his runs looks at his refinery in an entirely different manner than do managers who are not familiar with this technique. In fact, it is no longer possible for him to "go back" to the old ways of making production run decisions. Perhaps the most significant change is not the results from the computer runs of the linear program but this new way of looking at the production process. The competitive power of increased understanding and increased ability to measure, quantify, and analyze effectively is so great that all managers will sooner or later be caught up by it, just as the entire business world was caught up by double-entry bookkeeping.

The major impact of management science, in summary, has been to force management to face new kinds of decisions on a new level of decision making with new forms of information. One of the new required decisions is the establishment of rules for logical analysis. For example, a modern inventory system model requires—as old systems did not—that management set specific policies that define the operating parameters of the system.

Management science techniques coupled with effective computer systems provide today's managers with timely, accurate, and relevant information that permits them to cut through the complexities and uncertainties of business situations and thereby to select strategies and tactical courses of action and to exercise control with greater confidence in the outcome than ever before. Competitive advantages such as wider profit margins, lower costs, faster service or production, higher quality, and larger returns on investment are the payoffs from these improved information systems that rely on the combined power of a scientific approach and the capabilities of modern computing machinery.

23 WHAT IS MANAGERIAL OPERATIONS RESEARCH?*

William D. Brinkloe

The practicing manager at which this book aims knows his job well—or at least he thought he did. Lately, though, he has been getting a little uneasy. He reads of managerial revolutions and computerized information systems, and he hears predictions that those who have not seen the light are doomed to failure. The chilling automation study of one foundation predicts that growing numbers of managers will find themselves displaced, and he hopes they don't mean him. He overhears the easy jargon of those apparently in rapport with the computers, and wonders if he is somehow out of tune. He worries that he is missing the boat, and wishes he knew what there was in all this for him, but he doesn't know where to turn.

He *is* missing the boat. There is a great deal in all this for him. In the last few years, stimulated by the applicability of simple mathematics to wartime military problems, quantitative decision-making has invaded the executive suite. The simultaneous arrival of the digital computer, whose speed and growing simplicity of application make possible all sorts of helpful investigations, has accelerated this trend. Every executive want ad shows more corporations setting up operations research groups, and the hints are clear that line executives are more acceptable with a little quantitative know-how.

The aim of this book is to provide the practicing line executive with an understanding of operations research and related techniques that have become essential tools of modern business and industrial management.

OPERATIONS RESEARCH: A DEFINITION

Operations research is one name given to the broad and rather amorphous science of establishing mathematical or other explicit relationships that describe the key elements of some actual physical or administrative process with reasonable fidelity, and of drawing useful conclusions about the actual process through analysis of these relationships. (There are other names which may mean more or less the same thing: systems analysis, operations analysis, management science, quantitative method, and so on; sometimes, though, these terms have quite a different meaning, as when the computer programmer uses "systems analysis" to mean arranging a process into a sequence of steps so it can be accomplished on the computer.) The essence of operations research is that it puts aside the less significant factors and describes the way in which the key factors contribute to the key product.

A car dealer appraising a trade-in ignores hundreds of trivial factors—color, miles driven, condition of engine, type of use, former owner, make of tires, and so on—and makes his estimate in minutes on the basis of model, age, and appearance. He has learned that if he took days to examine each car minutely, in the long run the results would be very close to his on-the-spot judgment. Bank loan officers have devised the same short-cut method for loan approval, to the point where many banks turn the screening task over to computers.[1] Both of these procedures are representative of operations research techniques, in that they seek to peer through the thicket of facts and see the camouflaged trail through the forest; the operations research specialist is not needed, however, unless the path to a solution is less obvious than in the used-car case.

THE BACKGROUND OF OPERATIONS RESEARCH

Many scholars (and gamblers) have contributed to the underpinnings of operations research through the years, but the father of

* Reprinted by permission of the publisher from *Managerial Operations Research,* McGraw-Hill Book Company, 1969, pp. 1–13. Mr. Brinkloe is professor of management science at the University of Pittsburgh.

[1] See J. A. Vaughan and A. M. Porat, Managerial Reactions to Computers, *J. Am. Bankers Assoc.,* April 1967.

quantitative decision-making may be Frederick William Lanchester,[2] whose celebrated "N-square law" assessed the fighting power of opposing forces. When cavemen fought club against club, he reasoned, tactical concentration was precluded by the limited range of weapons; thus a Donnybrook between 1,000 "Red" and 1,400 "Blue" cavemen would end up with everyone dead except 400 Blues. When weapons range permitted tactical concentration (10 riflemen could concentrate on a single enemy), the *rate* of losses became proportional to the opponent's force—a rate that constantly increased for the weaker, as the stronger's relative advantage kept growing. The solution of Lanchester's resulting differential equations suggested that forces of equal man-for-man fighting power have overall strength proportional to the *squares* of their respective numerical strengths. Let the 1,000 Reds and 1,400 Blues be riflemen rather than cavemen, and since the square of 1,400 is approximately twice the square of 1,000, the Reds are annihilated with 1,000 victorious Blues still on the field.

Lanchester tested his theory against Admiral Nelson's Plan of Battle at Trafalgar. Nelson, calculating that the French would have 46 ships against his 40, divided his force into a main body of 32 ships to engage 23 ships in the French rear, and a second body of 8 ships to hold off the 23 downwind Frenchmen in the van until the rear 23 ships were defeated and his squadrons could join forces. Lanchester calculated Nelson's N-square strategy as follows:

FRENCH FIGHTING STRENGTH	ENGLISH FIGHTING STRENGTH
$(23)^2 = 529$	$(32)^2 = 1{,}024$
$(23)^2 = 529$	$(8)^2 = 64$
1,058	1,088

English margin of superiority $= \sqrt{1{,}088 - 1{,}058} = \sqrt{30} = 5\frac{1}{2}$ ships.

Nelson's strategy was exactly optimum according to Lanchester's theory; if he had divided his force any more evenly, say 31 and 9, his resultant strength would have been less than that of the French (only 1,042 versus 1,058), and if he had divided more unevenly, say 33 and 7, the weaker force might not have been able to carry out its initial assignment of holding off the French van without a battle. Perhaps this proves Nelson right because his strategy corresponds to the mathematical optimum; perhaps it proves Lanchester right because his theory confirms a professional's decision. The point is that Lanchester attempted to make explicit the underlying factors determining strategic choice, tested his "mathematical model" in a specific real-world case, and then offered it for general application to future cases. Ever since Lanchester, operations researchers have been trying to do precisely the same thing.

[2] F. W. Lanchester, *Aircraft in Warfare: The Dawn of the Fourth Arm,* Constable & Co., Ltd., London, 1916.

THE EVOLUTION OF OPERATIONS RESEARCH

The first application of our operations research concepts in this country appeared in the mid-1930s (although the term was not used at that time), when Congress was trying to assess the value to the nation of various river, harbor, and irrigation projects. Faced with the fact that there was no measurable payoff from these public projects, the government agencies and Congressional committees worked up techniques for estimating the equivalent social payoff. Irrigation water goes to the farmer free, but its imputed value is measured by estimating what the farmer would be willing to pay if it were not free. These techniques were expanded to include the side benefits of such projects: in addition to the navigational benefits of a canal system, what are the recreational benefits from any lakes thus created? Although these projects often were scorned as pork-barrel measures, the cost-effectiveness techniques they spawned foreshadowed the systems analysis developed in the Pentagon under Robert McNamara, and the program budgeting system now spreading to all government departments.

Operations research demonstrated its value on a large scale in World War II, as commanders needed help to comprehend the implications of intelligence collected over large theaters of operation. Some of its early triumphs were dramatic, partly because many of these unfamiliar operations provided such fertile fields for exploitation. When aircraft depth charges met with poor success in sinking submarines, analysis showed that their setting presupposed too fast a diving rate for submarines surprised on the surface, so that they were exploding too deep; halving the depth setting increased the kill rate dramatically with no increase whatsoever in resources allocated. Study of convoy operations showed that wolf-pack U-boats sank a relatively fixed number of freighters per attack, almost independently of convoy size; the resultant shift to fewer but larger convoys drastically reduced overall losses and marked the turning point in the Battle of the Atlantic.[3]

This wartime organization extended its usefulness in the Korean war, by which time the military commander had learned to work smoothly with the analyst assigned to his command. In planning an air strike on rail lines, for example, the analyst used data on bombing and navigational accuracy, effective damage radius of different bombs, probable enemy opposition, construction details of rail embankments, etc., to make the most effective choice of various attack modes utilizing equivalent resources (such as one 1,000-pound bomb versus ten 100-pound bombs). In the Vietnamese conflict these techniques extended to broad logistics analyses of a total theater such as simulating battlefield resupply of expendables and repair parts, using alternate transportation networks involving many routes with different capacities and ambushing probabilities.

After the war, business began to adapt these military innovations to its own operations. A well-publicized statistical-analysis group from the Air Force moved as a body to the Ford Motor Company; known as the "whiz kids," its members rose to top-management spots at Ford and later in other corporations. Initial business applications were transfers from military prototypes, such as finding the most effective combination of warehouses and shipping routes to minimize a corporation's overall cost of storing and shipping, or determining the cheapest combination of input factors to produce a required product meeting certain specifications. As business gained more experience with these techniques, it developed methods directly adapted to its own needs, such as analysis of marketing strategies for maximum profit, capital investment theory, and input/output analysis for industrial planning.

A formidable business contender today is the aerospace conglomerate, which in a sense has had the best of both worlds. Much of its research has been government-supported (and in exotic areas which have attracted some of the most capable scientists), it has been encouraged and often virtually forced to use advanced techniques in conducting analysis of weapons systems and similar projects, and it has lived in an environment of lively innovation in which the operations researcher's contributions have been accepted routinely.

These companies are expanding, by merger or broadening of product lines, into traditional consumer goods areas (plus the unfolding public sector), and they can be expected to make full use of quantitative management techniques in battling it out with the companies who hold the present markets.

Today few businesses of any size overlook at least some of the advantages of managerial operations research. A recent survey of such techniques, as used by management consultants of an accounting firm that deals with leading corporations, casts an interesting light on the relative popularity of the various areas. The following shows the extent to which recent consultant reports call on each of these techniques.[4]

General advice	18%
Critical path	16%
Inventory theory	14%
General statistical	11%
Linear programming	10%
Other forecasting techniques	7%
Simulation	5%
Methods and procedures	4%
Computer technology	4%
Decision theory	3%
Statistical regression	2%
Exponential smoothing	1%

THE BASIC CONCEPTS OF OPERATIONS RESEARCH

Specialists contribute two things: special information and special techniques. If you must know about tax law or tar sands, computer programming or colloidal chemistry, you need *information* from a professional in the field. But if a *technique* works in businesses or departments with problems like yours, just knowing this is half the battle; and where the technique is simple, you may be able to apply it yourself. If it is not this simple (and usually it will not be), you can consider which of several approaches fits the special characteristics of your problem, and call in the right specialist for the specific problem.

Quantitative methods work, not because numbers are smarter than you are, but because they can extract from past information about your operation (or another very like yours) the maximum guidance for your future actions. Some things have worked well in the past and some have not; barring changes in outside fac-

[3] An excellent review of the wartime operations research work done by the United States Navy is contained in P. M. Morse and G. E. Kimball, *Methods of Operations Research,* John Wiley & Sons, Inc., New York, 1951.

[4] Leland A. Moody of Arthur Andersen & Company, *Development of Management Sciences in the Public Accounting Profession,* presented at the 1966 meeting of Institute of Management Sciences.

tors, this pattern ought to continue. Even if outside factors do change, say in a way that raises or lowers gross sales, their effect is merely superimposed on the pattern of what has been happening before. The contribution of quantitative methods is their ability to separate these effects and associate them with their respective causes—to extract the hard facts hidden in disordered data.

Operations research draws on some basic relationships developed by economists, of which the following are representative:

The "marginal-analysis" concept provides to several claimants that last increment of resources which will bring to each the same unit measure of satisfaction. The family budgeteer, giving daughter \$2 for a folk record, Junior 10 cents for bubble gum, and Mother \$49.95 for a dress, hopes each purchase will bring equal pleasure per dollar. The company directors, apportioning capital investment funds to profit centers so as to produce equal return, are playing the same game.

The "standard-gamble" concept asks the decision-maker to evaluate each of his enterprises, with its estimated chance of payoff and the estimated profit or loss, against the certainty of some yardstick profit. "Would you rather spend \$5,000 to bid a contract that would bring you \$20,000 profit, and on which you have some specified chance of getting the award; or do business as usual with a 50–50 chance of making \$6,000 or \$7,000 for the same period?" If you can make realistic estimates of expected profits and associated odds, which is not easy, you have a systematic basis for an optimum choice.

Econometrics is a methodical attempt to weigh each payoff in proportion to its importance, so that you can evaluate an outcome in an important area as worth appropriately more than a similar outcome in a less important area. An econometrician would say that a manager who increases his supervisory ratio has decided that overhead deserves a higher coefficient in his profit equation.

The economist's "indifference curve" is an analytical concept whereby he can show you at what point in the evening you'd be just willing to forego that last drink in favor of a bus ticket home. (Any economics text will discuss indifference curves in the abstract, but few tell you how to construct one.)

THE ELEMENTS OF AN OPERATIONS RESEARCH ANALYSIS

Operations research has a host of applications, depending largely on what sort of person is using it. The administrator might employ it as a technique for applying the methods of science to administration, so that cause and effect can be predicted in the administrative sphere with something approaching the confidence with which this can be done in such "hard" sciences as physics or chemistry. Perhaps OR is understood best by describing the steps that go into the quantitative solution of a problem:

Determine Your Objective. Usually this is something more complex than "make the maximum profit." You operate under many constraints: working safely, maintaining your corporate reputation, staying within the law, and so on. Moreover, you won't elect to make the maximum profit in a specific case if the consequent course of action runs counter to a broader criterion in the long run—by neglecting maintenance or training, for example, or by concentrating on a few high-profit lines that may leave you dangerously undiversified in case of a shift in buying habits. But if you are to make your analysis quantitative, you can't translate all these qualifications and constraints into numbers; you have to select relatively simple objectives and live with them.

Determine A Performance Measure. If "maximum net profit" is your objective, the performance measure is simple: dollars of net profit. If your objective is more complex, a numerical measure of good performance is a little tougher. Nonetheless, you must pick one. And you must remember that your analysis really isn't measuring your achievement against your *objective,* but only against the performance measure you picked as proxy for the former. For example, if you are superintendent of a medical unit, and your objective is good performance on the part of your doctors, your *performance measure* may be the number of patients seen per day or something of the sort —which clearly isn't a foolproof proxy for what you really want, but may be the best you can devise.

Build A "Mathematical Model." This ominous-sounding device is nothing but a mathematical formula—as simple as you can make it—which contains the important variables or their limiting "parameters" and whose solution is the performance measure in numerical form. If your aim is net profits (P) and your two variables are number of items sold (n) and unit profit per item (p), then your mathematical model is nothing more than:

$$P = np$$

Note that, in building the model, you make use of theory insofar as you know it. In this example, the theory is obvious. In a more realistic case, you may have to do a great deal of hard thinking to decide how your parameters may be related. Furthermore, you will have to determine the coefficients that indicate how much each variable contributes to the performance measure.

It is well to become comfortable with problem-solving by means of models, for they are tremendous aids. We meet all sorts of models. A wind tunnel is a physical model; so is the wear simulator in a testing laboratory. The expression "He's a tiger!" is a symbolic model. An approximate mathematical model is the typical formula for current worth of an industrial building:

$$\text{Current worth} = [(\text{cost}) - (2\%\ \text{cost} \times \text{age})] \times \frac{\text{current price index}}{\text{original price index}}$$

Once you have decided, from evaluating many buildings, that the value of a building so many years old seems to correspond rather closely to this simple formula, it is economical to abandon the time-consuming estimates and depend thereafter on the formula—the model. Similarly, once you find that the arrival times and service times of customers can be represented by a model—slightly more complex but perfectly direct and understandable—you can use the model to simulate a wide variety of different procedures in a way that would be chaotic if you tried it on your real system. If you have seven repair centers, and from their operation you have constructed a mathematical model, you can operate your model to simulate nine repair centers, or five, or any number you want. And you can test the exact effect of each variable (average service or arrival time, number of servers, etc.).

THE ROLE OF THE EXECUTIVE

Never in history has the executive's task been tougher than it is today. Far from being displaced by supercomputers, the manager has been given more problems to solve. The burgeoning flow of management data has created pressures on management for action in new areas to exploit this data. "Computers can lessen the task of information-gathering," says an auto maker, "but they only increase the task of evaluation and recommendation."

It is surprising, in the face of these growing burdens, that much management makes so little use of quantitative managerial techniques. Its failure to exploit its own priceless operating statistics is astonishing. It guesses at developments when it could predict. Its "calculated risks" often are nothing of the sort, in the sense that there has been any analytical assessment of the probabilities and costs associated with various outcomes. It has fundamental misconceptions about samples or surveys—sometimes overestimating the validity of sample information, but more often buying too much data because it mistrusts conclusions inferred from samples of modest size. It does not appreciate how experience in one type of operation can be incorporated into some analytical structure that will provide synthetic experience about untried types of operation. If a number of factors are affecting its performance, it has little notion how their individual effects can be isolated and examined. It says "my tasks are different," ignoring the large core of regularity which makes prediction possible and can do away with the necessity for solving the same problems over and over again.

Why?

There are two reasons: communications and credibility. The line manager and the operations research specialist may speak such different languages that one really doesn't know what the other is saying; and often the mathematical approach seems to require such artificially limited assumptions as to be totally divorced from the untidy confusion of the real world. The manager feels that the operations research man knows very little about the totality of running a business, which is true; but he concludes therefore that the latter can be of no assistance, which is not true. The manager may accept assistance unhesitatingly in clearly defined specialist areas such as engineering or industrial hygiene, but feel that to call on a specialist in what apparently is the whole field of management smacks of abdicating the precise responsibilities for which he was hired.

Communications are hampered by the fact that you and the management scientist are different types of people. Your forte is making decisions in a hurry when you must; he might object on the grounds that there are insufficient facts for a good decision. You are intuitive, authoritative, inclined to weigh the human values; he is systematic, conservative, prone to dismiss personal factors as unmeasurable. You draw heavily on experience (even when it applies imperfectly) and instinctively weigh a fistful of imponderables to reach a swift decision; he leans on verifiable and repeatable factors, and hesitates to move before all the evidence is in—which it never is.

You don't have time to learn the mathematical foundations of operations research. If you had, you would know that when the OR man makes a statement he is not expressing his opinion but interpreting what the numerical indicators of your business are saying. His unsupported opinion of the action you should take is of little value, and you would be right to disregard it; his mathematical manipulations of data are (if he is competent) as valid as the information itself, and you should disregard it only if you consider the data suspect.

A good operations research specialist should not talk jargon. He should explain his assumptions and methods in reasonably understandable language, and if what he says sounds nonsensical, it probably is. But you must meet him halfway. You should have a notion what tools are in his kit, what sort of problem he can solve, what he needs to work with, and what are the general limitations of his methods. You should know when it would be helpful to call on him and when you ought to go it alone.

Indeed, you must meet him far more than halfway, if you are to take maximum advantage of quantitative management techniques. The operations research specialist is a staff man, who simply recommends; but yours is the responsibility for keeping the operation going, following up on decisions, and producing results in a highly competitive milieu. If you fail to call him in when you need him, or if you ask him to do the wrong things, you pay the price, not he. As each new method or device has entered the business world over the years, the executive has learned to understand it and turn it to advantage; when he has not, he has misused it and the business has suffered.[5] Quantitative management tools are so fundamentally intertwined with management itself that they must become basic to your managerial expertise.

You must learn to deal with measurement in management—not simply collecting data for decisions, but knowing how precise the numbers are, and how much they can be trusted. You must appreciate the value of complete and timely information about your operations, and how to collect it. You must have a feel for the underlying structure of a problem, and you must know the techniques for peeling away the nonessentials to lay bare the key variables that make the real difference. This is not to say you must perform your own multiple regression analysis, or find your way through an elaborate linear programming problem, but you need to know the uses and limitations of such techniques—and to do this you must have some comprehension of the theories that underlie them. If you do not, you will not know how to steer the specialist to the relevant facts, how and when to incorporate your executive judgment, or how to understand and use his recommendations.

[5] Companies who introduced computers without top-level understanding of their function, hoping to delegate the problem to specialists, are testimony to the folly and waste attending such an approach.

THE ROLE OF THE SPECIALIST

Where will the use of an operations research specialist pay off? Essentially the specialist deals with information that comes in (or can be put into) numerical form, and his particular skill lies in making recognizable order out of apparent disorder. Note that the disorder is only apparent—underneath the confusion there must be some systematic relationship or pattern which his quantitative methods can extract. Note, too, that some such information must exist, either in your operating statistics or in those of some other organization, which he can transfer to your problem; he cannot invent statistics.

If the disorder is almost total (if there is no underlying order to extract), his methods will not work and he probably cannot help; your managerial judgment will do a better job unaided. If there is little or no disorder (the information and its implications are clear-cut), his methods are not needed; you can see your way to the goal without specialist help. If his findings won't make any difference, it is foolish to use him. In a celebrated quantitative study, the analyst worked nearly two years to find out whether a price war with a competing product was desirable and to what extent; when he presented his findings to the board he learned that they wouldn't countenance a price war in any case, because it did not fit their corporate image.

You should not use the specialist unless you understand what you are asking him to explore, generally how he will do it, and how you will implement his possible recommendations. If one of his recommendations might be to undertake a major capital improvement program, either be prepared at the start to go after the funds for such a program or exclude it at the start from his list of alternatives. On the other hand, don't be too quick to tell him that certain alternatives are out of bounds; you may want to know the true benefits of a course of action, even though your present position is to exclude it from consideration, because the facts might change your mind.

Try not to let the specialist get too clear a picture of your hopes about the outcome. He is only human, and it is very tempting to produce and justify a recommendation known in advance to be highly acceptable. Remind yourself that you hope for such an outcome because of your present beliefs about the situation, and his findings may change some of those beliefs.

Steer him to the right sources of information, and give him all possible information on the relative reliability of such sources. If he thinks only a certain sort of information is available, he will extract the best conclusions from that much information; but if more is available, he can extract better information.

Give him all possible guidance on assumptions. The mathematical model he may build might strive to maximize some payoff for your organization; he may build such a model because he assumes that such a payoff constitutes the objective of your organization, but he may be very wrong. A new venture may be designed to penetrate a certain market rather than to turn maximum profit, or to achieve a certain quality level subject to attainment of some minimum profit, or to provide a training ground for budding executives even at some specified operating loss; he needs to be told this and not be made to guess, for differing goals lead to very different recommended actions.

Tell him the scope of the study. The operations researcher may not want to do a half-baked job, but he can accept close deadlines or fund limitations just as others can. If he knows you want the best conclusions he can reach by noon tomorrow, that's what you'll get—along with a statement of their shortcomings.

And remember, finally, that he is staff and you are line. His recommendations apply to that part of the problem amenable to quantitative analysis, but your judgment and your final decision apply to all of it. His findings arise out of the assumptions and data he used, which may constitute quite a limited view of the whole spectrum which you must consider. If he did a locational analysis for you, his estimate of annual volume would apply only if his assumed factors eventuated—if competing operations developed only where he said they might, if the future economic climate was as he postulated it, and if all the other intangibles followed his assumptions. If he did a good job, his assumptions are coupled with reasons why they should be legitimate, but you have yourself to blame if you slough over that part and imagine that he was predicting annual volume *come what may*.

It probably is a good deal more fun to be the manager than the specialist, but part of the fun lies in knowing your stuff—knowing enough about the specialist's work to second-guess him a bit and to bring out his very best performance. To be a generalist means to know something about everything—a tough assignment, but a challenging one.

24 HOW TO GROW A DECISION TREE*

Edward A. McCreary

The business schools, and a handful of bellwether companies, have a new device for long-range planning. Called a Decision Tree, this simple mathematical tool enables the planner to consider various courses of action, assign financial results to them, modify these results by their probability, and then make comparisons. It is the use of odds that distinguishes decision trees from conventional business decision-making and which sometimes produces a surprising result: the best business decision is not necessarily to prepare for the most likely event.

The clearest way to explain this is through an example. In this instance, a commonplace business decision is reduced to a decision tree:

• In the winter of 1967, Emperor Products Corporation, a medium-size electronics component manufacturer, had four semiautomatic assembly machines operating at full capacity for one of its products. Sales demand for this product was rising, and company officers were trying to decide whether to expand current production by installing a fifth production unit or putting its employees on overtime. Emperor's director of marketing backed the production vice president's bid for new equipment because, as he said: "I've been talking with key customers and the way things are going I'm confident we can get 20 percent more sales by fall."

The company treasurer, however, was less ebullient: "Maybe . . . I say, maybe . . . we can get a 20 percent sales increase. But with present tax and inventory prospects we have to look at the other side of the coin. Sales may go up, but there is also a good chance that we face a sales drop."

Over the course of the next week, after back-and-forth discussion on sales prospects, Emperor's president asked his treasurer, marketing director and their staffs to quantify and agree upon a joint estimate. The two groups agreed that while there was a 60 percent likelihood that sales would increase 20 percent, there was also a 40 percent chance that sales might drop by as much as 5 percent.

During this period, the company president had called for figures on the possible dollar consequences, over the next year, of the two decision alternatives: overtime v. new equipment; and of the two possible events, sales increase v. a sales decline. Moreover, since Emperor's growth had already strained its working capital, he asked for the figures in terms of net cash flow to the company. The figures he got were as follows:

	NEW EQUIPMENT ALTERNATIVE (NET CASH FLOW)	OVERTIME ALTERNATIVE
Event: 20 Percent Sales Rise	+\$460,000	+\$440,000
Event: 5 Percent Sales Drop	+\$340,000	+\$380,000

Obviously, in the event things went well and sales rose, the decision to install new equipment showed the greatest payout. But a sales decrease, if new equipment had been bought, would be more painful to the company than the elimination of overtime. The probabilities of the various events somehow had to be taken into account, so the president drew up the simple decision tree shown at the top of p. 195.

At the present moment in time the company was at the square box, or decision node, of a two-branched action fork. It could install new equipment or go to overtime. After it made either of these decisions the company would, sometime in the fall of the year, find itself in a circled event node of a two-branched *event* fork which would see sales either rise (60 percent probability) or drop (40 percent probability). The 12-month payout for each possible action-event branch was as illustrated.

To determine whether the new equipment or the overtime decision branch offered the better

* Reprinted by permission from *Think Magazine*, published by the International Business Machines Corporation, March–April, 1967, pp. 13–18. Mr. McCreary is on the staff of the International Business Machines Corporation.

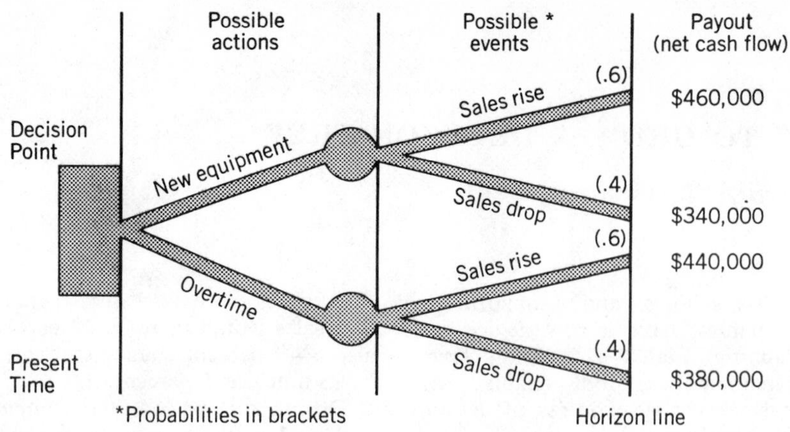

composite value of payout-as-modified-by-probability, the president did the following:

Starting at the horizon line or top of the decision tree, he multiplied each event branch "value" at the horizon line by the probability for this event. For example in the new equipment half of the diagram he multiplied the high sales probability (.60) by the payout for this event ($460,000) to get a composite figure of $276,000. Multiplying the lower sales probability (.40) times the payout for this event ($340,000), he got a figure of $136,000. He then added these two figures to get a total composite figure, a combined "value" at the event fork of $412,000.

Using the same technique for the overtime half of the diagram, he determined that the composite "value" of the high sales branch was $264,000, that the "value" of the low sales event branch was $152,000, and that the total probability-modified "value" for the overtime event fork was $416,000.

With this information he could simplify the decision diagram. He erased the event branches and end values at the horizon line. This left the two action branches (new equipment v. overtime) and the two combined "values" of $412,000 and $416,000 respectively. The decision diagram now looked as follows:

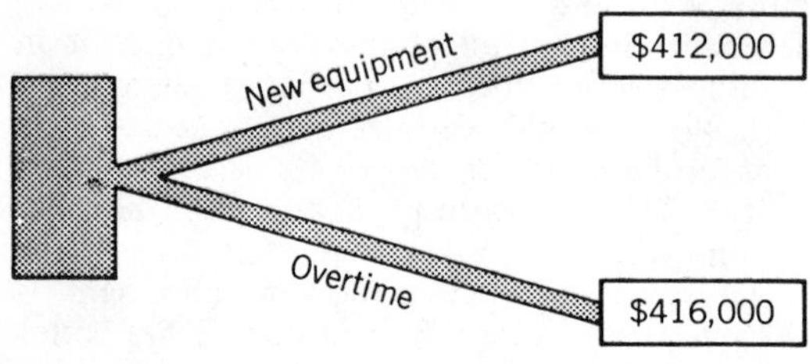

One glance at this simplified decision tree and the company president knew, considering the odds, that the best choice was overtime. It offered the highest total odds-modified value. The best decision, apparently, was to prepare for the less probable event. To complete the process the president erased the lower valued action branch which he now knew he did not wish to take, and his final decision diagram looked as follows:

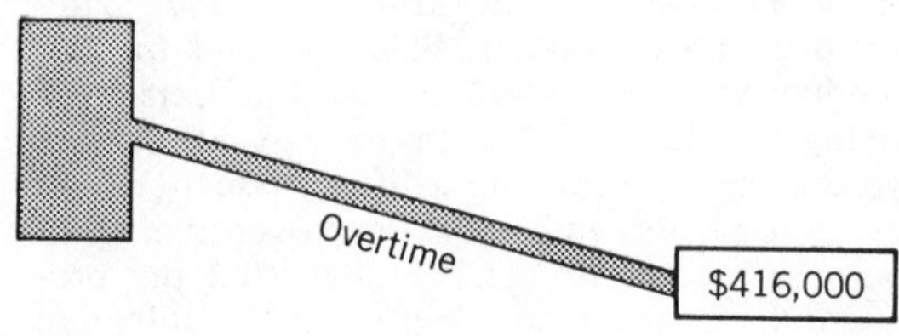

Later, in going through these numbers in order to try to explain their logic to his marketing director, treasurer and manufacturing vice president, the president noted, "Now I recognize that the $412,000 odds-modified 'value' for new equipment is something of an imaginary figure, but I'm not worried about that; I need it to compare with a similarly imaginary 'value' for the overtime alternative. Since the way the odds modify the payouts gives the overtime alternative the greater value ($416,000), I'm convinced that we should play it safe and stay with overtime. Later on, if our prospects look good, we can always add more equipment."

However, the company treasurer decided that it might be worthwhile taking that second look immediately, and extended the decision tree another year forward. After conferring with the marketing director, the treasurer decided he could safely assume that long-term trends for the component in question were excellent and that even if sales did drop 5 percent in 1967 and early 1968, the odds were 8-in-10 that sales would increase 20 percent in 1968 and 1969. The odds were 2-in-10 that sales would increase by at least 10 percent in 1968. Moreover, if sales rose in 1967, as hoped, the odds were 50-50 that they would further increase by either 20 percent or 10 percent in 1968.

With these probabilities in mind, the treasurer then drew up an extended two-year decision diagram of possible actions, events and payouts that looked as illustrated below.

After he had "rolled back" (i.e., simplified) his new decision diagram from the 12 points at its horizon line down to one basic decision point and preferred action branch, the treasurer, a bit embarrassed but also somewhat proud of himself, dropped in on the president.

"I was wrong," he said. "On a short-term basis it seemed best to go to overtime, but over the longer term we would be smarter to get that new equipment into production. Long-term growth is probably going to make up for any drops in volume that we might meet this spring."

Smiling as he pulled out his own extended two-year decision diagram, which showed the same conclusion, the president said, "Let's go

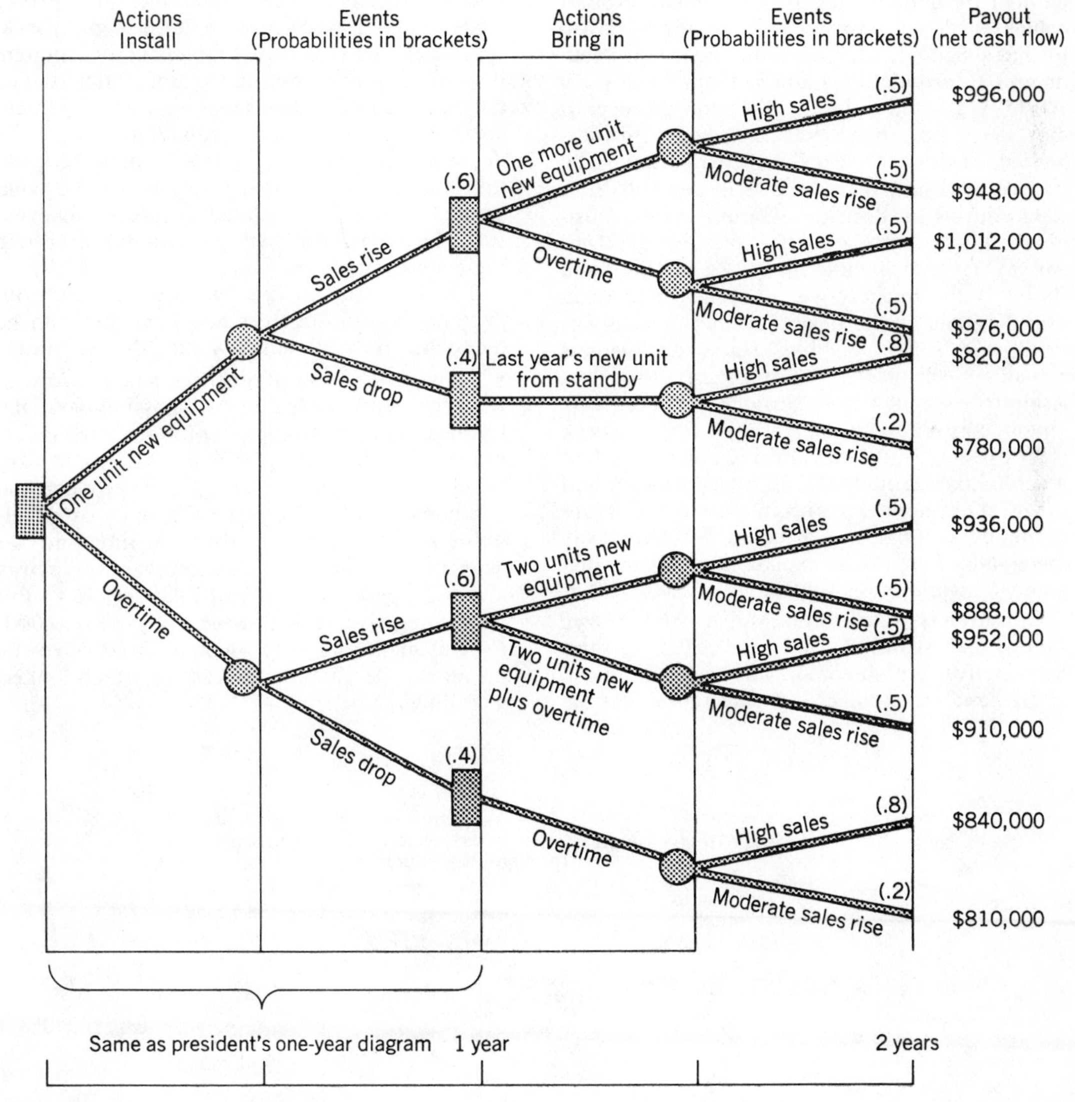

tell Harry down in Production." (Readers who may wish to work out the arithmetic by which the treasurer changed his mind can check their results with the probability-modified "values" for the various event fork junctions of Emperor's two-year decision diagram. Work from right to left using only the high value branch at any action fork.)

The above decision situations were simple enough so that, given the background information at each stage, most (but not all) executives would intuitively have made the decisions chosen by Emperor's management. What the decision trees did, however, was make abundantly clear what would have been debatable—and debated—in most companies.

Decision trees trace themselves through a number of mathematicians, such as Drs. Robert Schlaefer and Howard Raiffa at the Harvard Business School, and the late John von Neumann, a formidable mathematician and post-World War II developer of Game Theory. It may be indicative that Harvard Business School, revising its previous curriculum, now immerses its first-year students in two stiff, full-term courses on decision diagrams. Other business schools, among them Chicago, Stanford and MIT, are moving in the same direction. Probably the most active promulgator of decision diagrams to the business community is Dr. Paul A. Vatter of the Harvard Business School's Advanced Management Program. Aside from regular class sessions with relatively senior corporation managers in the six-week Harvard course, Vatter and his colleagues find much of their time taken up by lectures to, and program development with interested executives in major companies. "I could all too easily spend all of my time explaining decision diagrams or working on applications," says Vatter.

Consultants like John Magee and Gwyn Collins of Arthur D. Little, Inc., have also been active promoters of the systems. David Hertz and a number of his associates at McKinsey & Co. Inc., have similarly developed these and other techniques, and other consultants are joining the trend.

Exponents and developers of decision trees do note, however, that the internal logic of decision diagrams is sometimes difficult to get across to veteran managers. This, because, as one businessman student remarks, "Handling decision diagrams is a bit like learning parallel skiing: you have to override some deeply inlaid intuitions and instincts to make things click." The comparison is apt, for in parallel skiing a man, already on a steep mountainside, must lean far forward to bring his weight to the tips of his skis; only then will weight come off the backs of his skis to permit him control and maneuverability. A neophyte skier may accept all this intellectually, but on a steep slope every instinct yells for him to pull back.

Among businessmen, interestingly enough, it is often precision-prone mathematicians and engineers rather than sales and general managers who balk at the probability-logic of a decision tree. Their qualms, which tend to take the form of a sharp distrust of the composite "values" and related events at an event fork, have (within their limitations) a certain logical consistency.

The best way to illustrate the "logical" objections to decision trees and how they can be overcome is by a suitably altered case study:

• As part of an overall decision study involving research and development possibilities, the Pythagoras Parts Company of New York determined that for one particular $1,000,000 investment in a new process and product the company stood a 70 percent chance of developing high sales over a period of time and net cash flow of $4,000,000. However, there was also a 30 percent chance of relatively low sales and a negative cash flow of (—) $1,000,000. Project managers were anxious to get a yes or no on this decision, a diagram of which looked as follows:

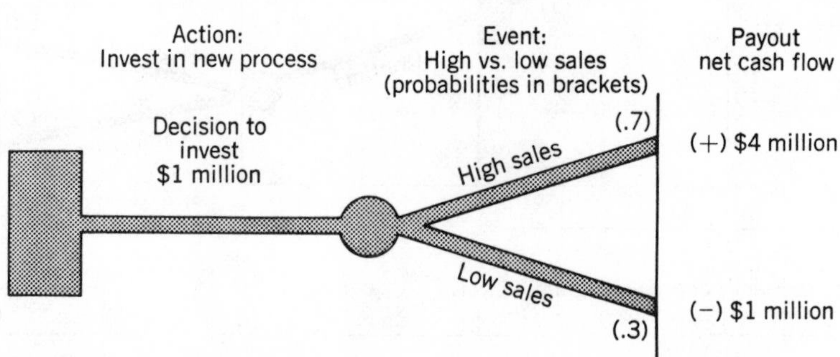

Via backwards induction, company analysts illustrated that the composite value of each branch was: .70 × \$4,000,000 = \$2.8 million, and .30 × (—) \$1,000,000 = (—) \$0.3 million. With these totals they determined a composite value of \$2.5 million for the event node (see diagram).

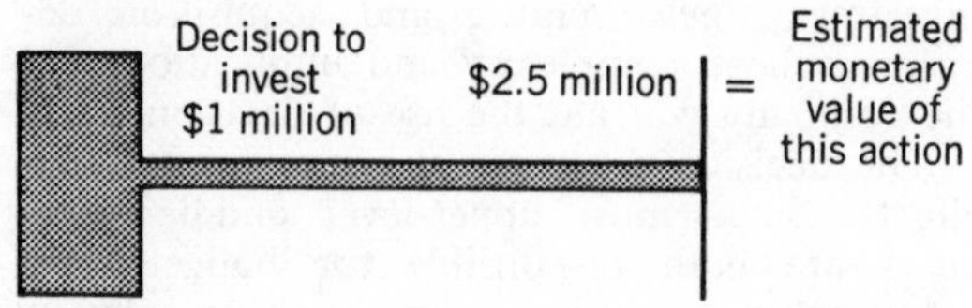

This was the first time some of the company executives had ever been presented with decision diagrams, and at this point in the presentation a number of executives began to balk.

"I agree that the odds are 70-30 for success or failure," one of them admitted, "but those are before-the-fact odds. In real life we won't get 70 percent success and 30 percent failure and some compromise average return. Once we get to making that product we are going to find sales bring in either plus \$4,000,000 or we are out \$1,000,000. We will either make money or lose it; there just won't be any in-between value like your \$2.5 million."

On this note the meeting ended. A decision on the project was postponed.

The next week, however, another development led Pythagoras managers to review decision values in a new light. A representative of Heisenberg Investments, Inc., a venture capital group, called on Pythagoras management. Heisenberg had heard of the new process from a Pythagoras director. The investment company "might" be interested in buying out the new process.

After a number of exploratory meetings, the senior Heisenberg representative began serious negotiations by announcing, "We agree that the odds on this project are 70 percent profitable and 30 percent unprofitable. We also recognize that your company is a bit tight on cash and dubious about taking a million-dollar gamble that might not pay off.

"Well, we can convert this situation from a gamble to a sure thing for you. We are willing to buy the process. In other words, we will take over the gamble. The question is, how much must we pay?"

Bargaining then got under way. Gradually, as the Heisenberg offer rose from a \$2 million starting point, the once purely "abstract" \$2.5 million composite value of Pythagoras' previous decision diagrams began to get very real. There was an in-between value after all, and not the strictly win-or-lose situation seen by one of the Pythagoras executives. In fact, when offered a sure \$2.5 million, the Pythagoras people found they were just about willing to give up the 70 percent chance at (+) \$4,000,000 and 30 percent chance at (—) \$1,000,000. They now saw \$2.5 million as the *value* of being in a position to take the 70-30 gamble for \$4,000,000 and (—) \$1,000,000 respectively.

Once a decision-maker can accept that position values at the nodes of a decision diagram are logical and meaningful, he can readily make use of decision trees. Any further difficulties will no longer be those of philosophy but of detail—though there may be plenty of these. Decision trees, while simple in essence, can get complex in application.

Take, for instance, any of the event forks in the Emperor Products illustration. In actuality, both at the action and the sales-event forks there might be a great many different possible actions and a whole spectrum of possible sales rises or drops after each possible different action. What we showed as simple event forks would be more accurately portrayed as event fans which make for a very complex, multiple-branched decision tree. Fortunately, under analysis some of the values of a given event fan can turn out to be much more likely to occur than others. In fact, there are times when event fans can be effectively treated as a single branch or as relatively simple two- or three-branch forks.

Such a rationalizing of event fans, of course, makes a decision tree more manageable. One of the main difficulties in analyzing decision trees is that even with simple two and three or four branch forks the trees can, as one analyst put it, "get so bushy they are hairy."

But there are useful techniques for thinning down bushy trees. Some involve simple common sense. For example, in a situation such as Emperor's the managers automatically eliminated two possible actions: do nothing, and raise price. In that case competitive factors and the possible entry of newcomers to the field would label both these alternatives, though possible, patently unrewarding. Then, too, for purposes of comparison between alternative branches, there are techniques for thinning a fork in a tree from, say, five down to a simpler two branches. With careful staff work it is usually possible to shape and trim a decision tree down to its principal branches before bringing it up for top management consideration.

The really difficult and vital element in the construction of a decision tree is the making of assumptions and setting of probabilities from which the "magic" numbers in a decision tree are developed. When decision trees are first introduced many managers go through strenuous verbal and mental contortions to avoid being pinned down to hard number estimates. When they do assign probability values to estimates, managers tend to be inconsistent; in dealing with related multiple events they often assign individual values that total more than 100 percent. Finally, with different managers involved in developing a given valuation of the probabilities of an event, it takes time and careful analysis to reach mutual agreement.

Moreover, the complexities that underlie even one simple-seeming probability number can be extensive. In some cases, an estimated probability may be the computer-simulated resultant of the interactions of four, five and more variables, plus a number of economic indices and a string of basic assumptions.

A reassuring aspect of decision trees, however, is that they are as easily adaptable to fairly rough calculations worked out by pencil and a hand calculator as to highly refined ones. And, as further reassurance, even at their most highly refined, decision tree numbers make no pretense of developing specific point values. They are intended only as a measure of the *relative* virtues of alternate action-event paths and of the various points on these paths.

Men with some exposure to a variety of decision diagram applications, such as Vatter of Harvard and Collins of Arthur D. Little, agree that within any one company there is an indeterminate band of applications where decision trees can be of value but outside of which they approach redundancy. For instance, if the decision problem is a relatively simple one in which the executives involved are well-practiced and which they can virtually handle in their heads, the use of decision trees, even as an introductory device, might be uneconomical. But there are many marketing, pricing, research investment, new venture and acquisition decisions whose complexity and implications for the company warrant the use of decision trees.

The decision diagrams also have useful side effects. Since most upper-level middle managers are both responsible for budgets and accountable to bosses, they tend to play a conservative game—and with good reason. If they run risks that pay off, fine. But one failure that generates losses can ruin or retard a career. The result, in most concerns, is a clustering of decisions at the lower payout, lower risk end of the spectrum. In other words, the company's best strategy and an individual manager's best strategy do not necessarily coincide.

If, however, the same manager makes a formal, decision tree analysis of the investment and gets agreement from above as to the relative risks and rewards of the project, he will be in a position to make the investment with much less likelihood of career suicide in the event of losses.

There is some danger in that managers, mesmerized by the logic of the numbers they see, may take the decision tree as an answer machine rather than carefully investigating the assumptions upon which the diagram's numbers are based. But valuating the risks versus rewards for decision trees finds the balance well in their favor.

E. STRATEGIES AND POLICIES

25 STRATEGY'S ROLE IN BUSINESS*

J. Thomas Cannon

Effective business strategy is an essential requirement for an outstanding company. Of all the contrasts between the successful and the unsuccessful business, or between the corporate leader and its followers, the single, most important differentiating factor is strategy. Differences in research achievements, in product development, in quality of manufacture, in sales penetration, in net profit, and in return on investment are all traceable in whole or in significant measure to the caliber of business strategy and its execution. Strategy is the catalyst, the main thread and thrust of the business. It is the dynamic element of managing which enables the company to achieve its results in the competitive marketplace over the long run.

Every business has a strategy, whether expressed or implied. It does not matter whether this strategy is consciously and deliberately developed or is largely intuitive, relying upon unusual leadership, chance, and timing for success. Either by design or by accident, the fine art of strategy is primarily responsible for the accomplishments of most success-sustaining companies. Conversely, the lack of effective strategy, either by design or by accident, explains the corporate declines or dissolutions which occur.

Since both the positive and adverse effects of strategy are long term and lasting rather than transitory, the strategic work of the business is fundamental to its longevity. Unfortunately, for so fundamental an aspect, too little is understood about its patterns. Competitors' future strategies are difficult to predict effectively. One's own strategic choices are made uncertain by the competitive environment and by the risks of technological and management obsolescence. Fortunately, a great deal more can be learned about the nature and types of business strategy and about the more deliberate means of developing winning strategies. The experience of every successful and not-so-successful company contains lessons to be learned and applied by tomorrow's management.

A fuller understanding of the concepts of strategy involves two questions: What? and How? What types of strategies are available to management? How can they help be developed more effectively to meet the competitive requirements of the business?

THE INGREDIENTS OF EFFECTIVE STRATEGY

The most successful business strategies can be selected on a number of tangible and intangible bases, including volume, dollars of profit, number of employees, image for innovation, technological accomplishments, and contribution to society. Perhaps the most meaningful measure of successful private enterprise is the company's return on capital, or its net profit as a percent of stockholders' equity. One recent snapshot of leading industrial concerns compared on this basis was taken by *Dun's Review* in conjunction with Moody's Investors' Service. The 1964 performance of twenty outstanding companies is summarized in Table 1.

The strategies employed by these concerns vary widely, even within the same industry. One of the most obvious contrasts to be drawn, for example, is that between the two cosmetic firms, Avon Products and Revlon, both of which have achieved impressive returns on investment, volume, and profit growth over the years, using markedly different approaches. Avon's entire strategy is built around its highly successful organization of sales ladies. Revlon relies upon brilliant execution of more commonly used methods of advertising and distribution, together with its own unique approach to product planning, brand names, and imagery.

The success of these contrasting marketing styles for Avon and Revlon is highly significant for the business strategist. Primarily, the contrast illustrates that there cannot be a single,

* Reprinted by permission of the publisher from *Business Strategy and Policy*, Harcourt, Brace & World, Inc., 1968, pp. 3–33. Mr. Cannon is an executive with the International Business Machines Corporation.

TABLE 1 Blue-Ribbon Earners in U.S. Industry, 1964

COMPANIES	RETURN ON EQUITY 1964	REVENUES 1964 (MILLIONS)	PERCENT-AGE INCREASE OVER 1959	NET INCOME 1964 (MILLIONS)	PERCENT-AGE INCREASE OVER 1959	PRINCIPAL BUSINESS
Xerox	70.5%	$268.0	745.4	$38.53	1,752.4	xerographic products
Louisiana Land & Explor.	47.4	62.4	61.2	32.08	65.7	oil and gas royalties
Avon Products	46.4	299.5	111.0	39.84	176.9	cosmetics and toiletries
Searle (G.D.)	45.4	86.5	150.7	24.24	232.1	ethical drugs
Royal Crown Cola	37.3	46.4	119.9	3.78	136.3	soft drinks
Smith Kline & French	36.0	218.2	61.8	38.69	54.7	ethical drugs
American Home Products	33.5	571.0	35.7	61.52	31.8	drugs, home products, foods
Bristol-Myers	32.5	265.0	101.5	23.09	159.7	toiletries and proprietary drugs
Gillette	31.0	299.0	42.9	37.67	20.9	shaving products and toiletries
Norwich Pharmacal	29.0	59.7	46.7	7.63	48.2	proprietary and ethical drugs
Caterpillar Tractor	28.6	1,161.0	56.4	123.83	166.2	earthmoving equipment
McGraw-Hill	28.1	193.4	82.8	15.17	85.2	book and magazine publisher
Beauty Counselors	27.5	13.1	33.7	1.14	16.3	cosmetics and toiletries
IBM	27.1	3,239.4	147.3	431.16	196.1	business machines
Magnavox	26.1	227.2	110.8	13.80	194.9	radio, TV and electronic equip.
Kellogg	26.0	349.1	44.0	32.61	68.7	ready-to-eat cereals
Square D	25.8	155.0	40.5	20.52	96.6	industrial control equipment
General Motors	25.7	16,997.0	51.3	1,734.80	98.7	automotive products
Revlon	25.6	197.2	56.9	15.08	39.1	cosmetics and toiletries
Sterling Drug	25.3	268.5	28.3	29.22	39.0	proprietary and ethical drugs

simple formula for strategic success, even within the same industry.

Similar comparisons can be made using either such long-established blue-chip firms as Procter & Gamble, Du Pont, U.S. Steel, IBM, and General Motors or such recent American success stories as Litton Industries, Polaroid, Xerox, and Indian Head. In every case, the questions may be asked: How did they get where they are? What will it take to keep them in the forefront of industry under increasing domestic and foreign competition? Effective business strategy is the best answer.

It is equally useful to examine the contrasting approaches of companies with negative achievement records, as portrayed in the analyses of corporate failures or in annually weakening status reports. Consider the New Haven Railroad and Packard Motors. What management action or the lack of it led the New Haven to the bankruptcy courts in the summer of 1961? Why are Packard and over 1,000 other makes of automobile no longer in the annual automotive shows displaying the coming models? What made success possible for the post-World War II phenomenon of corporate "raiders" who waged bitter proxy fights in their quest for idle cash or tax-loss carrybacks?

Obviously, a good many different factors have contributed to American industry's success stories and outstanding records of profits and sales growth. Likewise, no one factor can be held responsible for the numerous failures and slippages in profit and market positions. At or near the top of any analyst's list of requirements for success is the presence of outstanding leadership—people like Litton Industries' "Tex" Thornton and Roy Ash; IBM's Thomas J. Watsons (both Sr. and Jr.); Du Pont's succession of astute executives, including Pierre, Lamont, and Irénée Du Pont and Donaldson Brown; and Indian Head's James E. Robison.

Fortunate timing in discovering or tapping explosive potential demand is another factor contributing to success in modern business. Timing has been a particularly important feature in the strategies of such companies as Owens-Corning Fiberglas, Singer Sewing Machine, Cabincraft, and those companies that have catered successfully to the vast "leisure" markets. Appearing much less often than one might expect is an entirely new invention (e.g., the Gillette safety razor and the Polaroid Land camera).

To the student of business management, the many requirements for strategic success, such as leadership, timing, monopoly or patent protection, innovation, and research talent are familiar phenomena. Equally clear, on the other hand, is the difficulty of generalizing on a basic formula for success across the entire business spectrum. However, while the specific strategies of the hundreds of successful companies are highly individualized, there are patterns among them, even extending across industries, which can be reproduced or adapted by others. A look at one company in greater depth suggests the learning possibilities.

MINNESOTA MINING & MANUFACTURING: AN EFFECTIVE LONG-TERM STRATEGY

One of the numerous American enterprises whose strategic effectiveness has more than met the competitive tests of time is the Minnesota Mining & Manufacturing Company (3M). Founded in 1902, 3M had achieved annual sales of over $32 million and after-tax profits of $4.5 million by 1941. In subsequent years, both sales and profits continued to grow at an impressive rate.

Minnesota Mining & Manufacturing Company Performance

	SALES (IN MILLIONS)	NET PROFIT AFTER TAXES (IN MILLIONS)
1941	$ 32.4	$ 4.5
1946	75.2	9.9
1951	170.1	15.7
1956	330.8	38.7
1961	608.2	74.9
1966	1,152.6	138.4

SOURCE: *Moody's Industrials.*

In the twenty years following World War II, Minnesota Mining's sales rose to over thirty-five times their 1941 level, and its profits rose to more than thirty times their figure for this pre-War date. In recent years, 3M has consistently produced after-tax income of between 19 percent and 20 percent of stockholders' equity. This record of doubling sales and profits approximately every five years has been sustained through a consistent pattern of strategic decisions by an aggressive and change-oriented management team. The central theme of 3M's strategy throughout these years has been a continuing search for profitable new products and markets. Advancements have come through a combination of both internal research and development programs and acquisitions of going businesses.

3M Product Sales Distribution, 1965

	PERCENT OF SALES
Abrasives, adhesives, chemicals	12
Tape and allied products	14
Electrical products	16
Advertising services and protective products	11
Graphic systems	15
Photographic products and miscellaneous	10
International sales	22

SOURCE: *Moody's Industrials.*

The continuing success of this approach is evidenced by the fact that in 1965 "twenty-five percent of 3M's sales and thirty-five percent of profits came from items entirely new in 1960."[1] By the end of 1965, the company had twenty-two divisions in the United States and a rapidly growing international business. Sales were well diversified among six major product categories comprised of 40 product lines and over 35,000 individual products.

A number of the new products represented entirely new ventures for the company, but many came about as a result of astute extension or "chaining" of existing technologies into new product types, applications, or markets. Minnesota Mining's steady stream of new-product accomplishments is directly attributable to the climate for growth, innovation, and risk-taking which its leaders have unswervingly fostered, starting with William L. McKnight and continuing with Herbert P. Buetow and Bert S. Cross. The full list of significant participants and the total complement of strategic factors are, of course, considerably more numerous.

It is important for the student of business strategy to explore in full all key areas of the successful companies' experiences. There is a need to bring into better perspective the many

[1] "How To Be Happy With R & D," *Forbes*, July 1, 1966, p. 25.

complexities of strategy, often a most elusive aspect of business management. In the case of 3M, for example, just how much of its record can be explained by its inspirational and outstanding leadership? By its fortunate timing of entry into new markets? By well-selected acquisitions? By its monopoly of certain corporate resources? By patent protection or recurring research and engineering genius? What contribution was made by its highly effective marketing and distribution organization? And most important, how were these factors melded by 3M management into such an outstanding total result?

The truth of 3M's history is that all such factors have, in one way or another, been responsible for sales and profit growth, but overall success has decidedly been due to a shrewdly coordinated business strategy.

One measure of the effectiveness of this strategy is the fact that certain of 3M's successes came as a result of the company's recognizing and improving upon inferior product lines. For instance, during one early period it became apparent to management that the company was marketing an inferior sandpaper product to the automotive industry. Concern over this fact stimulated more careful attention to customer needs and led to new research and development decisions. The poor qualities of the paper, such as the dust hazard to the user, were eliminated and a waterproof paper was developed, which has led industry sales since its introduction.

As in most successful companies, 3M's resilience, resources, and strategic ability have overcome many such problems to keep moving the business ahead. More importantly, *new strategic challenges must never end* for any company which is to sustain a profitable growth. For 3M, among the most formidable strategic thrusts in its history was its aggressive, broadly-based plan of entrance into the photography, or image-formation, industry. This area had long been dominated in the United States by Eastman Kodak, with Polaroid, Bell & Howell, and General Aniline & Film as its principal, traditional competitors.[2] Employing a logical approach, 3M extended into direct competition with these companies first through its technologies in graphic arts, with pre-sensitized lithographic plates, and then through microfilming and office copying with Thermo-Fax. Subsequently, it acquired Revere Camera Company, Dynacolor Corporation, and Ferrania of Milan. (The latter is one of Europe's largest film manufacturers.)

[2] Robert Sheehan, "The Kodak Picture—Sunshine And Shadow," *Fortune*, May 1965, p. 127.

This type of strategic challenge, in an industry of tough and resourceful competition, dramatically illustrates two of the most elusive and intangible aspects of strategy: (1) the problems of guiding a company into new areas of unknown dimensions; and (2) the inherently high magnitude of risk-taking which accompanies such an undertaking. These considerations suggest why strategic management of the future will require much more than a reliance on intuitive leadership alone. One point of departure is to seek a more useful definition of business strategy than has heretofore been apparent.

DEFINITION OF BUSINESS STRATEGY

Business strategy is that area of management which calls the signals, or sets the direction, for the essential work of the company. A company's total (or composite) strategy is always a compound of many different action decisions, rather than a single plan of attack. It consists of a hierarchy of prime strategies and a background of supporting strategies. It is continuously in need of review and/or updating to keep it attuned to an ever-changing competitive environment. Consistent with these characteristics and conditions, the basic theme of this book derives from the following definition.

Business strategies are
the directional action decisions
which are required competitively
to achieve the company's purposes.

Each phrase of the definition requires amplification as a foundation for developing a useful conceptual framework for management.

Business Strategies Business strategies are not the ends, but rather the means for initiating the actions needed to achieve the ends or purposes of the company. Strategies, to be effective, must be based solidly upon, and be fully consistent with, such purposes. Therefore, they are subordinate to the company's purposes and, in turn, to its entire competitive environment. Strategies are subject to continuing formulation, change, and/or obsolescence through time.

These characteristics necessitate management's attention to strategic decisionmaking as a continuing, dynamic process rather than a chore to be undertaken at those few times each year when management meets to develop formal short- and long-range plans.

Directional Action Decisions This element of the definition includes all established and accepted objectives, plans, and policies, together with their implementing or "committing" decisions, which provide and initiate a direction for the business as a whole and for its essential functions. This includes the ever-present timing factor and the decision to take a step or adopt a set of objectives, plans, and policies. It excludes (but is nevertheless vitally interested in) the execution of the decision, which is tactical and/or administrative.

In this definition of directional action decisions, any business policies that provide directional action decisions are considered as having a similar role to that of strategies. In this context, strategies and policies will be treated as comparable entities.[3]

Distinctions between strategic and nonstrategic work, and between strategy, tactics, and administration, which are pertinent to usage throughout the text, will be explained in subsequent sections. No one source will be likely to satisfy all concerned with precise, airtight differentiations. Nevertheless, it is useful at this stage to note briefly the position taken, which is as follows:

Strategies	Directional action decisions for the company as a whole and for any function or area of the business.
Tactics	Implementation of the strategies, with emphasis normally confined to the direct-line functions of the business, such as sales and marketing, manufacturing, engineering, and research and development.
Administration	Management and operating work which is required to support, control, evaluate, and administer to the strategic and tactical aspects.

[3] Policies are guides to future decisions and actions. Their purpose is to provide a point of departure for future decisions or to approve in advance appropriate action to be taken in recurring situations. Thus, the use of policies facilitates decentralization of responsibility. Policies may be issued as written statements, or they may be derived as unwritten understandings of past actions (which may or may not have been aimed at establishing precedence or frames of reference for subsequent actions). The need for both major and minor policy guides exists at virtually all levels of the management structure. Therefore, business policies may be either strategic or non-strategic, depending on the extent of their influence on the basic direction of the business.

Strategic action decisions may either be planned or impromptu. They may also constitute either a new direction or a reaffirmation and continuation of a direction already being pursued. These opposing characteristics are particularly pertinent in relation to the competitive environment. Unforeseen activities and policies by competitors, new governmental actions or directives, explosive international situations, strikes in related industries, or the like, periodically warrant a rapid strategic response. This often entails making changes in basic strategy on more of a hasty or impromptu basis than management would prefer. Even if the decision is to maintain the status quo, communicating a reaffirmation of present strategies can have a stabilizing effect on the organization.

A management plan is not a strategy until it has been translated into a set of action decisions whereby the company's resources are either *committed* to or *"de-committed"* from a particular venture or course of action. Committing and de-committing decisions relate both to present competitive actions and to the assignment of development work leading to future competitive commitment. The essential point is that an action decision must be made before a plan qualifies as a strategy of the company. Too frequently, strategic planning remains a collection of alternatives left unresolved for an undetermined future date. In such instances, management is, in reality, hedging on the commitment decision. Application of the "hard" concept of directional action decisions instead of the frequently "soft" concept, which goes only as far as planning alternatives, is to be emphasized as a fundamental requirement of more effective strategic decisionmaking.

Competitive Requirements The company's strategies are at all times interdependent with competitors' actions, both present and prospective, and with all other forces and actions in the competitive environment. The changing setting of the business continuously confronts management with new choices of action to be identified, evaluated and selected, tabled, or rejected.

In its broadest sense, the company's total business environment encompasses at least eight spheres, or areas, of interest. Both the company's purposes and strategies must be realistic and consistent with the demands from each of these spheres. Just a few of the implications are suggested below. Many other requirements and issues in each sphere will no doubt occur to the reader.

Stockholders. Will the stock equity be protected and appreciate at an acceptable rate through time? Will the return on investment, earnings per share, and yield meet the needs and expectations of the stockholders? Are the purposes of the business and its directions consistent with the interests and intentions of the influencing or controlling stockholder groups?

Employees. Will there be adequate income appreciation and sufficient opportunities and incentives for self-development and self-realization of individuals and groups over the long term? Will the working environment necessitated by particular courses of strategic action be challenging and satisfying? Will the employees be able to identify with the purposes and directions as being worthwhile and as ends toward which they can contribute?

Customers and Prospects. Will the strategies keep or put the company in dynamic and growing markets? Will they provide the necessary basis for retaining present customers and creating new customers? Will they contribute to improving or innovating "user benefits" to these customers?

Suppliers and Middlemen. Will these groups, upon whom the company relies for outside services, be encouraged by on-going strategy to continue their support of the company's total effort? Will they be able to keep pace with the company's strategic timing?

Competitors. Will the strategies be aggressive and effective in relation to present and possible competitive courses of action? Will they leave gaps, soft spots, or opportunities for competitors to capture larger shares of the company's markets or to leapfrog ahead with new products, technologies, or policies?

The Community. Will the company's purposes and strategies be consistent with the best interests of the local communities in which it is a significant economic force or employment factor? Will they contribute to the growth and development of such communities and their people?

The National Interest. Will conflicts or restraints be avoided and compatibility be maintained in relation to basic national interests which affect the total business environment? Will the strategies be sensitive to social and civil rights programs and legislation? to labor-management relationships? to Justice Department and business regulatory requirements? to military and space efforts? to the country's ideological competition with communism?

International Market Interests. Will the company's strategies promote maximum development of its international market potential? Will they be consistent with the government's international trade development and balance-of-payment programs? Will they be sufficiently flexible to adapt to the differing requirements for business success in various parts of the world market?

The extreme complexity and interdependence of the various spheres of interest profoundly influence the scope and content of every company's total or composite strategic plan.

Company Purposes The company's purposes, the fourth key element of the strategy definition, are its basic corporate reasons for existing and for competing. These purposes must be consistent with the demands and opportunities of the various pertinent spheres of interest. The almost perpetual state of flux of the latter imposes a continuing requirement for review and updating of corporate purposes and strategies.

In the eyes of many stockholders, investment counselors, management consultants, top management, some enlightened union leaderships, and the Internal Revenue Department, the principal purpose of the American enterprise is profitability. This means fairly consistent profits year after year. No business practitioner or scholar would deny the prime role of profit motivation in achieving lasting corporate success. However, there is growing acceptance of the principle that profitability is not the purpose of business, but rather the prime measure of how well the business achieves its purposes.

Acceptance of this premise in no way diminishes the pressure for results provided by a profit target or requirement. Instead, it clears the way for more meaningful and substantive statements *re* the purpose of the business. For example, Peter Drucker, in his book *The Practice of Management,*[4] provided a profound clarification of company purpose when he said:

> If we want to know what a business is we have to start with its *purpose.* And its purpose must lie outside of the business itself. In fact, it must lie in society since a business enterprise is an organ of society. There is only one valid definition of business purpose: *to create a customer.*
>
> . . . What the business thinks it produces is not of first importance—especially not to the future of the business and to its success. What the customer thinks he is buying, what he considers 'value,' is decisive—it determines what a business is, what it produces and whether it will prosper.

Drucker provided industry with a significant new emphasis and a brand new point of departure for further refining the art of manage-

[4] Harper and Row Publishers, New York, 1954, p. 37.

ment. He shifted attention from the HOW to the WHAT of business principles, objectives, and management. His basic emphasis on "creating a customer" has stimulated elaboration of the market orientation theme. The marketing concept has become standard doctrine in many businesses, along with its "marketing myopia" converse, as first expressed by Theodore Levitt.[5]

Levitt said, in effect, that companies and entire industries were failing to grow because they defined their business purposes as product-oriented rather than market-oriented. Hence, the railroad industry was railroad-oriented rather than transportation-oriented. The petroleum companies were in the oil business rather than the energy business (which encompassed far more market alternatives, not only for fuels but also for other new end-uses and applications). Hollywood bowed to TV for a considerable period of time while it was in the business of "making movies." At the same time, TV was rapidly learning how to "provide entertainment." Ironically, by the mid-1960s, television was faced with re-examining its position to determine whether it was truly providing acceptable entertainment or whether it would need an even broader definition of its mission if it was to continue to grow and prosper.

The most meaningful extensions of Drucker's basic concept of business purpose—to create a customer—have been efforts by many businesses to define more fully just what they intend to do for their customers in terms of user benefits. Thus, IBM has stated that it is in the business of solving its customers' various information problems rather than merely selling computers. Lynn Townsend, President of Chrysler Corporation, stated on receiving the 1966 Marketing Statesman of the Year Award from the Sales Executives Club of New York that Chrysler's business was no longer that of making cars but rather that of "selling satisfactory transportation service for an extended period of time."

The task of defining corporate purpose in such a way as to motivate the organization toward fulfilling this purpose is more than just the skillful phrasing of a public statement, however. Much astute judgment lies behind Townsend's definition. At base is a fundamental understanding of the shifting nature of the automobile market, including changes in customer preferences; competitive styling and market approaches; the growing insistence of both dealers and consumers on greater guarantees of performance; emphasis on safety features and devices; plus many more trends and characteristics of the marketplace environment within which Chrysler operates. All of these factors heavily influence the nature of this company's strategic plan. A continuing understanding of the total competitive environment is essential to a meaningful updating of a company's purposes and strategies with respect to the passage of time and the inevitable industry and market changes that will occur.

A summary of the key points of each element of the business strategy definition is presented in Figure 1. The concept of strategy and its role in business is further clarified by distinguishing between strategy and tactics and by then identifying which of the general management functions of the executive are strategic in nature and which are not.

THE DISTINCTION BETWEEN STRATEGY AND TACTICS

The principal distinction between strategy and tactics is that strategy determines what major plans are to be undertaken and allocates resources to them, while tactics, in contrast, are the means by which previously-determined plans are executed. Beyond this, the difference between these two concepts reduces to matters of scope and timing, which are rarely the same for different industries. Our concern, therefore, is for the principal distinction, and here the military definitions of strategy and tactics add considerable understanding to the discussion.

Definitions of Military Strategy and Tactics

The Concise Oxford Dictionary states that "military strategy is the art of so moving or disposing the instruments of warfare (troops, ships, aircraft, missiles, etc.) as to impose upon the enemy the place, time and conditions for fighting preferred by oneself. Strategy ends, or yields to tactics when actual contact with the enemy is made." Tactics, on the other hand, are defined as the "art of disposing military or naval forces . . . in actual contact with the enemy."

Carl von Clausewitz, a Prussian army general and military scientist who helped found the German "General Staff" concept, similarly defined military strategy as "making use of battles in the furtherance of the war" and tactics as "the use of armed forces in battle."[6]

A successor to Clausewitz, Count von Moltke, was more lucid in his distinction be-

[5] Theodore Levitt, "Marketing Myopia," *Harvard Business Review*, July/August 1960, p. 45.

[6] Herman Foertsch, *The Art Of Modern Warfare*, Veritas Press, New York, 1940.

FIGURE 1 Definition of Business Strategies

Business strategies are ↓	The directional signals for the business Subordinate to the company's purposes, and in turn, to its competitive environment Subject to continuing formulation, change, and/or obsolescence through time
Directional action decisions ↓	Include all objectives, plans, and committing decisions which provide a direction for the business and its essential functions May be either planned or impromptu May constitute a new direction or a continuation of the present direction Are in force when the decision is made to commit (or decommit) the company's resources to: 1. Present competition 2. Development work leading to future competitive commitment Exclude the execution of the decision (execution is tactical or administrative)
Required competitively ↓	Interdependent at all times with 1. Competitive actions, both present and prospective 2. All other forces and actions of the business environment With continuing opportunities for new choices of action
To achieve the company's purposes	The basic corporate reasons for being and for competing Which relate to the entire competitive environment and all of the company's spheres of interest

tween strategy and tactics; in his definition he captures the uncertainty of the competitive environment.[7] He stated that "strategy is a system of makeshifts. It is carrying through an originally conceived plan under a constantly shifting set of circumstances. It is a matter of understanding correctly at every moment a constantly changing situation, and then doing the simplest and most natural thing with energy and determination.

"Strategy furnishes tactics with the opportunty to strike and with the prospect of success. It does this through its conduct of the armies and their concentration on the field of battle. On the other hand, however, strategy accepts the results of every single engagement and builds on them. Strategy retires when a tactical victory is in the making in order later to exploit the newly created situation."

[7] *Ibid.*

Moltke further defined the goal of military strategy: "to break the will of the enemy, deprive him of the means to fight, occupy his territory, destroy or obtain control of his resources . . . or otherwise make him submit." Moltke defines the goal of military tactics as success in a given action, which is only one part in a group of related military actions.

As the foregoing definitions imply, a major purpose, both in war and business, for carefully distinguishing strategy from tactics is to avoid delegating strategic decisionmaking responsibilities too low in the organization. Herman Foertsch, a colonel of the German General Staff in the twentieth century, diagrammed these differences on the scale shown in Figure 2. For many generations of warfare, this has been an accurate representation of the crossover point between strategy and tactics. To some extent the point has shifted with the advent of the so-called tactical nuclear devices

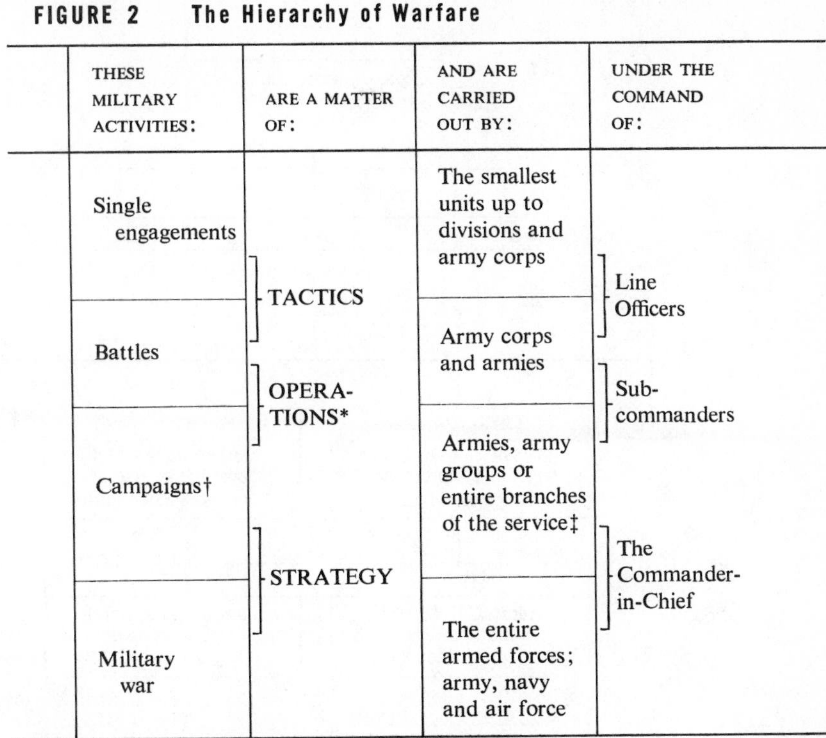

FIGURE 2 The Hierarchy of Warfare

THESE MILITARY ACTIVITIES:	ARE A MATTER OF:	AND ARE CARRIED OUT BY:	UNDER THE COMMAND OF:
Single engagements	TACTICS	The smallest units up to divisions and army corps	Line Officers
Battles	TACTICS / OPERATIONS*	Army corps and armies	Line Officers / Sub-commanders
Campaigns†	OPERATIONS* / STRATEGY	Armies, army groups or entire branches of the service‡	Sub-commanders / The Commander-in-Chief
Military war	STRATEGY	The entire armed forces; army, navy and air force	The Commander-in-Chief

* Strictly speaking, operations are the movements of armed forces preparatory to battle, but the fighting itself is usually also included in the concept.

† A connected series of battles in a single theater of war.

‡ Individual units may, of course, cooperate in engagements and battles, as, for instance, air forces in a land or naval battle.

SOURCE: Foertsch, Herman, *The Art of Modern Warfare* (New York: Veritas Press, 1940).

now in the hands of certain U.S. field forces on a very limited scale. Both their destructive physical potential and the political and moral implications of their use must now transfer even single engagements in such circumstances from tactical to strategic choices. But generally, the scalar differences of warfare shown in the diagram make a point which is equally valid for business: Do not unduly delegate the master strategy determination to echelons lower than those which possess the perspective required for the most effective decisions.

Characteristics which Make a Business Decision Strategic It is virtually impossible to define in advance of taking action all of the decisions which are strategic, as contrasted with those which are tactical. This differs widely by company and industry. However, it is important to make the effort in order to limit strategic work and to ensure that it is comprehensively planned.

Such work is distinguished from nonstrategic work in several ways: Strategic decisions are major choices of action which vary in scope, timing, emphasis, shifts in the allocation of key resources, and contributions to end-results. But what is major in one company may not be major in another. To illustrate this point, let us examine the classifications of a "decision ladder" for a hypothetical sales area, shown in Figure 3.

A major strategic decision (A) has been made to expand the present business rather than to diversify. The Figure shows some of the supporting decisions which are required to carry out the basic strategy. Among several moves which can be made at the B level to undertake the direction or course of action of A is B-2, setting higher volume goals. A number of decisions are adopted, in turn, at the C level which are still strategic in this situation because they involve basic questions of direction. Hence, the upgrading of the present sales force (C-2) is considered a strategic decision, because the company has never before hired college graduates for salesmen. In contrast, the steps D-2 and E-2 required for implementing

FIGURE 3 Strategic/Non-strategic Decision Ladder

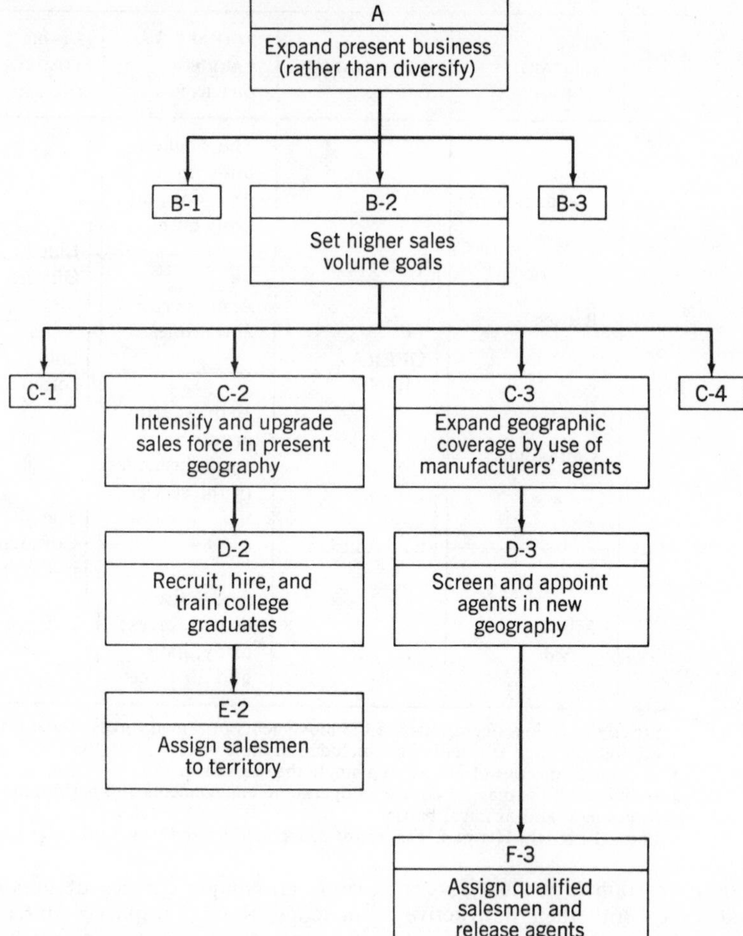

C-2 are tactical, since they only involve implementation of the previous decision which established the new direction for the business.

Similarly, C-3 was strategic, since the company had not previously used manufacturers' agents, but D-3 was not. Later replacement of the agents was a new strategic move. Ladder analysis of this type is equally useful in manufacturing, research and development, and other major line functions.

Additional characteristics of strategic decisions, which distinguish them from tactical decisions, include the following:

- They are likely to effect a significant departure from the established product-market mix. (This might involve branching out technologically or innovating in other ways.)
- They are likely to hold provisions for undertaking programs with an unusually high degree of risk relative to previous experience (e.g., using untried resources or entering uncertain markets and competitive situations where predictability of success is noticeably limited).
- They are likely to include a wide range of available alternatives to cope with a major competitive problem, the scope of these alternatives providing for significant differences in both the results and resources required.
- They are likely to involve important timing options, both for starting development work and for deciding when to make the actual market commitment.
- They are likely to call for major changes in the competitive "equilibrium," creating a

new operating and customer-acceptance pattern.

- They are likely to resolve the choice of either leading or following certain market or competitive advances, based on a trade-off[8] between the costs and risks of innovating and the timing vulnerability of letting others pioneer (in the expectation of catching up and moving ahead at a later date on the strength of a superior marketing force).

These characteristics illustrate that the differentiation of strategic from non-strategic work can never be quite as precise as some students of business would prefer. This limitation exists since judgement is still required to interpret what really does or does not constitute a directional action signal in a given situation. If there is still doubt, the wisest approach is to treat the decision as a strategy. In addition, further understanding of the areas of distinction is gained by classifying all of the major functions of the business and then isolating the strategic work within them. This also provides a conceptual framework for the classification of types of strategies.

[8] The process of balancing and choosing from among conflicting factors, requiring one to relinquish certain benefits in a choice of action in order to gain others considered to be more desirable.

CLASSIFICATION OF MAJOR FUNCTIONS OF THE BUSINESS

A profit-motivated company exists to develop a market. Its objectives, goals, and marketing concepts are oriented toward this purpose. In the broadest sense, all functions of the business are market-development functions. However, while this is an admirable attitude

FIGURE 4 Major Functional Areas of the Business

GROUPING	FUNCTION
1 Market development	Marketing research Sales and market planning Application development Channels of distribution planning Physical distribution Sales management Selling Sales promotion Advertising
2 Product development	Product planning Research Development Engineering Manufacturing Supply
3 Finance and administration	Finance Secretarial and legal services Personnel Industrial relations Public relations Control Administrative services
4 General management	Identification of opportunities Setting direction and goals Assigning basic work and allocating resources Developing resources Committing resources Evaluating results

to foster throughout the company, it is too fuzzy and idealistic a concept for strategic planning purposes. Thus, there are obvious advantages to sorting the functions into several categories according to their different roles and importance in strategic planning.

One useful approach is a four-way split into market development, finance and administration, product development, and general management functions. A possible grouping of specific functions on this basis is shown in Figure 4. With due allowances for corporate and industry differences, the first, second, and fourth areas generally include those functions which most often confront management with strategic choices. It is an exception when activities in the third area of finance and administration take on the same degree of strategic significance as the other three. However, at times strategic choices become extremely crucial in virtually every function designated here as financial or administrative.

It is the intent of the classification in Figure 4 to suggest a basic concept for planning both the over-all and the functional strategies of the firm. It is not expected to present a comprehensive listing of functions which will satisfy all concerned or suggest a method of organization. Regardless of how a business is actually organized, the utility of this conceptual separation of functions is that it recognizes several different types of work, standards of measurement, and decisionmaking requirements in the various areas.

Market Development Functions The market development functions embody all the various activities that go into identifying markets and marketing opportunities. They also specify the products to be offered and plan and accomplish their sale, distribution, and use in the market. Oversimplified, the functions of Area A are volume-oriented. The managers involved in them are anxious to give the market exactly what it wants, even if this means permitting many product variations and price concessions. Market development management is measured by how effectively market share increases.

One group of functions in this area *provides inputs* for strategic decisionmaking and clarifies strategy alternatives. For example, marketing research is mainly an input function. Sales and market planning is also a key input source, but is, in addition, the principal locus of *strategic market development decisions* on product, market, geographic and distribution-channel strategies, and on the marketing concept of the firm. The other functions of Area 1 contribute inputs to the strategic decision process, but they are primarily concerned with *implementation* of the established market development strategies.

Product Development Functions Area 2 of Figure 4 embraces a number of functional areas which contribute to developing and/or implementing the product strategies of the company. This involves the planning, design, engineering, and manufacture of the product as well as pure and applied research. The latter functions, in particular, carry the lead in identifying, evaluating, and developing new product and technological opportunities.

Product planning provides top management with a bridge from the plant and engineering laboratory to the market development area. It also establishes a crosscheck between the sales and manufacturing divisions. With sales and market planning on one side and product planning on the other, management is in the position of making trade-offs between the two points of view. There frequently are major conflicts between the sales and product management areas over the types of products sales has said the market requires and product management's views as to the economic, technical, and timing feasibility of providing them.

The conflict stems from marketing management's marketplace orientation and its interest in increasing market share. On the other hand, management of the product development functions, which must come up with the product, tends to want repetitive volume of a generalized line, expense efficiency, product quality, availability, and technical leadership. This implies that every company has two such counterbalancing forces, which often is not the case. The absence of a crosscheck is one of the major conditions which led Levitt to advance his previously noted marketing myopia thesis.

Finance and Administration Functions Area 3 of Figure 4 indicates a number of additional functions which are classified as financial or administrative, since they normally are not the key directional forces for the business. This composition of activities is narrower than that often used elsewhere in business practice and literature. The principal difference is that a number of the general management functions of the chief executive (Area 4) are often included in an administrative classification. The advantages of separating them in relation to the concept of strategy will become more apparent in the next section. The remaining administrative functions of Area 3 have a variety of supporting and controlling roles to play as backup to the basic line functions of the market and product development areas. In this regard, the administrative activities are somewhat analagous to the supporting staffs and logistical functions of the military which enable the development and execution of military strategy and tactics.

As indicated previously, most of the financial and administrative functions normally have a relatively limited strategic role. However, at one time or another virtually all of them do become involved in strategic alternatives and decisions. For example, the availability of suitable financial alternatives may be absolutely essential to the effective funding of a new set of decisions and programs. Similarly, strategic choices involving a basic directional decision periodically confront the chief executive in such areas as legal and patent considerations, personnel administration, industrial relations, and the choice of union representation.

Management cannot afford to ignore these exceptions and indeed, should be on the lookout for opportunities in such areas. Sometimes the need is obvious, after the fact. For instance, when the consumer buying strike suddenly erupted in the Fall of 1966, the Sperry & Hutchinson Company and other trading stamp concerns found themselves listed as being right in among the prime suspects in the public uproar over the high cost of food. Overnight the public relations function in these firms became an area of major strategic concern. The strategy lesson for management is whether the contingency could have been foreseen and major preventive action taken over a period of time.

General Management Functions General management provides the entrepreneurial force and emphasis for the business. It establishes the basic direction, provides the profit stewardship, and maintains the necessary motivation and leadership for success. Top management reconciles conflicting views in major functional areas, such as sales and manufacturing. It assures that all administrative areas maintain the needed support and/or control of the market development and product development areas.

Business writings contain literally dozens of frames of reference which are meant to describe the prime responsibilities of the head of the business. The most common of these is the three-step definition of *planning, execution,* and *control,* which is the classical basis for most guides to balanced business management. The classification of six broad aspects of management work, shown previously in Area 4 of Figure 4, offers another guide to executive responsibility. These six aspects are at the heart of the over-all strategic decisionmaking process. It is important to clarify which of the six are of greatest influence on the quality and timeliness of the company's strategic decisions and the execution.

THE STRATEGIC ASPECTS OF GENERAL MANAGEMENT

One of the principal shortcomings of management is its failure to separate work which is strategic from that which is not. Consequently, insufficient time and attention are given to the key matters, and a host of additional managerial problems are likely to flow from this central omission. Management tends to classify most of its decisionmaking activities and a large portion of its other work as strategic. The chance is great that some of this work is tactical rather than strategic and that the main body involves neither tactics nor strategy but is administrative in nature, involving such work as control, direction and motivation, review and development of supporting plans and programs, or even actual implementation and execution activities of the major operating functions. Some degree of participation in these areas is both desirable and essential. However, it is likely that the executive, by distinguishing too loosely between strategy and tactics detracts from the potential of sound business strategy.

Three conditions are usually responsible for a failure to isolate and concentrate on the strategic work which needs doing. *First,* senior management often has a desire to keep a hand in the operational, or on-the-job activities of the firm. Current operations are dynamic. They demand knowledgeable supervision. Orders must be given to keep things moving efficiently. The newly installed manager, particularly if he has come up through the ranks, is often prone to pay greater attention to operational activities (where his ability to second-guess is well-established) than he is to his general management functions. When this happens, the objectivity of the management team, required for effective strategic planning, is lessened.

Stemming from this natural inclination to keep operating is a *second* factor of inadvertancy. The pressures of serious current crises, sudden competitive moves, key personnel problems, and similar urgencies have a way of eroding management time. Clearly, the chief executive must attend to a number of these things. The cliche, "If I don't take care of today's problems, I won't be around to worry about next year's," is all too true. So the question is not either/or, but rather a matter of balance.

Balance is where the *third* factor comes in. Failure to isolate strategic work is often due to either an inadequate appreciation of what it is and what it is not, or, similarly, to a lack of understanding as to why it makes sense to separate the strategic work from the non-strategic. For this reason, it is helpful to examine the six functions of general management to see which are strategic and therefore deserve the special attention of top management.

Figure 5 emphasizes the six functions as a continuum for management and also classifies them as to their strategic or non-strategic emphasis.

FIGURE 5 Aspects of General Management

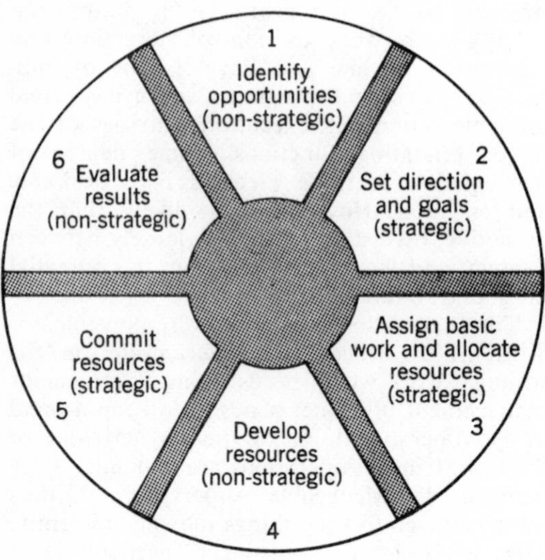

These six types of activities in the sequence shown (with sector 6 cycling back into sector 1) apply to essentially every kind of business endeavor, whether new or long-established.

For example, the engineers who splinter off from a major defense electronics contractor and start their own firm to launch a new product or component for space guidance systems must necessarily begin the process at 1 and then proceed through the other five stages in pursuit of their desired goals. New business ventures always start at 1, even though the opportunity-defining process quite often suffers because it is too informal, lacks thoroughness, or is optimistically distorted by the enthusiasm and fondness of the parent for his brain child.

Similarly, the going concern must follow the same six-step sequence, but with one very major difference. The new engineering splinter group initially has a simple one-track sequential progression through the six management functions. The going business may have a half-dozen or more strategic cycles working simultaneously, each in a different phase. The number of these cycles, and therefore the complexity of managing, varies in relation to two questions. First, how many different product-market strategies are in effect, regardless of whether they are well- or ill-defined? Second, how much difference is there in the timing and maturity of the various programs? In the complex situation, the annual planning and budgeting procedure actually can be a deterrent to balanced strategic decisions. It may unduly focus on sector 6, results evaluation, and lead management to project multiple-year goals based primarily on history to the exclusion of sector 1, opportunity definition.

The reverse of this can be equally bad. New opportunities can be pursued too much for their own sake. Consider, for example, the rash of diversification and acquisition studies pointed toward major changes in the character of the business, which could easily be proposed by an aggressive, growth-minded management team. Unfortunately, such diversification work all too often commences without an adequate assessment of its feasibility in relation to existing resources. Assessment of this type is part of the reason for sector 6.

The point to be made is that the six aspects of managing are a continuum, and each step may be applicable to a single strategic program at a different time. This means that the planning and review process cannot be pigeonholed arbitrarily into one fixed date or time period each year.

The typical strategic and non-strategic content of the six aspects of general management is further detailed in Figure 6. Strategy is particularly pertinent to three of the six aspects, 2, 3, and 5. These areas involve strategic decisions as to purposes, basic direction, the allocation of resources, and competitive commitment and de-commitment. Aspect 4 also gets involved in strategic de-commitment work. The other areas entail a combination of tactical implementation activities and a wide range of work which is administrative in nature.

FIGURE 6 Strategic and Non-strategic Aspects of General Management

BASIC FUNCTION	SELECTED ACTIVITIES	
	Strategic	*Non-strategic*
1 Identify opportunities		Audit competitive environment Research new customer needs and opportunities Specify market requirements Evaluate alternative objectives and strategies Test market
2 Set direction and purpose	Decide company purpose and mission Determine and define the company's markets Set basic objectives Set major policies	
3 Assign basic work and allocate resources	Determine and assign major strategies Allocate resources to functions and projects	Set up organization Assign functional responsibilities Develop formal plans and budgets
4 Develop resources	De-activate development projects	Implement development projects Control and measure Monitor for plan deviations
5 Commit resources	Commit new programs or resources to market De-commit programs and resources	Operate committed line functions Control Feed back plan results and deviations Recommend changes in plans and strategies
6 Evaluate results		Measure performance against plan Evaluate tests Audit development work-in-process Audit managerial effectiveness

An illuminating self-evaluation study for the general manager is to pick at random a previous month or quarter for which he can reconstruct a fairly accurate record of how he spent his time. He should then go through the calendar and classify how the time was distributed, first among aspects 1 to 6, and second between strategic and non-strategic aspects. If at least fifteen or twenty percent does not show up as strategic, and if this is a typical work-mix for him, he probably is headed for trouble. The disarming problem is that it is not likely to show up for a while, maybe not until it is too late.

The habitual "fire-fighter" has no easy way of escaping this dilemma. The first step is usually a conscious regimentation of his personal time to restore a sounder balance between current operations and strategic work. The second is a dynamic and realistic strategic decisionmaking process. A third approach is periodic practice in classifying actual management work as it progresses. This can sharpen the executive's effectiveness both in allocating his own work and time, and in directing the efforts of subordinates.

26 MANAGEMENT BY RULE AND BY POLICY*

M. Valliant Higginson

Few executives would suggest to their presidents that their companies abolish all rules and depend entirely on flexible directives. In all organizations the efficiency, safety, and well-being of employees are contingent on adherence to a few basic rules and inflexible directives. These rules and directives delineate what Wilfred Brown has called the "prescribed content of work" in a job—"the things that the occupant of the role must do if he is to avoid a charge of negligence or insubordination."

Yet most executives recognize that rules are not enough. An inflexible rule, or unconditional

* Reprinted by permission of the publisher from *Management Policies I*, American Management Association, New York, pp. 95–103, 1966. Miss Higginson is research associate with the American Management Association.

order, offers no guidance in the discretionary area of work which is "composed of all those decisions that we not only are authorized to make but also are held responsible for making."

But what do we mean when we use the word "rule"? Usually a rule is considered a directive whose major characteristics are precision and explicitness in bidding or forbidding action. An example of a rule that forbids action is "No Smoking!" and one that bids or prescribes action is: "Punch the Time Clock!" Instructions on work orders may also prescribe operating details in the form of rules.

Rules may serve as unconditional orders if they require complete and uniform compliance by everyone to whom they are directed. If they call for continued compliance in recurring situations, they may serve as standing orders. Although rules are usually found in plants, they can exist on any organizational level of a company.

Some executives assume that employee performance, on all organizational levels, can most effectively be directed and controlled by a system of rules or regulations, explicit procedures or instructions, and unconditional orders. With these directives they can establish and maintain highly centralized control, and run a tight ship by insuring that their plans and purposes are communicated precisely, in statements that will obtain the compliance necessary for uniformity of action and behavior. Only in this way, so the theory goes, can top management fully meet its responsibility to manage.

ADVANTAGES OF RULES

A clear-cut system of inflexible directives seems ideal to many supervisors. If sufficiently comprehensive and realistic, rules and instructions practically preclude the need for using judgment to decide whether subordinates are doing what top management expects. Inflexible directives can also assist in the setting of performance standards for employees.

There is no doubt that rules can protect the supervisor whose job is merely to transmit and enforce directives formulated by top management. A supervisor who goes by the book cannot easily be blamed when the performance of his subordinates produces results that do not measure up to expected standards.

Furthermore, if rules are clearly formulated so that they sharply delineate spheres of responsibility and authority and provide comprehensive controls, it is relatively easy for middle management to locate the source of trouble when something goes wrong—for example, when standards for quantity and quality of production are not being met. And in locating the origin of trouble, responsibility for inadequate performance can be fixed.

Anything as specific as a rule is relatively easy to put into words that can be understood by a person familiar with the subject. Thus members of middle management can develop proficiency in formulating rules that can be understood by supervisors, and they can count on the supervisors' communicating these rules to their employees with approximately the same meaning. When misunderstandings do occur, the trouble can usually be traced to carelessness or forgetfulness or to a deliberate intention to misconstrue the meaning of words.

When executives are managing by rule, they can exercise a relatively high degree of control over employees at the work level. In this way they reduce their dependence on the abilities of supervisors as leaders, planners, and potential managers.

WHAT'S WRONG WITH RULES?

But serious difficulties can arise when rules and regulations do not provide the anticipated results. There are eight major disadvantages associated with managing a company by rule.

1. Rules Limit Managerial Authority To some extent, this limitation is desirable. Whenever the well-being and safety of all members of the organization are involved, rules are appropriate. But when all administrative decisions are communicated in the form of rules and inflexible directives, the top executive is in effect bypassing intermediary administrators. They are reduced to the status of personal assistants.

Top executives need to recognize and respect the discretionary content of a subordinate's job if that subordinate is to retain the full authority to make appropriate decisions that match his organizational position.

2. Responsibilities Are Not Completely Separable The application of inflexible controls is often based on the theory that every manager has a separate set of functions and a sphere of responsibility for which he alone can be held accountable. However, the theory is not borne out by the facts.

In all organizational work, there are transition stages and interaction points of mutual responsibility and interdependence, at which the functions of two or more persons intermesh. Such situations occur in plants where laboratory research and pilot plant operations precede mass production. Efficiency depends on close cooperation between key personnel at all stages of the production process and on their feeling of responsibility for the ultimate success of their work.

Compartmentalization of attitude and of action hampers overall efficiency in most organizations. And rigid controls which overemphasize the separation of functions are at the same time underestimating the need for feelings of mutual responsibility.

3. Actions Lack Uniformity In addition to the undesirable effects on relationships, another unfortunate consequence of inflexible directives is that absolute uniformity of practice never really exists. Even though it is often a primary aim of management, it remains an ideal that can never be achieved. And when uniformity throughout an organization is preached but not practiced, employees have legitimate grounds for complaint.

In a nonunionized plant, complaints about arbitrary action and favoritism of managers may be expressed with some reluctance. But when the plant has a union, a well-founded dissatisfaction becomes a formal grievance and may develop into a costly arbitration.

4. Rules Cannot Cover All Cases Any manager who hopes to control his employees by rules is certain to fall short of success. No team of planners, however able, can foresee every contingency, and consequently directives that are supposed to be watertight will inevitably turn out to have some holes.

Experience has shown that effort to cover every foreseeable eventuality with a set of precise rules is frequently self-defeating. For example, a common difficulty is that unions, in contesting the enforceability of a rule, frequently argue that the rule as stated did not specify the particular contingency in question.

5. Rules May Be Inconsistent with Each Other Rules are usually developed over a period of time and as they are integrated into a company's system of directives, inconsistencies can creep in. This often happens when new rules are made to fit some new or unusual situation.

It can also happen when executives make rules which apply to their particular functions but do not take cognizance of those rules designed to meet other needs. For example, a rule that every injury must be reported to the medical department immediately may be inconsistent with a rule limiting time off for personal needs.

This difficulty can only be overcome if employees ignore one rule or the other. But anything which encourages employees to disregard rules not only weakens the effectiveness of the rules but also of management itself.

6. Rules Cause Delays and Confusion In maintaining tight control over employees without allowing for discretion by supervisors, management usually has difficulties with exceptions. A conscientious supervisor who goes by the book always contacts his boss when he encounters a situation not covered by the rules. But this practice causes delays and tends to weaken the authority of the supervisor when his subordinates discover that he does not make decisions in critical situations.

Another consequence is that manuals of rules and regulations tend to become increasingly complex, and eventually they are overloaded with so many rules that they become cumbersome. One executive commented that they have "a tendency to develop into mazes and hamstring the decision-making process. . . ."

In such an increasingly complex system of directives, the principles on which the first rules were based can become difficult to discern. Thus it sometimes happens that a rule or regulation intended to supplement an earlier one is incompatible with the aim of the original rule.

7. Independent Action Creates a Communication Barrier Not all managers are willing to ask the boss for a decision regarding every exceptional case. Some of them are more enterprising in responding to the "discretionary content" of their jobs, even though their bosses have emphasized the need to comply with specific directives and to inquire about exceptions. But independent exercise of judgment under a system of supposedly inflexible directives results in sub rosa slippages.

The immediate results of unplanned and unguided discretionary action by a supervisor may be excellent, but there are inherent disadvantages. For one thing, such departures probably will not be reported to top executives, particularly to those who are sticklers for rule enforcement. Open or tacit encouragement of deviation is unacceptable, since there is always the danger that it will ultimately lead to loss of control.

A manager usually will not run the risk of reporting independent action unless he has an especially good relationship with his superior. Furthermore, if he does report discretionary action and is rebuffed, he is unlikely to "stick his neck out again." But the most unfortunate consequence is that the effective executive who is discovered deviating from strict application of a rule has to contend with the feeling that he has been caught like a delinquent child—even if his boss is mollified by the results of his misdemeanor.

8. Management Development Is Limited Organizations that are managed primarily by rules tend to have more training programs than development programs. But training programs seldom promote the kind of self-education that helps a man develop his full potential as a leader. Only when the chief and other top executives recognize the "discretionary content" of jobs and encourage supervisors and employees to develop their abilities in this area can the company develop the managers needed to insure organizational continuity. In a company managed by rules, men who wish to exercise initiative are likely to decide that it is not the place for them to make a career. Others with less initiative and a stronger desire for security may remain, but gradually their ability to make independent decisions will atrophy.

WHAT CAN POLICIES DO?

When policies are stated with clear terminology and suitable explanatory information, they offer great advantages to management. Several of these benefits have already been suggested in the previous section which discusses the disadvantages of managing by rules. In brief, some of these advantages of policies are:

1. The need for close supervision is minimized.
2. Understanding of the company is greater.
3. Communication among executives is strengthened.
4. Management development is enhanced.

The basic characteristic of policies that differentiates them from rules is their flexibility. As flexible guides, policies serve to:

- Reflect a basic principle, purpose, or long-term objective that top management has established for the organization as a whole. (For example, a policy on travel expenditures and reimbursements states that "the individual traveler should *neither gain nor lose* personal funds as a result of travel assignments.")
- Present a statement of intent or a commitment that the organization and its members are to carry out the stated principle in a specific manner. (The travel policy made the commitment that "each traveler is to be fully reimbursed for all necessary and reasonable expenses. . . .")
- Indicate constraints or limits to be observed by all organizational members who are expected to use the policy as a guide for decisions. (The constraint suggested by the travel policy was that the traveler should make efforts to keep his expenses at a sensible minimum.)

In the travel policy quoted above, limits are indicated both for initial expenditures and for reimbursements, reflecting the principle of mutual responsibility.

A policy can also provide guidance by indicating the discretionary aspect instead of the constraints. For example, one company issued the following directive to its purchasing agents: "The company's reputation as a loyal customer is a priceless one and should be maintained. However, suppliers should be made aware that company sources will be changed whenever it becomes evident after consideration of all pertinent factors that a present supplier, regardless of prior adequacy for the company, is not necessarily the best in a current situation."

DIFFICULTIES AND PROBLEMS

Companies that want their policies to be clearly understood put them in writing. Sometimes the chief executive himself writes the statements, since he is responsible for insuring the consistency of directives throughout his company. Sometimes he delegates the job to an assistant. Occasionally policies are written by all of the executives who participate in their formulation. But, regardless of who actually writes policies, a number of difficulties may be encountered in their development and preparation. Six of these difficulties are listed.

1. Policies Are Not Easy to Express Although many executives are very articulate, few of them are accustomed to clarifying their concepts and ideas and expressing them in terminology that can be easily understood. Anyone who has ever tried to state a policy so that it is neither an optimistic, vague statement of aspiration nor an inflexible, dogmatic directive can attest to that difficulty. Every manager has read innumerable statements that have no clear-cut meaning, such as: "Our policy is to give a fair day's pay for a fair day's work."

Despite the problems and pitfalls, when an executive thinks through the fundamental principles, purposes, and objectives of his company to the point where he can put them into meaningful words, he is actually clarifying his own thinking. Among the executives who participated in this study there was general agreement that however difficult it may be to express policies, the very process of committing them to writing is an enlightening and valuable experience.

2. Policies May Not Be Consistent with Each Other Many executives have found that, when they formulate policies, they have a tendency to look at the whole, the conglomerate, or system rather than the individual directive. Therefore many companies revise all policies periodically, rather than modifying them singly. By contrast, rules are more often made one by one as the occasion arises.

There are two rather obvious reasons for this difference. First, policies are usually formulated on a higher level than rules, and the executives who formulate them have a broader view of the company. Secondly, by their very nature policies are more closely linked with the broad principles and long-term aims of the company, and as such their formulation is difficult unless there is a consistent management philosophy behind them.

3. Policies May Not Be Consistent with Other Directives Not only should policy statements mesh with each other and with the overall philosophy and principles of a company, but they should be consistent with both short-term and long-term objectives. In addition, since policies are general and flexible, they need to be supplemented by specific procedures, practices, and mandatory directives or rules, otherwise they will not be understood.

People who use policies want to know why the company has them and how they should be applied. The "how" frequently needs to be spelled out in detailed procedures; furthermore, rules are sometimes needed for cases in which discretion is not applicable.

In many organizations, however, policies, procedures, and rules have been issued and applied for years without ever being evaluated as a whole system of directives. Inconsistencies among them and even within them have continued to be perpetuated. Some companies have struggled along with only one type of formal directive. They have not yet realized that even policies are useless unless implemented by other directives that are both mutually consistent and consistent with the company's overall purposes and principles.

4. Policies May Not Be Consistent with Laws Associated with the internal factors that affect policy formulation is the need for consistency with environmental factors. Policies must reflect external constraints and therefore must be consistent with the laws and regulations of the state and Federal governments (as well as those of foreign governments if the company is located abroad). They must also reflect standards set by the government and by professional associations.

To insure that they are abiding by the laws, companies not only have to keep informed but must communicate certain of these laws to their employees. For this reason, many of them include government regulations and policies within their own policy statements. Although a policy statement can indicate that a company intends to do more than is required by law, it certainly cannot state that the company will do less. (Exhibit 1 shows the many internal and external factors that relate to company policies.)

5. Policies May Not Be Consistent with Contracts A company that has a contract with an outside organization—a union, the government, or another company—must also consider its contractual provisions. As with legislative enactments, a statement of policy can indicate that the company intends to do more, but not less, than it is committed to do.

When the company is under "shop law," it must be especially careful of the language it uses in policy statements that cover the same areas as those in contract clauses. Alert union leaders have often tried to gain additional benefits for their members by negotiating, as a matter of inflexible agreement or right, the greatest benefits permitted for an exceptional case by a liberal policy.

6. Policies Are Difficult to Communicate Even when a policy has been put in writing, it is not as easy to understand as a rule. And, although two-way communication about policies is advantageous, it would be unrealistic to deny that discussion about general ideas can be both time-consuming and vague.

From the time policies are initiated to the time they are used, there is always the danger of falling into generalities and pleasantries. The participation of executives in policy formulation is important and it can be a valuable experience, but it is only part of the process. Far more important is the implementation of the policies.

Unless the company is concerned about the extent to which policies actually serve as guides, and the degree of understanding which executives and employees have regarding policies, it is not really using them as directives in its management process.

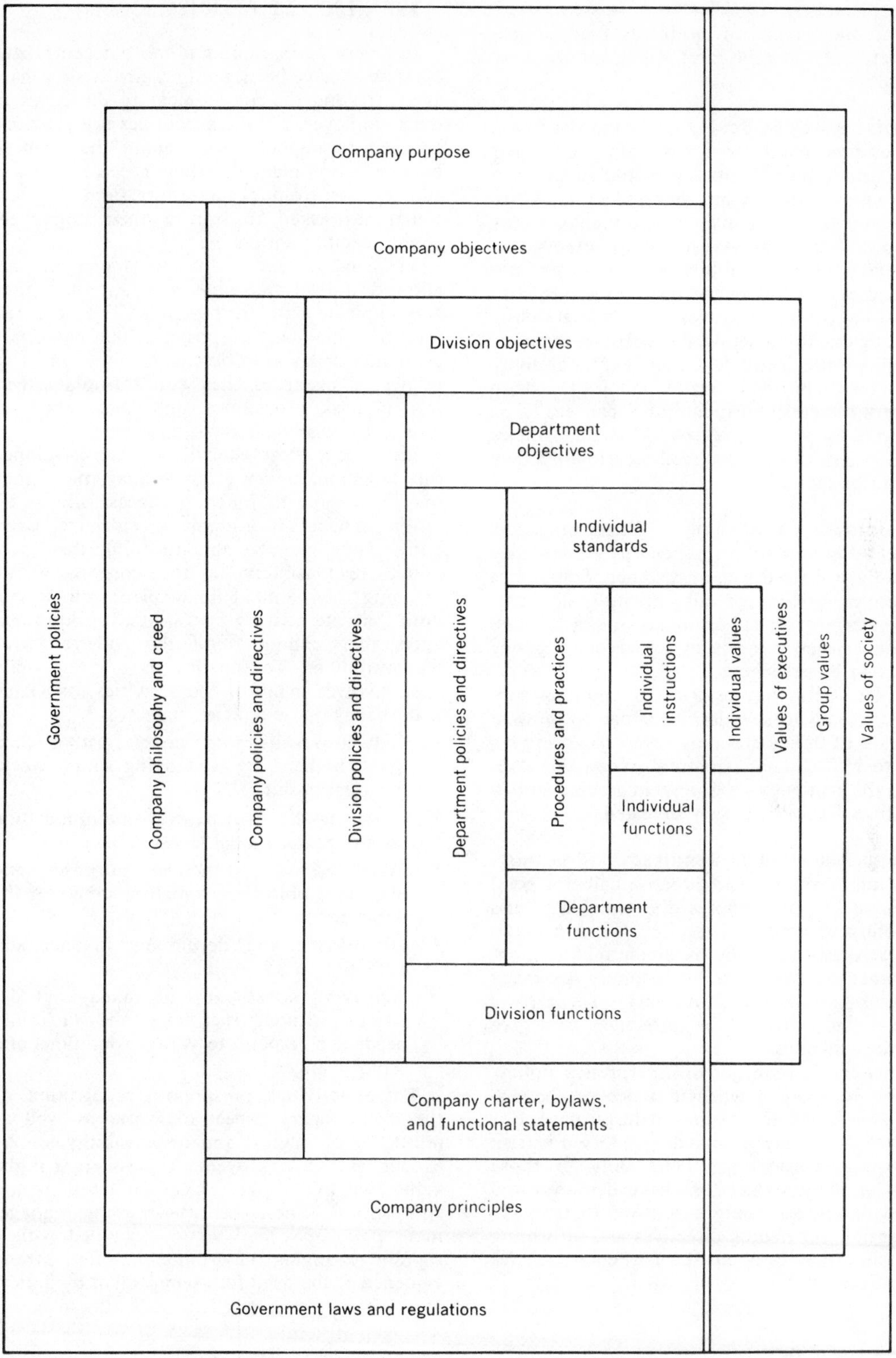

EXHIBIT 1 Company Statements and Directives within a Framework of Values and Constraints

Government policies

Company purpose

Company philosophy and creed

Company objectives

Company policies and directives

Division objectives

Division policies and directives

Department objectives

Department policies and directives

Individual standards

Procedures and practices

Individual instructions

Individual functions

Department functions

Division functions

Company charter, bylaws, and functional statements

Company principles

Government laws and regulations

Individual values

Values of executives

Group values

Values of society

Once written policies are disseminated, several other types of problems may be encountered. Among the most important are these difficulties:

1. Policies May Be Costly In the short run, policies may entail extra expenses, since their very latitude permits managers and supervisors to do more than they are required to do. Thus, there is always the danger that a manager may be more liberal than was originally intended.

Usually, the possibility of incurring unplanned expenses does not result in a long-term loss to the company—unless it fails to stand by its policies. In general, the extra margin of liberality may prove to be an excellent long-term investment. Any large loopholes that tend to permit excessive expenditures can easily be corrected by periodic review. After all, policies are like any other directive; occasionally they have to be revised.

2. Tolerance Is Needed When managers are learning how to use policies as guides, they probably will need some assistance. Sometimes executives discourage all attempts at independence by their subordinates or crack down on them when a decision based on a policy proves to be erroneous.

Under such circumstances a cautious subordinate tends to abandon his efforts to think at the level of policy and may revert to asking his boss to make major decisions. When this happens, the company's purpose in issuing policy directives has been largely defeated.

3. Good Judgment Is Required The interpretation of any flexible directive calls for good judgment. It presupposes the reliability and capability of people. Therefore, when a president delegates authority by giving middle management executives the opportunity to make decisions within the framework of company policies and other flexible directives, a degree of risk is involved.

Whenever a manager misinterprets a policy, or fails to apply it when it is needed, he distorts and dilutes top management purpose. For this reason, many companies reduce the risk by issuing corporate policies only to those levels of management that have demonstrated sound judgment. These executives in turn are responsible for issuing directives and informing their subordinates about the particular policies that affect them.

THE NEED FOR POLICIES

In recent years, more and more decentralized companies have been giving their division managers freedom in communicating directives to their employees. These executives are provided with corporate policies, often in the form of one or more manuals; they receive bulletins and memos from headquarters; and they are sometimes asked to inform their employees about specific matters.

In general, such division managers are allowed to determine what, when, and how they communicate with their people. They can use meetings, manuals, or posters; they can share as many or as few details as they wish; in numerous instances they can formulate their own policies, procedures, and rules. They are free to exercise their own judgment.

But unless these executives have developed this judgment under group management, they may be unable to function successfully as division managers in a highly decentralized company. They may be able to fulfill their economic responsibility to the corporation by reaching their annual financial objectives, but until they are actually operating as group managers they cannot fulfill the full range of responsibilities. To function as a group manager involves many of the activities associated with managing by policies, namely:

- Getting results with people rather than through them, by developing sound working relationships.
- Fostering effective two-way communication on all organizational levels.
- Clarifying basic principles, purposes, and long-term objectives for all members of the organization.
- Discovering and developing management potential on all levels.
- Achieving consistency of managerial decisions without sacrificing the flexibility needed to respond to varied conditions and rapid change.

These activities presuppose recognition of the discretionary aspect of work, as well as mutuality of interest and responsibility among executives and employees. Also inherent is the value that our society places on freedom and competition. These factors—present management philosophy and values—coupled with a rapidly changing environment, offer strong evidence of the need for management by policy.

27 CAN STRATEGIC PLANNING PAY OFF?*

Louis V. Gerstner, Jr.

One of the most intriguing management phenomena of the late 1960s and 1970s has been the rapid spread of the corporate or strategic planning concept. Except for the so-called computer revolution, few management techniques have swept through corporate and governmental enterprises more rapidly or completely. Writer after writer has hailed this new discipline as the fountainhead of all corporate progress. In 1962, one published report extolled strategic planning as "a systematic means by which a company can become what it wants to be" (Stanford Research Institute). Five years later, it was called "a means to help management gain increasing control over the destiny of a corporation" (R. H. Schaffer). By 1971, praise of strategic planning verged on the poetic; it had become "the manifestation of a company's determination to be the master of its own fate . . . to penetrate the darkness of uncertainty and provide the illumination of probability" (S. R. Goodman).

It is not surprising, therefore, that one company after another raced to embrace this new source of managerial salvation, and, as a result, most major companies today can boast a corporate planning officer, often with full attendant staff. It seemed appropriate to ask some CEOs whether strategic planning has lived up to its advanced billings. Three anonymous reactions were as follows:

> Strategic planning is basically just a plaything of staff men.
>
> It's like a Chinese dinner: I feel full when I get it, but after a little while I wonder whether I've eaten at all!
>
> Strategic planning? A staggering waste of time and money.

* Reprinted by permission of the publisher from *Business Horizons,* vol. 15, no. 6, pp. 5–16 (December 1972). Mr. Gerstner is a partner of McKinsey & Co., management consultants.

Some CEOs, of course, would disagree with these comments, and certainly few if any would agree publicly. But the fact remains that in the large majority of companies corporate planning tends to be an academic, ill-defined activity with little or no bottomline impact. Observations of many companies wrestling with the strategic planning concept strongly suggest that this lack of real pay-off is almost always the result of one fundamental weakness, namely, the failure to bring strategic planning down to current decisions. Before describing this problem and some possible ways to overcome it, I shall briefly define what I mean by the term strategic planning.

FORECASTS ARE NOT STRATEGIES

Many strategic planning programs begin with the extension of the annual operating budget into a five-year projection. This can be a valuable exercise, particularly for institutions that have operated on a yearly or even monthly planning cycle. Most companies, however, soon discover that five-year operational and financial forecasts, in and of themselves, are ineffective as strategic planning tools for a fundamental reason: they are predicated on the implicit assumption of no significant change in environmental, economic, and competitive conditions.

In other words, they are purely extrapolative projections, and, by practically everyone's standards, fall far short of real strategic planning. They offer no overview, no analyses of external trends, and no perceptive insights into company strengths and weaknesses—elements that both theorists and practitioners would agree are central to real corporate planning.

Forecast planning of the sort I have described can usually be identified by leafing through a company's planning documents. Pages and pages of accounting information, detailing five years of financial forecasts with little or no explanatory material, are one earmark. Graphs of projected future performance

FIGURE 1 The Basic Strategic Planning Concept

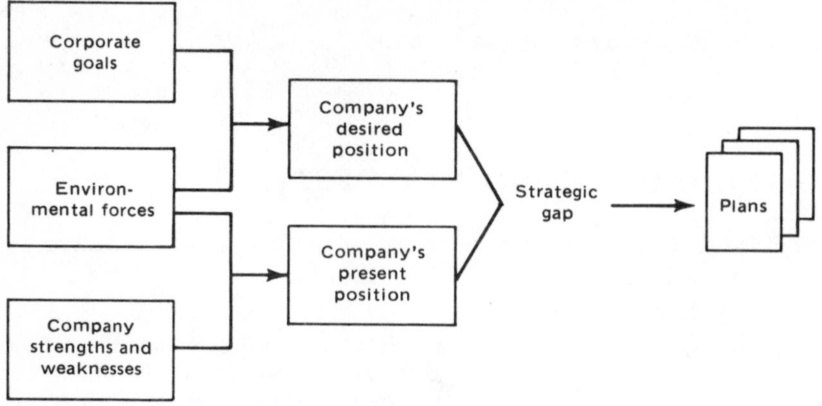

FIGURE 2 Elements of a Strategic Plan

ENVIRONMENTAL ASSESSMENT

1. Broad economic assumptions
2. Key governmental/regulatory threats
3. Major technological forces
4. Significant marketing opportunities/threats
5. Explicit competitive strategies for each major competitor

DIVISION'S POSITION

1. Statement of mission
2. Interrelated set of financial and nonfinancial objectives
3. Statement of strengths and weaknesses
4. Forecast of operations—profits and cash flow
5. Major future programs

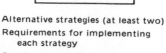

Strategic options

Alternative strategies (at least two)
Requirements for implementing each strategy
Contingency plans

also tend to follow a predictable pattern, that is, if recent performance has been good, the forecast calls for more and more of the same—on into eternity.

On the other hand, if performance has been poor, the forecast will allow for a year or two to effect the inevitable turnaround, and then—off to eternity. (The manager doing the forecasting hopes, of course, that he will get promoted before the two-year period is up.) Working with forecasts like this, executives tend to dismiss the second, third, fourth, and fifth years as irrelevant and continue to concentrate solely on the current year, that is, the annual budget. Most companies seem to have passed beyond forecast planning, and its weaknesses are fairly manifest—namely, a preoccupation with accounting data as the principal output of a planning program and the assumption that the future, at least in relation to general economic indexes, will closely resemble the past.

Recognizing these weaknesses, many institutions have introduced a more rigorous planning program aimed at defining or redefining the basic objectives, economics, competitive profile, and outlook of the company. These formal strategic planning processes show a distinct family resemblance. They usually begin with an assessment of environmental trends and an analysis of the company's strengths and weaknesses. A statement of corporate goals is then developed. From these three elements, a juxtaposition between the organization's present position and its desired position is derived; comparison of the two positions defines the well-known strategic gap. Finally, plans are developed to close the gap and bring the two positions together (Figure 1).

Of course, the steps required to arrive at

the statements of present and desired position are quite detailed. For example, one large U.S. company requires each of its more than fifty profit centers to include in its annual strategic plans all the information shown in Figure 2. For each profit center, the initial written output may run to a hundred pages. Such an effort is inevitably painful and time-consuming, but it may be necessary in the first planning cycle. Barring major changes inside or outside the company, subsequent plans can be considerably shorter. Since the specific elements of a good strategic plan have been described in many texts, I shall not dwell on them here. Instead, I shall move on to the central question of why strategic planning so often fails to pay off and what can be done about it.

MAKE DECISIONS—NOT PLANS

As mentioned earlier, the most fundamental weakness of most corporate plans today is that they do not lead to the major decisions that must be made currently to ensure the success of the enterprise in the future. All too often, the end product of present-day strategic planning activities is a strategic plan—period. Nothing really new happens as a result of the plan, except that everyone gets a warm glow of security and satisfaction now that the uncertainty of the future has been contained. Unfortunately, warm feelings do not produce earnings or capture market share. Neither do graphs of five-year earnings projections, gap charts, or complex strategy statements.

What does produce earnings are strategic decisions, and strategic decisions should be the ultimate output of a strategic planning program. That is, the strategic plan should clearly set forth the critical issues currently facing a company or division in terms of alternative courses of current action. If there are more than five or six issues, they are probably the wrong ones. If the decisions do not involve major risks or investments and/or changes in competitive posture, they are the wrong decisions. If the decisions do not have to be made now, they are wrong.

This is the creative leap that too many managements fail to make in strategic planning. They fail to ask, "What do we do now as a result of this plan?" They fail to recognize that the end product of strategic analysis should not be plans but current decisions. Some of the reasons why the leap to decisions is not made are important to understand:

It Is Risky. Probably the most significant reason is that stating plans in terms of decisions frequently requires an executive to take a personal stand on an important and controversial issue. In other words, it can often make or break his career. All of us can call to mind men who have staked their career and reputations on major strategic recommendations, for example, Learson leading IBM into digital computers, and Donaldson opening DLJ to public capital.

But most of us can also call to mind a few corporate casualties of such decisions—men who took a strong position as an adversary on a major strategic move and found themselves on the losing side. So the leap to decisions takes courage, and most executives prefer to play it safe. We can look at the top management teams of too many companies without finding any risk-taking, success-story managers.

It Is Difficult. Strategic planning, almost by definition, deals with the most complex questions facing a company. Just assembling the data to measure the variables is a considerable task. Moreover, once the data are in hand, the real job begins—the job of synthesizing critical issues and strategic options to resolve those issues. This is fundamentally a creative process. It cannot be programmed or systematized. To structure meaningful, practical action programs requires insight, wisdom, and perspective. Many executives find it an elusive, uncomfortable task.

It Requires Leadership. Most strategic decisions are controversial. The underlying issue being addressed is rarely new to the corporate executive team; typically, it has been debated within the company for some time. I use the word "debate" advisedly; these discussions tend to be problem-definition, opinion-swapping sessions. Because the issues they address have vital implications for individual careers, they soon become less than objective, and they almost never lead to action. In some companies propositions such as "We ought to liquidate that business" can bounce about in the executive committee for months or even years without any decisions being made. The missing ingredient is the leadership needed to push through tough-minded analysis and action on controversial matters.

I know of one company that has been facing a rather critical strategic problem for fully a year now—namely, survival. The underlying strategic issues were correctly identified and thoroughly analyzed over three years ago. A detailed action program was outlined. It is still valid, still ready for implementation, yet the company is headed for bankruptcy. The reason is simple: the CEO simply cannot bring himself to make some tough decisions. He is waiting and hoping that his key lieutenants will

FIGURE 3 Analysis for Overcoming Competitive Action. (a) Example of Strategic Issues and Decisions; (b) Assumed Strategies of Key Competitors

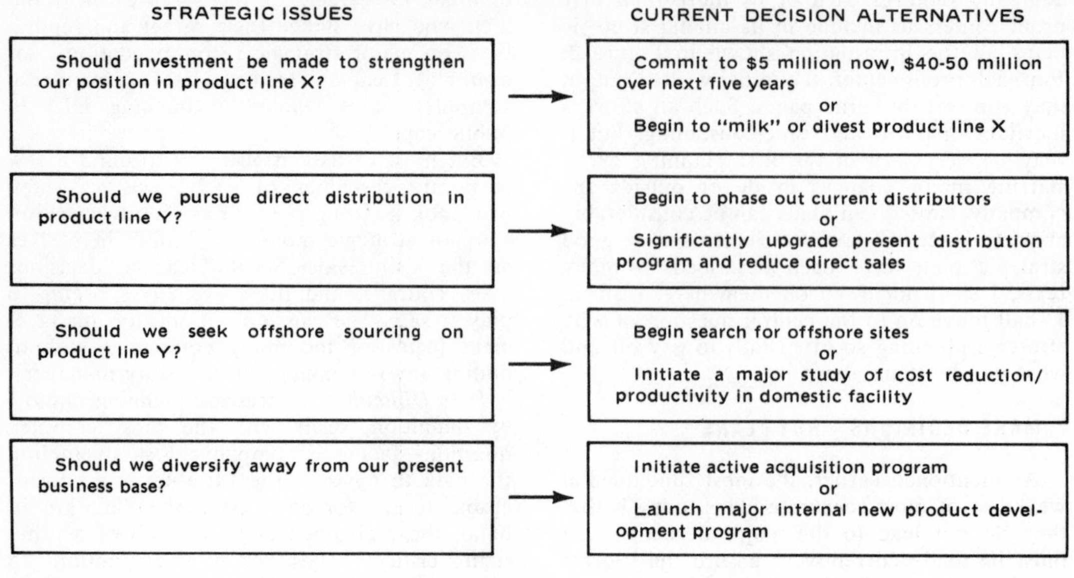
STRATEGIC ISSUES
CURRENT DECISION ALTERNATIVES
Should investment be made to strengthen our position in product line X?
Commit to $5 million now, $40-50 million over next five years
or
Begin to "milk" or divest product line X
Should we pursue direct distribution in product line Y?
Begin to phase out current distributors
or
Significantly upgrade present distribution program and reduce direct sales
Should we seek offshore sourcing on product line Y?
Begin search for offshore sites
or
Initiate a major study of cost reduction/productivity in domestic facility
Should we diversify away from our present business base?
Initiate active acquisition program
or
Launch major internal new product development program

(a)

		COMPETITORS A	B	C
Product line	Systems primarily		X	
	Components primarily	X		
	Systems and components			X
Markets	Domestic	X		
	Worldwide		X	X
	Domestic with foreign licenses			
Technology	Leader	X		X
	Follower		X	
Customers	Government		X	X
	OEM	X		X
	Direct		X	X
Profit economics	Mass production/high volume			X
	Specialized, high price	X	X	

(b)

reach a consensus. Given the nature of the decisions, this is impossible. In a situation of this kind only the CEO can exert the needed leadership, and this CEO is not the man to do it.

The Value System Works Against It. Too often a company's executive motivation system flies in the face of strategic decision making. This occurs for two reasons. First, good managers tend to be promoted so fast that they never have to live with the medium- to long-run outcome of their plans. Second, incentive compensation is often tied either to short-term earnings performance or to stock-price movements, neither of which has anything to do with strategic success.

DOWN TO THE "BOTTOM LINE"

As we have seen, the leap from plans to decisions is an entrepreneurial step that cannot be reduced to a routine. Making it happen is an educational, attitudinal task, but some concrete steps can be taken to facilitate the process.

Meet External Risks To begin with, the formal strategic planning program should be thoroughly reviewed to ensure that it requires a decision-oriented approach. Many planning systems simply are not designed to demand decisions as the end product. Instead, they produce forecasts of financial results or statements of objectives, or future action steps. This type of planning, which is basically "momentum" planning as opposed to dynamic planning that is attuned to the realities of external change, often results from excessive internal focus in the planning process. To overcome this problem, heavy emphasis should be given to three critical aspects of strategic analysis that are particularly important in identifying key issues and decisions: evaluating competitive strategies, developing contingency plans, and assessing environmental forces:

Evaluating Competitive Strategies. Too many corporate plans fail to give even minimal attention to the present and future action of competitive firms. They set out elaborate strategies without any real consideration of competitive reaction. Two examples of a simple analysis that can be extremely helpful in overcoming this weakness are shown in Figure 3 (note that 3b calls for a review of each major competitor's existing strategy). Figure 4 then attempts to evaluate the strength of the company's own strategy against that of each competitor. In most cases, analysis of this kind leads to the identification of opportunities or threats that call for current management decisions.

Contingency Plans. Most companies with active planning programs recognize the value of asking "what if" questions, taking important contingencies into account. Yet few really address this issue in a substantive way. A frequent excuse is that there are so many potential contingencies that it would take years to analyze them all.

The obvious answer to this objection is that one can and should be very selective, and deal only with the one or two possible contingencies that could upset the entire strategy. Here are two examples:

> An American packaging company selling a commodity product regularly reviews potential price changes by one of its smaller competitors. This competitor dropped prices sharply several years

FIGURE 4 Assessing Corporate Plans Against Each Competitor's Strategy

	KEY ELEMENTS OF OUR STRATEGIC PROGRAM			
COMPETITOR A'S BASIC STRATEGY	BUILD CONTINENTAL PRODUCTION CAPACITY	EXPAND CONTINENTAL SALES FORCE	"UNBUNDLE" SYSTEM PRICING	CONCENTRATE R&D ON APPLICATIONS
Component supplier	Effective	Neutral	Effective	Neutral
Domestic only	Neutral	Strong	Neutral	Neutral
OEM market	Neutral	Neutral	Effective	Effective
Leader in technology	Neutral	Neutral	Neutral	Weak
Specialized/high price	Weak	Neutral	Effective	Weak

ago, catching the market leaders by surprise and increasing its own market share significantly.

Last year, in speculating on the major contingencies they might face, the management of the packaging company asked, in effect, "What if they should do it again?" In view of the capacity situation in the industry, it was not an unrealistic question. Accordingly, the company meticulously planned a contingency program to be put into effect if and when its small competitor should move again. Early this year he did. The packaging company was ready and responded immediately and effectively.

An electronic components company depended on a single large customer for 30 percent of its sales. Management simply asked, "What if they should integrate backward?" There was no visible reason to believe that such a move was in the offing, and the question would probably not have surfaced as a serious issue without the forcing device of required contingency planning. But development of the contingency plan led to two real benefits. *First,* it brought out the need for some preventive medicine, and this became a continuing part of the company's relationship with its big customer. *Second,* it led to a detailed economic analysis of the risks and disadvantages to the customer of backward integration. One year later that analysis was instrumental in convincing the customer that a tentative step he had been about to take toward integration would be unwise.

Assessing Environmental Forces. We can all think of companies that have failed to anticipate important changes in their external environments. The U.S. automobile industry, with all its vast managerial and financial resources, was simply unprepared for the explosive issues of automotive safety and air pollutants. And during the late 1960s, stock brokers on Wall Street almost drowned in their own success because they had failed to anticipate the volume growth of the industry and its attendant "back-office" requirements.

Despite the difficulties of forecasting sociopolitical or even marketplace trends, the most aggressive companies are energetically taking steps to raise their present level of competence in this arena. These are some of the approaches they have found productive:

Drawing on the work of the so-called "futurologists," who seek to identify major developments emerging in the world. Their work is rarely directly applicable to a given industrial situation, but it can serve as a starting point for rigorous internal assessment of issues highly relevant to the corporation's future.

Building on broad economic forecasts. Here again it will be necessary to translate general trends into specific issues, but this simply requires thoughtful attention by corporate management and their advisors. A number of large companies annually prepare a general economic forecast to be used by all their operating units. These forecasts cover such subjects as government spending programs, expected major shifts in international trade and monetary policies, and potential new regulatory programs in ecology, safety, hiring, and so on.

Simply requiring a written assessment of critical environmental trends in every strategic planning document.

The assessment of environmental forces is not easy; nevertheless, the major issues (and therefore the strategic decisions) facing many institutions today are arising more and more in the external sociopolitical milieu. Merely being able to anticipate the issues (even if the "right" response is not clear) is a lot better than being caught completely unaware.

Provide Effective "Top-Down" Leadership

Since the purpose of strategic planning is to make basic decisions on the future course of the company, it is ultimately a responsibility of the CEO and his key lieutenants. In other words, top management cannot confine itself to perusing written plans and giving a perfunctory once-a-year approval. That would be abdication, not responsible delegation. To ensure that the right set of critical issues and decisions is in fact identified, top management must actively involve itself in the planning process. Even before the process of issue identification begins, the CEO should satisfy himself that the company's financial targets are properly integrated.

Most companies today include some statement of financial objectives in their corporate plans. Surprisingly often, however, these objectives fail to take into account the inherent interrelationships among most financial targets. Sales, earnings, and return-on-investment targets, which are of course inextricably interlinked, often are set apart from each other in the manner of a diner ordering a meal at a Chinese restaurant: one from group A, two from Group B. Since the objectives chosen are inherently inconsistent and thus worthless if not actually debilitating, the result is frequently a case of strategic indigestion.

FIGURE 5 Three Strategies to Achieve 15 Percent EPS

HIGH VOLUME APPROACH

	%
Sales growth	15.0
PBIT/sales	4.0
Asset turnover	3.5
Dividend payout	60.0
Debt/equity	50.0

HIGH ASSET UTILIZATION APPROACH

	%
Sales growth	7.0
PBIT/sales	4.0
Asset turnover	4.0
Dividend payout	60.0
Debt/equity	50.0

AGGRESSIVE FINANCING APPROACH

	%
Sales growth	10.0
PBIT/sales	4.0
Asset turnover	3.5
Dividend payout	40.0
Debt/equity	60.0

More important, too many companies fail to recognize the potential advantages of making trade-offs among various financial objectives. As Figure 5 shows, a company can choose widely different sets of financial and operating objectives and still achieve an identical over-all earnings per share target. Each set of objectives implies a fundamentally different way of operating the company, and each set is internally consistent.

Again, top management can vitally enhance the effectiveness of the whole strategic planning process by instituting a regular and rigorous process of *strategic review*. Most companies today accept without question the fact that operational planning is inseparable from operating control, that one without the other is meaningless. But too often they ignore the logical corollary in the strategic planning area and omit the vital follow-up linkage between planning and control. To be sure, top management conscientiously reads the strategic plans and sits through strategic planning presentations, but it rarely challenges the validity of the plans or their relevance to current decisions. This situation is dangerous, because a division manager cannot be both advocate and challenger of his strategic plan.

Strategic review should not be a mechanistic process. One of the most successful approaches I have seen is to get a few key members of the top management team out of the office for two or three days of informal but intensive review of the strategic options as set forth in the plan. Superb leadership by the CEO is required to keep the discussion centered on the critical problems and opportunities, keep it on an objective plane so that no one feels threatened, and come out with a set of actionable decisions as the end product. Given such leadership and adequate advance preparation by the participants, valuable results can be achieved.

Strategy review, of course, is not entirely a free-form creative process; it can be supported by an analytical framework. For example, one CEO has his staff subject the plans submitted by division managers to a set of validity tests designed to identify and evaluate the key assumptions underlying performance forecast in the plan (Figure 6). This top-down testing process ensures that issues and decisions that the division managers have failed to identify will be brought to the surface for top management consideration.

Provide Guidelines for Capital Deployment

As a company diversifies its activities, the task of capital allocation tends to emerge as the central function of the corporate CEO—the heart of strategic decision making in a multibusiness enterprise. Resource allocation or portfolio decisions arise because of the need to maximize over-all results by managing a collection of relatively independent operating units or product lines as a single portfolio. This means setting earnings targets and making investment decisions for any one division (or product line) within a framework that encompasses the whole enterprise. Of course, it can be argued that portfolio management is not a required function in a multibusiness company, since the pieces can simply be allowed to operate independently. But by that reasoning, a corporate management team is equally unnecessary, since if all the parts operate independently, there is no "value added" at the corporate or holding company level.

Too often, companies actually undermine their strategic planning programs by approaching major capital deployment decisions purely on a traditional capital budgeting basis. That is, in principle all requests for capital funds are filled no matter what division or product line they come from, provided only that they clear a single financial hurdle such as a pay-back or discounted cash-flow rate of return. Of course,

FIGURE 6 Testing Key Strategy Assumptions

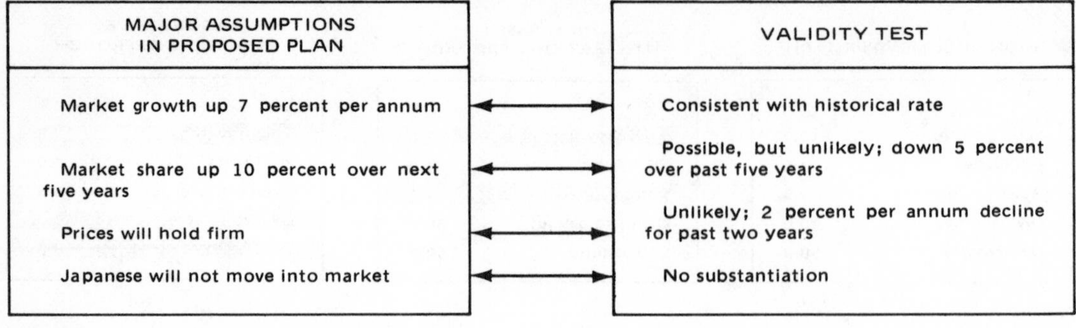

MAJOR ASSUMPTIONS IN PROPOSED PLAN
VALIDITY TEST
Market growth up 7 percent per annum
Consistent with historical rate
Market share up 10 percent over next five years
Possible, but unlikely; down 5 percent over past five years
Prices will hold firm
Unlikely; 2 percent per annum decline for past two years
Japanese will not move into market
No substantiation

NET ASSESSMENT

1. Plan is unrealistically optimistic.
2. Highly unlikely that market share can be increased without substantial price reduction.
3. Competitive threat from Japanese not adequately dealt with.

when the requests exceed the available resources, some ranking system is employed, but, in effect, the hurdle is simply raised and a new single-number decision rule is applied uniformly to all requests.

This approach fails to provide any portfolio assessment of the various parts of the enterprise considered as a group. Therefore, capital can flow to a mediocre division or product line at a rate that is the same as—or even faster than—the rate at which it flows to a high-potential division. This simply perpetuates the status quo, frequently negating the value of the strategic planning at the corporate level. In other words, the CEO's all-important decision of allocating capital is blurred and in fact abdicated.

One simple but powerful approach some multibusiness managers are using today is to sort their individual businesses into three broad portfolio categories: sources of growth (future earnings); sources of current and intermediate earnings; and sources of immediate cash flow. One of my colleagues has suggested that these categories relate directly to the so-called product life-cycle curve which can also, for these purposes, be termed a business life-cycle curve. When a company views its operations in this manner, some interesting implications for the capital allocation process may emerge.

Of course, change in capital allocation decisions is only one of the many management implications of multibusiness strategic planning. The impact of this broad perspective can and should carry over to every facet of management responsibility. For example, Figure 7 illustrates its impact on marketing planning and, more important, on decisions relating to the marketing mix.

The need for such top-down guidelines is perhaps most vividly apparent in the "pruning" or divesting activities of a multibusiness company, aimed at milking declining divisions or products for cash, which will then be redeployed in more attractive opportunities. (Hopefully, opportunities exist for redeployment, but this kind of analysis can bring to light imbalances at either end of this spectrum.)

While such a deinvestment program often makes eminent sense from a corporate point of view, it is a rare division or product manager who willingly plans himself out of business. Most managers will argue that the new growth is just around the corner; all they need to get the pay-off is a little more investment "up front." For this reason, strategic planning efforts rarely bring deinvestment-redeployment decisions to the surface, unless the CEO has provided explicit guidelines. He must find ways to create an environment in which different planning criteria and different performance criteria are not only acceptable but demanded.

This brings us to the human relations dimension of strategic planning, and the final action step needed to make it effective.

Target Responsibility and Reward Results

No strategic planning program will produce bottom-line results without careful attention to human motivations. This is a highly subjective

FIGURE 7 Impact of Multibusiness Strategic Planning on Marketing

	STRATEGY ADOPTED FOR DIVISION OR PRODUCT LINE		
MARKETING DECISION AREA	INVEST FOR FUTURE GROWTH	MANAGE FOR EARNINGS	MANAGE FOR IMMEDIATE CASH
Market share	Aggressively build across all segments	Target efforts to high-return/ high-growth segments Protect current franchises	Forego share development for improved profits
Pricing	Lower to build share	Stabilize for maximum profit contribution	Raise, even at expense of volume
Promotion	Invest heavily to build share	Invest as market dictates	Avoid
Existing product line	Expand volume Add line extensions to fill out product categories	Shift mix to higher profit product categories	Eliminate low-contribution products/ varieties
New products	Expand product line by acquisition, self-manufacture, or joint venture	Add products selectively and in controlled stages of commitment	Add only sure winners

matter, tied inextricably to the leadership style of the CEO, but two general recommendations apply almost universally.

First, involve the decision makers. In a decision-oriented planning environment, developing and implementing strategies can only be the responsibility of line managers. This does not mean that the CEO should do away with his planning staff and planning processes. Rather, it means that the output of such staffs and processes should only be an input to top management. It is top management's responsibility to weigh strategic issues, apply judgment, and make the decisions. Strategic planning may be a staff function, but strategic decision making is the responsibility of the CEO and his top management team. Several companies have underscored this point by requiring division managers to present and defend their strategies and plans in the absence of their staff planners. It seems to work.

Second, reward good strategic decision makers. If all promotions, bonuses, and other rewards go to the executives who meet or exceed short-term budget goals, without regard to the way they position their organizations for future success, then strategies and strategic plans will be no more than a charade. I am not suggesting that short-term performance measures should be eliminated; rather, I am saying that long-term performance milestones must be added and built into the annual performance review, particularly in companies where the best line managers get promoted every eighteen to twenty-four months.

An example of the sort of multidimensional performance appraisal system I have in mind is shown in Figure 8. The weighting factors shown are purely illustrative. They should be tailored for each individual operating unit to reflect the importance of short- versus long-term performance. To return to our earlier example, "building" criteria ought to be weighted more heavily in "future growth" units, while short-term goals should have most of the emphasis in "cash" units.

Following the widespread introduction of data processing in the 1950s, many companies sooner or later were obliged to recognize that the promise of this great management tool was stubbornly refusing to materialize. Real, tangible return on investment was low or nonexistent. Today, a great many companies have largely overcome this problem. Not without a

FIGURE 8 Performance Appraisal: Balancing Current and Future Needs

	CURRENT PERFORMANCE (0–100)			FUTURE BUILDING PERFORMANCE (0–100)				
DIVISION MANAGER	PROFITS % BUDGET	ROI VERSUS BUDGET	WEIGHT-ING FACTOR	SUCCESS IN IMPLE-MENTING LONG-TERM PROGRAM	QUALITY OF STRATEGY	QUALITY OF MAN-POWER	WEIGHT-ING FACTOR	OVER-ALL RATING
A	100	100	1	20	20	50	3	310
B	80	100	3	100	80	80	1	530
C	120	90	2	100	90	90	2	585
D	70	70	1	75	80	100	3	475

struggle, they have substantially brought their computer systems under control, and most of these managements are a good deal wiser for the experience. The most successful among them, I believe, would include at least the following among the lessons they have learned:

> The effort must be integrated directly into the important decision-making activities of the company. Each potential new project must pass the "so what" test.
>
> The chief executive holds the key to success; his commitment and leadership are absolutely necessary.
>
> The pay-off when it works is substantial, and it can be measured in dollars and cents.

All of these lessons apply to strategic planning. When it is focused on current decisions, under the leadership of a committed CEO, it works. And when it works, we may be sure that the pay-off will show on the bottom line.

28 HOW TO IMPROVE YOUR LONG-RANGE PLANNING*

George A. Steiner

Formal comprehensive business long-range planning is a phenomenon of the past twenty-five years. Today, virtually every large company throughout the world has some sort of formal planning system, and a large number of medium-sized and smaller companies also have such systems. Despite our relatively long experience with formal planning many managers voice dissatisfaction with their systems, although they are in the minority. Even among companies that are satisfied with their planning systems I have often heard managers express an interest in improving their systems. This paper is directed toward helping both groups.

There are a number of shortcomings I have observed in planning systems which, if not corrected, lead to dissatisfaction and poor performance. This paper presents ten of them. They are not in any particular order of importance and some can be considered subsets of others.

Before proceeding it is useful to comment briefly on the nature of planning, its relationships to management, and its contribution to company performance.

Long-range planning, as used here, is synonymous with formal planning, comprehensive planning, corporate planning, or similar words. It is a formalized system for hammering out long-range objectives, strategies, and detailed plans that make sure the strategies will achieve the objectives. It is a process of systematically identifying opportunities and threats in the company's environment so that management is in a position to make better current decisions to exploit the opportunities and to avoid the threats.

So important is this process in modern management that I no longer speak of it as a tool of management. It is a new way to manage. Some years ago corporate planners thought they had a new discipline, like accounting. It is now clear that long-range planning is not another tool or discipline but a new concept with its own principles and preferred practices and it is inextricably interrelated to the entire process of management. I call it management by structured foresight.

This does not imply any rejection of old tested principles and practices of management. Rather, it provides a new framework, a new approach, a new philosophy to management.

A company's success is not due to long-range planning but to the entire process of management. It is also useful to note that admirable management and or formal corporate planning cannot guarantee business success. It is my position, however, that the better both are the higher is the probability of success. Now, to ten ways to improve your formal planning system.

I. *The best planning is based on a thorough understanding of what long-range planning is, what it can do for you, and what you want it to do for you.*

Long-range planning is not likely to be effective if managers do not have a solid conceptual understanding of what it is, how to go about doing it, and how to use it. While there is no single way to do long-range planning we do know today as the literature will explain, what the essentials of an effective long-range planning system are. We know those principles and practices which must be followed for effective planning. If managers have only a vague, fuzzy and amorphous concept of this body of thought the resultant planning is not likely to be as effective as it should.

With this background a manager will know what long-range planning should be able to do for his company. He should know what basic questions should be asked and answered in the process. Then managers and their staffs are in a position to determine what they want to get

* Reprinted by permission of the publisher from *Managerial Planning,* vol. 23, no. 2, pp. 13–17, 28 (September–October 1974). Mr. Steiner is professor of management and public policy at the University of California, Los Angeles.

out of the long-range planning process, how to organize to do it, and how to use the results. This will differ from company to company.

Without this basic understanding, argument will be interminable and continuous, there will be abortive attempts at planning, doubts about what to do will impede planning, managers will become frustrated, and planning will be ineffective.

II. *Concentrate on finding good strategies rather than filling boxes with numbers.*

General Robert E. Wood once wisely said, when he was Chairman of the Board of Sears, Roebuck and Company, that "Business is like war in one respect, if its grand strategy is correct, any number of tactical errors can be made and yet the enterprise proves successful." Successful companies are those with successful strategies. Sears is a good illustration of a company that has had a series of brilliant strategies.

There are many parts of an effective planning system—developing information as premises for planning, formulating objectives, developing strategies, working out detailed medium-range plans, and making current budgets. While all parts of the process are important none is more critical than developing strategies. By strategies I mean the most significant decisions of a company that concern the acquisition, use, and deployment of its resources—capital and human. In a real sense the entire planning process, no matter how it is done, is a system to help managers develop better strategies and to make sure they are translated into current decisions.

It is not easy to devise successful strategies. There is no formula that is guaranteed to produce successful strategies. The more the concentration on strategy, in the planning process, however, the more likely successful strategies will be identified and implemented.

III. *There must be a proper climate in an organization if long-range planning is to thrive and be effective.*

The planning climate in a company should be congenial to stimulating the things required in good planning, such as having people enthusiastic about planning; creating an atmosphere which generates creativity, imagination, and innovation among managers and staff; assuring the proper blend of involvement of people; and developing a sense of commitment throughout the managerial levels that long-range planning is a necessary and good thing to do and should be done well.

Developing the proper climate must begin at the top of the company. Top management must realize that long-range planning is its responsibility. It must give the system its devotion and let others in the organization understand how fully committed it is to long-range planning. This does not mean, of course, that top management must do all of the long-range planning itself. It can and should delegate parts of it to others, both line and staff.

The climate for long-range planning will be gloomy, indeed, if top management publicly accepts formal planning but privately casts doubts about it or sharply criticizes it. The word soon gets around that top management is merely paying lip service to long-range planning and sooner or later it will wither and die.

The climate for planning will be improved if there is a general understanding that it is part of the entire process of management, that it is not something that is done once a year and then forgotten, and that it is a line and not a staff function. As noted above, staff can do much of the job but the final responsibility lies with line managers.

The climate for planning will be improved if conflicts between managerial judgment and the formality of long-range planning are reduced or eliminated. There are natural conflicts between the freewheeling intellectual life styles of many managers who depend upon their judgment and intuition for making decisions and the formalities involved in long-range planning. Such conflicts, however, are not necessary. The climate is better when it is recognized that the long-range planning system can help managers to sharpen their judgment and intuition. At least the system can give them more time for reflection. Furthermore, it must be recognized that there can be no effective planning without the injection of managerial intuition and judgment throughout the process. The best climate exists in that company where the blend of judgment and formality takes place in harmony rather than in tension.

The planning climate is best where there is encouragement to examine value systems of different executives, to honestly look for and evaluate potential major changes that lay ahead, and to appraise forthrightly the risks involved in meeting them. Doing these things is inherent in good planning. Very frequently, however, these matters are "sacred cows" at top management levels.

It is easy to understand how and why managers, especially those at the very top of a company, may be reluctant to accept examination of their value systems, or challenge of their judgments. But acceptable planning can proceed only upon the basis of top management values. If staff is to be helpful to top management it must have some understanding of these values. Long-range planning is a process which challenges judgments, those of top management as well as those of staff and lower levels of management. Top management must understand this. Staff, of course, must do this judiciously and with sensitivity to top management feelings. If top management severely restricts such intellectual processes, or if staff bungles the exchange, the climate for planning is badly strained.

Many managers do not want to think about unpleasant possibilities or harsh realities. They are reluctant to look disagreeable facts in the face. Nor do line managers want to plan for something that is very unpleasant but may not occur; they consider such planning to be nothing more than play exercises. These realities of human nature can be serious impediments to planning. Somehow, if there is to be better planning, such barriers to dealing with reality must be removed.

IV. *Make sure the system fits the unique characteristics of the company and avoid overplanning.*

Every company is unique and, therefore, the planning system of every company will differ from all others. The fundamental processes, principles, and practices will be similar, but the details will differ. I have never seen identical operational models of the long-range planning systems of two companies. Yet, I have never seen what I considered to be an effective planning system which did not have in it, implicitly or explicitly, every one of the parts of an acceptable conceptual model. Companies differ in terms of styles of top management, organization, problems, planning capabilities, complexity, size, product line, etc. The planning system must be tailored to fit such variables, not the other way around.

Overplanning occurs when the system involves too much paper work, too much staff and managerial time devoted to planning, too much formality, and too much procedure and ritual. The planning process should be as flexible as possible but have enough formality in it to make it apparent to everyone involved that there is a systematic process being pursued. Too much rigidity and ritual will tend to make the process routine. Then, it will become pedestrian and people will be more concerned with putting numbers in boxes than in trying to be creative. I shall return to this point later. On the other hand, too much looseness and informality can lead to sloppiness, fuzzy thinking, and neglect of long-range planning.

A major characteristic of modern long-range planning is that it is deliberate, comprehensive, systematic, and structured. There are, however, thousands of alternatives open to a company in organizing, doing, and using the results of planning. The best system has the "right" blend between formality and flexibility.

Line and staff must constantly look at the cost benefit equation for planning. I do not mean that this equation should be quantified because that is not possible. It is my suggestion that attention be given to the benefits from planning as well as to the costs of doing it. Costs in this context are broadly defined to include monetary, personal time, alternative costs, and any other expenditure, tangible or intangible, made in the planning process. If the cost benefit equation is considered by managers it is likely that benefits will exceed costs and overplanning will be avoided.

V. *Don't set fuzzy, pie-in-the-sky, or too many objectives.*

Objectives that are vague or described at high levels of abstraction are not too helpful in planning. For example, this objective is not likely to lead to effective planning: "We seek to make as much money as possible." Compare this with the following statement: "Our objective is to increase sales from $100 million today to $250 million five years from now." Objectives used in long-range planning should be as concrete and as specific as possible. As such they have much more guidance and provide much more direction to the planning process than vaguely defined objectives.

Some companies confuse basic company purposes with long-range planning objectives. Basic purposes are generally stated in broad terms and remain as written for long periods of time. For example, the following are basic company purposes: "To achieve the highest reliability and quality in our products and to be considered by the industry as the standard for comparison." Another: "To recognize and properly discharge our responsibilities for the welfare of our employees, the communities in which we do business, and society as a whole." These, of course, would be but two of a number of basic purposes one of which, of course, would concern profits. Such statements can be of high importance in a company and a fundamental basis for the development of a planning program. But for planning to proceed there must be objectives which rest under these broad aims which can guide more precisely the development of plans. These purposes cannot take the place of more concrete long-range planning objectives.

Pie-in-the-sky objectives are not helpful in planning. To say that we aim to increase our sales from $1 million today to $2 billion in five years is not helpful unless there is a creditable basis for setting such a target. Goals which are utterly impossible to achieve have no motivating or directive power. Goals which are too easy to reach also have little motivating power.

Too many objectives, no matter how well expressed, create problems. The more numerous are objectives the more opportunities exist for conflicts among them. The more conflicts are identified among objectives the more complex and frustrating the planning process becomes. There is no answer to how many objectives a company should have. That depends on the company. Generally, objectives should be set for activities of fundamental significance to the welfare of a company which the company wants to track and measure. A minimum would seem to be sales, profits, return on investment, and market share. But, in addition, objectives might pertain to employment, employee activities, facilities, distribution channels, acquisitions, divestment, etc.

VI. *Managers must not neglect long-range planning because of current problems.*

There is only one exception to this admonition. If current problems are so serious that bankruptcy is possible all efforts must obviously be devoted to getting the company out of this trouble. Two points should be made, however. Effective long-range planning can and should proceed along with efforts to resolve current problems.

Operating managers are faced with a Gresham's Law of planning: "short range problems drive out long-range thinking." It is easy to become engrossed in dealing with current problems. They are there, cannot be neglected, and give many managers a sense of fulfillment in dealing with them that does not derive from the more reflective processes of long-range planning.

When managers neglect long-range planning for short-term problems there will be at best an excessive delegation of the planning function to staff. At worst it can lead to dissatisfaction with the planning process and, in the end, a failure of it.

VII. *Stress should be placed on getting results from the planning process rather than upon following procedures.*

This point was mentioned previously but deserves further attention. Two types of results flow from long-range planning: the substantive conclusions and process-associated benefits.

First, planning should produce substantive results (especially strategies) of value to the company. There are some companies that establish objectives and then assume that by simply following a set of procedures there will be produced a usable plan to achieve the objectives. Rather than procedures, the planning process should stress the desirability of generating new ideas, of thinking about the basic questions with which long-range planning must deal, and of getting creditable and carefully developed objectives, strategies, and detailed plans which will assure that the strategies really will achieve the objectives sought. These substantive results then must be implemented by making proper current decisions.

Second, there are also ancillary or less tangible results which a company should seek from its long-range planning system. The military has an old saying: plans are sometimes useless, but the planning process is always indispensable. The reason, of course, is that the process itself has great value. To illustrate, the planning process can be a training ground for managers. It can perform this function because it forces managers to do the things good managers must do. I have in mind, for example, such things as asking fundamental questions and getting answers about what competitors are doing, product obsolescence, cash flow, objectives, strategies, etc.

The process also helps people to adjust to change. As such it helps them adapt better to unexpected events than when they have not had the experience of long-range planning. The process is also a communications system which, if created carefully, can be a great asset to a company. The process also makes it possible for people to participate in decision making, to have a piece of the action, so to speak. These days when employees want to contribute their talents to an organization in order to lead more fulfilling lives this potential for the planning system can be valuable to a company. The greater the effort to achieve these benefits, as distinct from simply following procedures, the more likely a company will profit from them.

VIII. *Planning is less effective than otherwise when procedures are dominant over personal interrelationships.*

Planning must stress economic analysis, capital allocation criteria, acquisition formulas, forecasts of experts, and other objective and bloodless data. But people think in other dimensions and to proceed without taking this factor into consideration will lead to less effective planning. Each person has a value system which differs from others. Judgments about what to do will vary among people, depending upon their value systems. The more authority a manager has the more important is his value system in the planning process. But value systems of all managers influence the system.

The point may be illustrated by considering the chief executive officer of a company who is interested solely in research and development in advanced technology. Another chief executive officer may wish to apply high technology to standard commercial products. A third may focus his interests on becoming the largest company in the industry. A fourth may aspire to see his firm become the largest and the technologically superior company in his industry. All these views flow from value systems, not demonstrable factual logic. The planning in each company must pay attention to such values of the chief executive office, or fail.

A planning process cannot proceed without problems of grave sorts if the interpersonal relationships of staff and line are not kept at a reasonably harmonious level. The top management of a company and the corporate planner, if there is one, must be compatible. Indeed, corporate planners must work agreeably with line and staff throughout an organization. Line managers are often highly practicable pragmatists, make quick decisions on the basis of personal judgments, are doers, and know how to work with and get things done with and through people. Staff planners, on the other hand, tend to be dispassionate observers, thinkers, researchers, and stand aloof from current crises. These are oversimplifications but point up the fact that when such differences exist they can cause personality conflicts. Many other opportunities for personality conflicts exist such as unnecessary confrontations between line and staff in the evaluation of plans, staff getting inappropriately involved in line affairs, or staff using top management authority in an unwise way to get line managers to do things the staff thinks should be done.

Harmonious relationships among people in an organization are more desirable than following procedures, if there is a choice between the two. It is easier to change procedures to fit personalities than the other way around.

IX. *When a company completes its long-range planning process the results should be used in making better current budget decisions.*

This seem obvious, yet there are instances where companies go through their planning process, or what passes for it, but the substantive results do not seem to get reflected in current budgets. The name of the planning game is better current decisions in light of their futurity. If better current decisions do not result the planning process is not complete and eventually will wither and become useless.

This does not mean that current budget decisions must be identical with those of the first year of the long-range plan. In some companies there is a tight linkage between numbers in the detailed functional plans and current budgets. In other companies the connection is loose and the numbers are not the same. In all cases, however, the budget decisions should reflect the results of the long-range planning effort.

X. *Long-range planning will not be done well by managers if their performance evaluations and bonuses are based strictly on a short-term profit return.*

This is especially true if top management does not conduct face-to-face sessions with managers to discuss their long-range plans. No manager will spend time on long-range planning if top management does not review his plans and give him some sort of feedback, and if his personal financial well being is based strictly on the bottom line of his annual profit and loss statement.

Companies are overcoming this problem by using a point system in calculating performance and bonus. Most points are scored for financial performance but merits are added for how well managers train their subordinates, meet community responsibilities, do effective long-range planning, and so on. The scores, of course, are based on subjective evaluations.

CONCLUDING COMMENTS

Despite extensive experience with comprehensive formal long-range planning there are many companies that are dissatisfied with their systems. This paper presented ten points which these companies may profitably consider to improve their planning systems.

Part 3
ORGANIZING

The purpose of organizing is to establish an intentional structure of roles by which people can know what their tasks and objectives are, how these fit with those of others, and how much discretion they and others have in making decisions to accomplish desired results. Organizing thus establishes a role environment for performance by individuals operating together in a formally structured enterprise. The pertinent readings related to this important function of managers are divided into six subject areas: The Span of Management; Departmentation; Decentralization; Line, Staff, and Functional Authority; Committees; and Organization Analysis and Effectiveness.

The existence of task and authority groupings, referred to as departments, and the hierarchy of organization structures are a result of the limitations imposed by the span of management. The editors believe that this important problem is best seen in terms of the influence of underlying variables. This point of view, along with an actual experience in applying this approach to practice, is reported in Harold Koontz' article "Making Theory Operational: The Span of Management."

Recent behavioral research has cast some interesting light on the existence of hierarchy and the problems of span of management. The paper by R. Carzo and J. N. Yanouzas, "Effects of Flat and Tall Organization Structure," examines empirical studies on this subject and reports on an original study of how levels and hierarchy influence performance. It is interesting that, in general, the researchers found better performance under tall structures than under flatter ones. In their paper, "Merging Management and Behavioral Theory: The Interaction between Span of Control and Group Size," R. J. House and J. B. Miner, drawing heavily from a wide variety of behavioral research, came to some helpful conclusions. Among these was that the optimal span is likely to be between five and ten persons, although this is affected by such variables as organizational level, technology, group cohesiveness, the nature and interdependence of tasks, and available leadership skills.

In practice, enterprises have developed various departmental patterns. The nature of these and their use in business enterprises is dealt with in Harold Stieglitz' article "On Concepts of Corporate Structure." The recent tendency to aim organization structures more toward supporting marketing efforts is effectively explained in Mack Hanan's paper on "Reorganize Your Company Around Markets."

As all enterprises have become increasingly concerned with end-results, organizational structures that cannot for various reasons be wholly designed to reflect these objectives have tended to develop variations of matrix organization. These are essentially structures which mix both functional and product (or project) patterns in a grid fashion. They have been widely used in engineering organizations and in marketing structures. Because these structures represent instances of dual command, certain elements of confusion and lack of responsibility have understandably tended to exist. The problems and suggested solutions of matrix management as applied to product management in marketing are ably presented by Robert M. Fulmer in his "Product Management: Panacea or Pandora's Box."

The problem of matrix organization has been complicated by the understandable desire of many companies to have persons with responsibility for developing plans and programs for reaching markets as well as the long-practiced attempts of placing responsibility in certain individuals for marketing a given product. This tends to give rise to a three-dimension matrix. The nature of this organizational development is explained in B. Charles Ames' article on "Dilemma of Product/Market Management."

One of the major developments in organizational practice and philosophy in the past five decades, a development which has allowed enterprises to grow large without loss of organizational effectiveness, has been decentralization of authority. This is more than the art and science of delegation, for it involves a philosophy and an art of dispersing authority without losing control. To a very great extent, successful decentralization is a matter of clarifying authority delegation. One of the most useful tools for so doing is the linear authority chart or management responsibility chart. This is explained in Robert D. Melcher's "Roles and Relationships: Clarifying the Manager's Job." Because control so often has been lost through decentralization, the editors have included the statement of another industrialist, John G. Staiger, "What Cannot Be Decentralized."

Among the most misunderstood and misapplied concepts in management is the line and staff concept, which the editors view as describing a kind of authority relationship rather than types of activities, people, or organizational units. In practice, misunderstanding of line and staff relationships has led to much friction and inefficiency. What the editors believe to be an accurate statement of the line and staff concept is found in Hall H. Logan's article "Line and Staff: An Obsolete Concept?"

Perhaps the most troublesome aspect of organizing in practice is the confusion existing in functional authority relationships. Functional authority exists when one department, usually operating in a staff or service capacity, is given authority in a given area over other departments not reporting to it. Fortunately, this long-neglected problem has been subject recently to some illuminating research. With respect to the personnel manager, Wendell French and Dale A. Henning have done such research in their "The Authority-Influence Role of the Functional Specialist in Management." With respect to the controller, light is cast in the research report of Dale A. Henning and R. L. Moseley, "Authority Role of a Functional Manager: The Controller."

Committees are special organizational forms designed for the undertaking of a task by a group, as a group, rather than by an individual. Cyril O'Donnell's summary article "Ground Rules for Using Committees" analyzes how to make committees work effectively. Alan C. Filley, by utilizing the results of small group and leadership research, gives novel and interesting implications for the nature, size, and operation of committees in his "Committee Management: Guidelines from Social Science Research."

In the final section of this part, two readings are presented which deal variously with with organization analysis and effectiveness. One of these is the perceptive analysis by D. R. Daniel of the problems of reorganizing and some of the pitfalls and difficulties encountered in recasting the organization structure. His article "Reorganizing for Results" is one of the most realistic and helpful papers that has been written on this subject. The final reading deals with the impact of technology on organizational structure. Raymond G. Hunt, relying heavily on a social psychological point of view and on research made by others, summarizes very well in his "Technology and Organization" the current findings concerning the impact of technology upon organizational structures.

A. THE SPAN OF MANAGEMENT

29 MAKING THEORY OPERATIONAL: THE SPAN OF MANAGEMENT*

Harold Koontz

One of the most striking phenomena of the latter half of the twentieth century is the belated search for a science of management. Not that the importance of effective group operation had theretofore gone unnoticed. One finds references to the problem in the Old Testament of the Bible, in the early Egyptian papyri extending back to 1300 B.C., in Confucius's parables, and in the writing of the early Greek philosophers. But the real awakening to the possibility that there might be an underlying science of managing is largely ascribable to the pioneering writings of the French industrialist Henri Fayol and the American engineer Frederick Taylor shortly after the turn of the twentieth century. Since World War II these slow beginnings have developed into a crescendo of thought, speculation, theory, research, trials and errors, and new techniques.

Despite the current interest in effective and efficient managing, management may be thought of as a science groping for useful knowledge. Managing is an art—but so is medicine, engineering, and baseball. Every art is made better if underlying it is a science—organized knowledge. Likewise, science has more practical meaning, if it has been structured around principles—significant predictive explanations of fundamental relationships.

What has been lacking in many areas of management theory is the means of translating available understanding into the most useful tools for the practitioner. While distilled management knowledge, summarized in concepts and principles, has already been found valuable as a guideline for practicing managers, it would be more useful if it could be translated into quantitatively or qualitatively verifiable tools.

To some extent this has been done. One of the major contributions of the mathematicians and systems theorists has been to bring the approaches of the physical sciences into the field of management. This has sharpened the understanding and techniques of management planning and control through the application of such techniques as operations research and critical path networks (PERT). Also, a major breakthrough in making managing subject to verifiable measures has taken place with the recently developed "results" approach to management appraisal. There are other, but still relatively few, techniques by which principles have been applied in a scientific way.

In the area of organizing—establishing an intentional structure of roles so that people can work effectively and efficiently together in groups—one has seen rather little development beyond the principles distilled from experience by such practitioners as Fayol, Alvin Brown, or Urwick. To be sure, the behavioralists have made progress in finding out some of the "people" problems in formally organized enterprise, but their researches still have not shed much light on what to do to establish a structural environment for performance.

One of the organizational areas which has been recognized as a difficult one at least since the time Moses organized to bring the children of Israel to the Promised Land[1] is that of the span of management.[2] The question of how many persons a manager should have reporting

* Reprinted by permission of the publisher from *The Journal of Management Studies,* vol. 3, no. 3, pp. 229–243, October, 1966. Mr. Koontz is Mead Johnson Professor of Management in the Graduate School of Management, University of California, Los Angeles.

[1] In Exodus 18:17–26 his father-in-law advised Moses to delegate and establish "rulers of thousands, and rulers of hundreds, rulers of fifties, and rulers of ten" so that these leaders could share the burdens of administration.

[2] In much of the literature of management, this is referred to as the "span of control." The writer and his co-author, Cyril O'Donnell, have preferred since 1955 to use the term of "span of management" as being more descriptive. See *Principles of Management,* McGraw-Hill, New York, 1955, p. 83. Other later writers have "coined" this phrase. See G. G. Fisch, "Stretching the Span of Management," *Harvard Business Review,* vol. 41, no. 5, pp. 74–85, September–October, 1953.

to him has long plagued managers. Yet, little progress has been made in answering this apparently simple question. However, as indicated by one company's approach to this question, referred to below, there is indication that progress can be made. This and other approaches may be crude and suffer from inexactness. They must, therefore, be used with care and judgment. But if they offer means for the manager to reach better answers than through intuition and trial-and-error, the gains are such that they are unquestionably justified.

THE SPAN OF MANAGEMENT: A PRACTICAL PROBLEM NEEDING CLARIFICATION

In looking over the literature, research, and programs of management, one cannot help but be impressed with the lack of real light cast on the question of span of management. This is particularly so when one notes the long concern over proper delegation of authority, over the need for having a work environment where people can perform, and over the impact of organization structure on the individual.[3] It is also surprising when only simple arithmetic will show that the difference between an average managerial span of, say four, and one of eight in a company of 4,000 non-managerial employees can make a difference of two entire levels of management and of nearly 800 managers!

Narrow spans cost money for salaries, fringes, space and other support. Perhaps even greater than the money cost is the cost of longer lines of communications, not only from the top down but from the bottom up. And these communications are significant in terms of plans made and transmitted, delegations made clear and effective, performance being known and evaluated, and control information being available and interpreted. In other words, organizational communication is far more complex than simply the ability to speak and be understood. Organization structure constitutes a decision-making communications network. Its task is to show the way, with respect to information that must be processed in the making of decisions, to whom one must communicate on what.

On the other hand, too wide a span of management may likewise be dangerous. The overburdened manager unable to arrive at and communicate decisions, with inadequate time and energy to select and appraise and teach his subordinates, and with too little time to plan and see that plans succeed may be the source of as much cost and frustration as the manager with too narrow a span.

The "Classical" Position on Span of Management Early theorists, generally placed in a school referred to as "classical," had only their experience or that of companies and managers they had observed to draw upon. Perhaps the most widely quoted authority on the span of management has been the eminent management consultant and scholar Lyndall F. Urwick. Reflecting on his experience and opportunities for astute observation, Urwick concluded that "no superior can supervise directly the work of more than five, or, at the most, six subordinates *whose work interlocks.*"[4] Placing heavy emphasis on the element of interlocking, Urwick readily admitted that the span may be much wider where the work of subordinates is not closely interrelated and managerial coordination is not required, or where a manager is well supported by staff, or where the requirements of leadership and morale do not require close and frequent face-to-face communication between the manager and his subordinates.

Other early writers on management advocate various spans. As summarized by one scholar,[5] these "classical" writers appeared to advocate a span of control of from three to seven or eight persons at the higher levels of organization and a span of up to twenty or thirty persons at the lowest echelon.

It is interesting that the so-called "classical" point of view is borne out in practice more often than is usually suspected. After extensive research on this point Healey found in a study of 620 industrial plants in Ohio that in 93.7 per cent of main plants and 84.2 per cent of the branch plants, the top executive had less than nine immediate subordinates and almost as high a percentage (76.3 per cent for main-plant executives and 70.3 per cent of branch plant managers) had from three through eight.

Substantially similar results were found by Dale in his study of 141 companies in 1951.[6] While he observed variations from one to twenty-four subordinates of chief executives in the companies, Dale found a median between eight and nine for the large companies

[3] See, among many others, the excellent work of Chris Argyris, reported most recently in his *Integrating the Individual and the Organization,* John Wiley & Sons, Inc., New York, 1964.

[4] "The Manager's Span of Control," *Harvard Business Review,* vol. 34, no. 3, p. 41, May–June, 1956.

[5] J. H. Healey, *Executive Coordination and Control,* The Ohio State University Press, Columbus, Ohio, 1956. See discussion on this point, pp. 11–15.

[6] E. Dale, *Planning and Developing the Company Organization,* Res. Rep. No. 20, American Management Association, New York, 1952, pp. 57–59.

and six to seven in the medium-sized companies. Comparable results were found by White in 1963 in a study of sixty-six companies.[7] In a much more narrowly based study, using a random sample, Fisch, on the other hand, discovered a tendency among very large (over $1 billion of sales) for a span of management at the top of more than twelve, with the span tending to be smaller as company size decreases.[8]

In a very real sense, none of these studies is truly indicative of the span of management actually practiced. For one thing, they only measure the span at the top of an enterprise. This is hardly typical of what the span may be throughout the enterprise, particularly since every organizer has experienced the tremendous pressure for a large number of functions of a business to report to the top executive. It is probable that the span below the top executive is much narrower. Indeed analysis of more than 200 companies of all sizes made by the author discloses a much narrower span in the middle levels of management than at the top.

In addition, the fact that apparently well managed companies have, as between them, and certainly within them, widely varying spans indicates that merely counting what is actually done is not enough to establish what a span *ought* to be. And this is true even if it could be assumed that, through trial and error, each company had reached an optimum span. It may only prove that underlying conditions vary.

The "Revisionist" or "Operational" School Position on Span of Management More recent management theorists have taken the position that there are too many variables in a management situation to conclude that there is any particular number of subordinates which a manager can effectively supervise.[9] It is concluded that there is a limit to the number of subordinates a manager may effectively supervise but the exact number will depend upon underlying factors, all of which affect the time requirements of managing.

In other words, the predominant current view is to look for the causes of limited span in individual situations, rather than to assume there is a given numerical limit generally applicable to all. If one can look at what it is that consumes the time of a manager in his handling of his superior-subordinate relationships and also ascertain what devices can be used to reduce these time pressures, the analyst has an approach helpful in determining the optimum span in individual cases. He also has a powerful tool to find out what can be done to extend the span without destroying effective supervision. There can be no argument that the costs of levels and supervision are such as to make it highly desirable for every individual manager to have as many subordinates as he can *effectively* supervise.

Identifying the Underlying Factors As a general proposition, the more subordinates an individual manager has, the greater the complexity of superior–subordinate relationships. That these can become astronomical is indicated by Graicunas' formula which discloses eighteen different human relationship situations existing when a manager has three subordinates, rising to 2,376 with nine subordinates, and 24,708 with twelve.[10]

What is more significant than the complexity and number of individual human relationship situations is their frequency and severity. In other words, how often do they occur and take the time of the superior, and, when they occur, how much of his time do they take? Certainly, time, itself, is the most limiting factor of all in the managerial task.

Looking at these underlying factors, the principal ones appear to be the following:

(1) *Training Required or Possessed by Subordinates.* The more a job requires training, the more training a subordinate must possess; the better trained a subordinate is, in relation to his job requirements, the less of a manager's time must be spent in teaching, in clarifying duties and desired results, and in correcting mistakes.

(2) *Clarity of Authority Delegations.* The greater the clarity of authority delegations (note: *clarity,* not detail), the less time of the manager needs to be taken in explaining a task, making decisions that the subordinate should make, and explaining to others what the subordinate's responsibilities are.

(3) *Clarity of Plans.* If plans (and particularly that part of plans encompassed in

[7] K. K. White, *Understanding the Company Organization Chart,* American Management Association, New York, 1963, pp. 60–61.

[8] G. G. Fisch, "Stretching the Span of Management," *Harvard Business Review,* vol. 41, no. 5, pp. 80–81, September–October, 1962.

[9] See, for example, H. Koontz and C. O'Donnell, *Principles of Management,* 3d ed., McGraw-Hill Book Company, New York, 1964, p. 229; also see H. Steiglitz, *Corporate Organization Structures,* Studies in Personnel Policy No. 183, National Industrial Conference Board, New York, 1961, p. 8.

[10] Although his formula is little more than an arithmetic truism, V. A. Graicunas found that the complexity of superior-subordinate relationships is given by the formula $n(2^n/2+n-1)$ where n equals the number of subordinates. See his "Relationship in Organization," in L. Gulick and L. Urwick (eds.) *Papers on the Science of Administration,* Institute of Public Administration, New York, 1937, pp. 181–87.

goals and policies) are clear (again, not necessarily detailed), the subordinate can proceed with his task, knowing where he is going and what is expected of him without continual checking with his superior; nor need the superior continually look over his subordinate's shoulder.

(4) *Dynamics of a Plan.* Understandably, if a company or a given plan is subject to a high rate of change, it is more difficult to keep plans up-to-date and clear and to maintain meaningful delegations; in this case, much more of a manager's time will be taken in supervision than where things move more slowly.

(5) *Extent to Which Adequate Controls Are Available.* Since a manager delegates none of his responsibility when he assigns a task to a subordinate and delegates authority to do it, he must necessarily make sure that task is being done and the authority is being used properly. This means control. The more effective his control devices, the less time he will be forced to spend to make sure that plans succeed.

(6) *The Quality of Communications Techniques.* An executive's task involves heavy time demands in communicating plans and instructions, teaching and interpreting delegations, and receiving information with respect to problems and progress against plans. Clearly, the more effective communications techniques are in making sure that information is transmitted accurately and quickly, the less time must be spent on communications, and, other things being equal, the wider a span of management he can handle.

(7) *Amount of Personal Contact Needed.* All managerial positions require a certain amount of face-to-face relationships. Many situations can be handled by written reports, others by special communications techniques not involving personal contact, but many require the manager spending time with people. Moreover, even where a matter might be handled without personal contact, situations of delicacy, cases where a "feel" of attitudes is necessary, and instances where simply the presence of a superior lends weight to a problem solution or a responsibility are among the many that make face-to-face relationships wise and necessary. Almost invariably these are time consuming.

While other factors might be noted, it has seemed that these are the principal ones which bear on the frequency and time severity of human relationship situations. It becomes readily apparent that, if a manager can solve the time demands involved in these, and still do an effective job of supervision, he should be able to handle a larger number of subordinates than otherwise.

Furthermore, the more a manager can have effective staff or line assistance to take over these time burdens, the more subordinates he should be able to manage. Note that the emphasis is upon "effective" assistance. There have been too many instances where an overburdened manager has tried to lower his load by use of staff or line assistants, only to find that he then spends more of his time with them or in undoing the problems and frictions they cause.

The Problem of Balance It can readily be seen that the span of management problem, like most in life, raises a difficult question of balance. In general, the narrower the span, the more complete the supervision can be, although there are many cases of very narrow spans where the superior, having too little to do, tends to oversupervise his subordinates. On the other hand, the narrower the span, the more the cost in terms of supervision and communications difficulties.

The exact optimum balance in any given situation depends upon underlying factors such as those outlined above. One thing is certain. The subordinate who cannot reach his superior when he must, or the superior who does not have time to guide his subordinate and remove obstacles to performance are just as much a source of cost and loss of morale and effectiveness as the problem of too much supervision and too many levels.

Need for Objective Standards In the case of the span of management, as in virtually every area of managing, there is an urgent need for objective standards. Even though one may identify accurately the underlying factors that determine the span, it is hardly possible to arrive at an optimum span until these factors can be given some degree of verifiable meaning.

This is necessary for determining the right span. It is also necessary if a superior is to find out whether a given technique, such as staff assistance, authority delegation, or special reports, are really helping or hindering him in the solution of the span of management. It may be too early to expect truly objective and verifiable measures of such factors as those involved in the span of management. It may be that such measures as can be used are crude. But it is reasonable to suspect that, if more effort were spent in finding methods of objectively verifying, progress might be made in management effectiveness comparable to the switch to verifiable planned results as the primary means of appraising managerial performance.

QUANTIFYING THE UNDERLYING FACTORS: THE LOCKHEED PROGRAM

One of the pioneering programs undertaken by an American company to give sharper meaning to the factors underlying the span of management was that introduced several years ago by the Lockheed Missiles and Space Company.[11] Although carried on as an experimental program and not presented here as a case of a completely proved approach to management problems, the originality and intelligence used by the company are admirable and could well show a way toward better seeing and solving span of management and other managerial problems.

Lockheed's Diagnosis of Its Span Problem

As many companies have discovered when they examine their organization structure, Lockheed found that the spans of management at the middle management level appeared to be too narrow. The span of the upper and top general manager and director level ranged from five to ten; the average spans of the first line supervisors ranged from fifteen to eighteen; but the spans of the middle management[12] averaged only 3.2, and ranged from 2.9 to 3.4.

As one might suspect, the analysis also disclosed that there were apparently too many levels of supervision. Surveys made in portions of the organization indicated that, in this company of some 4,000 persons, there were two levels of supervisors, four levels of managers, and a director, or seven levels in all. If direct line assistants were included as levels, these, in some cases, increased the total to eleven.

In examining the problem further, and feeling that a middle manager is better off if he does not have idle time to worry about his subordinates, the company observed that the narrow spans and excessive levels at the middle management level were apparently causing the following problems:

(1) *Decrease in Initiative and Morale.* There was a tendency not to delegate real authority, particularly at the first and second lines of supervision. This caused problems of accomplishing tasks and thwarted a feeling of accomplishment by many of these supervisors.

(2) *High Costs.* Narrow spans and added levels were increasing costs through multiplying supervisors, secretaries, space and service requirements.

(3) *Delay in Decisions.* A major problem encountered was delay in decisions in a company whose fast growth and highly dynamic product line required quick action. The added levels caused managers to review actions of levels below, causing delays, and in many cases implementing action was made more difficult because instructions had to be transmitted through many levels.

(4) *Decrease in Opportunities for Self-development.* The narrow spans at the middle management level limited managers to fewer activities and deprived them of the broadening knowledge of supervising related activities.

(5) *Over-management.* It was also found that managers were spending excessive time in reviewing and directing their subordinates in greater detail than necessary.

It became apparent that, if only the middle management group of the company where the span seemed obviously narrow were changed, significant reductions in levels could be attained. Starting with an average span of three at the middle management level, and with no other changes in first level or top level spans, it was calculated that an average span of four would reduce needed levels from six to five and total middle management employees in a major area of the company from 302 to 268. With a further widening of the span to six, the number of levels could be reduced to four and only 241 middle management employees would be required.

Critical Variables Underlying the Span of Management

If the span of management problem was to be approached intelligently, it was recognized that the underlying critical variables which determined the span would have to be examined. The analysts studied the inherent functions of each job and the actual activities needing direction in order to ascertain the complexity of managerial relationships. This analysis yielded seven factors which appeared to be closely related to an effective span of management or indicative in selecting an optimum span.

Although the underlying factors disclosed by

[11] For this section of the paper, the author is indebted to D. L. Harris who undertook extensive research of this program. Mr. Harris, in turn, received valuable assistance from Richard C. Anderson, Manager of Organization Analysis of the Company, who made available much of the data used in this paper. Likewise, the author is grateful to Herschel Brown, Executive Vice-President of the Company for permission to use Company records. The Lockheed program has been briefly reported in Harold Stieglitz, "Optimizing Span of Control," *Management Record,* vol. 24, no. 9, pp. 25–29, September, 1962; and in C. W. Barkdull, "Span of Control: A Method of Evaluation," *Michigan Business Review,* vol. 15, no. 3, pp. 25–32, May, 1963.

[12] Defined as all managers, except for department directors and general managers, having supervisory personnel reporting to them.

the Company's study are somewhat different from those outlined above as being generally applicable, it is interesting how fundamentally similar they are. Those that were determined to be most indicative were the following:

(1) *Similarity of Functions.* This factor refers to the degree to which functions performed by the various components or personnel reporting to a manager are alike or different. Its importance evolves from the fact that, as functions decrease in degree of variability, fewer factors and interrelationships must be kept in mind by the supervisor and the greater the number of persons he can effectively supervise.

(2) *Geographic Contiguity.* This factor refers to physical locations of units and personnel. The greater the geographic separation, the greater the difficulty in administration because of problems of communications.

(3) *Complexity of Functions.* This factor refers to the nature of the tasks done and involves a determination of the degree of difficulty in performing satisfactorily. Although admittedly a very difficult factor to measure objectively, Lockheed found that there was a high degree of coordination between what was generally believed to be complexity and the salary of a job.

(4) *Direction and Control.* In identifying this factor, the analysts had in mind the nature of personnel reporting directly to a superior, the amount of training required, the extent to which authority can be delegated, and the personal attention needed.

(5) *Coordination.* This is related to time requirements for keeping an organizational unit keyed in with other divisional or company-wide activities.

(6) *Planning.* This factor refers to the importance, complexity, and time requirements necessary to review goals, programs, and budgets, with particular emphasis on whether these planning functions are actually being performed by the manager or by others and whether the planning must be done on a continuing basis or merely once a year when budgets are approved.

(7) *Organizational Assistance.* This has to do with the extent and nature of assistance received from direct line assistants, assistants to, staff, or other personnel having planning, administrative, and control responsibilities.

The impact of the above factors on the span of management is easily perceived. The more similar the functions, the closer the geographic contiguity, and the more organizational assistance a manager has, the more people it might be expected that he could effectively supervise. The more complex functions are, the greater the need for direction, control and coordination, and the more difficult the planning, the fewer persons a manager might be expected to supervise. It will be noted, also, that the factors used by Lockheed, in general, deal with the same underlying variables as those outlined earlier in this paper.

Determining Degrees of Supervisory Burden within Span Factors Excluding the factor of the influence of organizational assistance, other span factors were spread over a spectrum of five degrees of difficulty, from the easiest situation (from the standpoint of span) to the most difficult. These were then assembled in a matrix as shown in Table 1. As will be noted presently, the element of organizational assistance was conceived of as a multiplier which reduced the span values derived from the other factors.

Determining a value for these other span factors was, as might be expected, a difficult task. After analysis of 150 cases at the middle management and director levels, to determine the span used and the underlying factors, preliminary weighting of the various factors were developed. These, in turn were checked against a number of comparative cases, with reference as a standard to those units regarded as well-managed. The weightings for each degree of difficulty of the six primary variables so derived are shown in Table 1.

To illustrate the way these burdens were analysed, a few examples may be noted:

Complexity of Functions—

(1) Simple repetitive duties which require little training (less than six months) and which follow simple well-defined rules and procedures. Examples would include typing, stock handling, mailing, simple assembly (generally in hourly grades 13–17 and professional grades 1–3).

(2) Highly complex duties which involve a wide variety of tasks and which require long training and experience (8–10 years). Abstract or creative thinking and/or necessity for consideration of many factors in arriving at courses of action would be typical. Examples: research scientist, engineering development (salary grades 18–20, professional grades 7–10).

Direction and Control—

Constant close daily supervision, instruction, and control. The closeness of the supervision could be the result of the type of work which requires constant attention from supervision,

TABLE 1 Degrees of Supervisory Burden within Span Factors. Numbers Show Relative Weighting

SPAN FACTOR	DEGREE OF SUPERVISORY BURDEN				
Similarity of functions	Identical 1	Essentially alike 2	Similar 3	Inherently different 4	Fundamentally distinct 5
Geographic contiguity	All together 1	All in one bldg 2	Separate buildings, one plant location 3	Separate locations, one geographic area 4	Dispersed geographic areas 5
Complexity of functions	Simple repetitive 2	Routine 4	Some complexity 6	Complex, varied 8	Highly complex, varied 10
Direction & control	Minimum supervision & training 3	Limited supervision 6	Moderate periodic supervision 9	Frequent continuing supervision 12	Constant close supervision 15
Coordination	Minimum relation with others 2	Relationships limited to defined courses 4	Moderate Relationships easily controlled 6	Considerable close relationship 8	Extensive mutual nonrecurring relationships 10
Planning	Minimum scope & complexity 2	Limited scope & complexity 4	Moderate scope & complexity 6	Considerable effort required guided only by broad policies 8	Extensive effort required; areas and policies not charted 10

such as very important and costly experiments, or it could be a result of the type of employees whose knowledge and skills are such that continual careful instruction and direction are required . . . typicaly, where regular rules, guides, or procedures for subordinates' conduct would be difficult or impossible to prepare.

The Supervisory Index After weighting the six primary span factors, the analysts undertook the development of a supervisory index. Admitting to a bias toward widening the span of management, the analysts used as a standard the cases of wider spans, which were generally considered to be effectively organized and managed, from a sample of 150 middle management positions. Against the standards and from the numbers derived by weighting the six underlying factors, the following supervisory indices were developed:

TABLE 2 Suggested Supervisory Index

TOTAL SPAN FACTOR WEIGHTINGS	SUGGESTED STANDARD SPAN
40–42	4–5
37–39	4–6
34–36	4–7
31–33	5–8
28–30	6–9
25–27	7–10
22–24	8–11

These indices, it was pointed out, were intended for middle managers only. However, upon the basis of their study the analysts concluded that the above data could be used for first line supervisors, by approximately doubling the span indicated above.

Correction for Organizational Assistance In arriving at a correction for organizational assistance, the analysts differentiated between types of assistants, as shown in Table 3. The multiplier factor value was determined again by reference to the 150 sample cases, with special emphasis, as standards, on those units with wider spans which were regarded as well organized and managed. In addition, these multipliers were checked through discussion with managers concerned. As can be seen, the more complete the organizational assistance, the lower the multiplier factor and the more a manager's initial supervisory index (not taking account the assistance) would be reduced downward.

TABLE 3 Adjustment to Span Index for Organizational Assistance

TYPE OF ORGANIZATIONAL ASSISTANCE PROVIDED	MULTIPLIER FACTOR
Direct line and staff activities	0.60
Direct line assistant (only)	0.70
Staff activities (administrative, planning *and* control functions)	0.75
Staff activities (administrative, planning *or* control functions)	0.85
Assistant to (limited duties)	0.95
For first line supervisors	
Number of leadmen	
1	0.85
2	0.70
3	0.55
4	0.40
5	0.25

Note: The numbers reduce total point values derived from Table I thus increasing the potential span of management.

Results under the Plan Although there were other variables that intervened after the program was instituted in 1962, such as a company austerity program in 1963, and even though the program was not applied throughout the company, there are clear indications that it did cause a widening of the span of management. It also led to a general reduction of one level of supervision.

In terms of costs and size of span, the following company-wide data indicate a significant change of span, particularly when it is realized that the program was not completely adopted and not too strongly pressed throughout the company:

	OCTOBER, 1961	JANUARY 1965
Total company personnel	25,846	23,236
Total managers*	672	575
Managerial ratio†	37.5	39.5
Total supervisory personnel	1,916	1,314
Supervisory ratio‡	12.4	16.7
Supervisory cost per employee§	$19.77	$14.98
Average span of management	3.4	4.2

* All managerial personnel above the supervisory level (supervisor is the title used at the lowest organizational level).
† Number of non-managerial personnel per manager.
‡ Number of non-supervisory personnel per supervisor.
§ Ratio of weekly supervisory payroll to the total number of non-supervisory personnel.

In addition to those apparent above, it should be remembered that the dollar cost savings are actually greater than shown. During the period involved, there were, of course, considerable pay rate increases. Moreover, the above results do not portray betterment in morale, reduction in over-supervision, and improvement in delegation believed by many observers to have occurred.

CAN QUANTIFICATION BE MEANINGFUL?

Although the Lockheed case is used as a practical instance where a well-managed company used ingenuity in an attempt to wrestle quantitatively with one aspect of management, the question may be asked, is it meaningful? Does this kind of approach show a practical way to approach certain management problems which cannot be reduced to the elegance of a complex mathematical model and the niceties of objective data and "answers"?

The Dangers of Pseudo-science There is, of course, a risk in approaches like this of giving the sanctity of numbers to phenomena that cannot accurately be quantified. In giving numerical weights to underlying variables and developing indices on the basis of standards of what is regarded as "good," there is indeed grave danger of falling into the trap of making a thing seem important and right merely because it is in numerical form.

On the other hand, if one were to rule out all such exercises in life, he would have to abandon cost accounting—even accounting itself (for what is *real* depreciation?), job evaluation programs based on point systems, and even most university grades. The question is not so much whether the numbers are real and accurate and free from question. It is rather several things. In the first place, are the values assigned reasonable and therefore useful for comparison? Does the breakdown of a problem into its component parts and the assignment of a system of numerical values and indices help in the understanding and analysing of a problem? Do the people who use the data so derived realize the elements of inaccuracy and subjectivity underlying them and realize that they should be used as aids and guides and not as iron-clad conclusive rules?

If the answers to these questions can be in the positive, as they can be in many areas of management, then such data should be used, at least until better information is available. And the dangers of pseudo-science tend to be more than offset by the advantages of greater visibility.

The Test of Results If even crude methods give such visibility and through doing so yield results, they can hardly be overlooked. In the Lockheed case, there is evidence that the system used did yield measurable results and that organization effectiveness was improved thereby.

Moreover, if problems such as those of the span of management are to wait until completely verifiable input data are available, those who must solve the realities of managing an enterprise would be deprived of much progress that can be made. Furthermore, if analysts and scholars of management are encouraged to search for data to give meaning to management problems, it is highly probable that more accurate and useful data can be developed. The approach of looking for answers to the span of management problem through analysis of the underlying contributing variables is certainly a step in the right direction. The additional attempt to give some quantitative meaning to these variables, even though crude by the objective standards of the more exact sciences, is a further significant step.

More experiments and studies should be made along these lines, not only with respect to the span of management, but in many other of the relatively unexplored areas of management. With the interest in managing which has risen in the past two decades and the examination of the management process by perceptive practitioners and those scholars who understand and deal with the realities of the managing art, we now have a reasonably operational understanding of the underlying variables in many aspects of managing. If there can be greater realization that, through effort and research, some progress can be made toward needed quantification of these variables, the usefulness of present management understanding can be greatly enhanced.

And it should not be overlooked by scholars who sneer at pseudo-science and by those responsible for the management of an enterprise that this effort would not be wasteful play. As indicated by the Lockheed program, there can be handsome rewards even for small progress with inexact data.

30 EFFECTS OF FLAT AND TALL ORGANIZATION STRUCTURE*

R. Carzo and *J. N. Yanouzas*

Empirical studies on the effects of organization structure have been mostly in field research. The purpose of this study[1] was to test the effects of organization structure in a laboratory experiment, specifically, tall and flat structures and their effects on organizational performance. A secondary purpose was to analyze the learning-curve patterns in the performance of organized groups.

THEORETICAL CONSIDERATIONS

Worthy's study (1950) of Sears Roebuck and Company was one of the first extensive and a widely accepted empirical study on the effects of flat and tall organization structure. Worthy argued that small organizations had better employee morale and productivity than large organizations. He stated that the advantages of small organizations could be incorporated into large organizations by using fewer levels of administration; that is, a flat organizational structure with a wide span of supervision rather than a tall or multilevel organization with a very narrow span of supervision.

At Sears, according to Worthy, the merchandising vice president had 44 senior executives reporting directly to him. The typical retail store at Sears had "forty-odd department managers reporting to a single store manager" (1959: 109). With this organization, the manager of a Sears department store did not have time to solve all the problems and was therefore forced to delegate decision-making authority to subordinates. When managers of departments were forced to manage, they learned to manage: "They cannot be running constantly to superiors for approval of their actions; they have to make their own decisions and stand or fall by the results. In the process, they make mistakes, but that, too, contributes to their growth and maturity" (Worthy, 1959: 110). The broad, flat type of organizational structure, according to Worthy, made it possible to do a better job and allowed individuals to develop and grow in ways that were not possible under the traditional tall organizational structure.[2]

While Worthy's views have gained wide acceptance, there has been empirical evidence that raises reasonable doubts about their validity. Meltzer and Salter (1960), for example, after studying completed questionnaires from 75 percent of all physiological scientists working in organizations in the United States, had serious doubts about the negative relationship between the number of organizational levels and productivity as stated by Worthy. A questionnaire study by Porter and Lawler (1964), on managerial attitudes, seemed to indicate that a tall structure was better in producing security and satisfaction of social needs, while a flat structure was better for self-actualization. Both studies concluded that there is no simple relationship between structure and performance and that a flat organization structure was not unequivocally superior to a tall organization structure. While these questionnaire studies do not settle the issues, they raise enough questions about the relation of structure and productivity to indicate a need for further research.

The need for further research is also indicated by the controversy that persists over the so-called principle of "span of supervision" or "span of control." Fayol (1949), Hamilton

* Reprinted by permission of the publisher from *Administrative Science Quarterly*, vol. 14, no. 2, pp. 178–191, June 1969. Mr. Carzo is professor of management at Temple University and Mr. Yanouzas is professor of management at the University of Connecticut.

[1] This research was supported by research grants from the Ford Foundation and two units of The Pennsylvania State University; the Central Fund for Research and the Center for Research of the College of Business Administration. The authors wish to acknowledge their indebtedness to Mr. Harsha B. Desai of The Pennsylvania State University, who collaborated on the formulation, implementation, and analysis of this study.

[2] Support for Worthy's conclusions was found in a small-group study by Jones (1966).

(1921), and Urwick (1956), to name only a few, have argued that man's available energy, knowledge, time and abilities are confined to narrow limits, he is unable to supervise the work of more than a few subordinates successfully. Graicunas (1937) hypothesized that the number of possible relationships that a supervisor might be required to manage increased exponentially with an arithmetic increases in the number of subordinates assigned directly to him. The conclusion, in traditional theory, is that supervisors should have a narrow span of supervision. Some writers are very specific about this prescription, as for example, "No supervisor can supervise directly the work of more than five or, at the most, six subordinates *whose work interlocks*" Urwick, (1956: 41).

The critics of the span-of-supervision principle emphasize that other, and perhaps more difficult, problems are created when the number of subordinates assigned to an executive is limited to a very few. For example, as an organization reduces the number of subordinates reporting to supervisors, it creates a tall organization by increasing the number of supervisory levels and supervisors. Corresponding administrative expenses for executive salaries, office space, and secretarial assistance also increase. Also, an increase in supervisory levels is said to cause communication problems. Communications in an organization are subject to different interpretation at each level. The more levels there are in an organization, the greater is the likelihood of distortion, so that the final recipient of a communication may get the wrong message or wrong emphasis. In addition, it takes longer to process information through the many levels of a tall structure. Many levels of supervision in an organization also dilute the influence of the most senior executive. The resulting administrative distance between top and lower-line officials may have a demoralizing effect on the latter. The critics essentially say that the decision and communication processes of a tall organization take longer and are of poorer quality than the processes of a flat organization.

Some of the hypothesized distortions in communications can be explained by the status differences of formal organization. The supervisor has two responsibilities, which conflict with each other. His decision-making responsibility requires that he be given adequate information by subordinates. However, his responsibility for evaluating the performance of subordinates means that he likely gets information that is not adequate or correct (Read, 1962). According to Hoslett, "The subordinate tends to tell his supervisor what the latter is interested in, not to disclose what he doesn't want to hear, and to cover up problems and mistakes which may reflect adversely on the subordinate. He tends to tell the boss those things which will enhance his position and indicate his success in meeting the problems of the day" (1951: 109). In addition to this distortion in the upward flow of communication, Hoslett points out that this status relationship creates a distortion in the downward flow of communication. In his efforts to maintain the status difference, the supervisor is not candid in his relationships with subordinates. He does not wish to admit mistakes or reveal conditions which would reflect adversely on his ability and judgment: "To do so would undermine his positions as a superior being in the formal organization" (Hoslett, 1951: 109).

As a solution to the problems caused by the tall organization with its narrow spans and many levels of supervision, critics such as Worthy offer the flat organization with relatively wide spans and few levels of supervision. However, there has been little research evidence to support the cases for either the flat or tall organization.

The field studies cited indicate that different organization structures produce significant differences in performance. Most of the literature on the theory of formal organization postulates that different structural arrangements produce significant differences in performance. However, several laboratory experiments on the effects of communication networks seem to indicate that the differences in performance on at least one variable, "time to complete an assigned task," are not significant.

One of the first to indicate nonsignificant differences in performance was the study by Guetzkow and Simon (1955). This research effort was a refinement of the empirical work of Leavitt (1951), who found that groups working in a wheel network took less time to complete tasks than groups in a circle network. Guetzkow and Simon made a distinction between: "(a) the effects of communication restrictions upon performance of the operating tasks; and (b) the effects of the restrictions upon a group's ability to organize itself for such performance" (1955: 233). The results supported their hypothesis that communication restrictions would only indirectly affect the efficiency with which the task was performed by "influencing the ability of the members to organize themselves for optimum performance in their line operation"

(Guetzkow and Simon, 1955: 238). Although different network groups had varying degrees of difficulty in achieving efficient organizational arrangements, there was no significant difference in time taken to complete the task after they reached an optimum organization.

If, as Guetzkow and Simon concluded, differences in performance were really a reflection of differences in the groups' ability to organize, then it should be possible to impose an organization structure, that is, eliminate the necessity for organizing, and produce nonsignificant performance results under different communication structures.

This possibility was realized in experiments by Carzo (1963), Yanouzas (1963) and Cain (1964). The purpose of these studies was to determine the effects of communication restrictions on group performance when an organization was imposed on the group. A seven-man group had a definite hierarchy of three levels. Each position in the organization had a specialized task and a title that was descriptive of the task. The central position, located at the top of the hierarchy, was occupied by a member responsible for coordinating all other tasks in the organization and making final decisions on the assigned problem from an overall analysis. Subordinate managers were responsible for decision making in their particular area of specialization.

Two different communication structures were tested. There was a highly restricted communication net called a "tight" structure in which subjects were allowed to communicate only through a chain of command. Communications under a less restricted loose structure was total; that is, each subject was allowed to communicate with every other member of the group.

During the early periods, it was found that the loosely structured groups were the fastest in time taken to make decisions, while the tightly structured groups showed a faster learning rate. During the second half of the experiment, there was no significant difference between the groups for the time required to make decisions. Therefore, even when organizing efforts were made unnecessary, groups still displayed the kind of behavior found by Guetzkow and Simon.

The present study is a modification of the studies just reported. In the previous experiments, the hierarchical relationships were held constant, while different communication networks were tested. In this study the communication network was the same for all groups, while two different hierarchies were tested, a flat structure and a tall structure, with each member of a group allowed to communicate with every other member.

RESEARCH DESIGN

Each organization had 15 members, the group size being arbitrarily determined by the researchers. The tall structure had four levels and a span of supervision of two. The subjects were seated spatially in a manner that approximated the relationships shown in the chart (Figure 1a). The flat structure had two levels, with all positions connected directly to the president's position, that is, the president had a span of supervision of 14 (Figure 1b). The subordinate subjects were seated in a semi-circle, each one approximately equidistant from the president.

Every position in each organization had a specialized task and a title that was descriptive of and commensurate with the task. There was a definite hierarchy in each organization with the president's office as the central position at the top of the hierarchy. The president was responsible for coordinating all tasks and for making final decisions on the assigned problem from an overall analysis. All subordinates to the president were responsible for decision making in particular market areas. The role of each subject was prescribed, but was different in the two organizations because the flat structure had no intermediate levels of supervision, although the overall size and task assigned were the same as in the tall structure.

Experimental Task The task of the experiment required that the organization produce ordering decisions in limited time periods. The organization sold one product in several market areas. Individual tasks were assigned, so that each market area received specialized attention. The subjects assigned to a market area were instructed to make a decision or recommendation on how much to order for that area. After this decision was made, it was passed up to the next higher level in the organization. The president was responsible for making a final decision for each area. He could accept the recommended decisions made at the lower levels or adjust the recommendations according to what he thought was best for the organization as a whole.

Subjects were asked to think of the organization as a business firm trying to produce decisions on a quantity of goods to order from its suppliers. Before making a decision on what to order, organization members first had to

FIGURE 1 Organization Chart of (*a*) Tall Organization and (*b*) Flat Organization

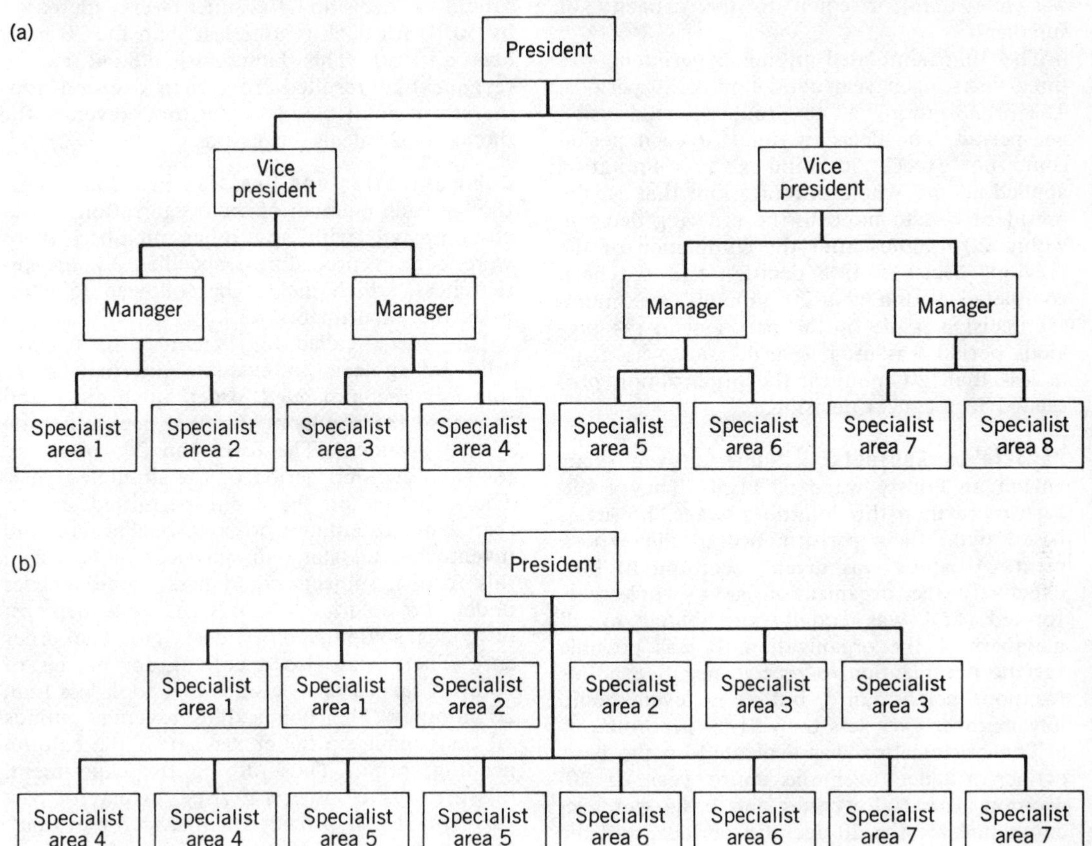

estimate demand. In practice, then, the task had two phases; the first phase involved a demand decision, and the second phase involved an ordering decision.

At the beginning of the experiment, each member of the organization was given a record of demand. The record contained a number of demand quantities, each with a probability of occurrence. For example, a hypothetical distribution for a specific market area might appear as shown in Table 1. The probability distribution was applicable in each decision period; that is, demand was a random variable with a given probability distribution.

TABLE 1 Example of a Record of Demand for a Market Area

Demand Quantity	7	8	9	10	11	12
Probability of occurrence	0.10	0.15	0.25	0.20	0.15	0.15

At higher levels, organization members had more inclusive probability distributions than at lower levels. Given this information, higher-level members were able to evaluate and adjust decisions made at lower levels. The president, for example, had a probability distribution that covered all the possible demand quantities for all market areas; so that he had the necessary data to make overall evaluations and decisions.

After estimating demand, subjects made the ordering decision. In making the ordering decision, they were asked to consider the following: (1) an estimate of demand, (2) inventories left from the previous period, (3) back orders from the previous period, and (4) a capacity restriction on the amount that could be ordered from suppliers. The capacity restriction applied only to the amount ordered by the president. Organization members at lower levels could order any amount they thought appropriate for their respective areas. The president then had to adjust the amounts recommended for the areas, so that the total amount ordered by the organization was less than or equal to the capacity of suppliers.

The time simulated in the experiment was three years, each year consisting of 20 periods. The organization had to produce one decision per period. The decision time for each period could not exceed 20 minutes. This limitation applied to the whole organization; that is, the president had to indicate the ordering decision within 20 minutes after the completion of the previous decision. If a decision had not been completed within the 20 minutes maximum, the decision made by the president in the previous period was used. If a decision was made in less than 20 minutes, the organization proceeded to the next decision.

Payoffs to Subjects Subjects were guaranteed an hourly wage of $1.50. They could earn more than this minimum wage, however, based upon their performance in the experiment. A bonus was given according to how effectively the organization as a whole performed, and was equally distributed to all members of the organization. It was possible for the organization to receive negative points for poor performance, but in no event could any member earn less than $1.50 per hour.

The organization was evaluated on the basis of performance over the entire year or 20-decision period. Revenues and costs were accumulated for the 20-decision periods, and the difference was the profit for the year. There was a single measure of performance (as far as subjects were concerned), the rate of return on sales revenue; for example:

Revenue for the year (20 periods)..........$50.00
Costs for the year (20 periods)........... 40.00
Profit for the year...............$10.00

Rate of return on sales revenue was ($10/$50) ×100 = 20 per cent.

Bonuses were paid on the basis of $0.70 per member for each percentage point earned on sales revenue. Thus, in the above example, each member of the organization would receive 20 percentage points times $0.70, or $14.00. The maximum that would be paid for any year was set at $15.00 per person. The minimum, as previously indicated, was the guaranteed $1.50 per hour rate. Subjects received the largest of the two amounts, that is, between the bonus and guaranteed rate. In the example, if the 20 decision periods had lasted four hours, each subject would receive $14.00 instead of the guaranteed amount of $6.00.

There was also a bonus to the organization for taking less than the allotted 20 minutes to submit a decision. Revenues were increased by $0.10 for each minute less than the 20 minutes allowed. This bonus was added to the revenue that resulted from each decision and, therefore, contributed to the total revenue for the entire 20 decision periods.

Communication and Decision Process Although each member of the organizations could communicate with any other member, there were certain procedures, specified by the researchers, which had to be followed to complete the experimental task.

One form, called the "memory form" was used by subjects to evaluate alternatives, to transmit recommended order quantities, and to record the results of the final decision made by the president. The form had 20 rows, one for each decision period of the simulated year. The columns of the form permitted entries for: demand, amount ordered, backorders, and inventories, all stated in physical units. From this record, subjects could make other entries under the column headings of: revenue, cost of goods sold, inventory cost, and backorder cost. There was also a column for entries of bonuses earned on decisions that took less than 20 minutes. This bonus, plus revenues, minus all costs made up the entries under the column heading, profit. Thus, during the experiment, this form gave subjects a visual display of past performance; it provided a means for evaluating alternative order quantities; and it was used as a device for transmitting information.

The only other form possessed by subjects was the probability distribution of demand quantities illustrated in Table 1. Every decision began with this form as subjects attempted to estimate demand for a period.

Flat Structure. As illustrated in Figure 2, the decision and communication process in the flat structure began with an estimate of demand. At the same time that subordinates 2 through 15 were estimating demand for their respective areas, the president was making an over-all demand estimate. The demand estimate and inventory and back order considerations served as a basis for evaluating alternatives and making decisions on the quantity to order. Subordinates recorded their decisions on the memory form and transmitted them to the president. After receiving these recommendations, the president compared their total with his own decision and the capacity restriction, and reconciled the differences by conferring with subordinates. His final decision was recorded and transmitted to the researcher, who then revealed actual demand, computed back orders, inventories, and units sold in each area, and the revenue, costs, and profits for the total organization on a blackboard visible to all members. From this information, organization members computed revenues, costs and profits for their respective market areas on another copy of the memory form. The process was then repeated for the next decision period.

Tall Structure. Figure 2 also shows that the communication and decision process in the tall structure was more complex than that in the flat structure. At the same time that subordinates 8 through 15 were estimating demand for their respective areas, intermediate supervisors 4 through 7, and 2 and 3, and the president were making more comprehensive demand estimates. The initial decision on the quantity to order for market areas was successively evaluated at each level of the organization until the president, in consultation with intermediate supervisors 2 and 3, made the final decision. Thereafter, the process was identical to the process of the flat structure, until it began again for the next decision period.

Experimental Design The experimental design for this project was a factorial treatment with two independent variables, one of these being organizational structure. The two levels on this variable were the tall structure and the flat structure.

It was assumed that performance would change as subjects gained experience with the experimental task, therefore, organizational experience was considered the other independent variable. Furthermore, it was expected that experience would be a factor in the outcome of each decision period. Thus, each of the 60 decision periods or trials was considered as a level of the independent variable, organizational experience.

Hypotheses Three measures of the dependent variable were used for this experiment. Decision time, the time taken by the group to make decisions, was considered as an indicator of the output of the system. The other two measures, profits and rate of return on sales revenue, were considered as indicators of the quality of the decision output of the system.

Industrial practice, as well as scientific research, has established that individuals and organized groups improve their performance after repeated exposure to a given task. Experiments with small groups such as those reported by Guetzkow and Simon (1955), Carzo (1963), Yanouzas (1963), Cain (1964), and Jones (1966) show a learning curve similar to that found in several industries (especially the aircraft industry: Andress, (1954), that is, an exponential decay function on the time taken to make decisions. This leads to the first hypothesis:

Hypothesis 1. As subjects gain experience with the experimental task, their performance, as measured by the time taken to make decisions, displays a pattern of improvement; i.e., a learning curve.

In addition, these same small-group experiments, seem to indicate that the way groups are organized has no significant effect upon the pattern of improvement in time required to make decisions; therefore:

Hypothesis 2. There is no significant difference in the patterns of improvement or learning curves, in decision time for different structures.

With respect to performance over all trials, past experience (e.g., Leavitt and Shaw) seems to indicate that different communication nets do produce significant differences in the time required to make decisions. On simple problems, Leavitt (1951) found that groups in a wheel pattern with one person in a central position completed tasks faster than groups in a circle pattern where all subjects were in equal positions. On complex problems, Shaw (1954) found that groups in the circle arrangement took less time to solve problems than groups in the wheel arrangement. Since the communication nets of this experiment were the same for all groups; that is, all groups used an "all channel" net, and assuming that structure has no effect on the time variable,[3] there should be no significant difference in the time required to make decisions; therefore:

Hypothesis 3. There is no difference in overall performance as measured by time taken to make decisions for the different structures.

The intermediate levels of a tall structure provide for repeated evaluation of decisions and, therefore, for more analysis than in a flat structure; consequently, the decisions should be better than decisions in flat structures. Specifically for this experiment, then, one can hypothesize as follows:

Hypothesis 4. Groups operating under a tall structure display better overall performance, as measured by profits and rate of return on sales revenue, than groups performing under a flat structure.

The quality of performance should also show a "learning-curve" effect, since there would be a pattern of improvement as subjects gained greater experience with the task; therefore:

[3] The basis for this assumption is explained in the "Discussion" section.

FIGURE 2 Procedure for Communication and Decision Making in Organizations with Flat Structure and Tall Structure

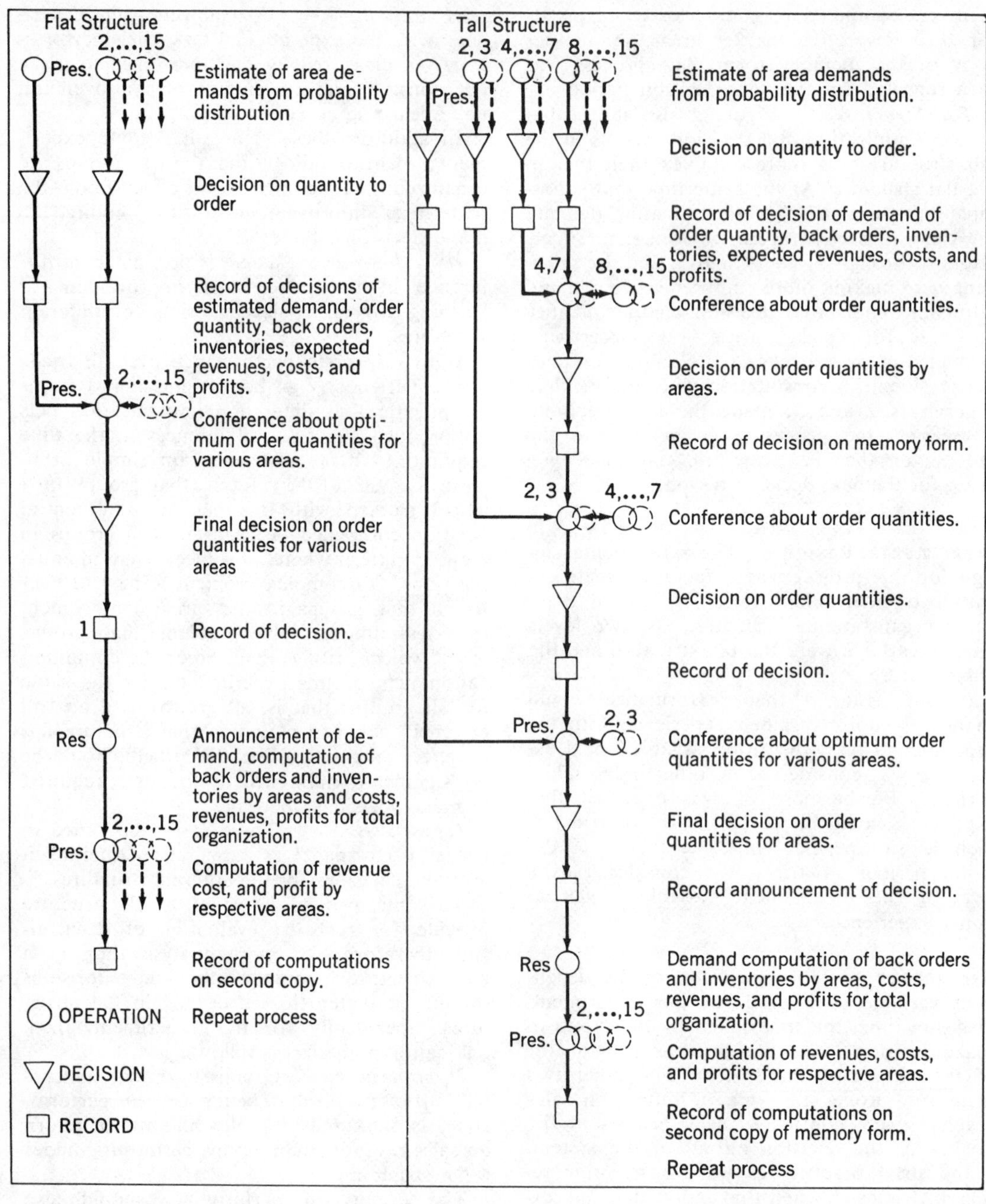

Hypothesis 5. As subjects gain experience with the experimental task, their performance, as measured by profits and rate of return on sales, shows a pattern of improvement; that is a learning curve.

Since the elements of the learning situation, that is, stimulus and reinforcement were not a function of structure but of the experimental task, and since the experimental task was the same for all groups, structure should not have a significant effect on the pattern of improvement; therefore:

Hypothesis 6. There is no difference in the pattern of improvement (learning curve) of profits and rate of return on sales for the different structures.

Test of Design Subjects were selected randomly from the male, junior and senior class enrollments of the College of Business Administration at The Pennsylvania State University. The flat and tall structures were assigned to the groups on a random basis. Four different groups of 15 subjects were selected, with two groups performing under each structure. Subjects were then assigned to each of the fifteen positions in the experimental organization on the basis of grade-point averages. Subjects with the highest grades were assigned to the president's position, the next highest to positions at the second level, the next highest to positions at the third level, and so on, until all positions were filled. It was easier to make assignments in the flat structure, since there were only two levels of organization.

Each group was tested on three successive evenings. For example, if a group was tested on a Monday evening, it would be tested on Tuesday and Wednesday evenings of the same week. Each group made twenty decisions in each evening. The problems for the second and third evenings were exactly the same as those faced by the group in the first evening.

Use of the same problems on successive evenings served as a basis for establishing the reliability of the testing instrument. An analysis of variance was used to estimate reliability, and gave the following coefficients of reliability on each of the performance variables: decision time, 0.954; profits, 0.837; rate of return on sales revenue, 0.831. An analysis of variance was also used to estimate validity. The performance of the groups operating under each structure was compared to determine whether the effect of structure was uniform. The results showed that the experiment was valid and that variations in performance of groups under their respective structures could reasonably be ascribed to chance.

RESULTS

For the variable, organizational structure, the focus was on whether it affected performance over all trials; for the variable, organizational experience, however, the focus was on the effect over successive trials. It was assumed that differences in performance found between trials were a result of difference in the amount of practice.[4] This learning effect is examined below in terms of variance, trend of means, degree of curvature, and cumulative average performance. The results of the analysis of variance for the performance variables are summarized in Table 2.

TABLE 2 **Summary of Analysis of Variance for Time, Profits, and Rate of Return**

VARIABLES	SS	D.F.	MEAN SQUARE	F RATIO
Time				
Structures	0.88	1	0.88	0.12
Error (a)	15.05	2	7.53	—
Trials	992.64	59	16.82	5.32*
Structures × Trials	205.19	59	3.48	1.10
Error (b)	372.57	118	3.16	—
Profits				
Structures	477.43	1	477.43	8.11†
Error (a)	117.74	2	58.87	—
Trials	4809.54	59	81.52	7.89*
Structures × Trials	2677.48	59	45.38	4.39*
Error (b)	1218.81	118	10.33	—
Rate of Return				
Structures	2000.46	1	2000.46	7.47‡
Errors (a)	535.64	2	267.82	—
Trials	23633.98	59	400.58	7.92*
Structures × Trials	13448.25	59	227.94	4.45*
Error (b)	6045.24	118	51.23	—

* Significant at 0.01 level.
† Significant at 0.12 level.
‡ Significant at 0.14 level.
Error (a) is variation due to groups within structures.
Error (b) is variation due to Trials × groups within structures.

Decision Time Decision time was defined as the amount of time required by a group to complete a communication and decision process. A decision period started when the researchers revealed the actual demand and results of a previous ordering decision; that is, revenue, costs, and profits, and the inventory and back orders that resulted from the previous decision. The decision period ended when the president indicated the amount ordered by the organization.

The analysis of variance summarized in Table 2 indicates that the F ratio for the structure effect on decision time is not significant. Thus, when decision time is analyzed over all the trials (decision periods), there is no significant difference for the different structures. This finding supports Hypothesis 3.

[4] We use "trend analysis" as discussed by Edwards (1960: 244–250).

FIGURE 3 For Each Session: (*a*) Average Decision Time; (*b*) Average Profits; (*c*) Average Rate of Return

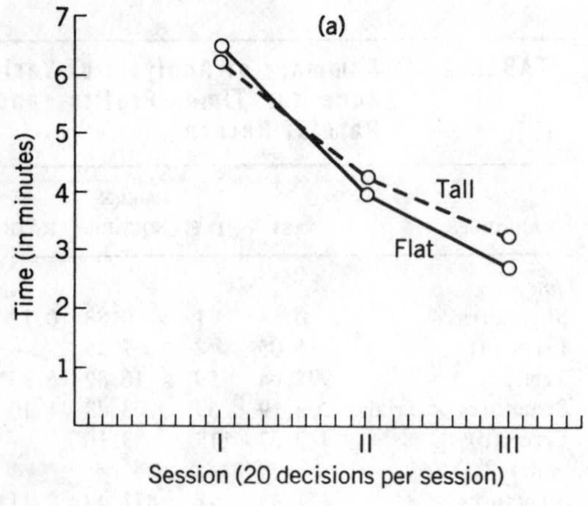

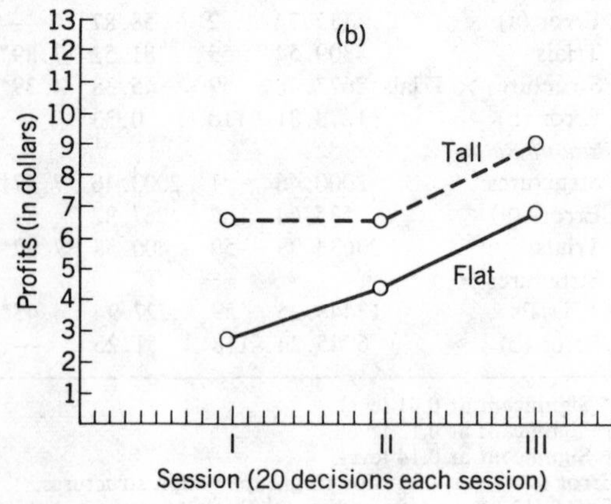

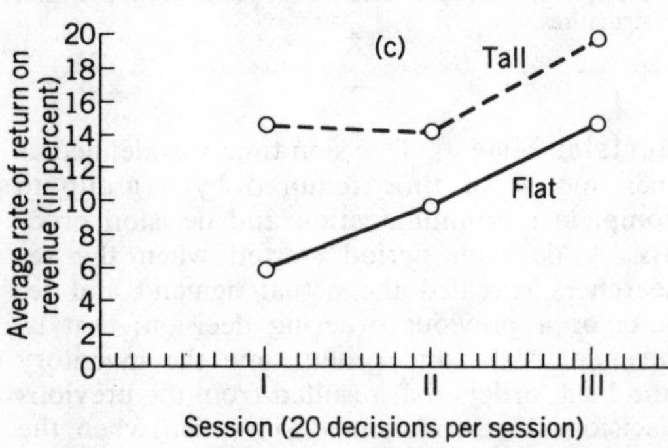

The F ratio for the effect of trials (decision periods) on decision time is significant; that is, when performance is analyzed over the two structures, there is a significant difference for the different trials. This finding indicates that performance changed as the result of practice or experience with the experimental task. When the decision times were averaged for each session (20 decisions for each session) and plotted, as shown in Figure 3a, the trend is downward and both curves appear to have a quadratic component. An analysis of variance of the trends, summarized in Table 3, indicates significant linear and quadratic components. The findings of a downward trend and a quadratic component support Hypothesis 1.

Next, it is possible to determine if the trend of means of the trials for the two structures is of the same form. The interaction effect, as shown in Table 2, is not significant; that is, the mean square, structure $\times$ trials indicates that the learning curves for the flat and tall structures are of the same form. This finding supports Hypothesis 2.

The conformity of the learning curves is supported by the nonsignificant interaction effect, shown in Table 3, for the linear component and for the quadratic component of the trends for the two structures. The similarity of the learning curves is illustrated even more vividly when decision times are averaged cumulatively and plotted as shown in Figure 4a.

Profits Profit was defined as the difference between total revenues and total costs. Table 2 indicates that when profits are analyzed over all the trials, there is a significant difference for the different structures. This result supports Hypothesis 4. Furthermore, when profits are analyzed over the two structures, there is a significant difference for the different trials. This finding indicates that there was also a significant change in profits as a result of experience with the experimental task. When profits were averaged for each session (20 decisions for each session) and plotted, as shown in Figure 3b, the trend is upward, and both curves seem to have a quadratic component. The analysis of variance of the trends (Table 3), indicates significant linear and quadratic components. The finding of an upward trend and a quadratic component supports Hypothesis 5. The interaction effect (Table 2), is significant, indicating that the trend of means for trials for the two structures is of a different form. This result does not support Hypothesis 6. The value of F in Table 3 indicates that the quadratic components of the trends for the two structures differ significantly. The curves for cumulative average profits are plotted in Figure 4b.

Rate of Return Rate of return on sales revenue was defined as the ratio of profits to sales revenue. The results for this were almost identical to the results found on profits; and

TABLE 3 Analysis of Variance for Linear and Quadratic Components on Decision Time, Profits, and Rate of Return

TRIALS	SS	D.F.	MEAN SQUARE	F RATIO
Time				
Linear Component	533.61	1	533.61	168.86*
Structures × Trials	9.15	1	9.15	2.90
Quadratic Component	136.87	1	136.87	43.31*
Structure × Trials	1.18	1	1.18	0.37
Higher-Order	322.16	57		
Structure × Trials	195.92	57		
Error (b)	372.57	118	3.16	—
Profits				
Linear Component	490.96	1	490.96	47.53*
Structures × Trials	7.98	1	7.98	0.77
Quadratic Component	352.77	1	352.77	34.15*
Structures × Trials	108.41	1	108.41	10.50*
Higher-Order	3965.81	57		
Structures × Trials	2561.09	57		
Error (b)	1218.81	118	10.33	
Rate of Return				
Linear Component	2587.0	1	2587.0	50.50*
Structures × Trials	75.53	1	75.53	1.48
Quadratic Component	1331.17	1	1331.17	25.98*
Structures × Trials	795.77	1	795.77	15.53*
Higher Order	19715.81	57		
Structures × Trials	12576.95	57		
Error (b)	6045.24	118	51.23	

* Significant at 0.01 level.
Error (b) is variation due to Trials × groups within structures.

since rate of return is a relative measure, it is considered as the more important indicator of over-all group performance.

The analysis of variance (Table 2), indicates a significant structure effect. This result supports Hypothesis 4. Table 2 also indicates that there is a significant trials effect. Thus, as the group gained greater experience with the experimental task, they improved their performance significantly on the rate of return. When the results for the rate of return are averaged for each session and plotted (Figure 3c), the trend is upward and both curves seem to have a quadratic component. The analysis of variance for the rate of return (Table 3), indicates both a significant linear component and a significant quadratic component. This result supports Hypothesis 5. The form of the two curves are significantly different as indicated by the significant interaction effect in Table 2. This result does not support Hypothesis 6. The F value in Table 3 indicates that the quadratic component of the trends for the two structures differ significantly. The cumulative average curves are shown in Figure 4c.

DISCUSSION

As expected from the results of past experiments and industrial practice with organized groups, subjects performing under the organizational structures of this experiment displayed a "learning-curve" behavior. Analysis of the data for this experiment indicates that this change in behavior was a result of practice with the experimental task. As subjects gained experience with the task, they improved their performance.

Decision Time Although experience affected behavior on the time variable, organizational structure had no significant effect on the time taken to make decisions or on the pattern of improvement. The absence of a structure effect on decision time does not seem to agree with the arguments presented earlier, that the deci-

FIGURE 4 Trials (Decision Periods 1-60): (*a*) Cumulative Average Decision Times; (*b*) Cumulative Average Profits; (*c*) Cumulative Average Rate of Return on Revenues

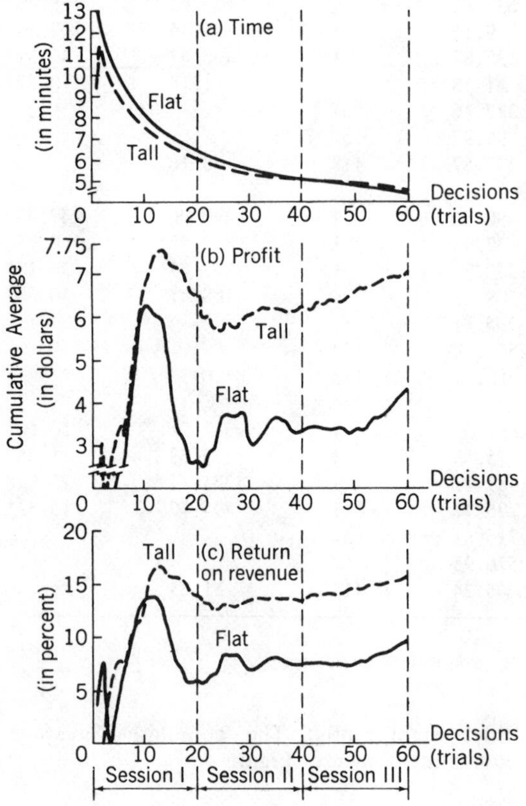

sion and communication processes of the tall organization take longer than the processes of the flat organization. The arguments and their applicability to this experiment are summarized below.

First, the greater number of levels between the top and bottom echelons in a tall structure interrupts the flow of information more frequently than in a flat structure in which there is a direct connection between top and bottom echelons. The delays caused by these interruptions in the tall structure supposedly extend the time required for decision making beyond that which is required by the flat structure. This argument was not supported by the results of this experiment.

Apparently, the disadvantages of a wide span of supervision in the flat structure offset the advantages of direct links between top and bottom echelons. The difficulties of a flat structure seemed to be most evident when the president rejected or altered the recommendations of subordinates and attempted to make a final decision on how to allocate orders among the seven market areas. After receiving recommendations from his 14 subordinates on how much to order in each market area, the president had to reconcile the total of recommended orders with the capacity restriction. Since total recommendations always exceeded capacity, the president was forced to scale down the requests of subordinates. Invariably, this led to much discussion with area specialists and debate among them.

In the tall structure there was the same problem of reconciling total recommendations with the capacity restriction; but the discussions were much more orderly and resolution was faster because the president and intermediate supervisors had to deal with only two subordinates. Also, many of the problems of allocation were resolved for the president as the recommendations filtered through the levels of the tall structure. The absence of a difference on the time variable, then, may be explained partly by the fact that the greater time required for decisions to pass through several levels of a tall structure is offset by the time required to resolve differences and coordinate the efforts of many subordinates in a flat structure.

Another reason given for impediments in the flow of information is the status differences among participants at different levels in the organization. It was argued that he has difficulty in obtaining information, because subordinates, realizing that he evaluates their performance, tend to report only information favorable to them. Such inadequate information flows tend to delay decision processes. For example, when problems at lower levels are not reported to higher-level officials, the decisions required to solve the problems will not be made. If information is inadequate, the decision maker must spend more time gathering the required information; if it is inaccurate, then decisions may be inappropriate.

The problem of status difference is more prevalent in tall structures, since there are more levels. Decision and communication processes should, therefore, require more time in a tall structure than a flat structure. However, in this experiment, there were practically no status differences between the levels of the organizations. Although the president and intermediate supervisors were placed in a higher position with regard to the importance of their jobs, they were not required to evaluate the performance of subordinates. Also, rewards were not distributed to members on the basis of the positions they occupied in the organization; rewards for organizational performance were distributed equally to each member of the organization.

The difficulties of processing information freely, where there are a number of levels and status differences, apply to downward communications as well as to upward communications. Again, the tall structure is supposed to be at a disadvantage. However, in the experiment this disadvantage was removed by providing instant feedback of results to all levels simultaneously. As soon as the president reported his decision, the researchers presented the results of this decision on a blackboard visible to all subjects; therefore, there was little need for downward communications in the experiment.

On the basis that status differences of the tall structure would be unimportant and that the advantage of a direct link between top and bottom echelons would be counteracted by the variety of activity in the flat structure, the researchers hypothesized, as stated in Hypothesis 3, that structure would not have a differential effect on average performance as measured by time required to make decisions. As noted, this hypothesis as well as Hypothesis 2 which stated that the learning curves would have the same form, were supported by the results.

Profits and Rate of Return On the two performance variables that were considered to be indicators of the quality of decisions, the groups displayed different patterns on each trial. As illustrated in Figures 4b and c, performance of the groups under each structure on the first 20 trials (Session I), was quite erratic. It appears as though they were going through a trial-and-error process in familiarizing themselves with the problem. From trials 21 through 40 (Session II), they appear to have learned and to have stabilized their performance. Thereafter, in trials 41 through 60, performance steadily improved. Considering their performance on Sessions I and II, and the fact that there was a limit on profits (cost of goods sold was fixed at 60 percent of each sales dollar), it is reasonable to assume that if the groups had continued for more than 60 decisions, their performance would have stabilized again or at least approached the limit.

On these two variables, there was a significant difference between the performance of the groups operating under the flat structure and those operating under the tall structure. The superior performance of the groups under the tall structure may be explained by the fact that their decisions were subjected to more analysis than the decisions of the groups under the flat structure. The intermediate supervisory levels apparently were an advantage to groups with the tall structure. They provided the means for repeated evaluation of decisions, and the output was of much better quality than the output of groups in the flat structure.

In addition, the narrow span of supervision in the tall structure permitted a much more orderly decision and communication process. Freed from the burdens that arise from having many subordinates, decision makers appeared to be able to develop a better understanding of the problem. Although the performance of groups with a tall structure was significantly better than with a flat structure, the design of the experiment did not include structural characteristics that seem to cause problems in communication, such as, status differences.

SUMMARY

In this study, four different groups of 15 subjects were organized—two under a flat structure and two under a tall structure. The flat organization structure had two levels, with 14 subordinates reporting directly to the president. The tall structure had four levels, with each supervisor limited to two subordinates. Each position had an assigned task which required decisions on a market-order problem. The president was responsible for making an over-all decision for the organization, which he made after receiving recommendations from subordinates on the amounts to order. His main task was to reconcile differences among recommended orders, a capacity restriction, and his own estimates of optimum order quantities. Group performance was measured on three variables: time taken to complete decisions, profits, and rate of return on sales revenue.

On all three performance variables, groups under each structure showed patterns of improvement as they gained experience with the experimental task. On the time variable, the pattern of improvement was not significantly different for the two structures; the patterns for decision time appeared to follow a function similar to learning curves found in industrial settings. For each structure, patterns for profits and rate of return on sales revenue were erratic on the first 20 decisions, and transient (that is, steadily improving on the stable pattern) on the third 20 decisions.

Structure had no significant effect on the decision time. This result was attributed to counteracting forces in the flat structure and to the elimination of some of the barriers to communication in the tall structure.

Structure did have a significant effect on performance as measured by profits and rate of return on sales revenue. Groups under the tall structure showed significantly better performance than groups under the flat structure. This result was explained by the fact that the tall structure, with a greater number of levels, allowed group members to evaluate decisions more frequently, and that the narrow span of supervision provided for a more orderly decision process.

REFERENCES

Andress, Frank J. (1954). "The learning curve as a production tool." *Harvard Business Review,* 32:88.

Cain, Geraldine S. (1964). "Some effects of organization structure on problem solving." Unpublished Doctoral Dissertation, The Pennsylvania State University.

Carzo, Rocco, Jr. (1963). "Some effects of organization structure on group effectiveness." *Administrative Science Quarterly,* 7:393–424.

Edwards, Allen L. (1960). Experimental Design in Psychological Research. New York: Holt, Rinehart and Winston.

Fayol, Henri (1949). General and Industrial Management. London: Sir Isaac Pitman.

Graicunas, V. A. (1937). "Relationship in organization." Pp. 52–57 in Luther Gulick and Lyndall F. Urwick (eds.), Papers on the Science of Administration. New York: Institute of Public Administration.

Guetzkow, Harold and Herbert A. Simon (1955). "The impact of certain communication nets upon organization and performance in task-oriented groups." *Management Science,* 1: 233–250.

Hamilton, Sir Ian (1921). The Soul and Body of an Army. New York: George H. Doran.

Hoslett, Schuyler Dean (1951). "Barriers to communication." Personnel. 28:109.

Jones, Halsey R. (1966). "The effects of the number of organization levels upon selected aspects of organization performance." Unpublished Doctoral Dissertation, The Pennsylvania State University.

Leavitt, Harold J. (1951). "Some effects of certain communication patterns on group performance." *Journal of Abnormal and Social Psychology,* 46:38–50.

Meltzer, Leo and James Salter (1960). "Organizational structure, and the performance and job satisfactions of physiologists." *American Sociological Review,* 27:351–362.

Porter, L. W., and E. E. Lawler, III (1964). "The effects of 'tall' versus 'flat' organization structures on managerial satisfaction." *Personnel Psychology,* 17:135–148.

Read, William H. (1962). "Upward communication in industrial hierarchies." *Human Relations,* 15:3–15.

Shaw, Marvin E. (1954). "Some effects of problem complexity upon problem solution efficiency in different communication nets." *Journal of Experimental Psychology,* 48:211–217.

Urwick, Lyndall F. (1956). "The manager's span of control." *Harvard Business Review,* 34:39–47.

Worthy, James C. (1950). "Organizational structure and employee morale." *American Sociological Review,* 15:169–179.

Worthy, James C. (1959). Big Business and Free Man. New York: Harper.

Yanouzas, John N. (1963). "The relationship of some organization variables to the performance of decision groups." Unpublished Doctoral Dissertation, The Pennsylvania State University.

31 MERGING MANAGEMENT AND BEHAVIORAL THEORY: THE INTERACTION BETWEEN SPAN OF CONTROL AND GROUP SIZE*

Robert J. House and *John B. Miner*

In an analysis of frequently cited books March (1965) documented the diverse origins of organization theory. He lists 33 ancestral books, each of which is widely cited in the literature of the field. These books can be readily classified as being part of either the management or the behavioral science literatures.

What March's analysis does not bring out, however, is the extent to which citations have concentrated within these two major segments, with relatively little overlap between them. Writings on management and organizations are differentiated into two schools of thought. Within each school, concepts, approaches, and citations are widely shared, but authors of both schools generally write as if the other literature did not exist.

This situation can generate confusion for business students and practicing managers. Faced with one set of practical problems, they are offered two different and totally unintegrated types of solutions. Even more important than these managerial reactions is the prospect that a merger of management and behavioral theories might yield a level of understanding far exceeding what has been possible with either segment alone.

This article first attempts to demonstrate that two distinct literatures dealing with the same kinds of basic problems exist, and then attempts to show how amalgamation can yield increased understanding. A merging of the management literature on span of control and the behavioral science literature on correlates of work group size illustrates this amalgamation process. A similar approach could be applied in other areas of management and behavioral science.

EVIDENCE OF SEPARATE LITERATURES

References and bibliographies in three management and three behavioral science textbooks have been studied to determine the degree of cross citation between the management and behavioral science segments. The analysis was limited to journal and serial publication citations because these can be more easily classified in terms of disciplinary origins than books. Each citation was considered as behavioral science if it referred to a sociological, psychological, anthropological, or political science publication; as management if it referred to a business, personnel, management science, public administration, management, economics, or general readership publication.

The books used were selected as representative of well-known, recent publications in the field. They also meet the requirement that there be considerable journal citation. The smallest number of articles noted was 62; the largest 513; the median 206.

Patterns of Citation The three management books are Dale (1965), Koontz and O'Donnell (4th edition, 1968), and Flippo (1966). All of these authors are professors of management in business schools. The three behavioral science books are Blau and Scott (1962), Katz and Kahn (1966), and Bass (1965). The authors of the first book are professors of sociology, of the second professors of psychology, and the author of the third has appointments both in psychology and management.

The data of Table 1 clearly fit our prediction. The first two management books cite very

* Reprinted by permission of the publisher from *Administrative Science Quarterly*, vol. 14, no. 3, pp. 451–465, September, 1969. Mr. House is professor of management at the University of Toronto, and Mr. Miner is professor of behavioral science at Georgia State University.

few behavioral science journals. The third was deliberately selected to represent the current tendency to include a behavioral science designation in the titles of management books. It is evident that the mere presence of the designation, "a behavioral approach," does not guarantee an extensive sampling of the behavioral science literature.

TABLE 1 Proportion of Citation to Management and Behavioral Science Literatures (in Percent)

BOOKS	MANAGEMENT	BEHAVIORAL SCIENCE
Management		
Dale (1965)	94	6
Koontz and O'Donnell (1968)	94	6
Flippo (1966)	77	23
Behavioral science		
Blau and Scott (1962)	7	93
Katz and Kahn (1966)	13	87
Bass (1965)	19	81

Although the data suggests a somewhat greater tendency to cite from the other literature among the behavioral scientists, especially among the psychologists, the figures of Table 1 may be slightly misleading in this respect. Many of the articles in management publications were in fact written by behavioral scientists. The reverse tendency is much less common.

One might have anticipated that with the influx of behavioral scientists into the business schools during the 1960's a more pronounced merging might have occurred, especially since over 50 percent of the courses taught by behavioral scientists in business schools appear to be in the management-organizational behavior area (Miner, 1963). In all probability the relatively high cross-literature citation rates of Flippo and Bass do reflect this change, although it is evident that a much greater amalgamation is possible.

Evidence of a Single Basic Problem Area These citation patterns would make considerable sense if there were two basic disciplines involved, each concerned with a separate and distinct area of knowledge. A check of chapter titles within the six books does not support this view, however. Such topics as decision making, leadership and supervision, change and innovation, communication, and organization are emphasized by practically all. Planning and control do appear to be stressed more in the management literature, but there is not a complete dichotomy. Chapter titles in both literature groupings include such words as motivation, policy, groups, and power.

In all the books the major objectives clearly are to provide an understanding of organizational functioning and to specify conditions for organizational effectiveness. These are the central problems of the field, whether approached from a management or a behavioral viewpoint. Unfortunately, the two segments show little tendency to integrate their combined knowledge into a single meaningful set of solutions to their mutual problems.

Treatment of Span of Control The evidence presented so far suggests that the span of control concept should receive major attention in the three management books and the three behavioral science books, with particular attention to correlates of group size in the literature of group dynamics. Furthermore, the hypothesis of two distinct literatures suggests that no amalgamation of span of control and group dynamics theories would appear in any of the six books.

Consistent with these expectations, all three management books do devote considerable space to discussions of the span of control concept. Dale, and Koontz and O'Donnell say little or nothing about group dynamics. Flippo does consider the group dynamics literature at some length, and even has several paragraphs dealing with correlates of group size. Yet some 200 pages separate this material from that on the span of control, and no amalgamation is attempted.

All the behavioral science books deal with group dynamics in considerable detail. However, only Bass among them gives any sizable attention to correlates of group size. Yet there is no mention of span of control in the index to Bass's book and the authors were unable to locate any references to the term in the text proper. Both Blau and Scott, and Katz and Kahn do note the span of control concept, although neither book gives it more than passing attention.

To the extent that this sample of six books is typical, the general tendency to divorce management and behavioral theory is reflected in the span of control and group size literatures. No attempt at amalgamation has been noted.

ORIGINS AND RECENT HISTORY OF THEORIES ON SPAN OF CONTROL

Theories on the span of control originally were based on casual observation by experienced managers and on deductive reasoning. Fayol (1949:98), who was probably the first to propose a "science of administration," stated that "whatever his level of authority, one head only has direct command over a small number of subordinates, less than six normally. Only the superior (foreman or his equivalent) is in direct command of 20 or 30 men, when the work is simple."

V. A. Graicunas (1937) applied deductive reasoning to the problem and demonstrated that arithmetic increases in the number of subordinates reporting directly to a manager are accompanied by potentially geometric increases in the number of personal relationships within the immediate work unit of the manager. Not only are there direct relationships between the executive and each of the men under his control, but there are also relationships among his subordinates. Thus, the addition of a single person to an executive's span of control not only adds the direct relationship between the new person and the manager, but also a larger number of potential relationships with others already reporting to the manager. Assuming that the number of different contacts that may be necessary between the manager and his subordinates, and among them, is a measure of the complexity of the manager's job, complexity will increase geometrically as the number of immediate subordinates increases arithmetically.

Graicunas classified the contacts that usually take place within a work unit into three categories: (1) direct single contacts that take place between superior and subordinate; (2) cross-contracts between two or more immediate subordinates without involvement of the superior; and (3) direct group contacts that take place directly between the superior and two or more subordinates. The increase in the potential number of contacts that accompanies an increase in the number of subordinates reporting directly to the manager can be expressed mathematically according to the following formula: $C = N\ (2^n/2 + N - 1)$, where C represents the total possible contacts and N represents the number of subordinates reporting directly to the manager. This relationship is shown numerically in Table 2, and graphically in Davis (1951:278). The graph illustrates clearly that the marginal increase in the potential complexity of the manager's job resulting from the addition of one subordinate is greatest beyond spans of five.

TABLE 2 Number of Relationships Possible with Varying Numbers of Subordinates

SUBORDINATES	POSSIBLE RELATIONSHIPS	SUBORDINATES	POSSIBLE RELATIONSHIPS
1	1	7	490
2	6	8	1,080
3	18	9	2,376
4	44	10	5,210
5	100	11	11,374
6	222	12	24,708

A number of other writers have presented similar mathematical estimates of this idea. Bossard (1945) has calculated that with each arithmetical addition to the primary group, the number of interpersonal relationships increases exponentially, as given by the formula $x = (n^2 - n)/2$. Finally, Entwisle and Walton (1961), have applied the coefficients of the binomial expansion as a model for the multiplication of intragroup combinations.

Several writers have qualified the general principle of span of control so as to make its application more precise. R. C. Davis (1951) has indicated a clear distinction between the executive span and the operative span. The former, which applies at middle and upper organizational levels, should vary from 3 to 9 depending on such conditions as the company's rate of growth and the nature of the work to be done. The operative span, which applies at the very lowest level, may increase to as many as 30 persons. To these two, Keith Davis (1962) has added the policy span to apply where subordinates are not supervised in the usual sense, but are subject only to general policy control. Under such circumstances a top executive might have from 6 to 15 other executives reporting to him.

More recently, the National Industrial Conference Board (Stieglitz, 1962) listed the following factors to be taken into account in determining the optimum span: (1) competence of the superior and the subordinate; (2) degree of interaction between the units of personnel being supervised; (3) extent to which the supervisor must carry out nonmanagerial responsibilities, and the demands on his time from other people and units; (4) similarity or dissimilarity of the activities being supervised; (5) incidence of new problems in the supervisor's unit; (6) extent of standardized procedure; and (7) degree of physical dispersion of activities.

Several criticisms may be leveled against

early theory. First, the theory seems to assume that the degree of interdependence between subordinates is not related to the size of effective span. If the work of the two units is so closely related that what one of them does has an immediate and important effect on the results achieved by the other, there must be constant coordination of their activities. If the relationship between the two is only intermittent, the superior will have to give it only occasional attention.

Second, in limiting the span of control to a definite number, writers appear to assume that all managers do nothing but manage. In practice, however, many of them do have other responsibilities. The sales manager who does some of the selling himself is an obvious example.

Third, Graicunas assumed that if there were two subordinates, A and B, there were two relationships between them: that which exists when A approaches B, and a second relationship when B approaches A. He also assumed that the superior's relationship with each was different when he talked to them together from the relationship with each when he consulted them separately. This, of course, may be disputed.

Even though there may be fewer relationships than those provided for in the Graicunas formula, the number of relationships is still large. Graicunas undoubtedly failed to note certain relationships that might have been included. The usefulness of the formula is clearly limited by the fact that it does not consider either frequency or intensity of contact. The number of relationships is probably less significant than the frequency with which they occur and the severity of the demands on a manager's time.

The classical theorists do not necessarily confine the spans at all levels to the same number. For example, both Urwick (1933) and Davis (1951) state that the ideal number for superior authorities is less than 4; at the lowest organizational level, the number may be 8 to 12 according to Urwick, and as many as 30 according to Davis. Others believe that the span of control should not necessarily be limited to any definite number in all cases but should depend on the situation and the type of supervision required. They would restate the principle as follows: "There is a limit to the number of positions that can be effectively supervised by a single individual."

A highly competent superior can manage more subordinates than one who is less competent, or perhaps less familiar with the details of the business. A highly competent subordinate or a subordinate whose task is merely to follow standardized procedures and who seldom encounters new problems on which he must seek advice may need little supervision. It is more difficult to supervise a number of dissimilar activities than a number of identical activities that require the same background knowledge, for there is a limit to what one person can know. Finally, managing geographically dispersed activities is usually more difficult than managing those concentrated in a single area, for the supervisor may lose a great deal of time in travel.

CONTROVERSY OVER THE SPAN OF CONTROL

Like many of the traditional principles of management, span of control has been the subject of substantial controversy. Some critics hold that while there may be a limit to the span, it is advantageous to make the spans a great deal wider than any of the numbers usually specified if the work is interrelated. Others believe that the idea is fallacious in itself in that it assumes what Likert (1961) calls the man-to-man form of supervision, rather than the man-to-group form.

One basis for advocating a broad span of control is the fact that a narrow span and the concomitant "tall" organization structure make for red tape and difficulties in communication; in addition, managers with short spans may tend to delegate less and to supervise more closely, thus damaging morale. For example, James Worthy (1950) has asserted on the basis of the findings of a questionnaire survey that the "flat" decentralized organization structure calling for wide spans at the middle and upper echelons is superior, as far as employee morale is concerned, to the "tall" centralized organization structure based on a narrow span of control. Golembiewski (1965) has argued that application of the span of control principle can be threatening since it limits the power of supervisors. They do not have enough control to make decisions of a nontrivial nature, management style tends to be authoritarian, and internal "politicking" is engendered.

W. W. Suojanen (1955), on the other hand, has argued that the entire notion of an optimum or "proper" span of control is meaningless, and that the principle has become a "fable." It was misappropriated from its birthplace in the military organization, he states, and has since been made obsolete by new decision-making processes (such as team management), by advanced communication techniques, and by insights offered by social scientists into the role of informal relationships in the formal organization. He cites Dale's (1952) report that the number of subordinates reporting to chief executives of successful companies was often much higher than the optimum spans advocated by classical theory.

In answer, Urwick (1956) has pointed out that Dale's measure includes all subordinates having access to the chief executive rather than only those reporting directly to him in the chain of command. This is an invalid measure of what is "exclusively a principle of formal organization concerned with responsibility for the immediate supervision of subordinate activities."

EMPIRICAL EVIDENCE

Empirical research in several areas throws light on the effects of various widths of spans, and thus provides some basis for assessing the validity of the span of control principle. First, evidence has been collected by management theorists and practitioners based on surveys of actual company practices.

Second, small group research dealing with the effects of group size is pertinent. The organizational unit, like any group, must be maintained by efforts of both leader and member. Through face-to-face contact, the group members establish a communication system, common values, and mutual expectations, and in this way the organizational unit becomes a cohesive group capable of co-operative performance. However, when the unit becomes so large that frequent face-to-face interaction among all the members becomes difficult, cohesiveness and performance may deteriorate. Thus, small group research dealing with concommitants of group size is relevant to a consideration of the validity of the span of control principle. Third, since the organization structure will generally be tall if the span of control is kept short, research on the effects of flat versus tall structures also bears on the principle.

Management Research Several attempts have been made by management researchers to determine the extent to which organizations actually observe the principle of the span of control, on the assumption that if successful organizations disregard it, it cannot be completely valid. Surveys on the subject have dealt mainly with the spans at the top level.

Dale (1952) in a survey conducted for the American Management Association found that the number of executives reporting to the chief executive in 100 large companies varied from 1 to 24, and in only 26 of the companies was the span as narrow as 6. The median was 9. In 46 medium-sized companies, the chief executives had from 1 to 17 immediate subordinates, the median being in the 6 to 7 range. Healey (1956) polled 620 managers and found that 93.7 percent of the plant executives had spans of 8 or less, while 84.2 percent of the branch managers shared a similar span. Entwisle and Walton (1961) in a study of colleges and small businesses, found median presidential spans of between 5 and 6 and of 5, respectively. A National Industrial Conference Board study (Janger, 1960) of 81 large companies found the range was the same as that reported in the Dale study. The median span was only 5, however.

The practices existing at a point in time in successful companies do not necessarily either prove or disprove the validity of the span of control principle. Some companies seem to be operating successfully with very wide spans at the top, but it is always possible that they would achieve even greater success with smaller spans.

One company has applied functional theory successfully in establishing managerial spans. Lockheed Missile and Space Company (Stieglitz, 1962) developed an analytical approach involving several factors considered important determinants of the span of control of their managers. Based on inductions from their previous experience and deductions from classical theory, they arrived at the conviction that seven factors should be weighed when determining the span of control. These factors were:

1. Similarity of function: the degree to which functions performed by the various components are alike or different.
2. Geographic contiguity: the physical location of the components and personnel reporting to a principal.
3. Complexity of functions: the nature of the duties being performed by the organization components or personnel. Takes into account the skills necessary to perform satisfactorily.
4. Direction and control: the nature of the personnel reporting directly to a principal. Includes the degree of the principal's attention which they require for proper supervision of their actions.
5. Coordination: the extent to which the principal must exert time and effort in keeping actions properly correlated and in keeping his activity keyed in with other activities of the company.
6. Planning: the importance, complexity, and time required to review and establish future programs and objectives.
7. Organizational assistance: the help received by the principal from direct-line assistants, staff activities, and assistants-to.

A weighted index was developed to measure these factors and then used to assist in organization design and planning in some of the

Lockheed units. One of the units extended the average span from 3.8 to 4.2 and reduced supervisory levels from 5 to 4; another broadened the average span of managers from 3.0 to 4.2 and cut levels from 6 to 5; and in a third case, the average span went from 4.2 to 4.8 persons and the levels dropped from 7 to 5. The reductions in managerial personnel on supervisory payrolls were reported as "substantial."

In a recent study, Udell (1967) attempted to determine whether the variables employed by the Lockheed Company actually did correspond to differences in span of control for the chief marketing and sales executives of 67 Wisconsin and Illinois manufacturing companies. This study investigated the relationship between the size of the span of control and the following variables: (1) managerial assistance to the marketing manager, either through an assistant-to position or supervision of subordinates by other members of the firm; (2) geographical contiguity of subordinates; (3) similarity of functions supervised; (4) need for coordination of subordinates; (5) need for close supervision of subordinates; (6) formalization of job relationships; (7) time available for supervision; (8) competence of the supervisor; and (9) competence of subordinates.

Classical theory and recent opinion (Dale, 1952; Barkdull, 1963; Stieglitz, 1962) argue that geographical separation of subordinates will result in smaller spans because of the difficulties and time consumed in supervision. In this study, geographical separation and functional similarity were found to be highly correlated with each other and also to be predictive of broad spans. It is possible that functional similarity of subordinates is a prerequisite for geographical separation and that subordinates whose functions are highly similar are easier to supervise, thus permitting a broader span for the executive; or it may be that geographical separation interferes with face-to-face supervision and therefore requires the executive to delegate more freely. Having delegated more authority, he is able to broaden his span further than if he were able to engage in more face-to-face supervision.

Although the research conducted by management theorists suggests some of the reasons for broadening or narrowing the span of control, none of the above studies relates the width of spans to criteria of organizational or supervisory effectiveness or to subordinate satisfaction or performance. Only two studies relate actual spans to a criterion of organizational success. Woodward (1965) found that companies that were economically successful could be differentiated from unsuccessful companies on the basis of their organization structure, if they were analyzed within three specific technological categories. The average span of control of first line supervisors in successful firms within each of three kinds of production technologies is different; successful companies closely approximate the traditional span only where continuous process technology—very large batch production or continuous flow production—exists. Woodward also reports that the span of control of chief executives increased directly with the degree of technological complexity, while spans at middle management levels decreased as technological complexity increased. Middle and top management spans were not analyzed in terms of organizational success, however.

Lawrence and Lorsch (1967) found that within the plastics industry production units tended to have narrow spans and many levels in the managerial hierarchy. Research units on the other hand had wider spans and fewer levels of hierarchy. Sales units were intermediate on the two variables, but tended more to the production pattern. Analyses relating these structural variables to organizational performance indexes indicated that companies which were closest to this industry pattern were the most successful. Thus, a narrow span in production units, a somewhat wider span in sales, and a considerably wider span in research was associated with the highest organizational performance levels. Other studies led the authors to conclude, however, that such differentiation of spans of control was not desirable in more stable, certain, and less diverse industries. Thus, in the container industry successful companies tended to have similar spans within the various units of the company.

Relevant Behavioral Science Research

Empirical research by behavioral scientists is relevant to a management principle if it deals with phenomena that are analogous to the phenomena described in the management principle: that is, if it concerns essentially the same properties. Some of the existing research findings on small group behavior deal with variables relevant to the span of control principle.

Research on small groups has dealt with such questions as: What is the effect of group size on group cohesiveness? on the ability of the members to arrive at a consensus? on the extent to which the members participate? on the satisfaction they feel with group activities? on their performance as individuals and as a group? on leadership behavior? Given that a manager, together with his subordinates, constitutes a decision-making or task-oriented group requiring teamwork, cohesiveness, coordination, communication and consensus, then research on the size of task-oriented or decision-making groups should have relevance to the principle of span of control. Also of direct relevance is the research on small group size where the leader is a formal leader rather than an informal or emergent leader. Studies of group size in which the leader is not formally appointed will be reviewed, although only indirectly pertinent to span of control theory. It will be shown that the findings of small group research are remarkably consistent for both those groups with formally and non-formally appointed leaders.

Natural Group Size. There have been at least four studies of groups that form spontaneously, and all four show that such "natural" groups tend to be fairly small.

In one of these studies, observations and records were used to determine the size of the groups naturally formed by pedestrians, shoppers, play groups, work groups, and Congressional committees. Group size appeared to be inversely related to the frequency with which the groups were formed, and groups of 5 or more seemed to be very unstable and to break down quickly into subgroups (James, 1951). In the second study, Fischer (1953) asked college students to describe groups to which they belonged that had frequent and continuing face-to-face contact and to rank these groups according to the intimacy of the members. Frequency, duration and intimacy of contact were found to be inversely related to group size. Hollingshead (1949) found that natural group size is related to the demographic characteristics of the members. Rural high school students form smaller groups, usually of about three persons, whereas city students are more likely to form groups of four or five. An early study by Thrasher (1927) suggests that the appropriate span of control may be different for urban as compared to rural organizations and by implication that other demographic variables may moderate the appropriate span of control. To the authors' knowledge there has been no research dealing directly with demographic characteristics of organizational members as they relate to span of control theory.

Effect of Group Size on Cohesiveness and on the Ability to Arrive at a Consensus. If a group is cohesive it does not break up into cliques or factions, and it is easier for members to arrive at a consensus on major issues concerning the group. Group size has been found to be significantly related to both cohesiveness and consensus in several studies.

Hare (1952) found that groups of 12 boy scouts had a greater tendency to break up into sub-groups than did groups of 5, and that groups of 5 members achieved significantly more consensus on discussion topics than groups of 12.

In another study, groups of various sizes—2 to 10, 11, 12, 14, 16, 18 and 20—were observed. A significant correlation of .77 was found between group size and the number of cliques, and group cohesiveness appeared to vary inversely with group size (Miller 1952).

Jennings (1960) approached the matter by asking people about the number of close associations they preferred on the job and in leisure time activities. She found that the generally preferred numbers were 8 on the job and 12 in social groups.

Thomas and Fink (1963) have argued that as group size increases, the number of possible relationships outgrows the number people need or want; hence they tend to form closer associations with some of the members than with others. Thus cliques and factions appear and members' ties to the group as a whole tend to lessen.

As group size increases, each member must talk less and listen more. In the study by Hare (1952) the members of the groups were aware of this limitation and reported that they had fewer chances to speak in the groups of 12 than in the groups of 5. Other studies have found that as size increases, an increased proportion of group members report feeling threatened and less willing to participate (Gibb, 1951); the proportion of members who speak decreases (Dawes, 1934); and the total number of verbal interactions between the members increases, while the ratio of actual to possible relationships decreases (Castore, 1962). Still other studies support the idea that as group size increases some members tend to withdraw from participation, either because they feel threatened or because they are not forceful enough to speak up against the competition (Bales *et al.,* 1951; Stephan and Mishler, 1952; Carter *et al.,* 1951).

These studies strongly suggest that where subordinates reporting directly to a manager exceed the conventional limits of the span of control, group member consensus and cohesiveness is likely to be lower. However, there are conditions under which managerial strategies to achieve consensus and cohesiveness are not worth their cost, and other conditions under which cohesiveness and consensus are actually not desired. When the work of subordinates is not highly interdependent and when team effort is not required because of the task technology, consensus and cohesiveness among members would not be functionally related to task achievement. When subordinates have attitudes that are anti-managerial, the provision of conditions that facilitate the emergence of group norms, consensus, and cohesiveness might actually mitigate the achievement of organizational objectives. Thus, appropriate span of control depends in part on the relationships between group cohesiveness and organizational outcomes.

Type of Participation and Group Size. The type of participation is also important, particularly in considering the optimum size of work groups and the number of subordinates under a single superior. An experimental study of groups of from 2 to 7 members revealed that as group size increased members gave information and made suggestions more frequently, but were less likely to ask for opinions, give their own opinions, or express agreement; and also that members tended to show less tension as group size increased, and to joke and laugh more (Bales and Borgatta, 1955).

Hare has interpreted these findings to mean that as group size increases, "there is a more mechanical method of introducing information, a less sensitive exploration of the point of view of the other, and a more direct attempt to control others and reach a solution whether or not all group members indicate agreement" (Hare, 1962:240). He also suggests that as group size increases the members feel less directly involved in task success.

However, consistent with the span of control principle, there seems to be a lower limit below which group size should not decline. Slater (1958) analyzed the interactions taking place within groups ranging from 2 to 7 members and concluded that there were inhibiting forces in the smallest group that prevented the expression of dissatisfaction and disagreement. Scores on an inhibition index were significantly higher in groups of 2, 3, and 4 members than in groups of 5, 6, and 7.

An experiment with groups of 3, 4, 6, 7, 9, and 10 members revealed that there was more disagreement in solving logical problems in the larger than in the smaller groups. This finding is consistent with the view that the reluctance to express dissatisfaction and disagreement is greater in the very small groups than in those as large as 5 to 7 members (Berkowitz, 1958). It is also consistent with the findings of experiments that showed that larger groups experienced less tension.

The amount of tension and disagreement to be expected within a group of subordinates can thus be partially predicted on the basis of the manager's span of control. Under conditions where supportive social interaction or anxiety-reducing efforts are required for effective performance or where problem solving is best accomplished through free exchange of information and opinions broader spans of control are appropriate. Finally, where the environment in which the group works is highly stress-inducing, small spans only exacerbate the situation by adding an additional source of stress.

Group Size and Individual and Group Performance. In evaluating the effect of group size on performance, it is necessary to specify criteria. In a review of 10 experimental studies (some of which have been discussed above), four such criteria were specified: quality of performance, speed, efficiency, and productivity (Thomas and Fink, 1963). Applying these criteria to individual performance, it was found that while group size is sometimes related to performance and individual problem solving, the direction of the relationship is highly dependent on group conditions other than size. The other conditions that facilitated individual problem solving were practice (Taylor and Faust, 1952) and leadership (Utterback and Fotheringham, 1958).

Other studies of individual performance, however, tend to show that individual performance is better, as measured by one of the criteria mentioned above, in the smaller groups. One such study showed that groups of 5 take less time on a group decision than groups of 12 (Hare, 1952); another, that there was a significant inverse relationship between individual productivity and the size of work group, ranging from 10 to 50 members (Marriot, 1949). Also, this study showed that factory workers' understanding of a payment plan was better among members of smaller groups.

As for group performance, various studies have indicated that a larger group may be able to solve a greater variety of problems because the variety of skills is likely to increase with group size (Watson, 1928; Gibb, 1951; Taylor and Faust, 1952).

Hare (1952) suggests that although additional members may increase the resources of the group and enable it to solve a variety of problems more effectively, there comes a point, which will vary with the task, after which the addition of new members brings diminishing returns. As group size increases, coordination of the group tends to become difficult, and thus it becomes harder for the members to reach a consensus. The negative effects on coordination are most pronounced when the task is one on which there is no clear and objective criterion for judging the quality of performance. If the task is a technical one with a clear criterion of correct performance, or if effective performance requires a specific resource such as a given level of intelligence or the ability to work quickly, a large group is more likely than a small one to contain some member who can find an answer easily acceptable to other group members.

Support for this hypothesis comes from several other studies. For example, when the task was one requiring modification of opinion without any objective criterion, groups of 6 took longer than groups of 3. But on "abstract" tasks, the groups of 6 were faster (South, 1927). In an experimental study Deutsch (1951) showed that a mathematical problem is likely to promote less coordination of effort and fewer attempts at communication than a "value-laden" human relations problem, and the latter results in more conflict (blocking, self defense, and aggression). From this Deutsch concluded that the objective nature of a mathematical problem minimized the differences between cooperative and competitive groups in some respects, while the subjective nature of human relations problems tended to maximize these differences.

These studies, when viewed collectively, clearly illustrate the importance of task technology and performance demands as a major consideration in the analysis of span of control theory. Broad spans are most effective when tasks require varied intellectual abilities for group problem solving, when there is adequate time to permit large groups to interact, when organizational policy and communication are not highly relevant to group performance, and where task outcomes are unambiguous and easily measured.

Group Size and Member Satisfaction. Since larger groups offer less opportunity for participation by all the members, member satisfaction is greater in smaller groups, both discussion groups (Hare, 1952; Slater, 1958) and groups of factory workers (Hewitt and Parfitt, 1953; Campbell, 1952).

Smaller groups tend to generate greater satisfaction than do larger ones. A number of studies of discussion groups at the college level have found that larger groups were less satisfying to both students and instructors (McKeachie, 1963). A number of studies of organizational behavior also show that smaller groups are more satisfying to their members and that satisfaction with the group is related to opportunities for participation, satisfaction of achievement and affiliation needs, the individual's position within the organization, and the extent to which he can grasp the organization's goals (Forehand and Gilmer, 1965).

There is greater opportunity for participation and for obtaining group recognition within small groups than in large ones; and large groups tend to break up into subgroups or to form cliques with goals somewhat different from overall group goals.

Group Size and Leadership Behavior. Another factor related to the span of control is whether the type of management skill needed is different for spans of different sizes.

In reviewing several studies, Forehand and Gilmer (1965) state that in dealing with larger groups, face-to-face techniques of management give way to dealing with subgroups within the larger unit in coordinating behavior. For example, in a study in the restaurant industry it was found that as organization size increased there was increasing difficulty in coordinating activities (Whyte, 1949).

A study by Homans (1950), and other studies mentioned previously, give evidence that clique formation increases with group size. Finally, Hemphill (1950) and Mass (1950) found that as groups became larger, demands on the leader became more numerous, more complex and more exacting, and the members of the group became more tolerant of highly structured and directive leadership.

Morale and the Long Chain of Command

Deduction suggests that a long chain of command and the consequent formalization of relationships would be detrimental to morale because people would feel like small cogs in a large machine. As mentioned, James Worthy (1950) does report survey research data showing that the "tall" hierarchical structure militates against good morale.

However, recent studies dealing with morale and organization structure indicate that the relationship is less clearcut and depends on the size of the entire organization. In one of these studies, 1900 managers were classified as belonging to tall, intermediate, or flat organizations and surveyed by questionnaire. From the responses it was evident that in organizations of 5,000 or fewer people managerial satisfaction was higher in the flat structure; however, in larger organizations the reverse was true (Porter and Lawler, 1964). A similar study of 2,976 managers in companies in 13 nations produced essentially the same results (Porter and Siegal, 1965). These findings suggest that at some point in the growth of an organization it may be desirable to formalize hierarchical relationships and establish limited spans.

CONCLUSIONS

The initial premise was that the literature on management and organization is separated into two divergent schools of thought, and that an amalgamation of this literature can yield increased understanding about organizational behavior and management processes. The preceding review of the literature concerning span of control and optimum group size illustrates both these points. Clearly, the initial theoretical position taken by Fayol and elaborated by Graicunas and others has been researched by both management theorists and behavioral scientists.

The contributions of the management theorists lie in their providing problem foci or hypotheses and in their examinations of current practices which show how the span of control principle can be made operational and useful. A major limitation of the work of the management theorists is their failure to relate various spans of control to dependent variables such as group cohesiveness, member consensus, satisfaction and productivity. On the other hand, while not concerned with current practice or even the determinants of span size, the behavioral scientists have studied the effects of group size on many dependent variables important to management and organization theory.

Research in group dynamics has revealed a negative relationship between group size and group cohesion, consensus, the extent of participation, and member satisfaction. These relationships are also indicated by several surveys conducted in natural settings. Yet there is likely to be a marked inhibition of emotional expression in the very smallest groups which can be dysfunctional. Although the relationship between performance and group size may be positive under certain circumstances, there is evidence to suggest a point of diminishing returns. In general, smaller work groups whose tasks require interaction are more productive.

Certain conclusions from the behavioral research are that as group size increases the manager's job normally becomes increasingly complex and coordination and control are made more difficult by a loss of group cohesion and the formation of cliques and factions. The number of member relationships increases rapidly, placing increased demands on the leader in coordinating group activity. Subgroups generate their own spokesmen and subgroup goals emerge which are frequently incompatible with the goals of the larger group. Member satisfaction and the average amount of participation per member decrease as group size increases, although very small groups may suffer from inhibition of expression. While larger groups make greater resources available for problem-solving and thus may result in improved group performance, this is often obtained at the price of decreased member satisfaction and increased difficulty in reaching a consensus.

Research on group size and leader behavior suggests that a more formal, structured approach to leadership is both required and preferred in large groups. Research on tall versus flat organization structures implies that limited spans are more satisfying in large organizations than small ones.

The implications for the span of control seem to be that (1) under most circumstances the optimal span is likely to be in the range 5 through 10; (2) the larger spans, say 8 through 10, are most often appropriate at the highest, policy-making levels of an organization, where greater resources for diversified problem-solving appear to be needed (although diversified problem-solving without larger spans may well be possible); (3) the breadth of effective spans of first line supervisors is contingent on the technology of the organization; and (4) in prescribing the span of control for specific situations consideration must be given to a host of local factors such as the desirability of high group cohesiveness, the performance demands of the task, the degree of stress in the environment, task interdependencies, the need for member satisfaction, and the leadership skills available to the organization. In particular, the degrees of stability, diversity and uncertainty in both the environment of the unit and of the organization appear to be important considerations.

These conclusions are at variance with some formulations of the span of control principle but support others. It seems that a consideration of the interaction of span of control and group size in its totality has served to extend understanding in this particular area. It also seems probable that a similar merging of management and behavior theory and research could achieve equally useful results in other areas. The theoretical contributions of Thompson (1967) and Lawrence and Lorsch (1967) certainly suggest that amalgamations of this kind may emerge as a significant "next phase" in the development of organization theory.

REFERENCES

Bales, R. F., and E. F. Borgatta (1955). "Size of group as a factor in the interaction profile." In A. P. Hare, E. F. Borgatta, and R. F. Bales (eds.), Small Groups-Studies in Social Interaction: 396–413. New York: Knopf.

Bales, R. F., F. L. Strodtbeck, T. M. Mills, and M. E. Roseborough (1951). "Channels of communication in small groups." *American Sociological Review,* 16:461–468.

Barkdull, C. W. (1963). "Span of control—a method of evaluation." *Michigan Business Review,* 15, No. 3:25–32.

Bass, B. M. (1965). Organizational Psychology. Boston: Allyn and Bacon.

Berkowitz, M. F. (1958). An Experimental Study of the Relation Between Group Size and Social Organization. New Haven, Conn.: Doctoral Dissertation, Yale University.

Blau, P. M., and W. R. Scott (1962). Formal Organizations. San Francisco: Chandler.

Bossard, J. (1945). "The law of family interaction." *American Journal of Sociology,* 50: 292–294.

Campbell, H. (1952). "Group incentive pay schemes." *Occupational Psychology,* 26:15–21.

Carter, L. F., W. Haythorn, B. Meirowitz, and J. Lanzetta (1951). "The relations of categorizations and ratings in the observation of group behavior." *Human Relations,* 4:239–254.

Castore, G. F. (1962). "Number of verbal interrelationships as a determinant of group size." *Journal of Abnormal and Social Psychology,* 64:456–458.

Dale, E. (1952). Planning and Developing the Company Organization Structure. AMA Research Report No. 20. New York: American Management Association.

Dale, E. (1965). Management, Theory and Practice. New York: McGraw-Hill.

Davis, K. (1962). Human Relations at Work. New York: McGraw-Hill.

Davis, R. C. (1951). The Fundamentals of Top Management. New York: Harper.

Dawes, H. C. (1934). "The influence of the size of kindergarten group upon performance." *Child Development,* 5:295–303.

Deutsch, M. (1951). "Task structure and group process." *American Psychologist,* 6:324–325.

Entwisle, D. R., and J. Walton (1961). "Observations on the span of control." *Administrative Science Quarterly,* 5:522–533.

Fayol, H. (1949). General and Industrial Management. London: Pitman.

Fischer, P. H. (1953). "An analysis of the primary group." *Sociometry,* 16:272–276.

Flippo, E. B. (1966). Management: A Behavioral Approach. Boston: Allyn and Bacon.

Forehand, G. A., and B. Gilmer (1965). "Environmental variation in studies of organizational behavior." *Psychological Bulletin,* 62: 361–382.

Gibb, J. R. (1951). "The effects of group size and of threat reduction upon creativity in a problem-solving situation." *American Psychologist,* 6:324.

Golembiewski, R. T. (1965). "Small groups and large organizations." In J. G. March (ed.), Handbook of Organizations: 87–141. Chicago: Rand McNally.

Graicunas, V. A. (1937). "Relationship in organization." In L. Gulick and L. Urwick (ed.), Papers on the Science of Administration: 183–187. New York: Columbia University.

Hare, A. P. (1952). "A study of interaction and consensus in different sized groups." *American Sociological Review,* 17:261–267.

Hare, A. P. (1962). Handbook of Small Group Research. New York: Free Press.

Healey, J. H. (1956). Executive Coordination and Control. Columbus, Ohio: Bureau of Business Research, Ohio State University.

Hemphill, J. (1950). "Relations between the size of the group and the behavior of 'superior' leaders." *Journal of Social Psychology,* 32: 11–22.

Hewitt, C., and J. Parfit (1953). "A note on working morale and size of group." *Occupational Psychology,* 27:38–42.

Hollingshead, A. B. (1949). Elmtown's Youth—The Impact of Social Class on Adolescents. New York: Wiley.

Homans, G. C. (1950). The Human Group. New York: Harcourt, Brace.

James, J. (1951). "A preliminary study of the size determinant in small group interaction." *American Sociological Review,* 16:474–477.

Janger, A. (1960). "Analyzing the span of control." *Management Record,* 22, Nos. 7 and 8: 7–10.

Jennings, H. (1960). "Sociometric choice processes in personality and group formation." In J. L. Moreno (ed.), The Sociometry Reader: 87–113. Glencoe, Ill.: Free Press.

Katz, D., and R. L. Kahn (1966). The Social Psychology of Organizations. New York: Wiley.

Koontz, H., and C. O'Donnell (1968). Principles of Management. New York: McGraw-Hill.

Lawrence, P. R., and J. W. Lorsch (1967). Organization and Environment—Managing Differentiation and Integration. Boston: Graduate School of Business Administration, Harvard University.

Likert, R. (1961). New Patterns of Management. New York: McGraw-Hill.

March, J. G. (1965). Handbook of Organizations. Chicago: Rand McNally.

Marriott, R. (1949). "Size of working group and output." *Occupational Psychology,* 23:47–57.

Mass, H. S. (1950). "Personal and group factors in leader's social perception." *Journal of Abnormal and Social Psychology,* 45:54–63.

McKeachie, W. J. (1963). "Research on teaching at the college and university level." In N. Gage (ed.), Handbook of Research on Teaching: 1118–1172. Chicago: Rand McNally.

Miller, N. (1952). "The effect of group size on decision-making discussions." *Dissertation Abstracts,* 12:229.

Miner, J. B. (1963). "Psychology and the school of business curriculum." *Journal of the Academy of Management,* 6:284–289.

Porter, L. W., and E. E. Lawler (1964). "The effect of tall versus flat organization structures on managerial job satisfaction." *Personnel Psychology,* 17:135–148.

Porter, L. W., and J. Siegel (1965). "Relationships of tall and flat organization structures to the satisfactions of foreign managers." *Personnel Psychology,* 18:379–392.

Slater, P. E. (1958). "Contrasting correlates of group size." *Sociometry,* 21:129–139.

South, E. B. (1927). "Some psychological aspects of committee work." *Journal of Applied Psychology,* 11:437–464.

Stephan, F. F., and E. G. Mishler (1952). "The distribution of participation in small groups: an exponential approximation." *American Sociological Review,* 17:598–608.

Stieglitz, H. (1962). "Optimizing span of control." *Management Record,* 24, No. 9:25–29.

Suojanen, W. W. (1955). "The span of control—fact or fable." *Advanced Management,* 20, Nov.: 5–13.

Taylor, D. J., and W. L. Faust (1952). "Twenty questions: efficiency in problem-solving as a function of group size." *Journal of Experimental Psychology,* 44:360–368.

Thomas, E. J., and C. F. Fink (1963). "Effects of group size." *Psychological Bulletin,* 60:371–384.

Thompson, J. D. (1967). Organizations in Action. New York: McGraw-Hill.

Thrasher, F. (1927). The Gang. Chicago: University of Chicago Press.

Udell, J. G. (1967). "An empirical test of hypothesis relating to span of control." *Administrative Science Quarterly,* 12:420–439.

Urwick, L. (1933). Organization is a Technical Problem: International Management Institute.

Urwick, L. (1956). "The span of control—some facts about the fable." *Advanced Management,* 21:5–15.

Utterbach, W. E., and W. C. Fotheringham (1958). "Experimental studies in motivated group discussion." *Speech Monographs,* 25: 268–277.

Watson, G. B. (1928). "Do groups think more effciently than individuals?" *Journal of Abnormal and Social Psychology,* 23:328–336.

Whyte, W. F. (1949). "The social structure of the restaurant." *American Journal of Sociology,* 54:302–310.

Woodward, J. (1965). Industrial Organization—Theory and Practice. London: Oxford University Press.

Worthy, J. (1950). "Organization structures and employee morale." *American Sociological Review,* 15:169–179.

B. DEPARTMENTATION

32 ON CONCEPTS OF CORPORATE STRUCTURE*

Harold Stieglitz

Just about 25 years ago, General Motors announced one of its most important products—the GM Formula. Its wage escalation clause negotiated then with the UAW provided for a 1¢ increase in hourly wages for each 1.14 point rise in the BLS index. Confronted with the inflationary period of Korea, many company negotiators copied GM and adopted the 1 for 1.14 formula for escalating wages. The fact that the formula had a specific relevance to GM's employees—that it reflected the ratio of average wages of the GM employees to the cost-of-living index at the time of adoption—seemed beside the point. The fact that a different formula might have more appropriately reflected the wage-cost-of-living relationship of their employees deterred few from just going ahead with 1 for 1.14. Evidently what was good enough for the sophisticates at GM was good enough for most of its emulators.

More than 50 years ago, however, GM had developed another product that proved to have an even larger impact. This was a management concept labeled "centralized coordination, decentralized administration"—or, "decentralization with coordination and control." While adoption of this concept came less rapidly, many companies turned to it—especially in the post-World War II growth period, when diversification and greater complexity characterized an increasing number.

In application, the concept meant reorganizing operations into divisionalized profit centers that operated with a high degree of decentralization; setting up corporate staffs to provide centralized coordination and control under corporate-wide policies. Initially, the ambiguities and vagaries of the concept were not seen as deterrents to its adoption. GM's success in the marketplace showed it must be doing something right. If "decentralization with centralized control" was good enough for GM, it was good enough for others.

Since the early 1920s, however, the concept was subject to adaptation and development at GM itself. Even during Alfred P. Sloan's tenure, changes in technology and the marketplace brought an ebb and flow to the degree of decentralization vs. centralized coordination—and, retrospectively, it's been more ebb than flow. But those who borrowed the concept sometimes missed the nuances of GM's later experience, so what seemed to work there didn't always work for them.

Emulation in structuring organization is not, of course, dead. Upon hearing of a major company that operates very effectively with a very small central staff, many a chief executive has envied the cost savings implicit in such a structure. Some have tried it. Similarly, the prospect of putting some young tigers at the head of their own decentralized profit centers has led others to reorganize. However, in more recent years, there is evidence that a more mature approach to organization planning has displaced such "me-too-ism."

THE REASONS FOR STRUCTURING ORGANIZATION

Sloan, the prime mover in the development and adaptation of GM's concept of organization, at the close of his long career, remarked, "An organization does not make decisions; its function is to provide a framework, based upon established criteria, within which decisions can be made."[1] The modifying phrase "based upon established criteria" is crucial, and maturity in corporate organization structuring has only developed as more top executives have been able to identify those criteria that condition the framework.

* Reprinted by permission of the publisher from *The Conference Board Record*, vol. 11, no. 2, pp. 7–13 (February 1974). Mr. Stieglitz is director of the management research staff of the Conference Board.

[1] Alfred P. Sloan, Jr., *My Years with General Motors* (New York, Doubleday, 1964).

Admittedly, many a pragmatic top executive denies that there are any basic criteria that dictate key elements of the organization structure. The "situation," the "personalities," the "management style," and a host of other factors are presumably enough to make each organization and its structure unique.[2] Over the long run, however, one may observe that constant reorganizations and adaptation tend to move the structure in directions that seem almost independent of particular personalities or styles or whims.

Demonstrably, the spectrum of organizational structures throughout industry remains quite broad. It stretches from companies that are organized virtually like holding companies to those that operate, basically, like one-man businesses. These are companies that operate in a highly centralized manner, others that are highly decentralized—and all shades in between. Similarly, some are functionally organized, some have certain elements set up as divisions, some are mixed. And staff within these companies come in all shapes and sizes.[3]

Still, the patterns of organization structure that have emerged indicate that there are company characteristics that are at the root of the developments, and they are primarily economic. Moreover, those that are evidently most influential in shaping organization structure can be specified:

- *Degree of diversification* in terms of the variety of goods and services produced and/or markets served.
- *Degree of interdependency,* integration or overlap among the diversified operating components.

Such other factors as economies of scale, dispersion, or absolute size are significant, but largely to the extent that they affect diversification and overlap.[4]

The extent to which a company is diversified tends to determine whether its major operating activities will be structured by division or function and the nature of the groups that come into existence.

[2] See *The Chief Executive and His Job,* Studies in Personnel Policy, No. 214 (The National Industrial Conference Board, 1969).

[3] For documentation of major organization trends see *Corporate Organization Structures,* Studies in Personnel Policy, Nos. 183 and 210 (The National Industrial Conference Board, 1961 and 1968), and *Corporate Organization Structures: Manufacturing* (1973). Also see *Organization Planning: Basic Concepts, Emerging Trends* (The National Industrial Conference Board, 1969).

[4] See, for example, *Staff Services in Smaller Companies: The View from the Top,* Report No. 592 (The Conference Board, April 1973).

The extent to which the operations overlap —in terms of markets, technology, sources of supply, etc.—emerges as the key determinant of the degree of decentralization and the types and role of corporate staff.

In short, the emergence of the divisionalized decentralized form of organization is less a matter of managerial sophistication, more a matter of economic necessity. In an organizational sense, sophistication amounts to recognition of the inevitable.

A CONTINUUM OF ORGANIZATIONS

Relating structure to economic variables is more readily seen when the varieties of types of companies and apposite key structural elements are arrayed. Looking at diversity and overlap of operations, it's quite evident, for example, that companies range from those engaged in the production and/or sale of one good or service to those involved in a multiplicity of related and unrelated businesses. Indeed, when so arrayed, it is clear that the myriad variations form a continuum with no real discontinuities.

A company at point 1 of the continuum may be substantially different from one at point 10, but to distinguish too sharply between companies at points 4 and 5 would be fatuous. Even so, the continuum, as represented in the chart, can be divided for analytical purposes into four categories—each of which, in itself, covers a spectrum of companies:

I *Single businesses*—one company producing a single or homogeneous product for a single or homogeneous market.

II *Multiple businesses, related*—one company producing a variety of products for a variety of markets, but with a high degree of overlap in markets for the various products and/or a high degree of integration in materials or technology involved in manufacturing the products.

III *Multiple businesses, unrelated*—one company producing a variety of products for a variety of markets, but the overlap is absent. There are virtually no common denominators—no overlap—in the markets served or the resources or technology employed in producing the variety of goods or services.

IV *Multiple businesses, unrelated (no corporate identity)*—one company but little or no attempt to manage the unrelated businesses; little or no attempt to project a company identity. This, of course, is the holding company defined by Sloan as "a central office surrounded by autonomously operating satellites."

A Continuum of Corporations and Related Organization Structures

ELEMENTS OF ORGANIZATION	SINGLE BUSINESSES I 1 2 3 4 5	MULTIPLE BUSINESSES RELATED II 6 7 8 9	MULTIPLE BUSINESSES UNRELATED III 10 11 12	MULTIPLE BUSINESSES UNRELATED (NO CORPORATE IDENTITY) IV 13 14 15 16
Structure of Operations	Functional	Divisionalized	Divisionalized	Divisionalized (subsidiaries)
Functional elements within divisions	—	Prod. & Sales little staff	Prod. & Sales more staff	Prod. & Sales more complete staff
Degree of Decentralization	More Centralized	Decentralized	Highly Decentralized	Highly Decentralized (virtual autonomy for divisions)
Corporate Staff Type	Administrative and Operational	Administrative and Operational	Administrative	Administrative (if any)
Role	Services Advisory Control	Advisory Control	Advisory (consultant)	—
Groups	—	Super-Divisions	Liaison	Unlikely

This continuum is not designed to suggest a strategy for growth. Nor does it imply that normal growth occurs through movement across the continuum. A company's growth pattern may keep it in Category I; move it from I to II; or from IV to III.

It bears repeating that the array is a continuum—there are no sharp discontinuities. For analytical purposes, a company can only be characterized as having "more or less" of the economic qualities of a particular category. Similarly, the key organizational elements that relate to these categories can also only be referred to in terms of degree—more or less—i.e., more or less decentralized, more or less divisionalized. Overall, the tendency to divisionalize increases as one moves from Categories I to IV; more significantly, the degree of decentralization decreases as one moves from IV to I. The major related structural elements—makeup of the divisions, types and roles of staff, nature of the groups—also vary.

FUNCTIONAL VS. DIVISIONAL FORM OF ORGANIZATION

It is no accident that companies, regardless of size, that fall into Category I tend to be organized on a functional basis. At the extreme left of the spectrum there is usually little basis for coordinating specialized activities in any other way. Thus, inasmuch as all manufacturing and engineering activities serve a common product, they are organized under one head. Inasmuch as all marketing activities are designed to promote one product, they too are most effectively coordinated by one head.

As the company finds either its product or market spectrum broadening—as it diversifies—it often is able to segregate either its production activities or its marketing activities by product or market. But in terms of who is accountable for what, it's still functional—until such time as increased diversity allows both marketing and production of a given product for a specified market to be linked.

This move to link production and sales of a given product under one head—thus divisionalizing and forming a "profit center," as opposed to a "cost center"—characteristically occurs in companies whose diversification efforts result in (a) more discrete technologies for each product, (b) more discrete markets for each product. Under these circumstances, whether diversification has come from internal product development or external mergers or acquisition, product divisions emerge as the more effective operating components. Again, it is no accident that companies whose operational characteristics are those of Categories II, III, or IV tend to organize them into product or so-called market divisions. In short, they divisionalize.[5]

However, the divisions that are so characteristic of the more diversified companies vary in terms of the more specialized functional components that are assigned or report to the division head. In Category II, for example, the divisions undoubtedly have their own production and sales units; they may very well have their own accounting and engineering units. But it is most likely that corporate units in various areas, e.g., marketing, manufacturing, purchasing, or research and development, will exist, in part, to supply certain services that are common to several divisions. Thus the divisions of companies in Category II tend to truncate; they are not complete in terms of all the functions necessary to carry on their operations.

The divisions that make up companies in Categories III and IV, on the other hand, tend to be more self-sufficient, less reliant on common services. Indeed, in Category IV, many of the operating components exist as virtually self-sufficient subsidiaries. Obviously, the greater interdependence and overlap of markets, technology and resources in Category II accounts for the more truncated divisions in this class; the lack of commonality between the divisions or sub-divisions of Categories III and IV makes for far greater self-sufficiency—at least in terms of functional components.

CENTRALIZATION-DECENTRALIZATION

Degree of overlap is even more closely related to the varying degrees of decentralization that is evident at various points in the continuum. Decentralization, in this context, has a specific meaning: the extent to which decision-making authority is delegated to lower levels of the organization and, by implication, the degree of constraint—of centralized control in the form, for example, of corporate-wide policies—that curtails the area of discretion left to lower-level managers.

Generally, it can be observed that three factors have a major effect on the degree of delegated authority and/or decentralization:

- *The confidence factor*—the confidence of superiors in the competence of subordinates.
- *The information factor*—the extent to which the organization has developed mechanisms to feed information to the decision-making points, and the extent to which feedback systems have developed that allow accountable managers to evaluate results of their decisions.
- *The scope-of-impact factor*—the extent to which a decision made by one unit head affects the operations of another unit.

It is this third factor—the scope-of-impact of decision—that, in the long run, becomes the key ingredient in determining the degree of decentralization. And, clearly, the scope-of-impact of decisions is directly related to the degree of integration, or overlap, or interdependence of the company's varied operations. With a greater degree of interaction, less decentralization is possible. As the operations become more highly varied and opportunities for operational synergy decrease, the greater the possible degree of decentralization, the greater the toleration of differences in approaches to personnel, customers, and the public.[6]

In terms of the continuum, it is evident that the operation of companies in Category I encourages a higher degree of centralized decision-making than takes place in Category II. Similarly, companies in Category III can, and do, tolerate more decentralization than those in Category II. And while the operations, or the divisions of companies, in Categories III and IV might be very similar in terms of diversity and minimum overlap, the fact that companies in Category IV are not intent on projecting a corporate identity—and thus can eschew corporate-wide policies—makes for a degree of decentralization that verges on virutal autonomy for the operating divisions or subsidiaries.

CORPORATE STAFF: FUNCTIONS AND ROLES

Size is undoubtedly a key factor that determines whether and when a particular staff unit will emerge within the corporation. Until there is a continuing need for a particular functional expertise, the company may well make use of outside or part-time consultants or services. But once the need is felt and a full-time staff unit is created, whether it be one person or a larger unit, the nature of the operations and the degree of decentralization tend to be strong determinants of the types of specialized staff that come into being and their role relative to the rest of the company.

For analytical purposes, it is useful to distinguish between: (a) administrative staff, the functional (staff) units that derive from the fact that a corporation exists as a legal and financial entity (the legal, financial, and public

[5] For a more complete analysis of divisionalization, see *Top Management Organization in Divisionalized Companies,* Studies in Personnel Policy, No. 195 (The National Industrial Conference Board, 1965).

[6] Ibid.

relations staff are typical) and, (b) operational staff, the functional (staff) units that emerge because of the peculiar nature of the companies' operations (e.g., manufacturing, marketing, purchasing and traffic).

An even more substantive distinction can be drawn between the various roles that characterize staff in its varied relationships. Again, for analytical purposes, whether it be administrative or operational staff, three roles can be distinguished.[7]

- *Advisory or counseling role*—the staff unit brings its professional expertise to bear in analyzing and solving problems. In this role, staff acts as a consultant; its relationship is largely that of a professional to a client.
- *Service role*—the staff unit provides services that can be more efficiently and economically provided by one unit with specialized expertise than by many units attempting to provide for themselves. Its relationship in this role is largely that of a supplier to a customer.
- *Control role*—because of its professional or specialized expertise in a given functional area, staff is called upon to assist in establishing the plans, budgets, policies, rules, standard operating procedures that act as major constraints on delegated authority; that set the parameters of decision-making at lower levels. And it sets up mechanisms to audit and evaluate performance vis-à-vis these controls. In exercising this role, its relationship to the rest of the organization is that of an agent for top management.

By combining the elements—type of staff and role—it is possible to draw a profile of corporate staff. And that profile tends to vary with companies in each of the four categories.

Thus the fact that Category I includes companies that are organized functionally, that are more centralized than decentralized, narrows the options for the character of staff units that come into being. Of necessity, staff units of both administrative and operational types become part of corporate structure—with the operational staff elements often reporting directly to the accountable operational head of manufacturing or sales. And while some staff units may be more service-oriented than advisory, others more advisory than control, the fact that the functional organization is virtually one large profit center makes advice, service and control a part of every staff unit's job.

[7] For a more complete discussion, see also *Top Management Organization in Divisionalized Companies* (op. cit.), especially Chapter 7, "Staff."

Among Category II companies, whose diversification has fostered divisionalization and greater decentralization, the profile of corporate staff changes. The change is largely one of role rather than type.

Because the divisional operations are interdependent and overlap, there may well be need for operational staff as well as administrative units at the corporate level. But divisions may also have their own staff units to provide services that are unique to the division. Thus, in a divisionalized company there may be, for example, R&D at both corporate and division levels, with divisional staff emphasizing development, corporate staff emphasizing longer range research. However, because more staff is created within the divisions of Category II companies to provide services locally, the service role of the corporate staff declines. As a result, the advisory and control roles of the corporate staff units assume primary emphasis.

However, this is not to suggest that the advisory and control role become dominant merely as residual factors. To the contrary, they gain emphasis because: (a) In companies with the economic characteristics of Category II, corporate top management becomes relatively more future-oriented; the divisions remain more oriented to the near term. The future emphasis underscores the corporate staff's advisory role in planning. (b) The decentralization occasioned by multiple profit centers heightens the need to discern areas of overlap as well as matters of overriding corporate concern that require consistency in decision-making, i.e., the generation of corporate policies. And it puts greater emphasis on discerning and establishing more sophisticated control procedures. Thus the greater emphasis on staff as an agency of control.

Moving to companies whose economic characteristics are those of Category III, the profile of corporate staff again changes—this time in both type and role. Because the operating divisions have little in common, they share no markets; they don't overlap in technology and resources; there is little need for corporate staff in operational areas. Rather, operational staff units are more often housed within the divisions or at the group level. The corporate staff units more often are those in the general areas of administration—financial, legal—and often those that are closely tied to future development of the corporation.

More significantly, the corporate staff's role as a control agency, prominent in both Categories I and II, fades among Category III companies. The far greater degree of decentralization possible in any such company is synonymous with fewer overall constraints in the form of corporate policies and procedures. This fact accounts for the change in role. For the most part, staff units in Category III companies, with the possible exception of finance and planning, are primarily advisory in role—captive consultants.

The diminished need for operational staff and the shift to a primarily consulting relationship that characterizes corporate staff in Category III companies becomes even more pronounced in Category IV. Indeed, it becomes difficult even to see corporate staff—in the sense so far discussed—in the company that operates like a holding company. The parent corporation may have a strong financial unit and legal unit, but these exist primarily to serve the parent. Since the divisions or subsidiaries are encouraged to operate in a manner that verges on autonomy, they establish their own controls, have their own staffs whose profile undoubtedly varies with the economic characteristics of the particular division or subsidiary. If there is such a thing as "corporate staff" in companies at the extreme of Category IV, it may very well exist as a separate "management service" subsidiary from which the other divisions may purchase services as required.

GROUP STRUCTURES

The increased use of groups, headed by group executives, is relatively recent. The increase has resulted largely from the proliferation of operating divisions within corporations. It's another level of management introduced to secure better coordination of several presumably separate divisions.[8] Almost by definition, the group mechanism is confined to the divisionalized companies of Categories II and III. But not quite.

There are ambiguities in the group concept and variations in the structure of groups that can be linked to the same factors accounting for variations in the role of corporate staff.

Starting with Category IV, in this instance, there is little evidence of attempts to link operating units into groups headed by a group executive. This seems consistent with the parent corporation's hands-off approach to the highly independent divisions or subsidiaries.

In Category III companies, on the other hand, diverse though the divisions may be, there is an attempt to link the operations more closely with guidance from the corporation. There is an attempt to devise a corporate strategy and to project a corporate identity. Divisions very often are assembled into groups. But for the most part, the divisions within the groups have little in common—other than that they serve the "industrial market" or "consumer market" or operate under some such similarly broad umbrella. The group executive, in such instances, may serve as an advisor, a reviewer of plans, an appraiser of performance. But he is essentially a link pin between the division and their objectives and the corporation. His primary function may well be to plug the communication gap that emerges when the proliferation of divisions has caused too broad a span of control for the chief executive. Chances are that such a group will have no staff at the group level, or possibly just a controllership function that reports to the group executive.

Move to Category II companies and the character of the group and the function of the group executive change. Here, the groups that emerge tend to be more closely knit, comprised of divisions that invite synergistic development. Indeed, in many such situations the group structure develops as a pragmatic mechanism for dealing with the fact that the "discrete and separate" divisions are not really all that discrete or separate. In many such companies, the divisions do share markets or do overlap in technology. The pulling together of these overlapping divisions makes it more possible to develop a business strategy for a total market, or to pool certain production facilities, or share common staff services.

The group, in such instances, actually becomes more of a super-division composed of truncated or even functional divisions. And the group executive, rather than providing liaison between a series of unrelated divisions, becomes the head of a more encompassing profit center.

In Category I companies, the definition of group seems to preclude its existence—except possibly at point 4 in the spectrum where beginning attempts to diversify may lead to the creation of a group that pulls together newer businesses emerging as product divisions. The closest approximation of the group executive in the functionally organized company is the high level executive who coordinates related staff and operating functions—e.g., an executive vice president whose domain covers manufacturing, engineering, R&D, and purchasing. However, he is still primarily a functional executive.

THE MODELS IN PERSPECTIVE

These major elements of structure, when assembled by category, reveal organizational profiles that are significantly different. Each structural model is rooted in the dominant eco-

[8] Ibid. Chapter 4, "Group Executives."

nomic characteristics of the corporation as a total entity. It is worth underscoring the point that each category in itself covers a spectrum. The "more or less" caveat referred to earlier applies to each as well as the overall continuum. The profile of a company at point 13 may be more like one at point 12 than one at 16; or 5 and 4 may be more similar than 5 and 8.

Developments in organization structure make clear that companies, structurally, are trending toward more congruence with the economic realities of their businesses. But obviously there are many companies whose current structures seem to be at odds with their economic models. Indeed, complete congruence is more an ideal than a realizable goal.

In some companies, shorter term pressures, or more immediate advantages take priority over what seems more logical in the longer term. Immediate pressure to penetrate special markets may induce a divisionalized structure even though there are longer term advantages to greater integration on a functional basis. Or one phase of the company's operations, accounting for perhaps the larger part of the company's total sales and profits, may be so significant that the overall structure is organized functionally to accommodate it. Or the lack of management talent may require higher level management to make more decisions and thus force a greater degree of centralization than seems warranted by the character of the operations. For these and many more highly practical reasons, the longer term optimum organization structure is less than optimum to those whose performance is evaluated in the short term.

However, there is another set of factors, equally real, that impede achievement of the best fit. These lie in the psyche of the human organization. The incumbent staff may be so thoroughly familiar with the more specific organization problems of various elements of the organization that they have difficulty seeing the total corporation because of its divisions.

Even more inhibiting to achievement of the optimum structure are the inertial factors that restrict any major organization change—the comforts of sticking with past habits and traditions, of applying past practice to new situations.[9] A company's growth may be of a character that it moves from Category I to Category II. But the operating and staff personnel who move with it know how to operate in the environment of a functional organization with greater centralization and don't willingly assume new roles. As a result, some of the more poignant managerial tragedies, particularly those of chief executives, can be traced to their inability to mate individual "management styles" with the economic verities of the total company.

[9] For elaboration, see *Organization Change—Perceptions and Realities,* Report No. 561 (The National Industrial Conference Board, July 1972).

33 REORGANIZE YOUR COMPANY AROUND MARKETS*

Mack Hanan

Throughout the 1960s, market orientation was such a dominant business concept that it is surprising to find, a decade later, that few companies have found a way to organize themselves so that their customers' needs consistently come first. In most companies, the divisional structures are still determined by regions, organized around products, or structured to commercialize a process technology. It has been only over the past few years that a small number of companies have come to realize that:

- There is no substitute for market orientation as the ultimate source of profitable growth.
- The only way to ensure being market-oriented is to put a company's organizational structure together so that its major markets become the centers around which its divisions are built.

Some leading companies are emphasizing growth by gearing their organizational structures to their markets' needs instead of to their product or process capabilities. IBM's data-processing operations are segmented organizationally according to key markets, such as institutions like hospitals and retail establishments like supermarkets. Xerox Information Systems Group, which sells copiers and duplicators, has converted from geographical selling to vertical selling by industry. General Foods has adopted a market-targeting organizational style. Even the strict product orientation of some scientific companies is gradually giving way to a combined product and market orientation. In its electronics product marketing, for example, Hewlett-Packard has created a sales and service group that concentrates separately on the electrical manufacturing market while another group serves the market for aerospace. Still other groups sell to the markets for communications or transportation equipment.

In other companies steps are being taken to orient businesses to their markets. At Mead, broad market clusters are coming into being to serve customer needs in home building and furnishings, education, and leisure. PPG Industries has been examining the benefits of systematizing the marketing of its paint, ceramics, and glass divisions through a home environment profit center whose product mix could resemble the pattern shown in *Exhibit I*. Monsanto has organized a Fire Safety Center that consolidates fire safety products from every sector of Monsanto and groups them according to the market they serve: building and construction, transportation, apparel, or furnishings. Revlon is engaged in "breaking up the company into little pieces": as many as six autonomous profit centers are being created, each of which is designed to serve a specific market segment.

General Electric is well along in constructing strategic business groups for its major appliance and power-generation businesses. For GE, the process of reorganizing from a product to a market orientation has been especially difficult. An average department contains three and one half product lines and may serve more than one business or, more frequently, only a part of a major business. Electric motors, for example, are divided among eight departments. Home refrigerators are split between two departments, even though the only significant product difference is the way the doors open. In such a setup, department managers have understandably become oriented to specific product lines rather than to the needs of a total market.

I use the term *marketcentered* (or market-centering) to describe the wide range of corporate organizational forms that make a group of customer needs, rather than a region, a product line, or a process, the center of a business division. These forms include General Foods's "strategic business units," National Cash Regis-

* Reprinted by permission of the publisher from *Harvard Business Review,* vol. 52, no. 6, pp. 63–74 (November–December 1974). Copyright © 1974 by the President and Fellows of Harvard College. All rights reserved. Mr. Hanan is managing director of the firm of Hanan & Son, Management Consultants.

EXHIBIT I Product Mix of a Business Marketcentered on the Home

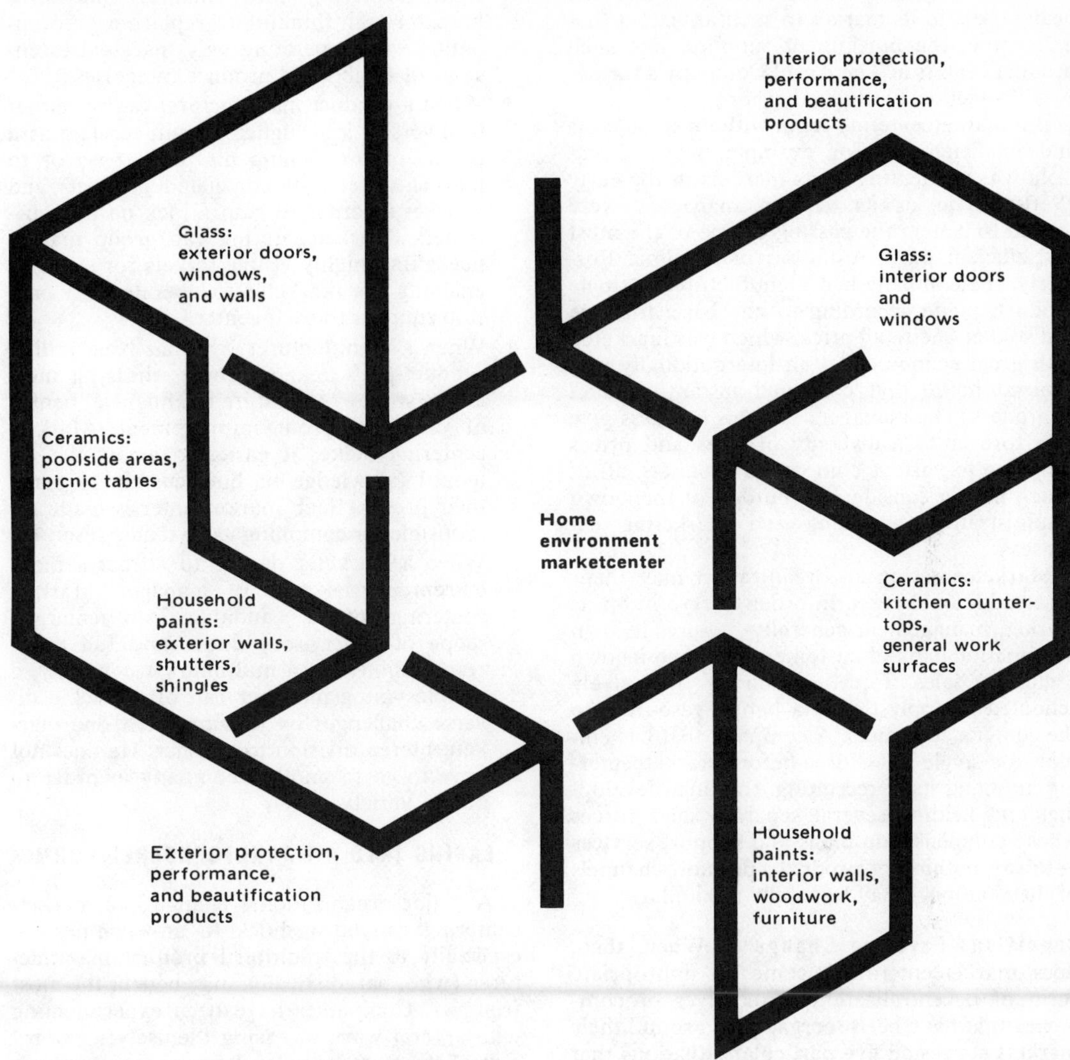

ter's "vocations," the "customer provinces" that some high-technology manufacturers are organizing as company-like units to concentrate on serving the needs of specific market groups, and the "financial need groups" through which some progressive banks serve the common financing needs of manufacturers of electronic systems, drugs, cosmetics, household products, and other items.

Marketcentering also describes the way some railroads are grouping their services around the common distribution needs of major customers so that they can provide a unique user-oriented service system for oil, chemical, and fertilizer shippers and a different system for grain shippers. These organizational formats are working so well that more railroads can be expected to adopt them.

WHEN SHOULD AN ORGANIZATION BE MARKETCENTERED?

Marketcentered describes an organization that is decentralized by markets—markets define the business. Organizing an enterprise in this way, which some companies think of as working backward from the points where they deal face to face with their customers, can yield many of the same benefits as decentralizing by processes, materials, or product lines. A marketcenter forms a natural profit center just as readily as does a materials center, such as Continental Can's Metal Operations group. A marketcenter may also be able to dominate the heavy users in its market to such an extent that it becomes the preeminent supplier, like such product centers as The Ansul Company's former Fire Protection Products division.

But marketcentering is not without some costs and inefficiencies. For example, when Coca-Cola was reorienting to its markets in the early 1960s, some of its veteran managers were moved to lament the passing of one of the most cost-efficient mass businesses of all time. Formerly, the company had manufactured a single product, made according to one basic formula and sold at one retail price, which was marketed with great economies in an internationally recognized bottle that conveyed instant product awareness. The managers saw this business give way forever to a diversity of sizes and prices and even to various companion products, all of which bore a considerable burden of their own administrative, operating and marketing expenses.

Marketcentering an organization may incur other additional costs. In order to zero in on its market, management generally requires its own information bank of customer needs and its own exclusive sales force, which is intensively schooled to apply the data bank's resources to the center's customers. A company that has employed a single sales force before marketcentering may find itself recruiting, training, developing, and fielding several separate sales forces whose compensation plans and support services —to say nothing of product lines and channels of distribution—may be totally dissimilar.

Conditions Favoring Change When, then, does marketcentering become an appropriate form of decentralization? Executives of companies that have been reorganizing around their markets suggested five particular situations that especially favor a marketcentered approach:

1. When market leadership is threatened by a competitor who has achieved sufficient product parity to deprive the leader of price superiority. Marketcentering can restore a competitive advantage with the more creative marketing techniques it develops from improved knowledge of customer, distributor, and retailer needs.
2. When new-product famine has afflicted the product-development function so that nothing, or only a crop of lemons, is being delivered, or when R&D has been foundering in its resource allocation because of a lack of market direction. Marketcentering can stimulate new-product winners by transmitting current knowledge of market life-styles or emergent needs to technical management. Marketcentering also enables innovative breakthrough thinking to replace a preoccupation with generating only marginal extensions of established product categories.
3. When a product manufacturer desires either to diversify into higher-margin services as a means of broadening his profit base or to market systems of correlated products and services in order to gain a lock on key customers. Marketcentering can group market needs into highly visible targets for systems, enabling the marketer to operate as a one-stop supplier to each center.
4. When a manufacturer who has been selling product-performance benefits shifts his marketing strategy to feature the financial benfits of customer profit improvement. Marketcentering makes it easier to amass the required knowledge of how customers make their profits. Each marketcenter is made responsible for compiling its own data resource.
5. When a marketer desires to attract a more entrepreneurial type of manager. Marketcentering offers candidates an enlarged scope of supervisory duties and full profit responsibility. In a multimarket company, a mobile young manager can often tackle diverse challenges by moving from one marketcentered division to another. He does not have to go to another company in order to obtain variety.

EASING INTO A MARKETCENTERED FORM

A major organizational change like marketcentering can be a shock to any company—especially to the traditional product manufacturer (who, paradoxically, may benefit the most from it). Companies have been experimenting with several ways of easing themselves toward a marketcentered approach, since the change is often best implemented by degrees. Along the way, a company can learn how much marketcentering it can stand at any given time and what particular form it should ultimately have. Three ways of beginning the transition have emerged thus far.

Marketcentering a sales force is the first way. It requires the least up-front commitment and the least alteration in the basic structure of a business. In addition, it succeeds in establishing the central relationship that earmarks all forms of marketcentered organizations: contact between customers with many varying needs and a sales force that can prescribe the most beneficial systems for those needs. In the romantic version of marketing, this interface takes place on a prolonged person-to-person basis in the marketplace. The reality, however, is that customer information is collected and analyzed at a data bank.

This is the approach that NCR has taken. Each sales staff is assigned a well-defined industry group to serve. The company's salesmen are trained to sell systems of different but interrelated products and services in a consultative manner. They consider market knowledge, rather than product knowledge, to be their principal resource.

General Foods has chosen a second way to ease into marketcentering. It has created a separate marketing division to serve each major market. This approach involves reclassifying major markets into new, more comprehensive groups and consolidating similar but differently manufactured products into product families to be marketed to each group. While the NCR salescentered approach requires a single salesman to serve most or all of a customer's needs with many different products and services, the General Foods approach coordinates a wide range of products that are essentially alike for a single user segment.

The third way is to begin with either the first or second step and then proceed to achieve a thoroughly marketcentered structure by integrating manufacturing and all marketing functions, including sales, into a single division. Both the NCR and General Foods examples lend themselves to this end result, which IBM and Xerox have perhaps most fully achieved.

In the following sections, I shall examine some of the major characteristics of the NCR and General Foods approaches. Then I shall describe the key criteria of a marketcentered organization, the role of the business manager, and the service systems needed to support that role.

NCR'S APPROACH—SEPARATE SALES FORCES

NCR has been reorganizing its traditional product-line sales approach into a strategy of "selling by vocation" on an industry-by-industry basis. Each vocation is a broad industry grouping which forms a specific market definable by reasonably cohesive needs. NCR is focusing a separate sales force on each of the following vocational markets: financial institutions, retailers, commercial and industrial businesses, and computer customers in medical, educational, and government offices.

NCR's marketcentered sales organization is enabling the company to be more competitive, especially in the marketing of systems. In each market, the NCR salesman assigned to it can sell coordinated systems of numerical recording and sorting products. Previously, each salesman could sell only his own product line. Also, the decision maker in the customer company could be involved with several NCR salesmen, no one of whom could know the sum total of the customer's numerical control needs, let alone serve them. Under the new system, the same retail industry salesman who sells an NCR cash register to a department store can also search out and serve the store's needs for NCR accounting machines, data entry terminals, and a mainframe computer. If he needs help, he can organize a team with other NCR salesmen that can bring the required strength to his proposal. The product groups he sells are still manufactured separately; the centralized sales approach is the innovation that makes the difference.

By selling groups or systems of products through a single salesman or sales team, rather than selling individual products through many uncoordinated salesmen, NCR believes it can help customers achieve greater profit improvement. It can prescribe systems that solve comprehensive problems which would otherwise remain immune to single product solutions. Management also believes it can expand its profitable sales volume by selling larger packages and insulating its position against competition.

Each vocational market's full range of recording and sorting needs is becoming better known to NCR personnel. In turn, by specializing in seeking out and serving these needs, each of NCR's vocational sales organizations can become known for expertise in its market, almost as if it were an independent specialist company. Moreover, every sales group can utilize the total financial and technical resources of the company for professional counsel and support in developing, prescribing, and installing product systems.

Operations & Options A vice president of marketing directs NCR's sales organization. The four vocational vice presidents report to him. Regional vocational directors supervise several states, giving a geographic underlay to the organization.

NCR's next step in marketcentering through its sales force is to specialize more precisely. This can logically lead to the appointment of retail specialists within the financial industry sales force, to mention one possibility. As additional ramifications of the new approach become apparent, NCR will be able to reorganize many other aspects of its corporate structure and operations, increasing its market orientation. Among the major options which will be open to the company are decentralizing staff services, bring-

EXHIBIT II Strategic Business Centers at General Foods

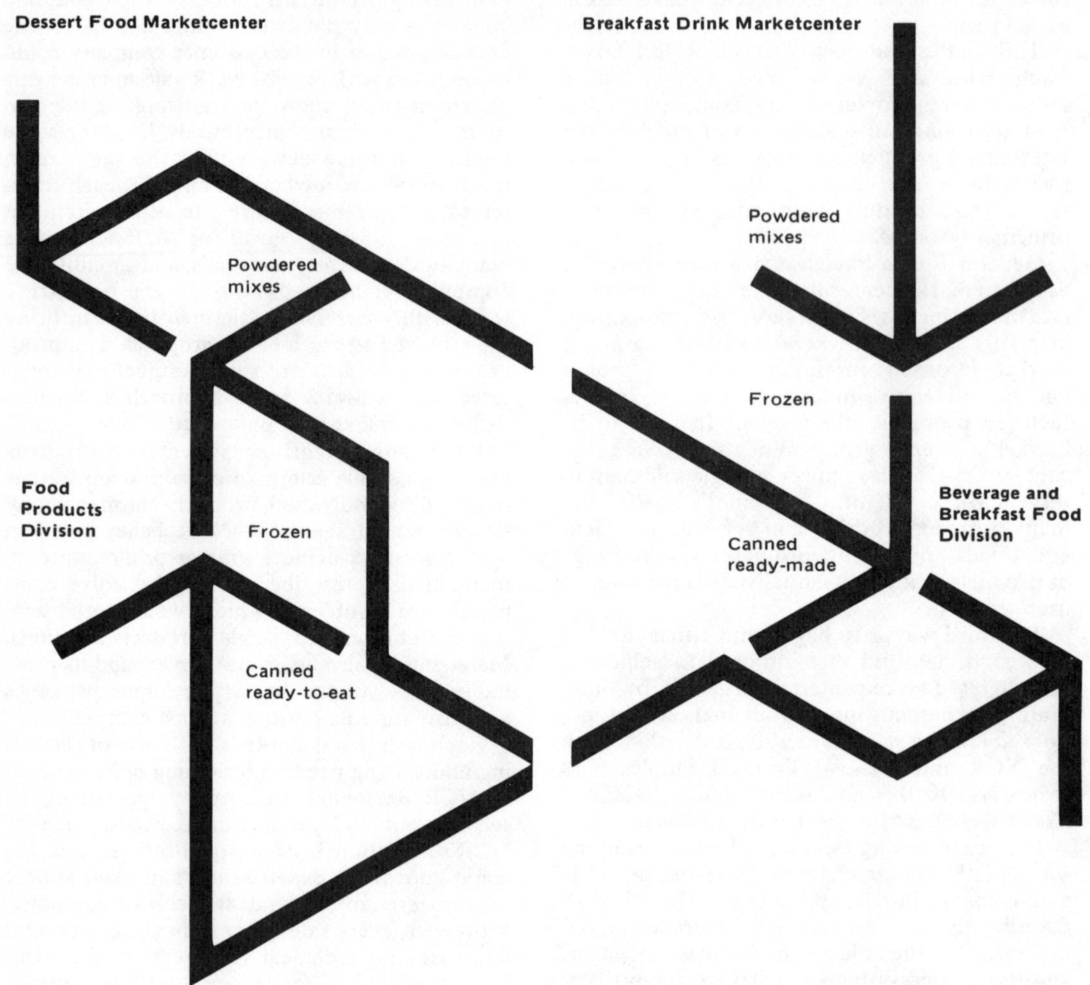

ing R&D and product development activities into closer vocational alignment, adding profit-making services to existing product systems, consolidating advertising and other promotional activities to appeal specifically to vocational needs, and combining the appropriate manufacturing and selling activities in marketcentered divisions.

GENERAL FOODS'S APPROACH—SEPARATE MARKETING DIVISIONS

While NCR has been stimulated to reorganize by the increasing preferences of its customers for systems and by the relentless competitive pressures of IBM, General Foods revised its approach because of internal strains and frustrations. In the early 1970s new product winners either stopped coming out of product development at their former rate or carried an unreasonable cost. Better knowledge of the needs of its consumers was obviously required if the company's product developers were to harmonize their technologies with the new life-styles influencing the demand for processed foods. At the same time, the needs of the company's customers at the retail level required new responses. Competitive brands were proliferating, clamoring for shelf and display space, while an increasingly attractive profit on sales was making private-label products more acceptable to the major supermarket chains.

These events combined to place unprecedented strains on the company's divisional structure, which was the legacy of a generations-old policy of acquisition. General Foods's major

EXHIBIT II (Continued)

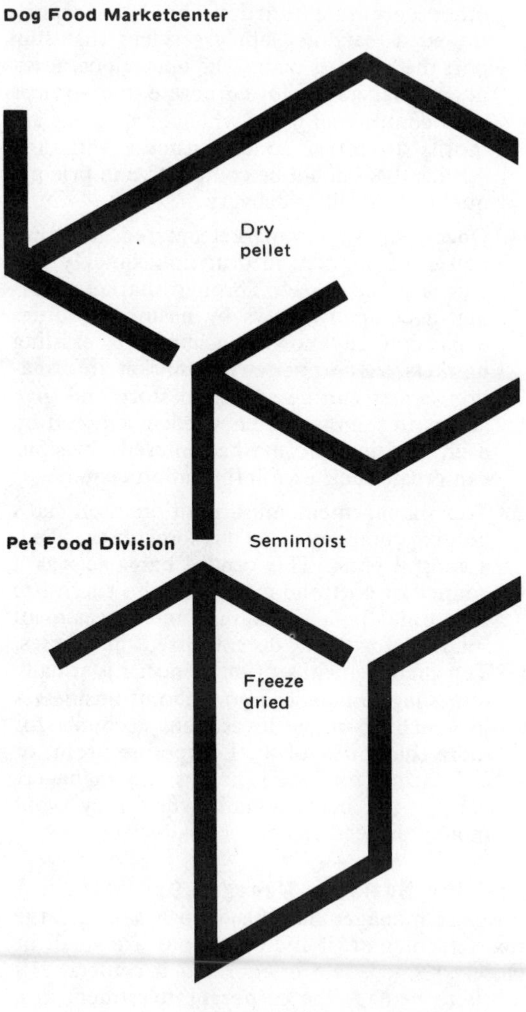

Dog Food Marketcenter

Dry pellet

Pet Food Division

Semimoist

Freeze dried

food divisions—Birds Eye, Jell-O, Post, and Kool-Aid—had evolved historically, each according to the process technology which it brought into the company. As the scope of each division's product categories grew, it was inevitable that one division's consumer provinces would be impinged on by other divisions, and that any given market would be served in a fragmented rather than a concentrated manner. Divisional sovereignties frequently made it impossible for the company to dominate a market that was served by two or more divisions with related product categories but with different styles and degrees of commitment.

Often more damaging for new-product development was the way in which division managers respected a no-man's-land between their provinces, leaving gaps in product categories that could give competitors a clear shot or deny the company a chance to establsh a position of category leadership. Beverages are a case in point. They were marketed by three divisions. If they were frozen, they were marketed by Birds Eye. If they were powdered mixes, the Kool-Aid division marketed them. Breakfast drinks had to come from Post. No centralized attack on consumer beverage needs could be made. In a similar fashion, puddings were marketed by two divisions: Birds Eye had jurisdiction over frozen puddings while Jell-O was the steward division for powdered mixes. The pudding market as such had no general representative within the company.

Relating Products to Market Needs The General Foods approach to marketcentering has been to reorganize its process-oriented divisional structure into separate marketing organizations known as "strategic business units" (SBUs). Each SBU concentrates on marketing families of products made by different processing technologies but consumed by the same market segment. As *Exhibit II* shows, the Food Products division coordinates the marketing strategy for all desserts whether they are in frozen, powdered, or ready-to-eat form. The exhibit also shows how the Beverage and Breakfast Food division markets breakfast drinks of three different processing techniques and how the Pet Food division centers the marketing of freeze-dried, dry pellet, and semimoist dog foods.

This scheme allows each SBU to take an overview of how an entire product family can best be related to the needs of both end users and retailers. Each SBU functions like a division and draws on the full range of corporate technologies. It also derives support services from a corporate pool where market research, production, personnel, new-product development, and sales are consolidated for use by all SBUs. A small amount of product-connected market research and new-product development is still left to the individual SBUs. But their primary mission is to engage in "pure marketing" as much as possible and to concentrate their resources on cultivating the market segments to which they have been assigned.

Among the benefits that General Foods believes it has gained so far from its form of marketcentering are an increasingly productive trade merchandising capability and improved ability to dominate a full consumer-need category at the point of sale—the supermarket. The company has also had better opportunities to aim multiple-product advertising at a single market, with the result that preferences for company brands have risen in certain product categories.

Another benefit has been that new products can be launched with fewer problems of stewardship than before. To take a hypothetical example, suppose that skin care products were to become part of the corporate growth scheme. If one proposed item were to be packaged in frozen form, it would not have to start its market life in the Birds Eye division, as presumably would have been necessary in the past, and therefore labor under the potentially negative connotations of having vegetable origins. Or, if the new skin care product were to be a premoistened patty or a water-soluable pellet, it would not have to be marketed under the umbrella of the Gaines pet food division.

GUIDELINES FOR DEVELOPMENT

In sketching the main guidelines that product- or process-centered companies can use to change to a marketcentered approach, I shall place special emphasis on two areas. One is the key criteria of marketcentering. The other is the role of the manager who runs a marketcenter and the unique aspects of his supportive service system.

Key Criteria When an organization is fully marketcentered, a market becomes the focal point of every one of the company's major operations. The objective of each business is to become its market's preferred center for fulfilling one or more principal needs. Such a business is the sum of its marketcentered divisions and should meet these five criteria:

1. It must be chartered to serve a market which is defined according to a system of closely related needs. This permits the market to be served by a diversified package of products and services that, taken together, supply a combination of closely related benefits. The business may market two or more related products in a single sale or market a package composed of products and their related services.
2. Because a marketcenter is operated as a profit center it should be administered by an entrepreneur. I like to call this executive the *business manager* of the organization. Unlike most product managers and brand managers, or even market managers who are merely profit-accountable, a business manager is fully profit-responsible. He enjoys considerable authority in running his business. He commands the key decisions. He sets prices, controls costs, and is charged with operating his marketcenter for a satisfactory profit.
3. Business managers are the chief line officers in their marketcentered organizations. All other corporate functions must be repositioned as satellite supply services that support the business managers' operations. Business managers employ corporate staff services on a contractual basis, which gives them authority to refuse to do business with any service that cannot be competitive in pricing, quality control, or delivery.
4. Once a division is marketcentered, its storehouse of market information quickly becomes its key asset. Through marketcentering, a company grows by basing its future expansion on knowledge about its existing markets. A corporatewide market information center can be set up to store and give access to the market knowledge required by each division, or marketcentered divisions can create their own information centers.
5. Top management must position itself as a holding company or, as it is sometimes called, a central bank. This central bank acts as a council of portfolio managers who centralize corporate policy making and investment funding for their decentralized businesses. Top management's prime concern is usually to manage a balanced portfolio of businesses in which no single investment accounts for more than 50% of total corporate profit, or at least not for long. The business managers consult the central bank when they want money or need advice.

How the Business Manager Operates A business manager may head up a single, large marketcenter or, if the operations are small or closely related, two or more such centers. His job is to manage the corporate investment in a center so that it will yield the maximum rate of return. At Textron, for example, a minimum pretax return on investment of 25% is mandated for every one of the company's businesses. At ITT, the manager's contribution must fall within the 10% to 12% annual range of increase in earnings.

As a result of his concentration on financial bogeys, a marketcenter's business manager tends to view himself as a profit creator rather than a curator of specific products or processes. He resists becoming addicted to any particular product line or acquiring a reverence for any technological process. "In my marketing mix, I recognize no such thing as an eternal product," one business manager told me. "Nor do I cherish any perpetual promotional appeals for them. Even the customer needs that I serve today will probably prove to be transient. Only my commitment to maximize the long-range profit of my marketcenter is everlasting."

Supportive Systems While marketcentering decentralizes the management of operations, it centralizes many of the staff services which business managers use. As *Exhibit III* shows, up to four consolidated service functions may revolve around each business manager.

Development services combine new-market research and development with new-product R&D under a single director. In this way, the market orientation of R&D—historically one of the chief stumbling blocks in raising a company's level of consciousness to its customers—is accomplished organizationally. New-market needs, new-process technology, and new-product development are able to interact harmoniously rather than competitively. With marketcentering, the traditional vice presidential functions for marketing and R&D can be subsumed under the director of development's functions. There is generally no need for a vice president of marketing in such an organization because the entire corporate structure is market-oriented and each business manager must act as his own chief marketing officer.

Control services do the basic research to evaluate the effectiveness of established product and service-system marketing. They also provide the necessary recruitment, compensation and motivation, training and development, legal, and financial functions. *Production services* coordinate engineering and manufacturing operations. And *promotion services* combine sales, advertising, and publicity.

These four groups of services are supplied by top management on an elective basis. Whether and when they are used depends on the business manager. Should he elect to contract with the internal services, he negotiates with the service managers as if they were outside suppliers.

Contracting for Service Any one, or all four, of his company's internal services may be retained, either in whole or in part, by a business manager. As the following position description indicates, the business manager is also chartered to employ outside services whenever he feels they can better help him meet his objectives:

> Through an annual contractual relationship with the director of production services, the business manager acquires a product supply to market. The business manager must, at minimal cost, negotiate for a dependable and sufficient supply of products, manufactured according to marketable specifications, that maintain maximum economies in production without impairing either market acceptance or corporate image.

Since the business manager has ultimate responsibility for profit, he must be free to negotiate with any strategic service that meets his product and market specifications at minimal cost. Much, if not most, of the time, these services will come from inside the company. But he can also buy them from outside and use them interchangeably with, or independently of, internal functions. In either case, the contractual form of doing business acts as his principal instrument of cost and quality control.

The service contract can also be an instrument of top management control. Making the use of internal services optional puts them squarely on their mettle. They must perform for the business managers, competing with alternate sources of supply in cost and quality terms, or be bypassed. If internal services are consistently selected by most business managers, top management can comfortably assume that they are competitive; if the services are rejected, that is a sign that they are not doing the job.

Ensuring Continued Service. From each business manager's point of view, being on the receiving end of a demand-feed schedule with contracted services is an almost ideal situation. Best quality at lowest price, every manager's dream, seems assured. But will there be chaos among the suppliers of services? To discourage an endless series of requests for custom-tailored variations in services, especially in production and promotion, a variance-request control system can be installed. Under this system, market-based justification can be required for all significant departures from contracted specifications.

However, it may be necessary to go further. What can be done to protect an internal supplier of services from having to react simultaneously to short-term strategy changes by several business managers? While a predictable problem area such as seasonal production peaks can be rather simply ironed out in advance, no service can fully anticipate a business manager's mid-cycle decision changes. He may need to alter his product mix in the face of sudden raw materials shortages. New corporate policies on allocating scarce ingredients or components may shut off his supply. Demand variations among his key customers may dry up one or more markets and force him to shift his product specifications to meet the needs of a previously less important customer group. Such stresses can disrupt R&D priorities, throw off manufacturing runs, scuttle cost estimates, and upset sales and advertising appropriations.

EXHIBIT III Supporting Services Available to a Business Manager

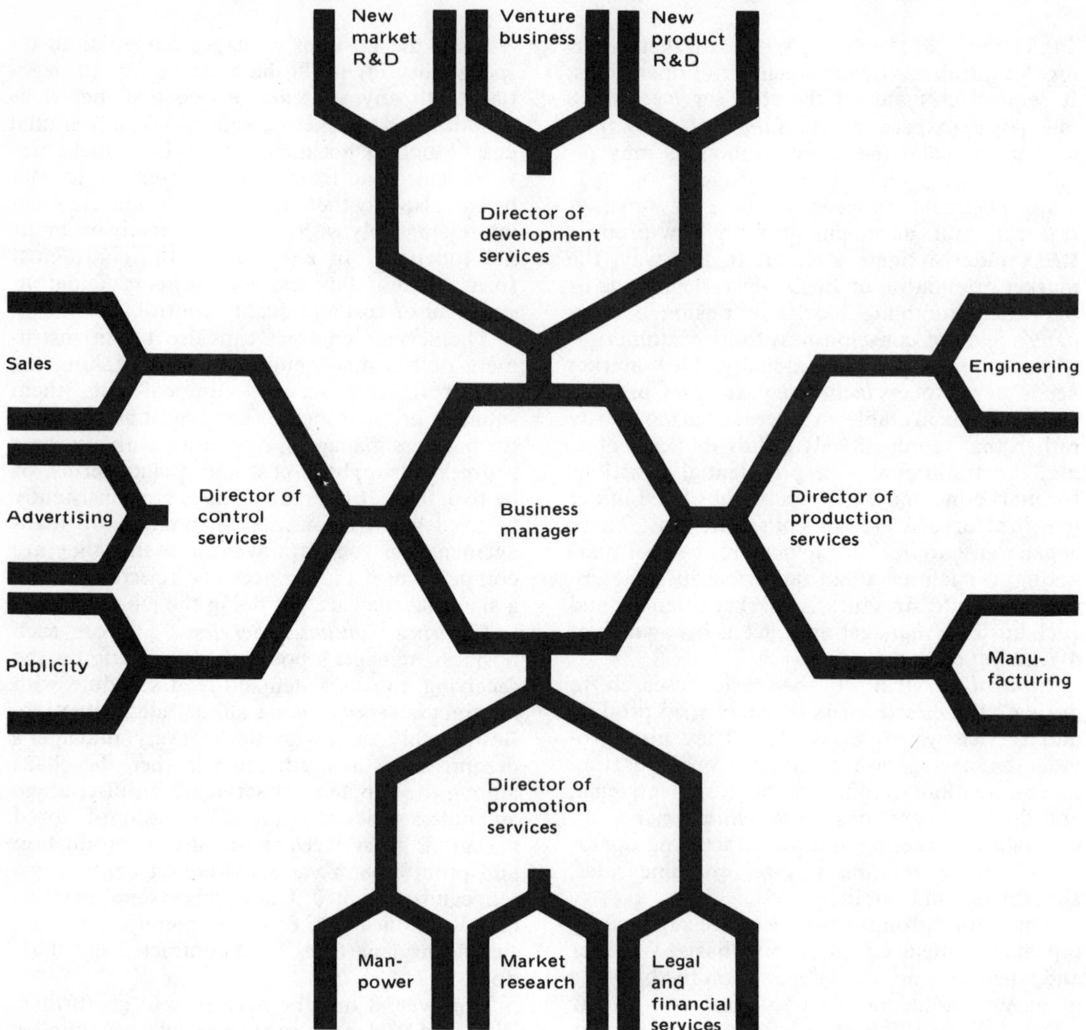

TWO-WAY GROWTH OPPORTUNITY

Some corporate executives feel that marketcentering may come to rank with Alfred Sloan's decentralization of General Motors along market-segmented lines. They see themselves regaining a customer focus that often became blurred by Procter & Gamble's brand management system. While contemporary with Sloan's market awareness, brand management directed the styles of many corporate formats away from customers and back to products. When product and brand management were imposed on the traditional organization of the manufacturing division and on the pyramidal organization chart, which was adapted for the needs of commercial business from Von Möltke's general staff concept, progress toward marketcentering slowed for half a century.

In the mid 1960s, the beginning of a new thrust toward the customer was signaled by the advent of free-form marketing groups. They were allowed to cut across corporate pyramids whenever unusual market sensitivity was demanded in an operation. A variety of problem-solving task forces and project management teams came into being for much the same reason; they represented jerry-built improvisations to defeat a product oriented or process centered organizational system. In other instances, managers have had to depart from the accepted corporate framework and to create highly decentralized conglomerates of market-targeted businesses.

Since it is probable that these dislocations will be with us for some time to come, methods for coping with them are under experimentation. Some companies are establishing resource allocation groups, composed of the directors of development, control, production, and promotion services, who recommend to top management the most favorable distribution patterns in times of materials short-falls. Their suggestions are based on the central criterion of close-in contribution to profit but are naturally conditioned by short- and long-term considerations, such as maintenance of the traditional market position, potential for future growth, and possible preemptive reactions from competitors.

Because a marketcentered company expands chiefly by serving new needs in established markets where it is well franchised, its growth is relatively safe. By asking and reasking the key question, "What *other* needs of the markets we know so well can we serve profitably?" management can develop new business on the basis of the strength of its existing businesses.

Marketcentering a company can give it two-way flexibility for growth. Each of its major markets can be served *intensively*, once it is established as the center of a business. When growth on a broadened profit base becomes desirable, the same markets can be served more *extensively* by searching out their closely related needs and centering new businesses around one or more of them. Through these two approaches, the basic growth strategy of a marketcentered company can be defined as meeting the greatest number of interrelated needs of every market segment it serves.

34 PRODUCT MANAGEMENT: PANACEA OR PANDORA'S BOX?*

Robert M. Fulmer

Despite its climb to popularity during the recent "marketing revolution," product management has failed to satisfy the hopes of some of its more optimistic adopters. The divergence between the highly touted theoretical potentials of product management and the conflict and confusion which occasionally followed its adoption has led some observers and practitioners to conclude that this organizational innovation is an impractical, unworkable, and unrealistic method of centering responsibility for the success of a product or product line. Yet, without question, there are several large, multiproduct companies where product management has provided a remarkably efficient method for coordinating and focusing the functional activities of the firm so as to gain a maximum amount of attention and activity for each product marketed.

How Can the Same Concept Be Both a Panacea and a Pandora's Box? A cursory analysis of published reports and empirical observations of product management in practice reveal that most of the difficulties mentioned revolve around the following problems: authority, selection, and definition.

Authority: How Much and What Kind? While it is impossible to give a universal answer to this question, it is unlikely that companies which exact responsibility for total product success without granting commensurate authority can expect the same results as a firm where the product manager is used as a coordinative center of authority to insure unified effort on behalf of each product. Similarly, it is doubtful that a staff assistant, salesman, or clerk can be as effective in working for a product's over-all success as the "president of a company within a company." Yet, positions with such varying degrees of authority are often discussed together under the heading of product management. This article will not attempt to provide an exact recipe for the authority and responsibility to be given product managers, but an overview of the existing spectrum of product-oriented positions will be given and conclusions drawn as to the practicality of this indiscriminate classification.

Selection: Traits or Training? Obviously, the ability to delegate authority and exact responsibility will depend on the talents of the employees involved and the degree to which these talents have been cultivated or utilized. There is no magic in the product management concept; consequently, the idea can be no more effective than the men who fill the positions.

Some companies find it desirable to recruit men expressly for development as product managers. Other firms feel that prior experience in one of the company's functional departments is essential. Certain general managerial traits such as the ability to accept responsibility, to think creatively and practically, to act quickly, and to work harmoniously with other departments are necessary. In every instance, a period of training directed toward the requirements of product management will increase effectiveness. Staffing problems are as unique as individual companies; therefore, any detailed analysis would be applicable only in the situation studied. The reservoir of available managerial talent certainly must be considered in any attempt to plan or evaluate the use of product management.

* Reprinted by permission from the *California Management Review*, vol. 7, no. 4, pp. 63–74, Summer, 1965. Mr. Fulmer is George R. Brown Professor of Management, Trinity University.

Definition: Does Everyone Understand? Almost every problem found in product management literature relates, in some way, to improper or misunderstood definitions. A primary step in the solution of difficulties connected with authority delegation and selection is a definite statement of the requirements of the position. With this as a foundation, authority can be delegated and individuals can be selected and trained in view of the requirements. While a general understanding of the terms used in discussing product management is important for all persons interested in this aspect of organization, the need for specificity is paramount for intrafirm understanding. In other words, if a term is misused, it can still prove of value if all personnel within a firm have the same understanding of its meaning.

I will attempt to move toward possible clarifications of these problems by analyzing the various ways in which different practitioners and scholars approach them, discarding the obviously incorrect, and discussing the relative merits of the acceptable theories.

A CONFUSING HISTORY

Origin of Product Management The history of product management provides an interesting insight into its initiating philosophy and can serve as a yardstick by which the later developments may be compared. Product management in its initial form appears to have first been practiced as brand management at Procter and Gamble nearly forty years ago. Since that time, product management has produced an outstanding genealogy (probably including such ramifications as project management, task teams, and, of course, brand management in its various forms). Some of these successors bear little resemblance to the original form of this organizational innovation. Perhaps the multiplicity of members in the product management family has made it difficult to pinpoint the exact birth of the idea. Certainly no aspect of this subject provides a better illustration of the misunderstanding and confusion which pervade the literature. Consider, for example, several absolute statements as to the origin of this idea.

- The concept of product management is not new. Probably it originated in the retail trade, in this case in the department stores.[1]
- Since the product manager concept was originally developed by General Electric in the early 1950's, most large companies have adopted the approach in one way or another.[2]
- The product manager originated accidentally —first as an assistant sales manager with an interest in a particular product or group of products.[3]
- An analysis of the concept's history will provide some clues. The product manager's job was created primarily to fill a critical need. In large, multiproduct companies, it has always been difficult to be certain that each product received the attention and support it merited from each of various functional activities of the business, especially manufacturing, marketing, and sales. . . . Therefore, to meet this need, the product manager form of organization was created.[4]
- It has been suggested that the rapid expansion of product lines and the need for developing specialized marketing strategies about specific products were the key points indicating a need for the product management function. . . . Initially the task of the product manager was one of a coordinator, trying to harmonize the manufacturing and marketing activities associated with his products. Gradually authority was delegated to him to make decisions regarding product improvement, packaging, pricing, field selling, advertising, etc. As authority was increased, the final responsibility for profits and market position was delegated to him.[5]
- Often mistakenly thought of as a comparatively new marketing creature, in Procter and Gamble, the brand manager goes back to 1931, when now-chairman Neil McElroy formalized that role in the company.[6]

It is possible that the idea of having one individual with primary responsibility for a group of products originated in the department store; however, the department head of a retail store is no more a product manager than is the production chief of a factory producing similar items or any manager with responsibility for some phase of the life cycle of one or more related products.

General Electric is often credited with ushering in the marketing concept with its reorganization in the early 1950's. While this distinction is somewhat dubious, without question there were companies employing product managers before the 1950's.

The position referred to as "product manager" in some companies may have evolved from "an assistant sales manager with an interest in a particular product or group of products." There is, however, little evidence that this title was so applied before 1928, and, as will be discussed later, there is reason to challenge the accuracy of using the title to describe specialized sales positions.

CREATION OF THE BRAND MAN

Although, and perhaps because, they lack any degree of specificity as to date and source of origin, it is difficult to question the statements cited from Ames or Schiff and Mellman previously quoted. There should be universal agreement that the job of product manager was created to fill the need to provide vigorous product-by-product leadership for multi-product companies. This view is supported in the *Printers' Ink* article of September 28, 1962, in which Procter and Gamble's Neil McElroy is credited with originating that company's brand-man organization in 1931. Actually the brand-man system began its evolution in this company even earlier. In January, 1928, Mr. C. C. Uhling was made Procter and Gamble's first brand manager when Lava soap was assigned to him. Later, brand-man assignments were made for Oxydol and Camay.[7] In 1931, the recommendation of McElroy was instrumental in refining the brand-man system and in making it a company-wide concept. This refinement consisted basically in the creation of the brand group hierarchy composed of an assistant brand man, who was to perform much of the detail involved in the management of a particular brand and to serve as an understudy of his superior; the brand man; and the brand-group supervisors, each responsible for reviewing the work of two to four brand managers, who reported to the head of the brand-promotion division.[8] To date, this company has enjoyed almost unparalleled success with little change in orientation or scope of the concept.

It is impossible to determine all the factors which influenced the thinking of those associated with the birth and development of this idea. However, it is possible that the reorganization of Du Pont and General Motors several years before had helped initiate the thought processes which led to this evolution by providing a working example of the product-oriented divisionalization. Ease of coordinating, by brand, the activities of advertising agencies was another possible contributing factor.[9] Certainly, the primary motivation appears to have been the desire to guarantee individual management for each of a number of products.

WHAT DOES THE TITLE MEAN?

What Is a Product Manager? Perhaps a portion of the problems besetting product management stem from a fundamental lack of understanding or confusion about what is meant by the term. There is a wide spectrum of meanings attached to this term which were not implied at its birth.

One extreme of the range is found in firms such as the National Biscuit Company where one product manager handles everything that pertains to the products except the actual selling—among his responsibilities are product quality, packaging, marketing, advertising, and promotion programs. One product manager handles these responsibilities for Dromedary cake mixes, nut rolls, pimientos, dates, fruits, and peels.[10] In essence this job could be accurately referred to as vice-president of a product division or simply as a division manager; the same holds true where the term "product manager" is used to describe General Electric's general managers. This is somewhat equivalent to calling the head of General Motor's Chevrolet Division a product manager. To avoid confusion, it is wise to differentiate between the titles of the executive who is in charge of a multiproduct division and the manager who has responsibility for a single product.

Examples of companies where real product or brand managers have extensive responsibility would include the following:

- At **Pillsbury,** the man who bears the title, brand manager, has total accountability for results. He directs the marketing of his product as if it were his own business. Production does its job, and finance keeps the profit figures. Otherwise, the brand manager has total responsibility for marketing his product. This responsibility encompasses pricing, commercial research, competitive activity, home service, and publicity coordination, legal details, budgets, advertising plans, sales promotion, and execution of plans.[11]
- Each of **Kimberly-Clark's** brand managers is responsible for drawing up complete marketing programs for his brand. . . . In addition (to serving as advertising manager for his product), the brand manager is responsible for recommending marketing objectives for his brand, planning marketing strategy, drawing proposed budgets, initiating new projects and programs, and coordinating the work of all functional units concerned with the production, financing, and marketing of the product.[12]
- At **Colgate-Palmolive,** product managers are responsible for developing plans and programs that will establish brand leadership and enlarge the current and long-range

share of market and profits for their brands. These plans include advertising and promotional programs and budgets, selection of distribution channels, forecasts of sales and inventory requirements, forecasts of manufacturing costs, and, as final objectives, projections of profit and share of market on the brands.[13]

- Men employed for this work (at **Procter and Gamble**) are trained to accept the responsibility for the effectiveness of the overall advertising and promotion effort on an important nationally advertised brand. . . . These positions involve working with many company departments, including research and development on product development, the sales department on the development of promotions and also with the advertising agency on all phases of consumer planning for the brand.[14]

At the other end of the spectrum from these consumer-oriented producers are some companies such as **Minneapolis-Honeywell** where:

> . . . the divisional executives in charge of selling temperature controls to the school market decided to appoint a "product manager" . . . who was charged with the broad responsibility of securing more business in this field. . . . Basically a salesman . . . sales management must select its man with great care.[15]

In his study of the semi-conductor industry, Bucklin observed that product managers were frequently required to spend 50 per cent of their time in calling on accounts.[16] Ames refers to an anonymous company where a product manager's role is really limited to maintaining sales statistics and performing a variety of high-grade clerical tasks.[17] Mauser makes the general claim that: "Sales managers for products may be given the simple title of product manager."[18]

R. H. Buskirk recognizes the divergent uses of the product manager title and asserts that: "The dimensions of his job vary widely from company to company, sometimes embracing all the activities of product management and sometimes being limited to the sales promotion of the products in his care."[19]

It appears that Professor Buskirk believes that a product manager does not necessarily handle the work of product management, for he defines product management as:

> The planning, direction, and control of all phases of the life cycle of products, including the creation or discovery of ideas for new products, the screening of such ideas, the coordination of the work of research and physical development of products, their packaging and branding, their introduction on the market, their market development, their modification, the discovery of new uses for them, their repair and servicing, and their deletion.[20]

From a descriptive standpoint, there is no doubt that in many companies "product managers" find their positions much more narrow than the description of product management. A normative view, however, should place considerable emphasis on bringing these two concepts together. The problem of management semantics, eloquently recognized by Col. Lyndall Urwick,[21] will continue to rear its ugly head and breed confusion and misunderstanding as long as commonly used terms such as these two have such a diversity of meaning and application.

While it is impossible to generalize from one article, a recent German publication[22] indicates that such confusion may not be so prevalent in that country. While the brand manager system is practiced only by some companies which are based in the United States and a few German firms in the food, detergent, and electrical industries, it is evidently practiced quite satisfactorily. If the German experience is indeed less chaotic than product management history in the United States, it may be due to the fact that United States companies are not likely to export the concept until they have eliminated most of the major difficulties in domestic practice. Consequently, a descriptive definition of product management in Germany should provide helpful insight into a type considered hardy enough to export. A review of the article suggests the following areas of product management activity:

1 / Marketing analysis (product, packaging, price, assortment, channels of distribution).

2 / Setting of marketing goals.

3 / Long- and short-range planning and budgeting.

4 / Coordination of work done by departments within a company as well as by "outsiders" (marketing research, selling, advertising, public relations, production, technical research, financing).

5 / Control.[23]

In a report prepared for the Financial Executives' Research Foundation, Schiff and Mellman describe the product manager as "the executive responsible for product management."[24] This definition may appear to be circular reasoning, but it may be expanded to say that a product manager must manage something; if he does not exercise the managerial functions of planning, direction, and control in relation to the entire scope of a product's immediate existence, he is something less than a product manager and should be appropriately renamed. Though overly simple, this is infinitely superior to saying that a product manager does not necessarily manage a product or that he may manage only one aspect of its existence. This definition does not require that all phases of a product's life cycle (from idea origination to termination of production) be exclusively the domain of one individual, but it does require management as one of the identifying characteristics of a product manager.

The Product Manager and His Authority

> The (product manager) concept is an organization anomaly in that it violates a proven management precept—that responsibility should always be matched by equivalent authority . . . (he is) a member of the management group with high level responsibility for getting a product to market without any line authority over the full range of activities required to get the job done.[25]

An equally extreme position concerning the product manager is taken by R. H. Jacobs who asserts:

> His is not, in essence, a management job but a staff job whose sole responsibility is to secure wider sales of one or more specific items in the line.[26]

Practically speaking, the major problem in applying the product-manager concept may well be how much and what kind of authority to delegate. The quotations cited above indicate that little, if any, line authority is available to the product manager to carry out his myriad responsibilities. Bucklin found that the lack of real authority was the basis for many of the problems encountered by product managers in the semi-conductor firms.[27] *Printers' Ink* reports that, at Merck & Co., "each product manager is a staff member whose primary function is to plan for the growth and profitability of his markets."[28] The same publication generalizes:

> Few companies sharply delineate the product manager's area of operations, as between line and staff function; most of them give him heavy responsibility, though not with commensurate authority.[29]

It is small wonder that the product manager concept has recently been receiving sharp criticism. It is impossible to imagine that a manager can coordinate and manage all aspects of the life cycle of a product with his hands tied in a manner such as described above. Fortunately, this situation is not universal. In those companies which give the product manager the responsibility for product management, there appears to be general agreement that such responsibility must be matched with comparable authority. At least the product manager is not always an "organization anomaly." Professor Edward Bursk has well summarized:

> We have reached the point where we need solid action that cuts across the traditional, functional lines of marketing, finance, manufacturing, research, and so on. Finance may have to consider the desirability of capitalizing initial heavy promotional expenses, manufacturing may have to build inventories faster than is apparently economical. . . . All in all, there must be one man or one office to see that all these steps are taken as part of a unified effort. . . . Those in charge may be merely in a staff capacity, or may have varying degrees of line authority depending on how far this concept (usually referred to as product or brand management) has developed.[30]

In a similar vein, Professor Hepner states that the product manager's job requires that he be endowed with authority to get things done:

> Product managers are a kind of "general manager." . . . The product manager, working under the general direction of a top manager or executive, decides how products shall be made, the quantities to be made, the chains of distribution for each, its packaging, pricing, advertising, and promotion. The product manager is more than a coordinator—he is the final authority whose decisions affect the profits to be made from his products.[31]

A previous attempt was made to define **product manager** so as to include only those individuals who were responsible for **product management.** At this point, it is proper to add to that definition the requirement that he should also possess adequate authority to handle the needs of his position. This apparently obvious truism has not been universally understood. While this authority cannot be absolute, unlimited, or unchecked, it must exist in sufficient quantity to allow use of the product manager's specialized knowledge and abilities. Bursk's poignant implication that the amount of line authority delegated is an indication of the degree to which the product-management concept has developed should provide real understanding of the product manager's job. There are clearly many companies where the concept, while supposedly employed, is in a state of considerable immaturity.

The Product Manager in Practice As employed in several companies, the product manager may have line authority in one specialized area of operation—advertising, sales, etc., or perhaps more commonly, general marketing—and functional authority (a slice of delimited line authority which cuts across organizational lines)[32] for the coordination of the activities of other departments **as they relate to his product.** For example, he might be directly in charge of advertising plans for the product and at the same time work closely with liaison members of the sales, market research, legal, art, production, merchandising, and sales promotion, packaging, and public relations departments. In his dealings with these departments, he is able to direct them to supply the services necessary to insure the maximum efficiency of the marketing program for his product. Under most circumstances, the representative of the service department works with several brand or product managers and, with proper planning, should be able to handle their various demands without undue conflict.

AN EXAMPLE

To illustrate, consider a typical situation where a sales force handles all of a division's six products. The very real problem of having all six product managers requesting special emphasis for their products' fall promotion could be handled by coordinative planning or appeal to a final authority. Promotional plans for the year should spell out which brands are free to promote in each selling period. At the time of plan formulation, questions and potential conflicts should be worked out between the individual product managers working in concert with their immediate superior and the division's sales manager. While the product manager focuses the coordination of the company's functional and service activities toward his product, in this case, the marketing division manager would probably hold the final power of decision to insure over-all coordination. Should situations arise during the year which forced deviations from the plan, the division manager would again serve as the ultimate appeal. Similar situations could, of course, be presented that would apply to relations with other functional or service departments.

From the foregoing discussion, it can be seen that, since he cannot hold total line authority such as is exercised by the president of a one-product company or by the division manager of a single-product division, the optimum use of the product manager should come when he is used as coordinating executive in charge of managing all component parts of the marketing mix of one particular product or brand and subject primarily to the final coordination of a superior in charge of the entire division or company.

LIMITS OF AUTHORITY

Functional authority is never absolute; therefore, the product manager does not have complete authority over all departments in the marketing program. In dealing with production, for example, his authority would have to be limited to the range of alternatives considered by production to be technically feasible. The legal department would, of necessity, determine limits to the potential activities of the brand; market research should be free to determine what research projects are practical and likely to provide the desired information; accounting would need the ability to limit activities to the financially feasible, etc. In other words, these departments could and should set parameters of operation within which the product manager should be free to work and, in turn, to request the services of and/or direct the activities of these departments within the limits which they themselves have set.

The authority level principle[33] (which implies that for any problem there is a level of authority at which a decision can be made for its resolution) provides one remedy for conflicts which might result from this reciprocal interdependence. Many problems can, however, be avoided by careful planning and definition of the product manager's tasks, authorities, and responsibilities.

The Product Manager—How Far from Ideal? Paradoxically, the perfect product manager is not a product manager at all. Probably the only person who would completely satisfy the definition given would be the president of a single-product firm. Obviously, the concept has wider applicability than this. Many firms have attempted to approach the ideal by adopting what is frequently referred to as the "little general manager approach." In these cases, however, there must be a "big general manager" to coordinate activities and to resolve conflicts arising from the divergent points of view held by various product managers. Other companies approach the problem by giving product managers authority only to advise. We have indicated in the preceding discussion, however, that staff specialists should not be considered in the same category as the true product manager.

As mentioned above, no product manager can possess final line authority if several executives are employed in this capacity. Similarly, if only staff authority is employed, the product manager is no longer able to manage his product. The answer obviously lies in the judicious delegation of functional authority.

While the specific responsibilities of the product manager will vary according to the needs of a particular situation or the interest of the individual company adopting the concept, the rule of thumb for allocating authority must be that the product manager should always have sufficient authority to discharge the responsibilities associated with or assigned to his position. Unless this basic tenet of management theory is recognized, the product manager can be nothing more than an "organization anomaly" completely incapable of satisfying the demands made of him. This places a large measure of the success of product management in the realm of position description; for without adequate definition at this level, commensurate authority cannot be made available.

A very similar organizational concept, although it usually has an engineering or production orientation rather than a marketing emphasis and is usually less permanent than product management, is project management. Basically,

> Project management is a general management activity encompassing planning, control, supervision, and the engineering or manufacturing involved in producing the end item. . . . The project manager has very specific objectives which, when achieved, mean the end of his function. He usually has no line authority over the organizations producing the items which he must deliver. . . . Communications must be very clear, prompt, comprehensive, and frequently cut across intercompany and intracompany lines.[34]

Baumgartner suggests that although project management had its origin during World War II, it was 1958 before companies began to set up organization structures which superimposed a horizontal project organization on vertical functional lines.[35]

Figure 1 shows such an organization cutting across functional lines in order to accomplish project objectives.

FIGURE 1 Organizational Structure

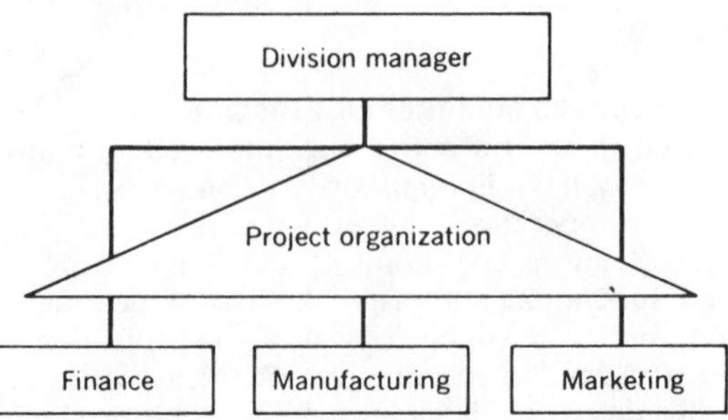

A more familiar method of showing the relationship of product and project managers to other departments is the so-called "grid management" approach shown in the simplest form in Figure 2.

FIGURE 2 "Grid Management" Structure

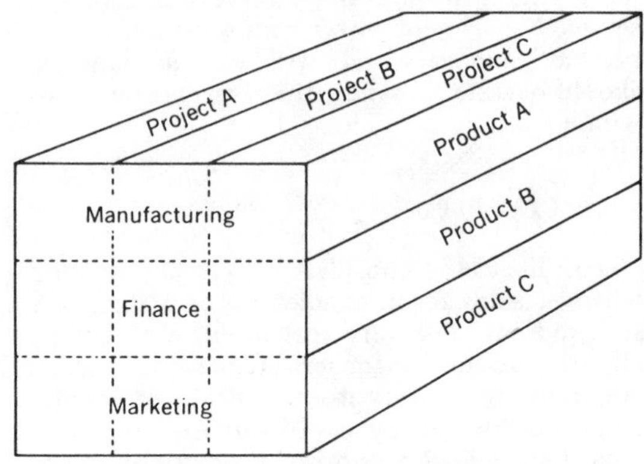

In project management, as with product management, it is impossible for complete authority to be granted in the various areas of responsibility. But at the same time, absolute responsibility cannot be exacted in these areas. It would bé incorrect to refer to a product manager as "ideal" only when he possesses complete line authority for each of his myriad responsibilities; in fact this would be chaotic even if it were possible. A situation is ideal when it functions efficiently in its particular environment.

MEANING VS. APPLICATION

Managers of Products, Markets, and Marketing Understanding of product management has been substantially clouded by an overlapping of several related terms. Articles referring to the concept have lumped together positions from sales promotion assistants to corporate vice-presidents under the general heading, product management. A primary emphasis of this paper has been to focus attention upon the disparity between the meaning of product management and the misapplication of this term throughout management literature. It is not enough, however, to say that the term has been incorrectly used, or to say that a spade should be called a spade. Some suggestion should be made as to the proper classification of those positions which have been shorn of the "product manager" appellation. Without attempting to use a currently popular buzzword to cover a multitude of positions and without particular emphasis on originality, why not merely call these positions what they are? For example, where one authority states, "Sales managers for products may be given the simple title of product manager,"[36] would it be too homely to refer to this position as a "product sales manager"? Similarly, would it not be preferable to refer to the executive in charge of selling to the school market as a "market manager" since he was "charged with the broad responsibility of securing more business in this field"?[37] Ames' reference to a product manager whose role was limited to keeping sales statistics and performing clerical tasks sounds very much like a "sales department staff assistant."[38]

While it is often correct to refer to a product manager as a marketing manager for a product, frequently his responsibilities are so broad that he is, in effect, the general manager of a "company."

> Companies have adopted the product division approach, centering, in effect, the general management of a "company within a company" on the shoulders of the product manager. He is generally given complete authority to the full extent of his responsibilities and is held accountable for the profit of his division.[39]

In instances such as the one illustrated, the title would more appropriately be "Marketing Manager-Product Division" or "Product Division Manager." (Since the authors had previously referred to the head of product divisions at General Foods, it is assumed that the manager is in charge of several related products. If only one product were in a division, the terms "product manager" and "division manager" could be used interchangeably. Although this situation would seldom occur, the status implication of the two terms would probably make "division manager" more desirable.)

The *Printers' Ink* product manager who "is interested in developing a broad line of products for use in his markets"[40] is not a true product manager because of his "broad line of products" and his market orientation. He is probably a divisional market manager. Again, the reference to a product manager with 203 products[41] probably refers to a division manager (the article does not indicate if he is a complete marketing manager or is oriented toward a single market).

From this discussion, it is possible to segregate the positions described in the section, "What is a product manager?" into the following titles:

1 / **Division manager**—The executive who has the authority and responsibility to manage (or as Buskirk would say, "plan, direct, and control"[42]) the life cycle of a group of related products. (See Exhibits I and II.)

2 / **Marketing manager**—The executive who has the authority and responsibility to manage all the marketing activities for the products in a company or division. (See Exhibits I and II.) In cases where the so-called "marketing concept" is employed, it is common for this official to have line authority over marketing activities and considerable functional authority over production and finance.

3 / **Product manager**—The previously mentioned Schiff and Mellman definition should be refined as follows: the executive with primary authority and responsibility for the planning, direction, and control of all phases of a product's current existence. (See Exhibit I.) This definition does not imply that the product manager has final or unrestricted authority or responsibility for all aspects of a product's life. Under the "marketing concept," however, functional authority belonging to the marketing manager is often delegated to the individual product managers for their products and is, of course, subject to review by the marketing manager.

4 / **Market product manager**—This position occurs when "the market manager may be so specialized that he devotes his attention to a single product for a single market."[43] This, however, is unusual. (See Exhibit II.)

5 / **Brand manager**—In most instances today,

EXHIBIT I Division Manager and Product/Brand Manager Organization

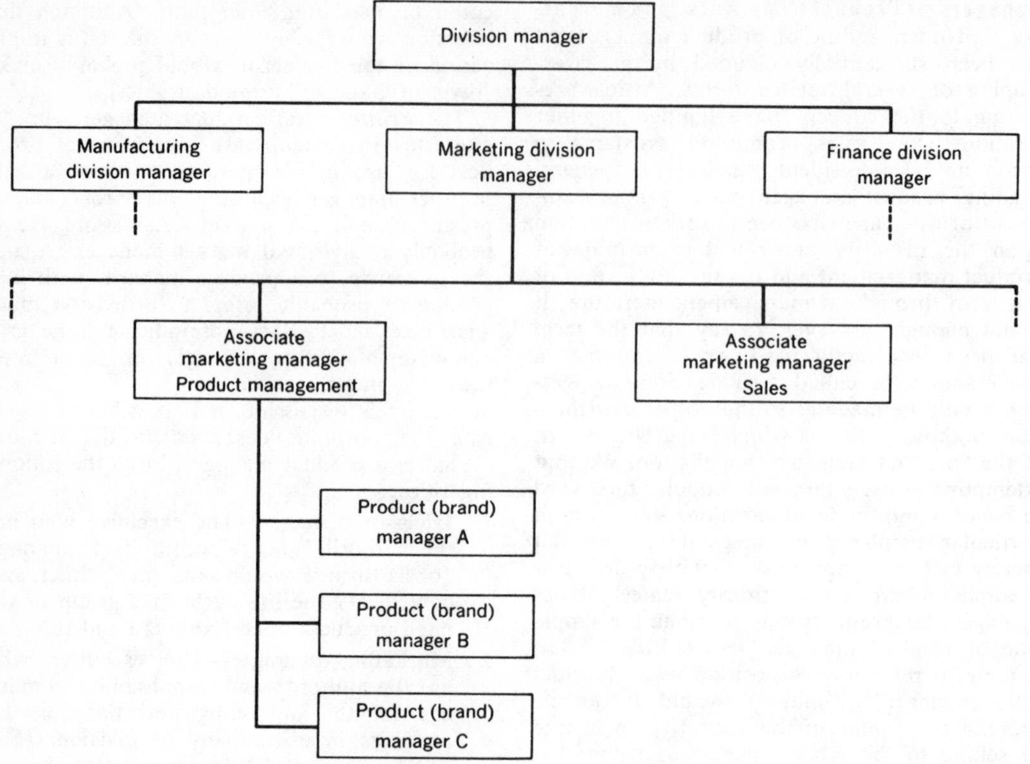

products are not sold but brands.[44] When purchases of products are made on the basis of brand preference, it is more accurate to refer to the executive responsible for managing the life cycle of the item as a brand manager. This is particularly true when one company markets competing brands within one product category. (See Exhibit I.)

6 / **Product specialist**—Unquestionably, there are instances where a staff position can be a valid way to insure individual attention and interest for each product in a company's line without creating the problems of company-wide coordination which the delegation of extensive functional authority may require. If an individual has only the authority to suggest the marketing program for his product and then must negotiate with the other areas of the company for services to implement these plans, he does not possess a manager's ability to take decisive action and should not be called a product or brand manager. Rather, it seems that the contributions which such a position can offer in some situations could be made with equal effectiveness (and less confusion) if it were recognized as a different variety and called "product specialist."

GUIDELINES

Product Management: Still No Panacea
Without doubt, the practice of product management is replete with potential pitfalls for the unskilled practitioner. The problem of the concept's scope has particularly manifested itself in the areas of authority, responsibility, and definition. A universal answer to the initial question of how much and what kind of authority the product manager should have can still not be given. A safe generalization, however, would be that sufficient authority must be granted to achieve the requirements of the position. A product or brand specialist with only staff authority lacks the quick, decisive power to act which can make the most effective use of his specialized knowledge and interest. Considerable functional authority is often given to the product manager because of his importance as a coordinating influence and be-

EXHIBIT II Division Manager, Market Manager, and Market Product Manager Organization

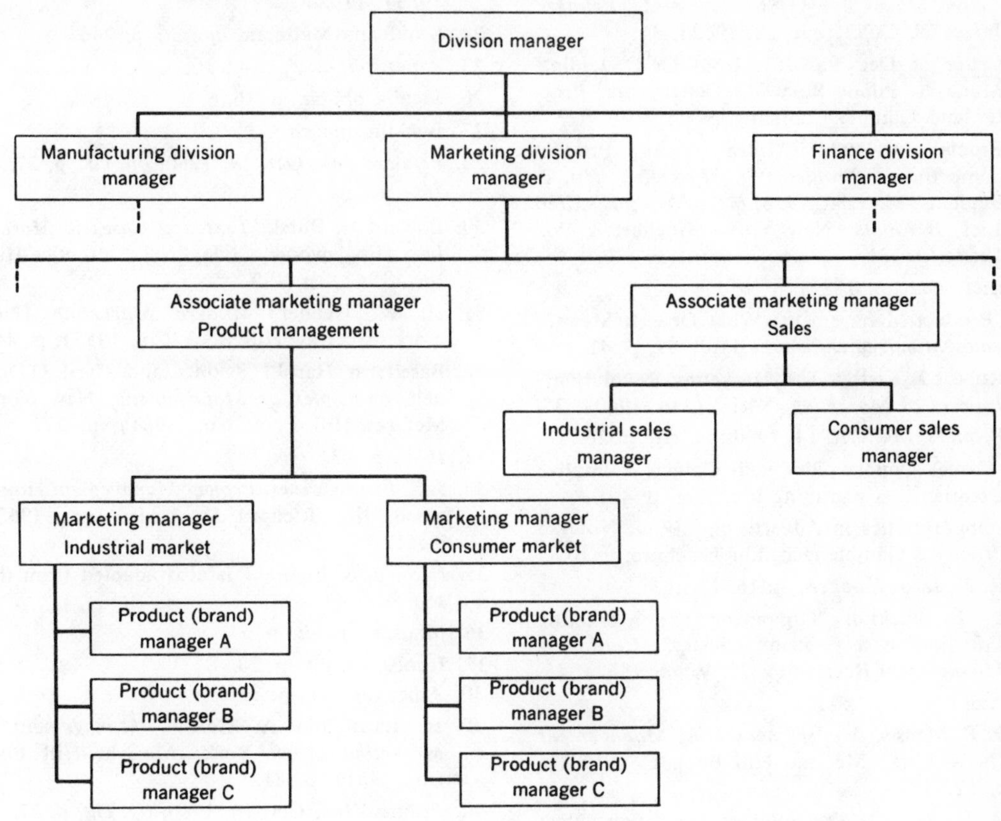

cause of the need to equate authority and responsibility. In order to avoid, or at least to minimize, conflict, functional authority thus delegated should be subject to over-all coordination one or, at the most, two levels immediately above the product manager.

Obviously, authority cannot be delegated, employees cannot be properly selected or trained, performance cannot be evaluated, and responsibility cannot be exacted until there is agreement on the meaning and scope of the position involved. An attempt has been made to evolve reasonable guidelines for classification of positions in the product management phylum. Operative definitions have been suggested as a means of revealing distinctions in the areas of activity and in the performance expected from various types of product-oriented organizations. Clarity is frequently a function of adequate understanding, and understanding begins with definition. This emphasis on semantics was aptly worded by Confucius: "If names be not used correctly, then speech gets tied up in knots; and if speech be so, then business comes to a standstill."[45]

REFERENCES

1. "Why Modern Marketing Needs the Product Manager," *Printers' Ink,* CCLXXIII (Oct. 4, 1960), 25.
2. Robert W. Lear, "No Easy Road to Market Orientation," *Harvard Business Review,* XLI (Sept.-Oct. 1963), 58.
3. R. H. Jacobs, "The Effective Use of the Product Manager," American Management Association, Marketing Series No. 97, 196, p. 31.
4. B. Charles Ames, "Pay Off from Product Management," *Harvard Business Review,* XLI (Nov.-Dec., 1963), 142.
5. Michael Schiff and Martin Mellman, *Financial Management of the Marketing Function* (New

York: Financial Executives Research Foundation, Inc., 1962), pp. 28–29.

6. "What Makes P & G So Successful," *Printers' Ink,* CCLXXX (Sept. 28, 1962), 31.
7. Letter of Dec. 9, 1963, from C. C. Uhling, Manager, Public Relations Department, Procter and Gamble Company.
8. Procter & Gamble, "Intra-company Product competition," *Problems in Marketing, No. 2,* Students' Material, 1956, p. 1. Also see Alfred Lief, *It Floats* (New York: Rinehart & Co., 1958), p. 181.
9. Lief, *ibid.,* p. 182.
10. "Product Management: What Does It Mean?" *Sales Management,* April 17, 1959, p. 42.
11. Robert J. Kieth, "The Marketing Revolution," *Journal of Marketing,* XXIV (Jan. 1960), 35.
12. *Printers' Ink,* Oct. 14, 1960, *op. cit.,* p. 26.
13. "Career Opportunities with Colgate-Palmolive Company," a recruiting brochure, p. 4.
14. "Opportunities in Advertising," *What Now?* a Procter & Gamble recruiting brochure, p. 10.
15. R. H. Jacobs, *op. cit.,* p. 16.
16. L. P. Bucklin, "Organizing the Marketing Function in a Growth Industry," *California Management Review,* IV:2 (Winter 1962), 45.
17. Ames, *op. cit.,* p. 141.
18. F. F. Mauser, *Modern Marketing Management* (New York: McGraw-Hill Book Co., 1961), p. 57.
19. R. H. Buskirk, *Principles of Marketing* (New York: Holt, Rinehart, and Winston, Inc., 1961), p. 623.
20. *Ibid.*
21. See Lyndall F. Urwick, "The Problems of Management Semantics," *California Management Review,* II:3 (Spring 1960).
22. E. R. Weger, *Die Absatzwirtschaft,* March 1963, pp. 131–134.
23. W. K. A. Disch, "Review of *Die Absatzwirtschaft,*" *Journal of Marketing,* XXVII (Oct. 1963), 116.
24. Schiff and Mellman, *op. cit.,* p. 246.
25. Ames, *op. cit.,* p. 142.
26. Jacobs, *op. cit.,* p. 16.
27. Bucklin, *op. cit.*
28. *Printers' Ink,* Oct. 14, 1960, *op. cit.,* p. 27.
29. *Ibid.*
30. Edward C. Bursk, *Text and Cases in Marketing* (Englewood Cliffs, N.J.: Prentice-Hall, Inc., 1962), p. 499.
31. H. W. Hepner, *Modern Marketing* (New York: McGraw-Hill Book Co., 1955), p. 448.
32. Based on Harold Koontz and Cyril O'Donnell, *Principles of Management* (New York: McGraw-Hill Book Co., 1964), p. 272.
33. *Ibid.,* p. 63.
34. J. S. Baumgartner, *Project Management* Homewood, Ill.: Richard D. Irwin, Inc., 1963), p. 112.
35. *Ibid.,* p. 6. Figure 1 is also adapted from this source.
36. Mauser, *op. cit.,* p. 57.
37. Jacobs, *op. cit.,* p. 20.
38. Ames, *op. cit.,* p. 141.
39. H. Lazo and A. Corbin, *Management in Marketing* (New York: McGraw-Hill Book Co., 1961), p. 81.
40. *Printers' Ink,* Oct. 14, 1960, *op. cit.,* p. 27.
41. *Ibid.,* p. 30.
42. Buskirk, *op. cit.,* p. 623.
43. Lear, *op. cit.,* p. 58.
44. See B. Gardner and S. J. Levy, "The Product and The Brand," *Harvard Business Review,* LIII (March-April 1955), 33–39.
45. Quoted by Lyndall F. Urwick, *op. cit.*

35 DILEMMA OF PRODUCT/MARKET MANAGEMENT*

B. Charles Ames

As companies have expanded into new product and market areas, they have changed their organizations to deal with the new complexities that have arisen in these areas. Over the past decade companies have responded to product/market growth by adding either product managers or market managers to their staffs.

Both positions were developed—and have been used successfully throughout industry—to provide the necessary market orientation and to ensure sound planning for various product/market segments. And the purpose of both has always been the same—namely, to safeguard the commercial health of the product/market business by ensuring that the necessary plans, decisions, and commitments made throughout the company effectively meet the changing needs of the marketplace.[1]

Nevertheless, the emphasis and appropriateness of each position differs with each company. Product managers have been used when a company has multiple products flowing into a common market through the same channels and to the same customer groups.

Market managers have been used in the reverse situation—when the company needs to develop different markets for a single product line. In this case, focus on developing the market rather than on taking the product to market has been the chief objective, and market managers have been used to provide this focus.

Both of these positions were designed to ensure that a single person had the full-time responsibility for planning the growth and development of each significant product/market segment. As long as a company has either a series of products that funnel into one market or a single product line that flows out into several markets, a single product manager or market manager can handle this responsibility. For, as shown in Exhibit I-A and I-B, it is relatively easy to carve out a discrete area of responsibility for such a manager under these fairly simple product/market conditions.

But because product/market proliferation has increased greatly in a large and growing number of industrial companies, many find themselves selling multiple products in multiple markets. When this happens, as Exhibit I-C shows, there is not a neat product/market match in most cases, but rather a crisscross of products and markets that dramatically increases the complexity of the planning and management job to be done.

At this point, planning from only one perspective—product or market—tends to be self-defeating. Neither one or the other can be downgraded or disregarded in the planning process without severe penalty.

THE DILEMMA

Let us consider the consequences of choosing one kind of manager over the other to do the planning in this crisscross product/market situation.

If product managers are chosen, each man is likely to have responsibility for one product line or area that is sold in several different markets, and, quite possibly through different channels. In most cases, it is simply impossible for one man to know enough about the characteristics and requirements of the different markets to plan for profitable participation and growth.

Thus the product manager is more than likely to concentrate on selling his existing products, rather than on determining what it takes to serve his markets more effectively. In so doing, he will probably miss important opportunities in related products and services. Even more important,

* Reprinted by permission of the publisher from the *Harvard Business Review,* vol. 49, no. 2, pp. 66–74 (March–April 1971). Mr. Ames is director of McKinsey & Company, management consultants.

[1] See my article, "Payoff from Product Management," HBR November–December 1963, p. 141.

EXHIBIT I Three Product/Market Business Situations

A. Product managers are the answer when multiple products flow into a single market

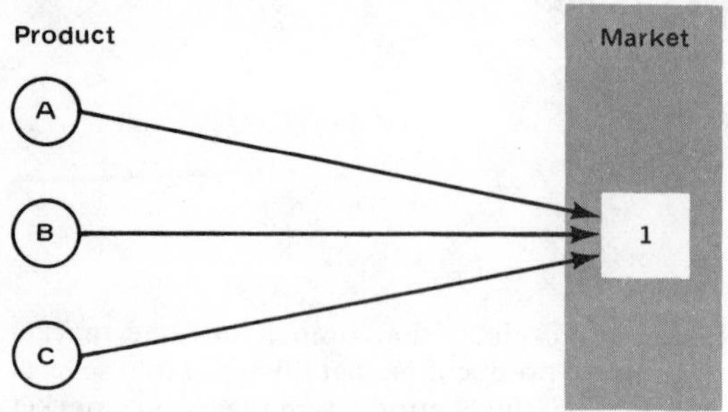

B. Market managers get the nod when a single product flows into multiple markets

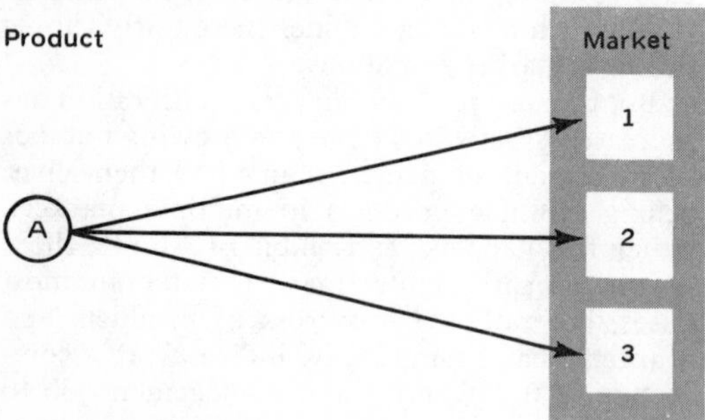

C. Neither approach is suitable when products and markets crisscross

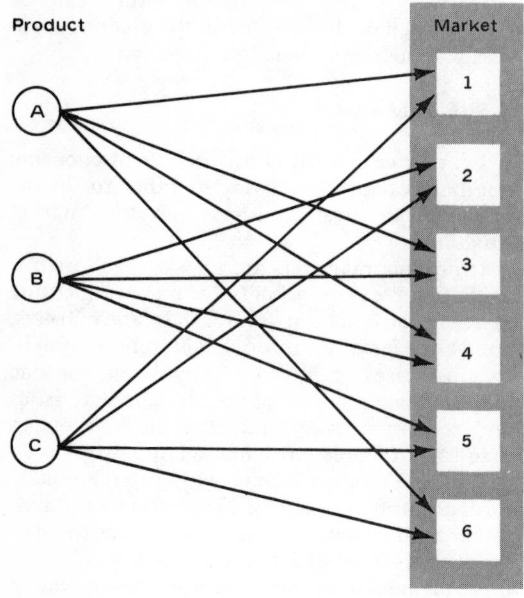

without sufficient focus on the market, the chances are good that his product line will lag behind competitive offerings, or even become obsolete, as he find himself unable to keep up with ever-changing user needs.

Alternatively, if market managers are selected, each manager will tend to focus on meeting the requirements of his assigned market without regard for the impact that his actions or recommendations may have on the company's ability to properly meet the needs of other market areas with the same product line. Thus, if a company has exceptionally strong or persuasive managers covering one or two market areas, it can very easily end up with product plans or actions in these markets that seriously jeopardize the company's positions in other market areas.

For these reasons, it becomes readily apparent that neither of these solutions is adequate in the crisscross situation. As I see it, meeting the requirements of this situation represents one of the most serious and complex organizational challenges that industrial management has had to deal with in a long time. It is serious because, unless an intelligent solution is found, the marketing planning effort is almost certain to be ineffective, causing both market position and profit growth to suffer. And it is complex because the only solution I know adds to overhead costs and sets up the potential for debilitating organizational conflict unless it is implemented properly.

Solution Is Difficult . . . How, then, can this challenge be faced? How does one ensure the right planning emphasis and balance in this kind of situation? A small but growing number of industrial companies have found that the only solution to this dilemma is to stop trying to decide between product or market managers and, instead, to use them both.

Under this dual arrangement, market managers have an external focus toward the market. They have the primary responsibility for developing a deep understanding of market needs and determining what the company could and should do to be more responsive to these needs.

Product managers, on the other hand, watch over their product areas in the same way any intelligent general manager would if his operation consisted of a single product flowing into several markets.[2] The product manager's job is to seek a balanced response to the needs and opportunities in certain markets without jeopardizing the company's position in others and without placing an unfair burden on manufacturing and engineering.

This dual approach positions the center of

[2] Ibid.

gravity for a particular product/market business between these two managers. In so doing, it provides the basis for achieving (a) the market orientation that is so essential to competitive success in any business and (b) a system of checks and balances to ensure that unbridled enthusiasm for market response does not wreak havoc within the business.

Admittedly, setting up two managers with joint responsibilities for product/market development is an organizational anomaly, and one could logically ask: Who is responsible for what?

While this is a good question for academic discussion, it does not represent a significant problem in practice. Product managers can be held accountable for all aspects of product line management, including long-term profitability. Similarly, market managers can be held accountable for long-term growth and profitability of their assigned markets.

Although neither manager would have line authority for decisions and actions that affect his areas of concern, both should be given full responsibility for using their superior knowledge and ideas about what is right and what is wrong for their areas to get the appropriate actions and decisions taken. If they assess and plan correctly, they will be successful in their roles; if they do not, they will not be successful. Thus both should be held accountable in this fashion to ensure the best planning and management job for each product/market segment.

Inevitable Conflict. It is clear that a dual management approach conceived this way offers a means of coping with the complex product/market situation that exists in many large-scale companies. However, it is important to bear in mind that when product and market managers are set up to work parallel with each other, a conflict situation is automatically created.

After all, the fundamental purpose of either of these two men is to fight for time and attention from engineering, manufacturing, and sales for their assigned products or markets. The potential for conflict is sharply brought out when both product managers and market managers are present in an organization. Let us look at the inner workings of this conflict more closely:

- The market manager's primary responsibility, on the one hand, is to identify his market's needs and to seek modifications in the existing product/service package or additions to it that will better enable him to meet the needs of the market. He has no interest in any other market or in the functional difficulties he may create.
- The product manager, on the other hand, has the basic responsibility for maintaining the integrity of his product line so that costs, design or performance characteristics, pricing policy, service and warranty arrangements, and so on, are broadly responsive to the needs of all the company's markets.
(Given this charge, it is clear that he cannot bend indiscriminately to the requirements any one market manager perceives. So, in addition to the conflict which he encounters in vying with his colleagues for functional time and attention, his major concerns often conflict with those of the market managers.)

Although it is inevitable, the conflict arising from the interaction of product managers and market managers should not be viewed as a negative factor. In fact, this kind of conflict is specifically what the dual management concept is designed to produce. It should be regarded as a positive force.

Moreover, if it is properly managed, the conflict should help uncover a multiplicity of market opportunities that would otherwise go unnoticed, and, at the same time, provide a mechanism for sorting through these opportunities so that the company's overall interests are best served. However, the key phrase is "properly managed." If not properly managed, the whole idea can turn into a two-headed monster.

Providing proper management places a heavy burden on the marketing head, since both product and market managers typically report to him. Thus he has the primary responsibility for ensuring that the conflict which develops is constructive and that it leads to better and more productive ideas. This means that he must ensure that these men work together as a team to blend their different points of view into better ideas for building the product/market business as a whole.

At times, of course, this means that the marketing head will have to decide between strongly contested alternatives. And he must do it in a way that avoids ruffling too many feathers or discouraging his managers from coming up with ideas and taking strong stands in the future.

. . . But Success Is Possible The reward has been well worth the effort for those companies that have built this concept into their organizations and made it work. Here are two actual examples of companies that adopted the dual management approach successfully and very profitably:

- An engine manufacturer found that his three product lines were losing ground in terms of both market and profit growth after a period of rapid expansion.

  The company president and his vice president of marketing agreed that they were missing the boat on too many sales opportunities because they were not getting the right kind of management attention on key products and markets. But they were not able to agree on how to organize to provide this management attention.

The president thought that setting up a product management group would be the answer. The vice president argued that market managers would be a better choice since the products were sold in three separate markets, and each had its own distinct characteristics and requirements.

Although the president saw the need for a market focus, he feared that using market managers would lead to product problems and pricing conflicts as each market manager sought to meet the needs of his particular market without regard for the others.

After a lot of give-and-take discussion, the president wisely concluded that both product and market managers were necessary to provide the proper attention to both products and markets. Within a few months, the market managers had developed a host of ideas for modifications in the existing product/service packages as well as several promising ideas for new product entries. The product managers then screened these ideas, and the two groups working together were able to help the company develop a stronger product/market strategy that significantly accelerated profit growth; volume gains and earnings per share were nearly doubled.

- A textile fibers company, confronted with a similar situation, actually made the shift from product managers to market managers as the key planning unit. This company sold three basic fibers in several end-use markets. Because the characteristics and requirements for these markets were significantly different, management reasoned that a market focus on planning was more appropriate than a product focus.

A chaotic situation arose, however, when plant and development managers discovered that they could not possibly respond to all of the requests coming to them from the market managers. As one plant manager put it: "Our production costs of Product 'X' have gone up by 12% because of all the short-run requests for additional stocking requirements. Also, we are running out of capacity for one of our most profitable products, and no plans are being formulated to add new capacity. It is a fine thing to be responsive to market needs. But someone had better watch out for product costs and capacity, or we will have a plant full of unprofitable business and will lose the chance to sell more of our profitable items."

Management then correctly decided to reinstate a product management group to work parallel with the market managers. The product managers quickly took hold of the product planning problems that had led to the chaotic situation in plant and development operations. And, at the same time, the market managers provided the end-user orientation so essential to success in the marketplace. As a result of product and market manager cooperation, the company struck a better balance between control of its manufacturing process and market response and achieved a short-term profit pickup of several hundred thousand dollars and a much stronger market share position.

THE REQUIREMENTS

While the dual management concept unquestionably requires careful thought and attention to implement successfuly, it does not require esoteric or ultrasophisticated management know-how. Rather, it simply demands attention to six management fundamentals.

Determine the Need First, management must make sure that there really is a need for this concept. In this already complicated world, it does not make sense to add complication unnecessarily, especially when it is costly and difficult to do so. Before deciding that an organization built around product and market managers is the best basis for planning and managing future growth, management should satisfy itself on these points:

- It should be certain that the crisscross flow of multiple products to multiple markets actually exists and that it is too complex for traditional approaches to the planning job.
- Even more important, management should assure itself that more concentrated or comprehensive planning for a larger number of discrete product/market segments will, in fact, provide the basis for accelerating profit growth.

Define the Roles Second, if management agrees that this dual management approach is appropriate, the next step is to decide how the roles of the two types of managers should be defined and structured. Of course, the specific responsibilities of either the market or the product managers will depend on the particular situation; but, by and large, their basic roles should be defined to include certain activities.

Thus *market* managers should concentrate their efforts on:

- Developing a comprehensive understanding of customer and end-user operations and economics and specifying ways that the existing product/service package can be improved to provide a competitive edge.
- Identifying related products and/or services that represent attractive opportunities for profitably enlarging the company's participation in the market through either internal development or acquisition.
- Drawing together at regular intervals an organized summary of the most attractive opportunities in the marketplace, specifying what must be done internally to capitalize on them, and recommending a first-cut strategy for the business.
- Developing a reputation for industry expertise among key customer and end-user groups and bringing this know-how to bear on the negotiation of major orders and on the training and development of field sales personnel.

In a similar vein, *product* managers should focus their efforts on:

- Protecting the pricing integrity of their product—that is, seeing to it that the pricing policies and practices in one market do not jeopardize the company's position or profit structure in another.
- Maintaining product leadership by making certain that product design, cost, and performance characteristics not only are broadly responsive to customer needs in all markets but also are not inadvertently altered to meet the needs of one market at the expense of the company's position in another.
- Ensuring that their product is responsive to market needs while at the same time protecting the engineering and production process from getting cluttered with a proliferation of small lot, custom, or special orders; in effect, they temper market managers' enthusiastic customer orientation with sober judgments on operating capability and economics.
- Ensuring that production scheduling and capacity are intelligently planned to profitably meet current and anticipated aggregate demands of various markets.
- Providing the in-depth technical and/or product knowledge required to support selling efforts on major and complex applications.

The broad activities just cited are always the core of the job for both market and product managers. However, the makeup and importance of the company's various products and markets should determine exactly how their jobs are structured. Product managers invariably function on a full-time basis but may, of course, be given responsibility for more than one product. There is little latitude in structuring this position.

The market manager's job, however, is quite a different matter. It may be structured in three different ways, depending on the number, importance, and geographic spread of the markets involved. Thus his role may be set up so he functions as (a) a full-time staff planner, (b) a full-time staff planner with line sales responsibility, or (c) a part-time staff planner. Consider:

- Most companies assign the market manager a full-time staff role, dividing the product/market planning job into two parts and setting up the two groups—product managers and market managers—in parallel, as shown in Exhibit II-A. This first approach is popular because it is a natural evolution from either product or market managers and is the easiest to introduce.

  Moreover, this setup is the right one to follow when all the markets are about equally important to the company and the number to be covered is relatively small, say, four to eight. Under these circumstances, it is economically practical to have a full-time staff planner for each one.
- Some companies have developed the market manager's job into a stronger full-time position, giving him line sales responsibility as well as the staff planning assignment, as shown in Exhibit II-B. This means that the market manager has direct responsibility for a group of salesmen that specialize in selling to the accounts that make up his market.

  Theoretically, this second approach is best, since it gives one man a combined responsibility for both planning and execution within each market area and thus makes it possible to hold him fairly accountable for results. It also ensures that he has a firsthand feel for customer and market requirements and helps him avoid ivory-tower planning.

  But, practically, its application is limited because it is often difficult to justify the degree of sales specialization inherent in this kind of arrangement. Although most companies can point to a cluster of accounts in certain geographic areas for which they could economically justify a specialist salesman, to get national coverage they must inevitably turn to the general salesman who sells all products to all markets. Accordingly, in most cases, it simply is not feasible to work out an arrangement where the sales force can be divided neatly under several market managers.

- Still other companies have adopted the third approach—that of a part-time planner—which gives them the market focus they are seeking without the added cost of full-time market managers. As we have noted, these companies add market planning assignments to the responsibility of senior salesmen, sales managers, or application engineers who have some expertise in a given end-use market. This compromise approach is normally followed by companies which deal in such a large number of markets that they simply cannot afford to provide full-time market manager coverage for each one.

  For example, one company identified over 30 markets that needed to be brought into focus. Even after considering various ways these markets might be combined into planning assignments, the number of full-time market managers required could not be justified. Consequently, the company gave market planning assignments to selected salesmen who had special experience or a concentration of accounts in key markets.

Although I have described these approaches to the market manager's job separately, they can be combined as necessary to meet the needs and structure of the marketplace. Thus, for example, one company was able to give two of its market managers line sales responsibility because there were groups of specialist salesmen that could logically be assigned to them. The company could also justify the appointment of two additional full-time market managers in a staff planning capacity. To complete its market coverage, the company gave half a dozen key salesmen part-time market manager assignments with the thought in mind that these positions could be upgraded to full-time assignments if the markets developed to any great extent.

Change the Systems Third, management must change the information and planning systems to reflect the existence and needs of both managers. On the information side, product managers need detailed operating information (e.g., engineering standards, production schedules, and cost breakdowns) to perform their jobs effectively. Market managers must have access to cost information for all products sold in their markets and to detailed market and customer information. And, ultimately, both managers should have profit and loss statements for their respective areas as a bench mark for evaluating their performance.

In many cases, the kind of cost, operating, and market information required for intelligent product and market planning either is not available or is in a form that is unusable. Correcting this situation may require a major effort (e.g., special research projects, restructuring of accounting information).

Moreover, modifying the information system also requires providing a close working relationship with engineering, manufacturing, and finance, so that managers can secure the assistance necessary to interpret much of this information in the correct manner. Regardless of the effort involved, the information and assistance must be provided or the concept does not stand a chance of getting off the ground.

On the planning side, two changes are necessary. One is a change in the way strategic plans are developed. Here market managers should be given the responsibility for developing an overview of their market and a no-holds-barred set of recommendations for capitalizing on the opportunities they see. They should then review their ideas with the product managers concerned with their markets to determine what is feasible and what is not—as well as to gain agreement on a going-in point of view that can be presented to other functional managers. From this point on, the process follows a normal planning pattern with all the functional managers collaborating to come up with a final recommendation for top management.[3]

The other change in planning affects the way top management reviews and responds to strategic recommendations. Basically, the planning system must be adjusted to cope with an increased amount of planning inputs. As discussed previously, if the dual management approach is successful, it should generate a vastly increased number of options and recommendations for building the business in various product/market segments.

For example, one company adapted this approach in a way that freed certain managers to focus full time on uncovering market opportunities. This, in turn, led to the generation of some 20 different strategic options for building just one product/market business and involved different levels of resource commitment and payoff expectations. To cope with this avalanche of ideas, the top managers had to draw extensively on their central planning staff and had to set aside substantial blocks of their own time to decide which options to accept and which to reject.

Admittedly this may be a unique situation, but bear in mind that the fundamental purpose of this dual management approach is to generate

[3] See my article "Marketing Planning for Industrial Products," HBR September–October 1968, p. 100.

EXHIBIT II Two Approaches To Meet the Needs of the Marketplace

A. Market manager in staff capacity only . . .

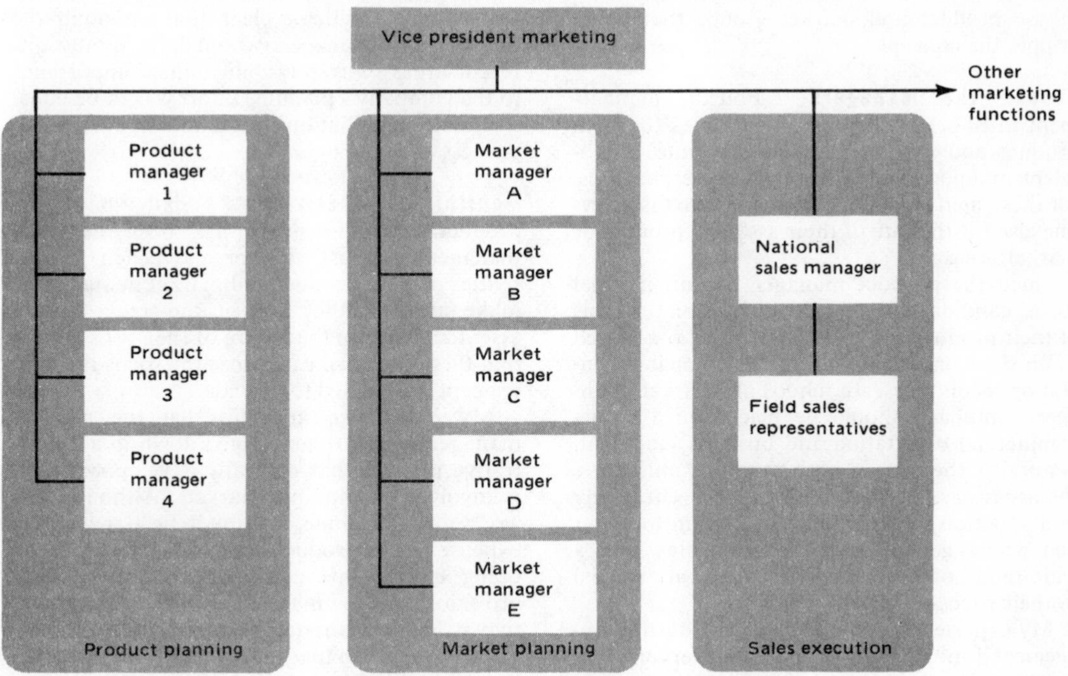

B. . . . and with combined line and staff responsibility

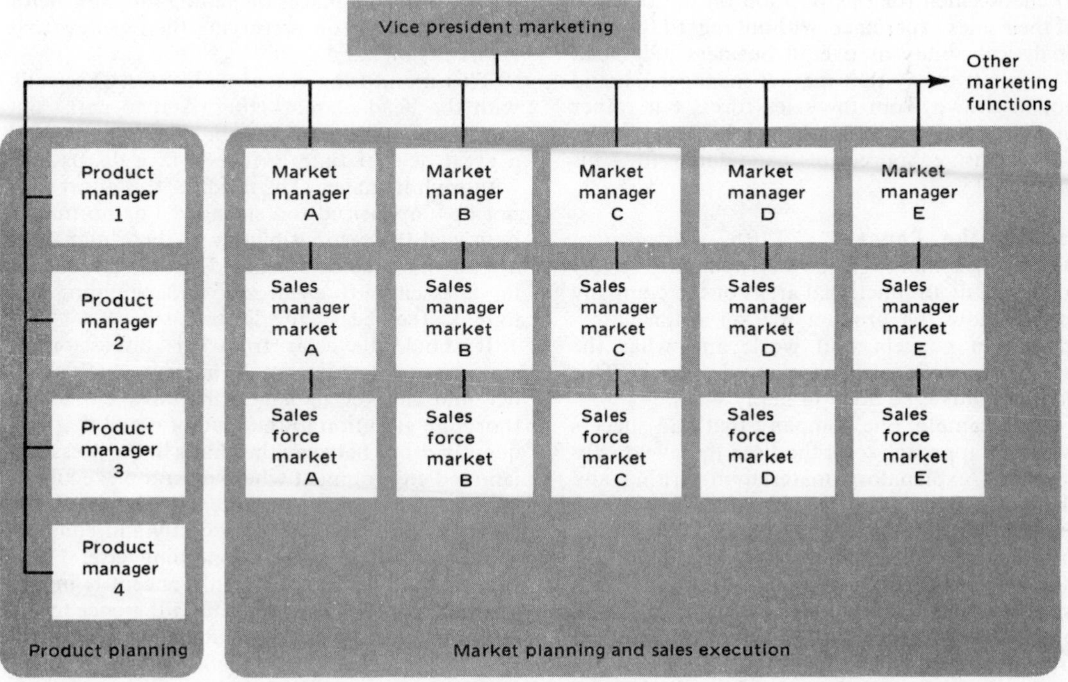

more ideas and recommendations for accelerating growth and profits. Top management must properly evaluate and respond to this flow of ideas to avoid frustration and discouragement in the product and market groups that could cripple the concept.

Choose the Managers Fourth, management must select the right candidates for both product and market manager positions. High-talent manpower is essential in these positions, for these men will be more responsible than anyone else for the fate of their assigned product or market areas.

Since the product manager has an internal focus, candidates should be selected on the basis of their product and technical know-how as well as on their understanding of the company's operating economics. In choosing market managers, emphasis should be placed on a strong commercial orientation and business judgment. Naturally, the men in both positions must have the necessary personal skills to work effectively in a situation where conflict is certain to occur and where good working relationships with a wide range of functional executives are crucial to their success.

My experience suggests that this fourth management fundamental is one that everyone will quickly agree with but few will take seriously enough, particularly when it comes to selecting market managers. There is a natural tendency to choose men for this position on the strength of their sales experience, without regard for their analytical ability or overall business judgment. This is not to say that market managers should not be drawn from the sales force, but rather that the sales force should not be regarded as the exclusive source of candidates for this position.

Explain the Concept Fifth, management has to do a thorough job of explaining to key managers in all functional areas of the company exactly how the product/market manager organization concept will work and what the underlying rationale is for moving to it. This can, of course, be done in many ways.

For example, one company that had success with this approach took the time to develop appropriate explanatory material in writing and then used it at a series of group meetings to explain the concept and respond to questions. In doing so, the company emphasized the distinctions between the roles that product and market managers would play in the management process and outlined the contributions expected from each type of manager.

Top management also went into some detail to explain how product and market managers would interact with other functional managers and executives and stressed the cooperative working relationships that were expected. And management made it clear that although the two types of managers would have totally different areas of responsibility, their importance to the company's planning effort was to be equal and their contributions to the total management process on a par.

Monitor the Activities Sixth, once the product/market concept has been installed, management must monitor and coach the activities of both product and market managers to make sure that they stay on the track. This is essential, because the nature of their jobs is such that these men can easily lose the focus the dual concept is intended to provide.

My experience indicates that the product manager seems to get bogged down in administrative matters that naturally develop when he is involved in multiple markets. Although this work must be done, it cannot be done at the expense of the product line planning and developing efforts—his core responsibilities. Thus provision must be made to give him administrative assistance as required.

The market manager can easily fall into the trap of looking for new fields to conquer before he has mastered his present business. If this occurs, the result could be a plan that places far too much emphasis on getting into new fields and not enough on preserving the business that is already on hand.

This monitoring responsibility rests basically with the head of marketing. And to carry out this job effectively, he must be prepared to spend a great deal of time in face-to-face discussions with each manager. The need for this effort cannot be emphasized too strongly. For no matter how well the responsibilities of these managers are documented or explained, on-the-job coaching is essential to ensure the understanding and to make the necessary adjustments.

It should be clear from this discussion of management fundamentals that using both product and market managers requires close and thorough attention to the kind of detail that frequently drops between the chairs in the pressure-jammed environment where most top executives operate. But unless this attention is given, the company will end up with a costly and cumbersome superstructure—and nothing else. However, if the dual management concept is implemented properly, with rigorous adherence to the requirements just discussed, it can be a powerful vehicle for accelerating profit growth in many companies.

CONCLUSION

As I see it, using both product managers and market managers provides a basis for achieving the kind of product and market planning necessary in most multibusiness companies. The concept unquestionably means added manpower, added expense, and greater complexity in the management process. And making the concept work will probably add problems for most companies.

But if a company with a crisscross of products and markets balks at attempting this organization approach simply because it sounds too complex or because it will add to marketing overhead, I strongly believe it is missing a real bet. For it has been the experience of those who have tried it that this concept can provide a significant payoff in increased market opportunities, strong competitive actions, and ultimately greater profits that far outweigh either the added costs involved or the difficulties of making it work.

C. DECENTRALIZATION

36 ROLES AND RELATIONSHIPS: CLARIFYING THE MANAGER'S JOB*

Robert D. Melcher

Far too many companies cherish the myth that the publication of organization charts and position descriptions will resolve the majority of problems relating to the role each manager plays in relationship to his work group and to the organization. The organization chart does show basic divisions of work and who reports to whom, but it does not depict detailed functions and how individuals relate to these functions; in other words, it does not show how the organization actually works. The position description delineates the detailed task to be performed, but it cannot show how the organization really functions, either. Position descriptions are far more concerned with defining an individual's tasks than with how, in carrying out his responsibilities, he interacts with his colleagues. The way in which management positions are described often indicates complete independence from other positions—and, more often than not, independent action instead of group participation is encouraged. As a result, there is no opportunity to build a framework that can be used to relate and integrate each manager and the work he does to the organization and its goals.

The human-relations approach to resolving problems relating to interpersonal and intergroup relations concentrates primarily on behavioral approaches and experiences involving sensitivity training sessions, group problem-solving and goal-setting courses, and similar techniques. The primary purpose of the behavioral approach is to develop an awareness within each individual of his own behavioral characteristics, to increase his understanding of the underlying cause of intergroup conflict, and to develop techniques and approaches that can in some way help improve the individual's working relationships.

Unfortunately, many of these human-relations approaches do not involve the work group. Even when the work group is involved, the subject matter seldom relates specifically to the various working roles and relationships of the members of the group. Hence there is little opportunity for the group to focus on their work interface problems and put to productive use the techniques and skills gained through human-relations training experiences —and when experiences cannot be put to use, their value is soon lost.

PLANNING AND PARTICIPATION

A sound and successful organization development process requires a planned, systematic approach that encourages management involvement and participation. In order to meet these criteria and strengthen the organization development process, a number of companies have utilized an approach that enables each manager to actively participate with his superiors, peers, and subordinates in systematically describing the managerial job to be done and then clarifying the role each manager plays in relationship to his work group and to the organization.

The tool that evolved has been called the Management Responsibility Guide. Its development was sparked by a linear charting technique, developed by Ernest Hijams and Serge A. Bern, that is used to relate management positions, functions, and responsibility relationships to each other. Although their Linear Responsibility Chart can be used to describe roles and relationships, its use seems to be somewhat limited, because the functions are not systematically structured and the approach does not actively involve members of the work group in resolving their roles and responsibility relationships. Without a planned and systematic approach, it is very difficult to group and relate

* Reprinted by permission of the publisher from "Roles and Relationships: Clarifying the Manager's Job," *Personnel*, vol. 44, no. 3, pp. 33–41, May–June, 1967. Mr. Melcher is president of Management Responsibility Guidance Corporation.

managerial functions in the manner best suited to aid an organization to objectively solve its organizational problems. And without the active involvement of the work group, there is little opportunity to actually resolve differences and improve communications. It was out of the recognition that the mating of a behavioral sciences approach to a systems framework was essential, if role and relationship resolution was to take place, that the Management Responsibility Guide approach evolved.

Within every organization there exist specialized managerial tasks or functions that must be acted upon if the organization is to attain its objectives and goals. At the higher management levels, these managerial functions tend to be described in objective-oriented terms; at each subsequent lower level, these functions are broken into more detailed functions and are defined in more task-oriented terms. To be meaningful, these functions must be structured and phrased in a manner that not only describes the managerial functions but highlights the role and relationship problems that need to be clarified and resolved by each work group. Only after the objective delineation and definition of these essential managerial functions have been completed should each manager's responsibility relationships be developed. How each manager's view of his responsibility relationship to each function and each person is resolved determines how effectively the organization works—or does not work.

SEMANTIC SOLUTIONS

One of the primary problems impeding the process of role and relationship resolution is that of developing a set of terms that describe the various responsibility relationships in a way that is meaningful and acceptable to the group. Although there are many responsibility relationship terms that could be developed for a specific organization, the following seven definitions seem to meet the communication requirements of most organizations and, along with the defined functions, serve as a common focal point for the work group:

A. *General Responsibility*—The individual guides and directs the execution of the function through the person delegated operating responsibility.

B. *Operating Responsibility*—The individual is directly responsible for the execution of the function.

C. *Specific Responsibility*—The individual is responsible for executing a specific or limited portion of the function.

D. *Must Be Consulted*—The individual, if the decision affects his area, must be called upon before any decision is made or approval is granted, to render advice or relate information, but not to make the decision or grant approval.

E. *May Be Consulted*—The individual may be called upon to relate information, render advice, or make recommendations.

F. *Must Be Notified*—The individual must be notified of action that has been taken.

G. *Must Approve*—The individual (other than persons holding general and operating responsibility) must approve or disapprove.

It is obvious that a format is required that can be used to relate the organization's managerial functions, positions, and responsibility relationships to each other—and this is where the Management Responsibility Guide format makes its contribution.

DEVELOPING THE GUIDE

How the Management Responsibility Guide is developed by the work group is as important to its successful completion as the elements that it comprises. The first and perhaps most important step pertains to how the work group views and relates to the process that is to take place. Ordinarily, someone outside the work group is needed to work with the group as a consultant in developing the functions and serving as a resource. More often than not, there is a high degree of skepticism within the work group regarding the role of the consultant and his ability to actually help them, as well as considerable concern on each person's part as to how his status will be affected. Because each member of the work group must be afforded the opportunity to understand the process and to express his feelings, a group briefing session should first be held to explain the entire process and ground rules. Questions about the process and its underlying concepts and purposes should be encouraged by the manager of the work group and the consultant.

The functions of the work group can now be developed. Each member of the group is individually interviewed and given the opportunity to describe his job and any problems he wants the consultant to be aware of. In this fact-gathering and problem-definition phase, it is essential that the focus be directed toward objectively describing and grouping managerial functions that logically belong or relate to the same family, regardless of who presently is responsible. If responsibility relationships are also discussed at this time, emotion and subjectivity enter the picture and the probability of objectively delineating what needs to be done is poor. When questions relating to responsibility relationships are raised, the person raising them should be advised that he will have the opportunity to express his views fully at a later stage in the process.

A DOUBLE CHECK

After the key functions have been defined to the satisfaction of each manager, the consultant reviews all the defined functions with the managers' superior and, if necessary, revises the definitions to the satisfaction of the superior and each of the subordinates concerned.

The point has now been reached where the responsibility relationships can be developed. Each individual within the work group is given, in the Management Responsibility Guide format, a list of all functions developed for the group and is requested to enter the relationship code or codes that best express what he thinks his responsibility relationship to each function should be. He is further instructed that if he assigns an operating responsibility (B) to himself for a function, he should enter what he thinks should be the responsibility relationship of all other managers who should have a relationship to that function. In addition, he is requested to review each function and make whatever change in the wording he deems necessary.

After the forms are completed, they are returned to the consultant and the various points of view are entered on a master copy. The chart in Figure 1 shows how the master copy might look after the views of all members of the group have been entered on it. (In this case, the group concerned is a large division of the company; other charts would break down each of the functions in more detail and would list managers at lower levels of the organization. This division, in turn, would represent one of the functions on a chart indicating top management's roles and responsibilities.) For each function, the top line of symbols represents the point of view of the person who has indicated that he holds operating responsibility (B) for that function. The symbols in the second line represent the point of view of the person whose position title appears at the top of the column. Since two people considered that they had operating responsibility for the function on line 10.8, the first two lines represent their points of view, and the third line represents the views of the individuals at the tops of the column. The symbols that are circled indicate major conflicts between the viewpoints of the person with operating responsibility and those at the tops of the columns.

RESOLVING CONFLICTS

After an analysis of the responses has been completed, a determination must be made as to how best to resolve any divergent points of view that have been brought to the surface. At this stage the personalities and backgrounds of the people in the work group influence what is to be done.

One approach is to allow each member of the work group to review the varying points of view, then bring them together at a group meeting to collectively clarify and resolve differences. This approach has the distinct advantage of getting the full participation and involvement of each member of the work group. Ordinarily, interpersonal differences related to the day-to-day job content never get aired; this process permits each member of the group to present his position, and more often than not the individuals themselves resolve differences without their superior's having to intervene or make a decision.

This process is highly educational; it gives each member of the group a better understanding of the interaction that must take place in order for the group to function effectively. Moreover, the superior has an opportunity to sit back and view how his organization operates and how the members of his staff relate to one another.

Of course, there may be sensitive situations that are better handled or resolved on a superior-subordinate basis, but, for the most part, group participation and involvement seem to be more effective. No matter what approach is taken, the objective should be to get differences into the open and encourage the individuals themselves to clarify and resolve their roles and responsibility relationships.

The same general approach is used to resolve differences between work groups. After the group members have reached agreement on their roles and responsibility relationships, other individuals or groups are asked to indicate what they think their responsibility relationships should be to each of the functions. As before, differences between the groups that have been brought to the surface can then be resolved, and copies of the form indicating the agreed-upon roles and responsibility relationships are then issued to each member of the work groups as well as to other members of management within the company. Figure 2

FIGURE 1

Number	Function	Vice-president Aerospace	Vice-president Manufacturing	Director Engineering	Manager Industrial technology	Manager Quality assurance	Manager Marketing	Manager Contracts	Manager Master scheduling	Manager Financial services
10.1	Coordinate division budgeting and financial planning activities and communicate financial information to division management	A A-F	E-F D-F	E-F E	E-F F	E-F F	E-F E-F	E-F E	E D	B
10.2	Develop project and program schedule requirements, establish, coordinate, and control schedules and report on status	A A	E-F D	E-F D	E-F D-F	E-F C	E-F D	E-F D	B	F
10.3	Direct contract activities and evaluate and approve contract provisions of all division sales proposals and contract documents	A A		E			E-F D	B	E-F D-F	F C
10.4	Plan and coordinate divisional marketing activities so as to secure the business necessary to maximize division's capabilities	A A-D	E-F F	E-F	E-F	E	B	D-F C-G	E-F C-D	F F
10.5	Develop and design new, and improve existing, electronic and electro-mechanical aerospace products and processes	A A-F	F E	B	E		E D-G			
10.6	Secure materials and tools, coordinate manpower, and manufacture products to specified quantity, quality, time, and cost requirements	A A	B	E	E	F C-D		E-F E	F	E-F E
10.7	Establish quality assurance policies, procedures, and controls to insure that products meet applicable standards and specifications	A A	D-F D-G	D-F E-F	E E	B	F E	E-F D	E-F	F
10.8	Develop and design proprietary products and processes utilizing proven technology specifically adapted to industrial automation	A A-F - - - A	D-F E-F - - - E	C B	B D-F	E	E - - - E-F	D E - - - D-F	F E - - - F	F F

Relationship code

A General responsibility
B Operating responsibility
C Specific responsibility
D Must be consulted
E May be consulted
F Must be notified
G Must approve

Organization identification Aerospace Aerospace division	Number 200	Management responsibility guide Approval	Date	Page No. 1 of 1

FIGURE 2

Number	Function		Vice-president Aerospace	Vice-president Manufacturing	Director Engineering	Manager Industrial technology	Manager Quality assurance	Manager Marketing	Manager Contracts	Manager Master scheduling	Manager Financial services	Treasurer and Controller	Vice-president Earth sciences	Vice-president Test laboratories	Manager Industrial relations		
		Management position															
10.1	Coordinate division budgeting and financial planning activities and communicate financial information to division management		A-F	E-F	E-F	E-F	E-F	E-F	E-F	D	(B)	D-F					
10.2	Develop project and program schedule requirements, establish, coordinate, and control schedules and report on status		A	D-F	D	D-F	D-F	E-F	E-F	(B)							
10.3	Direct contract activities and evaluate and approve contract provisions of all division sales proposals and contract documents		A-F	E	E	E	E	D-F	(B)	E-F	F	E-F					
10.4	Plan and coordinate divisional marketing activities so as to secure the business necessary to maximize division's capabilities	E-F	A-D	E-F	E-F	E-F	E	(B)	D-F	D-F	F	E-F	E	E			
10.5	Develop and design new, and improve existing, electronic and electro-mechanical aerospace products and processes	E-F	A	E-F	(B)	E		D-F				E					
10.6	Secure materials and tools, coordinate manpower, and manufacture products to specified quantity, quality, time, and cost requirements		A	(B)	E	E	D-F		E	E-F	E	E-F			E		
10.7	Establish quality assurance policies, procedures, and controls to insure that products meet applicable standards and specifications		A	D-F	D-F	E	(B)	E-F	D-F	E-F	F						
10.8	Develop and design proprietary products and processes utilizing proven technology specifically adapted to industrial automation		A-F	E	E	(B)	E	E-F	D-F	E-F	F						

Relationship code

A
General responsibility

B
Operating responsibility

C
Specific responsibility

D
Must be consulted

E
May be consulted

F
Must be notified

G
Must approve

Organization identification Aerospace Aerospace division	Number 200	Management responsibility guide Approval	Date	Page No. 1 of 1

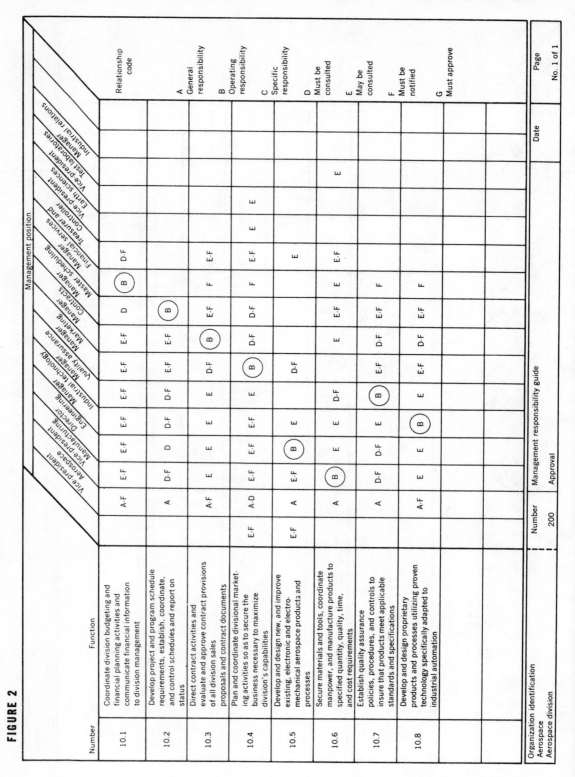

shows how the chart might appear after divergent views have been reconciled and the relationships with managers outside the work group have been entered.

The Management Responsibility Guide, as its name indicates, is only a guide; it reflects the work group's view as to how they agreed to work with one another at a specific point in time. Conditions continually change and the Management Responsibility Guide, like any other management tool, should be periodically review and updated.

SOME APPLICATIONS

Because the Management Responsibility Guide serves to clarify and resolve problems relating to working relationships, it can be a means of solving problems relating to duplication of effort and overlapping of responsibility; conversely, it can be used to identify responsibility gaps within the organization. It provides an objective way to bring sensitive relationship problems into the open and helps establish a common understanding of each function and each individual's or group's role in the organization.

The guide can also be used as a means of instituting managerial controls and pinning down responsibilities. Since objective consideration can be given to an individual's strengths and weaknesses, in relation to each function, management is able to tighten or loosen controls as well as clearly determine who is responsible for a given function.

As an organization analysis tool, there are a number of uses. For example, in a management audit, the Management Responsibility Guide can be analyzed to determine workload balance, pattern of delegation, and shifting of responsibility due to cutbacks, additions, or other changes in the workload. Since functions and responsibility relationships are delineated in an orderly and systematic manner, management is able to evaluate the impact of major staffing changes and, accordingly, can quickly realign functions and responsibility relationships.

EVALUATING PERFORMANCE

One of the more difficult aspects of evaluating performance is establishing the criteria on which performance is to be judged. Since functions and relationships are systematically delineated, it is possible to use the Management Responsibility Guide as a basis for evaluating performance. The systematic delineation of functions has similar advantages in the field of systems and procedures. At the lower echelons of an organization, functions tend to be described in task-oriented terms; hence, the job of the analyst is simplified, for with the clarification of responsibility relationships, the analyst need only describe the work in greater detail.

Position guides, at best, describe the general responsibilities of a position and generally do not consider organization levels or specific management relationships. Manually, or through the use of data processing techniques, a new type of "guide" can be prepared—one that can be updated instantly and that simultaneously considers organization level, functions, positions, and responsibility relationships. In a similar manner, programs relating to managerial experience inventories and the cross-referencing of similar or identical functions can be instituted.

PARTICIPATION IS THE KEY

Over the past five years, the Management Responsibility Guide has been used in some 30 organizations ranging from large to small, in industry and government, as an aid in solving a variety of management problems relating to managerial roles and relationships. One of the primary reasons for its success is the fact that managers at all levels were drawn into the process and actively participated in resolving problems in which they were personally involved. In each organization, this approach has provided a dynamic means of objectively describing the work to be done and clarifying the role each manager plays in it—and it has proved to be a major factor in improving management communications and interpersonal and intergroup relations.

37 WHAT CANNOT BE DECENTRALIZED*

John G. Staiger

Before a decision can be made as to what can or should be decentralized and what should remain centralized, certain questions must be answered. These can best be determined by first examining certain considerations.

When a company's organization plan is oriented to a single product or geographical marketing region, divisionalization often takes place, usually with some delegation of authority and decision-making responsibility. When, however, local management attention applies fairly equally to each of several products or geographical segments of the business, then decentralization rather than merely divisionalization has taken place.

The principle upon which decentralization is carried out is most often stated thus: "Authority to take or initiate action should be delegated as close to the scene of action as possible."

But decentralization is not merely a matter of delegation on paper. In our own organization manual we state:

> Delegation of authority must be real. It includes not only what a superior says to his subordinate, but also the way in which he acts. An important ingredient in delegation is the willingness to permit the subordinate to make a reasonable number of mistakes.

The question in delegation is: "When does delegation and permission to make mistakes become softness?" Within the broader context of company management, decentralization poses the question: "When does top management give up effective control of business?"

There are three practical considerations that determine the extent to which decentralization of decision making is possible and desirable: (1) The competence to make decisions on the part of the person to whom authority is delegated. A derivative of this must be his superior's confidence in the subordinate's competence. (2) Adequate and reliable information pertinent to the decision is required by the person making the decision. Decision-making authority, therefore, cannot be pushed below the point at which all information bearing on the decision is available. (3) The scope of the impact of the decision: if a decision affects more than one unit of the enterprise, the authority to make the decision must rest with the manager accountable for the several units affected by the decision.

Companies have not always paid attention to these limitations on effective decentralization. In particular, top managements often inadequately consider the scope of impact of the authority they are delegating, allowing operating executives to make decisions that have major effects on company profits.

In the July–August 1962 issue of *Harvard Business Review*, for example, there appears an article, "The Second Squeeze on Profits." This article comments, in part, on the excess capacity in many industries traceable to over-decentralization of decision making in regard to plant location, plant size, plant equipment and the products to be made in the plant. Therefore, I think it is fair to ask such questions as these: How often have unprofitable products, even entire product divisions, been carried because excessive decentralization had eroded profit-focused control? How often have profitability waned and staff costs multiplied while top management did only the long-range planning jobs?

MASSEY–FERGUSON'S EXPERIENCE

How do these general considerations apply to an individual company? On the assumption that one actual case study is worth a half-dozen hypothetical examples, I want to talk to you briefly about the company I know best—Massey-Ferguson, Limited. Massey-Ferguson is a Canadian company actively carrying on business in ten different countries. These are Australia, Brazil, Canada, France, Germany, India, Italy, South Africa, the United States and the

* Reprinted by permission of the publisher from *Management Record*, vol. 25, no. 1, pp. 19–21, January, 1963. Mr. Staiger is vice-president-administration, North American operations, Massey-Ferguson, Limited.

United Kingdom. We market farm equipment products in over 160 different world markets.

Structurally, the Massey-Ferguson organization plan for operating this worldwide business does not present noticeable differences from standard, textbook organizational plans. The organization chart shows a president with the usual, functionally identified, corporate staff to advise and assist him. At the operating level, there appear the following operating units: Australian, French, German, North American, Perkins and United Kingdom.

In addition, there are the Brazilian, Italian, South African and Indian operations which have recently been organized. While they develop organization strength and maturity, they will be the responsibility of the special operations function located within the corporate staff.

In the 160 regional markets our company sells in around the world, our business is handled by an export agency, which reports directly to the corporate staff marketing function.

A WORLDWIDE STRUCTURE

What is unique about our company is the concept by which these greatly dispersed operating entities are structured, managed and controlled. There is no foreign or international-operations division at Massey-Ferguson. We do not make a distinction between foreign and domestic operations. We sell in the world market and we give equal emphasis to each operating unit. Massey-Ferguson has a truly worldwide organization plan and structure.

In the Massey-Ferguson organization plan, the objectives of the company, the nature of the enterprise, and the geographic-political areas in which we operate have been the factors which determine the extent of decentralization. Three objectives, in particular, establish the limits of control. These are (1) to be worldwide in scope; (2) to have a full product line; (3) to be an integrated producer.

The world farm equipment industry is today a picture of vivid contrasts. It ranges from the highly competitive mature markets of North America to agriculturally undeveloped areas whose potential remains largely untapped.

There are marked differences from one market area to another with respect to type of agriculture, farming practices, equipment needs and distribution patterns. The rising tide of nationalism, the emergence of new countries and the formation of new trading blocs have all played a role in the shaping of this worldwide market.

From one region to another within this market, Massey-Ferguson's position fluctuates widely, ranging from a subordinate place in some areas to preeminence in others. To achieve the objective of becoming worldwide in scope means drastic upgrading in some areas while holding position in others. Success in this effort depends upon our ability to react appropriately and quickly to local marketing conditions. Marketing decisions must be made at local levels, and these are, therefore, always decentralized to local-operations-unit levels.

Manufacturing costs are substantially influenced by volume, mix and inventory "pipeline" considerations. To the extent feasible within the limits of broader worldwide requirements, control of manufacturing is decentralized to local-operations-unit levels.

To present a full line of agricultural machinery, it is necessary to coordinate the product needs of regional markets with available product-development funds and manpower. The goal is to develop a common unit that probably satisfies somewhat less than the total potential in each market, but achieves optimum worldwide market penetration and profitability.

Product decisions—product development decisions—are highly centralized in Massey-Ferguson because they involve a number of markets and a number of operational units.

As an example of what this control upon product development and product design can achieve, it might be noted that the North American tractor manufacturing operation in Detroit may use diesel engines from Perkins and transmissions from our tractor plants in the United Kingdom, rear axles from France, castings and machined components from Canada and, of course, the major complement of components from the United States. This can also be done in reverse: components can be sent from the Detroit factory to any location in the world and be mated with components from these other factories in such a way that we always get the same high quality and the same properly performing units.

AREAS OF CENTRAL CONTROL

Some other decisions that are made centrally are those determining what products will be manufactured, where and for whom. Since demand for certain products in many market areas is too small to support local manufacture, these decisions are centralized to ensure maximum use of facilities, cash and other such assets.

To achieve our objective to become an integrated producer, we require continual exploration for opportunities for acquisition and expansion. Since every additional integrated source of agricultural equipment can affect each Massey-Ferguson worldwide operation, facility-addition decisions that increase total integration are centralized. Of course, centralized planning and control of the product line, of product development and engineering, and of manufacture implies centralized controls upon capital expenditures and investments as well. They are complementary.

The international business environment, including such things as tariffs, exchange rates, import quotas and taxes, not to mention political situations that alter relationships between sources and markets, are obviously important to us. We are quite convinced that our success as an international enterprise depends in large part on our ability to react with maximum flexibility and speed to such changes. For this reason a central group constantly analyzes developments that influence the flow of trade within our world to ensure that all company operations create the most desirable cash flow and profits.

From the foregoing discussion of Massey-Ferguson's objectives and the nature of the worldwide farm equipment business, you can see that the organization plan that best serves our total requirements is a blend of centralized and decentralized elements. Marketing and manufacturing responsibilities, together with supporting service functions, are located as close as possible to local markets. Activities that determine the long-range character of the company, such as the planning and control of the product line, the planning and control of facilities and money, and the planning of the strategy to react to changes in the patterns of international trade, are highly centralized.

The board of directors of the company establishes basic policies and objectives. These are executed by the president and the corporate staff, who also play an important role in all major decisions that affect worldwide strategy in transactions between operations units.

The president is an active, participating executive, maintaining constant personal contact with heads of all operating units.

From all of these considerations we can draw up a list of those responsibilities that cannot be decentralized at Massey-Ferguson:

1. The responsibility for determining the over-all objectives of the enterprise
2. The responsibility for formulating the policies that guide the enterprise
3. The final responsibility for the control of the business within the total range of the objectives and policies, including control over any changes in the nature of the business
4. The responsibility for product design, where a product decision affects more than one area of accountability
5. The responsibility for planning for the achievement of over-all objectives and for measuring actual performance against those plans
6. The final approval of corporate plans or budgets
7. The decisions pertaining to the availability, and the application, of general company funds
8. The responsibility for capital-investment plans.

Truly, any such list must be custom tailored to the needs of each individual enterprise. It might include all, a few, or none of the kinds of items which I have listed.

D. LINE, STAFF, AND FUNCTIONAL AUTHORITY

38 LINE AND STAFF: AN OBSOLETE CONCEPT?*

Hall H. Logan

The concept that all functions or departments of a business enterprise are either "line" or "staff" is now so firmly entrenched in management theory that any attempt to dislodge it may well seem doomed to failure. Yet it is certainly pertinent to ask, how applicable to business today is this seemingly immutable principle of organization? Does it really serve any practical purpose—other than to add further confusion to the already complex system of interlocking relationships through which any company of any size actually achieves its goals?

Under the line-staff concept, as we all know, line departments are those directly engaged in producing or selling the goods or services the enterprise exists to provide. All other activities are staff—a definition that inevitably relegates staff people to positions of secondary or ancillary importance in the organization. This either-or theory may have some relevance for a company in its earliest stage of development, when there is usually little difficulty in distinguishing the people who are really bringing home the bacon from those whose activities clearly fall into the category of overhead. But as the enterprise grows and its operations become more and more complex, the demarcation between line and staff functions becomes progressively fuzzier until, in the typical large corporation, it is no longer possible to state unequivocally just who is directly engaged in furthering its objectives and who is not.

To take a simple example, who sells more beer—the market research and advertising people or the driver salesman on the beer truck? There can be little dispute as to who is closer to the final product; but a concept of organization that revolves around this matter of direct involvement in the fabrication or sale of the product overlooks the vast amount of work that has to be done before any sales are consummated, as, for example, in the consumer industries. Nor does it recognize the skill and precision that go into the evolution of a product long before it reaches the production stage.

WHAT KIND OF LABEL?

As an example of the latter, let's consider the case of a company operating under a prime or major secondary contract with the Department of Defense. In such companies, the responsibility for developing design concepts is usually assigned to the Advanced Design department. Once a concept has been sold, responsibility for designing the hardware then passes to the Product Design department. Next, it is up to the Tooling department to establish a manufacturing plan—determining the component breakdown, line stations, major fixtures, etc. This planning phase completed, Tooling then has the responsibility for designing and manufacturing all tools and fixtures.

What Kind of Departments Are These? The orthodox would call them "staff," because they never get their hands on the salable article. The more liberal element would say, "Well, if the company's objectives say 'design, manufacture, and sell,' Product Design is a 'line' department. But Advanced Design? Now that's research—or is it? Well, probably they will have to be 'staff.'"

Such answers are attempts to explain organizational relationships on the basis of the type of work performed by each unit of the enterprise. But organizational relationships—the relationships that management establishes between departments, groups, and individuals, and the degree of responsibility and authority it assigns to these various organizational units to meet the needs of the situation—are not determined by type of work per se. While some functions do rather consistently possess a certain kind of authority, modern practice has tended to spread authority more widely, particularly among the skilled functions. The attempt to establish authority by type of function is totally at variance with the relationships

* Reprinted by permission of the publisher from *Personnel*, vol. 43, no. 1, pp. 26–33, January–February, 1966. Mr. Logan is professor of management, University of Arkansas.

that actually exist in the modern corporation.

Later, I shall give some examples of the wide variations that can exist in organizational relationships. At this point, though, I should like to outline a concept of formal organization that portrays what really goes on in business these days.

The aim of formal organization is to insure singleness of purpose. A company's success in attaining its goals depends upon the skill with which management functions and authority are divided and, probably more important, how the divisions are integrated into unified action. In practice, this boils down to first assigning responsibilities and then trying to insure, as far as possible, authority co-equal with these responsibilities.

AUTHORITY SPELLED OUT

Particularly at the lower echelons of the organizational structure, authority relationships must be well established and thoroughly understood because of the heavy travel over these paths. There must be a clear understanding of who is responsible for what, as well as the degree of this responsibility. Relationships at the top echelons, between corporate staffs and multiplant managers, generally require less explanation, and are expressed in broader terms.

Organizational relationships take three basic forms: line, functional, and staff. Each type achieves its purpose through the exercise of its own kind of authority. Let's take a closer look at these different forms of authority. Here, though, a preliminary definition is called for: *Authority is the right or power to issue commands and to discipline for violation; an accepted source of information.* This definition must be firmly grasped if the three basic types of organizational relationships are to be clearly understood.

Line Authority This inheres in the relationship between superior and subordinate level. It is administrative authority, having the right and power to issue commands, to exact accountability, and to discipline for violations. Rarely, however, does it exist in a pure form. Over and above his line authority, a supervisor invariably has some degree of functional authority also. Line authority never crosses departmental lines horizontally, but is the scalar chain that, regardless of the type of work or function performed, links the lowest unskilled worker through successive echelons of supervision to the president.

Functional Authority This is the authority delegated by formal action of management to an "accepted source of information" or a specialist. Functional authority is the right and power of one department to issue orders or instructions to one, several, or all other departments in an enterprise, also with the right of accountability from the addressee. Functional authority is as binding as line authority, but it *does not carry the right to discipline for violation* (or even to threaten) in order to enforce compliance.

This authority to issue orders pertains to a single function, or to a limited number of functions in which the subject department is authorized to act. Functional authority should be formally established by agreement among the departments affected, preferably in written procedures that are approved by middle management and finally by the president, or at least by the manager who supervises all the departments concerned.

Functional authority also implies co-equality of responsibility. The department issuing the orders is responsible for the results of its directives, and thus shares in the total responsibility for other departmental tasks.

Functional authority is usually impersonal in nature. In larger companies, it takes the form of written orders, schedules, inspection reports, and the like. If, however, the individual exercising functional authority cannot, as I said, threaten, or take reprisals outside of his own department, where are the teeth? The prior agreement is the basis for the working relationship. Furthermore, the functional department usually issues periodic reports, or on an emergency basis if necessary, which go both to the supervisor directly concerned and to the next level of supervision above. This feedback permits each supervisor to evaluate the effectiveness of his performance in achieving prescribed targets or goals, and to take corrective action as required.

If management promotes a teamwork philosophy and the use of functional and staff organizations, employees will readily accept orders from authorized sources outside the linear chain of command. A supervisor will no more readily question or reject a functional order than he would one from his immediate superior. But if he honestly believes that he cannot carry out a particular order, he can and does question it, regardless of its origin.

A KEY DIFFERENCE

It is the right to reprimand that differentiates line from functional relationships and distinguishes today's organizational practices from Taylor's pure functional foremanship. Through functional authority, the benefits of functional specialization are attained while retaining unity of command—for each man, one person-to-person boss relationship.

Staff Authority This actually is a misnomer, for the person or department operating in a staff relationship has no authority to issue orders to other departments and no right to demand accountability. "Pure staff" personnel carry out their work through influence. Such relationships exist where the function is variable or intermittent in nature. For example, the industrial engineer may have the responsibility to develop better methods throughout the enterprise. It is usually deemed best to let the I.E. sell individual departments on the value of his proposals. However, in companies where centralized authority is a policy, the I.E. may have the authority to direct each department in how best to perform its work. In the latter situation, the I.E. would have functional authority. Here is one example of how different managements can establish different organizational relationships for what on their respective organizational charts might appear to be the same.

What should we call departments having line relationships, functional authority relationships, or staff relationships? In practice, because of their ambiguous meanings, the terms "line" and "staff" are rarely used to designate a department's exact relationship with other segments of the enterprise. In fact, as subsequent examples will show, departments do not operate with the same authority relationships in all phases of their work.

In their practical, day-to-day work, people are concerned only with how to carry out a particular job and who is involved in the process. In explaining the job to a new worker, the foreman does not say, "You are a line operator; I am a line man; the Production Control people are staff, and so are the Inspection and Process Control people." Most likely his remarks will go something like this: "You are responsible for making a good product, but to be certain that we have uniform quality and that all specifications are met, all parts must be approved by the inspector—that guy over there with the red vest. Orders and schedules come to us from Production Control. You have to make the exact quantity specified on the order and work according to the schedule. The required materials, tools, and engineering drawings are specified on the production order. You get these from the Production Control crib over there.

"And if the order calls for process instruction No. so-and-so, you'll find these instructions in this drawer, filed by number. They are prepared by the Process Control department and are like a part of the engineering design. You must follow them carefully. Now, if the tools won't produce a good part, come to me and we may have to call in the Tool Liaison man. Don't try to rework the tool yourself. That's Tooling's responsibility. . . ."

FUSING OF OPERATIONS

From the examples I have already cited, it should be clear that, in the modern corporation, the departments operating only through line relationships are by no means confined to the classic sales and production functions. Moreover, there are many functional departments whose activities cannot be reconciled with the proposition that production and sales are the only segments of the organization directly concerned with furthering its prime objectives. Let's consider some further examples bearing out these contentions.

We might begin by reconsidering the question I cited at the outset—the status of the Advanced Design department of a large defense contractor. Under the line-staff concept, this would be a staff department. Actually, in discharging its basic responsibility it will operate through line relationships only. It is unlikely to have any functional relationships, though its members might be called upon for advice on certain projects from time to time.

Inspection provides an interesting example of how a particular function's authority relationships can change with the changing demands of the situation. In some companies, Inspection may not even exist as a separate function, each foreman being directly responsible for the quality of the work he supervises. As operations expand, management may, however, permit the foreman to add one or more inspectors and an assistant foreman to relieve him of routine inspection duties. While this group would approve or reject all items produced, it would report to the foreman and thus serve, in the formal sense, as a staff unit.

Later on, quality control may be so crucial to the continued success of the company's overall operations that it becomes advisable to make it an independent operation. To insure the desired level of quality, Inspection, or Quality Control as it might henceforth be termed, will then have to have functional authority. It will be directly accountable to the vice-president of Manufacturing, or may even be independent of Manufacturing.

Accounting operates through all three types of authority. Usually, the accounting department has functional authority to prescribe the kind of input data it needs and to insure its timely collection or submission. But the ultimate purpose of both internal and external accounting reports is to inform the several levels of management, stockholders, and other interested parties of the results of the company's operations. This is an advisory function carried out through a staff relationship.

WEARING TWO HATS

Payroll and Accounts Payable perform a basic function of the business through line relationships only, insofar as their output is concerned. Nevertheless, these units exercise functional authority in the collection of time cards, invoices, receiving reports, and other supporting data needed to carry out their responsibility.

Depending on general management policy, Purchasing can operate through line or staff relationships. Thus, if Purchasing is completely subordinate to Production—a purely clerical operation that makes no independent decisions—it will have a staff relationship with the production departments. However, these days, Purchasing is mostly centralized, particularly in larger companies. Though a good purchasing agent will work with the technical departments in selecting suppliers, the actual contractual negotiations, placing of purchase orders, and follow-up are his responsibilities, and are carried out through normal line relationships.

As I earlier pointed out, Industrial Engineering can operate through staff or functional relationships, again depending upon general management policy. Occasionally, Industrial Engineering will be told to "take over and get the job done," after it has sold a proposal to another department. Some experts hold that this is assuming line authority, but it is not the case because, in such a situation, the I.E. does not have full authority of reprimand; he cannot fire or suspend an employee. He will discuss any serious disciplinary problem with the worker's regular supervisor, but leave it to him to take the necessary action. In short, I.E. has temporary functional authority.

Production Control is another function that can operate through staff or functional relationships. Thus, shop orders and schedules may be prepared by a production control group that reports to a superintendent. If all their work is subject to his formal approval, the clerks will have only staff authority even though most of their orders bypass the superintendent because of their routine nature. But a production control department that has clearly defined responsibilities, and reports to the works manager or the vice-president of Manufacturing, will issue orders and schedules directly to first-line supervision. This is a functional authority at this lower level.

In most mass production industries, Tooling carries out its authority through line relationships. It does not advise the shop, nor does it exercise functional direction or authority over it. In fact, since the advent of the numerical control process, responsibility for the accuracy and quality of the final product rests essentially in the tooling function.

The tape instructions are prepared by the tooling programmer. Theoretically, in any event, this reduces the shop operation to pushing a button on the console. If the man who pushes the button can be said to be "advancing the product," who, it must be asked, is more directly concerned with furthering the prime objectives of the business?

From the foregoing examples it is clear that the production and direct sales departments are not the only ones with line authority. There are a number of other departments that neither advise nor functionally direct other units, but operate solely through line relationships to discharge their responsibilities. Some of these are in the mainstream of the business—others are less so.

Then there are many other departments that exercise functional authority in their relations with other groups, thus diluting and sharing in the responsibility for the total activities and end products of the latter units.

On the other hand, "pure staff" personnel are relatively few and staff-type departments relatively fewer still.

This presents an entirely different pattern and proportional mix of authority relationships from that of the line-staff concept, about which, incidentally, studies have indicated that 50 percent of the total workforce in sample industries is engaged in staff work. (With present-day competition, can any enterprise afford the luxury of 50 percent "planners" and 50 percent "doers"?)

Regardless of what the theorists may say, in practice, as I have tried to show, working relationships are designed—or evolve—to meet the demands of the situation. In practice, also, the members of the enterprise pay little attention to "line" and "staff" labels. They are concerned only with the responsibility and authority of the persons with whom they associate in carrying out their jobs. As the situation was aptly summed up by one vice-president, "We aren't aware of many staff people around here. Everybody has a job to do and does it, no matter what you call him."

39 THE AUTHORITY-INFLUENCE ROLE OF THE FUNCTIONAL SPECIALIST IN MANAGEMENT*

Wendell French and *Dale A. Henning*

Traditional generalizations about the corporate personnel manager's authority are highly misleading. In none of the twenty-five firms examined was the personnel manager in an essentially advisory position. His authority varied from little or no authority in some aspects of the broad personnel management function to a high degree of unilateral authority in others.

Even when the personnel manager's job was broken into major components, such as wage and salary administration or employment, great differences in authority within each component were evident. For example, this study showed him to be highly authoritative in determining collective bargaining strategy but playing a very minor role in determining the maximum concession to be made in the bargaining.

In most aspects of personnel management the personnel manager was found to exercise a joint or shared authority. However, the personnel manager frequently perceived himself as having more authority than his superior or an executive peer perceived him to have.

We interviewed three top executives in each of twenty-five enterprises in a metropolitan area to find out how much authority the corporated personnel manager[1] was perceived to exercise. These executives were the corporate personnel manager, his superior, and one of his executive peers. The firms varied in size from approximately 100 to 15,000 employees. A variety of industries were represented including those in the retail, financial, educational, manufacturing, governmental health, and news media fields.

The general purpose of this research was to reduce a void in management literature relative to detailed factual descriptions of the authority-influence role of the functional specialist. The literature abounds with assumptions, definitions and conjecture about the role of such executives. Yet there is little empirical evidence underlying such discussion. As a consequence, researchers in business administration and the behavioral sciences may be building unrealistic models and developing unfruitful hypotheses.

A more immediate purpose was to analyze the authority-influence role of the corporate personnel director, who traditionally has been called a "staff" man in the literature. Unfortunately, the word "staff" has a wide variety of meanings, having been defined variously as "advisory," "auxiliary," "facilitating," "service," and more uniquely, as a role with which the corporation could dispense for a day or more. Traditional terminology and description, in our judgment, have not accurately portrayed the authority-influence role of this executive and have contributed nearly as much confusion as enlightenment.

The authors wish to emphasize the "pilot" or preliminary nature of this undertaking. The study is fraught with research difficulties of both conceptual and procedural natures.

Traditional research tools were simply inadequate to define the personnel manager's role with greater precision. Conceptual problems such as these pervaded the research: How are decisions of the personnel manager's subordinates to be treated? How does one treat the personnel manager's role when it is subdivided and performed by two, three or four persons at the same organization level? What constitutes an organizational peer? Is a decision unilateral if the decision-maker consults with his superior before implementing it?

Because decisions made in the resolution of these and similar problems lie hidden in the data, and because of the size and nature of the sample, the reader will, of course, wish to treat the conclusions presented here as tentative.

* Reprinted by permission of the publisher from *Academy of Management Journal*, vol. 9, no. 8, pp. 187–203, September, 1966. Mr. French and Mr. Henning are professors of management and organization at the University of Washington.

[1] Actual titles varied, but for convenience the term "personnel director" or "personnel manager" will be used throughout this study.

THE CONCEPTUAL FRAMEWORK

One of several conceptual models which we find helpful in organizational analysis is to view the enterprise as essentially a network of interdependent systems which facilitate flows of events (processes) toward predetermined objectives.[2] This process-systems model avoids the common pitfalls of viewing the organization as a group of vertically-oriented components (departments), and concentrates on the flow of decisions and other events that are actually taking place within the enterprise. The traditional view of such departments as semi-autonomous vertical units does not reflect the complexities of real life organizations where systems cross and crisscross departmental lines; where one person plays a role in a variety of different systems; and, where the other persons functioning within a given system "live" in another organizational unit.

Using this model, the broad personnel management activity in the enterprise is visualized as a network of subsystems pertaining to staffing, compensation, training and development, collective bargaining, and the like. These subsystems can be further described in terms of their various components—procedures, policies, devices—and the people involved in their management. For example, the employment system in most enterprises will typically involve such components as a recruiting procedure, the use of the application blank, interviews, the assignment of certain people to conduct the interviewing, the assignment of certain people to make the final employment decision, etc.[3]

With this conceptual framework in mind, we developed a patterned interview form to be used as a guide in talking with the personnel director, his superior, and one of the personnel director's executive peers. The questions were structured so that the resulting data would permit comparisons among the perceptions of the three executive groups, as well as permitting the calculation of "average" responses and the tallying of the frequency with which certain responses occurred.

The form which was developed included questions pertaining to (a) hiring, (b) promotions, transfers and demotions, (c) wage and salary administration, (d) collective bargaining, (e) training and development, and (f) "miscellaneous." Some examples of the specific items follow: "Who approves requisitions involving hiring from outside the firm for new positions?" "If written job specifications are used, whose approval was necessary before such specifications were adopted?" "Whose approval is necessary to employ a given applicant?" These questions, in effect, were designed to find out who exercised authority in the various components of these personnel subsystems.

The subject matter of the various questions is shown in Figure 1. The number of questions in each of the major categories was a function of the researchers' judgments as to what constituted an appropriate range from important to relatively unimportant decisions.

This list does not necessarily include all of the activities of the corporate personnel directors; nor is the list intended to suggest what activities these executives *should* be involved in, nor what activities might assume salient importance for the personnel director in the future. For example, organizational planning and executive appraisal are areas not covered in this study yet are areas the authors foresee as assuming greater importance in the future.

THE POWER PROFILE

An authority scale was then developed as shown in Figure 2. This scale permitted coding of responses as to whether the decision was made by: (1a) the personnel manager's superior with one or two other executives but without the personnel manager; (1b) the personnel manager's superior only; (1c) other executives with neither the personnel manager's superior nor the personnel manager; (2) the personnel manager in conjunction with his superior and with other executives; (3) the personnel manager and the superior jointly; (4) the personnel manager and other executives but without his superior; (5) the personnel manager plus one other executive but without the superior; and (6) the personnel director alone.

The designations from 1a to 6 on the authority scale were considered to be a rough index of the exercise of decision-making authority by the personnel manager. Items 1a, 1b, and 1c were grouped together because these categories represented decisions in which the personnel manager played no part. Items 2 through 5 were considered to reflect a higher and higher concentration of the personnel

[2] Wendell French, "Processes vis-a-vis Systems: Toward a Model of the Enterprise and Administration," *Academy of Management Journal* (March, 1963), pp. 46–58.

[3] For further description of the process-system model see Wendell French, *The Personnel Management Process: Human Resources Administration* (Boston: Houghton-Mifflin, 1964), pp. 44–58; and Leonard Sayles, *Managerial Behavior* (New York: McGraw-Hill, 1964), pp. 256–264.

FIGURE 1 Authority Areas Covered by the Investigation

DECISION NO.	HIRING
1a	Hiring requisitions (new positions)
1b	Hiring requisitions (present positions)
7*	Approving individual job specifications
9	Use of psychological tests
13	Physical examinations
15	Use of reference checks
16	Final approval in hiring
17	Initial hiring rates
	PROMOTION, TRANSFERS, DEMOTIONS
19	Promotions within a department
20	Promotions between departments
23	Approving transfers
25	Adopting transfer procedures
26	Approving pay/rank cuts
30	Adopting discharge procedures
31	Approving employee discharge
	WAGE AND SALARY ADMINISTRATION
33	Adopting wage level policy
35	Adopting special wage policies for special groups
37a	Jobs covered by evaluation program
37b	Method of job evaluation
37c	Approving job description
37d	Appointing evaluation committee
37e	Making actual job evaluation
39a	Coverage of wage incentive plan
39b	Type of wage incentive plan
39g	Determining profit-bonus ratio

DECISION NO.	WAGE AND SALARY ADMINISTRATION (Continued)
43	Grouping jobs for pay grades
44	Determining number of pay grades
46	Determining dollar amount of rate or range
47	Exceptions to rate or range
48	Using merit vs. seniority within grades
49	Using merit vs. seniority for promotion
50	Determining merit of individual employee
51	Granting extra time off
52	Granting fringe benefits exceeding policy
	COLLECTIVE BARGAINING
55	Maximum bargaining concessions
57	Determining negotiation goals
58	Determining bargaining strategy
60	Taking grievances to arbitration
	TRAINING AND DEVELOPMENT
62	Adopting training programs
63	Determining training objectives
64	Selecting employees for training
	MISCELLANEOUS
70	Allocation of budgeted funds
71	Determining areas or equipment unsafe
72b	Establishing output standards

* Items which have been excluded from this analysis are those involving: (a) questions directed only to personnel directors; (b) lead-in questions designed to find out if a certain practice or procedure was in existence in the responding firm; or, (c) questions which were applicable only to a small fraction of firms, e.g., production incentive plans.

manager's decision-making authority. The rationale for the order of items 3 and 4 was that the superior probably played a predominant role in bilateral decisions, and the personnel manager thus would be less authoritative in this instance than when he is making joint decisions with a peer.

All of the responses about a given decision were "averaged" as in the following example. If 20 personnel director respondents indicated a bilateral decision made with the superior (a "3" rating on the authority index) and 20 respondents indicated a bilateral decision made with a peer (a "4" rating on the authority index), the 40 responses would be "averaged" to show a "3.5" rating on the authority index.

It should be noted, of course, that profiles based on "averages" and "composites" can provide misleading images. In an oft used example, the man with one foot on a hot stove and the other in a bucket of ice cannot be considered to be "on the average" quite comfortable. Likewise, the personnel manager who makes a decision unilaterally in one instance and who is completely excluded from the decision making in the other instance cannot be considered "on the average" to participate jointly in the decision making. The most that can be said is that he makes the decision half of the time. In a sense, the authority scale

FIGURE 2 Authority Scale: The Personnel Manager

NO AUTHORITY			JOINT OR SHARED AUTHORITY				UNILATERAL AUTHORITY
DECISION MADE BY							
1a	1b	1c	2	3	4	5	6
The personnel manager's superior, with one or two others, but without the personnel manager.	The personnel manager's superior.	Others, with neither the superior nor the personnel manager.	Joint decision among the personnel manager, his superior and others.	Joint decision between the personnel manager and superior.	The personnel manager and others, without the superior.	The personnel manager plus one other person without the superior.	The personnel manager.

described above is subject to this shortcoming.

To complement these averages and to provide a composite image which is more accurate than averages alone, percentages were calculated relative to the frequency with which the personnel directors made certain decisions across the various organizations. Figure 3 shows in the left hand column the average ranking on the authority scale, as described above. In the right hand column are shown the percentage of respondents indicating the decision made by: (a) Others; (b) Jointly between the personnel managers and others; and, (c) the Personnel Manager unilaterally.

From this comparison of the ranking on the authority scale and the proportion of respondents indicating how the decision was made, it is possible to arrive at a clearer picture of the authority status of the personnel manager than has been available to us heretofore.

For example, question 1a, which deals with hiring people to fill new positions, is clearly a decision made by others, with very little participation on the part of the personnel director. The respondents indicated they never made this decision unilaterally. This is in keeping with the average ranking on the authority scale, which was 1.37—indicating relatively little authority in making this type of decision.

Decision number 55 (determining maximum concessions to be made in collective bargaining) is another good example. The ranking on the authority scale for this decision was 1.21—indicating the personnel manager to have very little authority. Of the respondents, 92 percent indicated that this decision was made by others; 4 percent indicated that the personnel manager participated in the decision with others; and, 4 percent indicated that he made the decision unilaterally. This decision, then, is one very clearly perceived as being made by persons other than the personnel manager.

Decision number 58 (determining collective bargaining strategy), on the contrary, was perceived by more than half of the respondents as being made by the personnel director. The corresponding ranking on the authority scale was 4.13—indicating substantial authority on this decision. By noting both the ranking on the authority scale and the proportion of respondents indicating unilateral or joint participation or non-participation, it is hoped that the interested reader can get a more accurate, if still imprecise, picture of just what decisions the personnel manager makes, participates in, or is excluded from.

HYPOTHESES

The central hypotheses of the study, implicit in the discussion above, is that the authority-influence role of the corporate personnel director is much more complex than the descriptions in the traditional literature, and that the word "staff" when applied to this role is symptomatic of a general lack of understanding of the role. More specifically, the following hypotheses were used to direct the course of the research:

(1) There are differences in authority exercised by the personnel director *within* the major personnel subfunctions.

FIGURE 3 Rating on Authority Scale and Percent of Respondents Indicating Unilateral and Joint Participation and Non Participation in Decision-Making

DECISION NUMBER	DECISION AREA	AVERAGE RANKING ON AUTHORITY SCALE SCALE IN 25 INDUSTRIAL FIRMS	PERCENT OF RESPONDENTS INDICATING DECISION MADE BY		
			OTHERS	JOINTLY	PERSONNEL MANAGER
1a	Hiring requisitions for new positions	1.37	79	21	0
1b	Hiring requisitions for present positions	2.92	47	33	20
7	Approving individual job specifications	3.24	25	65	10
9	Use of psychological tests	4.70	14	14	72
13	Physical examinations	2.78	50	29	21
15	Use of reference checks	4.10	29	13	58
16	Final approval in hiring	3.04	48	48	4
17	Initial hiring rates	3.17	48	17	35
19	Promotions within a department	2.45	50	50	0
20	Promotions between departments	2.48	48	52	0
23	Approving transfers	2.53	48	49	3
25	Adopting transfer procedures	3.69	45	10	45
26	Approving pay/rank cuts	3.02	50	50	0
30	Adopting discharge procedures	3.63	32	26	42
31	Approving employee discharge	3.16	37	50	13
33	Adopting wage level policy	1.33	80	20	0
35	Adopting special wage policies for special groups	1.36	78	22	0
37a	Jobs covered by evaluation program	2.84	32	45	23
37b	Method of job evaluation	3.83	19	43	38
37c	Approving job description	3.36	33	45	22
37d	Appointing evaluation committee	1.99	66	16	16
37e	Making actual job evaluation	3.78	11	73	16
39a	Coverage of wage incentive plan	1.36	67	33	0
39b	Type of wage incentive plan	1.67	40	60	0
39g	Determining profit-bonus ratio	1.28	71	29	0
43	Grouping jobs for pay grades	3.28	24	48	28
44	Determining number of pay grades	2.79	35	45	20
46	Determining dollar amount of rate or range	2.43	38	48	14
47	Exceptions to wage rate or range	2.34	61	27	12
48	Using merit vs. seniority within grade	1.89	58	37	5
49	Using merit vs. seniority for promotion	2.28	50	40	10
50	Determining merit of individual employee	1.75	75	18	7
51	Granting extra time off	2.31	65	21	14
52	Granting fringe benefits exceeding policy	1.55	79	14	7
55	Maximum bargaining concessions	1.21	92	4	4
57	Determining negotiation goals	2.27	48	39	13
58	Determining bargaining strategy	4.13	36	7	57
60	Taking grievances to arbitration	3.04	31	44	25
62	Adopting training programs	1.88	63	29	8
63	Determining training objectives	2.64	52	35	13
64	Selecting employees for training	2.88	48	40	12
70	Allocation of budgeted funds	4.11	20	20	60
71	Determining area or equipment unsafe	1.66	81	11	8
72b	Establishing output standards	1.90	0	75	25

(2) There are differences in authority exercised by the personnel director *between* the major personnel subfunctions.

(3) There are differences in the perceptions of the personnel director, his peers, and his superior as to the amount of authority he exercises.

FINDINGS

A very clear pattern emerges from the data in this study. This pattern is one in which the personnel manager exercises a joint or shared authority in decision making.

This joint or shared authority took two forms. In one form, the personnel manager took part in a decision that was made jointly by two or more persons with face-to-face participation. The second form of participation occurred when the personnel manager's concurrence was necessary for a decision to become effective or where the personnel manager made a decision and required someone else's concurrence before it could be implemented.

However, there were a large number of decisions which were made unilaterally by the personnel manager. Figures 3 and 4 indicate that the personnel manager exercises particularly strong unilateral action in the following areas: determining procedures and sources in the recruitment of potential employees, the use of psychological tests, establishing reference check procedures in employment, determining collective bargaining strategy, and expending departmental funds within broad budgetary guidelines.

On the other hand, there were certain areas where the respondents agreed the personnel manager took *no* unilateral action. For example, in no instance did the personnel manager unilaterally decide about promotions, nor did he ever unilaterally determine pay or rank cuts in any of the responding firms. Further, in no instance did the personnel manager make a unilateral decision about the level of company wages as related to community wages. Likewise, the personnel manager was excluded from unilateral action in all of the decisions that had to do with wage incentives and profit sharing.

Figure 5 indicates those instances in which the personnel manager made *joint* decisions. He appears to have a particularly strong decision-making role in the hiring, promotion, demotion, and discharge of employees. Based on the aggregate data, personnel managers played *some* role, either unilateral or joint, in all of the decisions investigated in the study.

Figure 6 indicates those instances where the personnel manager's authority was the weakest; namely, those where fewer than 25 percent of the respondents perceived him as participating either jointly in the decision making or making the decision unilaterally. Specifically, the decisions were: approving requisitions involving new positions granting fringe benefits exceeding stated policy, deciding on maximum bargaining concessions, and making equipment or areas inoperative for safety reasons. Figure 7 shows similar data for those decisions falling below the 50 percent level.

Differences of Authority *within* the Broad Personnel Management Function and *within* Its Major Components Figure 8 shows the average rating on the authority scale for each of the decisions in the study. The decisions are arranged in order from those wherein the personnel manager was most authoritative to those in which he had the least authority. There is a considerable range of authority, from 4.70 relative to the use of psychological tests to 1.21 in the case of decisions about maximum concessions in collective bargaining.

Thus, Figure 8 (and Figure 3, as well) give substantial evidence to support one of the basic hypotheses underlying this study, namely, that there are considerable differences in the authority exercised by the personnel manager from one decision area to another.

A further assumption provisionally accepted as a basis for investigation was that there would be considerable variation in the amount of authority exercised *within* each major component or sub-function of the personnel manager's position. This hypothesis has been confirmed by the results of this study. As one illustration, we find the personnel manager highly authoritative in deciding on the use of psychological tests and reference checks, but exercising little authority in approving requisitions for new organizational positions.

Authority Differences *between* Major Personnel Sub-Functions An additional hypothesis accepted provisionally as a basis for investigation was that the personnel manager would be more authoritative in one major component of his job than he would be in another. For example, he would be more authoritative in matters of wage and salary administration than he would be in matters of promotion, transfer and demotions. While the several subfunctions tended to cluster at the center of the authority index, differences between subfunctions were recorded as shown in Figure 9.

FIGURE 4 Unilateral Decision-Making by the Personnel Manager

STRONG UNILATERAL ACTION (50% OF RESPONDENTS AND OVER INDICATED UNILATERAL ACTION)	SUBSTANTIAL UNILATERAL ACTION (15% TO 49% OF RESPONDENTS INDICATED UNILATERAL ACTION)	WEAK UNILATERAL ACTION (1% TO 14% OF RESPONDENTS INDICATED UNILATERAL ACTION)	NO UNILATERAL ACTION (ZERO RESPONDENTS INDICATED UNILATERAL ACTION)
Decision Area:	*Decision Area:*	*Decision Area:*	*Decision Area:*
Use of psychological tests	Hiring requisitions (present positions)	Approving individual job specifications	Hiring requisitions (new positions)
Use of reference checks	Physical examinations	Final approval in hiring	Promotions within a department
Determining bargaining strategy	Initial hiring rates	Promotions between departments	Promotions between departments
Allocation of budgeted funds	Adopting transfer procedures	Approving employee discharge	Approving pay/rank cuts
	Adopting discharge procedures	Determining dollar amount of rate or range	Adopting wage level policy
	Jobs covered by evaluation program	Exceptions to rate or range	Adopting special wage policies for special groups
	Method of job evaluation	Using merit vs.-seniority within grades	Coverage of wage incentive plan
	Approving job description	Using merit vs. seniority for promotion	Type of wage incentive plan
	Appointing evaluation committee	Determining merit of individual employee	Determining profit-bonus ratio
	Making actual job evaluation	Granting extra time off	
	Grouping jobs for pay grades	Granting fringe benefits exceeding policy	
	Determining number of pay grades	Maximum bargaining concessions	
	Taking grievances to arbitration	Determining negotiation goals	
	Establishing output standards	Adopting training programs	
		Determining training objectives	
		Selecting employees for training	
		Determining areas or equipment unsafe	

FIGURE 5 Decisions Made Jointly by the Personnel Manager and Others

STRONG PARTICIPATION (50% OF RESPONDENTS AND OVER INDICATED JOINT DECISION-MAKING)	SUBSTANTIAL PARTICIPATION (15% TO 49% OF RESPONDENTS INDICATED JOINT DECISION-MAKING)	WEAK PARTICIPATION (1% TO 14% OF RESPONDENTS INDICATED JOINT DECISION-MAKING)
Approving individual job specifications	Hiring requisitions (new positions)	Use of reference checks*
Promotions within a department	Hiring requisitions (present positions)	Adopting transfer procedures*
Promotions between departments	Use of psychological tests*	Maximum bargaining concessions
Approving pay/rank cuts	Physical examinations	Determining strategy*
Approving employee discharge	Final approval in hiring	Determining areas or equipment unsafe
Making actual job evaluation	Initial hiring rates	
Type of wage incentive plan	Approving transfers	
Establishing output standards	Adopting discharge procedures	
	Adopting wage level policy	
	Adopting special wage policies for special groups	
	Jobs covered by evaluation program	
	Method of job evaluation	
	Approving job description	
	Appointing evaluation committee	
	Coverage of wage incentive plan	
	Determining profit-bonus ratio	
	Grouping jobs for pay grades	
	Determining number of pay grades	
	Determining dollar amount of rate or range	
	Exceptions to rate or range	
	Using merit vs. seniority within grades	
	Using merit vs. seniority for promotion	
	Determining merit of individual employee	
	Granting extra time off	
	Granting fringe benefits exceeding policy	
	Determining negotiation goals	
	Taking grievances to arbitration	
	Adopting training programs	
	Determining training objectives	
	Selecting employees for training	
	Allocation of budgeted funds	

* Areas of strong or substantial unilateral action by the personnel director.

FIGURE 6 **Decision Areas in Which the Personnel Manager's Participation (Either Unilateral or Joint) Was Limited Decisions Where Fewer Than 25 Percent of All Respondents Indicated the Personnel Manager Participated in Decision-Making**

QUESTION	DECISION AREA	PERCENTAGE
1a	Hiring requisitions (new positions)	21%
52	Granting fringe benefits exceeding policy	21%
55	Maximum bargaining concessions	8%
71	Determining areas or equipment unsafe	19%

FIGURE 7 **Decision Areas in Which Unilateral and Joint Action of the Personnel Manager Was Less Than "Strong" Decisions Where Fewer Than 50 Percent of All Respondents Indicated the Personnel Manager Participated in Decision-Making**

QUESTION	DECISION AREA	PERCENTAGE
1a	Hiring requisitions (new positions)	21%
33	Adopting wage level policy	20%
35	Adopting special wage policies for special groups	22%
37d	Appointing evaluation committee	32%
39a	Coverage of wage incentive plan	33%
39c-2	Establishing group sizes under wage incentive plan	33%
39g	Determining profit-bonus ratio	29%
47	Exceptions to rate or range	39%
48	Using merit vs. seniority within grades	42%
50	Determining merit of individual employee	25%
51	Granting fringe benefits exceeding policy	21%
55	Maximum bargaining concessions	8%
62	Adopting training programs	37%
63	Determining training objectives	48%
71	Determining areas or equipment unsafe	19%

It can be seen from Figure 9 that the personnel director is perceived as most authoritative in the hiring function followed closely by his authority in the area of promotions, demotions and transfers, and his authority in collective bargaining. On the average, he is seen as having less authority in training and development than in the above functions and the least authority in the area of compensation. Thus, our hypothesis about the existence of differences in authority between major sub-functions was confirmed.

Figure 10 repeats the data from Figure 9 and in addition shows that in general the personnel manager was perceived as having more authority with respect to decisions about blue-collar workers than about white-collar workers. The one exception to this general practice was in the area of collective bargaining, where the personnel manager appeared to play a stronger role relative to white-collar workers than to blue-collar workers.

Differences in Perception A third hypothesis was that there would be differences in the perceptions of the personnel director, his peers, and his superior about the amount of authority exercised by the personnel director. A general pattern of differing perceptions did appear.

In general, the personnel manager perceives himself to be more authoritative than he is perceived by either of the other two executive groups involved in the study. The personnel

FIGURE 8 **The Personnel Manager's Authority in Different Aspects of Personnel Management (Ranked from Most to Least Authority)**

QUESTION NUMBER	DECISION AREA	AVERAGE RATING ON AUTHORITY SCALE
9	Use of psychological tests	4.70
58	Determining bargaining strategy	4.13
70	Allocation of budgeted funds	4.11
15	Use of reference checks	4.10
37b	Method of job evaluation	3.83
37e	Making actual job evaluation	3.78
25	Adopting transfer procedures	3.69
30	Adopting discharge procedures	3.63
37c	Approving job description	3.36
43	Grouping jobs for pay grades	3.28
7	Approving individual job specifications	3.24
17	Initial hiring rates	3.17
31	Approving employee discharge	3.16
16	Final approval in hiring	3.04
60	Taking grievances to arbitration	3.04
26	Approving pay/rank cuts	3.02
1b	Hiring requisitions for present positions	2.92
64	Selecting employees for training	2.88
37a	Jobs covered by evaluation program	2.84
44	Determining number of pay grades	2.79
13	Physical examinations	2.78
63	Determining training objectives	2.64
23	Approving transfers	2.53
20	Promotions between departments	2.48
19	Promotions within a department	2.45
46	Determining dollar amount of rate or range	2.43
47	Exceptions to rate or range	2.34
51	Granting extra time off	2.31
49	Using merit vs. seniority for promotion	2.28
57	Determining negotiation goals	2.27
37d	Appointing evaluation committee	1.99
72b	Establishing output standards	1.90
48	Using merit vs. seniority within grade	1.89
62	Adopting training programs	1.88
50	Determining merit of individual employee	1.75
39b	Type of wage incentive plan	1.67
71	Determining area or equipment unsafe	1.66
52	Granting fringe benefits exceeding policy	1.55
1a	Hiring requisitions for new positions	1.37
35	Adopting special wage policies for special groups	1.36
39a	Coverage of wage incentive plan	1.36
33	Adopting wage level policy	1.33
39a	Determining profit-bonus ratio	1.28
55	Maximum bargaining concessions	1.21
44 Total		

FIGURE 9 Differences between Major Sub-Functions in Authority Exercised by Personnel Director

SUB-FUNCTION	RATING ON AUTHORITY INDEX
Hiring	3.166
Promotion, demotion and transfer	2.994
Collective bargaining	2.837
Training and development	2.466
Wage and salary administration	2.284

manager's superior sees him as having the least amount of authority, while the peer tends to have an in-between perception. The peer perceives the personnel manager as having more authority than his superior thinks he has, but less authority than the personnel manager perceives himself to have. This general pattern held in four of the five major sub-functions of the personnel manager's job.

Only in the collective bargaining activity was there a deviation from this general pattern. In the collective bargaining activity, both the superior and the peer perceived the personnel manager as having more authority than the personnel manager saw himself as having. The superior viewed him as having the most authority, the peer next, and the personnel manager saw himself with the least authority.

In rank order from most to least, the personnel director saw himself as exercising authority in the broad personnel sub-functions as follows: (a) promotions, demotions, and

FIGURE 10 Authority Exercised by the Personnel Manager: A Comparison between Major Personnel Sub-Functions

		PERSONNEL DIRECTOR RATING ON AUTHORITY INDEX	SUPERIOR RATING ON AUTHORITY INDEX	PEER RATING ON AUTHORITY INDEX	AVERAGE
Hiring	BC*	3.424	2.809	3.110	3.114
	WC**	3.328	2.710	3.035	3.024
	Both	3.510†	2.744	3.243	3.166
Promotion, Transfer, etc.	BC	3.416	2.586	2.580	2.861
	WC	3.226	2.423	2.384	2.678
	Both	3.561	2.633	2.787	2.994
Collective Bargaining	BC	2.440	2.976	2.194	2.537
	WC	2.082	3.230	2.692	2.668
	Both	2.262	3.588	2.660	2.837
Training and Development	BC	2.667	2.223	2.177	2.356
	WC	2.740	2.233	2.080	2.351
	Both	2.847	2.287	2.263	2.466
Wage and Salary Administration	BC	2.496	2.076	2.521	2.364
	WC	2.378	2.085	2.075	2.179
	Both	2.433	2.146	2.273	2.284

* "Blue-collar" employees.
** "White-collar" employees.
† It is possible for the "both" category to have a higher rating than either the Blue-collar or White-collar categories because of differences in the number and type of responses.

FIGURE 11 Relative Ranking of Personnel Manager's Authority in Major Sub-Functions

RANKING BY PERSONNEL DIRECTOR	RANKING BY SUPERIOR	RANKING BY PEER
Promotion, Demotion, and Transfer	Collective Bargaining	Hiring
Hiring	Hiring	Promotions and Transfers
Training and Development	Promotions and Transfers	Collective Bargaining
Wage and Salary Administration	Training and Development	Wage and Salary Administration
Collective Bargaining	Wage and Salary Administration	Training and Development

transfers, (b) hiring, (c) training and development, (d) wage and salary administration, and (e) collective bargaining (see Figure 11). His superior ranked his authority in these sub-functions as follows: collective bargaining; hiring; promotion, demotion and transfer; training and development; and wage and salary administration. His peers ranked his authority as follows: hiring; promotion, demotion and transfer; collective bargaining; wage and salary administration; and training and development.

Major Deviations from the Pattern of Perception As shown in Figure 12, there were 21 decisions which departed from the general pattern wherein the personnel manager thought himself to be most authoritative, the superior least, and the peer in-between. On 15 decisions (those marked with one asterisk), the superior saw the personnel manager as more authoritative than the personnel manager saw himself. On ten decisions (items marked with two asterisks) the personnel manager was caught in the middle with either a superior thinking he had *more* authority and his peer thinking he had *less* authority than he thought himself to have—or, conversely, the peer perceiving him to have more authority and the superior perceiving him to have less than he thought himself to have.[4]

There were ten instances where *both* the superior and the peer perceived the personnel manager as having more authority than he believed himself to have. In these cases, it could mean that they have expectations about how the personnel manager should act but the personnel manager's self-image might not allow him to act that way. In such circumstances, he is likely to be viewed as unwilling to take aggressive action or as indecisive and consequently as appropriately placed in a "staff" position since he seemed incapable of assuming a "real leadership" role.

Two of the decisions warrant special note since the magnitudes of the differences in perception were very great. These decisions were determining company strategy on collective bargaining issues (item 58) and deciding strategy with respect to the submission of grievances to arbitration (item 60). In these decisions, superiors thought the personnel manager to have a great deal of authority (5.4 and 4.4 respectively on the authority index) whereas the personnel managers perceived themselves as being considerably less authoritative (2.7 and 2.2 respectively).

SUMMARY AND CONCLUSIONS

The following general conclusions emerged from this study:

1. Traditional generalizations about the per-

[4] Some speculation might be in order as to the consequences of the superior perceiving the personnel director as more authoritative than the personnel manager perceives himself to be. The superior might then see his subordinate as a person "who won't take the initiative" or "who comes to me for advice when he should act himself." The peer, on the other hand, if he sees the personnel manager as being less authoritative than the personnel director's own perception of himself, may view the same man as "sticking his nose in where it doesn't belong" or "interfering with my men" or "throwing his weight around." In those cases where the peer perceived the personnel manager as more authoritative and the superior saw him as less authoritative, opposite pictures were likely to emerge. In those cases, it would be the superior who might view the personnel manager as overly aggressive and "grabbing for power" while the peer might view him as unwilling to make decisions or to take initiative and responsibility.

FIGURE 12 Sub-Functions in Which Peers and/or Superiors Perceive the Personnel Director as Having More Authority Than Directors Perceive Themselves to Have

QUESTION NUMBER	DECISION AREA	AVERAGE RATING ON THE AUTHORITY INDEX: PERSONNEL DIRECTOR	SUPERIOR	PEER
7	Approving individual job specifications	3.333**	2.375	4.0
13*	Physical examinations	2.333	[2.75]	[3.25]
15	Use of reference checks	4.89**	2.29	5.13
23	Approving transfers	2.58**	2.33	2.67
31	Approving employee discharge	3.09	4.00	2.40
34*		1.35**	1.50	1.13
35*	Adopting special wage policies for special groups	1.40**	1.67	1.00
37d*	Appointing evaluation committee	1.80	[1.83]	[2.33]
37e*	Making actual job evaluation	3.50	[4.00]	[3.83]
39g*	Determining profit-bonus ratio	1.00	[1.50]	[1.33]
43	Grouping jobs for pay grades	3.33**	3.00	3.50
44*	Determining number of pay grades	2.57	[2.67]	[3.14]
46*	Determining dollar amount of rate or range	2.00	[2.17]	[3.13]
48	Using merit vs. seniority within grades	1.88**	1.29	2.50
50*	Determining merits of individual employee	1.80**	1.89	1.55
51*	Granting extra time off	2.00	[2.67]	[2.25]
55	Maximum bargaining concessions	1.00	[1.50]	[1.15]
57*	Determining negotiation goals	2.22**	2.75	1.83
58*	Determining bargaining strategy	2.67	[5.40]	[4.33]
60*	Taking grievances to arbitration	2.20	[4.43]	[2.50]
62*	Adopting training programs	1.86	1.91	1.86

* Decision areas in which superior sees personnel director as more authoritative than the latter perceives himself to be.

** Decision areas in which superior and peer have perceptions on both sides of the personnel director's own perceptions.

□ Decision areas in which both superior and peer perceive the personnel director to have greater authority than he himself perceives.

sonnel manager's authority are highly misleading. Enough consistency emerges from this study to conclude that his authority varies from little or no authority in some aspects of personnel management to a high degree of unilateral authority in others.

2. Even when his job is broken into major components, such as wage and salary administration or employment, generalizations cover great differences of authority within each component. For example, this study shows him to be highly authoritative in determining collective bargaining *strategy* but to play a very minor role in determining concessions that can be made in the bargaining.
3. In most instances the personnel manager exercises a joint or shared authority. He is perceived as heavily involved in joint decision making over a wide range of personnel decisions within each of the major sub-functions.
4. The personnel manager appears to be particularly strong in terms of unilateral action (50 percent or more of respondents saw him as taking unilateral action) in decisions pertaining to the use of psychological tests, the use of reference checks in employment, and in determining bargaining strategy. He is seen as exercising substantial unilateral action (15 to 49 percent of respondents perceived him as acting unilaterally) over a wide variety of decisions within each of the major sub-functions except training and development.
5. The personnel manager plays a relatively

lesser role in decisions involving the creation of new positions, maximum bargaining concessions, granting unusual and additional fringe benefits, or declaring equipment or areas inoperative for safety reasons.

6. The personnel director is perceived as most authoritative in his hiring function, followed closely by his authority in the area of promotion, demotion, and transfer, and his authority in collective bargaining decisions. He is perceived as having less authority in training and development, and least in the area of wage and salary administration.
7. In general, personnel managers tend to perceive themselves as having more authority than their superiors or peers perceive them to have.

Finally, we would emphasize once more that over-simplification in describing the role of the personnel manager has led to erroneous impressions of what he is and what he does. Whereas the methodology and data in this study lead only to tentative conclusions, we feel confident that further research will corroborate rather than contradict its general findings. In this connection, we see as especially fruitful grounds for research the possible dysfunctional consequences that may arise from differential perceptions of the authority exercised by such functional executives as the personnel manager.

40 AUTHORITY ROLE OF A FUNCTIONAL MANAGER: THE CONTROLLER*

Dale A. Henning and *R. L. Moseley*

The complexity of most disciplines requires the extensive use of both classification and generalization. The field of management is no exception. Neither are those in this field exempt from the professional imperative to continuously examine and test the validity and usefulness of the concepts and constructs they employ. The widespread use of stereotype definitions of functional roles in organizations warrants their examination in particular.

French and Henning (1966) showed that the traditional definition of one functional role, the personnel manager, is misleading. Their study of the personnel manager in 25 firms revealed that (1) he does not have the same degree of authority in each area of his responsibility; (2) his authority varies from one type of decision to another even within a single area of responsibility; and (3) he and other executives in the organization do agree on the definition of the personnel manager's authority role.

The research findings reported in this article indicate that the role of the controller does not conform to traditional definitions either, and, in light of the French and Henning (1966) study, suggest that other functional specialist roles might also be inadequately understood.

An extensive literature describes the controller's duties and responsibilities and the techniques and tools associated with them (McDonald, 1940; Anderson and Schmidt, 1961; Heckert and Willson, 1963; Stott, 1964; Bradshaw and Hull, 1950; Hutton, 1962; Thomas, 1968). The traditional definitions and assumptions underlying this literature have inhibited the development of a more realistic and useful theoretical framework for analysis and normative proposals (Melcher, 1965). The Controllers Institute of America, now the Financial Executives Institute, has long recognized the need for "a comprehensive long-range plan . . . to bridge the gap between the theory and practice of controllership" (Bradshaw and Hull, 1950: vii).

This study attempts to clarify the real-life relationships involved in making important controllership decisions and to discern differences between the prescribed and perceived roles of the controller.

CONCEPTUAL FRAMEWORK

Traditional conceptual frameworks for research in management and organization fall into two main categories. The first approach focuses on behavior, for example, "conflict, poor communication, low motivation, difficulties of change, low productivity" while the second focuses on formal design, for example, "the design of the formal structure, physical-technical conditions, incentive systems or techniques of decision-making, directing, disciplining, planning" (Melcher, 1965: 130). Neither the formal design framework, which has dominated the study of controllership, nor the behavioral framework alone is adequate for examining the controller's role and relationships. Sayles (1964: 262) observed:

> For the most part, management theory and management principles stress abstract categories and entities rather than process. They are usually concerned with the nature of authority and its preservation (when there are multiple hierarchies and staff specialists) . . . Much is static description: the functions performed by typical controllers are surveyed and listed.
>
> As a result, management principles fail to deal with dynamic problems of human systems in action. For example, it is easy to say legalistically that staff advisors should not have authority because, lacking it, they will not destroy the principle of unitary command. But

* Reprinted by permission of the publisher from *Administrative Science Quarterly*, vol. 15, no. 4, pp. 482–489, December, 1970. Mr. Henning is professor of management and organization at the University of Washington, and Mr. Moseley is professor of management at Portland State University.

> . . . the actual conduct of an advisory relationship—the pattern and sequence of contacts and their quantitative characteristics—involve complex and subtle behavioral requirements.

Seeking a more useful analytical framework French and Henning (1966: 188) utilized a process-system model of the organization which described it as "essentially a network of interdependent systems which facilitate flows of events toward predetermined objectives." A system was defined as a particular linking of elements—people, raw materials, plans, policies, and so forth—designed to facilitate a particular process. A process was defined as a particular set of interrelated events or activities leading to some goal. Such processes were viewed as either administrative, such as planning, organizing, directing, or controlling, or operational, such as recruiting, hiring, training or promoting.

Using the French and Henning (1966) process-system model, controllership was described as such a set of processes or functions leading to the accomplishment of predetermined organizational objectives. For this study, the Financial Executives Institute's definitions of these processes were adopted, with the following modifications:

1. Evaluating and consulting, used by the Institute, was not used in the study.
2. Planning for control was divided into long-range budgeting and short-range budgeting.
3. Reporting and interpreting was divided into accounting reports and accounting systems.
4. Protection of assets was divided into internal control, internal auditing, and insurance adequacy.

The decision topics for each controller function were selected as representative of the types of decisions required in each function as described in the literature and by practicing controllers.

The controller was seen to carry out his responsibilities through direct participation as a member of the systems facilitating those processes or functions. The analysis centers on controllers' participation in the decisions relating to each of the decision topics.

MEASURING CONTROLLERS' AUTHORITY

The controllers' authority with respect to the various decision topics was initially identified in terms of how the controller typically participated in decision-making, that is, whether in committee or jointly with his immediate superior, and so on. Eleven such decision-making situations were utilized to categorize responses; these are listed in Table 1. A scale assigning authority values to the 11 types of decision-making situations was used to convert to a numerical value responses describing how a particular decision was made. This made it possible to arrive at a quantitative approximation of controllers' authority for any particular decision topic and, by aggregating, to arrive at a measure of authority for a controllership function.

TABLE 1 Authority Scale

DECISION SITUATION (WHO MAKES THE DECISION)	AUTHORITY INDEX SCORE
Controller	100
Controller jointly with one other Committee, controller chairs, superior not on committee	75
Controller jointly with two or more other members Committee, controller chairs, superior on committee Controller jointly with superior Committee, controller member, superior not on committee	50
Controller jointly with others and superior	35
Committee, controller member, superior is on committee Committee, controller member, superior chairs	25
Superior and/or others	0

To develop the values of the authority scale, a selected sample of 77 middle and top managers from both business and government organizations was asked to rank the 11 decision-making situations according to the degree of authority each would give to a hypothetical executive. A scaling procedure (Dunn-Rankin, 1965) was used to convert the resulting rank totals to a scale ranging from 0 to 100 and to identify decision situations with rank differences that were not statistically significant. Each of the resulting six categories consisted of decision-making situations not significantly different in rank from others in the same category, but significantly different in rank from decisions situations in other categories. By coincidence, the average value in each category turned out to be very close to the convenient values actually adopted for the scale, the added convenience clearly offsetting the minor loss in accuracy. The range in the scale scores did not exceed 9 in any category. The final authority scale is shown in Table 1. If a controller were perceived to make a certain type of decision by himself, he would be considered to have unilateral authority—index = 100. If he were perceived not to participate at all, he would have no authority—index = 0—insofar as that type of decision is concerned. Intermediate situations were handled in the same manner.

The controller, his superior, and a peer executive of the controller were interviewed in each of 25 medium-sized firms. In 14 of the 25 firms 2 or more executives, with such titles as treasurer, insurance supervisor, director of profit planning, financial vice president, and so on, shared the responsibility for the 10 controllership functions or processes studied. In those cases, each executive with responsibility for one or more of the functions, his superior, and a peer were interviewed. Each interviewee was asked how the controller participated in the making of the specific decisions in each of the controllership functions. Not every decision topic was relevant for every company.

FINDINGS

Authority Variations among the Functions

To determine whether there were differences in the degree of authority the controllers were perceived to exercise among controllership functions, null hypotheses were tested using the frequency distributions of responses among the authority categories for each function.

Hypothesis 1. There are no differences in controllers' degree of authority among the controllership functions, as perceived by controllers, superiors, or peers.

All three categories of respondents perceived controllers to have variations in their authority among the various functions. Chi-square tests were significant at $p < .01$ for controllers, superiors, and peers.

Controllers do not have homogeneous authority and the degree of their authority depends on the particular function in which they are engaged. As the authority scores in Table 2 show, this authority varies from almost unilateral authority in dealing with government reports and internal auditing to substantially shared authority in long-range budgeting, short-range budgeting, and accounting reports.

TABLE 2 Controllers' Authority Profile

FUNCTION	AGGREGATE AUTHORITY SCORE	RANGE OF AVERAGED DECISION TOPIC AUTHORITY SCORES	STANDARD DEVIATION OF AVERAGED DECISION TOPIC AUTHORITY SCORES
Government reports	90	15.0	8.7
Internal auditing	88	43.9	19.3
Accounting system	77	41.0	16.8
Economic appraisal	76	36.4	18.7
Tax administration	76	21.3	8.6
Insurance adequacy	76	22.6	9.5
Internal control	62	65.2	21.6
Long-range budgeting	52	83.7	27.4
Short-range budgeting	48	78.6	27.8
Accounting reports	48	69.2	21.5

Authority Variations among Decision Topics within Functions To determine whether there were differences in the controllers' degree of authority among decision topics within a function, the following null hypothesis was tested for each function by analysis of variance in a matrix of authority scores ascribed to the controller for each decision topic within that area:

Hypothesis 2. There are no differences in the controllers' degree of authority among the various decision topics within a function as perceived by controllers, superiors, and peers.

The differences in authority among decision topics were significant at $p < .01$ for all functions except economic appraisal and insurance adequacy. The results were significant at $p < .025$ for economic appraisal. For insurance adequacy the differences were not statistically significant. As shown in Table 2, by two measures of variation, range and standard deviation, these differences are not uniform among functions. For example, both measures indicate substantially greater variation in authority

TABLE 3 Authority Scores and Ranking of Decision Topics by Controllership Function

FUNCTIONS AND DECISIONS	RANK	AVERAGE AUTHORITY SCORES
Government reports		
Initiation of preparation of government reports	6	95.4
Directing preparation of government reports	7	95.2
Final approval of government reports	21	80.4
Internal auditing		
Auditing procedures	3.5	96.7
Frequency and timing of audits	9	93.3
Extensiveness of audits	3.5	96.7
Correcting problems revealed by audits	50	53.3
Petty cash audit	2	97.2
Accounting system		
Accounting source documents	25	76.6
Chart of accounts	11	90.8
Accounting procedures	14	85.8
Recording ambiguous transactions	10	91.3
Evaluation of purchased inventories	48	54.2
Evaluation of manufactured inventories	52	50.3
Capitalization rule	22	79.9
Depreciation method	51	51.8
Rate of depreciation	36	64.5
Economic appraisal		
Selection of economic indicators	19	82.0
Selection of sources of economic information	5	95.8
Forecasting economic conditions	44	54.4
Tax administration		
Extent of external tax consultation	31	74.0
Alternative ways of reporting income or expense	33	70.2
Final approval of tax returns	32	70.2
Minor tax negotiations	16	85.3
Major tax negotiations	39	64.6
Tax analysis of proposals	15	85.7
Insurance adequacy		
Determination of which assets and hazards to cover	46	57.6
Determination of amount of coverage	40	64.1
Special provisions and types of coverage	43	61.6
Major insurance decisions	23	79.2
Internal control		
Cash receipts control	30	74.1
Payroll control procedures	24	77.9
Shipment or delivery authorization procedures	45	56.8
Internal control (continued)		
Employee gate procedure	63	34.8
Approval of nonroutine purchases	56	42.5
Payment preaudit procedures	29	74.8
Establishment of petty cash funds	20	81.1
Access to data-processing programs	1	100.0
Long-range budgeting		
Timetable for long-range budgeting	26.5	76.2
Format of budget material for long-range budget	26.5	76.2
Long-range budget assumptions	53	49.2
Long-range sales forecast proposal	47	54.7
Long-range expense budget proposal	42	62.3
Long-range capital expenditure budget proposal	65	24.2
Long-range balance sheet and cash forecast	8	94.1
Long-range sales forecast approval	71	10.4
Long-range expenditure budget approval	70	15.4
Long-range capital expenditure budget approval	64	29.2
Long-range balance sheet and cash forecast approval	60	37.5
Short-range budgeting		
Timetable for short-range budgeting	17	84.2
Format of budget material for short-range budget	13	85.9
Short-range budget assumptions	57	41.4
Short-range sales forecast proposal	55	46.6
Short-range expense budget proposal	35	65.6
Short-range capital expenditure budget proposal	59	38.6
Short-range balance sheet and cash forecast	18	83.3
Short-range sales forecast approval	69	16.1
Short-range expense budget forecast	68	16.9
Short-range capital expenditure budget approval	72	7.3
Short-range balance sheet and cash forecast approval	62	36.7
Budgeting system changes	37	64.7

TABLE 3 (Continued)

FUNCTIONS AND DECISIONS	RANK	AVERAGE AUTHORITY SCORES
Accounting reports		
Income and expense report form and detail	54	48.4
Income and expense report comparisons	49	53.4
Definition of controllable costs	28	75.2
Allocation of factory overhead expenses	38	64.7
Allocation of general and administrative expenses	12	90.5
Critical size of deviations from expected	41	62.6
Causes of deviations	34	68.1
Adequacy of explanation of deviation	67	21.3
Analysis of proposed expenditures	61	37.4
Reports to stockholders	66	23.5
Financial reports to creditors and banks	58	40.3

among decision topics in long-range and short-range budgeting than among decision topics in insurance adequacy, tax administration, and government reports.

Table 3 presents a complete listing of decision topics with their respective authority scores and authority rankings among all topics. The overall range of scores is from 100, or unilateral authority, for access to data processing programs to 7.3, or almost no authority for short-range capital budget approval. One-sixth of the topics had scores of 90 or over and over two-thirds had scores of 50 or more. Fewer than one-third had scores of less than 50 and only one-ninth had scores of 25 or less.

These data suggest that controllers experience differing degrees of authority as they move among decision topics in a function and that this variation in authority is greater in some functions than in others. Overall, the pattern is one of strong, but shared authority.

Authority as Perceived by Controller, Superior, Peer To determine whether there were differences in the controller's degree of authority as perceived by the controller, his superior, and his peer, the following null hypothesis was tested for each functional area, by the analysis of variance in a matrix of authority scores ascribed to the controller by the controller, his peer, and his superior:

Hypothesis 3. There are no differences in the controller's degree of authority as it is perceived by controllers, peers, and superiors.

The differences in the perceptions of controllers, superiors, and peers were significant at $p < .01$ for the functions of long-range budgeting, short-range budgeting, accounting reports, accounting system, tax administration, and government reports and were significant at $p < .05$ for insurance adequacy. The differences in perceptions were not statistically significant for internal control, internal auditing, and economic appraisal. Figure 1 shows the patterns of controllers' authority as perceived by controllers, superiors, and peers for all decision topics. More controllers perceived controllers to have unilateral authority for more decision topics than did either superiors or peers. Peers perceived controllers to have unilateral authority for fewer decision topics than did superiors. The converse was true with respect to those decision topics in which controllers were perceived to have no authority.

These data suggest that controllers generally perceive themselves as having more authority than either their superiors or peers perceive them to have.

FIGURE 1 Authority of Controllers as Perceived by Controllers, Superiors, and Peers

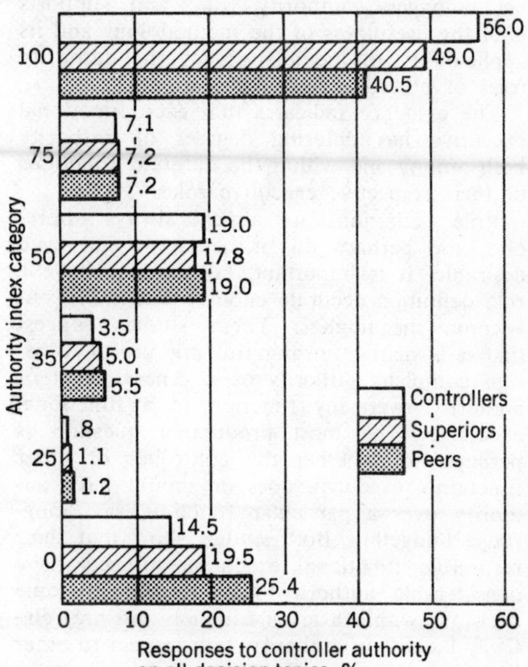

An analysis of the responses of company sets, that is, the controller, his superior, and a peer in the same organization, as to the controller's authority in specific decision topics is shown in Table 4. In less than half of the set responses did the controller, his superior, and peer all agree on the controller's degree of authority. Of specific import is the observation that the controller and his superior disagreed in their perceptions of the controller's authority for approximately one-third of the decision topics. Disagreement between the controller and peer occurred in almost 45 percent of the set responses and complete disagreement among the three executives in over 8 percent.

A more detailed breakdown of the data revealed further that in over two-thirds of the instances of some disagreement in the perception of the controller's authority, the controller perceived himself to have a higher or at least as high an estimation of his own authority as did his superior or peer. Only infrequently did the controller have a lower estimation of his own authority than either that of his superior or peer, and in only 51 of 885 response sets did he have a lower estimation than that of both his superior or peer.

TABLE 4 Agreement among Company Executives on Controller's Authority

CONTROLLER'S AUTHORITY	COMPANY RESPONSES	
	N	%
Controller, superior, and peer all agree	393	44.41
Controller and superior agree, but peer does not	190	21.47
Superior and peer agree, but controller does not	132	14.92
Controller and peer agree, but superior does not	94	10.62
Controller, superior, and peer all disagree	76	8.59

CONCLUSIONS

This study corroborates the general findings of French and Henning (1966) of the personnel managers' authority role, and supports both the usefulness of the methodology and its applicability to the analysis of the authority roles of other functional executives.

The evidence indicates that each functional executive has differing degrees of authority both among and within the different functions of their respective executive roles.

Role definitions are almost always imprecise, and perhaps this is necessary and even desirable. It is important, however, to have a role definition accurate enough that it will not become meaningless. These studies suggest that it is neither meaningful nor useful to assign complete authority or a general level of authority over any function to a functional executive. The most productive question is perhaps not whether the controller or other functional executive does or should have authority over a particular function, say, long-range budgeting. Both studies show that their respective functional executive subjects have considerable authority with respect to some decisions within a given function and are relatively lacking in authority with respect to other decisions. A more efficacious approach would appear to be the question of how much authority these functional specialists do have or should have with respect to specific types of decisions.

A comparison of the authority of controllers and personnel managers suggests the existence of overall differences in the authority of these functional specialists. In general, the controller has a stronger authority position than the personnel manager. He is perceived to have an average of unilateral authority in about 20 percent of the decision topics, whereas there are no decision topics in which the average perception indicates that the personnel manager has unilateral authority. Conversely, there is a smaller percent of decision topics falling in the lower end of the authority scale for the controller than for the personnel manager.

Both studies show that these are differences in the perceptions of the functional specialist, his peers, and his superior with respect to the authority of the specialist. Such differences in perception are conducive to misunderstanding and conflict. The importance of such differences has been suggested by Ghiselli and Barthol (1956: 241):

> The positions and the relationships of an individual are described in terms of prescribed and perceived roles. The prescriptions are either those of the individual himself or those of others in the organization. The difference in self descriptions reflect the qualities that distinguish the good supervisors from the poor supervisors . . . (the poor supervisor) persistently does the wrong thing, and this is possibly because he thinks these behaviors are expected of him.

Such differential perceptions of authority deserve further study.

The role of the controller appears to be much more complex than the literature suggests. He is assigned certain functional responsibilities, yet as he attempts to fulfill those responsibilities, he finds himself with differing degrees of authority as he moves from one function to another and from one decision to another. His superior, who has considerable say about his destiny, and his executive peers, with whom he must establish good relationships if he is to successfully fulfill his responsibilities, observe his behavior with different expectations about his authority. The controller might be looked upon in one instance by his superior as being too aggressive, and, at the same time, as not aggressive enough by his peers, or just the reverse. The profile of the controller is that of an executive with substantial authority in some functions and more limited authority in others; with varying degrees of authority in different decisions within a function, many times as making unilateral decisions and often sharing in the making of decisions; perceiving himself as having more authority than he is seen to have by his superior and his peers. He occupies a role with great opportunity, yet is both ill-defined and fraught with potential conflict.

The process-system model utilized in this study is the kind of framework which might provide an improved basis for analysis and prescription of the controller's and other functional specialist roles in relation to the achievement of organizational goals toward which their decisions are directed.

REFERENCES

Anderson, David, and Leon Schmidt (1961). Practical Controllership. Homewood: Richard D. Irwin.

Bradshaw, Thorton, and Charles Hull (eds.) (1950). Controllership in Modern Management. Homewood: Richard D. Irwin.

Dunn-Rankin, Peter (1965). The True Probability Distribution of the Range of Rank Totals and its Application to Psychological Scaling. Doctoral dissertation, Florida State University.

French, Wendell, and Dale Henning (1966). "The authority-influence role of the functional specialist in management." *Academy of Management Journal,* 9:187–203.

Ghiselli, E. E., and R. Barthol (1956). "Role perceptions of successful and unsuccessful supervisors." *Journal of Applied Psychology,* 40:241–244.

Heckert, J. Brooks, and James Willson (1963). Controllership. New York: Ronald Press.

Hutton, Clifford (1962). Controllership Function and Training. Working paper, Research Monograph No. 24. The University of Texas Bureau of Business Research.

McDonald, John (1940). Controllership: Its Functions and Technique. New York: Controllers Institute of America.

Melcher, Arlyn (1965). "Organizational structure: a framework for analysis and integration." In Edwin B. Flippo (ed.), Comparative Administration: 130–150. New York: Academy of Management.

Sayles, Leonard (1964). Managerial Behavior. New York: McGraw-Hill.

Stott, Alexander (1964). "Controllership in action." *Financial Executive,* 32:30–35.

Thomas, William E. (ed.) (1968). Readings in Cost Accounting Budgeting and Control. 3rd ed. Cincinnati: Southwestern.

E. COMMITTEES

41 GROUND RULES FOR USING COMMITTEES*

Cyril O'Donnell

A camel, someone has said, is a horse designed by a committee—and this is fairly typical of the current attitude toward this form of group activity. The use of committees has been criticized as a way of avoiding individual executive action, as a means of covering up managerial inadequacies, as a form of inefficient corporate "togetherness," and as a device for legitimizing procrastination and indecisiveness. What's more, every one of these accusations is justified, at least in many cases.

What is frequently overlooked, however, is that these are not valid criticisms of committees, but rather of the *misuse* of committees. For a committee that can be charged with any of these faults is not being employed as a committe should be used. Committees do have legitimate functions and, properly used, they constitute an invaluable management tool. The question is, how should they be properly used?

One common error is the confusion of committees with other kinds of joint action. Many people apply the term "committee" to any meeting of two or more people, but this definition is obviously too flexible and imprecise. It would necessarily include such diverse activities as business conferences, staff meetings, meetings of department heads, executive committee meetings, and even luncheon engagements, all of which are designed to serve quite different purposes. Conferences and typical staff meetings are primarily communication devices, utilized for economic purposes; a meeting of department heads may be called to clear up snags or overcome delays in some area that concerns all of them; meetings of an executive committee on which the president sits are held primarily for communication purposes. In none of these instances does a true committee exist.

THE TRUE COMMITTEE

What, then, is a committee? We might define it as *two or more persons appointed by their immediate superior for the purpose of acting or advising their superior about a subject that is not clearly within the competence of any of them.*

This implies that the superior does not sit in on the committee meetings; that the membership is confined to two or more of his immediate subordinates; and that the subject matter to be considered is not within the assigned duties of any individual member. Such a committee is properly considered an organizational device because it is performing an activity that, for various reasons, is not otherwise assigned. It may or may not have authority to take action, and it may be either an *ad hoc* group or a permanent committee.

BASIC REQUIREMENTS

The proper use of committees is based on two fundamental assumptions. In the first place, it assumes that the structure of the enterprise and the association of activities in this structure conform to the principles of good organization. Experienced business managers recognize that it is not possible, even in a well-organized company, to cover all types of activities or to assign all duties to specific individuals. Even when it is possible to make such assignments, they sometimes prefer not to do so. The important point is that the committee device is not a crutch for poor organization structure—it supplements good structure.

The second basic assumption is that the enterprise has effective managers. Too often the committee device is used to supplement

* Reprinted by permission of the publisher from the *Management Review*, vol. 50, no. 10, pp. 63–67, October, 1961. Mr. O'Donnell is professor of business organization and policy, emeritus, University of California, Los Angeles.

and buttress inefficient men. The use of a committee to support mediocrity in management is an extremely poor and even dangerous device. True, it may sometimes be necessary in the short run. But this situation should be clearly recognized, and vigorous effort should be made to achieve good organization and employ effective managers as quickly as possible.

The one time when a committee can be legitimately used—and the only circumstance in which its use can be justified—is when it can do a job better than a single manager. This means that the net effect must be superior in the light of such factors as cost, time, decisiveness, justice, and sound judgment.

Pooled Experience There are three situations in which a committee may meet this criterion. To begin with, a committee is a sound organizational device when it is used to obtain the considered views of subordinates about a subject beyond the experience of their superior. If the superior has the breadth and depth of experience represented by the members of a committee, it is obvious that he has no need of group action. Lacking this experience, the superior might conceivably ask for the advice of individual subordinates without organizing a committee. This is quite often done—as, for example, when an executive calls on a department or division manager for his views on a particular subject. Quite often, however, such an informal approach will result in the subordinate's giving views that are narrow in conception and not fully considered. As a member of a committee, the same subordinate would frame his views with an eye to potential questions or criticism of his fellow members, and he would thus be likely to be less extreme and insular in his viewpoint.

A good example of this kind of committee is the typical policy committee, whose purpose is to formulate policy to best fit the needs of the enterprise. For example, the question in the mind of the president may be, "Do we need a policy on pricing, and, if so, how should it be framed?" If he has come up through engineering or production, the president may lack the technical knowledge and experience required to decide a matter of this type. Consequently, he would find it advisable to refer the matter to his policy committee. The members of the committee would develop their views, not only with respect to special interests of the division or function they represent, but also from the viewpoint of the welfare of the company as a whole. Their considered views would result in a consensus which they would report to the president. In this instance, the committee would be acting in a staff capacity, and it would probably be a standing committee.

Too Much Power A second appropriate use of a committee as an organizational device is to exercise authority that is too great for any one man. The authority may be considered too great because it requires broader knowledge than any one man can be expected to have, because there is too much risk of bias or prejudice, or because it is difficult to find a person willing to exercise the authority. Good examples of such committees are investment committees, wage–and–salary committees, and boards of directors. It would be unusual to find a treasurer or a chairman of a board of directors who would be willing to take it on himself to decide how the surplus funds of a firm should be invested—and, indeed, it is likely to be too risky for the firm to rely on the judgment of any one man. Similar considerations are involved with respect to the wage–and–salary committee and the board of directors, which is a committee representing the stockholders. Committees of these types are standing committees that are delegated line authority. They make decisions on a majority basis and are true "plural executives."

Spreading Responsibility A third appropriate reason to use a committee as an organizational device is to diffuse responsibility among several executives. Very often it is undesirable to pinpoint responsibility for action on one person. A good example of this type of committee is the bonus committee, which determines the exact distribution of a fund among the qualified members or recipients. Although the total amount of a bonus fund may be expressed, in terms of a percentage of profits before taxes, the method of distributing the bonus is not always directly related to the salaries of the potential recipients; distribution is frequently made on the basis of an evaluation of their contributions to the company in the past year. One manager might well find the assignment of making this evaluation very uncomfortable, and he would be the target of complaints and accusations form those who felt that they were unfairly treated. When a committee is used for this purpose, responsibility is spread among the members, and disappointed recipients are less disposed to complain; they are more likely to be satisfied that no bias or prejudice was involved in the decision of a group.

A committee of this type is likely to be an *ad hoc* group, and it normally has a staff position with respect to the chief executive officer.

However, at the option of their superior, the committee may be delegated line authority to act in the situation.

COMMITTEE OPERATION

Three important elements are necessary to make committees truly and effectively operational. First, the purpose for which the committee is being established must be distinctly defined. A written statement will help to achieve clarity, and it will eliminate the need for committee members to spend time deciding exactly what they are supposed to be doing.

Second, the authority of the committee must be clearly specified. This is an easy matter, but it should be given careful attention. The committee may perform a staff function, having authority only to investigate and recommend to their superior, or it may be given authority to make decisions. Which is the case must be clearly determined and communicated.

Finally, the chairman of a committee should at all times be appointed on the basis of his ability to conduct an efficient meeting. Efficiency requires that the chairman prepare an agenda in advance so the members will have time to study the subject and consider their views. It means that the chairman must insure that all members are heard from, encouraging the reticent and keeping the loquacious in check. When all the contributions of the members are in, he should state the consensus of the meeting to be sure that he has properly understood it, and he should see that minutes of the meeting are distributed in rough form for correction and review prior to their final distribution.

If these points are given adequate consideration, management can be sure that its committees will operate effectively.

AN ANNUAL CHECKUP

It is an efficient practice for a company to make an annual audit of its committees, evaluating each one to determine whether it can be justified as an organizational device. If any existing group fails to meet one of the three basic purposes of committees, there is a serious question of its legitimacy.

As this audit is conducted from year to year, managers will gain a thorough understanding of the appropriate use of committees. They will shy away from using committees as crutches for inadequacies, as excuses for delay, or as devices to shift decision-making responsibility, and they will learn to use them to do the jobs for which they are uniquely suited.

When this has been accomplished, the committee will have attained its proper and respected place in the organization structure of the enterprise.

42 COMMITTEE MANAGEMENT: GUIDELINES FROM SOCIAL SCIENCE RESEARCH*

A. C. Filley

The committee is one of the most maligned, yet most frequently employed forms of organization structure. Yet despite the criticisms, committees are a fact of organization life. For example, a recent survey of 1,200 respondents revealed that 94 percent of firms with more than 10,000 employees and 64 percent with less than 250 employees reported having formal committees.[1] And, a survey of organization practices in 620 Ohio manufacturing firms showed a similar positive relationship between committee use and plant size.[2] These studies clearly indicate that committees are one of management's important organizational tools.

My thesis is that committee effectiveness can be increased by applying social science findings to answer such questions as:

- What functions do committees serve?
- What size should committees be?
- What is the appropriate style of leadership for committee chairmen?
- What mix of member characteristics makes for effective committee performance?

COMMITTEE PURPOSES AND FUNCTIONS

Committees are set up to pursue economy and efficiency within the enterprise. They do not create direct salable value, nor do they supervise operative employees who create such value.

The functions of the committee have been described by business executives as the exchange of views and information, recommending action, generating ideas, and making major decisions,[3] of which the first may well be the most common. After observing seventy-five conferences (which were also referred to as "committees"), Kriesberg concluded that most were concerned either with communicating information or with aiding an executive's decision process.[4] Executives said they called conferences to "sell" ideas rather than for group decision-making itself. As long as the executive does not manipulate the group covertly, but benefits by its ideas and screening processes, this activity is probably quite legitimate, for members are allowed to influence and to participate, to some extent, in executive decision-making.

Some committees also make specific operating decisions which commit individuals and organization units to prescribed goals and policies. Such is often the province of the general management committee composed of major executive officers. According to one survey, 30.3 percent of the respondents reported that their firms had such a committee and that the committees averaged 8.6 members and met 27 times per year.[5]

Several of the characteristics of committee organization have been the subject of authoritative opinion, or surveys of current practice, and lend themselves to evaluation through inferences from small-group research. Current practice and authoritative opinion are reviewed here, followed by more rigorous studies in which criteria of effectiveness are present. The specific focus is on committee size, membership, and chairmen.

COMMITTEE SIZE

Current Practice and Opinion The typical committee should be, and is, relatively small: Recommended sizes range from three to nine members, and surveys of actual practice seldom miss these prescriptions by much. Of the 1,658 committees recorded in the Harvard Business Review survey, the average membership was eight. When asked for their preference, the 79 percent who answered suggested an ideal committee size that averaged 4.6 members. Similarly, Kriesberg reported that, for the 75 con-

* Reprinted by permission of the publisher from *California Management Review*, vol. 13, no. 1, pp. 13–21, Fall, 1970. Mr. Filley is professor of business at the University of Wisconsin. Copyright 1970 by the Regents of the University of California.

ferences analyzed, there were typically five or six conferees in the meetings studied.[6]

Committees in the federal government tend to be larger than those in business. In the House of Representatives, Appropriations is the largest standing committee, with fifty members, and the Committee on Un-American Activities is smallest, with nine. Senate committees average thirteen members; the largest, also Appropriations, has twenty-three.[7] The problem of large committee size is overcome by the use of subcommittees and closed executive committee meetings. The larger committees seem to be more collections of subgroups than truly integrated operating units. In such cases, it would be interesting to know the size of the subcommittees.

Inferences from Small-Group Research

The extent to which a number is "ideal" may be measured in part in terms of the effects that size has on socio-emotional relations among group members and thus the extent to which the group operates as an integrated whole, rather than as fragmented subunits. Another criterion is how size effects the quality of the group's decision and the time required to reach it. Several small experimental group studies have evaluated the effect of size on group process.

Variables related to changes in group size include the individual's capacity to "attend" to differing numbers of objects, the effect of group size on interpersonal relations and communication, its impact on problem-solving functions, and the "feelings" that group members have about proper group size and the nature of group performance. To be sure, the effects of these variables are interrelated.

Attention to the Group. Each member in a committee attends both to the group as a whole and to each individual as a member of the group. There seem to be limits on a person's ability to perform both of these processes —limits which vary with the size of the group and the time available. For example, summarizing a study by Taves,[8] Hare[9] reports that "Experiments on estimating the number of dots in a visual field with very short-time exposures indicate individual subjects can report the exact number up to and including seven with great confidence and practically no error, but above that number confidence and accuracy drop."

Perhaps for similar reasons, when two observers assessed leadership characteristics in problem-solving groups of college students, the raters reached maximum agreement in groups of six, rather than in two, four, eight, or twelve.[10]

The apparent limits on one's ability to attend both to the group and the individuals within it led Hare to conclude:

> The coincidence of these findings suggests that the ability of the observing individual to perceive, keep track of, and judge each member separately in a social interaction situation may not extend much beyond the size of six or seven. If this is true, one would expect members of groups larger than that size to tend to think of other members in terms of subgroups, or "classes" of some kind, and to deal with members of subgroups other than their own by more stereotyped methods of response.[11]

Interpersonal Relations and Communication. Given a meeting lasting a fixed length of time, the opportunity for each individual to communicate is reduced, and the type of communication becomes differential among group members. Bales *et al.*[12] have shown that in groups of from three to eight members the proportion of infrequent contributors increases at a greater rate than that theoretically predicted from decreased opportunity to communicate. Similarly, in groups of from four to twelve, as reported by Stephen and Mishler,[13] size was related positively to the difference between participation initiated by the most active and the next most active person.

Increasing the group size seems to limit the extent to which individuals want to communicate, as well. For example, Gibb[14] studied idea productivity in forty-eight groups in eight size categories from 1 to 96. His results indicated that as group size increases a steadily increasing proportion of group members report feelings of threat and less willingness to initiate contributions. Similarly, Slater's[15] study of 24 groups of from two to seven men each working on a human relations problem indicated that members of the larger groups felt them to be disorderly and time-consuming, and complained that other members became too pushy, aggressive, and competitive.

Functions and Conflict. An increase in group size seems to distort the pattern of communication and create stress in some group members, yet a decrease in group size also has dysfunctional effects. In the Slater study check-list responses by members rating smaller groups of 2, 3, or 4 were complimentary, rather than critical, as they had been for larger groups. Yet observer impressions were that small groups engaged in superficial discussion and avoided controversial subjects. Inferences from post hoc analysis suggested that small group members are too tense, passive, tactful, and constrained to work together in a satisfying manner. They are afraid of alienating others. Similar results have been reported in other studies regarding the inhibitions created by small group size, particularly in groups of two.[16]

Groups of three have the problem of an overpowerful majority, since two members can form a coalition against the unsupported third member. Four-member groups provide mutual support when two members oppose the other two, but such groups have higher rates of disagreement and antagonism than odd-numbered groups.[17]

The data reported above are not altogether consistent regarding the reasons for dysfunctional consequences of small groups. The "trying-too-hard-for-agreement" of the Slater sfudy seems at odds with the conflict situations posed in the groups of three and four, yet both agree that for some reason tension is present.

Groups of Five. While it is always dangerous to generalize about "ideal" numbers (or types, for that matter), there does appear to be logical and empirical support for groups of five members as a suitable size, if the necessary skills are possessed by the five members. In the Slater study, for example, none of the subjects felt that a group of five was too small or too large to carry out the assigned task, though they objected to the other sizes (two, three, four, six, and seven). Slater concluded:

> Size five emerged clearly . . . as the size group which from the subjects' viewpoint was most effective in dealing with an intellectual task involving the collection and exchange of information about a situation, the coordination analysis, and evaluation of this information, and a group decision regarding the appropriate administrative action to be taken in the situation. . . .
>
> These findings suggest that maximal group satisfaction is achieved when the group is large enough so that the members feel able to express positive and negative feelings freely, and to make aggressive efforts toward problem solving even at the risk of antagonizing each other, yet small enough so that some regard will be shown for the feelings and needs of others; large enough so that the loss of a member could be tolerated, but small enough so that such a loss could not be altogether ignored.[18]

From this and other studies,[19] it appears that, excluding productivity measures, generally the optimum size of problem-solving groups is five. Considering group performance in terms of quality, speed, efficiency and productivity, the effect of size is less clear. Where problems are complex, relatively larger groups have been shown to produce better quality decisions. For example, in one study, groups of 12 or 13 produced higher quality decisions than groups of 6, 7, or 8.[20] Others have shown no differences among groups in the smaller size categories (2 to 7). Relatively smaller groups are often faster and more productive. For example, Hare found that groups of five take less time to make decisions than groups of 12.[21]

Several studies have also shown that larger groups are able to solve a greater variety of problems because of the variety of skills likely to increase with group size.[22] However, there is a point beyond which committee size should not increase because of diminishing returns. As group size increases coordination of the group tends to become difficult, and thus it becomes harder for members to reach consensus and to develop a spirit of teamwork and cohesiveness.

In general, it would appear that with respect to performance, a task which requires interaction, consensus and modification of opinion requires a relatively small group. On the other hand, where the task is one with clear criteria of correct performance, the addition of more members may increase group performance.

THE CHAIRMAN

Current Practice and Opinion. Most people probably serve on some type of committee in the process of participating in church, school, political, or social organizations and while in that capacity have observed the effect of the chairman on group progress. Where the chairman starts the meeting, for example, by saying, "Well, we all know each other here, so we'll dispense with any formality," the group flounders, until someone else takes a forceful, directive role.

If the committee is to be successful, it must have a chairman who understands group process. He must know the objectives of the committee and understand the problem at hand. He should be able to vary decision strategies according to the nature of the task and the feelings of the group members. He needs the acceptance of the group members and their confidence in his personal integrity. And he needs the skill to resist needless debate and to defer discussion upon issues which are not pertinent or where the committee lacks the facts upon which to act.

Surveys of executive opinion support these impressions of the chairman's role. The Harvard Business Review survey stated that "The great majority [of the suggestions from survey respondents] lead to this conclusion: the problem is not so much committees in management as it is the management of committees." This comment by a partner in a large management consulting firm was cited as typical:

> Properly used, committees can be most helpful to a company. Most of the criticism I have run into, while probably justified, deals with the way in which committees are run (or committee meetings are run) and not with the principle of working with committees.[23]

A chairman too loose in his control of committee processes is by no means the only difficulty encountered. Indeed, the chronic problem in the federal government has been the domination of committee processes by the chairman. This results from the way in which the chairman is typically selected: he is traditionally the member of the majority party having the longest uninterrupted service on the committee. The dangers in such domination have been described as follows:

> If there is a piece of legislation that he does not like, he kills it by declining to schedule a hearing on it. He usually appoints no standing subcommittees and he arranges the special subcommittees in such a way that his personal preferences are taken into account. Often there is no regular agenda at the meetings of his committee—when and if it meets . . . they proceed with an atmosphere of apathy, with junior members, especially, feeling frustrated and left out, like first graders at a seventh grade party.[24]

Inferences from Small Group Research. The exact nature of the chairman's role is further clarified when we turn to more rigorous studies on group leadership.

We shall confine our discussion here to leader roles and functions, using three approaches. First, we shall discuss the nature of task leadership in the group and the apparent reasons for this role. Then we shall view more specifically the different roles which the leader or leaders of the group may play. Finally, we shall consider the extent to which these more specific roles may be combined in a single individual.

Leader Control. Studies of leadership in task-oriented, decision-making groups show a functional need for and, indeed, a member preference for directive influence by the chairman. The nature of this direction is illustrated in a study by Schlesinger, Jackson, and Butman.[25] The problem was to examine the influence process among leaders and members of small problem-solving groups when the designated leaders varied on the rated degree of control exerted. One hundred six members of twenty-three management committees participated in the study. As part of an initial investigation, committee members described in a questionnaire the amount of control and regulation which each member exercised when in the role of chairman. Each committee was then given a simulated but realistic problem for 1.5 hours, under controlled conditions and in the presence of three observers.

The questionnaire data showed that individuals seen as high in control were rated as more skillful chairmen and as more valuable contributors to the committee's work.

The study also demonstrated that leadership derives from group acceptance rather than from the unique acts of the chairman. "When the participants do not perceive the designated leader as satisfactorily performing the controlling functions, the participants increase their own attempts to influence their fellow members."[26] The acceptance of the leader was based upon task (good ideas) and chairmanship skills and had little to do with his personal popularity as a group member.

The importance of chairman control in committee action has been similarly demonstrated in several other studies.[27] In his study of 72 management conferences, for example, Berkowitz[28] found that a high degree of "leadership sharing" was related inversely to participant satisfaction and to a measure of output. The norms of these groups sanctioned a "take-charge" chairman. When the chairman failed to meet these expectations, he was rejected and both group satisfaction and group output suffered. These studies do not necessarily suggest that committees less concerned with task goals also prefer a directive chairman. Where the committees are composed of more socially oriented members, the preference for leader control may be less strong.[29]

Leadership Roles. A second approach to understanding the leadership of committees is to investigate leadership roles in small groups. Pervading the research literature is a basic distinction between group activities directed to one or the other of two types of roles performed by leaders. They are defined by Benne and Sheats[30] as task roles, and as group-building and maintenance roles. Task roles are related to the direct accomplishment of group purpose, such as seeking information, initiating, evaluating, and seeking or giving opinion. The latter roles are concerned with group integration and solidarity through encouraging, harmonizing, compromising, and reducing conflict.

Several empirical investigations of leadership have demonstrated that both roles are usually performed within effective groups.[31] However, these roles are not always performed by the same person. Frequently one member is seen as the "task leader" and another as the "social leader" of the group.

Combined Task and Social Roles. Can or should these roles be combined in a single leader? The prototypes of the formal and the informal leader which we inherit from classical management lore tend to lead to the conclusion that such a combination is somehow impossible or perhaps undesirable. The research literature occasionally supports this point of view as well.

There is much to be said for a combination of roles. Several studies have shown that outstanding leaders are those who possess both task and social orientations.[32] The study by Borgotta, Couch, and Bales illustrates the point. These researchers assigned leaders high on both characteristics to problem-solving groups. The eleven leaders whom they called "great men" were selected from 126 in an experiment on the basis of high task ability, individual assertiveness, and social acceptability. These men also retained their ratings as "great men" throughout a series of different problem-solving sessions. When led by "great men" the groups achieved a higher rate of suggestion and agreement, a lower rate of "showing tension," and higher rates of showing solidarity and tension release than comparable groups without "great men."

When viewed collectively two conclusions emerge from the above studies. Consistent with existing opinion, the leader who is somewhat assertive and who takes charge and controls group proceedings is performing a valid and necessary role. However, such task leadership is a necessary but not a sufficient condition for effective committee performance. Someone in the group must perform the role of group-builder and maintainer of social relations among the members. Ideally both roles should probably be performed by the designated chairman. When he does not have the necessary skills to perform both roles, he should be the task leader and someone else should perform the social leadership role. Effective committee performance requires both roles to be performed, by a single person or by complementary performance of two or more members.

COMMITTEE MEMBERSHIP

The atmosphere of committee operations described in the classic literature is one where all members seem to be cooperating in the achievement of committee purpose. It is unclear, however, if cooperation is necessarily the best method of solving problems, or if competition among members or groups of members might not achieve more satisfactory results. Cooperation also seems to imply a sharing or homogeneity of values. To answer the question we must consider two related problems: the effects of cooperation or competition on committee effectiveness, and the effects of homogeneous or heterogeneous values on committee effectiveness.

Cooperation or Competition. A number of studies have contrasted the impact of competition and cooperation on group satisfaction and productivity. In some cases the group is given a cooperative or competitive "treatment" through direction or incentive when it is established. In others, competition and cooperation are inferred from measures of groups in which members are operating primarily for personal interest, in contrast with groups in which members are more concerned with group needs. These studies show rather consistently that "group members who have been motivated to cooperate show more positive responses to each other, are more favorable in their perceptions, are more involved in the task, and have greater satisfaction with the task."[33]

The best known study regarding the effects of cooperation and competition was conducted by Deutsch[34] in ten experimental groups of college students, each containing five persons. Each group met for one three-hour period a week for six weeks, working on puzzles and human relations problems. Subjects completed a weekly and post-experimental questionnaire. Observers also recorded interactions and completed over-all rating scales at the end of each problem.

In some groups, a cooperative atmosphere was established by instructing members that the group as a whole would be evaluated in comparison with four similar groups, and that each person's course grade would depend upon the performance of the group itself. In others, a competitive relationship was established by telling the members that each would receive a different grade, depending upon his relative contribution to the group's problem solutions.

The results, as summarized by Hare, show that:

> Compared with the competitively organized groups, the cooperative groups had the following characteristics:
>
> (1) Stronger individual motivation to complete the group task and stronger feelings of obligation toward other members.
>
> (2) Greater division of labor both in content and frequency of interaction among members and greater coordination of effort.
>
> (3) More effective inter-member communication. More ideas were verbalized, members were more attentive to one another, and more accepting of and affected by each other's ideas. Members also rated themselves as having fewer difficulties in communicating and understanding others.
>
> (4) More friendliness was expressed in the discussion and members rated themselves higher on strength of desire to win the respect of one another. Members were also more satisfied with the group and its products.
>
> (5) More group productivity. Puzzles were solved faster and the recommendations produced for the human-relations problems were longer and qualitatively better. However, there were no significant differences in the average individual productivity as a result of the two types of group experience nor were there any clear differences in the amounts of individual learning which occurred during the discussions.[35]

Similar evidence was found in the study of 72 decision-making conferences by Fouriezos, Hutt, and Guetzkow.[36] Based on observer ratings of self-oriented need behavior, correlational evidence showed that such self-centered behavior was positively related to participant ratings of high group conflict and negatively related to participant satisfaction, group solidarity, and task productivity.

In general, the findings of these and other studies suggest that groups in which members share in goal attainment, rather than compete privately or otherwise seek personal needs, will be more satisfied and productive.[37]

Homogeneity or Heterogeneity. The effects of member composition in the committee should also be considered from the standpoint of the homogeneity or heterogeneity of its membership. Homogeneous groups are those in which members are similar in personality, value orientation, attitudes to supervision, or predisposition to accept or reject fellow members. Heterogeneity is induced in the group by creating negative expectations regarding potential contributions by fellow members, by introducing differing personality types into the group, or by creating subgroups which differ in their basis of attraction to the group.

Here the evidence is much less clear. Some homogeneous groups become satisfied and quite unproductive, while others become satisfied and quite productive. Similarly, heterogeneity may be shown to lead to both productive and unproductive conditions. While the answer to this paradox may be related to the different definitions of homogeneity or heterogeneity in the studies, it appears to have greater relevance to the task and interpersonal requirements of the group task.

In some studies, homogeneity clearly leads to more effective group performance. The work of Schutz[38] is illustrative. In his earlier writing, Schutz distinguished between two types of interpersonal relationships: power orientation and personal orientation. The first emphasizes authority symbols. The power-oriented person follows rules and adjusts to external systems of authority. People with personal orientations emphasize interpersonal considerations. They assume that the way a person achieves his goal is by working within a framework of close personal relations, that is, by being a "good guy," by liking others, by getting people to like him. In his later work, Schutz[39] distinguished among three types of needs: *inclusion,* or the need to establish and maintain a satisfactory relation with people with respect to interaction and association; *control* or the need to establish and maintain a satisfactory relation with people with respect to control and power; and *affection,* or the need to establish and maintain a satisfactory relation with others with respect to love and affection.

Using attitude scales, Schutz established four groups in which people were compatible with respect to high needs for personal relations with others, four whose members were compatible with respect to low personal orientation, and four which contained subgroups differing in these needs. Each of the twelve groups met twelve times over a period of six weeks and participated in a series of different tasks.

The results showed that groups which are compatible, either on a basis of personalness or counter-personalness, were significantly more productive than groups which had incompatible subgroups. There was no significant difference between the productivity of the two types of compatible groups. As might be expected, the difference in productivity between compatible and incompatible groups was greatest for tasks which required the most interaction and agreement under conditions of high-time pressure.

A similar positive relationship between homogeneity and productivity is reported for groups in which compatibility is established on the basis of prejudice or degree of conservatism, managerial personality traits, congeniality induced by directions from the researcher, or status congruence.[40] In Adams' study, technical performance first increased, then decreased, as status congruence became greater. Group social performance increased continuously with greater homogeneity, however.

The relationship posited above does not always hold, however. In some studies, heterogeneous groups were more productive than homogeneous. For example, Hoffman[41] constructed heterogeneous and homogeneous groups, based on personality profiles, and had them work on two different types of problems. On the first, which required consideration of a wide range of alternatives of a rather specific nature, heterogeneous groups produced significantly superior solutions. On the second problem, which required primarily group consensus and had no objectively "good" solution, the difference between group types was not significant. Ziller[42] also found heterogeneity to be associated with the ability of Air Force crews to judge the number of dots on a card.

Collins and Guetzkow[43] explain these contradictory findings by suggesting that increasing heterogeneity has at least two effects on group interaction: it increases the difficulty of building interpersonal relations, and it increases the problem-solving potential of the group, since errors are eliminated, more alternatives are generated, and wider criticism is possible. Thus, heterogeneity would seem to be valuable where the needs for task facilitation are greater than the need for strong interpersonal relations.

Considering our original question, it appears that, from the standpoint of cooperation versus competition in committees, the cooperative committee is to be preferred. If we look at the effects of homogeneous or heterogeneous committee membership, the deciding factor seems to be the nature of the task and the degree of interpersonal conflict which the committee can tolerate.

SUMMARY AND CONCLUSIONS

Research findings regarding committee size, leadership, and membership have been reviewed. Evidence has been cited showing that the ideal size is five, when the five members possess the necessary skills to solve the problems facing the committee. Viewed from the standpoint of the committee members' ability to attend to both the group and its members, or from the standpoint of balanced interpersonal needs, it seems safe to suggest that this number has normative value in planning committee operations. For technical problems additional members may be added to ensure the provision of necessary skills.

A second area of investigation concerned the functional separation of the leadership role and the influence of the role on other members. The research reviewed supports the notion that the committee chairman should be directive in his leadership, but a more specific definition of leadership roles makes questionable whether the chairman can or should perform as both the task and the social leader of the group. The evidence regarding the latter indicates that combined task and social leadership is an ideal which is seldom attained, but should be sought.

The final question concerned whether committee membership would be most effective when cooperative or competitive. When evaluated from the standpoint of research on cooperative versus competitive groups, it is clear that cooperative membership is more desirable. Committee operation can probably be enhanced by selecting members whose self-centered needs are of a less intense variety and by directions to the group which strengthen motivations of a cooperative nature. When the proposition is evaluated from the standpoint of heterogeneity or homogeneity of group membership, the conclusion is less clear. Apparently, heterogeneity in a group can produce both ideas and a screening process for evaluating their quality, but the advantage of this process depends upon the negative effects of heterogeneous attitudes upon interpersonal cooperation.

REFERENCES

Based on A. C. Filley and J. Robert House, *Managerial Process and Organizational Behavior* (Glenview, Ill.: Scott-Foresman, 1969).

1. Rollie Tillman, Jr., "Problems in Review: Committees on Trial," *Harvard Business Review,* 38 (May–June 1960), 6–12; 162–172.

Firms with 1,001 to 10,000 reported 93 percent use; 250 to 1,000 reported 82 percent use.

2. J. H. Healey, *Executive Coordination and Control,* Monograph No. 78 (Columbus: Bureau of Business Research, The Ohio State University, 1956), p. 185.

3. "Committees," *Management Review,* 46 (October 1957), 4–10; 75–78.

4. M. Kriesberg, "Executives Evaluate Administrative Conferences," *Advanced Management,* 15 (March 1950), 15–17.

5. Tillman, *op. cit.*, p. 12.

6. Kriesberg, *op. cit.*, p. 15.

7. "The Committee System—Congress at Work," *Congressional Digest,* 34 (February 1955), 47–49; 64.

8. E. H. Taves, "Two Mechanisms for the Perception of Visual Numerousness," *Archives of Psychology,* 37 (1941), 265.

9. A. Paul Hare, *Handbook of Small Group Research,* (New York: The Free Press of Glencoe, 1962), p. 227.

10. B. M. Bass, and F. M. Norton, "Group Size and Leaderless Discussions," *Journal of Applied Psychology,* 35 (1951), 397–400.

11. Hare, *op. cit.*, p. 228.

12. R. F. Bales, F. L. Strodtbeck, T. M. Mills, and M. E. Roseborough, "Channels of Communication in Small Groups," *American Sociological Review,* 16 (1951), 461–468.

13. F. F. Stephen and E. G. Mishler, "The Distribution of Participation in Small Groups: An Exponential Approximation." *American Sociological Review,* 17 (1952), 598–608.

14. J. R. Gibb, "The Effects of Group Size and of Threat Reduction Upon Creativity in a Problem-Solving Situation," *American Psychologist,* 6 (1951), 324. (Abstract)

15. P. Slater, "Contrasting Correlates of Group Size," *Sociometry,* 21 (1958), 129–139.

16. R. F. Bales, and E. F. Borgotta, "Size of Group as a Factor in the Interaction Profile," in *Small Groups: Studies in Social Interaction,* A. P. Hare, E. F. Borgotta, and R. F. Bates, eds. (New York: Knopf, 1965, rev. ed.), pp. 495–512.

17. *Ibid.*, p. 512.

18. Slater, *op. cit.*, 137–138.

19. R. F. Bales, "In Conference," *Harvard Business Review,* 32 (March–April 1954), 44–50; also A. P. Hare, "A Study of Interaction and Consensus in Different Sized Groups," *American Sociological Review,* 17 (1952), 261–267.

20. D. Fox, I. Lorge, P. Weltz, and K. Herrold, "Comparison of Decisions Written by Large and Small Groups," *American Psychologist,* 8 (1953), 351. (Abstract)

21. A. Paul Hare, "Interaction and Consensus in Different Sized Groups," *American Sociological Review,* 17 (1952), 261-267.

22. G. B. Watson, "Do Groups Think More Efficiently Than Individuals?" *Journal of Abnormal and Social Psychology,* 23 (1928), 328–336; Also D. J. Taylor and W. L. Faust, "Twenty Questions: Efficiency in Problem Solving as a Function of Size of Group," *Journal of Experimental Psychology,* 44 (1952), 360–368.

23. Tillman, *op. cit.*, p. 168.

24. S. L. Udall, "Defense of the Seniority System," *New York Times Magazine* (January 13, 1957), 17.

25. L. Schlesinger, J. M. Jackson, and J. Butman, "Leader-Member Interaction in Management Committees," *Journal of Abnormal and Social Psychology,* 61, No. 3 (1960), 360–364.

26. *Ibid.*, p. 363.

27. L. Berkowitz, "Sharing Leadership in Small Decision-Making Groups," *Journal of Abnormal and Social Psychology,* 48 (1953), 231–238; Also N. T. Fouriezos, M. L. Hutt, and H. Guetzkow, "Measurement of Self-Oriented Needs in Discussion Groups," *Journal of Abnormal and Social Psychology,* 45 (1950), 682–690; also H. P. Shelley, "Status Consensus, Leadership, and Satisfaction with the Group," *Journal of Social Psychology,* 51 (1960), 157–164.

28. Berkowitz, *Ibid.*, p. 237.

29. R. C. Anderson, "Learning in Discussions: A Resume of the Authoritarian-Democratic Studies," *Harvard Education Review,* 29 (1959), 201–214.

30. K. D. Benne, and P. Sheats, "Functional Roles of Group Members," *Journal of Social Issues,* 4 (Spring 1948), 41–49.

31. R. F. Bales, *Interaction Process Analysis* (Cambridge: Addison-Wesley, 1951); Also R. M. Stogdill and A. E. Coons (eds.), *Leader Behavior: Its Description and Measurement,* Monograph No. 88 (Columbus: Bureau of Business Research, The Ohio State University, 1957); Also A. W. Halpin, "The Leadership Behavior and Combat Performance of Airplane Commanders," *Journal of Abnormal and Social Psychology,* 49 (1954), 19–22.

32. E. G. Borgotta, A. S. Couch, and R. F. Bales, "Some Findings Relevant to the Great Man

Theory of Leadership," *American Sociological Review,* 19 (1954), 755–759; Also E. A. Fleishman, and E. G. Harris, "Patterns of Leadership Behavior Related to Employee Grievances and Turnover," *Personnel Psychology,* 15, No. 1 (1962), 43–56; Also Stogdill and Coons, *Ibid.;* Also H. Oaklander and E. A. Fleishman, "Patterns of Leadership Related to Organizational Stress in Hospital Settings," *Administrative Science Quarterly,* 8 (March 1964), 520–532.

33. Hare, *Handbook of Small Group Research, op. cit.,* p. 254.
34. M. Deutsch, "The Effects of Cooperation and Competition Upon Group Process," in *Group Dynamics Research and Theory,* D. Cartwright and A. Zander, eds. (New York: Harper and Row, 1953).
35. Hare, *Handbook of Small Group Research, op. cit.,* p. 263.
36. Fouriezos, Hutt, and Guetzkow, *op. cit.*
37. C. Stendler, D. Damrin and A. Haines, "Studies in Cooperation and Competition: I. The Effects of Working for Group and Individual Rewards on the Social Climate of Children's Groups," *Journal of Genetic Psychology,* 79 (1951), 173–197; Also A. Mintz, "Nonadaptive Group Behavior," *Journal of Abnormal and Social Psychology,* 46 (1951), 150–159; Also M. M. Grossack, "Some Effects of Cooperation and Competition Upon Small Group Behavior," *Journal of Abnormal and Social Psychology,* 49 (1954), 341–348; Also E. Gottheil, "Changes in Social Perceptions Contingent Upon Competing or Cooperating," *Sociometry,* 18 (1955), 132–137; Also A. Zander and D. Wolfe, "Administrative Rewards and Coordination Among Committee Members," *Administrative Science Quarterly,* 9 (June 1964), 50–69.
38. W. C. Schutz, "What Makes Groups Productive?" *Human Relations,* 8 (1955), 429–465.
39. W. C. Schutz, *FIRO: A Three-Dimensional Theory of Interpersonal Behavior* (New York: Holt, Rinehart and Winston, 1958).
40. I. Altman and E. McGinnies, "Interpersonal Perception and Communication in Discussion Groups of Varied Attitudinal Composition," *Journal of Abnormal and Social Psychology,* 60 (May 1960), 390–393; Also W. A. Haythorn, E. H. Couch, D. Haefner, P. Langham and L. Carter, "The Behavior of Authoritarian and Equalitarian Personalities in Groups," *Human Relations,* 9 (1956), 57–74; Also E. E. Ghiselli and T. M. Lodahl, "Patterns of Managerial Traits and Group Effectiveness," *Journal of Abnormal and Social Psychology,* 57 (1958), 61–66; Also R. V. Exline, "Group Climate as a Factor in the Relevance and Accuracy of Social Perception," *Journal of Abnormal and Social Psychology,* 55 (1957), 382–388; Also S. Adams, "Status Congruency as a Variable in Small Group Performance," *Social Forces,* 32 (1953), 16–22.
41. L. R. Hoffman, "Homogeneity of Member Personality and Its Effect on Group Problem-Solving, *Journal of Abnormal and Social Psychology,* 58 (1959), 27–32.
42. R. C. Ziller, "Scales of Judgment: A Determinant of Accuracy of Group Decisions," *Human Relations,* 8 (1955), 153–164.
43. B. E. Collins and H. Guetzkow, *A Social Psychology of Group Process for Decision-Making* (New York: John Wiley and Sons, 1965), p. 101.

F. ORGANIZATIONAL ANALYSIS AND EFFECTIVENESS

43 REORGANIZING FOR RESULTS*

D. Ronald Daniel

Even the casual reader of the business press these days can hardly help noticing that organizational change—once a relatively infrequent phenomenon—has become something very much like a way of life in U.S. industry. Scarcely a day passes without an announcement of some major corporation's decision to subdivide, consolidate, or otherwise restructure itself. And even allowing for management's growing willingness to talk about such moves, it is certain that for every publicly acknowledged organizational realignment a good many others are quitely taking place without publicity.

The visible part of this iceberg is impressive enough. During the three-year period from 1962 through 1964, no fewer than 66 of the nation's top 100 industrial companies reported major organizational realignments to their stockholders—an average rate of one change per company every 54 months. Even though the scope of matters considered appropriate for discussion in the annual report has considerably broadened over recent years, there certainly must also be many unreported changes. My own observation as a consultant is that one major restructuring every two years is probably a conservative estimate of the current rate of organizational change among the largest industrial corporations. Our firm has conducted over 200 organization studies for domestic corporate clients in the past year, and organization problems are an even larger part of our practice outside the United States. And neither in the United States nor overseas is there any evidence of a leveling off in the immediate future.

CURRENT CHALLENGES

Where are these changes concentrated, and what are the principal forces motivating them? A closer look at the 1962–1964 figures suggests some answers:

- The bigger the company, the more likely it is to undergo a major change in a given period; 9 of the 10 largest companies, 16 of the top 25, and 27 of the top 50 were among the 66 corporations reporting change to their stockholders in this three-year period. Steel companies, automobile makers, and meat packers topped the other industries with respect to frequency of change.
- Commonest among the types of organization change were those relating to international operations, followed closely by establishment of group vice president positions, consolidation of product divisions into larger units, and rearrangement of marketing functions, in that order.

There is no mystery about the forces at work behind these changes. There are at least five:

1. The pressures of competition on margins and profits have put a premium on efficient organization structure. Overlapping departments are being combined, product divisions consolidated, and marginal units eliminated.
2. The booming internationalization of business has compelled more and more companies to supplant export departments by international divisions, to establish regional management groups, and to restructure corporate staffs.
3. Mergers and acquisitions—still apparently on the uptrend—have generated strong pressures for reorganization in parent companies as well as in newly acquired subsidiaries.
4. New developments in technology—such as the advanced management information systems made possible by recent progress in EDP hardware and software—often require new organizational arrangements to realize their ultimate potential for improving corporate performance.
5. Last, but not least, sheer growth is compelling many companies to amend time-

* Reprinted by permission of the publisher from the *Harvard Business Review,* vol. 44, no. 6, pp. 96–104 (November–December 1966). Mr. Daniel is managing director of the New York office of McKinsey & Company, management consultants.

honored organizational arrangements in order to cope with volume increases of as much as 20% a year.

Undoubtedly, the ability to plan organizational change wisely, implement it effectively, and realize its benefits promptly is becoming more and more essential to effective, competitive corporate performance. Indeed, the penalties for bungling a reorganization, both in terms of dollars and of competitive position, are getting higher every year.

How well is management equipped for the organizational challenges ahead? And how successfully has it managed organizational change to date?

During recent years, I have had a chance to discuss with hundreds of top executives the concepts, strategies, expectations, and results of dozens of reorganizations. The conclusion is as inescapable as it is serious: far too many of these organizational changes have *failed* to result in more vigorous competitive posture, greater profitability, or enhanced readiness for future growth.

Indeed, the record shows not only unfulfilled benefits, but unexepected troubles as well. In company after company where organizational change was seen as a solution to existing difficulties, it has only brought new ones. Momentum and continuity have been interrupted; confusion as to responsibility and decision-making authority has reigned; and, in some cases, organizational morale has been seriously damaged.

The purpose of this article is (a) to show the commonest reasons for these failures and, more importantly, (b) to outline an approach to designing and managing organization change that has proved remarkably successful *in terms of benefits realized* in a number of large companies with which I am personally familiar.

PITFALLS IN PLANNING

Among those companies where organization change has misfired, the great majority of fiascoes can be laid to one or more of five pitfalls in organization planning.

1. Theory & 'Principle' Perhaps the most conspicuous pitfall is the tendency to rely too heavily—or, rather, too exclusively—on theory and "principle" in organization design. The so-called principles of organization—those familiar universals dealing with span of control, reporting relationships, and so forth—frequently seem to be invested by organization planners with the authority of moral law. Certain organizational relationships, whatever their apparent practical merits, are damned because they commit the sin of violating these principles; others are favored mainly because of their theoretical purity.

Actually, of course, most of these principles are no more than generalizations about what has been observed *to work in practice,* based on past organizational experience. Being derived from experience, they are subject to revision in the light of new experiences and circumstances. It is as foolish to be totally bound by past experience as to ignore it.

The principles of organization, in short, are a double-edged sword. Employed with skill and with discretion, they can be useful in defining and refining an organization structure. Applied insistently and inflexibly, they can result in a rigid, bureaucratic organization structure poorly attuned to a company's unique needs.

Blind reverence for principle in organization planning is not confined to the classical school of thought, which considers organizations as mechanisms for the accomplishment of work. Much the same approach may be taken, with equally unfortunate results, by proponents of more contemporary theoretical approaches, such as these:

- The behavioral science school, which sees organizations in terms of the interactions of individuals and groups, takes personal development and satisfaction as its key parameters, and often seeks to remove structural constraints on this fulfillment.
- The management science school, which tends to view the organization as a huge man-machine system susceptible to modification in terms of mathematical models.

Both these schools, and others as well, have insights to contribute. But their adherents are so often preoccupied with one set of concepts that they deny the value of any insights generated by other approaches.

A classic example of the ill effects of theory-bound organization planning is the case of a well-known airline that decided some years ago to reexamine its organization structure:

> Its organization planner, a fervent believer in delegation of authority and the value of general manager positions for developing executive skills, designed a geographically decentralized organization for the airline that looked wonderful on paper. But it failed to recognize the absolute necessity for centralized decisions with respect to most of the key profit factors in air transportation, such as equipment acquisition, route planning, flight scheduling, maintenance and overhaul scheduling, and customer service standards.

> For years after the new organization structure was imposed, the regional managers—who were presumably accountable for profits, but were actually unable to function as anything more than public relations coordinators—slowed down critical decisions. Finally, top management, admitting that the new structure had been a mistake, reverted to the airline's traditional alignment of functional departments.

2. Imitative Pattern This common pitfall in organization planning is the tendency to replicate a particular organization pattern simply because it has proved successful for another company or companies. For example, the world-enterprise concept has been applied with poor results in situations where it was at best premature and at worst totally inappropriate.

Another example is the way the General Motors concept of profit-accountable product divisions coupled with a policy-making headquarters staff has been copied in countless instances. Admittedly, the concept is broadly applicable. But too many imitators have adopted the form without the substance. Lacking GM's depth of quality manpower and GM's finely tuned planning and control systems, some companies have found their divisionalized structures leading to abdication rather than delegation, and to anarchy rather than accountability. The imitative approach to organization planning, in my observation, accounts for a large share of the failures and disappointments encountered by some companies.

3. Unchanging Structure Reorganizations often miscarry because of a simple failure to allow for the dynamics of organizational change. In adopting a new organization structure, some managements are inclined to assume that the company has achieved its ideal, ultimate form. Actually, of course, the history of any successful enterprise does refute the notion that organization structures are permanent and unchanging. No matter how well-designed its present organization, changes in a company's human resources, in its size, geographical scope, or mission, can make changes in its structure not only desirable but essential.

This coin of dynamic evolution has another side—namely, the fact that radical changes in organization do tax the momentum and continuity of an enterprise. For this reason a prudent phasing of change in a sequence of evolutionary steps, possibly over several years' time, is sometimes the only way to fully realize the benefits promised by a different organization structure. For example:

> A number of years ago, one petroleum company began a succession of organizational moves to reach its present structure for its international operations. In 1959 the company announced a regional approach to the management of its overseas operations. In 1961 it moved these regional management units abroad to get them closer to affiliate operations. In 1965, after several successful years of intensive work by regional staffs to upgrade affiliate performance, certain regions were organizationally consolidated to simplify the structure.

The trouble is that for every company that times its moves so carefully, there may be three that reap disillusion by trying to reach equally ambitious organizational goals overnight.

4. Lack of Coordination Still another source of trouble in many of the organization changes of recent years has been the lack of attention to coordinating the organization structure and the company's philosophy of management. Ideally, structure and philosophy should be mutually reinforcing. At the very least, they must be compatible.

Where they are in conflict, only frustration can result. Consider a company, structured in profit-accountable divisions, whose chief executive retains authority on even low-level management appointments; or an organization with a newly established international division but still entirely dominated by domestic thinking; or a company whose top management is constantly preaching loyalty to the corporate interest while erecting impregnable organizational walls between functional departments. In all such situations where philosophy and structure are at odds, performance must inevitably suffer.

5. Poor Implementation A final inadequacy that has inhibited the effectiveness of many reorganizations is a lack of respect for the difficulties of implementing change. In some cases I have observed, top management almost seems to have assumed that switching formal reporting relationships—or adding, deleting, and rearranging boxes on the organization chart—was automatically going to change individual behavior overnight. In reality, established managerial habits usually tend to persist despite new organizational charts.

Where organization change has successfully influenced behavior, it is a safe bet that considerable thought has been given to the steps involved in implementation—announcing the changes, realigning executive personnel, timing the various moves, and securing the participation of those affected as a means of building understanding, acceptance, and commitment. Thus:

> One of the world's largest corporations, embarking on a massive reorganization in the early 1960's, assigned to eight senior executives the task of working out detailed schedules for implementing the new structure, and for carrying the objectives and concepts underlying the new arrangements to the rest of the organization. So that they could do the job properly, these eight top managers were relieved of their regular assignments for six months. Needless to say, implementation was thorough, and the reorganization "took" with exemplary effect.

KEY INPUTS

Against this background of constant changes in organizational structure, and evidence that these changes are often falling well short of their promise, I propose to outline a practical (and proven) approach to the determination of the right structure for any business organization, whether it be an entire enterprise or a specific segment. This approach, which among other things is designed to guard against the weaknesses I have reviewed earlier, rests on these basic notions:

- The right organization structure for a given enterprise is uniquely determined by four different inputs, which include: (1) the requirements for competitive success in the business; (2) the objectives and plans of the enterprise; (3) the "givens" of the present situation; and (4) tested organization theory.
- The definition (or validation) of a management philosophy consistent with the organization structure is an essential corollary step to any successful reorganization.

Let us examine each of the four input factors in turn.

1. Success Requirements Alfred P. Sloan, Jr. wrote, "Every enterprise needs a concept of its industry. There is a logical way of doing business in accordance with the facts and circumstances of an industry, if you can figure it out."[1] Careful analysis of the "facts and circumstances" of an industry is often needed to identify the basic requirements for success—namely, those few things that management must do exceedingly well if the company is to prosper. Some of these requirements are intuitively apparent:

- In auto making, the maintenance of a strong dealer organization; skillful, well-coordinated model year planning; and effective manufacturing cost control to keep the break-even point low.
- In petroleum, well-integrated planning of investment expenditures; and astute management of the logistics network that moves oil from wellhead to the ultimate customer of refined products.
- In the soap and detergent business, creative new product development; effective advertising and promotion; and a sound trade relations program.

In most cases, not all the success requirements of a particular company are as obvious as the examples above. In order to be able to identify and define all of them with precision, the analyst must evaluate products, markets, and marketing requirements; he must understand the manufacturing processes and the role of technology; he must learn the economics of the business in terms of the behavior of costs, prices, margin levels, capital requirements, and the like; he must appraise environmental forces, including the competitive picture; and he must identify the critical decision-making functions.

Whether the success requirements of a particular business are obvious or elusive, their implications for organization structure are easy to overlook. This is why I believe it is important to define the success requirements on the basis of a formal analysis, and then to consider explicitly how the organization structure can be set up to realize them.

Considered in this light, the success requirements provide insights into certain important aspects of a company's structure: (a) the soundness of the basic organizational arrangement, (b) the specific activities that must be carried on, and (c) the relative prominence of activities.

Basic Arrangements. To begin with, the success requirements will usually indicate the right fundamental organization pattern for the company—that is, whether it should be structured along functional, product, or geographic lines, or patterned on some other concept. Thus:

- Two important forestry products companies, each with a basically functional organization structure, merged. Promptly the new enterprise began to exhibit some classic symptoms of organizational malfunction—sluggishness in getting new products to market, inertia in the face of new profit opportunities, and a

[1] *My Years With General Motors,* edited by John McDonald with Catharine Stevens (Garden City, New York, Doubleday & Company, Inc., 1964), p. 58.

gradual decline in return on investment. Analysis showed that the company was really involved in four separate businesses: logging, wood products, pulp and paper, and packaging. Each of these had its own success requirements, and they were by no means wholly compatible. The company found it advisable to reorganize into four divisions, with two set up on a functional and two on a geographic pattern.

- A functionally structured cement company decided, after analyzing its success requirements, that the importance of transportation economics and local market contacts demanded a region-by-region approach to the business. The company restructured itself into geographic divisions with local profit accountability. Its return on investment has already improved markedly in the two years since the shift.

Critical Activities. Few businesses fail to give due organizational prominence to such basic functions as manufacturing, marketing, and finance. But without a clear definition of success factors, certain key activities can easily be overlooked in the organization structure. Thus:

- One of the truly critical factors in the performance of a food chain is pricing; no other variable has a greater impact on profitability. One major chain discovered, upon analysis, that it had in effect no real pricing function because the activity was fragmented among dozens of people in the organization. In the course of an organizational overhaul, each geographic division established a two-man pricing staff to analyze competitor's price strategies, to suggest different approaches to pricing (including store displays and feature advertising), and to work with stores in troubled trading areas where competitors' prices were especially low.
- A study of success requirements for an international farm equipment company showed that new product development was pivotal, because it provided the basic for keeping franchised dealers healthy and permitted premium prices by keeping products out of the "me too" category. Accordingly, the company, whose lead time to get new models to market had been dangerously long, set up special organization arrangements designed to ensure that the new product function was really productive. Activities that had been informally coordinated among sales, manufacturing, engineering, and research were made the responsibility of a Corporate New Product Development staff. Already, the lead time has been significantly cut.

Relative Prominence. Clearly defined success requirements also shed light on the relative prominence of various key activities. One sometimes hears it said, in connection with a particular company, "That's an old-line manufacturing business," or, "To get ahead in XYZ you really have to come up the sales route." Often a study of current success requirements will show that these functional emphases, historical in origin and perpetuated by habit, are in conflict with today's realities. Thus:

- Many airlines have concluded that the passenger service is the paramount factor in distinguishing a line and, hence, in building revenues. They reason that, since government regulation has equalized prices and made most routes competitive, a customer's selection is usually based on the quality of reservation service, baggage handling, food service, equipment cleanliness, stewardess service, and so on—functions that have historically been buried deep in other departments. Some lines have therefore consolidated all of these functions into a single Passenger Service department, under the direction of a senior executive, in order to give them new cohesion and importance.
- Oil companies have long had Supply and Distribution departments. But some companies, recognizing the logistics function as a crucial factor for profits, have upgraded S & D—once a clerically staffed expediting and balancing group—to a far more important, professionally managed coordinating agency for the company's total physical distribution operation. Its mission is to optimize the overall logistics system and to prevent the suboptimization of profits in individual segments of the total system.

In both of these cases, analysis of success requirements resulted in giving new organizational prominence to already established activities with rewarding results.

2. Objectives & Plans Although their importance seems to be self-evident, the objectives and future plans of the enterprise have been totally ignored in many reorganizations—perhaps because of the temptation to regard organization structure as an end in itself rather than as a tool to do a job.

Common sense tells us that a company is organized to do something—to achieve some goal. Structure is a means to this end, and changed ends often call for changed means. Thus companies that formulate new objectives will often find that supporting organizational moves are needed. To illustrate:

- A chemical coating company, which was ambitious to enter new fields, recently established a commercial development function as a first step. This department, free from day-to-day operating responsibilities, is a careful blend of individuals with technical and marketing skills. Its mission is to identify promising market opportunities and decide what arrangement—self-development, licensing, acquisition, or some other—is the best means of building the required technology. This particular department will manage fledgling new ventures until they can be turned over to the stewardship of an existing division or be set up on their own.
- Another instance is a diversified machinery company in the Midwest that decided to push aggressively into international markets, particularly in Europe. Its existing export division, selling modest amounts of equipment produced in the United States by over a dozen divisions of the corporation, would have impeded rather than facilitated direct manufacturing investments and intensified marketing activities on the Continent. Accordingly, the company developed a regional organization for Europe with a carefully defined role vis-à-vis the domestic product divisions. At a later stage, this company plans to dismantle its strong regional staff and give its product divisions world-wide responsibility.
- Again, General Foods determined several years ago to greatly strengthen its trade franchise. To help achieve this basic objective, the company adopted a new organizational concept. It consolidated the physical distribution and order-taking activities of all its product divisions in a single Distribution Sales Service Division. This move has greatly facilitated the attainment of GF's trade franchise objectives.

In each of these cases a company's objectives and future plans were an important input in designing a sound organization structure. Indeed, analysis of a company's success requirements and its objectives and plans will usually permit the *ideal* structure to be defined with some confidence. But the *ideal* structure and the *right* structure are only rarely one and the same. To bridge the gap between them, another critical input must be taken into account.

3. Range of 'Givens' This key input includes the entire range of "givens" that add up to the current situation of the enterprise. The givens that will influence organization design can be considered as (a) present structure, (b) present style of leadership, (c) present managerial processes, and (d) present manpower resources. Together, they define the position from which any changes must begin. Any or all of them may call for modifying the *ideal* structure into some different form that is more feasible to attain and more likely to be successful.

Present Structure. Is the current organization structure clearly defined? How well do top and middle management understand it? How closely is it adhered to? It is not unusual to find one structure documented on a chart, with a shadow organization, consisting of quite a different set of informal relationships, actually operating in practice. The existence of such shadow organizations is an important factor in the planning and design of any reorganization. In some instances they must be neutralized; in others, it is possible to capitalize on them.

Leadership Style. Every chief executive projects a style of leadership to his organization. This style or way of operating, which is often reinforced by other members of the top management group, is one component of a company's management philosophy (a subject to be taken up later in this article). It reveals itself in personal characteristics—assertiveness or reserve, conservatism or flamboyance, and so on—that others in the company tend to emulate. It also appears in the way a chief executive manages: his concept of staff work, his view of risk taking, his approach to decisions, his feelings about planning, and so forth. These often intangible, but nonetheless important, factors can greatly influence the design of the right structure for a particular organization. Ideally, the leadership style and the organization structure should effectively reinforce each other.

Managerial Processes. How plans are developed, how budgets are created, how decisions are made, how control is effected, and how performance is appraised, all must be considered in developing the right structure for a company. These processes most directly influence the ways in which individuals and groups in an organization do their jobs and spend their time.

On occasion, executive behavior can be modified faster, more easily, and more productively by changing the processes rather than the organization structure. Thus:

- An organization study of the headquarters staff of an international rubber company suggested that new approaches to planning and control were much more likely than structural changes to achieve the desired results—namely, greater profit contribution from the corporate staffs to the operating units. A careful review and overhaul of the company's planning and control mechanisms led to significantly improved performance while preserving the existing structure intact.

On the other hand, a change in structure may be designed primarily to strengthen a management process. Thus:

- Another international organization, a multiproduct chemical company, sought to accelerate management development—one of its most basic needs—by improving performance evaluation. By moving to a product division setup and giving individual general managers genuine profit accountability, problems of shared responsibilities and ambiguous authority, arising from the previous functional setup, were largely eliminated.

Manpower Resources. The quality, depth, and age and experience distribution of management personnel must also be evaluated in defining the right organization structure. Structural changes geared to capitalize on an individual's talents are often appropriate. In a number of cases, organization changes have been planned over a period of three to five years to permit the structure to shift in parallel with the complexion of executive resources. For example:

- A multibillion-dollar company wanted to structurally separate top-level policy making and day-to-day administration, but found it could not do so because of a shortage of senior executive talent. After considering and rejecting the possibility of outside recruiting, the chairman and the president decided they would have to share both roles until three group vice presidents could be developed within the company. Four years later, the shift was successfully made, and operations were explicitly assigned to the group vice presidents.
- Another company, having decided to move from a functional to a regional structure, discovered that it would need seven strong general managers to assume a significant degree of delegated authority. Since they were not available, the company sensibly conserved its limited talent for a number of years by retaining its functional structure, meanwhile developing some younger executives. It has now successfully regionalized its operations.

4. Tested Theory Once the right structure has been clearly defined, the so-called principles of organization can usefully be applied. As I have suggested earlier, the word "principles" is easily misunderstood. Far from being provable laws with universal applicability, the principles of organization are merely a set of ground rules distilled from experience. Some of the principles of organization invoked today are many centuries old. They can even be found in the Bible:

> *Exodus 18, 25:* "And Moses chose able men out of all Israel and made them heads over the people, rulers of thousands, rulers of hundreds, rulers of fifties and rulers of tens." (This would seem to be a pretty crisp definition of the scalar principle that results in the familiar pyramidal organization structure.)

> *Matthew 6, 24:* "No man can serve two masters: for either he will hate the one and love the other; or else he will hold to the one and despise the other." (Here is the equally familiar principle that every subordinate should report to one, and only one, superior—unity of command.)

One of the most unassailable principles is that authority and responsibility should be commensurate. It is true that either one without the other often leads to confusion and friction in organizational relationships. Were it not for challenges to this principle, however, two of the most successful contemporary organization concepts would never have evolved. Consider:

- The *product* manager, especially in the consumer package goods company, has substantial responsibility but usually little outright authority. He must secure the success of his product in terms of market share and profit contribution, but he lacks decision-making authority over several essential contributors to this success—the sales force, manufacturing plants, physical distribution operations, and so forth.
- In contrast, the *project* manager, as found most typically in aerospace and construction companies, has very specific delegation of authority, often without commensurate responsibility.[2] Thus the project manager is not responsible for the engineering of a new system or plant; but in order to keep his project on schedule or under estimate, he frequently makes unilateral decisions that can have a profound impact on engineering soundness.

Both of these concepts violate the letter of the principle.

[2] See John M. Stewart, "Making Project Management Work," *Business Horizons,* Fall 1965.

My point is not that the principles of organization are worthless, but rather that they must be challenged, applied with discretion, and never used to build the foundation of an organization. In too many cases I have seen them used as a diagnostic tool to scrutinize the established organization for supposedly improper structural arrangements and to rationalize proposed changes—an approach that tends to result in a rigid, oversimplified, and bureaucratic structure ill suited to the real complexity of the enterprise or its real business needs. On the other hand, I have seen the principles used in a number of highly successful reorganizations simply to check out contemplated organization changes for common-sense defects.

In short, the more pragmatic approach I am describing first builds the theoretical basis of the organization structure on an analysis of success requirements, objectives, and future plans, tempered by allowance for present conditions. Then the resulting structure is reviewed in the light of accepted organization principles. Where the structure is at odds with the principles, the reasoning behind the structure is reexamined for possible weaknesses. Where weaknesses are discovered, the structural arrangement is reconsidered; where not are found, it is of course allowed to stand.

MANAGEMENT PHILOSOPHY

The approach to organization problems described thus far is tied to an important complementary idea: no change in organization structure should be implemented until its consonance, or lack of consonance, with the enterprise's management philosophy has been evaluated.

A division manager I talked with recently put it more pungently. "The form and substance of this corporation are out of whack," he said. "On the surface, you'd think we had autonomous product divisions. But the way the man upstairs wants to run things, our divisionalized setup is a fiction."

Attitudes & Values If organization structures are designed to influence individuals and groups in an enterprise to do certain things in a certain way, then we should make sure that other sources of influence on behavior are not defeating the purpose of the structure. Whether tacit or explicit, a philosophy of management can be just as strong an influence as the organization structure itself on the way managers and workers function.

By management philosophy, I mean the beliefs, attitudes, values, and supporting actions that condition the way in which an enterprise is run. It comprises definable attitudes and values on such points as these:

- *Location of decision-making authority*—Is the company committed to a GE-like concept of decentralization, or is authority tightly held at the top?
- *Individual vs. group action*—Are decisions "syndicated"? In particular, are committee arrangements dominant? Or is personal accountability considered all-important?
- *Volume vs. profit*—What is the fundamental measure of accomplishment in the company? Is it sheer size? Return on investment, à la Du Pont? Or is it earnings per share? Indian Head Mills makes no bones on this score; President James Robison said in the company's 1960 Annual Report. "The principal objective of the directors and management of Indian Head Mills is to increase the intrinsic value of the company's common stock. To do this requires expansion of operating earning power per common share."
- *Character of personnel policies*—Are managers ever recruited from outside? What are the criteria for promotion? Is incentive compensation employed? Does seniority outweigh ability? Is the basic personnel philosophy one of paternalism, callous toughness, or something in between?
- *Holding company vs. operating company*—Are the company's departments, divisions, subsidiaries, and affiliates regarded simply as investments, or are they tightly managed and controlled in the interest of the total corporation?
- *Executive leadership*—What is the prevailing managerial style? How assertive, autocratic, dominant is it? How passive, democratic, supportive?
- *Facts vs. intuition*—How do facts stack up against executive "judgment" and "experience" when major decisions are at stake?
- *'Free wheeling' vs. 'formality'*—Are original thinkers and mavericks encouraged or repressed? Is the atmosphere charged with easy-going permissiveness or with protocol? Do people say what the boss wants to hear or what they really think?

Adjustment of Elements I have observed, as have my colleagues, countless cases where a company's viewpoint on issues such as these is a powerful influence on organization. A company's philosophy generally evolves over many years. In its core elements it directly reflects the personal convictions of top management and, therefore, is not subject to ready modification. But there are less central elements that can be changed. And in some cases the success requirements of the business may call for a readjustment in some elements of the philosophy, just as they may dictate a modification in structure. For example:

- The company which is involved in several different businesses will not only have to structure itself into product divisions but will also have to adopt a philosophy of decentralized decision making.
- The company in an industry with rapidly changing technology cannot safely give precedence to seniority if its long-service people fail to keep pace witsh technical advances.
- The company in a highly integrated and economically interdependent industry, such as international oil, must not allow concern for local interests to outweigh the corporate good.

Mutual adjustment of corporate philosophy and organization structure appears to be a hallmark of the most successful reorganizations. Without it the impact of structural changes on managers' behavior may be severely limited. On the other hand, a company whose philosophy and organization structure are mutually reinforcing possesses a powerful means for effecting constructive change.

44 TECHNOLOGY AND ORGANIZATION*

Raymond G. Hunt

In order to solve practical problems of organizational design, it is necessary initially to understand the many differences between types of organizations and the reasons that these differences exist. The fact that these aspects have not been considered until the mid-1960's is reflected by the independence of developments in organizational design and theory until this time.[1] However, recent progress in comparative analysis of organizations, together with integrative theory building, gives promise of altering this state of affairs, especially regarding the appreciation of technology as a main basis for differentiating organizational varieties and explaining organizational processes.

These recent developments are the foundation for this paper; first, we will outline the ways in which organizations may be classified, and then we will appraise the current understanding of the relationship between technology and organizational design.

CLASSIFYING ORGANIZATIONS

To be useful, a schema for distinguishing organizations must identify cogent parameters or dimensions that cut across particular cases and provide a basis for ordering those cases, even if it is only on a yes-no basis. Different schemas will be useful for different purposes, but since every organization can be construed as having: (1) a function in society; (2) a pattern of input; (3) a pattern of output; (4) a set of procedures for converting inputs into outputs (something to which we shall apply the term "throughput"[2]); and (5) a pattern according to which it is put together, it follows that any organization could be classified on any or all of these bases. Indeed, allowing for some mixed cases and some ambiguous ones, examples of all five kinds of classification can be found.

Classification by Social Function In Chapter 5 of their remarkable book, Katz and Kahn[3] present a "typology" of organizations based on "first-order" and "second-order factors." First-order factors describe "genotypic functions" that differentiate among all kinds of organizational systems and subsystems. Thus, in Katz and Kahn's typology there are productive or economic organizations (e.g., factories); maintenance organizations (e.g., those, like schools, specialized to socialize people); adaptive organizations (e.g., research labs); and managerial or political organizations. These first-order distinctions have to do principally with the part played by the organization in the larger society; thus, they can claim kinship with Parsons' social function criteria.[4] With regard to actual organizations, of course, these categories are not mutually exclusive. A particular organization could fall into more than one class: AT & T may be mainly an economic organization, but in its research labs it contains adaptive organizations.

Defined by its contributions to the larger social system, an organization's social function, unlike the other four of its facets, has to do with its *relations* with the society as a whole, not just with its own characteristics. Talking of an organization's social functions is to treat it (the organization) not so much as an integral system, but as a subsystem of a larger system. One might therefore infer that this essentially *exogenous* criterion for classification is different from and independent of the others. Katz and Kahn obviously think so with their distinction between first- and second-order factors (see

* Reprinted by permission of the publisher from *Academy of Management Journal*, vol. 13, no. 3, pp. 235–252, September, 1970. Mr. Hunt is professor of psychology in the State University of New York at Buffalo.

[1] R. M. Cyert and J. G. March, "Organizational Design," In Eds., W. W. Cooper, H. J. Leavitt and M. W. Shelly, *New Perspectives in Organization Research* (New York: Wiley, 1964), Chapter 29, p. 558.

[2] In this usage we are following the example of D. Katz and R. Kahn, *The Social Psychology of Organizations* (New York: Wiley, 1966).

[3] *Ibid.*

[4] T. Parsons, *Structure and Process in Modern Societies* (Glencoe, Ill.: Free Press, 1960).

also Pugh, footnote 9).[5] To be sure, an organization's social function is likely to influence its perceived social value which, in turn, may affect its access to societal resources, including technological ones which may help shape its other characteristics. But any such linkages depend entirely on the organization's embeddedness in the larger societal system. In any event, these linkages are complex and clearly not direct.

For very general purposes, classification by social function can be helpful. However, the variability within functional types is too great for them to afford much analytic power.[6] Katz and Kahn are aware of this, of course, as their positing of second-order factors implies. These second-order factors have more to do with input, output, or conversion methods (throughput), or else with design features.

Classification by Form or Pattern Pattern denotes the discernable "phenomenology" or anatomy of an organization—its characteristics or properties *qua* organization. This aspect of organizations we shall herein reference by the term "structure," or, when construed in a purposive sense, "design."

With its functional traditions, American scholarship has tended to pay more attention to operational than to structural properties of organization.[7] To be sure, structure is only revealed in the functions of organizations,[8] but structure there is nevertheless. We mean by it the varied patterns of interaction, intended or otherwise, that characterize an organization. To the degree these patterns are codified or standardized, we can speak of the organization as being formal. And "formal organizational structure" can be defined in terms of prescriptions regarding lines of authority, divisions of labor, and allocations of resources[9] that often can be found memorialized in such things as organization charts, job descriptions, and budgetary formulae. Such pointers are far from infallible guides to organizational reality, but even so it is essential to recognize that the nature of the formal organization has much to do with limiting and shaping organizational life (including whatever "informal" processes may be spawned therein). Moreover, the idea of formal structure is fundamental to rational organization design.

Our concept of structure in substance and in spirit approximates Anthony's idea of "system" as distinct from "process."[10] The latter has to do with the actual events and decisions that transpire within the organization, whereas the former represents the formal and informal framework within which these are done—the "formula," as it were, according to which the organization's tasks are specified, interrelated, performed, and controlled. Obviously this formula can be either explicit or not explicit.

As for the use of structural criteria for classifying organizations, it has long been traditional[11] to distinguish three basic forms of organization design: (1) line organization, (2) functional organization, and (3) line-staff organization. In line organizations everybody does essentially the same kind of work under the more or less immediate authority of a "man at the top." Some degree of internal specialization may lead to departmentalization of line organizations, but this does not necessarily change their fundamentals.

Pure functional organizations are scarce, apparently because they are based on the sensible but hard to implement idea that since it is difficult to combine all necessary managerial-supervisory skills in single individuals, it is wise to organize around functions—skills, activities, etc.—rather than people. The desire to include functional specialists within an organization while retaining unity of command is the basis for the widespread "compromise" development of line-staff organizations wherein supporting specialists work through particular line managers.

It is obviously possible to combine these models in various ways and mention might be made of such special cases as project organizations (which, in a sense, are temporary, special-purpose, line organizations) and matrix organizations (which are meldings of project and functional models calculated to satisfy institutional needs for permanence). Furthermore, other structural classifications are possible. Pugh, et al. stress a multidimensional characterization built around performance regulation, centralization of authority, and the

[5] D. Katz and R. Kahn, *Social Psychology*, "Dimension of Organization Structure," *Administrative Science Quarterly* 13 (1968), pp. 65–105.

[6] See, C. A. Perrow, "A Framework for the Comparative Analysis of Organizations," *American Sociological Review* (1967), 32, pp. 195–208.

[7] See, R. G. Hunt, "Review of Systems of Organization" by E. J. Miller and A. K. Rice, *Administrative Science Quarterly*, 1968, 13, pp. 360–362.

[8] D. Katz and R. Kahn, *Social Psychology*, Chapter 1.

[9] See, D. S. Pugh, et al., *"Dimensions"*; W. F. Whyte, *Organizational Behavior: Theory and Application* (Homewood, Ill.: Irwin-Dorsey, 1969).

[10] R. N. Anthony, *Planning and Control Systems* (Cambridge, Mass.: Harvard University Press, 1965).

[11] See J. Woodward, *Industrial Organization: Theory and Practice* (London: Oxford University Press, 1965).

degree to which operations are controlled by line management rather than by impersonal records and procedures generated from staff offices.[12] Burns and Stalker's well known distinction between "organic" and "mechanistic" management patterns is another somewhat similar example.[13] Organic organizations are characterized by less formalized definitions of jobs, by more stress on flexibility and adaptability, and by communication networks involving more consultation than command. Mechanistic organizations are more rigidly specialized functionally, and in general, define an opposite pole on an organic-mechanistic continuum. Finally, of course, distinctions between bureaucratic and nonbureaucratic organizations exemplify the classificatory use of structural or design criteria.[14]

Classification by Output Classifying organizations according to their output is a common practice that may involve one of two emphases. One, the kind or type of output (i.e., the product), is a standard basis for defining industries (e.g., automobile, motion pictures, etc.) and is too familiar to require further comment. But, output can also be viewed from the standpoint of the quantity or volume of whatever it is that is produced. For example, Woodward, although she thought of it more as a direct expression of technology, used to good effect classification of industrial firms as unit, small-batch, large-batch, and mass production.[15] The immediate meaning of unit, batch, and mass production is plain: it describes a scale of production quantities ranging from one of a kind through a few to very many.

W. F. Whyte makes use of these same distinctions, but only as subcategories within a broader, more heterogeneous system of classes.[16] Whyte's primary breakdown of organizations into "office, service, manufacturing, and continuous process" varieties clearly employs criteria other than output. Indeed it makes use of just about all criteria save social function. Office and service classes, for instance, appear to be distinguishable on the basis of the nature of their outputs, but they (and surely manufacturing and continuous processing) are classifications that also make use of other bases for categorization, notably throughout processes and, possibly, input as well.

Classification by Input Distinctions between organizations based on input rest on contrasts regarding the raw materials on which the system works. The possibilities here are at least as numerous as the vast number offered to classifications based on output. One input distinction that has received special attention in the literature, however, is that between organizations (such as prisons, schools, employment agencies) that deal mainly with people and those organizations that operate chiefly on things, objects, hardware, or the like. Erving Goffman has provided some especially exotic discussions of "people-processing" systems, and the topic is capable of generating more than a little emotion.[17] It is doubtless that such systems differ from others, if for no other reason than because their raw materials are "reactive" instead of passive. In fact, this reactivity can itself be made a basis for a distinction between organizations by focusing on the form of feedback controlling the system's operations. We shall illustrate this in the next section.

In the meantime, take notice of Thompson and Bates' use of a "ratio of mechanization to professionalization" to distinguish organizations.[18] By this they mean the extent to which technology is represented in human or nonhuman resources. But whether this is truly a classification based on input is questionable for, if Thompson and Bates stress the *locus* of technology, the notions of mechanization and professionalization seem to link the distinction closely to technology itself.

Classification by Throughput Conversion processes or throughput are the various things done, with or without tools and machines, to transform inputs into outputs. The term "technology" is usually applied to these processes.[19] Our own definition of technology encompasses the three facets of technology (1) operations, (2) materials, and (3) knowledge, differentiated by Hickson et al.,[20] and includes the

[12] D. S. Pugh, et al., "Dimensions."

[13] T. Burns and G. M. Stalker, *The Management of Innovation* (London: Tavistock Publications, 1961).

[14] See, e.g., D. Katz and R. Kahn, *Social Psychology*, Ch. 5; N. P. Mouzelis, *Organization and Bureaucracy* (Chicago: Aldine, 1967); W. F. Whyte, "Organizational Behavior," Ch. 1; W. Bennis, "Beyond Bureaucracy," *Transaction* (1965), 2, pp. 31–35.

[15] J. Woodward, *Industrial Organization*.

[16] W. F. Whyte, "Organizational Behavior."

[17] E. Goffman, *Asylums* (Garden City, N. Y.: Doubleday Anchor, 1961).

[18] J. D. Thompson, and F. L. Bates, "Technology, Organization, and Administration," *Administrative Science Quarterly* (1957), 2, pp. 325–342.

[19] For a useful discussion of definitional issues, see D. J. Hickson, D. S. Pugh, and D. C. Pheysey, "Operations Technology and Organization Structure: An Empirical Reappraisal," *Administrative Science Quarterly* (1969), 14, pp. 378–397.

[20] *Ibid.*

sequencing of activities involved in the conversion process, thereby including what Whyte, among others, refers to as "work flow."[21]

A straightforward throughput classification might be exemplified by J. D. Thompson's distinction between long-linked, mediating, and intensive technologies.[22] The first of these includes conversion processes (like those found in automobile assembly plants) involving serially interdependent operations, standard products, and constant, repetitive work rates. Mediating technologies link clients who "are or wish to be interdependent (as banks link depositors and lenders)." These, too, commonly employ standardization along with bureaucratic formats. Intensive technologies are those involving application of a variety of techniques to the change of some specific object, in which actual operations are determined by feedback from the object itself. This is clearly a "custom technology," and includes such examples as hospitals, schools, research projects, and tailor shops. Obviously a single organization might include within itself multiple technologies.

We have already mentioned that Whyte's classification of organizations included an admixture of output and throughput criteria; the same was true of Woodward's classification. Along with other categories defined by output, both Whyte and Woodward include in their schemas a "continuous process" category (e.g., a fully automated oil refinery) that indexes technology rather than output.[23]

It must be evident that input and output systems, as well as throughput systems, can be described in terms of the processes or technologies by which they are implemented. That is, the operations by which inputs—raw materials—are introduced into a system describe a technology, and the same is true on the output (product) side. This fact, plus the other consideration that conversion processes in an organization must be relative to the input and output to and from the system (e.g., knowledge of the raw materials and product specifications) strongly suggest that the input-conversion-output cycle represents a single basic technological sequence or organizational substrate. Thus, the crucial consideration may not be the particular properties of the inputs or the outputs per se, but the technologies according to which they are accomplished.[24] In any case, it seems clear that input, output, and technology (throughput) are inextricably joined. Taken together they constitute the basic *endogenous* operational properties of organizations and, when actualized, collectively describe what Anthony calls organizational "process" (or function) as distinguished from structure (system).[25]

There is, of course, nothing in these unifying assertions to preclude variation in technological manifestations at different points in the process cycle. Input and conversion operations might be highly routinized, for example, but output methods (e.g., marketing) might be quite nonroutine.[26] And certainly nothing prevents separate analyses of respective technological features of input, output, or conversion subsystems. The point here is that input and output criteria for classifying organizations may be structurally significant only insofar as they indirectly index technological phenomena.

Another thing that may have been evident in our exposition is the difficulty one has treating technology or process without making reference to structural or design aspects of the organization (see, e.g., the allusion to bureaucratic formats in the presentation above of Thompson's "mediating" technology). This is no accident of discursive formats. Indeed, we have taken notice of Anthony's proposition that system (structure) represents the formulae for organizational processes (input-throughput-output).[27] Certainly the two dimensions are intimately entwined, even if the nature and degree of that intimacy may not yet be altogether clear; furthermore, they are both technologies. Conversion processes, or, more generally, modes of production, constitute what Olsen has called "material technologies." He has described modes of organization as "social technologies."[28] Thus, from Anthony's perspective, exploring relations between "technology" and

[21] W. F. Whyte, "Organizational Behavior."

[22] J. D. Thompson, *Organizations in Action* (New York: McGraw-Hill, 1967).

[23] W. F. Whyte, "Organizational Behavior"; Woodward, *Industrial Organization*. Notice might be taken of Hickson, et al.'s incorporation of this category, along with unit production, mass production, and the others, into a throughput scale of "production continuity" (see Hickson, et al., "Operations Technology").

[24] For a related discussion with different conclusions see Hickson, et al., *Ibid.*, p. 380.

[25] R. N. Anthony, "Planning and Control."

[26] Distinction could be drawn, but throughout this discussion we shall use the basic terms "routine" (or "routinized") and "program" ("programmed") more or less interchangeably to mean the extent to which an organization's tasks can and have been specified and prescribed—formalized. Programming performance (as, to take an extreme example, in a robot) is difficult when tasks are vague, variable, or complicated, but the process can be generally regarded (with neither approval nor disapproval) as a broad organizational means of reducing operational uncertainty by eliminating operator discretion.

[27] Anthony, "Planning and Control."

[28] M. E. Olsen, *The Process of Social Organization* (New York: Holt, Rinehart, Winston, 1968).

"organization" resolves itself into an analysis of relations between system and process. From Olsen's standpoint, this amounts to tracing the linkages between material and social technologies. We should hardly be surprised to find a good deal of interdependence in these relationships. Indeed, the expectation is implicit in the now common characterization of organizations as sociotechnical systems. In a manner of speaking, then, describing relations between technology and organizational forms amounts to an extended definition of the meaning of the concept of the sociotechnical system. With that observation, a more explicit overview of technology and organizational patterns is in order.

TECHNOLOGY AND ORGANIZATION DESIGN

Beginning at least with Veblen and Marx, material technology has been regularly proposed as a major influence on organizational phenomena. Indications of its broad significance can be found in Toynbee's demonstration of changing forms of English social organization as new industrial technologies emerged during the 18th and 19th Centuries. Margaret Mead has provided vivid portrayals of interrelations between technological advances and social patterns.[29] More recently, Dubin[30] has nominated technology as the single most important determinant of work behavior and Mouzelis[31] has spoken at length of the determining effect of technological structures and processes on organizational interaction. Stinchcombe, too, in context with his discussion of "motives for organizing," mentions technology among the basic variables affecting organizing capacity,[32] and Olsen lists material technology as one of four primary factors underlying forms of social organization (the other three are the natural environment, population, and the human being).[33] Finally, in his excellent review of comparative studies, Udy points out two basic "causal mechanisms" that shape organizations. One operates via people to affect structures, and the other is *ecological* and deals with how activity is limited and channeled.[34] Together with the "social setting," which we are disregarding here, technology can be construed as imposing ecological limits on organizational properties.

In somewhat the same way, social technology can be looked upon as constraining material technology, as in the case of cultural or organizational resistance to change[35] or as in the extent to which a system is attuned to the receipt of inputs regarding new material technologies. Burns and Stalker, to cite a pertinent instance, found that firms adapting successfully to the electronics industry were characterized by a more global task model and a different communication process for innovative information than were the less successful ones. In the adaptive firms, technological or market information was introduced to reprogram routine operations, thus enhancing flexibility in a technologically changing environment.[36]

To undergird these contentions, a significant empirical literature has now emerged relating technology to various organizational matters. The most noteworthy examples are probably Woodward's seminal studies.[37] Her work and other relevant investigations have been well reviewed by Perrow, J. D. Thompson, and Hickson, et al., so there is no need for repetition here.[38] It will be sufficient to observe that, although the nature, degree, and conditions of its effect remain controversial,[39] technology has been shown to affect structure, to shape interaction, and to influence the personal characteristics of organizational members.[40]

Yet, as late as 1964, W. R. Scott felt constrained to mark the infrequency with which technological variables had been built into theory.[41] The reasons for this seem to reside partly in a preoccupation of organizational scholars with nonstructural human relations or "informal" processes.[42] and partly from the fact

[29] A. Toynbee, *The Industrial Revolution* (Boston: Beason, 1956); M. Mead, (ed.) *Cultural Patterns and Technological Change* (New York: New American Library, 1955).

[30] R. Dubin, *The World of Work* (Englewood Cliffs: Prentice Hall, 1958).

[31] N. P. Mouzelis, *Organization and Bureaucracy.*

[32] A. L. Stinchcombe, "Social Structure and Organization," ed., J. G. March, *Handbook of Organizations* (Chicago: Rand McNally, 1965. pp. 142–194).

[33] M. E. Olsen, *Social Organization.*

[34] S. H. Udy, "The Comparative Analysis of Organizations," ed., J. G. March, "Handbook of Organizations," pp. 678–710.

[35] See, e.g., M. Mead, "Cultural Patterns" for illustrations of such cultural disinclinations.

[36] T. Burns and G. M. Stalker, "Management of Innovation."

[37] J. Woodward, *Industrial Organization.*

[38] C. A. Perrow, "Framework for Comparative Analysis"; J. D. Thompson, "Organizations in Action"; D. S. Hickson, et al., "Operations Technology."

[39] Illumination of the controversy can perhaps best be found in Hickson, et al., "Operations Technology."

[40] One example of this last point, which is here mentioned only incidentally, may be found in R. Biauner's studies of alienation, e.g., *Alienation and Freedom* (Chicago: University of Chicago Press, 1964).

[41] W. R. Scott, "Theory of Organizations," ed., R. E. L. Faris, *Handbook of Modern Sociology* (Chicago: Rand McNally, 1964), pp. 485–530.

[42] See N. P. Mouzelis, *Organization and Bureaucracy,* for further discussion of the point.

that, although technological phenomena were widely recognized and sometimes even categorized, until recently there literally were no technological *variables* to build into theory.[43] Perhaps what is most important in the technology-organization literature of the past few years, therefore, aside from empirical explication, is that it has begun to give form to conceptualizations of manageable technological variables or dimensions. Prominent in this connection have been the work of Bell, Harvey, Perrow, Whyte, and Pugh and Hickson.

The Technology Variable It will be recalled from our earlier discussion that productive as it was empirically, the technology variable was ambiguous in Woodward's classification scheme. She regarded her entire scheme as a direct index of technology, even as a scale of technological complexity ranging from unit to mass to process modes of production. Harvey, however, has quite reasonably pointed out that the complexity scale could equally well be the reverse.[44] And Woodward's own findings that unit production and continuous process organizations tended to exhibit many common characteristics that contrasted sharply with other kinds of organizations, could imply a "circular" interpretation of the technological dimension underlying her classification.

The precise mechanisms linking technologies with organizational forms are still problematical in the literature, but, as a generality, the critical technological element to which organizational structure must respond seems best conceptualized as *complexity*. This is something that unit production organizations, for instance, may have in at least as long a supply as their continuous process counterparts —a moment's reflection on the many esoteric one-of-a-kind products produced under the American space program vindicates that assertion. To state it simply, this view of correlation between organization and technology signifies that the concrete manifestations of technology are less important than the essential complexity underlying them. Having said that, however, it is necessary to acknowledge immediately that complexity is an elusive concept that takes many forms.

Bell, for instance, has dealt explicitly with the matter of complexity and structure in his study of spans of control (ratios of personnel to supervisors) in a large hospital.[45] He defined complexity as:

(a) The degree of predictability of work demands;

(b) The discretion provided for in a position; and

(c) The responsibility of the job-holder (construed as the time lapse between decision and its supervisory review or assessment).

Bell then showed that as complexity increased with regard to either subordinates' or supervisors' roles, the span of control decreased.

Harvey, using Woodward's work as a point of departure, prefers to speak of a complexity dimension ranging from technical diffuseness ("made to orderness") to specificity.[46] He argues that one needs to take account not only of the *form* of technology (as Woodward tried to do), but also of the amount of "changefulness" *within* a form. As he puts it: A unit production firm might produce the same thing most of the time and thus be "specific." Or, it might vary its outputs and be "diffuse." Harvey postulated that whether the organization is specific or diffuse, it will have differential implications for its structural characteristics. He conceived three "sociotechnical types" (marriages of technology and internal organizational structure): (1) diffuse, (2) intermediate, and (3) specific (defined in terms of frequency of product change) and showed that when compared with specific types, diffuse types had fewer specialized subunits, fewer levels of authority, a lower ratio of managers and supervisors to total personnel, and a lessened degree of performance program specification.

Drawing mainly on the work of Woodward, Harvey, and Bell, together with his own experience, Whyte has gone about the detailed application of technological concepts to analysis of that basic organizational element, the span of control, asking what factors are responsible for its variations. He concludes that there are five factors:

(1) The complexity (in Bell's sense) of the job for the supervisor and subordinate;

(2) The visibility of results from performing the work;

(3) The interdependence and need for coordination among tasks;

(4) The degree to which interdependent activities require human rather than mechanical control; and

(5) The kinds of personnel required by the technology.[47]

Probably the most searching attempts at con-

[43] W. F. Whyte, "Organizational Behavior," (Chapter 3).

[44] E. Harvey, "Technology and the Structure of Organizations," *American Sociological Review* (1968), 33, pp. 247–259.

[45] G. D. Bell, "Determinants of Span of Control," *American Journal of Sociology* (1967), 73, pp. 90–101.

[46] E. Harvey, "Technology and the Structure."

[47] W. F. Whyte, "Organizational Behavior."

ceptualizing technology and relating it to organizational processes can be found in Perrow's work with his contingent, two-dimensional model that elaborates a distinction between routine and nonroutine technologies.[48] Perrow's emphasis is on classifying technologies regarding the frequency with which exceptional cases[49] are encountered and with reference to the nature of the search process (for solutions) that ensues when exceptions (problems) do occur. Using this general model, he relates task-structure to analogous control/coordination processes involving variations in individual or group discretion and the nature of the feedback mechanisms controlling performance (i.e., their degree of "programing"). Perrow also distinguishes three functional areas in management: (1) design and planning, (2) technical control and support of product, and (3) the supervision of production and marketing, each of which he ties in with the technological and task dimensions described. Finally, in a tentative way, Perrow undertakes to relate nontask-related (i.e., informal) interaction to the basic model.

In a later paper, Perrow refined his basic model and extended it to connect with the psychological processes of its human operatives.[50] He stresses a kind of "cognitive" conception of technology working as a system of cues (that may vary in clarity), which signal the initiation of performance routines (that also may vary in their degree of explicit "programming") and involve provision for handling exceptions that may be procedurally more or less routinized. The notable feature of this construction is that regardless of how complicated or elaborate, a system may be viewed as technologically routine to the extent that:

(1) The signals that initiate its processes are unambiguous;

(2) The performance processes so cued are programed; and

(3) When faced with exceptions not covered by regular performance routines, search processes and problem-solving methods are programed.

The properties of technology emphasized by other writers (e.g. Harvey's "changefulness" or Whyte's "human" vs "mechanical" control) can probably be treated in Perrow's formulation as either sources of cognitive complexity (exceptions) or as proxies for it.

Perrow's cognitive constructions rather closely parallel the much more general cybernetic model of human problem-solving due to Miller, Galanter, and Pribram.[51] These authors construe individual performance in relation to a cognitive Test-Operate-Test-Exit (TOTE) model which is based on the notion of "plan." A plan is defined as any hierarchical process controlling the sequence in which a set of operations is performed. They discuss a variety of ways that plans may differ (communicability, source, detail, flexibility, etc.) and also discuss plans for searching and solving, distinguishing between systematic and heuristic varieties.

Very briefly, their idea is that people have images of reality and an array of plans for dealing with it. As information in the form of environmental signals flows into a human performance system, it is "tested" for fit with existing plans which then may be put into operation. Results of action are appraised via feedback from the performance, and the system moves on either to another performance segment or, if a problem has arisen, to a more or less standardized search routine. Of course, the system could cycle into a search routine immediately if the initial "test" yielded no suitable performance program. From Miller, Galanter, and Pribram's presentation it is evident that when a search plan exists one may not even be aware of it, although it is necessary to perceive the exception—it is the function of the TOTE unit to guarantee that. Thus, regardless of how complicated it may be materially, at the behavioral level, technology can be defined in terms of an ordered set of skills or habits that differ mainly in their degree of routinization, integration, or mechanization. Complicated material technologies may be more difficult to program and they may place greater demands on human resources, but be that as it may, what counts operationally is behavioral routinization. We may say, then, that technological complexity is a function of the frequency with which problems (exceptions) confront organizational operations and the practical difficulty and degree of individual discretion or judgment required in resolving or finding solutions to them.

Performance vs Problem-Solving System

It may be concluded from the foregoing that it

[48] C. A. Perrow, "Framework for Comparative Analysis."

[49] I.e., tasks, decisions, etc. not covered, or perceived to be covered, by existing performance programs. Such exceptions define problems for which organizational solutions must be sought if the system is to function, or at least if it is to function smoothly.

[50] C. A. Perrow, "Technology and Structural Changes in Business Firms" (Paper presented at First World Congress, International Industrial Relations Assn, Geneva, September 1967).

[51] G. A. Miller, E. Galanter, and K. H. Pribram, *Plans and the Structure of Behavior* (New York: Holt, Rinehart, Winston, 1960).

is not material technology, per se, that presents organizational challenges, but the nature of the behavioral and problem-solving tasks confronting those operating the system at all its various levels. The extent to which an organization's task systems can be programmed and operational uncertainty thereby eliminated seem to be the critical circumstances. However, no performance program can anticipate every contingency; exceptions will occur. Even if it can be reduced, operational uncertainty cannot be totally eliminated. Consequently, as Perrow has maintained, the decisive structural determinants are apt to be associated with the handling of exceptions to task programs. The frequency of such exceptions, of course, will not be unrelated to material technology, but it still may not parallel it closely—very complicated material technologies may, for instance, be highly programmed. But, in any event, the more crucial consideration would seem to be the importance of exceptions to the viability of the organization and how these exceptions can be handled by it.

If paradoxical, then, it seems nevertheless reasonable to assume that the more a system depends upon its performance programs to control its outputs, the more seriously it must view exceptions to their application or breakdowns in their operation and, hence, the more it must be geared to deal with them if and when they occur. If problem-solving processes are routinized along with task performance, one could expect a different kind of organization from the one that would result when they are not. In an unpublished paper, Perrow has presented some data consistent with such an expectation.[52]

If this is sensible, a potential basis for the similarity found by Woodward between unit production and process organizations is discoverable via the simple expedient of conceiving, somewhat after the fashion of Burns and Stalker,[53] of two quite different kinds of organization: one geared chiefly to performance (as in a mass production factory or a modern bank) and the other one geared to problem-solving (as in a hospital or a design and development enterprise). In a unit production firm, the system deals almost entirely with exceptions, and its problem-solving modes are likely to be unroutinized, especially if it is technologically diffuse.[54] In automated continuous process organizations, whether exceptions are frequent or not, they will be critical when they occur so that such systems, too, are likely to be structured as problem-solving or trouble-shooting affairs. Thus, both unit production organizations (at any rate diffuse ones involved with complicated material technologies) and continuous process varieties are likely to be similarly structured—as organic problem-solving systems. Other operations, facing fewer exceptions and less vitally affected by ones that occur or are equipped with simple routines for solving the problems that ensue from them, are likely to be differently structured—as mechanistic performance systems. We shall not now go into the matter further, but it does seem likely that over the long run firms may tend to organize more and more as performance systems, whether or not it is good for them to do so.[55]

Organization-Level Analysis of Technology and Structure So far we have talked of relations between technology and structure mostly at the so-called level of the organization, treating the system largely as a unitary entity. Yet, we have mentioned the frequent internal technological diversity of organizations—a fact that confronts organizational-level analyses with thorny problems. In addition to complicating life, it prompts serious questions about suitable units of system analysis, for there is no inherent reason to expect technologically diverse organizations to be any less diverse structurally. Therefore, assessments of technology-structure correlations might profit from being based on homogeneous organizational subsystems instead of "forcing" aggregated total systems into statistically defined "types." Or, a system-level alternative might be to devise suitable indexes of technological diversity for use either as independent variables or as "test factors."

To illustrate the force of this point: it is possible that one reason Hickson, et al. found stronger relations between organizational size and structure than between technology and structure (leaving aside their definition of technology), is that size may well be correlated with diversity.[56] Small unit production firms (missing from Hickson, et al.'s research) are likely to be technologically more homogeneous (in the cognitive sense described above) than are very large firms (which were heavily represented in the Hickson, et al. investigation).

[52] C. A. Perrow, Working Paper on Technology and Structure (University of Wisconsin, 1970), mimeo.

[53] T. Burns and G. M. Stalker, "Management of Innovation."

[54] For data regarding this point, see E. Harvey, "Technology and Structure."

[55] Pertinent discussions of processes of bureaucratization can be found in N. P. Mouzelis, *Organization and Bureaucracy*, and in M. E. Olsen, "Social Organization," Ch. 17.

[56] D. J. Hickson, et al, "Operations Technology."

While no evidence exists bearing on the matter, actually, Hickson, et al.'s attempts to reconcile their findings with Woodward's are not too different from the present thesis. In any event, the issue is one which deserves attention in future research.

Designing Organizational Structures The design of an organization refers to the composition of its structure; moreover, "design" implies a purposive formulation legitimized by an organization's formal authority.[57] Certainly, presumptions of organizational rationality implicit in the idea of design connote a sense of organizational construction which is neatly adapted by managerial plan to the objectives and circumstances (technological or other) of a particular organization, adaptations optimized by careful analyses and the systematic application of "principles" of organization and management theory. Yet curiously enough, in her extensive studies, Woodward found firms, both successful and unsuccessful, to vary markedly in "organization consciousness." Even among firms "in which production systems were basically the same," considerable differences could be found regarding the extent to which they tried "to rationalize their production, in their awareness of technical developments, and in their use of techniques such as work study, methods engineering, and operations research."[58]

Woodward was led to the view that conscious organizational planning rarely is based on technical considerations; that it amounts mostly to implicit recognition of technologically constrained situational demands; and that it represents the institutionalization of prevailing organizational realities. Woodward did find process-type firms to be successful a little more often than any other kind, but, by and large she discovered that successful firms were mostly those organizations which were *typical* of their technological types. Successful large-batch firms, for instance, tended to be mechanistic (in Burns and Stalker's sense), whereas other successful firms tended to be organic. And, the same organizational characteristic associated with success among large-batch firms—formalization of roles—augured failure among process types. But, in Woodward's studies, the organizational designing was so "unconsicous" that most managers were not even aware of how their organizations compared structurally with others.

Findings like Woodward's suggest that planning is either absent (which it often surely is) or that it is more apparent than real (coming to little more than formalization of what already is). Undoubtedly, much ostensible organizational analysis and design does represent a sort of managerial doodling instigated by external affiliations,[59] motivated by managers' desires to display virtuosity, or motivated by their needs to "keep up with the Joneses." This analysis and design may also depend heavily upon having time to think about such things—on organizational "slack," as Perrow put it.[60] Furthermore, Blau, Scott, and V. A. Thompson have suggested that organizational elaboration often arises simply from desires on the part of those in power either to evade unpleasant tasks or to bolster the prevailing status structure,[61] or from some other consideration (e.g. empire-building) quite extraneous to technical requirements of organizational tasks.

Still, Woodward found too, that "organic" firms tended as a group to be low in organization-consciousness, thus implying that these things may not depend altogether on managerial caprice. And, while organization-consciousness was not always a mark of "mechanistic" orientations—organization charts sometimes poorly reflected what actually happened in the firm—consciousness did not seem to be altogether random regarding technology. In short, some technologies seem to prompt more concern with design than others. It follows that they would, from arguments like Udy's; that the salience of technology as an influence upon structure will decrease with its flexibility and that mechanization of technology will enhance the salience of group structure[62]—a proposition fully consistent with Cyert and March's assertion that questions of organizational design are meaningful only when alternative modes of performance exist.[63]

These issues have been well reviewed by J. D. Thompson who offers an array of propositions relating technology to organizational operations and thence to rational organizational design.[64] His book nicely illustrates both how operations depend on technology and how various principles of organizational design implicitly assume sustaining technologies. The

[57] See C. J. Haberstroh, "Organization Design and Systems Analysis", ed., J. G. March, *Handbook of Organizations*, pp. 1171–1213.

[58] J. Woodward, *Industrial Organization*, p. 42.

[59] See *Ibid.*, p. 21.

[60] C. A. Perrow, "Comparative Analysis."

[61] P. Blau and W. R. Scott, *Formal Organizations* (San Francisco: Chandler, 1962); V. A. Thompson, *Modern Organization* (New York: Knopf, 1961).

[62] S. H. Udy, "Analysis of Organizations."

[63] R. M. Cyert and J. G. March, "Organization Design."

[64] J. D. Thompson, "Organizations in Actions."

latter is a matter of overarching significance highlighted by Woodward's finding that success was associated with "textbook" management applications only among large-batch concerns;[65] this suggests the conclusion that management theory has been largely based on this technological model, without this fact having been understood. If that is true, application of standard managerial precepts in other technological contexts is likely to yield less than salutary consequences. Miller and Rice have made this point, commenting that classical theories of organization drew mainly on experience in industries representing only a narrow technological range.[66] They add that their own experiences support Woodward's implication that the models and principles derived do not fit either process or unit production industries. Hickson, et al. have also argued the relativity of design precepts to technological environments, though they appear to believe this is because technology is relevant mostly at "shop-floor levels" and, therefore, chiefly in small organizations "where nothing is far removed from the workflow itself."[67]

In any case, it follows, as Perrow also has said,[68] that there can probably be no "one best" organizational structure or managerial orientation—not participative management, not bureaucracy, not any single fashionable methodology. In this regard, one might call to mind Fiedler's persuasive arguments that effective leadership entails an adaption of "style" to organizational context.[69] In the same way, organizational success depends fundamentally upon meshing design (social technology) with the material technology out of which emerge the organization's tasks. It may be, as Woodward's work suggests, that organizations tend as a "natural" process to shape themselves into at least a loose match of technologies, but that does not mean that management design activity is irrelevant or that management ought to become passive and desist from efforts to plan and enhance operational effectiveness.[70] What follows is only that it must acknowledge the technological imperative.[71] Social and material technology must be mutually adapted in system designs. Admittedly, until more adequately differentiated social technological models become available from comparative studies this will be hard to do. But, who ever said management was easy?

CONCLUDING OBSERVATIONS

We have distinguished between two fundamentally different models for organization—performance and problem-solving. Analogous in conception to Burns and Stalker's mechanistic and organic management models, this distinction has the virtue of making management methods the means to ends—e.g. problem-solving—rather than inherently good or bad things. In any event, we have also suggested that most management theories pertain to performance models, not to problem-solving models of organization, but that, for various reasons, organizations tend to evolve toward performance models; i.e., they endeavor to increase routinization. It may be, as Olsen says, that such tendencies arise from the organization's continual efforts to rationalize its functioning in order to achieve its goals more effectively,[72] but nevertheless there are many times when such movement is premature and disfunctional. Consequently, it will sometimes require deliberate managerial effort to resist such evolution when it would compromise the flexibility and creativity of the system and defeat effective goal achievement.

Probably nowhere is this maxim more applicable than in research and development environments (whether in industry, universities, or wherever). Decentralized, organically operated project organizations have been effective vehicles for accomplishing goals in such contexts, but the moral of our story, paradoxically perhaps, is that centralized authority may be necessary to preserve their adaptive integrity in the face of "natural" forces toward bureaucratization. Udy, for instance, hypothesized that technological "complexity" stimulates concerns for coordination that tend to lead toward elaboration and formalization of administration.[73] Furthermore, the generation of inflexibility occasioned by predilections toward "empire building" within projects and by dispositions to assimilate project organizations to

[65] J. Woodward, *Industrial Organization.*

[66] E. J. Miller and A. K. Rice, *Systems of Organization* (London: Tavistock Publications, 1967).

[67] D. J. Hickson, et al, "Operations Technology," p. 396.

[68] C. A. Perrow, "Comparative Analysis."

[69] F. E. Fiedler, *A Theory of Leadership Effectiveness* (New York: McGraw Hill, 1967).

[70] I am indebted to John D. Senger for pointing out the possible analogy between this "natural" process and Darwinian evolution of form and its attendant costs. Managerial manipulation of organizational forms then might be considered an attempt to reduce the costs of evolutionary development, even if it might not always succeed.

[71] See Hickson, "Operations Technology."

[72] M. E. Olsen, *Social Organization*, pp. 300–301.

[73] S. H. Udy, "Analysis of Organizations."

functional (or administrative) divisions are familiar experiences in research and development environments.[74]

Finally, we should close by commenting that nothing in the foregoing should be interpreted to preclude various kinds of performance or information programming. Nor should it foreclose use of searching methods for systems analysis; the basic message is that these things must be employed in the service of a fundamental problem-solving model of organization. In brief, they should be means to ends and not devices for transforming the organizational design or for reducing it to some tepid least common denominator. One unfortunate (or fortunate, depending on your view) consequence of this policy, of course, is that it leaves the organization in a condition of heavy dependence on the commitment and competence of the people who run it—or at least those who manage it.

SUMMARY

Various means of classifying organizations are reviewed and the relevance of technology to the structure of organization is discussed. Developments in the operationalization of technological variables are traced, and the implications for purposive organizational planning considered. Emphasis is placed on a "cognitive" interpretation of technological complexity and on the role of uncertainty as a basic constraint upon organizational design. Two basically distinct organizational models are differentiated: one is oriented toward problem-solving and the other toward performance. It is concluded that most management theories pertain to the latter and not the former, and various consequences of that judgment are considered.

[74] See C. J. Haberstroh, "Organization Design," pp. 1208–1209 for a brief discussion of these issues.

Part 4
STAFFING

Staffing is the managerial function that has to do with providing personnel for the organization structure. It is thus the selection, inventory, appraisal, and training of people so that they can best assist in the accomplishment of enterprise objectives and obtain a high degree of satisfaction in doing so.

The staffing function logically proceeds from planning the future of an enterprise to planning the organization structure and the specification of the various roles to be filled. Of particular importance to students of management and given special emphasis in this part of the readings is the staffing of managerial positions. In order to make staffing effective, an essential requirement is manpower planning. Bruce P. Coleman offers a program for accomplishing this in his paper "An Integrated System for Manpower Planning."

There can be no doubt that actual selection of managers is a difficult and extraordinarily important task. And selection becomes more important the higher a manager is in the organization structure. In the first place, it is well accepted that, especially in the longer run, the quality of managers makes the difference in enterprise effectiveness. In the second place, it has been extremely difficult to appraise managers accurately and even more of a problem to know how an individual will perform in a new or higher job. A third consideration is that it may take considerable time before one can know how well a person is doing a job; by that time, not only is money lost in terms of salary and expenses, but, even more significant, time is lost. One of the prominent practitioners in this field, Robert N. McMurry, gives some valuable suggestions on how to deal with this problem in his "Avoiding Mistakes in Selecting Executives."

In the often misunderstood and misapplied aid to selection, psychological testing, J. Watson Wilson gives wise and practical advice in his article "Toward Better Use of Psychological Testing." One of the newer approaches to assessing managers as an aid to selection and promotion is the assessment center. In these centers, which have been used by companies with apparent success, trained assessors observe candidates in a variety of standardized activities, such as management games, in-basket exercises, and leaderless group discussions. From these, evaluations of current or future promotability, as well as needs for development, are made. This system is described and results from experience reported in Ann Howard's paper on "An Assessment of Assessment Centers."

Obviously, one of the keys to managerial planning is to have suitable replacements available, if at all possible, when positions are expanded or when managers are promoted or retire or die. For any enterprise to know what its needs are, means must be found for inventorying managers. This technique is the subject of Walter S. Wikstrom's "Management Inventory."

The key to management training, and perhaps even to management itself, is effective managerial appraisal. If management does not know the strengths and weaknesses of individual managers, it will have serious difficulty developing the most effective training program. Moreover, nearly every enterprise would like to have a group of effective managers, and this requires that managerial appraisals be as accurate as possible. Despite the importance of managerial appraisal, the editors were not impressed with the appraisal practices of most companies until they began to develop evaluations based upon predetermined objectives. When this is done, managerial appraisal becomes much less subjective; the manager is evaluated on the basis of what he does rather than of what people think of him. Thus the establishment of objectives becomes an integral part of the management process.

One of the clearest presentations on appraising managers against the setting and achieving of objectives is that made by Arch Patton in "How to Appraise Executive Performance." Some of the problems and difficulties in appraising managers against objectives are pointed out in Harold Koontz' paper on "Making Managerial Appraisal Effective." In this article he also makes a strong case for appraising managers, in addition, on their ability to manage and suggests some ways that this can be done.

In the area of managerial development, the editors introduce the subject in a paper by Walter S. Wikstrom published as "Developing Managers: Underlying Principles." These principles place managerial development in an accurate and proper perspective and can be usefully employed as standards against which to judge training programs. How to make managerial development effective in practice is also explained in the article by Charles E. Watson on "Getting Management Training to Pay Off."

One of the most widely used devices for managerial development has been sensitivity training or, as it is sometimes called, T-group or laboratory training. Because there are strong proponents and critics of this psychologically oriented technique, the editors have chosen to present Robert J. House's objective article "T-Group Training: Good or Bad?"

A fairly new and increasingly popular approach to training managers and to identifying and modifying behavior of people to help solve problems of unwanted frictions in an organization is referred to as organizational development, or "O.D." The nature of this approach and some of the issues involved are discussed in A. P. Raia's thoughtful paper on "Organizational Development—Some Issues and Challenges."

A. STAFFING AS A SYSTEM

45 AN INTEGRATED SYSTEM FOR MANPOWER PLANNING*

Bruce P. Coleman

During the past decade, industrial, academic, and governmental institutions have been giving more attention to manpower planning. Numerous organizations perform some manpower planning activities; scattered research has been done; and many kinds of federal and state government programs have been instituted. Pressures continue to build throughout the economy for the effective allocation and utilization of the manpower resource. Despite this interest and activity, there is little evidence that planning in this area is achieving sophistication in practice or is recognized for its potential as a major managerial activity that can make significant contributions to corporate strategy and operations.

If one uses the fund of literature as a barometer of the quality of theory and practice in a field, an analysis of the literature on manpower planning produces mixed conclusions. On the one hand, many contributions are positive; on the other, considerable fragmentation and confusion exist. The weaknesses lie in four primary areas.

First, manpower planning has widely different meanings. To some it applies only to particular types of personnel skills, usually managerial. It may include only forecasting activities rather than a full-range of planning functions. Second, many articles describe the experience of one firm in limited manpower planning activities and then draw generalizations for the field on the basis of that experience. Such generalizations are rarely justified; experiences are not usually transferable to different organizations with different needs. Third, few articles deal with the cost factors of manpower planning. As a result, manpower as an investment alternative or expense is not considered. Fourth, the integration of manpower planning and other planning activities of the organization is rarely attempted.[1]

The purpose here is to provide a conceptual but practical approach to manpower planning and programming. The approach is broad and comprehensive in order to present a total concept that serves the following purposes: to accommodate or expand upon divergent definitions as well as provide a set of suggested general definitions; to integrate the several functions of manpower planning into a system of planning and programming; to suggest the means for integrating manpower planning with other planning functions of the firm; and to provide the basis for the design of programs tailored to fit the specific needs of particular organizations.

Two key definitions are required before the manpower planning process can be examined. *Manpower planning is the process of determining manpower requirements and the means for meeting those requirements in order to carry out the integrated plans of the organization.* It includes determining types of skills and capabilities, numbers of people, and location and timing of manpower needs.

Given the manpower requirements and general policy direction, *manpower programming consists of structuring programs for providing the organization with the needed manpower.* It is the vital link between the definition of requirements and the placement and continual development of the individual on the job.

These are general definitions. As the discussion proceeds, it will become apparent how these can be made more specific with respect to particular activities involved in the process. In addition, these definitions can later acquire prefixes that will specify the type of manpower skill and the length of the planning period.

* Reprinted by permission of the publisher from *Business Horizons,* vol. 13, no. 5, pp. 89–95, October, 1970. Mr. Coleman is professor of management at Michigan State University.

[1] For additional comments and confirmation of the views presented here, see James W. Walker, "Forecasting Manpower Needs," *Harvard Business Review* (March-April 1969), pp. 152–54.

A FIVE-STAGE SYSTEM

Conceptually, the process of manpower planning can be viewed as a five-stage system (see the accompanying figure). The first stage is the determination of organizational objectives and plans for the planning period. In many instances, these may be taken as given for manpower planning, but, in other instances, they cannot. The second stage is the determination of gross manpower requirements for the planning period. These requirements constitute the total manpower needed for carrying out the integrated plans of the organization. Third, the manpower inventory, or current in-house capability is determined. The fourth stage is the definition of net manpower requirements for the planning period. These requirements are obtained by deducting the manpower inventory from gross requirements. The fifth stage consists of programming to meet the net manpower requirements. The programs may require expansion, contraction, or internal adjustment of the present work force.

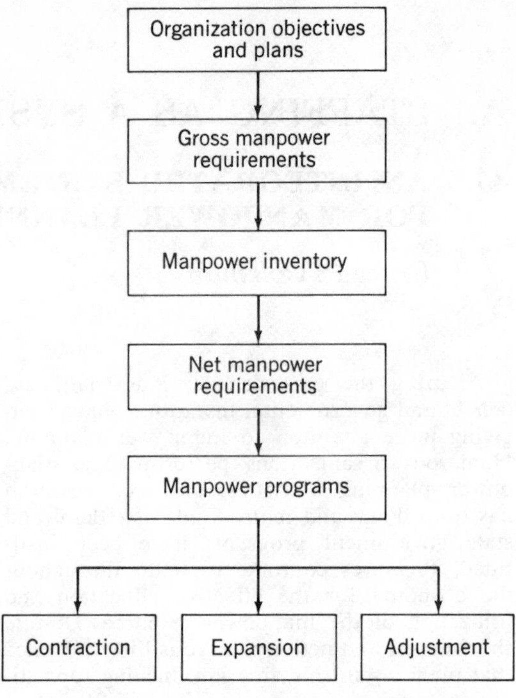

The remainder of this article develops and illustrates each of the stages in the process. The final section discusses integration of the stages and feed-back aspects of the total process.

Organizational Goals and Manpower The formulation of organizational objectives and plans and manpower planning are interdependent at all organizational levels. This interdependence is particularly apparent for long-range planning. A look at the two-way relationships should identify and illustrate this interdependence. The fundamental objective of manpower planning and programming is to provide the organization with the personnel to perform the activities that will achieve organizational goals. Consequently, objectives and plans at all levels of the organization provide the basis for defining manpower requirements.

Manpower data (availability of specific skills and numbers of people, for example) can be crucial inputs into the planning processes. The availability of the needed manpower may determine whether a specific project can be undertaken. In other instances, there are significant manpower implications for proposed programs such as mergers and divestitures.

In many instances, organizational objectives and plans may be taken as given for manpower planning purposes. Sales and production schedules may be the prime determinants of requirements for salesmen and production operative manpower. Unless significant exceptions to planned performance occur, little other than effective communication with manpower planners is necessary for the needed adjustments in those types of manpower skills.

But it may not be that simple. In an economic organization, manpower, like materials and facilities, should be considered as an investment alternative subject to similar cost, return, allocation, and control considerations given to other resources. Thus efficiency and effectiveness enter the picture in terms of minimum cost and effective utilization of manpower resources in order to obtain a respectable return on invested capital. Intimate knowledge of organizational plans and participation in the planning process can enhance efficiency and effectiveness. Close attention to the determination of manpower requirements and programming in terms of quality of skills, timing of their acquisition, utilization of skills, and their numbers and cost can yield significant returns in terms of investment and utilization of human resources.

Aside from the need to meet the firm's economic objectives, there are those programs that contribute less to the organization's profit picture, especially in the short run. These programs carry more social impact. At one extreme, a firm might be involved in attacking problems of transportation, housing, air and water pollution, or recreation. Clearly, participation in such programs diverts organizational resources from the primary economic mission.

An example of another set of special programs is the work of firms participating in the National Alliance of Business for the training and hiring of the hard-core unemployed. Such a program of training is a special case, but it is one that not only shows assumption of responsibility for a social problem, but also is one that can directly affect the economic mission of the enterprise.

If manpower planning is not integrated with total organizational planning, these programs run the risk of being harmful to the individual, the organization, and the economy. The skills being developed must be useful, challenging, and not subject to rapid obsolescence or displacement. The investment in these programs is substantially higher than for other kinds of employee training; consequently, the skills trained should be carefully defined as being required over time by the organization or the local economy. Quotas should be realistic and based on need, both in terms of the quality and the quantity of skills. No one benefits if skills are developed that no one needs two to five years hence.

These illustrations establish the position that the manpower expertise is just as much an essential element of corporate planning as marketing, manufacturing, financial, legal, and research expertise. Little formal research has been conducted to determine the essential relationships among manpower information inputs and other kinds of information inputs for total corporate planning. The research that has been done indicates that essential and identifiable relationships exist.[2]

Gross Requirements Gross manpower requirements encompass a complete definition of types, numbers, location, and timing of the manpower skills needed throughout the organization for the planning period. Most often neglected in organizations is this crucial determination of manpower requirements on a logical decision basis. Too often the emphasis is on programming—*given* an estimate of requirements.

While much of the manpower planning literature discusses this topic, little in the way of comprehensive analysis and integration of approaches has taken place. Methods for determining gross manpower requirements can be classified into categories for identification purposes. A useful classification borrowed from the defense industry is as follows:

Expert estimate: Estimation is made by a combination of systems familiarity, experience, and intuition on the part of the expert.

Historical comparison: Estimation is made by breaking the new system into subsystems similar to those already in existence. Data on known systems are retrieved from information libraries and provide the basis for the manning estimate of the new system.

Task-analytic: Estimation is made by a detailed analysis of the system requirements, establishment of mission profiles and ground equipment functions, definition of specific tasks, and a clustering of tasks.

Sovereign factors: Estimation is based upon identification of one or several factors that correlate highly with the item being estimated. It avoids the task of complex manipulation of multiple variables.

Modeling: Estimation is made by the use of decision models such as PERT, linear and dynamic programming, and multiple regression expression. It is typified by its objective and explicit nature.[3]

It has become quite apparent that the same method for determining gross requirements is not appropriate for all types of manpower skills. Attempting to visualize the organization chart of the future, with all its shortcomings, may be a useful method for anticipating managerial manpower requirements. Such an approach may yield insight into the numbers of managers required and the particular range of responsibilities and knowledge needed by the individual managers. The real danger of such an approach is that the planners may believe in the organization chart as projected, and it may become a restriction to progress rather than a catalytic agent.

For sales and manufacturing manpower, a method employing correlation analysis may be a highly effective first approximation of manpower requirements, particularly where products, territories, and production operations are not changing rapidly. In other organizations, however, where new and more complex products are marketed, new skills may be needed

[2] Bruce P. Coleman, *An Exploratory Study of Information for Manpower Planning* (Ann Arbor, Mich.: University Microfilms, Inc., 1967).

[3] Donald B. Haines and Sidney Gael, *Estimating Manning Requirements for Advanced Systems: A Survey of the Defense Industry* (Report No. AMRL-TDR-63-110; Wright-Patterson AFB, Ohio; U.S. Air Force, Air Force Systems Command, November, 1963).

in the sales force. The qualitative aspects of the problem then become significant. Where manufacturing operations are in a dynamic state, a similar situation exists; in addition, close attention to plans for facilities must be given to obtain realistic trade-offs among machines and manpower over time. Skills obsolescence among operative workers is a real danger.

Some types of manpower activities are more amenable to a method based on the function or mission of an organizational unit. For service functions such as a maintenance department, where heterogeneous groups of skills are utilized, manpower requirements can be based on work functions and work load factors. This method permits trade-offs among skill levels and types of skills.

None of these approaches is particularly satisfactory for determining requirements for technical and professional manpower. The more effective approach is a consultative method focused on qualitative requirements on a decentralized basis with managerial review at each level of operations. This is the basic approach taken by leading aerospace firms.

The point is this: no one method is appropriate for determining requirements for all types of manpower in an organization. Furthermore, the same method is not appropriate for determining requirements for a specific skill for all organizations. Each organization has its unique set of requirements, which is a function of its product, markets, facilities, operations, finances, and value systems. Consequently, the following general approach can serve as a guide:

Categorize types of manpower skills into homogeneous groups or functional units.

Calculate requirements utilizing the most effective method for each category for the planning period

Integrate these requirements centrally on a cost and performance basis

Ensure a free flow of information throughout the process.

Manpower Inventory Knowing with precision the existing manpower capability of the organization is the objective of the manpower inventory. The basic information needed is data relative to the knowledge and skills possessed by each individual in the organization. This includes not only his present duties, but all skills he possesses as indicated by past work experience and educational specialties. Other data, such as age, sex, and promotability, are desirable for planning purposes.

This information enables the firm to match the skills in the organization against gross manpower requirements. It is unlikely that it is economical to recruit, hire, and train additional people when the needed skills are already on hand somewhere within the organization. Often internal adjustments can be made satisfactorily at minimum cost. For example, a West Coast defense contractor reported hiring, at a high recruitment cost, an engineer with a specific type of knowledge and training. Later the company learned of two engineers and one technician, already on the payroll in the same division, who possessed—but were not utilizing in their present positions—that same specific background or some experience in the field. It was not until the organization developed the capability to know what skills and knowledge employees possessed and to retrieve that data that it could avoid such needless employment expense.

Having a manpower inventory is also essential to intelligent participation in total organizational planning. It provides the input for advice concerning the capability of the organization to undertake programs and for estimating the cost of acquiring additional manpower capabilities.

Firms that have failed to consider the manpower implications of acquisitions have learned an often expensive lesson. They found that they did not possess the managerial, technical, or operative manpower capability to exploit opportunities presented by the acquisition. They were unable to obtain the synergistic effects of the combined organizations because of the manpower drain on the parent organization and the time and cost involved in developing the needed manpower.

The inventory system need not be elaborate or expensive. Too much is made of the necessity for expensive computerized personnel data systems as necessary for skillful manpower planning. Many organizations cannot afford these systems nor do they need them; any system which provides the needed data will suffice. On the other hand, computerized personnel information retrieval systems tend to be underrated in terms of the cost/benefits accrued. These systems may well be the most significant development in personnel administration in decades. The potential applications are vast in terms of personnel research and manpower planning and control. Once the basic data bank is developed, its use for analysis and planning can be expanded as programs are developed. Thus the decision to computerize personnel data should be based on more than just information retrieval of basic employment data.

Net Manpower Requirements The definition of net manpower requirements becomes the manpower objective for the planning period and is the basis for action programs designed to effect changes necessary in the capability of this area in the organization. Basically, net requirements are the difference between gross requirements and the manpower inventory, but arriving at the net requirements is not simply a matter of addition and subtraction. Other factors enter into the structure of net requirements and affect the design of specific programs for obtaining personnel. For example, the timing of manpower needs will vary. Age and experience variations may well be built into the net requirements to achieve balance in the work force. Other qualitative factors such as sex and race may be important criteria in the definition of net requirements.

The planning lead time may greatly influence net requirements. In the short run, if immediate adjustments are necessary (and, in fact, no planning has likely occurred), qualitative criteria may be immaterial. Short-range fluctuations in the production schedule, for example, may trigger layoffs or hires. This occurs at a probable high cost, however, in terms of administrative and benefits costs caused by employment instability. When the lead time is lengthened through effective and intelligent planning, the definition of net manpower requirements serves as the basis for action programs, which can include qualitative manpower criteria as well as such criteria as minimum cost, effective manpower utilization, and efficient operation.

Action Programs Manpower programming permits, on a totally integrated basis, the design and implementation of action programs to assure that the manpower needs of the firm are met over time. These programs entail all of the traditional personnel functions, but the emphasis here is on the acquisition and development of manpower skills. Thus, the functions of employment (recruitment, selection, and placement) and education and training receive prime consideration.

Changes in manpower programs will take the form of expansion, adjustment, contraction, or a combination of these. A complete description of action programs to meet manpower requirements would be unrealistic since the possibilities are almost innumerable. Several examples and comments should suffice to illustrate possibilities and guidelines.[4]

An obvious starting place in programming is an analysis of present manpower capability. It is quite possible that some needs can be met through internal adjustment, such as transfers from skills in surplus to positions in shortage. Special skills and knowledge—in scientific and engineering manpower, for example—may reside in the organization at present. A transfer may permit complete internal adjustment or the hiring of a less expensive skill.

Action for periods of contraction is the most difficult for the individual. Allowing turnover and attrition to absorb cutbacks is desirable, and temporary layoffs and preferable to permanent layoffs and later rehiring. Economy and fairness should be primary criteria. Perhaps the most sensible action for alleviating difficult adjustments during times of contraction is effective long-range manpower planning itself. Surplus manpower is less likely to exist in the organization, and contraction can be better anticipated.

Education, development, and training constitute major action programs for meeting the skill requirements of the organization. The role of development for managerial skills and training for sales and production workers are firmly established in business. Other skills may be better and less expensively trained within the firm. Sometimes in-house training may be the only reasonable source of skills needed, but, again, these programs require advance thought and development.

The strength of taking a longer-range approach on a total organization basis is that needs, particularly changes in requirements, are anticipated in advance, and they can be met at minimum or optimum costs to the organization and of maximum benefit to the individual. In general, the longer the lead time, the greater the likelihood that programming will satisfy all the pertinent quantitative and qualitative criteria. However, the gestation period as well as acquisition and development costs vary for different types of manpower skills. Thus, the lead time will be substantial for managerial and highly skilled operatives and less for office and unskilled people. Programs must be designed specifically for different types of skills, and usually the programs will be highly dissimilar.

[4] For more illustrations see Eric W. Vetter, *Manpower Planning for High Talent Personnel* (Ann Arbor, Mich.: Bureau of Industrial Relations, The University of Michigan, 1967), Chapter 3.

INTEGRATION AND CONTROL

Several key points essential to the design and operation of the system, but not identified as stages in it, must be pointed out. These relate to integration and feedback and control. This process has been described as a set of stages or steps; in reality, it does not operate that way. It operates as an integrated system. For example, organizational objectives and plans determine and are determined by manpower data. Action programs are inseparable from net requirements and affect the manpower inventory, objectives, and requirements. The control process just described may affect any stage of the process.

For this process to operate effectively, there must be feedback and control. There must be continuous evaluation to assure that programs are being achieved, that programs are providing for requirements, and that they, in turn, are proper for providing personnel to meet organizational objectives and plans. Procedures must be designed to assure the flow of feedback information and its appraisal.

The position taken here is that manpower planning and programming must be upgraded significantly—both conceptually and operationally—if organizations are to meet the challenges of the future and if the nation is to utilize its manpower resource effectively. The approach has been to present a flexible, comprehensive concept of manpower planning which can serve as a basis for the design of specific corporate planning systems.

In addition, it has been the intent to stir the thoughts of executives to the development of an attitude toward manpower planning. Such an attitude would encompass an appreciation for the importance of developing the capability to plan, at the corporate level, the acquisition, development, and utilization of a critical and expensive resource—manpower.

B. SELECTION OF MANAGERS

46 AVOIDING MISTAKES IN SELECTING EXECUTIVES*

Robert N. McMurry

The viability of a business, that is, whether it will be a "thruster" or a "sleeper" (to use the interesting words of a British study[1]) is determined almost wholly by the competence, vision, and courage of a *small number of key executives.* A study conducted in Great Britain in 1966[1] embracing six quite disparate lines of business, makes an interesting distinction between the firms it designates as "thrusters" and those it characterizes as the "sleepers" in their industries. In all six of the areas researched, it found that one, two, or, at most, three producers dominated their markets, controlling in the aggregate from 60 to 80 percent of the total volume. These are the "thrusters." Supplementing these leaders, from 10 to 30 smaller, often marginal concerns, competed among each other for the remainder of their markets. These were designated as the "sleepers." Many parallels exist in the United States.

In many instances it is one man, the chief executive, operating at the apex of the business, and supplemented by a limited number of key subordinates, who is solely responsible for the status of the business. Actually, many of the greatest commercial successes in America can be attributed primarily to the genius of *one man,* e.g., General Motors to Alfred Sloane; Sears Roebuck to General Robert Wood; Pan American Airways to Juan Tripp, and the resurgence of Montgomery Ward to Robert Brooker. It is for this reason that the selection of the men to guide the destiny of an enterprise and administer its operation is of such critical importance.

QUALITIES OF A TOP EXECUTIVE

Competence as a top level executive is the product of a mix of both inherited and acquired qualities. However, given good health and adequate intelligence, most of the attributes which have led to his superior competence have been acquired in the course of his development, and reflect the influences to which he has been subjected and the mores and values of the culture of which he is a part. Thus, for example, *nearly all leading executives tend to subscribe to the values, principles, and goals characteristic of the Protestant or Puritan Ethic.* Nearly all of them believe in what are now disparagingly called by many the "bourgeois virtues" of hard work, perseverence, frugality, pride of craftsmanship, obedience to constituted authority, and loyalty to the employer. Their values are in marked contrast to those who hold the Mediterranean Ethic, i.e., a man should expend only enough effort to earn what he needs for enjoyment of the good life and such worldly pleasures as may appeal to him. Furthermore, most effective executives tend to be much more *inner* than *other* directed. They are more fixed in their conviction of the rightness of their beliefs; hence, less subject to influence by their peers. They have great confidence, albeit sometimes misplaced, in the essential rightness of what they are doing. They are also frequently men of unusual courage and self-assurance, who habitually exercise sound judgment, who ideally have an exceptional degree of creativity and imagination, and who are receptive to innovation and change. Since basic courage and decisiveness, coupled with imagination, a truly innovative spirit, and sound judgment, are very rarely encountered in the population as a whole, it is probable that not more than one person in 10,000 is qualified to head up an enterprise of any magnitude in today's demanding, highly technical, rapidly changing, and generally volatile milieu. (One of the major ironies of the world today is the fact that the leading Communist societies, Russia and China, are now the strongest advocates of their equivalents of the Protestant Ethic. It is the leaders of these societies who are now most vigorously attempting to remold their people's thinking in order to win their acceptance of the merits of industry, sobriety,

* Reprinted by permission of the publisher from *Michigan Business Review*, vol. 22, no. 4, pp. 7–14, July, 1970. Mr. McMurry is President of The McMurry Company, Consulting Industrial Psychologists.

[1] A PEP Report, *Attitudes of British Management* (more popularly known as "Thrusters and Sleepers"). Baltimore, Md.: Penguin Books, 1966.

pride of craftsmanship and a generally austere mode of life.)

DIFFERENT QUALITIES REQUIRED IN DIFFERENT POSITIONS

While certain attributes such as the foregoing are requisite for all executive positions, the specific combination of traits, attributes, etc., demanded by a particular opening in management will vary somewhat in terms of the level of the position and the nature of the industry to be served. For example, automobile manufacturing and chemicals tend to be much more volatile and demanding of top management than are utilities, banking, and insurance (as reflected in the differences in the compensation paid their key officers).

The degree to which the position is *structured,* i.e., the amount of control to which the incumbent is subjected, likewise plays an important role. An executive in a highly structured position is supported in his decision-making by precedents, rules, regulations, manuals, and the presence of a superior who is available to answer his questions. If necessary, the latter will even make his more difficult decisions for him. A well structured job usually demands few risk-taking decisions of the incumbent.

The *unstructured* job, on the other hand, has few or none of the foregoing supportive and protective features; the incumbent is largely on his own; his personal competence and courage determine whether he will sink or swim. Generally, the higher the position is in the hierarchy of management, the less the structure. Thus in most companies the chief executive has the least structured job. On the other hand, nearly all positions below the vice president or general manager level are totally or at least extensively structured. Line administrative positions, because the occupant "decides and acts," tend to be less comprehensively structured than are staff positions where the incumbent merely "recommends." In general, the less the position is structured, the greater the demands which will be placed on the incumbent. (It is of interest to note that there is an almost perfect negative correlation between degree of structure and level of compensation, i.e., the more all-inclusive the structure, the lower the pay.) This, of course, reflects the working of the law of supply and demand: there is an ample supply of candidates for activities demanding little risk taking: few for those which call for hard decisions.

THE PROBLEMS OF THE CHIEF EXECUTIVE

The most demanding of all management positions is that of the chief executive. This is because, in the final analysis, *he* carries the ultimate responsibility for the growth, profit and future of his enterprise. Furthermore, all of these responsibilities are centralized in *him.* To quote Harry Truman, his is the desk at which "the buck stops." He has no superiors to share the risks of his position, i.e., there is no one else to blame if things go wrong. In this sense, his role can be compared to that of the captain of a ship: he must accept ultimate responsibility for trouble even though personally he may not have contributed to it.

Several features of the chief executive's position can make it excruciatingly demanding. These are:

1. Although he has many to whom he can turn for advice and council, he cannot evade the fact that when the crunch comes, the sole responsibility is *his.*
2. Most, perhaps as many as 80 percent of his decisions, relate *to the future.* Hence he can never have complete and reliable information on which to base them. (Who can anticipate exactly how conditions will be from five to ten years hence?) Yet he must often deliver his answer *today.* In consequence, most of his business decisions must be in the nature of calculated risks.
3. As head of his company, he will almost invariably be the least informed of what is going on in his enterprise (he is the ultimate victim of poor internal communications, is often the recipient of slanted or wilfully inaccurate information, and, unfortunately, often has little control over any tendency on his part to be unreceptive to information which he does not wish to hear or believe). In view of this, even many of his day-to-day decisions must be based on incomplete or questionable information. In addition, many of them will be further contaminated by his biases, fears, and proneness to wishful thinking. In consequence, a number will be wrong. This will subject him to additional stresses.
4. While nominally he has total authority over his enterprise, he often discovers that his instructions are distorted or even blocked and that his ability effectively to influence his people is more theoretical than real. Few business organizations are genuinely well integrated and unified entities. Instead, many are highly pluralistic and rivalrous congeries of disparate functions each with competing goals and interests and with strong centrifugal tendencies. It requires a strong, sometimes ruthless leader to hold such groups together. Often their only point of commonality is their hostility to top

management. Hence, he can never expect to be universally loved.

5. If his organization is to grow, i.e., be a "thruster" and avoid obsolescence, he must constantly plan ahead and innovate. But, unfortunately, not all innovations prove successful. Actually only a small percentage of the new products or services placed on the market in any one year survive and far from all mergers and acquisitions prove to be productive and generally satisfactory.
6. In addition, the professional executive is faced with the difficulty of coping with potentially or actually threatening conditions over which he has little or no control, e.g., changes in his company's ownership, economic declines, the disappearance of markets, threats of acquisition by raiders, war, political upheavals and conflicts with other major elites, such as big government and big labor.

COURAGE AND DECISIVENESS, THE PRIME REQUISITES OF AN EXECUTIVE

Taking all of the foregoing factors into account, the role of entrepreneur-manager in a business enterprise, despite the prestige and earnings associated with it, is frequently filled with frustration, harrassment and anxiety. (As a rule, the least secure position in a company, unless he happens to own it, is that occupied by the president.) In consequence, it requires an unusual and uniquely well qualified individual to cope with its demands and problems. Hence, of all of the attributes demanded of the occupant of the top post in any undertaking, *courage, decisiveness, and self-confidence* are of the greatest importance. An executive can have every other qualification, but if he is lacking in these, he is almost certainly bound to fail. (This likewise applies in a lesser degree to all other major management positions.)

WHAT IT TAKES TO BE AN ENTREPRENEUR-MANAGER

Thus, using the position of chief executive as a prototype, the following personal attributes and qualifications, named roughly in descending order of their importance, are absolute prerequisites for success:

1. Courage, self-reliance, and freedom from dependence.
2. Sound judgment, i.e., common or "horse" sense, (a capacity for realistic thinking).
3. Creativity and constructive imagination, together with a receptivity to change and innovation.
4. Integrity (some executives have succeeded without it; nevertheless it is generally a valuable asset).
5. The ability to plan and organize and anticipate contingencies.
6. Energy and drive (the chief executive must often be the "spark plug" of his enterprise).
7. A fair but firm disciplinarian who does not fraternize with his subordinates and has no pets, favorites or strong biases.
8. A capacity to be ruthless when necessary (he may be called upon to close a plant, throwing 2500 people out of work).
9. He must, as noted, be essentially inner-directed and subscribe to the values characteristic of the Protestant Ethic, i.e., he must be convinced of the merits of industry, of frugality, of submission to constituted authority, of pride of craftsmanship, etc.

Ancillary qualifications for an entrepreneur manager include a knowledge of finance, training and experience in business principles and methods, empathy, and hopefully some degree of personal charm and magnetism ("charisma"). Obviously he must be above average in intelligence but he does not need to be a genius. (Actually, it is probably better for him not to be too intellectually inclined, since some "profound thinkers" have a tendency to lose contact with reality. They confuse "What should be" for "What can actually be done.") Likewise, as captain of his undertaking, it is best that he *not* be a specialist or technician in any particular field. He is ideally a generalist. His primary function is innovation and long-range planning. (As Peter Drucker puts it, "The basic postulate to entrepreneurship is the assumption that whatever is now being done is probably already obsolete.") Hence, the goal of the *thrusting* executive is not only to do it better, but to do it differently as well. He must also practice management by exception and leave the day-to-day administration of the business to his subordinates. Finally, he must be a skilled leader and be capable of *delegating authority as well as responsibility.*

THE ROLE OF THE VICE PRESIDENTS

For positions below that of the chairman or president and perhaps the executive vice president, the primary function of the executive staff is to *administer* the policies set forth by the chief executive and to run the business on a day-to-day basis. They are the *functional* heads of the enterprise. Most of their activities are well structured. Hence, at these levels, the primary emphasis in selection must be placed on *technical expertise* (experience, training, administrative skill, creativity and imagination). This is particularly true of staff specialists, whose primary function is *advisory*. Few of these have any significant decision or policy making authority but simply make recommendations within the fields of their expertise. Included in this group are the president's legal and tax advisers, financial experts, engineers, research and development personnel, public relations technicians, accountants, purchasing agents, medical staff, and personnel and labor relations specialists. All of the attributes enumerated above as prerequisite for success as a chief executive are desirable for any and all executive positions, except that a demand for courage and decisiveness diminishes with increasing job structure.

In addition to the qualities enumerated above, it is, of course, obvious that every candidate for an executive position must possess certain elementary personal qualities. Among these are the *habits* (values in action) of vocational stability, industry, ability to get along with others, perseverence, and appropriate vocational goals, needs and motivations. In addition, he must enjoy reasonable mental health, i.e., be free from mental quirks, idiosyncrasies, or peculiarities which will interfere with his productivity or cause him to be disruptive or abrasive in his dealing with others. Likewise, he must have a reasonably tranquil home environment; be compatible with his wife; not suffer unduly from distracting off-the-job problems such as debts or ill health and not engage excessively in activities which will interfere with his carrying out of his work, such as drinking, gambling, or the pursuit of women.

WHERE MANAGEMENT ERRS

Management's primary problems in the selection of executives lies in the fact that frequently *it neither understands the true nature of their jobs nor knows exactly what to look for in a candidate*. In consequence, it makes its most egregious blunders by over-weighting such elements as the candidate's experience, schooling, and technical expertise. (This is also in part because these qualities are relatively obvious and easily measured.) Likewise they do play important roles in *middle management*. What few managements recognize is the fact that executives seldom fail because of any deficiency in their *technical skills and expertise*. The majority who experience trouble do so primarily because *they lack courage, self-confidence, and decisiveness*. While most are loathe to admit it, they are "running scared" in their jobs.

Such frightened executives tend to become reactionary and reluctant to innovate (because they fear change); to become hostile and defensive (to deny their insecurities); to become indecisive (because they fear to accept responsibility); and to become autocratic and punitive, i.e., bullies and tyrants in dealing with their subordinates (to conceal their own feelings of inadequacy). These are among the executives who have been so aptly described by Laurence Peter and Raymond Hall in their book, *The Peter Principle*.[2] They are the men who have been advanced to their first or second "levels of incompetence." In popular terminology, these are the supervisors, managers and executives who have been "promoted over their heads."

A second common management error in the selection of executives is a tendency to be over-influenced by such superficial qualities as appearance, manner, and facility of verbal expression. Some men have been advanced into management primarily because they "look like executives." Sometimes they have also been qualified but not invariably so. Similar sources of error arise from an over-evaluation of the school the individual has attended or his social status, e.g., WASPs often tend to be specially favored. It is rather probable that if such an ugly person and prickly personality as the late Alfred Steinmetz were to apply for a position today, he would be accepted by few employers.

A third, almost universal error on the part of management, is to assume that because a man is performing well or has had long experience at one level of responsibility (and structure) he is equally qualified to advance to a higher and often far less well structured position. An example is the case of the star salesman who is unwisely promoted to sales manager. This is because his superiors do not realize that *managing* is not only a significantly different activity from *selling* but that it requires a considerably greater degree of stamina because *it is generally a less well structured position.* In short, the work of manager is usually more complex, the responsibilities and the pressures are greater and his job security is markedly less.

Unfortunately, the assessment of a man's courage, self-confidence, and decisiveness is complicated by three facts: first, the man on the street has little or no awareness of the acuteness of his needs for security, structure, and supportive supervision. It would conflict too brutally with his self-image. Hence if asked directly about his willingness and ability to take risks, make decisions, etc., he will, of course,

[2] Laurence J. Peter and Raymond Hall, *The Peter Principle*. New York: Bantam Books, 1969, p. 8.

report that he "loves a challenge." Second, there is no relationship between these factors and intelligence and schooling. A person may be a genius intellectually, and still have an acute need for security and structure. Third, *there are no psychological tests or similar measurement devices available to determine objectively how much self-confidence the subject has.* Because of these factors, the nature and importance of this trait and knowledge of the techniques available for its assessment in a candidate are often inadequately understood by management, as well as by many of those engaged in the conduct of "executive searches."

THE SEVEN STEPS TO EXECUTIVE SELECTION

In view of the foregoing factors, if men are to be properly chosen for key executive positions, particularly those of a line, administrative character, it is essential that their qualifications be carefully matched against the requirements of the job they are to fill. The following program describes the seven steps that are necessary to do this.

The first step, of course, is the determination in precise detail of the nature of the position to be filled. This requires answers to the following six questions, which cover the basic parameters of every executive position:

1. What will be the nature of the incumbent's duties, responsibilities, scope of authority, and reporting relationships?
2. How much and how will he be compensated?
3. What are the *technical* requirements of the position?
4. To what extent is it *structured*? (How much real autonomy will the individual have?)
5. What is the leadership style and what are the performance expectations, values, and tolerance for competition from subordinates of the prospective superior (to insure at least reasonable compatibility with him)?
6. What are the opportunities for advancement offered by the position?

The second step is to ascertain the candidate's *values* by asking him a series of open-ended, "knock out" questions, designed to cover:

1. His life goals and aspirations.
2. His opinions concerning the business or industry for which he is being considered. (For example, some persons are biased against the liquor industry.)
3. His attitudes toward all significant aspects of the job, e.g., his prospective duties and possible needs to relocate or to travel.
4. His financial expectations.
5. His aims with respect to his future with the company.
6. His values as they relate to the legitimacy of profits, the role of industry in the economy, etc.

The third step is to obtain relevant personal data about him, his make-up and his background by means of:

1. A comprehensive application form.
2. Transcripts of his school records.
3. A test of intelligence.
4. Various personality tests, e.g., the TAT, a sentence completion test and the Cornell Index.

The fourth step is to confirm the accuracy of the data already obtained from the applicant through the use of telephone or personal contacts with previous superiors and, when necessary, with schools. In addition, an assessment of the quality of his leadership skills (including self-reliance, courage, and decisiveness) is obtained by ascertaining from previous superiors the extent to which:

1. He has exhibited authentic leadership skills on or off previous jobs.
2. He has been sure of himself and decisive on his previous jobs, i.e., has made his own decisions, handled his problems on his own and has acted independently of his superiors. (The man who "leans" on his superiors or is prone to "second guess" them is usually also weak, insecure, and indecisive.)
3. He has shown a particular style of leadership in dealing with his subordinates, e.g., laissez faire, democratic-participative, manipulative, benevolently autocratic, or absolutely and bureaucratically autocratic. (If he is an autocrat, bureaucrat, or a tyrant, he is probably weak.)
4. He can delegate *authority* (weak men rarely do so).
5. He habitually takes flight into detail. (Men who are running scared often seek refuge in a preoccupation with petty detail.)
6. He has developed strong, competent subordinates. (Weak men often fear subordinates who may be potential threats to their personal job security.)
7. He has had pets and favorites or strong personal biases. (Weak men tend to look on their pets as sources of support for themselves.)
8. He has habitually accepted responsibility

for his own and his subordinates' errors. (Frightened men are prone to alibi and blame others.)

9. He can take protracted pressure without panicking or becoming disorganized. (Weak men often crack under pressure.)
10. He reacts negatively to criticism. (The weak man resents criticism and becomes defensive under it.)

The fifth step is to ascertain the candidate's habits, character make-up, principal motivations, and the extent of his emotional maturity and mental health by a one to two hour structured or patterned personal interview conducted in depth. This interview covers his:

1. Work and service experience.
2. Schooling.
3. Early home environment.
4. Present marital, social and domestic situation.
5. Finances.
6. Health.

Finally, by combining all of the foregoing data, it becomes possible to form an overall estimate of the candidate's:

1. Principal attitudes and values.
2. Technical experience and fields of expertise.
3. Chief character traits as revealed by his "track record," i.e., it is indicative of his:
   a. Vocational stability.
   b. Industry.
   c. Ability to get along with others.
   d. Perseverance.
   e. Loyalty.
   f. Leadership.
4. Primary needs and motivations.
5. Intelligence and mental health.
6. Self-reliance and capacity to work under relatively unstructured conditions.

This permits a measure of the extent to which he matches the requirements of the opening.

Sixth, he must be given a thorough physical examination.

VISITING THE CANDIDATE'S HOME

The seventh and final step is to visit the candidate's home and ascertain its probable influence, positive or negative, on his success. The object of this visit is to meet his family, to acquaint them with the nature of the position, to describe both its favorable and unfavorable aspects, and to determine:

1. Whether any special conditions exist, e.g., a retarded child, which might induce complications?
2. Who is dominant in the home, the candidate or someone else?
3. The nature of existing relationships within the home, i.e., the extent to which the wife and other family members are congenial and supportive or, in contrast, negative and a potential source of problems.
4. The family's attitudes toward:
   a. The nature of the activity, e.g., some families object to the liquor business or to insurance sales.
   b. The husband's travel schedules, the hours, etc.
   c. The amount and mode of compensation.
   d. The possibility of transfers or relocations.

With these data about the candidate, it becomes possible, with a surprising degree of effectiveness, to match his qualifications meaningfully against the opening for which he is being considered. To begin with, this procedure permits the ascertainment of his suitability in terms of each of the five parameters of the position. While the prediction of a candidate's *success* must, of necessity, be tentative because of contingencies which cannot always be anticipated, a prognosis of *failure* for him can be made with a high degree of assurance. This is because of a simple fact: *although it requires the combination of many skills, motivations and other attributes to insure success as an executive, a serious deficiency in any single trait or characteristic can almost invariably guarantee his failure.*

Effective steps for the evaluation of a candidate for an executive position, whether he be up-graded from within the company or recruited from outside, are inevitably involved, time-consuming and costly. Furthermore, many executives regard themselves as good judges of men. Hence, they can see little need for elaborate selection programs such as the foregoing for candidates for *management level positions.* (Paradoxically, they do accept "scientific selection procedures" for use in the hiring of factory, office and sales personnel and for members of middle management.) However, it is in the selection of senior managers and executives that the need for evaluation is greatest. This is because it is more difficult and the costs of an error are greater. Furthermore, these costs are not limited to those arising from the incumbent's outright failure. In some instances it may take from three to five years for an executive's inadequacies to become clearly manifest. Much damage can be done in the interim. Even lost time in finding a replacement can be expensive.

47 TOWARD BETTER USE OF PSYCHOLOGICAL TESTING*

J. Watson Wilson

As many a high school student can gleefully point out, none of our "laws" of aerodynamics is capable of explaining just how it is that the bumble bee flies. The fact of the matter is, according to some of these laws the bumble bee cannot possibly fly at all. Luckily, the bumble bee, as he blithely wings his way, knows nothing about aerodynamics and assuredly cares even less.

Psychologists occasionally find themselves in the same embarrassing position as the aerodynamicists, for there are some people who succeed brilliantly at jobs that psychological tests will "prove" they are unfitted for. This does not mean that the laws of psychometrics should be ignored any more than the case of the bumble bee means that there is something fundamentally wrong with the design of our airplanes. Rather, it indicates that we do not yet understand the laws of testing as well as we might. Unfortunately, the inadequacy of our present knowledge often leads to rashness, rather than caution, in the use of tests. Thus the flames of controversy over the value of testing, which have burned ever since tests were introduced into industry shortly after World War I, are stoked ever higher.

As in many controversies, atypical instances are frequently cited.

There is the example of the tense, shy young man who got the bright idea of becoming an insurance salesman in order to overcome his timidity and self-consciousness. His test scores, taking no account of his determination, predicted failure. Within three years, he joined the elite group of million-dollar producers.

Or take the case of a company that selected its salesmen by means of a very expensive mail-order testing program. The tests were accompanied by great claims to objectivity on the grounds that the people who interpreted them never saw the company or its candidates. They had objectivity to be sure, but some very elementary research proved that this particular company would have done better to hire men turned down by the tests than to hire those that the tests recommended, for the test scores showed a negative correlation with on-the-job performance.

Some years ago—to take just one more example—the agency vice president of a large insurance company offered a psychologist $100,000 to study one of its salesmen, who had sold more than a million dollars' worth of life insurance in his first ten months of employment. All the psychologist had to do for his tidy fee was to find out what made this man a million-dollar producer and devise a test that would uncover others just like him. The psychologist was flattered, but had to refuse the offer. Similar performance on the part of different individuals, he explained, may stem from very different personality characteristics—especially as one moves up the occupational scale from the more specific jobs to the more abstract, or creative, ones.

These anecdotes illustrate some of the more basic things that need to be said about tests and testing.

THE IMPORTANCE OF INDIVIDUAL DIFFERENCES

The most important point is that it is people who are being tested, and people differ. They differ in such general abilities as intelligence. They differ in aptitudes and talents, both general and specific. They differ in interest and temperament and motivation. Moreover, what accounts for one man's success or failure may be very different from what accounts for another's, and the ways in which a

* Reprinted by permission of the publisher from *Personnel,* vol. 39, no. 3, pp. 55–62, May–June, 1962. Mr. Wilson is managing partner of Nordli, Wilson Associates, of Westport, Connecticut.

certain individual differs from other people may be an asset or a liability to his employer, depending on the job he is in, the nature of the difference, and the degree of the difference.

Psychological tests, as part of a selection or appraisal program, may be a very important tool for managers, a means of helping them identify and understand individual differences and thereby perform their functions better. Tests cannot, however, be substituted for managerial judgment, or action, and they have limited value except insofar as they help the manager to judge well. Any manager who treats them as ends in themselves is guilty of abdicating his responsibilities.

In passing, it should be noted that the old concept of putting "square pegs" into "square holes" is quite obsolete. There are, of course, some people in this world who just cannot find a place for themselves. Generally speaking, however, people aren't square and neither are jobs. There are many things that any one individual can do and do well; hence, there are many people who can competently perform more than one kind of job. For this reason, tests ought never to be used for pigeonholing people, and their results ought never to be considered a final verdict on anybody.

GROUND RULES OF TESTING

If you are using tests or contemplating their use—and every company of any size should at least consider them—there are certain ground rules you should observe:

1. *The test data should be weighed in the context of the subject's history.* There are many tests whose results cannot be validly interpreted without consideration of other information about the person being tested. Trying to interpret these results in a vacuum is like trying to diagnose a man's physical condition on the basis of his height, weight, pulse rate, and blood pressure without knowing anything about his medical history.

> Take, for example, personality tests, which are very popular and can be highly useful in many situations. A so-called adverse score on an emotional scale may mean any number of things. One person with such a score may find it hard to hold a job because his emotional problems lead to difficulty in getting along with other people; this will be reflected in a history of frequent job changes. Another person with an adverse emotional pattern may take his feelings out on himself rather than others and may have a history of ulcers or some other physical disorder. Still another with such a score may manage his emotions in a way that does not affect either his health or his job history and may even make him a more diligent worker. Thus the personal history makes the bare test score meaningful.
>
> The same holds true of interest tests, which are commonly used for uncovering vocational preferences. To interpret these tests properly, one must know whether the picture the individual has presented in his responses describes him as he really is or as he would like to be. The extroverted young man who sold magazines as a child and was a leader all through school will probably score high, naturally enough, in persuasiveness—but so may the introverted young man who wishes he were more outgoing. Only by interpreting the test data in light of the individual's history can you know what such a score really means.

2. *Know the job in question. Have valid and adequate job descriptions and analyses.* How specific or detailed your testing program is should be determined to a very large degree by job analysis. After all, tests are tools, and should therefore be chosen for their suitability to the particular selection job to be done. Whether you should use a typing aptitude test or a typing achievement test depends on whether you want to train your personnel within the company or to hire them fully trained. Whether you should use a test of clerical aptitude or one of general intelligence depends on whether the tests involved in the particular job at issue are highly standardized or not.

Unless your company is a very unusual one, it will not be able to find one test, or even one battery of tests, that can yield adequate information about all its jobs and all its applicants. This may sound too obvious to be worth mentioning. Yet I know one New England company where all prospective employees are given a test originally intended to select butter wrappers. As it happens, this company doesn't make butter, and its product is rarely wrapped.

3. *Know your tests—what they will do and what they won't do.* It is constantly amazing how little some people know about the tests they use daily. Yet every test worth using comes with a carefully prepared manual that describes its use, gives its reliability rating and probably its validity rating as well, and tells how the scores on the test usually run. Never —and I can't be too emphatic about this— never use a test that is not accompanied by information of this kind. Furthermore, don't use any test until you have mastered the material given in its manual.

A brief explanation of the terms "reliability" and "validity" is probably in order. A test is reliable if the person taking it today scores the same (or almost the same) as he would have scored last week or as he would score next week. Reliability is measured on a scale running from zero to 1. Perfect reliability is very hard to achieve, but ratings of .86 to .92 are fairly common in good tests. A rating of .24, for example, would be an indication of poor reliability.

The importance of reliability is obvious, and reliability ratings are easy to come by, for every good test is accompanied by such data. Yet one test that is now among the most widely used instruments for selecting salesmen has a reliability of only .14. Apparently, companies that will spend hundreds, and even thousands, of dollars evaluating the reliability of a machine they are thinking of buying will hardly give a second thought to the tools with which they propose to choose people to run the machine or sell its products—though on the basis of tests like the one just mentioned they make decisions that may cost thousands of dollars in salaries, advances, and the like.

Along with their reliability ratings, many good tests are accompanied by validity data. Broadly speaking, validity is an index of the degree to which a test measures what is it supposed to measure. A validity rating answers the question how well test scores correlate with job performance. To the degree that a sales test, say, is valid, the best salesmen will get the highest scores, the worst salesmen will get the lowest scores, and so on. Incidentally, all sales talks and rationalizations to the contrary, it is unlikely that a test with low reliability will have significant validity either.

Generally speaking, reputable test builders and publishers determine the validity of their tests by analyzing the scores of people whose productiveness or effectiveness is known. They publish the results of these analyses either in the test manuals or in separate research studies. *Don't use tests about which such data are not available unless you are prepared to do your own validity research.* Remember, in these test-happy days there are many patent medicines. Some are good, some are indifferent, and some are downright harmful.

Not too long ago, for example, the research department of a trade association conducted a validity study on a test used by many of its member companies. The test scores, it found, showed a negative correlation with on-the-job performance. Here too, the companies would have been better off in hiring the people who "failed" the test than they were in hiring those who did well on it. And yet, despite the published research of their own association, many of these companies are still using this test, which is, incidentally, a fairly expensive one. This sort of thing, which happens over and over again, is not only poor management; it is also a grave injustice to the people who must take the tests.

4. *Insofar as possible, use tests that have both general and specific norms.* Test builders who approach their work scientifically often provide data on the scores of different population groups. This enables the test user to compare his candidates not only with people in general but also with people performing the same job in companies like his own. Since we live in a competitive society, both comparisons may be important. The first one tells you how your candidates compare with the man in the street, and the second tells you how they compare with the people selected by other companies—perhaps your competitors.

One eastern manufacturing company has a policy of selecting only those candidates whose test scores are 50 per cent higher than the selection norms of other companies in the same business. The result is that its costs are lower, and its profits higher, than those prevailing in the industry, and the company itself is more stable than its competitors.

On the other hand, I know of another company that only recently installed a testing program. Management was appalled to discover that the employees scored much lower than people performing the same jobs in other companies. No wonder this company's unit cost was higher than that of its competitors.

5. *Don't confuse recruiting and selection.* The chances are, your testing program will be of little avail if you too readily move your hiring standards up and down to suit the market—particularly if you ignore test data when people are hard to come by. In times of a tight labor market, it is much better to intensify your recruiting efforts than to adapt your standards to the pressures of the situation. Once you have established sound and realistic test norms, stick by them; you'll find that the people you select will stick by you when the going is really rough.

A couple of examples will serve to illustrate the point.

One company, dissatisfied with the performance of the people it was hiring, installed a new testing program with norms that were correlated with what it considered satisfactory performance and were as high as those of other companies in the industry. When it began to give the tests to applicants, it found that only one out of twelve met the new standards—a far smaller ratio than it had been accustomed to. The tests quickly became "impractical," "unrealistic," and a lot of other things. The fact of the matter was, of course, that the tests had begun to highlight glaring inadequacies in the company's recruiting program. Management had not counted on this turn of events and, unable to face up to it, used the tests as a scapegoat.

Another company takes quite a different attitude toward the problem of selection standards. Its standards are high, and it refuses to lower them. When things get tougher, it recruits harder. Not long ago, the company went through a slate of 25 applicants to find one acceptable candidate. "We can afford to spend money on recruiting," one of its executives has remarked, "but we cannot afford to hire incompetent or marginal people."

6. *Have as high a "selection ratio" as you possibly can.* The "selection ratio" is the number of candidates available for each job to be filled. With or without tests, you don't really *select* when you decide whether or not to accept the only candidate you have. Genuine selection takes place when you have several candidates to choose among—and it is then that testing is most useful. It can be shown statistically that even a test of only moderate validity can be very helpful if you administer it to a large number of candidates—in other words, if you have a high selection ratio. Conversely, the most valid and reliable test in the world will be of limited value if your selection ratio is very low.

One company, recognizing the importance of the selection ratio, has a rule that at least three candidates must be considered for every position, be it the job of machine operator or that of vice president. In the latter case, the number of candidates considered may run as high as 50. The money this company invests in its recruiting program is returned many times over, as one can see from its balance sheet.

7. *Before adopting any test, try it out on your own employees.* Though this is often expensive and time consuming, it is an essential part of the testing program. There are two reasons for this:

First, trying out each test on a known quantity—your own personnel—will help you to choose the tests you need. You should never assume that because a test is applicable in some situations it is necessarily applicable in yours. Its usefulness may be affected by any number of subtle, easily overlooked differences in the job or the environment. There are, for example, dozens of clerical aptitude tests; some situations call for one test, others for a different test. In prescribing various tests, the trained psychometrician makes educated guesses that are usually right. Their rightness, however, should always be carefully and accurately tested in the situation in question.

Second, try-outs of all tests under consideration may yield valuable information about your present employees and even about your recruiting and selection processes. If the companies using the invalid sales test mentioned earlier had done some elementary research before adopting it, they probably would not have become so emotionally involved that they continued to use it despite its poor reliability and its complete lack of validity.

8. *Have your testing program installed by experts.* Approach the installation of a testing program with the same enlightened skepticism that the head of an accounting department would use in selecting bookkeeping equipment. Remember that knowing how to administer tests is one thing, knowing how to interpret them is another, and knowing how to install a testing program is yet a third. Unless you are training in psychometrics, or are willing to spend years learning psychological principles and statistics, don't make this a do-it-yourself project.

In one southern company, do-it-yourself installation has led to increases in the turnover and accident rates. The personnel man was eager to save money by cutting the amount of time new employees spent in learning their jobs. Reasoning that the smarter men are, the quicker they learn, he set high standards of intelligence for *all* the company's jobs. What he did not realize is that in many jobs too much intelligence is as bad as too little. Employees whose intellectual capacities are greatly above those needed for their work will soon become bored and will either begin looking for more stimulating jobs or become so inattentive that they are likely to have accidents.

9. *Avoid the role of counselor.* The minute some people see test data, they are unable to resist the urge to manage other people's lives.

Our world seems to be filled with people who mistakenly think that tests furnish the answer to every human problem. If your testing program is well designed, it may help you decide how well a certain person can do a particular job in your own company. Don't ask it to do more. The testing done for purposes of selection is very different from testing done for purposes of guidance—educational, emotional, or vocational.

> Not long ago, a young man who had taken a battery of tests in applying for a factory job consulted a psychologist to check the advice given him by the factory's employment manager. Among other things, the employment manager had suggested that, in the light of his ability, he should take advantage of the G.I. Bill and go to college rather than take a training position in a factory. The employment man had also told him that when he finished college he should study medicine. What the tests didn't show was that the young man was color-blind and had a history of fainting at the sight of blood.

All this adds up to the simple conclusion that psychological tests, like any other tool, can be effective only when they are handled well. Unfortunately, testing is so often misused that it is scarcely any wonder that its value is a matter of constant controversy.

Many companies, having begun by expecting too much of tests in the first place and ended by getting less from their programs than they might have done, may well be tempted to write off the entire testing movement as a bad mistake. Experience shows, however, that companies that choose their tests as carefully as they choose their equipment and do not delegate to tests the management function of making basic decisions will find them a valuable aid in the complicated task of making the best use of industry's most valuable asset—its human ones.

48 AN ASSESSMENT OF ASSESSMENT CENTERS*

Ann Howard †

As anyone familiar with the traditional psychometric literature can corroborate, the whole idea of assessment centers is preposterous. The basic principle requires that candidates, usually for management positions in organizations, go through a series of individual and group tests and exercises in one concentrated period while being evaluated by a group of assessors. The absurdity is that most of the procedures used to predict future job success are the very ones experience has demonstrated do not work. For example:

1. Clinical, not actuarial, predictions typically are relied upon, although most studies have shown the latter to be more accurate.[37, 41]
2. Multiple predictors are used in spite of evidence that clinical prediction may be worse with the inclusion of more than a few variables.[2]
3. Projective tests may be included, although their reliability and validity are highly questionable.[31]
4. An interview is usually an integral part of the process, in spite of its dubious validity.[35]
5. Personality tests are often included, although it has been claimed that they have little or no value for personnel selection.[27]
6. Situational tests are relied on most heavily, although they are still in an embryonic stage compared to classical psychometric tests and failed dismally at predicting the performance of clinical psychologists.[30]
7. Managers are asked to integrate all this information and predict behavioral traits as well as potential success, even though psychologists are still struggling to demonstrate that even they can do it well.[15, 37]

Where did such an extravagant idea as assessment centers come from? The credit is usually given to the Germans, from whom it was copied by the British and then by the Americans in World War II for use in selecting candidates for the Office of Strategic Services.[40] And did it work for the OSS? The war ended and everyone went home, so no one really knows.

This would be an appropriate place to end this assessment except for one intriguing fact. Psychologists involved in these endeavors over the last few years have been thoughtfully and professionally demonstrating that assessment centers work. How is this possible? A combination of weak psychometric methods cannot be expected to lead to strong predictions any more than an accumulation of weak materials can be expected to produce a substantial building. The purpose of this review is to examine the structure of assessment centers, study the data concerning their uses and efficacy, and try to discover how such an apparent contradiction of psychometric experience can function successfully.

THE ARCHITECTURE OF ASSESSMENT CENTERS

Although the use of multiple assessment methods has been reported previously,[15, 42] this review is confined to those operations which have been designated specifically as assessment centers. This means not merely multiple methods of assessment but the inclusion of situational tests and the use of multiple assessors. The "center" is really more a set of procedures than a physical location, and the "architecture" described here refers to the design of the components of those procedures.

* Reprinted by permission of the publisher from the *Academy of Management Journal,* vol. 17, no. 1, pp. 115–134 (March 1974). Ms. Howard is a doctoral student at the University of Maryland and Director of Research for L. F. McManus Co., Inc.

† The helpful comments of C. J. Bartlett, Irwin L. Goldstein, and Benjamin Schneider are much appreciated. The contribution of unpublished and prepublication articles as well as personal remarks by the following persons are gratefully acknowledged: Stanley R. Acker, V. Jon Bentz, Marvin D. Dunnette, Robert B. Finkle, Allen I. Kraut, Thomas A. Jeswald, Herbert H. Meyer, Joseph L. Moses, A. J. Schaffer, and George C. Thornton, III.

The first industrial use of an assessment center is generally attributed to AT&T,[6] and other centers have been more or less variations on AT&T's theme, as Finkle puts it.[21] A highlighting feature is that candidates are evaluated not on what they have done in present or past jobs but on how they are likely to cope with a new type of position. This involves using various situational tests as well as incorporating some of the more classic selection procedures, such as aptitude tests and interviews. Assessments are conducted at least partially in groups, which permits observing group interactions as well as obtaining peer ratings.

The organization of an assessment center typically follows a prescribed set of steps. The similarities and diversities in centers are explored below as these steps are described. Information on the various centers was compiled from a review of published articles and solicited unpublished material.

The Objectives of the Program The original industrial experimentation with assessment center techniques at AT&T was research-oriented and designed to follow the development of managerial personnel. The first applied use of the assessment methods was in the selection from current employee populations of candidates for either first level or higher level management. The selection function is being expanded gradually to include areas other than management, such as sales, engineering, and revenue agents and auditors.[16] Expectations are that the application of these methods to rank-and-file employees will also be investigated in the future.[7] As the centers have progressed, the possible advantages of the procedures for the training and development of both assessors and assessees have become more apparent, and some programs have changed their objectives to reflect this additional purpose.

The Dimensions to be Assessed Among programs to assess managerial candidates, the number of dimensions of effective performance in the companies studied here varied from about 10 to 52. Serveral companies have factor analyzed criteria to try to explicate the most important constructs. Generalizing from the managerial dimensions selected and factored, the following seem to be important: (a) leadership, (b) organizing and planning (c) decision making, (d) oral and written communications skills, (e) initiative, (f) energy, (g) analytical ability, (h) resistance to stress, (i) use of delegation, (j) behavior flexibility, (k) human relations competence, (l) originality, (m) controlling, (n) self-direction, and (o) overall potential.

Tests and Exercises to Tap the Dimensions

A unique contribution of assessment centers is the inclusion of situational tests in the assessment battery. The rationale behind using such exercises is that they simulate the type of work to which the candidate will be exposed and allow his performance to be observed under somewhat realistic conditions. Contrary to the aptitude test approach, samples, not signs of behavior, are used for prediction.[44]

Situational tests measure more complex or dynamic behavior rather than aptitudes or traits isolated by more traditional psychometric tests; for example, interpersonal skills, leadership, and judgment. Videotapes or films may be used to help capture these dynamics for evaluation purposes. The stated intention of the OSS staff[40] was to measure the Gestalt, or whole, integrated personality. The modern extension of this idea, in process-oriented terms, is that the whole personality is observed in interaction with simulations of the future job environment.

The In-Basket. This simulation is one of those most frequently used in assessment centers and is usually considered the most important.[8] Although commercially prepared in-baskets are available, the most relevant simulations are developed from actual in-basket items in the appropriate offices of the participating company. Typically, the candidate is faced with an accumulation of memos, reports, notes of incoming telephone calls, letters, and other materials supposedly collected in the in-basket of the job he or she is to take over. The candidate is asked to dispose of these materials in the most appropriate manner by writing letters, notes, self-reminders, agenda for meetings, etc.

In many companies completion of the in-basket exercise is followed by a questionnaire or an interview by one of the assessors, in which the candidate is asked to justify his decisions, actions, and nonactions. Ratings of performance may be subjective evaluations or highly standardized checklists.

The Leaderless Group Discussion. The participants in the leaderless group discussion are usually given a discussion question and instructed to arrive at a group decision. Topics may include such things as promotion decisions, disciplinary actions, or business expansion problems. Sometimes participants are given a particular point of view to defend, although they know the group must eventually come to a mutually agreeable decision. Dimensions that can be revealed in the leaderless group discussion include interpersonal skills, acceptance by the group, individual influence, and leadership.[10]

Management Games. Management games usually require participants to solve problems, either cooperatively or competitively. Stock market tasks, manufacturing exercises, and merger negotiations are common. Selection of games, whether commercial or homemade, should be geared to the level of the job concerned. The games often bring out leadership, organizational abilities, and interpersonal skills.[10] Some games also permit observations under stress, especially when conditions suddenly change or when competition stiffens.

Individual Presentations. Subjects are often given time to make an oral presentation on a particular topic or theme. Presentations are typically short, 5 to 10 minutes, but they allow the assessors to observe oral communications skills, persuasiveness, poise, and reaction to the stress of making a group presentation.[10]

Objective Tests. All types of paper and pencil tests of mental ability, personality, interests and achievement (reading, arithmetic, general knowledge) are used. The tests are generally standardized, marketed instruments, although a few companies have developed their own. Usually two companies will not use the same combination of tests or even duplicate single tests.

Projective Tests. Although only a few companies use projective tests, sentence completion and TAT cards are the most popular. The projectives are used to get at some of the more obscure behavioral characteristics, such as need for achievement or originality.[21]

Interview. Most centers have an interview between at least one assessor and the participant. Current interests and motivation as well as general background and past performance are sought.[10] Interviews vary between companies in terms of structure, standardization of interpretation, and the general climate in which they are conducted.[21]

Other Techniques. Written exercises, such as autobiographical essays or open-ended history questionnaires, may be required of participants before entering the center,[10] or creative writing assignments may be made. Some companies have a mock interview between the participant and an applicant for employment or an employee in an appraisal situation. Since such interviews are often an important part of a manager's job, their inclusion in the assessment process has some face validity. The assessor can observe such things as interpersonal skills and empathy and attitude toward the job and the company.[10]

One of J. C. Penney's exercises is the "Irate Customer Phone Call," in which the assessee must display tact and diplomacy to handle a customer's unreasonable demands. A company may also use informal meetings, such as lunches or cocktail parties, to gather information about participants.

The Assessors A typical assessment center will have four to six assessors in anywhere from a 4:1 to 1:1 ratio to assessees.[10] The assessors may be psychologists, members of management, or both. Management members usually are two or three levels above the position for which the candidates are being assessed and not in a supervisory capacity over them.

Most importantly, the assessors are trained for their job. They become familiar with the exercises by participating themselves, watching videotapes, or observing actual performances as nonvoting members of the assessment team. The behavioral dimensions to be assessed are defined, and assessors are given practice and instruction in how to recognize these behaviors. Assessor training varies widely in duration, from brief orientations to two or three weeks of intensive training. Companies highly interested in training managers in appraisal techniques will change assessors frequently, while those most interested in producing a stable selection program or in saving money on training will make changes less often.

The Assessees Typically, assessees are in their first management position or are being considered for management. Candidates for other jobs are rapidly being included in assessment programs, however. Assessees are usually nominated by their supervisors to attend the center. There is some contradiction in this, since a basic purpose is to find a better way of rating potential than reliance on the supervisor's judgment.

Operating the Center The time to run a center varies from a day to about a week, including time for assessor evaluations and report writing. The length of assessment ordinarily should increase with the responsibility level of those being assessed.[9] Group exercises usually are run with a maximum of six candidates per group, and at least two assessors observe each group. Schedule rearrangements and alternating assignments of assessors can allow the processing of two six-candidate groups at one time.

The Evaluations Peer and self-ratings and rankings may be part of the evaluation process. The official assessors typically write reports, skill by skill, exercise by exercise, and candidate by candidate according to their respective assignments. The reports are read aloud in a final evaluation meeting where each assessee is rated by every assessor on each predefined behavioral dimension. Meaningful differences of opinion are discussed and either resolved or noted. Final reports usually are written in a narrative style, relating remarks to specific behaviors and specifying the candidate's strengths, weaknesses, and developmental needs.

Feedback Feedback of results to candidates is handled differently in various organizations according to the original objectives of the program. Those highly concerned with management development emphasize the directions in which the candidate should move in the future. Others concerned with training may stop in the middle of the assessment program and offer feedback and discussion of particular exercises. Oral feedback is much more frequent than written. Line management or assessment center personnel may provide it either automatically or on request only.

Research Research on the effectiveness of the program is critical, since programs constantly need to be reviewed, critiqued, and improved if they are to be effective. This final step in the architectural design of an assessment center could be the one which determines the applicability of all of the other steps.

STRUCTURAL SUPPORT: WILL THE BUILDING STAND?

The basis of acceptance for any selection and classification procedure must be its reliability and validity. An examination of research on these two questions follows.

Reliability In many assessment center exercises and in the final evaluations each participant is evaluated by more than one assessor. Accordingly, interrater reliability becomes a matter of some importance, in addition to the reliability of individual measures. A summary of reliability data is shown in Table 1.

It should be noted that the AT&T studies

TABLE 1 Summary of Interrater Reliability Studies of Assessment Procedures

SOURCE	COMPANY	VARIABLES	ASSESSORS	INTERRATER RELIABILITY
Thomson (43) (N = 71)	SOHIO	13 dimensions	2 psychologists	Ratings, .73-.93, $\bar{r}$ = .85[a]
Thomson (43) (N = 71)	SOHIO	13 dimensions	3 managers	Ratings, .78-.95, $\bar{r}$ = .89[a]
Thomson (43) (N = 71)	SOHIO	Potential	2 psychologists	Ratings, .89[a]
Thomson (43) (N = 71)	SOHIO	Potential	3 managers	Ratings, .93[a]
McConnell & Parker (36) (N = 12)	AMA client	a) 12 categories b) Potential	5 managers 5 managers	Ratings, .64-.90[a] Ratings, .83[a]
McConnell & Parker (36) (N = 12-48)	6 AMA clients	Overall mgt. ability	5 managers	Ratings, .85-.98[a]
Greenwood & McNamara (26) (N = 288)	IBM	a) Task force game b) Leaderless group c) Mfg. problem	All pairs of 3 alternating observers	a) Ratings, .70; Rankings, .71 b) Ratings, .66; Rankings, .64 c) Ratings, .74; Rankings, .75
Bray & Grant (6) (N = 355)	AT&T	a) Leaderless group	2 psychologists	Ratings, .75; Rankings, .75
		b) Mfg. problem	2 psychologists	Ratings, .60; Rankings, .69
		c) In-basket	2 psychologists	Ratings, .92
Grant, Katkovsky, & Bray (25) (N = 355)	AT&T	9 variables from protective tests	2 psychologists	Ratings, .85-.94[a]
Grant & Bray (24) (N = 355)	AT&T	18 variables from interview data	2 psychologists	Median = .82 college, .72 non-college[a]

[a] Internal consistency estimates, correction for number of assessors.

of the in-basket, projective tests and interviews probably had inflated reliability estimates, since the interrater reliability was determined for the written report of a procedure, not the procedure itself. Two raters in high agreement on what a report says is a far less potent finding than two raters in high agreement on how a candidate performs in a situational exercise. The reliability coefficients do indicate, however, that the reports presented clear evaluations from which consistent ratings could be made.

In summary, based on the data available, interrater reliabilities for assessment evaluations and for several assessment components seem sufficiently high to support their further use. There appear to be no advantages of ratings vs. rankings or psychologists vs. managers in terms of reliability.

Validity of Overall Assessment Ratings

What must be regarded as "The Study" in assessment center validity is AT&T's Management Progress Study,[6] which was predictive and "uncontaminated"; i.e., results were retained for research purposes only and not released to management to influence promotion decisions. The researchers administered the assessment procedure to 422 male employees of six Bell Telephone companies beginning in 1956, stored the results, and waited eight years before pursuing information on the assessees' progress in the company. While many may view eight years of waiting as an almost unbelievable display of forbearance, the authors admit that by their own standards they were impatient—they had intended to wait ten years. Comparisons made in 1965 of management level achieved by men assessed six to eight years previously are shown in Table 2. Validity for the assessment predictions was amply demonstrated.

Point biserial correlations were .44 for the college group and .71 for the non-college group. Of the total number of men who reached middle management, 78 percent were correctly identified by the assessment staff. In contrast, among those in both groups who had not progressed further than first level management, the assessors predicted that 95 percent would not reach middle management within ten years. Note that these predictions still had two years to run; later communications from the company indicate that even greater accuracy was achieved.

Correlations between assessment ratings of general effectiveness and salary increments were also given for four samples of individuals who had at least six years of tenure in management since being assessed: (a) Company A, 54 college men, $r = .41$; (b) Company C, 27 college men, $r = .51$; (c) Company B, 83 non-college men, $r = .45$; (d) Company C, 39 non-college men, $r = .52$. All correlations were significant at $p < .01$. Combined with the data in Table 2, the usefulness of AT&T's overall assessment ratings for predicting management success seems well established.

Another AT&T study with newly hired candidates for sales positions also used an uncontaminated, predictive validity paradigm.[5] The primary criterion of performance was a six-month field review by an experienced team from AT&T headquarters which regularly makes such inspections. Where the assessment judgment was "more than acceptable," 100 per-

TABLE 2 Relationship Between AT&T Assessment Staff Prediction and Management Level Achieved

PREDICTION IF MAKE MIDDLE MANAGEMENT WITHIN 10 YRS	STATUS IN JULY, 1965		
	% 1ST LEVEL MANAGEMENT	% 2ND LEVEL MANAGEMENT	% MIDDLE MANAGEMENT
		College[a]	
Yes (N = 62)	2	50	48
No or ? (N = 63)	11	78	11
		Non-College[a]	
Yes (N = 41)	7	61	32
No or ? (N = 103)	60	35	5

Note: Adapted from Bray and Grant (6).
[a] χ^2 significant at $p < .001$.

cent of the salesmen met the review standards. Comparable success figures for those judged "acceptable," "less than acceptable," and "unacceptable" were 60 percent, 44 percent, and 10 percent, respectively, producing a chi-square value of 24.19 ($p < .001$). Again the predictive validity of AT&T's overall assessments was evident, this time for the job of salesman and over a short time interval.

Problems of criterion contamination have confounded predictive validity studies other than those described above, since assessment ratings were used in promotional decisions. Where assessment ratings were used primarily to make the first promotion, the effect on later promotions was not felt to be large, however. A summary of these contaminated criterion studies is shown in Table 3.

From the studies done to date, overall ratings of potential or performance from assessment center procedures generally have shown impressive predictive validity, especially for managerial jobs. Unfortunately, use of the ratings for decision making about assessees' careers somewhat restrains an overwhelming acceptance of the findings. Nevertheless, "clean" predictive validity has been demonstrated, but only in two studies with both at the same company.

Validity of Predictions of Multiple Criteria One of the few companies to report prediction of multiple criteria was SOHIO. In three studies,[14, 22, 43] five groups of subjects, ranging in size from 72 to 122, were assessed on 12 behavioral traits in addition to overall potential. The assessment committees' ratings of participants on these dimensions were compared with follow-up job ratings on the same dimensions by two independent supervisors. All but a few of these 60 behavioral validity coefficients reached statistical significance, with median correlations per group of .23 ($p < .05$), .26 ($p < .01$), and .36, .38 and .42 (all $p < .001$). The amount of criterion contamination is not known, however. While the rating of potential in nearly every case was a much better predictor ($r =$ about .64 for each group), the data did indicate that assessors were able to predict a variety of behavioral criteria.

An exploration of whether or not these correlations merely represent a halo effect was made by Thomson,[43] who put the correlations of ratings of assessor-psychologists, assessor-managers, and supervisors in a multitrait-multimethod matrix.[11] Very good evidence for discriminant validity was found for the two assessor groups, but not for the untrained supervisors. It was concluded that the assessment center method was able to predict multiple criteria fairly well, but that the poor quality of criterion measures probably reduced the convergent validity coefficients.

The Sears battery has included hundreds of predictors and criteria and many assessment techniques. One report of assessment validities included 33 pages of *significant* validity coefficients.[4] Suffice it to say that some type of validity has been shown for all Sears assessment components predicting many criteria. Attempts to analyze the data and refine the basic program are proceeding continuously.[3]

Contributions of Various Program Components The contribution of the components of assessment programs has been evaluated in two different ways; first, how much each influenced assessors' overall ratings and, second, the degree to which each component related to measures of job success. The first method is of interest from a process viewpoint, but the latter is the more direct way of establishing the validity of the component. No matter how impressed an assessor may be with a particular assessment component, its validity should be established empirically before it is accepted as an integral part of a program.

The various AT&T studies have emphasized the importance of overall assessment ratings and situational tests, the latter primarily because of their influence on the former, which have shown high predictive validity. Positive support has been shown for interview and projective results, but the data provide a less positive view of mental ability and other personality tests.

At SOHIO, ten individual tests, some personality but most cognitive, correlated with managers' ratings of potential, but r's ranged from .20 to .48 compared to the full committee correlation of .65 with the same criterion. The assessment committee at SOHIO apparently was highly influenced by the projective tests, and the projective rating of potential correlated .39 with the supervisory rating of potential.[22] The interview reports showed 9 significant correlations out of 12 with ratings of individual behavioral criteria by managers, the correlations ranging from .20 to .36 with an N of 122.[14] In summary, the SOHIO data point to the superiority of the overall assessment ratings but would not eliminate any single category of assessment components.

At IBM, significance in relation to the criterion of change in position level was attained with 9 of the 12 assessed behavior ratings, 8 personality scales, 1 of 2 scales of the biographical inventory, 2 of the 3 group exercises, and 1 individual exercise (in-basket). The

TABLE 3 Summary of Validity Studies of Overall Assessment Ratings Where Ratings Were Used for Promotions

SOURCE	COMPANY	CRITERIA	TIME	VALIDITY
Wollowick & McNamara (45) [N = 94 men, lower and middle management]	IBM	Position code	3 yrs.	$r = .37$***
Dodd (18) [11 groups, various jobs, N = 11-72]	IBM	Position level & salary	1-4 yrs.	Significant for 8 of 11 groups; r .29 to .63
Kraut & Scott (34) [N = a) 67 Sales, b) 141 Service, c) Admin., 1st line mgt.]	IBM Office Products Division	% promoted to 3 higher levels of management	up to 5 yrs.	a) $\chi^2 = 16.18$** b) $\chi^2 = 10.60$* c) $\chi^2 = 6.66$ *ns*
Thomson (43) [N = 71]	SOHIO	Ratings from supervisors' interviews	6-27 mos.	$r = .64$***
Finley (22) [N = a) 109, b) 119]	SOHIO	Supervisors' ratings, potential	30-62 mos. 9-29 mos.	a) $r = .65$*** b) $r = .63$***
Carleton (14) [N = 122]	SOHIO	Supervisors' ratings, potential	2½-5 yrs.	$r = .65$***
Moses (39) [N = 5,943]	AT&T	a) 2 or more promotions b) Management level	7 yrs.	a) $\chi^2 = 12.39$*** b) $r = .44$***
Campbell & Bray (13) [N = 471 1st-level supervisors, assessed vs. nonassessed]	AT&T	Last appraisal + ratings & rankings from interview (performance)	Several years	55% of those promoted before center installed rated "above average performers" vs. 68% of those assessed "acceptable."*
Campbell & Bray (13) [N = 471 1st-level supervisors, assessed vs. nonassessed]	AT&T	Last appraisal + ratings & rankings from interview (potential)	Several years	28% of those promoted before center installed rated "high potential" vs. 50% of those assessed "acceptable."*
Byham & Thornton (10) [N = 37 supervisors processed by assessment vs. 27 supervisors placed traditionally]	Caterpillar Tractor Co.	Job performance	—	*ns* (small N + restriction of range of criterion).

* $p < .05$.
** $p < .01$
*** $p < .001$

mental ability tests and the Leadership Opinion Questionnaire were not related to the criterion measure. Multiple *R*'s computed from the best of the three types of assessment components (tests, exercises, and rated characteristics) showed neither to be superior.[45]

One of the most comprehensive examinations of the in-basket test was conducted at General Electric,[38] where several types of analyses showed that the in-basket was primarily a valid predictor of planning-administrative ability. Age, education, and experience had relatively little influence on in-basket validity, which seemed to indicate that the test was measuring managerial ability or aptitude and not just managerial experience.

In conclusion, the ratings of candidates based on the totality of assessment procedures seemed to have validity superior to any of the specific components. Since the situational tests represented a unique contribution to the process and were relied upon heavily, it was usually assumed that these were what made the difference, although specific data often were not reported. The in-basket's contribution usually was considered critical, although it mainly tapped administrative skills and was thus more narrow in scope than some of the other exercises. Other situational tests were so varied and data were so seldom reported on them that conclusions are difficult to draw. The mental ability tests seemed to work for some companies but not for others; personality tests showed moderate to little success, but they continue to be used. The projectives and interviews were more successful than expected from their past reputations. More research evidently is needed on the various components of assessment centers and their integration.

Validity Compared with What? Prior to the assessment center approach, there were three primary methods of selecting the managers of the future from current employees:

Manpower Inventories by Private Consultants. Consultants' evaluations have tended to be clinical predictions based on interviews and various test scores but without situational tests. The validity of these predictions has not been established precisely, but the literature on clinical vs. actuarial prediction has not been especially encouraging, as previously noted.

Performance Appraisals. Kraut[33] has offered some convincing arguments as to why assessment centers should be superior to the typical performance appraisal system in selecting higher level managers. In the first place, multiple raters are used rather than one manager, and the yardsticks are common to all assessors rather than left to one individual's idiosyncracies. Furthermore, the assessors are given training in making judgments, their mode of observation is attentive rather than distracted, and skills are observed in simulations of future jobs rather than on the current job.

On the other hand, Hinrichs[28] showed that assessment ratings of overall potential for a group of 47 college males in marketing jobs were correlated .46 ($p < .001$) with similar independent ratings by experienced managers who reviewed their personnel records. Hinrichs argued from this study that the expensive two-day assessment program may be unnecessary when much of the same information can be obtained so much easier. Interpersonal relationships seemed to be a relatively untapped area in the traditional system, however. Dunnette[20] also disputed Hinrichs' conclusions in that his correlation of .46 still left nearly 80 percent of the assessment ratings' variance unaccounted for.

To this writer, the real test would seem to be how well personnel records or performance appraisals vs. assessment ratings can predict future managerial performance, not how well personnel records can predict assessment ratings.

Psychometric Tests and Scored Inventories. According to a broad study by Ghiselli,[23] average validity coefficients of paper and pencil tests of abilities or personality traits for first level or higher level managers are not exceptionally high, usually ranging in the .20's. Korman[32] noted that personal history data seem to have some predictive validity for first level supervisors but are less productive for higher level management. Leadership questionnaires have shown little or moderate predictive validity (seldom over .30).

Compared with the alternatives for selecting higher level managers, then, assessment centers look promising. Nevertheless, the research on them, though positive, is sparse, comes from too few sources, covers too many variations in components, lacks replication, and is usually plagued by methodological problems such as criterion contamination.

ARCHITECTURAL AESTHETICS AND BLEMISHES

Aesthetics Many have claimed that there are additional benefits to be obtained from assessment centers beyond selection and placement of employees. These "architectural aesthetics" include the following benefits.

Help with the Criterion Problem. Installation of assessment procedures may force better job analyses and identification of the important criteria for success on a job. Such a rigorous process has been aptly described in connection with an analysis of the job of foreman.[1] Another way assessment centers may help with the criterion problem is by training assessors to evaluate more accurately the performance, behavior, and potential of others. Assessors have been shown to have greater agreement in ratings of different assessee traits,[43] but it has not yet been demonstrated that assessors will experience a transfer of training in rating subordinates under the unstandardized conditions of the normal work experience.

Training Assessors. Benefits of assessor training have been claimed not only in the form of a partial solution of the criterion problem but through (a) improvement in interviewing skills, (b) broadening of observation skills, (c) increased appreciation of group dynamics and leadership styles, (d) new insights into behavior, (e) strengthening of management skills through working with simulations, and (f) broadening one's repertoire of responses to problems. No well-designed training studies have validated these promises, however; as has been pointed out previously, firms do considerably more management research on selection than on training and development.[12]

Development of Assessees. Since many exercises, like the in-basket and oral presentations, were used formerly as training exercises, many assume they serve such purposes in assessment centers, even without immediate feedback of results.[10] Again, evidence supporting this training benefit has not been convincingly provided. Claims for increased self-insight[9] have not been evaluated with pretests or control groups, and statements by assessees that they felt the program was informative and useful for self-development[33] cannot be accepted as firm empirical demonstrations of the developmental value of assessment centers.

Minority Group Selection. Recent government interest in the fairness of selection tests for minorities has stressed that selection procedures must be job related, and the simulated aspects of assessment centers do have face validity in this respect. One study bearing on this problem at AT&T[39] demonstrated that there were highly significant correlations between performance in a one day approximation of the company's longer Personnel Assessment Program and performance in the latter, regardless of race or sex. The research design in this study more closely resembled alternate-form test reliability that predictive validity, however; thus the minority group fairness question for assessment centers is not yet sufficiently answered.

Face Validity. The simulation exercises in particular have high face validity, and the whole process has been claimed to be received favorably by managers, especially those who may be mistrustful of tests.[21] Some assessee questionnaires have also indicated that the majority consider the procedures useful and objective.[16, 33]

Attitude Changes. It has sometimes been claimed that assessees may change their attitudes in the direction of a clearer understanding of some of the problems facing the manager and the necessity for making some unpopular decisions,[10] but so far the evidence is anecdotal.

In summary, the bonus benefits, or architectural aesthetics, of assessment centers sound promising but are largely without research support.

Blemishes On the other side of the coin, there are those who cite "architectural blemishes" in the process, or possible negative outcomes for both individuals and organizations. These include:

The "Crown Prince or Princess." Those who do outstandingly well in assessment centers may find that they have become a crown prince or princess. Management may treat them so well that their future success becomes a self-fulfilling prophecy, the morale of those without royal status may decline, and the validity coefficients for the assessment center process may become inflated. No research has substantiated these potential coronation effects, however.

The "Kiss of Death." A candidate who does poorly at an assessment center may feel that he has been given the kiss of death as far as his future with the company is concerned. This could result in some undesirable attrition, since the candidate may be quite competent in the job he is now performing. Research on turnover of assessees so far has been inconclusive.

Stress. If a candidate gets the impression that his entire career is on the line based on a few days "on stage," the stress effects could be quite strong. It would seem important that the data from the procedure not be made of the pass-fail variety or kept too long in an employee's file. On the other hand, defenders of the procedures reply that since stress is a typical part of a manager's job, a candidate should be stressed to see how he copes with it. It would still seem important to keep stress in the exercises within limits.

The Nonnominee. The feeling that an individual may be part of the "out group" if he or she has not been selected to participate in the assessment process (which may become a status symbol) is another dimension of employee attitudes that needs to be empirically tested.

The "Organization Man." Some have raised the issue of whether or not assessment centers may not proliferate the model of the conforming organization man and serve to eliminate the unusual or imaginative managers that are believed to be needed in the future. A study at SOHIO showed that assessments correlated negatively with conformity for one small sample, however.[14] An IBM study indicated that supervisors may nominate those higher on conformity and lower on independence, but that the assessment procedure itself does not select this type of individual.[19] The organization man may be the other side of the nonnominee problem; the most able and not the least able may be denied access to the assessment center. The implication is that it is the nomination procedure and not the assessment procedure that creates the organization man syndrome. The supervisory nominations should perhaps be supplemented by self-nominations, peer nominations, personnel records, or assessment of everyone at a job level if numbers are not too large.

Costs. Estimates of costs have ranged from the price of a few meals to $5,000 per candidate, exclusive of staff salary.[10] Installation costs are the highest, but to these must be added assessors, assessees', and psychologists' time, travel, accommodations, and meals, plus materials, from rating sheets to videotapes. Various cost saving devices might include completing all possible procedures before arrival at the center, conducting exercises on company property over weekends, and combining small companies with similar jobs in a multiple company center, perhaps in a synthetic validity paradigm. In the end, these costs must be weighed in the context of current selection ratios against the possible gains in selection and training in some kind of a utility model.

In summary, the architectural blemishes, or possible negative outcomes of assessment centers, have much the same status as the architectural aesthetics; they appear reasonable, but for the most part they lack supporting data.

BUILDING BETTER CENTERS

Assessment centers may look promising, but they certainly raise some questions about the past and the future.

Has the Psychometric Literature Been Proven Wrong? If assessment centers do indeed violate much of the past psychometric literature, as indicated in the introduction to this review, does that mean the findings in the literature have been proven wrong? In this writer's opinion, not at all. The assessment center concept seems much more evolutionary than revolutionary. Techniques developed in the past, from mental ability tests to management games, are combined in one package, but more than just a simple summation is involved. Perhaps because of the expense, psychologists have tried to develop assessment centers in more than a haphazard way. Close attention has been paid to criterion development; tests and exercises have generally been chosen with a definite predictive purpose in mind; and, thanks to AT&T, research has begun properly and is continuing.

The projectives probably worked better in assessment centers because they were deliberately oriented to management variables rather than to deeply clinical ones and because results were described in terms of organizationally relevant constructs. For example, after an initial try with projectives, SOHIO refined its procedures for writing projective protocols and was able to predict more than twice as many behavioral dimensions in supervisors' appraisals.[22]

The interview may have been more successful because those conducting the interviews understood what was to be covered and those rating the information knew exactly what they were looking for. Similarly, the situational exercises were appropriate to the job and the organization. The in-basket, in particular, is a straightforward sample of work from the job and company involved.

The assessment center approach has not necessarily demonstrated the superiority of clinical over actuarial combination of data, however. What the research has shown is: (a) Clinical interpretation of tools such as projective tests and interviews can make a contribution; that is, clinical *measurement* can work, as found by Sawyer;[41] and (b) clinical combination of data into an overall prediction of success can work. What the data have not shown is that clinical combinations of data or clinically oriented tools are the *best* selection procedures.

One of the most interesting studies in the assessment center research[45] measured the contribution of the various procedures separately and in various combinations. For 94 lower and middle managers who had gone through the IBM program about three years previously, three types of predictors yielded highly similar multiple correlations with degree of increases in managerial responsibility: the best test composite (ascendancy + vigor scales) had an R of .45; the best exercise composite (in-basket + cooperative group exercise) had an R of .39;

TABLE 4 Stepwise Multiple Regression for Assessment Variables of 94 IBM Managers and Degree of Increase in Managerial Responsibility

ASSESSMENT VARIABLE	R	R^2
Ascendency (test)	.39	15%
+ In-basket (exercise)	.46	21%
+ Administrative ability (rating)	.51	26%
+ Cooperative group performance	.59	35%
+ Interpersonal contact (rating)	.60	36%
+ Biographical inventory test scale	.62	38%

Note: Adapted from Wollowick and McNamara.[45]

and the best ratings composite (self-confidence + written communications skills + administrative ability) had an *R* of .41. A stepwise multiple regression, presented in Table 4, shows how the types of predictors alternated in building incremental validity.

The overall staff rating (clinical) correlated .37 with the criterion, accounting for 14 percent of the variance; but using all the assessment data in an actuarial fashion produced a multiple correlation of .62, accounting for 38 percent of the variance. Unfortunately, this multiple *R* was not cross-validated, but independent application of a shrinkage formula[33] indicated no drastic reduction was likely.

Again we find a demonstration of the usefulness of clinical measurement but the superiority of mechanical combination of data.[41] Although one study cannot be generalized to all assessment centers, it certainly appears advisable for other centers to research the hypothesis that mechanical combination of data may improve predictions even more. Should this prove true, once the research costs were recovered, the unit cost savings of reducing assessors' time could be substantial.

The psychometric literature thus has not been disproved. The critical lesson from assessment centers has been learning how to use all these techniques most appropriately for a given situation. Rather than throwing away old tools, psychologists have learned to reexamine them, use them better, and use them together.

Research Needs A number of issues have been raised in this review that need to be researched, and undoubtedly there are many more. A brainstorming session at the Center for Creative Leadership of the Smith Richardson Foundation produced a list of over 100 relatively unresearched questions concerning assessment centers.[29] All the components of the process and their integration can be studied more intensively, as can the potential uses of assessment procedures with such organizational problems as personnel selection, training, motivation, job analysis, job satisfaction, and organizational climate.

Aside from the as yet unexplored research questions, the importance of situation related validation research for those attempting to use assessment centers should be emphasized. Because their initial industrial development was grounded in research, it is often casually implied that therefore any assessment center will work. It is true that AT&T laid a solid basic foundation in its pioneering predictive validity research. Some other large companies have also contributed to the foundation of the assessment center building. But each situation will probably require a little different architecture, just as a building in California should ideally be earthquake-proof, while one in New England had better be well-insulated. How many variations in design and style the present foundations can support is open to question.

For each organization, the key to raising its ideal building will be solid, individualized construction by well-qualified masons and carpenters. Moreover, there must be maintenance of an open system that will allow for refinements and improvements. The plumbing must be kept clear or the pipes will clog with outdated and invalid components. Constant monitoring with continuous research would seem to be of the utmost importance, or one of these days, as so often happens with behavioral science techniques, a Big Bad Wolf may blow the house down.

REFERENCES

1. Acker, S. R., and M. R. Perlson. *Can We Sharpen Our Management of Human Resources?* (Olin Corporation, June, 1970).
2. Bartlett, C. J., and C. G. Green. "Clinical Prediction: Does One Sometimes Know Too Much?" *Journal of Counseling Psychology*, Vol. 13 (1966), 267–270.
3. Bentz, V. J. "The Sears Longitudinal Study of Management Behavior." Paper presented at the 79th Annual Convention, American Psychological Association, 1971.
4. Bentz, V. J. "Validity of Sears Assessment Center Procedures." Paper presented at the 79th Annual Convention, American Psychological Association, 1971.
5. Bray, D. W., and R. J. Campbell. "Selection of Salesmen by Means of an Assessment Cen-

ter," *Journal of Applied Psychology,* Vol. 52 (1968), 36–41.

6. Bray, D. W., and D. L. Grant. "The Assessment Center in the Measurement of Potential for Business Management," *Psychological Monographs,* Vol. 80, No. 17 (1966), Whole No. 625.
7. Bray, D. W., and J. L. Moses. "Personnel Selection," in *Annual Review of Psychology* (Palo Alto, Calif.: Annual Reviews, 1972).
8. Byham, W. C. "Assessment Centers for Spotting Future Managers," *Harvard Business Review,* Vol. 48, No. 4 (1970), 150 ff.
9. Byham, W. C. "The Assessment Center as an Aid in Management Development," *Training and Development Journal* (December, 1971), 10–22.
10. Byham, W. C., and G. C. Thornton, III. "Assessment Centers: A New Aid in Management Selection," *Studies in Personnel Psychology,* Vol. 2, No. 2 (1970), 21–35.
11. Campbell, D. T., and D. W. Fiske. "Convergent and Discriminant Validation by the Multitrait-multimethod Matrix," *Psychological Bulletin,* Vol. 56 (1959), 81–105.
12. Campbell, J. P., M. D. Dunnette, E. E. Lawler, III, and K. E. Weick, Jr. *Managerial Behavior, Performance and Effectiveness* (New York: McGraw-Hill, 1970).
13. Campbell, R. J., and D. W. Bray. "Assessment Centers: An Aid in Management Selection," *Personnel Administration,* Vol. 30, No. 2 (1967), 6–13.
14. Carleton, F. O. "Relationships Between Follow-up Evaluations and Information Developed in a Management Assessment Center." *Proceedings of the 78th Annual Convention, American Psychological Association,* 1970.
15. Cronbach, L. J. *Essentials of Psychological Testing,* 3rd ed. (New York: Harper & Row, 1970).
16. DiCostanzo, F., and T. Andretta. "The Supervisory Assessment Center in the Internal Revenue Service," *Training and Development Journal* (September, 1970), 12–15.
17. Dodd, W. E. "Will Management Assessment Centers Insure Selection of the Same Old Types?" *Proceedings of the 78th Annual Convention, American Psychological Association,* 1970, pp. 569–570.
18. Dodd, W. E. "Summary of Assessment Validities." Paper presented at the 79th Annual Convention, American Psychological Association, 1971.
19. Dodd, W. E., and A. I. Kraut. "The Prediction of Management Assessment Center Performance from Earlier Measures of Personality and Sales Training Performance. A Preliminary Report." (IBM Corporation, April, 1970).
20. Dunnette, M. D. "Multiple Assessment Procedures in Identifying and Developing Managerial Talent," in P. McReynolds (Ed.), *Advances in Psychological Assessment,* Vol. II (Palo Alto, Calif.: Science and Behavior Books, 1971).
21. Finkle, R. B. "Managerial Assessment Centers," in M. D. Dunnette (Ed.), *Handbook of Industrial and Organization Psychology* (in press).
22. Finley, R. M., Jr. "Evaluation of Behavior Predictions from Projective Tests Given in a Management Assessment Center." *Proceedings of the 78th Annual Convention,* American Psychological Association, 1970.
23. Ghiselli, E. E. *The Validity of Occupational Aptitude Tests* (New York: Wiley, 1966).
24. Grant, D. L., and D. W. Bray. "Contributions of the Interview to Assessment of Management Potential," *Journal of Applied Psychology,* Vol. 53 (1969), 24–34.
25. Grant, D. L., W. Katkovsky, and D. W. Bray. "Contributions of Projective Techniques to Assessment of Management Potential," *Journal of Applied Psychology,* Vol. 51 (1967), 226–232.
26. Greenwood, J. M., and W. J. McNamara, "Interrater Reliability in Situational Tests," *Journal of Applied Psychology,* Vol. 31 (1967), 101–106.
27. Guion, R. M., and R. F. Gottier. "Validity of Personality Measures in Personnel Selection," *Personnel Psychology,* Vol. 18 (1965), 135–164.
28. Hinrichs, J. R. "Comparison of 'Real Life' Assessments of Management Potential with Situational Exercises, Paper-and-Pencil Ability Tests and Personality Inventories," *Journal of Applied Psychology,* Vol. 53 (1969), 425–432.
29. Jeswald, T. A. "Research Needs in Assessment —A Brief Report of a Conference," *The Industrial Psychologist,* Vol. 9, No. 1 (November, 1971), 12–14.
30. Kelly, E. L., and D. W. Fiske. *Prediction of Performance in Clinical Psychology* (Ann Arbor: University of Michigan Press, 1951).
31. Kinslinger, H. S. "Application of Projective Techniques in Personnel Psychology Since 1940," *Psychological Bulletin,* Vol. 66 (1966), 134–149.
32. Korman, A. K. "The Prediction of Managerial Performance. A Review," *Personnel Psychology,* Vol. 21 (1968), 295–322.
33. Kraut, A. I. "A Hard Look at Management Assessment Centers and Their Future," *Personnel Journal,* in press.
34. Kraut, A. I., and G. J. Scott. "The Validity of

an Operational Management Assessment Program," *Journal of Applied Psychology,* Vol. 56 (1972), 124–129.

35. Mayfield, E. C. "The Selection Interview—A Re-evaluation of Published Research," *Personnel Psychology,* Vol. 17 (1964), 239–260.
36. McConnell, J. H., and T. C. Parker. "An Assessment Center Program for Multiorganizational Use," *Training and Development Journal* (March, 1972), 6–14.
37. Meehl, P. E. *Clinical versus Statistical Prediction: A Theoretical Analysis and a Review of the Evidence* (Minneapolis: University of Minnesota Press, 1954).
38. Meyer, H. H. "The Validity of the In-Basket Test as a Measure of Managerial Performance," *Personnel Psychology,* Vol. 23 (1970), 297–307.
39. Moses, J. L. "The Early Identification of Supervisory Potential," *Personnel Psychology,* in press.
40. Office of Strategic Services (OSS) Assessment Staff. *Assessment of Men* (New York: Rinehard, 1948).
41. Sawyer, J. "Measurement *and* Prediction, Clinical *and* Statistical," *Psychological Bulletin,* Vol. 66 (1966), 178–200.
42. Taft, R. "Multiple Methods of Personality Assessment," *Psychological Bulletin,* Vol. 56 (1959), 333–352.
43. Thomson, H. A. "Comparison of Predictor and Criterion Judgments of Managerial Performance Using the Multitrait-multimethod Approach," *Journal of Applied Psychology,* Vol. 54 (1970), 496–502.
44. Wernimont, P. F., and J. P. Campbell. "Signs, Samples and Criteria," *Journal of Applied Psychology,* Vol. 52 (1968), 372–376.
45. Wollowick, H. B., and W. J. McNamara. "Relationship of the Components of an Assessment Center to Management Success," *Journal of Applied Psychology,* Vol. 53 (1969), 348–352.

49 MANAGEMENT INVENTORY*

Walter S. Wikstrom

Developing is essentially an individual process. For a company, however, it is the total management development effort and the total results that count. From this broad and impersonal perspective it makes little difference whether John Doe or Richard Roe is promoted to the presidency as long as the one who gets the job is fully prepared to assume the responsibilities.

Thus, one responsibility of the management development function is to keep track of needs of the company and the progress being made to develop managers capable of fulfilling the needs. This information must be summarized in a form that provides responsible company officials with an over-all view of the corporate program. With such an overview, they are in a position to assess the company's ability to withstand the shocks of personnel and organizational changes.

Information about the company's present and future needs for managers is the starting point for preparing a management inventory. Data on the present organization and its needs is obtained from such sources as position guides and organization charts. The future needs of the firm may be estimated from organization plans and market forecasts. Research or engineering may provide data concerning new products or new production processes. The impact of changes in the economy or changes in management methods may be estimated in determining future needs for managers.

Information on individual managers is obtained from many sources within the firm; personnel records, performance appraisals, and records of manager's progress with their individual development activities. The data that has significance for management development purposes includes such things as a man's specialized education and training, his work experience, and his performance. Age, health, family circumstances, or other personal matters may be noted if they have a bearing upon a man's availability for promotion or transfer. It is a common practice to include tentative judgments about a man's ability to handle larger responsibilities than those he now has; these may be specifically identified, with a notation added about additional training he may need to be prepared for them.

The specific types of data included in the summary reports of the inventory differ considerably from one company to another, depending upon the needs of individual firms. One company may be concerned about a poor age distribution in its management group; a large number of its managers may be due for retirement in a brief span of years. In this case, the inventory forms may highlight managers' ages because this would be an important factor for that company to consider in making promotions and transfers. In another firm the specific technical training and experience of its managers may be a vital factor to consider in assigning responsibilities; this company might emphasize these factors on its inventory records.

It is obvious from what has been said that managers in almost every function and at many levels in the company supply the data and judgments that go into the management inventory. The contribution of the management development function is the compilation and analysis of this data in terms of its impact on management manpower.

MANAGEMENT INVENTORY FORMS

The data that is gathered is usually summarized on forms designed to highlight those factors that are most pertinent for control of the over-all management development program. These are essentially inventory records. They may be organized on the basis of individual managers or individual positions. Some firms cross-file the data both ways.

Exhibit 1 is quite typical of the records that

* Reprinted by permission of the publisher from *Developing Managerial Competence: Changing Concepts, Emerging Practices*, Studies in Personnel Policy No. 189, National Industrial Conference Board, New York, pp. 95–100, 1964. Mr. Wikstrom is on the staff of the National Industrial Conference Board.

are used when an inventory of managers is maintained. It provides a good deal of information about a fictional manager, Mel Murray. His age (which would indicate his retirement date as well as his maturity) and his date of employment are noted. His present position and length of service in it are given. The record indicates that Mr. Murray is doing a good job and it points out some of his specific strengths and weaknesses His efforts to develop even greater management ability are recorded.

In planning for possible changes in the organization, the lower two sections of the form are particularly meaningful. They indicate positions to which Mr. Murray might move, the dates when he would probably be ready to assume the responsibilities and the training that he might need.

Position Replacement Forms Some firms maintain their management inventories on the basis of jobs rather than men. A typical example of this type of form is Exhibit 2. Here the key factor is the job—the sales manager's position—rather than the incumbent manager, Mel Murray. This form tells little about Murray but a good deal about the men who might replace him when he vacates the job. It shows that there are two possible replacements, one who is ready now and one who will probably be able to take over in two years. The form shows the salaries of these men in relation to what Murray is being paid. It gives a little information about their present positions and their history with the company. This form, too, describes the training that they might need to be ready to fill this position.

Of course, companies do not use these records as blueprints for future changes. For instance, there would be no guarantee that either Renfrew or Storey would succeed Mel Murray, even though their names appear on Exhibit 2 as likely candidates. Companies that make use of management inventories still consider each promotion and transfer carefully at the time it is made. But the judgments and planning that the inventory forms reflect increase the chance that there will be men ready for consideration when a decision must be made. Many companies consider their inventories more valuable in the preparation for changes than in the making of them.

However, many firms say that their inventories also play an important role in the early stages of the actual selection. More rapid and comprehensive searches for candidates can be made because the pertinent information on each manager has been collected in one place. To speed this process, a number of companies have put their inventory information on machine-sorted cards or tape. Thus, no one is accidentally overlooked; the entire management group can be reviewed in culling out the names of candidates qualified for a particular opening. And it provides those making the selection with the broadest group of qualified candidates from which to choose. This has been particularly helpful in very large or geographically scattered

EXHIBIT 1 Management Inventory Card

This form is a composite of a number of company forms in The Conference Board's files.

Name	Age	Employed
Murray, Mel	47	1945
Present position		**On Job**
Manager, sales (House Fans division)		6 years
Present performance		
Outstanding—exceeded sales goal in spite of stiffer competition.		
Strengths		
Good planner—motivates subordinates very well—excellent communication.		
Weaknesses		
Still does not always delegate as much as situation requires. Sometimes does not understand production's problems.		
Efforts to improve		
Has greatly improved in delegating in last two years; also has organized more effectively after taking a management course on own time and initiative.		
Could move to		**When**
Vice-president, marketing		1963
Training needed		
More exposure to problems of other divisions (attend top staff conference?) Perhaps university program stressing staff role of corporate marketing versus line sales.		
Could move to		**When**
Manager, House or Industrial Fans division		1964-1965
Training needed		
Course in production management; some project working with production people; perhaps a good business game somewhere.		

EXHIBIT 2 Detailed Position Replacement Card

Position			
Manager, sales (House Fans division)			
Performance Outstanding	**Incumbent** Mel Murray	**Salary** $22,000	**May move** 1 year
Replacement 1		**Salary**	**Age**
Earl Renfrew		$17,000	39
Present position		**Employed:** Present job	Company
Field sales manager, House Fans		3 years	10 years
Training needed			**When ready**
Special assignment to study market potential for air conditioners to provide forecasting experience.			Now
Replacement 2		**Salary**	**Age**
Bernard Storey		$16,500	36
Present position		**Employed:** Present job	Company
Promotion manager, House Fans		4 years	7 years
Training needed			**When ready**
Rotation to field sales Marketing conference in fall, 1963			2 years

companies where the selecting managers may not know personally every possible candidate.

THE REPLACEMENT CHART

In many cases the data on individual inventory forms is further summarized, for major company units, on a replacement chart. These charts present only the information that the firm considers most significant for management manpower planning. In a sense, the replacement chart serves the same purpose for a unit that a coded symbol on the chart serves for an individual manager—they both indicate readiness for changes in responsibility. The symbol may indicate whether or not a particular manager can take on changed or increased duties; the chart indicates how well the total unit can absorb such changes in its management group.

Exhibit 3 is the current chart for a portion of the Whiteside Manufacturing Company, a firm manufacturing and marketing household and industrial fans. It serves to illustrate some of the ways in which companies use inventory forms and replacement charts to assist in planning and controlling management development activities. The Whiteside Company is a fictitious company but the chart is similar to the replacement charts used by a number of companies that cooperated in THE CONFERENCE BOARD's survey.

The chart bears a strong resemblance to the Whiteside organization chart and is, in fact, an expansion of it. The reason is that in many cases promotion and transfer follow the lines of formal authority. The lines then represent routes of progression as well as reporting relationships. An organization chart, in a sense, is a very simple replacement chart.

One difference from most organization charts becomes apparent as soon as one looks at Exhibit 3. It shows a position that does not now exist. The Whiteside Company is considering expanding into the air-conditioning field. No decision has yet been reached but a thorough study is being made. Part of this study is concerned with the company's ability to staff the new division. The chart shows that there is a man already in the company, Ray Jarvis, who is thought capable of taking charge of operations if the company does expand.

As far as current operations are concerned, the household fans division appears to be in pretty good shape. Two of the men have "satisfactory" ratings on present performance and three are rated "outstanding." There is a ready replacement for each of the men and two men are considered ready to replace Mr. Snow, the division manager, if he should be moved. All in all, Dan Snow can take pride in this part of his manpower planning. It probably helps to account for his own outstanding performance rating since, as division manager, he has the over-all responsibility for manpower planning for his division.

In the industrial fans division, however, the situation is not so good. Only the production manager, Mr. Jarvis, is doing an outstanding job while the performance of one of the incumbent managers needs improvement. There are ready replacements for two managers, but there is no one who is thought capable of replacing Mr. Piper, the manager of accounting—and it seems possible that Mr. Piper will have to be replaced. With a situation like this in his division. Ed Farley, the division manager, must be doing a very good job in other areas to achieve an over-all rating of "satisfactory."

Replacements in Depth? On one score the chart seems to be encouraging. The company has "replacements in depth." Most positions have two replacements identified. For ten of the fifteen jobs at least one of the replacements is ready now. It appears that the future is secure.

Suppose, however, that two things happen. The Whiteside Company decides to expand into air conditioning. Henry Grady, the executive vice president, retires early because of poor health. Neither of these would be unusual events. A number of shifts could then take place.

Jarvis would most likely be promoted from the industrial fans division to head the new division and Pitts would probably move up to replace him in the production department. Snow might well become executive vice president with Joe James moving up from the production manager's job to head the household fans division. Long would probably replace James. What depth would remain after these shifts?

Seven jobs would have only one man identified as a replacement. Instead of ten, only five of the fifteen jobs would have someone ready to take over immediately. For the key job of manager of household fans, James would have no backstop at all.

If Farley, manager of the industrial fans division, should be disgruntled over missing the chance for the executive vice presidency and leave the company, the situation would become even worse. Goland, the sales manager, would probably have to move into Farley's old job, with Ramos replacing Goland, even though neither is considered ready for a move without

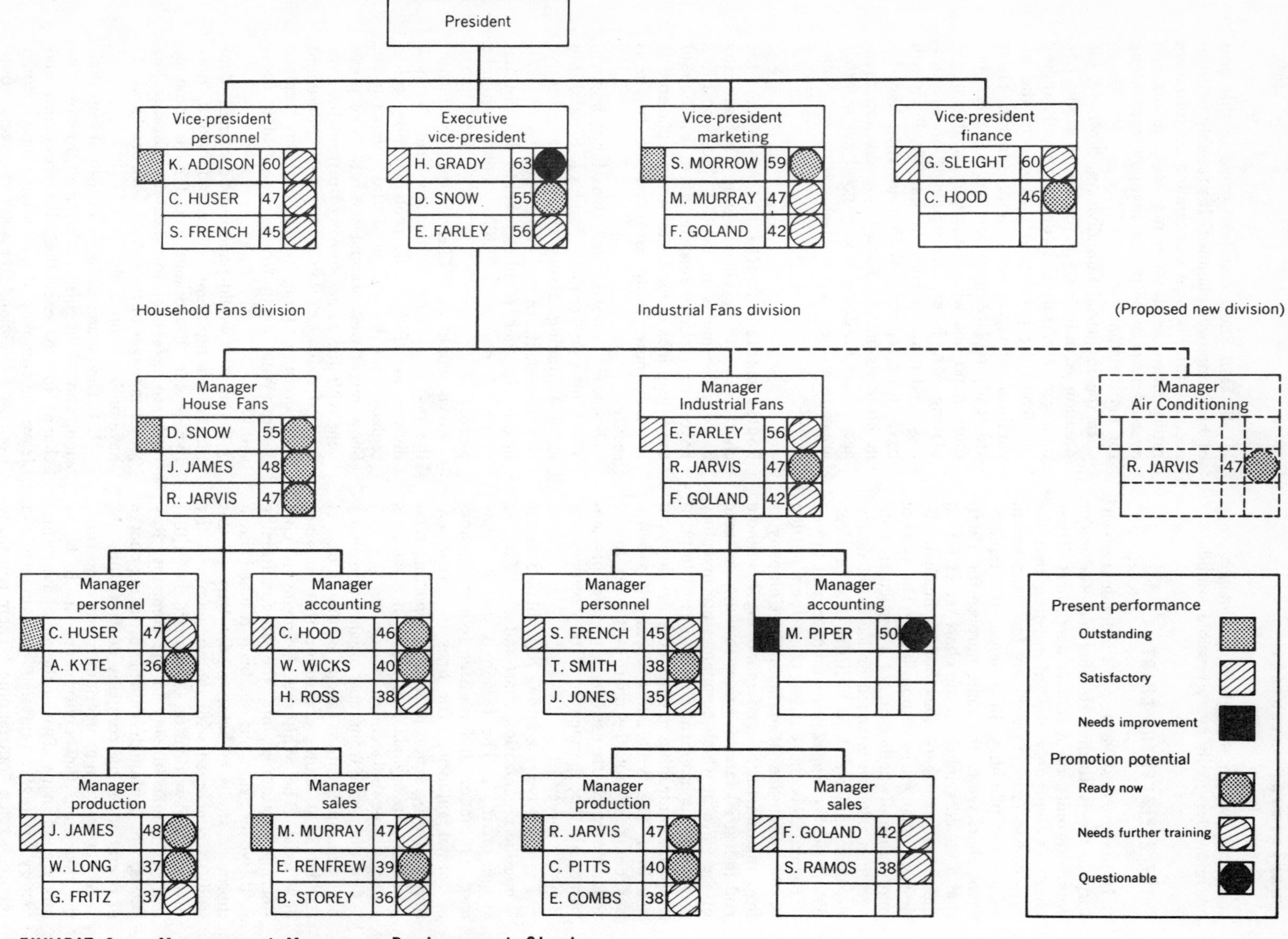

EXHIBIT 3 Management Manpower Replacement Chart

more training. Then there would be no backstop for the executive vice president, the division managers, or accounting or sales in the industrial fans division. When shifts have to be made, depth can become shallow very quickly.

This does not mean that even greater depth must be planned for each job. Companies consulted by the Board agree that it is unwise to have too many men in the line of succession for any job. But the hypothetical situation does underscore the need for advance planning and the constant search for managerial talent to be developed. It takes time to develop adequate reserves, and constant attention to keep the number adequate.

THE INVENTORY IN DEVELOPMENT PROGRAMS

Inventory forms and replacement charts are valuable tools in the corporate management development effort. But companies emphasize that they are tools; they are not a development program in themselves. The most impressive forms or beautifully color-coded charts are of little value if the company has not determined its objectives and policies, planned its organization structure to achieve these goals, provided challenging jobs and other opportunities for learning how to manage, or created an atmosphere in which men are encouraged to develop. These conditions are the important ones for management development. The mechanics of the management inventory are only an aid.

The value of these mechanics, it is stressed, lies in the fact that they permit a division manager or corporate executive to see at a glance the general outline of a unit's preparations for management continuity. They can highlight danger spots, so that corrective action can be taken. And, they can reassure top management that the objective of management development is being carried out—with the result that men are prepared to carry out their present and future responsibilities. That is, after all, the real test of a management development program.

C. APPRAISAL OF MANAGERS

50 HOW TO APPRAISE EXECUTIVE PERFORMANCE*

Arch Patton

What makes an executive successful? Why does one man forge his way to the top, while another, equally trained, fails to live up to company expectations? How can we better understand the process by which executives develop?

In hopes of finding answers to these important questions, one of the country's largest corporations made a survey, a few years ago, of the educational, economic, and social backgrounds of more than 100 top-echelon executives. The objective of the study was to discover if the early life experiences of this demonstrably successful group of men had common elements that could be used to improve the corporation's executive selection and development process.

AS DIVERSE AS AMERICA

The research team carefully studied the early family life of each top-management executive, including his family's financial and social status, the extent of his formal education, subjects studied, marks received, and his early work experience. When the results of the survey were reviewed, it was found that the environment of the company's key executives during their formative years tended to be as diverse as America itself. These highly successful executives came from poor as well as wealthy families, some had Master's degrees while others failed to finish high school, and outstanding and average students were found in equal numbers.

Only one common historic relationship was discovered: *within two years after joining the company, the compensation of each executive topped the average for his age group, and this pay differential above the average widened at an accelerating rate throughout his career.*

The results of this study underscore the dangers inherent in a recruiting process that slavishly follows preconceived ideas of what it takes to make an outstanding executive. The results indicate, furthermore, that intelligence, courage, aggressiveness, and other qualities making for business success are incubated in virtually every conceivable early environment.

The most significant contribution of the survey may turn out to be a better understanding of the executive development process. For if we cannot prejudge the *capacity* of the individual with any certainty, it follows that we must assign critical importance to the ability to judge on-the-job *performance*. This performance appraisal is a never-ending process, for individuals reach the peak of their ability, or willingness, to accept responsibility at different stages in their careers. As every top executive knows, many apparently well-endowed individuals reach "plateaus" of arrested development early in their careers, while others seem able to draw indefinitely on hidden reserves of strength to take on ever larger responsibilities.

In effect, this means that the soundest basis for judging an individual's ability to handle a higher level job is how well he is dealing with similar problems in his present job. Or, to put it another way, an executive's past and present performance is the most reliable key to his future performance. This being the case, the ability of management to judge an individual's performance is basic to the continuing success of the enterprise.

EARLY APPRAISAL EFFORTS

The need for sound appraisals of executive performance has been recognized in industry for many years. The first efforts in this direction tended to have psychological overtones and usually consisted of appraisals of traits that were deemed important to a successful executive. Thus, these early approaches did not appraise performance in terms of the results stemming from decisions made or influenced by an individual, but rather in terms of pre-

* Reprinted by permission from *Harvard Business Review*, vol. 38, no. 1, pp. 63–70, January-February, 1960; © 1960 by the President and Fellows of Harvard College; all rights reserved. Mr. Patton is a director of McKinsey and Company, Inc., management consultants.

conceived characteristics that management personnel were presumed to have. Particularly in the years following World War II, performance appraisal was often looked on as an integral part of an executive development program.

Subjective Approach Unfortunately, the executive characteristics appraised in development programs—leadership, initiative, dependability, judgment, getting along with people, ambition, and so on—do not necessarily measure a man's *effectiveness* on the job. Indeed, all too often judgments of performance under such plans reflect what is *thought* of the man rather than what he *does*.

The great weakness in this approach has proved to be the lack of performance criteria that are related to job responsibilities. Such concentration on personality traits ignores the more objective measures of on-the-job performance that are developed from budgets and accounting reports. This highly subjective approach, in turn, has made it difficult for management to communicate its judgment of an executive's performance to the man who has been evaluated. It is the rare individual who will concede that he does not display executive characteristics, and an even rarer boss who can comfortably explain shortcomings of so personal a nature to his subordinate. By contrast, the more objective criteria—rising or falling sales, profit margins, scrap losses, employee turnover, absenteeism, machine down time, and the like—are more readily understood by the subordinate and easier to explain because they are in quantitative terms that are part of the operating language of the business.

Another factor that tends to obsolete trait-oriented appraisals in recent years has been the increasing use of executive incentive plans in industry. More and more companies have found their bonus plans "in trouble" because eligible executives do not believe that incentive payments based on subjective appraisals reflect their individual efforts. This belief apparently results from an instinctive revulsion among executives to having their compensation largely dependent on what senior executives *think* of them. First, they suspect favoritism, and second, they exhibit a subconscious desire to have their performance measured by yardsticks that are based on more tangible, quantitative targets they have learned to understand and trust.

Mathematical Approach Some companies have taken steps to overcome the "popularity contest" aspects of subjective appraisals and to meet the growing need for judging performance in terms of individual targets. Often, however, such procedures have swung to the other extreme in bonus plan administration: setting individual goals for the year in quantitative terms (e.g., increase sales 10% or cut scrap losses 7%) and paying off on "performance" directly keyed to those goals. This approach has the great advantage of eliminating subjective judgment as the determinant of an individual's bonus. Furthermore, it does measure performance, and in terms that are understandable to the individual.

But the experience of many companies that have adopted this mathematical approach indicates that it, too, has serious shortcomings. The most important weakness revolves around the fact that once the individual targets have been established, mathematics takes over the basic responsibility of management to manage. If the individual goals set at the beginning of the year are not consistent between divisions, or between functions within divisions, the mathematically derived payoff at the year's end, undoubtedly, will be unfair. Some executives will be overpaid and others underpaid as a result of forces beyond the control of the individual. An unexpected price war, for instance, may seriously reduce profit margins in one division, while margins in another division benefit from the liquidation of a competitor. With mathematics deciding who gets what bonus, such basic economic shifts go unrecognized.

Then, too, the mathematically derived payoff that results from preset goals permits no adjustment in rewards for the *difficulty* of accomplishment. A manufacturing department, for example, may have surmounted major problems in fulfilling commitments that were easily attained by the sales department, or vice versa. But unless the program permits the *judgment* of management to reflect the difficulty of accomplishment, great incentive values are lost to the inflexibility of mathematics.

Because unfavorable results frequently stem from these relatively extreme approaches to performance appraisal—the wholly subjective and the mathematically determined evaluations—a number of leading companies have blended the best of the two into what appears destined to become a formidable management tool. The remainder of this article will examine in some detail the philosophy underlying the new concept, the administrative problems encountered, and the benefits derived from its use.

PLANNED PERFORMANCE

Essentially, this composite approach to appraisal is aimed at providing a sound basis for judging the relative performance of executives, expressed in terms of their individual responsibilities. It establishes annual targets for the individual that are implicit in the job he holds. And it provides for *judging* performance in terms of these targets rather than a purely mathematical measurement. In addition, it relates these individual targets to the short- and long-term goals of the enterprise. This means that each member of the management team is working toward the same agreed-on objectives of the company or division and will be judged by how well he performs these tasks.

Company Goals This approach is called by a variety of names: programed management, management by objective, or planned performance programing. But whatever the title, its users have a common objective: that individual performance be judged in terms of agreed-on tasks reflecting the goals of the business. The first step, therefore, involves the development of long- and short-range company goals. The longer-term objectives are useful in "stretching" executive thinking—in making managers think "bigger"—but are also valuable as a guide to the practicability of the forecast targets:

> Let as assume, for instance, that a single-product manufacturer, after considerable study, sets a five-year goal of doubling his unit volume. As a result, he has decided how much must be added to current sales in the first, second, and later years to attain this goal. The practicability of these estimates, of course, needs to be checked against the ability of the company to manufacture, sell, and finance such increases in volume. It makes no sense, for example, to set goals beyond the company's ability to provide funds at reasonable cost, or to agree to sell more of a product than facilities can be expected to turn out.
>
> Once it is decided that a 15% increase in company volume is a realistic target for the first year, the next step is to determine what must be accomplished by each functional group in order to attain such a goal. To do so necessitates a careful assessment of interfunctional relationships. For instance, perhaps it is possible for the sales department to develop 15% more business by a greater utilization of salesmen's time; but if this is accomplished, new facilities might be needed by manufacturing in order to meet this goal. (These new facilities, in turn, would obviously have to be considered in relation to the forecast needs of future years as well.)
>
> On the other hand, production facilities might be adequate to attain the necessary volume, but the sales department might have to introduce a new line of products in order to reach this figure. If this occurs, of course, other functional areas are likely to be involved. In addition to changes that a new line might necessitate in the sales department, i.e., the introduction of a specialized sales force, the engineering department would be expected to design the new line, credit standards might have to be tightened or loosened, transportation costs or lead times might need alteration, and so on.

Functional Tasks Experience has shown that translating short-term company objectives into 12-month goals for individual functional executives is best done by setting up both quantitative and qualitative tasks to be accomplished during the period. In other words, executive responsibilities include (a) those that can be *measured*, such as sales, behind-schedule production, or credit losses, and (b) those that must be *judged*, made up of the intangibles that arise when an executive develops a new process, establishes a training program, improves the quality of engineering candidates, and the like.

The advantage of separating qualitative and quantitative tasks lies in the very human tendency among executives to "let the numbers decide." It appears to be much easier for a superior to point out shortcomings to a subordinate when he can blame such an unpleasant conclusion on the results of a quantitative evaluation. Explaining weaknesses that must be *judged* impressionistically, while frequently more important to the training process, causes greater discomfort to the superior. The separation of the two induces a deeper awareness of the importance of both elements.

Further, these tasks need to be set up for both line and staff positions—a process that has proved to be a serious stumbling block to performance appraisal programs. Trouble results largely from line-oriented senior executives finding it difficult to visualize the possibility of setting realistic targets for staff jobs. There appears to be an unfortunate tendency among some senior executives to write off the entire approach because of this blind spot where staff is concerned. Thus:

> Dislike of this approach frequently occurs when the responsibilities of staff functions are vague, and their contribution to the management process has not been adequately developed. The senior executive subconsciously questions the value of the staff function, yet has come to believe that "staff is a hallmark of modern management." He remembers the time, a few years ago, when his company had two vice

presidents—sales and manufacturing. Today, there may be vice presidents for finance, engineering, personnel, administration, and so on, but the senior executive does not have the same "feel" for these jobs that he has for the line sales or manufacturing jobs with which he grew up.

This problem has been reduced, however, as top management more and more recognizes the need for spending as much *time* in establishing company and functional goals at the outset as it spends in appraising performance at the end of the year. This more thoughtful approach to task setting results in a better understanding of staff activities, as well as a more practical evaluation of the contributions that can be made in this area.

A number of techniques have been found helpful in cutting the problem down to size. If the tasks of the line organization are worked out first, for example, the process of thinking through the supporting goals of the staff functions is simplified. Similarly, there appears to be an advantage in setting up quantitative goals first and, subsequently, building the qualitative tasks on this foundation. One company has developed a master list of general goals for each functional area, some quantitative and some qualitative. While individual tasks will vary, of course, from year to year, these general goals have been found to be worth keeping in mind.

Examples of annual tasks developed as a basis for appraising the performance of a division head, a personnel executive, and a manufacturing executive are shown in Exhibits I, II, and III. The tasks in these examples are obviously fewer than would be the case in real life, but they are adequate to show the kind of tasks that can be used as a basis for appraising the performance of top line and staff executives.

Lower Level Tempo The annual tasks established for the key functions naturally set the tempo for executives below the top functional level. The goals of subordinates are necessarily tied in with the targets set up for the boss. However, some confusion has crept into the picture at this point. There are those who regard goal setting as the job of the subordinate, with the supervisor merely helping the subordinate relate his own tasks "to the realities of the organization," as one commentator put it. The great advantage of this method, in the eyes of its supporters, is psychological. The executive sets his own tasks, hence paces his own development.

My experience indicates that it is unrealistic to expect middle-management executives to be broad-gauged enough to set their own tasks. They do not fully comprehend the goals that have been established for their boss by top management in order to maintain integration between functions. Further, there is little evidence that lower echelon executives (those without full functional responsibility) are likely to set personal targets that fully "stretch" their capabilities. The political environment in most

EXHIBIT I Planned Performance Targets for Division Manager

Annual target plans

List of major accomplishments needed this year to meet corporation, division, or department goals.

Quantitative targets

Objectives for the year ahead that can be appraised in terms of *how much;* for example, "increase return on investment from 12% to 15%."

1. Increase billings by 17%, maintaining a 50%-30%-20% product mix in Departments A, B, and C.
2. Increase over-all profits (BT) by 35%.
3. Increase asset turnover from 1.3 times a year to 1.5 times.
4. Increase return on total assets from 18% to 21%.
5. Increase inventory turnover from 6.1 to 5.8 months.
6. Expand market share from 21% to 24%.

Qualitative targets

Objectives that can best be appraised in terms of *how well;* for example, "improve technical appraisal program," or "make more effective use of budgetary control."

1. Develop a new line of motors for introduction in 1961. Complete engineering phase, start production engineering.
2. Develop a more effective basis for testing candidates for supervisory positions, with particular reference to individual aptitudes for specific positions.
3. Increase the number of promotable executives by better training methods, including the introduction of job rotation and the establishment of a special assignment program designed to broaden the skills of outstanding men.
4. Start weekly department head meetings as a training and information medium.

EXHIBIT II Planned Performance Targets for Director of Personnel

Annual target plans

List of major accomplishments needed this year to meet corporation, division, or department goals.

Quantitative targets

Objectives for the year ahead that can be appraised in terms of *how much;* for example, "increase return on investment from 12% to 15%."

1. Reduce clerical costs of operating the employment function (recruiting and screening applicants) 60%.
2. Reduce cafeteria operating loss 3%.
3. Increase the typing pool from 25 to 30 employees.
4. Reduce the number of secretaries in headquarters staff by 15.

Qualitative targets

Objectives that can best be appraised in terms of *how well;* for example, "improve technical appraisal program," or "make more effective use of budgetary control."

1. Develop a safety training program for the operating divisions.
2. Simplify and reduce the number of clerical salary classifications.
3. Complete the management inventory.
4. Develop an approach to executive performance appraisal that will improve bonus plan administration.
5. Speed up new-employee indoctrination procedure (estimated target—one hour).
6. Develop a program to provide the negotiating group with information that anticipates union demands more accurately.
7. Work with the manufacturing function to eliminate "assistants to" general foremen and plant superintendents within five years.

companies is such that it is very important for executives to "hit the target" they have agreed on. Since "stretched" goals are more difficult to attain, the incentive to play it safe is frequently overwhelming.

This does not mean that lower level executives should not have an important voice in their job targets. The record indicates they should. But since their tasks are keyed directly to the goals of the functional executive, the latter must determine the targets of a subordinate, virtually in self-protection. Indeed, many of the tasks of the top functional executive are delegated directly to the subordinate:

- For example, when a chief engineer has responsibility for reducing the number of motor frames in the product line, he almost certainly delegates this particular chore to someone on his staff.
- When the top manufacturing executive is charged with cutting 20% off the lead time in component purchases, this too will be passed along if he is a good executive.

Thus, the tasks of this lower level group are much like those of their superiors. The main

EXHIBIT III Planned Performance Targets for Director of Manufacturing

Annual target plans

List of major accomplishments needed this year to meet corporation, division, or department goals.

Quantitative targets.

Objectives for the year ahead that can be appraised in terms of *how much;* for example, "increase return on investment from 12% to 15%."

1. Cut lead time on component purchases from 120 to 100 days.
2. Reduce WDC to 70% in terms of present prices.
3. Manufacturing's phase of the cost reduction program for the division is one third of the $1,500,000 excess saving over last year.
4. Improve delivery schedule performance by 5 percentage points (to 83%).
5. Reduce spoilage ratio by 2% net from 1959 figure.
6. Improve net allowed hours ratio by 3%.

Qualitative targets

Objectives that can best be appraised in terms of *how well;* for example, "improve technical appraisal program," or "make more effective use of budgetary control."

1. Speed up the recognition and utilization of suggestions developed in the suggestion system.
2. Improve production planning on the assembly floor to reduce the need for stand-by stocks of sub-assemblies.
3. Restudy the manufacturing process now used for product "X" to reduce the direct labor needs.

difference is in the number of special, short-term assignments that do not appear in any job description because they change so rapidly.

Judging Performance With job targets set up for top and middle-management executives, the next step involves determining where each executive's performance of agreed-on tasks falls in the spectrum from outstanding to poor.

Companies doing the best job of appraising the performance of their executives appear to have a number of points in common. For one thing, most of them have incentive bonus plans. The existence of this constant prod to developing better appraisal techniques seems to pay off in good results. Perhaps this reflects top management's willingness to spend more time on something involving a lot of money.

Another common attribute of such companies is top management's recognition that in the most important aspect of the entire appraisal process lies in the identification of outstanding and poor performers. Many appraisal programs bog down because of the time spent trying to identify minuscule differences in performance among the middle 60% to 70% of the executive group whose performance approximates the average! As a result of the effort spent in this direction, the 30% to 40% of the executives who are either outstanding or poor performers receive inadequate attention. Naturally, this becomes a critically important roadblock to success if the appraisal program includes an unwieldy number of executives.

In this connection, a technique so simple that it hardly seems worth mentioning has proved of considerable value. The outstanding performer and the poorest performer are first identified; then, in pairs, the second most outstanding and the second poorest are determined; and so on in pairs until it becomes difficult to distinguish between the performance of individual executives. Thus, a sense of proportion and reality is built into what otherwise tends to be a swampy morass.

One of the most difficult problems in judging performance lies in the values to be assigned line verus staff contributions. A few companies have developed an approach that appears helpful and sounds practical. While its use seems to be limited to those with incentive plans, there is no apparent need for such a limitation. This approach involves appraising the performance of fully profit-responsible executives (such as division managers) first, line executives (sales and manufacturing) second, and staff executives only after tentative values have been set for the profit-responsible and line executives. In other words, the performance of staff executive is "slotted" around already established relationships among the line executives.

This technique makes sense. The performance of the fully profit-responsible executive can be measured with a good deal of accuracy, by means of share-of-market, return-on-investment comparisons, and the like. Yardsticks for appraising sales and manufacturing executives are also good. However, measures of the staff executive's performance still leave much to be desired, and the evaluation of his performance should benefit from being tied in to the more tangible landmarks used for line executives.

The risk, of course, is that staff executives will be "slotted" on a position-in-the-hierarchy basis, or, in other words, judged by their position on the organization chart rather than by their performance. But a hardheaded judgment of the relative value of the tasks agreed on, as well as a careful assessment of performance will go a long way toward protecting against this risk.

Action Needed Having determined where individual performance falls in the continuum from outstanding to poor, it is necessary to do something about these findings. One of the recurring problems in appraisal programs is that lower echelon executives come to believe "nothing happens" as a result of the admittedly time-consuming appraisal effort.

An obvious first step is to see that the individual knows what is thought of his performance, and why. Since management's judgment of his performance is based on results racked up in the attainment of specific tasks, the individual's weaknesses and strengths are clearly delineated, and the supervising executive can discuss reasonably concrete "hits and misses" with the subordinate. This overcomes the natural reluctance among executives to criticize purely personal traits in their subordinates. Further, it focuses attention on specific opportunities for improvement. The planned performance approach, therefore, provides a basis for self-development on the part of the individual, as well as an assessment of "how he is doing."

For performance appraisal to be firmly rooted in a company's way of life it should play a key role in promotions, merit increases, and bonus payments. The outsider reviewing corporate administration practices all too frequently finds top performers, as measured by the appraisal program, doing no better than the average performer where bonuses, merit increases, and promotions are concerned. It may not make sense, but the rationalizations are plentiful. For instance, a top performer will be passed over for a merit increase "because his bonus was boosted this year"; or his bonus will be held unchanged despite outstanding performance "because he recently received a merit increase."

The point is this: if performance appraisal is worthwhile, it should provide the backbone for executive personnel administration.

Early Problems To date at least, only a handful of companies have seriously attempted to set up such a programmed approach to performance appraisal. Because most of these pioneering efforts were started in the past few years, it is too early to look for success stories. However, the top executives of companies that have tackled task planning are almost uniformly enthusiastic with results achieved so far. The principal accomplishment, in their view, is the establishment of a task-oriented way of life. Job objectives are morely clearly defined and, therefore, better coordinated. Individual executives know what is expected of them and can target their activities more effectively. Last but certainly not least, the annual review of "hits and misses" between superior and subordinate becomes more realistic and more productive of improved future performance.

Needless to say, there have been problems. It is significant, however, that the major problem areas follow a reasonably consistent pattern from company to company. For example:

1. The detailed probing of individual job responsibilities essential to this approach takes a great deal of time and necessitates some highly creative thinking. Since executives are human, many of them tend to resist both the effort and the thought processes that are involved. For this reason, it is essential that that the chief executive be solidly behind the project. If, for instance, executives come to suspect that their own bonuses may suffer from any neglect of the necessary time and thought requirements, so much the better.
2. Another common problem of successful performance programing is the need for a competent and creative "control function." Executives who are to be rewarded or penalized. in part at least, on results developed by the budgeting and accounting function should have great confidence in the control techniques used, as well as the skill and honesty of this group. It is relatively simple to devise yardsticks, but the objectivity and courage of the top control executives must be respected at all levels if these measures are to be effective. Executives need to have faith that tasks set for the various functions are equally difficult, and that figures are not going to be juggled to protect someone's favorite.

   The judgment of individual performance in terms of agreed-on tasks (such as those in Exhibits I, II, and III) requires maturity of a high order at the top level. One of the great advantages of the approach is the coordination of effort that results from its thoughtful, orderly task-setting process. If top management is overly arbitrary in its judgments, understandable problems develop. The chief executive who looks only to the results, without a careful weighing of the difficulties encountered in the accomplishments, is storing up future trouble.
3. The planned performance approach also calls for a personnel staff of unusual competence. This group necessarily plays a key role in advising top management when an imbalance occurs between functions. Several appraisal programs have suffered because the top personnel executives were unwilling or unable to convince top management of developing problem areas. In one instance, the personnel executive knew that the annual tasks set for one functional group were consistently more difficult to attain than were those of other groups. As a result this group had lost about 25% in bonus income over a four-year period. Top management became aware of the problem only after several promising young executives quit, and a subsequent study disclosed the source of the trouble.

   Since this approach to performance appraisal is most effective when confined to executives who importantly influence company profits, many personnel executives find themselves dealing with new and complex problems when an executive appraisal program is adopted. As one personnel vice president put it, "I used to spend 95% of my time on problems dealing directly or indirectly with moves having union overtones. Now, more than half my time is spent on the recruitment, development, organization, and motivation of executives!"

   Many personnel executives have found it difficult to effect a changeover. Thus, top management faces a serious handicap, since a strong, capable personnel group is a major ingredient in a successful appraisal program.
4. The "cutoff point" of executives to be included in the appraisal program has proved to be another problem area. If too many are

included, the programing task becomes monumental. The most effective course appears to involve starting off with a relatively limited group of key executives whose profit impact is unmistakable, and adding levels of executives to the program as its usefulness "proves out." The temptation to include too many, however, is almost overwhelming and needs to be consciously restrained.

Results to date indicate that the programed approach to performance appraisal is not for the laissez-faire management. It is a new way of life—and as difficult as it is rewarding.

CONCLUSION

The planned performance approach provides several important advantages over earlier attempts at executive appraisal:

- The long- and short-term objectives of the enterprise become an integral part of the performance appraisal process
- The job responsibilities of executives provide the basis for setting individual targets. As a result of the necessity for thinking through the interrelationships between job activities, there is a more effective targeting of individual effort
- The outstanding and poor performers receive primary attention, spotlighting those eligible for promotion or merit increases and those requiring training or elimination
- Personality plays a less important part in the final evaluation of performance, for the focus is on what a man does rather than what is thought of him. Thus, subjective criteria are replaced by objective ones
- Mathematics is put in its proper role, providing guidelines rather than final decisions.

Companies using this appraisal approach believe its greatest contribution stems from the disciplines it imposes on the management process. Planned performance forces a company:

- To think hard about its objectives and review them constantly.
- To study the responsibilities involved in individual positions and determine their relative importance to the business
- To set practical work tasks for individuals and hold them accountable for their attainment
- To take whatever action is called for by the information presented to it, in order to build a more effective management team.

In a sense, therefore, such a program involves a down-to-earth executive development program. Since people learn by doing, on-the-job training has great advantages over the more formal executive development programs that bloomed in profusion after the war.

The planned performance approach requires an enormous investment of top management's time in its early years. Since it usually involves a more disciplined way of life in the management process, it needs strong support from the chief executive and those directly under him. Because of the great time demands involved, companies have found it advantageous to limit the number of positions included in the program to those having a clearly recognizable impact on profits.

The approach also requires unusually skilled and resourceful control, market, and economic research functions. Because quantitative yardsticks play a major role in establishing targets and judging performance, they must be demonstrably good or executive belief in the fairness of the process will be undermined. It should be recorded, however, that the performance of executives is subject to constant scrutiny, for decisions bearing on promotions, merit increases, and bonuses are being made by top management almost daily. The question is whether the planned performance approach is worth the time and the effort that are needed to make it effective.

Companies that have worked hardest to develop their skill in this area believe it to be a major improvement over earlier efforts. And the fact that these concerns are pacesetters in industry implies that the competitive pressure exerted by their success with this new management tool will force an ever-widening circle of companies to think in similar terms about executive performance appraisal.

51 MAKING MANAGERIAL APPRAISAL EFFECTIVE*

Harold Koontz

The development of valid appraisals of managers over the past quarter century has been slow, in spite of the giant strides of the management revolution. Yet few would deny that appraisal is the key to management development and that, at least in the long run, the quality and vigor of managing make the difference in the success or failure of any organized enterprise. Without meaning to downgrade the importance of entrepreneurial genius and the profit-making potential of such non-managerial talents as marketing, production or engineering, no company can expect to enjoy prosperous growth for long without strong management. There are many companies that have been poorly managed, but have made high profits through special talents in marketing, production, or engineering. However, there is evidence that genius in these functional operating areas does not usually bring *long run* success unless the company, as a total system, is well managed. Moreover, it is well known that such non-business operations as government agencies and universities often fail in achieving their goals efficiently because of managerial shortcomings.

Perhaps the most exciting development in managing generally and in managerial appraisal in particular has been the growing use of management by objectives in the past decade. However, even this sensible and promising approach to management is often poorly conceived and implemented. Despite the excitement generated by it, by far the majority of business, government, and other organizations still evaluates managers on the basis of out-moded and discredited trait or work-quality appraisals. And even where management by objectives is done well—as in a very small percentage of organized enterprises—appraisal of performance does not necessarily measure how well a man is doing *as a manager*.

WHAT SHOULD BE MEASURED?

Managerial appraisal should measure performance as a manager in meeting goals for which a *manager,* in whatever position he occupies, is responsible. Obvious as this is, examination of a large number of appraisal systems used by business, government, and other organizations discloses a lack of understanding of this truism, or at least an unwillingness or inability to translate understanding into practice.

Appraisal should measure both *performance* in accomplishing goals and plans and *performance* as a *manager*. No one would want a person in a managerial role who appeared to do everything right as a manager but who could not turn in a good record of profit-making, marketing, engineering, or whatever his area of responsibility might be. Nor should one be satisfied to have a performer in a managerial position who cannot operate effectively as a manager. Performers are sometimes "flashes in the pan" and many have succeeded through no resources of their own.

Performance in Achieving Goals In assessing this aspect of the manager's job, the newer systems of appraising performance against preselected verifiable goals represent the best means that have yet been devised. The criteria of this aspect of performance are a manager's goals (including the intelligence with which he selects them), the programs he devises to accomplish them, and his success in achieving them. Many who have operated under this system of appraisal have claimed that these are adequate standards and that, in the course of evaluation, elements of luck or other factors beyond the manager's control can be considered in arriving at an appraisal. To some extent this may be true.

* Reprinted by permission of the publisher from the *California Management Review,* vol. 15, no. 2, pp. 46–55 (Winter, 1972). © 1972 by the Regents of the University of California. Mr. Koontz is Mead Johnson Professor of Management at the University of California, Los Angeles.

But there are too many cases of the sparkling performer being promoted despite these factors and the performing failure being inaccurately blamed.

Performance as a Manager I would urge that performance in selecting and achieving goals be supplemented by an appraisal of a manager as a *manager*. One must grant that a manager at any level undertakes nonmanagerial duties and these cannot be overlooked. The primary purpose for which a manager is usually hired and against which he should be measured, however, is his performance as a manager and not his work as an engineer, accountant, or salesman. Therefore, one of the major bases on which he should be appraised is how well he understands and practices the managerial functions of planning, organizing, staffing, directing, leading, and controlling. For standards in this area we must turn to the fundamentals of management.

REQUIREMENTS FOR AN EFFECTIVE MANAGERIAL APPRAISAL SYSTEM

The following are requirements for an effective program of managerial appraisal:

1. *The program should measure the right things.* As pointed out above, the effective program must weigh both performance in accomplishing managerial goals and performance as a manager. It is also entirely possible that the evaluator might wish to measure a manager's expertise in non-managerial skills and knowledge. But a manager who does well on the two standards of goal performance and managerial performance can draw upon expertise in non-managerial areas.
2. *The program should be operational.* The most effective appraisal program will not be an exercise separate from the operations of the individual manager. It should be operational in the sense that it evaluates what a manager does in his job and not, as has been the case with traditional appraisal programs, what raters *think* of the man and his work habits.
3. *The program should be objective.* Any appraisal program gains as it becomes more objective: both appraisers and the appraised prefer objectivity. Verifiability, the key to objectivity, is present if, at the end of the period, it can be said with certainty that something has or has not been accomplished. The better programs of management by objectives accomplished this largely by making goals verifiable either in quantitative terms (for example, dollars of sales or profit or percentage of scrap reduction) or in qualitative terms (for example, a marketing program having certain characteristics to be completed by a certain date). But even in these programs, as well as in the management appraisal program below, complete objectivity has not yet been achieved.
4. *The program should be acceptable.* Any management technique or program that people do not understand and accept is likely to be ineffective. If forced to, people will give lip service and fill out forms. However, if they understand and believe in a program and see it as a means of helping them accomplish their own personal desires through contributing to group goals, they will use it and feel a sense of commitment to it.
5. *The program should be constructive.* An effective managerial appraisal program should be constructive by helping individuals to improve their abilities and work. An effective appraisal program will not only determine how well an individual meets position requirements, an important requisite, but it should also point to his errors, weaknesses, or failures, and by giving him an understanding why these occurred, teach him or open his eyes to his training or learning needs.

DEFICIENCIES OF TRADITIONAL APPRAISAL SYSTEMS

Despite the fact that any knowledgeable manager knows his defects, for many years, and even commonly today, managers have been evaluated against the standards of personal traits and work-oriented characteristics. A typical system might list ten to fifteen personal characteristics such as leadership, ability to get along with people, industry, judgment, initiative, and others. It might also include such work-oriented characteristics as job knowledge, ability to complete assignments, production or cost results, or seeing that instructions and plans are carried out. Given these standards, the rater is then asked to evaluate his subordinates on the basis of one of five or six ratings ranging from unacceptable to outstanding.

The practical problems of these programs are well known. Ratings are highly subjective. Serious fair-minded managers are reluctant to affect a person's life or career on such subjective standards. Any subordinate who receives less than a top rating is likely to feel that he has been unfairly dealt with. The basic assumption of these appraisal systems, that there is a connection between performance and traits or work qualities, is also highly questionable.

The results of such deficiencies are predictable. Most managers dislike making such appraisals and see it as a paperwork exercise that must be done because someone has ordered it done. Raters understandably tend not to be very discriminating. It is hardly surprising that a study of ratings of Naval officers a few years ago found that of all officers of the U.S. Navy rated over a period of time, 98.5 percent were "outstanding" or "excellent" and only 1 percent were "average"!

Many attempts have been made to strengthen these rating systems. Traits have been carefully defined. For example, in one form, "judgment" was defined as "how capable is he of differentiating the significant from the less significant in arriving at sound conclusions?" Other systems encourage open-ended comments by the rater whereby he is asked to supply evidence on performance he feels is pertinent for appraisal. However, the results have been disappointing in terms of light cast and discrimination shown. Attempts have been made to improve the rating process by forcing the rater to rank his subordinates, forced choice questionnaires, and requiring listing of critical incidents. Even having ratings made by peers, subordinates, superior's superiors and groups have not been very successful, since the standards themselves are essentially nebulous.

APPRAISING AGAINST OBJECTIVES: THE FIRST MEANINGFUL APPROACH

The most promising tool of managerial appraisal yet practiced is the system of evaluating managerial performance against the setting and accomplishing of verifiable goals. Once a program of managing by objectives is operating effectively, appraisal is a fairly easy step. What is involved is seeing how competently a manager sets his objectives, their relationship and contribution to objectives of the enterprise and its parts, and how well performance against them is achieved.

To a very great extent, advantages of appraising cannot be separated from the benefits of managing by objectives. Clearly, to appraise performance against objectives is to assume that objectives have been established and that the person being appraised has been working toward their attainment. The most important advantage of such a system is that it can result in much improved managing. Actionable objectives cannot be established without planning—and results-oriented planning is the only kind that makes sense. Managers are forced to think of planning for *results,* rather than merely planning *activities* or *work*. It also requires a manager to think of the way he will accomplish given results, the organization and personnel he will need to do it, and the resources and interdepartmental assistance he will require.

A major strength of a system of managing by objectives is the almost certain clarification of organizational positions and structure. It dramatizes the fact that delegation should be done in accordance with results expected and goal assignments should, if possible, be consistent with a position that carries clear responsibility for their accomplishment.

Coordination of planning and budgeting is assisted. As many companies have found out, in addition to a need to understand superiors' and subordinates' objectives, managers should know the goals and achievements of those in other departments who affect their own goal accomplishment. The production manager, for example, would be foolish not to have his objectives coordinated with those of marketing or research and development.

One of the great advantages of a system of managing by objectives is that it elicits commitment for performance. No longer is a man just doing work, following instructions, and waiting for guidance or decisions—he now has a clearly defined purpose. Furthermore, he has had a part in actually setting his objectives, has had an opportunity to put his ideas into the making of plans, now understands his area of authority and has hopefully been able to get a number of decisions from his superior at the time goals are agreed upon to assure that he can accomplish his goals. When managing by objectives has been done well, a man becomes master of his own fate and feels a real sense of commitment to his goals.

One of the frustrating problems of effective control is selecting those critical points in any situation that a manager must watch if he is to be assured that his actions are conforming to plans. In cases of effective management by objectives, this problem is often solved. Now the manager knows what he should watch and has standards against which to measure his progress. Indeed, there has probably been no development in management that has contributed so much to improving the quality of control and pinpointing information needs.

Thus, appraisal is an operational "fallout," as is shown in Table I, from a system of managing. It need not be a world of forms and reports separate from managing. Information on what a man has done against what he agreed was a reasonable target is readily available. Moreover, it is available in an atmosphere of the superior working with and helping his subordinate, not sitting in remote judgment of him.

TABLE I The System of Managing and Appraising by Objectives[1]

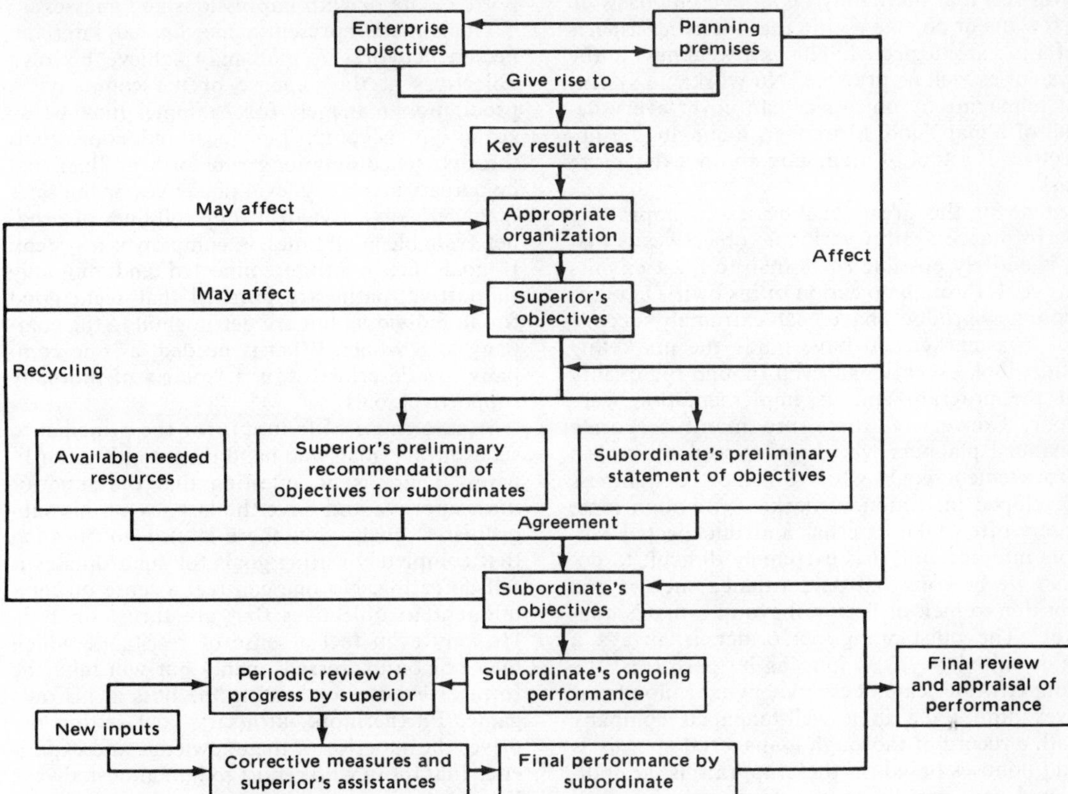

THE PROBLEMS OF APPRAISING AGAINST OBJECTIVES

In spite of its being promising and sensible, appraising against objectives is not the easy answer to evaluating managers. Even the best operating program has limitations—there are great difficulties and weaknesses in practice. Since it measures only end-result performance, it overlooks how effective a manager is as a manager.

Deficiencies in the System Even with considerable analysis, study, and supervision, goals with the right degree of "stretch" or "pull" are difficult to set year in and year out. Characteristic of all planning is the uncertainty inevitable in anything intended to operate in the future. More work and study is needed to establish verifiable and actionable objectives, rather than to develop many typical plans which only lay out work to be done. Objectives must not be too easily attainable. Experience has shown that, at least in the earlier days of a program, most people set goals too high. Later, when goal achievement becomes a major standard of appraisal and sometimes a determinant of compensation or promotion, there is a natural tendency for subordinates to understate goals to assure that they will exceed them. Goal appropriateness can be determined only by an experienced superior, although this good judgment can be developed in the manager only with time and trial and can become highly objective in instances where goals of other managers in similar positions are available for comparison.

In almost all systems of management by objectives—particularly where goals are used for appraisal—goals are usually short-term, seldom longer than a year and often quarterly or less. There is a danger that emphasizing short-term planning and results may be at the expense of the longer term. The need to get short-term performance, say one or two years, may undermine long-range plans. This can be particularly dangerous if managers rotate to other positions. Meeting this danger requires that short-term goals be carefully and specifically geared to long-term plans and objectives and that the appraiser never lose sight of this need. For companies that have longer-range plans and objectives, this should not be difficult.

Critics of programs of managing by objectives feel that there may be an overemphasis on a few major objectives and that the other aspects of a job are neglected. This is a weakness in the system as well as practice. No workable system of managing by objectives can cover every detail of a man's job. Moreover, managing by objectives is a tool of managing and not the entire task.

One of the great weaknesses in appraising performance against verifiable objectives is that it is entirely possible for a man to meet or miss his goals through no action of his own. On occasion, new products have been extremely successful in a market and have made the marketing effort look exceptional, even though the quality of the program and its implementation were poor. Conversely, there are many corporate financial planners who have missed their cash procurement goals when unexpected tightness developed in a money market. Although most raters often take external and unexpected factors into account, it is extremely difficult to do. Can we be sure that performance success was not due to luck or factors beyond a man's control? The outstanding performer is always a "fair-haired boy," as long as he performs; the nonperformer cannot escape having a cloud cast over him. Even in a well-managed company with a record of thorough managerial appraisals and bonuses based on these appraisals, an individual rose rapidly to the corporation's presidency following a period of success based almost entirely on changes in consumer tastes which were beyond his control.

Weaknesses in Practice Analysis of programs of managing and appraising by objectives has also disclosed many difficulties and weaknesses in practice. Learning the system is difficult. For one thing, those who have been accustomed to planning find it difficult to shift to developing actionable objectives. Because of the difficulties in learning the system, it is urgent that people who are expected to operate under it understand the nature and philosophy of the program—what it is, how it works, why it is being done, how appraisal will work, and, above all, how everyone will benefit. Like most other worthwhile programs it cannot be installed by edict and distributing forms and instructions with an order to participate.

A major reason why managing by objectives, as well as planning and budgeting, does not work is the lack of adequate guidelines. People must have some planning premises and some understanding of company policies and the directions of other plans and objectives to do their planning effectively. No one can plan in a vacuum. How will the planner fill the vacuum—with supportive data or with impressions and guesses?

Goals must represent a coordinated, interconnected network. A man may achieve his own objectives at the expense of the company. A production manager, for example, may be so zealous in accomplishing cost reduction goals through scheduling long runs of a product that he defeats inventory level objectives or the sales manager's objective of having full lines of product available at all times. A company is a system. If goals are not interconnected and mutually supportive, paths are pursued that seem good for an individual but are detrimental to the company as a whole. What is needed, as one company has described it, is a "matrix of mutually supportive goals."

A sure cause of failure is for the principal to set arbitrary goals and hand them to his subordinates. There is no question that the superior must approve and have the last say on his subordinates' goals—but there is also no question that completely setting goals for subordinates is self-defeating. No one can feel a sense of commitment to objectives that are thrust on him. He may even feel a sense of resistance which may not be expressed openly but will take the form of excuses or beating the boss at his own game. Furthermore, arbitrary goal setting deprives the superior of the knowledge and experience that those who report to him almost always have.

It is clear that, if goals are to be meaningful and are to be used as a standard of appraisal, they must be verifiable in either a quantitative or qualitative way. Because goals expressed in numbers are the most verifiable, there is too often insistence on quantities and numbers. We should not forget that not every worthwhile end result can be expressed quantitatively. Lower and middle management programs have been known to fail because of the expression of their goals in numbers. The management by objectives program in such a situation becomes a "numbers game" and the more intelligent subordinates beat their bosses at it.

Particularly where quantitative goals are used, there has been a natural tendency to set up company-wide targets for somewhat similar positions and use these as a standard of appraisal. But this can be dangerous. National standards in an unusual operation, even when applied to similar managerial roles, would not be applicable to managers operating in dissimilar markets and environments. In one company where such standards were used, the result was frustration, resistance, no real sense of commitment, filling in forms, and playing the numbers game.

There are still other deficiencies in practice. As in budgeting, some companies are inflexible and do not change objectives during a period of time, normally a year. It is true that if objectives can be changed easily and often they cease to be meaningful. However, if goals are materially obsolete, there is no sense in keeping them.

In many programs, progress toward goal accomplishment is not adequately monitored. Particularly where goals can only be achieved in a period of a year or more or where a company is accustomed to setting goals annually, there is a danger that a principal, for fear of interfering with his deputy, may sit back and fail to keep track of progress during the period. While not taking over the task from his subordinate, or interfering with his operation, the superior should, of course, have information to watch progress, should counsel with his subordinate, and give him assistance in solving problems and removing obstructions to his performance. Managing and appraising by objectives cannot become abdication of responsibility.

Perhaps the major problem in practice arises from seeing management by objectives only as an appraisal program instead of a way of managing. Even though search for a better appraisal method did give managing by objectives its strongest impetus, it is likewise true that the system is not likely to work if only used as a device for appraisal. Management by objectives must be a way of managing, a way of planning, as well as the key to organizing, staffing, directing, and controlling—it is then a part of managing, a summary of what has been done, and not a difficult separate operation.

SUPPLEMENTING APPRAISAL BY OBJECTIVES: APPRAISING MANAGERS AS MANAGERS

As encouraging as appraisal of managerial performance against verifiable objectives is, it still leaves much to be desired. No one interested in long-term enterprise success would want managers who could not accomplish goals, nor would they want performers in a managerial role who could not manage.

A few companies have recognized the importance of evaluating the quality of managing. Some have asked for appraisal in such broad areas as planning, organizing, coordinating, leading, motivating, and controlling. Others have broken down these areas into broad subcategories such as, in the case of organizing, job assignments, clarity of responsibilities and authorities, and delegation effectiveness. Even fewer companies have gone farther. The St. Regis Paper Company has aided managers in their appraisals by preparing and distributing a booklet called *Guidelines for Managing,* which is really a brief summary of basic principles of management. However, the standards thus far used for appraising managers, as managers, have been too broad and too susceptible to general and subjective judgment.

The program suggested here is a somewhat experimental step toward appraising managers as managers.[2] However, it has been tested by presentation to a number of executives in both business and government, and, above all, it has been tested by experience. In one company with three domestic divisions and five wholly owned subsidiaries overseas, it has been used as a major method of appraising middle- and top-level managers for five years. Coupled with a program of appraising managerial performance against verifiable objectives, it has not only been the means of evaluating managers but also the basis for bonuses paid to them.

The Program The program involves taking each function of a manager in accordance with standard managerial analyses (planning, organizing, staffing, directing, and controlling) and setting up checkpoint questions under each to reflect basic principles of management. As imperfect as the basic principles of management may be and as much judgment as may be required for their use in practice, they do give the evaluator bench marks to determine whether persons understand and are following the basics of management. Even though application of principles to an individual manager's operations requires a degree of subjective judgment, this is far more meaningful than the general questions often used as standards of appraisal. They at least focus attention on what may be expected of a manager *as a manager*.

While the total list of seventy-three questions is too extensive to be repeated here, some samples are given. In planning, for example, a manager may be rated by such check questions as the following:

- Does he set for his departmental unit both short-term and long-term goals in verifiable terms that are related in a positive way to those of his superiors and his company?
- Does he understand the role of company policies in his decision-making and assure that his subordinates do likewise?
- Does he check his plans periodically to see if they are consistent with current expectations?
- In choosing from among alternates, does he recognize and give primary attention to

those factors which are limiting or critical to the solution of a problem?

In the area of organizing, such questions as the following are asked:

- Does he delegate authority to his subordinates on the basis of results expected of them?
- When he has delegated authority to his subordinates, does he refrain from making decisions in that area?
- Does he regularly teach his subordinates or otherwise make sure they understand, the nature and operation of line and staff relationships?
- Does he distinguish in his operations between lines of authority and lines of information?

In the area of controlling, such questions as the following are asked:

- How effectively does he tailor his control techniques and standards to reflect his plans?
- Does he develop controls that point up exceptions at critical points?
- Does he keep abreast of, and utilize, newer techniques of planning and control?
- Does he help his subordinates develop control techniques and information that will show them how well they are doing in order to implement "control by self-control"?

Other questions are asked in these areas as well as in the areas of directing (leadership) and staffing. Furthermore, in order to solve the problem of semantics and understanding of terms and techniques so prevalent among managers, those who have used this system are strongly urged to use a standard book on management with page references for each question. Without repeating each of the seventy-three checkpoint questions, along with the explanations required for effective use of the program, the subject matter areas may be seen in Table II. It should be pointed out that any summary does not clearly reflect emphasis on an area since experience has shown that certain critical questions may shed as much light as a number of questions in certain areas.

In developing this system, it was hoped to make ratings highly objective by designing the checkpoints and questions to be "go-no-go": the manager being rated either did or did not follow the basics involved. However, this was not found to be practicable and degrees of "how well" had to be inserted on each question, with rankings from 0 (inadequate) to 5 (superior).

In order to give the numerical ratings for each question some rigor, each is defined. "Superior," for example, is defined as "a standard of performance which could not be improved upon under any circumstances and conditions known to the rater." Other attempts to reduce subjectivity and lack of discrimination in rating include (1) the requirement in the final annual appraisal that a narrative with incident examples be given to support ratings; (2) a review of ratings by the superior's superior; and (3) making the evaluation of raters dependent in part on the discrimination and care shown in their evaluations. A degree of objectivity is also introduced by the number and specific nature of the checkpoint questions. Also, it was found that encouraging self-rating and comparison with the superior's rating served to elicit discrimination. Moreover, as is often the case, per-

TABLE II.

BASIC SUBJECT AREAS	NO. OF QUESTIONS
Planning	
Goal Setting	3
Furnishing and utilizing planning guidelines	4
Quality of decision making	7
Total	14
Organizing	
Appropriate structure	3
Delegation	6
Line, staff, functional authority, and service departments	4
Committee and group meetings	2
Organizational Planning and operations	4
Total	19
Staffing	
Exercise of staffing responsibility	1
Training and development	5
Appraisal	3
Selection and promotion	2
Compensation	1
Total	12
Directing and Leading	
Motivation	2
Communication	3
Participation	4
Leadership skills and practices	3
Total	12
Controlling	
Tailoring controls	4
Control information	4
Control action	3
Effective budgeting	2
Utilizing newer techniques	3
Total	16
Total checklist questions	73

sons rating themselves tended to be more severe on themselves than their superior was.

Advantages of the Program Clinical experience with the program has shown certain advantages. By focusing on the essentials of management, this method of evaluation gives operational meaning to what managing really is. One upper level manager, who was in fact a good manager, declared after discussing his first ratings with his superior that, despite having read many books on management and having attended many seminars, this was the first time he really understood what managing is. By use of a standard reference text for interpretation of concepts and terms, much of the semantic and communication difficulties so commonly encountered are removed. Such things as "verifiable objectives," "staff," and "delegation" take on consistent meaning. Likewise, management techniques and their proper application become uniformly understood.

The program has also proved to be a tool for management development by calling to a manager's attention certain basics that he may have long disregarded or had not understood. In addition, the approach has been found useful in pinpointing areas where weaknesses exist and toward which development efforts should be aimed. Furthermore, as intended, the program acted as a supplement and a check on appraising managers with respect to their effectiveness in setting and achieving goals. If a manager had an outstanding performance in goal accomplishment but was found to be deficient as a manager, those in charge were encouraged to look for the reason. Normally, one would expect a truly effective manager to be also successful in meeting goals.

Weaknesses in the Program There are some shortcomings in the program. The program applies only to managerial aspects of a given position and not to such technical abilities as marketing and engineering that might also be important. These, however, should be reflected in the goals selected and achieved. There is also the problem of the apparent complexity of the total of seventy-three checkpoints; to rate on all of these does take time, but it was believed that the time was well spent.

Perhaps the major defect of the program is the unavoidable element of subjectivity remaining. However, it still has a fairly high degree of objectivity and is certainly far more objective than the practice of having managers appraised in broader areas of the managerial functions as has been common in the few cases where serious attempts have been made to evaluate managers as managers. At least the checkpoints are specific and go to the essentials of managing.

MOVING TOWARD MORE EFFECTIVE APPRAISALS

After many years of frustration from utilizing trait and work-oriented qualities as standards of managerial appraisal, there is at last some hope that our more alert and intelligently managed organizations are moving toward more meaningful evaluation of those to whom we trust the responsibilities of managing. Certainly, appraisal based on selection and achievement of verifiable objectives is a tremendous step in the right direction. It is such a breakthrough, however, only if it is applied with care and intelligence. It concentrates, as it should, on what a manager *does* rather than on what someone subjectively thinks of him. When coupled as a standard of evaluation with appraisal of a manager as a manager, there is hope that we can, at long last, begin to approach the area of evaluating managers logically and effectively.

But devices and approaches will not solve the problem. There is ever the danger that top managers will adopt techniques and forms without accompanying them with an understanding of the philosophy in back of them, without the tools and assistance subordinates need, and without the hard work, time, commitment, and leadership necessary to make them work. No management technique is self-actuating and many have failed through executive malnutrition, particularly from the top.

In the area of managerial appraisal, the results should be worth the effort required. Few would deny the strategic importance of the quality of managing in every level and in every kind of enterprise. It is probably true that managerial appraisal has been the weakest link of the entire chain of the management process. While the proposals suggested here may not completely solve this problem, they are believed to be important steps in the right direction.

SUGGESTIONS FOR FURTHER READING

R. B. Finkle and W. S. Jones, *Assessing Corporate Talent* (New York: John Wiley and Sons, Inc., 1970).

C. H. Granger, "How to Set Company Objectives," *Management Review* (July, 1970), pp. 2–8.

R. A. Howell, "A Fresh Look at Management by Objectives," *Business Horizons* (Fall, 1967), pp. 51–58.

J. W. Humble, *Improving Business Results* (London: McGraw-Hill Publishing Company, Ltd., 1970).

J. W. Humble, *Management by Objectives in Action* (London: McGraw-Hill, 1970).

A. F. Kindell and J. Gatza, "Positive Program for Performance Appraisal," *Harvard Business Review* (Nov.–Dec., 1963), pp. 153–160.

H. Koontz, *Appraising Managers as Managers* (New York: McGraw-Hill Book Company, 1971).

H. Levinson, "Management by Whose Objectives?" *Harvard Business Review* (July–Aug., 1970), pp. 125–134.

D. McGregor, "An Uneasy Look at Performance Appraisal," *Harvard Business Review* (May–June, 1957), pp. 89–94.

G. S. Odiorne, *Management by Objectives* (New York: Pitman Publishing Corporation, 1965).

A. Patton, "How to Appraise Executive Performance," *Harvard Business Review* (Jan.–Feb. 1960), pp. 63–70.

A. P. Raia, "A Second Look at Goals and Controls," *California Management Review* (Summer, 1966), pp. 49–58.

E. C. Schleh, *Management For Results* (New York: McGraw-Hill Book Company, 1961).

H. L. Tosi and S. J. Carroll, "Managerial Reaction to Management by Objectives," *Academy of Management Journal* (Summer, 1968), pp. 70–78.

H. L. Tosi, J. R. Rizzo, and S. J. Carroll, "Setting Goals in Management by Objectives," *California Management Review* (Summer, 1970), pp. 70–78.

T. L. Whisler and S. F. Harper (eds.), *Performance Appraisal: Research and Practice* (New York: Holt, Rinehart and Winston, Inc., 1962).

W. S. Wikstrom, *Managing By- and With- Objectives* (New York: National Industrial Conference Board, Inc., 1968).

REFERENCES

1. Harold Koontz, *Appraising Managers as Managers* (New York: McGraw-Hill Book Company, 1971).
2. *Ibid.*, chapters 5–6.

D. MANAGERIAL DEVELOPMENT

52 DEVELOPING MANAGERS: UNDERLYING PRINCIPLES*

Walter S. Wikstrom

Management development often appears to be a chaotic field. The literature reports in glowing terms one new training method after another. Some firms stick doggedly with one or only a few development practices, while others seem to play the field, trying any new method that comes along. With all this confusion, is anything being accomplished, has anything been developed?

One thing that has developed is a growing body of "principles" that guide the planning of development programs. The use of a wide variety of training methods has sometimes led companies into unproductive, blind alleys, but it also has provided a rich body of experience. As development specialists have shared these experiences, through management literature and in their professional associations, they have been able to generalize their own particular experience and to use these generalizations as a basis for more productive efforts in the future. While some company programs still appear to be a formless collection of methods and techniques, closer examination often reveals the shrewd application of this growing body of principles.

These "principles," however, are not considered statements of natural law governing human behavior. Rather, they are a set of guidelines. And as with any body of empirically derived knowledge, acceptance of individual ideas varies widely; some are acknowledged by everyone; others are adhered to by only a few men.

This article discusses eight of the most widely accepted guidelines. Their almost universal acceptance will be understandable when they are stated, for they seem so obvious as to need no statement. However, the company development specialists who have analyzed the results they have achieved, and the failures they have encountered, say that it *is* important to state them, for beyond their apparent obviousness lie implications that profoundly affect the development of men as managers.

ALL DEVELOPMENT IS SELF-DEVELOPMENT

This truism is the most widely accepted of these "principles." Many of the others are derived from it. It is obvious that John Doe cannot expect some training man to accomplish his development for him; this is one job that Doe cannot delegate to any subordinate, however capable. If John Doe is going to develop, *he* must develop.

The significance of the statement goes beyond this obvious interpretation, however. In helping a man develop as a manager, a firm cannot start from scratch; the man already has developed to some degree. He has his own personality, a unique combination of abilities, potentials, needs, desires, fears, and values. Some of his characteristics may be assets for his development as a manager; others may be liabilities; and still others may be relatively neutral. But these characteristics cannot be ignored; they are the raw materials he has to work with in any further development.

For instance, if a hard life has taught John Doe that the world is a pretty risky place where the chances of failure are great and the rewards are usually slim, it obviously will be difficult for him to develop into an entrepreneurial risk taker. On the other hand, if an equally hard life has convinced Richard Roe that life is an exciting series of challenges and opportunities to be seized, he is well on his way toward seeking the risks and responsibilities of business leadership.

According to some theorists, even such basic attitudes toward life may be modified somewhat if time and proper methods are used. No change, however, can be effected if existing personality structures are ignored in planning the developmental experiences needed by John Doe and Richard Roe.

Just a few of the personality characteristics

* Reprinted by permission of the publisher from *Management Record*, vol. 24, no. 11, pp. 14–18, November, 1962. Mr. Wikstrom is on the staff of the National Industrial Conference Board.

that can play a role in determining the direction and extent of the individual's development as a manager will serve to illustrate the complexity of the problem. The individual's personal goals and ideals affect his motivation to develop in any particular direction. His tolerance of ambiguity (or need for the reassurance of demonstrable factual truth) can determine whether he chooses to develop as a physical scientist or a personnel specialist. His ability to admit the need for further growth, and the consequent admission of some degree of present inadequacy, can help determine whether he even undertakes to develop as a manager. And his tolerance of frustration is a factor, especially when no progress seems to be taking place.

These, and many more factors, present to some degree in each person, interact to make a unique personality. None of them is "good" or "bad" in itself. However, they do affect the possibilities for further growth. They call for different approaches to each man to prompt and assist his development of greater managerial competence. From this fact follows the second widely accepted guideline used in planning management development programs.

ACTIVITIES SHOULD BE TAILORED TO THE MAN

Since development specialists agree that "what is one man's meat is another's poison," they argue that a total corporate development program must be flexible enough to include a variety of development activities sufficient to accommodate each individual's needs and learning abilities. In a sense, this guideline declares, an ideal corporate program includes an individual "program" for each manager, a set of activities and experiences that are based upon *his* background, *his* present needs, and *his* prospects for future assignments in the company.

This, of course, does not preclude a unified coordinated corporate program, nor does it rule out all group-training methods. In developing managers, as in other company activities, carefully planned and well-coordinated programs increase the chances of success. Further, group-training methods are often efficient ways of meeting the common development needs of a number of men. What this guideline *does* rule out, however, is dependence upon a single lockstep program that attempts to provide completely identical experiences to all the managers who are expected to benefit from it.

The following hypothetical situation may serve to illustrate the need for flexibility. A firm may decide that its managers need to do a better job of planning. It may announce this as a major development objective and assign responsibility for a development program to some specific unit, perhaps the staff training department. That group might come up with a lecture and discussion course on the general concepts of planning and on specific methods of analysis and projection. This course might be scheduled for all managers.

Thus far, the corporate program could be quite useful in helping with the general problem of increasing the planning competence of each manager. There might be danger, however, in complete reliance upon this single approach.

Some managers may be poor planners simply because they don't know enough about it. The course could be of great benefit to them. Others may know all about planning, but not consider it very important. Again, the course might help by convincing them that the company considered planning to be an important part of their jobs.

Still other managers may believe that planning is important and have an intellectual grasp of the concepts, but have very little skill in applying what they know. A lecture and discussion course might add little to their development; guided practice in the application of the concepts under discussion would probably be more useful to them.

Again, some managers may have all the knowledge and skill but may be so harrassed by superiors who do not look ahead that they have learned to play every situation by ear. Their development as planners requires that their bosses learn more about managing and the importance of planning.

Yet another man may be a poor planner because his job is so structured that he does not have access to all the information he needs to plan his work intelligently. Obviously, he cannot further develop his planning ability until there has been a change in his job structure.

These examples should be sufficient to illustrate that the reasons men have certain deficiencies as managers may be as varied as the men themselves. A total company development program that does not recognize the possibility of these individual differences cannot cope with them. Clearing away the particular obstacles that block each man's progress permits him to make use of the available development opportunities.

DEVELOPMENT REQUIRES ACTION

It is said that one learns from experience. It is also said that, in the same length of time, one man will have ten years' experience while another will have only one year's experience while another will have only one year's experience repeated ten times.

The difference, of course, lies in what the men have learned from their experience and this probably depends not on what happened to them but on what *they did* with what happened to them.

If a person develops, he changes. Yet nothing changes by itself; change is produced by some cause. In human change—development—the cause lies within the person. It is true that external events are a factor in human growth, but these are only the stimuli for change. The change in personality (which includes competencies as well as traits, attitudes and all that makes each person unique) comes about because of the person's perception of and reaction to events. Development is an extremely personal process, not a purely mechanistic one.

Thus, development takes place because of some action or reaction on the part of the learner. This is not necessarily observable overt action. It is often the covert action involved in the weighing and testing of a new idea or attitude. It may be the assimilation of new information into one's existing store of knowledge, relating what is being learned to what is already known. It may, of course, be such overt action as the practicing of a new manual skill. When the learner interacts with the stimulus, whether this be the contents of a course, training simulation, a problem situation or what-have-you, his personality changes—he develops.

That is why management courses, and educational programs generally, seek to involve the learner. Involvement is indispensable to effective learning. If a developing manager can be induced to become interested in some subject matter for its own sake, or because mastery of it will help him achieve his personal goals or reduce a sense of inadequacy caused by some weakness—if in any way he can be moved to really react to the material being taught—the chance of his really learning and retaining will be greatly increased. He can make the new material part of himself, tie it to his previous knowledge, his perceptions, his attitudes, his whole personality.

Increasingly, company management development programs provide actual practice in applying management knowledge and actual use of management skills on the job. Otherwise, specialists say, a man might learn all *about* managing without ever learning really *to manage*. The payoff, for the company and for the developing manager himself, comes with management ability and not mere management knowledge.

CONTROL CAN AID DEVELOPMENT

Soundly based management development, like other well-managed activities, requires the use of controls. This is true whether one thinks of the total corporate program or the activities of a particular manager.

It seems self-evident that the total management development program calls for carefully defined objectives, planned procedures, a known time schedule and attention to costs. These would be the controls against which the activities of the total company program could be measured.

Control, however, can contribute to the development of individuals too. The individual can learn more effectively if he knows what he is trying to learn, what type of information he needs to acquire and what sort of skills he must master. He can benefit from having a set of priorities for attacking his development tasks and some idea of a reasonable time schedule for achieving his goals. A review of the resources he can call upon, in the company, in the community, and in himself can help his planning. These individual development plans become his personal controls for his own development activities.

The existence of these bench marks evidently has an important influence on the man's ability to sustain motivation. Changing one's ways of thinking or behaving can be very hard and frustrating work. At times little progress may seem to be taking place. Unexpected difficulties can appear. At such times a review of the goals and of the progress to date will usually show that *something* has been accomplished, *some* headway has been made. This can buoy up the spirits of a manager just about to give up the struggle. He can adjust his plans, perhaps develop a more feasible line of attack and concentrate his attention upon those areas that appear most apt to produce the results he seeks. On the other hand, if a manager does not really know what he is trying to do, or if he gets no feedback as to what, if anything, he is accomplishing, his difficulty in sustaining any real effort becomes understandable. Thus while the management development specialist requires information on the plans and progress of the firm's individual managers in order to do his own job of controlling the total corporate program, the crucial need is for each developing manager to have the information he requires to control his own development.

COMPANY "CLIMATE" AFFECTS DEVELOPMENT

"Climate" is the perception employees have of their company. It encompasses the company's organization, its procedures and its policies—the way it actually operates. It is not necessarily the organization drawn on the charts; it may not be the procedures in the manual or the statements engraved on the wall plaques. It is the total impression employees gain from their daily experiences in working for the firm. "Climate" is what a man is talking about when he says: "That's the way things are around here."

"The way things are around here," so far as management development is concerned, inevitably is one of the principal determinants of how managers will develop. Men learn from doing; most companies recognize that a man learns to do those things he sees others doing or that he is required to do himself.

Companies concede that some of their notable failures in attempting to develop managers occur when the climate of the firm does not complement its development program. Thus, if a company wishes its managers to adhere to high standards in dealings with customers, suppliers and employees, it must clearly define and explain these standards. Beyond this, however, it must adhere to them unswervingly in order to demonstrate that it means what it says. In short, a company cannot train its managers to operate "by the book" if it doesn't follow the book in its daily work. Of course, Emerson said it better in his terse: "What you do speaks so loud, I cannot hear what you say."

Classroom discussion of the principles of sound organization and their importance to success as a manager cannot offset a chaotic organization climate. When job responsibilities have been poorly defined or not defined at all, when it is unclear what authority has been delegated to any particular position, when the relationships among positions have not been delineated, companies find that they cannot convince their men that organization planning is a central part of their work as managers. Rather, the men often learn to give lip service to the principles while grabbing whatever responsibilities they want, ducking whatever accountability they can, and using the general confusion for departmental empire building or personal advantage.

A company's acceptance of change is an important aspect of its management development climate. Successful managers do not all perform their jobs in the same way. Sometimes different ways of doing things can be anticipated, but sometimes they cannot. If a company does not let its managers try out different approaches, its claims that it wants to develop management men who are innovators will not be taken very seriously.

A company can say in many subtle ways that it really does not want its men to develop. The man who starts to experiment with different ways to produce or sell the product, different ways to reach decisions, may soon begin to sense that he is considered an upstart who had better keep his mouth shut for twenty years or so until he gains a little real know-how. "We've always done it this way" may be the climate. In such an atmosphere good men develop, but only frustration and ulcers.

Thus, development specialists maintain that if there is discrepancy between what the firm says it wants its men to learn and the way it actually operates, top management had better rethink its management development objectives. If improved—and therefore different—management is really desired, these specialists say that top officials must make unmistakably clear to everyone concerned that a bootstrap operation is in progress, and that managers are expected to learn how to do a better job and expected to apply what they learn day-to-day on the job.

INFLUENCE OF BOSS IS CRUCIAL

A sixth widely accepted guideline is a special instance of the fifth, namely *a man's boss is apt to be a key influence upon his development.*

For most employees, the immediate boss is the chief ingredient in the company's climate. It is the boss who represents the firm's formal authority and who defines or interprets its policies and objectives. It is the boss who determines the employee's assignments and his opportunities to learn on and from his job. The boss plays a crucial role in determining an employee's—particularly a manager's—future in the company. It follows that it is the boss whose management methods, whose attitudes, whose "style" is most apt to be observed and imitated.

This is borne out by research in a number of companies where successful high-level managers have been asked to name the influences that they believe account for their own success. Repeatedly such men have said that the most important influence upon their careers has been one of their bosses. "He let me try new ideas." "He always demanded good work from me and set an example by doing an excellent job himself." "He always had time to help me work out my own problems; he didn't jump in with suggestions every time some little thing went wrong." These paraphrases are typical of the comments reported in studies of the careers of successful managers.

DEVELOPMENT IS A LINE RESPONSIBILITY

This is really a corollary of the preceding guideline, for if a boss influences his subordinates' development, obviously he has a responsibility for properly using this influence. No manager who had a guiding influence upon product design would try to deny responsibility and accountability for the product; a man whose actions affect sales volume would not deny responsibility for sales. Similarly, no manager may reasonably argue that he is not responsible and accountable for the development of his subordinates and for their future usefulness to the company, for he is a prime influence upon their development.

Some years ago, Frederick R. Kappel, president of the American Telephone and Telegraph Company, was addressing a group of management men on a variety of technical matters. Toward the end of his discussion he said: "But in my judgment, all of these activities, valuable as they may be, can only be effective as an aid to growth in the right kind of climate, and for that the boss is everlastingly responsible. . . . We will do the best job, I'm sure, when, and only when, every boss acts on the understanding that an indispensable part of his assignment is to do everything he thoughtfully and reasonably can to encourage the growth of his subordinates."

Development specialists agree that this does not mean that every boss must do all the training personally. In carrying out this responsibility, as in the case of other duties, the boss is a manager first and a direct worker second. He may, if he has the skills and the personality, directly coach and guide and teach his subordinates. If he is not a good teacher himself, he can call upon staff services for instructional assistance. He remains responsible, however, for seeing to it that needed services are provided. He is responsible for ensuring that his subordinates' jobs and assignments are such that they have opportunity to grow in them. He is responsible for motivating them toward growth. He is responsible, also, for setting an example that will help, or at any rate will not hinder, their development as competent managers.

Inevitably, every boss is responsible for these duties because in most cases he is in the best position to carry them out and in many cases he is the only man with the continuous influence over the subordinates necessary to carry them out effectively.

DEVELOPMENT IS A LONG-RANGE PROCESS

Development is a process of growth and change. No process occurs instantaneously; all occur over some period of time. The process of human change usually takes a fairly long period of time if the change is of any magnitude and if it is to persist.

It is true that some men seem to change very rapidly—to become new men overnight. But beneath the surface, masked by their customary behavior, the process of gradual change has been going on, preparing the way for the sudden appearance of new courses of action. Very few, if any, men can change appreciably overnight.

This has implications for management development programs and for the payoff that management can expect. When reliance has been placed upon training fads and quickie gimmicks to bring about substantial improvement in performance, rapid changes in behavior have sometimes been brought about. These, however, have usually proved to be merely temporary adaptive responses to the pressure for quick results. The men usually became their old selves, managing in their old ways, as soon as the pressure was off.

Most development specialists agree that the continued growth and development of a man as a manager is very like his growth as a boy. It is generally slow, often imperceptible, with occasional spurts of rapid development. A boy can't be made to mature faster. A parent or teacher can only attempt to motivate him toward wholesome growth, provide inspiration and example, insure his access to information and provide him with opportunities to explore his own abilities and to practice his skills. If a parent or teacher does this, most children will grow, slowly perhaps but steadily, toward maturity.

Development specialists believe that if a company does these things, it—like the parent or the teacher—can be confident that most of its managers will steadily develop ever-increasing managerial competence.

53 GETTING MANAGEMENT TRAINING TO PAY OFF*

Charles E. Watson

Over the past twenty-five years, the number of management training programs in government and business has increased enormously. As a result, many people have improved their knowledge and understanding of management. Unfortunately, many of the potential benefits these educational experiences can bring are never fully realized because the participants in management training courses and seminars frequently apply only a small part of their increased knowledge when they return to their jobs. One promising approach to overcoming this problem is a method of continuing—on the job—the learning begun in the formal training program. This approach consists of helping managers apply in their daily work the management theories and principles learned in the program.

The understanding and acceptance of management principles can be generally advanced to satisfactory levels during a formal training program, but the ability to be consistently successful in applying them typically cannot. It is extremely difficult for practicing managers to acquire the adequate skills and competence necessary to apply management theories and principles anywhere but on the job.

In this article several examples are presented of how first and second level supervisors of the Anaconda Company's mining and forest operations have learned to apply management principles on the job. After attending a management course, managers encounter problems when they attempt to apply on the job what they have recently learned. Brief descriptions of the typical problems are presented. Finally, useful methods for overcoming these problems are described and integrated to form a comprehensive system for helping practicing managers learn how to apply management theories. Although the illustrations presented here are of first and second level supervisors, the available evidence indicates that the same basic approach works for middle and executive level managers also.

THE PAYOFF: APPLYING PRINCIPLES

During a two-week supervisory management course in the Anaconda Company's western operations, each participant was given the assignment of identifying a problem, applying the appropriate principles and concepts learned at the course to solve it, and reporting on the results. Here are some examples from actual reports of how several of these supervisors were successful in applying what they had learned.

Clarence H. found that goal setting and motivation go hand in hand. When Clarence returned to work after participating in the first week of the supervisory management program, he began communicating the importance of goals to his people. He discussed how well his group had been reaching goals in the past and posted daily the goals for each day of the upcoming month.

At the end of the first day, his group produced 14 percent below the established goal of 17,000 board feet per shift, but the next few days showed improvement. On the last day of the first week, his men produced only 2.9 percent below the goal for that day. And then, halfway through the second week, his group surpassed their daily goal by 0.5 percent.

Clarence reported that goal setting lifted the morale and motivation of his people and increased their interest in production. Frequently they ask, "How are we doing? Are we going to make our target today?" Clarence believes that within a few more months his people will be ready and able to set their own production goals and suggest improvements in how to reach them more easily and economically.

* Reprinted by permission of the publisher from *Business Horizons,* vol. 17, no. 1, pp. 51–58 (February 1974). Mr. Watson is a faculty member in management and director of executive development programs, Temple University.

Ben P. applied the concepts of work planning, communications, motivation, and group participation in the overhaul of a Harnischfeger, Model 2100, 15 yard shovel. In his report Ben stated, "The whole principle of this project was to encourage everyone involved—salary bosses, five-day bosses, and the men—to work together to reach one goal—to overhaul the shovel in thirty-eight days."

Ben worked out an initial plan to overhaul the shovel using the Gantt Chart technique. He then gathered his people together to enlist their ideas and suggestions. He wrote, "I held a meeting with all of my bosses and explained the complete plan to them. They were not only very interested but volunteered all of their help and cooperation required in order to make the project succeed. Next, I called in the men who would be working on this project and explained the details of this plan to them. They were told that if they needed further information not to be afraid to come in and talk it over. It was quite surprising how the men took to this. When a question was raised, they came in and talked it over. As the project continued, the chart was plotted from day to day." Progress was reported to the men periodically, and meetings were held to discuss problems.

The results of Ben's approach were fantastic. The average down-time for overhauling this type of shovel had been sixty days. Ben's initial plan cut the time to thirty-eight days. Amazingly, his people beat this plan by eight days. Thus, Ben got the shovel back into operation in thirty days instead of the normal sixty. When operating at full capacity, this machine will dig an average of 12,000 to 16,000 tons of material per hour. Ben's efforts amounted to a savings of well over $90,000.

Jim F. was successful in helping two of his men who had excessive absences. One man had been absent for 51 out of the last 305 shifts, or about one day in six. Talking with each man privately, Jim started out by having them tell him about any of their personal problems that would cause them to be absent from work. He did not judge what they said by telling them their excuses were "no good." Rather, he let them tell him how they felt. Using communications skills, he allowed these men to express their feelings, and, by so doing, he conveyed his sincere interest in them.

After having had the opportunity to express their feelings, the men were ready to hear what Jim had to say. Jim calmly explained to each man the importance of his job. He showed them how they fitted into the operation and the important roles they played. Next, he turned to another important matter—money. Using simple arithmetic, Jim showed each man how much money they lost as a result of their absences. They were surprised.

Jim reported seventeen weeks later that their absences had fallen to only two to three days each over the past four months. He reinforced this good behavior by telling these men what the change has meant to them in terms of dollars and to the company in terms of production.

Jim B. was successful in orienting a new employee. Knowing that a new man was to be assigned to him, he prepared himself by reading over the recommended procedures for orientation. In the changehouse before work the next day, he introduced the new man to those with whom he would be working. Then, on the way to the job, he found out about the new man's background, including his past jobs and interests. Jim explained to the new man what he would be doing and how this work fitted into the overall mission.

Jim knew that there were too many new things for the man to learn in one day and that the first day for any new person is confusing. So Jim focused his efforts on reducing the new man's anxiety, giving him encouragement, and creating a climate where he would feel free to ask questions. Jim took several days for this, and followed up by asking the new man's coworkers how he was coming along. The results were as could be expected. The man fitted in well and has been doing a good job from the start.

Claude H. found that a good way to build motivation is to recognize good work. Claude was using a well-established principle from psychology—the law of effect. This is a principle formulated by Thorndike. It says, in part, that people will tend to continue to behave in those days in which they are rewarded.

One of the underground miners working for Claude had done an especially fine job of timbering, and Claude took the time to look over the work and compliment him on it. Claude reported that this individual really brightened up. He told Claude, "That's the first time anyone ever did that. Nobody ever cared before." Claude reported that the man's motivation and morale showed definite signs of improvement from that time on.

PROBLEMS OF APPLICATION

Unlike the performance of manual skills, the practice of management does not require precision in following rather specific, well-defined procedures. Instead, it involves the application of subtle, complex concepts and theories in real situations where psychological barriers and human factors are often present. If this were not the case, the teaching of management would be considerably easier and involve nothing more than having people learn to perform prescribed routines. Some of the most common reasons why the application of recently learned management theories and principles are so difficult are illustrated in the problems discussed below.

Identifying Applications When hearing or learning about management theories and principles, managers frequently ask, "Where can they be applied?" Although they can grasp a concept or theory, they often have difficulty in identifying the particular situations in their own work in which they should apply the knowledge they possess and understand. There are no simple solutions to this problem. Every situation is, to some extent, unique, and the particular circumstances surrounding it will determine when and how a theory or principle can be applied successfully.

Beyond the problem of determining when a principle should be applied in a particular situation lies another stumbling block. This is, how do you make a theory operational? What are the things you must do in the process of applying it? Participants in management training programs generally feel that time spent answering these questions is worthwhile.

Identifying Principles Another difficulty many managers have after completing a management course is to identify specific principles, theories, or concepts that were covered. At best, they can vaguely identify only a few. Their responses to the question, "What principles did you learn at the seminar that you can apply?" are usually broad, such as: "Managers should always be working toward goals, I should listen more, being tough isn't the best way to motivate people, and planning is important." If training is to cause changes in behavior, learners must know the specific theories and principles that they can and should apply. For this reason, it seems advisable to devote some portion of the formal training program to identifying the specific theories and principles covered.

Anyone planning and coordinating a management seminar should spend some time during the seminar and especially at its conclusion to obtain feedback from participants to discover how well they can identify the specific principles or generalizations covered. In most cases, the results from this exercise will be valuable aids for seminar leaders. They will be able to better understand the learning that has taken place, and they will be able to improve future seminars.

Lack of Drive, Understanding, Willingness The lack of drive and persistence to follow through and complete tasks is one of the most common human failings. The manager returning from a training program will have to overcome this tendency to procrastinate if he is to do a conscientious job of applying his newly acquired knowledge. In addition, he is faced with the distraction of everyday problems and concerns, which further distract and divert his attention and energies from systematically applying the theories he has recently learned.

Under pressure, people generally revert to working and coping with problems as they have in the past. It is generally when people are free from pressure or are completely convinced that their familiar methods for solving problems are not effective that they will experiment with new approaches.

An adequate level of understanding of theories and principles is necessary for their correct and successful application. Ideally, this is accomplished in the formal training program. However, this end might not be completely achieved for every principle which an individual might wish or need to apply. In these cases, or in situations where a person's understanding is dimmed over time, there should be a continuation of the learning program.

Some managers may be unwilling to implement recently learned management theories and principles because they lack the self-confidence needed to successfully apply these concepts. Others may be unwilling because they are not convinced that the theories and principles they learned will actually work. This is especially true if there is a conflict between the theories and the manager's values and attitudes. It is also true if these managers have been relatively successful in their jobs by using methods considerably different from the ones they have just learned.

Negative Attitudes The challenge posed by negative attitudes held by superiors, peers, subordinates, and even the learners themselves toward newly acquired knowledge and attempts at its application can be formidable. Negative attitudes often give rise to social pressure which can be an extremely strong force in controlling and modifying behavior. This type of social pressure can discourage or block a person's attempts to apply new ideas. Here are some of the more common ways in which negative attitudes toward a manager's application of newly acquired knowledge can arise:

Superiors and peers may develop negative attitudes toward a person's training if they feel that they have been ignored by higher management and will not have the same or similar opportunity to attend a training program.

Superiors might feel insecure if their subordinates have attended management development programs and they have not. In these situations, supervisors often feel that subordinates have learned about recently developed mangement theories and practices which they do not yet know.

Negative attitudes can also develop if those receiving the training return to work and openly discuss new ideas and concepts which superiors and peers neither understand nor agree with.

Subordinates of individuals who have attended a management training program might suspect that their bosses have learned devious ways to manipulate them. This can create negative attitudes which might be reflected in uncooperative behavior.

Subordinates can develop negative attitudes toward their boss if he attempts to apply his newly acquired knowledge too quickly or abruptly.

Obvious actual negative attitudes do occur, but they are not nearly so common as the imagined ones. In one Anaconda operation all first and second level supervisors (about 120) completed a two-week supervisory management course. Afterwards, a survey of the training's impact was conducted. In the course of the survey the remark, "I'd like to apply what we discussed but my boss keeps me from it," was encountered on numerous occasions. Each time, the speaker was asked, "Tell me, how does your boss prevent you from applying what you learned at the program?" Not a single one of the men interviewed had an answer. Most simply replied, "I don't know." Each was then asked, "Have you ever tried applying what you learned and found either direct or indirect disapproval from your boss?" None had.

One conclusion that might be drawn is that imagined disapproval from one's superior can be just as effective in modifying behavior as actual, outright disapproval. Subordinates, interested in building and preserving a favorable image of themselves in the boss's eyes, will often be sensitive to their superior's methods and opinions.

It is hard to believe that this conclusion fully explains the existence of imagined negative attitudes. Perhaps the men's statements claiming disapproval from superiors was an excuse for their lack of motivation to practice what they learned rather than an identification of an influence over which they had no control. Or it might be their own resistance to recently learned theories and principles. Some men, unable or unwilling to reject publicly the content of a training session, resist the actual application. They show their rejection to the idea by refusing to apply the learning. They say, "It's all theory. It won't work here."

Discouragement The skillful application of management theories and principles is not easy. Many repeated attempts at applying any particular theory or principle are often needed before mastery is reached. This can be discouraging in the early stages of learning and may even lead people to the incorrect conclusion that the principle failed because it is not valid. People returning from management training programs should be prepared to encounter initially only partial success at applying their new knowledge. Moreover, they should be prepared to overcome discouragement and to learn from their own mistakes.

A SYSTEM FOR TEACHING

One system which has been found successful for teaching application of management theory and principles consists of three distinct elements: formal seminar training, procedure to follow for applying principles on the job, and providing assistance and support to the managers. This system contains a variety of methods specifically aimed at overcoming the problems described in the previous section. It is also designed to provide a framework and climate to stimulate and promote ongoing learning and application of good management practices.

Formal Seminar Training The training seminar is the first step in this learning process. At the formal classroom seminar, participants not only learn about principles and theories, but also learn to accept and believe in them. For this to occur, the practical value of the theories and principles must be convincingly illustrated so that learners can accept them as being superior to their old methods of managing. In addition, the following should occur at the training seminar so that participants will be enabled to apply the concepts taught:

The teaching of each topic must contain illustrations, similar to the ones in this article, of how other managers have applied the concepts being taught.

Part of the formal seminar should include opportunities for participants to think about and discuss how they might apply the principles and theories. Participants should be permitted to practice applying their new knowledge in simulated exercises during the formal seminar.

Principles should be specifically identified. This can be done by the program coordinator, by the discussion leaders, or, better still, by the participants themselves. Suggestions and aids for on-the-job applications of each principle should be provided also. The list of principles and suggestions for their application (see the accompanying table) should be reproduced and distributed at the end of the formal program.

It should be emphasized that there are definite limits to which these guides can and should be relied upon. They should be presented and used only as suggestions and not as required prescriptions. Management is a complex process and should be understood as such by those who practice it. It cannot be boiled down to a set of tidy principles and corresponding easy-to-follow recipes. On the contrary, the application of management concepts and principles must be adjusted to fit the unique circumstances of every situation.

One of the objectives of any management training program should be to enable learners to bridge the gap between understanding the theory and its application in a wide variety of unique situations. Guides (such as the ones in this article) suggesting how to apply theories should not be set forth as the only way in which theories can be applied. It is unrealistic to suggest there is a best way to apply a concept or theory. Also, if guides are heavily relied upon, learners might be restricted in developing their ability to identify and understand unique parameters of given situations and in creatively developing appropriate approaches for implementing management theories. Rather, sugggestions for the application of management principles should be used to assist managers in their initial attempts to apply recently learned knowledge.

Management training opportunities should be periodically available to all who want them. No one should be left out. It is advisable that executives at or near the top levels of the organization participate first in formal training programs.

Applying Principles on the Job Beginning attempts at applying newly learned theories and principles will be more successful if the managers have a well-structured procedure to follow. This can provide helpful guidance and motivation by making the process easier and less confusing. One approach consists of an eight-step assignment. Part of any management training program should include this exercise:

- Identify a work problem to solve through the application of the appropriate principles and concepts covered in the formal management seminar.
- Report to the other participants at the seminar the work problem and the principles you intend to apply to solve it.
- Study the problem; define exactly what the problem is. Isolate and analyze its causes. Identify the appropriate principles to be used to solve it. Study these principles by reviewing your notes and readings. If your boss and/or peers are familiar with the principles, discuss with them the problem and the solution you have worked out.
- Plan the steps you will take to solve the problem.
- Execute the plan.
- Carefully observe and record the results.
- Analyze the results. Ask yourself what you learned from the assignment. What did you do well? What should you have done differently? How should you handle problems like this or apply this principle in the future?
- Prepare a report that describes your treatment of the project to be delivered to the seminar participants.

Assistance and Support Assistance and support consist of motivational incentives and methods for overcoming negative attitudes, forgetting, fear, and discouragement. Assistance and support from training and development specialists and from higher level managers help learners complete assignments and encourage continued efforts. This phase involves the following:

There should be recognition of and sympathy for the problems typically encountered by returning participants who will attempt to apply what they have learned. Near the conclusion of the formal program, these problems should be discussed so that the participants will be prepared to face them. These include the challenge to continue to learn about and to believe in the concepts and theories; the challenge of dealing with possible negative attitudes (real or imagined) of superiors, peers, and subordinates; and the challenge to live with and learn from failures.

The program participants should be encouraged to gather informally when they return to their jobs (at lunch, for example) to discuss problems, share experiences, and learn from

Principles and Suggestions for Application

PRINCIPLE

SETTING MANAGEMENT OBJECTIVES

Management should be goal-oriented. Without objectives there is no logical basis for actions. Therefore, objectives should be established.

SUGGESTIONS FOR APPLICATION

HOW TO ESTABLISH OBJECTIVES

- Identify the major missions of your organizational unit by identifying why it exists, the purpose it serves, and role it should play within the total organization.
- Identify each specific end result (future condition) which your organizational unit is responsible for accomplishing.
- Carefully think through each future condition which you would like to see prevail to see what these should be like.
- Describe each of these desired future conditions in writing. These should be:
- *Realistic*—A future condition that should logically be caused to exist by your organizational unit
- *Attainable*—Within reach but challenging
- *Specific*—Clear not confusing or ambiguous
- *Measurable*—Written in quantifiable terms or established professional standards.

PRINCIPLE

DECISION MAKING

To decide is to choose. But it is not easy to make the "best" choice. The best decision is the one that best serves to advance or achieve the goals of the organization. It is a choice that will bring the greatest profit, the highest productivity, the surest gain, and the least cost.

SUGGESTIONS FOR APPLICATION

HOW TO MAKE A DECISION

- Always keep the goals of your organization in mind when confronted with a decision, no matter how small.
- Try to develop all the possible alternative solutions, courses of action, and choices. If appropriate, seek assistance from your subordinates and peers.
- Identify the probable consequences for each alternative.
- Rank the probable consequences in the order of their desirability.
- Select the course of action that best serves to advance or achieve the goals of your organization as determined in step four.

PRINCIPLE

EMPLOYEE INDUCTION AND TRAINING

It is important that new employees be started off on the right foot. Their attitudes toward you, their work, and the company can go sour if they are not inducted properly and vice versa.

SUGGESTIONS FOR APPLICATION

HOW TO INDUCT A NEW EMPLOYEE

- Learn all you can about the new person, his skills, interests, experience, past work, and so on.
- Tell him what is expected—rules, policies, work expectations, standards, and so on.
- Tell him how his job fits into the overall operation and acquaint him with it. Stress the importance of his job.
- Assign a sponsor for the new person.
- Keep in close contact with the new person. Talk over his progress with him in a helpful way.
- Encourage him to talk about any problems he may have and do your best to see that they are solved.
- Deal with discipline problems before they become bad habits.
- Reduce the new person's anxiety by telling him his chances for being successful are quite good and encouraging him to ask questions.

PRINCIPLE

COUNSELING EMPLOYEES

Nondirective counseling can release potent forces of change within the individual who receives it.

SUGGESTIONS FOR APPLICATION

HOW TO COUNSEL AN EMPLOYEE

- Treat the other person with genuine kindness and respect.
- Be ready for the person to make unpleasant, confused statements or be reluctant to talk. Do not act startled at what you may hear.
- Listen for his feelings and attitudes in addition to his logic. Do not criticize or argue but be neutral. Do not agree or disagree.
- Try to feel like he feels. Reflect his feelings, not his logic, to his satisfaction. Do not try to reason with him or ask questions which are suspicious.

each other how and where principles can be applied.

To continually update their knowledge, people should have periodic opportunities to attend training programs and seminars of their choice.

Through coaching and counseling, training managers, personnel managers, and bosses should help learners carry out the application assignment and the continued systematic application of principles.

Top management should be aware of the assignment to apply principles and should communicate its support of this exercise.

Success stories, such as the ones at the beginning of this article, should be written, based on reports generated. These can be reproduced and distributed, printed in house organs, or included in management newsletters.

Top management should recognize outstanding successes, perhaps by writing letters of congratulation. A recognition dinner may even be held once a year to honor the most outstanding successes of the participating managers.

Training programs provide immediate and tangible benefits when they include on-the-job application of management principles and theories and when they receive strong support from top management. The specific methods for doing this, as described in this article, have been successfully applied in industry.

Moreover, this approach to training has become popular in a few company training programs and in university executive development programs. CPC International, Inc. now includes the teaching of applying principles by having the participants in their middle management program follow the eight step application assignment. The University of Illinois' Executive Development Program and Temple University's program also have similar assignments for their participants.

54 T-GROUP TRAINING: GOOD OR BAD?*

Robert J. House

T-Group training, perhaps one of the most discussed innovations in management development today, is a technique that has its foundation in the discipline of social psychology and, more specifically, the study of group behavior, technically referred to as group dynamics. T-Group training is really only one aspect of the whole field of sensitivity training. However, it happens to be one area of training in which a great deal of social science research and evidence is now being produced. It is the purpose of this article to review the results of research on T-Group training, advance several conclusions based on the evidence, and raise several questions for consideration by the practicing manager.

For the purposes of this article, the definition of Laboratory Training advanced by Paul Buchanan will be used. Buchanan defines Laboratory Training (T-Group Training is synonymous with Laboratory Training) as follows:

> Laboratory Training methods have in common the attempt to use behavioral science concepts (personality theory, group dynamics, organizational and social change theory, and learning theory) by applying them in the design and conduct of experiences which the laboratory participant undergoes. This is in contrast to other methods which rely more on 'practical sense' theory, or on other-than-experimental means of utilizing concepts, such as group discussions, lectures, case methods, etc.
>
> Training approaches meriting the name of laboratory utilize: (a) a face-to-face, largely unstructured group as a primary vehicle for learning (some variation of the "T-Group"); (b) planned activities involving interaction between individuals and/or between groups; (c) systematic and frequent feedback and analysis of information regarding what happened in the here-and-now and what effect it had; (d) dilemmas or problems for which 'old ways' of behaving for most of the participants do not provide effective courses of action (and thus for which innovative or 'search behavior' is required); and (e) generalization, or reformulation, of concepts and values based upon the analysis of direct experiences.
>
> A second way in which training laboratories differ is in the strategy of their use. In some, the goal is development of the participant as a person—to help him become more mature and to enhance his ability to act effectively and with satisfaction in concert with others.... In other laboratories, the concern is to help the participants become more effective in their work in a given organization—as when a person's attendance is sponsored by his organization... or when a company conducts a laboratory as part of its management-development program. ... In still others, the concern is to facilitate the development or improvement of an intact organization or major unit thereof, as when a laboratory is used as one phase in an organization development.[1]

THE RECENT CONTROVERSY

In recent years, controversy has developed concerning T-Group training. This controversy has resulted partially from the fact that the people involved come from different schools of thought with different training, and therefore hold different biases, and also partially because these people have witnessed different events resulting from their own T-Group or Laboratory Training experiences.

The most well-known figures involved in the T-Group controversy are George Odiorne of the University of Michigan and Chris Argyris of Yale University. The two debated the problem at a Cornell University conference conducted in 1963. Odiorne stated that T-Group training is not training, since the objectives and process have not been well-defined, are not

* Reprinted by permission of the publisher from *Business Horizons*, vol. 12, no. 6, pp. 69–78, December, 1969. Mr. House is professor of management of the Bernard M. Baruch College of the City University of New York.

[1] P. C. Buchanan, unpublished paper presented at a seminar on "Applying the Behavioral Sciences to Management Skills," American Management Association, New York City, Feb. 24–26, 1964.

well understood as yet, and are not within the control of the instructor. The implication was that the feedback process—the critical analysis of each other's behavior that goes on within the T-Group—sometimes gets out of control. It was also implied that this process becomes harmful to some of the individuals. A second criticism advanced by Odiorne was that the process has been known to result in serious mental disturbances to the participant; Odiorne reported having witnessed such a disturbance as a result of participation in a T-Group.

In rebuttal, Argyris stated that only four nervous breakdowns have occurred among 10,000 students, and that "all of these people had previous psychiatric histories." He stated further that "a trainer can only go so far in preventing destructive experience"; the important thing is that people in T-Group training "Can decide how much they want to pay psychically" for what they are learning.

T-Group training is defended on the grounds that it is not psychotherapy, though it does aim to change behavior. It is only fair to recognize that many T-Group training proponents, including Argyris, have conducted a substantial amount of research in the field to test their own assumptions and hypotheses. Some of this research has resulted in less than what they would like. It is to their credit that they have continued to publish their findings, criticize their own efforts, and revise their own procedures and position on the issues.

Recently, Argyris wrote: "In recent years, there has evolved a new way of helping executives develop new inner resources which enable them to mitigate . . . organizational ills." Here he is referring to such ills as:

A tendency for dynamic, flexible, and enthusiastic teams to become sluggish

The loss of intrinsic challenge of executive's work, overtime, and the tendency to become motivated largely by wages and executive bonus plans

The tendency for executive conformity as companies grow older and bigger. The tendency for executives to resist saying what they truly believe—even when it is in the best interest of the company

The difficulty in developing a top management team that is consistently innovating and taking risks

The belief that we get things done only when we create crises, check details, arouse fears, and penalize and reward in ways that inadvertently create 'heroes' and 'bums' among our executive group.

For the solution of these ills and this dilemma, Argyris recommended T-Group training and published a claim to a successful T-Group training experience which he conducted and researched.[2]

SIGNIFICANCE OF THE CONTROVERSY

There appear to be three important reasons why this controversy is significant for students and practitioners in the field of management. First, a tremendous amount of resources is currently being allocated to T-Groups. For example, several graduate schools of business are now including this training as an important part of the total curriculum, both in their graduate programs and in their advanced management programs for practicing executives. As of 1963, Mathew Miles reports that 4,000 people had attended T-Group training programs sponsored by the National Training Laboratories, that approximately 900 persons attend NTL labs each year, and that several large organizations sponsor their own laboratories in the United States and in as many as eleven other nations.[3] Recently, the American Management Association inaugurated and is conducting T-Group training on a rather large scale. Several universities require business students to attend a session as part of their academic work, and several universities include the experience in their management-development programs. A recent survey of the nation's largest firms disclosed that 35 percent send executives to T-Group programs.[4]

A second reason concerns the alleged psychological damage. Although there is little evidence of such damage reported in the literature, there seems to be some reason to believe this damage is possible as a result of the nature of the T-Group itself and the properties that it intentionally brings into being and causes to react. This reason will be discussed in more detail later in this article.

The third reason why the controversy is significant is that it concerns matters of professional ethics. Opponents of the movement argue that since validity of the method has not

[2] Chris Argyris, "T-Group Training for Organizational Effectiveness," *The Harvard Business Review* (March–April, 1964), p. 60.

[3] M. B. Miles, "Human Relations Training: Current Status," in I. R. Weschler and E. H. Schein (eds.), *Issues in Training* (Washington: The National Training Laboratories, National Education Association, 1962).

[4] H. Rush and W. Wikstrom, "The Reception of Behavioral Science in Industry," *The Conference Board Record* (September, 1969), pp. 15–54.

been demonstrated, and since the possible damages could be severe, it is unethical to offer T-Group training on a commercial basis, and to make claims that it will result in greater awareness of oneself, greater sensitivity to the needs of others, and, in general, improved human relations and management practices. The opponents further argue that the training is a form of manipulation involving a methodology which is an invasion of personal privacy and not the proper concern of employer-employee relations or of consulting firms, business schools, or management scholars.

To date, approximately one hundred different research studies have been concerned with what happens during and after participation in T-Group programs. Many of these studies are based on anecdotal evidence such as post-training reports of participants for which there is little confirmation. Approximately thirty of the studies meet the minimum requirements for acceptable social science research acceptability.[5] The requirements are these:

> The study must be based on tests of hypotheses and criteria stated before conducting the experiment.
>
> The study must be expressed in some quantitative assessment, such as statistical significance measures, scaled results, or straight count of the incidents reported.
>
> The variables studied must be isolated through the use of statistical or experimental controls or else verified by replication in several studies.

To help clarify the issue and to provide a basis on which one might evaluate the pros and cons, the studies that meet these requirements will be reviewed. Using these rather rigorous criteria for the admission of evidence, we immediately eliminate anecdotal evidence, such as self-reports of participants, or post-training reactions of participants which are likely to be biased by selective perception (the eye of the beholder), or selective recall that cannot be confirmed or denied.

The following sections deal with two major questions: first, what happens to the participant throughout the T-Group training experience? second, what effect does the training have on the participants when they return to their work environment?

STUDY RESULTS

Four studies that meet the above criteria of evidence are relevant to the first question.[6] These studies are based primarily on diaries mantained by people in the T-Group or intermittent samplings of participant opinions and observations throughout the process. The participants reported their experiences and in some way gave quantitative evidence (accounts of their significant experiences) as to whether they were going through happy, satisfying experiences, or anxious, unsettiing, and traumatic periods. Although these studies lack rigor in some respect and are therefore subject to some question, there is a great deal of consistency among their findings. These studies strongly suggest that people almost inevitably experience high levels of anxiety as a result of the T-Group during the middle of the process, and that they get unsettled and uncomfortable about their own opinions and the comments made to them by others. As the experience continues, this anxiety recedes. If we were to chart these findings on a conceptual graph, all the data follow the same pattern in that anxiety rises during the middle of the T-Group and then declines.

This is not surprising, and few T-Group proponents would disclaim this or state that it is either unexpected or undesirable. For example, Burke and Bennis state in a review of some of the theoretical issues involved in T-Group training that:

> The usual factors we associate with organization life are conspicuously absent at the outset of the T-Group. . . . It is hoped that this ambiguous and anxiety-producing situation will create an atmosphere in which the individuals can identify and consciously diagnose the interpersonal and group problems which emerge, as

[5] For technical reports of these studies see: J. P. Campbell and M. D. Dunnette, "Effectiveness of T-Group Experience in Managerial Training and Development," *Psychological Bulletin*, VII (August, 1968), pp. 73–104. and R. J. House, "T Group Education and Leadership Effectiveness: a Review of the Empiric Literature and a Critical Evaluation," *Personnel Psychology*, XXII (Spring, 1967), pp. 1–32. Also see a bibliography of research reported in *Explorations in Applied Behavioral Science* (New York: Institute of Applied Behavioral Science, 1967).

[6] These studies are: Bradford and Mallison, reported by L. P. Bradford in *Exploration in Human Relations Training* (Washington: National Education Association, 1953); D. Stock and H. A. Thelan, "Changes in Work and Emotionality During Group Growth," *Emotional Dynamics and Group Culture* (Washington: National Training Laboratories, 1957, August, 1968); R. Tannenbaum, I. R. Weschler and F. Massarik, *Leadership and Organization* (New York: McGraw-Hill Book Company, 1961); B. M. Bass, "Mood Changes During a Management Training Laboratory," *Journal of Applied Psychology*, XLVI (1962), pp. 361–64.

well as gain deeper understanding of their own reactions toward authority figures, colleagues, needs for controls, intimacy, belonging, etc.[7]

Thus we see that anxiety is deliberately introduced into the T-Group session as a means of stimulating emotional learning as opposed to intellectual learning. The findings suggest that the deliberate induction of anxiety bears the results desired, at least during the process. Knowing this, we might now ask, "What happens to the participant when he returns to the job?"

Twenty-one studies concerned with changes in participant behavior, perceptions, attitudes, or personality meet the criteria of acceptability stated above. Of these studies, nine deal with measurement of the effect of T-Group training on managerial behavior in the post-training job situation. All nine were conducted with acceptable rigor, employing scaled measures of results and control groups to isolate the effect of training. Furthermore, all are based upon changes which the participants have made in their own behavior as judged by their subordinates. These studies lend strong support to the proposition that T-Group training is capable of bringing about changes in job behavior. Four of these studies demonstrate positive effects of T-Group training; four demonstrate both positive effects and undesirable effects; and one study shows no measurable change.[8]

The remaining twelve studies that meet the above criteria of evidence concern the effect of T-Group training on the perceptions, attitudes, subjective opinions, and personality characteristics and behavior in training tasks rather than the job behavior. Seven studies reveal the intended effect of training, four reveal no measurable effect, and one reveals a negative effect.[9]

From these studies, the following conclusions seem apparent:

- T-Group training is not only capable of inducing anxiety, but very likely to do so.
- The anxiety may have an unrewarding effect, such as causing the people to be highly frustrated, unsettled, and upset.
- It can also have the intended effect of helping people to be more considerate of subordinates and less dependent on other people in the organization, causing them to demand less dependence from other persons, and be more sensitive, better communicators, and better listeners.

[7] H. L. Burke and W. G. Bennis, "Changes in Perception of Self and Others During Human Relations Training," *Human Relations*, XIV (1961).

[8] The four demonstrating positive effects are: Chris Argyris, "Explorations in Interpersonal Competence—I," *Journal of Applied Behavioral Science*, I (1965), pp. 58–63, and Chris Argyris, *Organization and Innovation* (Homewood, Ill.: Richard D. Irwin, 1965); M. B. Miles, "Human Relations Training: Processes and Outcomes," *Journal of Counseling Psychology*, VII (1960), pp. 301–306; M. B. Miles, "Changes During and Following Laboratory Training," *Journal of Applied Behavioral Science*, I (1965), pp. 215–45.

The four describing both positive and undesirable effects are: W. J. Underwood, "Evaluation of Laboratory Method Training," *Journal of the American Society of Training Directors*, XIX (1965), pp. 35–40; study by Boyd and Eliss, reported in P. C. Buchanan, "Applying the Behavioral Sciences to Management Skills"; J. R. Gibb and J. M. Allen, "Experimental Comparison of Two Methods of Management Training," unpublished (mimeographed); and D. R. Bunker, "Individual Applications of Laboratory Training," *Journal of Applied Behavioral Science*, I (1965), pp. 131–48.

The one study showing no individual change was N. L. Gage and R. V. Exline, "Social Perception and Effectiveness in Discussion Groups," *Human Relations*, VI (1953), pp. 381–96.

[9] The studies revealing the intended effect are: H. L. Burke and W. G. Bennis, "Changes in Perception of Self and Others During Human Relations Training," *Human Relations*, XIV (1961); B. M. Bass, "Reactions to Twelve Angry Men as a Measure of Sensitivity Training," *Journal of Applied Psychology*, V (1962); P. S. Smith, "Attitude Changes Associated With Training in Human Relations," *British Journal of Social and Clinical Psychology*, II (1964), pp. 101–12; D. R. Bunker and E. S. Knowles, "Comparison of Behavioral Changes Resulting From Human Relations Laboratories of Different Lengths," *Journal of Applied Behavioral Science*, XXX (1967), pp. 505–23; R. Harrison and B. Oshry, "The Impact of Laboratory Training on Organizational Behavior: Methodology and Results," unpublished manuscript, National Training Laboratories, Washington, D. C., 1969; M. B. Miles, "Learning Processes and Outcomes in Human Relations Training: a Clinical-Experimental Study," in E. Schein and W. Bennis (eds.), *Personal and Organizational Change Through Group Methods* (New York: John Wiley & Sons, Inc., 1965), pp. 244–54; and W. W. Sikes, "A Study of Some Effects of a Human Relations Training Laboratory," unpublished doctoral dissertation, Purdue University, 1964.

Studies showing no measureable effect are: chapter by R. Harrison in Chris Argyris, *Interpersonal Competence and Organizational Behavior* (Homewood, Ill.: Richard D. Irwin, 1962); study of Massarik and Carlson reported by M. D. Dunnette, in P. R. Farnsworth (ed.), *Annual Review of Psychology* (1962), p. 285; J. Kernan, "Laboratory Human Relations Training—Its Effects on the 'Personality' of Supervisory Engineers," unpublished Ph.D. dissertation, Department of Psychology, New York University, 1963; N. D. Bowers and R. S. Soar, "Evaluation of Laboratory Human Relations Training for Classroom Teachers," U. S. Office of Education, Contract No. 8143 (Columbia: University of South Carolina, 1961).

The one study revealing a negative effect is S. Deep, B. M. Bass, and J. A. Vaughan, "Some Effects of Business Training on Previous Quasi T-Group Affiliations," Tech. Report 12, O. N. R. (Pittsburgh: Management Research Center, University of Pittsburgh, 1966).

QUESTIONS FOR THE MANAGER

In light of the above evidence, we might ask some questions pertinent to the practice of personnel management or to the practice of top management when faced with the questions: should we use T-Group training? Following are seven questions intended to help the manager decide whether this kind of training is appropriate for him or members of his organization. These questions are grouped into two categories: those concerning effective use of T-Groups and those concerning ethical issues.

Questions Concerning Effective Use The following four questions are intended to guide the manager in determining whether T-Group training is appropriate for his particular circumstances.

Question 1. Are the changes that an effective T-Group is likely to produce the ones that are needed in the organization to improve managerial performance?

We have seen that T-Group training can result in better listening, more supportive behavior, more considerate managers, more sensitive people, and less need for dependence. Research indicates that these values are associated wtih effective managerial performance for certain kinds of organizations and certain kinds of subordinates. There is evidence that these values, however, do not always lead to more effective organizational performance. For example, one might ask whether combat sergeants should have these characteristics to effectively command in the field? We know from a vast amount of evidence that there are situational factors which determine the kind of leadership and followership required.

Fundamental to the determination of effective leadership practices are the immediate superior of the leader, the expectations, attitudes, and abilities of the followers, and the nature of the organization in which the leadership is to be exercised. Studies by the Ohio State Leadership Group and the University of Michigan Institute of Social Research, to name only a few, demonstrate that sensitivity is only one of the many variables which determine leadership effectiveness, and this characteristic is by no means universal.[10] In regard to this point, Warren Bennis, a proponent of T-Group training, states that:

> It is not possible at this point to be certain whether these new organizational values lead to improved performance. . . . for example, these new change-induction processes emphasize openness rather than secrecy, superior-subordinate collaboration rather than dependency or rebellion, internal rather than external commitment, team leadership rather than a one-to-one vertical relationship, authentic relationships rather than direction or coercion, and so on. What then happens to status or power? What about those individuals who have a low need for participation and/or a high need for structure and independence? And, what about those personal needs which seem to be incompatible with these models, such as a high need for power or aggression? In short, what about those needs which can be expressed and best realized in a bureaucratic mechanism? Are these people expected to be changed through some transformation of needs, or are they expected to yield to a concept of human nature incompatible with their own needs?[11]

Thus, while T-Group training is a powerful tool for inducing change, the change may be either beneficial or detrimental to both the organization and the individuals involved. If we make a few members of an organization independent and considerate and they return to an organization which does not reward independent and considerate behavior, what would happen to these people? Will they be more or less effective, satisfied, and accepted?

Question 2. Can the organization tolerate the change in the individual if the T-Group is successful?

A likely result of a successful T-Group experience is that the participants develop new role definitions and individual expectations. It seems that the assumption that the resulting change will always be tolerated by the organization and beneficial under these circumstances requires some consideration.

Management training has been found to cause changes in attitudes and perceptions that were incongruent with the attitudes and perceptions of superiors and other members of the participant's organization. Both conventional training methods and T-Group training have induced changes which resulted in role conflict for the subordinate and undesirable consequences for the organization, such as loss of key personnel or the need to demote key

[10] Ohio State Leadership Group—C. L. Shartle, *Executive Performance and Leadership* (Englewood: Prentice-Hall, Inc., 1956).
University of Michigan Institute of Social Research —Martin Patchen, "Supervisory Methods and Group Performance," *Administrative Science Quarterly*, VII (December, 1962); D. C. Pels, "Leadership Within a Hierarchical Organization," *Journal of Social Issues*, VII, No. 3 (1951); V. Vroom, *Some Personality Determinants of the Effects of Participation* (New York: McGraw-Hill Book Company, 1961).

[11] W. C. Bennis, "Bureaucracy and Social Change: an Anatomy of a Failure," *Human Organization* (Special monograph series: Fall, 1963).

personnel.[12] For example, Buchanan reported that "less than a year after [the T-Group training study was conducted] the program was discontinued, the head of the department was replaced, and the organization development staff [T-Group trainers] accepted jobs in other companies. Why? So far as could be determined, it was because the style of management and the approach to problems which were emerging from the development effort came into conflict with that practiced at higher levels of the company."

Question 3. Can the candidate tolerate the anxiety involved in the process?

Here we must consider the fact that we are dealing with people who have gone through the adjustment processes involved in adolescence and early adulthood, and are already settled in their ways. They have well-established behavior patterns, habits, responses, values, emotional reactions, and defense mechanisms, all of which have now become meaningful to them, and which allow them to operate in their own environment. The T-Group experience is a very soul-searching process; it requires the individual to become introspective, to look at his own values and his own emotions, to ask himself whether and why he likes them, and whether he wishes to live the way he has.

After a person is established in his way of life, two things must be considered: first does he have the general ability to tolerate the anxiety involved in this kind of soul-searching? second, is he at this time going through some other stress experience, such as adjusting to the change in life on the part of himself or other members of his family or meeting difficult financial obligations? To prevent avoidable emotional disturbances, it is recommended that admission to a T-Group should be based on careful screening designed to ensure that the participants are able to withstand and profit from the anxiety induced in the process.[13]

Question 4. What are the credentials of the trainers? Perhaps this question should be restated. Is the person who leads the T-Group qualified to conduct group emotional-learning processes (as opposed to cognitive learning)?

As mentioned previously, many of the T-Group properties deal with complex psychological and sociological variables. The group is designed to induce anxieties and to stimulate interpersonal feedback, introspection, and self-evaluation. Although some may claim that the process is not therapeutic, within the latitude of group emphasis are methods which closely approximate methods utilized in overtly therapeutic practice. This being the case, it seems imperative (at least to the writer) that T-Group leaders have psychological training equivalent to that required for professional clinical practice.

The question of trainer qualifications is of concern because today there are training directors, personnel managers, business consultants, and members of business school faculties who have no formal psychological training and who are engaged in conducting T-Groups. Are these people not going beyond the area in which they were trained and might they not induce anxieties or problems which they are not qualified to treat?

Questions Concerning Ethical Issues The questions raised so far are not easy to answer, and depend on some knowledge of the candidate, some knowledge of the organization, the kind of behavior desired of the manager, and how much behavioral change the organization can tolerate. Although these are difficult questions, continued research may eventually yield quite conclusive answers.

There is yet another set of questions which will not be answered on the basis of factual information alone, because they deal with ethical values and questions of the manager's respect, responsibility, and authority for the personal well-being and privacy of his subordinates. These questions are offered here with the recognition that there is room for disagreement among both reasonable and sincere men.

Question 5. Is it within management's prerogative to direct an employee to attend a T-Group?

Many proponents of the method argue that it is not therapy, and many opponents claim that it is. However, it is clear that it at least involves some of the properties of psychotherapy, namely, induced anxiety, interpersonal feedback, introspection, and self-reevaluation. Should a manager assume the authority to order people to engage in a soul-searching process which involves interpersonal feedback and which requires him to undergo introspection under conditions of induced anxiety? It is recommended not only that precautions be

[12] See, for example, studies by J. A. M. Sykes, "The Effects of a Supervisory Training Course in Changing Supervisor's Perceptions and Expectations of the Role of Management," *Human Relations* (1962), and E. A. Fleishman, E. Harris, and H. Burtt, *Leadership and Supervision in Industry* (Monograph 33; Columbus: The Ohio State University, Bureau of Educational Research, 1955).

[13] Only recently has research suggested the participant characteristics that permit a fruitful T-Group experience. For a study concerning these characteristics, see B. J. Oshry and R. Harrison, "Transfer From Here-and-Now to There-and-Then," *Journal of Applied Behavioral Science*, II (1966), pp. 185–98.

For an opinion on participant requirements see *Interpersonal Competence and Organizational Behavior.*

taken to screen out those who are likely to be seriously disturbed by the experience in the first place, but that entry should be strictly voluntary, since what will be discussed in the group is a matter of personal feelings (and perhaps personal problems).

Let us restate this question: may the manager ethically order (or subtly suggest) that people who work for him and depend on him or the organization for their livelihood engage in this kind of activity, or must participation be strictly voluntary? How is such suggestion or direction different from ordering an employee to undergo treatment from a company-paid psychologist or psychiatrist? Certainly psychological treatment may be warranted, but should not the choice to accept such treatment be left to the individual if it is not to be an invasion of privacy, and if it is to be consistent with the values of free choice, on which our political and economic systems rest?

Question 6. If it is concluded that it is not within management's prerogative to order a person to attend T-Group training, one can ask: what are the conditions required to ensure that attendance is made on a strictly voluntary basis? If no superior suggests it to him, attendance could become strictly voluntary. On the other hand, if the personnel manager, the representative of management, or his superior, suggests that the employee attend such a training session, and even if they tell him he should exercise his own choice as to whether or not he will attend, the suggestion may be well interpreted as a subtle order.

Because the organization possesses the power to reward and punish its employees, and because the man is dependent upon the organization, he may think he must attend; therefore, the element of coercion is a possibility. If people volunteer to go to a T-Group, there is less of an ethical problem, but can a superior suggest attendance to the individual and be sure that it is strictly voluntary?

Question 7. Can "organizational family" T-Groups be called voluntary? It is not uncommon practice in industry today to have sessions for entire departments or organizational units. Under these circumstances, it can hardly be said that attendance is voluntary. If a man and all of his subordinates are scheduled to go to a T-Group, anyone who declines to go is declining under some coercion. First, there is usually pressure for social conformity within organizations; second, his boss sets an example by attending; and third, the T-Group is sponsored by the organization.

The choice to attend or not to attend is made by top management and enforced both by the social pressures of the managerial group and the reward and punishment system of the organization. To expect one to refuse to attend any series of meetings suggested and paid for by the top management of the firm seems to ignore almost all of what we know about social persuasion.

RECOMMENDATIONS

It seems clear that T-Group training is a powerful tool for changing behavior. Such changes may be beneficial to both individual and organization alike, or they may be detrimental to both, depending on the circumstances. Therefore, it is recommended that it be offered under conditions that minimize risk of harm to the individual and on terms that make attendance strictly voluntary.

To accomplish this, the following practices are recommended:

- *Careful selection of participants* to ensure those admitted do not have psychiatric case histories, symptoms of emotional instability, and low tolerance of anxiety.
- *Careful study of performance requirements* before choosing to use T-Group training to ensure that the changes induced are changes required for effective performance and changes which the organization will support when the individual returns to the job.
- *Careful selection of the T-Group leader* to ensure that he has adequate training to conduct group emotional-learning sessions which deliberately induce anxiety, interpersonal feedback, intrapersonal introspection, and experimentation with new methods of behavior.
- *Continued research to determine the participants' characteristics and conditions required* for using T-Group training to bring about individual and organization improvement.
- *Careful explanation to those selected for participation* of the goals and the process of training, in order to allow withdrawal of any individual who prefers not to invest psychically in the program, and to provide a mental framework that will facilitate the learning process of those who attend.
- *Provision of reserve precautionary procedures* to be instituted in the event that a program, once begun, fails to fulfill the expectations of either the organization or members of the group. Such precautions would include alternative methods for accomplishing the desired changes, as well as provisions for the safety and well-being of individuals enrolled in an organization-sponsored program of behavioral training.

55 ORGANIZATIONAL DEVELOPMENT—SOME ISSUES AND CHALLENGES*

Anthony P. Raia

A growing body of knowledge has evolved in the last decade. It concerns the ways in which organizations can better adapt to the challenges of a modern society, with its new values, new technologies, and increasing rate of change. This new and rapidly evolving discipline has been labelled **organizational development.** OD focuses on innovation and planned change in organizations. Its technology consists of an increasing body of knowledge, methods, and techniques derived primarily from the applied behavioral sciences. Because organizational development is a relatively new discipline, its form and potentiality have not yet been clearly identified. The problem is further complicated by the wide variety of OD approaches and activities, ranging from "canned" techniques to highly creative programs and strategies.[1]

A number of authors have attempted to define the field of organizational development in operational terms. Warren Bennis, for example, describes OD as "a response to change, a complex educational strategy intended to change the beliefs, attitudes, values, and structure of organizations so that they can better adapt to new technologies, markets, and challenges, and the dizzying rate of change itself."[2] When viewed as an educational strategy, the technology of organizational development generally evolves around the use of laboratory method to bring about cultural or climate change. Richard Beckhard provides a somewhat broader view of OD as a change strategy which is "(1) *planned,* (2) *organization-wide,* (3) *managed* from the top, to (4) increase *organization effectiveness* and *health* through (5) *planned interventions* in the organization's *processes,* using *behavioral-science* knowledge."[3] The planned interventions, regardless of the technology used, generally result from an action research process which involves the generation and collection of data, their feedback to the client-system, and sound organizational diagnosis. Still another dimension is added by Wendell French, who describes OD as "a long-range effort to improve an organization's problem solving capabilities and its ability to cope with changes in its external environment with the help of external or internal behavioral-scientist consultants, or change agents, as they are sometimes called."[4] The use of third parties to facilitate organizational learning and change is an important aspect of many existing programs. It is important to note at this point that most OD consultants are behavioral scientists who share a philosophy and common set of values concerning the nature of man and the quality of life in organizations.

The emphasis of organizational development, then, is on planned change and is generally directed toward improving system effectiveness. In addition to learning new ways of dealing with complex internal and external relationships, the organization also learns to view change as a natural rather than an extraordinary phenomenon. Most efforts involve the use of consultants who work in an action research mode to guide and facilitate the process of change. Consequently, OD strategies and programs are usually based upon a set of assumptions and values concerning man in organizations which have a "humanistic" quality to them.[5] The impact of these underlying values cannot be underestimated. They determine not only the nature of programs, but the kinds of data collected, the techniques for their collecting, and the nature of the planned change interventions into the organization's processes. In short, humanistic values provide the basis, guidelines, and directions for *what* will be undertaken in an organizational development effort and *how* the program will evolve and be sustained.

The number of organizations engaged in OD activities is increasing at an accelerating rate.

* Reproduced by permission from the *California Management Review,* vol. 14, no. 4, pp. 13–20 (Summer, 1972). Copyright 1972 by the Regents of the University of California. Mr. Raia is professor of management, University of California, Los Angeles.

Business firms, school systems, government agencies, religious institutions, and a variety of other large and small organizations, both here and abroad, have become involved in organizational development to some degree. The widespread use of OD programs and techniques has brought to the surface a number of significant issues and unsolved problems. Several of them are perhaps characteristic of any new and emerging discipline. Others, however, appear to be unique to the field. Dealt with here are some of the major issues and challenges confronting the theory and practice of organizational development today. For present purposes they are discussed around five major themes:

- the use of laboratory method
- the need for professionalism in the field
- the use of OD consultants
- the overemphasis on personal-cultural change
- the limitation of OD technology and models of change to hierarchical systems.

THE USE OF LABORATORY METHOD

One of the most controversial issues in the field of organizational development evolves around the use of laboratory method, frequently called sensitivity training or T-Groups. Its opponents charge that sensitivity training in management education is at best inconsistent with the business world in which we live. Some fear that its use in organizations constitutes an invasion of privacy, or worse, that participation in T-Groups can result in serious psychological damage to the individual.[6] Charges such as these have raised a number of ethical questions for the practice of management. Despite the controversy, however, the use of laboratory method in management training and organizational development appears to be growing at an increasing rate.

Laboratory training, one among many possible OD interventions, generally reflects only *part* of the overall strategy for change in an organization. Lab interventions may be used in a wide variety of ways and for a number of different reasons. For example, stranger labs (participants from different organizations) may be used to "seed" the organization with the kinds of values and behavioral norms that help pave the way for team-building and other types of interventions. Cousin labs (participants from the same organization, but not the same work group) may be used to begin changing the organization climate and culture. Family labs (participants from the same work group) may be used to change group values and norms, as well as to improve group effectiveness. In any event, the use of laboratory training in organizational development requires *both* pre-lab and post-lab activities to ensure that the learning is organizationally relevant and to facilitate its transfer to work environment.[7]

A number of important distinctions need to be made between sensitivity training per se and the use of laboratory method in organizational development. It may be useful to compare them along a number of different dimensions—the participants, the group, and the activity itself:

The Participants Voluntary participation is one of the distinguishing characteristics of T-Groups. Individual members are generally free to decide for themselves, first, if they want to participate and, second, the level and extent of their participation. When used as an OD intervention, however, there may be some real question about participation being voluntary or not. Another difference evolves around expectations and behavior. Since participation in T-Groups is normally voluntary, both the expectations and behavior of members are more apt to be consistent with the values and goals of sensitivity training. This may not obtain when it is used in organizational development. The expectations and behavior of members generally reflect organization values and norms which, more often than not, may be in direct conflict with T-Group values and goals. A final distinction evolves around the element of risk. Participants in stranger labs, for example, can afford to be more open and confronting since they may have less to lose than participants in either cousin or family labs.

The Group There are a number of significant differences along this dimension. Perhaps most important is the fact that T-Groups are generally unstructured and have no previous history together. Variables such as group culture, values, norms, structure, and processes are actually established by the group during the training sessions. In most OD efforts, however, these variables are changed by the work group. Both the structure and the history of the group must be dealt with. The group (or team) is generally structured in terms of authority, power, or status; functional and role relationships exist; group processes have been internalized; distinctive group values and norms have been established. While sensitivity training attempts to *build* these group variables, organizational development attempts to *change* them. There is another important difference: T-Groups tend to be temporary systems. Participants can more easily deal with issues in the here and now. Organization groups, on the other hand, are more permanent. Members have considerably more concern for both the past and the future. They are more apt to deal with issues in the there and then. And finally, laboratory training as such involves small groups and deals primarily with interpersonal relationships within that group. In organizational development, however, laboratory training involves much larger and more complex systems and is concerned with intergroup as well as intragroup relationships.

The Activity There are also a number of significant differences in terms of learning goals and the laboratory activity itself. Sensitivity training is aimed at changing individual behavior. The focus is on developing interpersonal skill through greater awareness of self and others. In organizational development, on the other hand, laboratory training is aimed at increasing the effectiveness of the system. The focus is on changing both individual relationships and group processes. Perhaps more important, however, T-Groups are primarily social systems. As such, activities and learning are appropriately focused on human behavior. This is not the case in organizational development where the emphasis is placed on integrating the technological, administrative, and human systems.

Needless to say, the above differences have some serious implications for the use of sensitivity training in organizational development. These may be summarized as follows:

1. Sensitivity training can only be *part* of an overall OD strategy. There is little chance that T-Groups, in and of themselves, will induce organization change without meaningful pre-lab and post-lab activities.
2. The objectives of the training need to be made clear and explicit to all concerned and, to the extent possible, should be consistent with the expectations of the participants.
3. Laboratory method and design must take into consideration existing culture, values, and norms. The focus of activities should be on changing individual and group behavior in the work environment.
4. A considerable amount of time and energy must be devoted to the problem of transfer. Learning and change should be organizationally relevant and transferable.
5. The focus of training activities should be on *integrating* the technological, administrative, and human systems.
6. A longer time commitment is required on the part of all concerned. Meaningful organizational change usually requires more than just a few days of sensitivity training.
7. Finally, given the above differences, laboratory trainers must expand their knowledge and skills to include a broader base of management theory and practice.

The issue as I see it, then, is not whether laboratory training is an appropriate intervention or not. Experience tells us that it is a potentially powerful facilitator of organization change and development. The real challenge confronting OD practitioners involves expanding the technology and learning how to use it more effectively.

THE NEED FOR PROFESSIONALISM

There are also a number of issues and challenges concerning professionalism, or the lack of it, in organizational development. The degree of respectability normally attributed to a profession is directly related to a variety of characteristics, including the existence of such things as a specialized body of knowledge and technology, adequately trained and certified practitioners, ethical standards to guide professional conduct, and a representative organization with professionalization as its goal. Professionalism in OD, if these guidelines are relevant, has barely begun.

To begin with, there is currently no systematic body of knowledge that can be clearly identified as the theory of organizational development. There are, in fact, a wide variety of theories and approaches. Each practitioner seems to apply his own brand of OD. Although many of the applications are indeed based upon sound theory, they have not been derived from a common body of clearly defined and interrelated concepts and techniques. This may be due to the fact that, up to this point at least, practice still outstrips research in the field. A number of factors may be responsible for this. First, there is no unifying framework or way of adding to a common body of knowledge and techniques. Science is advanced primarily by the systematic accumulation of research data. Second, it is extremely difficult to identify and control the large number of interdependent variables present in most organization systems. The complexity and dynamics of organizational life do not lend themselves to the rigorous demands of scientific method. And, finally, organizational development by its very nature is a process that continues over an extended period of time. There has been little interest to date in long-term OD research projects. Sound professional practice is generally based upon a specialized body of knowledge and techniques derived from cumulative research. In this regard organizational development still has a long way to go. Perhaps the first step must begin with the reconciliation and integration of the existing theories and approaches into a meaningful conceptual scheme.

Closely related to the above issue is the problem of training competent OD practitioners. There is an alarming lack of formalized methods for acquiring the necessary knowledge and skills. Our universities have not yet responded to the increasing need for qualified people in the field. The few courses and programs currently available are severely limited in terms of both quantity and quality. Some organizations, like the California-based TRW Systems Group, have developed their own in-house training programs. But these too are limited in the sense that they generally reflect the organization's own experience with OD and lack the level of sophistication and insights that might come from external sources. The development of competent and ethical practitioners is one of the great challenges confronting any emerging discipline.

In summary, then, organizational development cannot emerge as a respectable profession until its theory and practice develop in a way that encourages the formulation of a specialized body of knowledge and techniques through systematic research. Formalized methods of acquiring OD knowledge and experience must also be developed. This will require collaboration between our universities and a variety of participating organizations. The current respectability of OD as an emerging discipline is due largely to the creative efforts of a limited number of highly talented individuals. Unless we can learn to train and develop future generations of competent and ethical practitioners, organizational development may indeed turn out to be just another passing fad on the management scene.

THE USE OF CONSULTANTS

As already indicated, organizational development makes extensive use of consultants to facilitate the process of change. In many cases the consultant is an objective third party who is external to the client system. An increasing number of organizations, however, are developing their own internal resources. The availability of both external and internal consultants raises the issue of when and how to use them most effectively.

The advantages of using an external consultant are fairly obvious. To begin with, he is generally an "expert" in the field. This means that he has had formal training in behavioral science, possesses an array of sophisticated tools, and brings an action research orientation that is useful in most OD efforts. He can also provide a new and fresh approach to old problems. Perhaps most important, however, he possesses the objectivity required to enhance his effectiveness in the client system. An external person can often see blocks to effectiveness that have become so much a part of the culture that organization members are blind to them. He generally exerts a great deal of influence on organization members. This is due not only to his expertise, but because he is seen as not having a vested interest or an axe to grind. Finally, the external consultant can take greater risks since he is not dependent (presumably) upon the organization's reward and penalty system.

There are, on the other hand, some potential disadvantages to using external consultants. It takes both time and effort to acquire an understanding of how a large and complex organization functions. The external consultant must spend a good deal of his time becoming familiar with the organization's structure and processes and acquiring an intimate knowledge of its culture, values, and norms. And unless he is in constant touch with the client system, he must also spend some time getting up to speed on current problems and issues. Organizational development requires constant attention. The problems and issues are both persistent and complex. If his relationship is temporary or sporadic, the external consultant can play only a limited role in OD activities.

Some of the potential problems resulting from the use of external consultants have encouraged organizations to develop their own internal resources. The internal consultant is thoroughly familiar with the way in which the organization functions. He understands its structure and processes; he has intimate knowledge of its values and norms; he is available to provide continuous attention to the process of change; he is generally on top of current problems and issues; and he is in a position to provide continuing thrust and support for OD activities. Perhaps most important, he provides the organization with internal OD expertise in the sense that he has essentially the same knowledge and skills possessed by the external consultant.

Using internal resources, however, also has its potential disadvantages. The internal consultant may not be able to influence the client system because other members of the organization may not see him as an expert. They are more apt to see him as having a vested interest. In this respect he may truly be a prophet without honor in his own country. If he in fact has a vested interested in the outcome, he may be both biased and subjective. Internal consulting resources also depend upon the organization's reward and penalty system and, consequently, may not be in a position to confront the system or to take the risks they otherwise might. Finally, there is the tendency of management to delegate the responsibility for organizational development to internal consulting resources much in the same way that management delegates functional responsibility to specialists in other areas. Management must remain committed to and involved with OD activities. It is a responsibility that cannot be delegated.

In summary, then, organizations must learn to use external and internal consultants in more effective ways. Perhaps the best approach involves the use of both. External consultants can bring objectivity, expertise, and fresh approaches to organization problem-solving. Internal consultants can provide knowledge and understanding of organizational processes, information about current issues, and continuity of effort. Together they possess the knowledge and skill required to deal with the complex and continuous nature of organizational development. Perhaps most important, however, the collaborative relationship provides an opportunity to transfer the external consultant's skills to the client-system. The training and development of internal resources is an extremely important activity since, in the final analysis, the capacity for organizational development must ultimately rest within the organization.

OVEREMPHASIS ON PERSONAL-CULTURAL CHANGE

Theoretically, organizational development represents a systems approach to change in organizations. The application of systems theory to management is not new. The major elements, or subsystems, have been generally identified as: (1) the *technical,* or task system, which includes the flow of work, the design of jobs, the required task roles, and a number of other technological variables; (2) the *managerial,* or administrative system, which includes such things as the organization structure, policies and procedures, the ways in which decisions get made, and a large number of other variables designed to facilitate the management processes; and (3) the *human,* or personal-cultural system, which is primarily concerned with organization culture and values, the informal organization, the behavioral norms, the satisfaction of personal needs, and the motivational level and attitudes of members. It is the interaction among these three major subsystems that produces the role relationships and behavioral patterns that impact on organizational effectiveness.

Although most OD practitioners recognize the technical and managerial subsystems, their efforts tend to focus on personal-cultural changes. The majority of planned interventions which presently come under the OD label are generally aimed at changing group values, norms, and processes. Their focus tends to be on changing the culture and improving the climate in an organization; on increasing the effectiveness of some of its internal processes; on changing individual attitudes and interpersonal relationships; or on improving intragroup and intergroup relationships. The emphasis on these personal-cultural aspects of organizational life can be seen in the limited number of techniques that have been developed in the field to date and, more importantly, in the way in which they are generally applied. The extensive (and almost exclusive) use of "sensing" techniques, organization "mirrors," laboratory training, team development activities, and intergroup building reflects an emerging bias in the existing technology and the present state of the art.[8]

The reality is that there are a number of other important and effective ways to change organizations.[9] A change in the flow of work or in the nature of the work itself can increase individual and organizational performance. Current approaches to job design take technology as the operant variable and, as a consequence, are concerned with the interaction between personal and organizational needs as manifested in the jobs.[10] Performance can also be improved by modifying the managerial system. A change in the organization structure, the implementation of a "Management by Objectives" system, or the application of any number of other manage-techniques may be both an appropriate and an effective vehicle for improving effectiveness. The point here is that there are any number of alternative but related change strategies available to the OD practitioner. Too frequently, however, the choice tends to be biased toward a narrow and limited range of interventions into the personal-cultural system.

If organizational development is truly to represent a systems approach to effectiveness and change, it must further develop and expand its technology to include interventions into all of the major subsystems. It must also provide the means for integrating them in a more meaningful way. Perhaps most important, however, OD techniques must be applied as a *means* to improved performance and not as an *end* in themselves. Planned change interventions should result from sound organizational diagnosis rather than individual biases and preferences.

THE LIMITATION TO HIERARCHICAL SYSTEMS

The theory and practice of organizational development has so far focused on innovation and planned change within formal organizations. These are essentially "closed" hierarchical systems in the sense that they include common purpose, which is generally (but not always) reflected in a hierarchy of goals and sub-goals, centralized power from which to exercise control over individuals, a management hierarchy of coordinating authority, and a common system of values and norms. Formal organizations generally reflect collaborative models of human behavior. The need for interdependence between the various parts of the organization is relatively high, as is the requirement for collaboration among its members. These conditions are clearly reflected in the strategies and models which have been developed in the field to date.

For the most part, existing OD technology attempts to create "win-win" situations and conditions under which conflict can be creatively resolved, generally in a climate of openness and trust. The underlying assumption is that there exists both the need and the desire for collaboration. Perhaps more important, however, present strategies and models are based upon a set of assumptions that man is rational and reasonable; that he can be influenced by logic and knowledge; that he is responsible and will respond to the truth; and that he is loving, caring, and trusting of others.

The fundamental "truth-love" models of change used by most OD practitioners may be indeed appropriate under these conditions.[11] They appear to be especially successful in smaller systems. To my knowledge, however, they have been less successful (if at all) when applied in larger, nonhierarchical systems where power is diffused and the need for interdependence and collaboration are not clearly evident to those concerned. There are presently no OD models for dealing on a large scale with relationships between nations, between political parties, between the races, between students and police, or even between management and labor unions. There are presently no OD models which can function for any length of time in a climate of distrust. And there are presently no OD models that consider the possibility that *some* men at least are not rational and reasonable, do not respond to the truth, and are not loving, caring, and trusting of others.

One of the major challenges confronting both practitioners and theoreticians, then, is to develop more appropriate technology and models of change that can be applied successfully in large-scale "open" systems; that is, in nonhierarchical systems where there are pluralistic power and authority systems; where there are diverse and often conflicting goals; where there are different systems of values and norms; and where there is often violence and hate. Organizational development will be severely limited as an instrument of change in our society unless this challenge is squarely met.

SUMMARY

The field of organizational development promises to make an important contribution to management theory and practice. As an emerging body of knowledge and techniques, it represents an innovative and refreshing approach to increased effectiveness and planned change in organizations. It appears to be especially suited to meet the present and future demands of our society. There are, however, a number of issues and challenges which must be met if OD is to take its place as a relevant and useful discipline for practicing managers.

Laboratory method, which has provided the backbone and thrust for many early OD efforts in this country, must first of all involve more than sensitivity training for organization members. The focus of the activity must be on changing behavior in the work environment in a way that improves individual and group performance. Laboratory training can at best represent only part of an overall strategy for organizational learning and change. Although considerable progress has been made in this regard, the real challenge lies in expanding laboratory technology beyond team development and intergroup building activities.

A second major challenge evolves around the need for professionalism in the field. The current respectability of organizational development is due largely to the innovative efforts of a limited number of highly talented and creative individuals. The evolution of OD as a bona fide profession rests on the ability to develop a body of specialized knowledge and techniques, primarily through systematic research, as well as formalized methods for training and certifying future generations of practitioners.

The use of consulting resources offers still another challenge in the field. Client-systems must learn to use OD consultants more creatively. They must also learn to develop more effective working relationships between their external and internal resources. Perhaps more important, however, is the need to develop an internal capability to the point that OD becomes a way of life among line managers.

A fourth challenge can be found in the need to modify and expand the technology of organizational development. Although the technology for making interpersonal interventions is developing nicely, OD practitioners have tended to neglect interventions into the managerial and technological systems. The existing technology must be expanded to include new change strategies and new ways of intervening in organizations and systems in a more holistic way.

REFERENCES

1. See Richard Beckhard, *Organization Development: Strategies and Models* (Reading: Addison-Wesley, 1969); Robert R. Blake and Jane Mouton, *Corporate Excellence Through Grid Organization Development* (Houston: Gulf Publishing, 1968); Edgar H. Schein and Warren G. Bennis, *Personal and Organization Change Through Group Methods* (New York: Wiley, 1966); and Sheldon A. Davis, "An Organic Problem-Solving Method of Organizational Change," *Journal of Applied Behavioral Science,* 3:1 (1967), 3–21.
2. Warren G. Bennis, *Organization Development: Its Nature, Origins, and Prospects* (Reading: Addison-Wesley, 1969), 2.
3. Beckhard, 9. (Italics in original)
4. Wendell French, "Organization Development: Objectives, Assumptions, and Strategies," *California Management Review,* XII:2 (Winter 1969), 23.
5. In addition to above references see Sheldon A. Davis and Robert Tannenbaum, "Values, Man, and Organizations," *Industrial Management Review,* 10:2 (Winter 1969), 67–86.
6. For critical assessments see, for example, Robert J. House, "T-Group Education and Leadership Effectiveness: A Review of the Empiric Literature and a Critical Evaluation," *Personnel Psychology,* XX (Spring 1967), 1–32; John P. Campbell and Marvin D. Dunnette, "Effectiveness of T-Group Experiences in Managerial Training and Development," *Psychological Bulletin,* LXX (August 1968), 73–104; and essays by M. D. Dunnette, J. P. Campbell, and Chris Argyris, "A Symposium: Laboratory Training," *Industrial Relations,* VIII (October 1968), 1–45.
7. For illustrations of the application of laboratory training in organizations see, for example, Chris Argyris, "T-Groups for Organizational Effectiveness," *Harvard Business Review,* 42:2 (March–April 1964), 60–74; Michael G. Blansfield, "Depth Analyses of Organizational Life," *California Management Review,* V:2 (Winter 1962), 29–42; and Davis, 3–21.
8. Descriptions of the application of these techniques can be found in Davis, 3-21. For more detailed illustrations of team development and intergroup building see, for example, Richard Beckhard, "The Confrontation Meeting," *Harvard Business Review,* 45:2 (March–April 1967), 149–155; Robert T. Golembiewski and Arthur Blumberg, "The Laboratory Approach to Organizational Change: Confrontation Design," *Academy of Management Journal,* 11:2 (June 1968), 199–210; and Newton Margulies and Anthony P. Raia, "People in Organizations: A Case for Team Training," *Training and Development Journal,* 22:8 (August 1968), 2–11.
9. An excellent survey of the approaches to change in organizations can be found in Harold J. Leavitt, "Applied Organizational Change in Industry: Structural, Technological, and Humanistic Approaches," in James G. March, ed., *Handbook of Organizations* (Chicago: Rand McNally, 1965), 114–1170.
10. For example, see Louis E. Davis, "The Design of Jobs," *Industrial Relations,* 6:1 (October 1966), 21–45.
11. For a more detailed description of the truth-love model and the politics of change, see Warren G. Bennis, "Unsolved Problems Facing Organization Development," *Business Quarterly,* 34:4 (Winter 1969), 82.

Part 5
DIRECTING AND LEADING

Directing and leading comprise the managerial functions of guiding, overseeing, and leading people. It is preeminently, therefore, that portion of the management process which involves personal relationships, even though the reader will recognize that all aspects of managing must be designed to make it possible for people to cooperate effectively. But directing and leading as a function goes peculiarly outside of the formal organization and the enterprise for its roots, since people are necessarily a product and a part of a culture far wider than any undertaking or its immediate industrial environment. The editors have therefore chosen to group readings dealing with this function of managing into "The Area of Human Relations," "Motivation," "Leadership," and "Communication."

Because the handling of people is central to directing and leading, the study of human relations has been of major interest to management, particularly since the famous Western Electric Hawthorne experiments more than four decades ago. This widespread interest in and study of human relations has resulted in illuminating research on the one hand and many excessive claims on the other. In the summary "Changing Concepts of Human Relations," a chapter from one of Carl Heyel's books, the author skillfully and accurately traces the development of human relations concepts in management, emphasizing the major research and objectively dealing with various concepts as they have changed over the years.

Of particular value—especially seeing that many managers in the period since World War II have perhaps become overly enthusiastic about "practicing human relations"—is Malcolm P. McNair's incisive "What Price Human Relations?" McNair's paper has, in the editors' view, been of tremendous influence in removing from management teaching and practice some excessive and impractical notions.

Much fruitful research and experimentation have been done in the area of "Motivation," and the editors regret that they cannot reprint more than the four selections included here. But four outstanding articles are reprinted in this section. The relationship between leader behavior and subordinates' motivations are presented by Martin G. Evans in his paper on "Leadership and Motivation: A Core Concept."

To make easily available the findings on motivation of an outstanding scholar and practitioner in the field, an excerpt on executive motivations has been selected from the book by Arch Patton, *Men, Money, and Motivation.* Patton feels that most of the studies by psychologists on motivations of individuals have not dealt adequately with the factors especially applicable to executives. Although, in their fundamentals, there seems to be little difference between Patton's findings and those of prominent students of motivation, he does place them in the credible framework of actual experience and noteworthy examples.

The various approaches to explaining motivation are further discussed by Fred Luthans and Robert Ottemann in their paper on "Motivation vs. Learning Approaches to Organizational Behavior." These authors emphasize the relationship of human motivations, particularly those aroused by positive reenforcement, to management practice and to what they refer to as organizational behavior modification ("O.B. Mod.").

One of the more popular approaches to motivating people, especially those at the operating level, is to enrich jobs by making them more meaningful and challenging. Experience with a number of job enrichment programs is analyzed by the prominent industrial engineering management consultant, Mitchell Fein, in his report on "Job Enrichment: A Reevaluation." This paper is interesting, not only in giving a review of many job enrichment programs, but also in showing their weaknesses and the problems encountered. Fein contributes a sense of reality to this exceptionally interesting method of motivating people and shows that many programs of job enrichment are not proving as promising or as easy to implement as some people believe them to be.

Because it is hoped that managers may be effective leaders, and indeed, those who manage well are virtually certain to become leaders, a considerable amount of writing and research concerning leadership has been undertaken. The trends in leadership theory and research are ably summarized by a longtime and respected scholar in the field. The editors are happy to present Ralph M. Stogdill's summary paper on "Historical Trends in Leadership Theory and Research."

One of the Harvard Business Review's classics, a pioneer discussion of leadership, has recently been reprinted by the Review. The editors are happy that they can include the paper by Robert Tannenbaum and Warren H. Schmidt on "How to Choose a Leadership Pattern," along with the authors' comments on their essay that first appeared in 1958. As perceptive scholars of management will realize, these authors recognized the contingency approach to leadership nearly two decades ago.

One of the most active and respected researchers in the field of leadership is Fred E. Fiedler. He has been particularly well known for his research and approach to measuring leadership style. The editors are glad that they can present a recent paper by Fiedler on "The Contingency Model—New Directions for Leadership Utilization."

The ability to communicate is obviously important to managers in every aspect of their interpersonal relationships. This important topic is dealt with concisely and clearly in the selection "Ten Commandments of Good Communications," issued some years ago by the American Management Association. One of the rare empirical studies of managerial communications is reprinted in the perceptive research of A. K. Wickesberg, "Communications Networks in the Business Organization Structure." Working with a group of ninety-one business managers, Wickesberg identified the dimensions, purposes, directions, and network characteristics of communications patterns and disclosed how extensively actual communications take place outside the lines of organization.

A. THE AREA OF HUMAN RELATIONS

56 CHANGING CONCEPTS OF HUMAN RELATIONS*

Carl Heyel

A man who was trying to read his newspaper was continually interrupted by his small daughter as she played on the floor beside him. In desperation, he persuaded her to try her older sister's jigsaw puzzle. He was quite certain that the puzzle, picturing a map of the world, was difficult enough to keep her occupied indefinitely. To his surprise, after but a few minutes she tugged at his arm and showed him the completed map.

"How on earth did you do it so fast?" he exclaimed.

"Well, you see," she replied, "there was a picture of a man on the other side. I put the man together in the box lid and flipped it over. When the man was right, the whole world came out right too!"

The moral, of course, is obvious in our threatened age. But it applies with special aptness to the individual plant and departmental situation—when the man is right, the department and the company are right too.

Ever since the late 1920's, and intensified by the social problems of the Great Depression, advanced management has increasingly been preoccupied with the human side of its operations. Prior to that time, industrial engineers had been seeking most of the answers to efficient operation in improved production processes and more refined budgeting for cost controls and the like. Even in the stress and strain of World War II production, the question of employee morale and motivation was always of high-priority concern. "Put the worker at his ease" was a prime injunction of JIT, the Job Instructor Training program of the War Manpower Commission's Training Within Industry Division; and human relations was further stressed in its JRT, or Job Relations Training, program.

Human relations has been much belabored in supervisory training courses. "How to Get Along with People," "How to Motivate," "How to Handle Grievances" are stock titles in all such training programs—to say nothing of the shelves of books and stacks of magazine articles on the same subjects. What more should be said about "new concepts in human relations" here?

The fact is that there have been some wide pendulum swings in management attitudes on the subject ever since the famous "Hawthorne experiments" of the Western Electric Company in 1923–26 and 1927–32 triggered the so-called "human relations movement." Some pages of review and perspective are therefore in order. . . . Our purpose here, . . . will be to see if we can attain a balanced view. . . .

SOME BACKGROUND

The Hawthorne experiments had such a profound effect in ushering in the new preoccupation with worker motivation, participation, satisfaction, and the like that it may be well to tell the story again briefly, despite the risk of familiarity. These experiments represent the most ambitious single investigation ever attempted up to and since that date to determine what factors significantly influence the efficiency and productivity of working groups.

> The investigators began what they at first thought would be a more or less routine study of the effect of illumination on production. A test group of employees was chosen, and a suitable assembly operation was set up. Conditions were standardized, and it was found that production did indeed increase as illumination increased. But when the analysts *decreased* the illumination within very broad limits, they found to their surprise that production still continued to go up! Obviously, some variable or variables were at work that were more important than illumination.
>
> As a result of the unexpected findings a second, more ambitious research study was undertaken. This experiment consisted of an exhaustive investigation of the production of five girls who were continuously engaged in the

* Reprinted by permission of the publisher from *Management for Modern Supervisors*, American Management Association, New York, 1962, pp. 44–67. Mr. Heyel is a prominent writer and lecturer on management topics.

repetitive assembly of small electrical relays. The girls were subjected to all sorts of changes in their working conditions. They took six rest pauses a day, worked without rest pauses, worked short hours and long hours. They were switched around in their chairs, and given different kinds of relays to assemble. Detailed records were kept on such factors as the weather outside and whether the girls came to work tired after parties or fresh after a good night's sleep. There were changes in the form of incentive payments and in the quality of supervision.

The results of all these observations were again unexpected. No matter what the changes were, total output continued to rise throughout the period of the experiments, reaching a total increase of 30 per cent. The conclusion reached was that the increases in output were due, not to any of the changes in tangible working conditions, but rather to the *social relationships* of the girls and *their attitude toward supervision.*[1]

The girls were interviewed in depth and were asked to reply to detailed questionnaires. The investigators, in their final explanation of the results, placed great emphasis on the apparent influence of the *sense of participation and belonging.* The girls knew that they were taking part in an interesting experiment, and they were consulted on details that affected them. They realized that they were part of something that management considered important, and this affected the pride they took in their work. The investigators also concluded that the informal organization and social relationships which the girls developed by working together were as important as the formal organization.

The final report stated that "the operators have no clear idea as to why they are able to produce more in the test room; but as shown in the replies to the questionnaires, there is the feeling that better output is in some way related to the distinctly pleasanter, freer, and happier working conditions." Professor Elton Mayo stated that "comment after comment from the girls indicates that they have been relieved of the nervous tension under which they previously worked. They have ceased to regard the man in charge as a 'boss.'" The social influences were rated as being of more significance than physical factors and changes in pay.

The study of the relay-assembly girls was followed by a study of 14 male operators in a bank wiring room with a view to obtaining more exact information about social groups within the company. This second study reinforced the findings from the relay test room.

Following the Hawthorne experiments there was a tremendous swing by management to a deep preoccupation with the human and social aspects of work. In industrial relations literature and from the platforms of management gatherings the Hawthorne findings were quoted extensively ("interminably," as one commentator has since put it). This is not, of course, to say that the swing was due solely to this work—but the findings did provide an apparent scientific basis for the arguments that were increasingly being advanced by socially conscious spokesmen for government, business, and academic circles. These arguments held that human relations had been a neglected factor in productivity; that too much attention had been given to money incentives and to impersonally engineered standards of performance; that management in general and supervisors in particular had to be much more concerned with "what made people tick," with problems of informal organizations in any working group, and with problems of *communication, participation,* and *understanding.*

This new trend in management thinking had a marked influence on the type and content of supervisory training programs—and in many cases the preoccupation with the human reactions on the job led to rather extreme emphasis on psychological and even near-psychiatric approaches. While there has been a justified reaction against giving analysis and advice to subordinates on alleged personality defects and a concomitant swing back to stressing performance on the job, the net result has been a salutary concern in getting supervisors to think about what constitutes constructive leadership on the job; about effective techniques of communication and teaching, overcoming resistance to change, instilling pride in work, and achieving identification with company objectives.

Another direct result of the Hawthorne experiments was the impetus they gave to "undirected" employee counseling. This was carried to great lengths by the Hawthorne management, which made a skilled interviewer available to each shop department. As soon as he felt that he had a fairly good knowledge of the special human problems in question, this interviewer began meeting with individual employees in a special room. Complete confi-

[1] The experimental room was devised and maintained by the Western Electric Company. Much of the analysis was done by Prof. T. N. Whitehead and his associates at the Harvard Graduate School of Business Administration, under the direction of Prof. Elton Mayo. The story is told by F. J. Roethlisberger and W. J. Dickson, *Management and the Worker,* Harvard University Press, Cambridge, Mass., 1939.

dence was absolutely guaranteed. Nothing the employee could say could shock the interviewer—and the interviewer never argued and never gave advice. Management felt that the interviews were eminently worthwhile, even though the interviewer actually did nothing!

Under this philosophy, whatever corrective action takes place comes about through increased understanding, through thinking and self-help stimulated by the questions. Not many companies, of course, could afford the luxury of such an elaborate setup, but the techniques of this form of counseling—that is, largely listening—are now widely applied as part of formal employee and executive appraisal plans.[2]

NEW INSIGHTS INTO MOTIVATION

In the years under our review, a great deal of attention has been given to the question of human motivation. Social scientists have sought to develop theories about the motivation of people at work on the basis of their own observations in industrial situations, the results of studies by clinical psychologists, the reactions under controlled experiments of nonindustry groups such as school children and military units, and the "living examples" furnished by the practitioners of work simplification and by programs such as that of the Lincoln Electric Company.

We shall come back to all of these later. At this point, however, we should mention some ideas about motivation advanced by A. H. Maslow.[3] These ideas have since won general acceptance by psychologists and provide valuable insights to anyone concerned with getting the best out of people in our industrial society today.

Dr. Maslow postulates five basic needs which, he says, are organized into successive levels. For example, hunger is a basic physiological need. But when there is plenty of food, higher needs emerge. When the higher needs are satisfied, newer and still higher needs come to the fore, and so on. Thus gratification becomes as important a concept in motivation as deprivation. A want that is satisfied is no longer a want.

Below we give, necessarily simplified, these levels of basic needs, starting with the lowest. (It should not be assumed that a need must be entirely satisfied before the next one emerges. Most normal people are partially satisfied in all of their basic needs at the same time.)

1. *The physiological needs.* These are hunger for food, sexual gratification, and shelter.

2. *The safety needs.* If the physiological needs are relatively satisfied, a set of needs emerges for protection against danger and threats. In an ordered society a person usually feels safe from extremes of climate, tyranny, violence, and so on. Expressions of safety needs are thus seen in preferences for job security, insurance, and the like. Other manifestations are preferences for the familiar rather than the unfamiliar, the known rather than the unknown. These are normal reactions. Arbitrary management actions giving rise to uncertainty can have an adverse effect at any level in the organization. The tendency toward resistance to change is human and universal.

3. *The love needs.* (Some writers term these "social" needs.) If the physiological and safety needs are fairly well taken care of, the needs for love and affection and "belongingness" will emerge, and the cycle will repeat itself with this new center. The person now seeks affectionate relations with people in general, a place in his group. If he is deprived of these goals, he will want to attain them more than anything else in the world, and, in Dr. Maslow's words, "he may even forget that once, when he was hungry, he sneered at love." In our society, the thwarting of these needs is the most common cause of severe psychological maladjustment.

4. *The esteem needs.* Practically everyone has a need for self-respect and for the esteem of others. This results in the desire for strength, adequacy, confidence, independence, reputation or prestige, recognition, attention, and appreciation. These "egoistic" needs are rarely completely satisfied. They are of special importance in our discussion because the typical industrial and commercial organization does not offer much opportunity for their satisfaction to employees at the lower levels. It is the recognition of these needs that has focused so much attention upon ways to provide employees with a sense of participation. Extreme advocates call for very broad participation indeed, covering even allocation of work and setting of the work pace, and criticize "scientific management" as deliberately thwarting these esteem needs.

5. *The need for "self-actualization," for self-fulfillment.* Even if all the needs thus far men-

[2] That this was no short-lived enthusiasm at Hawthorne is indicated by the fact that the counseling procedure was in force for 20 years, 1936 to 1956. Since then the program has been curtailed, and the counseling techniques have been incorporated into Western Electric's general supervisory development programs.

[3] A. H. Maslow, "A Theory of Human Motivation," *Psychological Review*, vol. 50, 1943.

> tioned are satisfied, we can still expect that a new discontent and restlessness will develop unless the individual is doing what he is fitted for. Dr. Maslow writes: "A musician must make music, an artist must paint, a poet must write, if he is to be ultimately happy. What a man can be he must be. This need we may call self-actualization." The clear emergence of these needs rests upon prior satisfaction of the physiological, safety, love, and esteem needs. People who are satisfied in these needs are basically satisfied people, and it is from these that we can expect the fullest and healthiest creativeness.

An important point about these basic needs is that in the average person they are more often unconscious than conscious. A supervisor who is aware of them will often obtain a clarifying insight into seemingly contradictory behavior. ("We agreed to their wage demands—now why can't we get productivity?")

"DEMOCRATIC" VERSUS "AUTHORITARIAN" SUPERVISION

All the foregoing ties in with the continuing emphasis that has in recent years been given by many industrial psychologists and others interested in the industrial application of the social sciences to the advantages of so-called "democratic" versus "authoritarian" supervision and to more "participative" management in general. A supervisor who is "democratically oriented" is one who thinks of himself as a coordinator of his group rather than "boss." He believes subordinates should have more voice in running the department and listens to ideas and suggestions from them. He passes adequate explanations on to his subordinates when changes are made and is prepared on occasion to give in to a subordinate if there is disagreement on how something should be done.

The advocates of democratic supervision contend that with all that is now known about the reactions of people in groups, about individual motivations, and about worker satisfaction, an entirely new theory of management is called for, one that permits more self-fulfillment or self-actualization by the worker.

Under this concept, the supervisor is seen not so much as the directive head of his group but rather as its representative in the next higher group in the organization. The supervisor and the members of his work group are interdependent, whereas under the authoritarian system the supervisor's authority and the subordinate's dependency are emphasized. The latter view is considered unrealistic by the proponents of democratic supervision, since, they point out, in many situations the superior must depend on his subordinate. The principle is illustrated by what Rensis Likert has called the "linking pin" concept of supervision, illustrated in Exhibit 1.[4] In (*a*), loops are drawn around each individual and his boss, indicating that the pairs represent the primary working and communication relationship. In (*b*), illustrating the "linking pins," loops are drawn around each supervisor and all of his subordinates.

INCENTIVE PLANS AND THE NEW CONCEPTS OF MOTIVATION

It is understandable that developments such as those discussed thus far would cause many people to question individual incentives or piecework plans. By the beginning of the "human relations movement" such plans had been brought to a point of wide application in industry, and they are still very widely used. (We include under the term any system of wage payment under which the earnings of an employee or a small group of employees are directly related to output by means of a formula linking their measured performance to a predetermined standard.)

These plans, of course, rely practically altogether on a single motivation—additional monetary reward for additional effort—and if recognized industrial engineering procedures are followed, the production standards against which individual performance is measured are set by a professional methods department. In management literature there has been increasing advocacy of replacing such plans with group bonus plans and companywide profit-sharing plans, relating the bonus either to company profits or company savings as a whole or to departmental savings effected by voluntary group effort. These, it is claimed, are much more conducive to harmonious relationships, continuing productivity, and dedication to the objectives of the enterprise as a whole.

In an attempt to support this view industrial psychologists and others have cited numerous

[4] Rensis Likert, "Developing Patterns in Management," in *Strengthening Management for the New Technology*, American Management Association, General Management Series, no. 178, New York, 1955; and *Changing Patterns and Concepts in Management*, American Management Association, General Management Series, no. 182, New York, 1956, part 2.

EXHIBIT 1 "Man to Man" (*a*) and "Linking Pin" (*b*) Concepts of Supervisory Relationships

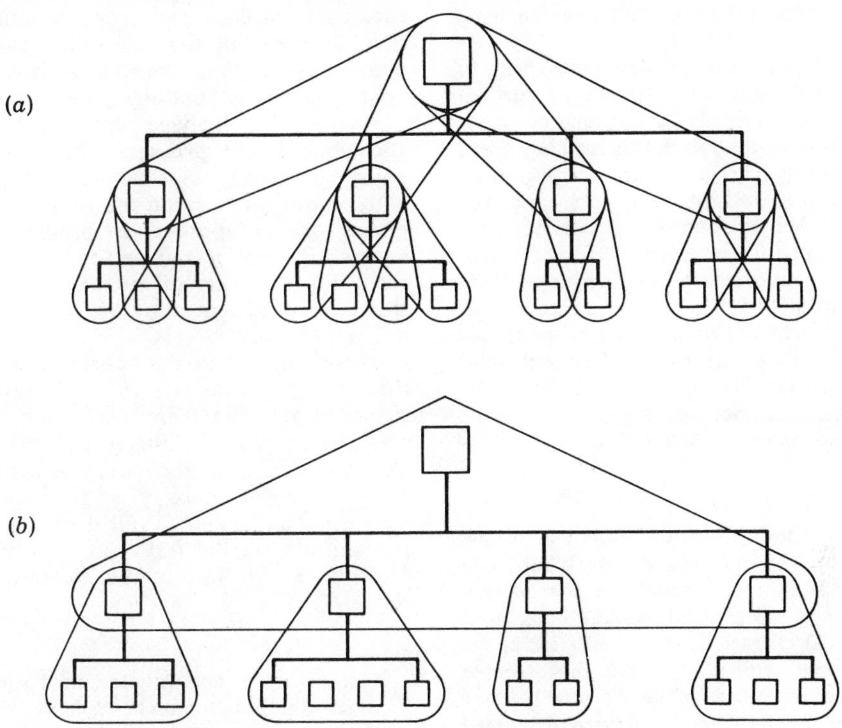

case study examples of worker opinions polled in specific plants, showing shortcomings of engineered performance standards and incentive systems or citing beneficial results when the newer philosophies of participation, group cohesiveness, and the like were applied. We cannot take the space to review the literature extensively; but, to give the flavor of the general nature of these reports, we offer two examples as typical. Presently we shall comment on the validity of such criticisms if an incentive plan is soundly engineered and installed in such a way as to achieve employee cooperation. . . .

Our first example, as related by William Foote Whyte,[5] concerns a paint room, where women spray-painted wooden toys and hung them on hooks which carried them into a drying oven. The girls were expected to reach engineered performance standards in six months.

But there was a serious problem of absenteeism and turnover. The girls claimed that the standards were impossible, and many hooks went into the oven empty, They complained of the oven heat, fumes, and general messiness. The foreman decided to meet with the girls and discuss their problems. They claimed that the room was poorly ventilated and too hot and asked for some large fans. The foreman got management approval to install three fans.

The girls' attitude was so improved that the foreman arranged for another meeting. The girls then complained that the time study men had set the conveyor too fast. They asked to be allowed to control the conveyor speed themselves—to be able to vary it during the day.

After meetings between the foreman and the standards men, it was decided to try the girls' idea, and a control was installed, containing a dial for "low," "medium," and "fast." Medium speed was just a little above standard. The girls experimented with this and established the following pattern: For the first half-hour each day the control was set at slightly above medium. The next two and a half hours were at high speed. For a half-hour before and after lunch the speed was set at low. Thereafter the control was again changed to high and left there until the last 45 minutes, when it was changed to medium.

The girls now reported that the pace was comfortable. Scarcely a hook went by empty,

[5] William Foote Whyte, *Money and Motivation,* Harper & Row, Publishers Incorporated, New York, 1955.

and rejects leveled off. Two months before the end of the six months' learning period, production was 30 to 50 per cent above standard, and the girls were collecting base pay, learner's bonus, and regular bonus.

This story typifies case studies purporting to show the possibilities, even in fairly mechanized operations, of applying the new concepts of participation—although in this instance there was a sad ending. The girls were earning more money than many skilled workers, and the latter knew it. Whyte reports that without consultation the superintendent revoked the learning bonus and returned the painting operation to its original status: The hooks again moved at a constant speed, production dropped, and within a month all but two of the girls had quit. The foreman stayed for several months but then left for another job.

Our second example is from Douglas McGregor:[6]

> The practical logic of incentives is that people want money, and that they will work harder to get more of it. . . . Incentive plans do not, however, take account of several other well demonstrated characteristics of behavior in the organizational setting: (1) that most people also want the approval of their fellow workers and that, if necessary, they will forego increased pay to obtain this approval; (2) that no managerial assurances can persuade workers that incentive rates will remain inviolate regardless of how much they produce; (3) that the ingenuity of the average worker is sufficient to outwit *any* system of controls devised by management.
>
> A "good" individual incentive plan may bring about a moderate increase in productivity (perhaps 15 per cent), but is also may bring a considerable variety of protective behaviors—deliberate restriction of output, hidden jigs and fixtures, hidden production, fudged records, grievances over rates and standards, etc. It generally creates attitudes which are the opposite of those desired.

THE REACTION

The cumulative effect, in some companies, of all the emphasis on human relations was to swing the pendulum pretty far—to a "dogooder's" philosophy of personnel administration. Inevitably, there were second thoughts. Was all this talk about the human factor in industry taking on the aspects of a fad? Was "democratic" supervision simply "soft" supervision? (As one executive put it, "Are we running a pink-tea party, or operating a business?") Were all the interesting case studies nothing more than anecdotes—isolated casebook material without any general significance?

Participative management is all well and good, but should girls really be allowed to set conveyor speeds? Are we overly concerned with patting workers on the head, giving them expressions of approval to bolster their self-esteem? Do engineered performance standards really rob a worker of human dignity? Where should management draw the line in giving up its prerogatives?

These implied doubts were accentuated by the recession of the late 1950's. Cost-conscious managers felt that there were many frills that could be cut from industrial relations practices, and many felt that they were in a position to adopt somewhat more of a "get tough" policy with organized labor. Typical of the questioning attitude are the following observations by Malcolm P. McNair in the *Harvard Business Review*.[7]

> My quarrel is not with the solid substance of much that is comprehended by the phrase "human relations," but rather with the "cult" or "fad" aspects . . . which are assuming so much prominence.
>
> . . . The world's work has to be done, and people have to take responsibility for their own work and their own lives. Too much emphasis on human relations encourages people to feel sorry for themselves, makes it easier for them to slough off responsibility, to find excuses for failure, to act like children. When somebody falls down on a job or does not behave in accordance with accepted codes, we look into his psychological background for factors that may be used as excuses. In these respects the cult of human relations is but part and parcel of the sloppy sentimentalism characterizing the world today. . . .
>
> It has become the fashion to decry friction, but friction has its uses; without friction there are no sparks, without friction it is possible to go too far in the direction of sweetness and light, harmony, and the avoidance of all irritation. . . . The overemphasis on human relations, with all its apparatus of courses, special vocabulary, and so on, tends to create the very problems

[6] Douglas McGregor, *The Human side of Enterprise*, McGraw-Hill Publishing Company, New York, 1960.

[7] Malcolm P. McNair, "Thinking Ahead: What Price Human Relations?" *Harvard Business Review*, March–April, 1957.

that human relations deals with. It is a vicious circle. You encourage people to pick at the scabs of their psychic wounds.

THE SEARCH FOR PROOF

To seek answers to questions such as those raised above, there have been numerous attempts by social scientists to put a somewhat firmer scientific base under all the admonitions to encourage participation, to provide scope for individual goal setting, to consider social relationship, and the like. To see whether such human relations practices could actually be tied in to increased production, a number of controlled experiments were undertaken, incorporating as much as possible of the rigor employed in experiments in the physical sciences.

But, before discussing such experiments, let us note that in this search for hard-boiled evidence, the sacrosanct Hawthorne experiments themselves came under some critical review. In 1953, 20 years after the original Hawthorne reports, a British social scientist, Michael Argyle, published a paper entitled "The Relay Assembly Test Room in Retrospect."[8] He carefully re-examined all the reported results, subjecting them to tests for statistical significance, evaluated the types of controls that had been set up, and reconsidered all the possible influences on the final measurements. He flatly stated:

> The conclusion drawn was that the reported increase of output was not due to the experimental periods, to the wage change, or to certain other physical factors, but to social changes, and in particular to the new attitude of the girls toward supervision. . . . It is clear that the three groups of physical factors considered [rest periods, shorter hours, changes in pay] could easily have been responsible for the whole of the observed increase of output, although there is insufficient evidence to show whether they were or not. . . . It was concluded that only about half of the 30 per cent increase was due to the method of payment. This figure was arrived at by comparison with two control groups, but no conclusions can be based on comparisons of single case studies where there is no control of other important conditions. . . . It is thus not possible to say how much increase was due to the wage change. . . . There is no quantitative evidence for the conclusions for which this agreement is famous—that the increase in output was due to a changed relationship to supervision.

It is interesting to note that this British paper has as yet apparently made no impression upon American management literature.

THE HARWOOD MANUFACTURING CORPORATION STUDY

Getting back to the laudable efforts to assemble quantitative data under controlled conditions, we can remark that carefully controlled statistical studies are still relatively few in number. One of the most widely quoted is that of the Harwood Manufacturing Corporation.[9] The company manufactures clothing, chiefly pajamas, and at the time of the study employed 500 women and 100 men.

When girls were transferred to new work because of, say, a change of style, their output dropped below the 60 units per hour standard for fully trained workers and tended to stay down, even after a reasonable readjustment period and even when the changes were quite small. Those who succeeded in regaining standard did so slowly, taking longer than a "green" worker. There was also a good deal of conflict with supervisors, time study men, and management generally.

To test the effect of allowing the girls to participate more in a needed change, the company developed a series of experiments when four groups of girls had to be transferred to new work. The work was all about equally difficult, and the changes were of about the same magnitude. One of the groups was used as a control, and for it the customary transfer procedure was used.

For the other groups, meetings were set up at which a manager discussed the need to cut costs. He showed two seemingly identical pairs of pajamas. The one had been made the year before, and the other was made by the new method at half the cost. Animated discussion ensued. The workers agreed that cost reductions were possible and necessary and came foreward with suggestions. Management then presented its plan for making a job study and training operators for the new job and explained how the new rate would apply.

The control group showed all the typical symptoms found in previous transfers. Its output after transfer averaged only about 50, with

[8] Michael Argyle, "The Relay Assembly Test Room in Retrospect," *Occupational Psychology*, vol. 27, 1953.

[9] L. Coch and J. P. French, Jr., "Overcoming Resistance to Change," *Human Relations*, August, 1948.

close standardization of output around the average. In the first 40 days of the experiment about 17 per cent of the group left the company. The rest caused trouble with supervisors and time study men and brought in the union to dispute the new rate.

Results with the participating groups showed a remarkable contrast. Output not merely recovered, but climbed quickly to about 70. Interest and cooperation shown in the initial discussions carried over to the jobs. Workers referred to "our job" and "our rate." There were no difficulties with supervisors and no major grievances, and none of the workers left the firm. The investigators reported that intergroup competition quickly developed and sped the process of achieving higher output.

A further experiment was then made: When the first group had adequately proved the deficiencies of the old procedure, it was broken up, and its members were scattered to other departments. Several left the firm. Later, the 13 surviving members were reassembled and once more launched on a new job under the "total participation" procedure. This time there was no question of their output sticking at around 50: Like the others, it quickly rose to and stayed at 70.

THE NORWEGIAN SHOE FACTORY

A group of Norwegian investigators[10] was impressed with the Harwood findings but felt they should be confirmed by a more detailed study which would be more closely controlled and would employ more refined methods of statistical analysis to be sure that the results could be attributed to the variables under study and not to random or unknown causes. They chose for their study a shoe factory in southern Norway, with 1600 employees. The department studied employed 400 men and women organized in almost identical work groups. Nine four-employee groups took part in the experiment, because they were going to be assigned to work on a new product.

Four areas of decision making were used: (1) allocation of articles to be produced, (2) length of training, (3) division of labor, and (4) assignment of jobs. Two of the experimental groups were allowed "moderate participation," and the other three were allowed only "weak" participation—that is, they participated only in allocating the articles. The control group was permitted *no* participation. Detailed production records for all groups were supplied by management. Each of the five experimental groups met with its foreman and representatives of the planning department to decide which of the five new products should be assigned to it. The two groups with greater participation held additional meetings in which they helped decide about the division of labor into four jobs, the assignment of these jobs to group members, and the training for the new jobs.

Ten weeks after the training, extensive post-experimental questionnaires were answered by the group members. The variations in the production of the groups, and in the answers to the questionnaire, were subjected to extensive statistical-significance analysis to determine the statistical probability that the results could have been due to other factors than the ones under review.

As far as tangible results—actual production—were concerned, the experimental groups did *not* differ significantly from the control groups. All kept fairly close to standard. However, the two groups that had been permitted the greater amount of participation took a relatively shorter time to reach the standard level of production. One of these groups increased beyond the level but took 15 weeks to do so.

This experiment must be disappointing to anyone who wants to make an open-and-shut case for participation in terms of increased productivity. With respect to attitudes toward management and job satisfaction in general, the authors concluded from the questionnaire analysis that they had adduced statistical support for their hypothesis (which might appear obvious) that the effects of participation hold only for subjects who experience only as much participation "as they consider right and proper" and that the effects of participation increase with decreasing resistance to the methods adopted by management to assure participation.

We have, of course, given only the bare bones of these Norwegian results, limiting ourselves to the tangible effects on production. The authors speculate on participation in general and on employee attitudes revealed by the questionnaires. They find moderate support for relating participation to feelings of satisfaction, and to labor/management relations. Despite the apparent inconclusiveness of this much more statistically refined version of the Harwood experiment, the authors surprisingly conclude that it seemed to yield consistent results, but that "the American experimental manipulation was more relevant to production and hence produced stronger forces affecting production."

[10] John P. French, Jr., Joachim Israel, and Dagfinn As, "An Experiment in Participation in a Norwegian Factory," *Human Relations,* no. 1, 1960.

UNIVERSITY OF MICHIGAN STUDIES

Another widely quoted source of quantitative analytical data on human relations in industry is the University of Michigan Research Center. In recent years this group has conducted extensive research into the effect on productivity of various organizational variables, with emphasis on the type of supervision. Included are studies of 72 foremen in charge of maintenance gangs for the Baltimore and Ohio Railroad; 224 Prudential Insurance Company office supervisors; over 300 supervisors in the Caterpillar Tractor Company; and employees of The Detroit Edison Company. The general conclusion of the investigators is that "democratic" supervision, as against close or "autocratic" supervision, is related to higher output. Job satisfaction on the part of employees is also reported as generally greater under democratic leadership. In the Prudential study, an average difference of 10 per cent in production was found between matched departments under different supervisors. The studies seemed to indicate that pressure for production on the part of the supervisors was completely unrelated to productivity, even to be inversely related to it. Surprisingly, when other data of the studies were analyzed, the evidence indicated that the foremen who spent more time on supervision had more productive sections, even though the same studies showed that close supervision was related to low output. It was concluded that to obtain high output a foreman had to tread a narrow path, spending a lot of time on supervision and yet not supervising too closely!

THE INDUSTRIAL CONTROLS CORPORATION

Industrial Controls is the disguised name of a medium-sized company (1,000 employees) in which a group of investigators from the Harvard Business School made an exhaustive six months' study, in 1955, of a department with 45 industrial workers. The stages of this research, including selection of the company, collection of preliminary data, and processing and reporting upon the data, extended over more than two years.[11] The study was designed to test a large number of hypotheses about factors which were thought to determine the behavior of any work group and the individuals in it. Findings were subjected to elaborate statistical tests for significance.

Eighteen basic hypotheses and resultant predictions are discussed in detail in the published report. The researchers had established these on the basis of prior studies and speculations by themselves and other social scientists. The hypotheses ranged over a wide field, covering the effects on productivity and worker satisfaction of such factors as acceptance by the group, differences in social and educational background, degree of interaction required by the job, rewards by management, and differences in social and educational background of an individual as compared with the norms of the group. They also covered observations about informal leadership, factors determining acceptance by the group, tensions arising from confusion as to "status" with the group, and the like.

Statistically speaking, the results of this detailed study were decidedly mixed. In the words of the authors:

> A document of some 200 pages was prepared which recorded our hits, our near-misses, our gross errors, etc. It compared the actual results with the results we had predicted from each hypothesis as well as from the combination of hypotheses we had used. . . . In some few cases we were right "on the nose"; in some more cases we were not "on the nose" but in "the right direction"; and then there were a substantial number of cases in which we were "way off." In some cases the actual behavior in terms of productivity and satisfaction was at a variance of 180 degrees from the behavior we had expected and predicted.

But the published study is valuable, nevertheless, in terms of the insights into motivation and behavior which are provided by the speculations and extended discussions of the authors in which they glean illuminating perspective out of varying and sometimes contradictory results. . . .

ARGYRIS'S "PLANTS NO. 5 AND 6"

Professor Chris Argyris of Yale has long been attempting to find laws of organizational behavior. In recent publications[12] he has documented in detail his interpretations of observations and depth interviews in "Plants No. 5 and 6" of a worldwide corporation. Both plants

[11] A. Zaleznik, C. R. Christensen, and F. J. Roethlisberger, *The Motivation, Productivity, and Satisfaction of Workers: A Prediction Study*, Harvard University, Division of Research, Graduate School of Business Administration, Boston, 1958.

[12] Chris Argyris, "Organizational Effectiveness Under Stress," *Harvard Business Review*, May–June, 1960; and *Understanding Organizational Behavior*, Dorsey Press, Inc., Homewood, Ill., 1960.

were approximately similar in size (500 employees), type of employees, products manufactured, and type of corporate controls and management leadership.

The management of Plant No. 5 had always paid the highest wages in the community. It had instituted liberal employee benefits long before the unions championed them. Indexes such as turnover, absenteeism, and grievances were very low. Excessive scrap and waste did not exist; stealing, gambling, rule breaking, late arrival, and refusal to work overtime on short notice hardly ever occurred. Surprisingly, after his detailed probings, Professor Argyris arrived at the following conclusion, despite the observed results which any factory manager would yearn to achieve:[13]

> The traditional indexes of low absenteeism, low turnover, low grievance occurrences, and high productivity are questioned. Given such indexes, management should not assume that it also will have employees who desire to be identified with the company . . . to worry about making the company more effective, to feel some responsibility for the over-all health of the company. . . . Such a climate will develop few employees who want to promote themselves into positions of responsibility. . . . The employees . . . will slowly become "simplified" human beings.

Two years later, Professor Argyris had the opportunity to round out his study by going into the "Siamese twin," Plant No. 6. Here management had just begun a drive to cut costs. Pressure was applied to cut production waste, errors, and down time and to increase quality. New control procedures were introduced. One of the "tightening up" actions of management was the elimination of what appears to have been an unusually loose feature of the incentive pay system—a so-called "kitty"—and much of Professor Argyris's discussion of worker attitudes and resentments has to do with the kitty's demise. Briefly, an employee could restrict his reported production by holding back work tickets, "banking" them in his kitty until a day when he was assigned a tough job, when he was not feeling well, or when his machine broke down. (There is no report as to the effect of this informal system on production scheduling and inventory control!)

Professor Argyris does not present any results of Plant No. 6's "pressure" in terms of output or costs, but he does give some adverse results in terms of absenteeism, turnover, and quality. The high-skill departments had a considerably poorer record on quality than the low-skill groups, although no control figures are given for the period preceding the study.

Like the Norwegian experiment, this exhaustive study under almost ideal experimental conditions (two like plants, one subject to stress, the other available as a control) must be considered disappointing to anyone seeking positive proof supporting theories on human relations. It produced few quantitative results that one can sink his teeth into.

WHAT IT ALL ADDS UP TO

What we have been saying in this chapter may be summed up as follows:

1. Studies at the Western Electric Company some 30 years ago got everyone to thinking much more than before about the human relations factor in industry. There was a great swing toward human relations skills in supervisory training and in executive development programs. Great stress has been laid on the findings that social relationships within a working group and the attitudes of employees toward their supervisors were actually more important than physical aspects of the job and often more important than pay. "Democratic foremanship" rather than "authoritarian direction" has been advocated. There has been emphasis on the need of employees to participate in decisions affecting their work, to give them a sense of belonging.

   In their concern about allowing people in industry to work as mutually helpful members of groups rather than as highly competitive individuals, some loud voices have been raised against piecework and other individual-incentive plans. Many case examples have purported to show that better results are obtained when groups of employees are allowed to set their own pace.
2. In more recent years, there have been a number of attempts at scientifically controlled experiments to get a quantitative basis for the assumptions made about the beneficial effects (in terms of tangible increases in productivity or production-related reductions in worker dissatisfaction or reductions in problems of quality, turnover, absenteeism, and so on) of a management policy of permitting a high degree of participation, providing a sense of belonging, and exercising democratic supervision.

   As a whole, the results are not statisti-

[13] Chris Argyris, "The Organization: What Makes It Healthy?" *Harvard Business Review*, November–December, 1958.

cally impressive, and some of the interpretations have been challenged. But, even where the results seem quite inconclusive, many conductors of experiments apparently are uninfluenced by their own findings and remain stanch advocates of the "human relations thesis," on the basis of side speculation flowing from their work rather than on quantitative proof.

3. In recent years there have been some strong criticisms of the emphasis on human relations and even some critical review of the original Hawthorne studies. There has been a tendency in many executive appraisal programs and supervisory development courses in industry to return to an emphasis on tangible performance results. This has implied a more "hard-boiled" approach to achieving engineered performance standards by employees with less concern for subtle motivations and formally "structured" human relations.

SIGNIFICANCE FOR THE SUPERVISOR

What should the balanced appraisal be? The following remarks are offered as a guide to the supervisor who is confronted with practical problems of output and quality but who also has an awareness of the importance of the individual human being in every production group.

1. There is as yet no exact science of human relations. It is not possible to predict the specific results in terms of *worker output* to be obtained by extending the degree of participation by employees, improving their "job satisfaction," clarifying their attitudes toward management, and so on.
2. The supervisor will be well advised to take heed of the swing toward greater stress on cost and immediate output as measures of his supervisory effectiveness and insist upon results from his people without too many qualms about friction and harmony and the workers' liking for him as a person. But this does not mean that he should dismiss as "bunk" all the preoccupation with human relations that has become increasingly prevalent over the past few decades. Without trying to develop a host of formalized techniques, he should take the commonsense view that "treating people like people" results in a more responsive working force.
3. Putting real thought into overcoming resistance to change, into effective communication, into putting workers at their ease when instructing them or checking on them, into getting them to work as a team for the objectives of the company—all of these are definitely part of good supervision. At the same time, it will be well to beware of going overboard on some of the notions advanced about seeking employee views on every change, about allowing employees to allocate work or set their own pace, and the like.
4. The concept of "democratic supervision" is sound—within limits. Yes, if it means careful indoctrination of the worker by the supervisor on what is expected of him, careful teaching of methods, solicitation of suggestions, voice for the employee *to the extent feasible* in work allocation, and then a minimum of "breathing down the employee's neck." Yes, *if by his experience in his own department* he knows that his people are ready for it. No, if he has "green" help, or if methods in his department have undergone a significant change, or if the quality record is poor, or if there has been a past record of poor management/employee relationships. Of course, the application of the principle depends upon the type of operation. Supervisors of highly creative departments (such as research and development) are the best candidates for the "linking pin" concept and are most effective when they consider themselves largely as representative of the employees to higher management rather than as strict directors of their efforts. The same could be true in almost any highly skilled, low-turnover department.
5. Contrary to much of the human relations literature, individual-incentive systems, *properly engineered* and installed in a way to achieve full employee understanding and cooperation, are still a powerful motivator. As recently as October 1960, Arthur A. Rath, a pioneer in the field, had this to say:[14]

> Based on observation in hundreds of plants, large and small, in every type of industry, it is my conviction that nothing will stimulate an employee to perform at his top capacity as will individual incentives—a system of compensation which links his reward as directly as possible with his *own efforts*. This position is based not only on 40 years of personal contact with problems of worker productivity, but also on parallel profes-

[14] Arthur A. Rath, "The Case for Individual Incentives: Management's Most Potent Motivational Tool," *Personnel Journal*, October, 1960.

sional experience of others, the testimony of operating executives, and by confirming evidence of published surveys.

It goes without saying that the supervisor must be thoroughly acquainted with the workings of the plan in force (and the plan must be one that adheres to modern industrial relations principles). The attitude cannot be that an individual-incentive system is "automatic" and requires less skilled supervision. (The "kitty" with which Professor Argyris is so preoccupied would not be tolerated in advanced practice.)

6. Employee participation should be encouraged *in matters which are within the employees' province.* They should be given ample explanation about changes, and their opinions and suggestions should be welcomed. Key employees will often have good ideas on how work can be done better, and, as is advocated by the practitioners of work simplification, the supervisor can use these ideas in supplementing the work of the professional methods and systems people in plant or office. Management should have a policy of paying well for any usable ideas. However, management should not step away from its right and duty to manage. The supervisor should be wary of those who advocate that workers set the pace of their work. This is something for engineers to determine. Even James F. Lincoln, famous for the "incentive management" system he instituted at the Lincoln Electric Company,[15] centers all his motivational philosophy around instilling a sense of belonging and participation in employees and flatly attests, "It is the responsibility of management to find the most efficient way of doing any job. This is not the responsibility of the operator."

   With engineered performance standards in use, the opportunities for democratic supervision are, if anything, enhanced. Since methods and expected output are established, the supervisor can leave conscientious employees to be their own taskmasters and concentrate on planning for and servicing the department.

7. There is no conflict between the concept of *participation,* as exemplified in successful group incentive plans, and the drive of *individual competition,* as shown in the success of individual-incentive plans—as long as there is ingrained acceptance of the idea of individual responsibility for performance. To be successful, group plans require that employees be ready for them. Engineered group incentives can, with proper management philosophy, develop a feeling of solidarity, of individuals helping one another. Perhaps the Lincoln Electric plan is the best example of combining the drives of *both* individual competition and teamwork: Every encouragement is given, by dividing a fair share of profits among employees, to constructive efforts by them as members of a group, and to fostering pride in belonging to the group. But *within* each group each man is judged individually and given individual recognition so that he can benefit both ways. As Mr. Lincoln puts it, "All men want to be part of a group—but they still want to be outstanding in that group. . . . Competition and pride are fundamental urges."

8. Even though there is no solid statistical evidence correlating job satisfaction with tangible output, the supervisor should not forget about satisfaction and concentrate solely on output. The conclusion to be drawn from research is that we should revise a fundamental notion about job satisfaction: It is not the *cause* of something (for example, increased production) but rather the *result* of something (the conditions under which the work is done). Hence, job satisfaction is an *output,* not an *input.* But it should always be a desired output, and for long-run operating efficiency it is intelligent to take the position that a balance may well be struck which sacrifices some productivity for job satisfaction.

[15] James F. Lincoln, *Incentive Management,* Lincoln Electric Company, Cleveland, 1951.

57 WHAT PRICE HUMAN RELATIONS?*

Malcolm P. McNair

In 1956 the Inland Steel Company appointed a vice president of human relations. The Inland Steel Company, of course, is big business; but little business is not being neglected, for I note that the McGraw-Hill Book Company, Inc., is publishing a book on *Human Relations in Small Industry*. The Harvard Business School has had a chair of Human Relations since 1950; by now the number of courses in Human Relations in schools and colleges throughout the country has multiplied substantially. Even more marked is the rapid growth of executive development programs, some in schools, some in industry, but almost all of them placing emphasis on human relations.

Doctoral theses increasingly carry such titles as "A Case Study of the Human Aspects of Introducing a New Product into Production," "An Intensive Study of Supervisory Training in Human Relations and Foreman Behavior at Work," "A Case Study of the Administration of Change in the Large Modern Office," and "Emergence of Leadership in Manufacturing Work Groups." And recently the *Harvard Business Review* has reprinted a dozen articles on human relations, under the title "How Successful Executives Handle People, 12 Studies on Communications and Management Skills," which include such intriguing subjects as "Making Human Relations Work," "Barriers and Gateways to Communication," and "The Fateful Process of Mr. A Talking to Mr. B."

It is obvious that human relations is very much the fashion in business thinking today. And fashions in business thinking are not a novelty; there have been many others. I can well recall that when I first joined the Harvard Business School faculty, the reigning vogue in business thinking was scientific management. Only a few years later, however, the grandiose claims of scientific management were sharply debunked. What was of solid worth remained —but a considerable amount of froth had been blown off the top.

Must we go through the same process—with all its waste and possible damage along the way—to get to what is worthwhile in human relations?

My quarrel is not with the solid substance of much that is comprehended by the phrase "human relations," but rather with the "cult" or "fad" aspects of human relations, which are assuming so much prominence.

There can be no doubt that people are of absorbing interest to other people. To verify this fact you have only to look at what makes headlines in the newspapers. There is a fascination for most of us in speculating about people and their behavior. So it is not surprising that human relations has assumed so much prominence as a fashionable mode of thinking. But, as with any kind of fashion, it can be carried to the point where people accept it without questioning—and certainly this can be dangerous when we are dealing with such an important segment of man's activity.

Therefore, just because the tide has gone so far, I must make my points in the most emphatic manner possible. Though I feel I have not distorted the picture, I do not care whether businessmen accept my interpretation in full, or even in large part, *so long as they get stirred up to do some critical thinking of their own.*

Before going any further let me try to indicate the things in this area of human relations which are really basic and with which there is no conceivable quarrel. In the first place, there can be no dispute with research in the social sciences, including the behavioral sciences. Obviously such research is highly important to business management and to business educa-

* Reprinted by permission from *Harvard Business Review*, vol. 35, no. 2, pp. 15–23, March-April, 1957; © 1957 by the President and Fellows of Harvard College; all rights reserved. Mr. McNair is Lincoln Filene Professor of Retailing, emeritus, at the Harvard Business School.

tion. Business management and education must seek to understand the behavior of people as workers, the behavior of people as members of organizations, and, of course, the behavior of people as consumers. In all these areas we need more and better understanding of human behavior.

Neither is there any dispute in regard to the things that are important for a man's conduct in relation to his fellow men. The foundation is good Christian ethics, respect for the dignity of the individual human being, and integrity of character. On these we should stand fast. Personally I have always liked this paraphrase of what Theodore Roosevelt once said in a commencement address: "On the Ten Commandments and the Sermon on the Mount, uncompromising rigidity; on all else, the widest tolerance."[1] But between acceptance of high moral principles and the exigencies of day-to-day conduct of affairs there can be, with the best intentions, a very wide gap. This is the gap which by better understanding of human motivation we should try to fill.

Also there can be little dispute about the observations on the behavior of people at work which Professor Fritz J. Roethlisberger, the leader of the human relations group at Harvard, summed up half a dozen years ago:

> People at work are not so different from people in other aspects of life. They are not entirely creatures of logic. They have feelings. They like to feel important and to have their work recognized as important. Although they are interested in the size of their pay envelopes, this is not a matter of their first concern. Sometimes they are more interested in having their pay reflect accurately the relative social importance to them of the different jobs they do. Sometimes even still more important to them than maintenance of socially accepted wage differentials is the way their superiors treat them.
>
> They like to work in an atmosphere of approval. They like to be praised rather than blamed. They do not like to have to admit their mistakes—at least, not publicly. They like to know what is expected of them and where they stand in relation to their boss's expectations. They like to have some warning of the changes that may affect them.
>
> They like to feel independent in their relations to their supervisors. They like to be able to express their feelings to them without being misunderstood. They like to be listened to and have their feelings and points of view taken into account. They like to be consulted about and participate in the actions that will personally affect them. In short, employees, like most people, want to be treated as belonging to and being an integral part of some group.[2]

In other words, "People behave like people." They have feelings. They don't always behave logically. The concept of the economic man can be a dangerous abstraction. Every individual wants to feel important, to have self-esteem, to have "face." Everybody likes to feel that he is "wanted." He likes to have a "sense of belonging." Group influences and group loyalties are important. The desire for psychological "security" is strong. People don't always reveal their feelings in words.

That all these human attitudes have important consequences for management is likewise not open to dispute. It is well accepted in management thinking today that leadership has to be earned, it cannot be conferred; that authority comes from below, not from above; that in any business unit there will be "social" groups which will cut across organization lines; that good communication involves both the willingness to listen and the ability to "get through" but not by shouting.

Dean Stanley F. Teele of the Harvard Business School recently made the statement,

> As we have learned more and more about a business organization as a social unit, we have become increasingly certain that the executive's skill with people—or the lack of it—is the determining element in his long-range success or failure.[3]

Here we are down to the nub of the matter. What is this skill? Can it be taught? Are there dangers in the teaching of it? Is skill an appropriate concept?

Perhaps I can give a clue to the line of thought which I am developing when I say that I am essentially disturbed at the combination of *skill* with *human relations*. For me, "human relations skill" has a cold-blooded connotation of proficiency, technical expertness, calculated effect.

[1] From Farida Wiley (ed.), *Theodore Roosevelt's America,* The Devin-Adair Company, Inc., New York, 1955, Introduction, p. xxi.

[2] Fritz J. Roethlisberger, "The Human Equation in Employee Productivity," Speech before the Personnel Group of the National Retail Dry Goods Association, 1950.

[3] Stanley F. Teele, "The Harvard Business School and the Search for Ultimate Values," Speech at the presentation to the *Harvard Business Review* of a citation from The Laymen's Movement for a Christian World, New York, Oct. 25, 1955.

There is no gainsaying the fact that a need long existed in many businesses for a much greater awareness of human relations and that, in some, perhaps in a considerable number, the need still exists. The very avidity with which people prone to fashionable thinking in business have seized on the fad of human relations itself suggests the presence of a considerable guilt complex in the minds of businessmen in regard to their dealings with people. So it is not my intent to argue that there is no need for spreading greater awareness of the human relations point of view among many businessmen. Nevertheless it is my opinion that some very real dangers threaten.

The world's work has to be done, and people have to take responsibility for their own work and their own lives. Too much emphasis on human relations encourages people to feel sorry for themselves, makes it easier for them to slough off responsibility, to find excuses for failure, to act like children. When somebody falls down on a job, or does not behave in accordance with accepted codes, we look into his psychological background for factors that may be used as excuses. In these respects the cult of human relations is but part and parcel of the sloppy sentimentalism characterizing the world today.

Undue preoccupation with human relations saps individual responsibility, leads us not to think about the job any more and about getting it done but only about people and their relations. I contend that discipline has its uses in any organization for accomplishing tasks. And this is especially true of self-discipline. Will power, self-control, and personal responsibility are more than ever important in a world that is in danger of wallowing in self-pity and infantilism.

Most great advances are made by individuals. Devoting too much effort in business to trying to keep everybody happy results in conformity, in failure to build individuals. It has become the fashion to decry friction, but friction has its uses; without friction there are no sparks, without friction it is possible to go too far in the direction of sweetness and light, harmony, and the avoidance of all irritation. The present-day emphasis on "bringing everybody along" can easily lead to a deadly level of mediocrity.

We can accept the first part of a statement by Peter Drucker:

> The success and ultimately the survival of every business, large or small, depends in the last analysis on its ability to develop people. . . . This ability . . . is not measured by any of our conventional yardsticks of economic success; yet it is the final measurement.

Drucker, however, goes on to add a further thought, which opens more opportunity for debate. He says,

> Increasingly from here on this ability to develop people will have to be systematized by management as a major conscious activity and responsibility.

In this concept there is the familiar danger of turning over to a program or a course or an educational director a responsibility that is a peculiarly personal one.

The responsibility for developing people belongs to every executive as an individual. No man is a good executive who is not a good teacher; and if Drucker's recommendation that executive development be "systematized by management as a major conscious activity" is interpreted as meaning that someone trained in the new mode of thinking should be appointed as director of executive development, then the probable outcome will be simply another company program in human relations. While this may be good for some of the executives, no long-run contribution to the development of good people will be made unless the good individuals personally take the responsibility for developing other individuals.

Please do not misunderstand me. I am not talking about old-fashioned rugged individualism or the law of the jungle, and I am not holding up as ideals the robber barons of the nineteenth century, or even some of the vigorous industrialists of the early twentieth century. But I ask you to consider whether some of today's business leaders, well known to all of us—Clarence Randall, Gardiner Symonds, Neil McElroy, Tex Colbert, Earl Puckett, Fred Lazarus, and so on—are not primarily products of a school of friction and competitive striving. We need more men like them, not fewer. It may be appropriate here to cite the recent observations of Dean Teele on "inner serenity" and "divine discontent":

> Any realistic approach to the nature of top business management, and therefore to the problems of selection and development for top business management, makes abundantly clear that the balance between these two [attributes] is perhaps the most important determinant of success in top business management. Let me elaborate.
>
> Psychiatrists, psychologists, and religious advisers join with ordinary lay observers in noting

> how often human efficiency is greatly reduced by sharp inner conflicts—conflicts which usually center around value judgments. That is to say, conflicts as to basic personal purposes and objectives, as to the values to be sought in life, are far more often the barriers to effective performance than intellectual incapacity or lack of necessary knowledge. The goal then from this point of view is the development of that inner serenity which comes from having struggled with and then resolved the basic questions of purpose and values.
>
> On the other hand, in business as in the world generally, discontent is an element of the greatest importance. Dissatisfaction with oneself, with one's performance, is an essential for improvement. So important to the progress of the world is discontent on the part of the relatively few who feel it, that we have come to characterize it as divine discontent. Here . . . the need is for both inner serenity and divine discontent—a need for both in a balance between the two appropriate for the particular individuals.[4]

To keep that important balance of inner serenity and divine discontent in our future business leaders, we need to focus educational and training programs more sharply on the development of individuals than is the fashion today. What is important for the development of the individual? Obviously, many things; but one prime essential is the ability to think, and the nurturing of this ability must be a principal objective of all our educational effort.

In the field of business education this ability to think, to deal with situations, to go to the heart of things, to formulate problems and issues, is not an innate quality. It has to be cultivated, and it requires long and rigorous and often tedious practice in digging out significant facts in weighing evidence, foreseeing contingencies, developing alternatives, finding the right questions to ask. In all business education, whether at the college or graduate level or at the stage of so-called executive development, we must not omit the insistence on close analysis, on careful reasoning and deduction, on cultivation of the power to differentiate and discriminate.

There is a very real danger that undue preoccupation with human relations can easily give a wrong slant to the whole process of education for business leadership. For one thing, it tends to give a false concept of the executive job. Dealing with people is eminently important in the day's work of the business executive, but so are the processes of analysis, judgment, and decision making. It takes skill and persistence to dig out facts; it takes judgment and understanding to get at the real issues; it takes perspective and imagination to see the feasible alternatives; it takes logic and intuition to arrive at conclusions; it takes the habit of decision and a sense of timing to develop a plan of action.

On the letterhead of the general policy letters that are sent periodically to the managing directors of all 80-odd stores in the Allied Stores Corporation there is this slogan:

> To LOOK is one thing.
> To SEE what you look at is another.
> To UNDERSTAND what you see is a third.
> To LEARN from what you understand is still something else.
> But to ACT on what you learn is all that really matters, isn't it?

An executive's ability to see, to understand, to learn, and to act comprises much more than skill in human relations.

Awareness of human relations as one aspect of the executive's job is of course essential. But, in my view, *awareness of human relations* and the *conscious effort to practice human relations on other people* are two different things, and I think this is crucial.

As soon as a man consciously undertakes to practice human relations, one of several bad consequences is almost inevitable. Consciously trying to practice human relations is like consciously trying to be a gentleman. If you have to think about it, insincerity creeps in and personal integrity moves out. With some this leads by a short step to the somewhat cynical point of view which students in Administrative Practices courses have described by coining the verb "ad prac," meaning to "manipulate people for one's own ends."

A less deliberate but perhaps even more dangerous consequence may be the development of a yen for managing other people's lives, always, of course, with the most excellent intentions. In the same direction the conscious practice of human relations leads to amateur psychiatry and to the unwarranted invasions of the privacy of individuals.

Hence I am disturbed about the consequences to business management of human relations blown up into pseudoscience—with a special vocabulary and with special practitioners and experts. In fact, to my mind there is something almost sinister about the very term

[4] Stanley F. Teele, "The Fourth Dimension in Management," Address to the American Management Association, New York, May 25, 1956.

"human relations practitioner," though I am sure that all sincere devotees of human relations would vigorously disclaim any such imputation.

For me much of the freshness and the insight which characterized a great deal of the earlier work in this field—exemplified by the quotation from Professor Roethlisberger which I cited in my introductory statement—has been lost as the effort has progressed to blow human relations up into a science—something to be explored and practiced for its own sake.

I realize that many people in the human relations field—Professor Roethlisberger in particular—are also disturbed about this trend, and about its unintended repercussions. But it was almost inevitable that other people would run away with such a fruitful concept, and set it up as an idol with appropriate rituals of worship (usually called "techniques"). Once you throw yourself into trying to "listen," to "gain intuitive familiarity," to "think in terms of mutually independent relationship," and so on, you can easily forget that there is more to business—and life—than running around plying human relations "skill" to plumb the hidden thoughts of everybody with whom you come in contact, including yourself.

This is the same mistake that some consumer motivation researchers make, as Alfred Politz has pointed out—trying to find out the attitudes, opinions, and preferences in the consumer's mind *without regard* to whether these factors are what determine how he will act in a given buying situation.[5] In his words, the "truth" that such researchers seek—and he always puts the word in quotes—is not only of a lower order than the scientifically established facts of how consumers react in real life, but it is also of less use to managers in making marketing decisions.

The whole things gets a little ridiculous when . . . foremen are assumed to have progressed when they have gained in "consideration" at the expense of something called "initiating structure"—yet such was the apparent objective of one company's training program.[6]

From the standpoint of developing really good human relations in a business context, to say nothing of the job of getting the world's work done, the kind of training just described seems to me in grave danger of bogging down in semantics and trivialities and dubious introspection. I am totally unable to associate the *conscious practice of human relations skill* (in the sense of making people happy in spite of themselves or getting them to do something they don't think they want to do) with the *dignity of an individual person created in God's image.*

Apparently this "skill" of the "human relations practitioner" consists to a considerable degree of what is called "listening." The basic importance of the ability to listen is not to be gainsaid; neither is it to be denied that people do not always reveal their inward feelings in words. But in the effort to blow human relations up into a science and develop a technique of communication, some of the enthusiasts have worked up such standard conversational gambits as "This is what I think I hear you saying," or "As I listen, this is what I think you mean."

No doubt there are times when a silent reaction of this kind is appropriate, but if the human relations practitioner makes such phrases part of his conversational repertoire, there are times when these cute remarks may gain him a punch in the nose. Sometimes people damn well mean what they are saying and will rightly regard anything less than a man-to-man recognition of that fact as derogatory to their dignity.

That a group of foremen who were given a course emphasizing human relations and thereafter turned out to be distinctly poorer practitioners than they had been before taking the course, as in the above case, would not, to my mind, be simply an accident. I think it a result that might well be expected nine times out of ten. In other words, the overemphasis on human relations, with all its apparatus of courses, special vocabulary, and so on, tends to create the very problems that human relations deals with. It is a vicious circle. You encourage people to pick at the scabs of their psychic wounds.

In evaluating the place of human relations in business, a recent incident is in point:

> At a luncheon gathering Miss Else Herzberg, the highly successful educational director of a large chain of stores in Great Britain, Marks and Spencer, Ltd., described at some length the personnel management policies of that concern and the high state of employee morale that existed. Throughout her description I was listening for some reference to human relations. I did not hear it, and when she had finished I said, "But, Miss Herzberg, you haven't said anything about human relations." Immediately

[5] Alfred Politz, "Science and Truth in Marketing Research," *Harvard Business Review*, January–February, 1957, p. 117.

[6] Kenneth R. Andrews, "Is Management Training Effective? II. Measurement, Objectives, and Policy," *Harvard Business Review*, March–April, 1957, p. 63.

she flashed back, "We live it; we don't have to talk about it."

In point also is a recent remark of Earl Puckett, chairman of the board of Allied Stores Corporation, when in discussing a particular management problem he said, "Of course you treat people like people."

And so, although I concede that there is still too little awareness of human relations problems in many business organizations, I think that the present vogue for human relations and for executive development programs which strongly emphasize human relations holds some real dangers because it weakens the sense of responsibility, because it promotes conformity, because it too greatly subordinates the development of individuals, and because it conveys a one-sided concept of the executive job.

I turn now more specifically to the dangers to business education at the college level which seem to me inherent in the present overemphasis upon human relations. Business executives should have as much concern with this part of the subject as teachers—perhaps more, because they must use the young men we turn out; furthermore, they represent the demand of the market and so can have a real influence on what the educators do.

The dangers to the education of young men, in my opinion, are even more serious than the dangers to business executive development programs for mature men. After all, we are well aware that businessmen follow fads, and so fairly soon the human relations cult in business will begin to wane and operations research or something else will become the fashion. Also, as remarked earlier, there is still a substantial need in business for greater awareness of human relations, and more businessmen are sufficiently adult to separate the wheat from the chaff. Thus in advanced management training programs for experienced executives there is no doubt greater justification for courses in Human Relations than there is in collegiate and immediate graduate programs.

From the general educational standpoint perhaps the first question is whether human relations can be taught at all. I do not deny that something can be learned about human relations, but I do maintain that direct emphasis on human relations as subject matter defeats the purpose. When things must come from the heart, the Emily Post approach won't do; and if behavior does not come from the heart, it is phony. Clarence Budington Kelland, that popular writer of light fiction, in a recent *Saturday Evening Post* serial entitled "Counterfeit Cavalier," makes one of his characters say:

> A very nice person has to start by being nice inside and have an aptitude for it. . . . They don't have to learn. It comes natural. No trimmings, but spontaneous. . . . If you have to think about it, it is no good.[7]

Good human relations do not lend themselves to anatomical dissection with a scalpel. How do people normally acquire good human relations? Some of course never do. In the case of those who do enjoy success in human relations and at the same time retain their sincerity, the result, I am convinced, is a composite product of breeding, home, church, education, and experience generally, not of formal Human Relations courses.

Hence in my view it is a mistake in formal education to seek to do more than develop an awareness of human relations, preferably as an integral part of other problems. This does not mean, of course, that the results of research in human behavior should not be utilized in the teaching of business administration. Certainly such results should be utilized (with due circumspection to avoid going overboard on theories that are still mostly in the realm of speculation). To take account of human relations in marketing problems and in personnel management problems and in labor relations problems and industrial management problems, and so on, of course makes sense. What I am decrying is the effort to teach human relations as such. Thus, I applaud the training of personnel managers, but I am exceedingly skeptical of training human relations practitioners.

I should like also to venture the personal opinion that human relations in its fairly heavy dependence on Freudian psychology is headed the wrong way. In the long history of mankind, the few centuries, dating perhaps from the Sumerian civilization, during which we have sought to apply an intellectual and moral veneer to man the animal are a very short period indeed as compared with the time that has elapsed since our ancestors first began to walk erect; and it seems to me that a large part of the job of education still must be to toughen and thicken this veneer, not to encourage people to crack it and peel it off, as seems to have been the fashion for much of the last half century. I suspect that modern psychiatry is in a vicious circle, that some of the principal causes of increased mental disease lie in morbid introspection, lack of strong moral convictions, and leisure that we have not yet learned how to use.

[7] Clarence Buddington Kelland, *Counterfeit Cavalier*, *Saturday Evening Post*, May 26, 1956, p. 24.

I believe that one of these days a newer school of thought in these matters will reemphasize the importance of will power, self-control, and personal responsibility. I can well recall hearing Charles William Eliot, on the occasion of his ninetieth birthday, repeat his famous prescription for a happy life: "Look up, and not down, look forward and not backward, look out and not in."

Our present preoccupation with the emotional and nonlogical aspects of life seems to me in many ways responsible for the prevalent wishful thinking of the American people. As a higher and higher proportion of American youth goes to college, it might be supposed that intelligently realistic ways of looking at things would be on the increase, but the contrary seems to be true. As people we are more prone than ever to let our desires color our thinking. More and more the few people who have the courage to present realistic viewpoints on national and world affairs find that the public will not listen to what it does not wish to hear. Why isn't education bringing us a more intelligent outlook on life?

Can it be that one of the reasons is that education itself has surrendered so far to the ideas that are concerned primarily with the current fashionable interest in the emotional and nonlogical aspects of living? In reviewing Joan Dunn's book, *Why Teachers Can't Teach —A Case History,* E. Victor Milione remarks, "Our educational system has substituted training in life adjustment for education."[8] Obviously there are many analogies between the doctrines of the progressives in education and the over-emphasis on human relations. Personally I prefer a more rigorous educational philosophy. I can well recall a remark of A. Lawrence Lowell that "the business of education is making people uncomfortable."

In any event, I think it is the job of education to push for more and not less emphasis on logics and morals in dealing with social problems. The following quotation from C. C. Furnas, chancellor of the University of Buffalo, makes much sense to me:

> We must recognize, of course, that it takes much more than pure intellect to answer social questions. Great problems involving many people are usually handled in an atmosphere of high emotion and the participants often show but little evidence of being rational human beings. But, even though it acts slowly, it is certainly true that intelligence can and does have some influence in shaping mass emotions. It is in this slow modification of mass emotional patterns that the average intelligent person can and should play a continuing role within his own sphere of influence.[9]

How can we do this if we encourage immature minds to regard the nonlogical aspects as the most important? Not that teachers necessarily intend it this way—though I am sure some have been carried so far—but simply that putting so much explicit emphasis on the emotional and irrational makes the student feel it is all-important. No protestation to the contrary can undo that impression—that perhaps *nonlogical* impression—which is exactly what an understanding of human behavior ought to lead us to expect in the first place.

But perhaps my principal quarrel with the teaching of human relations has to do with timing. Discussion of such problems as what men should learn, and how they should learn it, is probably as old as education itself, but much less attention has been given to the question, "When should men learn?"

The whole modern development of adult education has brought into disrepute the old adage that you can't teach an old dog new tricks. In fact, in the area of business administration it is quite plausible that teaching of certain managerial skills is best accomplished in later years, after men have gained considerable experience in business activities. William H. Whyte, Jr., the author of *Is Anybody Listening?* and *The Organization Man,* in discussing the Alfred P. Sloan Fellowship Program at the Massachusetts Institute of Technology, has this to say:

> But on one point there is considerable agreement: to be valuable, such a course should be taken only when a man has had at least five years' business experience. The broad view can be a very illusory thing. Until a man has known the necessity—the zest—of mastering a specific skill, he may fall prey to the idea that the manager is a sort of neutralist expediter who concerns himself only with abstractions such as human relations and motivation. Those who study these subjects after ten years or so of job experience have already learned the basic importance of doing a piece of work; in the undergraduate business schools, however, the abstractions are instilled in impressionable minds before they are ready to read between the lines and to spot the vast amount of hot air and wishful thinking that is contained in the average business curriculum.[10]

[8] E. Victor Milione, *The Freeman,* March, 1956, p. 59.

[9] *Ibid.,* p. 24.

[10] William H. Whyte, Jr., *Fortune,* June, 1956, p. 248.

Among those managerial skills the specific teaching of which had better be left to later years is the handling of human relations. Thus I should not only rewrite the old adage in the form, "There are some tricks you can teach only to an old dog," but I should go on to the important corollary, "There are some tricks that you had better not try to teach to young dogs." The dangers in trying to teach human relations as such at the collegiate or immediate graduate level are substantial. Indeed, by developing courses in human relations for college graduates in their early twenties without previous business experience we are essentially opening Pandora's box.

Such courses lead to a false concept of the executive's job. There is a de-emphasis of analysis, judgment, and decision making. Someone has said that the job of the modern executive is to be intelligently superficial. This statement is true in the sense that when a man reaches an important executive post, he does not have time to go to the bottom of every problem that is presented to him, and he certainly should not undertake himself to do the work of his subordinates. If he does these things, he is a poor executive. But if an executive has not learned at some stage to go to the bottom of problems in one or more particular areas, he will not in the long run be a successful manager.

Human relations expertise is not a substitute for administrative leadership, and there is danger in getting young men to think that business administration consists primarily of a battery of experts in operations research, mathematics, theory of games, and so on, equipped with a Univac and presided over by a smart human relations man. Undoubtedly many of the new techniques are substantial aids to *judgment*, but they do not fully replace that vital quality. One of the great dangers in teaching human relations as such at the collegiate or immediate graduate level is that the student is led to think that he can short-cut the process of becoming an executive.

The study of human relations as such also opens up a wonderful "escape" for the student in many of his other courses. Let's admit it: none of us is too much enamored of hard thinking, and when a student in class is asked to present an analysis of some such problem as buying a piece of equipment, or making a needed part instead of buying it, he frequently is prone to dodge hard thinking about facts in favor of speculation on the probable attitudes of workers toward the introduction of a new machine or new process.

For some students, as for some businessmen, the discussion of human relations aspects of business management problems can even lead to the development of the cynical "ad prac" point of view, which assumes that the chief end of studying human relations is to develop skill in manipulating people; this perhaps is the present-day version of high-pressure selling.

A different but equally dangerous result occurs in the case of the student who becomes so much interested in human relations that he turns himself into an amateur psychiatrist, appraises every problem he encounters in terms of human relations, and either reaches an unhealthy state of introspection or else develops a zeal for making converts to human relations and winds up with a passion for running other people's lives.

The sum of the matter is this. It is not that the human relations concept is wrong; it is simply that we have blown it up too big and have placed too much emphasis on teaching human relations as such at the collegiate and early graduate level. A sound program in business education, in my opinion, will of course envisage research in human behavior; it may, with some possible good results, venture on offering specific courses in Human Relations for mature executives; but for students in their twenties who have not yet become seasoned in practical business activities we should keep away from specific courses in Administrative Practices and Human Relations, while at the same time inculcating an awareness of human relations problems wherever they appropriately appear in other management courses. In other words, let us look closely enough at what we are doing so we can be sure that the gains we make in this area turn out to be *net* gains.

Finally, to express a personal conviction on a somewhat deeper note, I should like to refer again to Dean Teele's comments, cited earlier, on "inner serenity." The attainment of that all-important goal, in my opinion, is not to be sought through the present vogue of interest in human relations. Inner serenity is an individual matter, not a group product. As Cameron Hawley puts it, "A man finds happiness only by walking his own path across the earth."[11]

Let's treat people like people, but let's not make a big production of it.

[11] Cameron Hawley, "Walk Your Own Path!" *This Week Magazine,* Dec. 11, 1955.

B. MOTIVATION

58 LEADERSHIP AND MOTIVATION: A CORE CONCEPT*

Martin G. Evans

The question of whether a leader's behavior has an impact upon the job satisfaction and performance of the subordinate has been subjected to considerable empirical exploration. This, however, has been on a broad front rather than in any great depth. There has been a great deal of replication of Fleishman's[1] original finding that supervisory *initiation of structure* and *consideration* have an impact upon worker behavior and satisfaction. Originally it was found that satisfaction was positively related to consideration, while performance was positively related to initiation of structure. However, even in this early study, differences appeared between different types of work groups—the results were stronger for those foremen in production departments than for those in non-production departments. Additional work in the area has added to the confusion. A variety of studies has shown little consistency in the strength or even direction of the relationships observed.

Among the few studies that have attempted to go below the surface of the observed relationships to try to discover the conditions under which either positive or negative relationships are observed is that of Fiedler.[2] This has been a significant contribution. However, his use of a model of leadership which implies that the consideration and initiation of structure styles are the two extremes of a single continuum rather than being two orthogonal continua may have restricted its utility. Nevertheless, he found that the relationship between employee performance and supervisory behavior was moderated by aspects of the "favorableness" of the situation for the supervisor. Highly favorable situations were characterized by:

a) High formal power of the supervisor

b) High degree of liking for the supervisor by the work group

c) Highly structured task

Highly unfavorable situations were characterized by:

a) Low formal power of the supervisor

b) Dislike of the supervisor by the work group

c) Unstructured task

Fiedler found that in highly favorable and in highly unfavorable situations the more task-oriented (initiating structure) the supervisor then the more effective were the subordinates. Only in moderately favorable/unfavorable situations was the relationship reversed so that the more person-oriented (considerate) the supervisor the more effective the subordinates. This research has defined one set of external conditions that influence the nature of the relationship between leader and follower.

It is our purpose here to attack the problem from a slightly different angle. We are interested in the problem of motivation and in the way in which the behavior of the supervisor can change the motivational state of the individual. In order to explore this, we must develop and test:

a) a working theory of motivation, and

b) a theory concerning the nature of the articulations or junction points between supervisory behavior and the motivational state of the worker.

A WORKING THEORY OF MOTIVATION

In recent years, two strands of theory concerning motivation have been drawn together. The first, developed by Maslow[3] and applied

* Reprinted by permission of the publisher from *Academy of Management Journal*, vol. 13, no. 1, pp. 91–102, March, 1970. Mr. Evans is professor of management at the University of Toronto.

[1] E. A. Fleishman, E. F. Harris and H. E. Burtt, *Leadership and Supervision in Industry* (Columbus, Ohio: Bureau of Educational Research, Ohio State University, 1955).

[2] F. E. Fielder, "Engineer the Job to Fit the Manager," *Harvard Business Review* (1965), 43, 5, pp. 115–122.

[3] A. H. Maslow, *Motivation and Personality* (New York: Harper, 1954).

to the organizational scene by McGregor[4] and others, concerns the nature of the needs and goals of the individual and the interrelationship between these needs. This strand of theory describes in some detail the nature of the goal space of the individual, its complexity, and the relative importance of the various goals. Briefly, this theory suggests that the individual has a set of quite basic needs and that these are arranged in a hierarchy shown as:

- Self-actualization,
- Esteem from self and others,
- Social: Love and Belongingness,
- Security, and
- Physiological.

Initially, the needs at the base of this hierarchy are important in motivating behavior; the individual tries to have his physiological needs gratified. However, once such needs are relatively well satisfied they *cease to be important* as motivators of behavior and the next higher need becomes important. This continues up the hierarchy: each need becomes important as the one below it is satisfied and then in turn declines in importance as it itself is satisfied. When Self-Actualization is reached as the important need, it is assumed to continue as the important need, for by its nature full gratification cannot be attained. This picture of the rise and decline of the importance of a need is of necessity overdrawn. In reality, the individual is motivated by several of these needs with varying degree of importance. Such a variety of sources of motivation must be accounted for in our theory.

The second strand in motivation theory concerns the interrelationship between the action or behavior of the individual and his goal attainment and need satisfaction. This has been called the *Path-goal* approach to motivation. As a basic premise, the assumption is made that the individual is basically goal directed; in other words, that he will actively strive to engage in actions that he perceives as leading to his important goals. This is a simplification of the actual state of affairs; for the individual presumably has a set of goals (see above), all of which may be of importance to him, so that his choice of actions will be such as to satisfice this set of goals. However, this does not alter the basis whereby action decisions are made; i.e., the actions taken by the individual will be consistent with his perception of their instrumentality for goal attainment.

At this point we should emphasize that our initial concern is with the individual's *perception* of whether or not a particular activity helps or hurts him in the attainment of the goal. Such a perception may or may not be based upon the reality of the situation; nevertheless, the action decisions of the individual will be based upon these perceptions of path-goal instrumentality. We may, therefore, introduce the core concept of *Path-Goal Instrumentality* which is defined as the degree to which the individual perceives that a given path will lead to a particular goal.[5] We are now in a position to make some predictions about an individual's motivation to engage in specific behavior. This will be a function of the instrumentality of the behavior for his goals; and the relationship will be stronger for the more important goals of the individual. This can be summarized:

1. Motivation to engage in specific behavior = $f \sum^{\text{goals}}$ (Behavior's perceived Instrumentality for goal × Goal importance)

The actual frequency with which paths are followed by the individual will be a function not only of the individual's motivation to follow it, but also of the constraints on him in his choice of behavior (such as: his ability, the nature of the task, etc.).[6]

2. Frequency with which a path is followed = f (Motivation to follow paths/Ability, freedom, etc.)

This can be taken one step further; the extent to which a path is followed will, in combination with the actual path-goal instrumentality, affect the degree to which an individual's goals are attained. In other words, by frequently taking paths which actually lead to an individual's goals there is a strong likelihood that these goals will be attained; more formally:

3. Degree of Goal Attainment = $f \sum^{\text{paths}}$ (Path Frequency × Actual Path Instrumentality)

We suggested earlier that perceived path-goal instrumentality (which is the basis of a choice of paths) might or might not be based upon actual situations. In the ongoing organization, it is to be expected that as a result of experience, people will develop realistic perceptions

[4] D. McGregor, *The Human Side of Enterprise* (New York: McGraw-Hill, 1961).

[5] This position has been outlined most recently (with slightly different terminology) in V. H. Vroom, *Work and Motivation* (New York: Wiley, 1964).

[6] A multiplicative relationship has been suggested by Vroom, *op. cit.*, for the moderating effect of ability: Frequency of behavior = f (Motivation × Ability).

of the path-goal instrumentalities; though we should be aware that both organizational and individual factors may inhibit the process of verification.[7]

The first strand of motivation theory helped us to understand the kinds of needs and goals that are relevant for motivating individual behavior. This second strand in motivation theory provides us with the relationship between action and goal attainment. This indeed sheds some light on the thorny problem of the relationship between job satisfaction and job performance.[8] In Figure 1, this is outlined diagrammatically. First, the path-goal instrumentality, in conjunction with goal importance, determines the level of motivation to follow a given path; second, this motivation level, in conjunction with environmental factors, determines the actual frequency with which a path is followed; third, path frequency, in conjunction with path-goal instrumentality, determines the level of goal attainment, which is a partial measure of job satisfaction. We can, therefore, see that the individual will choose a level of performance that is perceived as instrumental for the attainment of his goals. If the individual sees low performance leading to his goals, then he will be a low performer; if he sees high performance as leading to his goals, then he will be a high performer; if he is able to choose paths that lead to his goals, then he will be satisfied; if he is unable to do so, then he will be dissatisfied.

ARTICULATION BETWEEN SUPERVISORY BEHAVIOR AND THE MOTIVATION MODEL

If the outline presented above is an accurate description of the motivational patterns in human behavior then the concept of *perceived path-goal instrumentality* becomes a crucial point at which influence can be exerted on the individual. To be sure, there are a variety of factors that can affect path-goal instrumentalities, but, in certain conditions, the behavior of the supervisor can be one of the most potent. In this section, we shall consider aspects of the supervisor's behavior that impinge upon the subordinate's perceptions of the instrumentalities of his paths for his goal attainments.

Fleishman and his associates identify two major components of supervisory behavior (*initiation of structure and consideration*) that

[7] For example organizational complexity, organizational change, and managerial policies on secrecy may contribute to creating ambiguity in an individual's role requirements and hence in his perception of path-goal instrumentalities, R. L. Kahn, M. Wolfe, R. P. Quinn, J. D. Snoek, and R. A. Rosenthal, *Organizational Stress: Studies in Role Conflict and Ambiguity* (New York: Wiley, 1964); while central individual beliefs about whether the environment is essentially random in its rewards or whether such rewards are contingent upon behavior will distort the individual's perception of actual path-goal instrumentalities, J. B. Rotter, "Generalized Expectancies for Internal Versus External Control of Reinforcements," *Psychological Monographs* (1966), 80, 1 whole number 609.

[8] L. W. Porter and E. E. Lawler, "What Job Attitudes Tell About Motivation," *Harvard Business Review* (1969), 46, 1, pp. 118–126.

FIGURE 1 Motivation Model

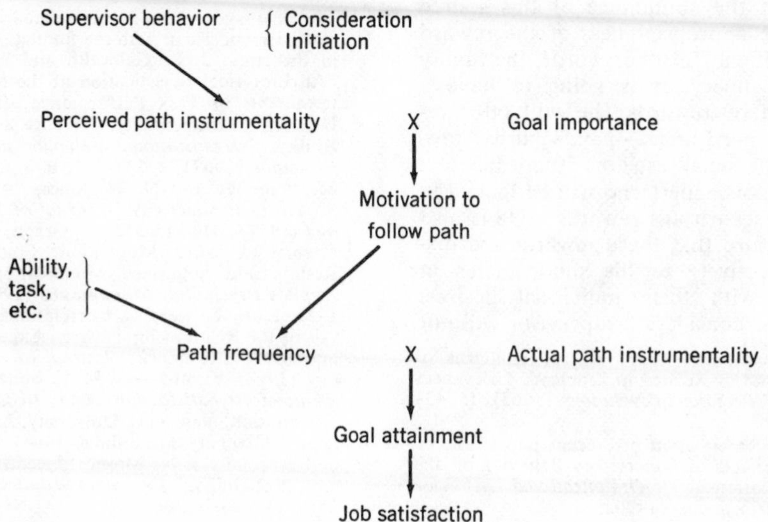

seem to result in different patterns of subordinate behavior (in terms of both job performance and job satisfaction). These are defined as:

- *Consideration* which includes behavior indicating mutual trust, respect and a certain rapport between the supervisor and his group. This does not mean that this dimension reflects a superficial "pat-on-the-back," "first name calling" kind of human relations behavior. This dimension appears to emphasize a deeper concern for group members' needs and includes such behavior as allowing subordinates more participation in decision-making and encouraging more two-way communication.
- *Initiation of Structure* which includes behavior in which the supervisor organizes and defines group activities and his relation to the group. Thus, he defines the role he expects each member to assume, assigns tasks, plans ahead, establishes ways of getting things done, and pushes for production. This dimension seems to emphasize overt attempts to achieve organizational goals.[9]

Path instrumentality is the subordinate's expectation that a specific goal will be attained by following a specific path; so that, in trying to effect path-goal instrumentality, it would appear that there are three aspects involved:[10]

1. The subordinate must perceive that it will be possible for him to attain his goals. In other words, he must envisage a situation in which there exists a supply of rewards and punishments. In most formal organization situations, the supervisor is one of the sources of such a supply. It would appear that the level of *consideration* exhibited by the supervisor would affect the abundance of this source and also the appropriateness of the reward to the individual. In other words, the highly considerate supervisor is going to have a larger range of rewards (he will offer rewards in all need areas—pay, security, promotion, and social esteem) than his less considerate colleague (who will be locked in on pay and security as rewards). He is also going to ensure that these rewards are distributed selectively to his subordinates in accordance with their individual desires, while the less considerate supervisor will not make such sophisticated discriminations among his subordinates.
2. The individual must see that his rewards and punishments (whether from an abundant and sophisticated source, or from a meagre and simplistic one) are coming to him as the result of his specific behavior. In other words, there must be a perceived connection between his behavior and the rewards or punishments that he receives. It is here that *initiation of structure* by the supervisor has its impact. The supervisor who is high on initiation indicates to the subordinate the kinds of paths that he (the supervisor) wants followed and links his reward behavior to a successful following of the path. The supervisor who is low on this dimension does not indicate which paths should be followed and distributes his rewards without reference to the successful following of a path.
3. Implied in this is a third way in which supervisory behavior affects the strength of the path of instrumentality. Through his initiation of structure, the supervisor indicates those paths or activities that he thinks are appropriate to the role of the subordinate. It may be that the type of path that the superior deems appropriate is a function of the supervisor's *consideration*. This last impact is going to be very much a function of the path: presumably all supervisors see good performance as an appropriate activity for workers; whereas only those with high consideration might see "helping fellow workers" as an appropriate activity.

SUMMARY AND EVIDENCE[11]

The implications of the motivation theory and the theory of articulation between leader

[9] E. A. Fleishmann and E. F. Harris, "Patterns of Leadership Behavior Related to Employee Grievances and Turnover," *Personnel Psychology* (1962), 15, 43–56.

[10] This section is based upon my recent paper: M. G. Evans, "The Effects of Supervisory Behavior on the Path-Goal Relationship," *Organizational Behavior and Human Performance* (1970, 5).

[11] The results are given in more detail in Evans, *op. cit.* They are consistent with the findings of other workers in this area: J. R. Galbraith and L. L. Cummings, "An Empirical Investigation of the Motivational Determinants of Task Performance: Interactive Effect Between Instrumentality—Valence and Motivation—Ability," *Organizational Behavior and Human Performance* (1967), 2, 237–257; B. S. Georgopoulos, G. M. Mahoney and N. W. Jones, "A Path-Goal Approach to Productivity," *Journal of Applied Psychology* (1957), 41, 345–353; G. Graen, "Instrumentality Theory of Work Motivation: Some Experimental Results and Suggested Modifications," *Journal of Applied Psychology Monographs* (1969), 53, 2 part 2, 1–25; E. E. Lowler, "A Correlational—Causal Analysis of the Relationship between Expectancy Attitudes and Job Performance," *Journal of Applied Psychology* (1968), 52, 462–468; M. E. Spitzer, *Goal Attainment, Job Satisfaction, and Behavior* (Doctoral Dissertation, New York University, Ann Arbor, Michigan: University Microfilms, 1964) No. 64–10, 048; and especially J. N. Mosel, "Incentives, Supervision, and Probability," *Personnel Administration* (1962), 25, 9–14.

behavior and subordinate motivation are clear. Supervisory behavior will only have an impact upon worker behavior and satisfaction if the two following conditions are met:

a) Supervisory behavior is related to the path instrumentalities perceived by the worker.
b) Path instrumentalities are related to satisfaction and performance.

A recent study that we carried out attempted to investigate these relationships. In two organizations (a utility and a hospital) we asked members of the work force the following:

a) to describe their supervisors in terms of initiation of structure and consideration.
b) to evaluate their own level of goal attainment and goal importance for such goals as: respect from supervisor; respect from fellow workers; doing a good job; improving skills and abilities; pay and fringe benefits; job security; serve other people (hospital only); respect from doctors (hospital only).
c) to indicate the degree to which they engaged in specific behaviors such as: do high or low quality work; do high or low production; help fellow workers; give suggestions to the boss or do what the boss tells you.
d) to indicate whether, in their opinion, following each of the paths helped them or hindered them in the attainment of their goals (Path-Goal Instrumentality).[12]

The results indicated support for our position:

1. In the Utility

a) Supervisory initiation and consideration were related to Path-goal Instrumentalities. When the supervisor exhibited high consideration or initiation of structure, the subordinates saw that following such paths as high quality, high production, and helping fellows led to their goals while following such paths as low quality, low production, led away from their goals. There are a possible 60 Path-goal instrumentalities; consideration and/or initiation are related to 42 of them; it is unlikely that chance could account for such a high proportion of significant relationships.
b) Goal attainment was related to the product of Path Frequency and Path-goal Instrumentality (Equation 3). For all goals except that of job security, these products account for between 10 percent and 25 percent of the variance in the attainment of the remaining goals.
c) Path frequency was related to motivation (Path-goal Instrumentality times Goal importance—Equations 1 and 2). For the paths of high and low performance, the product accounted for about 12 percent of the variance in frequency.
d) Supervisory behavior was related to goal attainment, although contrary to our expectations it was not related to the frequency with which quality and quantity paths were followed. For the goal of respect from supervisor, initiation and consideration accounted for about 40 percent of the variance in goal attainment. Results for other goals were somewhat lower: doing a good job—18 percent; respect from fellows—11 percent; improve skills and abilities—10 percent; job security—4 percent. (We would not expect this to be strong, as the goal attainment/product of path frequency and Path-goal instrumentality relationship were not significant).

2. In the Hospital

a) Supervisory initiation and consideration did not relate strongly to Path-goal instrumentalities—other aspects of the organization must be inhibiting the relationship. These are a possible 70 Path-goal instrumentalities. Consideration and Initiation of Structure only account for significant variance in 21 of these cases.
b) Goal attainment relates to the product of Path Frequency and Path-goal instrumentality. For all goals except doing a good job and pay and fringe benefits, these products account for between 16 percent and 25 percent of the variance in the attainment of the remaining goals.
c) Path Frequency was related to motivation; i.e., the product of Path-goal Instrumentality and Goal Importance. For the paths of high and low performance, the product accounted for about 12 percent of the frequency.
d) Supervisory behavior was *not* related to goal attainment nor to path frequency. Only for the goals of respect from head nurse and job security did initiation and consideration account for any variance—11 percent and 19 percent respectively. The fact that significant relationships exist for only two out of seven goals suggests that little relationship exists.

[12] The *Perception* of Path-Goal Instrumentalities was the only measure taken. It was used as the operational definition of both perceived and actual Path-goal instrumentality. Such a procedure rests on the assumption that the individual has an accurate perception of his situation.

These results are impressive in their consistency. Both sets of results support the suggestion that two conditions have to be met if supervisory behavior is to have any relationship with worker satisfaction and performance. In the utility, both conditions are met and supervisory behavior is related to worker satisfaction (though not to performance). In the hospital, the first condition *is not* met, the second condition *is* met, there is *no* relationship between supervisory behavior and worker satisfaction and performance.

These results illustrate how a variety of relationships have emerged between supervisory behavior and worker performance and satisfaction, and the theoretical position indicates that such variety is feasible.

IMPLICATIONS FOR MANAGEMENT

For a management that wishes to bring about changes in the organization so as to improve worker motivation, performance, and satisfaction, and wishes to do so through the changing of leadership behavior, the initial strategy depends upon whether the two conditions are met; i.e., that a strong relationship exists between supervisory behavior and the Path-goal instrumentalities *and* a strong relationship exists between Path-goal instrumentalities and behavior and satisfaction.

If both conditions are met, then a relatively simple strategy will suffice. Any change in leadership behavior should have direct consequences for Path-goal instrumentalities and hence on worker performance and satisfaction.

If the first condition is not met (there is no relationship between leadership behavior and Path-goal instrumentalities), the organization must investigate other aspects of the system, explore to see what variables have an impact on Path-goal Instrumentalities or inhibit the effect of supervisory behavior on Path-goal Instrumentalities—such things as the formal reward and penalty system or the nature of the work group might have this sort of impact. The organization may then decide that one of these variables is salient and that changes in this can bring about greater worker motivation; or it may decide that supervisory behavior is still salient and undertake to bring about two changes.

a) create the conditions for a strong relationship to exist between supervisory behavior and Path-goal instrumentalities by change of the other inhibiting organizational variables, and
b) if necessary, bring about changes in supervisory behavior with resulting changes in worker motivation.

If the second condition is not met, the organization must be examined to find out what factors inhibit the appearance of this relationship. Here such variables as individual ability, the nature of the task, etc. are likely to be crucial. The procedure is then to undertake such changes as to strengthen the relationship in the second condition prior to undertaking any changes in leadership behavior.

Too many programs of organizational development and change are based upon an inadequate appreciation of the relevant variables. The position outlined above provides us with a method for examining which of all possible variables are the relevant ones—they are those that either have a strong relationship with path instrumentalities or inhibit the relationship between other variables and path instrumentalities, or between path instrumentalities and performance and satisfaction. Only when these have been identified can the difficult task of designing a change program begin.

SITUATIONAL CHARACTERISTICS

We have suggested a model whereby the effects of supervisory behavior on worker performance and satisfaction are contingent upon two intervening relationships:

a) Supervisory behavior is related to Path-goal instrumentalities, and
b) Path-goal instrumentalities are related to job performance and satisfaction.

It might be useful to sketch out some of the factors that might affect the likelihood of these two relationships existing in an organization. Such factors might include Fiedler's situational variables:

Favorableness of Situation
  Task specificity
  Liking for supervisor
  Supervisor's power

and other aspects such as:

subordinate's role set
subordinate's abilities
supervisor's upward influence

Such a list is not exhaustive, but is sufficient to give an example of the kind of effects that situational variables might have on our basic model.

In dealing with the dimensions of "situational favorableness" suggested by Fiedler, we run into a problem—that the dimension of *leader power* and *subordinate liking for the leader* are unlikely to be independent of the supervisor's behavior; as Campbell has suggested:[13]

> important aspects of the leadership situation will be changed over time by a leadership style which reduces stress, improves internal group relations and contributes to improved leader-member relations. Likewise, any style of leadership which improves performance can lead to increased position power.

He is even of the opinion that task-centered leadership can lead to a structuring of initially unstructured tasks; though our understanding of Fiedler's position is that the nature of the task does provide organizational imperatives that are independent of supervisory behavior. Recent work suggests that this is indeed the case.[14] The nature of the task provides constraints upon the individual's choice of path, and hence upon the actual path instrumentality/performance relationship. In highly structured tasks it is suggested that the individual's choice is highly restricted so that he only has a narrow range of possible activities; in such a case, the relationship between path instrumentalities and performance will be weak—whatever the path instrumentalities, all are constrained to perform in the same way. On the other hand, in the unstructured situation, the individual has freedom of choice so that the relationship between instrumentalities and behavior will be high.

In a similar fashion, the individual's own abilities provide constraints upon the paths that he is free to choose. The high ability individual has a wide range of choices; that of the individual with minimal abilities is lower.

The role-set in which the individual is embedded is going to have an effect both upon the relationship between supervisory behavior and Path-goal instrumentalities and on the path instrumentality/performance relationship. Where the individual is engaged in highly inter-dependent tasks—those in which the individual cooperates either sequentially or concurrently with others—the relationship between Path-goal instrumentality and performance will be lower than it would be if the individual was engaged in an independent task.[15] Where the individual is in interaction with a wide variety of others the centrality of the supervisor for providing rewards or for creating conditions where other rewards are available will be reduced so that in such a situation, the relationship between supervisory behavior and *Path-goal* instrumentalities will be weak.[16] Finally, the upward influence of the supervisor will affect the relationship between supervisory behavior and Path-goal instrumentalities. Where upward influence is low, the most considerate supervisor may be unable to deliver the rewards that were implicitly promised; therefore Path-goal instrumentalities will be unrelated to supervisory behavior. The suggestion is in line with the work of Pelz who found that subordinates were only satisfied if the supervisor was a) considerate and b) had high influence. If he was considerate but had low upward influence, the subordinates were quite dissatisfied.[17]

[13] R. N. Campbell, Review of F. E. Fiedler, *A Theory of Leadership Effectiveness* (New York: McGraw-Hill, 1967).

[14] See J. Woodward, *Industrial Organization: Theory and Practice* (New York: Oxford University Press, 1965); P. R. Lawrence and J. W. Lorsch, *Organization and Innovation* (Boston: Division of Research, Harvard Business School, 1967).

[15] Most industrial jobs have a somewhat interdependent characteristic. However, it should be possible to distinguish between different degrees of interdependence, and thus test this supposition.

[16] This, perhaps, typifies the ward situation in the hospital where the nurse rather than the headnurse may be the "Linking-Pin" between the patient and a variety of hospital services—doctor, headnurse, therapy units, dieticians, laboratories, etc.

[17] D. C. Pelz, "Influence: A Key to Effective Leadership in the First-Line Supervisor," *Personnel* (1952), 29, 209–217.

59 THE MOTIVATIONS OF AN EXECUTIVE*

Arch Patton

I

Surprisingly little has been written about executive motivations.[1] A review of the literature uncovers only a limited number of articles and books on the subject, with the academic world accounting for virtually all this material.

Even a casual perusal of the available writings indicates that few of the authors have more than a nodding acquaintance with the decision-making process in industry. This undoubtedly results from the academician's relatively limited exposure to the industrial environment, but it has the effect of giving some of the writers' conclusions an aura of unreality. For example, the stresses and strains involved in the climb up the organizational ladder tend to be treated in a classical vein that leaves much to be desired as a practical evaluation of executive motivations during this process.

However, a study of compensation administration necessarily involves at least a reasonable understanding of executive motivations to put financial rewards in perspective vis-à-vis the other motivational elements that make a man tick, for the value of money as an incentive has declined steadily with rising income taxes. Furthermore, the freedom of management to reward outstanding performance has been restricted by the increasing proportion of the total payroll that accrues to the individual simply because he is an employee. The cost of fringe benefits (pension, vacation, sick leave, insurance, etc.) has approximately trebled in the past 20 years. In the bellwether steel industry, for instance, fringe costs soared from 8 percent of payroll in 1940 to 26 percent in 1958. In the light of rising taxes and restrictions on current financial rewards due to deferral in income, the importance of nonfinancial motivations to the executive group has obviously increased.

The assessment of executive motivations made in this chapter is a personal one. Certainly from the psychologist's viewpoint, it is unscientific. However, it is based on more than a decade of experience in wrestling with industry's compensation and organization problems and observing top management at work. To this extent, it should provide a reasonable background of executive compensation administration.

Let us recognize at the outset that some of the motivations discussed herein are environmental forces that flow from the quality of leadership, for instance, or the characteristics of the industry. However, it seems to me that such environmental forces *are* motivations, in a practical sense, and should be treated as such. Furthermore, we will be talking about *individual* motivations as though they were separable from each other. I doubt that they are. The mix of the several motivations varies considerably from person to person and may well vary widely from one time to another in an individual's career. But each of us is probably subject to all these motivations to some degree at any stage in our career.

No effort is made to explore group motivation as distinct from individual motivation; yet the chances are that group motivation offers a far greater opportunity for future development of management skills. This inconsistency is more apparent than real. In the first place, we know so little about group motivations in industry that a reasonable evaluation at this time is impractical. More important, while we know quite a bit about individual motivations, we probably must know a great deal more than we do to realistically study group motivations.

* Reprinted by permission of the publisher from *Men, Money, and Motivation*, McGraw-Hill Book Company, New York, 1961, chap. 2, pp. 17–37. Mr. Patton is a director of McKinsey and Company, Inc., international management consultants.

[1] Mason Haire, one of the outstanding industrial psychologists, in the book *Social Science Research on Business: Product and Potential* says: "The area of motivational studies is surprisingly lacking—the study of the motivation of management. . . . The emphasis on social and egoistic need satisfactions at work has been primarily on the hourly worker, as if he alone had the sensibilities to avoid the rigid determinism of economic motivation. . . . But there is virtually no work in psychology on prestige and status as springs of action in the management structure."

The reason, of course, is that individual motivations may well provide the foundation upon which group motivations must be built.

Finally, there is a reasonable body of evidence that many of us are not fully aware of important aspects of our work motivations. They are frequently deeply hidden and extremely difficult to isolate. An executive may appear motivated by an interest in people to work in the personnel department, for example, whereas the real reason is his fear of facing the competitive environment in a line job. On the other hand, there is the executive who says he prefers the line job because he is "doing things," whereas his real reason may be that he prefers the repetitive nature of the problems in a selling or manufacturing job to the constant need for thinking through problems "on his own" in a staff job.

We are not concerned here with an evaluation of the importance of these motivations, for this is subject to an almost endless succession of variables. The objective is to explore these motivations to the point of establishing that each of us is subject to a variety of such pressures that influence our on-the-job performance. This, in turn, will help us put the financial motivations with which we are concerned in a reasonable perspective.

II

One of the basic executive motivations is the challenge each of us finds in our work. Thorstein Veblen shrewdly termed this the "instinct of workmanship." Essentially, we are motivated to do increasingly better work for the sheer satisfaction of accomplishment.

If the effectiveness of this deep-seated motivation is to be maximized, however, the executive must know the purpose and scope of his assignment. Thus if he is responsible for sales, he should know his authority over the product line, pricing, the selection and training of salesmen, organizing the headquarters and field selling effort, etc. With this knowledge, he is in the position of the professional—the doctor or lawyer—to steadily improve his competence in the fundamentals of his profession. He is not placed in the position of jockeying for power with his right hand while doing his job with his left. (When this occurs, the chances strongly favor maximum effort being expended in the power struggle, at the expense of the job itself.)

The chief executive who refuses to use organization charts, for instance, because "they limit an executive's interest in the total picture," is undermining this potent motivation by making it difficult for the individual to understand the scope of his responsibility and authority. So is the president who thinks it necessary "to put every man in business for himself." The end result, in both instances, is to unleash an internal power struggle. When the boundaries of responsibility and authority are ill-defined, the power grabber takes over. (Few executives would want the boundaries specified in a deed to their property equally vague!)

Implicit in the optimum use of job challenge as a motivation are clearly defined job responsibilities. Enthusiasm for such individual job charters has been somewhat dimmed by experience with the traditional "job descriptions." These "descriptions" have been widely adopted incidental to job-evaluation programs and have frequently proved to be of minimal value. My own exposure to many such "scraps of paper" —as one president termed his company's job descriptions—indicates that they have a number of weaknesses:

1. They rarely recognize the critical elements in the enterprise that make for profit or loss.
2. They often ignore the decision-making and decision-influencing process.
3. They do not discriminate between important and unimportant responsibilities.
4. They rarely deal effectively with joint responsibilities.
5. They have inherent difficulties in dealing with the changes that are essential to progress.

These weaknesses can be rectified. And if this is done, not only is the job-challenge motivation strengthened, but management's understanding of the economics of its business is normally improved in the process.

A final word on job challenge. To maximize the effectiveness of this motivation, an executive should not only know the limits of his responsibility and authority but he should also have a reasonable understanding of the quality of work expected of him. Many an executive coasts along doing so-so work because his superior has set no clear-cut performance standards. The president of a large company was shocked to find the management of a major division considered its 6 percent return on assets to be adequate—for he had never told them otherwise! An executive should be *expected* to make mistakes—this is critical to the learning process—but his boss needs to have established reasonably clear limits of "failure tolerance" in advance.

An intangible motivation that is closely related to job challenge is the individual executive's belief in the value of the work he is doing. The most widely recognized example of this particular motivation is the doctor. It is not to add to his income that he leaves a comfortable bed at 3 A.M. in answer to a phone call. He simply feels responsible for the well-being of his patient. The only conceivable reward for such dedication is a personal satisfaction of doing a supremely important job well.

This sense of mission is also found in a well-led company and is enormously effective in maintaining a sharp competitive cutting edge. The late Thomas J. Watson, as president of IBM, provided his associates with the belief—that had an almost religious fervor—in the punch card's ability to solve virtually any clerical problem. The effectiveness of IBM's sales force in "saving" the world from being buried under mountains of paperwork is legendary, and their messianic zeal often left competitors numb.

The potency of this motivation flows from the emotional identification of the individual with a worthwhile objective and the increased creative energy this imparts to his efforts. The development of such an environment in an industrial company takes leadership of a high order. It requires that top management supply the organization with an emotional basis for transforming a dollar-and-cents business transaction into a "cause," as Thomas J. Watson did so effectively.

This motivation is obviously easier to develop in some businesses than in others. The products of an ethical drug manufacturer cure our aches and pains; therefore executives have a built-in identification with improving the lot of mankind. The same can be said of executives making propellants for our missile program; on the quality of these propellants may hinge our national survival. But the top executives of a cosmetics company, or a candy manufacturer, or a toy plant are not so fortunate. They have to develop the basis for this motivation from scratch, using imaginative leadership as their principal tool.

Outstanding leadership can build belief in the value of work into some rather improbable situations. My first job interview after completing school was with the sales vice president of a company that the employment agency said "manufactured games." In my discussion with this man it became evident that the company's products were primarily crooked dice, marked cards, and electrically controlled roulette tables for the professional gambling fraternity.

Sensing my reluctance to give the proffered job serious consideration, the vice president said, "Someone is going to make equipment for the gamblers, and we're the largest manufacturers in the field because we make the best damn crooked dice, cards, and roulette wheels in the business." He sincerely believed in his own work, though it might appear offbeat to me. His boss, the owner of the business, had done a good job of developing a "sense of mission," however misguided his efforts.

The need for the individual to believe in his work occasionally creates some problems. Many a corporate research function has lost a prized researcher to the teaching profession because he felt uncomfortable in what he regarded as a "commercial" environment. In many such instances, the university job paid substantially less than the company laboratory.

A somewhat similar situation crops up when a staff man feels the need to prove that he can handle line responsibility. Many management consultants, for example, take jobs running client companies for reasons that can seldom be explained by any increase in income they can keep. It is usually a more subtle desire to do more than advise, to wield the authority of decision rather than the authority of ideas.

Status has been a powerful motivation for centuries in the church and military, not to mention the government. The intensity of the struggle among the early princes of middle Europe to become Pope, the jockeying among England's nobility to be First Lord of the Admiralty, and the wealth expended in political campaigns in an effort to become an ambassador to some important country all attest the potency of this aspect of status as a motivation.

However, industry has recognized this motivation only in comparatively recent years. Prior to the Civil War, for example, titles such as executive vice president, vice president, general manager, division manager, and director of research were rarely if ever used. The owner ran his own business with little managerial help; hence there were few chances to develop job-status symbols.

The growing complexity of industry, however, provided this opportunity. Indeed, the inflation in job-status symbols in recent decades may well have exceeded that occurring in compensation. The advent of the executive airplane, the country club membership, the luxurious office, the "executive" secretary, and similar accoutrements of status involved a sort of Parkinson's law all their own!

Status motivation has many facets. For example, a young executive may be motivated to strive for a promotion that carries eligibility in the executive bonus plan more because of the status satisfaction implicit in becoming "a member of management" than the financial rewards that also accrue. More than one company loses much of the impact of this powerful motivation by not letting lower-echelon executives know where bonus-plan eligibility begins in the organization structure. What a man does not know about, he cannot aspire to!

Promotion offers a dual motivation—financial reward and status—that is often poorly utilized. Thus when a vice president-manufacturing retires, for instance, and his successor immediately inherits the vice presidential title, top management has lost an opportunity to keep up the motivational pressure on the individual. The two-stage promotional process is effectively used by many companies as a "complacency deterrent"; the vice presidential *title* is conferred only after the promotee has proved himself on the job.

The individual promotion also has companywide motivational implications of great importance. For example, when a young executive of high competence is promoted over the head of a senior executive with a so-so performance record, other executives are quick to recognize the message: Performance will be rewarded in this company. On the other hand, a chief executive who promotes the so-so senior executive in such a situation can talk about performance until he is blue in the face; his actions speak so loudly that his words are not heard.

Many companies have been slow to fully accept status as a motivational element. For example, the railroad and steel industries have what is called a "chief clerk." This job generally carries reasonably important responsibilities; yet the status implicit in the title is hopelessly negative and impinges on the quality of men willing to take the job. A similar anachronism is the title "general manager" for a man directing the efforts of some 25,000 or more people. Such a job is much bigger than the title indicates.

One of the most important executive motivations is the urge to achieve leadership. This inner drive compels a man to scramble up the organizational ladder, often at the expense of his fellows, his family, and even his own health. As in the case of other motivations, the urge to leadership covers a broad spectrum of intensity. At one extreme is the executive about whom Alfred P. Sloan, Jr., the long-time president of General Motors, was talking when he answered the question: 'What does it take to be a top executive at G.M.?" Mr. Sloan replied: "Naturally such a man has superior talents, drive, and is ready to work hard. But, more importantly, he must be willing to pay the price of being a top executive, by putting company interests ahead of everything else, including a comfortable home life."

This is the motivation that keeps the 75-year-old company president, many times a millionaire, working from 8 until 6 on the endless minutiae of a large business. Having reached full flower, the will to lead is one of the most powerful motivations in industry's arsenal. While the grasping of power for power's sake is undoubtedly an ingredient in this motivation, my experience has been that relatively few executives are devotees of sheer power as an end in itself.

The leadership motivation, however, is a frail flame. It burns brightly in many a young executive on the lower rungs of the executive ladder but flickers and, all too frequently, dies under the increasing buffetings of competition on the higher rungs. The stronger the flame, of course, the greater its chances of survival.

But many a flame has been snuffed out on the lower rungs by poor leadership higher up. For example, a promising young executive turned down a promotional opportunity involving transfer because of the probable consequences of the change on the health of his little daughter. This ruined his future chances in this particular company, and he has gradually settled into a rut far below his capacities. Another executive, with limited experience but great ambition, was made manager of a relatively small division. Ill-equipped for the job and receiving no guidance from top management, his mistakes cost the company over $7 million in less than three years. This flame was extinguished by exposure to the gale winds of profit responsibility without the necessary protection of experience.

Thus there is another aspect of leadership that has important motivational values: the quality of the leadership itself. Since men have repeatedly shown their willingness to follow a leader to virtually certain death, the quality of leadership must of necessity provide the most powerful of motivations. To be sure, an unwillingness to break with the disciplines of the group may be a factor in emotional exuberances such as the Charge of the Light Brigade, but it is unrealistic to discount the great influence of the leader on individual behavior for this reason.

Ralph Waldo Emerson expressed this leadership credo in a sentence in his essay on self-reliance that every chief executive would do well to have framed in large type on his desk: "The institution is the lengthened shadow of the individual."

The top man sets the pattern for the group. If he is competitive, profit-conscious, aggressive, and an innovator, these qualities will usually be present among his subordinates. If they are not, such a leader eventually will find someone who does have these characteristics as a replacement. By the same token, if the chief executive is tolerant of poor results, "protects" weak executives, makes expedient decisions, and does not work very hard himself, company environment will reflect his image.

The steady procession of outstanding leaders that General Motors brings to the top of the corporation—despite such losses as Ernest Breech and several hundred lesser executives to the Ford Motor Company—reflects the policies and practices developed by Alfred P. Sloan, Jr., during his 23 years as president. General Motors today is the "lengthened shadow" of this man who is sometimes called the father of modern corporation management.

Incidentally, Mr. Sloan's long tenure as chief executive of the big automobile manufacturer underscores an important point about the shadow cast by a leader; it takes *time* for this image to clarify. If Mr. Sloan had only run General Motors for four or five years, the shadow he projected would not have been as strong or as permanent. When a company has five chief executives in 11 years—as in the case of one large concern—the "shadow" becomes very thin indeed.

What are the principal elements of leadership that provide motivation for the led? The answer to this question will vary with the experiences of the respondent, but the applicability of these leadership characteristics should be reasonably consistent in all manner of situations.

One of the critical responsibilities of leadership is establishing goals and seeing to it that they are attained. These goals run the gamut from work habits (such as getting to work on time), to acquiring a company that rounds out a product line, to upgrading the quality of employees. The executive who does not know what is expected of him frequently sets easily attained—hence less productive—goals for himself. The leader who sets *specific* goals—be they qualitative or quantitative—is likely to get better results. Similarly, targets that "stretch" the capacity of the individual have higher motivational values than those permitting a more relaxed effort.

The setting of high goals and high performance standards is consistent with another key motivational element: the will to excell. The "four-minute mile" became reality only when Roger Bannister, a good miler, had to prove he was a great miler to win a race—and in so doing broke the four-minute barrier for the first time.

The lash of competition is also effective as a developer of outstanding performance in the business world. There can be little question that executives develop faster and more solidly in an environment that encourages the full utilization of an individual's capacity. Certain industries lend themselves to the development of such a competitive environment. However, the most competitive companies in *any* industry generally have a highly competitive chief executive. In effect, his organization is "the lengthened shadow" of himself—the leader.

The public utility industry is essentially noncompetitive, and the environment of many utilities reflects this condition. However, a number of companies have developed highly competitive internal relationships despite this handicap. The president of one of this latter group of companies has accomplished this by pitting the two major segments in his company against one another. Each unit knows the sales, construction, and maintenance costs, profits, etc., of the other. The "low man" is constantly being prodded to do better by every means at the disposal of the chief executive. Another president, having no major units to provide competition for each other, has devised ingenious statistical yardsticks on a regional basis to accomplish the same result. He uses these to whip up competitive efforts between regions to increase sales and reduce costs, with the result that the company record is consistently better than that of similarly situated utilities.

Many companies undermine their competitive environment by directly or indirectly setting up "crown princes" who receive preference in promotions. This sometimes results from having *one* executive vice president, or *one* assistant sales manager, or some other one-over-one reporting relationship that *automatically* results in the promotion to a higher job. What happens when this condition prevails broadly within a company, of course, is that the incentive for other executives—the "non-crown princes"—to make the all-out effort to fit themselves for the job in question is weakened. This, in turn, dulls the sharp cutting edge of the will to perform at peak capacity.

Recognizing this problem, many companies organize their activities so that there will be several candidates available for each promotional opportunity, when this is possible. If the corollary principle is also applied—that every promotion will go to the best qualified candidate—the executive "stretching" process goes on at all levels in the organization.

One of a leader's key responsibilities is to encourage his followers. This simple, but highly effective, instrument of leadership is widely ignored. A pat on the back at the right moment has a magic all its own. With this in mind, the army permits spot promotions in the field for heroic performance, and the navy has its own laconic "well done" for the most daring of exploits.

The other side of this coin, which is also often overlooked, is discipline. As parents, we recognize the training value involved in punishing a child when he or she has done something wrong. But many an executive ignores or makes light of sloppy work by a subordinate on the premise that to make an issue of it hurts teamwork and morale. In fact, he may simply be avoiding the discomfort of calling a spade a spade and risking his subordinate's displeasure. I suspect that in our secret heart each of us is a little contemptuous of the boss who takes this course, however comforting it is to have our mistakes overlooked.

The navy also has a phrase for discipline: "A taut ship is a happy ship." Men are *expected* to do their jobs well; hence they accept punishment as a natural consequence of poor work. To be sure, this means that FEAR is a critical ingredient in discipline. Men may do their work simply because they do not relish the consequences of doing it poorly. Thus those men who do not find sufficient motivation in the challenge of their job to do it well may, as an alternative, turn in at least acceptable work rather than risk disciplinary action.

Fear is a powerful motivation for improvement. Dr. Will Menninger, of the Menninger Psychiatric Clinic, commented to a recent seminar of top-management executives that "anxiety is a major motivation in producing change." Unfortunately, most of us prefer to do things the way we have been doing them until fear of the consequences of continuing in this course impels us to accept new methods. In other words, discipline—based on fear, which in turn produces anxiety—is a spur to progress.

Fear as a motivation is something of an "ugly word" in the lexicon of many executives. Somehow, fear is presumed to depress morale, which in turn is supposed to interfere with effective teamwork. This point of view gained fairly wide credence during the boom years following the war, when the magic wand of a seller's market effectively concealed poor decisions. The fear element in discipline, of course, can be overdone. Many companies lose valuable ideas and internal drive because a highly placed executive misuses his authority to punish or is irresponsible in dealing with the hopes and fears of his subordinates.

But, in the final analysis, the learning process demands that mistakes have their consequences. When a pitcher loses control, he is benched. When an army officer disobeys orders, he is court-martialed. So too with the business executive who fails to carry out his role; his bonus may be reduced, promotion may be denied, he may even be fired. Indeed, if these penalities are *not* exacted, a sort of incentive-in-reverse develops. Many a company asks hard work and difficult accomplishments of their divisional management, only to have the enthusiasm to make this effort dulled by the presence of a few widely recognized featherbedding nonentities on the headquarters staff. A large divisional concern has "taken care" of two ineffective divisional executives by "promoting" them to the top corporate functional staff. This has not only downgraded the value of the corporate staff—for the two were widely recognized as ineffective—but has removed promotion to the headquarters group as a motivation for divisional management. As a partial consequence, three good division executives have left the company in less than 18 months.

Financial motivation is the final item on this brief motivational agenda. This is not intended to minimize its importance but rather as an acknowledgement of the complexity of the "money motive" and the fact that its administration is so closely interrelated with the other key executive motivations.

The psychologists tell us that money is not the most potent motivation on the industrial scene. More often than not, they nominate "the approval of associates" as the number-one motivation. Each executive, according to the "approval" thesis, will tailor his actions to meet the environmental standards important to his associates. For example, if a company prides itself on promotion-from-within, it is the rare executive who will go "outside" for a replacement. This would be an admission of weakness in "developing people"; hence his standards of acceptable performance are likely to be reduced to fit the available personnel rather than recruit outside the company. (In fact, one of the great weaknesses of the 100 percent promotion-from-within concept is that no basis is available for comparing the quality of internal versus external performance.) A return-on-investment-conscious management, in another situation, may be so tightfisted about expenditures for office space and equipment that they unwittingly invite unionization of office personnel rather than "waste" money on what the group considers a frivolous investment in office improvement.

Important as group approval is as a motivation, the psychologists frequently overlook the fact that money is the generally recognized yardstick by which this approval is expressed. In other words, money is a motivation that has many facets and means many things to its recipient. Money not only serves as the wherewithal by which we keep up with the Joneses, pay for our youngsters' schooling, buy houses and the other artifacts of modern living, but it also is an important measure of where we stand with our associates. The man who has done outstanding work *expects* to be financially rewarded. Poor work—lack of approval—is penalized by fewer and smaller merit increases and smaller bonuses. To be sure, promotion is an important measure of "approval"—the most important, because of its status implications—but it occurs infrequently compared with merit increases or bonus payments, hence is not so readily available as a measure of approval.

There are some curious aspects to the money motive. For example, there is the instance of the newly elected company president, whose "other" income from securities approximated $125,000, demanding a salary of $100,000. When asked why he did not take a $50,000 salary and defer the other half of his salary until after retirement at a sizable tax saving, he replied, "I want my salary to be in six figures when it appears in the proxy statement." He found some sort of status symbol in being "a $100,000-a-year man."

Then there is what the executives of one large company call "the numbers game." Take the case of two executives, both paid salaries of $100,000. One receives a bonus of $100,000; the other gets only $85,000. The difference in the spendable income between these bonuses is probably only 8 percent of $15,000, or $1,200. Yet the executive receiving the smaller bonus *knows* his performance is regarded as being below that of his peer and that this is a none-too-gentle hint that he had better do better the next time.

When executive compensation appears on the proxy statement or the "grapevine" is particularly sensitive—and it usually is—"the numbers game" can provide a powerful incentive among highly paid executives.

But the greatest impact of the money motivation on the executive group results from consistent administration of promotion, salary, and bonus to reflect the performance of individuals. If this is done effectively, compensation administration becomes an instrument for targeting the efforts of individual executives on the objectives of the business, as well as a stout ally in the executive developmental process.

III

It is reasonable to expect that the individual executive's reaction to the various motivational elements varies widely at different stages in his career. The young executive reacts strongly to direct financial incentives that only mildly motivate the executive in the final decade of his active years. On the other hand, the status implications of being made a vice president at little or no increase in pay is likely to prove a powerful incentive to the senior executive, whereas the youthful executive may be tempted to snort that "management is trying to pay me off in titles."

Executives who have fallen behind those in their age group on the organizational ladder frequently do outstanding work when given encouraging leadership. For example, a man who had been a divisional plant superintendent for 10 years, suddenly, at the age of 52, started a meteoric rise that lifted him to the executive vice presidency of the company at 59. His superior assesses the phenomenon in these terms: "Bill suddenly realized that men who started with the company when he did were leaving him behind, and he made a tremendous effort to catch up that optimized his capacities to a degree I have rarely seen in my years as a corporation executive."

I suspect that the motivational adrenalin injected into such a man consists largely of the fear that he will "lose face" with his contemporaries. And this, in turn, spurs him to make an all-out effort to reestablish himself in their eyes—and his own. However, if company leadership does *not* encourage an environment that offers such an opportunity, the rehabilitation or optimizing process may never start. Thus if the president of this company had assumed that Bill's long period of inactivity meant he had reached his ceiling, he might still be a divisional plant superintendent rather than executive vice president.

The deeply rooted urge to be a leader is subject to significant influences that result from environment. For example, the executive who has always worked in a committee-run company tends to lose touch with the need for leadership to maintain discipline, to hold individuals accountable for their actions. After all, a committee decision is no *one* person's responsibility but the shared responsibility of all. The executive who has worked in the shadow of a boss who made *all* the decisions, on the other hand, frequently does not recognize that leadership requires a willingness to take action.

If environmental characteristics do work subtle changes in the individual's concept of leadership, the chief executive should be aware of the probable effects of his method of operation on executives. The president of a large company was disappointed in the performance of a man he had put in charge of the division from which he himself had been promoted. "I don't understand it," he commented, "George seemed to do good work for me when I ran the division."

Subsequent study showed that this president made all key decisions in what he termed the operating committee, a practice he had followed as division manager. By so doing, he made it possible for an executive with a highly developed political instinct to jump aboard the proper bandwagon at the right moment without fully understanding the economics or basic strategy on which the decision turned. Thus a politically oriented executive—like the weak division manager about whom the president complained—could *sound* good during a discussion of a business problem by asking questions designed to "explore the situation" without committing himself.

This environment not only made it difficult for the chief executive to judge the ability of the committee member but it also minimized the individual's opportunity to learn by doing, by being permitted to make mistakes in his early years so that he became acutely aware of their consequences before it was too late.

Most chief executives use the various motivational elements instinctively rather than consciously. This is not to imply that such leadership is any less effective. The chances are that the instinctive leader plays on individual motivations more successfully than the leader who makes a deliberate effort to harness these incentives. However, there is growing evidence that competition is forcing a more effective utilization of all executive motivations, both financial and nonfinancial. And, since the demand for industrial leadership far outstrips the supply of "born" leaders, the need for *a conscious* use of these motivational elements is developing rapidly.

60 MOTIVATION VS. LEARNING APPROACHES TO ORGANIZATIONAL BEHAVIOR*

Fred Luthans and *Robert Ottemann*

Motivation theory has played the dominant role in the emerging field of organizational behavior. Both content and process theories of motivation have been considered. Initially, content theories, such as Maslow's hierarchy of needs and Herzberg's two-factor approach, were widely accepted by management scholars and practitioners.

These two well-known theories attempted to identify specific variables which would energize or motivate organizational behavior. The Maslow theory inferred that esteem and self-actualization would motivate organizational participants; Herzberg's motivators included recognition, advancement, responsibility, growth, and achievement. Unfortunately, neither of these content theories has been satisfactorily substantiated by research or practice.

PROCESS APPROACH TO MOTIVATION

In search of alternatives to the simplistic content theories, many management scholars have begun to develop and test more complex process theories of motivation. These theories attempt to explain the process of how organizational behavior is activated, directed, sustained, and extinguished. The two major approaches are oriented toward drive and expectancy. Drive theory has its roots in hedonism and Thorndike's classic law of effect, but its modern development starts with the work of Clark Hull. In the 1940s and 1950s he identified the variables of drive strength, habit strength, and incentive, which he said combined in multiple ways to produce behavior.

Similar to this past-oriented drive approach but of more direct relevance to understanding organizational behavior are the "forward oriented" expectancy theories of the motivational process. The expectancy theories of Victor Vroom and of Lyman Porter and Edward Lawler are becoming increasingly accepted. Vroom postulates that motivation is a function of the interactions among effort-performance expectations, performance-outcome instrumentalities, and outcome valences.

Porter and Lawler have a somewhat more elaborate expectancy model that relates the nine variables of value of reward, perceived effort-reward, effort, abilities and traits, role perceptions, performance, instrinsic rewards and extrinsic rewards, perceived equitable rewards, and satisfaction. The expectancy motivation theories have stimulated numerous research questions and have begun to provide an explanatory framework for organizational behavior. To date, research has generally supported expectancy motivation models.[1]

The process approach to motivation seems to hold much more promise for understanding organizational behavior than the simplistic content approach. For example, expectancy models now are providing explanations of how expectancies and instrumentalities are acquired and modified.[2] To the degree that these motivational processes affect subsequent behavior, investigation of the interaction between the organizational environment and individual perceptions will contribute to the understanding of organizational behavior. Yet practitioners will subscribe primarily to content models of motivation. There is a great deal of surface logic to the content approach, and it can be easily adapted to practical application.

Even though the expectancy models of motivation are similar to operant models when oper-

* Reprinted by permission of the publisher from *Business Horizons,* vol. 16, no. 6, pp. 55–62 (December 1973). Mr. Luthans is professor of management, University of Nebraska, Lincoln, and Mr. Ottemann is professor of management, University of Nebraska, Omaha.

1 Charles N. Greene, "The Satisfaction-Performance Controversy," *Business Horizons,* XV, No. 5 (October 1972), pp. 31–41.

2 George S. Graen, "Instrumentality Theory of Work Motivation: Some Experimental Results and Suggested Modifications," *Journal of Applied Psychology Monograph,* LIII, No. 2 (1969), pp. 1–25.

ationalized in actual practice, operant learning as a theoretical base for organizational behavior has been almost completely ignored. In the behavioral sciences as a whole, however, the new, exciting breakthroughs in understanding, predicting, and controlling human behavior are based on learning, not motivation theory. The dramatic impact that behavior modification techniques derived from operant learning theory have had on the mental health and education fields is a case in point. Is it possible to use the same theoretical framework in the field of organizational behavior? It is the authors' contention that operant learning theory can add a necessary dimension to the process theories of motivation in understanding organizational behavior.

In particular, the authors feel that the operant model and behavior modification techniques may prove to be more successful in predicting and controlling organizational behavior than have been the content motivational models and techniques. The term O.B. Mod. (organizational behavior modification) is used to represent this operant approach to the management of human resources.[3]

MOTIVATION

Motivation is a basic psychological process which involves needs (deprivations) that set up drives (deprivations with direction) to accomplish goals (alleviation of needs). In this process, needs stem from within the person and drive him to search for goals that will satisfy his needs. This "motivated" behavior is purposive and means-ends oriented. It must be remembered, however, that no one has ever actually observed this motivational process. It is merely a hypothetical construct or intervening variable or "black box" concept that is used by all sciences to explain the unexplainable. The term "motivation" refers to unobservables which are inferred from observable behavior.

A motive can be thought of as an intervening variable or hypothetical construct that is often inferred from observable behavior. When motivation is used to explain organizational behavior, there is always the risk of using a given motive as an explanation of the observed organizational behavior from which it was inferred. For example, when a worker is highly productive or a manager works diligently on a project, it is easy to explain this behavior by inferring that the person has a motive, for example, a high need for achievement.

[3] Fred Luthans, *Organizational Behavior* (New York: McGraw-Hill Book Company, 1973), pp. 521–23.

Although this may be descriptive of the behavior, it certainly does not explain the causes of the productive or diligent behavior. It cannot automatically be assumed that the worker or manager has a high need for achievement. The same observable behavior may be produced by controlling the environment.

Operant learning theory emphasizes that behavior is greatly influenced by environmental consequences, not just by unobservable inner states such as achievement motivation. Most behavior, including achievement motivated organizational behavior, is learned behavior. Accordingly, organizational behavior can be considered to be a function of its consequences and not merely a hypothetical construct called motivation.

DEPRIVATION AND SATIATION

Obviously, not all motivated behavior can be explained by its consequences. For example, deprivation and satiation have two major effects on behavior which cannot be fully explained by learning alone. First, primary or unconditioned reinforcers such as food, water, sex or sleep will be reinforcing only if the person has been deprived of them. Deprivation increases the relative value of these reinforcers while satiation diminishes their value. A second major effect of deprivation-satiation involves purposive means-ends behavior. As deprivation of a need increases, the person will exhibit those behaviors that have in the past led to reinforcement. The deprived person is purposive and efficient in his reward-seeking behavior while the satiated person tends to be nonpurposive and inefficient.

The deprivation-satiation of primary reinforcers have been a central concern of traditional motivation theorists in psychology. However, in organizations these primary needs and drives have little relevance to more complex human behavior. Of greater importance to organizational behavior are the conditioned or secondary reinforcers. Conditioned reinforcers acquire their rewarding value as a result of learning or experience. Objects or events which were initially neutral in value acquire rewarding properties by being paired with other reinforcers. In addition, most conditioned reinforcers become discriminative and generalized. A conditioned reinforcer may serve as the means to the end of an unconditioned reinforcer or another conditioned reinforcer.

Some conditioned reinforcers, because they have been paired with many other reinforcers and because they have served as a means to many other ends, often become ends in themselves. Conditioned reinforcers, such as money, social approval, attention, praise, and responsibility, probably fit this latter category for most organizational participants.

Because of their almost universal reinforcing properties, these generalized conditioned reinforcers have often been assumed to be subject to the same deprivation-satiation effects as the primary reinforcers. This assumption has led to explanations of complex human behavior in terms of various underlying constructs such as motivation, attitudes, and other internal states that are difficult if not impossible to observe, measure, and operationally define. These vague explanations have tended to discourage the active search for antecedent (stimulus conditions) and consequent (reinforcers) factors in organizational behavior.

The motivational construct still has a definite place in understanding human behavior as a whole. For example, deprivation and satiation determine the relative reward value of primary or unconditioned reinforcers. On the other hand, it is not these primary reinforcers that are most important and relevant to the prediction and control of organizational behavior. The organizational environment factors which act as positive or negative reinforcements for participants are mainly conditioned or secondary reinforcers. For example, an increase in responsibility, a salary raise, or praise from the boss acquire rewarding value from past learning or experience.

These conditioned reinforcers are not subject to the same deprivation-satiation effects as the primary reinforcers. Complex organizational behavior is much more concerned with conditioned than with primary reinforcers. Therefore, consequences of behavior and the administration of this consequent behavior through schedules of reinforcement, timing of reinforcement, and the determination of reward value of reinforcement become relatively more important than deprivation-satiation in understanding, predicting, and controlling organizational behavior.

APPLICATION OF O.B. MOD.

One learning theorist has bluntly stated that "all of the phenomena that have been called motivational can be translated, without loss, into phenomena of reinforcement" and the result is that "what can be said in the language of motivation can be said as well in the language of reinforcement."[4]

This proposed importance of reinforcement is justified on the basis that observable stimuli control and reinforce behavior, whereas motivations merely explain behavior in terms of unobservable inner states. Reinforcement, or more specifically O.B. Mod., attempts to name, without reference to unobservable intervening variables, the conditions and the processes by which the environment controls human behavior. The behavior itself is always dealt with directly.

A motivational approach to organizational behavior infers that the practicing manager should attempt to define and manipulate such vague internal states as desire, satisfaction, and attitude. Under the O.B. Mod. approach, the manager determines the organizational goals he wants participant behavior to accomplish, the organizational stimuli available to control the behavior, and the types and schedules of reinforcement that can be applied to the consequent behavior. In other words, under O.B. Mod., organizational behavior is subjected to *observable* analysis so that the stimulus conditions and reinforcing consequences can be determined and administered by management.

Stimulus Control Organizational stimulus control is derived from observable analysis made by management. Such control is accomplished when a certain response is reinforced in the presence of a discriminative stimulus, and this response is not reinforced when the stimulus is changed or absent. A specific organizational example can be found in a stamping mill. The operator must occasionally stop the mill to sharpen and reset the dies. If the operator is consistently reinforced for stopping the process and resetting the dies when the product is off-standard, then the presence of the defect will control the occurrence of the chosen response. This chosen response (resetting the press) will occur when the discriminative stimulus (defect) is present, but not when the discriminative stimulus is changed or absent.

In this example, stimulus control has been achieved. Adam and Scott note that, "A supervisor could either implement an avoidance procedure in which a negative reinforcer such as criticism or a threat is made contingent upon not stopping the press and cleaning the die in the presence of the defect, or he could make a positive reinforcer contingent upon stopping the press and cleaning the die. The end result will be the same in that the defect will come to evoke the . . . behavior, but the relationship between the supervisor and the operator may be quite different."[5]

[4] Robert C. Bolles, *Theory of Motivation* (New York: Harper and Row, 1967), p. 434.

[5] Everette E. Adam and William E. Scott, "The Application of Behavioral Conditioning Procedures to the Problems of Quality Control," *Academy of Management Journal,* XIV, No. 2 (June 1971), p. 184.

Punishment Managers and supervisors typically depend upon various forms of threat or punishment in attempting to change subordinates' behavior. Learning experts acknowledge that punishment does have an immediate effect on stopping an undesired response. On the other hand, they are careful to point out that punishment also has several undesirable side-effects. Most prominent is the fact that, although punishment will suppress an undesired response, it does not normally extinguish it. When the punishing agent is removed or the punishment discontinued, the behavior is likely to reoccur.

An additional negative effect of punishment occurs if no acceptable alternative to the punished response is provided. Punishment only leads to the suppression of one response and leaves the punished person in a conflicting state between habit and inhibition. Unless the punished person is given an alternative response to the situation, he does not know what to do the next time he is in the situation where his previous response was punished. A third possible negative effect is that the punished response may not be made under conditions deemed more appropriate. For example, a project manager may assume additional responsibility on a project that he is heading. This behavior may be punished by his boss who feels the manager is overstepping his bounds. The punishment may generalize to the point where his initiative to assume additional responsibility may be inhibited in all cases, even those projects where his boss feels he should assume more responsibility.

Finally, the administration of the punishment may become associated through conditioning with the punishment itself and take on accompanying negative properties. Since the punisher is also most often the source of reinforcement, the two roles become incompatible, and there is a loss of effectiveness as either a punisher or a rewarder.

Positive Reinforcement A vital task for management is to learn to use O.B. Mod. techniques which do not have the negative side-effects of punishment. Positive reinforcement should be used whenever possible. Positive reinforcement in O.B. Mod. is operationally defined as a response followed by a reward, which will strengthen the response and increase the probability that the response will be repeated. In other words, behavior is a function of its consequences.

Positive reinforcement has wide generality and great practical significance to the practice of management. For instance, positive reinforcement principles can be applied to job and organizational design, wage and salary administration, training, supervisory techniques, and overall organizational development. However, it is not easy to readily identify specific events that are rewarding to organizational participants. Since human behavior is so highly dependent upon positive reinforcement, the key for the prediction and control of organizational behavior is to find the conditions or contingencies of reinforcement. Learning principles such as the one developed by David Premack would seem to be especially valuable in this effort.

THE PREMACK PRINCIPLE

The Premack principle of reinforcement is an accepted part of operant learning knowledge. The principle simply states that the opportunity to perform a response of high probability can be used to reinforce less probable responses. Stated more precisely, the Premack principle says that one event is capable of reinforcing another event if the reinforcing event has a higher probability of occurrence and its occurrence is made contingent upon emission of a lower probability behavior. Any response A will reinforce any other response B as long as the independent response rate of A is greater than that of B.

Thus far, concepts from learning theory like the Premack principle have not been applied to the theory or practice of management. Yet if organizational behavior is largely controlled by its consequences (ranging from pay to a pat on the back), then concepts like the one proposed by Premack seem directly applicable. In modern organizations with participants who are not physiologically deprived, traditional reinforcers tend to lose their reward value. This means that either organizational participants have simply lost their capacity to be reinforced or that they no longer value the normal reinforcers provided by management. Management could analyze this situation by providing employees with a wide variety of different possible reinforcers. Then by using the Premack principle management could determine which of these reinforcers are truly reinforcing.

The first step would be to determine the participants' independent rates of response for the various possibilities and then rank the responses in terms of frequency. Since reinforcement is relative rather than absolute, the more frequent responses of the set will reinforce all other lower responses. By the same token, the least probable responses will not reinforce any of the other higher response rates in the set. In other words, the reinforcing properties of the various responses will depend upon the responses to which they are paired. Based upon the Premack principle, the guideline would be that, to have reinforcing properties, a response must be more probable than that of the response to be reinforced.

There seem to be many direct applications of the Premack principle to the management of human resources. For example, the first step in job design would be to determine the independent rates of several of the employee's responses and rank them in terms of frequency. This procedure would result in a reinforcement "menu." Generally, such a menu contains many possible reinforcers which were not even considered. Also of great significance to cost conscious management is the fact that most of these reinforcers are nonfinancial. Since the employee is able to select his own reinforcers, the most effective ones are immediately programmed into his work environment. This helps to ensure that the consequences of his behavior will in fact increase the frequency of desired behavior (for example, productive performance and goal attainment).

After the activities the employee wants and does not want to do are determined, management should permit him to do the desired activities, provided he first performs the less desired but necessary activities. All employees like or dislike particular aspects of their jobs. A salesman may like to travel in a certain part of his territory. According to this approach, he would first be required to travel in a less desirable part of his territory or he might be required to demonstrate proficiency in a tedious training exercise. Another example would be an assembler on a production line who performs a single, monotonous operation all day. This job could be made self-rewarding by increasing the number of tasks the assembler performs and then making the performance of the tasks with the higher response rate contingent upon the performance of the task with the lower response rate.

This type of job design would seem to be mutually beneficial to both employee and organization. The employee is being continually reinforced by natural reinforcers in the immediate work environment, and the organization is getting needed tasks performed at a minimum cost. With this approach, there is no need to explore the underlying motives of the employee. Management simply asks the employee what parts of his job he prefers and then schedules the work accordingly.

CONCLUDING COMMENTS

The content motivational approach to the management of human resources has primarily relied upon job enrichment, which will presumably lead to increased performance and goal attainment. The approach is based on the assumption that the feelings of responsibility or achievement will affect job satisfaction, which in turn will improve job performance. This explanation is in terms of internal, nonobservable states. The operant-based O.B. Mod. approach suggests that a simpler and more direct alternative explanation for improved performance is possible. Job enrichment increases the number, type, and variety of tasks available to the employee. This increased set of tasks can serve as potential reinforcers for the employee.

Since each task has an independent rate of response, Premack's principle suggests that a task with a higher rate of response will reinforce a task with a lower rate of response. Thus, the impact from job enrichment can be better explained in terms of the greater number of reinforcers and how they are sequenced rather than by unobservable motivational changes on the part of the employee. From the viewpoint of O.B. Mod., the organization is a potential source of a great many positive reinforcers, including job enrichment.

The Premack principle represents only one tool in the O.B. Mod. approach that can be used by management in today's complex organizations. Even punishment, if properly administered and the negative side-effects are avoided, can be effectively used.[6] O.B. Mod. has been taught to and successfully applied by supervisors in managing their workers. The authors, along with David Lyman, conducted an O.B. Mod. program for a medium-sized manufacturing plant.[7] Rather than participating in traditional human relations training, the group of supervisors were trained to manage their workers contingently. The trainers served as supervisory behavior models and contingently reinforced the desired behavior with valued rewards. As a consequence, the supervisors learned to use the principles of O.B. Mod. to analyze and solve human performance problems in their departments.

The O.B. Mod. approach in this situation was basically to identify behavioral events that need to be changed, measure the frequencies of behavior to be changed, perform functional analysis by examining antecedents and consequences,

[6] Fred Luthans and Robert Kreitner, "The Role of Punishment in Organizational Behavior Modification: (O.B. Mod.),"*Public Personnel Management,* II, No. 3 (May–June 1973), pp. 156–61.

[7] Fred Luthans and David Lyman, "Training Supervisors to Use Organizational Behavior Modification (O.B. Mod.)," *Personnel,* L (September–October 1973), pp. 38–44.

develop intervention strategies that stress positive reinforcement, apply the strategy contingently, and evaluate. In this manner, every supervisor was able to improve the performance of at least one worker in his department, and most were able to effect the change of several workers. In all cases, overall departmental performance improved. The O.B. Mod. program resulted in considerable cost savings to the company in terms of improved performance.

In the area of sales training, Edward Feeney, then of Emery Air Freight, developed a program utilizing operant conditioning in the training of supervisors. Evidence indicated that new salesmen who participated in the program were more effective and comfortable in developing client relationships.

In addition to the examples cited, there seems to be a natural alliance between an O.B. Mod. approach and the currently popular job enrichment and management by objectives approaches to organizational development. A strict motivational approach to the understanding, prediction, and control of organizational behavior has not proved to be sufficient. With operant learning theory serving as the base, what has been termed here as O.B. Mod. may prove to be a much needed new dimension to the understanding and, even more important, to the prediction and control of organizational behavior.

61 JOB ENRICHMENT: A REEVALUATION*

Mitchell Fein

INTRODUCTION

The quality of working life, work humanization, job enrichment, restructure of work, and other such concerns are increasingly the subject of discussions and articles in the management literature and the press. A vocal school of social scientists is pressing government officials, legislators, and management to give serious attention to the signs of unrest in industry. Their proposals are summarized in *Work in America,* a study written for the Department of Health, Education, and Welfare.[1]

To a large extent this article disagrees with the findings of that study. In the first part of the article, the theory of job enrichment is examined in detail. It is suggested that job enrichment does not work as well as has been claimed. The second part of the article develops a more balanced framework for thinking about worker motivation and job enrichment.

THE THEORY BEHIND JOB ENRICHMENT

According to the study *Work in America,* the primary cause of the dissatisfaction of white and blue-collar workers is the nature of their work. ". . . significant numbers of American workers are dissatisfied with the quality of their working lives. Dull, repetitive, seemingly meaningless tasks, offering little challenge or autonomy, are causing discontent among workers at all occupational levels."[2] The study reports that the discontent of women, minorities, blue-collar workers, youth, and older adults would be considerably less if these Americans had an active voice in decisions at the work place that most directly affect their lives. "The redesign of jobs is the keystone of this report, . . ."; work must be made more meaningful to the workers.[3] The presumption is that blue-collar employees will work harder if their jobs are enriched or expanded to give them greater control over the order of their work or its content, or to allow them more freedom from direct supervision. Far too many variations on the theme of job enrichment have appeared in the last ten years to attempt to describe even a small proportion of them. The following discussion therefore assumes that the reader is familiar with the basic ideas of job enrichment.

DO THE STUDIES SUPPORT THE THEORY?

Claims for the success and usefulness of job enrichment are based primarily on a number of job enrichment case histories and studies conducted over the past ten years. These studies attempt to prove that workers really want job enrichment. However, when they are examined closely, it is found that:

1. What actually occurred in the cases was often quite different from what was reported to have occurred.
2. Most of the cases were conducted with hand-picked employees, who were usually working in areas or plants isolated from the main operations and thus did not represent a cross section of the working population. Practically all experiments have been in nonunion plants.
3. Only a handful of job enrichment cases have been reported in the past ten years, despite the claims of gains obtained for employees and management through job changes.
4. In *all* instances the experiments were initiated by management, never by workers or unions.

A review of some of the more prominent studies illustrates these points.

* Reprinted by permission of the publishers from *Sloan Management Review,* vol. 15, no. 2, pp. 69–88 (Winter, 1974). Mr. Fein is a prominent industrial engineering consultant.

[1] See *Work in America* [24].

[2] See *Work in America* [24], p. xv.

[3] See *Work in America* [24], p. xvii.

Survey of Working Conditions[4] This large scale study of workers' attitudes toward work and working conditions, conducted for the Department of Labor by the Survey Research Center at the University of Michigan, is cited in numerous articles and is a mainstay of the HEW study. When examined closely, however, several errors are revealed which cast serious doubt upon the validity of its conclusions.

In the study, the workers polled were asked to rank twenty-five aspects of work in order of importance to them. They ranked interesting work first; pay, fifth; and job security, seventh. The researchers neglected, however, to indicate that these rankings averaged together the survey results for all levels of workers, from managers and professionals to low skilled workers. The researchers created a composite image that they called a "worker." The study, however, was based on a cross section of the United States work force rather than just lower-level workers.

When separated into the basic occupational categories and analyzed separately, the data show that blue-collar workers rank pay and job security higher than interesting work. Interesting work was ranked so high in SRC's results because the responses of managers, professionals, and skilled people were averaged with the responses of lower-level workers.[5]

It seems reasonable to suspect that the attitudes of managers and professionals toward their jobs might be different from those of factory workers, and that there also might be differences between skilled and unskilled workers' attitudes within occupational groupings. When the data were compiled by SRC, each subject's occupation was identified, but the results presented in the final report were lumped together for all subjects.

The new data obtained by reanalyzing the SRC data by occupational categories is supported by a large scale study that was conducted abroad. In the first phase of a study covering 60,000 people in more than fifty countries (excluding the Communist bloc), Sirota and Greenwood found that there was considerable similarity in the goals of employees around the world and that the largest and most striking differences are between jobs rather than between countries. Most interestingly, the security needs of people in lower-skilled jobs were found to be highest.[6] The final phase of the study is even more illuminating because the data include the full range of occupations, from managers to unskilled workers, reported separately by seven occupational groups. Unskilled workers in manufacturing plants abroad ranked their needs in this order: physical conditions first, security second, earnings third, and benefits fourth. A factor labeled "interesting work" was not included, but there were several which in total encompass this factor. These were ranked far below the workers' top four needs.[7]

General Foods-Topeka General Foods-Topeka has been widely cited to show how, when jobs are enriched according to organization development principles, productivity and employee satisfaction will rise. However, Walton's reporting of this case omits critical information which greatly affects the interpretation of what actually occurred and why.[8]

Walton attributes the success of the Topeka plant to the ". . . autonomous work groups . . . integrated support functions . . . challenging job assignments . . . job mobility and rewards for learning . . . facilitative leadership . . . managerial decision making for operations . . . self-government for the plant community . . . congruent physical and social context . . . learning and evolution . . ." which were established for the employees.[9] He does not mention that the sixty-three Topeka employees are a group of very special people who were carefully selected from 700 applicants in five screening interviews. The fourth screening was an hour long personal interview, and the fifth was a four-hour session that included a complex two-hour personality test.[10]

General Foods-Topeka is a controlled experiment in a small plant with conditions set up to achieve desired results. The employees are not a cross section of the larger employee population, or even of Topeka. The plant and its operations are not typical of those in industry today. The results obtained are valid only for this one plant. What are other managers to do? Should they screen out nine of ten possible candidates and hire only from the select group that remains? What happens to the other nine who were not selected?

If the investigators had shown how they converted a plant bursting with labor problems into one where management and employees told glowingly of their accomplishments, the study would truly merit the praise it has received. Instead they turned their backs on the company's parent plant in Kankakee, which has many of the problems of big city plants. Even worse, they tantalize management with the prospect that, in building a new plant with new

[4] See "Survey of Working Conditions" [26].
[5] See, for example, Fein [4].
[6] See Sirota and Greenwood [18].
[7] See Hofstede [9].
[8] See Walton [27].
[9] See Walton [28], p. 9
[10] See King [12], p. 9.

equipment, carefully selected employees, and no union, productivity will be higher.

Many managers have dreamed of relocating their plants in the wheat fields or the hills to escape from the big city syndrome. Is this Walton's message to managers in his article, "How to Counter Alienation in the Plant?"[11]

Writers who extol the GF-Topeka case do not understand that what makes this plant so unique is not only the management style but the workers themselves, who were hand-picked. These are highly motivated workers who were isolated from the mainstream of workers and now are free to do their work in their own way. One wonders how these hand-picked workers would produce without any changes at all in management practices.

Procter & Gamble Procter & Gamble is cited by Jenkins. "Without doubt the most radical organizational changes made on a practical, day-to-day basis in the United States have taken place at Procter & Gamble, one of America's largest companies, well known for its hard-boiled, aggressive management practices."[12] What generally is not mentioned in any of the laudatory articles about P&G's organizational development practices is that P&G is an unusual company with a history of concern for its employees that is matched by few other firms in this country. In 1923 William C. Procter, then president of the company, recognized that the workers' problems were caused in large part by seasonal employment, and he established genuine job security. He guaranteed forty-eight weeks of employment a year. P&G has a long history of good wages and working conditions; they also have pioneered in old age pensions and profit sharing. Since P&G has a good reputation among workers, its plants attract some of the best workers in their areas. In seeking the reasons for P&G's success, one must not overlook their excellent bread and butter policies, among the best in the nation. Would their organizational development and job enrichment practices work without such policies?

Other Studies on Job Enrichment

Texas Instruments. The intensive job enrichment efforts of Texas Instruments management is unequalled in this country. Since 1952 the TI management has tried diligently to gain acceptance of its enrichment program by its workers. In 1968 the management announced that its goal was to involve 16 percent of its employees in job enrichment. Their data show that the actual involvement was 10.5 percent.[13] This is far from the huge success claimed in the numerous articles describing the program.

Polaroid Corporation. Experiments involve only job rotation, not job enrichment. Foulkes reports that from 1959 to 1962, 114 employees out of 2000 were involved in changing their jobs.[14] Although management had guaranteed that employees could change their jobs and be assured of a return to their original jobs if they wished, less than 6 percent of the employees actually became involved. It does not appear that the employees favored the plan or that it was broadly successful.

Texas Instruments Cleaning and Janitorial Employees. The version of this report in *Work in America* states that when Texas Instruments took over the cleaning work formerly done by an outside contracting firm, the employees were ". . . given a voice in planning, problem solving, and goal setting for their own jobs . . . the team [had the] responsibility to act independently to devise its own strategies, plans, and schedules to meet the objective . . . the cleanliness level rating improved from 65 percent to 85 percent, personnel . . . dropped from 120 to 71, and quarterly turnover dropped from 100 percent to 9.8 percent . . . cost savings for the entire site averaged $103,000 per annum."[15]

What was not reported by the study was that the outside contractor's employees received only $1.40 per hour. When TI took over the program, the starting pay was raised to $1.94 per hour for the first shift, with $.10 extra added for the second shift and $.20 extra added for the third. The janitorial employees were given good insurance programs, profit sharing, paid vacations, sick leave, a good cafeteria, and working conditions similar to those of other employees at Texas Instruments. *Work in America* does not mention that in raising the pay by 46 percent and adding benefits worth one-third of their pay, TI was able to recruit better qualified employees. Yet the study insists on attributing the improved performance to job enrichment. The omission of this pay data is strange, since the data appear prominently in the report from which the HEW task force obtained the case material.[16]

American Telephone and Telegraph. Space does not permit a discussion of the various cases reported by Robert Ford.[17] To a large degree, he redesigned jobs at AT&T which had been ineffectively set up in the first place. To label

[11] See Walton [27].
[12] See Jenkins [10].
[13] See Fein [2].
[14] See Foulkes [7].
[15] See *Work in America* [24], p. 100.
[16] See Rush [15], pp. 39–45.
[17] See Ford [5].

such changes "job enrichment" is to render the phrase meaningless.

The Scandinavian Experience. *Work in America* suggests that worker initiative is inhibited by a lack of democracy at the work place. The study points to Europe and especially to the Scandinavian countries as examples of productivity gains through democracy in the plants.[18] The assumption is that European experience in industrial relations is directly transferable to this country. In fact, it may not be. Nat Goldfinger, Research Director of the AFL-CIO, believes "... that industrial democracy was not needed in America: 'The issue is irrelevant here. I would suspect that most of the issues that are bugging Europeans are taken care of here in collective bargaining.' "[19]

The study of worker participation councils covering fifty different countries cited earlier supports this position. It shows clearly that this movement is the European workers' way of institutionalizing union plant locals and of establishing collective bargaining on the plant floor. It is not a new form of worker democracy as described by the behaviorists.[20]

The examples discussed above are only a sampling of the job enrichment studies. Many more could be cited, but most of them are subject to criticisms already voiced. Only lack of space prevents a fuller discussion.

Job Enrichment or Common Sense? Admittedly there are some cases where jobs have actually been productively enriched. Much more common, however, is the masquerading of common sense as job enrichment. Many studies have simply involved the elimination of an obviously bothersome problem, which hardly warrants the use of the term job enrichment. This paper is not directed toward the common sense applications of job enrichment. Rather this analysis is aimed at the broader claims of job enrichment success.

LIMITS TO JOB ENRICHMENT

One reason that job enrichment has not been widely implemented is that there are many factors operating within the work place to constrain its applicability. Several of these factors are discussed below.

Technology The structure of jobs in American industry today is dictated largely by the technology employed in the production process. The size of the parts used, the equipment required for the operations, and the volume of production are all important determinants. When the blacksmith of a century ago shaped a piece of metal, his only capital equipment was a forge. He was the operator and the forge press. Today there are even larger, specialized machines for parts which are viewed under a microscope. Much of the job redesign called for by proponents of job enrichment neglects the constraints imposed by technology.

There are few decisions on what to do in mass production. A piece is put into a press and hit. Two pieces or fifty are assembled in a given manner, simply because the pieces do not fit together in another way. In typing a letter or keypunching, the operators strike certain keys, not just any they wish. Even in the highly praised experimental Volvo plant where a small team assembles an engine, the workers have no choice in the selection of parts to be installed, and they must assemble the parts in a given sequence. While they may rotate their jobs within the group and thus obtain variety, this is not job enrichment or autonomy but job rotation.

In most instances it is impossible to add to jobs decision making of the kind that job enrichment theorists call for, simply because of the technology of the work. The job shops which produce only a small number of an item can provide true decision making for many of its employees, but these shops have not attracted the attention of job enrichers. They are worried about the mass production plants where work has been grossly simplified.

Another view of the technological constraints on job enrichment is offered by workers themselves. A full page article in a union newspaper recently denounced attempts by General Electric to combine the tasks of a thirty-two operator line producing steam irons into a single work station, with a headline: "Makes no difference how you slice it, it's still monotony and more speed up." Jim Matles, an officer of the United Electrical Workers, derides management's efforts, pointing out that, "As monotonous as that job was on that continuous assembly line, they were able to perform it practically without having to keep their minds on the job ... they could talk to each other. On the new assembly line, however, the repetitiveness of the job was there just as much, but ... they no longer could do it without being compelled to keep their minds on the job." Another Union leader in the plant said, "I've finally been able to show [management] that the more repetitive or rhythmic the job, the less unhappy the worker. On jobs where the rhythm is broken and unrepetitive, the employ-

[18] See *Work in America* [24], pp. 103–105.
[19] See Jenkins [11], p. 315.
[20] See Roach [14].

ees are unhappy and must constantly fight these jobs [rather] than do them by natural reflex."[21]

It is not intended that technological constraints be thought of as structural barriers to job enrichment. In the long run technology can be changed. Workers and managers are by no means forever locked into the present means of production. At the very least, however, proponents of job enrichment have neglected badly the immediate problems posed by technology. At their worst they have intentionally ignored them. The purpose of this section is to restore a more balanced perspective to the relationship of technology to job enrichment.

Cost Giving workers job rotation opportunities or combining jobs can increase costs. This occurred recently at the General Motors Corporation Truck and Coach Division. Early this year they initiated an experiment using teams of workers to assemble motor homes. *Business Week* reported that, "Six-member teams assembled the body while three-member teams put the chassis together. The move was an attempt to curb assembly line doldrums and motivate workers. Last month, the experiment was curtailed. The complexity of assembly proved too difficult for a team approach, which was too slow to meet GM's production standards."[22]

Increased costs from combining jobs and in job rotation also occurred in a case reported by Louis E. Davis, a prominent advocate of job redesign. He made studies to compare the levels of output obtained with a mechanically-paced conveyor line, a line with no pacing, and a line with individuals performing all of the jobs as a "one-man line." Using the average output of the nine-operator paced line as 100 percent, Davis found that the same non-paced line operated at 89 percent, and the "one-man line" operated at 94.0 percent. Translated into unit costs, the non-paced line cost 12.4 percent more and the individual line 6.4 percent more than the conventional paced line.[23] Suppose that the workers liked the non-pacing or the built up job better (although this did not happen to be true). Would the consumer be willing to pay the additional cost?

Relative Levels of Skill The possibility of making enriching changes in jobs increases with the skill level of the jobs. However, relatively few jobs have a high skill content, and relatively few workers occupy these jobs. If widespread benefits are derived from job enrichment, these are most needed for workers in the low level jobs, where boredom presumably is highest. The work of skilled workers already has challenge and interest built into the jobs, requiring judgment, ingenuity and initiative. Adding job enrichment responsibilities in some cases may only be gilding the lily. What are managers to do with low-skilled workers who make up the great majority of the work force? That is the essence of the problem confronting managers. When tested in the plant, enrichment programs do not operate as predicted. They usually can be applied only to the wrong people, to those who do not need them because their jobs potentially provide the necessary enrichment.

Work Group Norms Studies from around the world, including the communist countries, demonstrate that the concepts of McGregor and Herzberg regarding workers' need to find fulfillment through work hold only for those workers who *choose* to find fulfillment through their work. Contrary to the more popular belief, the vast majority of workers seek fulfillment outside their work.[24] After almost twenty years of active research in job enrichment, it is clear that only a minority of workers is attracted to it. These workers are mostly in the skilled jobs or on their way up. However the social pressure in the plant from the workers who are not involved in job enrichment sets the plant climate, and they apparently oppose job changes. The effect of this opposition is minimal on the active minority, because they find their enrichment by moving up to the skilled jobs where they have greater freedom to exercise their initiative. Obviously, the isolation of small groups of workers is not possible in the real world industry. In the main plant, the pervasive social climate controls what goes on, and job enrichment may not be permitted to work.

Contrasting Employer and Employee Goals Proponents of job enrichment often forget that management and workers are not motivated in the same direction; they have different goals, aspirations, and needs. The fact of life which workers see clearly, but which often is obscured to others, is that *if workers do anything to raise productivity, some of them will be penalized.*

Job enrichment predicts that increased job satisfaction will increase motivation and raise productivity. However workers know that if they increase production, reduce delays and waiting time, reduce crew sizes or cooperate in

[21] See Matles [13].

[22] See "GM Zeroes in on Employee Discontent" [8], p. 140.

[23] See Davis and Canter [1], p. 279.

[24] See, for example, Fein [2].

any way, less overtime will be available, some employees will be displaced, and the plant will require fewer employees. The remaining workers will receive few financial benefits. What employee will voluntarily raise his production output, only to be penalized for his diligence?

This phenomenon does not occur with "exempt" employees, the executives, administrators, professionals, and salesmen. Have you ever heard of a manager who worked himself out of a job by superior performance? Have you ever heard of a salesman whose security was threatened because he sold too much or an engineer who caused the layoff of other engineers because he was too creative? These employees usually can anticipate rewards for their creativity and effectiveness.

When workers excel and raise productivity, the company benefits and management is pleased, but the workers usually do not benefit. On the contrary, in the short term their economic interests may be threatened; some suffer loss of income. When exempt employees are more effective, they cover themselves with glory; their economic security is enhanced not threatened. Ironically, the relationship between workers and management actually provides workers with the incentive not to cooperate in productivity improvement. Most companies offer their employees the opportunity to reduce their earnings and job security as they raise productivity. Management does not, of course, intend such results, but the system often operates that way in this country.

A recent study by the Harris organization, conducted for the National Commission on Productivity, provides support for this contention.

> Nearly 7 in 10 feel that stockholders and management would benefit a lot from increased productivity, compared with scarcely more than 1 in 3 who see the same gains for the country as a whole.
>
> The term 'increased productivity' does not have a positive connotation for most people who work for a living.
>
> A majority believes the statement 'companies benefit from increased productivity at the expense of workers.' Hourly workers believe this by 80–14 percent.[25]

Is it any wonder that workers are alienated from their work? Would company executives improve the effectiveness of their work if they believed it would not benefit them, and more, that it would reduce their income and even cause their layoff?[26]

DO MANAGERS SUPPORT THE THEORY?

If job enrichment were the panacea it is so often claimed to be, then somewhere in this country some aggressive, farsighted manager should have been able, in the past ten years, to have made it operational on a large scale basis. The claims that large productivity gains will be made through job redesign should have spurred many companies to implement it. Yet there are few successful examples. Given this lack of acceptance, it is reasonable to assume that managers do not support job enrichment.

DO THE WORKERS SUPPORT THE THEORY?

Those advocating that work should be redesigned start with the premise that such changes are socially desirable and beneficial to workers. Curiously, however, these investigators are not supported in their claims by many workers or unions. There is a sharp difference of opinion between what workers say they want and what proponents of job enrichment say workers should want.[27]

Workers' opinions on the enrichment of jobs are expressed by William W. Winpisinger, Vice-President of the Machinist Union.

> In my years as a union representative and officer I've negotiated for a lot of membership demands. I've been instructed to negotiate on wages . . . noise . . . seniority clauses; fought for health and welfare plans, . . . and everything else you find in a modern labor-management contract. But never once have I carried into negotiations a membership mandate to seek job enrichment. In fact, quite to the contrary, working people want management to leave their jobs alone.[28]

The question of job enrichment and boredom on the job was discussed at last year's United Auto Workers convention and significantly was not made an issue in the following auto negotia-

[25] See the Harris Survey published in *The Record* (Bergen, N.J.), 19 February 1973, p. A-3.

[26] A most ironic turn of events has occurred in plants with supplementary unemployment benefits (SUB). Unions are asking that layoffs occur in *inverse seniority*, with the highest seniority employees going first. By inverting seniority and giving the senior employees a choice, a layoff under SUB becomes a reward, not a penalty. For working diligently and working himself out of a job, a worker is rewarded by time off with pay.

[27] This divergence of opinion is explored in more detail by Fein [3].

[28] See Winpisinger [301].

tions. Leonard Woodcock, President of the UAW, was sharply critical of the HEW report and a number of its suggestions. "Mr. Woodcock was very outspoken in his denunciation of government officials, academic writers and intellectuals who contend that boredom and monotony are the big problems among assembly workers. He said 'a lot of academic writers . . . are writing a lot of nonsense' . . . [he] expressed resentment over a recent government report on work as 'elitist' in its approach, describing assembly line workers as if they were 'subhumans'."[29]

A similar attitude on the part of European workers is reported by Basil Whiting of the Ford Foundation. He visited Europe to study their job enrichment efforts ". . . in terms of the experiments on job redesign: By and large all these experiments were initiated by management. We found no cases where they were initiated by unions and other forces in society."[30]

Despite the urgings for increased participation by workers, Strauss and Rosenstein also found that workers all over the world have failed to respond: " 'Participation' is one of the most overworked words of the decade. Along with 'meaningful' and 'involvement' it appears in a variety of forms and context." "Participation in many cases has been introduced from the top down as symbolic solutions to ideological contradictions," especially in the countries with strong socialist parties.[31] "In general the impetus for participation has come more from intellectuals, propagandists and politicians (sometimes all three combined) than it has from the rank-and-file workers who were supposed to do the participating."[32] There is obviously a lack of worker interest in participation despite claims by intellectuals that the work place is dehumanizing.

A MORE BALANCED APPROACH TO WORKER MOTIVATION AND JOB ENRICHMENT

Studying satisfied and dissatisfied workers, job enrichment theory contends that the intrinsic nature of the work performed is the main cause of the differences between them. The job enrichment theorists propose to change the work of the dissatisfied workers to more closely resemble the work performed by the satisfied workers. There is, however, a large "if" to this approach. What if the nature of the work is not what primarily satisfies all satisfied workers? Restructuring the work and creating work involvement opportunities may ignite a small flame under some people, but to what extent is the nature of the work the determinant of a person's drive? *The simple truth is that there are no data which show that restructuring and enriching jobs will raise the will to work.*

The essential assumption of job enrichment theory is that the nature of the work performed determines to a large extent worker satisfaction or dissatisfaction. It is argued here that this is not always so. *The intrinsic nature of the work is only one factor among many that affect worker satisfaction.* Moreover, the available evidence suggests that its influence is very often subordinate to that of several other variables: pay, job security, and job rules. The inconclusive performance of job enrichment to date stems largely from those programs that have neglected to consider these factors.

A useful starting point in understanding how workers feel about their jobs is to look at how they choose their jobs. A "natural selection" model of job choice proves very fruitful in examining this process.

A "NATURAL SELECTION" MODEL OF JOB CHOICE

There is greater selection by workers of jobs than is supposed. The selection process in factories and offices often occurs without conscious direction by either workers or management. The data for white- and blue-collar jobs show that there is tremendous turnover in the initial employment period, which drops sharply with time on the job. Apparently what happens is that a worker begins a new job, tries it out for several days or weeks, and decides whether the work suits his needs and desires. Impressions about a job are a composite of many factors: pay, proximity to home, the nature of the work, working conditions, the attitude of supervision, congeniality of fellow workers, past employment history of the company, job security, physical demands, opportunities for advancement, and many other related factors. A worker's choice of job is made in a combination of ways, through evaluating various trade-offs. Working conditions may be bad, but if pay and job security are high, the job may be tolerable. There are numerous combinations of factors which in total influence a worker's disposition to stay on the job or not.

There is dual screening which culls out those who will be dissatisfied with the work. The worker in the first instance decides whether to stay on the job, and management then has the opportunity to determine whether to keep him

[29] See "UAW Indicates It Will Seek to Minimize Local Plant Strikes in Talks Next Fall" [22].
[30] See his testimony before the Senate Subcommittee on Employment, Manpower, and Poverty [23].
[31] See Strauss and Rosenstein [21], pp. 197, 198.
[32] See Strauss and Rosenstein [21], p. 199.

beyond the trial period. The combination of the worker's choice to remain and management's decision that the worker is acceptable initially screens out workers who might find the work dissatisfying.

INTRINSIC AND EXTRINSIC JOB CHARACTERISTICS

As a result of this selection process, workers are able to exert much control over the nature of the work which they finally accept. They can leave jobs that they do not like and only accept jobs which they find rewarding. The major constraint on the variety of work available to them is the intrinsic nature of the work itself. However, if there are no intrinsically rewarding jobs but a worker still must support his family, he will have to take an intrinsically unsatisfactory job.

Unlike the intrinsic nature of the work that he accepts, the worker has much less control over the extrinsic characteristics of his job. There may be many different kinds of jobs for which he is qualified, but most of them will pay about the same maximum salary or wage. Similarly, there will be few options regarding the different kinds of job security and work rule combinations which he can find. The suggested hypothesis is that the influence of extrinsic factors, particularly pay, job security, and work rules, on worker satisfaction has been obscured and neglected by job enrichment. Undoubtedly some workers are distressed by the highly routinized work that they may be performing, but to what extent is dissatisfaction caused by the intrinsic nature of their work? What proportion is caused by their insufficient pay? Would workers have a greater interest in the work if their living standards were raised and they could see their jobs as contributing to a good life?

Individual Differences in Job Preference

Work that one person views as interesting or satisfying may appear boring and dissatisfying to another. There are significant differences among workers, and their needs vary. Some workers prefer to work by rote without having to be bothered with decisions. Some workers prefer more complicated work. It is really a matter of individual preference.

There would undoubtedly be far greater dissatisfaction with work if those on the jobs were not free to make changes and selections in the work they do. Some prefer to remain in highly repetitive, low skill jobs even when they have an opportunity to advance to higher skill jobs through job bidding. A minority of workers strives to move into the skilled jobs such as machinists, maintenance mechanics, set-up men, group leaders, utility men, and other such positions where there is considerable autonomy in the work performed.

The continued evaluation of workers by management and the mobility available to workers to obtain jobs which suit them best refine the selection process. A year or two after entering a plant, most workers are on jobs or job progressions which suit them or which they find tolerable. Those who are no longer on the job have been "selected" out, either by themselves or by management. Given the distinction between intrinsic and extrinsic job characteristics and the greater degree of control which workers exert over the former, those who are left on the job after the selection process can be expected to be relatively more satisfied with the nature of their work than with their pay, job security, or work rules. In fact this prediction proves to be correct.

WORKERS' ATTITUDES TOWARD THEIR WORK

Work in America cites a Gallup Poll which found that 80 to 90 percent of American workers are satisfied with their jobs.[33] A more recent poll found that from 82 to 91 percent of blue- and white-collar workers like their work. The workers were asked, "If there were one thing you could change about your job, what would it be?" Astonishingly, very few workers said that they would make their jobs " 'less boring' or 'more interesting'."[34]

In a recent study, David Sirota was surprised to find that the sewing operators in one plant found their work interesting. Since the work appeared to be highly repetitive, he had expected that they would say they were bored and their talents underutilized.[35] These workers' views are supported in a large scale study by Weintraub of 2535 female sewing machine operators in seventeen plants from Massachusetts to Texas. He found that "Most of the operators like the nature of their work. Of those who were staying (65%), 9 out of 10 feel that way. Even of those who would leave (35%), 7 out of 10 like their work."[36]

[33] See *Work in America* [24], p. 14.
[34] See Sorenson [20].
[35] Personal communication.
[36] See Weintraub [29], p. 349. The auto workers' jobs have been cited by many writers as the extreme of monotonous and dehumanizing work. However, a recent study of auto workers in the United States, Italy, Argentina, and India by W. H. Form found that "Most workers believe that their work integrates their lives . . . that their jobs are satisfying. Nowhere did assemblyline workers dwell upon monotony . . . Machine work does not make workers more unhappy at any industrial stage. Nor do workers heed the lament of the intellectuals that the monotony of the job drives them mad" (See Form [6], pp. 1, 15).

For the most part workers are satisfied with the nature of their work. What they find most discomforting is their pay, their job security, and many of the work rules with which they must cope. They can find their work engrossing and still express dissatisfaction because of other job related factors such as pay, working conditions, inability to advance, and so on. When a person says his work is satisfying, he implies that his work utilizes his abilities to an extent *satisfactory to him*.

EXTRINSIC DETERMINANTS OF WORKER SATISFACTION

As the studies cited above indicate, most workers appear relatively more satisfied with the intrinsic nature of their jobs than with the extrinsic job factors. The major extrinsic factors are examined below.

Pay Pay is very important in determining job satisfaction. This is hardly a novel observation, but it is one that is too often overlooked or forgotten in job enrichment programs. Sheppard and Herrick, both of whom served on the *Work in America* task force, analyzed the SRC and other data and provided a cross section of feelings by workers about their jobs. The following quotations concerning pay are from their study.[37]

> It was found that dissatisfaction with work decreases steadily as pay rises. When earnings exceed $10,000 per year, dissatisfaction drops significantly.

If we knew why this occurs, we would probably have a major part of the answer to the question of why there is dissatisfaction at the work place. There is a cause and effect relationship involved in which it is difficult to evaluate how the various factors affect the employee. The higher the social value of the work performed, the higher is the pay. The higher the skill required of the employee, the higher is his opportunity for involvement in his work. As pay rises, to what extent does the pay level produce higher satisfaction with the affluence it brings? To what extent does the interesting content of the work cause higher satisfaction?

Construction workers are the highest paid of the blue-collar workers and have unexcelled benefits. Many professionals and managers earn less than construction workers. These workers are among the last of the craftsmen who still largely work with their hands and still may own their own tools. Their satisfaction may well come from their creative work, but to what extent does their high pay influence their attitudes?

> In the managerial, professional and technical occupations only 1 in 10 were dissatisfied.

Is it the attraction of their work or their pay which affords them their satisfaction?

> Slightly less than 1 in 4 manufacturing workers were dissatisfied. The data for workers in the service occupations and the wholesale-retail industry are about the same.

In 1971, Bureau of Labor Statistics data for blue-collar workers showed that 58.7 percent earned less than $150 per week, 24.6 percent earned from $150 to $199, and 16.8 percent earned over $200. In 1971, the BLS "lower level" budget for a family of four was $7214 per year.[38] The SRC data showed that 56.2 percent of the subjects reported having inadequate incomes. Considering the earnings statistics, it is a wonder that more workers are not dissatisfied.

Experience reveals that increasing the availability of interesting work will not compensate for a desire for increased pay, whereas increasing pay can go far to compensate for poor working conditions. This was vividly demonstrated by the workers who collect garbage in New York City. They perform their work in all kinds of weather. Their job is highly accident-ridden and is not held in high esteem by society. Ten years ago few people were interested in the job. Then the pay scale was raised to $10,500 per year with good benefits, and a long waiting line formed for the jobs. The nature of the work had not changed. It was the same dirty, heavy work, but now the pay was attractive.[39]

Job Security A second critical component of the work environment is job security, the continuity of income. Pay must be not only sufficiently high but also fairly regular. No one can budget for a family if he is not reasonably sure of his income for some time into the future. Most people become distressed when faced with a layoff. Reduced employment affects the morale of everyone in the organization. When employment finally is stabilized and the threat of further reductions passes, fears and memories still linger.

Because it is such an important component of the work environment, *job security is an*

[37] See Sheppard and Herrick [16].

[38] See *Handbook of Labor Statistics* [25].

[39] The average annual pay is now $12,886.

essential precondition to enhancing the will to work. While the idea is not new that economic insecurity is a restraint on the will to work, its effect often is minimized by managers, behavioral scientists, and industrial engineers involved in productivity improvement. Job security is as vital to productivity improvement as advanced technical processes and new equipment.

What happens to feelings of identity and loyalty when employees see their increased productivity contributing to their layoff? It is hard to conceive of a manager who would cooperate in designing his own job out of existence, as might occur when several managerial jobs are combined and one person is no longer required. When managers consider their own job security, they quite expectedly have empathy for James F. Lincoln's truism: "No man will willingly work to throw himself out of his job, nor should he." Yet managers do not extend this obvious logic to their work force.

Managers must view job security not only in the social sense of how it affects workers' lives, but as absolutely essential to high levels of productivity. In the plants without job security, workers stretch out the work if they do not see sufficient work ahead of them.[40] They will not work themselves out of their jobs. When workers stretch out their jobs, though it is hidden from view, it is reflected in costs.

Managers historically have considered job security as a union demand to be bargained as are other issues. This has been a tragic error because whenever job security is lacking, labor productivity is restrained. Paradoxically, job security must be established as a demand of *management* if it hopes to increase productivity. What would happen in contract negotiations if management started off by demanding that the new contract include job protection for the employees? This radical act might encourage profound changes in employees' attitudes.

Unduly Restrictive Plant Rules There are many other factors beside the work itself which affect workers' attitudes. In many companies workers still are considered "hands," hired by the hour with little consideration given to their needs and desires as "people." Some managers find it easier to lay workers off with four to eight hours notice than to plan production and avoid plant delays. In many plants, the plant rules, which management calls its prerogatives and guards jealously, are insulting to human sensibilities.

[40] In a very fundamental way, work *does* expand to fill time (Parkinson's Law).

A worker's self-esteem is affected by how he is treated and how he rates with the others around him. Increasingly, workers want fair treatment for everyone. However, the "hands" concept still separates the white-collar from the blue-collar workers. White-collar workers are generally paid a weekly salary and often do not punch a time clock. They have more leeway in lateness and often do not lose pay when absent. Most factory workers have few of these benefits. A white-collar worker often has a telephone available and can make personal calls during the day. Factory workers have great difficulty in making calls. Receiving calls usually is reserved for extreme emergencies. When a worker has a problem, he stays out.

The penned-in feeling of workers, which is stylishly called their blues, comes in large part from their inability to take care of these daily personal problems and needs. Any job enrichment program which hopes to succeed must effectively address the problems posed to workers by plant rules. Until now very few programs have acknowledged their importance.

WHAT SHOULD BE DONE?

Everyone will accept the idea that improvement of the quality of working life is a desirable social goal. However, how should this be done? David Sirota provides a concise statement of the problem. "I can't get it through some thick skulls that [many] people may want both—that they would like to finish a day's work and feel that they had accomplished something and still get paid for it."[41] A logical approach to formulating the problem must begin with a determination of who is now dissatisfied and why and with the recognition that people have individual needs and desires.

The *Work in America* task force believes that, ". . . pay . . . is important," it must support an 'adequate' standard of living, and be perceived as equitable—but high pay alone will not lead to job (or life) satisfaction.[42] They conclude that work must provide satisfaction and must be restructured to become the *raison d'etre* of people's lives. Their statement of the problem is correct, but their conclusion that work alone must provide satisfaction is wrong. Satisfaction can come from wherever people choose. It need not be only from their work.

The blues of many workers are due less to the nature of their work and more to what their

[41] Panel discussion between Louis E. Davis, Mitchell Fein, and David Sirota, Annual Convention of the American Institute of Industrial Engineers, 24 May 1973.

[42] See *Work in America* [24], p. 95.

work will not bring them in their pay envelopes. Increasingly, workers also want freedom on their jobs. Some workers prefer enriched jobs with autonomy. Most workers want more freedom to act on personal things outside of their work place. Some may want the freedom to just "goof off" once in a while. In short, workers' blues are not formed solely around the work place. Blues are partly a work place reaction to non-work related problems.

Solving problems in the plants must start with the question why should workers want enriched jobs? It is readily apparent that management and the stockholders benefit from increased worker involvement which leads to reduced costs. For their part, if all the workers get is reduced hours or even layoffs, they must resist it. It is futile to expect that workers willingly will create more for management without simultaneously benefiting themselves. *The most effective productivity results will be obtained when management creates conditions which workers perceive as beneficial to them.* The changes must be genuine and substantial and in forms which eventually are turned into cash and continuity of income. Psychic rewards may look good on paper, but they are invisible in the pocketbook. If workers really wanted psychic job enrichment, management would have heard their demands loud and clear long ago.

Change must start with management taking the first steps, unilaterally and without *quid pro quo*. There must not be productivity bargaining at first. Management must provide the basic conditions which will motivate workers to raise productivity: job security, good working conditions, good pay and financial incentives. There must be a diminution of the win-lose relationship and the gradual establishment of conditions in which workers know that both they and management gain and lose together. Labor, management, and government leaders are very concerned that rising wages and costs are making goods produced in this country less competitive in the world markets. Increasingly all three parties are engaging in meaningful dialogue to address these problems.[43]

There are unquestionably enormous potentials for increased productivity which workers can unleash—if they want to. The error of job enrichment is that it tries to talk workers into involvement and concern for the nature of their work when their memories and experiences have taught them that increased productivity only results in layoffs. Only management can now create conditions which will nullify the past.

Companies which are experimenting with new work methods probably will increase their efforts. As viable methods and approaches are developed, more companies will be tempted to innovate approaches suited to their own plants. The greatest progress will come in companies where workers see that management protects their welfare and where productivity gains are shared with the employees.

In the ideal approach, management should leave to workers the final choice regarding what work they find satisfying. In real life, this is what occurs anyway. Workers eschew work that they find dissatisfying or they find ways of saying loudly and clearly how they feel about such work. We should learn to trust workers' expressions of their wants. Workers will readily signal when they are ready for changes.

[43] See, for example, the articles on the experimental negotiating agreement in the basic steel industry by I. W. Abel and R. Heath Larry, in this issue.

REFERENCES

1. Davis, L. E., and Canter, R. R. "Job Design Research." *The Journal of Industrial Engineering* 7 (1956): 275–282.
2. Fein, M. "Motivation for Work." In *Handbook of Work, Organization and Society,* edited by R. Dubin. Chicago: Rand McNally, 1973.
3. ———. "The Myth of Job Enrichment." *The Humanist,* September–October 1973, pp. 30–32.
4. ———. "The Real Needs of Blue Collar Workers." *The Conference Board Record,* February 1973, pp. 26–33.
5. Ford, R. N. *Motivation Through Work Itself.* New York: American Management Association, 1969.
6. Form, W. H. "Auto Workers and Their Machines: A Study of Work, Factory, and Job Satisfaction in Four Countries." *Social Forces* 52 (1973): 1–15.
7. Foulkes, F. K. *Creating More Meaningful Work.* New York: American Management Association, 1969.
8. "GM Zeroes in on Employee Discontent." *Business Week,* 12 May 1973, pp. 140–144.
9. Hofstede, G. H. "The Colors of Collars." *Columbia Journal of World Business,* September–October 1972, pp. 72–80.
10. Jenkins, D. "Democracy in the Factory." *The Atlantic,* April 1973, pp. 78–83.
11. ———. *Job Power: Blue and White Collar Democracy.* New York: Doubleday, 1973.
12. King, D. C. "Selecting Personnel for a Systems 4 Organization." Paper read at NTL Institute

for Applied Behavioral Science Conference, 8–9 October 1971.

13. Matles, J. "Humanize the Assembly Line?" *UE News,* 13 November 1972, p. 5.
14. Roach, J. M. "Worker Participation: New Voices in Management." The Conference Board, Report 594, 1973.
15. Rush, H. M. F. *Job Design for Motivation.* New York: The Conference Board, 1971.
16. Sheppard, H. L., and Herrick, N. Q. *Where Have All The Robots Gone?* New York: New Press, 1972.
17. Sirota, D. "Job Enrichment—Another Management Fad?" *The Conference Board Record,* April 1973, pp. 40–45.
18. Sirota, D., and Greenwood, J. M. "Understand Your Overseas Work Force." *Harvard Business Review,* January–February 1971, pp. 53–60.
19. Sorcher, M. "Motivating the Factory Workers." In *The Failure of Success,* edited by A. J. Morrow. New York: American Management Association, 1972.
20. Sorenson, T. C. "Do Americans Like Their Jobs?" *Parade,* 3 June 1973, pp. 15–16.
21. Strauss, G., and Rosenstein, E. "Workers Participation: A Critical View." *Industrial Relations* 9 (1970): 197–214.
22. "UAW Indicates It Will Seek to Minimize Local Plant Strikes in Talks Next Fall." *Wall Street Journal,* 20 February 1973, p. 5.
23. U.S., Congress, Senate, Subcommittee on Employment, Manpower, and Poverty, Labor and Public Welfare Committee, *Worker Alienation, 1972,* 92d Cong., 2d sess., S. 3916, July 25 and 26, 1972.
24. U.S., Department of Health, Education, and Welfare. *Work in America.* Report of a Special Task Force to the Secretary of Health, Education, and Welfare. Prepared under the Auspices of the W. E. Upjohn Institute for Employment Research. Cambridge: MIT Press, 1973.
25. U.S., Department of Labor. *Handbook of Labor Statistics 1972.* Bulletin 1735. Bureau of Labor Statistics. Washington, D.C.: Government Printing Office, 1972.
26. ———. "Survey of Working Conditions, November 1970." Prepared by the Survey Research Center of the University of Michigan. Washington, D.C.: Government Printing Office, 1971.
27. Walton, R. E. "How to Counter Alienation in the Plant." *Harvard Business Review,* November–December 1972, pp. 70–81.
28. ———. "Work Place Alienation and the Need for Major Innovation." Paper prepared for a Special Task Force to the Secretary of Health, Education, and Welfare (for *Work in America*), May 1972. Unpublished.
29. Weintraub, E. "Has Job Enrichment Been Oversold?" Address to the 25th Convention of the American Institute of Industrial Engineers, May 1973. Reprinted in the technical papers of the convention.
30. Winpisinger, W. P. Paper presented to University Labor Education Association, 5 April 1973, at Black Lake, Michigan.

C. LEADERSHIP

62 HISTORICAL TRENDS IN LEADERSHIP THEORY AND RESEARCH*

Ralph M. Stogdill

Jazz is not the only native American contribution to world culture. Leadership as a body of theory and research is distinctly an American creation. Its development probably can be attributed to two aspects of the democratic tradition in the United States. Elected officials are expected to lead rather than govern. Leaders are held accountable to followers to a greater degree than in countries that have experienced centuries of aristocratic rule. Also, formal barriers between different status levels are less strictly observed. As a result, granting followers the right not only to observe their leaders but also to describe their behavior as it is perceived is not regarded as a threat to the status or authority of leaders. Thus, leaders in industrial, military, educational and governmental organizations make themselves readily available as subjects of research, while long traditions of formality and status distinctions discourage such research in most countries.

American theory and research in leadership as a branch of social psychology has drawn heavily upon concepts and models originated by European philosophers, psychologists and sociologists. However, a strong empirical tradition has resulted in the transformation of speculation into a science of interpersonal relations. Practical demands arising from two world wars stimulated new trends and the development of new methodologies. In fact, World Wars I and II mark the boundaries among three major stages in the study of leadership.

Unfortunately, it is not possible in a brief review to acknowledge the contributions of all of the more than 3,000 scholars and researchers who have addressed themselves to the leadership problem. In the following pages, only the earliest or the most frequent publishers are mentioned.

* Reprinted by permission of the publisher from *Journal of Contemporary Business,* vol. 3, no. 4, pp. 1–17 (Autumn, 1974). Mr. Stogdill is professor of behavioral science at the Ohio State University.

BEGINNINGS: DEFINITIONS AND TYPES OF LEADERSHIP

The earliest literature consists primarily of speculative writings on definitions, types and origins of leadership. At that time, one school of thought sought by definition to remove any ground for justifying the domination of followers by their leaders. On the other hand, a second school sought by definition to legitimize leader control of the follower group. Later schools, less extreme in their orientation, have sought to avoid the political and moral implications present in the earlier definitions and to establish a basis for value-free theories.

Leadership in the earliest definitions was regarded as a focusing of group processes. Cooley stated that "the leader is always the nucleus of a tendency, and, on the other hand, all social movements closely examined, will be found to consist of tendencies having such nuclei."[1] In this and similar definitions, leadership is conceived as a resultant of group processes and member interactions. The leader, although a necessity, is merely an instrument of group purpose and action. No theoretical grounds are provided for imposing the will of the leader upon the follower group.

Bundel represented another school of thought and defined leadership as "the act of inducing others to do what one wants them to do."[2] Conclusions based on this and similar definitions sought to ease the task of the leader by establishing a theoretical base for his or her exercise of authority and control.

More recent definitions regard leadership as an aspect of role differentiation in a group; leadership is viewed as the act of initiating and maintaining role structure. These definitions seek to provide a basis for explaining the origin and maintenance of leadership in newly created, as well as in long established, groups. They contribute little toward a theoretical justification of either democratic or authoritarian doctrines of groups control.

Along with the definition of leadership, early theorists sought to identify the various types of leaders that are to be found in a society. Six types of leaders were observed: the *authoritative* seeks to dominate and impose his or her will upon the follower group; the *democratic* leader acts as an instrument of group purpose and seeks to further the welfare of the group; the *persuasive* leader is a crowd arouser and seeks to gain a following by appealing to the sentiments of the follower group; the *representative* acts primarily as a spokesman for the group as a whole; the *executive* is found primarily in formally structured organizations and is valued for his or her administrative abilities; and the *intellectual* leader is an eminent person who has a following of individuals and groups who find his or her ideas appealing. These different types of leaders and the basis for leadership positions are discussed more thoroughly in a few broad theoretical frameworks.

THEORIES OF LEADERSHIP

Various attempts have been made to develop theories of leadership, explaining the emergence or maintenance of leadership or the relationship between leader behavior and follower response. A brief review of the theories is presented below.[3]

In *trait* theories, the leader is conceived as a great man whose superior endowments induce others to follow him/her. *Environmental* theories explain leadership on the basis of situations and crises that provide opportunities for capable people to propose solutions or exhibit heroic actions that place them in positions of leadership. *Personal-environmental* theories maintain that characteristics of the leader, the followers and the situation interact to determine who will be a leader. *Exchange* theories suggest that group interaction represents an exchange process in which leadership is conferred upon the member whose efforts appear most likely to reward other members for their effort on behalf of the group. *Humanistic* theories are based on the hypothesis that groups will be more effective and members will be better satisfied when the leader allows followers freedom to satisfy their needs for achievement and self-actualization. *Expectational* theories maintain that leadership is most likely to be achieved by the member who succeeds in initiating and reinforcing the expectation that he or she will maintain the role structure and goal direction of the group.

It is proposed in *contingency* theories that a given pattern of leader behavior will lead to effective group performance in some circumstances and to ineffective performance in others. *Path-goal* theories suggest that certain patterns of leader behavior facilitate the clarification of group goals while other patterns of behavior stimulate effective instrumental responses in the follower group.

Each of these theories is concerned with a small subset of the total leadership problem. A complete theory of leadership should explain: (1) the emergence of leadership in initially unstructured groups, (2) the maintenance of leadership once a role structure has been developed and stabilized, (3) the relation of leader personality and behavior to follower and group response and (4) the conditions under which specific patterns of leader personality and behavior are effective. No such theory is presently available.

WORLD WAR I AND TRAIT RESEARCH

At the beginning of World War I the American Psychological Association appointed a committee of eminent psychologists to assist the U.S. Army in screening and selecting military personnel.[4] Among the notable achievements of the committee were the development of the Army Alpha test of intelligence; the Woodworth-Wells test of personality; the classification of military specialties; manning tables; and an officer qualifications rating scale. The demonstrated usefulness of these methods in a military emergency suggested that they might also be applied in the industrial situation, and they were quickly adapted to industrial use after the end of the War.

The personnel testing movement gave rise to research on leadership. It was hypothesized that leadership should be acquired by the individual who is most fortunately endowed with various aspects of physique, intelligence and personality. Nutting was one of the first to publish empirical results on the characteristics of leaders.[5] Other studies followed which reviewed the literature on leadership traits.[6] A wide variety of traits classified as: physical, social background, intelligence and ability, personality and social and task orientation, was found to differentiate leaders from followers and effective leaders from ineffective leaders.[7] However, all of the above reviewers were in agreement that use of tests for measuring the various traits has not proved very useful for the selection of leaders.

There are several reasons why test scores are not consistently predictive of later leader effectiveness. Traits do not operate singly, but in combination, to influence followers. In addition, a rise to a position of leadership in formal organizations usually is the result of severe screening processes that reduce differences between the candidates for a given position. But most important is the fact that numerous studies have shown that leader characteristics which are effective in one situation may not be effective in other situations.

The finding that trait measures are not predictive of leader effectiveness has been used by several writers as a basis for arguing that personality is unrelated to leadership. This view is in error. More recent research has shown that personality and behavior are factors in emergence of the leadership role and in leader-follow relations. However, the trait theories of leadership don't tell us how and when the traits are most effective. Disenchanted with the trait approach, researchers began to emphasize the importance of behavior and personal interaction in the study of leadership. Shartle suggested the development of scales for measuring different dimensions of leader behavior.[8] Research initiated by Hemphill identified two factors—Consideration and Initiating Structure—that appear repeatedly in studies of military, business, educational and other samples.[9] Since then, other scales have been developed that appear to be factorally independent.[10]

WORLD WAR II AND POST-WORLD WAR II SMALL GROUP RESEARCH

German military psychologists during World War II used leaderless group problems for the selection of men for assignments requiring initiative, resourcefulness and leadership.[11] These methods were adapted and greatly refined by American and British psychologists.[12] Bass reviewed his own program of research on leaderless group discussion and the work of other experimenters, relying heavily on observations of behavior rather than on measures of personality characteristics.[13]

The work of Lewin and Lippitt, Lippitt, and White and Lippitt was highly influential in stimulating experimental studies of leadership.[14] Adult leaders of children's recreational groups were trained to exhibit either an autocratic, democratic or laissez-faire pattern of leader behavior. Data obtained from observers' reports show that in groups under democratic leadership, higher degrees of cohesiveness, freedom of action, initiative, morale and quality of project work were exhibited. Children under autocratic leadership were more dependent and productive but less well satisfied and less likely to remain in the group. Children under laissez-faire leadership tended to be bewildered and dissatisfied and to ask for direction, system and guidance.

Two lines of research developed rapidly following World War II: (1) the controlled group experiment and (2) the survey of formal organizations. The controlled group experiment was largely concerned with (1) emergence of the leadership role, (2) factors in leader-follower interaction and (3) the relation of leader behavior to group performance. The survey of formal organizations was concerned to some extent with leader-follower interactions, but largely with the relation of leader behavior to follower satisfaction and group productivity. The two lines of research tend to produce mutually confirming results when they converge. Small group research has been far more sophisticated than the survey, not only in the exercise of experimental controls, but also in the system of variables that it has investigated. A large program of studies sponsored by the Office of Naval Research did much to stimulate both lines of investigation.[15]

Emergence of the Leadership Role

Leadership is an aspect of role differentiation in a group. Bales, Bales and Strodtbeck and Borgatta and Bales demonstrated that role differentiation takes place in progressive stages.[16] The first stage is concerned with task orientation and getting acquainted. The second stage, involving a relative high degree of emotional tension, is critical for the differentiation of the leadership role. Norms and cohesiveness are developed in the third stage, while the fourth stage is concerned with productivity.[17] Thus, a group cannot engage in effective task performance until it has solved its problems concerned with role differentiation and cohesiveness.

Bales and Slater observed that two different types of leader roles tend to emerge in certain groups; one was identified as a task maintenance role and the other as a socioemotional role.[18] Borgatta, Couch and Bales demonstrated that groups are more effective when a leader combines both the task and socioemotional functions in the same role.[19]

Several factors have been identified which are associated with the emergence of leadership in initially unstructured groups. The individual who talks the most is likely to emerge as a leader, particularly if his or her speech is supportive of the group and contributive to task performance.[20] Task ability and the possession of task-relevant information facilitate emergence as a leader.[21] Jennings, as well as Polansky, Lippitt and Redl, observed that spontaneity which stimulates spontaneity in others, tolerance of freedom of action for others and acceptance of group members aid in emergence as leader.[22] Research results also suggest that as a group member exhibits leadership acts, he or she arouses the expectation in others that he or she should continue in the same role. Acquiescence of the group reinforces the expectation that this person should continue to lead—leadership comes about as a result of the reinforcement of intermember expectations.[23]

Schachter, Gerard, Berkowitz, Raven and others demonstrated that groups develop norms of behavior and exert pressures on deviant members in order to bring their behavior into conformity with the norms.[24] Numerous studies indicate that the leader tends to incorporate and support these norms. However, once the leader has consolidated the leadership position, he or she is granted greater latitude to deviate than is allowed other members.[25] Leaders also exhibit greater concern for group goals and for goal direction than do followers.[26] In summary, leaders emerge through the interaction process by the use of either task or interpersonal skills. Once positioned, they uphold the norms, clarify goals and provide direction for the group.

Conditional Relationships in Leader-Follower Interaction The trait approach assumed that the personality of a leader and its effect on followers was relatively constant in all situations. However, research with experimental groups suggests that the behavior of a leader may change under different situational demands and the personality of followers affects their reactions to the leader.

Haythorn and others studied different combinations of authoritarian leaders and followers.[27] Low authoritarian leaders and followers were rated as more equalitarian and more sensitive than those high in authoritarianism. However, high authoritarian subjects rated themselves and were rated by observers as less productive and less well satisfied with their leaders than low authoritarians. Calvin, Hoffman and Harden studied groups that differed in member intelligence and leader authoritarianism-permissiveness.[28] Dull members under authoritarian leadership were more effective than dull members in permissive groups and the performance of bright members did not differ under authoritarian and permissive leadership.

Bass observed different types of followers under coercive and persuasive leadership.[29] Task-oriented followers were more productive under persuasive leadership. Interaction-oriented followers were more productive under a directive style of leadership. Task satisfaction of followers was higher under a directive than under a persuasive interaction-oriented leader, but lower under a directive than under a persuasive task-oriented leader. Shaw and Blum found that groups perform more effectively under directive than under nondirective leadership when the task is highly structured.[30] Tasks of low and medium structure were performed more effectively under nondirective leadership.

Evans and House have advanced path-goal theories of leadership which suggest that leader Initiating Structure clarifies path-goal relationships for followers.[31] Leader Consideration is seen as a moderator of the relationship between leader Initiating Structure and follower satisfaction. When tasks are ambiguous and the group norms are not well developed, leader Initiating Structure will clarify path-goal relationships and increase follower satisfaction. Under the same conditions, leader Consideration results in increased group cohesiveness and team effort. Leader Initiating Structure under routine and clear task conditions and under well-developed group norms leads to dissatisfaction because structure is already present in the situation.[32]

Fiedler conducted an extensive program of research on the leader's perception of his or her least preferred co-worker (LPC).[33] A high LPC score indicates a tendency to perceive other persons in favorable terms. High-LPC individuals tend to be person-oriented; low-LPC individuals to be task-oriented. The low-LPC leader tends to lead more effective groups when the situation is very favorable or very unfavorable and the high-LPC leader tends to lead more effective groups when the situation is intermediate in favorability. But more recent research has revealed an additional complication; the high-LPC leader tends to be low in person-oriented behaviors and high in task-oriented behaviors in favorable situations.[34] Person-oriented behaviors increase and task-oriented behaviors decrease as it becomes increasingly difficult to exercise leadership in the group. On the other hand, the low-LPC leader tends to become more task-oriented and less person-oriented as he (she) experiences increasing difficulty in the exercise of leadership in the group. Fiedler's results tend to support a contingency theory of leader effectiveness.

Research on conditional relationships indicates that the personality of the leader interacts with the personality of the follower group to determine satisfaction and performance. For example, task-oriented followers were more productive under directive leadership, while interaction-oriented followers were more productive under permissive leadership. Groups of dull followers performed better under directive than permissive leadership, while bright followers performed equally well under the two patterns of behavior. Directive leader behavior resulted in better group performance for structured tasks, but nondirective leader behavior resulted in better performance when tasks were low or medium in structure. Job autonomy tends to moderate the relationship between leader behavior and follower satisfaction and performance. Leader Consideration and Initiating Structure facilitate follower performance and satisfaction under conditions of low job autonomy, but not under conditions of high job autonomy.

The relationship between leader behavior and group performance is contingent upon the ease or difficulty experienced in exercising leadership. The task-oriented leader tends to become increasingly task-oriented, while the person-oriented leader becomes more person-oriented as the difficulty of the leadership situation increases. The task-oriented leader facilitates group productivity in very easy and very difficult situations, while the person-oriented leader contributes most to group performance when he or she experiences an intermediate degree of difficulty.[35]

These findings suggest that the behavior of the leader is not fixed in all situations. Rather, the leader, consciously or unconciously, changes behavior in response to changing situational demands. The effectiveness of a given pattern of leader behavior depends on the personality of the leader, the personality and competence of the followers, the nature of the task, the difficulty of exercising leadership and probably on other unidentified variables. In view of the complexity of the factors that determine the relationships between leader behavior and group performance, it is apparent that no simple recipe for leader effectiveness will be applicable in more than a small proportion of situations encountered.

Leader Behavior and Group Performance

Leadership is of little significance except as it affects the performance and satisfaction of the group of followers. Thus, the real criterion of leader effectiveness is group performance. Publications on the relation of leader behavior to group performance appear to be divided into two major schools of thought—the propogandists and the researchers. The propogandists appear determined to demonstrate that a human relations style of leadership fosters high group productivity, group cohesiveness and follower satisfaction in most situations. The researchers seem more willing to acknowledge the validity of experimental findings which suggest that the effectiveness of a given pattern of behavior depends on the nature of the situation.

McGregor and Argyris as advocates of the human relations approach perceived a fundamental conflict between the demands of the organization and the needs of followers.[36] Whereas the organization imposes demands for routinized behavior and conformity to rules and norms, individuals exhibit dominant needs for creative expression, initiative and self-actualization. A human relations style of leader behavior that fosters the satisfaction of these basic follower needs is most likely to result in high degrees of organizational productivity and morale. Blake and Mouton found that organizations are more effective under leaders who are high in both person-oriented and task-oriented behaviors.[37] Halpin found that the most effective groups had leaders who were high in both Consideration and Initiating Structure.[38]

Katz and others, in one of the pioneering studies of group performance, found that railroad section gangs were more productive when their foremen exercised leadership rather than surrendering leadership to a worker; when the foremen spent more time in supervision and less time in production work; when the foremen were perceived as taking a personal interest in their men and when they felt free of pressures for production from superiors.[39] Mann and Hoffman found that factory workers were better satisfied when their supervisors were perceived as being considerate of feelings, recognizing good work, being reasonable in their expectations, getting workers' ideas about the job and standing up for their workers.[40] Seashore reported that the productivity and cohesiveness of work groups is positively related under high support by management; without management's support, high productivity is related to low cohesiveness.[41] Likert obtained results which support the hypothesis that a supportive attitude toward workers and belief in the group method of supervision, combined with high group loyalty to the organization, is associated with high productivity and desire for responsibility.[42] Productivity steadily increased under a style of supervision that emphasized human relations and fostered high performance goals. Finally, Comrey, High and Wilson studied supervisors and workers in an aircraft factory.[43] Supervisors of more productive groups were characterized by adequate authority, good communication with followers, lack of arbitrary behaviors and lack of hypercritical attitudes.

There are a number of research studies that present a more complex view. Stogdill, in a study of 27 organizations, found supervisor Consideration to be consistently related to group drive and follower satisfaction with freedom of action. Supervisor Initiating Structure was related to group cohesiveness and follower satisfaction with the organization.[44]

Stogdill analyzed more than 170 studies of the relation of leader behavior to group productivity, group cohesiveness and follower satisfaction.[45] In general, an impersonal style of leadership was found to foster group productivity more often than a personal style of supervision. A follower-oriented style of behavior was more highly related to productivity than democratic, permissive, participative or considerate styles were. Among the impersonal styles, socially distant (low-LPC), directive and structured leader behaviors more often were related to productivity than were autocratic, restrictive or task-oriented patterns of behavior. Personal, rather than impersonal, styles of leader behavior tend to strengthen group cohesiveness. However, leader Initiating Structure, an impersonal style, consistently was related to high group cohesiveness. All personal styles of leadership, except permissiveness, tend to foster follower satisfaction. Impersonal styles, with the exception of Initiating Structure, tend to be associated with follower dissatisfaction or to be unrelated to satisfaction. This analysis considered only those studies which reported a direct relationship between leader behavior and group response and ignored conditional studies which indicate that the relationship of leader behavior to group performance is affected by a variety of situational factors.

Research results indicate that not all varieties of personal and impersonal leader behavior are equivalent. Behaviors that facilitate group productivity do not necessarily strengthen group cohesiveness or follower satisfaction. In general, personal patterns of behavior (follower-oriented, participative and considerate) tend to foster group cohesiveness and follower satisfaction. Impersonal patterns of behavior (socially distant, directive and structured) tend to facilitate group productivity. Initiating Structure also tends to be associated positively with group cohesiveness and follower satisfaction.

But various situational factors as well as follower personality moderate the relationship between leader behavior and group performance. For example, task-oriented followers have been found to be more productive under directive leadership, while interaction-oriented followers respond in a more productive manner to persuasive leadership. Socially distant, task-oriented leaders have groups that are more productive when the situation is very favorable or unfavorable for the leader. Socially warm, person-oriented leaders have more effective groups when the leadership problem is moderately favorable. Thus, it is difficult to prescribe a single pattern of behavior that will be effective in all situations.

SUMMARY AND DISCUSSION

The beginnings of leadership research during World War I were concerned with the identification and measurement of traits that differentiate leaders from followers. Although such traits were discovered, they proved to be disappointing in that they did not contribute to the selection and placement of persons for positions of leadership. Among the several possible reasons for this outcome, two appear to be particularly important. First, traits act in combination, not singly, to affect group performance. Second, an effective pattern of behavior in one situation may not be effective in other situations.

World War II marked the development of two major new trends in leadership research. The first was concerned with the emergence of leadership in initially unstructured groups. The second sought to identify patterns of leader behavior associated with follower satisfaction and effective group performance.

Research with leaderless groups revealed that the member who talks the most contributes the most to group problem solving, keeps the group goal in mind and shows the most promise of maintaining group role structure is most likely to emerge as a leader. Capacity to interact effectively with a wide range of personalities, ability to adapt behavior to changing demands, concern for the comfort and welfare of followers and provision of follower freedom of action are personality qualities that facilitate emergence as a leader. The leader tends to incorporate and espouse the norms of the group but often is granted greater freedom to deviate from group norms, particularly when such deviation is necessary for effective action on behalf of the group.

Person-oriented patterns of leader behavior tend to contribute to group cohesiveness and follower satisfaction. One such pattern of behavior, Consideration, tends also to be associated with group drive and follower satisfaction with freedom of action. Task-oriented patterns of leader behavior tend to facilitate group productivity. One such pattern, Initiating Structure, tends also to be associated with group cohesiveness and follower satisfaction with the group or organization.

However, no one pattern of behavior is equally effective in all situations. The socially distant, task-oriented leader contributes most to group productivity when the situation is extremely easy or extremely difficult for the exercise of leadership. The socially close, person-oriented leader tends to lead more effective groups when the leadership problem is moderately difficult. Thus, the pattern of leader behavior that contributes to effective group performance is contingent upon the situation.

Groups that accept task committment tend to develop differentiated role structures. Groups cannot engage in effective task performance without such structure. The leader plays a critical role in developing and maintaining role structure. Thus, the essential functions of leadership are to preserve role structure, maintain group norms and goal direction, provide for follower freedom in task performance and foster follower welfare and group cohesiveness. Because all of the outcomes provided by these functions are dependent upon at least a moderate degree of structure, leadership is best defined as the initiation and maintenance of structure in expectations and interaction. Thus, leadership is defined in terms of the critical factors that give rise to the leadership role and grant it legitimation by the group members.

The task of the leader is indeed complex and attended by numerous conflicting demands, arising from differences in follower personality, ability and value commitment, changes in task requirements and changes in pressures that impinge upon the group. The most effective leaders appear to exhibit a degree of versatility and flexibility that enables them to adapt their behavior to the changing and contradictory demands made on them.

REFERENCES

1. C. H. Cooley, *Human Nature and Social Order* (New York: Schribners, 1902).
2. C. M. Bundel, "Is Leadership Losing Its Importance?" *Infantry Journal,* 36 (1930), pp. 339–349.
3. R. M. Stogdill, *Handbook of Leadership: A Survey of Theory and Research* (New York: The Free Press, 1974).
4. Adjutant General's Department, *The Personnel System of the United States Army* (Washington, D.C.: U.S. Army, 1919).
5. Ruth L. Nutting, "Some Characteristics of Leadership," *School and Society,* 18 (1923), pp. 387–390.
6. C. Bird, *Social Psychology* (New York: Appleton-Century, 1940); W. O. Jenkins, "A Review of Leadership Studies with Particular References to Military Problems," *Psychological Bulletin,* 44 (1947), pp. 54–79; R. M. Stogdill, "Personal Factors Associated with Leadership: A Survey of the Literature," *Journal of Psychology,* 25 (1948), pp. 35–71; R. D. Mann, "A Review of the Relationships between Personality and Performance in Small Groups." *Psychological Bulletin,* 56 (1959), pp. 241–270; T. O. Jacobs, *Leadership and Exchange in Formal Organizations* (Alexandria, Va.: Human Resources Research Organization, 1970).
7. R. M. Stogdill, *Handbook of Leadership.*
8. C. L. Shartle, "Leader Behavior in Jobs," *Occupations,* 30 (1951), pp. 164–66; ———, *Executive Performance and Leadership* (Englewood Cliffs, N.J.: Prentice-Hall, 1956).
9. J. K. Hemphill, *Situational Factors in Leadership* (Columbus, Ohio: Ohio State University, Bureau of Educational Research, 1949).
10. R. M. Stogdill, O. S. Goode and D. R. Day, "The Leader Behavior of Corporation Presidents, *Personnel Psychology,* 161 (1963), pp. 127–132.
11. H. L. Ansbacher, "German Military Psychology," *Psychological Bulletin,* 39 (1942), pp. 370–392.
12. C. A. Gibb, "The Principles and Traits of Leadership," *Journal of Abnormal and Social Psychology,* 42 (1947), pp. 267–284; Office of Strategic Services, *Assessment of Men: Selection of Personnel for Office of Strategic Services* (New York: Rinehart, 1948); H. Harris, *The Group Approach to Leadership Testing* (London: Routledge and Kegan Paul, 1949); M. C. Knowles, "Group Assessment in Staff Selection,"*Personnel Practice Bulletin,* 19, 2 (1963), pp. 6–16.
13. B. M. Bass, "The Leaderless Group Discussion," *Psychological Bulletin,* 51 (1954), pp. 465–492.
14. K. Lewin and R. Lippitt, "An Experimental Approach to the Study of Autocracy and Democracy: A Preliminary Note, *Sociometry,* 1 (1938), pp. 292–300; R. Lippitt, "An Experimental Study of the Effect of Democratic and Authoritarian Group Atmospheres," *University of Iowa Studies in Child Welfare,* No. 3 (1940), pp. 43–95; R. K. White and R. Lippitt, *Autocracy and Democracy: An Experimental Inquiry* (New York: Harper, 1960).
15. H. Guetzkow, *Groups, Leadership and Men: Research in Human Relations* (Pittsburgh: Carnegie Press, 1951).
16. R. F. Bales, *Interaction Process Analysis* (Reading, Mass.: Addison-Wesley, 1950); R. F. Bales and F. L. Strodtbeck, *Phases in Group Problem-Solving* (1951) E. F. Borgatta and R. F. Bales, "Task and Accumulation of Experience As Factors in the Interaction of Small Groups," *Sociemetry,* 16 (1953), pp. 239–252.

17. B. W. Tuckman, "Developmental Sequence in Small Groups," *Psychological Bulletin,* 63 (1965), pp. 384–399.

18. R. F. Bales, *Interaction Process;* P. E. Slater, "Role Differentiation in Small Groups, *American Sociological Review,* 20 (1955), pp. 300–310.

19. E. F. Borgatta, A. S. Couch and R. F. Bales, "Some Findings Relevant to the Great Man Theory of Leadership," *American Sociological Review,* 19 (1954), pp. 755–759.

20. B. M. Bass, "The Leaderless Group Discussion"; T. W. Harrell, Lucy E. Burnham and H. E. Lee, *"Correlations between Seven Leadership Criteria,* TR No. 4 (Stanford, Calif.: Stanford University, 1963).

21. L. Carter and Mary Nixon, "Ability, Perceptual, Personality and Interest Factors Associated with Different Criteria of Leadership," *Journal of Psychology,* 27 (1949), pp. 377–388; E. P. Hollander, *Leaders, Groups and Influence* (New York: Oxford University Press, 1964); M. E. Shaw, "Some Effects of Varying Amounts of Information Exclusively Possessed by a Group Member upon His Behavior in the Group," *Journal of Genetic Psychology,* 68 (1963), pp. 71–79; J. K. Hemphill, et al., "The Relation between Possession of Task-Relevant Information and Attempts To Lend," *Psychological Monographs,* No. 414 (1956).

22. Helen H. Jennings, *Leade.ship and Isolation* (New York: Longmans, Green, 1943); N. Polansky, R. Lippitt and F. Redl, "The Use of Near-Sociometric Data in Research on Group Treatment Process," *Sociometry,* 13 (1950), pp. 39–62.

23. G. Gardner, "Functional Leadership and Popularity in Small Groups," *Human Relations,* 9 (1956), pp. 491–509; B. Mausner and Barbara L. Bloch, "A Study of the Additivity of Variables Affecting Social Interaction," *Journal of Abnormal and Social Psychology,* 54 (1957), pp. 250–256; R. L. Hamblin, K. Miller and J. A. Wiggins," Group Morale and Competence of the Leader," *Sociometry,* 24 (1961), pp. 295–311; A. H. Hastorf, "The Reinforcement of Individual Actions in a Group Situation," in L. Krasner and L. P. Ullmann, eds. *Research in Behavior Modification* (New York: Holt, Rinehart and Winston, 1965); M. W. York, "Reinforcement of Leadership in Small Groups," *Dissertation Abstracts International* 30 (4B), (1969), p. 1643.

24. S. Schachter, "Deviation, Rejection and Communication," *Journal of Abnormal and Social Psychology,* 46 (1951), pp. 190–207; H. B. Gerard, "The Effect of Different Dimensions of Disagreement on the Communication Process in Small Groups," *Human Relations,* 6 (1953), pp. 249–271; L. Berkowitz, "Effects of Perceived Dependency Relationships upon Conformity to Group Expectations," *Journal of Abnormal and Social Psychology,* 55 (1957), pp. 350–354; P. H. Raven, "Social Influence on Opinion and the Communication of Related Content," *Journal of Abnormal and Social Psychology,* 58 (1959), pp. 119–128.

25. E. P. Hollander, *Leaders, Groups and Influence.*

26. A. Zander, *Motives and Goals in Groups* (New York: Academic Press, 1971).

27. W. W. Haythorn, et al., "The Effects of Varying Combinations of Authoritarian and Equalitarian Leaders and Followers," *Journal of Abnormal and Social Psychology,* 53 (1956), pp. 210–219.

28. A. D. Calvin, F. K. Hoffmann and E. D. Harden, "The Effect of Intelligence and Social Atmosphere on Group Problem-Solving Behavior," *Journal of Social Psychology,* 45 (1957), pp. 61–74.

29. B. M. Bass, "Social Behavior and the Orientation Inventory: A Review," *Psychological Bulletin,* 68 (1967), pp. 260–292.

30. M. E. Shaw and J. M. Blum, "Effects of Leadership Style upon Group Performance As a Function of Task Structure," *Journal of Personality and Social Psychology,* 3 (1966), pp. 238–242.

31. M. G. Evans, "The Effects of Supervisory Behavior on the Path-Goal Relationship," *Organizational Behavior and Human Performance,* 5 (1970), pp. 277–298; R. J. House, "A Path-Goal Theory of Leader Effectiveness," *Administrative Science Quarterly,* 16 (1971), pp. 321–338.

32. R. J. House, *Path-Goal Theory.*

33. F. E. Fiedler, *A Theory of Leadership Effectiveness* (New York: McGraw-Hill, 1967).

34. F. E. Fiedler, "Personality and Situational Determinants of Leader Behavior," in E. A. Fleishman and J. G. Hunt, eds., *Current Developments in the Study of Leadership* (Carbondale: Southern Illinois University Press, 1973).

35. F. E. Fiedler, "Validation and Extension of the Contingency Model of Leadership Effectiveness: A Review of Empirical Findings," *Psychological Bulletin* 76 (1971), pp. 128–148.

36. D. McGregor, *The Human Side of Enterprise* (New York: McGraw-Hill, 1960); C. Argyris, *Integrating the Individual and the Organization* (New York: Wiley, 1964).

37. R. R. Blake and Jane S. Mouton, *The Managerial Grid* (Houston: Gulf, 1964).

38. W. Halpin, "The Leader Behavior and Effec-

tiveness of Aircraft Commanders," in R. M. Stogdill and A. E. Coons, eds., *Leader Behavior: Its Description and Measurement* (Columbus: Ohio State University, Bureau of Business Research, 1957).

39. D. Katz et al., *Productivity, Supervision and Morale Among Railroad Workers* (Ann Arbor: University of Michigan, Institute for Social Research, 1951).
40. F. C. Mann and L. N. Hoffman, *Automation and the Worker: A Study of Social Change in Power Plants* (New York: Holt, 1960).
41. S. E. Seashore, *Group Cohesiveness in the Industrial Work Group* (Ann Arbor: University of Michigan, Institute for Social Research, 1954).
42. R. Likert, *New Patterns of Management* (New York: McGraw-Hill, 1961).
43. A. L. Comrey, W. S. High and R. C. Wilson, "Factors Influencing Organizational Effectiveness, VIII. A Survey of Aircraft Supervisors," *Personnel Psychology,* 8 (1955), pp. 245–257.
44. R. M. Stogdill, *Managers, Employees, Organizations* (Columbus: Ohio State University, Bureau of Business Research, 1965).
45. R. M. Stogdill, *Handbook of Leadership.*

63 HOW TO CHOOSE A LEADERSHIP PATTERN*

Robert Tannenbaum and *Warren H. Schmidt*

- "I put most problems into my group's hands and leave it to them to carry the ball from there. I serve merely as a catalyst, mirroring back the people's thoughts and feelings so that they can better understand them."
- "It's foolish to make decisions oneself on matters that affect people. I always talk things over with my subordinates, but I make it clear to them that I'm the one who has to have the final say."
- "Once I have decided on a course of action, I do my best to sell my ideas to my employees."
- "I'm being paid to lead. If I let a lot of other people make the decisions I should be making, then I'm not worth my salt."
- "I believe in getting things done. I can't waste time calling meetings. Someone has to call the shots around here, and I think it should be me."

Each of these statements represents a point of view about "good leadership." Considerable experience, factual data, and theoretical principles could be cited to support each statement, even though they seem to be inconsistent when placed together. Such contradictions point up the dilemma in which the modern manager frequently finds himself.

NEW PROBLEMS

The problem of how the modern manager can be "democratic" in his relations with subordinates and at the same time maintain the necessary authority and control in the organization for which he is responsible has come into focus increasingly in recent years.

Earlier in the century this problem was not so acutely felt. The successful executive was generally pictured as possessing intelligence, imagination, initiative, the capacity to make rapid (and generally wise) decisions, and the ability to inspire subordinates. People tended to think of the world as being divided into "leaders" and "followers."

New Focus Gradually, however, from the social sciences emerged the concept of "group dynamics" with its focus on *members* of the group rather than solely on the leader. Research efforts of social scientists underscored the importance of employee involvement and participation in decision making. Evidence began to challenge the efficiency of highly directive leadership, and increasing attention was paid to problems of motivation and human relations.

Through training laboratories in group development that sprang up across the country, many of the newer notions of leadership began to exert an impact. These training laboratories were carefully designed to give people a first-hand experience in full participation and decision making. The designated "leaders" deliberately attempted to reduce their own power and to make group members as responsible as possible for setting their own goals and methods within the laboratory experience.

It was perhaps inevitable that some of the people who attended the training laboratories regarded this kind of leadership as being truly "democratic" and went home with the determination to build fully participative decision making into their own organizations. Whenever their bosses made a decision without convening a staff meeting, they tended to perceive this as authoritarian behavior. The true symbol of democratic leadership to some was the meeting —and the less directed from the top, the more democratic it was.

* Reprinted by permission from the *Harvard Business Review*, vol. 51, no. 3, pp. 162–180 (May–June 1973). Mr. Tannenbaum is professor of behavioral science and Mr. Schmidt is senior lecturer in behavioral science at the University of California, Los Angeles. This article, an "HBR classic," was originally published in 1958.

Some of the more enthusiastic alumni of these training laboratories began to get the habit of categorizing leader behavior as "democratic" *or* "authoritarian." The boss who made too many decisions himself was thought of as an authoritarian, and his directive behavior was often attributed solely to his personality.

New Need The net result of the research findings and of the human relations training based upon them has been to call into question the stereotype of an effective leader. Consequently, the modern manager often finds himself in an uncomfortable state of mind.

Often he is not quite sure how to behave; there are times when he is torn between exerting "strong" leadership and "permissive" leadership. Sometimes new knowledge pushes him in one direction ("I should really get the group to help make this decision"), but at the same time his experience pushes him in another direction ("I really understand the problem better than the group and therefore I should make the decision"). He is not sure when a group decision is really appropriate or when holding a staff meeting serves merely as a device for avoiding his own decision-making responsibility.

The purpose of our article is to suggest a framework which managers may find useful in grappling with this dilemma. First, we shall look at the different patterns of leadership behavior that the manager can choose from in relating himself to his subordinates. Then, we shall turn to some of the questions suggested by this range of patterns. For instance, how important is it for a manager's subordinates to know what type of leadership he is using in a situation? What factors should he consider in deciding on a leadership pattern? What difference do his long-run objectives make as compared to his immediate objectives?

RANGE OF BEHAVIOR

Exhibit I presents the continuum or range of possible leadership behavior available to a manager. Each type of action is related to the degree of authority used by the boss and to the amount of freedom available to his subordinates in reaching decisions. The actions seen on the extreme left characterize the manager who maintains a high degree of control while those seen on the extreme right characterize the manager who releases a high degree of control. Neither extreme is absolute; authority and freedom are never without their limitations.

Now let us look more closely at each of the behavior points occurring along this continuum.

- The manager makes the decision and announces it.

In this case the boss identifies a problem, considers alternative solutions, chooses one of them, and then reports this decision to his subordinates for implementation. He may or may not give consideration to what he believes his subordinates will think or feel about his decision; in any case, he provides no opportunity for them to participate directly in the decision-making process. Coercion may or may not be used or implied.

- The manager "sells" his decision.

Here the manager, as before, takes responsibility for identifying the problem and arriving at a decision. However, rather than simply announcing it, he takes the additional step of

EXHIBIT I Continuum of Leadership Behavior

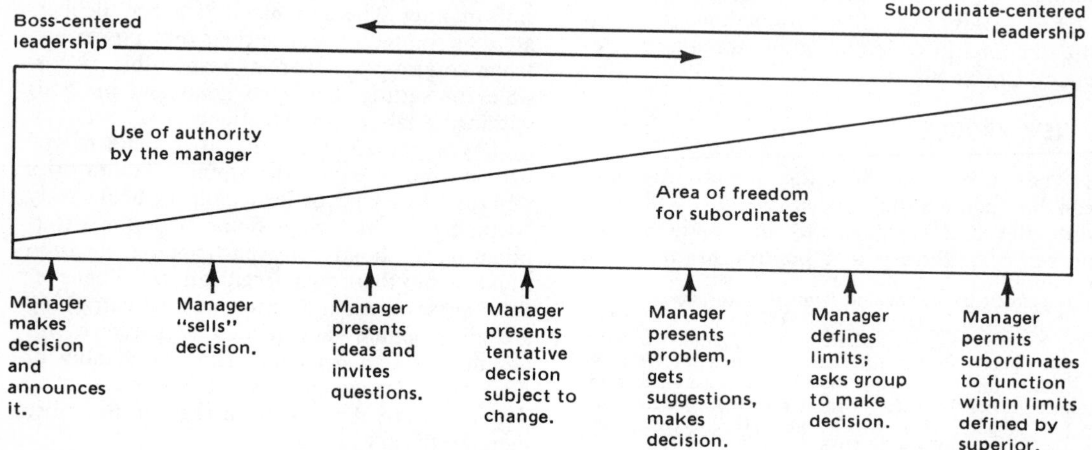

persuading his subordinates to accept it. In doing so, he recognizes the possibility of some resistance among those who will be faced with the decision, and seeks to reduce this resistance by indicating, for example, what the employees have to gain from his decision.

- The manager presents his ideas, invites questions.

Here the boss who has arrived at a decision and who seeks acceptance of his ideas provides an opportunity for his subordinates to get a fuller explanation of his thinking and his intentions. After presenting the ideas, he invites questions so that his associates can better understand what he is trying to accomplish. This "give and take" also enables the manager and the subordinates to explore more fully the implications of the decision.

- The manager presents a tentative decision subject to change.

This kind of behavior permits the subordinates to exert some influence on the decision. The initiative for identifying and diagnosing the problem remains with the boss. Before meeting with his staff, he has thought the problem through and arrived at a decision—but only a tentative one. Before finalizing it, he presents his proposed solution for the reaction of those who will be affected by it. He says in effect, "I'd like to hear what you have to say about this plan that I have developed. I'll appreciate your frank reactions, but will reserve for myself the final decision."

- The manager presents the problem, gets suggestions, and then makes his decision.

Up to this point the boss has come before the group with a solution of his own. Not so in this case. The subordinates now get the first chance to suggest solutions. The manager's initial role involves identifying the problem. He might, for example, say something of this sort: "We are faced with a number of complaints from newspapers and the general public on our service policy. What is wrong here? What ideas do you have for coming to grips with this problem?"

The function of the group becomes one of increasing the manager's repertory of possible solutions to the problem. The purpose is to capitalize on the knowledge and experience of those who are on the "firing line." From the expanded list of alternatives developed by the manager and his subordinates, the manager then selects the solution that he regards as most promising.[1]

- The manager defines the limits and requests the group to make a decision.

At this point the manager passes to the group (possibly including himself as a member) the right to make decisions. Before doing so, however, he defines the problem to be solved and the boundaries within which the decision must be made.

An example might be the handling of a parking problem at a plant. The boss decides that this is something that should be worked on by the people involved, so he calls them together and points up the existence of the problem. Then he tells them:

"There is the open field just north of the main plant which has been designated for additional employee parking. We can build underground or surface multilevel facilities as long as the cost does not exceed $100,000. Within these limits we are free to work out whatever solution makes sense to us. After we decide on a specific plan, the company will spend the available money in whatever way we indicate."

- The manager permits the group to make decisions within prescribed limits.

This represents an extreme degree of group freedom only occasionally encountered in formal organizations, as, for instance, in many research groups. Here the team of managers or engineers undertakes the identification and diagnosis of the problem, develops alternative procedures for solving it, and decides on one or more of these alternative solutions. The only limits directly imposed on the group by the organization are those specified by the superior of the team's boss. If the boss participates in the decision-making process, he attempts to do so with no more authority than any other member of the group. He commits himself in advance to assist in implementing whatever decision the group makes.

Key Questions As the continuum in Exhibit I demonstrates, there are a number of alternative ways in which a manager can relate himself to the group or individuals he is supervising. At the extreme left of the range, the emphasis is on the manager—on what *he* is interested in, how *he* sees things, how *he* feels about them. As we move toward the subordinate-centered end of the continuum, however, the focus is increasingly on the subordinates—on what *they* are interested in, how *they* look at things, how *they* feel about them.

When business leadership is regarded in this way, a number of questions arise. Let us take four of especial importance:

[1] For a fuller explanation of this approach, see Leo Moore, "Too Much Management, Too Little Change," HBR January–February 1956, p. 41.

1. Can a boss ever relinquish his responsibility by delegating it to someone else?

Our view is that the manager must expect to be held responsible by his superior for the quality of the decisions made, even though operationally these decisions may have been made on a group basis. He should, therefore, be ready to accept whatever risk is involved whenever he delegates decision-making power to his subordinates. Delegation is not a way of "passing the buck." Also, it should be emphasized that the amount of freedom the boss gives to his subordinates cannot be greater than the freedom which he himself has been given by his own superior.

2. Should the manager participate with his subordinates once he has delegated responsibility to them?

The manager should carefully think over this question and decide on his role prior to involving the subordinate group. He should ask if his presence will inhibit or facilitate the problem-solving process. There may be some instances when he should leave the group to let it solve the problem for itself. Typically, however, the boss has useful ideas to contribute, and should function as an additional member of the group. In the latter instance, it is important that he indicate clearly to the group that he sees himself in a *member* role rather than in an authority role.

3. How important is it for the group to recognize what kind of leadership behavior the boss is using?

It makes a great deal of difference. Many relationship problems between boss and subordinate occur because the boss fails to make clear how he plans to use his authority. If, for example, he actually intends to make a certain decision himself, but the subordinate group gets the impression that he has delegated this authority, considerable confusion and resentment are likely to follow. Problems may also occur when the boss uses a "democratic" façade to conceal the fact that he has already made a decision which he hopes the group will accept as its own. The attempt to "make them think it was their idea in the first place" is a risky one. We believe that it is highly important for the manager to be honest and clear in describing what authority he is keeping and what role he is asking his subordinates to assume in solving a particular problem.

4. Can you tell how "democratic" a manager is by the number of decisions his subordinates make?

The sheer *number* of decisions is not an accurate index of the amount of freedom that a subordinate group enjoys. More important is the *significance* of the decisions which the boss entrusts to his subordinates. Obviously a decision on how to arrange desks is of an entirely different order from a decision involving the introduction of new electronic data-processing equipment. Even though the widest possible limits are given in dealing with the first issue, the group will sense no particular degree of responsibility. For a boss to permit the group to decide equipment policy, even within rather narrow limits, would reflect a greater degree of confidence in them on his part.

Deciding How To Lead Now let us turn from the types of leadership which are possible in a company situation to the question of what types are *practical* and *desirable*. What factors or forces should a manager consider in deciding how to manage? Three are of particular importance:

- Forces in the manager.
- Forces in the subordinates.
- Forces in the situation.

We should like briefly to describe these elements and indicate how they might influence a manager's action in a decision-making situation.[2] The strength of each of them will, of course, vary from instance to instance, but the manager who is sensitive to them can better assess the problems which face him and determine which mode of leadership behavior is most appropriate for him.

Forces in the Manager. The manager's behavior in any given instance will be influenced greatly by the many forces operating within his own personality. He will, of course, perceive his leadership problems in a unique way on the basis of his background, knowledge, and experience. Among the important internal forces affecting him will be the following:

1. His value system.

How strongly does he feel that individuals should have a share in making the decisions which affect them? Or, how convinced is he that the official who is paid to assume responsibility should personally carry the burden of decision making? The strength of his convictions on questions like these will tend to move the manager to one end or the other of the continuum shown in Exhibit I. His behavior will also be influenced by the relative impor-

[2] See also Robert Tannenbaum and Fred Massarik, "Participation by Subordinates in the Managerial Decision-Making Process," *Canadian Journal of Economics and Political Science*, August 1950, p. 413.

tance that he attaches to organizational efficiency, personal growth of subordinates, and company profits.[3]

2. His confidence in his subordinates.

Managers differ greatly in the amount of trust they have in other people generally, and this carries over to the particular employees they supervise at a given time. In viewing his particular group of subordinates, the manager is likely to consider their knowledge and competence with respect to the problem. A central question he might ask himself is: "Who is best qualified to deal with this problem?" Often he may, justifiably or not, have more confidence in his own capabilities than in those of his subordinates.

3. His own leadership inclinations.

There are some managers who seem to function more comfortably and naturally as highly directive leaders. Resolving problems and issuing orders come easily to them. Other managers seem to operate more comfortably in a team role, where they are continually sharing many of their functions with their subordinates.

4. His feelings of security in an uncertain situation.

The manager who releases control over the decision-making process thereby reduces the predictability of the outcome. Some managers have a greater need than others for predictability and stability in their environment. This "tolerance for ambiguity" is being viewed increasingly by psychologists as a key variable in a person's manner of dealing with problems.

The manager brings these and other highly personal variables to each situation he faces. If he can see them as forces which, consciously or unconsciously, influence his behavior, he can better understand what makes him prefer to act in a given way. And understanding this, he can often make himself more effective.

Forces in the Subordinate. Before deciding how to lead a certain group, the manager will also want to consider a number of forces affecting his subordinates' behavior. He will want to remember that each employee, like himself, is influenced by many personality variables. In addition, each subordinate has a set of expectations about how the boss should act in relation to him (the phrase "expected behavior" is one we hear more and more often these days at discussions of leadership and teaching). The better the manager understands these factors, the more accurately he can determine what kind of behavior on his part will enable his subordinates to act most effectively.

Generally speaking, the manager can permit his subordinates greater freedom if the following essential conditions exist:

- If the subordinates have relatively high needs for independence. (As we all know, people differ greatly in the amount of direction that they desire.)
- If the subordinates have a readiness to assume responsibility for decision making. (Some see additional responsibility as a tribute to their ability; others see it as "passing the buck.")
- If they have a relatively high tolerance for ambiguity. (Some employees prefer to have clear-cut directives given to them; others prefer a wider area of freedom.)
- If they are interested in the problem and feel that it is important.
- If they understand and identify with the goals of the organization.
- If they have the necessary knowledge and experience to deal with the problem.
- If they have learned to expect to share in decision making. (Persons who have come to expect strong leadership and are then suddenly confronted with the request to share more fully in decision making are often upset by this new experience. On the other hand, persons who have enjoyed a considerable amount of freedom resent the boss who begins to make all the decisions himself.)

The manager will probably tend to make fuller use of his own authority if the above conditions do *not* exist; at times there may be no realistic alternative to running a "one-man show."

The restrictive effect of many of the forces will, of course, be greatly modified by the general feeling of confidence which subordinates have in the boss. Where they have learned to respect and trust him, he is free to vary his behavior. He will feel certain that he will not be perceived as an authoritarian boss on those occasions when he makes decisions by himself. Similarly, he will not be seen as using staff meetings to avoid his decision-making responsibility. In a climate of mutual confidence and respect, people tend to feel less threatened by deviations from normal practice, which in turn makes possible a higher degree of flexibility in the whole relationship.

Forces in the Situation. In addition to the forces which exist in the manager himself and in his subordinates, certain characteristics of the general situation will also affect the man-

[3] See Chris Argyris, "Top Management Dilemma: Company Needs vs. Individual Development," *Personnel,* September 1955, pp. 123–134.

ager's behavior. Among the more critical environmental pressures that surround him are those which stem from the organization, the work group, the nature of the problem, and the pressures of time. Let us look briefly at each of these:

1. Type of organization.

Like individuals, organizations have values and traditions which inevitably influence the behavior of the people who work in them. The manager who is a newcomer to a company quickly discovers that certain kinds of behavior are approved while others are not. He also discovers that to deviate radically from what is generally accepted is likely to create problems for him.

These values and traditions are communicated in numerous ways—through job descriptions, policy pronouncements, and public statements by top executives. Some organizations, for example, hold to the notion that the desirable executive is one who is dynamic, imaginative, decisive, and persuasive. Other organizations put more emphasis upon the importance of the executive's ability to work effectively with people—his human relations skills. The fact that his superiors have a defined concept of what the good executive should be will very likely push the manager toward one end or the other of the behavioral range.

In addition to the above, the amount of employee participation is influenced by such variables as the size of the working units, their geographical distribution, and the degree of inter- and intra-organizational security required to attain company goals. For example, the wide geographical dispersion of an organization may preclude a practical system of participative decision making, even though this would otherwise be desirable. Similarly, the size of the working units or the need for keeping plans confidential may make it necessary for the boss to exercise more control than would otherwise be the case. Factors like these may limit considerably the manager's ability to function flexibly on the continuum.

2. Group effectiveness.

Before turning decision-making responsibility over to a subordinate group, the boss should consider how effectively its members work together as a unit.

One of the relevant factors here is the experience the group has had in working together. It can generally be expected that a group which has functioned for some time will have developed habits of cooperation and thus be able to tackle a problem more effectively than a new group. It can also be expected that a group of people with similar backgrounds and interests will work more quickly and easily than people with dissimilar backgrounds, because the communication problems are likely to be less complex.

The degree of confidence that the members have in their ability to solve problems as a group is also a key consideration. Finally, such group variables as cohesiveness, permissiveness, mutual acceptance, and commonality of purpose will exert subtle but powerful influence on the group's functioning.

3. The problem itself.

The nature of the problem may determine what degree of authority should be delegated by the manager to his subordinates. Obviously he will ask himself whether they have the kind of knowledge which is needed. It is possible to do them a real disservice by assigning a problem that their experience does not equip them to handle.

Since the problems faced in larger or growing industries increasingly require knowledge of specialists from many different fields, it might be inferred that the more complex a problem, the more anxious a manager will be to get some assistance in solving it. However, this is not always the case. There will be times when the very complexity of the problem calls for one person to work it out. For example, if the manager has most of the background and factual data relevant to a given issue, it may be easier for him to think it through himself than to take the time to fill in his staff on all the pertinent background information.

The key question to ask, of course, is: "Have I heard the ideas of everyone who has the necessary knowledge to make a significant contribution to the solution of this problem?"

4. The pressure of time.

This is perhaps the most clearly felt pressure on the manager (in spite of the fact that it may sometimes be imagined). The more that he feels the need for an immediate decision, the more difficult it is to involve other people. In organizations which are in a constant state of "crisis" and "crash programming" one is likely to find managers personally using a high degree of authority with relatively little delegation to subordinates. When the time pressure is less intense, however, it becomes much more possible to bring subordinates in on the decision-making process.

These, then, are the principal forces that impinge on the manager in any given instance and that tend to determine his tactical behavior in relation to his subordinates. In each case his behavior ideally will be that which makes possible the most effective attainment of his immediate goal within the limits facing him.

Long-run Strategy As the manager works with his organization on the problems that come up day by day, his choice of a leadership pattern is usually limited. He must take account of the forces just described and, within the restrictions they impose on him, do the best that he can. But as he looks ahead months or even years, he can shift his thinking from tactics to large-scale strategy. No longer need he be fettered by all of the forces mentioned, for he can view many of them as variables over which he has some control. He can, for example, gain new insights or skills for himself, supply training for individual subordinates, and provide participative experiences for his employee group.

In trying to bring about a change in these variables, however, he is faced with a challenging question: At which point along the continuum *should* he act?

Attaining Objectives. The answer depends largely on what he wants to accomplish. Let us suppose that he is interested in the same objectives that most modern managers seek to attain when they can shift their attention from the pressure of immediate assignments:

1. To raise the level of employee motivation.
2. To increase the readiness of subordinates to accept change.
3. To improve the quality of all managerial decisions.
4. To develop teamwork and morale.
5. To further the individual development of employees.

In recent years the manager has been deluged with a flow of advice on how best to achieve these longer-run objectives. It is little wonder that he is often both bewildered and annoyed. However, there are some guidelines which he can usefully follow in making a decision.

Most research and much of the experience of recent years give a strong factual basis to the theory that a fairly high degree of subordinate-centered behavior is associated with the accomplishment of the five purposes mentioned.[4] This does not mean that a manager should always leave all decisions to his assistants. To provide the individual or the group with greater freedom than they are ready for at any given time may very well tend to generate anxieties and therefore inhibit rather than facilitate the attainment of desired objectives. But this should not keep the manager from making a continuing effort to confront his subordinates with the challenge of freedom.

CONCLUSION

In summary, there are two implications in the basic thesis that we have been developing. The first is that the successful leader is one who is keenly aware of those forces which are most relevant to his behavior at any given time. He accurately understands himself, the individuals and group he is dealing with, and the company and broader social environment in which he operates. And certainly he is able to assess the present readiness for growth of his subordinates.

But this sensitivity or understanding is not enough, which brings us to the second implication. The successful leader is one who is able to behave appropriately in the light of these perceptions. If direction is in order, he is able to direct; if considerable participative freedom is called for, he is able to provide such freedom.

Thus, the successful manager of men can be primarily characterized neither as a strong leader nor as a permissive one. Rather, he is one who maintains a high batting average in accurately assessing the forces that determine what his most appropriate behavior at any given time should be and in actually being able to behave accordingly. Being both insightful and flexible, he is less likely to see the problems of leadership as a dilemma.

RETROSPECTIVE COMMENTARY

Since this HBR Classic was first published in 1958, there have been many changes in organizations and in the world that have affected leadership patterns. While the article's continued popularity attests to its essential validity, we believe it can be reconsidered and updated to reflect subsequent societal changes and new management concepts.

The reasons for the article's continued relevance can be summarized briefly:

- The article contains insights and perspectives which mesh well with, and help clarify, the experiences of managers, other leaders, and students of leadership. Thus it is useful to individuals in a wide variety of organizations—industrial, governmental, educational, religious, and community.
- The concept of leadership the article defines

[4] For example, see Warren H. Schmidt and Paul C. Buchanan, *Techniques that Produce Teamwork* (New London, Arthur C. Croft Publications, 1954); and Morris S. Viteles, *Motivation and Morale in Industry* (New York, W. W. Norton & Company, Inc., 1953).

is reflected in a continuum of leadership behavior (see Exhibit I in original article). Rather than offering a choice between two styles of leadership, democratic or authoritarian, it sanctions a range of behavior.

- The concept does not dictate to managers but helps them to analyze their own behavior. The continuum permits them to review their behavior within a context of other alternatives, without any style being labeled right or wrong.

(We have sometimes wondered if we have, perhaps, made it too easy for anyone to justify his or her style of leadership. It may be a small step between being nonjudgmental and giving the impression that all behavior is equally valid and useful. The latter was not our intention. Indeed, the thrust of our endorsement was for the manager who is insightful in assessing relevant forces within himself, others, and the situation, and who can be flexible in responding to these forces.)

In recognizing that our article can be updated, we are acknowledging that organizations do not exist in a vacuum but are affected by changes that occur in society. Consider, for example, the implications for organizations of these recent social developments:

- The youth revolution that expresses distrust and even contempt for organizations identified with the establishment.
- The civil rights movement that demands all minority groups be given a greater opportunity for participation and influence in the organizational processes.
- The ecology and consumer movements that challenge the right of managers to make decisions without considering the interest of people outside the organization.
- The increasing national concern with the quality of working life and its relationship to worker productivity, participation, and satisfaction.

These and other societal changes make effective leadership in this decade a more challenging task, requiring even greater sensitivity and flexibility than was needed in the 1950's. Today's manager is more likely to deal with employees who resent being treated as subordinates, who may be highly critical of any organizational system, who expect to be consulted and to exert influence, and who often stand on the edge of alienation from the institution that needs their loyalty and commitment. In addition, he is frequently confronted by a highly turbulent, unpredictable environment.

In response to these social pressures, new concepts of management have emerged in organizations. Open-system theory, with its emphasis on subsystems' interdependency *and* on the interaction of an organization with its environment, has made a powerful impact on managers' approach to problems. Organization development has emerged as a new behavioral science approach to the improvement of individual, group, organizational, and interorganizational performance. New research has added to our understanding of motivation in the work situation. More and more executives have become concerned with social responsibility and have explored the feasibility of social audits. And a growing number of organizations, in Europe and in the United States, have conducted experiments in industrial democracy.

In light of these developments, we submit the following thoughts on how we would rewrite certain points in our original article.

The article described forces in the manager, subordinates, and the situation as givens, with the leadership pattern a resultant of these forces. We would now give more attention to the *interdependency* of these forces. For example, such interdependency occurs in: (a) the interplay between the manager's confidence in his subordinates, their readiness to assume responsibility, and the level of group effectiveness; and (b) the impact of the behavior of the manager on that of his subordinates, and vice versa.

In discussing the forces in the situation, we primarily identified organizational phenomena. We would now include forces lying outside the organization, and would explore the relevant interdependencies between the organization and its environment.

In the original article, we presented the size of the rectangle in Exhibit I as a given, with its boundaries already determined by external forces—in effect, a closed system. We would now recognize the possibility of the manager and/or his subordinates taking the initiative to change those boundaries through interaction with relevant external forces—both within their own organization and in the larger society.

The article portrayed the manager as the principal and almost unilateral actor. He initiated and determined group functions, assumed responsibility, and exercised control. Subordinates made inputs and assumed power only at the will of the manager. Although the manager might have taken into account forces outside himself, it was *he* who decided where to operate on the continuum—that is, whether to announce a decision instead of trying to sell his idea to his subordinates, whether to invite questions, to let subordinates decide an issue, and so on. While the manager has retained this clear prerogative in many organizations, it has been challenged in others. Even in situations where he has retained

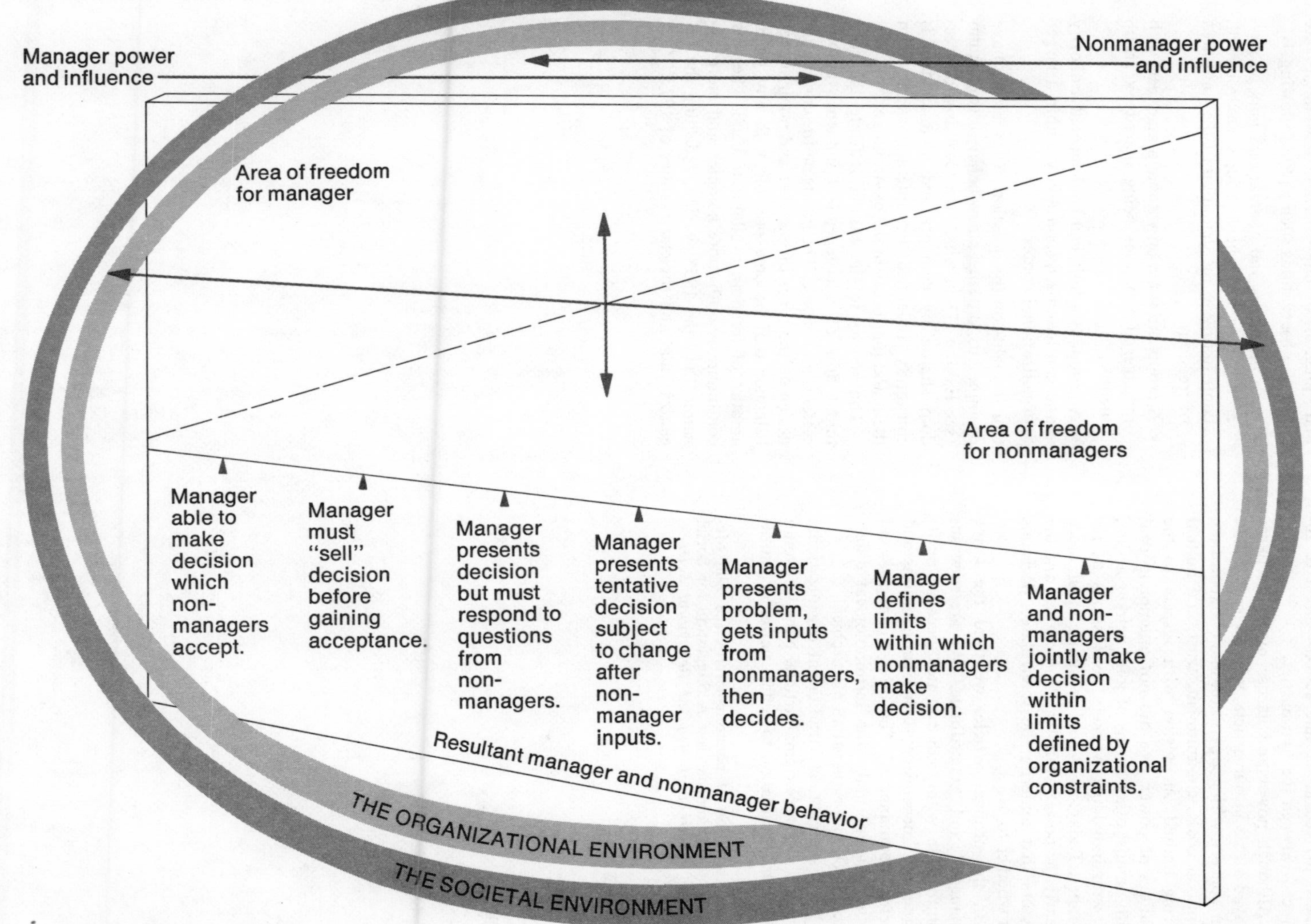
Manager power and influence
Nonmanager power and influence
Area of freedom for manager
Area of freedom for nonmanagers
Manager able to make decision which non-managers accept.
Manager must "sell" decision before gaining acceptance.
Manager presents decision but must respond to questions from non-managers.
Manager presents tentative decision subject to change after non-manager inputs.
Manager presents problem, gets inputs from nonmanagers, then decides.
Manager defines limits within which nonmanagers make decision.
Manager and non-managers jointly make decision within limits defined by organizational constraints.
Resultant manager and nonmanager behavior
THE ORGANIZATIONAL ENVIRONMENT
THE SOCIETAL ENVIRONMENT

EXHIBIT II **Continuum of Manager-Nonmanager Behavior**

it, however, the balance in the relationship between manager and subordinates at any given time is arrived at by interaction—direct or indirect—between the two parties.

Although power and its use by the manager played a role in our article, we now realize that our concern with cooperation and collaboration, common goals, commitment, trust, and mutual caring limited our vision with respect to the realities of power. We did not attempt to deal with unions, other forms of joint worker action, or with individual workers' expressions of resistance. Today, we would recognize much more clearly the power available to *all* parties, and the factors that underlie the interrelated decisions on whether to use it.

In the original article, we used the terms "manager" and "subordinate." We are now uncomfortable with "subordinate" because of its demeaning, dependency-laden connotations and prefer "nonmanager." The titles "manager" and "nonmanager" make the terminological difference functional rather than hierarchical.

We assumed fairly traditional organizational structures in our original article. Now we would alter our formulation to reflect newer organizational modes which are slowly emerging, such as industrial democracy, intentional communities, and "phenomenarchy."* These new modes are based on observations such as the following:

- Both managers and nonmangers may be governing forces in their group's environment, contributing to the definition of the total area of freedom.
- A group can function without a manager, with managerial functions being shared by group members.
- A group, as a unit, can be delegated authority and can assume responsibility within a larger organizational context.

Our thoughts on the question of leadership have prompted us to design a new behavior continuum (see Exhibit II) in which the total area of freedom shared by manager and nonmanagers is constantly redefined by interactions between them and the forces in the environment.

The arrows in the exhibit indicate the continual flow of interdependent influence among systems and people. The points on the continuum designate the types of manager and nonmanager behavior that become possible with any given amount of freedom available to each. The new continuum is both more complex and more dynamic than the 1958 version, reflecting the organizational and societal realities of 1973.

* For a description of phenomenarchy, see Will McWhinney, "Phenomenarchy: A Suggestion for Social Redesign," *Journal of Applied Behavioral Science,* May 1973.

64 THE CONTINGENCY MODEL—NEW DIRECTIONS FOR LEADERSHIP UTILIZATION*

Fred E. Fiedler

Leadership research has come a long way from the simple concepts of earlier years which centered on the search for the magic leadership trait. We have had to replace the old cherished notion that "leaders are born and not made." These increasingly complex formulations postulate that some types of leaders will behave and perform differently in a given situation than other types. The Contingency Model is one of the earliest and most articulated of these theories;[1] taking into account the personality of the leader as well as aspects of the situation which affect the leader's behavior and performance. This model has given rise to well over one-hundred empirical studies. This article briefly reviews the current status of the Contingency Model and then discusses several new developments which promise to have considerable impact on our thinking about leadership as well as on the management of executive manpower.

THE CONTINGENCY MODEL

The theory holds that the effectiveness of a task group or of an organization depends on two main factors: the personality of the leader and the degree to which the situation gives the leader power, control and influence over the situation or, conversely, the degree to which the situation confronts the leader with uncertainty.[2]

Leader Personality The first of these factors distinguishes leader personality in terms of two different motivational systems, i.e., the basic or primary goals as well as the secondary goals which people pursue once their more pressing needs are satisfied. One type of person, whom we shall call "relationship-motivated," primarily seeks to maintain good interpersonal relationships with coworkers. These basic goals become very apparent in uncertain and anxiety provoking situations in which we try to make sure that the important needs are secured. Under these conditions the relationship-motivated individual will seek out others and solicit their support; however, under conditions in which he or she feels quite secure and relaxed —because this individual has achieved the major goals of having close relations with subordinates —he or she will seek the esteem and admiration of others. In a leadership situation where task performance results in esteem and admiration from superiors, this leader will tend to concentrate on behaving in a task-relevant manner, sometimes to the detriment of relations with immediate subordinates.

The relationship-motivated leader's counterpart has as a major goal the accomplishment of some tangible evidence of his or her worth. This person gets satisfaction from the task itself and from knowing that he or she has done well. In a leadership situation which is uncertain and anxiety provoking, this person will, therefore, put primary emphasis on completing the task. However, when this individual has considerable control and influence and knows, therefore, the task will get done, he or she will relax and be concerned with subordinates' feelings and satisfactions. In other words, business before pleasure, but business *with* pleasure whenever possible.

Of course, these two thumbnail sketches are oversimplified, but they do give a picture which tells us, first, that we are dealing with different types of people and, second, that they differ in their primary and secondary goals and, consequently, in the way they behave under various conditions. Both the relationship-motivated and the task-motivated persons may be pleasant and considerate toward their members. However, the task-motivated leader will be considerate in

* Reprinted by permission of the publisher from the *Journal of Contemporary Business,* vol. 3, no. 4, pp. 65–80 (Autumn, 1974). Mr. Fiedler is professor of psychology, University of Washington.

situations in which he or she is secure, i.e., in which the individual's power and influence are high; the relationship-motivated leader will be considerate when his or her control and influence are less assured, when some uncertainty is present.

These motivational systems are measured by the Least Preferred Coworker score (LPC) which is obtained by first asking an individual to think of all people with whom he or she has ever worked, and then to describe the one person with whom this individual has been able to work least well. The description of the least preferred coworker is made on a short, bipolar eight-point scale, from 16 to 22 item-scale of the semantic differential format. The LPC score is the sum of the item scores; e.g.:

Friendly

:____:____:____:____:____:____:____:____:

1 2 3 4 5 6 7 8

Unfriendly

Cooperative

:____:____:____:____:____:____:____:____:

1 2 3 4 5 6 7 8

Uncooperative

High-LPC persons, i.e., individuals who describe their LPC in relatively positive terms, seem primarily relationship-motivated. Low-LPC persons, those who describe their least preferred coworker in very unfavorable terms, are basically task-motivated. Therefore, as can be seen, the LPC score is not a description of leader behavior because the behavior of high- and low-LPC people changes with different situations

Relationship-motivated people seem more open, more approachable and more like McGregor's "Theory Y" managers, while the task-motivated leaders tend to be more controlled and more controlling persons, even though they may be as likeable and pleasant as their relationship-motivated colleagues.[3]

Current evidence suggests that the LPC scores and the personality attributes they reflect are almost as stable as most other personality measures. (For example, test-retest reliabilities for military leaders have been .72 over an 8-month period[4] and .67 over a 2-year period for faculty members).[5] Changes do occur, but in the absence of major upsets in the individual's life, they tend to be gradual and relatively small.

The Leadership Situation The second variable, "situational favorableness,"[6] indicates the degree to which the situation gives the leader control and influence and the ability to predict the consequences of his or her behavior.[7] A situation in which the leader cannot predict the consequences of the decision tends to be stressful and anxiety arousing.

One rough but useful method for defining situational favorableness is based on three subscales. These are the degree to which (a) the leader is, or feels, accepted and supported by his or her members (leader-member relations); (b) the task is clear-cut, programmed and structured as to goals, procedures and measurable progress and success (task structure); and (c) the leader's position provides power to reward and punish and, thus, to obtain compliance from subordinates (position power).

Groups then can be categorized as being high or low on each of these three dimensions by dividing them at the median or, on the basis of normative scores, into those with good and poor leader-member relations, task structure and position power. This leads to an eight-celled classification shown on the horizontal axis of Figure I. The eight cells or "octants" are scaled from "most favorable" (octant I) to the left of the graph to "least favorable" (octant VIII) to the right. A leader obviously will have the most control and influence in groups that fall into octant I; i.e., in which this leader is accepted, has high position power and a structured task. The leader will have somewhat less control and influence in octant II, where he or she is accepted and has a structured task, but little position power, and so on to groups in octant VIII, where control and influence will be relatively small because the leader is not accepted by his or her group, has a vague, unstructured task and little position power. Situational favorableness and LPC are, of course, neither empirically nor logically related to each other.

The Personality-Situation Interaction

The basic findings of the Contingency Model are that task-motivated leaders perform generally best in very "favorable" situations, i.e., either under conditions in which their power, control and influence are very high (or, conversely, where uncertainty is very low) or where the situation is unfavorable, where they have low power, control and influence. Relationship-motivated leaders tend to perform best in situations in which they have moderate power, control and influence. The findings are summarized in Figure I. The horizontal axis indicates the eight cells of the situational favorableness dimension, with the most favorable end on the left side of the graph's axis. The vertical axis indicates the *correlation coefficients* between the

FIGURE I

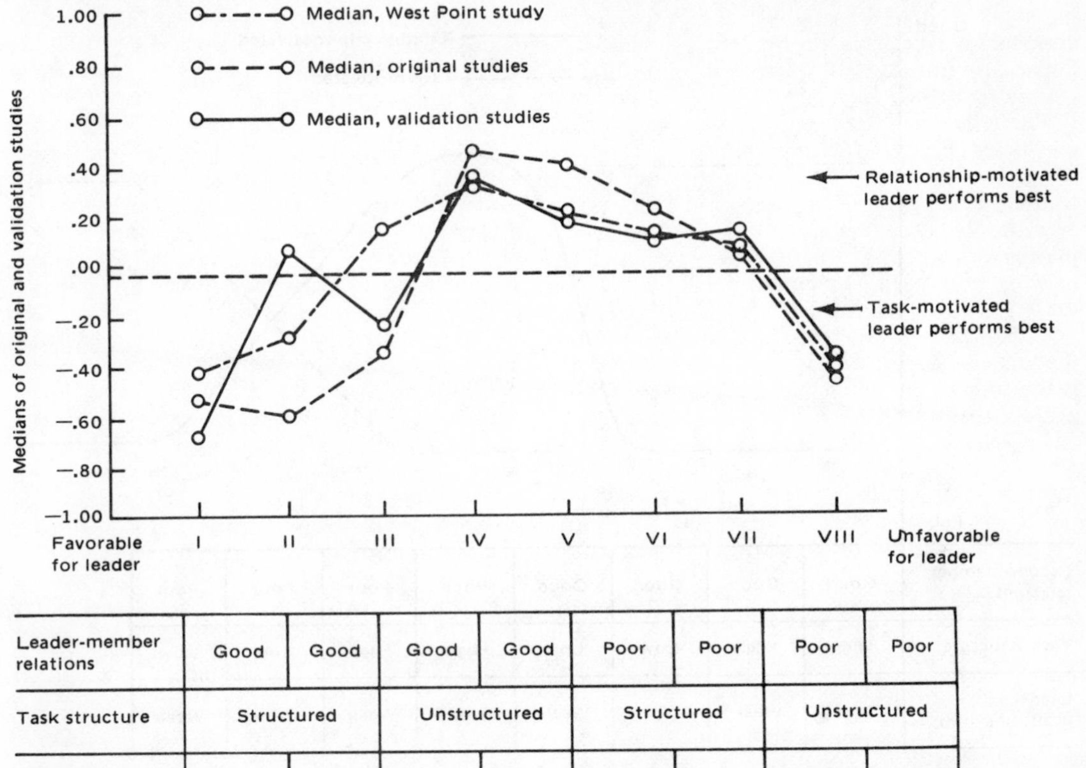

	I	II	III	IV	V	VI	VII	VIII
Leader-member relations	Good	Good	Good	Good	Poor	Poor	Poor	Poor
Task structure	Structured		Unstructured		Structured		Unstructured	
Leader position power	Strong	Weak	Strong	Weak	Strong	Weak	Strong	Weak

leader's LPC score and the group's performance. A high correlation in the positive direction, indicated by a point above the midline of the graph, shows that the relationship-motivated leaders performed better than the task-motivated leaders. A negative correlation, shown by a point which falls below the midline of the graph, indicates that the task-motivated leaders performed better than relationship-motivated leaders, i.e., the higher the LPC score, the lower the group's performance.

The solid curve connects the median correlations within each of the octants obtained in the original studies (before 1963) on which the model was based. The broken line connects the median correlations obtained in various validation studies from 1964–1971.[8] As can be seen, the two curves are very similar, and the points on the curves correlate .76 ($p < .01$). Only in octant 2 is there a major discrepancy. However, it should be pointed out that there are very few groups in real life which have a highly structured task while the leader has low position power, e.g., in high school basketball teams and student surveying parties. Most of the validation evidence for octant II comes from laboratory studies in which this type of situation may be difficult to reproduce. However, the field study results for this octant are in the negative direction, just as the model predicts.

The most convincing validation evidence comes from a well-controlled experiment conducted by Chemers and Skrzypek at the U.S. Military Academy at West Point.[9] LPC scores as well as sociometric performance ratings to predict leader-member relations were obtained several weeks *prior* to the study, and groups then were assembled in advance, based on having the leader's LPC score and the expressed positive or negative feelings of group members about one another. The results of the Chemers and Skrzypek study are shown in the figure as a dotted line and give nearly a point-for-point replication of the original model with a correlation of .86 ($p < .01$). A subsequent reanalysis of the Chemers and Skrzypek data by Shiflett showed that the Contingency Model accounted for no less than 28 percent of the variance in

FIGURE II **The Performance of Relationship- and Task-motivated Leaders in Different Situational-Favorableness Conditions**

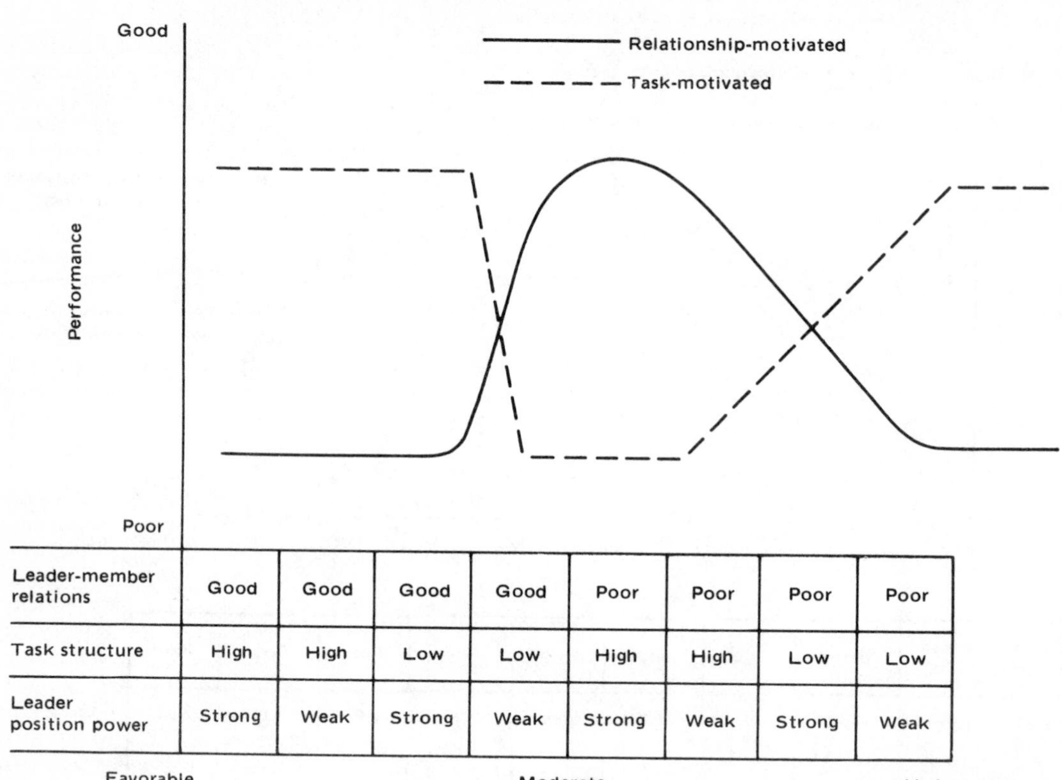

group performance.[10] This is a very high degree of prediction, especially in a study in which variables such as the group members' intelligence, the leader's ability, the motivational factors of participants and similar effects were uncontrolled. Of course, it is inconceivable that data of this nature could be obtained by pure chance.

A different and somewhat clearer description of the Contingency Model is presented schematically in Figure II. As before, the situational favorableness dimension is indicated on the horizontal axis, extending from the most favorable situation on the left to the relatively least favorable situation on the right. However, here the vertical axis indicates the group or organizational performance; the solid line on the graph is the schematic performance curve of relationship-motivated (high-LPC) leaders, while the dashed line indicates the performance of task-motivated (low-LPC) leaders.

These curves show, first of all, that both the relationship- and the task-motivated leaders perform well under some situations but not under others. Therefore, it is not accurate to speak of a "good" or a "poor" leader, rather, a leader may perform well in one type of situation but not in another. Outstanding directors of research teams do not necessarily make good production foremen or military leaders, and outstanding battle field commanders, like General Patton, do not necessarily make good chiefs of staff or good chairmen of volunteer school picnic committees.

The second major implication of Figure II is that leader performance depends as much on the situation to which the organization assigns him (her) as on his or her own personality. Hence, organizational improvement can be achieved either by changing the leader's personality and motivational system—which is at best a very difficult and uncertain process—or by modifying the degree to which the situation provides the leader with power and influence. It should be obvious from the graph that certain leaders perform better with less rather than more power, i.e., some leaders let the power "go to their heads," they become cocky and arrogant, while others need security to function well.

Extensions of the Contingency Model

Two important tests of any theory are the degree to which it allows us to understand phenomena which do not follow common-sense expectations and, second, the extent to which it predicts nonobvious findings. In both of these respects, the Contingency Model has demonstrated its usefulness. We present here several important findings from recent studies, and then discuss some implications for management.

Effects of Experience and Training One of the major research efforts in the area of leadership and management has been the attempt to develop training methods which will improve organizational performance. However, until now the various training programs have failed to live up to their expectations. Stogdill concluded that:

> "the research on leadership training is generally inadequate in both design and execution. It has failed to address itself to the most crucial problem of leadership—. . . [the] effects of leadership on group performance and member satisfaction."[11]

The Contingency Model would predict that training should increase the performance of some leaders and also decrease the performance of others. However, it raises the question of whether any current method of training logically can result in an across-the-board increase in organizational leadership performance.[12]

As pointed out before, a group's performance depends on the leader's personality as well as the degree to which the situation provides him or her with control, power and influence. If the leader's power and influence are increased by experience and training, the "match" between leader personality and situational favorableness would change. However, increasing the leader's power and influence is exactly the goal of most leadership training. For example, technical training increases the leader's expert power; coaching and orthodox training programs which use the case study and lecture method are designed to increase the structure of the task by providing the leader with methods for dealing with problems which, otherwise, would require him or her to think of new solutions. Human relations training is designed to develop better relations with group members, thus enabling the leader to exert more personal influence or "referent power."

For example, let us take a newly promoted supervisor of a production department in which he has not worked before. As he begins his new job, some of the tasks may seem unfamiliar and he will be unsure of his exact duties and responsibilities. He also may be uncertain of the power his position provides—how, for example, will the group react if he tries to dock an old, experienced worker who had come in late? Is this type of disciplinary measure acceptable to the group even though it may be allowed by the union contract? He may wonder how he should handle a problem with a fellow supervisor in the plant on whom he has to depend for parts and supplies. Should he file a formal complaint or should he talk to him personally?

After several years on the job, our supervisor will have learned the ropes; he will know how far he can go in disciplining his workers, how to troubleshoot various machines and how to deal with other managers in the organization. Thus, for the experienced supervisor the job is structured, his position power is high and his relations with his group are probably good. In other words, his situation is very favorable.

When he first started on the job, his leadership situation probably was only moderately favorable. If you will recall, relationship-motivated leaders tend to perform best in moderately favorable situations, while task-motivated leaders perform better in very favorable situations. Therefore, a relationship-motivated leader will perform well at first before gaining experience (e.g., by using the resources of group members and inviting their participation); a task-motivated leader will perform well after becoming experienced. In other words, the relationship-motivated leader actually should perform less well after gaining experience, while the task-motivated leader's performance should increase with greater experience.

A substantial number of studies now support this prediction.[13] A good example comes from a longitudinal study of infantry squad leaders who were assigned to newly organized units.[14] Their performance was evaluated by the same judges shortly after they joined their squads and, again, approximately 5 months later after their squads had passed the combat readiness test. As Figure III shows, the data are exactly as predicted by the Contingency Model. Similar results have been obtained in studies on the effects of training and experience of post office managers, managers of consumer cooperatives, police patrol supervisors and leaders of various military units.

The effect of leadership training on performance also was demonstrated by a very ingenious experiment conducted at the University of Utah.[15] ROTC cadets and students were assembled *a priori* into four-man teams with high- and low-LPC leaders. One-half of the team leaders were given training in decoding cryptographic messages, i.e., they were shown

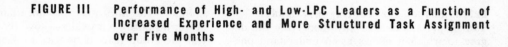

FIGURE III Performance of High- and Low-LPC Leaders as a Function of Increased Experience and More Structured Task Assignment over Five Months

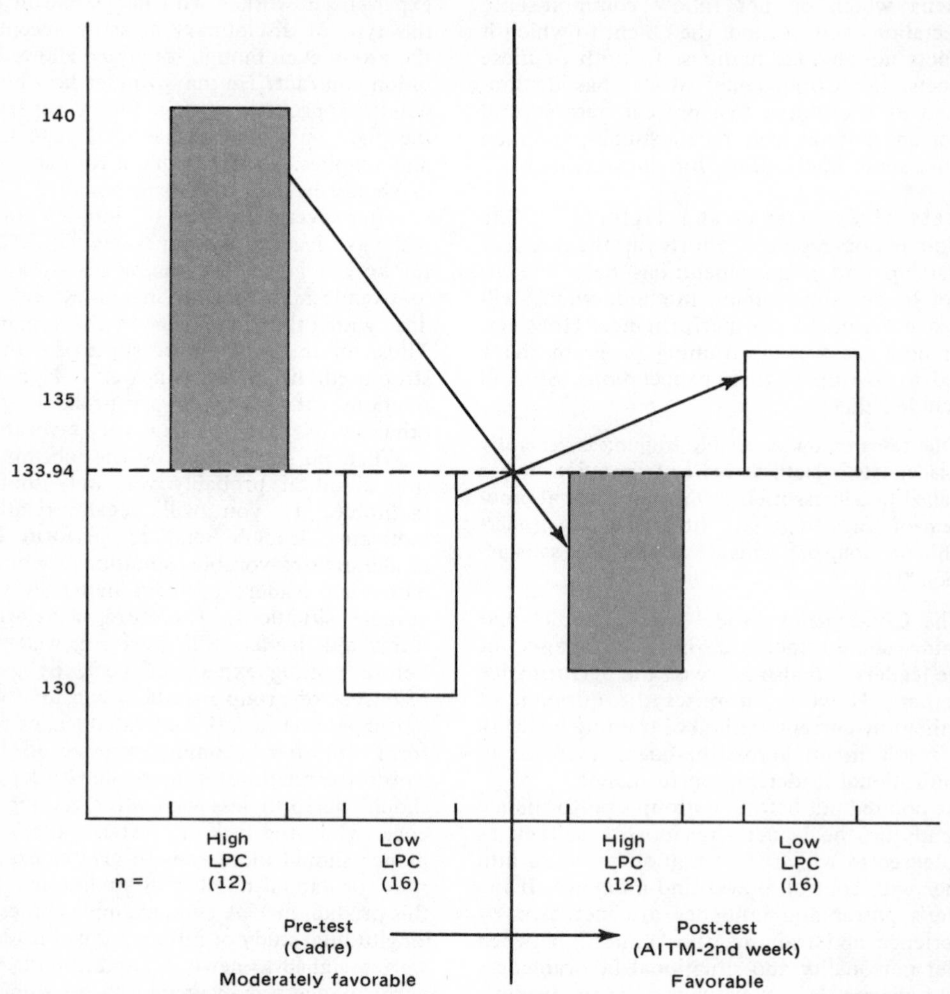

how to decode simple messages easily by first counting all the letters in the message and considering the most frequent letter an "e." A three-letter word, ending with the supposed "e" is then likely to be a "the," etc. The other half of the leaders were given no training of this type. All teams operated under a fairly high degree of tension, as indicated by subsequent ratings of the group atmosphere. Because the task is by definition unstructured, the situation was moderately favorable for the trained leaders but unfavorable for the untrained leaders. Therefore, we would expect that the relationship-motivated leaders would perform better with training, while the task-motivated leaders would perform more effectively in the unfavorable situation, i.e., without the benefit of training. As can be seen in Figure IV, the findings support the predictions of the model.

FURTHER IMPLICATIONS

Selection It seems highly likely from these and similar findings that we need to reconsider our management selection strategies. Obviously, the old adage calling for "the right man for the right job" is not as simple as it once appeared. The right person for a particular job today may be the wrong person in 6 months or in 1 or 2 years. As we have seen, the job which presents a very favorable leadership situation for the experienced leader presents a moderately favorable situation for the leader who is new and inexperienced or untrained. Hence, under these con-

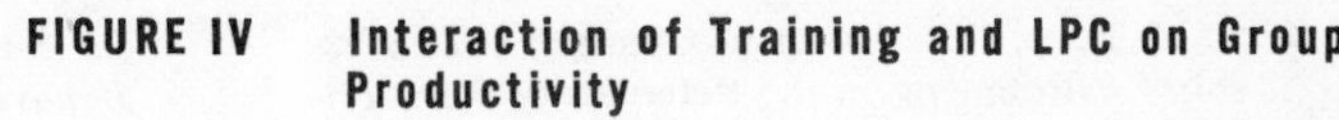

FIGURE IV Interaction of Training and LPC on Group Productivity

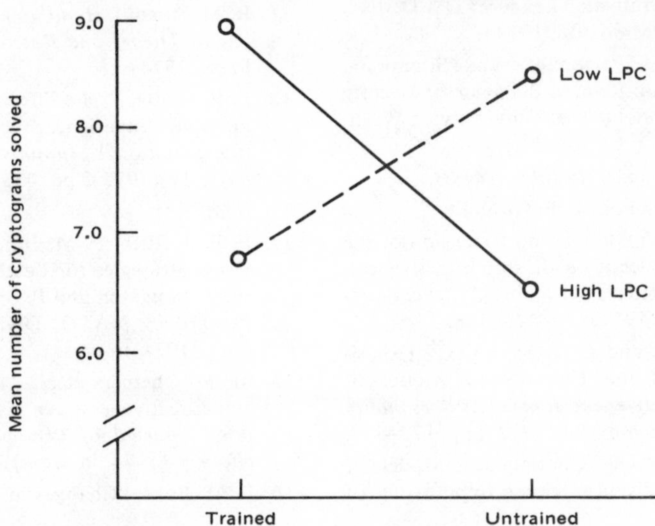

ditions a relationship-motivated leader should be chosen for the long run. The job which is moderately favorable for the experienced and trained leader is likely to represent an unfavorable leadership situation for the inexperienced leader. Hence, a task-motivated leader should be selected for the short run, and a relationship-motivated leader should be selected for the long run.

Rotation Figure IV suggests that certain types of leaders will reach a "burn-out point" after they have stayed on the job for a given length of time. They will become bored, stale, disinterested and no longer challenged. A rational rotation policy obviously must be designed to rotate these leaders at the appropriate time to new and more challenging jobs. The other types of leaders, e.g.. the task-motivated leaders represented in Figure IV, should be permitted to remain on the job so that they can become maximally efficient.

Most organizations and, in particular, the military services, have a rotation system which (at least in theory) moves all officers to new jobs after a specified period of time. Such a rigid system is likely to be dysfunctional because it does not properly allow for individual differences which determine the time required by different types of people to reach their best performance. Recent research by Bons also has shown that the behavior and performance of leaders is influenced by such other organizational changes as the transfer of a leader from one unit to a similar unit and by a reorganization which involves the reassignment of the leader's superiors.[16]

The Contingency Model clearly is a very complex formulation of the leadership problem. Whether it is more complex than is necessary, as some of its critics have claimed, or whether it is still not sufficiently complex, as others have averred, remains an open question. It is clear at this point that the theory not only predicts leadership performance in field studies and laboratory experiments, but also that it serves as a very important and fruitful source of new hypotheses in the area of leadership.

REFERENCES

1. F. E. Fiedler, "A Contingency Model of Leadership Effectiveness," in L. Berkowitz, ed., *Advances in Experimental Social Psychology* (Academic Press, 1964); Also *A Theory of Leadership Effectiveness* (New York: McGraw-Hill, 1967); F. E. Fiedler and M. M. Chemers, *Leadership and Effective Management* (Glenview, Ill.: Scott, Foresman & Co., 1974).
2. D. Nebeker, "Situational Favorability and Environmental Uncertainty: An Integrative Study," *Administrative Science Quarterly* (1974, in press).
3. L. K. Michaelsen, "Leader Orientation, Leader Behavior, Group Effectiveness and Situational Favorability: An Empirical Extension of the Contingency Model," *Organizational Behavior and Human Performance,* 9 (1973), pp. 226–245.

4. P. M. Bons, "The Effect of Changes in Leadership Environment on the Behavior of Relationship- and Task-Motivated Leaders" (Ph.D. diss., University of Washington, 1974).
5. Joyce Prothero, "Personality and Situational Effects on the Job-Related Behavior of Faculty Members" (Honors thesis, University of Washington, 1974).
6. F. E. Fiedler, *Leadership Effectiveness.*
7. D. Nebeker, "Situational Favorability."
8. F. E. Fiedler, "Validation and Extension of the Contingency Model of Leadership Effectiveness: A Review of Empirical Findings," *Psychological Bulletin,* 76 (1971), pp. 128–148.
9. M. M. Chemers and G. J. Skrzypek, "Experimental Test of the Contingency Model of Leadership Effectiveness, *Journal of Personality and Social Psychology,* 24 (1972), pp. 172–177.
10. S. C. Shiflett, "The Contingency Model of Leadership Effectiveness: Some Implications of Its Statistical and Methodological Properties, *Behavioral Science,* 18 (1973), pp. 429–441.
11. R. M. Stogdill, *Handbook of Leadership: A Survey of Theory and Research* (New York: Free Press, 1974).
12. F. E. Fiedler, "The Effects of Leadership Training and Experience: A Contingency Model Interpretation," *Administrative Science Quarterly,* 17 (1972), pp. 453–470.
13. *Ibid.*
14. F. E. Fiedler, P. M. Bons and L. L. Hastings, "New Strategies for Leadership Utilization," in W. T. Singleton and P. Spurgeon, eds., *Defense Psychology* NATO, Division of Scientific Affairs (1974, in press).
15. M. M. Chemers et al., "Leader LPC, Training and Effectiveness: An Experimental Examination," *Journal of Personality and Social Psychology* (1974, in press).
16. P. M. Bons, "Changes in Leadership."

D. COMMUNICATIONS

65 TEN COMMANDMENTS OF GOOD COMMUNICATION*

As a manager, your prime responsibility is to get things done through people. However sound your ideas or well-reasoned your decisions, they become effective only as they are transmitted to others and achieve the desired action—or reaction. Communication, therefore, is your most vital management tool. On the job you communicate not only with words but through your apparent attitudes and your actions. For communication encompasses all human behavior that results in an exchange of meaning. How well you manage depends upon how well you communicate in this broad sense. These ten commandments are designed to help you improve your skills as a manager by improving your skills of communication—with superiors, subordinates, and associates.

1. *Seek to clarify your ideas before communicating.* The more systematically we analyze the problem or idea to be communicated, the clearer it becomes. This is the first step toward effective communication. Many communications fail because of inadequate planning. Good planning must consider the goals and attitudes of those who will receive the communication and those who will be affected by it.

2. *Examine the true purpose of each communication.* Before you communicate, ask yourself what you *really* want to accomplish with your message—obtain information, initiate action, change another person's attitude? Identify your most important goal and then adapt your language, tone, and total approach to serve that specific objective. Don't try to accomplish too much with each communication. The sharper the focus of your message the greater its chances of success.

3. *Consider the total physical and human setting whenever you communicate.* Meaning and intent are conveyed by more than words alone. Many other factors influence the over-all impact of a communication, and the manager must be sensitive to the total setting in which he communicates. Consider, for example, your sense of timing—i.e., the circumstances under which you make an announcement or render a decision; the *physical setting*—whether you communicate in private, for example, or otherwise; the *social climate* that pervades work relationships within the company or a department and sets the tone of its communications; *custom and past practice*—the degree to which your communication conforms to, or departs from, the expectations of your audience. Be constantly aware of the total setting in which you communicate. Like all living things, communication must be capable of adapting to its environment.

4. *Consult with others, where appropriate, in planning communications.* Frequently it is desirable or necessary to seek the participation of others in planning a communication or developing the facts on which to base it. Such consultation often helps to lend additional insight and objectivity to your message. Moreover, those who have helped you plan your communication will give it their active support.

5. *Be mindful, while you communicate, of the overtones as well as the basic content of your message.* Your tone of voice, your expression, your apparent receptiveness to the responses of others—all have tremendous impact on those you wish to reach. Frequently overlooked, these subtleties of communication often affect a listener's reaction to a message even more than its basic content. Similarly, your choice of language—particularly your awareness of the fine shades of meaning and emotion in the words you use—predetermines in large part the reactions of your listeners.

6. *Take the opportunity, when it arises, to convey something of help or value to the receiver.* Consideration of the other person's interests and needs—the habit of trying to look at things from his point of view—will frequently point up opportunities to convey something of immediate benefit or long-range value to him. People on the job are most responsive to the manager whose messages take their own interests into account.

* Reprinted by permission of the *American Management Association.* Copyright, 1955.

7. *Follow up your communication.* Our best efforts at communication may be wasted, and we may never know whether we have succeeded in expressing our true meaning and intent, if we do not follow up to see how well we have put our message across. This you can do by asking questions, by encouraging the receiver to express his reactions, by follow-up contacts, by subsequent review of performance. Make certain that every important communication has a "feed-back" so that complete understanding and appropriate action result.

8. *Communicate for tomorrow as well as today.* While communications may be aimed primarily at meeting the demands of an immediate situation, they must be planned with the past in mind if they are to maintain consistency in the receiver's view; but, most important of all, they must be consistent with long-range interests and goals. For example, it is not easy to communicate frankly on such matters as poor performance or the shortcomings of a loyal subordinate—but postponing disagreeable communications makes them more difficult in the long run and is actually unfair to your subordinates and your company.

9. *Be sure your actions support your communications.* In the final analysis, the most persuasive kind of communication is not what you say but what you *do.* When a man's actions or attitudes contradict his words, we tend to discount what he has said. For every manager this means that good supervisory practices—such as clear assignment of responsibility and authority, fair rewards for effort, and sound policy enforcement—serve to communicate more than all the gifts of oratory.

10. *Last, but by no means least: Seek not only to be understood but to understand—be a good listener.* When we start talking we often cease to listen—in that larger sense of being attuned to the other person's unspoken reactions and attitudes. Even more serious is the fact that we are *all* guilty, at times, of inattentiveness when others are attempting to communicate to us. Listening is one of the most important, most difficult—and most neglected—skills in communication. It demands that we concentrate not only on the explicit meanings another person is expressing, but on the implicit meanings, unspoken words, and undertones that may be far more significant. Thus we must learn to listen with the inner ear if we are to know the inner man.

66 COMMUNICATIONS NETWORKS IN THE BUSINESS ORGANIZATION STRUCTURE*

A. K. Wickesberg

In recent years there has been an increasing interest in the detailed workings of organization structure with particular reference to communications patterns. Harold J. Leavitt[1] and more recently Guetzkow and Dill[2] and others have constructed laboratory experiments in which communications patterns such as the "wheel," the "chain," and the "star" are artificially imposed to restrict communications ability and the effect on task performance noted. Another group of researchers, Burns,[3] Sayles,[4] Ponder,[5] and Walker, Guest, and Turner,[6] have sought to record communications as they occur in actual business conditions. A principal contribution stemming from these latter studies is the indication of the substantial amount of time individuals spend in communicating with others in the organization.[7]

The bulk of the studies outside the laboratory setting, however, deal with factory (assembly) environments and record single firm experience. Data are lacking on what communications nets occur for what purposes, how many persons comprise any one individual's own communications network, and what differences there are between such networks for managers and for nonmanagers.

To secure some preliminary insights into the dimensions of individual network membership, a study was undertaken at the University of Minnesota to investigate the composition and nature of the several subnets, and the breadth of individual contacts throughout the firm as the individual builds his total communications net to carry out his task assignment. Ninety-one businessmen in Minnesota's Executive Master of Business Administration program recorded all communications, oral and written, issued or received, over a sample five-day period which consisted of Monday from Week I, Tuesday from Week II, Wednesday from Week III, Thursday from Week IV, and Friday from Week V. In all, 35 organizations in the Twin Cities were represented from a wide range of industrial, transportation, educational, retailing, and financial organizations. Participants were almost equally divided between managerial (those with subordinates formally assigned to them) and nonmanagerial positions. While occupational titles ranged widely, the principal functional areas of marketing, production, finance, engineering, and research and development were represented in about equal proportions.

No superior-subordinate pairs were present, nor were there any communications pairs among the participants. To include communications pairs (both issuer and receiver of a given communication) creates problems in analyzing the data to avoid double counting of a communication as received by one individual and reported as issued by another. Absence of communications pairs also serves to in effect double the size of the reporting group.

Each participant maintained a daily log of his communications including information on the nature or purpose of the communication,

* Reprinted by permission of the publisher from *Academy of Management Journal*, vol. 11, no. 3, pp. 253–262, July, 1968. Mr. Wickesberg is professor of management at the University of Minnesota.

[1] Harold J. Leavitt, "Some Effects of Certain Communication patterns on Group Performance," *Journal of Abnormal and Social Psychology* (1951), pp. 38–50.

[2] H. Guetzkow and W. R. Dill, "Facets in Organizational Development of Task-oriented Groups," *Sociometry*, XX (1957), 175–204.

[3] Tom Burns, "The Direction of Activity and Communications in a Departmental Executive Group," *Human Relations*, VII (1954), 73–97.

[4] Leonard R. Sayles, *Managerial Behavior* (New York: McGraw-Hill, 1964).

[5] Quentin Ponder, "Supervisory Practices of Effective and Ineffective Foremen" (unpublished Ph.D. dissertation, Columbia University, 1958).

[6] Charles R. Walker, Robert H. Guest, and Arthur N. Turner, *The Foreman on the Assembly Line* (Cambridge: Harvard University Press, 1956).

[7] Robert Dubin, "Business Behavior *Behaviorally* Viewed," *Social Science Approaches to Business Behavior*, ed. George Strother (Homewood, Ill.: Richard D. Irwin, 1962), pp. 11–55.

whether written or oral, the amount of time taken for each entry, and to whom or from whom the communication was issued or received. The log contained a brief description of the subject matter as well as a purpose code. In addition to the log, each participant provided the researcher with an organization chart and a brief statement pointing out any unusual features in his communications patterns for the period studied plus any other information he felt would contribute to better understanding of that individual's communications behavior.

DIMENSIONS OF THE COMMUNICATIONS NETWORK

Examination of the data suggests the following as major categories for classifying the different purposes of the reported communications:

1. information received or disseminated,
2. instructions given or received,
3. approval given or received,
4. problem-solving activities, and
5. nonbusiness related communications or scuttlebutt.

General Purposes for Which Communications Take Place The five categories into which data are grouped to study the purposes for which communications occur indicate several general conclusions (see Table 1). First, communications separate into four frequency levels with transmission of information by far the highest, followed by instruction and problem-solving in middle position, and with scuttlebutt and approval showing lowest frequency levels. In addition, there is little variation between manager and nonmanager in the frequency composition of his communications subject matter. While one might expect such frequencies to be identical where the participants consist of communications pairs, where such pairs are lacking and where the respondents range widely over both position and industry categories, closeness of the data for each category is indeed of interest. It should also be noted that the findings showing the high frequency of information over other categories of communications are consistent with other research reports and with intuitive reflections on organization practice.

Direction of Communications Flow In an organizational context, communications may be transmitted vertically up or down the scalar chain, horizontally to one's peers either within or outside one's own organizational unit, or diagonally to or from an organizational unit and hierarchical level outside the reporter's own formal organizational location. The data suggest very little difference between managers and nonmanagers in terms of the direction of communications flow analyzed by purpose with the exception of scuttlebutt or nonbusiness related communications. Nonmanagers restrict nonbusiness communications to horizontal

TABLE 1 Communications Frequency Classified by Purpose and Position

PURPOSE	POSITION	PER CENT OF TOTAL COMMUNICATIONS	FREQUENCY LEVEL
Information	Manager	53.5	Level I
	Nonmanager	54.2	
Instruction	Manager	22.4	Level II
	Nonmanager	21.3	
Problem-solving	Manager	11.1	Level III
	Nonmanager	12.5	
Scuttlebutt	Manager	6.6	Level IV
	Nonmanager	8.2	
Approval	Manager	6.2	
	Nonmanager	3.8	

TABLE 2 Direction of Communications Flow as Per Cent of Total Entries for Each Purpose and for All Communications

DIRECTION	INFORMATION	INSTRUCTION	APPROVAL	PROBLEM-SOLVING	SCUTTLEBUTT	ALL COMMUNICATIONS
Horizontal:						
Manager	31.0	25.1	21.5	33.3	43.1	30.2
Nonmanager	41.3	43.7	33.4	45.6	67.9	44.7
Vertical:						
Manager	29.7	38.7	42.2	31.3	23.5	32.8
Nonmanager	22.8	23.2	34.5	22.8	19.1	23.1
Diagonal:						
Manager	39.4	36.1	35.8	35.4	33.3	36.9
Nonmanager	35.9	33.0	32.2	31.5	13.1	31.7

organizational relationships to a far greater extent than do managers (see Table 2).

Of particular interest is the proportion of communications for all five purposes which utilizes *diagonal* relationships. Considerable contact between individuals regardless of position and unit takes place in the performance of the day-to-day activities related to their task assignment.

Managers and nonmanagers alike seek out contributors to their task effectiveness and in so doing direct approximately one-third of their communications to persons in units and organizational levels other than their own. To the superior-subordinate and peer contacts reported in the literature, one must add and not overlook the presence and significance of the diagonal component.

Data on initiation of communications were submitted by 47 of the 48 managers and by 39 of the 43 nonmanagers. While perceptions undoubtedly differ on who is the initiator and who is the receiver, the data provided in the reporter logs clearly demonstrate that nonmanagers as well as managers initiate not only information and scuttlebutt but also play a sizeable role in the managerial communications activities of instruction, approval, and problem-solving. These nonmanagers, as their communications networks indicate, are engaged in man-

TABLE 3 Acceptance or Rejection of the Hypothesis That Significant Differences Exist between Managers and Nonmanagers in the Proportion of Individuals Initiating Communications for All Purposes to Selected Organizational Unit-level Cells*

	ORGANIZATIONAL UNIT INITIATED TO:			
ORGANIZATION LEVEL INITIATED TO:	TO OWN UNIT	OUTSIDE UNIT, TO OWN DEPARTMENT	OUTSIDE DEPARTMENT, TO OWN DIVISION	OUTSIDE DIVISION, TO OWN FIRM
to one level up	reject	reject	reject	accept
at own level	reject	reject	reject	reject

* Using chi square test with acceptance at .05 level.

aging the accomplishments of those duties and tasks assigned to them regardless of where in the organization such activities may take them.

Of course, managers differ from nonmanagers in that nonmanagers have no opportunity for downward communications, for they are by definition the lowest members of the organizational hierarchy. In those organizational levels to which both managers and nonmanagers communicate, however, the bulk of these communications contacts occur at their own organizational level and at the level immediately above them. At these two levels, there are seldom any significant differences between managers and nonmanagers in the proportion of individuals in each category initiating communications for all five purposes. And the communications so initiated are directed by both managers and nonmanagers vertically, horizontally, and diagonally to every major segment of the organization at those two levels (see Table 3).

Questioning of respondents indicates that few horizontal or diagonal relationships are prescribed in the formal authority statements or procedures. This may be a function of the kinds of positions and the nature of the industries represented by the reporters. That such movement is so widespread, however, suggests that individuals move wherever in the organization information, advice, counsel, and expertise may be found to assist in gaining satisfactory accomplishment of the goals assigned. Managers and nonmanagers are alike in this behavior. Formal organization boundaries and levels yield to the demands of the task and situation.

Network Membership The composition of a communications network for a given individual may be considered in terms of (1) the total number of individuals with whom he communicates and their unit location in the organization, (2) the organizational level of these individuals in terms of communicating vertically, horizontally, or diagonally, and (3) the nature or purpose of the communication.

The data indicate that both managers and nonmanagers have communications network members who total far more than traditional spans of management or control would indicate and which are in excess of what one would conclude from examination of the organization charts and prescribed procedures alone (see Table 4). Furthermore, the scope of these networks varies only slightly between manager and nonmanager. The very large proportion of members outside one's own immediate organizational unit should be noted. This amounts to 80 per cent for managers and 85 per cent for nonmanagers and confirms Leonard Sayles' experience.[8]

This sizeable component of net membership occurring outside one's own organizational unit and the substantial amount of communications movement regardless of formal organization and hierarchy boundaries are further supported in Table 5. Relatively few persons are present from the scalar chain, the vertical structure. The bulk of the network membership is to be found among one's peers in other units (the horizontal structure) and in persons at higher or lower levels in units other than the reporter's home base (diagonal structure). Taking into consideration the fact that nonmanagers have no subordinates and are at the lowest level in the hierarchy so they can have no "vertical down" or "diagonal down" communication, there is again close correspondence between managers and nonmanagers both in the total network size and in the network composition classified by direction of communication.

In addition to network membership examined in terms of organization location of the mem-

[8] Sayles, *op. cit.*, p. 39.

TABLE 4 Number of Members in Average Individual Network (by Organization Unit)

	WITHIN OWN UNIT	OUTSIDE UNIT, IN OWN DEPT.	OUTSIDE DEPT., IN OWN DIV.	OUTSIDE DIV., IN OWN FIRM	OUTSIDE FIRM	TOTAL NET MEMBERS
Manager	7	9	9	9	2	36
Nonmanager	4	6	10	6	2	28

TABLE 5 Number of Members in Average Individual Network (by Direction of Communication)

	VERTICAL UP	VERTICAL DOWN	DIAGONAL UP	DIAGONAL DOWN	HORIZONTAL	TOTAL
Manager	2	5	5	10	14[a]	36
Nonmanager	2	—	10	—	16[b]	28

[a] in own unit—1; outside unit—13.
[b] in own unit—2; outside unit—14.

bers and the direction of flow of communications issued or received, membership may be analyzed according to the function or purpose served by the individual network member (see Table 6). As in the case of communications frequency (see Table 1), network membership shows a predominance of individuals who serve the information function. The next highest number of members is less than one-half the number engaging in the information function. At this second level, the number of individuals in a network for instructional purposes is similar to those present for the problem-solving activity. The similar number of individuals for these latter two purposes departs from their volume characteristics as displayed in Table 1 where the number of instructional communications exceeds substantially the frequency of problem-solving items. As in Table 1, however, the approval and scuttlebutt purposes show the fewest number of subnet members. The magnitude for these two purposes is again less than one-half the number at the next higher level. Thus, with the exception of problem-solving and instruction, there is close correspondence between the functional frequency of communications and the number of net members participating in the performance of that function.

TABLE 6 Number of Members in Average Individual Network* (by Type of Communication)

COMMUNICATION TYPE	POSITION	NUMBER OF MEMBERS
Information	manager	25
	nonmanager	19
Instruction	manager	11
	nonmanager	9
Problem-solving	manager	10
	nonmanager	7
Approval	manager	4
	nonmanager	2
Scuttlebutt	manager	4
	nonmanager	4

* Any one individual may be a member of more than one subnet.

While some network members are present for multiple communications purposes, it is of interest to note that a substantial proportion of a given network membership is present to service but a single function (see Table 7). In the average managerial network, 22 individuals (approximately 60 per cent) participate in one function alone while for nonmanagers 16 persons (approximately 58 per cent) are single-function participants. Once again, the information category has the highest proportion of persons present for a single activity.

QUALITATIVE OBSERVATIONS FROM REPORTER LOGS

The large number of instances where communications take place outside the scalar chain indicates a substantial task orientation in the companies represented in the study. Such communications across organizational boundaries and in directions other than vertical suggest the existence of procedures regulating the flow of such communications. Little evidence, however, exists in the comments of participants to support the presence of formally prescribed procedures governing communications channels in the day-to-day activities. For the most part, reporting individuals were left to seek out and establish those network relationships which they believed to be useful or essential in the performance of their tasks.

The predominance of inter-unit and inter-level network membership and the substantial role of the nonmanager in initiating communi-

TABLE 7 Number of Members Serving Single Purpose Only in Average Net

	INFORMATION		INSTRUCTION		APPROVAL		PROBLEM-SOLVING		SCUTTLE-BUTT		TOTAL MEMBERS
	THIS ONLY	TOTAL	THIS ONLY	TOTAL	THIS ONLY	TOTAL	THIS ONLY	TOTAL	THIS ONLY	TOTAL	
Manager	13	25	3	11	.7	4	4	10	1	4	36
Nonmanager	11	19	3	9	.3	2	1	7	1	4	28

cations in all five purpose categories may well be a reflection of the high component among the reporters of professional or technical competence, of a sample bias toward aggressive, ambitious, younger individuals, and of a large component of so-called staff positions. At the same time, regardless of one's position title, his organization unit, his location in the hierarchy, and the presence or absence of formal structure, the qualitative as well as the quantitative data reflect the day-to-day emphasis on effective and economical task performance unrestricted by formal limits.

While one might feel that "staff" individuals would of course range widely through the organization, attempts at identification of "line" versus "staff" positions and relationships prove of little value. Position titles are of minor help in such classifications and give few clues as to the actual relationships existing between individuals in a network. As one might suspect, examination of the communication itself provides the best indicator of the character of such relationships. And the data fail to provide any clear-cut distinction between "line" and "staff" or between "manager" and "nonmanager" based on the communications themselves. Any individual regardless of position title or organization location could be a member of either group depending on the time and the situation.

CONCLUSIONS

Several conclusions stem from the quantitative and qualitative data. First, the extent of the total communications network and therefore the range of individual contacts in an organization are far wider for both manager and nonmanager than one would gather from such traditional concepts as formal structure, span of management, and superior-subordinate relationships. This is illustrated in the large proportion of horizontal and diagonal contacts which exist outside the formal prescriptions of structure and procedure.

Second, on a day-to-day basis, the concept of manager should be expanded to include all individuals performing managerial functions whether or not these persons have subordinates assigned in the formal organizational hierarchy. Both managers and nonmanagers perform activities which are essentially managerial in planning for, implementing, and controlling those tasks assigned to them. Without recognition of the managerial characteristics of those traditionally classified as nonmanagerial individuals, these persons often are denied the official resources to perform satisfactorily and must rely primarily on their expertise and persuasive abilities to obtain from others those contributions necessary for effective goal attainment.

Performance of managerial functions by persons historically considered as nonmanagerial coupled with the substantial crossing of organizational boundaries and surmounting of hierarchical levels by both managers and nonmanagers suggest the growing contribution of informal relationships developed by individuals to further task accomplishment. This is a phenomenon which increases as complexity and sophistication of organizational requirements increase. Greater efforts must be made in the assignment or resources better to serve the activities and contributions of these informal relationships. More effective resource allocation is essential if informal relationships are to be relied upon to an ever-larger degree in solving complex tasks and in drawing to the maximum on the expertise present wherever it may be found in the organization.

That these are observations based on data from highly qualified professional reporters does not reduce their relevance for the nontechnical or less professionally dominated organization membership. These are observations drawn from individuals in organizations many of which are at the forefront of technological advance and therefore are indicators of structural changes and relationships likely to develop in any organization as its level of technology and the general expertise of its membership advance.

It is therefore suggested that management scholars and practitioners alike give greater attention to achieving organization balance by more carefully identifying the resource needs and structural relationships arising *de facto* from task requirements, project objectives, and individual expertise and initiative. Resource allocation based on formal power structures embedded in traditional concepts of superior-subordinate relationships, unit boundaries, and organizational hierarchy is no longer sufficient in meeting the demands produced by increasing levels of technology and higher levels of member competence.

Part 6
CONTROLLING

Controlling is the management function of making sure that plans succeed. In other words, it is the measuring and correcting of activities of subordinates to ensure that these activities are contributing to the achievement of planned goals. The reader can see, of course, that planning and controlling are very closely interrelated. He will note also that effective controlling implies more than measuring. In many instances it requires revised planning, additional organizing, improved staffing, and better methods of directing. It is thus a means of "closing the loop" in the entire management process. In this part, readings on controlling are arranged into the following sections: "The Process of Controlling," "Information for Planning and Controlling," "Techniques of Planning and Controlling," and "Controlling Overall Performance."

The controlling process is regarded by the editors as one of establishing standards against which performance can be measured, measuring performance, and correcting deviations from the standards or plans. In "The Meaning of Control," Douglas S. Sherwin points out that controlling is an important responsibility of every manager, and he emphasizes the significance of information, particularly forecasting, to effective controlling. The second article, by Harold Koontz and Robert W. Bradspies, suggests that management control can be made more fruitful if it is based on a future-directed system and applies engineering principles of feedforward control. This concept is outlined in their article on "Managing Through Feedforward Control."

Because of the importance of information to both planning and controlling—and because electronic data processing has made information available in unprecedented amounts—the editors have selected three articles on information. One of these is the insightful paper by G. Anthony Gorry and Michael S. S. Morton on a "Framework for Management Information Systems." These authors suggest a framework built around planning and decision making to replace the general practice of building new information systems on old patterns of information. A helpful attempt is made to relate management information systems to the management process and to the needs of profitability in Bertram A. Colbert's article "The Management Information System." In this reading, the author describes what an information system is, and how it differs from traditional systems, and he depicts graphically the part information systems play in the management process. The relationship of information systems to the computer and essential steps and requirements for developing a practical information system are discussed in Robert W. Holmes's "Developing Better Management Information Systems."

A number of techniques, both improvement of old tools and the development of new ones, have been applied to assist managers in better planning and controlling. All these techniques have elements of furnishing an environment for performance, that is in being means whereby the manager can and will carry on these two closely related functions more effectively. One of the interesting and promising developments to improve the application of traditional techniques is tying in variable budgeting with the accounting system of direct costing. Certainly, both require and use the same basic data, and their combined use is mutually supportive. This subject is presented in Howard B. Burdeau's paper "Variable Budgets and Direct Costing."

Perhaps the most exciting development in the area of planning and control by government agencies has been program budgeting, introduced into the Department of Defense by former Secretary of Defense Robert McNamara in 1961. This technique really represents what budgeting ought to be—in the first place a planning tool leading toward the accomplishment of preselected goals. The original idea for program budgeting came from the Rand Corporation, and perhaps the originator was David Novick, who was for years head of that company's cost section. It is therefore particularly fortunate that the editors can include from Novick's book on program budgeting an excerpt titled "What Program Budgeting Is and Is Not."

Among the newer techniques for planning and controlling which have grown out of recognition that systems theory, long used in the physical sciences, can be applied with great profit in management are program evaluation and review technique (PERT) and PERT/COST. These should be thought of as additions to the operations research techniques already dealt with in the part on planning. Indeed, it is difficult to see control techniques as separate from planning since the latter necessarily furnishes the standards for control.

On the subject of PERT, the editors include the article by R. W. Miller, "How to Plan and Control with PERT," which outlines a general description of this technique. To cast further light on this network approach to managing through its application to cost as well as time, the editors have reprinted the analysis by Peter P. Schoderbeck, "PERT COST: Its Values and Limitations."

Because usual sources of information may not furnish managers adequate means for control and because direct personal observation may not be feasible in many areas, operations auditing has come into growing use. This technique operates by having a staff of trained auditors whose task it is to review, it is hoped, in a friendly and constructive way, various operations in an enterprise and call attention to significant deviations from what is intended. The nature and requirements for effective operations auditing are discussed by Roy A. Lindberg in his "Operations Auditing."

One of the major aspects of controlling is the measurement of overall performance of a company or an integrated division thereof. Perhaps the most widely used device for measuring such overall performance has been the rate-of-return-on-investment method, developed in the du Pont Company in 1914 and used by it since as a major means of divisional controlling. This concept, with its logic, problems, and means of application, is treated in Maurice S. Newman's "Return on Investment: An Analysis of the Concept." Additional analysis of the rate-of-return concept and practice, particularly with a view to dealing with criticism of this technique, is found in the article by J. Fred Weston on "ROI Planning and Control." Weston emphasizes that the rate-of-return technique must be used in a flexible and dynamic way, rather than woodenly and without reference to the total task of managing.

One of the pioneering areas of management control is the still experimental approach to measuring and monitoring the human resources of an enterprise. The feeling is completely accurate that human assets are of major importance to an ongoing operation, that they represent a large investment, and that we should have better ways of making sure they do not waste away or are not neglected. The original research in this area has been done by Rensis Likert and his staff at the Institute of Social Research at the University of Michigan. A summary of the nature and a review of the progress that has been made in accounting for human resources are found in Geoffrey M. N. Baker's article on "The Feasibility and Utility of Human Resource Accounting."

A. THE PROCESS OF CONTROLLING

67 THE MEANING OF CONTROL*

Douglas S. Sherwin

"What exactly do you mean by management control?" When this question was asked of a number of managers, in both Government and industry, the answers showed a surprising lack of agreement—surprising, since in a field for which theory has been developed to the extent it has in business management, terms should be precise, specific, and unambiguous. The literature, as one might expect, reflects about the same variety of views as entertained by management men themselves, and so does little to clarify the situation.

Is it important that managers have a clear understanding of this concept? The question almost answers itself. A manager who does not understand management control cannot be expected to exercise it in the most efficient and effective manner. Nor can staff men whose duty it is to design systems and procedures for their organizations design efficient systems unless they possess a clear understanding of management control. And certainly (though the truth of this is seldom sufficiently appreciated) anyone who is subject to control by others has to understand clearly what that means if he is to be contented in that relationship.

Indeed, when management control is *not* understood, good management is a very improbable result. This is especially true when—as frequently it is—control is identified with management, or is confused with certain devices of management, such as objectives, plans, organization charts, policy statements, delegations of authority, procedures, and the like. The manager who believes managing and controlling are the same thing has wasted one word and needs a second to be invented. And one who believes he has provided for control when he has established objectives, plans, policies, organization charts, and so forth, has made himself vulnerable to really serious consequences. A clear understanding of control is therefore indispensable in an effective manager.

Understanding control really means understanding three principal things about it: What is control? What is controlled? And who controls? By proposing answers to these questions, I will try to frame a concept of control that will be useful to practitioners of the managerial art.

The conception of control which I advocate can be simply and briefly stated as follows:

The essence of control is action which adjusts operations to predetermined standards, and its basis is information in the hands of managers.

We have a ready-made model for this concept of control in the automatic systems which are widely used for process control in the chemical and petroleum industries. A process control system works this way. Suppose, for example, it is desired to maintain a constant rate of flow of oil through a pipe at a predetermined, or set-point value. A signal, whose strength represents the rate of flow, can be produced in a measuring device and transmitted to a control mechanism. The control mechanism, when it detects any deviation of the actual from the set-point signal, will reposition the valve regulating flow rate.

BASIS FOR CONTROL

A process control mechanism thus acts to adjust operations to predetermined standards and does so on the basis of information it receives. In a parallel way, information reaching a manager gives him the opportunity for corrective action and is his basis for control. He cannot exercise control without such information. And he cannot do a complete job of managing without controlling.

As mentioned earlier, some students of management have defined control as what results from having objectives, plans, policies, organization charts, procedures, and so forth; and they refer to these elements of the management system, consequently, as controls or means of control. It is not difficult to understand why

* Reprinted by permission of the publishers from *Dun's Review and Modern Industry*, pp. 45ff., January, 1956. At the time the article was written, Mr. Sherwin was assistant coordinator, Rubber Chemicals Division, Phillips Chemical Company.

these devices of managing are so described by proponents of this point of view. Without objectives, for example, we all know results are likely to be other than desired, so it is assumed they function to control the results. And so it is with the other elements of the system.

Nevertheless, these elements are neither controls nor means of control. They do have, however, as we shall see later, an important role to play in a control *system*, and we can therefore examine them now in a little detail.

Certainly, to accomplish a task except through accident, people must know what they are trying to do. Objectives fulfill this need. Without them, people may work quite industriously yet, working aimlessly, accomplish little. Plans and programs complement objectives, since they propose how and according to what time schedule the objectives are to be reached.

But though objectives, and plans and programs are indispensable to the efficient management of a business (or, for that matter, to the management of almost any human endeavor) they are not means of control. Control is checking to determine whether plans are being observed and suitable progress toward the objectives is being made, and acting, if necessary, to correct any deviations.

Policy is simply a statement of an organization's intention to act in certain ways when specified types of circumstances arise. It represents a general decision, predetermined and expressed as a principle or rule, establishing a normal pattern of conduct for dealing with given types of business events—usually recurrent. A statement of policy is therefore useful in economizing the time of managers and in assisting them to discharge their responsibilities equitably and consistently.

POLICY VERIFICATION

Nothing in these advantages, however, makes policy a means of control. Indeed, by their very nature, policies generate the need for control; they do not fulfill that need. Adherence to policies is not guaranteed, nor can it be taken on faith. It has to be verified. Without verification, there is no basis for control, no control, and incomplete managing.

Organization is often cited as a means of control. This detracts both from its own significance and from the concept of control.

Organization is part of the giving of an assignment. The organization chart, for example, is a first crude step in the defining of assignments. It gives to each individual, in his title, a first approximation to the nature of his assignment, and it orients him as accountable to a certain individual. But it is not in a fruitful sense a means of control. Control is checking to ascertain whether the assignment is being executed as intended—and acting on the basis of that information.

The relation between 'internal check' and 'internal control' is likewise not well understood. The two terms refer to quite different aspects of the managerial system. 'Internal check' provides in practise for the principle that the same person should not have responsibility for all phases of a transaction. This makes it clearly an aspect of organization, rather than of control. For how do we provide for internal check? We provide for it through segregating the duties of recording and those of custodianship and assigning them to different employees or groups of employees.

Assigning duties is, of course, the very essence of organizing, and thus internal check is simply organizing in a special way in order to realize special objectives. Internal control, on the other hand, observes the actual performance of duties as against the assigned duties and acts, where necessary, to correct deviations of the actual from the assigned.

Internal check and internal control are obviously both very necessary in an enterprise. But they operate differently. The objective of internal check is to reduce the opportunity for fraud or error to occur. The objective of internal control is to restore operations to predetermined standards. Internal check is thus static or built-in; it is provided before-the-fact; and its operation is preventive in its effect. Internal control, in contrast, is active and continual; it is exercised after-the-fact; and its operation is corrective in its effect.

Assignments are far from defined, however, by the preparation of an organization chart. Among the ways we have for supplementing the titles and lines of authority of an organization chart are delegations of authority. Delegations of authority clarify the extent of authority of individuals and in that way serve to define assignments. That they are not means of control is apparent from the very fact that wherever there has been a delegation of authority the need for control increases, and this could hardly be expected to happen if delegations of authority were themselves means of control.

MANAGER'S RESPONSIBILITY

Control becomes necessary whenever a manager delegates authority to a subordinate, because he cannot delegate, then simply sit back and forget all about it. A manager's accountability to his own superior has not diminished one whit as a result of delegating part of his authority to a subordinate. It is therefore incumbent upon managers who delegate authority to exercise control over actions taken under the authority so delegated. That means checking results as a basis for possible corrective action.

The question whether budgets are a means of control does not yield a straightforward answer because budgets perform more than one function. They perform three: they present the objectives, plans and programs of the organization and express them in financial terms; they report the progress of actual performance against these predetermined objectives, plans, and programs; and, like organization charts, delegations of authority, procedures, and job descriptions, they define the assignments which have flowed down from the chief executive.

In expressing the objectives and plans of the organization, budgets are of course not means of control, for reasons examined earlier when objectives and plans were considered. Nor do budgets qualify as means of control in their function of defining assignments. Though this service of budgets is frequently overlooked, defining an assignment, as I have suggested previously, is neither a means of control nor the exercise of control.

Budgets are a means of control only in the respect that they report progress of actual performance against the program,—information which enables managers to take action directed toward bringing actual results into conformity with the program.

In the previous paragraphs I have tried to show that objectives, plans and programs, organization charts, and other elements of the managerial system are not fruitfully regarded as either 'controls' or 'means of control.' They nevertheless do bear a very important relationship to the control function. They are the pre-established standards to which operations are adjusted by the exercise of management control.

It may seem unfamiliar to some to view these devices of management in that light. Perhaps 'standards' is not the very best word. Yet these elements of the system are standards in a very real sense, for they have been laid down by competent authority as models or standards of desired performance.

These standards are, of course, dynamic in character, for they are constantly altered, modified, or revised. But for a moment let us give our attention to their static quality.

An objective is static until revised; a plan or program is static until it is abandoned. They possess a kind of temporary durability or limited permanence. They are in force until superseded. This same static quality inheres also in the other elements of the managerial system we spoke of. Policies, organizational set-up, procedures, delegations, job descriptions, and so forth, are, of course, constantly altered and added to. But, like objectives and plans, they retain their force until they are either abandoned or revised.

Suppose, for convenience, we use the phrase 'framework of management' to mean all the elements of the managerial system taken together—objectives, plans and programs, policies, organization, and the like. Doubtless, a more descriptive phrase could be invented, but this one at least suggests the notion that there is something of a semi-permanent nature in the managerial system. Now we can in a new way identify what is controlled. Managers control adherence to the objectives, plans, policies, organizational structure, procedures, and so forth, which have been laid down. In brief, managers control adherence to a predetermined 'framework of management.'

Now we can turn to the very important question that must be answered: "Who should act?"

It has become almost axiomatic as a management principle (which is unfortunately not always given effect in practise) that that person should act who is responsible for the results. 'Results' has to be interpreted here in a broad sense. For results include not only profits and costs—obvious items—but the conformity of all operations with all standards. Hence, whoever had responsibility for specifying and establishing a particular standard has to be ultimately responsible for controlling adherence to it and responsible, therefore, for such corrective action as is necessary. Of course, those below him in the chain of command may help him, but they cannot relieve him of final responsibility for control. Therefore, authority for managers to establish standards should be delegated as far down in the organization as practical wisdom permits. It then becomes their responsibility to control adherence of operations to the system they establish.

It is not only a responsibility, but a right; and it is asking for trouble to place in anyone else's hands the responsibility for controlling results in the operating manager's sphere of responsibility.

If the basis of control is information in the hands of managers, 'reporting' is elevated to a level of very considerable importance. Used here in a broad sense, 'reporting' includes special reports and routine reports; written, oral, and graphic reports; staff meetings, conferences, television screens, and any other means whereby information is transmitted to a manager as a basis for control action. Even the non-receipt of information, as where management is by exception, can be informational and imply the existence of control.

We are often told that reports should be timely and designed to meet the needs of managers. We are in a better position to appreciate this when we realize the important role that reporting plays in the control function. Certainly if it is to be the basis for control, information should be assembled with that objective in view. It should exclude material extraneous to the problem of control and must be placed at the disposal of managers quickly so that operations do not deviate any further from the desired norm—or for a longer period—than can be avoided.

That control occurs after the fact is a point that sometimes troubles managers. It should not —since this is simply part of the nature of the concept. The situation is entirely comparable in the process control system described earlier. In that system the detecting device continuously evaluates results and transmits them back to the control mechanism, which, sensing the difference between the actual and the desired results, acts to restore results to the desired value. The results, just as in management control, precede the exercise of control. Control systems, human or mechanical, deal with transfers of energy and a transfer of energy takes time. We learn from this—and it underscores the importance of speed in reporting—that all we can do for the management problem is to minimize the time lag between results and action.

CONTROL SPECTRUM

There is another sometimes troublesome aspect of control, namely, that control over some things must be relinquished as successively higher echelons of management are reached. This again we must simply face. Managers in the first echelon require certain information as their basis for controlling. But in the next higher echelon, the character of required information changes; some information is dropped, some is added. There is thus a kind of 'control spectrum.' For the process of fading out and shading in of information is continued as you move up the pyramid until, just as in the visible spectrum the colors at one end are wholly unlike those at the other, the information reported to the top is wholly different from the information reported to first line managers.

This would hardly be worth pointing out except that some managers are burdened with a persistent sense of insecurity which undermines their self-confidence and ability to do the job, because they are unable to keep track of all the details under their management. Of course, they should not be able to keep track of all the results, or more accurately, should not allow themselves to do so. Relinquishing control over some operations is a calculated risk, taken so that managers can assume more important tasks.

It will bear mentioning that information serves other purposes than as the basis for control. The notion of a 'framework of management,' which we suggested earlier, is helpful in describing one of these purposes. This 'framework,' we said, is constantly undergoing change in one or another of its aspects. Such change takes place, not accidentally, but following conscious decisions for change by those responsible for such decisions. And decisions for changes in the framework are based on information that is conceptually different from information used for controlling adherence to the framework.

WHERE FORECASTS FIT

Forecasts and projections, for example, have no place in the problem of control (since control is after-the-fact while forecasts are before) but they are very important for setting objectives and formulating plans. Of course, information for aiming and for planning does not have to be before-the-fact. It may be an after-the-fact analysis proving that a certain policy has been impolitic in its effect on the relations of the company with customer, employee, or stockholder; or that a certain plan is no longer practical; or that a certain procedure is unworkable. The prescription here certainly would not be 'control' (since in these cases control would simply bring operations into conformity with obsolete standards), but the establishment of new standards—a new policy, a new plan, and a new procedure—to be controlled to.

Besides furnishing evidence of a need for reconstructing the managerial framework, information is, of course, the basis of all communication. But since that subject is one of the most discussed in the management field to-day, there is no need to discuss it further here.

Control, we have seen, means something quite specific in the managerial art. This is certainly as it should be in an area of thought as well developed as business management. For in any field for which theory has been developed to an appreciable extent, terms should be precise and unambiguous. Control, when used in a management context, should mean one thing and one thing only. I have suggested that it means action directed toward bringing operations into conformity with predetermined standards and goals; that it is exercised by managers; and that its basis is information in their hands after-the-fact.

In addition to being a specific part of managing, control is also, quite evidently, an extremely important part of managing. In organizations, therefore, where the responsibility for control is not placed in the hands of managers, or not accepted by them, difficulties are certain to arise. Managers must control. Staff members of the organization may, by furnishing information, help a manager discharge this responsibility, but may not share in it. Where this philosophy is adopted by top management as the policy of the organization, the probability is enhanced that the energies of the organization will be channeled in fruitful directions.

TERMINOLOGY

Control is admittedly a term with emotional connotations. The denotation of the term, however, suffers from no such objection. Control is not supervision. Experienced managers perceive that as their authority is broadened, their superiors must place increased reliance on control as a means of safeguarding their own accountability. But at the same time, supervision of their activities by superiors becomes less close. There seems every reason to believe, therefore, that as the real nature of control becomes better understood, managers will come to recognize that their being subject to it in increasing measure is as sure a sign as any of their progress in the organization and in the fulfillment of their position.

Managerial Control

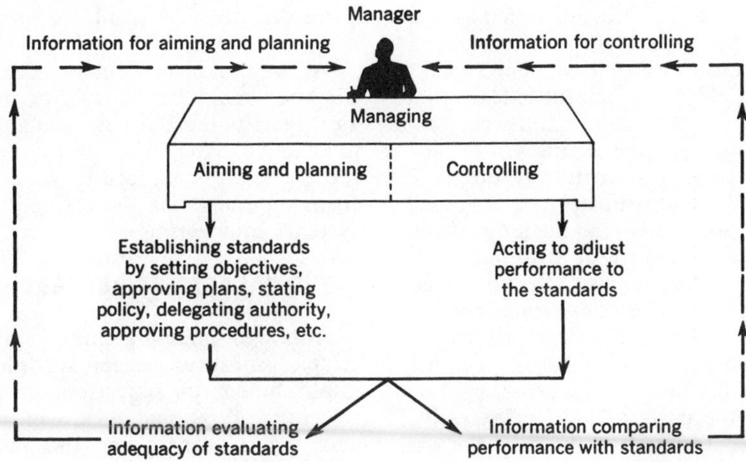

68 MANAGING THROUGH FEEDFORWARD CONTROL*

Harold Koontz and *Robert W. Bradspies*

Managers have long been frustrated by making the occasional discovery—*too late*—that actual accomplishments are missing desired goals. Anyone responsible for an enterprise or any department of it has suffered the discomfiture of realizing that typical control reports merely inform him what has already happened and that most control analyses are really post-mortems. It does, indeed, do little good to find out late in December that inventory levels were too high at the end of November because of something that happened weeks or months before. Nor is it helpful to learn that a program is behind schedule or incurring excessive costs because of past events.

Most current control systems rely on some form of feedback. Unfortunately, a feedback loop must sense some error or deviation from desired performance before it can initiate a correction. This is, of course, after the fact. Moreover, since correction takes some time to become effective, the deviation tends to persist. The costs incurred, in many cases, increase directly with the duration of the error.

For example, the costs of holding excessive inventory are proportional to the time the excess inventory is held. The time slippage in a program may continue until correction is applied, and the costs of making up for the time lost usually seem to rise at an increasing rate. It is not surprising, therefore, that most managers consider the problem of control to be one of early recognition of deviations so that correction can be applied promptly. Although many managers have solved this problem to some extent through careful planning, simulative techniques, and network systems of control (PERT/CPM), truly effective control has rarely been achieved.

* Reprinted by permission of the publisher from *Business Horizons,* vol. 15, no. 3, pp. 25–36 (June 1972). Mr. Koontz is Mead Johnson Professor of Management and Mr. Bradspies is a doctoral candidate at the University of California, Los Angeles.

To achieve more effective control, it is necessary to reduce the magnitude of the error. To avoid the problems inherent in the response time of a feedback system, deviations should be anticipated. The only way to do this, short of using a crystal ball, is to monitor the critical inputs to a program. If we watch changes in inputs, we can determine whether these would eventually cause failure to achieve desired goals. Time will then be available to take corrective action.

At first glance, it may seem that such a method would be difficult to use in practice. Fortunately, there is now available an approach to effective managerial control through adapting the principles of feed-forward control. This form of control is increasingly being used in systems engineering.

THE PROCESS OF CONTROL

Although planning and control are closely related, most managers see planning as the establishment of objectives or goals and the selection of rational means of reaching them, and regard control as the measurement of activities accompanied by action to correct deviations from planned events. It may thus be perceived that the function of managerial control is to make sure that plans succeed.

It is obvious that any system of controls requires plans, and the more complete, integrated, and clear they are, the better control can be. This simple truth arises from the fact that there is no way one can know whether he is going where he wants to go—the task of control—unless he first knows where he wants to go—the task of planning.

Control also requires an organization structure that is complete, integrated, and clear. The purpose of control is to detect and correct deviations in events; this must necessarily be done through people responsible for them. It does little good for a manager to be aware of

FIGURE 1 Management Control as a Cybernetic System

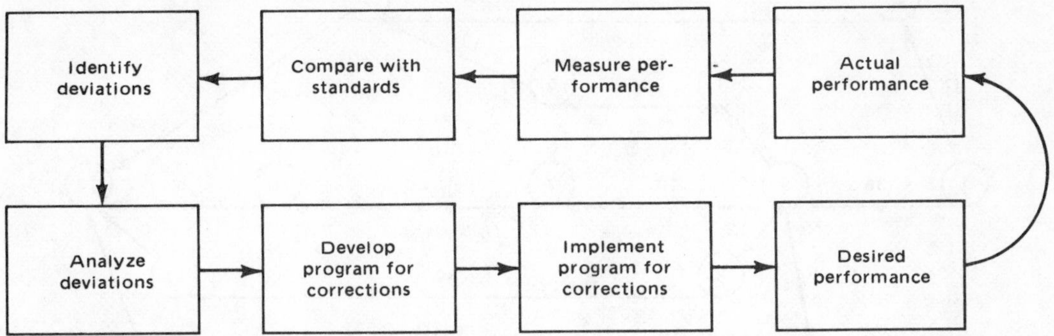

variances but not know where in the organization structure the responsibility for them lies.

Given these prerequisites, any type of control and any control technique fundamentally involves the same basic process. *First,* standards must exist. While an entire plan can be used as the standard of control, the inability to watch everything usually forces a manager to select relatively few critical points that will reasonably measure how planned accomplishments are proceeding. *Second,* the logic of control requires measurement of performance against standards. *Third,* the process calls for taking action to correct deviations from plans.

Shortcomings and Needs Control is really not this simple in practice, however, especially in management. Its basic features should be regarded as a cybernetic system as outlined in Figure 1. These steps represent the kind of feedback system that is involved in the simple room thermostat or the myriad of other control devices that one finds in mechanical and electrical control systems. But it dramatizes what every manager knows so well and many feedback engineers do not consider when they attempt to apply their thinking to management problems.

Simple feedback is not enough. Even the much-heralded ability of electronic data processing specialists to furnish information in real time, that is, as events are happening, is seldom good enough for management control. The fastest possible information may measure actual performance, may often be able to compare this measurement against standards, and may even be able to identify deviations. But analysis of deviations and the development and implementation of programs for correction normally takes weeks or months, if the correction can be made at all. Moreover, during this time lag, variances often continue to grow.

An inventory above desired levels may take months to analyze and correct. A cost overrun on a project may not even be correctible. A delay in an aspect of engineering or production, if recoverable at all, may be remedied only by an expensive crash program. Feedback is not much more than a post-mortem, and no one has found a way to change the past.

Need for Future-directed Control Intelligent and alert managers have recognized that the only problems they can solve are those they see, and the only way they can exercise control effectively is to see the problems coming in time to do something about them. In 1956, the senior author of this article identified future-directed control as one of the major principles of managerial control: "Since the past cannot be changed, effective control should be aimed at preventing present and future deviations from plans."[1] At this time it was emphasized that control, like planning, must be forward-directed and that it is fallacious to regard planning as looking ahead and control as looking back.

The simple principle of future-directed control is largely disregarded in practice, mainly because managers have been so dependent on accounting and statistical data instead of forecasts of future events. They have been too preoccupied with decimal accuracy, which can only be attained—if at all—from history. In the absence of any means to look forward, reference to history, on the assumption that what is past is prologue, is admittedly better than not looking at all. But no manager attempting to do an adequate job of control should be satisfied with using historical records, adequate as they are for tax collection and reporting on stewardship of assets to stockholders.

[1] Harold Koontz, "A Preliminary Statement of Principles of Planning and Control," *Academy of Management Journal,* I (April 1958), p. 45–61. (Paper presented in 1956.)

FIGURE 2 Simple PERT Network*

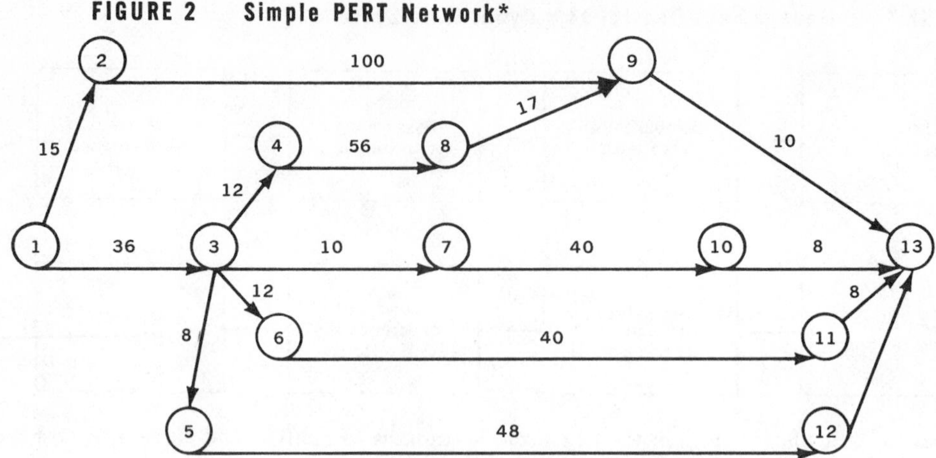

*Circled numbers are measurable or verifiable events, and numbers on arrows are estimates of days required to complete an event.

As a matter of fact, Norbert Wiener, the father of cybernetics, recognized the deficiencies of common feedback. He pointed out that, where there are lags in a system, corrections (the "compensator") must predict, or anticipate, errors. Thus, what he referred to as "anticipatory feedback" is often needed, particularly in human and animal systems. However, judging by the slowness in developing future-directed controls or anticipatory feedback in management control systems, there is little evidence that this variation of feedback has had the impact on thinking and practice that might have been expected.

Techniques of Future-directed Control

Relatively few techniques of future-directed control have been devised. Perhaps the most widely used is the continual development and revision of various kinds of forecasts, utilizing current expectancies to forecast probable results, comparing these with performance desired, and then developing programs to avoid undesired forecast events. Many managers, for example, after realistically working out their sales forecasts may be disappointed with the anticipated results; they then may review their programs of product development or marketing to see where changes can be made.

Cash forecasts are also a widely employed kind of future-directed control. Because banks do not normally honor checks without funds in an account, companies seldom can risk waiting until late November to find out whether they had adequate bank balances for checks written in October; instead, they engage in future-directed control by assuring that cash balances will be adequate to absorb charges.

One of the best approaches to future-directed control in use today is the formalized technique of network planning, which is exemplified by PERT networks. In PERT/TIME the discrete events required to accomplish a given program result are depicted in network form (since few programs ever are linear in the sense that one portion of it is sequentially followed by another), and the time required to finish each event is contained in the network. As will be recalled, when this is done, the planner can determine which series of events will have the least slack time.

The simple PERT network shown in Figure 2 will illustrate this long-used technique and how the most critical path—the one with the least slack—can be identified. A major advantage of this tool is that, through careful planning and measurement of progress in each event, any time slippage becomes evident long before the program is finished. The time available to finish the remaining events is one of the inputs to those events; if it is more than the minimum desired time, steps can be taken to accelerate any event along the critical path that lends itself to speed-up at minimum cost.

If, for example, there is no slack time on the critical path of events "1-3-4-8-9-13" (in other words, if delivery has been promised in 131 days), the manager knows that if event "3" is ten days late the entire project will be late unless something is done now. Although PERT has tended to become so complex in practice that its use for actual managerial control has

FIGURE 3 Comparison of Feedback and Feedforward Control Systems*

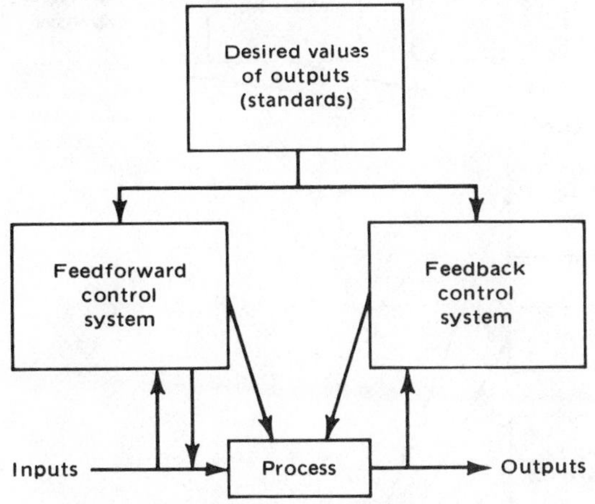

* In a feedback system, correction of outputs are fed back into the process. In a feedforward system, undesired variations of inputs are fed into the input stream for correction or into the process before outputs occur.

declined, it is basically the best single device of future-directed control that has yet been put into practice.

FEEDFORWARD IN ENGINEERING

As early as 1928, U.S. Patent No. 1,686,792 was issued to H. S. Black on a "Translating System," which incorporated the principle of feedforward control in engineering systems. However, the application of feedforward in electrical and process systems did not come into common use until a few years ago.[2]

In its essence, engineering feedforward control aims at meeting the problem of delay in feedback systems by monitoring inputs and predicting their effects on outcome variables. In doing so, action is taken, either automatically or by manipulation, to bring the system output into consonance with a desired standard before measurement of the output discloses deviation from standard. Thus, while feedback control relies on detecting errors in controlled variables as system outputs, feedforward is based on detecting and measuring system disturbances, and correcting for these before the system output change occurs. The basic concept of a feedforward and feedback system is outlined in Figure 3.

Feedforward has had wide application in the chemical and petroleum processing industries. It has been found particularly valuable where constant temperatures of material flow, exact mixtures, and various forms of chemical reactions require the precision that ordinary feedback, with its normal cycling, cannot achieve.

Perhaps the simplest form of feedforward control is contained in a system to maintain a fixed temperature of hot water leaving a heat exchanger where cool water inputs are heated by steam inputs. A thermostat on the water outlet would hardly be adequate, particularly with intermittent and variable uses of hot water; sudden changes in water output would probably cause bursts of cold water and steam inputs with resultant cycling of the water temperature.

To solve this problem, a systems design would provide a controller that would adjust the opening of the steam valve slightly. As the hot water usage starts to increase, the steam will be on its way into the tank before the water temperature drops below standard. A second feedforward loop might monitor the steam temperature and increase the rate of steam usage if its temperature should fall, in order to maintain the same heat input. By typing mathematical calculations into a computer that translates information to the input control valves, the oscillations characteristic of simple feedback systems can be reduced or entirely avoided.

However, even the most enthusiastic proponents of feedforward control admit that, if input variables are not known or unmeasurable, the system will not work. Therefore, for the best control, the use of feedback for output variables is also suggested.

FEEDFORWARD IN HUMAN SYSTEMS

The feedforward applications one finds in everyday life are far simpler than engineering applications. A motorist who wishes to maintain a certain speed does not usually wait until he notes that his speedometer has fallen below this speed as he goes up a hill. Instead, knowing that the incline represents a disturbing variable in the system of which he is a part, the driver

[2] See, for example, L. F. Lind and J. C. C. Nelson, "Feed Forward: Concept in Control System Design," *Control & Instrumentation,* (April 1970), pp. 39–40; F. G. Shinskey, *Process Control Systems* (New York: McGraw-Hill Book Company, 1967), Chapter 8; F. G. Shinskey, "Feedforward Control of pH," *Instrumentation Technology* (June 1968), pp. 69ff.; J. A. Miller, P. W. Murrill, and C. L. Smith, "How to Apply Feedforward Control," *Hydrocarbon Processing* (July 1969), pp. 165–72.

A review of engineering literature discloses a few references to feedforward control early in the 1960's, but the real volume of writing has occurred since 1967.

FIGURE 4 Input Variables for a Cash Plan

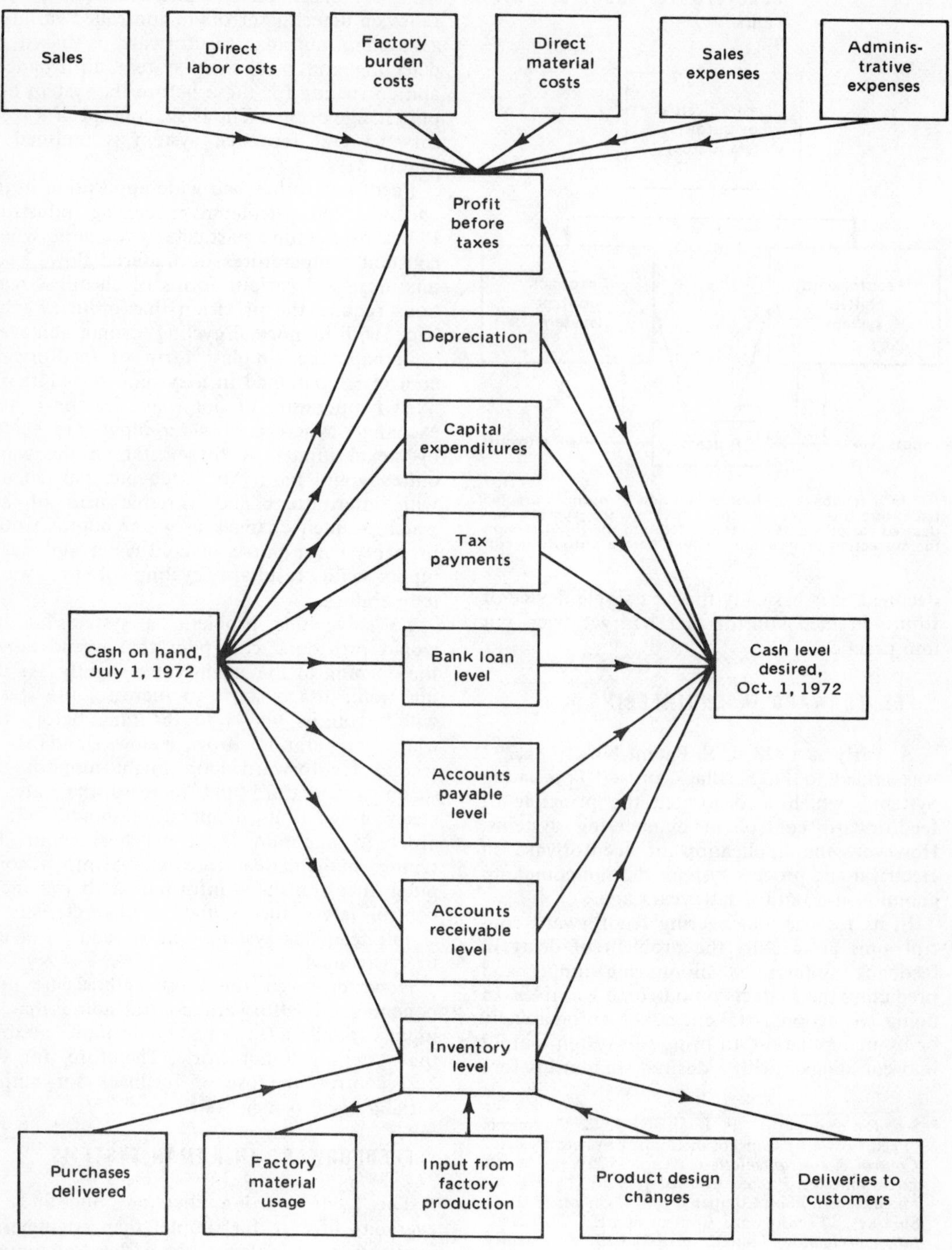

is likely to start correcting for the expected decrease in speed by accelerating in advance.

Similarly, the average person does not wait until a rainstorm actually feeds back to him the need for an umbrella before he carries one. Nor would a successful hunter aim his gun directly at a flying bird; he would "lead" it to correct for the delay in his own system, his reactions, the gun, and the shot velocity.

It is, therefore, surprising that more thorough and conscious feedforward techniques have not been developed in management, particularly since the delay factors in ordinary feedback correction are so long. As mentioned previously in this article, this has been done by such means as forecasting end results and PERT/CPM networks. But a little analysis and ingenuity could result in much wider use of effective controls and even the future-directed controls now in existence could be greatly improved.

A number of illustrations of how the principles of feedforward might be used in management may be given. Many require development of mathematical models of the system so as to provide managers information of forthcoming trouble in time for correction, but space does not permit the display of such models here. The approach of feedforward can be shown by several simple schematic models. For this purpose, the cases of control of cash, inventories, and new product development will be presented.

Feedforward in Cash Planning Since cash forecasting lies at the base of cash planning and control, this widely used technique of control is one of the best for revealing the application of feedforward to management. The basic inputs and construction of a cash control system may be seen in Figure 4. As can be noted, a number of input variables account for a desired future cash level. This model, representing a fairly simplified prototype of reality, shows that if any of the input variables differ from those premised when the cash plan was made, the desired cash level for the future will be affected.

As can be seen, many of these variables can have either a negative or positive effect on cash flow and the desired cash level at a given time in the future. It is readily apparent that normal feedback techniques are not adequate, and constant monitoring of the various input variables, with a feedforward of their influence on cash, is necessary for careful cash control. Of course, one way to avoid the problem of shortages is to have available a ready bank line of credit. But what is likely to happen in this case is that the enterprise will keep unnecessarily high balances of cash, with resultant avoidable interest costs or loss in investment income.

It is also clear from cursory examination of this feedforward system that a mathematical model programmed to a computer can readily trace the influences of changes of input variables on cash flow and availability. Neither this nor careful monitoring of input variables should be very difficult to do in practice.

Feedforward in Inventory Control One of the most difficult problems in business is the proper control of inventories. Many enterprises incur large and often unexpected cost increases, as well as sizable demands for cash because of inadequate control of inventories. Moreover, as experience continually teaches us, an inventory discovered to be out of control on the high side is extremely difficult to get under control except, of course, through that most costly of all solutions—writing off excess stocks.

Also, the costs of carrying inventory, due to expenses from handling and storage, interest, property taxes, and possible obsolescence, are higher than generally assumed; 25 percent of inventory value per year is often regarded as a reasonable estimate. Nor should it be overlooked that inventory shortages often have high costs because of missed sales or lost customers.

In recent years, operations researchers have presented a vast array of mathematical inventory models and refinements. There can be no question that they have contributed greatly to effective planning and control of inventories, and many can be used as the basis for effective feedforward in inventory control. The difficulty with many models is that they tend to concentrate unduly on such matters as economic order quantities and safety stock levels. These may be appropriate for a mass production operation, but may not take into account the many other input variables, such as obsolescence or property taxes, that make effective inventory control so difficult and important.

Any company will do well to develop its own inventory model, using, of course, the many standard algorithms and techniques available, but taking into account as many as possible of the variables that may influence actual inventory accumulation.

The schematic diagram shown in Figure 5 reveals the complexity of inventory control. Once a desired inventory level is established in a way that minimizes costs in the light of demands for adequate inventory, the total (whether expressed in dollars or days of sales) tends to be used as a standard. Actual results are compared to it through feedback with little or no monitoring of the input variables on which the desired level was determined.

The attempt is normally made to maintain

FIGURE 5 Effect of Increases in Input Variables on Determining Desired Inventory Level

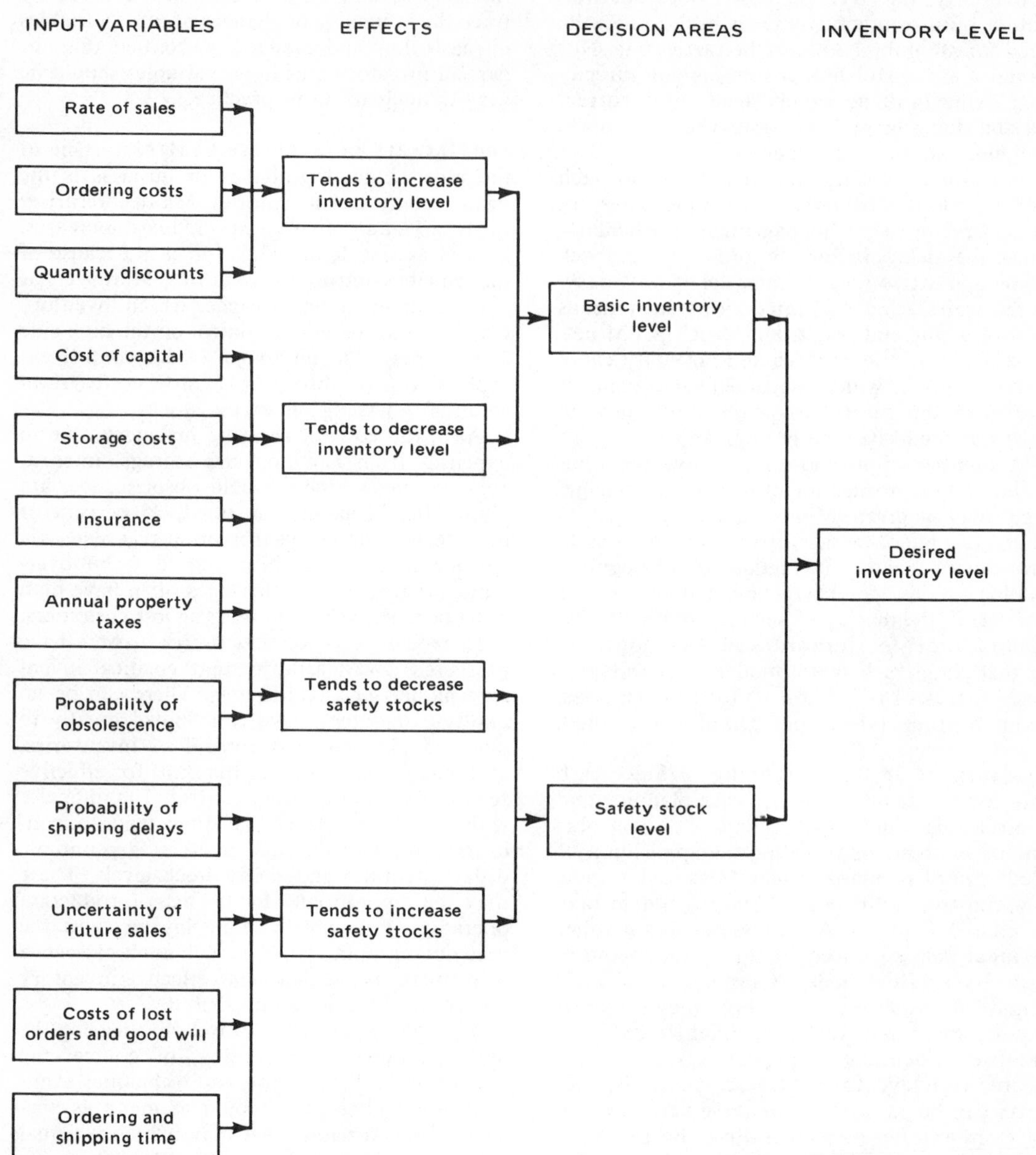

the inventory within desired limits by using only reorder point, economic order quantity, and maximum inventory level. In the simplest manual system, when a withdrawal is noted on a stock record, the balance is compared with the reorder quantity. When the balance on hand falls below this level a purchase order is issued. All of this may take place without considering the predictive changes of the original inputs.

The effect of such action may be to allow inventory to go out of control and raise costs. For example, if the rate of sales increased for a particular item, a company could find itself reordering too frequently or even running out of stock, thus increasing costs unnecessarily. Conversely, if sales decrease, a company could find that it was wasting cash by holding excess inventory. If sales declined further and a company continued reordering, it could find itself with a large obsolete stock.

If, instead, a company regularly monitored input variables, inventory levels could be adjusted by feedforward control by following the original decision paths and adjusting inventory purchases. In a company that used a manual inventory control system, for example, a simple monitoring system could be devised. It need only consider significant changes in input.

However, it must be admitted that a more sophisticated computer-controlled inventory system would be able to adjust more accurately for the effects of smaller changes in input variables and thereby reduce over-all operating costs by keeping inventory under control.

In reviewing the various input variables, it can easily be seen that different departments within the company would have to be responsible for feeding information (probably into a central inventory planning and control unit) on the variables within its field of knowledge. For example, ordering costs, economic order quantity, and quantity discounts are usually best known by the purchasing department; shipping time and unscheduled delays in shipping are data that could be reguarly expected from the traffic department.

Given a recognition of the types of input variables and a system for regularly collecting information on them, it should be easy to anticipate what is likely to happen in inventory. In feeding forward this information, it should be practicable to develop a kind of inventory control that is truly future directed.

Feedforward in New Product Development The typical new product development program is, in the first instance, a system of interlocking contributory programs, as shown in Figure 6. It can be readily seen that this is similar to a PERT planning and control network. If times and costs are estimated for each program event in the network, the accomplishment of each subsidiary program becomes an input variable by which it is possible to feedforward the probable delays and costs of the completion of the program.

Moreover, each of the major programs in this network can be further broken down into a system of input variables so that completion of the total program can be forecast. Action can be taken in time to make necessary corrections and keep it under control. For example, within the product research program, there will normally be a number of subsidiary programs or events. These may include establishment of design definition and specifications; preliminary design of the product; development of a breadboard model; and testing the model.

Each of the other programs can be broken down into a number of subsidiary events or programs. These, in turn, constitute input variables to the individual programs necessary for the completion of a total product development program; their monitoring can feedforward both time and cost factors against the standards desired for the total program.

In addition, analysis can disclose a number of other possible, and usually unplanned, input variables that may affect a desired end result. There are likely to be many of these, including such influences as delay in obtaining needed parts; failure of some part in a test; illness or departure of a key engineer; interference of a higher priority program; or change in a customer's desired specification. While not all of these can be carefully estimated in advance, and some may even be unforeseen, feedforward control can recognize the impact of such disturbances and provide for action in time to avoid program failure.

Change of Goals In feedforward control systems in engineering, the systems are almost inevitably designed to correct input variables so that a given standard or goal may be achieved. In its application to managerial problems, the same approach can be used, but it should not be overlooked that the system may lead to changes in goals.

By placing emphasis on input variables, both those foreseen as a part of the program and those unforeseen, feedforward applications can furnish a means of regularly reviewing program goals themselves. A material change in interest rates, for example, may make a review of inventory goals desirable. Or a new development in product technology or market tastes may require a reevaluation of a product program. Managers must always keep in mind that goals and programs may become obsolete.

FEEDFORWARD CONTROL GUIDELINES

Although many other examples of application of feedforward to management control might be given, it is hoped that the transfer of engineering principles to management situations will be clear enough to help open the way toward the systematic application of feedforward in many areas. This can be done more easily than it may first appear. But in doing so several guidelines should be kept in mind.

1. *Thorough planning and analysis is required.* As in all instances of management control, thorough and careful planning is a primary prerequisite. But, especially in applying feedforward, this planning must be as thorough as feasible. Input variables should not only

FIGURE 6 Feedforward through a System of Interlocking Contributory Programs of a New Product Program

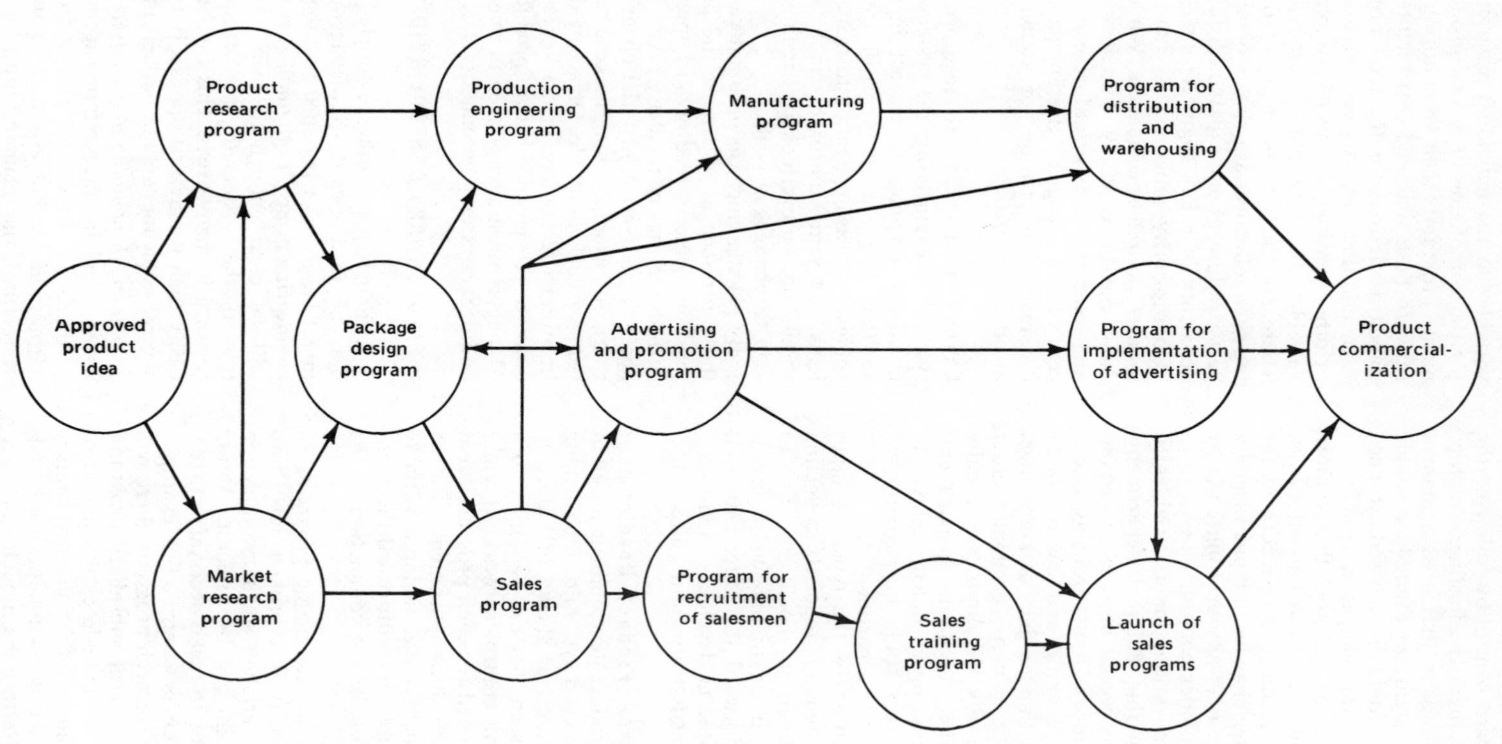

be identified but seen in their relationship and impact on desired end results.

2. *Careful discrimination must be applied in selecting input variables.* Since not all variables that *may* have some effect on output can be identified and monitored in typical management systems, it is essential that only the more critical variables be selected for watching. This is, of course, one of the key requirements of the managerial art—to identify those elements that make a material difference in the operation of a plan.
3. *The feedforward system must be kept dynamic.* There is always the danger that input variables will be identified in the analysis stage and only these will be monitored. The alert manager will, of course, watch for new influences, either within or outside the control system, which might seriously effect a desired output. New technology, unexpected changes in loan rates and availability, changes in customer tastes, and even unanticipated changes in social or political pressures are examples of input variables that may not have been foreseen.
4. *A model of the control system should be developed.* Clearly, if a feedforward system is to be utilized, the area in which such control is desired must be defined, with the various significant input variables identified and their effects on desired goals analyzed.

   This model may be a simple schematic drawing. It is far better, of course, to use an appropriate mathematical model that can be programmed in a computer. This way, the manager can take into account a larger number of input variables, more accurately calculate their impact on program goals, and be able more quickly and accurately to take corrective action.
5. *Data on input variables must be regularly collected.* Feedforward control is, of course, not possible without regular collection of pertinent data concerning the input variables so that the impact of this information can be carefully weighed. It is in this area that fast information availability is highly desirable and real-time information could have much meaning for control.
6. *Data on input variables must be regularly assessed.* No purpose can be served if input data are not regularly and carefully assessed to ascertain their influence on future program results. Barring unforeseen and unprogrammed variables, a computerized system can deliver this assessment quickly. However, for many feedforward systems the experienced eye and judgment of a top analyst may be good enough to point toward future deviations from planned results.
7. *Feedforward control requires action.* Few, if any, techniques or systems of management control are self-activating. All the system can do is to surface information that indicates future troubles, hopefully in time for something to be done to avoid them. This, of course, requires action. But if the system can be designed with enough lead time for a manager to take action, that is all that can be expected. And astute managers ask for nothing more than to be able to see their problems in time to do something about them.

There can be no doubt that feedforward is largely an attitude toward the analysis and solution of problems. It is the recognition that feedback information is just not adequate for management control and that a shift must be made away from emphasis on quickly available data on final results to quickly available data on those inputs variables that lead to final results. It is a means of seeing problems as they develop and not looking back—always too late—to see why a planning target was missed.

B. INFORMATION FOR PLANNING AND CONTROLLING

69 A FRAMEWORK FOR MANAGEMENT INFORMATION SYSTEMS*

G. Anthony Gorry and *Michael S. S. Morton*

INTRODUCTION

A framework for viewing management information systems (MIS) is essential if an organization is to plan effectively and make sensible allocations of resources to information systems tasks. The use of computers in organizations has grown tremendously in the 1955 to 1971 period, but very few of the resulting systems have had a significant impact on the way in which management makes decisions. A framework which allows an organization to gain perspective on the field of information systems can be a powerful means of providing focus and improving the effectiveness of the systems efforts.

In many groups doing MIS work, this lack of perspective prevents a full appreciation of the variety of organizational uses for computers. Without a framework to guide management and systems planners, the system tends to serve the strongest manager or react to the greatest crisis. As a result, systems activities too often move from crisis to crisis, following no clear path and receiving only *ex post facto* justification. This tendency inflicts an unnecessary expense on the organization. Not only are costly computer resources wasted, but even more costly human resources are mismanaged. The cost of systems and programming personnel is generally twice that of the hardware involved in a typical project, and the ratio is growing larger as the cost of hardware drops and salaries rise.[1] Competent people are expensive. More importantly, they exist only in limited numbers. This limitation actively constrains the amount of systems development work that can be undertaken in a given organization, and so good resource allocation is critical.

Developments in two distinct areas within the last five years offer us the potential to develop altogether new ways of supporting decision processes. First, there has been considerable technological progress. The evolution of remote access to computers with short turnaround time and flexible user interfaces has been rapid. Powerful mini-computers are available at low cost and users can be linked to computer resources through inexpensive typewriter and graphical display devices. The second development has been a conceptual one. There is emerging an understanding of the potential role of information systems within organizations. We are adding to our knowledge of how human beings solve problems and of how to build models that capture aspects of the human decision-making processes.[2]

The progress in these areas has been dramatic. Entirely new kinds of planning and control systems can now be built—ones that dynamically involve the manager's judgments and support him with analysis, models, and flexible access to relevant information. But to realize this potential fully, given an organization's limited resources, there must be an appropriate framework within which to view management decision making and the required systems support. The purpose of this paper is to present a framework that helps us to understand the evolution of MIS activities within organizations and to recognize some of the potential problems and benefits resulting from our new technology. Thus, this framework is designed to be useful in planning for information systems activities within an organization and for distinguishing between the various model building activities, models, computer systems, and so forth which are used for supporting different kinds of decisions. It is, by definition, a static picture, and is not designed to say anything about how information systems are built.

* Reprinted by permission of the publisher from the *Sloan Management Review*, vol. 13, no. 1, pp. 55–70 (Fall, 1971). Mr. Gorry and Mr. Morton are professors at the Massachusetts Institute of Technology.

[1] See Taylor and Dean [9].

[2] See Scott Morton [6] and Soelberg [8].

In the next section we shall consider some of the general advantages of developing a framework for information systems work. We shall then propose a specific framework which we have found to be useful in the analysis of MIS activities. We believe that this framework offers us a new way to characterize the progress made to date and offers us insight into the problems that have been encountered. Finally, we shall use this framework to analyze the types of resources that are required in the different decision areas and the ways in which these resources should be used.

FRAMEWORK DEVELOPMENT

The framework we develop here is one for managerial activities, not for information systems. It is a way of looking at decisions made in an organization. Information systems should exist only to support decisions, and hence we are looking for a characterization of organizational activity in terms of the type of decisions involved. For reasons which we make clear later, we believe that an understanding of managerial activity is a prerequisite for effective systems design and implementation. Most MIS groups become involved in system development and implementation without a prior analysis of the variety of managerial activities. This has, in our opinion, prevented them from developing a sufficiently broad definition of their purpose and has resulted in a generally inefficient allocation of resources.

In attempting to understand the evolution and problems of management information systems, we have found the work of Robert Anthony and Herbert Simon particularly useful. In *Planning and Control Systems: A Framework for Analysis,*[3] Anthony addresses the problem of developing a classification scheme that will allow management some perspective when dealing with planning and control systems. He develops a taxonomy for managerial activity consisting of three categories and argues that these categories represent activities sufficiently different in kind to require the development of different systems.

The first of Anthony's categories of managerial activity is *strategic planning: "Strategic planning* is the process of deciding on objectives of the organization, on changes in these objectives, on the resources used to attain these objectives, and on the policies that are to govern the acquisition, use, and disposition of these resources."[4] Certain things can be said about strategic planning generally. First, it focuses on the choice of objectives for the organization and on the activities and means required to achieve these objectives. As a result, a major problem in this area is predicting the future of the organization and its environment. Second, the strategic planning process typically involves a small number of high-level people who operate in a nonrepetitive and often very creative way. The complexity of the problems that arise and the nonroutine manner in which they are handled make it quite difficult to appraise the quality of this planning process.

The second category defined by Anthony is *management control:* ". . . the process by which managers assure that resources are obtained and used effectively and efficiently in the accomplishment of the organization's objectives."[5] He stresses three key aspects of this area. First, the activity involves interpersonal interaction. Second, it takes place within the context of the policies and objectives developed in the strategic planning process. Third, the paramount goal of management control is the assurance of effective and efficient performance.

Anthony's third category is *operational control,* by which he means "the process of assuring that specific tasks are carried out effectively and efficiently."[6] The basic distinction between management control and operational control is that operational control is concerned with tasks (such as manufacturing a specific part) whereas management control is most often concerned with people. There is much less judgment to be exercised in the operational control area because the tasks, goals, and resources have been carefully delineated through the management control activity.

We recognize, as does Anthony, that the boundaries between these three categories are often not clear. In spite of their limitations and uncertainties, however, we have found the categories useful in the analysis of information system activities. For example, if we consider the information requirements of these three activities, we can see that they are very different from one another. Further, this difference is not simply a matter of aggregation, but one of fundamental character of the information needed by managers in these areas.

Strategic planning is concerned with setting broad policies and goals for the organization. As a result, the relationship of the organization to its environment is a central matter of concern. Also, the nature of the activity is such that predictions about the future are particularly

[3] Anthony [2].
[4] Anthony [2], p. 24.
[5] Anthony [2], p. 27.
[6] Anthony [2], p. 69.

TABLE 1 Information Requirements by Decision Category

CHARACTERISTICS OF INFORMATION	OPERATIONAL CONTROL	MANAGEMENT CONTROL	STRATEGIC PLANNING
Source	Largely internal	⟶	External
Scope	Well defined, narrow	⟶	Very wide
Level of Aggregation	Detailed	⟶	Aggregate
Time Horizon	Historical	⟶	Future
Currency	Highly current	⟶	Quite old
Required Accuracy	High	⟶	Low
Frequency of Use	Very frequent	⟶	Infrequent

important. In general, then, we can say that the information needed by strategic planners is aggregate information, and obtained mainly from sources external to the organization itself. Both the scope and variety of the information are quite large, but the requirements for accuracy are not particularly stringent. Finally, the nonroutine nature of the strategic planning process means that the demands for this information occur infrequently.

The information needs for the operational control area stand in sharp contrast to those of strategic planning. The task orientation of operational control requires information of a well-defined and narrow scope. This information is quite detailed and arises largely from sources within the organization. Very frequent use is made of this information, and it must therefore be accurate.

The information requirements for management control fall between the extremes for operational control and strategic planning. In addition, it is important to recognize that much of the information relevant to management control is obtained through the process of interpersonal interaction.

In Table 1 we have summarized these general observations about the categories of management activity. This summary is subject to the same limitations and uncertainties which are exhibited by the concepts of management control, strategic planning, and operational control. Nonetheless, it does underscore our contention that because the activities themselves are different, the information requirements to support them are also different.

This summary of information requirements suggests the reason why many organizations have found it increasingly difficult to realize some of their long-range plans for information systems. Many of these plans are based on the "total systems approach." Some of the proponents of this approach advocate that systems throughout the organization be tightly linked, with the output of one becoming the direct input of another, and that the whole structure be built on the detailed data used for controlling operations.[7] In doing so, they are suggesting an approach to systems design that is at best uneconomic and at worst based on a serious misconception. The first major problem with this view is that it does not recognize the ongoing nature of systems development in the operational control area. There is little reason to believe that the systems work in any major organization will be complete within the foreseeable future. To say that management information systems activity must wait "until we get out operational control systems in hand" is to say that efforts to assist management with systems support will be deferred indefinitely.

The second and perhaps most serious problem with this total systems view is that it fails to represent properly the information needs of the management control and strategic planning activities. Neither of these areas *necessarily* needs information that is a mere aggregation of data from the operational control data base. In many cases, if such a link is needed, it is more cost effective to use sampling from this data base and other statistical techniques to develop the required information. In our opinion, it rarely makes sense to couple managers in the management control and strategic planning areas directly with the masses of detailed data required for operational control. Not only is direct coupling unnecessary, but it also can be an expensive and difficult technical problem.

For these reasons it is easy to understand why so many companies have had the following

[7] See, for example, Becker [3].

experience. Original plans for operational control systems were met with more or less difficulty, but as time passed it became increasingly apparent that the planned systems for higher management were not being developed on schedule, if at all. To make matters worse, the systems which were developed for senior management had relatively little impact on the way in which the managers made decisions. This last problem is a direct result of the failure to understand the basic information needs of the different activities.

We have tried to show in the above discussion how Anthony's classification of *managerial* activities is a useful one for people working in information systems design and implementation; we shall return later to consider in more detail some of the implications of his ideas.

In *The New Science of Management Decision,* Simon is concerned with the manner in which human beings solve problems regardless of their position within an organization. His distinction between "programmed" and "nonprogrammed" decisions is a useful one:

> Decisions are programmed to the extent that they are repetitive and routine, to the extent that a definite procedure has been worked out for handling them so that they don't have to be treated *de novo* each time they occur. . . . Decisions are nonprogrammed to the extent that they are novel, unstructured, and consequential. There is no cut-and-dried method of handling the problem because it hasn't arisen before, or because its precise nature and structure are elusive or complex, or because it is so important that it deserves a custom-tailored treatment. . . . By nonprogrammed I mean a response where the system has no specific procedure to deal with situations like the one at hand, but must fall back on whatever *general* capacity it has for intelligent, adaptive, problem-oriented action.[8]

We shall use the terms "structured" and "unstructured" for programmed and nonprogrammed because they imply less dependence on the computer and more dependence on the basic character of the problem-solving activity in question. The procedures, the kinds of computation, and the types of information vary depending on the extent to which the problem in question is unstructured. The basis for these differences is that in the unstructured case the human decision maker must provide judgment and evaluation as well as insights into problem definition. In a very structured situation, much if not all of the decision-making process can be automated. Later in this paper we shall argue that systems built to support structured decision making will be significantly different from those designed to assist managers in dealing with unstructured problems. Further, we shall show that these differences can be traced to the character of the models which are relevant to each of these problems and the way in which these models are developed.

This focus on decisions requires an understanding of the human decision-making process. Research on human problem solving supports Simon's claim that all problem solving can be broken down into three categories:

> The first phase of the decision-making process—searching the environment for conditions calling for decision—I shall call *intelligence* activity (borrowing the military meaning of intelligence). The second phase—inventing, developing, and analyzing possible courses of action—I shall call *design* activity. The third phase—selecting a course of action from those available—I shall call *choice* activity. . . . Generally speaking, intelligence activity precedes design, and design activity precedes choice. The cycle of phases is, however, far more complex than the sequence suggests. Each phase in making a particular decision is itself a complex decision-making process. The design phase, for example, may call for new intelligence activities; problems at any given level generate subproblems that in turn have their intelligence, design and choice phases, and so on. There are wheels within wheels. . . . Nevertheless, the three large phases are often clearly discernible as the organizational decision process unfolds. They are closely related to the stages in problem solving first described by John Dewey: 'What is the problem? What are the alternatives? Which alternative is best?'[9]

A fully structured problem is one in which all three phases—intelligence, design, and choice—are structured. That is, we can specify algorithms, or decision rules, that will allow us to find the problem, design alternative solutions, and select the best solution. An example here might be the use of the classical economic order quantity (EOQ) formula on a straightforward inventory control problem. An unstructured problem is one in which none of the three phases is structured. Many job-shop scheduling problems are of this type.

In the ideas of Simon and Anthony, then, we have two different ways of looking at managerial activity within organizations. Anthony's

[8] Simon [7], pp. 5–6.

[9] Simon [7], pp. 2–3.

FIGURE 1 Information Systems: A Framework

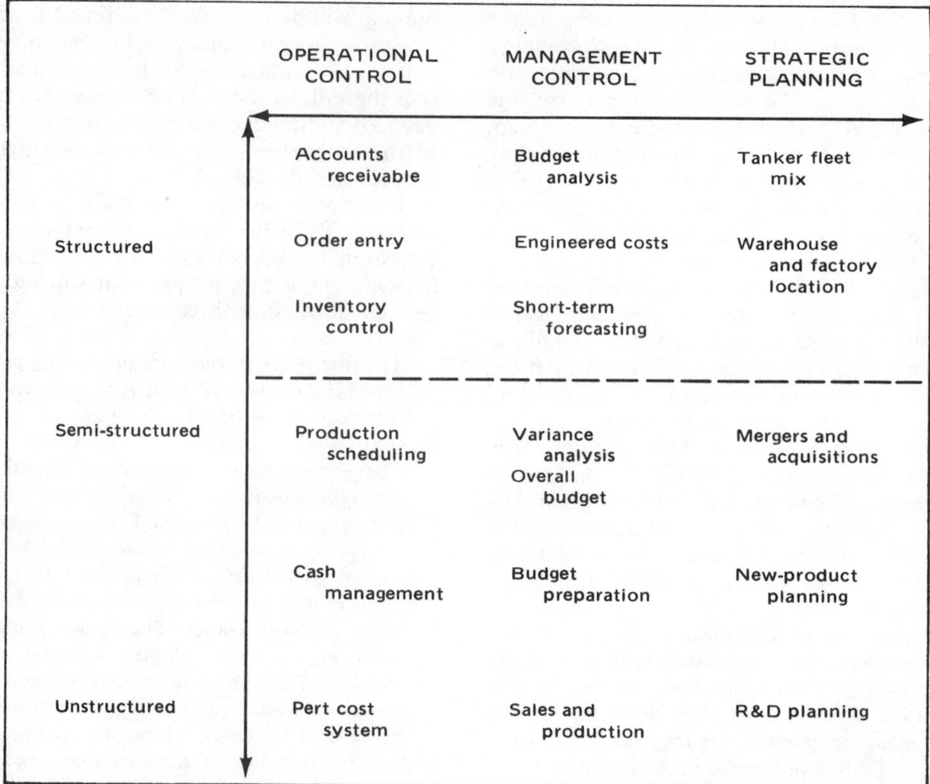

categorization is based on the purpose of the management activity, whereas Simon's classification is based on the way in which the manager deals with the problems which confront him. The combination of these two views provides a useful framework within which to examine the purposes and problems of information systems activity. The essence of this combination is shown in Figure 1. The figure contains a class of decisions we have called "semi-structured"—decisions with one or two of the intelligence, design, and choice phases unstructured.

Decisions above the dividing line in Figure 1 are largely structured, and we shall call the information systems that support them "Structured Decision Systems" (SDS). Decisions below the line are largely unstructured, and their supporting information systems are "Decision Support Systems" (DDS). The SDS area encompasses almost all of what *has* been called Management Information Systems (MIS) in the literature—an area that has had almost nothing to do with real managers or information but has been largely routine data processing. We exclude from consideration here all of the *information handling* activities in an organization. A large percentage of computer time in many organizations is spent on straightforward data handling with no decisions, however structured, involved. The payroll application, for example, is a data handling operation.

In Figure 1, we have listed some examples in each of the six cells. It should be stressed, however, that these cells are not well-defined categories. Although this may sometimes cause problems, the majority of important decisions can be classified into their appropriate cell without difficulty.

DECISION MAKING WITHIN THE FRAMEWORK

Planning and Resource Allocation Decisions An immediate observation can be made about the framework we have presented. Almost all the so-called MIS activity has been directed at decisions in the structured half of the matrix (see Figure 1), specifically in the "operation control" cell. On the other hand, most of the areas of greatest concern to managers, areas where decisions have a significant effect on the company, are in the lower half of the matrix. That is, managers deal for the most part with unstructured decisions. This implies, of course, that computers and related systems which have so far been largely applied to the structured operational control area have not yet had any real impact on management decision making. The areas of high potential do not lie in bigger and better systems of the kind most companies now use. To have all the effort concentrated in only one of the six cells suggests at the very least a severe imbalance.

A second point to be noted on the planning question is the evolutionary nature of the line separating structured from unstructured decisions. This line is moving down over time. As we improve our understanding of a particular decision, we can move it above the line and allow the system to take care of it, freeing the manager for other tasks. For example, in previous years the inventory reordering decision in most organizations was made by a well-paid member of middle management. It was a decision that involved a high degree of skill and could have a significant effect on the profits of the organization. Today this decision has moved from the unstructured operational control area to the structured. We have a set of decision rules (the EOQ formula) which on average do a better job for the standard items than most human decision makers. This movement of the line does not imply any replacement of managers since we are dealing with an almost infinite set of problems. For every one we solve, there are 10 more demanding our attention.

It is worth noting that the approach taken in building systems in the unstructured area hastens this movement of the line because it focuses our analytical attention on decisions and decision rules. We would therefore expect a continuing flow of decisions across the line, or at least into the "grey" semi-structured decision area.

Through the development of a model of a given problem solving process for a decision in one of the cells, we can establish the character of each of the three phases. To the extent that any of these phases can be structured, we can design direct systems support. For those aspects of the process which are unstructured (given our current understanding of the situation), we would call on the manager to provide the necessary analysis. Thus a problem might be broken down into a set of related subproblems, some of which are "solved" automatically by the system and the remainder by the user alone or with varying degrees of computational and display support. Regardless of the resulting division of labor, however, it is essential that a model of the decision process be constructed *prior* to the system design. It is only in this way that a good perspective on the potential application of systems support can be ascertained.

Structured/Unstructured Decisions

Information systems ought to be centered around the important decisions of the organization, many of which are relatively unstructured. It is therefore essential that models be built of the decision process involved. Model development is fundamental because it is a prerequisite for the analysis of the value of information, and because it is the key to understanding which portions of the decision process can be supported or automated. Both the successes and failures in the current use of computers can be understood largely in terms of the difficulty of this model development.

Our discussion of Structured Decision Systems showed that the vast majority of the effort (and success) has been in the area of structured operational control where there is relatively little ambiguity as to the goals sought. For example, the typical inventory control problem can be precisely stated, and it is clear what the criterion is by which solutions are to be judged. Hence we have an easily understood optimization problem. This type of problem lends itself to the development of formal "scientific" models, such as those typical of operations research.

Another important characteristic of problems of this type is that they are to a large extent "organization independent." By this we mean that the essential aspects of the problem tend to be the same in many organizations, although the details may differ. This generality has two important effects. First, it encourages widespread interest and effort in the development of solutions to the problem. Second, it makes the adaptation of general models to the situation in a particular organizational setting relatively easy.

The situation with regard to areas of management decision making is quite different. To the extent that a given problem is semi-structured or unstructured, there is an absence of a routine procedure for dealing with it. There is also a tendency toward ambiguity in the problem definition because of the lack of formalization of any or all of the intelligence, design, or choice phases. Confusion may exist as to the appropriate criterion for evaluating solutions, or as to the means for generating trial solutions to the problem. In many cases, this uncertainty contributes to the perception of problems of this type as being unique to a given organization.

In general, then, we can say that the information systems problem in the structured operational control area is basically that of implementing a given general model in a certain organizational context. On the other hand, work in the unstructured areas is much more involved with model development and formalization. Furthermore, the source of the models in the former case is apt to be the operations research or management science literature. In the latter case, the relevant models are most often the unverbalized models used by the managers of the organization. This suggests that the procedure for the development of systems, the types of systems, and the skills of the analysts involved may be quite different in the two areas.

Although the evolution of information systems activities in most organizations has led to the accumulation of a variety of technical skills, the impact of computers on the way in which top managers make decisions has been minimal. One major reason for this is that the support of these decision makers is not principally a technical problem. If it were, it would have been solved. Certainly there are technical problems associated with work in these problem areas, but the technology and the technological skills in most large organizations are more than sufficient. The missing ingredient, apart from the basic awareness of the problem, is the skill to elicit from management its view of the organization and its environment, and to formalize models of this view.

To improve the quality of decisions, a systems designer can seek to improve the quality of the information inputs or to change the decision process, or both. Because of the existence of a variety of optimization models for operational control problems, there is a tendency to emphasize improvement of the information inputs at the expense of improvement in the decision making process. Although this emphasis is appropriate for structured operational control problems, it can retard progress in developing support for unstructured problem solving. The difficulty with this view is that it tends to attribute low quality in management decision making to low quality information inputs. Hence, systems are designed to supply more current, more accurate, or more detailed information.

While improving the quality of information available to managers may improve the quality of their decisions, we do not believe that major advances will be realized in this way.[10] Most managers do not have great informational needs. Rather, they have need of new methods to understand and process the information already available to them. Generally speaking, the models that they employ in dealing with this information are very primitive, and as a result, the range of responses that they can generate is very limited. For example, many managers employ simple historical models in their attempts to anticipate the future.[11] Further, these models are static in nature, although the processes they purport to represent are highly dynamic. In such a situation, there is much more to be gained by improving the information processing ability of managers in order that they may deal effectively with the information that they already have, than by adding to the reams of data confronting them, or by improving the quality of those data.[12]

If this view is correct, it suggests that the Decision Support Systems area is important and that these systems may best be built by people other than those currently involved in the operational control systems area. The requisite skills are those of the model building based on close interaction with management, structuring and formalizing the procedures employed by managers, and segregating those aspects of the decision process which can be automated. In addition, systems in this area must be able to assist the evolution of the manager's decision making ability through increasing his understanding of the environment. Hence, one important role of a DSS is educative. Even in areas in which we cannot structure the decision process, we can provide models of the environment from which the manager can develop insights into the relationship of his decisions to the goals he wishes to achieve.

In discussing models and their importance to systems in the DSS area, we should place special emphasis on the role which the manager assumes in the process of model building. To a large extent, he is the source upon which the analyst draws. That is, although a repertoire of "operations research" models may be very valuable for the analyst, his task is not simply to impose a model on the situation. These models may be the building blocks. The analyst and the manager in concert develop the final structure. This implies that the analyst must possess a certain empathy for the manager, and *vice versa.* Whether the current systems designers in a given organization possess this quality is a question worthy of consideration by management.

This approach in no way precludes normative statements about decision procedures. The

[10] See Ackoff [1].

[11] See Pounds [5].

[12] See Gorry [4].

emphasis on the development of descriptive models of managerial problem solving is only to ensure that the existing situation is well understood by both the analyst and the manager. Once this understanding has been attained, various approaches to improving the process can be explored. In fact, a major benefit of developing descriptive models of this type is the exposure of the decision-making process to objective analysis.

In summary then, we have asserted that there are two sets of implications which flow from our use of this framework. The first set centers on an organization's planning and resource allocation decision in relation to information systems. The second set flows from the distinction we have drawn between structured and unstructured types of decisions. The focus of our attention should be on the critical *decisions* in an organization and on explicit modeling of these decisions prior to the design of information systems support.

The second major point in relation to the structured/unstructured dimension that we have raised is that the kinds of implementation problems, the skills required by the managers and analysts, and the characteristics of the design process are different above and below the dashed line in Figure 1. In discussing these differences, we have tried to stress the fundamental shift in approach that is required if Decision Support Systems are to be built in a way that makes them effective in an organization. The approach and technology that have been used over the last 15 years to build information systems in the structured operational control area are often inappropriate in the case of Decision Support Systems.

IMPLICATIONS OF THE FRAMEWORK

System Design Differences The decision categories we have borrowed from Anthony have a set of implications distinct from those discussed in connection with the structured and unstructured areas. The first of these has to do with the systems design differences that follow from supporting decisions in the three areas.

As was seen earlier, information requirements differ sharply among the three areas. There are few occasions in which it makes sense to connect systems directly across boundaries. Aggregating the detailed accounting records (used for operational control) to provide a base for a five-year sales forecast (required for a strategic planning decision) is an expensive and unnecessary process. We can often sample, estimate, or otherwise obtain data for use in strategic planning without resorting to the operational control data base. This does not imply that we should *never* use such a data base, but merely that it is not necessarily the best way of obtaining the information.

This point is also relevant in the collection and maintenance of data. Techniques appropriate for operational control, such as the use of on-line data collection terminals, are rarely justified for strategic planning systems. Similarly, elaborate environmental sampling methods may be critical for an operational control decision. In looking at each of the information characteristics in Table 1, it is apparent that quite different data bases will be required to support decisions in the three areas. Therefore, the first implication of the decision classification in our framework is that the "totally-integrated-management-information-systems" ideas so popular in the literature are a poor design concept. More particularly, the "integrated" or "company-wide" data base is a misleading notion, and even if it could be achieved would be exorbitantly expensive.

Information differences among the three decision areas also imply related differences in hardware and software requirements. On the one hand, strategic planning decisions require access to a data base which is used infrequently and may involve an interface with a variety of complex models. Operational control decisions, on the other hand, often require a larger data base with continuous updating and frequent access to current information.

Differences in Organizational Structure

A second distinction is in the organizational structure and the managerial and analyst skills which will be involved across the three areas. The managerial talents required, as well as the numbers and training of the managers involved, differ sharply for these categories. The process of deciding on key problems that might be worth supporting with a formal system is a much smaller, tighter process in the strategic planning area than in the operational control area. The decision to be supported is probably not a recurring one and will normally not involve changes in the procedures and structure employed by the remainder of the firm. Because it is a relatively isolated decision in both time and scope, it need not involve as many people. However, the process of defining the problem must be dominated by the managers involved if the right problem and hence the best model formulation are to be selected. Similarly, the implementation process must be tightly focused on the immediate problem. The skills required of the managers involved are analytical and reflective, rather than communicative and procedural. In the strategic planning case, the manager must supply both the problem definition and the key relationships that make up the model. This requires an ability to think logically and a familarity with models and computation. In the case of operational control, the particular solution and the models involved are much more the concern of the technical specialist. This is not to say that in unstructured operational control the manager's judgment will not be involved in the process of solving problems. However, his role in *building* that model can be much more passive than in the strategic area.

The decision process, the implementation process, and the level of analytical sophistication of the managers (as opposed to the staff) in strategic planning all differ quite markedly from their counterparts in operational control. The decision makers in operational control have a more constrained problem. They have often had several years in which to define the general nature of the problem and to consider solutions. In addition, to the extent that these managers have a technical background, they are more likely to be familiar with the analysis involved in solving structured and unstructured problems. In any event, the nature of the operational control problem, its size, and the frequency of the decision all combine to produce design and implementation problems of a different variety. The managers involved in any given problem tend to be from the decision area in question, be it strategic planning, management control, or operational control. As a result, their training, background, and style of decision making are often different. This means that the types of models to be used, the method of elucidating these from the managers, and the skills of the analysts will differ across these three areas.

As the types of skills possessed by the managers differ, so will the kinds of systems analysts who can operate effectively. We have already distinguished between analysts who can handle structured as opposed to unstructured model building. There is a similar distinction to be made between the kind of person who can work well with a small group of senior managers (on either a structured or unstructured problem) and the person who is able to communicate with the various production personnel on an unstructured job-shop scheduling problem, for example.

In problems in the strategic area, the analyst has to be able to communicate effectively with the few managers who have the basic knowledge required to define the problem and its major variables. The skills required to do this include background and experience which are wide enough to match those of the line executives involved. Good communication depends on a common understanding of the basic variables involved, and few analysts involved in current MIS activity have this skill.

A breadth of background implies a wide repertoire of models with which the analyst is familiar. In the operational control area, an analyst can usefully specialize to great depth in a particular, narrow problem area. The depth, and the resulting improvement in the final system, often pays off because of the frequency with which the decision is made. In the strategic area the coverage of potential problems is enormous and the frequency of a particular decision relatively low. The range of models with which the analyst is familiar may be of greater benefit than depth in any one type.

In addition to the managerial and analyst issues raised above, there is a further difference in the way the information systems group is organized. A group dealing only with operational control problems would be structured differently and perhaps report to a different organizational position than a group working in all three areas. It is not our purpose here to go into detail on the organizational issues, but the material above suggests that on strategic problems, a task force reporting to the user and virtually independent on the computer group may make sense. The important issues are problem definition and problem structure; the implementation and computer issues are relatively simple by comparison. In management control, the single user, although still dominant in his application, has problems of interfacing with other users. An organizational design that encourages cross functional (marketing, production, distribution, etc.) cooperation is probably desirable. In operational control, the organizational design should include the user as a major influence, but he will have to be balanced with operational systems experts, and the whole group can quite possibly stay within functional boundaries. These examples are merely illustrative of the kind of organizational differences involved. Each organization has to examine its current status and needs and make structural changes in light of them.

Model Differences The third distinction flowing from the framework is among the types of models involved. Again looking at Table 1 and the information differences, it is clear that model requirements depend, for example, on the frequency of decisions in each area and their relative magnitude. A strategic decision to change the whole distribution system occurs rarely. It is significant in cost, perhaps hundreds of millions of dollars, and it therefore can support a complex model, but the model need not be efficient in any sense. An operational control decision, however, may be made frequently, perhaps daily. The impact of each decision is small but the cumulative impact can involve large sums of money. Models for the decision may have to be efficient in running time, have ready access to current data, and be structured so as to be easily changed. Emphasis has to be on simplicity of building, careful attention to modularity, and so forth.

The sources of models for operational control are numerous. There is a history of activity, the problems are often similar across organizations, and the literature is extensive. In strategic planning, and to a lesser extent management control, we are still in the early stages of development. Our models tend to be individual and have to come from the managers involved. It is a model creation process as opposed to the application of a model.

In summary then, we have outlined implications for the organization which follow from the three major decision categories in the framework. We have posed the issues in terms of operational control and strategic planning, and with every point we assume that management control lies somewhere in between the two. The three major implications we have discussed are the advisability of following the integrated data base path; the differences in managerial and analyst skills as well as the appropriate forms of organizational structure for building systems in the three areas; and differences in the types of models involved. Distinguishing among decision areas is clearly important if an organization is going to be successful in its use of information systems.

SUMMARY

The information systems field absorbs a significant percentage of the resources of many organizations. Despite these expenditures, there is very little perspective on the field and the issues within it. As a result, there has been a tendency to make incremental improvements to existing systems. The framework we suggest for looking at decisions within an organization provides one perspective on the information systems issues. From this perspective, it becomes clear that our planning for information systems has resulted in a heavy concentration in the operational control area. In addition, there is a series of implications for the organization which flows from the distinction between the decision areas. Model structure and the implementation process differ sharply between the structured and unstructured areas. Data base concepts, types of analysts and managers, and organizational structure all differ along the Strategic Planning to Operational Control axis.

We believe that each organization must share *some* common framework among its members if it is to plan and make resource allocation decisions which result in effective use of information systems. We suggest that the framework that has been presented here is an appropriate place to start.

REFERENCES

1. Ackoff, R. "Management Misinformation Systems," *Management Science,* Vol. 11, no. 4 (December 1967), pp. B147–B156.
2. Anthony, R. N. *Planning and Control Systems: A Framework for Analysis.* Boston, Harvard University Graduate School of Business Administration, 1965.
3. Becker, J. L. "Planning the Total Information System." In A. D. Meacham and V. B. Thompson (eds.), *Total Systems,* pp. 66–73. New York, American Data Processing, 1962.
4. Gorry, G. A. "The Development of Managerial Models," *Sloan Management Review,* Vol. 12, no. 2 (Winter 1971), pp. 1–16.
5. Pounds, W. F. "The Process of Problem Finding," *Industrial Management Review,* Vol. 11, no. 1 (Fall 1969), pp. 1–20.
6. Scott Morton, M. S. *Management Decision Systems.* Boston, Harvard University Graduate School of Business Administration, 1971.
7. Simon, H. A. *The New Science of Management Decision.* New York, Harper & Row, 1960.
8. Soelberg, P. O. "Unprogrammed Decision Making," *Industrial Management Review,* Vol. 8, no. 2 (Spring 1967), pp. 19–30.
9. Taylor, J. W., and Dean, N. J. "Managing to Manage the Computer," *Harvard Business Review,* Vol. 44, no. 5 (September–October 1966), pp. 98–110.

70 THE MANAGEMENT INFORMATION SYSTEM*

Bertram A. Colbert

What has information to do with profitability? Every chief executive knows it has a great deal to do with it. Information plays a major, usually a crucial, role in achieving profits—the profits which are one of the main indexes of successful business operations in our economy.

Obviously, the manager must understand and evaluate a wide range of information about his operations in order to reach sound, profitable decisions. Concise, complete, and timely management information thus forms the basis for effective planning, decision making, and control.

As the complexity and magnitude of business decisions have increased, the typical corporate manager has found that existing systems do not have the capability to deliver the significant data required at the time they are required. Too often the manager has found himself overwhelmed with masses of data or long listings of historical information which were of little help in the decision making and planning processes.

The need for a better way was clearly evident. Therefore, many companies, both large and small, are seeking ways to improve their information and data flow and its end use—the generation of profit. The result has been the group of techniques called the management information system.

Let us consider some basic questions:

What is a management information system? How does it differ from such existing systems as accounting, sales, or production? Should you have one? What is its value? How do you obtain one or put one in a specific company?

This article attempts to answer these questions, to show graphically the management process and the part information plays in it, and finally to provide a frame of reference within which each executive, by further analysis, can obtain more complete specific answers, tailored to his company's needs.

* Reprinted by permission of the publisher from *Management Services*, vol. 4, no. 5, pp. 15–24, September–October. Copyright 1967 by the American Institute of CPAs. Mr. Colbert is a principal of Price Waterhouse & Company.

We may begin by noting the functions of management: to plan, to organize, to direct, and to control, as indicated in Chart 1 and by illustrating the role which information plays in this process (Chart 2). Information which is internal is necessary to provide communication in the management process. Information which is external is necessary to assure that management is aware of, first, the outside events which may influence the plan and, second, the effect of the operation on this outside world. As information is received, we may recycle through the management process: RE-plan, RE-organize, RE-direct, with the measurement in the control process.

To provide a framework for discussion, let us consider the organization of a typical company (Chart 3). The company has five principal functions: administration, marketing, research and development, manufacturing, and finance. The relationship to the board of directors and the specific departments which we might find in each function are depicted in Chart 3.

MANAGEMENT INFORMATION SYSTEM

A management information system, simply, is an organized method of providing each manager with all the data and only those data which he needs for decision, when he needs them, and in a form which aids his understanding and stimulates his action.

Such as system

1. Considers the full effect of a decision in advance by supplying complete, accurate, and timely data for use in the planning and decision making processes
2. Eliminates from the planning and decision making processes the problems associated with the use of inconsistent and incomplete data by providing a means for preparing and presenting information in a uniform manner
3. Uses common data and methods in the preparation of long-range and short-term plans

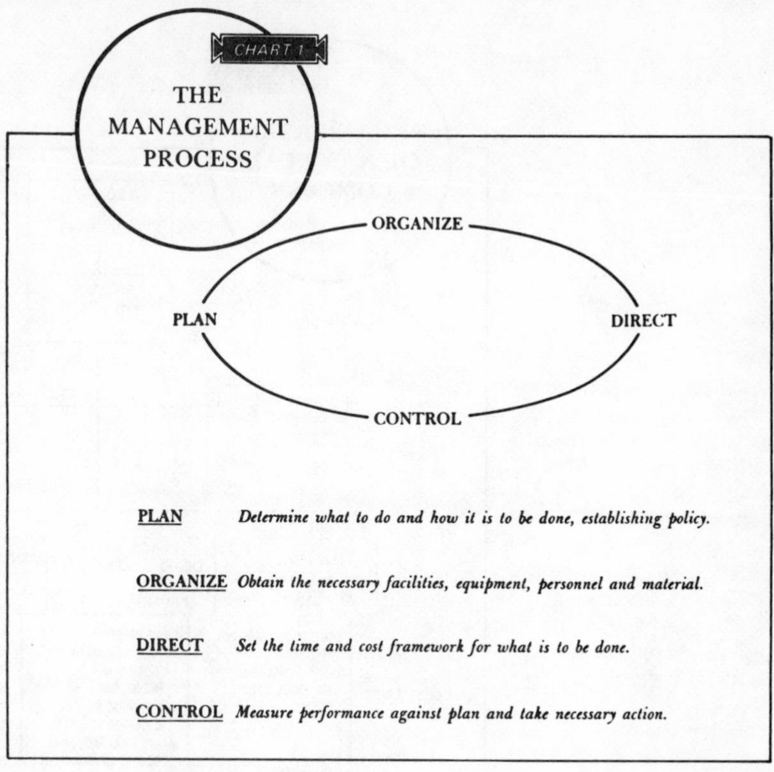
CHART 1
THE MANAGEMENT PROCESS
ORGANIZE
PLAN
DIRECT
CONTROL
PLAN Determine what to do and how it is to be done, establishing policy.
ORGANIZE Obtain the necessary facilities, equipment, personnel and material.
DIRECT Set the time and cost framework for what is to be done.
CONTROL Measure performance against plan and take necessary action.

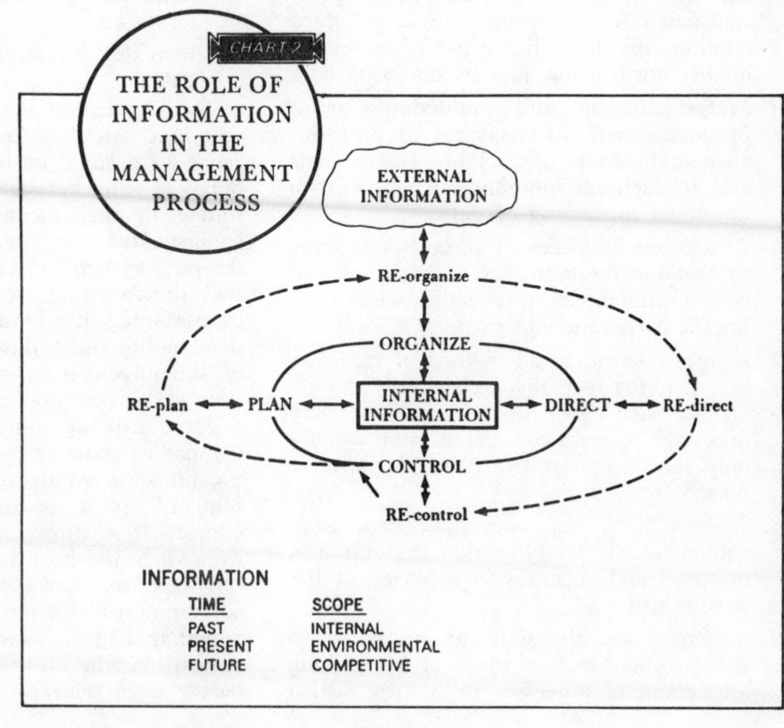
CHART 2
THE ROLE OF INFORMATION IN THE MANAGEMENT PROCESS
EXTERNAL INFORMATION
RE-organize
ORGANIZE
RE-plan
PLAN
INTERNAL INFORMATION
DIRECT
RE-direct
CONTROL
RE-control
INFORMATION
TIME
PAST
PRESENT
FUTURE
SCOPE
INTERNAL
ENVIRONMENTAL
COMPETITIVE

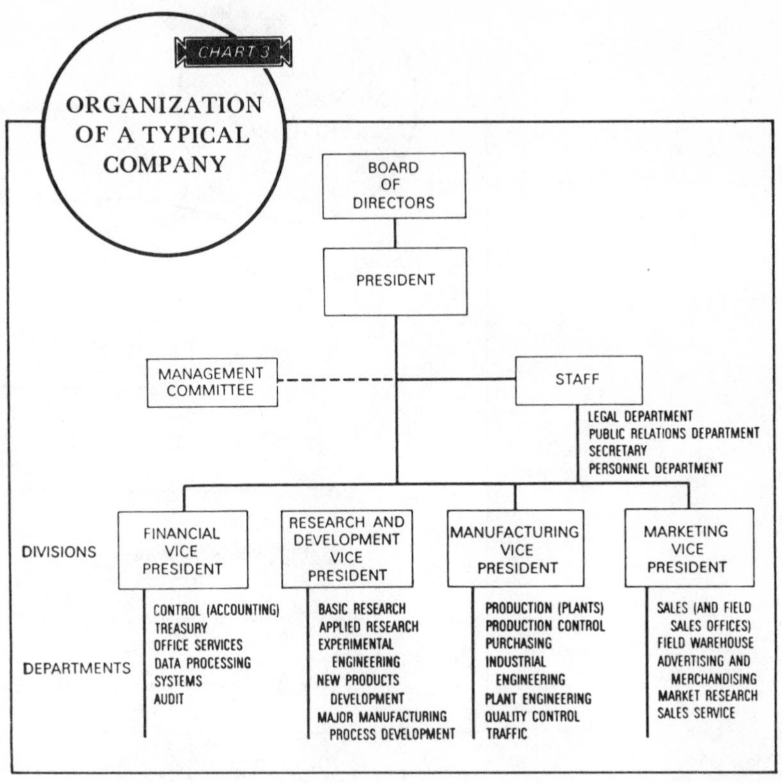

4. Identifies, structures, and quantifies significant past relationships and forecasts future relationships through the use of advanced mathematical techniques in analyzing data
5. Merges financial and production data to produce significant measures of performance to facilitate control of present costs and to facilitate planning decisions with minimum processing of data
6. Recognizes the needs of all corporate units so that the requirements of each are met with a minimum of duplication while serving the corporation as a whole
7. Reduces the time and volume of information required to make decisions by reporting to each level of management only necessary degrees of detail and usually only the exception from the standard or norm
8. Utilizes personnel and data processing equipment effectively so that the optimum in speed and accuracy is achieved at the lowest cost
9. Requires that the data be presented to those responsible for the decision making and planning processes in a form which minimizes the need for analysis and interpretation
10. Provides flexibility and adaptability to change.

The concept of management information is one that would be equally valid if the company were small or large or if the data were obtained and processed through the most simple manual means or through the most sophisticated computer. Management must, to design a system, select at each level of control only the data that are required. The data must be presented in a manner which facilitates understanding and action and provides a measure of the effectiveness of the action which has been and is being taken.

Most growing companies and many mature companies show certain symptoms or clear indications of what we can call "information hunger." Some of these symptoms may, of course, arise simply from poor management, even when the information system is adequate, but we have listed them here because they are so common and often so baffling even to competent managers. Many managers just do not realize that the information on which they are basing even their most routine decisions may be dangerously inadequate or misleading because their information system is not geared to the needs of their company. Let us turn to Chart 4 and consider the 25 symptoms any or any combination of which may indicate an inadequate information system.

In the operational aspect of the business, they range from large inventory adjustments to a sterile R&D program; in the human aspect, from inability to note the significance of certain financial indicators to overloaded briefcases and poring over reports at midnight.

Any executive will do well to study these symptoms and note whether his organization exhibits one or more of them. A study of the present scope of management information in the typical enterprise (as shown in Chart 5) and a comparison of the typical management informational efforts with the values to be received through each (shown in Chart 6) shows that in the typical organization management is either using its information facilities too narrowly or has not developed facilities of the necessary scope and significance to ensure the enterprise's future. As indicated, most managements devote 90 percent of their efforts to obtaining information which will enable them to operate and control and only about 5 per cent of their efforts to obtaining the necessary information to meet competition and another 5 per cent to obtaining the information needed to meet future needs. These proportions do not make the organization adaptable to change and may lead to such stagnation or such poor prep-

OPERATIONAL	PSYCHOLOGICAL	REPORT CONTENT
Large physical inventory adjustments	Surprise at financial results	Excessive use of tabulations of figures
Capital expenditure overruns	Poor attitude of executives about usefulness of information	Multiple preparation and distribution of identical data
Inability of executives to explain changes from year to year in operating results	Lack of understanding of financial information on part of nonfinancial executives	Disagreeing information from different sources
Uncertain direction of company growth	Lack of concern for environmental changes	Lack of periodic comparative information and trends
Cost variances unexplainable	Executive homework reviewing reports considered excessive	Lateness of information
No order backlog awareness		Too little or excess detail
No internal discussion of reported data		Inaccurate information
Insufficient knowledge about competition		Lack of standards for comparison
Purchasing parts from outside vendors when internal capability and capacity to make is available		Failure to identify variances by cause and responsibility
Record of some "sour" investments in facilities, or in programs, such as R & D and advertising		Inadequate externally generated information

SYMPTOMS OF AN INADEQUATE MANAGEMENT INFORMATION SYSTEM CHART 4

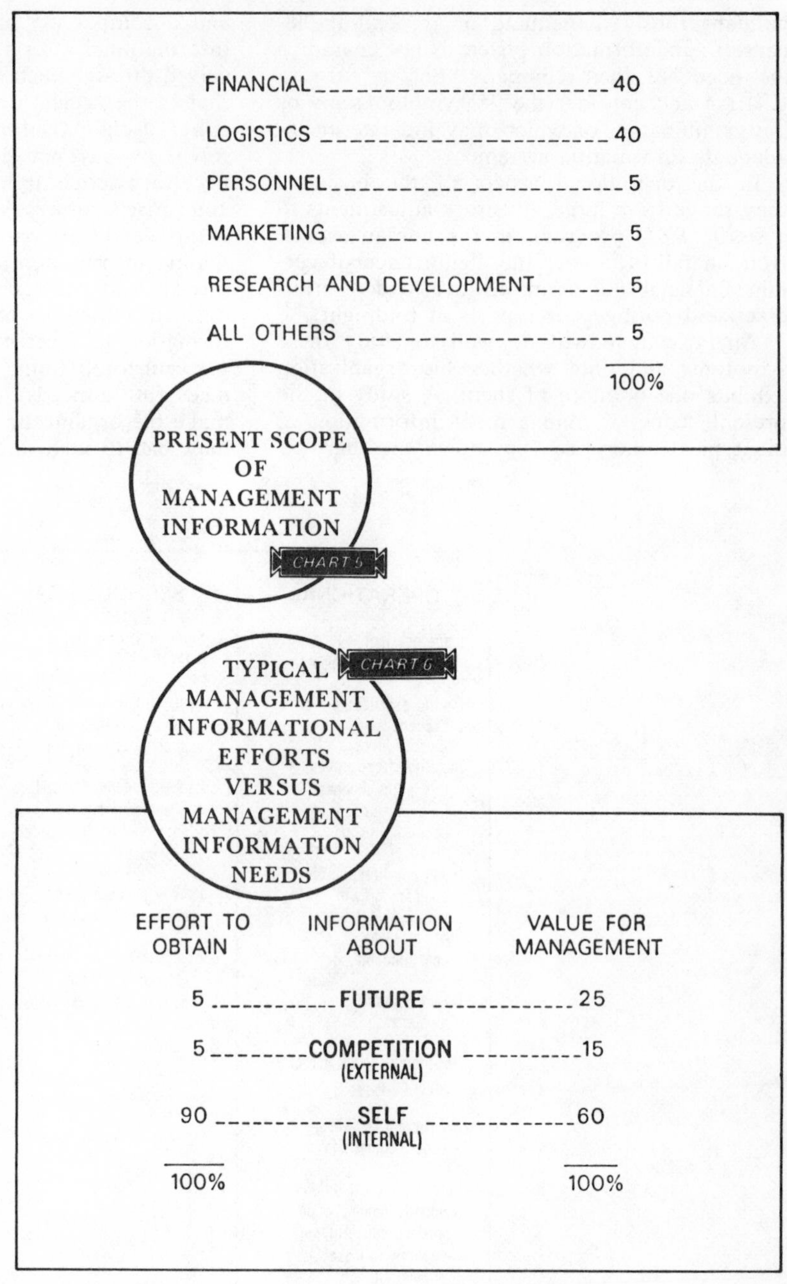

aration that a competitor's new product or a change in consumers' tastes and needs may knock the enterprise right out of the ball game.

FINANCIAL 40
LOGISTICS 40
PERSONNEL 5
MARKETING 5
RESEARCH AND DEVELOPMENT 5
ALL OTHERS 5
100%
PRESENT SCOPE OF MANAGEMENT INFORMATION
CHART 5
CHART 6
TYPICAL MANAGEMENT INFORMATIONAL EFFORTS VERSUS MANAGEMENT INFORMATION NEEDS
EFFORT TO OBTAIN
INFORMATION ABOUT
VALUE FOR MANAGEMENT
5 FUTURE 25
5 COMPETITION (EXTERNAL) 15
90 SELF (INTERNAL) 60
100%
100%

KINDS OF INFORMATION NEEDED

What, then, are the kinds of information which managers need? They can be grouped into three major categories: information which various company executives require for operation and control, information required to assess future action, and information required to assess or compare performance by the company in competition or within the industry.

Let us look first at information required for management operation and control. A great deal has been written on this subject, and most organizations of any size or sophistication have developed fairly good and reliable information-generating systems for operations (production, inventory, efficiency). Where they often fall down is in the selection, organization, and processing of this information. The best method of employing such information is that of rigid selection by need—that is, sending key information to executives, information processed purely for the management requirements as indicated and requested by the recipients. A system called *Key Item Control* (described in MANAGEMENT SERVICES, January-February, '67 p. 21) gives a detailed discussion of such a method.

Control, of course, is obtained by comparing actual performance for each given activity with preestablished goals set at each level. The principal value of presenting key items to management using exception techniques is that it focuses management attention on the important areas of operation which require action. A typical operating report of this type (Chart 7) shows how the tabular information normally presented in a company could be re-presented to enhance understanding and provide data for decision. This is done through a blending of narrative, graphic, and tabular techniques of presenting information. The overall highlights of the operations are given in a narrative summary. Graphs present comparisons of present performance with planned performance in the framework of trends to provide current perspective, and tables provide key figures of detail information.

Let us now suggest the kinds of information which should be generated in two key areas, financial and research and development (Chart 8 and Chart 9). Some 23 items are suggested in the financial area in Chart 8, and 15 in the R&D area in Chart 9. It can be seen that the data vary widely from an analysis of sources and availability of capital in the financial area to a research personnel analysis in the R&D segment. Nevertheless, top management must consider all the kinds of information its operations require and then turn to the task of processing this information to achieve maximum use from it.

The financial information available to management is usually quite complete. Often, however, the accounting data are not as integrated with operating control information as would be practical or desirable. Frequently the chart of accounts provides information for audit, internal control, or tax purposes but not specifically for management control. Often major improvement would result from integrating operating management information with cost management information. In this approach, the source documents used to provide information for operating statistical purposes would provide cost and financial management information as direct products.

TECHNIQUES OF IMPROVEMENT

Substantial improvement in most companies' management information would result from the following:

1. Increased use of ratios to provide improved understanding of the effects or results of operations, including graphic presentations of the ratios to provide analysis of both short-term and long-range trends. The data would also provide an improved basis for forecasting probable future events, particularly in the cost area.
2. Use of information developed from using work sampling, work measurement, and work simplification techniques. This would provide improved measures of the effectiveness of personnel in the clerical and production groups. In addition, these techniques would permit costs of specific operations to be determined and would enable management to determine the most efficient and least costly way to perform them. A further benefit of using such techniques would be the development of cost data which would be integrated with operating statistical data and thus improve management information.
3. Increased use of network techniques of presentation. Specifically, this would place in focus all of the events that would be involved in a particular management activity and would define their relationship to each other. This technique could be of great value in determining the chain of events which must take place in order to implement a management decision which was made on the basis of improved management information. It would also provide understanding of the time and personnel which would be involved in such an implementation.
4. Increased use of PERT techniques in the cost system. The PERT technique places cost information in relation to the event occurrence. This approach would incorporate the principles of flexible budgeting.
5. Increased use of incremental cost concepts. These would improve the decision making related to costs of operating facilities at various production levels. This cost concept would provide management with an improved tool for determining the cost effect of operating a given facility at different specific levels or volumes of production by measuring the cost effect in major steps or

increments rather than only by an average slope or trend.

6. Increased use of data processing equipment as the means of securing vital data in a timely and effective manner to implement the new concepts involved.
7. Increased attention to the development of a simulating incentive which would serve as a motivation to management to take action on the basis of the information provided by an improved management information and control system.

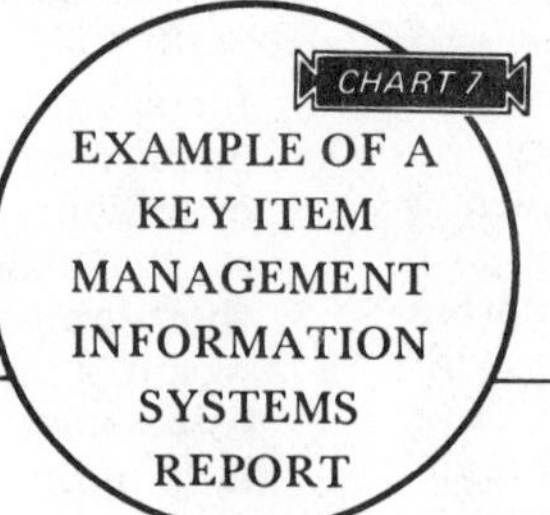

CHART 7
EXAMPLE OF A
KEY ITEM
MANAGEMENT
INFORMATION
SYSTEMS
REPORT

PERIODIC MANUFACTURING REPORT

PERFORMANCE HIGHLIGHTS

Shipments increased as expected this month. However, Herron Manufacturing Co., one of our principal motor suppliers, was on strike until four weeks ago. Accordingly, we were not able to build inventory as planned in preparation for the added shipments. As a result, we had to go to a partial third shift for the assembly department and add a number of new employees throughout the plants this month. The inexperience of the new employees and the lack of adequate supervision on the partial third shift led to decreased delivery performance and labor productivity, particularly in the machining department. These problems have been largely corrected and we expect improved performance next month.

KEY INFORMATION

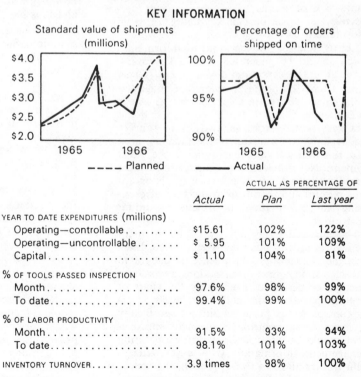

Standard value of shipments (millions)

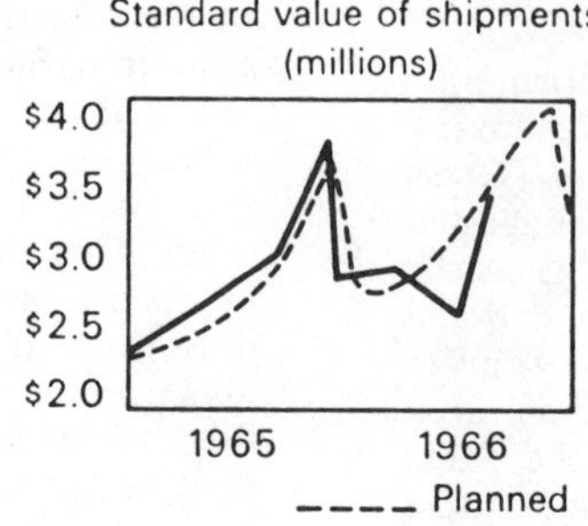

Percentage of orders shipped on time

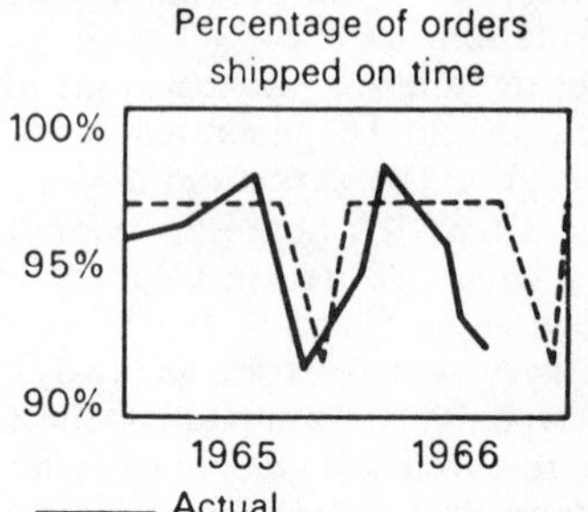

---- Planned ——— Actual

	Actual	ACTUAL AS PERCENTAGE OF Plan	Last year
YEAR TO DATE EXPENDITURES (millions)			
Operating—controllable.........	$15.61	102%	122%
Operating—uncontrollable.......	$ 5.95	101%	109%
Capital......................	$ 1.10	104%	81%
% OF TOOLS PASSED INSPECTION			
Month......................	97.6%	98%	99%
To date.....................	99.4%	99%	100%
% OF LABOR PRODUCTIVITY			
Month......................	91.5%	93%	94%
To date.....................	98.1%	101%	103%
INVENTORY TURNOVER...............	3.9 times	98%	100%

CHART 8

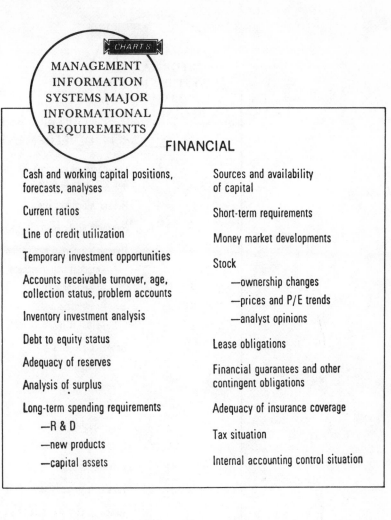

MANAGEMENT INFORMATION SYSTEMS MAJOR INFORMATIONAL REQUIREMENTS

FINANCIAL

Cash and working capital positions, forecasts, analyses	Sources and availability of capital
Current ratios	Short-term requirements
Line of credit utilization	Money market developments
Temporary investment opportunities	Stock —ownership changes —prices and P/E trends —analyst opinions
Accounts receivable turnover, age, collection status, problem accounts	Lease obligations
Inventory investment analysis	Financial guarantees and other contingent obligations
Debt to equity status	Adequacy of insurance coverage
Adequacy of reserves	Tax situation
Analysis of surplus	Internal accounting control situation
Long-term spending requirements —R & D —new products —capital assets	

RANGE OF INFORMATION

Each chief executive represents a different company of different size in a different location. To a large extent, his problems are individual. He does, however, operate within the framework of a certain industry and can make decisions based on analysis of the data in a specific industry.

To illustrate the range of information which might be significant to the management of a typical company, let us now turn to a study of information of the second category: information required to assess future action. For our purposes let us call our illustrative company Company X (although they do not make the well known "Brand X"). This company markets a product in the consumer industry and is affected by consumer patterns of spending. What kind of information would management review to plan and assess future action? Let us consider the following data:

POPULATION GROWTH EFFECT

First, management might look at the effect of growth in population (Chart 10). In 1910 the population of the United States was about 90 million people. The population now is close to 200 million; the population has doubled in less than the lifetime of most managers. As you can see from the projection for 1975, population is expected to increase another 30 percent to 40 percent in this shorter time. We are in an era of rapidly changing, rapidly increasing population.

This growing population has very interesting characteristics for our Company X. Perhaps the most significant is shown in Chart 11. This is a measure, since 1900, of per capita disposable

CHART 9

MANAGEMENT INFORMATION SYSTEMS MAJOR INFORMATIONAL REQUIREMENTS

RESEARCH AND DEVELOPMENT

Knowledge of research discoveries and advances in existing knowledge

Research opportunities

Research goals and balance of effort

Research proposal evaluation
- —product improvements
- —new products
- —new materials
- —process improvements

Research projects
- —status—technically
- —status—cost

Research personnel
- —qualifications
- —experience

Scientist support

Research space/person

Research cost as % of sales

Historical evidence of value of research to company

personal income. Income for the individual has gone from less than $1,000 per person in 1900 to almost $3,000 per person and is rising at an increasing rate; it is expected to approach $4,000 by 1980. Such predictions have often proved to be conservative. We have a rising population which is living better.

Now Company X management might consider the effect of this increase in per capita income and the additional increase in the working population as reflected in per household disposable income (Chart 12). As noted, this income has gone from $4,000 to $6,000 per household since 1939 and is expected to exceed $10,000 in ten years. Gross national product, which has nearly tripled since 1950, is likely to pass the $1,000-billion mark by 1975 (Chart 13). Next, management of Company X can note that, in the period since 1950, our total of consumer expenditures in the United States has gone from $200 billion to $400 billion (Chart 14). The population in this period has not doubled, but our per capita income has just about doubled.

What does this mean for Company X? It means people have much more money to spend individually and, therefore, in total. One of the most interesting things is that, with this in-

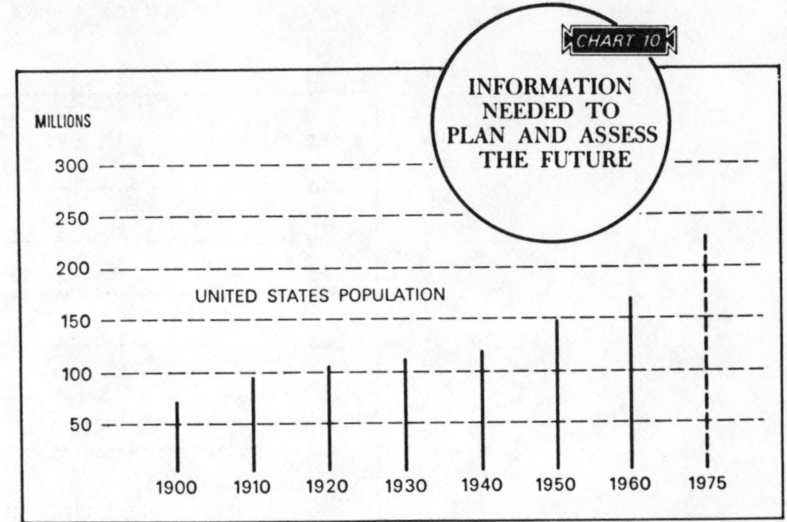
CHART 10
INFORMATION NEEDED TO PLAN AND ASSESS THE FUTURE
MILLIONS
300
250
200
150
100
50
UNITED STATES POPULATION
1900
1910
1920
1930
1940
1950
1960
1975

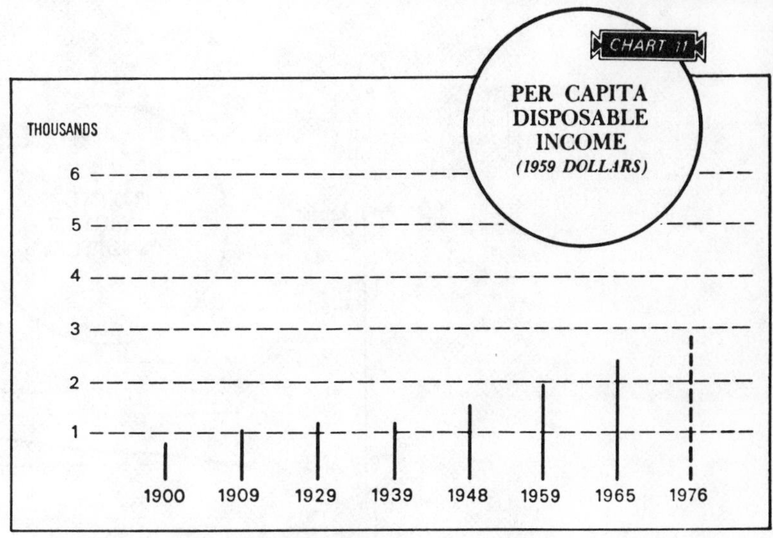
CHART 11
PER CAPITA DISPOSABLE INCOME
(1959 DOLLARS)
THOUSANDS
6
5
4
3
2
1
1900
1909
1929
1939
1948
1959
1965
1976

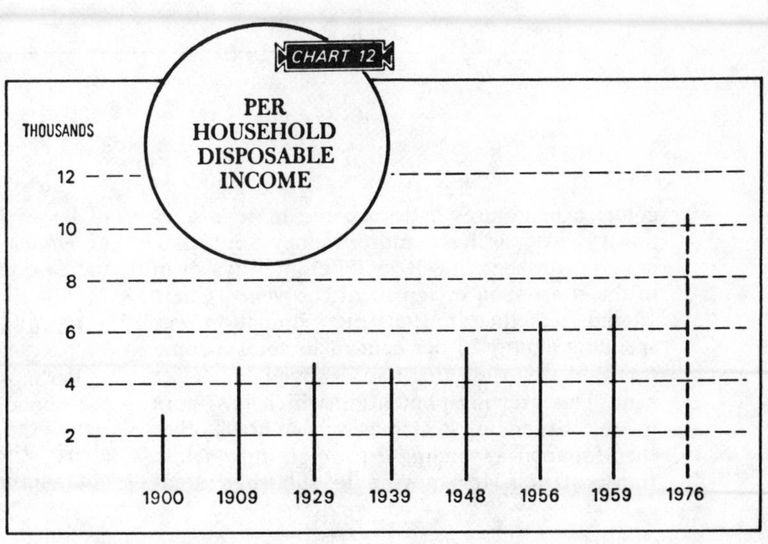
CHART 12
PER HOUSEHOLD DISPOSABLE INCOME
THOUSANDS
12
10
8
6
4
2
1900
1909
1929
1939
1948
1956
1959
1976

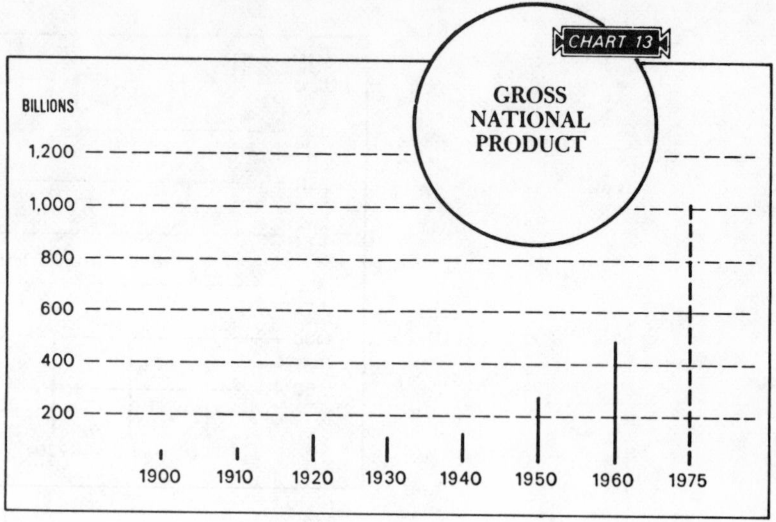

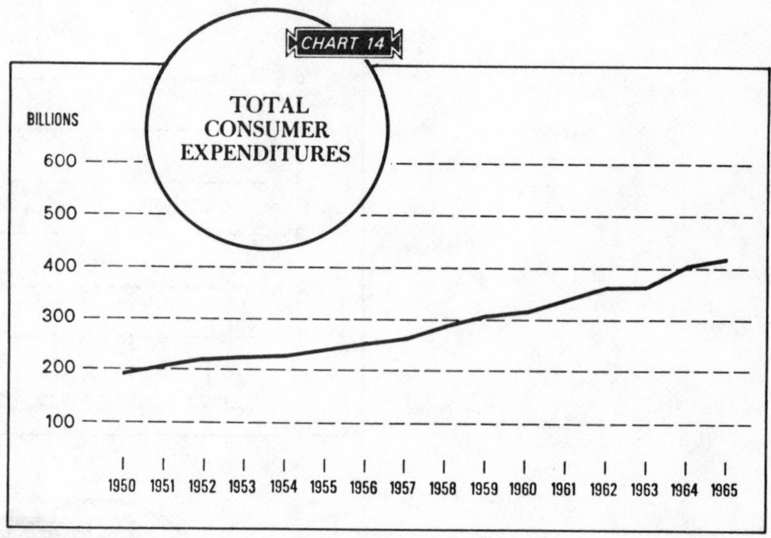

come, expenditures have become more discretionary. People have more money, but they have begun spending it in different ways even in the short span of ten to fifteen years. Chart 15 indicates that in 1950 our population was spending almost 23 per cent of its total income for food. By 1962 this had dropped to 19 per cent. This growing population which has more money is spending it increasingly in areas other than for food—spending it for clothing, shelter, transportation; for moving to suburban areas of larger homes where people have an average of almost two cars per family; spending it on increased recreation—on better living.

RECREATION EXPENDITURES

Perhaps the most significant characteristic of the economy for the industry in which Company X operates is shown in Chart 16, which charts the expenditures on recreation. This chart indicates that these expenditures have in-

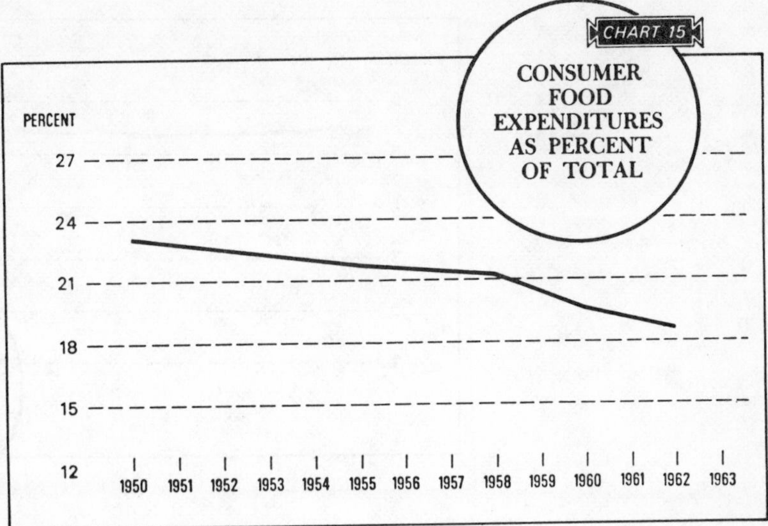

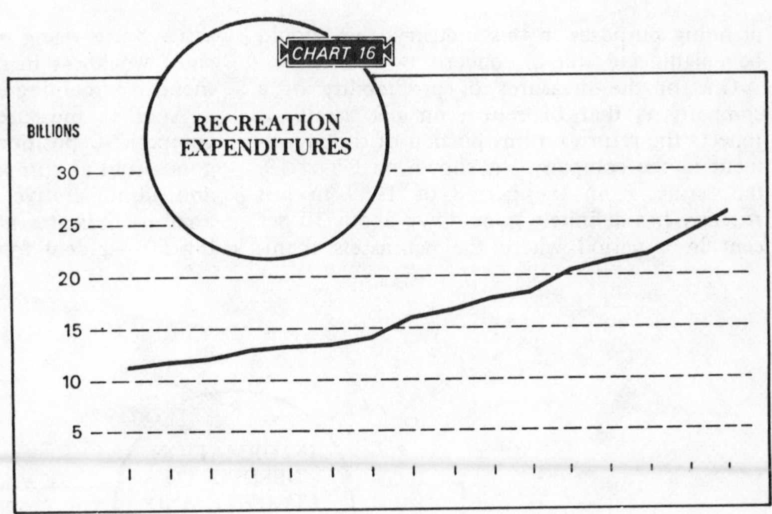

creased from about 12 billion to 27 billion dollars, more than doubling in the past 15 years.

As Chart 17 indicates, in this period the consumer expenditures on recreation as a per cent of total expenditures have risen from 5 per cent to over 6 per cent as a result of the shift in consumer interests.

We now come to that third category of information—the information needed to compete in an industry and to obtain a fair share of the market. Here we present some of the kinds of information in this category and show how the managers of our Company X might use it to place themselves in the industry.

We can start with some calculations for Product X made by our company showing the expenditures for Product X as a per cent of total recreational expenditures (Chart 18). This ratio indicates that, while there was a rise from the 1950 to 1959 period, there has been a downward trend in the past six years, with a reduction from 12 per cent to 9 per cent, or almost a 25 per cent change in the ratio. For

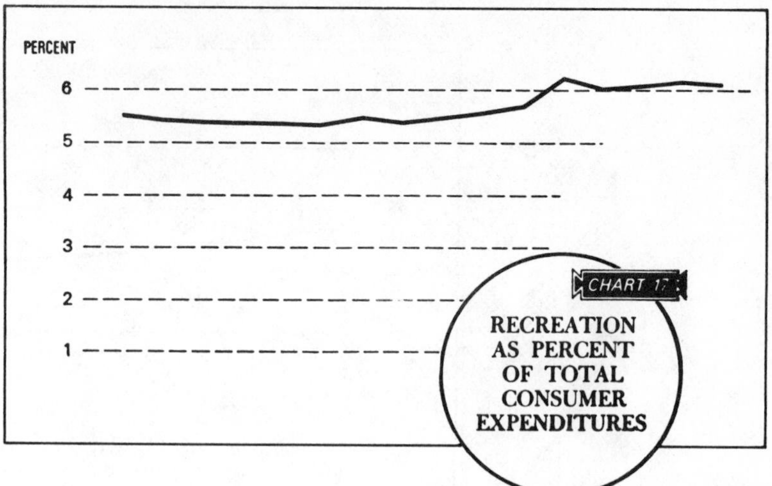

planning purposes in this industry, this should be a significant area of concern.

One of the measures of profitability of a company is that of return on net assets. It reflects the return on this portion of the investment in the company. As shown on Chart 19, the return from the period of 1959 to just recently has definitely gone down about 30 per cent in a period where the net assets themselves were rising over 50 per cent. This indicates weakness in cost control, a key requirement in remaining competitive.

Another measure which might well affect competitive position is the change in cost of goods sold as compared to selling, distribution, and administrative expenses (Chart 20). This analysis indicates a significant increase exceeding 50 per cent for the period, with the trend

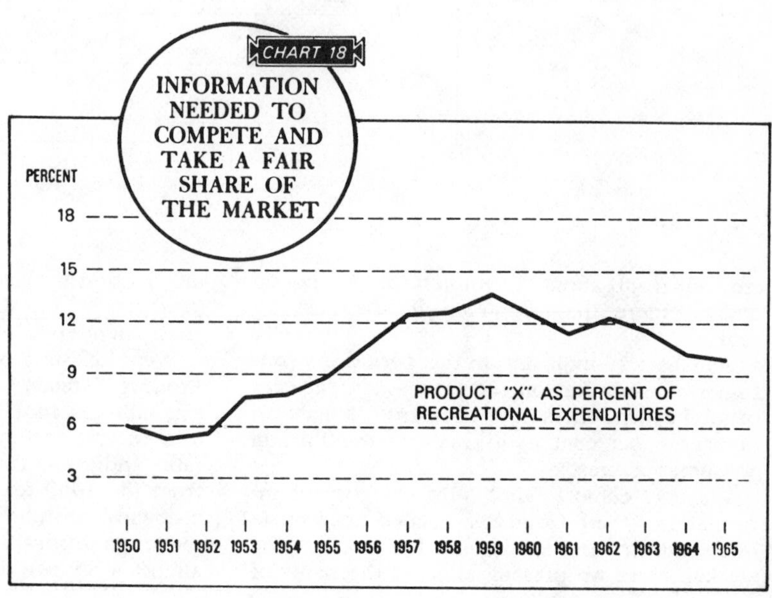

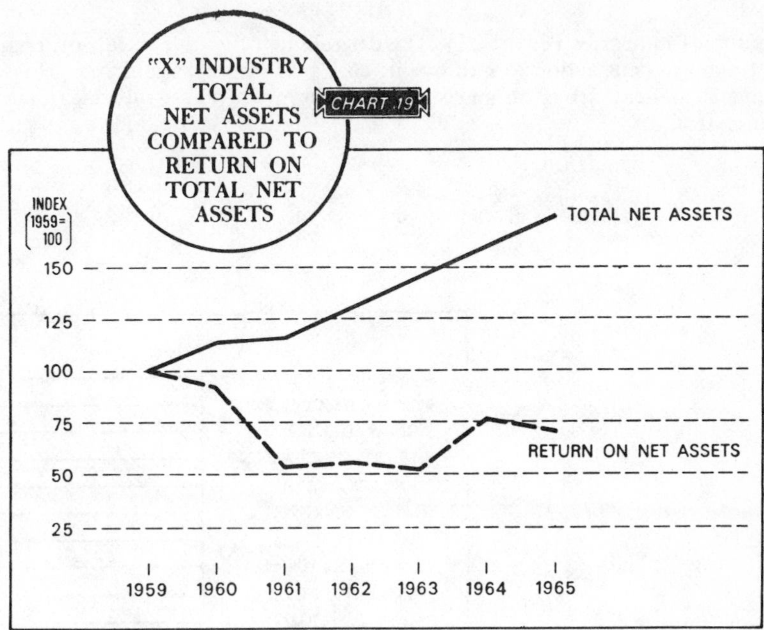

increasing for the overhead costs in relation to factory costs. This indicates a need for review of manpower utilization and distribution cost controls.

A third measure might be the pre-tax earnings as a per cent of sales for the "X" industry compared to twelve major industries for the past year (Chart 21). The chart indicates that in relative ranking, the "X" industry has the lowest per cent of earnings.

Fourth, measurement might look at the annual inventory turnover rate for the same

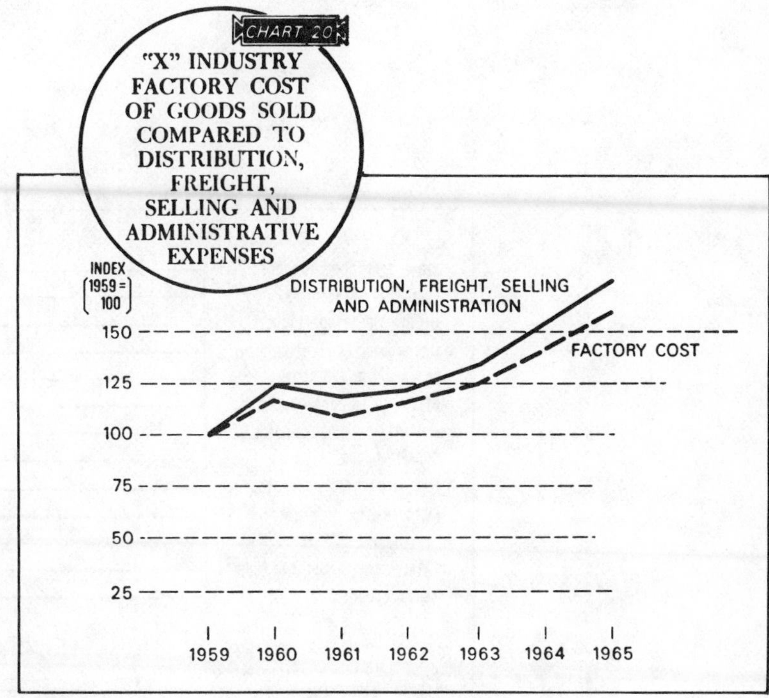

group of industries (Chart 22). The desirability of management action to improve its cash position as indicated by this measure of performance is clear.

Next let us observe the measure of sales change from 1964 to 1965 (Chart 23). The chart indicates that "X" industry is average as compared to the group.

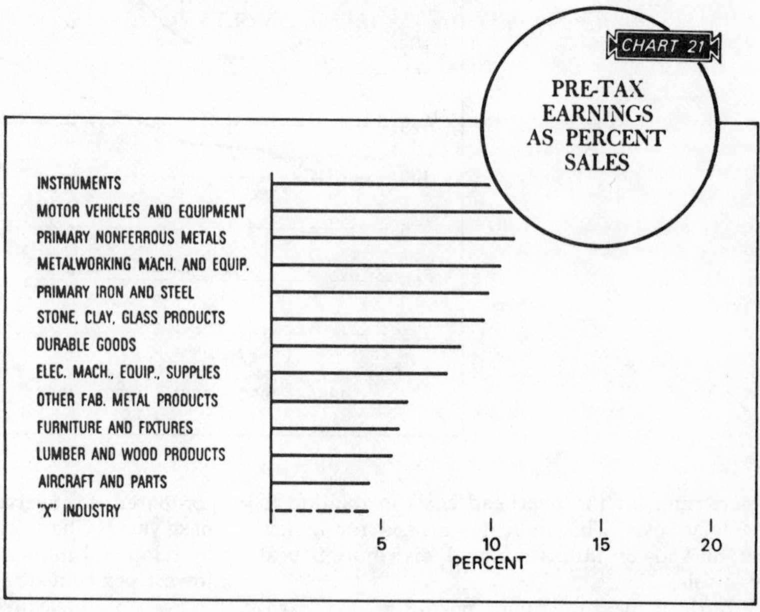

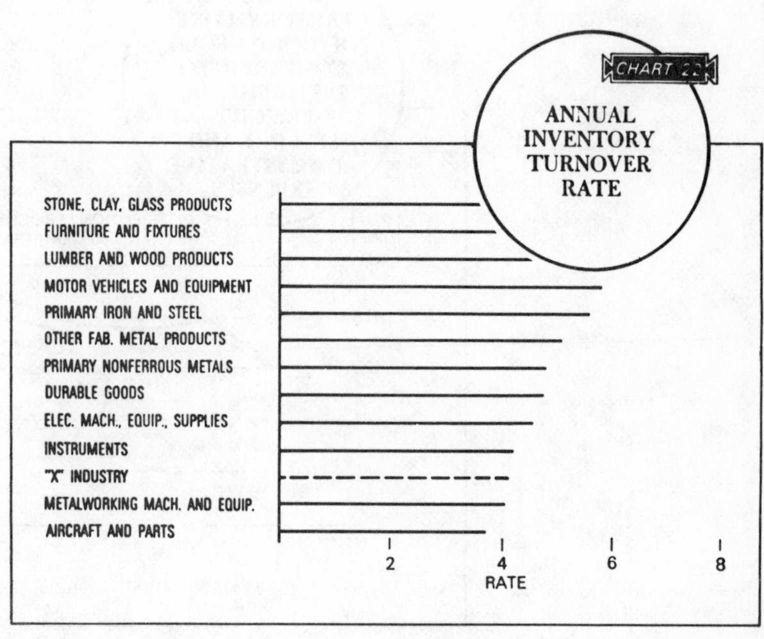

MOVING OUT AHEAD

Up to now we have been speaking generally about industry averages. Perhaps the most significant item noticed in Company X's relationship with companies in its industry is the effect of individual management ability and action. One can go along with the crowd. A company can become profitable as its industry becomes profitable, or it can lose money as the industry loses money if it acts only as the average company does. There have been dramatic instances which show that when management of a specific company takes dynamic, aggressive action, it can (despite what has happened on the average to the industry in general) make its company more profitable than average. It can use the information in an improved management information system for management action.

Let us then consider the case of Company X as an instance of this kind of action. To protect the identity of our illustrative company, we will not identify specific years or the specific industry.

Let us look, however, at this actual industry and Company X. Chart 24 shows industry average sales for a recent eight-year period compared with sales for Company X. The industry sales increased through the period as shown in previous charts, rising 20 per cent in the eight-year period. The sales of Company X doubled in the same period as a result of the policy that it had adopted.

Turning to the ratio of net profits on sales for a recent four-year period in Chart 25, we note that industry profit on sales has stayed generally about 2 per cent, declining slightly as shown in earlier charts. Profit on sales for Company X, however, rose from 2 percent to almost 5 per cent in the same period as a result of the individual actions which management in that company had taken.

In the ratio of net profit to invested capital (Chart 26), the industry in the recent four-year period has shown a rate of about 10 per cent and slightly decreasing. The profit picture of Company X is considerably more attractive than the industry average, increasing from 17 per cent to almost 25 per cent in the same period.

With regard to the ratio of current assets to current liabilities (Chart 27) for a recent three-year period of Company X as compared with eight individual companies representative generally of companies in the industry, the ratio of assets to liabilities for the companies in the industry has changed very little, while in the three-year period Company X has rapidly increased its ratio to a more and more attractive figure.

These charts show clearly the effect when individual management takes action, based on information available through its information system—when a company does not merely follow the trends in the industry, but makes its own trend. There are many factors to consider in improving profits. By itself, no system, no

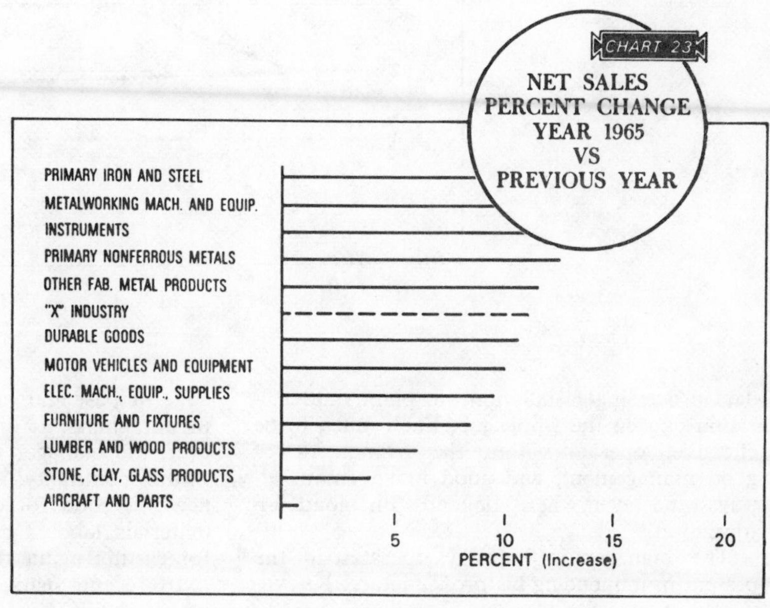

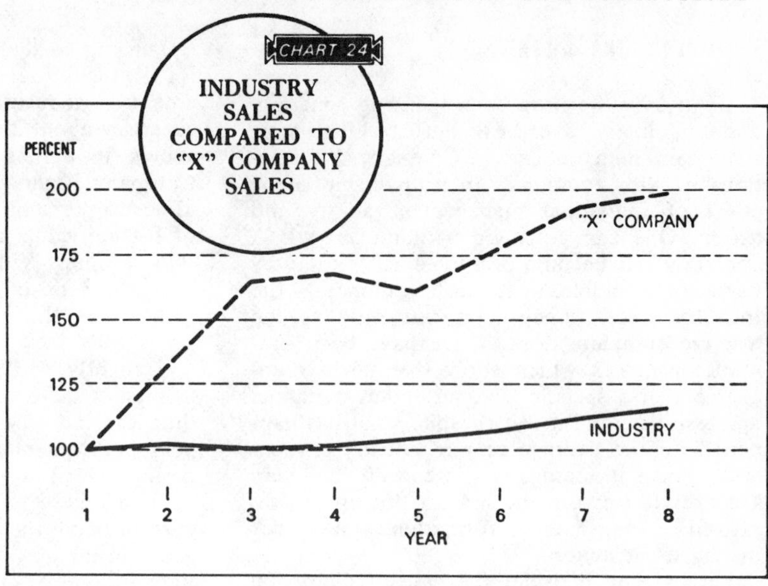

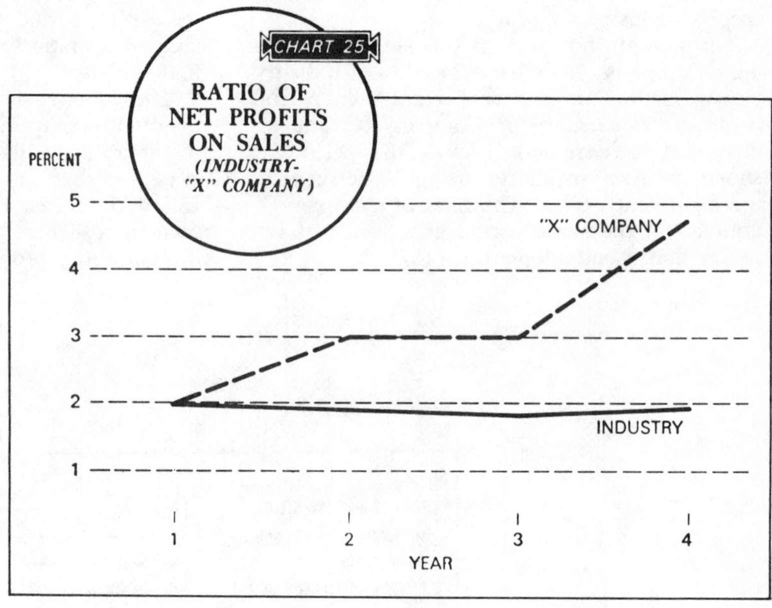

data processing installation, no plant modernization can do the whole job. Each must, to be effective, operate within the framework of good management, and good management always and everywhere depends on good information.

The manager in industry operates in the present in influencing his profit picture. Knowledge of past and present operations, as shown in our charts, is one of his basic tools. However, the manager must plan for the future to assure continuity of profits. To do this, he needs a good forecast of future demands on materials, labor, facilities, and capital, and good forecasting again requires good information.

In recent years, tools for prediction have

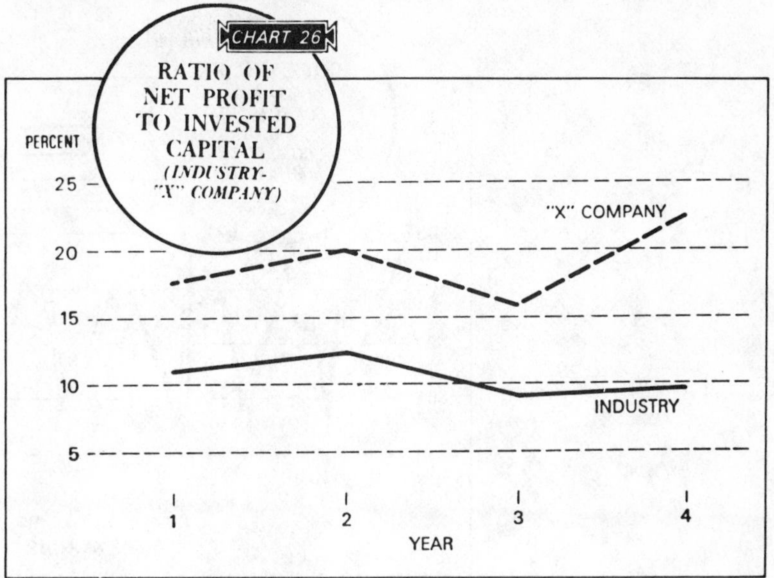

been greatly improved. The use of mathematical techniques for quantifying and analyzing probability have provided important contributions to the management decision making process. Increasingly, the use of computers for rapid solution of mathematical "models" of business problems has provided a tool which can increase profitability of operations.

To illustrate, in Chart 28 results are shown which were obtained from forecasting using a simulation technique recently developed by a Price Waterhouse & Co. mathematician, J. L. Ray. The solid line shows the actual price index for the 128-month period from 1953 to mid-1963. The dotted line shows the price index forecast by the model three months in advance of the actual month.

The computer program is designed so that, for example, at month 40, the computer reviews the predicted price index for month 40,

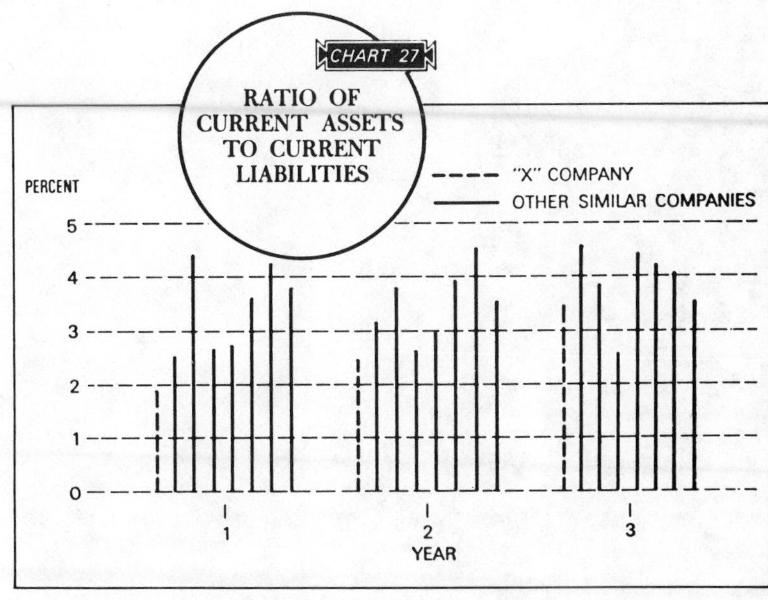

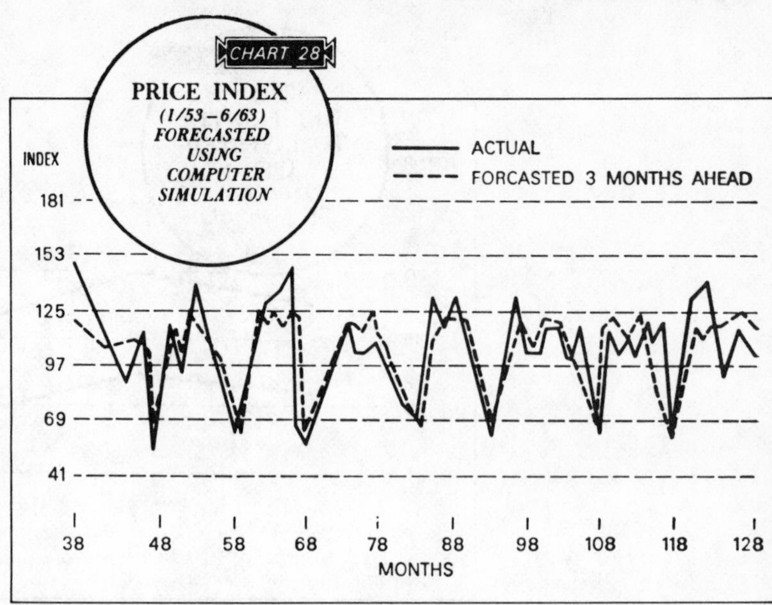

the actual price index reported for month 40, the deviation from prediction for month 40, and the deviation pattern for each previous month of actual to forecast. The program then calculates the best prediction for month 43 based on all past history. This forecast simulator is a general purpose tool which has proven to be remarkably effective in a wide variety of predictions. It provides the manager of today a technique for improvement of his decision making.

In summary, the profit picture in any company in the future will be to a significant extent a result of the gathering and intelligent use of good information. Each company should be concerned that it is providing its managers with the kind and quality of information they need to do their job well.

71 DEVELOPING BETTER MANAGEMENT INFORMATION SYSTEMS*

Robert W. Holmes

Computer systems directed to management planning and assistance in making decisions for most companies are still a myth. Executives failing to exploit the computer are facing a grim future, and they are well-advised to investigate in depth the reasons for their failure with the computer and to profit from the successes of others.

Impressive MIS achievements of many large companies have received wide exposure and publicity, and they should serve as models of what can be accomplished through the computer. For each instance of noteworthy achievement, however, there has been a multitude of unsatisfactory results, ranging from minor dissatisfaction to serious lack of progress and, finally, to complete failure.

Management generally has not come to associate high profit return directly with strong information capability. (By "information," I refer to all computer output after its conversion from raw data input by computer processing.) The definition of MIS put forth by the Management Information Systems Committee of the Financial Executives Institute makes clear the relationship between the two. The definition is, in part, as follows:

> MIS is a system designed to provide selected decision-oriented information needed by management to plan, control, and evaluate the activities of the corporation. It is designed within a framework that emphasizes profit planning, performance planning, and control at all levels. It contemplates the ultimate integration of required business information subsystems, both financial and non-financial, within the company.
>
> A successful management information system must consider the current and future management information needs of the administrative, financial, marketing, production, operating, and research functions. It will have the capacity to provide environmental (competitive, regulatory) information required for evaluating corporate objectives, long-range planning (strategy), and short-range planning (tactics).

The development of MIS within a company is a continuous process, phase by phase, all blending together, with additions made as required to meet the needs of management.

By and large, senior management has been unable to come to grips with the organization and operation of its information processing function. Well-defined objectives of the function are almost nonexistent. Major applications have been hurriedly computerized, piecemeal, without over-all plans, without concern for management's needs, and without updating basic systems.

Current writings reveal the strong trend toward turning over data processing activities completely to outside service organizations for facilities management. Large and small companies alike are using this escape hatch. The complexities of the computer itself, high costs with poor return on investment, shortage of qualified technicians, and problems which seem to defy solution are exhausting a disproportionate amount of top management's time and patience.

Passing off the facilities management or operational problems, however, attacks only the portion of the iceberg above water. Management is still faced with a very basic problem which extends beyond systems development and operation: the organization and management of information technology for maximum competitive leverage.

The real advantages that can be gained from computers come from the operating intelligence it provides to assist management. A sensitive and quick-acting intelligence/information system can arm a company with a most formid-

* Reprinted by permission of the publisher from "Areas to Investigate for Better MIS," *Financial Executive*, vol. 38, no. 7, pp. 24–31, July, 1970. Mr. Holmes is president of Lincoln Institute, consultants in information systems.

able competitive weapon. Such a system can figure in a company's present and future strength as forcibly as the more exotic influences, like acquisitions, product research and development, new product lines, market development, and manufacturing process breakthroughs. In the present period of extraordinary high costs, management leverage through information becomes the most significant factor in insuring a maximum return on invested capital. Timely, relevant information enables management to make key decisions and to take action promptly with minimal risk. The outcome of decisions can be predicted with reasonable accuracy before they are implemented, and knowledgeable choices can be made between many alternatives.

To use outside facilities management could have the regrettable impact of allowing management to continue in its failure to exploit the computer. Management is better advised to investigate thoroughly and to deploy constructively the factors contributing to the success of a management information system. These factors, largely nontechnical, will vary with the viewpoint of the person assessing them. They are listed in the order of their importance.

Investigation of these factors will illuminate the causes of any unsatisfactory condition and, more importantly, will ascertain the proper responses leading to desired improvements.

12 Areas to Investigate for Better MIS

1. Top management's involvement with the system
2. Management's ability to organize the MIS function
3. The use of a master-plan
4. The attention given to human relations between functions involved
5. Management's ability to identify its information needs
6. Management's ability to apply judgment to information
7. The condition of basic accounting, cost, and control systems
8. The degree of confidence generated by accuracy at the input level
9. The frequency of irrelevant or outdated data provided
10. The competence of systems technicians and their grasp of management problems
11. The justification for projects undertaken
12. Reliance on equipment vendors

TOP MANAGEMENT'S INVOLVEMENT WITH THE SYSTEM

Computer failures have caused disillusionment and management withdrawal at times when greater management involvement is needed. Some managers even consider the computer an encroachment on and a threat to their traditional decision-making rights. Perhaps they feel this way because the presence of decision-oriented information—specific facts and figures—can force management to take action in distasteful situations which they are otherwise able to ignore. General knowledge does not trigger action, but facts and figures cannot continually be ignored.

Management's abdication has been interpreted by technicians as a complete delegation to them of the active direction of computer systems concepts, applications, and more importantly, of implementation. This unfortunate delegation of great responsibility to technicians usually does not correspond with their skills in human relations. In fact, the technicians have tended to hammer their systems creations through, sometimes against all odds. As a result, almost all implementation problems or failures are traceable to the human element.

It is interesting to note some of the impressions of top management held by persons down the line involved with systems creation, design, and implementation.

- Management has not made itself aware of the computer's capacity for developing relevant information directed toward problem solving.
- Management normally cannot define problem areas clearly, yet it quaintly regards the computer as a challenge to its decision-making prerogative.
- Management does not understand the absolute necessity of securing accurate input data to insure the success of a system, and the difficulties in accomplishing this.
- Management does not understand or appreciate the time span required to implement a system properly.

It is clear that management must come to realize much more fully the competitive significance of information systems and that, with the proper approaches, eminently successful systems can be developed. Further, management must gain a much broader knowledge of computer systems, possible applications, and implementation problems than it now possesses. With this knowledge, it can confidently demand specific information that is relevant, fresh, accurate, and obtainable.

Management should not feel incapable of understanding computers nor should it fear that computer technology challenges its decision-making rights. The computer is a valuable aid and can remove much of the guesswork and risk. The overall decision-making function, however, remains the province of management.

Finally, it is absolutely certain that any softening in interest, involvement, or support demonstrated by top management will flow freely down through all segments of the organization and present a major handicap to the success of any information system.

Members of senior management have felt that they should not try to grapple with the technical mysteries and complexities of computer systems. Computer technicians, to a large extent, have added to the confusion by failing to assist those outside technical circles in understanding the capabilities and limitations of the computer, thereby making what is a relatively simple problem unnecessarily complex.

MANAGEMENT'S ABILITY TO ORGANIZE THE MIS FUNCTION

Limited understanding of information systems coupled with the dynamic nature of systems have made it difficult for management to deal with policy formulation, organization, and control of this critical resource. The sum presents a continuing, nagging, and major problem for senior management.

Management is groping for answers to such questions as what skills, qualifications, and background should the head of information systems possess? Where should information systems report in the top organization? How much in the way of resources should be devoted to the function? Who should participate heavily in the planning and development of objectives? How should the function be staffed?

Another element often contributing to the problem is the incumbent head of the established information system who continually strives to convince his management that his policies, objectives, and qualifications are the best obtainable and should not be challenged. Management, in not resisting this kind of persuasion, allows the old and largely ineffectual methods to linger on.

The cornerstone of effective MIS organization and performance is the link between senior management and the personnel which form the technical staff. The individual serving as this link must have special qualifications. He must have a heavy background in upper management practices and good knowledge of computer systems and operations, and he must enjoy the confidence and cooperation of both the senior management group and the technical staff. Such qualifications are exceedingly rare, a fact which may help to explain why this position has undergone more failures in recent years than any other key management position. A common mistake has been to assign a person with only a systems background to a managerial position. In other instances, the position has been filled at a time of crisis by someone in the company not remotely qualified.

There are no hard and fast rules for guidance in setting organizational relationships. The function can report to the chief financial officer, to an "independent" executive, such as the head of administration, or directly to the president. Experience has shown that all can work successfully. The key, again, is the ability of the MIS head to gain the confidence and cooperation of senior management as a group. Likewise, the matter of centralization is dependent upon company organization, concepts of profit responsibility, and degree of commonality of the segments of the business.

THE USE OF A MASTER PLAN

Setting over-all company objectives and planning to meet those objectives still leaves much to be desired in most companies. The real orphan within such imperfect planning is the information gathering system. Management's abdication of MIS leadership has required the system's technical staff to proceed with applications of its own selection. The more simple, low-risk applications have, therefore, tended to be selected on a piecemeal basis. Management information needs have been largely ignored. The result has been the failure to tap MIS' full potential.

Planning for information systems by involving management, other users of the service, technicians, and related clerical staff can save an enormous amount of backtracking, opposition, time, and expense. The full economic impact of charging ahead without planning can never be completely quantified. The costs of applications never completed, of other lost opportunities and poor decisions, however, are often painfully real. The more subtle effects of poor planning, on the other hand, usually lie hidden and manifest themselves only in general dissatisfaction and lack of steady progress.

Planning must start by setting long-term company objectives followed with a detailed profit plan. Information needs within the plan must then be determined and provided for in the creation of the data bank. All separate subsystems should be coordinated into one integrated system. Planning should cover the gathering, transmission, and dissemination of data as well as its processing. Never should individual major applications be started without a complete integrated plan. Above all, the matters of systems concepts, goals, and long-range planning must not be left to the discretion of the technical staff, but assumed entirely by top management.

Individual project planning should assign responsibilities, time schedules, and a means for project progress reviews and project monitoring.

THE ATTENTION GIVEN TO HUMAN RELATIONS BETWEEN FUNCTIONS INVOLVED

People problems in information systems cause disappointments and failures to a much greater extent than do technical problems. The lack of participation by users of the service or by related clerical staffs can result in a deficiency of interest which alone can cause the system to fail. Forcing service upon users that they neither ordered nor helped to conceive may cause the system to die. Clerical personnel, who must make the system work, will not be predisposed toward cooperation if they are brought aboard only in the final implementation stage. Sloppy input, arising out of clerical indifference, leads to erroneous information that can destroy all confidence in the system.

The success of any information system is dependent largely upon the effective use of behavorial sciences *well in advance* of the application of systems techniques. It must be realized that an effective system is composed of a preponderance of nontechnical factors—concepts, attitudes, acceptance, and enthusiasm.

How can human relations techniques be better applied to modern information systems with success? What are the approaches which should be taken to assure success? These requisites can be categorized as follows:

- All functional management as well as information systems management serve on the planning and review committee,
- Active participation by all users of the service,
- Clear support of technical staff by management,
- Involvement of related clerical persons in all planning and implementation as it affects them.

The following are comments applicable to each of these requisites.

Planning and Review Committee In order to achieve its maximum benefit, an information system must fulfill the needs of all company functions. In fact, to ignore certain functions is to risk aborting the effort of the entire system. A good human relations approach must be premised on a clear delineation of the technicians' role: that they should serve operating management; they are the specialists to whom management looks for technical tools. But their technical expertise must be tempered with consideration, humbleness, and patience. A group of systems managers and functional managers working together in harmony can accomplish amazing results. Comprehensive forward planning and a united implementation effort will insure a high rate of success.

The committee preferably should consist of the head of each function which reports to the chief executive or another high-level executive with decision-making authority. Information systems representation should consist of the MIS head and project managers. The committee should meet regularly, reshaping ultimate goals, assigning new major applications, and reviewing progress on existing applications. Priorities should be changed where beneficial.

Participation by Users of Service After objectives and priorities for major applications are set by the planning and review committee, individual projects are set up within the context of an over-all plan. It is at this juncture—establishing individual projects—that the systems technicians and the specific users of the information must be joined in the effort. Again, if projected goals are set or a new system is originated without complete user participation, failure is practically guaranteed. In many instances, the users do not make any outstanding contribution to the formulation process. If, however, their participation has been invited, they will view the system somewhat as a creation of their own and will be more likely to support it enthusiastically.

The degree of user satisfaction is probably the most useful index of measuring the success or effectiveness of an information system. A mediocre system can be eminently successful when supported by user participation, while a model technical system, without such support, can be a dismal failure. Human relations has much greater impact here than is generally realized; it at least equals technical expertise in importance.

Support of Technical Staff The enthusiasm and interest with which technicians approach their assignments appears almost in direct relationship to the support openly demonstrated by higher management. Management interest cannot lie on the surface; to be influential, it must be deep-rooted.

Support means involvement—active participation in both application assignments and application reviews. It means honest discussions, knowledgeable commentary, and substantial ideas. Support, above all, means commendation where appropriate.

It is virtually impossible in today's competitive market to retain the loyalty of capable computer technicians where they feel a lack of direction or interest from upper management. The choice, therefore, is to give full support or to settle for an inferior technical staff.

Involve Related Clerical Persons This is the area in which information system delays and ultimate failures are very prevalent. In the development of a system, extensive data must be gathered and considered. Omission of any relevant, although seemingly unimportant, particulars can create the need for extensive redesign and costly delays. Complete involvement of clerical personnel gives them the opportunity to make important contributions and encourages their support of the system, thus helping to assure its successful operation. All approaches should emphasize the objective of work simplification for them.

The time of change is time for crucial added attention to human relations. Change means resistance (usually hidden) and often creates much deeper people problems than it does technical problems. Change upsets stable routines and threatens security. The benefits of change must be shared with those affected wherever practicable. When understanding, pride of accomplishment, and job satisfaction are added to the particular skills of an individual, his efforts can be astounding.

MANAGEMENT'S ABILITY TO IDENTIFY ITS INFORMATION NEEDS

Management chronically deplores that it "does not have enough information to go on." This criticism, more often than not, is entirely correct. Yet management often has not identified its needs, nor has it demanded that these needs be identified by subordinate staff members. Human judgment alone must decide what questions to ask.

A logical approach to defining management's information needs is to review the adequacy of the present information received. Much of this will be excellent. Management certainly will not want any major overhaul that might jeopardize what it presently finds useful.

To determine its information needs, management must review the types of decisions it is called upon to make, the frequency of these decisions, and the specific information that might assist in securing the ultimate success of the decisions. Companies well advanced in MIS can logically use their present cost of capital as a focal point for information requirements, initially comparing this to the present return on investment rate. Relative return on assets employed can be used to evaluate segments of the business. In any case, the information flow can be directed to identify problem areas and to propose solutions. Information should give deep insight into all operating areas so that necessary action is clear and timely.

MANAGEMENT'S ABILITY TO APPLY JUDGMENT TO INFORMATION

The span of answers that modeling techniques can develop under differing situations is infinite, but human judgment must make the final selections. Present-day practices of making such selections can be dramatized by the example of the senior executive faced with a major decision who, surrounded by stacks of computer runoffs, closes his door and flips a coin.

To a great extent, seasoned management believes that decisions, even the critical ones, must be made on pure judgment and intuition alone. Many very successful businesses have been built with this type of management. And budget-minded management members are leary of the cost to produce management-oriented information. Applications using the management sciences tend to appear exotic and are not considered to be economically sound.

Thus, the practicality of using scientific techniques, management sciences, and operations research is always a problem. Companies with basic data processing problems, including organizational problems, usually are not remotely interested in the more abstruse facilities of the computer. Management's attitudes toward the utility of simulation, risk analysis, and the relative weighting of alternatives have a strong bearing on the final successes of the scientific techniques applied. Finally, the nature of the particular business, such as the need to make frequent decisions under a multiplicity of uncertain conditions, also has a large role in determining company needs.

On the whole, company management is beginning to realize that scientific management approaches, including financial models of the company or parts of the company, are important to future success. The next few years should witness rapid growth in the use of these techniques. To exploit fully the computer and the leverage derived from information obtained by the computer, management must learn more about the computer, its power, and what it can do to serve management's information needs.

THE CONDITION OF BASIC ACCOUNTING, COST, AND CONTROL SYSTEMS

Computer-based information systems are not a solution to outmoded and deficient accounting, cost, and budgetary control systems. There is some tendency to concentrate attention on MIS and to neglect these basic systems. An alarmingly large number of companies today are using antiquated basic systems that have not changed to meet the needs of a dynamic business—systems that produce inaccurate and irrelevant data. Job costing on repetitive production is expensive to administer; often the cost fluctuations reported are not meaningful. To make matters worse, the causes for excess costs cannot be determined because the excesses simply flow in an unidentified cost and are neither isolated nor reported in accounts under a standard cost approach.

Overhead expense accounts are commonly not sufficiently particularized to be meaningful. Account codes are not clear, and considerable cost is reported erroneously. The principles of responsibility reporting are neglected many times. Losses in the work-in-process production flow are not currently reported and cannot be detected until inventory. For many companies, special price quotations are vital to obtaining business: yet their quotation cost data is deplorable.

Budgetary controls using historical data as the principal basis for evaluating new budgets can be most detrimental when grounded on inaccurate data.

Such deficiencies can make the most carefully developed MIS fail. Until basic foundation systems are effective, bad decisions continue to be made based on bad data fed through the computer at a faster rate. A major problem in correcting outmoded basic systems is, again, people. Changes here disrupt their ingrained working patterns and are most subtly resisted.

Continual review by qualified individuals is necessary to assure that the basic systems are meeting the changing needs of the business. Encouraging participation by the users of the systems and the systems specialists is again the most fruitful approach. Fresh and independent viewpoints by outside specialists are usually very helpful.

THE DEGREE OF CONFIDENCE GENERATED BY ACCURACY AT THE INPUT LEVEL

Well-conceived and well-designed technical systems can fail miserably with poorly directed implementation. During implementation, inaccurate careless input can produce data so erroneous that the users lose all confidence in the entire system. Moreover, the memory of failure becomes so fixed that successful operations and enthusiastic support can be set back for years. The presence of the computer has created new disciplines for obtaining accurate data. Clerical errors traditionally have prevailed in abundance. The contemporary use of formal systems for handling data on a mass basis and the recent sophistication acquired by the information user have required that much greater attention be given to input.

Important involvement of the clerical personnel and a thorough testing of the system followed by adequate training—all contribute to successful implementation. Most important, going on-stream cannot be rushed, and all inaccurate output must be traced back to its source. Data isolation and correction devices are helpful in preventing bad data from causing damage or delay.

The successful operation of major applications involves substantial time, sometimes years. The high cost of development and implementation over such long periods wears management's patience thin. They demand "something from the system." If such demands are unreasonable, compliance will assure failure or setback.

THE FREQUENCY OF IRRELEVANT OR STALE DATA PROVIDED

It is unbelievable under present-day concepts of exception reporting to find stacks of machine runoffs being delivered to senior executives. Sometimes the user finds the appropriate pages to keep, but more often all is discarded. It is not uncommon to find deliveries of the data lagging three to four weeks behind the period being reported.

In these instances, it is obvious that the system technicians are completely insensitive to the process of management, and management simply goes along for the ride. Often the unfortunate consequence of this indifference is the effort by members of management, unable to deal with the situation, to set up their own informal information systems. Such independent efforts on the part of management are not isolated cases; they are appearing with alarming frequency.

For a system to be effective, MIS managers must observe the principles of exception reporting and reporting by appropriate levels. Top management cannot accept less than this.

THE COMPETENCE OF SYSTEMS TECHNICIANS AND THEIR GRASP OF MANAGEMENT PROBLEMS

In the section covering problems of organization, the importance of the qualifications of the head of MIS was discussed. The casualty rate in MIS reaches into all levels of the technical staff. In particular, the MIS managers, including the systems project leaders and data processing supervisors, have a high turnover.

Although the most serious failings by technical personnel have been related to human relations aspects, there have also been serious technical deficiencies in much of the systems work. Such deficiencies stem largely from the absence of a clear understanding of management's desires and objectives. Systems men do not know what they are expected to accomplish, and they usually do not have a keen sensitivity to management's needs and problems.

To a lesser extent, technical deficiencies are traceable to outright incompetency. Technical qualifications are often overlooked due to the tremendous demand for skilled senior systems designers and programmers resulting from the explosive growth of computer sciences. In spite of the shortage, however, it is usually prudent to defer systems project work until fully qualified personnel can be assigned. Continuous upgrading of the staff has been necessary in most companies to pursue a solid constructive effort. Close coordination with company management has broadened the skills of technicians and has assisted them in better understanding of management. A very successful policy has been to select highly qualified accounting supervisors and train them for systems work.

THE JUSTIFICATION FOR PROJECTS UNDERTAKEN

A policy of economic justification for all major projects provides for the allocation of resources and for maximum payoff, and prevents time and cost from being expended beyond the reach of practical application. As an example, the basic data required might not be in the data base, or even worse, it might not be obtainable by any reasonable means. A clear disclosure of what a project will accomplish prevents subsequent controversies.

In charging ahead without a master plan, many companies undertake major projects without sufficient formalized justification. All major projects should be analyzed under the following criteria:

- Strategy for profit return maximization and investment considerations,
- Planning and decision-making information for management,
- Improved service to customers and other company units,
- Improved short- and long-term processing of data, and
- Direct cost reduction.

All assignments should be approved by the head of MIS. Major projects should be approved by an operating committee.

Projects undertaken without a sophisticated evaluation of benefits versus cost can very likely cause negative payback and abandonment soon after implementation.

RELIANCE ON EQUIPMENT VENDORS

Until recently, systems and programming support service was supplied on a limited basis by all equipment vendors. This service, being "free" under the equipment rental arrangements, has been used extensively to save on in-house staffing. Equipment companies have tended to oversell their limited services and have dampened interest in developing ambitious MIS programs. As a result of the intense competition between equipment vendors, some sales representatives have put a gloss on the capabilities of their hardware. Smaller companies are frequently the victims of such a sales pitch. Many times the false confidence inspired by sales representatives has resulted in serious delays and temporary failures. Fortunately, the hardware capability problem has become less critical now that more companies have the skills necessary to review hardware proposals with a realistic approach. Reviews excluding equipment vendors' representatives are most necessary, and full reliance for equipment selection must be placed on in-house staff.

Opportunity to Exploit the Computer Is Enormous Many of the larger, well-managed, forward-looking companies have taken advantage of modern techniques and the computer's power enabling management to plan, control, and enhance the company's future return on investment. All these companies have dealt with the factors discussed here, but they have been able to profit from past errors. Problem identification must precede problem solving.

As a business continues to grow and more blind spots appear, management tends to reach out for assistance. Positive action toward acceptance of facts, figures, and probabilities using computer systems is still a critical point and a difficult step. Realization that members of management will make the final decisions with or without MIS—but with greater chances of success with MIS—should facilitate acceptance of the new concepts.

There is enormous opportunity to profit through the exploitation of the computer's capabilities, and the degree of opportunity will intensify in the future. Although past problems and failures have generally manifested themselves as being technical in nature, very often they are not. The key to computer opportunities, optimum costs, and maximum profit leverage through information will be realized only by management involvement, solid planning, and over-all company coordination.

C. TECHNIQUES OF PLANNING AND CONTROLLING

72 VARIABLE BUDGETS AND DIRECT COSTING*

Howard B. Burdeau

The term "annual operating budget" can best be described as the "action plan of management." Budgeting is not a new technique, for it has been used for many years as a management practice of major importance in some companies, while it may merely be a routine clerical process in others.

In recent years, with the great improvement in management information systems (total systems), communications, electronic data processing, quantitative management techniques, budgeting is fast becoming the focal point for more effective management processes. Therefore, the integrated budgetary system is the most effective method to help accomplish the overall objectives of management.

The growth of large and complex industrial organizations and the decentralizing of management has led the individual manager of the various divisions to optimize his individual operations. The different objectives of the various divisions of a concern are often inconsistent with each other and frequently come into direct conflict.

The vast sums spent on product research in recent years has led to the development of many new products which have to be manufactured, sold, and the entire operation financed. This has led to major decisions concerning plant capacity, production processes, marketing strategy, and foreseeing the action of competitors. In planning we must identify the various conditions of uncertainty we find, study the potential impact of these rapidly changing conditions and we must develop our proposed reactions to these conditions. Our company must be able to react quickly to a changing business environment.

The budget is management's answer to the query whether it has the capacity to handle and respond to change. Planning is the action by top management and supervisory personnel at all levels to decide on objectives, to identify the market areas in which to sell, and to react to the current business conditions. This plan of action is a quantitative technique that results in specific programs for the future growth of the business. The operating plan, once developed, is not static, but must be flexible (variable), so that it will change with the ever-changing business conditions.

To review briefly the mechanics of the budget process, we first start with the sales budget, which has a relation to the advertising, promotion, and research budgets. As the sales budget sets the contemplative activity level of the company, it is used to some extent to develop the selling, distribution, and administrative expense budgets. The sales budget provides information to establish the finished goods inventory budget, which also takes into account the optimum inventory levels as adjusted for production requirements. The finished goods requirements are used to establish the production budget. The production budget leads to the development of the purchase budget for direct materials, and also to the development of direct labor requirements. The manufacturing overhead budgets for both the production and service departments are developed by the responsible managers with assistance from the budget officers staff. After these various individual budgets are summarized, reviewed, and finally approved by top management, we have our plan (the operating budget).

Management control is the effort to follow the budget plan, so that organizational requirements are met and the ultimate goals of our organization accomplished. Management control utilizes the feedback of information so that the manager can compare the actual results of his department with what should have been attained under the actual operating conditions. These performance reports are sent to the line manager responsible for a particular operation and they highlight the differences between the actual results and the desired results that should have been realized if expected levels of efficiency were achieved in internal operation. The manager responds to the unfavorable variances

* Reprinted by permission of the publisher from *Managerial Planning*, vol. 19, no. 4, pp. 4–11, January–February, 1971. Mr. Burdeau is professor of accounting at California State College, San Bernardino.

by attempting to correct the underlying cause, and, in some instances, sends higher echelon a report of what actions are to be taken to correct the situation requiring attention.

After this brief review of planning and control, let us turn our attention to variable budgeting to control overhead expenses. Variable budgets are schedules of costs that indicate for each subdivision of the company, how each expense should change with volume, output, or activity. They express short-term costs—volume relationship within the narrow relevant range of volume. We are dealing with the concept of cost variability, which holds that cost can be related to output or activity. Costs then are primarily the result of two factors (1) passage of time and (2) activity.

Our first task in developing the variable budget is to analyze cost behavior. Under proper control, every cost will follow some definite pattern of behavior—although this pattern may not always be the expected one. Assumptions on cost behavior can be dangerous.

It cannot be presumed that certain costs will fluctuate with volume in some definite manner or remain constant because of their nature. Only through scientific analysis, drawing upon the skills of the industrial engineer, mathematician, statistician, economist, and production personnel, can the answer be found.

To simplify our examination of cost behavior patterns, let us classify cost in accordance with the concept of cost variability into the three categories as (1) nonvariable, (2) variable, and (3) semi-variable.

(1) Nonvariable costs, or fixed costs, are those items of cost which do not vary with volume or productive activity—they remain constant in amount regardless of the production activity within the relevant range of activity. Nonvariable costs can be classified as (a) committed costs, which are related to the provision of a capacity to do business, and (b) programmed, or managed costs, which are related to the utilization of the capacity provided. The amount of fixed costs remains the same over the relevant range of activity, but the unit cost varies inversely with activity. Step-fixed costs are those which remain constant only for a limited range of activities. The average step-fixed cost will decrease as production increases within the range. It may actually increase on a per unit basis as the next range of activity is reached, but usually only a portion of the new range, and then decrease as production activity is increased within that range. An example of a step-fixed cost is that one lead man can control fifteen (15) employees. As the number of employees increases to sixteen (16) and up to thirty (30) employees, a second lead man is required.

(2) Variable costs are those items of cost that vary directly with volume or productive capacity. For if there is no productive activity, the variable cost is zero. If the activity increases fifty percent, the variable cost increases the same percentage. The variable cost is variable in amount, but the cost per unit remains the same.

(3) Semi-variable, or mixed costs, are those items of cost that increase or decrease as volume or activity increase, but not in proportion thereto. These costs possess some of the characteristics of both fixed and variable costs. As the level of activity changes, the amounts incurred will change but not in direct proportion to activity changes. With an increase in activity, the average cost will decrease because the variable portion remains constant on a per unit basis, while the fixed portion will decrease on a per unit basis. Therefore, we are faced with a fixed element which represents the minimum cost of supplying the service and a variable portion which is influenced by changes in activity.

There are various methods of determining cost variability with the majority of the methods involving an analysis of historical costs. First, we would carefully study each expense account in a department and isolate those expenses which can be identified as either fixed or variable. The mixed cost must be further studied to identify the fixed and variable components of cost.

To understand how an expense varies for different activity levels, we can draw a graph, with the Y axis indicating the expense and the X axis indicating a measure of activity (which can be units produced, direct labor hours, direct machine hours). Exhibit A presents graphs of basic cost behavior patterns. By changing the measure of activity, a recognizable pattern of cost behavior may become apparent on the graph.

Basically there are three methods of determining cost variability for the mixed expenses, which can be described as (1) direct estimate method, (2) arithmetic approach, and (3) statistical correlation methods.

The direct estimate method is not normally used for routine expenses, and is utilized for

EXHIBIT A Basic Cost Behavior Patterns

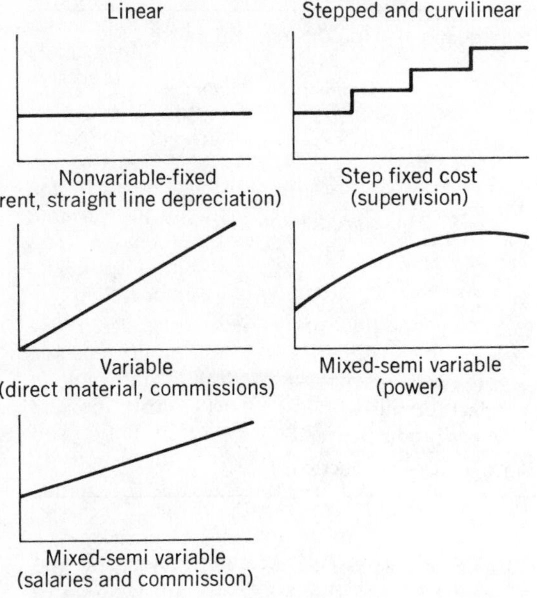

EXHIBIT B Tabulation by Months of Indirect Material Cost and Units Produced

MONTH	INDIRECT MATERIAL COST (Y VALUE)	PRODUCTION ACTIVITY UNITS (X VALUE)
January	$ 1,250	100
February	1,500	150
March	1,680	200
April	1,750	250
May	1,900	300
June	1,375	125
July	1,600	180
August	1,680	200
September	1,750	250
October	1,700	225
November	1,650	200
December	1,260	100
	$19,095	2,280

particular cost problem areas. One technique of this method is industrial engineering studies, which utilizes engineering studies based on analysis and direct observations of the manufacturing operations and often provide the most reliable cost estimates of certain expenses. Also engineering studies should be undertaken to check the results obtained from historical cost data. Such studies provide rates of material consumption, labor requirements, waste and spoilage allowances among others. The engineering approach to cost analysis is one of the more preferable techniques, but the expense of using it for all expenses year after year can be prohibitive for a concern. A National Association of Accountants Research Report dealing with industrial engineering describes some of the uses of engineering studies.

The information used to explain the arithmetic approach is shown in Exhibit B. Here we have a tabulation by months of a mixed expense, (indirect material cost) and the activity index (units produced).

The high and low method basically develops for each item of expense two budget allowances at two different levels of activity. The fixed and variable components are simply computed on an arithmetic basis assuming a straight line relationship. The calculations to employ this method are shown in Exhibit D. After the computations are made we have separated the mixed expense into its variable and fixed components and can express the results as a budget formula as follows:

Fixed	Variable
Indirect Material Cost 9.25	3.25 per unit of production

Correlation and statistical methods are widely used in the analysis of costs. These methods use historical data to determine how costs have varied in the past to estimate how costs should vary in the future. An example of this method is the use of scatter charts. This method involves the use of scatter graphs in order to determine visually the fixed and variable components of cost. The data from Exhibit B is plotted on a graph, Exhibit D, with the cost on the vertical scale (Y axis) and volume on the horizontal scale (X axis).

A visual trend line is drawn through the plotted points, and the point at which the trend line intersects the vertical scale (zero volume) indicates the fixed element while the slope of the trend line represents the variable rate. The variable component can be found by subtracting the nonvariable component from the total cost at any volume.

For example, the total cost of 300 units is

EXHIBIT C High and Low Method for Determining the Budget Formula for Mixed Expenses Using Data from Exhibit B

1. Select the HIGH and LOW activity months for the relevant range of activity and list.

	Maximum	*Minimum*	*Difference*
Budget allowance	\$ 1,900	\$ 1,250	\$ 650
Volume (units)	300	100	200

2. Compute the rate of variability.

$$\frac{\text{Difference in allowance}}{\text{Difference in volume (activity)}} \quad \frac{650}{200} = \$3.25 \text{ per production unit}$$

3. Compute the fixed cost.

Total cost at volume level of 300 units	\$ 1,900
Variable expense 300 units × \$3.25	975
FIXED COST	\$ 925

4. Express the results as a variable budget formula.

Cost	Fixed	Variable per production unit
Indirect Material	\$925	\$3.25 per unit of production

\$1,900; the variable cost then is \$975, or \$3.25 per unit, determined as follows:

Total cost of 300 units	\$1,900
Less nonvariable component	925
	\$ 975

EXHIBIT D Scattergraph Separating Variable and Nonvariable Components of a Mixed Cost Trend Line Fitted by Inspection (See Exhibit B for Source Data)

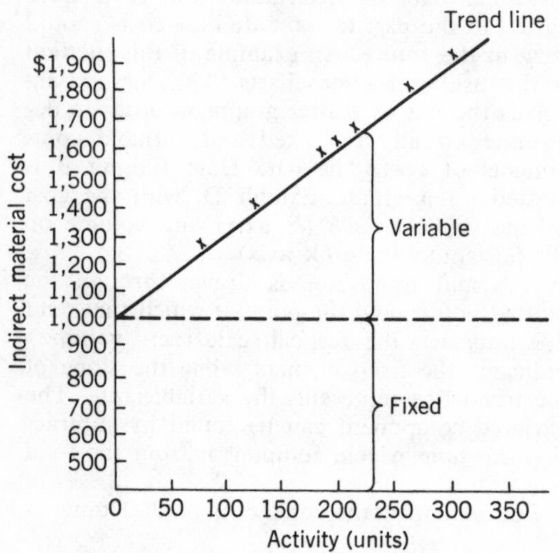

Variable cost per unit—\$975 divided by 300 units = \$3.25. Exhibit E gives an example of this method.

This procedure provides a simple comprehensible look at the interrelationships. It can be critized in that no two individuals would draw the same trend line through the points, but the margin of error is usually within acceptable limits.

The statistical method of least squares is a technique that is used for computing the trend line. This method is based on the formula for a straight line, $y = a + bx$, where y represents the dependent variable, a the constant factor, b the slope of the trend line, and x the independent variable. Simply, (a) expresses the portion of the line and (b) the slope of the trend line. Exhibit E shows the computations required for fitting a regression line to the data previously used.

After having examined our cost behavior and decided which expenses are nonvariable, variable, and mixed, we can now develop our variable budget for our service and production departments. An example of a variable (flexible) budget formula for a production department is shown in Exhibit F, part A.

Now let us assume that for the month of January, 10,000 direct machine hours were actually incurred. The variable budget for the month of January is computed in part B of Exhibit F.

After the variable budget is computed for a month based on actual activity (in this case, direct labor hours), it is compared with actual

EXHIBIT E Computations Required for Fitting a Regression Line Statistical Method of Least Squares

MONTH	INDIRECT MATERIAL COST (y Value)		PRODUCTION ACTIVITY UNITS (x Value)		x^2		xy
J	$ 1,250		100		10,000		125,000
F	1,500		150		22,500		225,000
M	1,680		200		40,000		336,000
A	1,750		250		62,500		437,500
M	1,900		300		90,000		570,000
J	1,375		125		15,625		171,875
J	1,600		180		32,400		288,000
A	1,680		200		40,000		336,000
S	1,750		250		62,500		437,500
O	1,700		225		50,625		382,500
N	1,650		200		40,000		330,000
D	1,260		100		10,000		126,000
Σy	$19,095	Σx	2,280	Σx^2	476,150	Σxy	3,765,375

1. Convert the formula for a straight line ($y = a + bx$) into two simultaneous equations which are the same as those developed by using the method of least squares:

$$\Sigma y = Na + b\Sigma x \text{ (N is the number of items in the listing)}$$
$$\Sigma(xy) = a\Sigma x + b\Sigma x^2$$

2. Substitute the values into the equations.

$$19{,}095 = 12a + 2{,}280b$$
$$3{,}765{,}375 = 2{,}280a + 476{,}150b$$

3. Solve for a (fixed portion) and for b (variable portion), resulting in the following:

Fixed portion – a = 984
Variable portion – b = 3.20

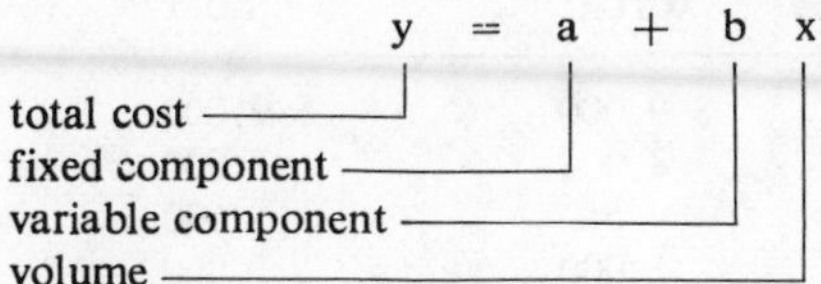

costs and a performance report prepared by the Accounting Department and sent to the manager responsible for Production Department One. Exhibit G shows the performance report for Department One.

Performance reports of this type for internal use constitute an important part of a comprehensive budget system. Every firm should design for itself an integrated cost report system constructed around (a) the organizational structure, (b) the budget objective, and (c) the exception principle. It must be remembered that the control reports must be suited to the individual user, for the different levels of management have different responsibilities and these frequently call for different kinds of information. We find a detailed report, similar to our performance report (Exhibit G) going to the lower levels of management (supervisors and foremen) to facilitate the control of current

EXHIBIT F Variable Budget for Production Department #1

PART A. BUDGET FORMULA

	FIXED	VARIABLE (PER 100 DIRECT MACHINE HOURS)
Supervisory salaries	$ 9,000	$ 0
Indirect labor	6,000	15.00
Maintenance parts	500	1.00
Depreciation	1,000	
Insurance and taxes	200	
Miscellaneous	300	2.00
Total	$17,000	$18.00

PART B. VARIABLE BUDGET FOR MONTH OF JANUARY
(10,000 direct machine hours were actually incurred in January)

	FIXED	VARIABLE CALC.	TOTAL
Supervisory salaries	$ 9,000	0	$ 9,000
Indirect labor	6,000	15 × 100 = $1,500	7,500
Maintenance parts	500	1 × 100 = 100	600
Depreciation	1,000		1,000
Insurance and taxes	200		200
Miscellaneous	300	2 × 100 = 200	500
Total	$17,000	$1,800	$18,800

EXHIBIT G Performance Report for Production Department #1. The Muncie Manufacturing Company Performance Report January 1969

DEPARTMENT: PRODUCTION DEPT. #1 SUPERVISOR: J. SMITH

	ACTUAL	BUDGET	VARIANCE (OVER) OR UNDER BUDGET
Supervisory salaries	$ 9,000	$ 9,000	$ —
Indirect labor	8,000	7,500	(500) Unfavorable
Maintenance parts	550	600	50 Favorable
Depreciation	1,000	1,000	—
Insurance and taxes	200	200	—
Miscellaneous	575	500	(75) Unfavorable
Total	$19,325	$18,800	($525) Unfavorable

NOTE: The activity level for the month was 10,000 direct machine hours.

operations. Budget reports for middle and top management would be summary in nature. If the variation is significant, it should result in an investigation to determine the underlying causes, because the cause rather than the result provides the basis for corrective action.

Although an adequate budget program can be developed without using cost-volume-profit techniques, these techniques can add to the understanding and usefulness of budget procedures and forecasts, as well as providing us with information for many types of managerial decisions.

This technique can be used, of course, with

EXHIBIT H Cost, Volume, Profit

A. BASIC INFORMATION. MUNCIE MANUFACTURING COMPANY BUDGETED INCOME STATEMENT YEAR ENDED DECEMBER 31, 1969

Sales		$100,000	100%
Variable costs to manufacture and sell			
Material-direct	$10,000		
Direct labor	25,000		
Indirect manufacturing expenses	15,000		
Selling and administrative expenses	10,000	60,000	
Contribution margin (P/V ratio)		$ 40,000	40%
Nonvariable (fixed costs)			
Indirect manufacturing expenses	$ 5,000		
Selling and administrative expenses	20,000	25,000	
Net income before taxes		$ 15,000	

B. BREAKEVEN CHART

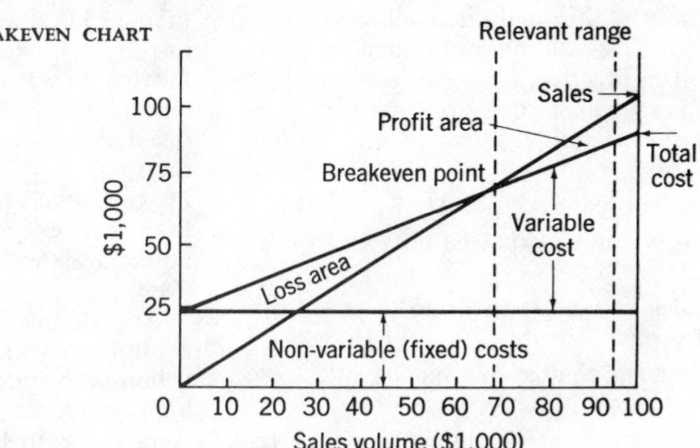

EXHIBIT H Schedule 1: Breakeven Computations

1. Breakeven formula:

$$\frac{\text{Nonvariable cost} \quad \text{Desired net income}}{\text{P/V ratio (contribution margin \%)}} = \text{B.E. sales in dollars}$$

2. Breakeven point for the Muncie Manufacturing Company (Exhibit I)

$$\frac{\$25,000}{.40} = \$62,500$$

3. What sales are required to make a net income of $11,000?

$$\frac{\$25,000 + \$11,000}{.40} = \$90,000 \text{ sales}$$

4. For our company, variable expenses increase to $80,000 (80%) due to rising material and increased wage rates. The nonvariable expenses remain the same. The P/V ratio is now 20%.

$$\text{B.E.} = \frac{\$25,000}{.20} = \$125,000$$

5. We plan a plant expansion which will increase production capacity 30% which will increase nonvariable costs to $60,000. The variable costs will not change, and, therefore, the P/V ratio remains at 40%.

$$\text{B.E.} = \frac{\$60,000}{.40} = \$150,000$$

6. Our sales manager requests an advertising campaign which will cost $3,000 per year. How much additional sales must be generated to cover this expenditure?

$$\text{Sales required} = \frac{\$3,000}{.40} = \$7,500$$

(Just a few of the applications for breakeven analysis).

historical data, but can make a greater contribution to management planning when used for future estimates based on the budget. The use of this technique depends upon the valid identification of cost variability with volume. That is the identification of cost as nonvariable and variable, which we have previously discussed.

In our discussion concerning cost-volume-profit analysis, we will take a simplified presentation of a complex subject and, it must be remembered that this concept must be used with care. It is a static representation of a dynamic set of data and its application is restricted by the assumption on which it is based. These assumptions are valid for limited periods of time and only within a limited relevant range of activity. Cost-volume-profit analysis has proven itself in practice.

What management questions can be answered by this technique? Just a few of these questions are:

1. What is the breakeven point?
2. What profit can be expected on a given sales volume?
3. What sales volume is required to produce a desired profit?
4. How would a change in capacity affect the profit potential?
5. What additional sales volume would be required to cover the increase in wages that the labor union is demanding?
6. What effect would a change in selling prices have on profits?

The profit of a business is dependent on three basic factors:

1. Selling price of the product
2. Cost of manufacturing and distributing the product
3. Volume of sales.

No one factor is independent of the others because cost determines the selling price to arrive at a desired rate of profit. The selling price affects the volume of sales, and the volume of sales directly influences the volume of production. The volume of production, in turn, influences the cost. The cost-volume-profit relationship is influenced by five factors, or a combination of them. They are:

1. Selling price
2. Volume of sales
3. Product mix
4. Variable cost per unit
5. Total fixed cost.

To permit effective profit planning, management must foresee the part that each of these factors plays, or will play, in changing the net income, the breakeven point, and the return on investment for the firm. To illustrate this technique, let us assume the following budget figures for our firm as shown on Exhibit H.

Management is interested in the sales volume to which the company breaks even; that is, the point at which sales revenue equals the cost to make and sell the product and no profit or loss is reported. Cost-volume-profit analysis lends itself to graphic representation on a breakeven chart, as shown in Exhibit H, part B. Sales volume is plotted along the X axis; cost and revenue related to this volume are plotted along the Y axis. The nonvariable line was drawn first, $25,000 at all volumes. The variable cost line was drawn next, starting at $25,000 and moving upward uniformly with volume at the rate of 60 percent of sales. Finally the sales revenue line was plotted. The intersection of the total cost line with the sales revenue line is the breakeven point. The wedge to the right of the breakeven point represents the profit potential; the wedge to the left represents losses.

An examination of this chart will reveal that a company with a high fixed cost and low contribution margin (P/V ratio) will have a very high breakeven point. The breakeven point of a company with low fixed costs and high contribution margin will be low. The company with the higher contribution margin has the higher profit potential. We can compute the breakeven point mathematically by using the following formula as shown on Exhibit H, Schedule 1. Also on this schedule is shown the answers to certain questions management might ask.

It can be seen where cost-volume-profit analysis can be developed with a reasonable degree of accuracy they can be of considerable value as a managerial tool. It is a technique that proves insight into the economic characteristic of a firm and can be used as we have seen to determine the approximate effect of various alternatives. Although the results we obtain from this analysis are not precise, it is a "slide rule" approach that can be used to develop and test, with a minimum of effort, the appropriate effect on costs and profits of several types of managerial decisions.

As we have reviewed variable budgets, the nature of cost-volume-profit relationships and breakeven analysis, we can see the usefulness of this type of data for profit planning, cost control, and decision making.

Direct costing is concerned with integrating and incorporating into the accounts a group of related techniques which include the variable budget, breakeven chart, and contribution margin analysis.

Under the conventional (absorption) costing, all factory costs are treated as product costs. Factory overhead which includes variable and fixed costs is applied to items produced. Income is not affected by fixed factory overhead until the products are sold.

The essential difference between direct costing and conventional costing relates to the treatment of fixed factory overhead. Under direct costing, fixed factory overhead costs are treated as period costs rather than product costs. They are written off during the period in which they are incurred.

Therefore, under direct costing, fixed factory overhead is excluded from inventories of work in process and finished goods. Under direct costing, all variable costs, including selling and manufacturing, are deducted from the selling price, resulting in the contribution margin toward fixed costs and profits.

Exhibit I presents a partial income statement comparing conventional (absorption) and direct costing. On the conventional income statement the Cost of Goods Sold is deducted from the Sales to obtain the Gross Profit. You will notice that all manufacturing expenses are deducted, which include the fixed and variable overhead. The inventory is costed out at the Total Manufacturing Cost which includes fixed overhead. In the direct costing statement all variable costs, which include manufacturing, selling, and administrative expenses, are deducted from the Sales to obtain the contribution margin. The inventory is costed out at the total variable manufacturing expenses.

Exhibit J gives a comparative effect on income and inventories under conventional and direct costing. The income statement under direct costing is rearranged to emphasize the contribution margin, that is, the excess of sales revenue over variable production, selling, and administrative costs. All the fixed costs are deducted in full as period costs. A study of these two costing methods shows that the income varies substantially under the two methods. What caused this difference? It is due to costing the inventories under conventional costing at their full factory cost of $70.00, while under direct costing, inventories are costs of $50.00.

Income will always be lower under direct costing when sales lag behind production and

EXHIBIT I Comparison of Conventional (Absorption) and Direct Costing: Partial Income Statements

CONVENTIONAL COSTING		
Selling Price (per unit)		$90
Factory cost		
Direct material	$13	
Direct labor	19	
Variable factory overhead	18	
Fixed factory overhead $400,000/20,000 units	20	
Cost to make		70
Gross profit before selling and admin. expenses		$20

DIRECT (VARIABLE) COSTING		
Selling price (per unit)		$90
Total variable costs		
Direct material	$13	
Direct labor	19	
Variable factory overhead	18	
Variable cost to manufacture	50	
Variable selling and admin. expenses	5	55
Total variable		
Contribution margin		$35

EXHIBIT J Comparative Effects on Income and Inventories under Conventional and Direct Costing

January activity data:		
Production (normal activity 20,000)	20,000	
Sales units	21,000	
Opening finished goods inventory (units)	3,000	
Closing finished goods inventory (units)	2,000	

CONVENTIONAL COSTING

Sales	21,000 at $90	$1,890,000
Cost of sales	21,000 at $70	1,470,000
Gross profit		420,000
Selling and administrative expenses		165,000
Net income		$ 255,000

DIRECT COSTING

Sales	21,000 at $90		$1,890,000
Variable costs			
Direct material	21,000 at 13	$273,000	
Direct labor	21,000 at 19	399,000	
Variable			
Factory 0/0	21,000 at 18	378,000	
Selling & admin.	21,000 at 5	105,000	
Total variable			1,155,000
Contribution margin			$ 735,000
Period (fixed) costs			
Fixed factory overhead		$400,000	
Fixed selling and admin.		60,000	460,000
Net income			$ 275,000

INVENTORY VALUATION

	Conventional	*Direct*
Opening inventory	$210,000	$ 150,000
Closing inventory	140,000	100,000

Reconciliation of difference in net income

Net income direct costing	$275,000
Net income conventional costing	255,000
Difference	$ 20,000

Difference between ending and beginning inventories (1,000) times fixed factory overhead unit cost $20. = $20,000.

the company has accumulated a large inventory at the end of the period than at the beginning of the period. Under direct costing, profits vary more directly with sales, while under conventional costing, profits are dependent on the level of production as well as sales.

Although direct costing has its shortcomings it is far better suited to the needs of management than conventional costing. Management requires a knowledge of cost behavior patterns under various operating conditions. Planning and control are more concerned with nonvariable and variable costs than with full costing under the conventional method. Under direct costing, the cost data needed for profit planning and decision making are readily available from the accounting records and statements. Cost-volume-profit relationships and the effect of changes in sales volume on net income can be readily computed from the direct costing income statement. Profits and losses reported under direct costing bear a relationship with sales revenue and are not affected by inventory or production variations. The full impact of nonvariable costs on net income is brought to the fore by the presentation of costs on an income statement prepared under direct costing.

Direct costing is preferred over conventional costing in analysis of relative profitability of products, territories, and other segments of a business. Direct costing concentrates on the conventional costing in analysis of relative profitability of products, territories, and other segments of a business. Direct costing concentrates on the contribution that each segment is making to the recovery of nonvariable costs which will not be altered by decisions to make and sell.

Direct costing provides valuable data for short term decision making—for in the short run period costs are not relevant. Direct cost data are also useful in capital investment and make or buy decisions which depend on direct cost data. A few examples of decision making which utilize the direct costing information are:

1. Selection among alternative uses of production facilities
2. Selling versus additional processing of manufactured items
3. Optimizing the production mix
4. Determining the inventory levels
5. Selective selling decisions.

I have briefly discussed the concept of direct costing and I do not want to get into the controversy between the adherents of conventional and direct costing. Simply stated, direct costing has its merits, and for internal reporting with its separation of nonvariable and variable costs, it is better adapted to managerial uses in profit planning and decision making. Direct costing should be judged solely on its merits.

73 WHAT PROGRAM BUDGETING IS AND IS NOT*

David Novick

During the 1960s the concept of program budgeting generated substantial interest, speculation, experimentation and literature in business and at all levels of government throughout the western world. With the widespread introduction of this new management idea that started in the middle of the decade, many and varied activities have been undertaken in its name. Most of them have included some or all of the major features of this new management system. However, some of the new proposals bear little resemblance to it other than the use of the words Program Budgeting as part of an argument for management changes that really are not at all program budgeting or the Planning-Programming-Budgeting System (PB, PPB or PPBS).

WHAT PROGRAM BUDGETING IS

Program Budgeting is a management system that has ten distinctive major features. These are:

1. Definition of the organization's objectives in as specific terms as is possible.
2. Determination of programs, including possible alternatives, to achieve the stated objectives.
3. Identification of major issues to be resolved in the formulation of objectives and/or the development of programs.
4. An annual cycle with appropriate subdivisions for the planning, programming and budgeting steps to ensure an ordered approach and to make appropriate amounts of time available for analysis and decision-making at all levels of management.
5. Continuous re-examination of program results in relationship to costs and anticipated outcomes to determine need for changes in stated programs and objectives as originally established.
6. Recognition of issues and other problems that require more time than is available in the annual cycle so that they can be explicitly identified and set apart from the current period for completion in two or more years as the subject matter and availability of personnel require.
7. Analysis of programs and their alternatives in terms of probable outcomes and both direct and indirect costs.
8. Development of analytical tools necessary for measuring costs and benefits.
9. Development each year of a multi-year program and financial plan with full recognition of the fact that in many areas resource allocations in the early years (e.g., years one through five) require projections of plans and programs and their resource demands for ten or more years into the future.
10. Adaptation of existing accounting and statistical reporting systems to provide inputs into planning and programming as well as continuing information on resources used in and actions taken to implement programs.

THE GENERAL APPROACH

To carry out the major objectives of program budgeting, three general areas of administrative and operational activities are involved. These are:

(1) The Program Format which identifies the organization's objectives, programs established to meet them, and the program elements through which the operations are carried out. This identification of the overall activity in program terms is sometimes referred to as the "format or structural phase" to distinguish it from the analytical and informational parts of the total which are described below.

* Reprinted by permission of the Rand Corporation and David Novick from *Program Budgeting 1970* by David Novick, pp. 1 to 19, a Rand Corporation-sponsored research study published in 1972. Mr. Novick is a member of the Research Council of the Rand Corporation and is generally credited as the originator of program budgeting as applied to government.

Program budgeting for an organization begins with an effort to identify and define objectives and to group the organization's activities into programs that can be related to each objective. This is the revolutionary aspect of this new management system since it requires groupings by end product or output rather than as in traditional budget practice by line items of input arranged in terms of administrative organizations or activities. The new method allows us to look at what we produce—output—in addition to *how* we produce or *what* inputs we consume.

The program budgeting summary document presents resources and costs categorized according to the program or end product to which they apply. This contrasts with traditional budgets that assemble costs by type of input—line item—and by organizational or activity categories. The point of this restructuring of budget information is that it aids the planning by focusing attention on competition for resources among programs and on the effectiveness of resource use within programs. The entire process by which objectives are identified, programs are defined and quantitatively described, and the budget is recast into a program budget format, is called the format or structural phase of Program Budgeting (PB) which also is frequently termed the Planning-Programming-Budgeting System (PPBS).[1]

One of the strengths of the program budgeting process is that it cuts across organizational boundaries, drawing together the information needed by decisionmakers without regard to divisions in operating authority among jurisdictions. Bringing everything together has its obvious advantages because a program can be examined as a whole, contradictions are more likely to be recognized, and a context is supplied for consideration of changes only made possible by cutting across existing agency line barriers.

An outstanding feature of program budgeting is the emphasis on analysis at all stages of activity. Although it is sometimes not recognized, the development of the appropriate format or structure in and of itself requires analysis. In fact, just examining an organization's objectives and identifying its programs and program elements in and of itself can constitute a major contribution to improvement of management in the organization even when the more complete analytical capability contemplated in the program budget is not fully developed.

One product of the structural phase is a conversion matrix or crosswalk from the budget in program terms to the traditional line-item, organization and activity budget. In program budgeting, organization gives way to program, and line-item detail is aggregated into summary figures more appropriate to decisionmaking.

For example, the wages and salaries figure for Environment Program in Fig. 1 is not only the sum of personnel service payments in the program elements which, constitute environment-oriented activities in water, air, land, pollution, etc., but also an aggregation of pieces of the wages and salaries data in each operating department whose activities contribute to environmental control. If Fig. 1 were not space-limited, the illustration would extend to include the contributions from other departments and supporting services like central electronic data processing. Detail is not the objective, however, and such activities are instead grouped into a general support program.

To aggregate the multitude of line items in the traditional budget or even its operating department summaries into their program element contributions or costs, allocations must be made and some of them may be rather arbitrary ones. The important features of the crosswalk are (1) to have the two documents balance no matter what the dimensions of the classifications, and (2) to ensure that decisionmakers and reviewing entities can identify next year's traditional budget in program terms and vice versa.

Through the crosswalk we also are able to translate existing methods of record keeping and reporting into data for program planning. It permits program decisions to be translated into methods already in use for directing, authorizing, controlling, recording and reporting operations. If the management methods now being used in any of these areas are inadequate or unsatisfactory, they should be upgraded and improved, whether or not the organization has a program budgeting system. In any case, the program budget must derive its information and relationships from existing management records and practices and must rely on them for the implementation of the programs.

(2) The second area of the general approach is Analysis. The program budgeting method of decisionmaking subsumes a systems analysis capability with which the resource and cost implications of program alternatives and their expected "outputs" or accomplishments may be estimated, ex-

[1] PPBS is the more common usage in the United States. In England, Australia, Canada and New Zealand and most other countries Programme Budgeting is favored. In France, it is "Rationalization des Choix Budgetaires" (RCB). Program Budgeting (PB) will be the preferred usage herein.

FIGURE 1 Crosswalk: Traditional Line-item Budget to New Program Budget

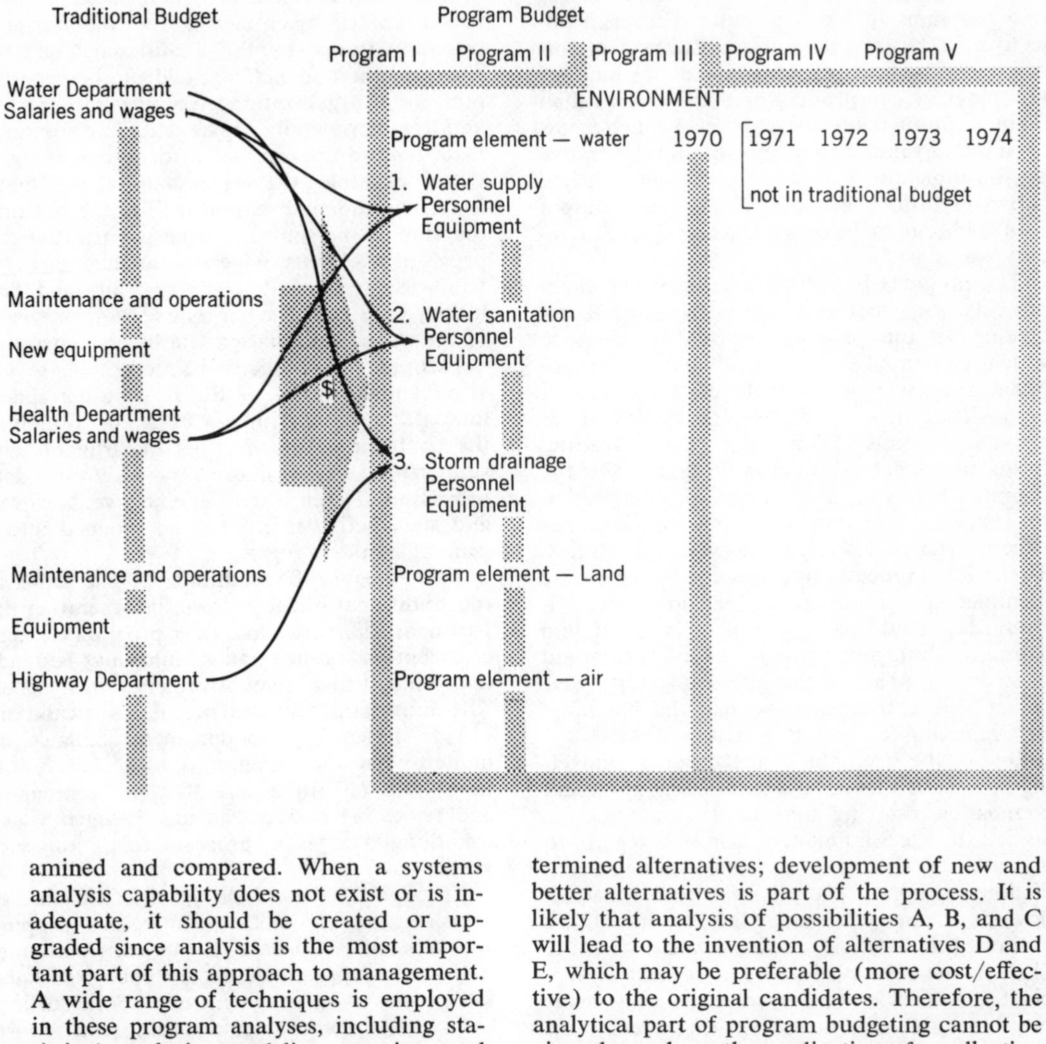

Traditional Budget
Water Department
Salaries and wages
Maintenance and operations
New equipment
Health Department
Salaries and wages
Maintenance and operations
Equipment
Highway Department
$
Program Budget
Program I
Program II
Program III
Program IV
Program V
ENVIRONMENT
Program element — water
1970
1971 1972 1973 1974
not in traditional budget
1. Water supply
Personnel
Equipment
2. Water sanitation
Personnel
Equipment
3. Storm drainage
Personnel
Equipment
Program element — Land
Program element — air

amined and compared. When a systems analysis capability does not exist or is inadequate, it should be created or upgraded since analysis is the most important part of this approach to management. A wide range of techniques is employed in these program analyses, including statistical analysis, modeling, gaming and simulation, operations analysis and econometric techniques. The analysis examines both the resource/cost side and the benefit/effectiveness side of program consequences.

Quantification is sought wherever possible but many of the effects or outcomes involved do not readily lend themselves to quantitative measurement. In these instances, qualitative analysis is required. In every case, whether the analysis is quantitative, qualitative, or an appropriate mixture of the two, there is explicit identification of the problem, the alternative ways of resolving it and an attempt to measure the cost and effectiveness of each possibility.

Program analysis is not confined to predetermined alternatives; development of new and better alternatives is part of the process. It is likely that analysis of possibilities A, B, and C will lead to the invention of alternatives D and E, which may be preferable (more cost/effective) to the original candidates. Therefore, the analytical part of program budgeting cannot be viewed merely as the application of a collection of well-defined analytical techniques to a problem. The process is much more flexible and subtle, and calls for creativity by the managers and the analysts and interaction between analysts and decisionmakers during the process.

(3) The third part of the program budgeting system deals with Information and Reporting. This covers identification through the accounting and related statistical reporting systems of information on all of the activities of the organization. This does not call for the creation of either new accounting or new statistical reporting systems. Instead, it means re-identification or structuring in the existing systems so that their product can be utilized in the plan-

ning and programming parts of the activity. When program determinations are made, the reporting requirement imposes on existing systems the need to provide continuing information (usually monthly and/or quarterly) on the use of resources and the operational steps taken in the implementation of the programs.[2]

Although the accounting and statistical reports of necessity are carried on in terms of actions in the current calendar, the reporting provision must require and provide specific identification of current activities in terms of impact in both the balance of the current year and the future years of the multi-year plan.

A brief summary that relates the areas of operation to the major features of program budgeting and to the kinds of documents the system produces may be useful at this point. This is sketched in Fig. 2.

REASONS FOR PROGRAM BUDGETING

The primary reason for program budgeting is that it provides a formal, systematic method to improve decisions concerning the allocation of resources. Obviously, these allocation problems arise because available resources usually are scarce in relation to demand. This leads to a need for making choices amongst demands in terms of: what to do, how much to do, and when to do it.

Program budgeting is designed to open up debate and put discussion on a new basis. It does this by requiring explicit identification of all actions—ongoing or new proposals—in terms of programs related to stated objectives. This enables the top decisionmakers to act in terms of the total organization rather than on the basis of ideas limited by individuals or operating units. The orientation of this new method is planning the future in both near-term and long-range aspects, and making decisions on what is to be done.

A second reason for program budgeting is that planning should be carried on with adequate recognition of both what is to be done and what it will cost. When an organization's plans call for more resources than it has or is likely to have available to it, then planning becomes a game not played for "keeps." When an organization is unable to carry the costs of its objectives, then it should revise its objectives or otherwise it will be wasting some of its substance. Resource considerations introduce realism into planning.

Since we should examine as many alternative plans as we have imagination to construct at the planning level, resource considerations should be in highly aggregated terms. We should use "in the ball park" estimates of costs to facilitate examining a large number of possibilities in a reasonably short period of time. In program budgeting the name of the game is "alternatives" and we seek the longest possible menu.

When we have selected the most promising plans from that menu, we analyze them in a less aggregative but still not completely detailed form. This is programming. Here activities are identified and feasibility is established in terms of capability, resource requirements, and timing of each one of the alternatives. The

[2] Complete enumeration on a periodic basis is not always required. For example, sample surveys might be used.

FIGURE 2 Sketch of Program Budgeting

MAJOR FEATURES	OPERATION AREAS	REPRESENTATIVE DOCUMENTS
Define objectives Determine programs Assign activities to programs Establish plan-program-budget cycle	Structural Aspect	Multi-year program and financial plan
Develop cost/benefit measurement methods Identify and evaluate alternatives Develop and apply criteria	Analytical Aspect	Program memoranda including alternatives Issue Analysis Special studies
Use existing reporting system Update programs	Data and Information Aspect	Accounting and statistical reports Program change proposals

selection is linked to a budget-like process because the final budget decisions determine the allocation of resources not only for next year but also in many cases make commitments for many years into the future.

To formulate a single program requires that we make decisions on feasibility, resource demands and timing. Even so, data used for programming are still not in the complete detail of next year's budget. The budget is an operating and financial plan and as such must be in great detail for inputs like personnel, supplies, equipment, etc., and assignment of such resources to administrative units. That kind of detail overwhelms and makes unmanageable a process designed for choosing between alternatives—even a limited number of them.

The third basic reason for program budgeting is to choose between available and feasible alternatives, which choice takes place at the conclusion of the programming. At that point we have illuminated the issues involved and the decisionmakers can exercise their judgment and experience in an appropriate and informed context. They can make the important decisions on "what to do" in the multiyear program and financial plan on the basis of program information that is not in the massive detail of next year's budget.

Given these decisions, the detail of operations and expenditures can then be laid out so that the final and less important budget decisions are on "how to do it." This is the point at which performance budgeting, management by objective, work measurement, and other methods of improving efficiency take over. In program budgeting the objective is annual allotments of funds that allow the next step to be taken along a path the general direction of which has been thoughtfully set by policymakers at all levels. Probably more important, the direction of the path and the distance to be covered in the next year will have been established after considering a number of possible futures for the entire government or business organization.

Program budgeting was not designed to increase efficiency in the performance of day-today tasks, nor was it designed to improve control over the expenditure of funds. It is instead a recognition of the fact that more money is wasted by doing the wrong thing efficiently than can be wasted by doing the right thing inefficiently. In short, the focus of the program budget is the decisionmaking process; that is, the determination of what to do, how much to do, and when to do, rather than deciding on how to carry on day-to-day operations, decisions which are best made by those who are closest to the activity.

WHAT PROGRAM BUDGETING IS NOT

In both government and business, responsibility for the work required to accomplish a coherent set of objectives is divided among a number of organizations. In government, for example, programs with objectives for health and education are each fragmented among a dozen bureaus and independent agencies and levels of government—in the United States; e.g., federal, state and local units. The activities of each one are sometimes complementary, sometimes contradictory, or in conflict with those of the others. As a result, there is no overall coordination of the resource allocations relevant to program objectives in, for example, health and education.

Since program budgeting cuts across organization and administrative lines, there are cases where this has been translated to mean that the activity is limited to the structural phase and resultant reorganization to fit the new identification of programs. This is not only an incomplete view of what is involved but also a most undesirable one.

It should be recognized, as indicated in No. 9 above, that this management concept calls for continuous re-examination of program results and for re-identifying and restructuring programs and objectives. Normally, this would be done on an annual basis. One can readily visualize the chaos that could result in administration and operations if organization changes were required for every change in program format.

The program budgeting system is not a reorganization plan nor does it seek or require changes in organization to fit the program structure.

In the same way, the information and reporting requirement of program budgeting, with its emphasis on accounting and recurring statistics, has sometimes been translated into the need for the development of a new accounting system or a major change in the existing one. As indicated in the just-preceding discussion of organization, programs can be expected to change or, at a minimum, be modified on a recurring basis. This makes it not only unnecessary but undesirable to change the accounting or the reporting systems to the currently identified program structure.[3]

The emphasis on maintaining existing accounting and reporting systems derives from the recognition of two major factors. First, temporary change is always undesirable and since programs and objectives are both continuously subject to change, molding them to

[3] This is especially true if sample surveys can be used.

fit the format developed at any one point in time provides only limited advantage and has all the disadvantages that will be encountered when they must be changed to fit the next development of the format. The second reason is that both the operators and decisionmakers are knowledgeable about the existing system and therefore will find it more comfortable to operate in a situation in which changes have been kept to a minimum and are of a kind that will be made essentially once and for all time.

Another reason for not making changes is that in providing information for the inputs into the planning and programming process, and in reporting on actions taken in the execution of programs, the emphasis on detail changes from that in traditional line-item budgets. As we move through the process from the lowest level of operation and decision up through the higher levels of executive decisionmaking, there is a steadily increasing need to present aggregated instead of detailed information. The important new development for accounting and statistical reporting is to ensure that, as we move up the ladder and aggregate the data, the units of record do not lose integrity through the continuing introduction of judgment or "fudge factors."

What is needed is an examination of both the accounting records and the basic records from which statistical reports are drawn to ensure that these can in fact be translated into the required inputs in planning, programming, and budgeting activities as well as in recording and reporting. This means an emphasis on units of account that are "pure"; that is, ones that can be carried upward in the accounting or statistical reporting system "as is" and do not require the introduction of adjustments when accumulated into more aggregative units of information.

Program budgeting is not a new accounting system nor does it require changes in the existing accounting and statistical reporting systems to fit the program structure.

Management Information Systems have also come into fashion. As a result, in many cases the development of program budgeting has been regarded as synonymous with the installation of a new computer system and the related techniques for making management data more readily available and nothing more. Although a good MIS is always desirable and can be used to very good advantage in the working of a program budgeting system, it should be obvious that the MIS may lack the planning emphasis on structure, and surely does not include the appropriate recognition of the development of programs, the analysis of alternatives, and the development of all of the related analytical activities and tools that are so important to the total concept of program budgeting.

Program budgeting is not a Management Information System even though a good MIS is very useful to its operations.

Although program budgeting, because of its emphasis on analysis, frequently calls for individuals with an analytical approach and/or training, the requirement for analysts does not mean that program budgeting requirements are met just by introducing elaborate new personnel recruiting, education or training efforts. For the most part, what is required is some redirection of existing personnel and the kind of education and training essential for this purpose. On the other hand, the program requirements will not be met just by the introduction of sweeping new personnel policies and activities.

The word "budget" in program budgeting—or the planning, programming, budgeting system—sometimes leads to the assumption that, if the title Program is introduced into the existing budget documents, the result is in fact a program budget. Obviously, the word "program" is available for anyone to use in any manner that he sees fit.

The emphasis on program in this new system is on output, or end-product measurement rather than on the inputs as they are emphasized in traditional budgetmaking. Therefore, whether the existing budget is the straight line-item type, performance oriented, or based on organization and function, adding the word program in selected places or in the title does not make them program budgets. Introducing the words "program" or "major program" into the groupings used in traditional budgets in no way accomplishes the purpose of program budgeting.

It is especially worth noting that program budgeting is not performance budgeting. Performance budgeting developed mainly in the 1930s and has had a major impact, particularly at the state and local government levels. It has also been used extensively in business. The performance budget is a way of choosing between a series of alternative ways of "how to do" a specific task. It does not provide for evaluation of the importance of the task in terms of either the total program or individual programs designed to meet a set of goals. In short, it is a way of choosing among alternative means available for doing a task rather than a way of determining whether the task should be performed at all or, if it is to be included, the amount of it that is required for a program.

Program budgeting recognizes the need for administrative and organizational budgets as well as performance budgeting and does not contemplate that these should be abandoned or relabelled. Instead, it requires that through the crosswalk they be used in conjunction with it.

The program budget has a time element that extends beyond the typical next-year's budget. The multi-year program and financial plan lays out not only next year's budget but also the budgets that would be required for future years on the basis of decisions already made when the final action is taken. In this sense, next-year's budget is an important first step in the operation of the multi-year program.

This does not mean making fundamental changes in existing budget practice. In the traditional line item, performance, or organization and function budget, there is a need for detailed identification by object or activity classes which requires more detail than is either necessary or possible to use as the program budget moves upward in the decision process. For this reason, the primary change is the addition of program budgeting to the ongoing annual budget process. This permits the development of the multi-year financial plan at a high level of aggregation from which a "crosswalk" can be made to the traditional line-item budget by object class.

SUMMING UP "WHAT IT IS" AND "WHAT IT IS NOT"

In short, program budgeting is characterized by an emphasis on objectives, programs, and program elements, all stated in output terms. Cost, or the line items of the traditional budget, is treated at an appropriate level of aggregation which ensures that plans and programs are developed with adequate recognition of their resource implications.

Analysis and the use of a large variety of analytical techniques are the backbone of this new system of management. It requires explicit identification of assumptions, the development and as complete treatment as time and personnel availability permit of all relevant options and alternative outcomes. It is in the process of analysis that we are forced to recognize the organization and operation line-cutting features of programs. In the same way, the analytic process forces translation of broad goals like better education, into operational terms like courses, students, teachers, libraries, etc. that identify both the purposes of the education process and the resources that can reasonably be made available for it. Analysis takes many forms and places substantial emphasis on the use of tools like computers and mathematical models. However, the computer and the model are simply part of the kit of tools for analysis rather than either the analytical process or the decision-making process.

Program budgeting also places a new emphasis on continuous reporting of both the accounting and statistical type, including ad hoc data collection methods when appropriate. This is for the purpose of providing inputs into the next planning and programming cycle as well as providing a measure of how the determinations on resources and programs are being carried out.

New organization charts, accounting systems, personnel recruitment and training systems, management information systems, or the generous use of the word program in traditional budgets are not program budgeting. Although all of these kinds of activities have been undertaken in the current vogue for program budgeting, from the foregoing they can easily be identified as not fitting into the context described above or promising the improvement in decisionmaking that is the primary goal of the program budgeting process.

74 HOW TO PLAN AND CONTROL WITH PERT*

R. W. Miller

The last three years have seen the explosive growth of a new family of planning and control techniques adapted to the Space Age. Much of the development work has been done in the defense industry but the construction, chemical, and other industries have played an important part in the story, too.

In this article we shall consider what is perhaps the best known of all of the new techniques, Program Evaluation Review Technique. In particular, we shall look at:

- PERT's basic requirements, such as the presentation of tasks, events, and activities on a network in sequential form with time estimates.
- Its advantages, including greatly improved control over complex development and production programs, and the capacity to distill large amounts of data in brief, orderly fashion.
- Its limitations, as in situations where there is little interconnection between the different activities pursued.
- Solutions for certain difficulties, e.g., the problem of relating time needed and job costs in the planning stage of a project.
- Policies that top management might do well to adopt, such as taking steps to train, experiment with, and put into effect the new controls.

LEADING FEATURES

The new techniques have several distinguishing characteristics:

1. They give management the ability to plan the best possible use of resources to achieve a given goal, within over-all time and cost limitations.
2. They enable executives to manage "one-of-a-kind" programs, as opposed to repetitive production situations. The importance of this kind of program in the national and world economy has become increasingly clear. Many observers have noted that the techniques of Frederick W. Taylor and Henry L. Gantt, introduced during the early part of the century for large-scale production operations, are inapplicable for a major share of the industrial effort of the 1960's—an era aptly characterized by Paul O. Gaddis as the "Age of Massive Engineering."[1]
3. They help management to handle the uncertainties involved in programs where no standard cost and time data of the Taylor-Gantt variety are available.
4. They utilize what is called "time network analysis" as a basic method of approach and as a foundation for determining manpower, material, and capital requirements.

CURRENT EFFORTS AND PROGRESS

A few examples may serve to indicate for top management the current status of the new techniques:

- The Special Projects Office of the U.S. Navy, concerned with performance trends in the execution of large military development programs, introduced PERT on its Polaris Weapon Systems in 1958. Since that time, PERT has spread rapidly throughout the U.S. defense and space industry. Currently, almost every major government and military

* Reprinted by permission from *Harvard Business Review*, vol. 40, no. 2, pp. 93–104, March-April, 1962; © 1962 by the President and Fellows of Harvard College; all rights reserved. Mr. Miller is Director of Management Science for the Raytheon Corporation.

[1] See "Thinking Ahead: The Age of Massive Engineering," *Harvard Business Review*, January–February, 1961, p. 138.

agency concerned with Space Age programs is utilizing the technique, as are large industrial contractors in the field. Small businesses wishing to participate in national defense programs will find it increasingly necessary to develop a PERT capability if they wish to be competitive in this field.

- At about the same time the Navy was developing PERT, the DuPont company, concerned with the increasing costs and time required to bring new products from research to production, initiated a study which resulted in a similar technique known as CPM (Critical Path Method). The use of the Critical Path Method has spread quite widely, and is particularly concentrated in the construction industry.
- A very considerable amount of research now is taking place on the "extensions" of PERT and CPM time-network analysis, into the areas of manpower, cost, and capital requirements. As an ultimate objective, "trade-off" relationships between time, cost, and product or equipment performance objectives are being sought. This research is being sponsored in two ways—directly by the military and privately by large companies. Anyone familiar with the current scene will be impressed by the amount of activity taking place in this field. For example, at least 40 different code names or acronyms representing variations of the new management controls have come to my attention.
- Applications of the new techniques, beyond the original engineering-oriented programs for which they were developed, are increasing every day. The PERT approach is usefully introduced in such diverse situations as planning the economy of an underdeveloped nation or establishing the sequence and timing of actions to effect a complex merger.

WHAT IS PERT?

Now let us turn to PERT in particular. What are its special characteristics and requirements?

The term is presently restricted to the area of time and, as promulgated by the Navy, has the following basic requirements:

1. All of the individual tasks to complete a given program must be visualized in a clear enough manner to be put down in a *network,* which is comprised of *events* and *activities.* An event represents a specified program accomplishment at a particular instant in time. An activity represents the time and resources which are necessary to progress from one event to the next. Emphasis is placed on defining events and activities with sufficient precision so that there is no difficulty in monitoring actual accomplishment as the program proceeds. Exhibit I shows a typical operating-level PERT network from the electronics industry.
2. Events and activities must be sequenced on the network under a highly logical set of ground rules which allow the determination of important critical and subcritical paths. These ground rules include the fact that no successor event can be considered completed until all of its predecessor events have been completed, and no "looping" is allowed, i.e., no successor event can have an activity dependency which leads back to a predecessor event.
3. Time estimates are made for each activity of the network on a three-way basis, i.e., optimistic, most likely, and pessimistic elapsed-time figures are estimated by the person or persons most familiar with the activity involved. The three time estimates are required as a gauge of the "measure of uncertainty" of the activity, and represent full recognition of the probabilistic nature of many of the tasks in development-oriented and nonstandard programs. It is important to note, however, that, for the purposes of computation and reporting, the three time estimates are reduced to a single expected time (t_e) and a statistical variance (σ^2).
4. Depending on the size and complexity of the network, computer routines are available to calculate the critical path through it. Computers can also calculate the amount of slack (viz., extra time available) for all events and activities not on the critical path. A negative slack condition can prevail when a calculated end date does not achieve a program date objective which has been established on a prior—and often arbitrary—basis.

Time Estimates Interpretation of the concepts of optimistic, most likely, and pessimistic elapsed times has varied over the past few years. The definitions which, in my opinion, represent a useful consensus are as follows:

- *Optimistic*—An estimate of the *minimum* time an activity will take, a result which can be obtained only if unusual good luck is experienced and everything "goes right the first time."

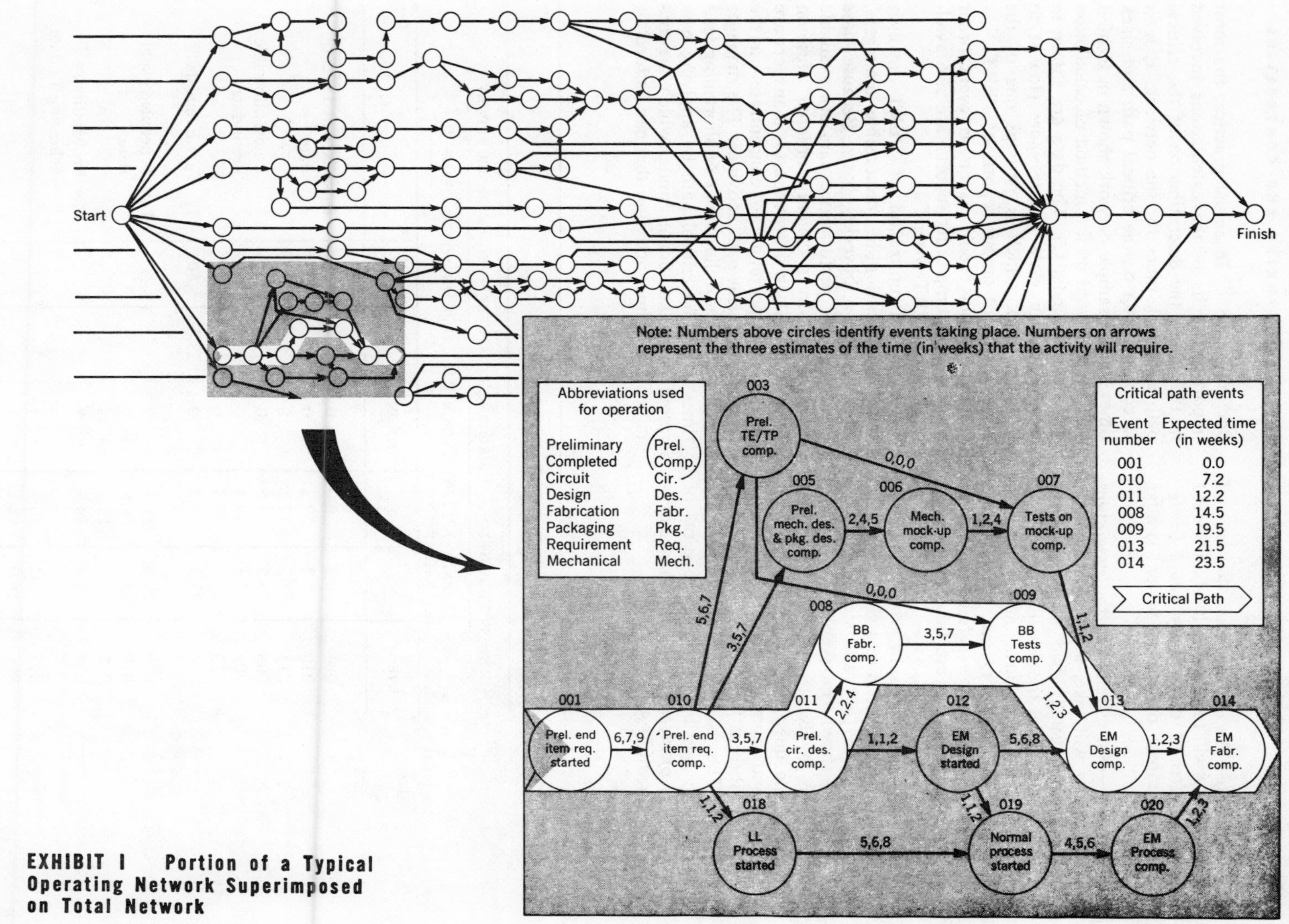

EXHIBIT I   Portion of a Typical Operating Network Superimposed on Total Network

• *Most likely*—An estimate of the *normal* time an activity will take, a result which would occur most often if the activity could be repeated a number of times under similar circumstances.

• *Pessimistic*—An estimate of the *maximum* time an activity will take, a result which can occur only if unusually bad luck is experienced. It should reflect the possibility of initial failure and fresh start, but should not be influenced by such factors as "catastrophic events"—strikes, fires, power failures, and so on—unless these hazards are inherent risks in the activity.

The averaging formulas by which the three time estimates are reduced to a single expected time (t_e), variance (σ^2) and standard deviation (σ) are shown in Appendix A. The approximations involved in these formulas are subject to some question, but they have been widely used and seem appropriate enough in view of the inherent lack of precision of estimating data. The variance data for an entire network make possible the determination of the *probability of meeting an established schedule date,* as shown in Appendix B.

Critical Path In actual practice, the most important results of the calculations involved in PERT are the determination of the critical path and slack times for the network. Exhibit II contains data on the critical path and slack times for the sample network shown in Exhibit I (they are based on the method of calculation given in Appendix C). The data are shown in the form of a *slack order report* (lowest to highest slack), which is perhaps one of the most important output reports of PERT.

Other output reports, such as event order and calendar time order reports, are also available in the PERT system.

The actual utilization of PERT involves review and action by responsible managers, generally on a biweekly basis. Because time prediction and performance data are available from PERT in a "highly ordered" fashion (such as the slack order report), managers are given the opportunity to concentrate on the important critical path activities. The manager must determine valid means of shortening lead times along the critical path by applying new resources or additional funds, which are obtained from those activities that can "afford" it

EXHIBIT II Slack Order Report

PERT SYSTEM AIRBORNE COMPUTER — SLACK ORDER REPORT

DATE 7/12/61 WEEK 0.0 TIME IN WEEKS PAGE 1

EVENT	T_E	T_L	$T_L - T_E$	T_S	P_r	
001	0.0	0.0	0			T_E = Expected event date
010	7.2	7.2	0			
011	12.2	12.2	0			
008	14.5	14.5	0			T_L = Latest allowable event date
009	19.5	19.5	0			
013	21.5	21.5	0			
014	23.5	23.5	0	23.5	.50	$T_L - T_E$ = Event slack
020	20.6	21.5	+ .9			T_S = Scheduled event date
019	15.6	16.5	+ .9			
012	14.4	15.3	+ .9			
018	9.4	10.3	+ .9			P_r = Probability of achieving T_S date
007	18.2	20.3	+2.1			
006	16.0	18.1	+2.1			
005	13.2	14.3	+2.1			
003	14.2	19.5	+5.3			

because of their slack condition. Alternatively, he can re-evaluate the sequencing of activities along the critical path. If necessary, those activities which were formerly connected in a series can be organized on a parallel or concurrent basis, with the associated tradeoff risks involved. As a final, if rarely used, alternative, the manager may choose to change the scope of work of critical path activities in order to achieve a given schedule objective.

It should be pointed out that the PERT system requires constant updating and reanalysis; that is, the manager must recognize that the outlook for the completion of activities in a complex program is in a constant state of flux, and he must be continually concerned with problems of re-evaluation and reprograming. A highly systematized method of handling this aspect of PERT has been developed. An example of the input transaction document involved is given in Exhibit III.

BENEFITS GAINED

Perhaps the major advantage of PERT is that the kind of planning required to create a valid network represents a major contribution to the definition and ultimate successful control of a complex program. It may surprise some that network development and critical path analysis do, in fact, reveal interdependencies and problem areas which are either not obvious or not well defined by conventional planning methods. The creation of the network is a fairly demanding task, and is a sure-fire indicator of an organization's ability to visualize the number, kind, and sequence of activities needed to execute a complex program.

Another advantage of PERT, especially where there is a significant amount of uncertainty, is the three-way estimate. While introducing a complicating feature, this characteristic does give recognition to those realities of life which cause difficulties in most efforts at planning the future. The three-way estimate should result in a greater degree of honesty and accuracy in time forecasting; and, as a minimum, it allows the decision maker a better opportunity to evaluate the degree of uncertainty involved in a schedule—particularly along the critical path. If he is statistically sophisticated, he may even wish to examine the standard deviation and probability of accomplishment data, which were mentioned previously as features of PERT. (If there is a minimum of uncertainty in the minds of personnel estimating individual activity times, the single-time approach may, of course, be used, while retaining all the advantages of network analysis.)

And, finally, the common language feature of PERT allows a large amount of data to be presented in a highly ordered fashion. It can be said that PERT represents the advent of the management-by-exception principle in an area of planning and control where this principle had not existed with any real degree of validity. An additional benefit of the common language feature of PERT is the fact that many individuals in different locations or organizations can easily determine the specific relationship of their efforts to the total task requirements of a large program.

This particular benefit of PERT can represent a significant gain in the modern world of large-scale undertakings and complex organizational relationships.

COPING WITH PROBLEMS

A new and important development like PERT naturally is attended by a certain amount of confusion and doubt. PERT does indeed have its problems. However, they are not always what businessmen think they are, and often there is an effective way of coping with the restrictions. In any event, it is time to compare the situations in which PERT works best with situations in which real (or imagined) troubles occur.

Uncertain Estimates One key question concerns the unknowns of time and resources that management frequently must contend with.

In PERT methodology an available set of resources including manpower and facilities is either known or must be assumed when making the time estimates. For example, it is good practice to make special notations directly on the network when some special condition (e.g., a 48-hour rather than a 40-hour week) is assumed. Experience has shown that when a well-thought-through network is developed in sufficient detail, the first activity time estimates made are as accurate as any, and these should not be changed unless a new application of resources or a trade-off in goals is specifically determined. A further caution is that the first time estimates should not be biased by some arbitrarily established schedule objective, or by the assumption that a particular activity does not appear to be on a critical path. Schedule biasing of this kind, while it obviously cannot be prevented, clearly atrophies some of the main benefits of the technique—although it is

EXHIBIT III Input Transaction Document

PERT
REPORT OF TIME INTERVAL
ESTIMATES & PROGRESS

CLASSIFICATION:

REVISION NO. 2
13 FEBRUARY 1959

FROM: (NAME & LOCATION OF CONTRACTOR)

TO:

FLOW CHART NO.

CONTRACT NO.

REPORT PERIOD
FROM:
TO:

FOR OFFICE USE ONLY (A)			ACTIVITY IDENTIFICATION		TIME INTERVAL ESTIMATES			COMPLETION DATE	REMARKS
			BEGINNING EVENT NO.	ENDING EVENT NO.	OPTI-MISTIC (WEEKS) *	MOST LIKELY (WEEKS) *	PESSI-MISTIC (WEEKS) *		
(1)	(2) (3)	(4)	(B)	(C)	(D)	(E)	(F)	(G)	(H)
12	13 — 16	17	18 — 26	34 — 42	44 — 47	48 — 51	52 — 55	60 — 65 MO. DAY YR.	
1			010	003	5.0	6.0	7.0	— — —	New Activity
1			003	007	0	0	0	— — —	New Activity
1									
2			010	018	2.0	1.0	1.0	— — —	Re-estimated Activity (Change)
2			018	019	5.0	6.0	8.0	— — —	Re-estimated Activity (Change)

SIGNATURE OF RESPONSIBLE OFFICIAL:

DATE SIGNED:

CLASSIFICATION:

* Columns D, E, and F. These estimates should be given for the full activity even though the activity has already started.

more quickly "discovered" with PERT than with any other method.

Because of the necessity for assumptions on manpower and resources, it is easiest to apply PERT in *project-structured* organizations, where the level of resources and available facilities are known to the estimator. PERT does not itself *explicitly* resolve the problem of multiprogram planning and control. But there is general recognition of this problem, and considerable effort is being devoted to a more complete approach to it. Meanwhile, in the case of common resource centers, it is generally necessary to undertake a loading analysis, making priority assumptions and using the resulting data on either a three-time or single-time basis for those portions of the network which are affected. It should be pointed out, however, that in terms of actual experience with PERT, the process of network development forces more problems of resource constraint or loading analysis into the open for resolution than do other planning methods.

Although PERT has been characterized as a new management control approach for R & D effort, it has perhaps been most usefully applied in those situations where there is a great deal of interconnection betweeen the activities of a network, or where there are interface connections between different networks. Certainly, network development and critical path analysis are *not* too appropriate for the pure research project, where the capabilities of small numbers of individuals with highly specialized talents are being utilized at a "constant rate" and where their activities have no significant dependence on other elements of the organization.

Justifying the Cost One of the most frequently raised objections to PERT is the cost of its implementation. A fundamental point to examine here is whether or not a currently established planning system is giving value commensurate with its cost—or perhaps more basic still, whether the system is used at all effectively to pinpoint and control problem areas. It is quite true that, by the very nature of its logical requirements for networking, the PERT approach calls for a higher degree of planning skill and a greater amount of detail than is the case with conventional methods. In addition, the degree of detail—or the "level of indenture," as it is called—is a function of:

1. What is meaningful to the person or persons who will actually execute the work.
2. The depth of analysis that is required to determine the valid critical path or paths.

It is perhaps more appropriate to view the implementation of PERT as costing *initially* something in the order of twice that of a conventional planning system. This figure will vary significantly with such factors as:

- The degree of planning capability already available.
- The present effectiveness and homogeneity of the organization.
- The amount and quality of PERT indoctrination given.

The advocates of PERT are quick to point out that the savings achieved through better utilization of resources far outweigh the system's initial implementation costs. This better utilization of resources is achieved through concentration on critical path activities—for example, limiting overtime effort to these key activities as opposed to across-the-board use of overtime. Even more important are the "downstream" savings which are achieved by earlier and more positive action on the part of management to resolve critical problems.

Use of Standard Networks Because of the considerable impact of PERT on many organizations where detailed planning has not had major emphasis, a trend has recently developed which can be characterized as "model or standard networking." This has to do with efforts to use the typical or established pattern of carrying out a new program in a particular industry. Model networking has many advantages (particularly in handling the large amounts of data involved in PERT), but it may also compromise one of the real objectives of PERT—i.e., *obtaining a valid network which is meaningful to the person or persons who will actually execute the work*. In the area in which PERT is used most effectively no two programs are ever exactly the same, and no two individuals will have exactly the same approach to the development of a network. Therefore, model networks should be introduced with this caution: management should always allow for the possibility of modifications which will match the realities of the program.

In addition, the introduction of so-called "master plan networks" and the top-down structuring of networks for large programs involving many different firms, while very necessary from the point of view of long-range planning and the ultimate management of such programs, should be handled with a philosophy of flexibility. The cardinal principle is that a management control structure is no better than the adequacy and accuracy of the data at its base. In the future, the top-down structuring approach—which is already evident on some major defense and space programs—will probably increase; but internal objectives, at least, will be subject to reconfirmation or realignment at the level of industry, depending upon the development of actual operating networks. The top-down structuring approach is necessary, however, in order to preserve the mechanics of *network integration;* it is important that the data from lower level networks be properly and meaningfully summarized into higher level management data.

Application to Production A final problem, and one that is often viewed as a disadvantage of the PERT technique, is the system's lack of applicability to all of the manufacturing effort. As has been stated, PERT deals in the time domain only and does not contain the quantity information required by most manufacturing operations. Nevertheless, PERT can be, and has been, used very effectively through the preliminary manufacturing phases of production prototype or pilot model construction, and in the assembly and test of final production equipments which are still "high on the learning curve." After these phases, established production control techniques which bring in the quantity factor are generally more applicable.

Note, however, that many programs of the Space Age never leave the preliminary manufacturing stage, or at least never enter into mass production. Therefore, a considerable effort is going forward at this time to integrate the techniques of PERT within some of the established methods of production control, such as line-of-balance or similar techniques that bring in the quantity factor.

Computer or No Computer As a result of the Navy's successful application of PERT on the Polaris program, and other similar applications, there is a common impression that the technique is only applicable when large-scale data-processing equipment is available. This is certainly true for large networks, or aggregations of networks, where critical path and slack computations are involved for several hundred or more events. It is as desirable to have a computer handle a PERT problem when a large volume of data is involved as it is to use a computer in any extensive data-processing assignment.

Probably equally significant is the fact that several ingenious manual methods have been developed in industry by those organizations which have become convinced of PERT's usefulness. These manual methods range from simple inspection on small networks to more organized but clerically oriented routines for determination of critical path, subcritical path, and slack times on networks ranging from fifty to several hundred events.

This is sufficient proof that PERT can be applied successfully to smaller programs wherever the degree of interconnection and problems of uncertainty warrant it. For those organizations practiced in the technique, both the creation of small networks and the formation of time estimates and their reduction to critical path and slack analyses can be done in a matter of hours. Exhibit I shows the network for a relatively small electronics program. Developed in less than a day, the whole network required only two hours for manual computation.

It seems clear that the small business organization which wishes to participate in national defense and space programs, or to improve its own internal schedule planning and control, should not hesitate to adopt PERT merely because it does not possess large-scale data-processing equipment.

PERT Extensions Variations of PERT to accommodate multi-project and manufacturing situations have already been mentioned, and these are merely representative of a basic movement to *extend* the approach into the areas of manpower, cost, and the equipment performance variable. The ultimate objective of these efforts is to quantify the trade-off relationships which constantly come up in development programs but are rarely acted on with explicit data in hand.

Though none of these extensions have as yet attained as much maturity and acceptance as PERT, anyone familiar with the current scene will be impressed by the amount of effort being given to them throughout the country in both the military and industry. One healthy offset to this particular trend is the fact that the U.S. Air Force has withdrawn its code name PEP (Program Evaluation Procedure), which was an equivalent for PERT. There remains, however, a great need for government agencies to standardize input and output requirements of basic PERT time before uniformly effective extensions can be made into the area of PERT cost.

COST OF PERT

Much of the research effort on the new management controls which has taken place throughout the country is concentrated on the problem of manpower and cost. This is probably a reflection of certain facts well known to most managers of complex development programs:

- The job-costing structures generally found in industry on such programs need a great deal of interpretation to relate *actual costs* to *actual progress*. They are rarely, if ever, related in any explicit manner to the details of the scheduling plan.
- Cost constraints, either in the form of manpower shortages or funding restrictions, have a great deal to do with the success with which a program of this type can be managed.

It seems clear that both of these problems must be solved in any valid PERT cost approach.

Solutions Required The first problem means that an explicit relationship must be established between the time network and the job-cost structure, either on a one-to-one basis for each network activity, or for a designated chain of activities. As a minimum, it seems clear that more detailed job-cost structures are required than are currently in general use, although this requirement should present no serious limitation for organizations which possess modern data-processing methods and equipment.

With regard to the development of actual cost figures *from the time network*, an estimate of manpower requirements, segregated by classification, is usually considered the easiest place to start, since these requirements were presumably known at the time the network was established. In fact, however, the actual summation of such data often reveals a manpower or funding restriction problem, and forces a replanning cycle if no alternatives are available. (The summation may also reveal inefficiencies in personnel loading which can be removed by proper use of slack activities.)

Two other problems that should be mentioned are:

• *Handling of nonlabor items*—The costs for these items are often aggregated in a manner quite different from that which would result from analysis of a time network. For example, there is a tendency to buy common materials on one purchase order for a number of different prototypes, each one of which represents a distinct phase of progress in the program. A refined allocation procedure may be needed to handle this problem.

• *Coordination and control efforts* (e.g., those carried out by project or systems engineering[2])—These are often not indicated on time networks unless they result in specific outputs. For PERT costing, the network in all cases must be complete, i.e., it must include all effort which is charged to the program. This is one of the areas of deficiency in many present-day networks, and one which must be overcome before an effective PERT cost application can be made.

Each of the foregoing problems can be handled if the underlying network analysis is sound and subject to a minimum of change. As a result, a number of different approaches are being attempted in the development of costed networks which have as their objective, the association of at least one cost estimate with a known activity or chain of activities on the network.

The ultimate objective of all this is not only improvement in planning and control, but also the opportunity to assess possibilities for "trading off" time and cost, i.e., adding or subtracting from one at the expense of the other. It is generally assumed that the fundamental relationships between time and cost are as portrayed in Exhibit IV. Curve A represents *total direct costs* versus time, and the "U" shape of the curve results from the assumption that there is an "optimum" time-cost point for any activity or job. It is assumed that total costs will increase with any effort to accelerate or delay the job away from this point.

Some companies in the construction industry are already using such a time-cost relationship, although in a rather specialized manner:

> In one application, an assumption is made that there is a *normal* job time (which might or might not coincide with the theoretical optimum), and that from this normal time, costs increase linearly to a *crash* time, as indicated in Exhibit IV. This crash time represents the maximum acceleration the job can stand. On the basis of these assumptions, a complete mathematical approach and computer program have been developed which show how to accelerate progress on a job as much as possible for the lowest possible cost. The process involves shortening the critical path or paths by operating on those activities which have the lowest time-cost slopes.

Challenge of Cost Data Making time-cost data available for each activity in usable form is one of the fundamental problems in using

[2] See Clinton J. Chamberlain, "Coming Era in Engineering Management," *Harvard Business Review*, September–October, 1961, p. 87.

EXHIBIT IV Assumed Time-Cost Relationships for a Job

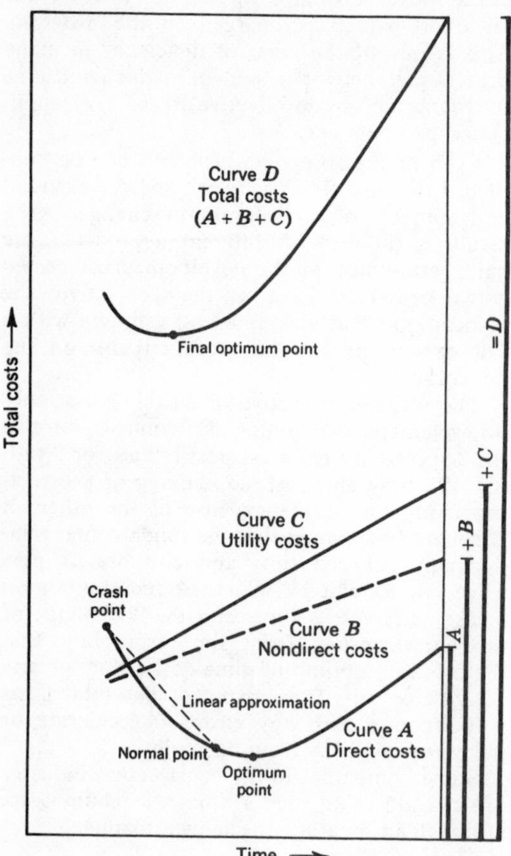

PERT in development programs. At the planning stage, in particular, it is often difficult to determine time-cost relationships in an explicit manner, either for individual activities or for aggregates of activities. (There are often good arguments for characterizing time-cost relationships at this stage as nonlinear, flat, decreasing, or, more likely, as a range of cost possibilities.) If alternative equipment or program objectives are added as a variable, the problem is further compounded. While posing the problem, it should be pointed out that solutions for the technical handling of such data, in whatever form they are obtained, have recently been developed.

Curve B of Exhibit IV indicates *total non-direct costs,* which are assumed to increase linearly with time. Clearly, accounting practices will have to be reviewed to provide careful (and probably new) segregations of direct from non-direct costs for use in making valid time-cost trade-off evaluations.

Curve C is a representation of a *utility cost curve,* which is needed to complete the picture for *total time-cost* optimization (indicated as the final optimum point on Curve D). The utility cost curve represents a quantification of the penalty for *not accomplishing the job at the earliest possible time,* and is also shown as a linear function increasing with time.

The difficulties of determining such a curve for many programs, either in terms of its shape or dollar value, should be obvious. But it is significant to note that in certain industrial applications such utility cost data have already been developed, typically in the form of "outage" costs or loss-of-profit opportunities, and used as the basis for improved decision making. Further, in the military area, utility cost is the converse of the *benefit* concept in the *benefit-cost* ratio of a weapon system; this factor varies with the time of availability of a weapon system, even though judgments of benefit are made difficult by rapidly changing circumstances in the external world.

CONCLUSION

It is clear that there are difficulties yet to be overcome in advancing the new management controls—particularly in the new areas into which PERT is being extended. Yet it is equally clear that significant progress has been made during the last few years. Assuming that developments continue at the rate at which they have taken place up to this time, what position should top management adopt *today* with regard to its own internal policies on the new management controls? Here are the most important steps:

1. Management should review its present planning and scheduling methods and compare their effectiveness with that of the PERT system. (I refer here to time networks only —not time-and-cost networks.) If the company has no direct experience with PERT, it will certainly want to consider training and experimentation programs to acquaint the organization with the technique. Management may even decide to install PERT on all of its development programs (as some companies have done), even though it has no contractual requirement to do so.

2. Management may wish to enter directly into research efforts on the new management controls or, if such efforts are already underway in the organization, place them on a higher priority basis. As a minimum, it will probably want to assign someone in the

organization to follow the numerous developments that are taking place in the field.

3. Executives should consider carefully the problem of organization to make the most effective use of the new management controls. They should consider the responsibilities of the level of management that actually uses PERT data in its working form, and the responsibilities of the levels of management that review PERT in its various summary forms. Clearly, the usefulness of the new management controls is no greater than the ability of management actually to act on the information revealed. It should be realized that problems of "recentralization" will probably accompany the advent of the new tools, particularly when applied to the planning and control of large projects throughout an entire organization.
4. Finally, management may wish to assess the longer range implications of the new management controls, both for itself and for the entire industrial community, since the forces calling for centralization of planning and control within the firm can apply equally well outside it. In the Age of Massive Engineering, the new controls will be utilized to an increasing extent in the nation's defense and space programs, which are in turn increasing in size and complexity. It seems clear that the inevitably closer relationships between government and industry will require the establishment of new guidelines for procurement and incentive contracting where these management control techniques are used.

APPENDIXES

Readers interested in applying PERT may find it helpful to have a more precise formulation of certain calculations mentioned earlier in this article. The mathematics involved is basically simple, as the following material demonstrates.

Appendix A. Expected Time Estimate In analyzing the three time estimates, it is clear that the optimistic and the pessimistic time should occur least often, and that the most likely time should occur most often. Thus, it is assumed that the most likely time represents the peak or modal value of a probability distribution; however, it can move between the two extremes. These characteristics are best described by the Beta distribution, which is shown in two different conditions in the figures that follow.

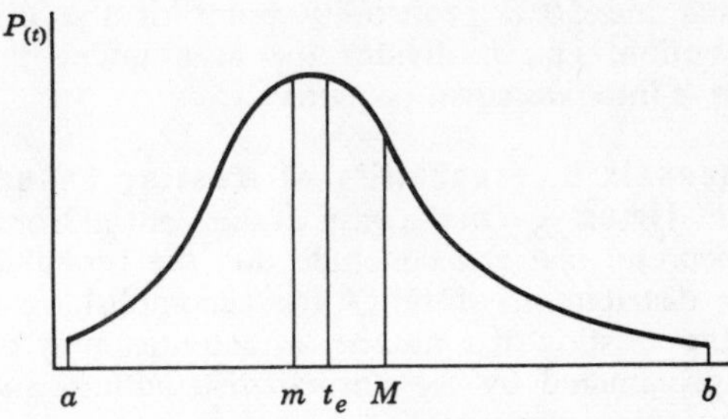

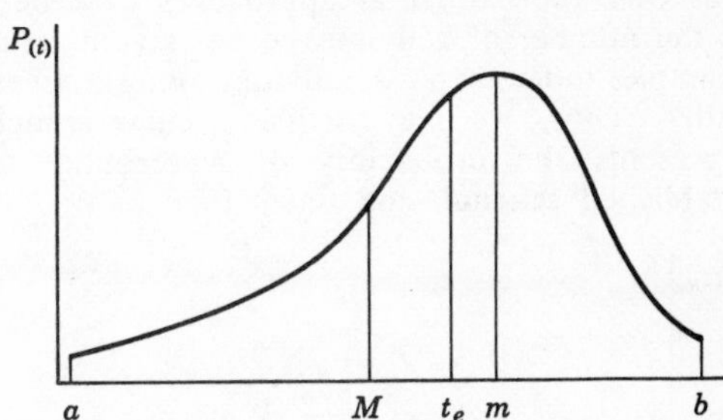

where:

$$a = \text{optimistic time}$$
$$m = \text{most likely time}$$
$$b = \text{pessimistic time}$$
$$M = \text{mid-range}\left(\frac{a+b}{2}\right)$$
$$t_e = \text{expected time}$$

As a result of analyzing the characteristics of the Beta* distribution, the final approximations to expected time (t_e), variance (σ^2), and standard deviation (σ) were written as follows for a given activity:

$$1. \quad t_e = \frac{1}{3}(2m + M) = \frac{1}{3}\left(2m + \frac{a+b}{2}\right) = \frac{a + 4m + b}{6}$$

$$2. \quad \sigma^2 = \left(\frac{b-a}{6}\right)^2$$

$$3. \quad \sigma = \frac{b-a}{6}$$

The first equation indicates that t_e should be interpreted as the weighted mean of m (most likely) and M (mid-range) estimates, with weights of 2 and 1, respectively. In other words, t_e is located one third of the way from the modal to the mid-range values, and repre-

* Note: The Beta distribution is analyzed in the PERT Summary Report, Special Projects Office, Department of the Navy, Washington, D.C., Phase I, July, 1958.

sents the 50% probability point of the distribution, i.e., it divides the area under the curve into two equal portions.

Appendix B. Probability of Meeting Schedule Times On the basis of the Central Limit Theorem, one can conclude that the probability distribution of times for accomplishing a job consisting of a number of activities may be approximated by the normal distribution, and that this approximation approaches exactness as the number of activities becomes great (for example, more than 10 activities along a given path). Thus, we may define a curve which represents the probability of a meeting on established schedule-end date, T_S:

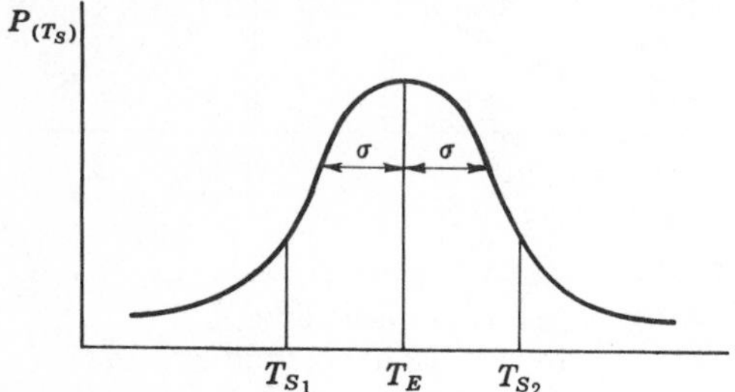

where:

$$T_E = \Sigma t_{e_1} + t_{e_2} + \cdots t_{e_n}$$
$$\sigma^2(T_E) = \Sigma\sigma^2(t_{e_1}) + \sigma^2(t_{e_2}) + \cdots \sigma^2(t_{e_n})$$
T_{S_1} = Scheduled Time (earlier than T_E)
T_{S_2} = Scheduled Time (later than T_E)

The probability of meeting the T_S date when given T_E and σ^2 for a chain of activities is defined as the ratio of (1) the area under the curve to the left of T_S to (2) the area under the entire curve. The difference between T_S and T_E, expressed in units of σ, is:

$$\frac{T_S - T_E}{\sigma}$$

This will yield a value for the probability of accomplishing T_S by use of the normal probability distribution table. Thus:

$$\frac{T_{S_1} - T_E}{\sigma} = -1.2\sigma,\ P_r\ (\text{accomplishment of } T_{S_1}) = .12$$

$$\frac{T_{S_2} - T_E}{\sigma} = +1.2\sigma,\ P_r\ (\text{accomplishment of } T_{S_2}) = .88$$

Appendix C. Determining Critical Path and Slack Times The computation steps required to determine the critical path and slack times for the network shown in Exhibit I are as follows:

Step 1. Determine t_e for every activity on the network in accordance with the equation:

$$t_e = \frac{a + 4m + b}{6}$$

Step 2. Starting with Event No. 001, determine T_E (or cumulative T_E) for all succeeding events by summing small t_e's for each activity leading up to the event, *but choosing the largest value for the final T_E figure in those cases where there is more than one activity leading into an event.* For example, Exhibit I indicates three activities leading into Event No. 013 (EM design complete). The three preceding events are No. 007 (test on mock-up complete), No. 009 (breadboard tests complete), and No. 012 (EM design started). The cumulative T_E figures for these three preceding events, as can be seen from Exhibit II, are 18.2 weeks for Event No. 007, 19.5 weeks for Event No. 009, and 14.4 weeks for Event No. 012. Now, add the respective activity times between these three events and Event No. 013 and examine the results:

EVENT NO.	T_E	ACTIVITY TIME T_E TO EVENT NO. 013	TOTAL WEEKS
007	18.2	1.2	19.4
009	19.5	2.0	21.5
012	14.4	6.2	20.6

The largest figure, which represents the longest path or earliest time at which Event No. 013 can be completed, is 21.5 weeks, and this path leads through Event No. 009. As will be noted from Exhibit I, Event Nos. 009 and 013 are on the critical path, since the T_E values of all other paths leading into final Event No. 014 are smaller.

Step 3. Having determined the critical path through the network of Exhibit I to be 23.5 weeks, we can now set the final date of Event No. 014 at 23.5 weeks, or we can use some arbitrary scheduled time. The process covered in Step 2 is now reversed. Starting with the final event, we determine the *latest allowable time*, T_L, for each event so as not to affect critical path event times. For example, Event No. 007, with a T_E of 18.2 weeks, can be delayed up to a T_L of 20.3 weeks, before it will affect critical path Event No. 013.

Step 4. The difference between T_L and T_E, known as slack, is next computed for each event. These computations are shown in Exhibit II in the form of a slack order report, i.e., in order of lowest to highest values of *positive* slack. Note that along the critical path there is zero slack at every event, since by definition there is no possibility of slippage along the critical path without affecting the final event date. In this example, if the end schedule date of Event No. 014 were set at 23.0 weeks rather than at 23.5 weeks, there would be 0.5 weeks of negative *slack* indicated for every event along the critical path.

Step 5. The computation of variance and of standard deviation for this network is optional and involves adding the variances for each activity along the critical path, which are obtained from the formula:

$$\sigma^2 = \left(\frac{b - a}{6}\right)^2$$

The interested reader may verify that the variance for final Event No. 014, with a T_E of 23.5 weeks, is 1.46 weeks.

75 PERT COST: ITS VALUES AND LIMITATIONS*

Peter P. Schoderbeck

PERT, network diagraming, critical path scheduling, and similar planning and control techniques have proved highly useful in the scheduling and controlling of the time elements of large projects. Only recently, however, has a system been evolved to integrate both time and cost on a common framework.

The PERT/Cost system was developed in 1962[1] for the specific purpose of integrating time data with the associated financial data of project accomplishment. Schedule slippages and the consequent cost overruns of many projects had made it necessary to add the resources dimension (manpower, materials, machines) to PERT/Time. Although PERT/Time provided the means of monitoring, coordinating, and controlling a project's time progress at various levels, it provided no means of measuring the project's financial status along with its physical accomplishment.

PERT/Cost is not yet old enough to have won a firmly established place in project management. Although it seems to have real potential as a means of cost control, it is more difficult to apply than PERT/Time. A number of problems have arisen in actual use. Some of them may disappear as users gain more experience with the technique and its application. Others may prove to be inherent limitations, however.

The use of PERT/Cost unquestionably has many advantages. It greatly facilitates the assessment of project status in relation to financial planning. It highlights the interrelationships of time and costs and the financial effects on the project of possible changes in resources and/or schedules. It permits evaluation of progress from multiple sources of information, and it provides a single set of reports for appraising both the financial and the physical status of a project.

Other Values PERT/Cost also aids in conceptual planning by financially quantifying the project tasks to be performed and by assessing the adequacy of funding requirements for meeting total project costs. It provides a means for comparing time schedules and resource estimates of different departments or of different contractors. For example, with it the project manager can combine detailed information from engineering and manufacturing or fuse summary cost data from one contractor with in-house data and still have consistent program output information. Its outputs for net-

* Reprinted by permission of the publisher from *Management Services*, vol. 3, no. 1, pp. 29–34, January–February, 1966. Mr. Schoderbek is associate professor of management at the University of Iowa.

What PERT Is

PERT (Program Evaluation and Review Technique) is a method for planning, controlling, and monitoring the progress of complex projects. The emphasis is on time scheduling. A project is broken down into its component steps. These steps are represented graphically in the form of a network showing the dependencies among them. The times required to complete each step are estimated and potential bottleneck steps are identified. Then the planner is in a position to reassign manpower and resources to speed up the steps that might cause the project to fall behind schedule.

PERT, originated to coordinate the work of a large number of subcontractors engaged in the development of the Navy's Polaris missile, is credited with having cut two years off the time span of that project. Because PERT incorporates a method for estimating the time it will take to do something that has not been done before—and for which, therefore, no time standards exist—it is particularly useful in the scheduling of research and development projects. It has been widely applied in the space and defense industries.

PERT works this way:

All the individual tasks required to complete a given project must be identified and put down in a network. A network is composed of events and activities. An event represents a specific project accomplishment at a particular point in time. An activity represents the actions required to progress from one event to another.

Events and activities are sequenced on a network diagram. Activities are represented by arrows connecting two events. The direction of the arrow shows which event must precede the other. For example, on the sample network shown on this page, Events 2 and 3 both precede Event 4; Events 6, 7, 9, and 10 must precede Event 11; and Events 8, 11, and 12 must precede Event 13.

Sample Pert Network

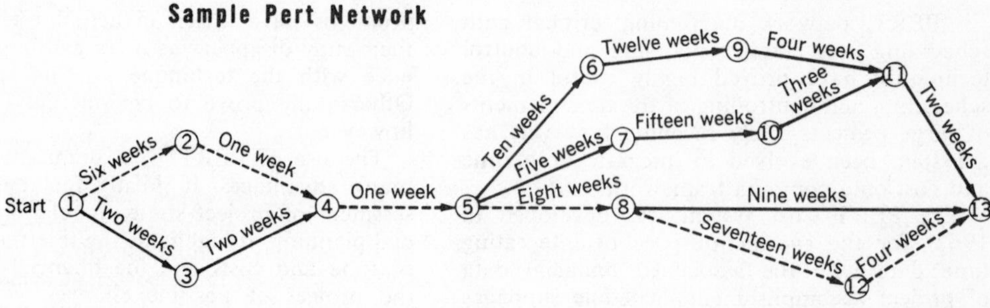

Sequencing must follow a rigorous set of rules. No successor event can be considered completed until all of its predecessor events have been completed. No "looping" is allowed; that is, no successor event can be a predecessor of one of its predecessors.

Time estimates are made for each activity on the network. Because completion times are assumed to be uncertain, three time estimates are sometimes made for each activity—optimistic, pessimistic, and most likely—and the expected time is calculated from these by means of a probability formula.

Once expected activity times are recorded on the network, it is easy to see the critical path (the dashed lines in the illustration). The critical path is the sequence of events that will require the greatest expected time to accomplish. Activities not on the critical path have slack time, which means that it would be safe to delay them somewhat by shifting resources from them to critical activities.

On a research project, for example, manpower can be shifted from Activities 1–3 and 3–4 to speed up Activities 1–2 and 2–4. Similar slack in Activities 5–7, 7–10, and 10–11 can be utilized to shorten the critical path 5–8, 8–12, and 12–13.

What PERT/Cost Is

PERT/Cost is an extension of PERT for planning, monitoring, and controlling the cost progress as well as the time progress of a project. Cost classifications are based upon project work breakdowns so that costs can be identified with the activities on the PERT network. The breakdowns serve as vehicles for both estimating and accumulating costs. Thus the PERT network, with costs tied to its activities, can be used for planning and performance evaluation in terms of both costs and time.

In addition, PERT/Cost provides a method of comparing the costs of alternative course of action. The cost penalty as well as the time benefit of transferring resources to the critical path can be determined. And the lowest-cost allocation of resources among individual activities can be determined—for comparison with the least-time allocation.

work areas are useful even if one section is given in summary form and another in detailed network form.

By integrating PERT/Time and PERT/Cost one can determine whether the various-level managers are meeting their schedule commitments, cost estimates, and technical performance standards and, if not, decide how resources can be recombined so as to minimize costs.

In measuring the progress of a project, the sum of actual costs to date can be compared directly with funds authorized and the estimated cost of completion of the project. Such a comparison will reveal potential cost overruns and/or underruns and will pinpoint the segments of work that require cost control action.

Limitations While PERT/Cost undoubtedly provides a substantial measure of cost control for large, complex projects, there are, nevertheless, shortcomings that somewhat limit its applicability.

Although the splintering up of large, unwieldy projects into smaller, more manageable units permits the sharing of exacting responsibility and the more precise delineation of multiple efforts, it also increases the overall problem of departmental coordination. Top management, of course, is concerned chiefly with summary reports. Much of the requisite on-the-spot control is delegated to departmental heads who have vested interests in the type and amount of information presented to top management. Just as time estimates in PERT/Time tend to be used for firm schedules (although they should not), so cost estimates in PERT/Cost eventually end up as budgets, and, despite the fact that cost estimates are subject to revision, there is a tendency to inflate the budget in the initial planning stage.

Padding This tendency to "pad" does not necessarily represent any willful attempt to convey fraudulent or erroneous information but rather that all too human desire to "play it safe." Since time and cost are directly related, and since engineers tend to be somewhat pessimistic about time estimates, there is concomitant hedging on the cost side as well.

No department head wants to encounter cost overruns, which would reflect adversely on his performance. As a result, he is naturally tempted to pad the cost estimates so as to compensate for any possible error in the time estimates.

This problem is by no means limited to PERT/Cost systems, of course. It is always a hazard in budget formulation, regardless of the control technique employed.

It is ordinarily impractical to have each cost estimate independently recalculated—or have its components independently verified—by someone outside the department responsible for preparing the estimate. However, several steps can be taken to discourage "fudging."

Complete work packages or specific activities within a work package can be selected at random for review and verification by the project manager. This review can be performed either during the planning stage of the project, in which case the validation is of time and cost estimates, or during the execution stage of the project, in which case actual times and costs may be available for comparison with estimates. These checks provide clues to estimator bias; they also act as psychological deterrents to fudging.

This review by the project manager is itself a kind of audit. However, it is also possible to have an internal audit by an accounting department or some other independent staff, performed randomly on work packages or at a summary level. On some government projects an external government agency routinely performs such an audit. An internal audit helps to provide control since it measures deviations from a standard; more important, however, the threat of an audit or close review "disciplines before it acts."

Changes in Estimates Usually, as a project develops, changes are made in the product or system under design because unforeseen technical difficulties are encountered or because it becomes evident that certain modifications would increase the stability, reliability, or economy of the product or the system. Indeed, it has been suggested that out of thousands of government projects fewer than one per cent fail to undergo significant alterations.

Cost estimates, of course, change accordingly. Such changes are particularly characteristic of cost-plus government contracts, for under such contracts there is little or no penalty for underestimation of costs. Thus, contractors tend to understate costs in order to win the contracts and then make little effort to control costs.

Cost-plus Psychology This tendency to understate costs seems to be the rule rather than the exception. Reports of final incurred costs tend to play down or omit earlier cost estimates, thus making it difficult to verify the original estimates. Revisions partially absolve the individual responsible for the original estimates since the final costs are really for a new program, not for the one whose cost estimates he formulated. Furthermore, by the time the project is completed, it is usually impossible to demonstrate what the original program would have cost if it had not been altered.

On many projects the margins of error have been significant, even startling. Cost increases of 200 to 300 per cent and extensions of development time by one-third to one-half are not uncommon.[2] The degree of error in estimates depends to some extent on the type of program. Programs that incorporate many new technological innovations are particularly subject to large margins of error. For instance, on six missile projects in which The Rand Corporation played a major role, the actual cumulative costs ranged from 1.3 to 57.6 times the initial projected costs,[3] with a mean of 17.1; in other words, the final costs were on the average 17.1 times as great as the earliest available estimates.[4]

Cost Uncertainties Even if changes in cost estimates are not forced by external or project changes, they are likely to become necessary as a project moves along and estimating errors become apparent. Because PERT by its very nature deals so much with uncertainties, it is difficult to extrapolate from previous cost patterns. Nor do project costs always react in a linear fashion.

Thus, the assumption that a particular course of action will result in a least-cost situation may prove highly unrealistic. It is true that a computer can theoretically minimize costs and optimize resource allocation. In actual application, however, many of these costs are so difficult to estimate that the optimum allocation of resources remains a guess.

In the stage of project planning when entire networks are being visualized and computer programs are being prepared, it is often too early to subject cost patterns to precise mathematical determination. This is not to imply that costs are not predictable for discrete situations or that PERT/Cost does not provide a sound framework for cost control. But the difficulty of obtaining reliable cost estimates is certainly a limitation on the effectiveness of the technique.

Allocations Cost allocation is a major problem. Work packages are usually made up of activities involving several different departments. An engineering department, for example, is frequently involved in many aspects of a program, while the production department may be concerned with the major assemblies only. It is frequently difficult, it not impossible, to assign departmental expenses accurately among projects, and for control purposes an arbitrary allocation is about as useful as none.

Sometimes on large projects it is possible to break the work packages down in the planning stages in such a way that each department with a major contribution to make to the project can be assigned a specific criterion to be met, for example, $100,000 or three months' effort. The assumption implicit in this technique is that the necessary resources for the execution of the work packages are present and available.

So long as departments operate on tight budgets, however, the haphazard reporting of labor classifications is likely. Suppose, for example, that the engineering department has ten man-months allocated for one work package, and it actually requires only five man-months. If a second work package begins to show signs of slippage, then it is to be expected that engineering resources will be traded off accordingly. Department heads are often indifferent about which accounts their costs are charged to so long as they stay within their own over-all budgets. Thus, the seeming definiteness associated with the PERT/Cost system may be only an apparent one, for there is always ample scope for flexibility and manipulation in the reporting of cost figures.

Whatever the reason for the misallocation of costs, there always remains the danger that these misleading figures will be used as a basis of estimating the costs of future work packages of similar nature. Obviously such forecasting, based on false or at best dubious premises, is likely to prove highly erroneous.

Actually, of course, these problems are not unique to PERT/Cost. They existed before it was developed, and they continue to plague project managers and controllers whatever the management and control techniques used. The particular problem with PERT/Cost is that it seems to be so scientific and its results seem so definitive that managers may be tempted to forget that no control technique is any better than the data upon which it rests.

Evolution PERT/Cost is not, after all, a complete departure from earlier techniques. Most of its elements existed before, often under other names. For example, the cost-to-complete estimates do not differ greatly from reports formerly titled future cost to be incurred, costs to terminate, or simply recosting. The organization status reports have been in use for years under the name of department work sheets or department budget reports. The manpower loading report goes back to the older manpower requirement report or the jobs skills form. Thus, most of the components of PERT/Cost are evolutionary rather than revolutionary; i.e., pre-existing ideas of management and control have been refined and linked with the use of new data processing equipment and computers.

One of the chief advantages of this evolution is increased speed. However, although the PERT/Cost reporting system is relatively rapid, it still may not be fast enough to be really useful.

While it is relatively easy to gather historical costs, it is much more difficult to estimate the costs of physical progress for projects in various stages of completion. The rule that the value of work performed to date is measured by the actual costs, divided by the latest estimate to complete, times the budget to date is not an accurate guide for evaluation, especially if progress is not on target. By this formula, increasing the budget for a work package automatically increases the value of work performed—which is patently fallacious.

Thus, while PERT/Cost does aid in assessing the financial progress of activities, it is not an infallible guide. For many projects costs can be accurately reported only after completion.

Future Despite these limitations, there is no doubt that PERT/Cost has added a new dimension to the field of operations control. It has brought management closer to the ultimate goal of total systems control. As PERT/Time provides timely information helpful in achieving goals more rapidly, so PERT/Cost provides information that facilitates achieving these goals not only promptly but also efficiently and economically.

Although it is premature to pass final judgment on the success or failure of PERT/Cost, most companies that use it feel that it provides true management control by focusing attention on significant deviations from set goals. Just as operating personnel are forced by PERT/Time to examine schedule dates and accomplishments in detail, so PERT/Cost forces personnel to be equally cognizant of resources. This awareness of direct labor hours, material costs, computer time, and the like in turn aids in setting objectives for departments and managers at various levels of management.

PERT/Time and PERT/Cost will not make decisions for the manager. They will, however, aid him by revealing schedule and cost segments of programs that require his special attention. They also will pinpoint "crash" areas where acceleration may be essential if the project is to be completed on the target date.

Like other control techniques, PERT/Cost is no panacea. Its usefulness is directly dependent upon the usefulness of the data fed into the system, and this in turn depends upon the efficiency of the operating personnel. If unreliable data are fed into the PERT/Cost program, then haphazard information will be received from the computer.

Many of the current efforts to improve the PERT/Cost system are aimed at alleviating the difficulties in cost estimating, at tying cost reports more closely to time schedules, and at introducing other mechanical devices to complement the system. More attention, however, should be devoted to increasing the capabilities of the operating personnel who are responsible for the day-to-day functioning of the PERT/Cost system. Technical problems will—and should—not be neglected, but the need to solve more of the problems of human engineering apparently far outweighs any of the mechanical deficiencies of PERT/Cost.

One promising area of further development of the PERT/Cost system is that of Time/Cost estimating procedures. It may soon be possible to place manpower needs and costs directly on the detailed project networks. This would facilitate the control function by enabling the operations manager to formulate a more realistic program initially instead of making continual readjustments. Although many time and cost schedule revisions result from changes in the program objectives and from unexpected contingencies involving resource availability and the like, a substantial number are due to misestimations by PERT personnel in the first place.

REFERENCES

1. Available at the present time are many manuals on PERT/Cost issued by private industries using PERT or by government agencies or departments. See especially U.S. Defense Department and National Aeronautics and Space Administration, *DOD and NASA Guide, PERT Cost, Systems Design,* U.S. Government Printing Office, Washington, D.C., 1962, and U.S. Department of the Navy, *An Introduction to the PERT/Cost System for Integrated Project Management,* Special Projects Office, Bureau of Naval Weapons, Washington, D.C., 1962. The following articles have also proved helpful: Richard E. Beckwith, "A Cost Control Extension of the PERT System," *IEEE Transactions of Engineering Management,* EM-9, December, 1962, pp. 147–149; Roderick W. Clarke, "Activity Costing—Key to Progress in Critical Path Analysis," *IRE Transactions on Engineering Management,* EM-9, September, 1962, pp. 132–136; Roland Frambes, "PERT and PERT/Cost in the RFP," *Aerospace Management,* V, May, 1962, pp. 24–26; J. Sterling Livingston, Willard Fazar, and J. Roland Fox, "PERT Gains New Dimensions," *Aerospace Management,* V, January, 1962, pp. 32–36; and Hillard W. Paige, "How PERT/Cost Helps the General Manager," *Harvard Business Review,* VI, November-December, 1963, pp. 87–95.
2. A. W. Marshall and W. H. Meckling, *Predictability of the Costs, Time and Success of Development,* 2d ed., Rand Corporation, Santa Monica, Calif., 1959, p. 11.
3. *Ibid.* The above figures are unadjusted both for price level changes and, more important, for modifications that have been made since the initial cost estimates. For example, on the above-mentioned missile project where the latest cost estimate was 57.6 times the initial one, this would be reduced to 14.7 if adjusted for the above factors. Even this margin of error is highly significant, this writer feels.
4. In an effort to stimulate the profit motive and to cut costs for the government, "incentive" contracts have made a policy for the Department of Defense since January, 1964. It is still too early to judge the effects of this policy. (See article in *The Wall Street Journal* which states that a "limited number of incentive contracts showed costs running about 50 per cent more than anticipated." See also "McNamara Cuts Costs, but Officials Wonder if Gain Is Exaggerated," *The Wall Street Journal,* June 11, 1964.) Some writers think that cost overruns will cease to be a problem with the advent of "incentive" contracts. However, while incentive contracts have undoubtedly reduced cost overruns in many instances, success has been far from complete; i.e., the controversial TFX project is currently expecting an overrun of about $.5 billion.

76 OPERATIONS AUDITING*

Roy A. Lindberg

A new management technique, operations auditing, has come into being because the traditional sources of information do not fully supply the requirements of managers in current forms of organization. Specifically, operations auditing arises out of the need of managers responsible for areas beyond their direct observation to be objectively, fully, and currently informed about conditions in the units under their control.

The traditional sources of information are no longer sufficient because the nature of business and the managerial role have been changing in recent years. Among the changes, companies have been growing larger and managers' spans of responsibilities have been broadening and diversifying.

More and more managers are operating out of sight of the activities they are responsible for. One result is that the capacities of the familiar tools of management are being strained and, in some cases, exceeded, and profit-absorbing procedures have become organizational fixtures in many companies. The aim of operations auditing is to seek out and define such practices. OA provides every manager with a means for readily identifying and accurately defining emerging problems before they become institutionalized. The manager with diversified responsibilities in a highly differentiated structure, particularly, has need for operations auditing.

CONFUSION

One of the problems plaguing OA today is that some of its sponsors confuse it with more traditional management tools and tend, therefore, to use it as the other tools are used. When this takes place, something other than operations auditing is being done. Either OA has a definite work content, or there is no justification for performing other work in its name.

* Reprinted by permission of the publisher from *Management Review*, vol. 58, no. 12, pp. 2–9, December, 1969. Mr. Lindberg is manager of the management services department of J. H. Cohn & Company.

Until recently the main sources of knowledge about what was going on in a unit were:

- The unit's manager.
- Staff assistants or assistants to the manager.
- Regular performance reports.
- The operating of controls.
- Studies, reviews, surveys.

In today's operations, however, these sources suffer from the following shortcomings:

- The manager or executive in large-scale enterprises usually has too large a span of responsibility and too little time or incentive to act primarily as information gatherer and problem finder.
- Extensions of the manager, in the person of staff assistants and assistants to the manager, are normally used more for information transmission than for information generation and analysis. Even where they are qualified to act as knowledge centers (a rare circumstance), they usually have vested interests that prevent them from being fully objective.
- Performance reports in the form of accounting statements, internal audit reports, performance appraisals, and so on are historical in nature and, even where combined into extrapolations such as extensions of trend and the like, fail to provide insight into the particular problem developing somewhere in a unit.
- Controls, when they operate, give notice of a failure or irregularity, but are so specific in activity coverage that they fail completely as barometers of environmental conditions.
- Studies, reviews, and surveys are excellent sources of information on which the manager can act, but the analyses they are based on take a great deal of time, cost a good deal of money, and are infrequently performed.

None of these sources of information provides all managers with the means by which they can readily, conveniently, and frequently have the assurance that things are either proceeding according to plan or accepted standards, or that they know what, where, and how things are going wrong. Operations auditing has come into being to provide such knowledge, and it fills the gap created by modern business conditions in the traditional range of information-supplying devices.

A SEPARATE TOOL

The major difficulty in applying operations auditing successfully is the failure to establish a separate role for it. When OA is made into a dolled-up version of well-established managerial information sources, it has the same deficiencies as the traditional sources and fails its mission entirely—which is to create confidence that things are going according to plan and/or to find the problems on the basis of efficient and nondisruptive research.

The above considerations make it apparent also that OA, unlike some of the traditional information sources, is not a useful tool in all situations. Its usefulness is related to organizational and managerial circumstances. Because OA is a tool of managers who need to be informed about areas out of their sight (that is, who operate in highly differentiated organizations), it is a "complex situation" tool. This may be an oversimplification, depending upon the construction placed upon the term "complex," but it is certainly true that where the managers of the business operate in a broad role (vertically and horizontally), there is little need to maintain an OA function internally.

This is not to say that smaller or less differentiated companies cannot benefit from OA. It is entirely possible that an independent appraisal carried out by an OA staff from the outside will produce benefits, such as confirmation of internally held views of performance or the discovery of problems unseen because of familiarity. But the company that cannot employ an OA staff almost continuously in audit work may find it economically preferable to have the work done by outside sources.

DEFINITION

Recognizing that operations auditing has arisen in response to the distinctly modern need for a performance-gauging tool that costs relatively little, is nondisruptive, and identifies problems before they have gotten old or out of hand, makes it possible to establish a definition. Following is one that encompasses the foregoing points:

"Operations auditing is a technique for routinely and systematically appraising unit or function effectiveness against corporate and industry standards, utilizing nonspecialist (in the area of study) personnel, with the objective of assuring a given management that its aims are being carried out, or identifying conditions capable of being improved through more intensive and specialized attention."

Like any tool, OA has to be used properly if it is to produce satisfactory results. In many cases, OA is not being properly used. Consequently, it is being threatened with discard in many of the companies now trying it out.

The main reason for this is that the tool, in the hands of unthinking or overzealous men, is being applied to tasks for which it was not designed or being used without regard to its limitations. One indication of this practice is given by the following words from a recently issued promotional brochure:

> An inadequate sales forecast leads to more trouble than you may think. Operational auditing found out such forecasts make it impossible to:
>
> 1. Schedule production economically.
> 2. Keep inventories at a minimum but effective level.
> 3. Determine staffing requirements, both current and future.
> 4. Schedule production adjusting for seasonal and cyclical variation.
>
> Problems of this nature are too critical to go undetected. Discovering them and suggesting solutions is exactly what operational auditing is designed for.

On the contrary, suggesting solutions is exactly what operations auditing is *not* designed for.

Following is a statement by Peter A. Phyrr, which appeared in an article in the May, 1969, *Financial Executive,* that typifies the urge to make OA into an instrument of execution:

> Operational auditing is a review and appraisal of operations and operating procedures. It carries with it the responsibility to discover and inform top management of operating problems . . .

So far so good, but the statement goes on to say:

> . . . but its chief purpose is assisting management to solve problems by recommending realistic courses of action.

With the addition of that idea, the OA concept starts to come apart at the seams.

PROPER ROLE

It is no accident that this tool has been labeled with the word "auditing." Attest auditing rose in response to the need for a *convenient* and *efficient* means of verifying that the equity of an enterprise hasn't been tampered with. In the furthest stretch of the audit assignment, statements may be issued that assets are not being used to the best advantage. But direct suggestions of how to use assests more productively (in the sense of recommending by name institutions in which to invest funds) are definitely irregular and out of keeping with the audit assignment. The operations audit has similar characteristics. Its prime job is to ascertain, verify, and report—not to recommend or implement solutions. These qualities alone favor applying the term "auditing" to the operational as well as custodial function.

Look at it from another viewpoint; it has often been said that the prime job of the manager is to find problems, not to solve them. If this is true, then the main objective of OA also is to find problems (if they exist), because OA is an instrument of management intelligence. Nor does this "flatten" OA into a thin, narrowly useful instrument. Finding, identifying, and accurately describing a real business problem is no easy task. When this has been accomplished, finding the solution is relatively simple.

The insistence that the operations auditor recommend solutions to the problems he finds opens the door to other things OA should not be doing, such as:

- Appraising employees.
- Implementing recommendations.
- Making management's decisions.
- Departing from standards (that is, arbitrarily choosing new evaluation guides).

Operations auditing should not do any of these things. For example, it can appraise the effectiveness with which goals are met or work is done, but not whether a man is being effective or not; it can find problems using limited methods, but cannot be sure of finding the best solutions; it can report problems, but is in no position to say that the time is ripe for dealing with them. OA is a problem-finding tool, and its job ends when it has located, tested, and accurately defined the problem.

It is, therefore, misleading to say, as some persons do, that operations auditing focuses on the finding of improvements, and thus on the future. Rather, OA focuses on things as they are in the present. The executive branch focuses on improvement and on the future.

Taking this position does not place restrictions on the range of operations auditing investigations. OA can and should be used in every area of corporate activity. The statement does, however, place restrictions on the extent of operations auditing activities.

USE OF STANDARDS

The definition given earlier states that appraisal in operations auditing is made against standards. This is so because standards are the only forms of reference with sufficient stability and universality to permit comparisons between units and periods of time.

Standards used by OA are of two kinds—corporate and industry. For corporate standards, OA relies heavily upon documentation of the unit being audited. Some performance yardsticks are:

- Objectives, goals, plans.
- Budgets.
- Historical performance.
- Policies, procedures, directives, and so on.

For industry standards, OA relies upon the common body of knowledge of sound business practices and an analysis of industry statistics provided by association and governmental sources.

Preparation of standards is a significant part of the OA manager's responsibility. Developing a body of standards against which a given unit's performance can be soundly measured is a time-consuming, painstaking task. The effort is more than justified, however, because it is probable that no single factor goes further toward ensuring success in the performance of operations audits.

One of the reasons it is commonly held that OA should include the finding and recommending of solutions is the belief that every effective manager has, in his own way, been doing OA for years. This idea is attractive to managers, but it simply is not true.

It is true that every good manager instinctively takes frequent measures of the effectiveness of the units within his ken—whether under his direction or not—but to say OA is just another version of this does it an enormous disservice. It is because the manager requires something more dependable than his own informal pulse-taking that OA came into being. Operations auditing differs from the manager's appraisals mainly by being consciously and systematically carried out against acceptable standards. In other words, it is a formal activity with a definite work content.

USE OF QUESTIONNAIRES

OA, to be systematic and efficiently performable, involves the use of checklists in the form of questionnaires. The use of questionnaires tends, in many minds, to cast doubt on the value of OA, but this is also a mistaken view. OA cannot fulfill its mission without using questionnaires, regardless of the caliber of personnel employed in the audit. A questionnaire lends uniformity to the performance of the audit and acts as a checklist to ensure that the audit covers all subjects.

Using questionnaires has many important benefits outside performance of the audit itself. In the first place, it helps depersonalize the audit by visually signaling the fact that there is form to the audit, and where there is form there is equal treatment. Thus, personnel who are interviewed will not be so tempted to feel they have been singled out for investigation. Secondly, the questionnaire offers a basis for developing audit time standards. The questionnaire involves a specific amount of work, and the time involved in performing it can be used as a measure of the amount of time needed to do the audit next time. Finally, the questionnaire forces management to deal with OA in a practical way. OA can only operate successfully in a supportive environment, and giving it a franchise to operate in a specific way requires management to examine it in detail and be faced with the realities involved. Nothing can be more destructive to OA or the operations auditor than being given an open-ended assignment, and few devices focus attention more efficiently on what is involved than a questionnaire.

A PATHFINDER FUNCTION

Every company has renewal (maintenance, immunity) resources. In the company these resources take the form of managerial, specialist, and consulting personnel, often among the most experience of all personnel. It needs these to survive, but it cannot survive if it does not use these people efficiently. What is needed is a device for efficiently locating problems that the specialist forces can work on. This is one of the important services OA can perform. The trouble is that, in their haste to gather in greater authority and prestige, many operations audit personnel get the operations auditing role mixed up with the work of renewal. (There is a Parkinsonian tendency among many auditors to arrogate to themselves, through the agency of operations auditing, the broadest range of functions and responsibilities.) This is extremely dangerous.

The tendency of some auditors to assume responsibilities beyond operations appraisal is not hard to understand. Established renewal resources fail to meet all the requirements of current organizational forms. Operations auditors, therefore, feel impelled by moral and knowledge factors to contribute to the maintenance of the enterprise of which they are a part. This tendency, however, is deadly to the spirit and purpose of OA. It destroys independence and implies a virtuosity and expertise at odds with the economics of the operations auditing function. Plainly, what is needed are additions to the renewal tools at hand, not extension of operations auditing into activities almost certain to destroy it as a management tool.

QUALIFICATIONS FOR AUDITORS

Because OA developed out of financial auditing, there is a marked tendency to staff operations auditing projects with internal auditors. This is not a mistake—financial auditing is a good background for anyone doing OA work. But OA projects can be staffed from many sources. There are no standards for operations auditors in terms of experience or training—only in capabilities.

Operations auditors, if anything, are "experts in asking questions." They should also, of course, have analytical minds, aptitude with figures, and communicating skill. They can be identified by their breadth of knowledge and their reflective thinking.

Staffing is vitally affected, of course, by whether attest auditing and operations auditing are combined. OA can be combined with the financial audit, or it can be performed separately, with benefits from either practice. Obviously, if the two forms of auditing are to be performed by the same people, these people must be skilled in financial audit work. This constitutes a constraint that, added to the other qualities needed in an operations auditor, markedly reduces the number of persons available for OA work.

OA is a valuable training device. The work offers rich opportunities to obtain bird's-eye views of the corporation and of the administration process. Some companies recognize these benefits and seek to extract as much advantage as possible from them by rotating the assignment of auditors to departments each year.

Operations auditing is, of course, a great source of personnel for reassignment. A man who does a good job of OA is prized for the qualities that make him competent in the field. The compensation paid operations auditors is far below the average earnings of managers and specialists, so OA tenure tends to be short.

ESTABLISHING FRIENDLY RELATIONS

Because the operations auditor is an intruder in the unit he is sent to audit, defenses begin to be thrown up as soon as he makes his appearance. One of the commonest defenses is to call into question the qualifications of the auditor to appraise effectiveness in "this unit." The auditor must be trained to see that his mission justifies his presence in an area. If he comes in as a healer, the attack on his competence becomes viable. If he comes in as a fact-finder, he is beyond attack.

There is necessity to be factual, to maintain independence—but there is also a need to create acceptance, keep fear to the minimum. The operations auditor understands, therefore, the need to establish friendly relations, to be thought of as a source of help, rather than a threat. This suggests progress reports to unit management and the need for an exit meeting or debriefing.

Frequency of the operations audit varies according to the unit involved. The amount of resources employed is one factor. The nature of operations is another. Frequency of audit will, of course, relate to rate of change likely to be or actually incurred in the unit—especially as a result of a previous audit. The need to follow up, to appraise the effects of major changes, usually suggests earlier than normal return to a unit.

D. CONTROLLING OVER-ALL PERFORMANCE

77 RETURN ON INVESTMENT: AN ANALYSIS OF THE CONCEPT*

Maurice S. Newman

Effective use of capital is vital to a company's success. Measuring that success by "earnings per share" is not always satisfactory on a short-term basis, but there is a highly persuasive presumption in favor of the use of this standard on a long-term basis. The cost of capital must be recognized, and capital must be used where it will produce the best possible return on the investment.

Return on investment is employed as a measure of performance in two broad areas. The phrase is used to refer to the overall return on the overall investment in a company, division, or product group and also to the specific return on a specific investment in merchandise, buildings, or other types of assets.

The first area, which embraces the second, is the one in which the term "return on investment" or "return on capital employed" was first applied. It reconciles the financial or accounting viewpoint with the operating or engineering viewpoint and thus contributes to unified effort toward the achievement of overall company objectives.

Use of the term "return on investment" in the second area is semantically correct, but the area is of interest only to those with a specific problem. The introduction of actuarial principles and "cost of money" in these latter calculations often makes it difficult to relate the indicated return on a specific investment to the subsequent transactions appearing in the financial statements and accounting records because the premises are different. In this article, unless otherwise indicated, the term will be used in the broader sense.

Return on investment is being used increasingly as an objective test of planning and as a measure of performance. Its use has been given a substantial boost by the trends toward diversification through mergers and acquisitions and toward the decentralization of profit responsibility.

One of the reasons for its widespread application is that it translates a financial objective into such operating terms as selling prices, profit margins, sales turnover, production costs, and capital equipment, which are easily understood by sales and production personnel. However, return on investment is not always easy to calculate. When two businesses are operating independently, the income of each can be matched with the investment in each to give a reasonable indication of the return on investment. If these entities are merged and various administrative functions are shared jointly, it becomes more difficult to determine the contribution of each to the overall profits of the company. The same is true when there are various divisions or product groups within a company competing for the available capital resources.

Thus, there is a considerable difference of opinion on exactly how and where the return on investment concept should be applied. Nevertheless, there is a fairly general agreement that it is a useful measure of management stewardship at various levels.

"My Years with General Motors" by Alfred P. Sloan, Jr., (parts of which were published in *Fortune*) gives a good perspective on this concept and its working. The return on investment approach was brought to a high degree of development within General Motors Corporation by Donaldson Brown as a result of Mr. Sloan's stress on incentive compensation and the consequent need to determine the effectiveness of the various operating segments of the corporation.

Other companies—for example, DuPont and Monsanto—also have refined the return on investment concept to the point where it has become a highly effective management tool. The DuPont reporting system was described in the published *Proceedings* of the annual conference of the National Association of Accountants held in June 1952. Shortly thereafter a

* Reprinted by permission of *Management Services*, vol. 3, no. 4, pp. 15–27, July–August, 1966. Copyright 1966 by The American Institute of CPAs. Mr. Newman is a partner of Haskins & Sells, international accounting firm.

similar treatment of Monsanto's reporting system was published by the American Management Association. Other articles on this subject have appeared in various accounting publications. Many of these articles deal with the practical problems encountered in applying this logical analysis to the financial and operating statements of individual companies.

UNDERLYING LOGIC

The beauty of the return on investment concept lies in the pure simplicity of its logical accounting analysis as shown in the exhibit. By exploding the end result into the many business components that influence the final answer, it clearly relates the earnings to the manifold operations of the business. Step by step, it shows how the return on stockholder investment can be affected not only by the amount of net income but also by the amount of equity.

For instance, if the earnings after preferred dividends are retained in the business illustrated in the exhibit rather than paid out in common dividends, the equity would increase to $8,250,000. For the rate of return to remain the same the following year, the net income would have to increase by $75,000. If the additional funds are required in the business and can earn at least the same return on equity that the funds already invested in the business are earning, it would be in the interest of the stockholders to have the funds remain there. If the funds are not needed or cannot produce a comparable return, dividends paid to the stockholders will have a favorable influence on the rate of return.

It should be emphasized that the rate of return on equity may not be the same as the rate of return on a single stockholder's investment. Most stocks are traded in the market at prices that are entirely different from their book values.

Nor is the rate of return on equity the same as the rate of return on assets employed. Essentially the difference is represented in the accounting equation of "Assets = Liabilities plus Equity." An adjustment to the righthand side alone, such as increasing liabilities and reducing equity by the same amount, or vice versa, would not affect the return on assets but would affect the return on equity.

This is the domain of the financial officer, who, given the same operating income, may influence the return on equity favorably by several different actions. Among these would be redeeming preferred stock, buying in common stock, using cash balances effectively, deferring taxes, and paying larger dividends. Some of these actions would increase income or reduce expenses; other actions would reduce the equity. To the extent that funds were made available when needed to carry out operations and that excess funds were converted into earning assets when not required elsewhere, any of these actions would have a favorable effect on the return on equity and yet might affect the rate of return on assets employed only slightly or not at all.

It should also be noted that the return of 17 percent on assets employed is a product of two other factors: the percentage of operating income to sales and the sales volume in relation to the total investment. A glance at the equation (5 times 3.4 percent = 17 percent) makes it quite clear that a change in either component will affect the result. While this is axiomatic, it is surprising how much attention is given by most managements to the "percentage on sales" and how little to the turnover of investment. As the exhibit indicates, reduction of any component of the investment would have just as favorable an effect on the rate of return as would an increase in sales or in the profit margin.

Any $1,000 reduction of expenses would be equivalent to a $30,000 increase in sales, which might be harder to get. Considerable attention has been paid to the "product cost" component of the "cost of sales." However, a reduction in "period costs" would have an equally favorable effect on the rate of return. Furthermore, this reduction might be easier to accomplish.

It is up to each member of the management group to consider just what he can do to influence the overall return on the overall investment. Inventories could be reduced; accounts receivable could be collected more promptly; capital expenditures could be made prudently—all of which would tend to minimize the investment. These are areas to which the average production manager or marketing manager often fails to pay sufficient attention even if he holds stock options that may be adversely affected.

There are distinct advantages to using the return on investment concept in planning the future performance of a company. Changes in any one of a number of factors can have an effect on net earnings. By planning with all of these factors in mind and then measuring performance against the plans, a management may see where to take action that will increase net earnings. Furthermore, the return on investment concept allows management to plan and measure performance in a way that is under-

Components of Return on Investment

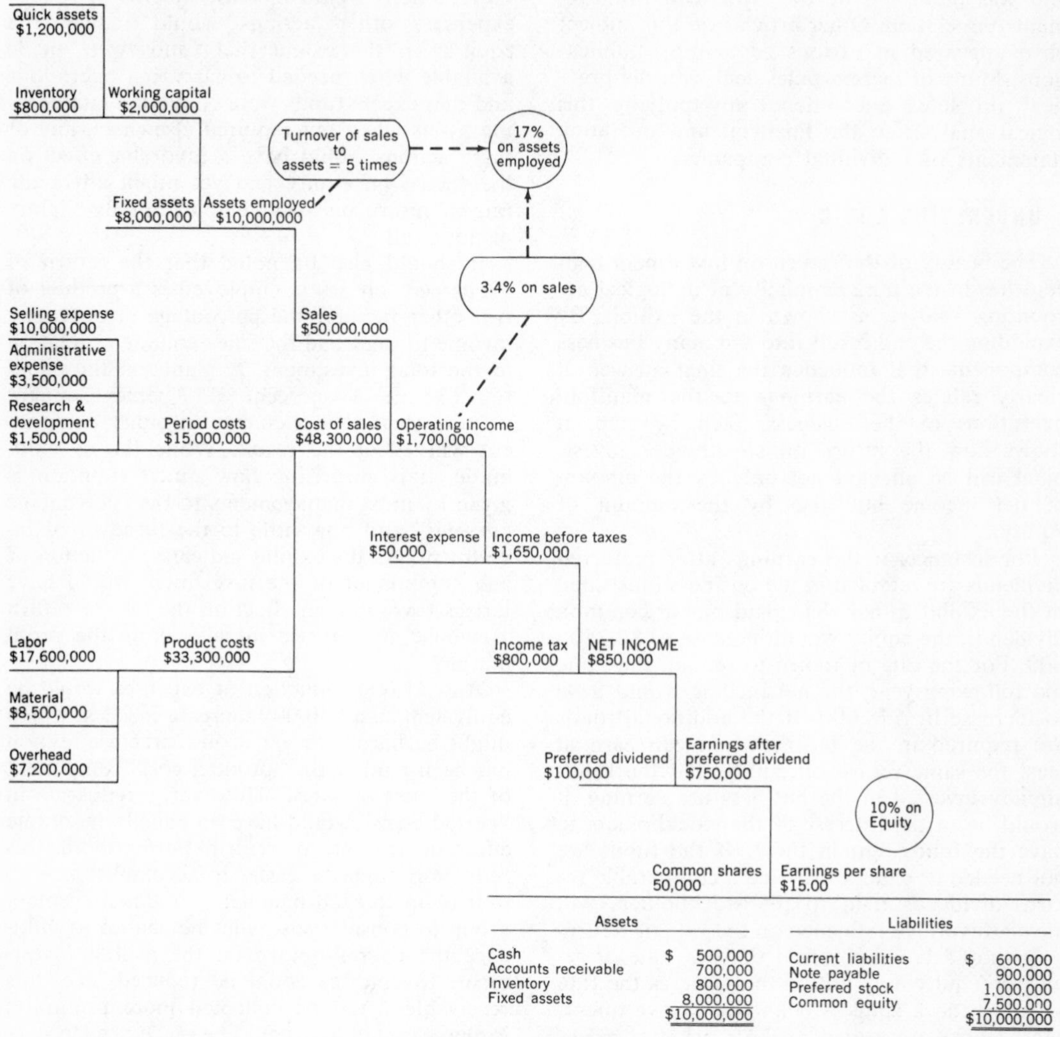

standable to the bankers and investors from whom the company must seek the capital required to finance growth.

Setting aside for the moment the complications that arise in actually applying "return on investment" principles to financial statements and management reports, the value of the concept is that it is clear and easy to understand. It reflects a basic responsibility that executive management has to its stockholders for an adequate return on the capital invested by them. This responsibility is keenly felt, as was indicated by a survey conducted some years ago. The executive officers of more than 200 companies were asked what single financial indicator they regarded as most symptomatic of the basic present fortunes of their companies. To this question more than half replied, "Net return on equity."

If this is accepted by a majority of chief executives as the basic measure of their performance, it would seem no more than reasonable to use this same criterion for planning operations on both a companywide and a divisional basis and also as a measurement of divisional performance.

CAPITAL EMPLOYED

There is general agreement that the performance of operating management should be measured by the return on the total capital employed rather than on stockholder equity, which involves financial management. There is less agreement, however, on how to compute capital employed. For instance, should fixed assets be valued at original cost, at estimated replacement value, or at their depreciated book value? Although undepreciated cost or replacement values might be more realistic, depreciated book values are often used since they are reflected in the financial statements and thus are more readily accepted by those whose profit performance will be judged. Questions can also be raised on the consideration to be given to such items as LIFO inventory values, current liabilities, and leased equipment in computing the amount of capital employed.

An essential tenet of the return on investment concept is that, in total, there should be a reasonable return on the total amount of the business investment in tangible and intangible assets. A company may be required to make certain expenditures from which no income will be received except perhaps in terms of employee morale or well-being. These expenditures are nevertheless part of the total investment, and the income from the remaining assets will have to be a little higher to offset the lack of income from the nonearning assets.

On a short-term basis, money spent for buildings and equipment or research and development may not begin to produce profits immediately but may assure adequate profits in later years. Similarly, amounts spent for preventive maintenance may reduce the present earnings but may at the same time lead to greater earnings in future years. The need for adjustment in these areas does not invalidate the concept but emphasizes that it needs to be carefully applied to individual situations.

OUTSIDER'S VIEW

Bankers, financial analysts, and company treasurers are primarily concerned with the return on equity. Financial analysts work generally from the published financial statements or similar sources. They are interested in such matters as debt service, cash flow, dividends paid, and the utilization of retained earnings.

Adjustment may have to be made before the return on investment of one company can be compared to that of another. One company may price its inventory on a LIFO basis, valuing it considerably below its market value in a period of rising prices, whereas another company may use FIFO, with the opposite result. One company may lease a considerable portion of its assets; another may own them. It could be argued that some capital assets held for future income such as undeveloped land or growth stocks should be eliminated from the capital employed base before any comparisons are made. Depreciation policies vary from company to company, and this factor must be considered. Unusual capital gains or losses on nonrecurring items have to be allowed for in any comparison.

MANAGEMENT'S VIEW

When a company is measuring its performance against its own predetermined standards, it has more freedom in the choice of ways of making this measurement, and its management may change any of the factors involved to what it considers to be a realistic measure of operating performance. Management is interested not only in the financial aspects of the situation but also in the comparative performance of various operating divisions of the company. While this operating performance will eventually be reflected in the financial statements, certain financial factors can be separated out so that the performance reports may be more easily understood by operating personnel.

For instance, it is a fairly general practice for companies to use income before taxes in calculating the return on investment so as to avoid the effect of such tax adjustments as carrybacks, carry forwards, and the investment credit. Some companies add back depreciation to the operating income when gross assets are used for assets employed. Interest on funded dept or other long-term obligations may also be excluded from consideration since operating management has little to do with such financial matters.

Similarly, total assets, rather than total stockholder invested capital, are often used for internal measurement purposes, and this is sometimes referred to as "total capital employed." The theory is that divisional managements have been provided with certain assets on which to earn profits and it is of no concern to them whether these are being financed by creditors, bondholders, or investors in common stock.

There is, however, much less agreement on whether the assets should be valued at book value, at original cost, or at replacement value. Replacement value is rarely used because of the difficulty of determining such a figure, although some companies use insurance appraisal figures for this purpose and others adjust their fixed asset and depreciation reserve values by the use of index numbers. Of the various methods, replacement value would probably be the most useful if a realistic figure could be obtained, but in practice the choice is usually narrowed down to either book value or original cost. For internal measurement of the performance of a company as a whole as against divisional performance measurement, it appears that the most common practice is to use net book value as it appears in the financial statements.

Although it is not accepted practice for a company to write up its assets in its financial statements, it may be useful to include certain assets in the investment base of an operating division at current market value. This is helpful for two purposes: one, measuring the operating department against realistic standards and, two, indicating those situations where alternative decisions might be made, for example, where valuable land and depreciated buildings might be sold and a new plant constructed elsewhere on less valuable land. There are many operations that earn a fairly good return on the book value, because the property was purchased many years ago, but earn a negligible return on the current market value.

The elimination from the operating reports of financial matters beyond the control of plant and division managers will make the reports more appropriate for these managers, who must deal with the situations they reveal. It is fundamental that these people should understand the computation of the rate of return if their performance is to be measured by it. It is fundamental that they should be charged only with the capital and those costs over which they have direct control. If for other purposes allocations are made of administrative expense over which they have no control, it may be desirable to compute the operating return both before and after such charges.

What is a reasonable rate of return for a company to adopt as a predetermined standard? This depends upon the nature of the business, the risk of capital employed, the investment basis used, and many other factors, but several manufacturing companies have established a return of 20 percent before taxes as a reasonable objective.

There seems to be a fairly general assumption that if a company is to earn over-all, say, 20 percent before taxes, each division should also earn a 20 percent return on the capital employed. This may be true where the operating divisions are similar in nature, but it is not always possible in a highly diversified organization. After all, a lower return should be expected where there is little risk entailed and a higher return where the hazards of capital loss are greater.

DIVISIONAL ANALYSIS

Applying the return on investment concept to operating divisions of the company is a different problem and often calls for a different type of measurement. The emphasis is more likely to be on operating performance and on comparison with other divisions.

This can be accomplished, in an accounting sense, by setting up a separate corporate division to carry the various investments and long-term liabilities and receive interest, dividends, or other income of a like nature as well as to absorb interest expense and other miscellaneous expenses. Such a division might possibly rent buildings and equipment to the operating divisions. This would avoid the problem that may arise when some divisions are housed in leased buildings and others are quartered in company-owned buildings. A higher return could normally be expected from a division that leased real property than from a division that owned a considerable amount of real property since lower rates are usually available on capital secured by real estate than on other risk capital. Management should review each situation objectively and arrive at rates of return for the division that will produce, on a composite basis, the desired overall company return.

Standards also need to be set for such things as preventive maintenance and the size of inventories. A plant manager who understands the basis on which he is being measured might embark on a program of cost cutting or inventory reduction that could have a spectacular short-term effect on his return on investment but start a long-range decline in the division's operating efficiency. If such reductions can be made wisely, however, everything possible should be done to encourage them.

One of the first questions that arise in divisional analysis is once again the valuation to be placed on the fixed assets. There seems to be fairly general agreement among those companies using return on investment to measure divisional performance that gross assets should be used as to value the investment. This avoids the variations in net return that may occur when one division has a brand new plant and another has one that is almost fully depreciated; in such circumstances the return may range widely. A further argument for using gross assets is the fact that when plants are built they are expected to produce income over their entire life expectancy. Furthermore, since companies have various depreciation policies at their disposal and different procedures may be used in various divisions, stating assets at net book value would certainly complicate relative comparisons unless corrective adjustments were made.

One of the arguments for using gross assets cited in most of the literature on this subject is that this value is closer to replacement value than the depreciated book value. This would seem to indicate that these authors would prefer to use replacement value if they could but have found considerable difficulty in determining it—whereas original cost is usually available from the books of record. These assets will eventually have to be replaced, if the business is to survive, at much higher prices. Using gross assets in the capital employed base provides one way of injecting a higher return into the pricing formulas to provide sufficient capital for the eventual replacement of these assets. This could also be accomplished by planning for a higher return on depreciated original cost, but there is always the possibility that the problem of replacement in an inflation-ridden economy will be overlooked.

If a company can develop fairly reliable present values, such as can be derived from insurance appraisals or from construction indices, there is considerable advantage to using such values, particularly in making divisional analyses. There is movement in this direction. In some utility rate hearings regulatory commissions have authorized rate increases that would produce a rate of return of approximately 6 percent on an investment based on current dollars, even though this would be equivalent to a higher return based on original cost.

Obviously the use of replacement values in divisional performance measurement would present problems if these values were not generally accepted by division managers. However, it would seem that management planning would be on a sounder basis if some approximation of replacement value could be used for the valuation of fixed assets in measuring company and divisional performance.

The real difficulty, of course, lies in the fact that the mechanical application of index numbers, price indices, or appraisal figures will rarely give the desired economic result. What is actually needed is the theoretical investment required to maintain the present capability of the existing plant and equipment, assuming that this can be defined in terms of units of physical output or other appropriate measurement. Since very few companies would be interested in identical replacement of their present plant and equipment, for the purpose of determining return on investment the replacement value of the existing plant could be quite meaningless. A possible compromise would be to use historical cost as the basis of computing the return at the level of operating responsibilities and then, in recognition of the price level problem, make a second computation on the basis of present values, dealing with this as a general policy matter.

Another question about which a difference of opinion may develop in divisional analysis is whether the total assets should be used with or without any allowance for current liabilities. In most cases it does not appear to make too much difference since liabilities are usually incurred more or less proportionately by the operating divisions, but there are certain businesses whose inventories are almost entirely financed by their suppliers; in these cases it does make a difference. When one division is in a business of this type and the others are not, it would seem necessary to give that division full credit for the working capital so obtained. This might be effected by reducing, by this amount, the value of the inventories included in the total assets.

Questions also may arise concerning plant and equipment not yet in full production, real estate held for future growth, and other such items on which a satisfactory current return cannot always be expected.

Whereas financial statements are prepared for financial purposes and must conform to generally accepted accounting principles, operating statements should be prepared for operating purposes and should be based on sound operating principles, even though these may seem to conflict with generally accepted accounting principles. Operating results should not be obscured by entries made primarily for tax accounting purposes, such as the use of LIFO valuation for inventories.

Eliminating this type of accounting entry from the operating statements prepared for the divisions and putting greater emphasis on measuring assets at their current market values, to the extent that these can be determined, might enable the division managers to concentrate more heavily on other factors, such as sales volume, prices, and product mix, which could materially improve the return on the assets entrusted to them.

EQUIPMENT REPLACEMENT

There has been considerable semantic difficulty in the application of the return on investment concept to capital equipment replacement. The most important goal of capital planning is an adequate return on the total investment. It is possible to use the return on investment concept as a guide in selecting those projects for which capital expenditures will be made. Confusingly, however, there are other methods for computing the expected return on the amount of capital invested in individual projects.

The traditional favorite is the payout method, by which the number of years required to recoup the original investment is determined. More recently the "discounted cash flow" concept has been advocated for this purpose; although it is rather complicated, it has considerable merit. The formula developed by the Machinery and Allied Products Institute, which has come to be known as the MAPI formula, takes certain actuarial factors into consideration in determining whether equipment that may have outlived its economic life but may still appear to have a useful physical life should be replaced.

The discounted cash flow concept is based on the actuarial formula for determining the rate of an annuity with a stated present value and certain specified payments. In other words, if we expect from our initial investment certain annual cash returns, which may vary from time to time, and if we know the present cost of the investment, what will the effective interest rate be? If this rate should prove to be 7 percent, we would then, under this concept, have a 7 percent return on the investment in the equipment. If this rate of return is higher than the cost of the capital required for this investment, it would presumably be advantageous to spend the money in this way—although whether the company should purchase or lease the asset is another factor to be considered.

There is a significant difference between the discounted cash flow concept and the return on investment concept as generally expressed in financial statements. The latter concept does not give weighted consideration to the time period in which the money is returned. This is a characteristic—perhaps a weakness—of the usual pro forma financial projections; they are on an annual basis and do not usually take into consideration the years in which profits will probably accrue. A dollar earned this year is given no more weight than a dollar earned two years from now. Obviously, if the same amount of cash is to be returned over a period of, say, five years, the investment that would return the greater part of the amount in the earlier years should be preferable to one that would return the greater part of the amount in later years. As a practical matter, however, most investments do tend to return cash fairly evenly over a long period so that the differences between the discount theory and the financial statements may be more theoretical than practical.

PRODUCT PROFITS

Another valuable use of the return on investment concept is in pricing individual products or product groups for a profit. It is true that sales prices are often determined by competitive conditions. However, a company does not have to promote actively the sales of any product that it cannot make and sell at a fair profit; it would perhaps be better advised to use the capital elsewhere.

The concept can be applied both to manufactured products and to products purchased and resold. A different approach may be required in each case, but with a reasonable amount of effort some valuable conclusions can be drawn from such an application.

The significant thought added to product profitability analysis by the return on investment concept is the effect of capital turnover. When products are turned over more rapidly, a somewhat lower percentage of profit on sales can be justified. This, in turn, may be effective in increasing the turnover. Just what constitutes capital investment in a particular product may be somewhat hard to define, but in product profitability studies this is generally a relative problem. So long as the same basis is applied consistently to each product, the relative percentages of return on investment will tend to highlight the more profitable products.

For manufactured products generally, the capital employed would normally be the various inventories, such as raw materials, work in process, and finished goods, together with the accounts receivable and such plant and equipment as can be readily attributable to the product. In retailing, a very satisfactory result can be obtained by using just inventories and receivables. Mathematical formulas can be developed for making such profit analyses, on an individual product basis, with the aid of electronic computers. Calculations of the profitability of individual products can be improved if the product gross profits are reduced by standard allowances for warehousing costs and selling commissions.

Product profitability analysis is a relatively unexplored area and one in which much might be done to increase a company's overall profits. The effect of turnover on profits is not well understood by many company managers. In addition to sales volume and sales price, there are many other factors, such as product design and mix, material and labor rates, administrative costs, and equipment replacement, that can have a considerable effect on the profitability of individual products or product groups.

This article has reviewed a number of ways in which the return on investment concept can be applied to assist company management in intelligent planning and in performance measurement. The concept can be used for measuring the performance of a company against that of others with which it can be usefully compared, and it can be used within a company for measuring the performance of the company as a whole and the performance of the separate divisions. It can be used in planning for the use of capital—both of the total amount to be spent in any given period and of the way in which the total should be distributed, as among divisions or products. It can also be used to evaluate the use of capital for individual equipment purchase commitments or for the establishment of higher inventory levels.

It is not necessary to use the same bases for all these purposes; both the bases and the definition of return can be adjusted to suit the individual circumstances. In external comparisons it is desirable to stay fairly close to the published financial statements, both in the definition of return and of investment. For internal company comparisons it may be desirable to eliminate certain items of a financial or miscellaneous nature. For divisional purposes it may be logical to use operating profit rather than net profit and gross assets rather than net assets. In product profitability studies gross profit may be used instead of operating profit, and certain assets may be eliminated from the investment base. Finally, in retail product profitability studies the investment may be reduced to a bare minimum of the inventory and accounts receivable applicable to each product.

There are many ways in which the return on investment concept may be applied, and there are no hard and fast rules about the choice of method, particularly when the comparisons are used for internal purposes. When relative, rather than absolute, measurements are sought, the results are useful whatever the bases used. There is no question that return on investment analysis is a valuable tool for managerial purposes and that it will be used in many more companies and in many more applications by progressive company managers of the future.

78 ROI PLANNING AND CONTROL*

J. Fred Weston

The problem of departmentation, involving the grouping of activities and the use of specialist expertise, is a problem faced by firms of all sizes. A very small firm that has not yet grouped or specialized its activities faces the question in seeking to improve the efficiency of operations. A related continuing issue, regardless of the firm's size, is whether to buy specialist expertise as required through the external market place or to obtain the flow of services through a generalized contractual relationship.

Indeed, the organization and management questions involved are applicable to all purposive organizations. The basic issue is the general problem of seeking optimal production functions by effective grouping of activities and utilization of specialist expertise.[1] In turn, this raises a number of problems concerning the delegation of authority while achieving effective control of decentralized operations.

One widely used method of divisional control is the return on investment (ROI) technique, which has been widely criticized. Economists have regarded ROI objectives as indicative of market control. Management specialists have described defects in the method for achieving effective control of decentralized operations, and behaviorists and accountants alike have questioned the motivational consequences of such control.

Field surveys of corporate resource allocation policies have developed evidence that many of the criticisms are directed against a static concept of the ROI control system with inadequate recognition of its dynamic process characteristics. This proposition will be developed in three parts: first, the prevailing description of ROI and the criticisms made of it; second, the nature and significance of ROI as a dynamic process; and third, an evaluation of the criticisms of ROI control in the framework of its actual characteristics.

THE STATIC FORM OF ROI

Short-term business planning as reflected in the financial budgeting process has been referred to in the literature as "planning and control for profit," "management by objectives," or "the du Pont system."[2] The du Pont Company pioneered the ROI system, widely used by divisionalized firms as well as by effectively managed small firms. Surprisingly, although du Pont began to develop and utilize the system before 1910, there was no description in the literature of the system's details until after the late 1940's. Even the early presentations covered only the mechanical aspects of the system. The concepts were not really brought alive until Alfred Sloan's book in 1964.

In addition to confusion about its implications, there is also misunderstanding about the system itself. This is reflected in Dearden where the "case against ROI control" is directed against its static, not its dynamic, elements.[3]

The static form of the du Pont system focuses on a formula chart showing the relationship of factors affecting ROI, which is the end focus of the chart. This is shown as the product of the turnover of investment multiplied by the margin on sales, to emphasize that the ROI can be

* Reprinted by permission of the publisher from *Business Horizons,* vol. 15, no. 4, pp. 35–42 (August 1972). Mr. Weston is professor of finance at the University of California, Los Angeles.

[1] Compare R. H. Coase, "The Nature of the Firm," *Economica* (1937), pp. 336–38, and J. Hirshleifer, *Investment, Interest, and Capital* (Englewood Cliffs, N.J.: Prentice-Hall, Inc., 1970), pp. 11–12.

[2] The reference to "planning and control for profit" has caused confusion by such writers as J. K. Galbraith in associating planning with control. This article will seek to clarify the relationship.

Management by objectives (MBO) involves processes similar to ROI planning and control.

[3] John Dearden, "The Case Against ROI Control," *Harvard Business Review,* XLVII (May–June 1969), pp. 124–35.

increased either by minimizing investments per dollar of sales, or by controlling costs so that the profit margin on sales is improved. The formula chart then fans into details of all the elements of operating investment: cash, receivables, inventories, and fixed assets (gross). The income statement provides details for all of the factors affecting the profit margin, with emphasis on the nature and behavior of the cost elements.

Even in its static form, the ROI method of control has a number of positive attributes, which have been summarized effectively by Dearden. First, it is a single, comprehensive measure, influenced by everything that has happened which affects the financial status of the divisions. Every item in the du Pont chart is related to its effect on either turnover or profit margin, and through either of these to its effect on ROI. If an alternative organization of the financial planning and control system is desired, the required information for doing so has been assembled.

The second advantage is that ROI measures how well the division manager has used his resource allocations, thereby providing a means for detailed post-auditing capital investment proposals. A third advantage is that ROI is a common denominator so that comparisons can be made directly among divisions within the company, with outside companies or with alternative investment of funds generally. Fourth, it is also claimed that since the manager is evaluated on his ability to optimize ROI, he will be motivated to do so.

Criticisms of this method of control have also been expressed. A list of technical defects is well covered in the Dearden article.[4] These include oversimplification of a complex decision-making process, failure to distinguish the required rate of ROI in common assets used in different divisions that may have different ROI targets, and difficulties arising out of accounting methods measuring ROI. A review of these technical defects suggests that many of them are arbitrary procedures not inherent in the method. Many criticisms of this method of planning and control stem from the predilection of accounting systems for recording the expiration of historical costs, and hence reflect the limitations of traditional accounting methods.

A second difficulty is that of assigning responsibility. Inherently, many decision areas involve the joint participation of a number of divisions and different levels of authority. Consequently, assigning responsibility for results is difficult under a static method.

[4] Dearden, "The Case Against ROI Control."

The third and most fundamental criticism is that any static control system is likely to have motivational defects. *Any* static control method will invite a wide range of practices for beating the system. In addition, there are important additional positive values not captured by the static concept. Therefore, it is important to view the du Pont system in its correct exposition—the du Pont planning and control system as a dynamic process.

ROI AS DYNAMIC PROCESS

In its dynamic aspects, the du Pont system represents the creation of a significant addition to management technology. Detailed analysis of operations is provided in a series of individual charts on each element of investment, revenue, or cost. It is in connection with review of these individual charts that a dynamic process is generated. For each asset or investment account, historical data are provided on an annual basis for five years with the sixth or current year presented on an annual basis to date and on a forecast basis for one year.

In addition, data are provided on a monthly basis for the previous year and for the current year to date. Periodic forecasts are made for four quarters into the future. The forecast is repeated periodically. When the forecast and review are on a quarterly basis, the one-year forecast is expressed by month for the proximate quarter and by quarter for the remainder of the year.

Thus, on a quarterly forecast and review basis, each quarter will have been projected and reviewed four times before the actual events are experienced. (In highly dynamic departments the forecast review may be monthly and even weekly.) Similar analysis is made of expenses expressed as a percentage of sales and transfers. Expenses as a percentage of sales are placed in perspective by showing production as a percentage of capacity since volume influences per unit cost.

The mechanics of the du Pont planning and control system have been described. The review process makes this a dynamic system with three main elements: the review itself, process rather than goal orientation, and the adaptive learning process.

The Review Process The process begins with periodic meetings of the firm's finance committee when divisional proposals for funds are presented. The prospective ROI represents one of the criteria used to evaluate the alternative investment opportunities and to allocate corporate resources. Initial projections are related to the potentials for the individual areas. The subsequent analysis compares performance to projections. A periodic presentation is made by the responsible managers of divisions or departments to a review committee comprised of men with years of experience in diverse areas of operations of the company. The committee as a whole has experience covering a range so wide that the review of any department is an *informed* review.

The data are a vehicle for the significant aspect of the process—the review of the data and the adjustment of policies. Performance is related to potential and not to any absolute standard. Thus the evaluation system provides a two-way information flow in an effective communication system. In its evaluation of an individual division or department, the review committee takes into account not only optimization for that segment, but also over-all optimization for the firm. Analysis of the data and comparisons of forecasts with actual results lead to policy modifications.

A reward and penalty system closes the loop in this process of stimulating, guiding, and motivating effective managerial performance. A salary and bonus committee allocates promotions, salary adjustments, and bonuses by departments. This committee typically includes members of the finance committee responsible for the original-allocation or resources, and members of the review committee engaged in a continuing evaluation of performance.

Three aspects of the review process represent a dynamic system. First, there is a detailed information flow on key decision areas. This provides feedback in the information system loop. Second, the review process represents a monitoring of the data and other forms of information. Third, on the basis of the information, review, and discussion, policies and decisions are adjusted in the attempt to improve performance. Thus, the entire process represents a method of adjusting to changes in the total economy, the industry, and actions of competitors.[5]

Goals vs. Process The ROI system must properly be seen as a process. Managers are not evaluated on the basis of the size of the ROI their division earns. Performance evaluation is related to the potential for the division, and not to any absolute standard. A manager who is able to limit the loss in a division in a product market characterized by severe excess capacity may be rated higher than a manager who achieves a positive 20 percent return in a product market area where at least temporarily the sales/capacity relations may have made possible a 30 percent return.

Similarly, if the risks of a divisional operation are high, there will be a minimum screening standard or investment hurdle rate that will be higher than for a less risky division. For example, the ROI for oil exploration will be higher than that on the investment in the land on which a filling station is located; obviously, the results of the operations of the filling station are more predictable than the outcome of oil exploration. Or a company contemplating the establishment of a manufacturing operation in a foreign country, subject to a wide range of political as well as commercial and foreign exchange fluctuation risks, will require a greater return on that activity than the return on expanding its capacity to produce and sell through established channels a staple consumer nondurable good.

Information and Adaptive Learning The review process focuses on the difference between the actual performance of a division and the projection that the managers had made. This comparison is more important than specific goal orientation because errors in forecasts in either direction result in misallocation of resources. In the corporate allocation of resources by the finance committee, a project may promise a 10 percent return, resulting in an allocation of $1 million for that investment. But if the expected return had been 20 percent, perhaps a $4 million investment would have been allocated. Hence, errors in either direction result in a misallocation of resources.

But it would be inaccurate to characterize the ROI system as emphasizing that results conform to budgets or forecasts. The dynamic ROI system recognizes important variables external to the firm: changes in the economy and competitive conditions, elements of costs change, and so on. Such changes are taken into account in evaluating managerial performance. The informed review process thus provides a basis for achieving an efficient two-way information flow.

The forecasting, information flow, review and adjustment process provides for both formal and informal multiple flows of information. The evaluations are not mechanical. The review discussions aim at an informed evalua-

[5] In their research on implementation of the management by objectives approach, Carroll and Tosi found that frequency of review is highly related to goal clarity and indexes of organizational effectiveness. Their attempts to quantify the quality of the review process yielded less conclusive results. See S. J. Carroll, Jr., and Henry L. Tosi, "The Relationship of Characteristics of the Review Process to the Success of the 'Management by Objectives' Approach," *Journal of Business* XLIV (July 1971), pp. 299–305.

tion of performance. This increased understanding provides a basis for a dynamic adaptive learning process. The fundamental objective of the ROI system as a dynamic process is to shorten reaction time to change or error, thereby making the firm an effective learning and adaptive mechanism.

EVALUATION OF THE DYNAMIC PROCESS

Most of the criticisms of the ROI control method are applicable only to the static formulation. The use of any type of static control system develops incentives in the wrong direction, leads to the development of devices for beating the system, and results in the wrong motivations. But in the dynamic management control system described, this major defect of the static ROI method is eliminated. Particularly, the informed review process and the two-way information flow system make for good communication and understanding. The process then becomes a vehicle for continued improvements and provides strong motivations in the proper directions.

A major problem in the utilization of the ROI method of control is the failure of companies to adopt its dynamic elements. One reason for this failure is that so many firms came to the method relatively late. The systematic literature on the "principles of management" developed after the mid-1950s. Particularly, the literature on long-range planning did not appear until after 1955. The emergence of second-generation computers with their increased information processing and retrieval capabilities gave impetus to formal methods of planning and control.

Widespread adoption of decentralized responsibility utilized the device of profit centers. Implementation of the profit center concept involves determination of the amount of profit and relating it to some base to determine a profitability rate. Thus, to some degree, the development of measures of performance of investment centers represents an index of the extent to which an important development in planning and control activities had taken place.

As of mid-1965, 60 percent of 2,658 respondents indicated the use of investment centers.[6] Of those firms not using investment centers, about two-thirds indicated that they did not have two or more profit centers or that capital assets were relatively less significant in determining the performance of their business. It is difficult to assess whether the firms not employing profit centers should have done so for effective planning and control of their operations.

Perhaps of greater significance is the timing of the adoption of investment centers in performance measures of decentralized divisions. Of 851 large American firms that responded to an inquiry with respect to how they utilized the analysis of investment center performance, 60 percent indicated that they had adopted the method after 1955, and over 37 percent had adopted the method after 1960. When the learning aspects of the dynamic control system are taken into account, it is sobering to reflect upon persistent differentials in organization effectiveness that may have been caused by the lag in the adoption of modern management control methods in a large number of American corporations.

Hence, one reason why the ROI method of control is used in its static form may stem from its late installation by so many large companies. In its static form, the method is relatively mechanical in its installation and operation. It is thus easier to understand and easier to install. Furthermore, the review and information flow process cannot be installed as an ongoing dynamic system from the very beginning. There is an important learning element involved. This may require various forms of experimentation by companies in order to superimpose a dynamic control system on the methods of management control processes then in use.

Indeed, the difficulties of applying the ROI method in a flexible and dynamic way appear to have been experienced at the du Pont Company itself. The key element has been relations with the review committee, which plays the critical role in the effective functioning of a dynamic planning and review process. The review committee at du Pont is the executive committee, consisting of the president of the company and eight vice-presidents. Some recent changes in its methods of functioning have been described:

> The committee meets each Wednesday. It receives monthly reports from department managers, and every quarter each manager appears to discuss what happened, why, and the outlook.
>
> For decades, these reports were illustrated by a series of financial charts hung from movable overhead trolleys. A man from the treasurer's office presented the data in a stylized manner while the general manager waited for questions. The crucial charts focused on the department's return-on-investment, a very rigid concept.
>
> All this has changed. The trolleys and the

[6] John J. Mauriel and Robert N. Anthony, "Misevaluation of Investment Center Performance," *Harvard Business Review* XLIV (March–April 1966), pp. 98–105.

chart room are gone. Instead of sitting theater-style, the executive committee now sits around an oval table. The charts are at hand in page form, but, 'unless we have a question or unless the general manager wants to talk from them, we don't pick them up. . . .' The old system looked backward rather than forward. Now, the thrust is to the future.

Apparently, an effective information and review process could not be achieved by the periodic presentations to the total executive (review) committee. An important organizational change was, therefore, made:

> Last spring, McCoy broke with another du Pont tradition by giving each executive committee member an assignment as liaison man to a department to improve the connection between the operating groups and the policy level, and to give us better understanding of our problems.

The advantage of this new approach was expressed by one of the general managers in the following terms: "Instead of worrying about keeping nine men informed . . . I can clue my man anytime. He deals with the committee and I have more time to run my business."

Another important development was a more flexible approach to the application of the ROI concept:

> Now, return-on-investment is redefined every so often, says economist Charles L. Reeder, to accept reality. Where once the minimum was fixed, today it varies—higher when the risks are greater, lower when the results are more certain (a tribute to venture analysis techniques now permeating the company) or when an investment supports an established business.[7]

The implication that a fixed minimum ROI rate had been a rigid requirement of all types of opportunities, regardless of the degree of risk, suggests the application of the method in a mechanistic way. The du Pont experience emphasizes the requirement of a dynamic, flexible continuing review process rather than a bureaucratic application. Further, strategic planning was not effectively integrated with operations planning and control at du Pont.

But the recent du Pont experience offers no evidence that the failure to integrate financial planning and control with long-range or strategic planning is inherent in the ROI system. There is nothing in the method that inhibits a firm from effective integration. Indeed, Sloan emphasized that bringing the du Pont system to General Motors in the early twenties facilitated the development of long-range strategy. The installation of the du Pont system in General Motors at a time of financial crises in the early 1920s enabled Sloan and his management team to bring the operation under control. They were then able to take the long-term view in developing a strategy for increasing their share of the market.[8]

THE ROLE OF ROI CONTROL

Defects in the application of the ROI planning and control method have been disclosed by its originator, du Pont. Even worse errors were observed in a large number of firms that adopted planning and control efforts relatively late. Direct interviews with a number of these companies indicated three major types of difficulties.

First, the most widespread errors involved a static approach to planning and control. A related error has been the reflection of the emphasis of classical management theory of a strict top-down planning approach in which the standards of performance were imposed from above. The resulting rigidity has resulted in continuing conflicts between the corporate office and the operating divisions. Second, these problems have been aggravated by the domination of short-term budgeting operations by traditional accounting practices. The third major defect was the closed systems approach in which budgeting was carried out without effective integration with strategic or long-range planning.

None of the observed errors is inherent in the ROI method. The central error is in the confusion of goals and process. But both businessmen and theorists have committed the error of treating these objectives as ends in themselves. Without a full understanding of the dynamics of planning and control systems, business firms have installed ROI or other forms of management information systems, using the targets and standards bureaucratically.

Economists have also misinterpreted targets as goals rather than as instruments for coordination of decentralized divisions. Specific management function areas such as a marketing or engineering departments are likely to place greater emphasis on the importance of targets

[7] "Lighting a Fire Under the Sleeping Giant," *Business Week* (Sept. 12, 1970), pp. 40–41. The first quotation suggests that the process orientation of the effective utilization of ROI planning and control has become bureaucratized and mechanized at du Pont.

[8] Alfred P. Soan, Jr., *My Years With General Motors* (Garden City, N.Y.: Doubleday & Company, 1964).

than the general office executives. In surveying such departments an exaggerated impression of the role of targets may be obtained.

But the targets and standards by which managers seek to make the goals of the firm operational are not ends in themselves. Rather, they should be viewed as management instruments for engendering healthy processes in the firm. Targets and standards can be employed to contribute to an information and feedback process that is dynamic in quality, has favorable effects on the development of the firm's personnel, and can facilitate fast reaction time to change.

The ROI system of planning and control is a useful vehicle for assembling relevant information. It is not critical whether that information is focused on ROI or other "organization objectives." ROI is useful in providing information on every element of the balance sheet and income statement as a basis for further analysis. As a vehicle for a dynamic communication, feedback, and adjustment process, ROI, as well as other management information systems appropriately employed, can potentially be a useful system for developing healthy processes in successfully functioning firms.

79 THE FEASIBILITY AND UTILITY OF HUMAN RESOURCE ACCOUNTING*

Geoffrey M. N. Baker

Accountants have attracted much criticism for omitting any valuation of human capital in balance sheets. For example, R. Lee Brummet *et al.* state:

> A favorite cliche for the president's letter in corporate reports is 'our employees are our most important—our most valuable—asset.'. . . looking to the remainder of the report, one might ask, 'where is this human asset . . . What is the value of this most important . . . asset? Is it increasing, decreasing or remaining unchanged?'[1]

At times critic's views may be taken to attribute, not only misleading omissions, but also misanthropy to the accounting profession, involving disastrous effects on employee commitment.[2]

It thus seems necessary to underline that accounting statements are not intended to display the brotherly love of their compilers; but rather information useful to their readers in decision making. Mere detection of an omission is not, as such, a valid criticism.

Rational (that is, goal oriented) behavior requires the selection of strategy and this, in turn, requires information as to the strategies open to the subject and their likely outcomes. Apart from problems of uncertainty generally, and of the assimilative and cognitive capacity of the individual, difficulties arise because reality presents a mass of unstructured data, most of which is irrelevant to a particular decision.

The aim of information services in general and of accounting in particular, has therefore been to present models to minimize these difficulties. The models are necessarily and designedly incomplete portrayals of reality. They seek to present, in a readily digestible form, only data relevant and appropriately weighted, to a particular class of decision-makers' needs. To this end, there have evolved a number of accounting practices and techniques, appropriate to a particular model presentation. However, as regards both the models and the practices underlying them, the specificity to a particular purpose and the inappropriateness to other purposes may easily be overlooked. Growing sophistication of business information requirements enhances the need to consider the appropriateness of the basis of presentation.

Thus, for example, conservatism in general and in particular, largely ignoring intangible assets not saleable per se, admirably meets the needs of collateral-minded creditors for whom balance sheets were originally primarily intended. Conservatism is also well suited to the desire to postpone profit recognition and, hence, tax payment. Equally obviously, however, it tends to distort income measurement and efficiency appraisal based thereon.

Similarly, actual historic cost records are objective (particularly because they are admissible as evidence) and, as such, ideal for checking on agents' defalcations. However, in a period of inflation, statements based on them will tend to overstate growth and profits and understate assets, again impeding efficiency appraisal.

Objectivity may certainly have been given undue weight. Says Billy Goetz:

> In the recent past, accountants . . . have often behaved as if relevancy were irrelevant and the criterion of objective verifiability alone had any significance. The obsessive preoccupation with historical original cost seems to support this judgment conclusively.[3]

Fairer comments might be:

- it is virtually impossible to devise a standardized statement appropriate to the needs of differently motivated users in different decisional contexts; and
- accordingly, the need to modify established

* Reprinted by permission of the publisher from *California Management Review*, vol. 16, no. 4, pp. 17–23 Summer, 1974). Copyright 1974 by the Regents of the University of California. Mr. Baker is professor of accounting, University of New Brunswick.

practice or supplement information portrayed to meet newer user needs should be considered.

The specific area which it is the purpose of this article to examine is the feasibility and desirability of different treatments of expenditure on, and valuation of, human resources. In keeping with the above indicated treatment of intangibles, expenditure on recruiting, hiring, training, and developing employees is usually immediately written off. However, other approaches have been proposed. Rensis Likert claimed all such expenditure should be regarded as of a capital nature, stating,

> Accounting procedures at present ignore a substantial proportion of the income-producing assets of firms . . . , all levels of management are handicapped by the inadequate and at times inaccurate information now available . . . The wrong decisions are made too often on such questions as:
>
> - What system of management is most productive and hence should be used by the firm?
> - What strategies of cost control yield the lowest costs?
> - What system of managerial compensation yields motivation and behavior most nearly in the best interest of the entire organization?[4]

It remains to consider the existing state of the art, alternative treatments proposed and the extent to which any of these would ameliorate the weaknesses alleged by Likert, or otherwise prove of value.

HUMAN RESOURCE ACCOUNTING IN PRACTICE

Pioneers in adoption of Human Resource Accounting (HRA) were, and still are, the R. G. Barry Corporation of Columbus, Ohio. The 1967 Annual Report described its inauguration as "just the first step in the development of sophisticated measurement and accounting procedures that will enable us to report accurate estimates of the human assets of the organization."

Costs were accumulated in individual subsidiary accounts for each manager under seven main heads, namely, recruiting, acquisition, formal training and familiarization, informal training and familiarization, investment building, experience, and development. A full description of the nature of expenses so analyzed is given by R. L. Woodruff.[5]

Costs were amortized over expected working lives of individuals or shorter, and unamortized cost written off on, for example, an individual leaving the company, his experience becoming obsolete, or his health impaired, on recommendations of operating managers from their quarterly review of their staff balances.

In explaining the reasons for selection of the historic cost approach to employee valuation, the Vice President of Personnel (Mr. R. L. Woodruff, Jr.) indicated it was rather a dictated choice, stating:

> We feel that this cost-of-the-outlay approach is the best approximation at this time that we have of determining the value . . . [of an employee to the company] . . . Now we realize that it is not the true value of the employee, but we say it is one approximation of the value. We have not yet come to grips with identifying value with individual employees; we have talked about a number of ways but we have felt that this kind of information necessitates a good deal of judgment, and if individual values are placed on employees then we could have a more threatening situation than we wish . . .[6]

Further, despite the above quoted ambitions in the 1967 report, Woodruff implied that they might adhere to this basis even if other measures became available:

> As to the value question I am not sure that we will ever get to the point where we will want to place a (future oriented) value on an individual even though we are now collecting the outlay cost data on individuals.

Advantages of the historic cost approach include (a) its relative objectivity; (b) its facilitation of comparison on levels of human resource investment on a basis consistent with accounting treatment of other assets; and (c) at least debatably, a fairer matching of benefits exhaustion with expense in particular time periods.[7]

However, it has all the traditional weaknesses of this basis of asset valuation, notably the invalidity of the stable dollar assumption. These are aggravated by the much greater degree of subjectivity in the detection and write-off of abortive expenditure, and the absence of independent valuation check, in that the asset is not saleable as such. Moreover, in the absence of any measure of the value of the employee to the undertaking, there is no direct indication of the soundness of the investment in human resources.

It therefore seems pertinent to examine other bases of valuation, available to supplement data of the type extracted by Barry. A number of these have been adumbrated in theory, although not yet adopted in practice, and these are briefly surveyed below.

ALTERNATIVE VALUATION BASES FOR HUMAN RESOURCES

Proposals fall broadly into three categories: replacement cost; present value of future earnings; and present value to the undertaking (that is, profit contribution) which are considered below, seriatim.

1. Replacement Cost. This has been suggested by Likert[8] to include recruitment, training and development expenditure together with the income foregone during the training period. However substitution of replacement for actual cost appears to do little more than update the valuation, at the expense of importing considerably more subjectivity into the measure.

Eric Flamholtz[9] has pointed out that it is easier in practice to estimate replacement cost than market value, and the former might therefore be adopted as a surrogate measure of the latter. The greater ease of establishing the measure does indicate the greater feasibility of the method, but is far from validating it as a close approximation to market value or demonstrating usefulness. The principal decisional context in which such data would be relevant would be that of dismissal and replacement of staff. Here, the decision makers are already aware of the nature of the costs. There seems some room for doubt, firstly, whether the above described data will be of sufficient precision to be very influential in the decision and, secondly, whether such decisions are so frequent as to build into the accounting system the regular production of such data on all employees.

2. Present Value of Future Earnings. Baruch Lev and Aba Schwartz[10] have proposed an economic valuation so based, adjusted for the probability of death. They seek to enhance the objectivity of their measure by using very widely based statistics (census income returns, mortality tables, and so on). However, this approach, giving a value of the average rather than any specific group, drastically limits the usefulness of the measure. In particular, for example, it would be valueless to monitor the efficiency of an individual firm's investment in employee development, in that the investment would have little or no impact on this valuation.

More fundamental objections were expressed by James Hekimian and Curtis Jones[11] who rejected any such earnings capitalization as an indicator of human asset value on grounds, inter alia, of the low correlation between a man's salary and his value.

If despite their findings, this or any other formulation based on present values of an employer's future outgo, is regarded as a fair appraisal of the individual's economic worth to the undertaking, then:

a. (subject to any profit expectancy built into the discount rate applied) that worth is equal to the future cost, that is, the employing organization is indifferent as to whether the employee is retained or not;
b. insofar as "earnings" exclude fringe costs, the organization is indeed better off without this resource; and
c. consequently the value of past recruitment and development of the employee is zero in (a) or negative assuming (b).

3. Value to the Undertaking. Hekimian and Jones[12] proposed that where an undertaking had several divisions seeking the same employee, he should be allocated to the highest bidder and the bid price incorporated into that division's investment base.

This idea seems to have some merits but the circumstances in which it would be operative are relatively rare. If an opportunity cost evaluation is the intention, presumably the appropriate inclusion in the investment base is the highest unsuccessful bid. Finally, of course, the soundness of the valuation depends wholly on the information, judgment and impartiality of the bidding divisions.

Roger Hermanson has outlined[13] an aggregate valuation approach, involving establishing the net present value of expected wage payments (discounted at the economy rate of return on owned assets for the latest year); and applying to this a weighted efficiency ratio, being the rate of income on owned assets for the current year against the average rate of income on owned assets for all firms in the economy.

Use of such broadly based statistics appears to diminish precision of these calculations in general and, in particular, to import unrelated risk factors into the efficiency ratio calculation. Moreover, human resources so valued would apparently subsume all other intangible assets of a goodwill nature.

This last criticism seems also applicable to Likert's proposed Causal Variables Method,[14] although the position is there more obscure. Likert traces a connection between "causal variables" (independent variables alterable by the organization and its management, being such things as structure, management policies, business and leadership strategies) through "intervening variables" (the internal state and health of the organization) to "end-result variables" (productivity, costs, scrap loss, earnings, and so on). Discounting forecast earnings (end variables) would give the value of the organization and, hence, some suggestion of the contribution thereto of earlier variables in the causal chain.

DESIRABILITY OF ADOPTION OF HUMAN RESOURCE ACCOUNTING

Too often data producers' enthusiasm for enlarging their "sales" and empires has precluded adequate review of the cost or value of the information "sold." Information users may hesitate to reveal their ignorance by querying data supplied, and thus more than ever lose control of the information system they should have. Reed Powell and Paul Wilkens comment:

> Researchers must now extend their thinking beyond the design of data collection systems and begin considering the utilization of this information, such as providing it for specific managers.[15]

Here and elsewhere, there seems little real recognition of the incongruity—the tail-wagging-the-dog aspect—in data processing preceding consideration of its utility. The result tends to be a flood of irrelevance drowning reception of the relevant.

Advocates of HRA make a reasonable case for the need for this information, but tend to confuse information, which is available, with dollar labels for it, which are not. Thus, for example, Brummet *et al.* state.

> Managerial effectiveness may be viewed as a function of the ability to acquire, develop, allocate, maintain and utilize resources. This requires resource information of many kinds. Managers presently receive extensive information concerning physical and financial resources but relatively little about their organizations' human resources.[16]

It remains obscure what improvement in the "wrong decisions" of which Likert complains would follow adoption of HRA.

Some claims are made. For example, Patrick Kehoe and Ciaran Brennan have suggested:

> Capital budgeting, which compares actual performance against the budgeted plan can be used to monitor the investment in, and expenditure on, existing employees and on new employees . . . [and] indicate the efficiency of the personnel function . . . in considering alternative investment decisions, make or buy decisions . . . a more practical idea of both the benefits and the costs is obtained.[17]

No substantiation is offered for these claims. The sole adopter of HRA has expressed doubts on the acceptability of other than cost based methods even if they became less nebulous than they currently are. For cost based methods the claims seem quite invalid. Budgetary comparison can be practiced whether expenditure is classified as capital or revenue. Past recruitment and development expenditures are sunk costs and, as such, irrelevent to alternative investment and make or buy decisions.

Accounting may have clung to practices appropriate to earlier user requirements, but misleading in other decisional contexts. However, advocates of change are bound to establish that: (1) a specific need exists; (2) there are feasible means to meet it; and (3) the value of meeting the need exceeds the cost of so doing. Judged on this basis, HRA advocates make a fair case on (1), a hitherto strikingly inadequate case on (2) and no attempt on (3).

They have a legitimate criticism of standard accounting treatment of intangibles violating the matching of expense to time periods (a violation originally dictated by the need to produce balance sheets appropriate to collateral-minded creditors). Conventional accounting methods often penalize managers of the future, treating their long-range plans as if they were short-range. One can remove this penalty by giving advantages to managers of the future. This one advantage is, to a large extent, otherwise obtainable by appraisal of managers having regard to the nature of expenses incurred by them.

The converse system of judging managers *solely* by the net profit figure attributed to them is so naive as to be ineffective no matter what curious arithmetical rites are performed for it by the accounts department. Moreover, a different modification of accounting practice, to value goodwill, seems nearer feasibility state, and would more comprehensively meet these objections.

More widespread planning and the faintly discernible trend to more incorporation of future-oriented information in published financial statements might generate information permitting inclusion of meaningful estimates of goodwill in final accounts becoming the norm. This more realistic treatment of intangibles would restore some measure of meaningfulness to the old title "net worth" as applied to the owners' equity section of balance sheets. Goodwill fluctuations might then afford some means of monitoring the effectiveness of investment in intangibles (including human resources) thereby enhancing the usefulness of measuring these investments.

This would be in keeping with the AAA recommendations:

> External users may wish to know the degrees of employee morale, customer satisfaction, product quality and reputation of a given entity. If quantification of these were possible, a substantial amount of additional relevant information could be provided the external users. The accountant must constantly be alert to the possible applications of new measurement methods to develop additional quantifiable information for external users.[18]

The only quantification basis immediately suggesting itself is the present value of future profit streams attributable to the specified sources (which may not be amenable to differentiation inter se). Obligatory goodwill disclosure should stimulate further management attention to the accuracy of profit forecasts, on which these goodwill estimates are thus based.

As the situation now is, while the desirability of HRA information seems reasonably established, meaningful quantification does not seem practicable. Good management is already aware, qualitatively, of factors affecting their decisions regarding human resources. Attempted quantification of these, on the bases hitherto explored, would seem to achieve more in misleading (by reason of the uncertainty absorption in the specious precision of their calculations) than in clarification. The best predictor psychologists have established for managerial success, is a high tolerance for uncertainty. The enforced reliance on qualitatively derived decisions on human resources currently appears one more area in which that high tolerance needs to be exercised.

SUMMARY AND POSSIBLE RESEARCH IMPLICATIONS

HRA has been extensively advocated as a management decision aid. In the sense in which internal or external users normally now call for accounting information, the above casts considerable doubt on whether HRA has any significant value. One can much more readily see a negative value, namely, the scope for profit manipulation by syphoning charges from expense to human resource development.

All the objections to asset omission or, the other side of that coin, income distortion by premature expensing, would seem better, more comprehensively and more feasibly met by goodwill valuation (to subsume intangible assets generally). Moreover, this would do much to encourage more future orientation in management behavior.

Research in this direction would therefore appear much more promising than the current impractical and overly narrow focus on human resources alone. Energy now devoted to the latter might reflect no more than the almost mystical desire to quantify the unquantifiable. This quality has been noted in humanity in general by William Vatter[19] and in social scientists in particular by Stanislav Andreski.[20] Social scientists' doubtful methodology in "quantifying trivia" was further commented on by David Banner and Kenneth Zapp.[21]

It seems likely, however, that more is involved than this. In that assumptions are not spelled out, one can only seek to infer them. The attempt appears to be to divert resources to employee development, by modifying accounting practice such that the diversion involves less impact on short-run profit. Thus, William Pyle commented on the Barry experience:

> Appropriate personnel costs are now formally recognized as long lived assets which need not be justified as operating expenses, hence make it easier for a manager to secure funds for . . . developing human resources.[22]

Elaborating on this inferred real reason for HRA advocacy, its possible genesis is:

- humanity is universally desirous of fulfilling its psychological needs in the work environment;
- the desire can be met and resource diversion to employee development will assist this; and
- accounting practice should be changed so that this diversion "need not be justified as operating expenses" (or as anything else until it is too late to change).

If this is the thinking, research might be better addressed to the extent to which the premises are established, which tends to be much exaggerated. Some of the research tending to confirm them is suspect in that: (1) the methodology tends to imply emotionally satisfying conclusions of the ubiquity of personal growth desires, arrived at in advance of the evidence . . . questionnaires then producing the latter as a self-fulfilling prophecy; and (2) in particular, samples examined may be biased since they are both genuinely imbued with above average growth desires, and are likely to exaggerate these in responses demonstrating company loyalty.

Several studies, including those of George

Strauss[23] and Robert McMurray[24] have cast doubt on how widespread are desires for challenge, responsibility, participation and accompanying ulcers.

Further, continually advancing technology and possible decline in consumerism may dictate satisfaction of psychological needs being shifted from work to leisure environments. On the individual employer scale, accelerating market and technological change (especially automation) and increased labor mobility all limit the extent of possible loyalty and commitment by organization of employee or vice versa.[25]

The capacity to meet growth desires is further limited by the continuance (however regrettable this may be) of jobs of an inevitably substantial monotony content. Training and developing such job holders beyond the capacities they require merely augments their frustration, and is a disservice both to them and their employing organization. Robert White has suggested[26] a much more widely diffused psychological need—possibly the only one almost universally held—is for a sense of competence in mastering the world facing the individual, including work tasks. *Reduction* in the challenge may then minister to this need.

Frederick Herzberg has produced an encouraging case for the scope for job enrichment and the successfulness of this as a motivator[27] . . . but that scope is necessarily limited.

It is not here argued that the assumptions inferred as underlying HRA advocacy are quite unsound. It is, however, suggested that they are of more limited application than is commonly supposed. Research toward defining those limits and hence desirable behavioral change in management would seem much more promising than seeking to open the flood gates of "easier" fund procurement for human resource development. One might then more clearly perceive, and pursue, the goal of individual development —a goal legitimate in itself not merely as a means of profit. In planning and monitoring progress to this goal, a modified HRA may find a usefulness, which is only very faintly and peripherally discernable in current literature.

REFERENCES

1. R. Lee Brummet, Eric G. Flamholtz, and William C. Pyle, "Human Resource Measurement: A Challenge for Accountants," *Accounting Review,* Vol. 43 (April 1968), p. 217.
2. Reed M. Powell and Paul L. Wilkins, "Design and Implementation of a Human Resource Information System," *MSU Business Topics,* Vol. 21, Iss. 1 (Winter 1973), pp. 21–28.
3. Billy E. Goetz, "Transfer Prices: An Exercise in Relevancy and Goal Congruence," *Accounting Review,* Vol. 42 (July 1967), p. 435.
4. Rensis Likert, *The Human Organization, Its Management and Value* (New York: McGraw-Hill, 1967), p. 115.
5. R. L. Woodruff, Jr., "Human Resources Accounting," *Canadian Chartered Accountant,* Vol. 97 (September 1970), pp. 156–61.
6. ——— *et al.,* "Discussion R. G. Barry Human-Resource Accounting" in Thomas J. Burns (ed.) *The Behavioral Aspects of Accounting Data for Performance Evaluation* (Columbus, Ohio: College of Administrative Science, Ohio State University, 1970), p. 35.
7. R. Lee Brummet, *et al., loc. cit.*
8. Rensis Likert, *op. cit.,* pp. 146–7.
9. Eric G. Flamholtz, "A Model for Human Resource Valuation: A Stochastic Process with Service Rewards," *Accounting Review,* Vol. 46 (April 1971), pp. 253–267.
10. Baruch Lev and Aba Schwartz, "On the Use of the Economic Concept of Human Capital in Financial Statements," *Accounting Review,* Vol. 46 (January 1971), pp. 103–112.
11. James S. Hekimian and Curtis H. Jones, "Put People On Your Balance Sheet," *Harvard Business Review,* Vol. 45 (January–February 1967), pp. 107–113.
12. *Ibid.*
13. Roger H. Hermanson, *Accounting for Human Assets* (Occasional Paper No. 14) (East Lansing, Michigan, Bureau of Business & Economics Research, Graduate School of Business Administration, Michigan State University, 1964).
14. Rensis Likert, *loc. cit.*
15. Reed M. Powell and Paul L. Wilkens, *op. cit.,* p. 23.
16. R. Lee Brummet, Eric G. Flamholtz and William C. Pyle, "Human Resource Accounting—A Tool to Increase Managerial Effectiveness," *Management Accounting,* Vol. 51, Iss. 2 (August 1969), p. 12.
17. Patrick T. Kehoe and Ciaran Brennan, *When the Assets Go Marching By* (unpublished research paper, 1972), p. 5.
18. A.A.A., *A Statement of Basic Accounting Theory* (American Accounting Association, 1966), p. 29.
19. William J. Vatter, "Tailor-making Cost Data for Specific Uses," *N.A.(C.)A. Bulletin, 1954 Conference Proceedings.*
20. Stanislav Andreski, *Social Sciences as Sorcery* (London: Andre Deutsch, 1972).

21. David K. Banner and Kenneth Zapp, *Radicalism and Tomorrow's Industrial State* (prepublication edition, 1972), ch. 1.
22. William C. Pyle, "Human Resource Accounting," *Financial Analysts Journal* (September, October 1970).
23. George Strauss, "The Personality Versus Organization Theory" in Sayles (ed.) *Individualism and Big Business* (New York: McGraw-Hill, 1963).
24. Robert N. McMurray, "The Case for Benevolent Autocracy" in Shepard (ed.), *Organizational Issues in Industrial Society* (Englewood Cliffs, N.J.: Prentice-Hall, 1972).
25. B. O. Saxberg, "Obsolescence of Employee Loyalty Under Automation," *European Business* (April 17, 1968), pp. 59–65.
26. Robert W. White, "Ego and Reality in Psychoanalytic Theory," *Psychological Issues,* Vol. III, No. 3 (New York: International Universities Press, 1963).
27. Frederick Herzberg, Bernard Mausner and Barbara Snyderman, *The Motivation to Work* (New York: John Wiley & Sons, 1959).